# CHICKADEES, TITS
# NUTHATCHES
# & TREECREEPERS

# CHICKADEES, TITS
# NUTHATCHES
# & TREECREEPERS

## Simon Harrap and David Quinn

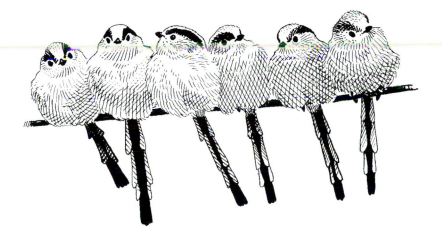

Princeton University Press

Princeton, New Jersey

Published by Princeton University Press, 41 William Street,
Princeton, New Jersey 08540

ISBN 0-691-01083-8

**Library of Congress Cataloging-in-Publication Data**

Harrap, Simon
    Chickadees, tits, nuthatches & treecreepers / Simon Harrap and
David Quinn.
        p.      cm.
    Includes bibliographical references and index.
    ISBN 0-691-01083-8 (cloth   :   alk.   paper)
    1. Chickadees.   2.  Titmice   3.  Nuthatches.   4.  Creepers  (Birds)
    I.  Quinn, David,   1959-       II.  Title.
    QL696.P2615H37  1995
    598.8′2- -dc20                                         95-30342
                                                                    CIP

This book has been composed in Optima

Printed in Singapore

10  9  8  7  6  5  4  3  2  1

# CONTENTS

## FAMILY SITTIDAE
### Subfamily Sittinae: 'True' Nuthatches

### Subfamily Tichodromadinae: Wallcreeper

## FAMILY CERTHIIDAE
### Subfamily Certhinae: Tribe Certhiini: 'Typical' Treecreepers

### Tribe Salpornithini: Spotted Creeper

## FAMILY PARIDAE
### Subfamily Remizinae: Penduline Tits

## Subfamily Parinae: 'True' Tits

### Subgenus *Poecile*

### Subgenus *Periparus*

### Subgenus *Pardaliparus*

### Subgenus *Lophophanes*

### Subgenus *Melaniparus*

### Subgenus *Parus*

# FAMILY AEGITHALIDAE: LONG-TAILED TITS

# INTRODUCTION

This book brings together under one cover the members of several disparate families (or subfamilies: see Family Introductions), but, whilst scientists may argue over their relationships, they do have several things in common. They are all small Passerine birds and almost all of them are non-migratory, or undertake only limited and irregular movements. Many are common birds within their range, and throughout the temperate parts of the Northern Hemisphere many live in close association with man. Whether it be to 'birdtables' in Europe or to 'feeders' in North America, some of the commonest, cheekiest and best-loved visitors are likely to be tits and chickadees. And, when winter has gripped the northern woodlands, roaming bands of tits, nuthatches and treecreepers are among the few songbirds to remain, much to the delight of birdwatchers.

These common denominators in the biology of tits, nuthatches and treecreepers have produced some startling consequences. Being small and non-migratory many have adapted, in terms both of their physiology and their behaviour, to withstand extremes of cold (and, in some cases, extreme heat). Moreover, as non-migratory species, often with vast ranges, many have undergone a strong radiation in terms of their appearance, resulting in the description of many subspecies (or geographical races). Some of these races are poorly marked and barely distinguishable in the museum, let alone in the field, but others exhibit pronounced variations. Indeed, so well marked are the differences between some populations that there is an ongoing (and increasingly complex) debate over the limits of many species. For example, a 'standard' work such as 'Peters' (*Check-list of Birds of the World*: Snow 1967) lists 46 species in the family Paridae (the 'true' tits), compared with the 32 species recognised by Eck (1988) and 53 listed by Sibley & Monroe (1990). In this book, we recognise 57 species (and could have gone further; there are at least another three good candidates). There can be few, if any, other groups of birds where there is such a wide discrepancy in the number of species recognised.

The abundance of some of the tits and nuthatches, as well as their close association with man, has made them the favourite subjects of research for many ornithologists. In Britain and Europe the Great Tit has found most favour, and must surely claim the title of the most-studied bird in the world, with over 700 papers published on various aspects of its life in the period 1979-1993 (synthesised in an eminently readable and authoritative monograph by Andrew Gosler (1993)). Work on the Great Tit has perhaps concentrated on population dynamics and vocabulary, and in North America, the Black-capped Chickadee has similarly attracted attention, again resulting in a monograph, by Susan M. Smith (1991). Research on this species has concentrated on its vocabulary, with some remarkable results (the Black-capped Chickadee may have a language). Paradoxically, however, many species of tits, nuthatches and treecreepers are poorly known, especially those in Africa and southern Asia, and it is the latter region that holds the greatest diversity of species.

The aim of this book is to summarise many of the fascinating aspects of the biology and evolution of tits, nuthatches and treecreepers. Identification is, of course, covered fully, but a significant amount of detail is also given on vocalisations, distribution, general biology, breeding behaviour, plumages, moults, geographical variation and the relationships between and within the various species. This highlights just how much we know about some species, and how poorly known others are. If it stimulates a greater interest in an absorbing group of birds, thus helping to fill some of the gaps, it will have served its purpose.

So much has been written about the tits, nuthatches and treecreepers that it is difficult to keep up with the literature, and the author (c/o the publishers, A & C Black) would be grateful to receive any information which corrects or updates the information in this book for use in future editions.

# ACKNOWLEDGEMENTS

No book covering 110 species could claim to be the work of just two people, and we have drawn heavily on the work of hundreds, if not thousands, of ornithologists, birdwatchers and collectors. Holding a specimen of White-browed Tit from the Tibetan plateau, or reading a short paper on ecology and vocalisations, it is all too easy to forget the hundreds of hours of effort that have already been invested by the bird's collector or the paper's author. Our greatest debt is thus owed to those who have gone before us.

During the course of our work of the text and plates a great many people gave us assistance, advice and information. Very special thanks go to Mike Wilson for his considerable help in translating Russian references and in tracking down some obscure data. Special thanks, too, go to Jochen Martens for many useful data, references and discussion, Duncan Brooks for kindly providing advance proofs of volume VII of *BWP*, and Mike Crosby for much information from BirdLife International's Biodiversity Project. Craig Robson also provided information from the Biodiversity Project, and helped to track down many obscure localities and references. Michael Rank kindly translated several Chinese references and Peter Harrap assisted with the translation of some long French papers. Help with translations also came from David A. Christie, Daniela Ford, Nick Gardner, Yvonne Harrap, Erik Hirschfeld and Arakdy Semyonov.

We are indebted to the staff of the Natural History Museum, Tring, especially Peter Colston, Mark P. Adams and Michael Walters, for assisting with access to the national collections and assisting with loans. Dr Clem Fisher, Dr Malcolm Largen and Tony Parker facilitated use of the collections at the National Museums and Galleries on Merseyside. Colin and Pauline Dalton and Graham and Carol Green provided much-needed hospitality on numerous visits to Tring. Specimens were loaned by the following institutions: American Museum of Natural History (Mary LeCroy, who also arranged for specimens to be photographed), Carnegie Museum of Natural History (Dr Kenneth C. Parkes), Field Museum of Natural History (David E. Willard), Manchester Museum (Dr Mike Hounsome), Muséum National d'Histoire Naturelle (Francis Roux and Dr J.-F. Voisin), National Museum of Natural History, Washington (J. Phillip Angle and M. Ralph Browning), Natural History Museum of Los Angeles County (Kimball L. Garrett), and Rijksmuseum van Natuurlijke Historie (G.F. Mees, who also advised on some specimens in his care); and Raymond A. Paynter at the Museum of Comparative Zoology arranged for photographs of specimens, and helped with the description of Yellow-billed Nuthatch and the identification of some Chinese tits.

Thanks to Linda Birch of the Alexander Library at the Edward Grey Institute, Oxford, and Effie Warr at the Natural History Museum, Tring, for considerable time and effort expended in providing copies of numerous references. Thanks to Mike Wilson and the *BWP* team for access to material in preparation for revised edition of *BWP*.

Special thanks to Derek Scott, who provided much information on Iran, to Steve N.G. Howell for advance information from *A Guide to the Birds of Mexico and Northern Central America*, and to Dr J.S. Ash for information on Ethiopia, Steve Madge on Afghanistan and treecreepers, Dave Farrow on Russia, Guy M. Kirwan on China, Craig Robson on breeding behaviour and much information on oriental ornithology, Robert Clay on Brown Creeper, and Lars Svensson, Jan H. Christensen, Roger Norman and A.D.W. Tongue for comments on treecreeper identification. Thanks also to Michael Frankis for much advice on plant nomenclature and to Roy Robinson for assistance with the maps. J. Laurens Barnard, D.T. Lees-Smith, Frank Rozendaal and Lester Short advised on various points.

The following individuals kindly answered specific queries: Humayun Abdulali, Per Alström, Mark Beaman, Arnoud B. van den Berg, Seb Buckton, P.A. Clancey, C.F. Clinning, Millicent S. Ficken, Annika Forsten, Frank B. Gill, Brian Henshaw, Phil Holder, Jesper Hornskov, Carol Inskipp, Alan Knox, Steve Madge, Dr Clive F. Mann, Pete Morris, V.A. Nechaev, Nigel Redman, Tom Roberts, C.S. Roselaar, Sheldon R. Severinghaus, Rob Simmons, Warwick Tarboton, Mick Turton and Effie Warr.

The following very kindly read and commented upon various drafts of the species accounts: Per Alström, Dr J.S. Ash, Mark Beaman, Nik Borrow, Mark Brazil, Carla Cicero, Professor Keith L. Dixon, Dr Stephen Ervin, Lincoln Fishpool, Michael Frankis, Steve Gantlett, Peter Gooden, Dr Andy Gosler, Annie Harrap, Steve Howell, Erik Matthysen, Rod Martins, Dr Kenneth C. Parkes, Dr Olof Persson, Iain Robertson, Craig Robson, Anne Starling and Mark Van Beirs.

For providing provided photographs which were used in preparation of the plates and text, we are grateful to Claus Yding Andersen, Arnoud B. van den Berg, Ted Brett, Dave Cottridge, Martin Davies, Jon Eames, Richard Fairbank, David Henderson, Paul Holt, Allen Jeyarajasingam, John Knowler, Volker Konrad, Pete Morris, Paul Noakes, Michael Køie Poulsen, Nigel Redman, Don Roberson, Chris Rose, Steve Smith, Ray Tipper, Mark Van

Beirs, Walter Warburton, Steve Whitehouse and Johan Wallender.

In addition to the commercially available sound recordings listed at the end of the Bibliography (p. 445), several people made recordings available. Special thanks go to Richard Ranft at the National Sound Archive of the British Library, who provided copies of many recordings, often at short notice (recordists Dr B.C.R. Bertram, Clide Carter, B.B. & L.C. Coffey, F. Dowsett-Lemaire, Nicolai Formosov, Dr Axel Gebauer, Alan Greensmith, Tom Gullick, Nigel Lindsey, Dr Liou, H. Lütgens, R. McVicker, W.M. Meriwether, Phil Riddett, Richard Ridgway, J.C. Roché, Per Schiermacher Hansen, R. Stjernstedt, A. Wassink and Christopher Watson). Thanks also to Paul Holt and Jelle Scharringa, who both provided many recordings from Asia, as well as Per Alström, Bas van Balen, Arnoud B. van den Berg, Nik Borrow, Dave Farrow, Vladimir Loskot, Steve Madge, Rod Martins, Pete Morris, Nigel Redman, Tom Roberts, Iain Robertson, Craig Robson, Phil Round, Steve Smith, Steve Whitehouse and Mark Van Beirs, and to the Borror Laboratory of Bioacoustics (Ohio State University; recordists Sandra L.L. Gaunt and D. Archibald McCallum), and the Library of Natural Sounds, Cornell Laboratory of Ornithology (recordists E.W. Cronin Jr and Dr Ben King).

Finally, a very special word of thanks to Jo Hemmings for helping to initiate the project and to Robert Kirk at A & C Black for his constant help, encouragement and patience, and considerable assistance with the maps. David A. Christie translated many German references and gave much useful advice, as well as enduring the painful task of copy-editing the text, and Anne Starling gave much patient support and encouragement in the final and most time-consuming stages of the project.

# CLASSIFICATION

## Higher Classifications

Note that I follow, purely for convenience, Sibley & Ahlquist (1990) in the classification of the higher taxonomic categories.

All birds are members of the Animal Kingdom, and within that Kingdom are placed in the Class Aves. The Class Aves is further divided into about 23 Orders, which are the most fundamental divisions of the world's birds. The tits, nuthatches and treecreepers are all members of the order Passeriformes, that is Passerines or perching birds. This is a vast assemblage of well over 5,000 species, accounting for over half of the bird species in the world. The order Passeriformes is divided into two Suborders, the Tyranni (or 'suboscines') and the Passeri (or 'oscines'). The Tyranni reach their greatest diversity in South America and are poorly represented in the Old World.

The Passeri include all of the tits, nuthatches and treecreepers, and this Suborder is in turn divided into two Parvorders, the Corvida and the Passerida. The Corvida is a largely Australasian group, although it also includes vireos, shrikes, crows etc. The Passerida includes the tits, nuthatches and treecreepers, and is divided into three superfamilies, the Muscicapoidea (comprising thrushes, chats, flycatchers, starlings and their allies), Sylvioidea (including swallows, bulbuls, warblers and babblers) and the Passeroidea (comprising the sunbirds and flowerpeckers, sparrows, pipits, accentors, finches, buntings, New World warblers, tanagers etc.). The tits, nuthatches and treecreepers are all members of the superfamily Sylvioidea, and are divided among four families, the Sittidae, Certhiidae, Paridae and Aegithalidae. These families are, in turn, divided into subfamilies (and these sometimes into tribes).

Thus, the Parvorder Passerida, superfamily Sylvioidea, includes, among others, the following families:

Family Sittidae
> Subfamily Sittinae, nuthatches
> Subfamily Tichodromadinae, Wallcreeper

Family Certhiidae
> Subfamily Certhiinae
>> Tribe Certhiini, typical treecreepers
>> Tribe Salpornithini, Spotted Creeper
> Subfamily Troglodytinae, wrens
> Subfamily Polioptilinae, gnatcatchers and gnatwrens

Family Paridae
> Subfamily Remizinae, penduline tits
> Subfamily Parinae, typical tits

Family Aegithalidae, long-tailed tits

Covered here are all members of these families, with the exception of the Troglodytinae (wrens) and Polioptilinae (gnatcatchers and gnatwrens). See Family Introductions for further details.

## Species Limits

Unfortunately, despite having received considerable attention, the taxonomy of the genus *Parus* is something of a mess. Studies based on a traditional taxonomic approach, using an analysis of plumages and measurements, have produced widely differing results, largely dependent on the philosophy of the taxonomist. These approaches may be equally valid, but they are not directly comparable.

Taxonomy is, however, in the midst of a revolution, with new techniques and technologies producing an ever-increasing flow of information, some of it conflicting. Information on vocalisations is used with growing frequency by taxonomists. Good portable tape recorders and microphones and the increasing ease of travel (especially within the former USSR and China) have made the documentation of the songs and calls of obscure tits and nuthatches almost routine. Sonagrams (see below under Voice, p. 25) allow such sounds to be analysed and compared with mathematical precision, and playback experiments can be conducted to gauge the responsiveness of a tit in China to the song of its cousin in Germany.

The latest advance is the use of high-tech biochemistry to compare the genetic material of different birds. A variety of techniques has been developed, some allowing quite fine discrimination of DNA samples from different populations. These will never tell us whether birds are separate species, but can, for example, give a guide as to how long populations have been separated. Research into genetics is however, still expensive and very specialised.

Despite these new techniques and technologies, the problem for the taxonomist nevertheless remains essentially the same. How much weight should be attached to the various pieces of data? Which of the characters examined reflects the history of the bird concerned (and thus can be used to deduce its relationships), and which is an adaptation, perhaps relatively recent, to life in a particular environment? The solution to this problem has unfortunately, also remained the same. Taxonomists tend to attach most weight to the characters and methods with which they are most closely involved personally. A student of morphology plots wing length against tail length and uses this to produce a list of species, while a 'voice expert' studies sonagrams and declares populations to be conspecific if they produce similar geometric patterns on the sonagram, or conducts playback experiments and declares that these are the most important clue to relationships. The net result is that the ordinary birdwatcher is thoroughly confused, and that it is impossible to produce a list of tits and nuthatches which would satisfy every interested party.

## 'Splitting' and 'Lumping'

Widely differing criteria have been applied to the more difficult questions as to whether to 'split' populations into different species or to 'lump' them into just one. There are two particular problems.

The first is when populations are *allopatric* (i.e, their ranges do not overlap or come into contact). An example is Red-breasted, Corsican and Chinese Nuthatches. These are found in North America, Corsica, and the Far East, respectively, with many thousands of kilometres separating their breeding ranges. They look remarkably similar, however, occupy similar habitats and even sound rather similar. Should they be treated as one species, with several far-flung populations, or as three distinct species? The former option was favoured earlier in the 20th century, whilst the latter is now the universal treatment. The birds themselves have not changed, but our conceptions have.

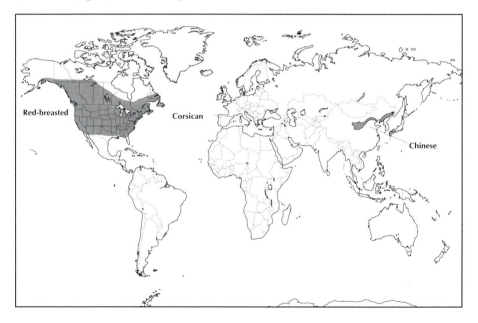

*The ranges of Red-breasted, Corsican and Chinese Nuthatches are well separated, with no overlap (they are allopatric). They look and sound very similar, but should they be treated as one, two or three species?*

Taxonomists studying these groups have speculated what would happen should these birds meet in the wild. Would they recognise each other as the same species, and if so, would they be able to interbreed *successfully?* (Even though they may initially hybridise, the hybrids produced may in some way be less 'fit' than pure-bred birds, so that in time selection would favour those individuals that did not hybridise. Isolating mechanisms would develop and they would then be able to coexist as two distinct species.) In the case of the smaller nuthatches, work by Hans Löhrl established that the 'location call', an innate vocalisation used by begging fledglings to attract their parents, differed between Corsican and Red-breasted Nuthatches (there was no information on Chinese Nuthatch) and hence he concluded that any hybrid juveniles would give the 'wrong' call and probably starve. These small nuthatches are therefore split into three species (see p. 13 for more details).

In the case of most allopatric populations, however, such good evidence is not forthcoming. It has to be admitted that the decision whether to split or lump then boils down to the taxonomist's (or checklist author's, or field-guide author's) personal preferences and gut feelings. The current trend is to split, and to treat the various populations as members of a 'superspecies' (see below).

The second major problem is the case of two populations that meet and hybridise. In the long term, these questions will resolve themselves. If the hybrids are as 'fit' (i.e. as successful) as or even fitter than the parent populations, they will survive as well as pure-bred birds, and individuals that mate with the 'wrong' form will be at no disadvantage. The hybrid zone will gradually expand outwards and eventually the two populations will merge in a continuous distribution. There will be no question that they are the same species. Alternatively, the hybrids are not so 'fit' as pure-bred birds if individuals that enter into hybrid liaisons will be selected against, because their genes are not so likely to be passed on to future generations. Behavioural mechanisms will probably develop to keep the two populations apart: for example, different songs or different courtship rituals will act as 'isolating mechanisms' and allow the two to overlap (that is, to become *sympatric*) without interbreeding. Clearly, they will have become distinct species.

Such processes, however, may occur over thousands of generations, and taxonomists cannot wait that long. At present, we have a 'snapshot' of various hybrid zones, presumably showing various stages of the processes of intergradation or separation, but which is which? Even evidence collected over the 150 years of modern ornithology may not give us enough data to deduce the dynamics of and within the hybrid zone, to work out which way things are going. Various detailed studies have been undertaken (e.g. on Black-capped and Carolina Chickadees, Tufted and Black-crested Titmice, Coal and Spot-winged Tits), but even these have not been able to provide unambiguous results.

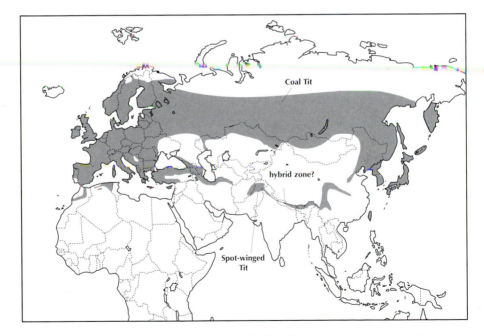

*Coal Tit and Spot-winged Tit meet and presumably hybridise in a very narrow zone in western Nepal. Should they be treated as one or two species?*

The consequence is that in the case of hybridising populations, as in allopatric forms, the final decision is often somewhat arbitrary. Differing standards have been applied, resulting in some species being split and others lumped, depending on where in the world they happen to live. In undertaking this global review, I have attempted to apply

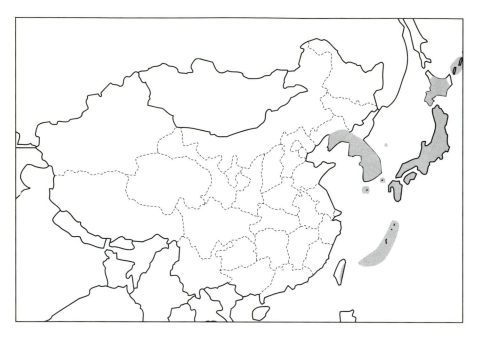

*The range of Varied Tit spans many islands in the Far East, and a number of subspecies have evolved, some very distinct.*

a uniform policy, and have decided to split in the majority of cases, resulting in a longer list of relevant 'species' than given in any other checklist. There are four reasons for this decision:

1. After a long period of lumping, the current fashion is to split.
2. By splitting, I hope to draw attention to the problems and encourage further study.
3. By splitting, the material can be presented in a more easily digestible form, and gaps in our knowledge highlighted. Filling these gaps in our understanding of distribution, habitat, vocalisations and breeding biology may produce much useful information.
4. By splitting, various populations are elevated to species level and automatically assume a greater conservation priority. Few would care if the race *victoriae* of the widespread White-tailed Nuthatch were extinct?, but the fate of White-browed Nuthatch, *Sitta victoriae*, endemic to a single mountain in Burma, will generate far more concern. In turn, concern for this species may go a little way towards conserving an extremely valuable forest community, with a whole host of endemic plants and animals.

## Superspecies

One way of dealing with the problem of closely related species that are allopatric is to invoke the term 'superspecies'. This is used for two or more 'allospecies' (allopatric species) which are closely related and are thought to have relatively recently *evolved from a common ancestor*. It is thus a 'halfway house' for those species that are obviously very closely related, but too different (or too widely separated) from each other to be easily accommodated as races of a single species. I prefer to use the term superspecies only where it involves *allopatric* species (or those that meet and do not overlap, but hybridise in a narrow zone, e.g. Coal and Spot-winged Tits, Black-capped and Carolina Chickadees). The allocation of many tits and nuthatches to a superspecies has up to now been largely based on similarities in their plumage and structure, and sometimes in vocalisations. Research into genetics may well challenge some of these allocations, and produce some surprising results.

The term 'species group' can be used for a group of species which may not necessarily be so closely related, and may overlap, often substantially (i.e. that are sympatric).

## Subspecies and Clines

Many species are divided into geographical races or subspecies. These may differ from one another only subtly in coloration and size (sometimes only on average measurements) and it may be difficult to distinguish them, even with a range of specimens to hand. There may be considerable disagreement as to whether some of these subtle races are worth recognition at all. Others differ in very obvious ways, so much so that birdwatchers may take some convincing that they are the same species.

Subspecies are presumably the product of a process whereby each population adapts subtly to local environmental conditions, and several 'rules' have been proposed to govern these processes (e.g. 'Gloger's Rule' states that in a given species races occupying warm and humid areas tend to be darker and more heavily pigmented than those in cool and dry regions, and 'Bergmann's Rule' that body size tends to be larger in cooler regions and smaller in warmer areas).

A few subspecies occupy discrete geographical areas, such as islands. These 'islands' may be geographical islands, or they may be environmental islands, such as an isolated forest region or a patch of desert well separated from other deserts. Such discrete populations, whether recognised as distinct subspecies or not, are the building blocks of evolution, for a given population can begin on the process of speciation only when it is separated from other populations of the same species.

Among the tits, nuthatches and treecreepers, however, most subspecies are part of a broader, continuous distribution. In Europe and Asia in particular, several species have unbroken ranges across thousands of kilometres from the Atlantic to the Pacific (e.g. Willow Tit). Because the distribution is continuous, variation is also usually continuous, and it becomes an arbitrary decision as to where one subspecies ends and the adjoining subspecies begins (some taxonomists like to give a name to every perceptible stage in variation, whilst others may wish to name only the extremes). In such cases, variation is said to be *clinal*. A 'cline' is where there is a geographical gradient in a particular character: e.g. there may be a cline of increasing colour saturation, that is, a continuous and gradual increase in the intensity of pigmentation of the species concerned, or there may be a cline of increasing size. Importantly, different characters, such as overall size, bill dimensions and coloration, may show clinal variation *independently* of each other.

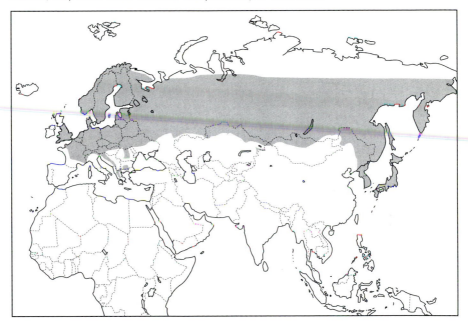

*The range of Willow Tit spans the whole of northern Europe and Asia, as well as the British Isles and Japan. There are few gaps in the continental range, and among most of the continental subspecies variation is clinal.*

# FAMILY INTRODUCTIONS

## Family Sittidae

This relatively small family comprises 25 species in two genera: the 24 species of typical nuthatches in the subfamily Sittinae and the Wallcreeper in the subfamily Tichodromadinae.

### Subfamily Sittinae: the typical nuthatches

The typical nuthatches are a very homogeneous group, and, once one is familiar with one species, all the others will be instantly recognised as nuthatches.

Nuthatches are relatively small and compact, with a sturdy, long, straight and pointed bill. Their legs are short, with strong toes and rather long claws. The wings are relatively short, with ten primaries, and the tail is short and square, with 12 feathers. Typically, the upperparts are blue-grey, there is a long and broad black eyestripe (and sometimes a pale supercilium and/or black cap), and the underparts are white, variably washed with buff, orange or rufous. Some have distinct lilac tones. The sexes are rather similar, but they do differ, usually in underpart coloration (especially the rear flanks and undertail-coverts), and these differences may already be apparent in nestlings. On the other hand, juveniles and 1st adults are very similar to adults, and nuthatches are often difficult to age, even in the hand.

Nuthatches feed on insects, spiders and other invertebrates, and also on seeds and nuts. They forage almost entirely on the surface of the trunks and branches of trees (and their feet are 'scansorial', specialised for climbing), with two species, the rock nuthatches, being adapted to feeding in a similar fashion on rock faces and sometimes buildings. The strong legs and feet are used for climbing, one foot being kept high to hang from, the other low for support, and they move in a series of jerky hops. They do not use their tail for support (unlike woodpeckers and treecreepers) and are adept at climbing down trunks and rocks head-first.

Larger food items, such as bigger insects and seeds, are wedged into cracks and crevices in bark or rocks and then hammered open with the bill. Indeed, nuthatches gain their name from this habit of hacking open seeds and nuts. They do not use their feet to hold down large prey items. Brown-headed Nuthatch has been recorded using bark scales as a tool to pry off bark in search of food. Many (all?) species of nuthatch store food, usually seeds and nuts; these are 'scatter-hoarded' singly in cracks and crevices.

All nuthatches nest in cavities, usually holes in trees or, in the case of rock nuthatches, in or among rocks. Many reduce the size of the entrance hole and seal up cracks with mud, whilst the rock nuthatches build more elaborate flask- or bottle-shaped structures around the entrance to their holes. At least two species have unusual practices, thought to be anti-predator strategies: Red-breasted Nuthatch daubs the entrance to its nest with sticky tree resin, and White-breasted Nuthatch sweeps around its nest hole with noxious-smelling insects.

Nuthatches are typically very vocal, with a variety of loud whistles, calls and trills, but their songs are rather simple, and often not very distinct from the calls.

Nuthatches are found throughout the Northern Hemisphere in the Nearctic, Palearctic and Oriental Regions, but reach their greatest diversity in southern Asia, where 15 of the 24 species can be found.

### Subfamily Tichodromadinae: Wallcreeper

This subfamily contains just one species, the elegant and enigmatic Wallcreeper. About the size of a Eurasian Nuthatch, it has a long, slender, downcurved bill which strongly recalls that of a treecreeper. The tarsus is rather weak, with long and slender toes and long, slender, sharply curved claws. Its wings are relatively long, with ten primaries, but, like a nuthatch, the tail is rather short and comprises 12 feathers. Generally blue-grey above, the wings are spectacularly marked with red, white and black. The underparts are grey-white, variably marked with blackish on the throat and breast depending on season and sex: unlike any nuthatch, Wallcreeper has distinct breeding and non-breeding plumages, the former acquired by a partial pre-breeding moult (also exhibited, but in a much reduced form, by some nuthatches). Males and females are easily separable, and the juvenile is relatively distinct.

Wallcreepers are specialist feeders, foraging on vertical rock faces. They constantly flick their wings when climbing, but do not use the tail for support. In the winter some descend from their montane breeding areas, and they may then be found on level rocky riverbeds. Wallcreepers feed on insects and other small invertebrates, extracted from cracks and crevices by the tweezers-like bill, but they do not use their feet to hold prey items, and are not known to store food.

The nest is placed in a crack or hole in a rock face, but the entrance is not walled up, daubed or decorated in any way. Generally rather silent, they do have a short, melodious song. Wallcreepers are found throughout the mountain regions of southern Europe and Asia.

The exact relationships of this species have long been debated, with opinions divided as to whether it is closer to the treecreepers or to the nuthatches. Although traditionally placed with the treecreepers, and having a similar slender, curved bill, Wallcreepers are actually closer to nuthatches. This relationship was confirmed by an analysis of structural and plumage characters (Vaurie 1957d) and behavioural studies (Löhrl 1964); and, whilst DNA-DNA comparisons show that nuthatches and Wallcreeper are not very closely related, they are nevertheless each other's closest relatives (Sibley & Ahlquist 1990). Wallcreeper is thus placed in a subfamily of the Sittidae, but could equally be put in a family of its own, the Tichodromadidae (e.g. Cramp & Perrins 1993, following Voous 1977; Voous stated that 'The extraordinary adaptations to extreme mountain conditions ... might not immediately have justified the recognition of a family of its own, but they surely mark the arrival at a new structural and ecological level with promising possibilities.').

## Other unrelated 'nuthatches'

In birds, as in other animals, form is often dictated by function. Thus, several species have evolved to fill a similar niche to that of the nuthatches, foraging on the surface of the trunk and branches of trees, and have also become rather similar in outward appearance in a process of 'convergent evolution'. In many of the older systems of classification these species were associated with the Sittidae. They include the Nuthatch Vanga *Hypositta coral-lirostris* of Madagascar and the sittellas *Daphoenositta* of New Guinea and Australia. The present consensus is that the Nuthatch Vanga is a member of the Vangidae/Vangini, a small family/tribe endemic to the Malagasy region (Parvorder Corvida, family Corvidae, subfamily Malaconotinae, tribe Vangini: Sibley & Ahlquist 1990). DNA-DNA comparisons show that the sittellas are members of the old endemic Australo-Papuan assemblage that includes whistlers and shriketits (Parvorder Corvida, family Corvidae, subfamily Pachycephalinae, tribe Neosittini: Sibley & Ahlquist 1990). They are thus extremely distantly related to nuthatches, and are not considered further.

# Family Certhidae

Depending upon which criteria are used, this is a small family comprising just seven species in two genera (the 'typical treecreepers, *Certhia,* and the Spotted Creeper, *Salpornis*), or a large amalgamation of around 100 species in 22 genera.

Traditionally, the treecreepers of the genus *Certhia* have been placed in their own family, the Certhiidae, with debate centring upon which of a miscellaneous group of other 'creepers' (including the Spotted Creeper) ought also to be included in this family (see below). The Certhiidae was widely assumed to have a close relationship with the nuthatches Sittidae and tits Paridae, despite differing in many aspects of structure, plumage and behaviour.

Recent DNA-DNA comparisons have indicated that the treecreepers *Certhia* may be members of a large family comprising 22 genera divided into three subfamilies, the wrens Troglodytinae, the gnatcatchers and gnatwrens Polioptilinae (also including the Verdin, see p. 237) and the treecreepers Certhiinae (Sibley & Ahlquist 1990). In this classification, the enlarged family Certhiidae still maintains its place between the Sittidae and the Paridae. I follow this classification here for convenience, but the members of the other subfamilies, the wrens, gnatwrens and gnatcatchers, are not covered by this book.

## Subfamily Certhinae

### Tribe Certhiini: the 'typical' treecreepers

This is a small group of just six species, all of which are very similar. Treecreepers have intricately patterned upperparts in which a combination of black, brown, buff and white markings acts as excellent camouflage, although the rump is contrastingly brighter and more rufous. The feathers are thick, long and soft (quite different from those of nuthatches and Wallcreeper). They have a paler supercilium, and the underparts are whitish, variably washed with grey or buff. The sexes are similar, and juveniles and 1st adults differ only slightly from adults. The bill is long, slender and decurved and the legs rather short, with long toes and strong, long and curved claws. The wings are short and rounded, with ten primaries. The tail is very specialised, being rather long and graduated and with the 12 feathers stiffened and pointed, the shafts projecting from the vane at the tip. The tail is used as a support when climbing, as in woodpeckers. Unlike all other Passerines, in which the tail feathers are moulted from the centre outwards ('centrifugally'), treecreepers retain the central pair until all the others have been replaced. This maintains the usefulness of the tail as a support throughout the moult, and a similar moult strategy is used by woodpeckers.

Treecreepers forage almost exclusively on trees, only occasionally on stone walls and very rarely on the ground. The typical foraging method is to fly to the bottom of a tree, creep jerkily up and around the trunk in a spiral pattern, and then fly to the bottom of the next tree to repeat the performance. They readily work along the underside of branches, but only very rarely creep downwards, head-first. They feed on insects and spiders, and in winter sometimes also on small seeds. Prey items are extracted from the substrate with the fine bill, and, unlike nuthatches, treecreepers do not hack away bark to reveal prey. They do not use their feet to hold prey, and are not known to store food.

The nest is typically placed behind flaps of loose bark, although occasionally in deep crevices in trees or walls, or behind ivy or other dense, tangled vegetation. All treecreepers are quite vocal, but their rather high-pitched and thin calls are often overlooked by bird-watchers. Their songs are either rather fine sweet warbles or cadences, or harder and flatter rattles.

Treecreepers are found throughout the forested regions of Europe and Asia, extending south into the Oriental Region in South-East Asia. One species, the Brown Creeper, breeds in North America and penetrates south into the Neotropical Region in Central America. As with nuthatches, the highest diversity is found in southern Asia, with four species occurring in the Himalayas.

## Tribe Salpornithini: Spotted Creeper

This tribe contains just one species, the Spotted Creeper. Bearing a strong resemblance to treecreepers, its upperparts are cryptically marked with brown and white, with the wings and tail strongly barred and a long pale supercilium. The underparts are whitish, variably tinged buff, and marked with blackish bars or spots. The bill is long, slender and decurved, and the legs are long with partly fused toes and strongly curved claws. The wings are relatively pointed, with ten primaries. The tail is short and slightly rounded and comprises 12 feathers, but, unlike in typical treecreepers, the tail feathers are not stiffened. The sexes are similar, and juveniles are rather similar to adults.

Their foraging methods are similar to those of treecreepers, although their short tail is held clear of the trunk and not used for support. They feed on insects and spiders.

Spotted Creepers build cup-shaped nests which are placed in the open, typically in the fork of a tree where a horizontal branch goes off the main trunk. Like the bird itself, they are beautifully camouflaged. The calls and song are rather high-pitched.

The Spotted Creeper has an unusual distribution, with several disjunct populations in Africa and another population in central India. Although favouring relatively dry forest, its current range is probably a relict of a wider distribution in the past in periods when a more humid climate prevailed and suitable habitat was found across southwest Asia in Pakistan, Iran and Arabia.

The relationships of the Spotted Creeper have long caused debate, and it has sometimes been placed with the Sittidae (e.g. Mayr & Amadon 1951), sometimes with the Certhiidae, and sometimes in its own family, the Salpornithidae or Salpornidae (e.g. Vaurie 1957d). Recent DNA-DNA comparisons show that the Spotted Creeper is the closest relative of *Certhia* (Sibley & Ahlquist 1990), hence its inclusion as the tribe Salpornithini in the sub-family Certhiinae.

## Other unrelated 'creepers'

The 'Certhiidae' has often been enlarged to embrace some other 'creepers', including the three species of Philippine creeper *Rhabdornis* and the seven Australo-Papuan treecreepers of the genera *Climacteris* and *Cormobates*. Even when these have been classified in separate families or subfamilies, they have been placed next to the Certhiidae in the taxonomic sequence. DNA comparisons have shown, however, that the Australo-Papuan treecreepers are members of the Parvorder Corvida, family Climacteridae, and thus only very distantly related to the treecreepers of the tribe Certhiini, their superficial similarity being due to convergent evolution to fill a similar niche (Sibley & Ahlquist 1990). There have been no biochemical studies of the Philippine creepers, and their relationships are very obscure. Indeed, they only superficially resemble a treecreeper and seldom 'creep' (rather, they prefer to loaf on dead snags and branches, perching crosswise, and when foraging walk along branches in the canopy; unlike treecreepers, they are rather gregarious). Probably closest to Babblers Timaliidae, the Philippine creepers are not considered further in this work.

# Family Paridae

The English name 'tit' is an abbreviation of 'titmouse', a Middle English word which can be traced back to at least the 14th century. 'Titmouse' is a combination of *tit*, apparently of onomatopoeic origin, meaning a small animal or object (although 'titmouse' is an older word than 'tit' on its own), and *mose,* an Old English word of obscure origin for a kind of bird (and becoming 'mouse' only as a corruption rather than because of any connection with small mammals). Thus, a 'tit' is simply a 'small bird'.

In terms of scientific nomenclature, the family Paridae is sometimes restricted to include just the 'true' tits in the genera *Parus*, *Sylviparus* and *Melanochlora* (e.g. 'Peters', Voous 1977) and sometimes enlarged to include three subfamilies, the Parinae, the penduline tits Remizinae and the long-tailed tits Aegithalinae (e.g Mayr & Amadon 1951).

The penduline tits are often treated as a distinct family, Remizidae (e.g. Cramp & Perrins 1993, Voous 1977), and placed near to the true tits Paridae or allied with the flowerpeckers Dicaeidae, but biochemical evidence indicates that at least the African penduline tits in the genus *Anthoscopus* are distant from the flowerpeckers and close to the true tits, the two forming subfamilies of the Paridae (DNA data from the 'typical' penduline tits *Remiz* is lacking, but they are probably very close to *Anthoscopus*.) Following Sibley & Ahlquist (1990), the Aegithalidae are maintained here as a separate family.

## Subfamily Remizinae: penduline tits

The Remizinae are a diverse assemblage of *c.* 13 species in five genera, and further research may result in one or more species being shifted to other families. Indeed, the Verdin, here treated as a member of the subfamily Remizinae, is placed by Sibley & Ahlquist (1990) in the subfamily Polioptilinae of the family Certhiidae (see p. 237). Also, the Fire-capped Tit, another species currently placed in Remizinae, has a very distinct plumage pattern and breeding biology, suggesting that it, too, may find a new home.

Reflecting the fact that they are a diverse assemblage, the details of structure, plumage and biology differ among the various genera and they are outlined separately, although the bill is typically short, conical and pointed in all species.

The **'typical' penduline tits** *Remiz* of Europe and northern Asia are found in lowland areas where reeds and bushes form a mosaic, and also in upland regions in riverine willows, poplar plantations etc. Some populations are migratory, and at least two species have undergone major range expansions in recent years. They all have a pale grey head with a variably extensive dark mask (sometimes a hood), chestnut upperparts with blackish wings and tail, and whitish, pink-washed underparts. The sexes are rather similar, but juveniles are very distinct. The post-juvenile moult is partial, incomplete or complete, and 1st adults are often difficult to age. The wing is short and rounded, with ten primaries, and the tail is short and slightly forked, with 12 feathers. The bill is short, conical and sharply pointed, with a straight culmen ridge. The legs and feet are long and strong in European and Black-headed Penduline Tits, but short and slender in White-crowned and Chinese Penduline Tits.

All species feed on insects and other invertebrates, and also on small seeds. Their foraging methods are similar to those of the 'true' tits, but they are even more acrobatic, and able to climb easily along the underside of branches. Unusually, they 'pry' open prey items, inserting the closed bill and then opening the mandibles (like a starling Sturnidae, and unlike the Parinae). The foot is used to hold larger food items 'clamped' against a perch (the item held by the front toes); the food is then eaten piecemeal. Less frequently, they use a foot to 'grasp' prey, holding it in one foot, using all the toes, whilst the standing on the other leg; willow buds may thus be picked off with the bill and then grasped in one foot whilst being picked at with the bill. Another example of their dexterity is the use of one foot to grasp foliage and pull it towards their bill for inspection.

The nest is a ball beautifully constructed from soft materials and often suspended, 'pendulous', from a tree fork, and the European Penduline Tit is known to have a complex mating system. The calls are high-pitched and lisping, but the song is relatively rich and trilling, sometimes almost finch-like.

The **African penduline tits** *Anthoscopus* of sub-Saharan Africa are found in a wide variety of habitats, from tropical evergreen forest to arid thorn-scrub, and members of the genus are sometimes known as the 'kapok tits'. They are occasionally 'lumped' with the genus *Remiz,* but comprise a group of singularly drab tits, typically uniformly coloured above and yellow or whitish below, with no conspicuous plumage features except for a contrastingly patterned or spotted forehead. The sexes are similar, and in all species the juvenile is just a little duller than the adult. The post-juvenile moult is inadequately known for most, but is probably usually incomplete. Structurally, they are close to *Remiz.*

*Anthoscopus* species feed on insects and some fruit, and are agile, but their foraging techniques are poorly known. The nest is a pendent pouch of soft felted material with the entrance to the side. The nests also have 'false entrances', presumably to confuse predators, and, with the dexterity typical of the Remizinae, *Anthoscopus* uses one foot to 'unzip' the real entrance. The calls are high-pitched, and the songs (if indeed they are songs) are usually rhythmic or mechanical, including buzzes and trills.

The **Fire-capped Tit** *Cephalopyrus flammiceps* breeds in southern Asia in moist temperate forest. Some populations, at least, are migratory. The upperparts are yellowish-olive with a yellower rump and the underparts off-white, yellower on the belly. In breeding plumage, the forecrown, chin and throat become reddish-orange in the male, but duller and yellower in the female. The juvenile is rather similar to the non-breeding adult. The wings are relatively pointed, with a minute outermost primary, and the tail is short. The bill is rather spike-like, a slender elongated cone with a sharply pointed tip.

Feeding on insects, buds and possibly pollen and sap, they are acrobatic and hold prey items 'clamped' under one foot whilst dealing with them with the bill; larger insects are opened thus and the contents extracted (as in *Parus*, but they apparently do not break the whole object into bits as do the true tits). As in *Remiz*, they also 'pry' objects open, are able to climb freely along the underside of branches, and will use one foot to grasp foliage and pull it towards the bill. The Fire-capped Tit is, however, highly anomalous in building its nest in a tree hole and in laying dull blue-green eggs. The calls are soft and recall true tits Parinae, and the song is high-pitched and sometimes trilling. The relationships of this species are obscure; its breeding biology is unlike that of any other member of the Remizinae, but its feeding behaviour is similar to that of the penduline tits *Remiz*.

The **Tit-Hylia** *Pholidornis rushiae* is found in the evergreen forests of West and Central Africa. The upperparts are streaked and scalloped brown and dull white, with a yellow rump. The throat and breast are streaked, grading into full yellow underparts. The sexes are similar, differing in eye coloration, but the juvenile is relatively distinct. The bill is slender, pointed and slightly decurved. The species' habits are poorly known, but it hammers at twigs, woodpecker-like, and also flycatches, and appears to have the dexterity typical of the Remizinae. The nest is a domed bag of felted material, with the entrance hole opening downwards to one side; it may be pendent, or wedged among the vegetation. The song is well structured and trilling. The affinities of the Tit-Hylia have long been debated, and it has, at one time or another, been placed in seven different families. DNA comparisons are not available, but several aspects of its behaviour, structure and voice (especially the nest structure) suggest that it is a penduline tit.

The **Verdin** *Auriparus flaviceps* is found in desert scrub in southwest North America. It is grey above and whitish below, with a yellow-olive tone to the head and chestnut lesser coverts. The sexes are very similar, but the juvenile is distinct, as is the 1st adult (in the hand) after the incomplete post-juvenile moult. It feeds on insects, spiders and fruit and, like *Remiz* and Fire-capped Tit, will use one foot to grasp twigs and pull them towards it, and will 'grasp' leaves. Similarly, prey items are 'clamped' under one foot and torn apart with the bill (and as in the Parinae, but unlike Fire-capped Tit, they are *completely* consumed). The nest is a ball of thorny twigs with the entrance to one side, placed near the tip of a low branch in a thorny tree or shrub. The calls are loud and sharp and the song is a repetition of whistled notes. The relationships of the Verdin are disputed, and Sibley & Ahlquist place it in the Certhiidae (see p. 237 for details).

## Subfamily Parinae: 'true' tits

The Parinae includes 57 species divided among three genera. The typical tits of the genus *Parus* account for 55 of these, with two aberrant monospecific genera, the Sultan Tit *Melanochlora sultanea* and Yellow-browed Tit *Sylviparus modestus*.

Despite the size of the genus Parus, it is relatively homogeneous. All of its members are small or medium-small songbirds, varying from the Coal Tit, 110 mm in length and weighing *c.* 10 g, through the Great Tit at 140 mm and *c.* 18 g, to the Tufted Titmouse, a relative giant at 155 mm in length and *c.* 21.5 g. All have a relatively short, pointed bill, often stout and conical, and the legs and feet are short and strong. The wing is short and rounded, with ten primaries, and the tail is typically square or slightly notched, with 12 feathers.

Although there is a tremendous variety of plumage patterns, there are common themes. The upperparts are typically uniform and brown, grey, greenish or bluish, and the wings and tail dark brown or blackish, often with white wingbars and white outer tail feathers. The underparts are whitish, grey, yellow, buff or rufous, and the head is usually contrastingly marked with black and white (often with white cheek patches and a black bib). Some species are crested. The sexes are usually quite similar, but can be distinguished with care in the hand by the overall duller and less glossy appearance of the female. A minority of species show more marked differences between the sexes (e.g. Yellow-bellied, Palawan and Elegant Tits and some of the African black tits). Juveniles are distinct, being duller and often showing a distinct yellow tone to the plumage, with any black markings shown by adults much reduced. 1st adults can usually be aged in the hand after the partial-incomplete post-juvenile moult by careful examination of the wings and tail for moult contrasts.

All tits feed on insects and other invertebrates, supplemented to a greater or lesser extent by seeds and fruits. Very agile, they often hang upside-down, using one foot, or more usually both feet, to cling on. All are versatile and 'clever', and Blue and Great Tits have been recorded using tools held in the bill to obtain hidden food. Otherwise food is always first obtained with the bill, and, in all tits, larger and tougher items are 'clamped' with the feet to a perch (either with one foot or, in the case of larger items, with both feet) and hammered with the bill, the tit breaking off bits to be eaten piecemeal. 'Grasping', in which food is held up in one foot, is rather infrequent (and food is never raised to the bill with the feet). Many tits store food, hiding prey items singly with the bill.

Almost all tits are forest birds, both deciduous and coniferous, lowland and montane, and many have adapted to man-altered habitats and, indeed, they usually form a conspicuous part of the suburban avifauna. Some have, however, adapted to more arid regions, such as semi-desert scrub in southern Africa and the harsh Tibetan Plateau. Tits are found throughout the forested regions of Europe, Asia, North America and Africa, extending south to the islands of Indonesia and to southern Mexico. In Europe, Great and Blue Tits are abundant birds, but in other regions tits are not so numerous. Most species are resident, but some northern breeders are migratory or undertake irregular 'irruptive' movements, and most montane breeders descend to lower altitudes in winter. Specialist adaptations, both behavioural and morphological, allow some to tolerate extremes of cold.

All tits nest in cavities, usually in trees, but sometimes in stone walls or among the roots of trees. One species, the White-browed Tit, uses rodent holes in the ground. Some will excavate their own holes in rotten wood, and many take readily to nestboxes. The cavity is filled with a mass of soft material, often moss, upon which the lining is placed; many species will reduce the size of very big cavities by filling them with a mass of nesting material. Incubating females often react to disturbance on the nest by emitting a loud hiss, snapping the bill closed and knocking their wings against the sides of the cavity. Most tits have a wide repertoire of loud calls, often used in complex combinations, and also distinct songs, but these are usually rather simple stereotyped *repetitions* of notes or groups of notes or motifs (exceptions include Blue and Rufous-naped Tits); this simple song construction is unusual among the Passerines.

The allocation of its various members to the genus *Parus* has been straightforward, and there is little or no debate as to what is a tit and what is not (as any birdwatcher can testify). Debate has usually centred upon how the various peripheral groups (penduline tits, long-tailed tits, nuthatches etc.) are related to the *Parus* core.

Although a very homogeneous group, there are several distinct subgroups within *Parus*, and in other groups of Passerines such subgroups have often been treated as distinct genera (e.g. the small chats *Luscinia*). Recent biochemical studies have supported the elevation of at least some of the subgenera to the status of a full genus, and in recognition of these sugroups I have followed the division of the genus *Parus* into the following ten subgenera (roughly following Thielcke 1968):

**Subgenus *Poecile*** A group of 15 black- or brown-capped species comprising Marsh and Willow Tits and their allies. Relatively dull; many excavate their own nest holes. Most have complex 'chick-a-dee' calls (the North American members of this group are known as 'chickadees').

**Subgenus *Periparus*** Coal Tit and its allies, comprising four species.

**Subgenus *Pardaliparus*** Three species from China and the Philippines, characterised by marked sexual dimorphism. Probably close to *Periparus*.

**Subgenus *Lophophanes*** The two crested tits of northern Eurasia.

**Subgenus *Melaniparus*** A hotchpotch of all 15 African tits, this group may be better divided into four (the black tits, Dusky Tit, Rufous-bellied Tit and its allies, and the grey tits).

**Subgenus *Parus*** Includes the Great Tit and its allies, totalling six species. Unlike all other tits (except subgenus *Cyanistes*), they do not, as far as is known, store food.

**Subgenus *Machlolophus*** Containing just one species, Yellow Tit, whose affinities are obscure.

**Subgenus *Cyanistes*** Comprising the three species of the Blue Tit complex. Like subgenus *Parus*, they do not store food, and the two subgenera could well be combined.

**Subgenus *Sittiparus*** Two Far-Eastern tits united by the possession of a long bill and white forehead.

**Subgenus *Baeolophus*** Includes the four North American crested tits, all known as 'titmouse'. Perhaps the best candidate on the basis of present knowledge for treatment as a separate genus, *Baeolophus*.

The two odd-ones-out in the subfamily Parinae are both found in the Oriental Region. The Yellow-browed Tit is a dull olive species with no conspicuous plumage features (recalling a warbler); it is sometimes considered to represent a 'primitive' stage in the evolution of the genus *Parus*. The large and gaudy Sultan Tit, although clearly a tit, has no obvious affinities. Both are hole nesters and appear to be typical tits in all known aspects of their biology.

# Family Aegithalidae: long-tailed tits

This family comprises eight species in three genera, *Aegithalos, Psaltriparus* and *Psaltria*. All three genera are very similar and they can be considered together (although the correct placement of the Pygmy Tit *Psaltria exilis* is still open to question).

Long-tailed tits are typically very small, with very short wings and, as the name suggests, disproportionately long tails. The bill is short, conical and altogether stubby, and the legs are long and slender. The contour feathers are rather loose, giving these birds the appearance of tiny balls of fluff. Often the eyes are contrastingly pale, and some have vividly coloured eyerings. Most species are grey or brown above, sometimes tinged pink, with a white rim to the tail and prominent black and white markings on the head. The underparts are white, often with a black or brown bib or collar and a tinge of pink or buff on the flanks. The sexes are similar, but juveniles are distinct, although they undergo a complete post-juvenile moult (unusual among temperate-zone passerines), and 1st adults are identical to adults.

They feed on insects and other small invertebrates, and they are very acrobatic, often gleaning from the terminal branches of shrubs and trees, hanging from one or both feet. They may use one foot to 'grasp' food (see above) while hanging upside-down from the other foot, the bill being lowered to the prey item (rather than the foot lifting the food to the bill). They are not known to store food.

Typically, long-tailed tits live in small groups which defend group territories. The nest is an intricate ball constructed from soft material, with the entrance to one side near the top. Although pairs are monogamous, there is a tendency towards cooperative breeding, with 'helpers' (probably members of the winter flock) assisting the breeding pair. Rather vocal, group members keep contact with a variety of notes, often soft, clipped monosyllables and short silvery trills. At best however, the song is a rambling amalgamation of the calls.

The Bushtit *Psaltriparus minimus* breeds across the southwest USA and through Central America to Guatemala, whilst the typical long-tailed tits of the genus *Aegithalos* are distributed across Europe and Asia, extending into the Oriental Region in China and South-East Asia. In a distributional quirk, the enigmatic Pygmy Tit is confined to Java. All species are highly sedentary and, as with all the families covered here, long-tailed tits reach their greatest diversity in the Himalayas and western China.

At various times the Aegithalidae have been treated as a subfamily of the Paridae, but it has frequently been noted that long-tailed tits differ significantly from the 'true' tits in several important aspects, including their nest structure and complete post-juvenile moult, and in certain structural details. DNA-DNA comparisons have confirmed that the Aegithalidae are rather distinct from the Paridae, hence their treatment as a distinct family. There are, however, some structural, biochemical and behavioural similarities with the babblers Timaliidae (especially the parrotbills), and there may yet be changes to the classification of this intriguing group.

# PLUMAGES AND TOPOGRAPHY

The following terminology has been followed (the equivalents in the Humphrey/Parkes system, widely used in America, are given in parentheses):

## Plumages
**Juvenile** The first plumage worn after fledging (Humphrey/Parkes equivalent: 'Juvenal').
**1st adult** The plumage worn following the post-juvenile moult ('1st adult' is preferred to the more frequently used 'first winter', as many of our species breed in the tropics and several in the Southern Hemisphere, where seasons do not correspond with those in the north) (Humphrey/Parkes equivalent: 'First Basic').
**Adult** The plumage that, once attained, does not change with age (Humphrey/Parkes equivalent: 'Definitive'). Almost no tits, nuthatches or treecreepers have distinct breeding and non-breeding plumages, but 'Breeding' and 'Non-breeding' are added in the few cases where this is appropriate (Humphrey/Parkes equivalents: 'Alternate' and 'Basic').

## Moults
**Post-juvenile** The moult from juvenile to 1st-adult plumage (Humphrey/Parkes equivalent: 'First Pre-Basic'). This is usually partial in our species.
**Adult pre-breeding** The moult from non-breeding or 'winter' plumage to breeding or 'summer' plumage (Humphrey/Parkes equivalent: 'Pre-Alternate'). This moult is rather infrequent among our species.
**Adult post-breeding** The moult after the breeding season. This is complete in all our species (Humphrey/Parkes equivalent: 'Pre-Basic').

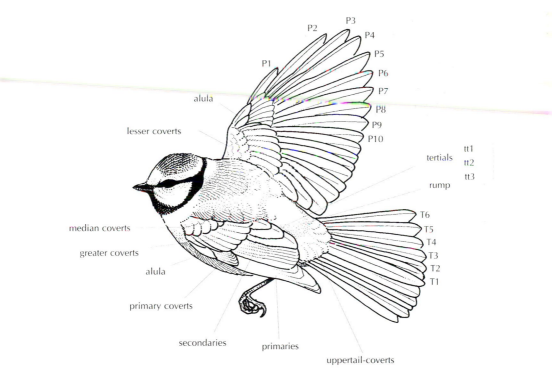

23

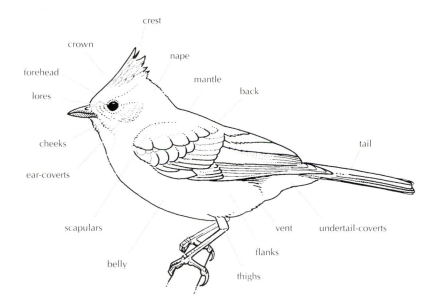

crest

crown

forehead

lores

nape

mantle

back

cheeks

ear-coverts

tail

scapulars

vent

undertail-coverts

flanks

belly

thighs

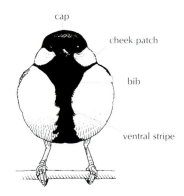

cap

cheek patch

bib

ventral stripe

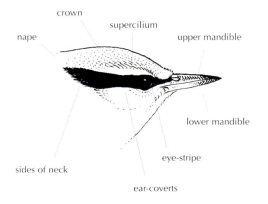

crown

supercilium

nape

upper mandible

lower mandible

sides of neck

eye-stripe

ear-coverts

# NOTES ON THE SPECIES ACCOUNTS

The sequence of species follows Sibley & Monroe (1990), with additional 'splits' being inserted as appropriate. This sequence is followed purely for convenience, as this is the most up-to-date world checklist.

The accounts are headed with the preferred **English name** for the species. Whilst most species in Europe and North America have well-established English names, those in Africa and Asia often labour under several aliases, many rather cumbersome or confusingly similar. I have attempted to choose the best and most appropriate of the existing names and, for those species which have recently been 'split', have generally followed Sibley & Monroe (1990, 1993). Under the heading '**Other names**' we list alternative English names as used in regional handbooks or field guides, but the plethora of names recently proposed in various world checklists is *not* included.

The English name is followed by the **scientific name**. Full citations for the scientific name, with author, date and place of publication, and type locality are not included. These can be found, together with a complete list of synonyms (essential in any nomenclatural research), in 'Peters' (Paynter 1967). A few names were omitted in error from 'Peters' or have been proposed since its publication; in these cases, the author and date of publication are included in the main text, whilst the full reference can be found in the Bibliography.

Each species is given a number, allowing easier cross-referencing between the plates and the text. These are purely for the purposes of this book, and have no other function.

## Identification

This section starts with a measurement of overall length, but it should be noted that this is somewhat arbitrary and is a guide only. The figure is in millimetres (mm), followed by the approximate equivalent in inches (in). A brief description of the species is then given, followed by a discussion of the important identification features, if necessary including mention of vocal characteristics. Likely confusion species are also highlighted.

## Sex/Age

The differences between males and females and between juveniles and adults are summarised here; this is not a repetition of the information given under Description, but rather a synthesis of the important points. Some general points apply to juveniles of all species. In the hand, they often have looser and more 'fluffy' plumage, especially the undertail-coverts. They may appear 'blotchy', especially on the mantle, neck and underparts, where the weaker and looser contour feathering does not form a uniformly opaque covering over the dark underdown. Their tail feathers and primary coverts may be a little narrower and more pointed than an adult's (and their primary coverts a little duller), and, when very recently fledged, juveniles show yellow gape flanges which may be visible in the field. Considerable space is also given to the ageing of 1st-adult birds, which is generally possible only in the hand. Where juveniles undergo a complete post-juvenile moult, 1st adults are indistinguishable from adults; but, where this moult is only partial or incomplete, ageing may be possible, using the contrast in the wing between the old juvenile feathers, which are usually duller and, being weaker, wear and fade more quickly, and the newer, brighter and stronger 1st-adult feathers. Similar contrasts may sometimes be shown in the tail, but these are usually more difficult to perceive. (For further information on the specialised techniques of in-the-hand ageing and sexing, such as the presence or absence of a brood patch, cloacal protuberance or skull ossification, see Jenni & Winkler 1994, Pyle *et al.* 1987 and Svensson 1992.)

It is important to remember, when considering sex and age variation (and also geographical variation), that every bird is an individual and that there will always be a certain amount of individual variation. Whilst most will 'fit' into a particular age or sex category, some may not, and these are better left unsexed or unaged (rather than forcing a square peg into a round hole).

## Voice

A range of calls is described first, and then the song. In most passerine birds, the song is more complex than the calls and is used in territorial advertisement and pair formation. In many tits, however, perhaps especially the chickadees (subgenus *Poecile*), this division is often not clear-cut. Some have rather simple songs, used to advertise their territory, but in other situations, often aggressive encounters with members of their own species, use groups of calls that are structurally far *more* complex

This was one of the most difficult sections (if not *the* most difficult) to write, and may not be easy for the reader to understand fully. The verbal description of bird sounds will never be satisfactory, especially when the vocalisations are complex, as in most of the tits. After

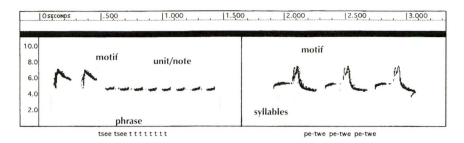

Two examples of sonagrams. The left-hand figure represents a song phrase given by a Blue Tit (with a verbal transcription below); on the right, a song phrase from a Coal Tit (both recorded in Norfolk, England by Simon Harrap). Such graphical representations are near-essential in the analysis of vocalisations, but can seldom convey what the bird actually sounds like.

careful thought, I decided not to use sonagrams for more than just a handful of species. These are graphic representations of bird sounds (see figure above), and for all but specialists, are virtually meaningless. I have attempted to produce consistent verbal descriptions for all species based on a careful analysis of tape recordings (obtained for all but Beautiful Nuthatch, Black-headed Penduline Tit, Cinnamon-breasted Tit and White-throated Tit). No two works on bird vocalisations use the same terminology, but the following terms (adapted from Cramp (ed) 1988) have generally been used (see also figure below):

* **motif** a short succession of sounds that produces a continuous or near-continuous trace on a sonagram, usually changing appreciably in frequency; generally more complex than a note or unit, but similarly combined with other motifs or units to form a phrase.
* **note** generally a rather looser term used to indicate shorter, simple utterances; may be interchangeable with 'unit'.
* **phrase** a combination of motifs and/or units to form a distinct utterance, separated from other phrases by an appreciable time gap (alternatively, a 'song phrase'); generally combined with other phrases to form a complete 'song'.
* **repertoire** the total vocabulary of an individual, but often confined to the song; thus, the song repertoire comprises all the different song phrases given by that individual.
* **sonagram** an abbreviated term for a sound spectrogram, in which the sound frequency of the vocalisation is plotted against time, and the loudness or intensity of the sound is shown by the depth of the shading (the darker and more solid the trace, the louder and more powerful the sound).
* **song** the sum total of all phrases or other utterances given in a particular bout of singing; generally has a recognisable pattern unique to a particular species and, in tits, unique to a population or even to an individual. Properly, the term 'song' is applied only to those vocalisations used in territorial advertisement, and this function is sometimes hard to define among the tits and nuthatches.
* **syllable** a subdivision of a motif.
* **unit** a simple discrete subdivision of a motif or phrase, generally not changing appreciably in pitch.

## Distribution and movements

A detailed account of the range is given. Each country is emboldened for easy reference, as often are also the major regions, provinces or states of the larger political units. These accounts supplement and amplify the information given on the maps which face the colour plates. As most tits, nuthatches and treecreepers are resident and non-migratory, their ranges often have precise limits. The information presented here should enable the observer to decide whether a particular species is likely in an area and hence to gauge the significance of any observations. Note that the Distribution and Movements section should always be read in conjunction with Geographical Variation if the finer details of distribution are required, as the precise limits of range may sometimes be given under the appropriate subspecies. Only references for the most significant, new or controversial data are cited, so as not to burden the text with references. Throughout, National Park is abbreviated NP.

Throughout, I have attempted to use names (and spellings) found in the *Times Atlas of the World. Comprehensive Edition (7th)*. Some alternatives may be given in parentheses, and geographical coordinates may be given for localities not easily traced.

Details of any known migrations are given, with dates of occurrence, propensity to cross water etc., and records of vagrants are listed by country.

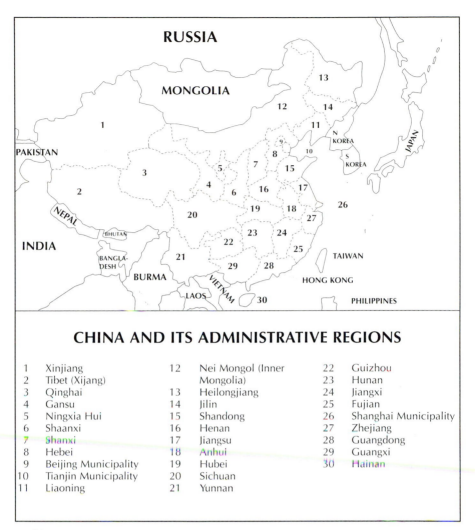

## CHINA AND ITS ADMINISTRATIVE REGIONS

| | | | | | |
|---|---|---|---|---|---|
| 1 | Xinjiang | 12 | Nei Mongol (Inner | 22 | Guizhou |
| 2 | Tibet (Xijang) | | Mongolia) | 23 | Hunan |
| 3 | Qinghai | 13 | Heilongjiang | 24 | Jiangxi |
| 4 | Gansu | 14 | Jilin | 25 | Fujian |
| 5 | Ningxia Hui | 15 | Shandong | 26 | Shanghai Municipality |
| 6 | Shaanxi | 16 | Henan | 27 | Zhejiang |
| 7 | Shanxi | 17 | Jiangsu | 28 | Guangdong |
| 8 | Hebei | 18 | Anhui | 29 | Guangxi |
| 9 | Beijing Municipality | 19 | Hubei | 30 | Hainan |
| 10 | Tianjin Municipality | 20 | Sichuan | | |
| 11 | Liaoning | 21 | Yunnan | | |

## Habitat

An attempt has been made to give accurate descriptions of habitat requirements, which are taken from the literature tempered with personal experience. Scientific names for all plants mentioned are given in Appendix B. Altitudinal range is given special attention, as this is of crucial importance for understanding the distribution of many species.

## Population

Gives an indication of abundance, any changes or trends, and conservation status if appropriate, using the categories adopted by BirdLife International. Any statement on abundance is, however, very subjective. Thus, in European field guides the Blue Tit is often described as 'common', whilst in southern African guides the Southern Grey Tit is also 'common', yet in objective terms Blue Tits are many times more abundant than Southern Grey Tits, and the probabilities of finding one when birdwatching in suitable habitat are very different. An attempt has been made to use a more or less uniform terminology, and this has been easiest for North American species, for which the terms used in DeSante & Pyle (1986) have been used throughout.

## Habits

A summary of social behaviour, territoriality, roosting habits, food and foraging is given. These are of varying length, and serve to highlight gaps in our knowledge. Little or no information is given on displays, however, either sexual or territorial, dominance etc. This is

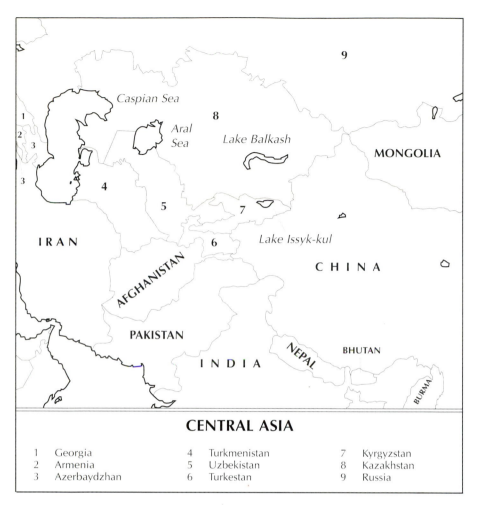

## CENTRAL ASIA

| 1 | Georgia | 4 | Turkmenistan | 7 | Kyrgyzstan |
| 2 | Armenia | 5 | Uzbekistan | 8 | Kazakhstan |
| 3 | Azerbaydzhan | 6 | Turkestan | 9 | Russia |

because different terminologies have been used by various researchers, and a concise and understandable verbal summary is difficult or impossible to achieve.

## Breeding Biology

Gives a summary of breeding behaviour in a standard format, and aims to highlight gaps in published information. The 'season' indicates the months during which egg-laying has been recorded. By extrapolating forwards, the periods during which incubation, feeding of young, fledging and juvenile dispersal take place may the be calculated. Details of the site and of materials used in nest construction are also given, with the height in metres (m) above ground that nests have been found; if a larger range is given in parentheses, this refers to rarer or more exceptional records. Similarly, clutch size is given, occasionally qualified geographically, and a figure in parentheses indicates less frequent values. Egg descriptions are summaries taken from the literature, as are egg dimensions, which are mean length and width in millimetres (mm); the subspecies concerned may be given.

## Description

If the species is polytypic, the name of the subspecies to be described is given (it is not necessarily the nominate subspecies, as this may not be the most widespread or 'typical', or sometimes a better range of specimens may have been available for the race described). The description of the **Adult Male** is given first, with, where possible, an indication of when *fresh plumage* may be expected. At the end of the description is a summary of any differences in *worn plumage* (together with dates to be expected). The description of the **Adult Female** follows the same patterns as for the male, although concentrating on the differences, as do those of the **Juvenile**, **1st Adult Male** and **1st Adult Female** (but, when these are very different from the adult male, they are described in full).

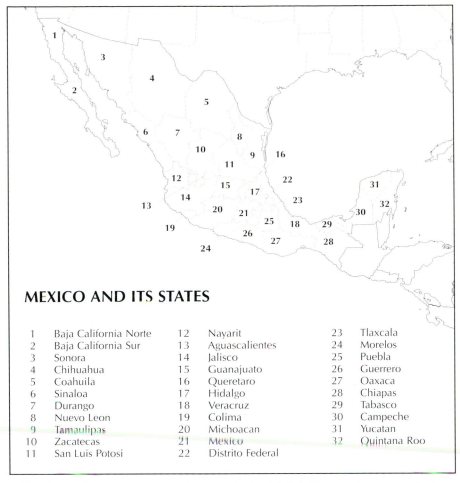

# MEXICO AND ITS STATES

| | | | | | | |
|---|---|---|---|---|---|---|
| 1 | Baja California Norte | 12 | Nayarit | 23 | Tlaxcala |
| 2 | Baja California Sur | 13 | Aguascalientes | 24 | Morelos |
| 3 | Sonora | 14 | Jalisco | 25 | Puebla |
| 4 | Chihuahua | 15 | Guanajuato | 26 | Guerrero |
| 5 | Coahuila | 16 | Queretaro | 27 | Oaxaca |
| 6 | Sinaloa | 17 | Hidalgo | 28 | Chiapas |
| 7 | Durango | 18 | Veracruz | 29 | Tabasco |
| 8 | Nuevo Leon | 19 | Colima | 30 | Campeche |
| 9 | Tamaulipas | 20 | Michoacan | 31 | Yucatan |
| 10 | Zacatecas | 21 | Mexico | 32 | Quintana Roo |
| 11 | San Luis Potosi | 22 | Distrito Federal | | |

The descriptions of every species (except Algerian Nuthatch) were taken personally from specimens. In some cases, an initial description was summarised from the literature (notably *BWP:* Cramp & Perrins 1993), but this was always controlled and duly modified after a careful examination of specimens. To achieve consistency, the *Naturalist's Color Guide* (Smithe 1975) was used as a colour standard, although the nomenclature used in this guide has not been followed, as it is largely meaningless without reference to the colour charts ('Paris Green', 'Smalt Blue' and 'Spinel Pink' are just some of the names used by Smithe). I have nevertheless attempted to use the same colour terms throughout, most of which should be self-explanatory, but some of which demand explanation:

* **buff** is the colour of a manila envelope or a clean chamois leather;
* **chestnut** is brown tinged with red (slightly darker and browner than rufous);
* **cinnamon** is the colour of raw cinnamon sticks (not ground cinnamon);
* **cream** is the colour of full cream, i.e. distinctly yellowish;
* **drab** is a dull light brown, tinged greyish-pink (in fashion terminology, 'taupe' is close in coloration);
* **flesh** is the colour of raw salmon flesh (and *not* of human skin);
* **grey** comes in various shades, and following Smithe (1975) these proceed from the darkest, 'blackish-grey', through 'dark grey', 'mid grey' and 'light grey' to 'pale grey';
* **olive** is the colour of a green olive, hence essentially dull green with a hint of grey, rather than any shade of brown;
* **rufous** is red tinged with brown;
* **vinaceous** is the colour of red wine, or, more specifically, of red wine when spilled on to a white cloth.

In compound colours, the dominant colour is placed last. Thus, 'greenish-brown' is browner than 'brownish-green'.

Unless otherwise indicated, 'crown' includes the forehead, 'throat' includes the chin, 'greater', 'median' and 'lesser coverts' refer to the greater, median and lesser secondary coverts respectively, and 'primary coverts' refers to the greater primary coverts.

Throughout the text, the **primaries** are numbered 'ascendently', i.e. from the outside of the wing towards the body, P1 being the outer and P10 being the innermost. All the species treated in this book have ten primaries (although the outermost, P1, may be rather small, and the innermost, P10, may be similar in size and shape to the secondaries). The secondaries are occasionally numbered, ascendently (ss1 to ss6), and the tertials are sometimes numbered, too, from the innermost, tt1, to the outermost (and longest), tt3. The tail feathers are numbered by pairs centrifugally, from the centre pair, T1, to the outermost, T6 (all tits, nuthatches and treecreepers have 12 tail feathers in total).

The coloration of the **Bare Parts** is given in the sequence of iris, bill, legs, feet and, if appropriate, claws. These are taken from the literature and from specimen labels. An attempt has been made to rationalise the description of bare-part coloration, rather than merely repeating a long list of variant descriptions. This often requires an educated guess as to what the author of a specimen label or textbook meant by, for example, 'horn-brown' or 'plumbeous-blue'. When recently fledged, juveniles of all species typically show traces of yellow gape flanges, so this has not been mentioned in the individual species accounts.

**Measurements** gives details of the measurements of the form described. All linear measurements are in millimetres (mm). They are taken from the literature, notably Cramp & Perrins (1993), Vaurie (1950a,b, 1957a,b,c,d, 1959, 1972) and Svensson (1992), as well as from many museum specimens measured personally (using the methods detailed below). This introduces several problems:

1. Even using the same techniques, different individuals may record slightly different measurements from the same specimen.
2. A variety of slightly differing techniques is used to measure specimens (e.g. the wing may be measured flattened or unflattened). In many publications, the method used is not specified.
3. Specimens shrink very slightly over time, especially in the wings and tail (museum specimens are c. 2–3 % smaller in wing length than living birds; most of the measurements refer to museum specimens).
4. Sample sizes are very variable, from just one individual to several hundred birds.

In view of the variety of sources, it would be misleading to attach too much precision to the figures and, with a few exceptions, only the range, from the lowest to the highest figure, is given (e.g. 75–90, 16.2–18). If the measurements from only one or two individuals are available, they are given separately.

Even simple statistical analysis (mean, standard deviation, significance tests) would be misleading when applied to such heterogenous material. Assuming that the range of variation shows a normal distribution, however, the mean, median and mode will all have the same value. Thus, the middle of the given range should approximate to the mean (or average) figure, this being increasingly probable as the sample size increases.

**Wing** is the distance between the carpal joint and the tip of the longest primary with the wing *flattened* and *straightened*. For some North American species a value is also given for the unflattened wing or minimum chord ('chord'); this method is favoured in America, and most measurements in the literature on American birds are taken using this method (but note that, when measurements are given as chord, these are taken from the literature and *do not refer* to the same sample of birds as the basic set of measurements, and hence the two values may not correspond closely). If the information is available, wing measurements are given separately for male and female, and all are rounded to the nearest 0.5 mm (in some cases a range for male and female combined may also be given; this may be greater than the range for the individual sexes, reflecting a different source). Wing lengths are perhaps the most reliable and reproducible measurements taken from birds, either living or specimens.

**Tail** measurements are also given separately for male and female, and are rounded to the nearest 0.5 mm. As with the wing, several different methods are used to measure tails, and details are very seldom given in published sources. For those measurements taken personally (from specimens), the method employed was to insert the point of the pair of dividers between the shafts of the central tail feathers and push it gently to their base, then measuring the distance to the tip of the longest feather. Even with care, tail measurements are less reproducible than wing lengths and should be treated with a certain amount of caution.

**Bill** measurements are given to the nearest 0.1 mm and the sexes are combined (any differences between the sexes are usually small and are swamped by the varied source material being used). Again, a variety of methods may be used, with the bill being measured to either the *nostrils* (assumed to be distal edge, but often unspecified), the *feathering* or the *skull*. I use the bill length as measured to the skull with a pair of dial callipers (occasionally other methods are used, and this is specified). Despite the impression sometimes given by rows of tables and complex statistical analysis, bill measurements of very small passerines such as tits are difficult to make with precision.

**Tarsus** measurements are given to the nearest 0.1 mm and the sexes are combined. The tarsus is measured from the notch on the back of the intertarsal joint to the lower edge of the last complete scale before the toes divide.

**Weight** is given in grams (g) and combines the sexes. The data come from a variety of published sources and, although (given an accurate balance) they are less open to variation, the weight of a bird varies both through the day and from season to season. If figures are not available for the form described, another race may be substituted, and this is indicated.

## Moult

Details of the moult regime of each species are given under this heading. In every species, the **Adult post-breeding** moult is 'complete', and every feather is shed and replaced. The primaries are moulted 'descendently', the innermost (P10) being shed and replaced first and the outermost (P1) last. This moult (as measured by the duration of the primary moult) typically lasts 65–90 days.

The **Adult pre-breeding** moult, if present, is 'partial', and is associated with those species which have a distinctive breeding plumage (hence it is well documented for Wallcreeper). Conversely, it may be difficult to detect where there is no seasonal difference in plumage pattern. It usually involves the replacement of a limited number of body feathers, usually the cheeks, throat and/or the breast, and occasionally a few feathers of the upperparts. A pre-breeding moult is absent in all of the well-studied typical tits Parinae in the Western Palearctic and North America, but may well occur in some species from Asia or Africa (e.g. White-naped Tit). Otherwise, it is recorded for some nuthatches, Wallcreeper, occasionally Bushtit and possibly European Penduline Tit. Information on this moult is usually scant, and for most species it is impossible to give any information at all; even the existence or not of a pre-breeding moult may be uncertain. Similarly, the **First pre-breeding** moult, which would normally occur in the second calendar-year, is obscure. Unless adult pre-breeding or first pre-breeding moults are specifically mentioned, no information is available on either their presence or their absence.

The **Post-juvenile** moult is the most variable moult regime, and a clear understanding of this moult is an essential first step in the ageing of many birds. The post-juvenile moult may be complete (i.e. as the adult post-breeding) or partial, in which only the body feathers, lesser and median coverts, and sometimes some or all of the alula, greater coverts, tertials and tail feathers are replaced. In a few species, it may be more extensive, and such 'incomplete' moults involve the replacement of some of the flight feathers (usually some secondaries); incomplete moults appear to be more frequent among species living in tropical or subtropical environments. If the post-juvenile moult is partial or incomplete, 1st adults will usually show 'moult contrasts' in the wings or tail between the older, retained juvenile feathers and the younger, fresher 1st-adult feathers.

For each moult, the dates in parentheses indicate the period when it has been recorded, qualified in some cases by a geographic location (as dates may vary from place to place).

## Geographical Variation

All subspecies recognised in this work, together with details of their range and how they differ from one-another, are listed. For those named since the publication of 'Peters', or omitted from 'Peters' in error, the author and date of publication are included, which will lead to the full citation for the work in the References. The range of each form may be given precisely, or may refer merely to a region of a state or country if this is all that is necessary to delineate it from other races (full details of the range will then be given under Distribution and Movements). Some measurements are also given, generally the wing and tail lengths, but also sometimes the bill and tarsus if these vary significantly; these measurements are usually taken from the literature.

An attempt has been made to assess, by the examination of specimens, the validity of all the subspecies listed and to apply uniform standards in deciding which to recognise. This has not, however, been achieved. Specimens of some races have not been available, and for many others only very limited material has been examined. I have therefore had to rely heavily on the literature, and for Palearctic birds Vaurie's *Birds of the Palearctic Fauna* (1959) has proved invaluable, whilst for North American species Phillips's *Known Birds of North and Middle America* (1986) has also been extremely useful. It has become clear in the course of this work that many named races are based on differences that are barely perceptible, even in the museum, this being especially true of North American birds. In contrast to the treatment at the species level, I have tended to suppress or 'lump' subspecies wherever this seemed reasonable. Some of these are still mentioned briefly, and their name placed in inverted commas.

## Hybrids

Where appropriate, mention is made of any known hybrids, their prevalence and appearance. Hybrids are unknown among the nuthatches (and probably also the treecreepers). They are also rare among the tits, with the exception of Blue and Azure Tits and species such as Tufted and Black-crested Titmice, Black-capped and Carolina Chickadees and Coal and Spot-winged Tits, where the existence of a permanent hybrid zone has continually thrown doubt on their status as distinct species.

## Relationships

The relationships of the species are discussed, with reference to any subgenus or super-species as appropriate. As a number of the species in this book have more usually been 'lumped', that is treated merely as subspecies or subspecies groups belonging to another species, these cases are discussed in some detail. The significance of any instance of regular hybridisation (as detailed under Hybrids) is also given particular mention.

## References

This lists the major references used in the preparation of the species account. It does not list every reference used, but rather those from which the bulk of the source material was taken.

# NOTES ON THE COLOUR PLATES, CAPTIONS AND MAPS

## Plates

All 110 species of tits, nuthatches and treecreepers are illustrated in colour. Where there are significant differences between males and females, adults and juveniles, and the various subspecies, these are illustrated separately. The colour plates have been carefully prepared, using field sketches, photographs and museum specimens as reference material. Of the 110 species illustrated, we were able to examine specimens of all but one, the recently described Algerian Nuthatch, for which photographs form the major reference.

All the birds on the plates are adults in fresh plumage unless specified in the caption.

All the major figures on each plate are to scale. Occasionally, additional minor figures have been inserted, and these are obviously not to scale.

## Captions

These give a very brief outline of the species' range (and that of the subspecies, if appropriate). The main features separating each species from any similar tit, nuthatch or treecreeper are highlighted, as are the distinguishing features of females, juveniles and any races illustrated. In most cases, reference to the text is recommended, as, for reasons of space, only essential details can be given in the caption.

## Maps

Each species has a range map (some have more than one map). The maps include national boundaries and, for larger political units (such as the USA) state boundaries. Owing to the small scale of the map, they should, however, be perused in conjunction with the Distribution and Movements sections in the main text.

On the maps, the areas where the species can be found year-round are indicated in **green**. In these regions the species is normally resident, but in a few cases the local breeders may move south, to be replaced by migrants from further north. Some species breed at high altitudes and winter at lower levels, but these seasonal movements cannot be indicated on the maps. A dashed green line indicates the southern limit of sporadic breeding. A solid green or magenta line may be used to enclose a number of isolated breeding localities (e.g. small islands or the scattered known colonies of Chinese Penduline Tit).

Areas to which the species is a summer visitor only are indicated in **red/magenta**.

Areas where it is found only outside the breeding season (i.e. usually winter) are shown in **orange-yellow**. For some irruptive species, the extreme southern limits of winter wanderings are indicated by a broken orange-yellow line.

Green, yellow or magenta **arrows** are used to highlight the smaller areas of distribution (which may not be obvious owing to the scale of the maps), or regions where the range just creeps across a political border. Black arrows are used to indicate migration routes, and black **stars** are used to indicate isolated records of wanderers or vagrants.

Within the given range, the species may be sparsely, locally or abundantly distributed. Reference to the Population section in the main text is recommended.

# PLATES 1–36

PLATE 1    EURASIAN NUTHATCH

# 1  Eurasian Nuthatch *Sitta europaea*          **Text page 109**

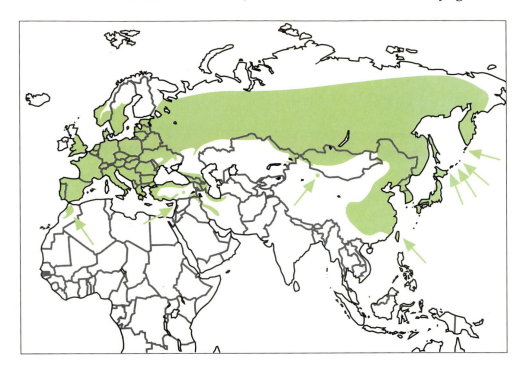

Distinctive over most of the range, but in SE Europe and SW Asia may be confused with the rock nuthatches, but note Eurasian's prominent white tail spots. A more difficult problem is separation from Chestnut-vented in SW China.

**S. e. caesia** Britain and western and southern Europe.

a  **Male**: Chin whitish, cheeks, ear-coverts and throat white, tinged buff, merging into dull orange-buff underparts; flanks and rear vent brick-red, undertail-coverts whitish, broadly fringed brick-red.

b  **Female**: Eyestripe slightly browner and less well defined; flanks etc. rufous-orange, showing reduced contrast with breast and belly.

c  **Male**: In flight from below and above. Note blackish under primary coverts.

**S. e. persica** SW Iran.

d  **Male**: Rather pale, with white forehead and supercilium; throat white, remainder of underparts creamy, tinged orange-buff.

**S. e. europaea** Scandinavia and northern Europe.

e  **Male**: Underparts whitish, flanks etc. extensively chestnut.

f  **Female**: Underparts faintly washed buff, flanks etc. relatively pale, more rufous-buff.

**S. e. asiatica** NE Europe, Siberia and northern Japan.

g  **Male**: Rather smaller, with fine, sharply pointed bill. Upperparts pale, forehead and supercilium often white, greater coverts tipped white when fresh; underparts pure white, with paler and more restricted flank patch.

**S. e. bedfordi** Cheju island, Korea.

h  **Male**: White throat and breast well demarcated from orange-buff belly.

**S. e. sinensis** Central and eastern China. For separation from Chestnut-vented Nuthatch see text (p.114).

i  **Adult**: In fresh plumage coloration as *S. e. caesia*, but ear-coverts cinnamon-buff, concolorous with underparts, only chin and cheeks whitish.

j  **Adult**: In worn plumage underparts duller, may show a faint drab-grey wash.

PLATE 2    LARGER ORIENTAL NUTHATCHES 1

## 4  Chestnut-bellied Nuthatch  *Sitta castanea*          **Text page 119**

Relatively well-defined white cheek patches, richly coloured underparts, lacking contrast between flanks and belly, and scalloped undertail-coverts distinctive. Three groups of subspecies.

**The plains group** *S. c. castanea* Northern and central India, also Western Ghats of peninsular India. Small, with short, slender bill. **a Male**: Crown and nape generally paler than mantle, black eyestripe expands broadly at rear. Underparts brick-red, undertail-coverts centred mid grey. **b Female**: Underparts dull beige; undertail-coverts fringed pinkish-cinnamon.

**The foothills group** Four rather similar races in foothills of Himalayas, NE India, SE Yunnan, NW Vietnam, and Doi Hua Mot, Thailand. Large, with long, deep, broadly tipped bill. Crown only marginally paler than mantle; underparts slightly paler and more orange than nominate *castanea*, undertail-coverts grey to slaty-black with broad white subterminal band and fine chestnut fringes. *S. c. cinnamoventris* Eastern Himalayas, NE India, NE Burma, western Yunnan and (formerly?) Bangladesh. **c Male**: Underparts chestnut-brown (darkest in group). *S. c. koelzi* SE Arunachal Pradesh, Nagaland and north Cachar (Assam). **d Female**: Underparts pinkish-cinnamon, marginally darkest and pinkest of females in group, cheeks and sides of throat speckled blackish.

**The *neglecta* group** *S. c. neglecta* Lowlands of Burma, Thailand, Laos, Cambodia and southern Vietnam. Relatively small and slender-billed, with reduced dark eyestripe and paler and more orange underparts; cheek patch often washed buff. Undertail-coverts dark grey with broad whitish subterminal bands. **e Male**: Underparts dull orange-rufous. **f Female**: Underparts pale drab-orange.

## 2  Chestnut-vented Nuthatch  *Sitta nagaensis*          **Text page 114**

Contrastingly dark rufous flanks usually distinctive, but for separation from Eurasian Nuthatch in China see text (p. 114).

*S. n. nagaensis* NE India and western Burma. **a Male**: In worn plumage, underparts, including chin, ear-coverts and sides of neck very pale grey, only faintly washed buff, contrasting with brick-red rear flanks. Undertail-coverts rusty with tear-shaped white spots. *S. n. montium* Western China, SE Tibet, eastern Burma and NW Thailand. **b Male**: Ear-coverts and underparts dull pale buff with slight grey wash (this is a rather buff example), chin and cheeks only slightly paler (not forming contrasting whitish patch), rear flanks contrastingly deep brick-red. Undertail-coverts rufous with a line of broad white scallops down each side. **c Male**: In worn plumage, underparts pale dirty grey-buff (thus flanks more contrasting), but even when very worn still shows traces of buff.

## 1  Eurasian Nuthatch  *Sitta europaea*          **Text page 109**

*S. e. sinensis* Central and eastern China (cf. Chestnut-vented Nuthatch; see also Plate 1). **j Adult**: In worn plumage, underparts cinnamon, sometimes faintly washed drab-grey.

PLATE 3    LARGER ORIENTAL NUTHATCHES 2

## 3  Kashmir Nuthatch  *Sitta cashmirensis*                 **Text page 117**

Eastern Afghanistan to western Nepal. Undertail-coverts uniform as on White-tailed Nuthatch, but larger and longer-billed.
    **a Male**: Ear-coverts and chin form conspicuous but rather ill-defined silver-grey cheek patch (better demarcated than on White-tailed); breast cinnamon, flanks and vent chestnut. **b Female**: Cheek patch tinged buff (but still whiter than on White-tailed), contrasting less with underparts (i.e more like White-tailed); breast and belly paler and more uniform than male, flanks hardly contrasting. **c Spread tail**: Lacks white base to *central* tail feathers.

## 5  White-tailed Nuthatch  *Sitta himalayensis*             **Text page 123**

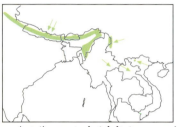

Himalayas, NE India, western Burma and SW China (Yunnan); scattered records in SE Burma and northern Laos and Vietnam. Undertail-coverts uniform, chin and cheeks (sometimes also throat) white, *grading* into underparts, ear-coverts (at least *rear* ear-coverts) cinnamon-orange; white bases to central tail feathers diagnostic when visible (but see White-browed Nuthatch).
    **a Adult**: Black eyestripe expands broadly at rear, may show indistinct off-white supercilium above and behind eye. Cheeks and throat whitish, grading to cinnamon-orange on breast and fore flanks, and to darker orange-cinnamon on the belly, vent and undertail-coverts. **b Adult**: In worn plumage, whitish feather bases may show on nape and upper mantle, eyestripe more extensive, especially at rear, wings darker and sootier, and underparts paler, sometimes buff-white on breast and belly. **c Spread tail**: Showing extent of white on central tail feathers and tail corners.

## 6  White-browed Nuthatch  *Sitta victoriae*                **Text page 125**

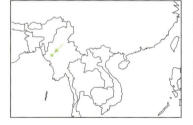

Endemic to Mount Victoria, SW Burma. White forehead and supercilium, well-defined black eyestripe, and white throat and breast contrasting with orange-rufous flanks, vent and undertail-coverts distinctive.
    **a Adult**: Supercilium often extends downwards at rear, where broken by eyestripe. **b Spread tail**: Shows white at base of central tail feathers as on White-tailed Nuthatch, also known from Mount Victoria.

## 23  Giant Nuthatch  *Sitta magna*                          **Text page 169**

SE Burma, NW Thailand and SW China. Very large and comparatively long-tailed; crown noticeably paler than mantle.
    **a Male**: Crown, nape and upper mantle light grey, variably streaked black and enclosed by long, broad black eyestripes (may appear hooded). Upperparts contrastingly darker bluish-grey. Cheeks and throat off-white, underparts pale grey, undertail-coverts rufous with large whitish spots or scallops. **b Female**: Eyestripe duller, slightly less contrast between cap and upperparts, breast washed buff, and flanks, belly and vent washed cinnamon. **c In flight from above**: Broad, butterfly-like wings. **d In flight from below**: Contrast between black carpal and white base to flight feathers.

3a

3c

3b

5a

6b

5c

5b

6a

23a

23c

23d

23b

PLATE 4    AMERICAN NUTHATCHES

## 16  White-breasted Nuthatch  *Sitta carolinensis*    **Text page 150**

White face with isolated dark eye distinctive.

**S. c. carolinensis** Eastern North America. **a Male**: Cap glossy black, upperparts light grey (the palest race), with a marked contrast in wings between black feather centres and pale fringes. Undertail-coverts marked orange-rufous. **b Female**: Cap often (but not always) duller and greyer, black band on upper mantle much narrower, upperparts slightly paler, faintly tinged brown. Face and underparts duller, variably washed buff. **c Juvenile male**: Paler and duller. Cap dull black, upperparts may be faintly barred, fringes to secondaries washed buff, and underparts washed dull buff. **S. c. nelsoni** Rocky Mountains (northern Montana to northern Mexico). **d Male**: Upperparts rather dark, with reduced contrasts in wings, underparts clean white. Bill long and slender **S. c. mexicana** Central and southern Mexico. **e Female**:Upperparts washed olive-brown, rusty tinge to fringes of wing feathers, underparts extensively washed drab.

## 7  Pygmy Nuthatch  *Sitta pygmaea*    **Text page 127**

Small size unique (separated by range from Brown-headed).

**S. p. pygmaea** Coastal California (Mendocino to San Luis Obispo Cos.). **a Adult**: Cap brownish-olive, lores and eyestripe sooty-brown (ill-defined behind eye). Chin, cheeks and ear-coverts off-white, darkening to pale buff on sides of neck, throat and upper breast and buff on remainder of underparts. **b Adult**: In worn plumage, cap a little paler and greyer, contrasting more with eyestripe, nuchal spot more obvious, and underparts dirty grey-white, buff tones much reduced. **c Juvenile**: Cap rather greyer (lacking the brown tone of worn adult), hardly contrasting with upperparts, which are also greyer. Nuchal spot faint or absent (but may have paler area on upper mantle). Greater coverts fringed brownish, and underparts whitish (near worn adult). Note extensive pale base to lower mandible. **S. p. brunnescens** SW Mexico in southern Jalisco and Michoacan. **d Adult**: Cap averages slightly browner (olive-brown), nuchal spot slightly more prominent, tinged yellow-buff.

## 8  Brown-headed Nuthatch  *Sitta pusilla*    **Text page 130**

Small size distinctive (separated by range from Pygmy Nuthatch).

**S. p. pusilla** Continental USA (excluding peninsular Florida). **a Adult**: In late summer and early autumn, cap warm pale brown with whitish nuchal spot visible at close range. Cheeks, ear-coverts and sides of neck whitish, darkening to buff on underparts. **b Adult**: In worn plumage, cap mottled/frosted rather paler, with contrastingly darker eyestripe. Nuchal spot more obvious, underparts paler, buff tones reduced. **c Juvenile**: As adult, but less contrast between slightly greyer cap and browner mantle. Nuchal spot less conspicuous, greater coverts and fringes to tertials and secondaries fringed buffish. Underparts as fresh adult, but with slight rosy flush and browner flanks.

## PLATE 5    SMALLER WEST PALEARCTIC NUTHATCHES

## 10  Algerian Nuthatch *Sitta ledanti*                    Text page 135

Endemic to four sites in Petite Kabylie in NE Algeria, where it is the only nuthatch.
  **a Male**: In worn summer plumage, well-defined black forecrown, prominent white supercilium and black eyestripe. **b Female**: In fresh autumn plumage forecrown and eyestripe concolorous with upperparts (feathers tipped blue-grey, concealing dark bases), blackish confined to diffuse area on forehead at base of bill. **c 1st-adult female**: In worn summer plumage supercilium mottled grey, blue-grey feather tips of forecrown and eyestripe rather broad, with only limited black mottling on forehead. **d Juvenile (female?)**: Cap and eyestripe blue-grey, concolorous with upperparts, supercilium very poorly marked, upperparts paler and less blue than adult, underparts also paler.

## 9  Corsican Nuthatch *Sitta whiteheadi*                    Text page 133

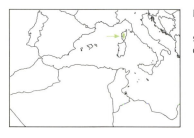

Restricted to Corsica, where it is the only nuthatch.
  **a Male**: Cap and eyestripe black. **b Female**: Cap blue-grey, eyestripe grey, rather poorly defined behind eye (in worn plumage, dark grey feather bases may show on forehead and forecrown).

## 11  Krüper's Nuthatch *Sitta krueperi*                    Text page 138

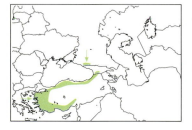

Confined to Turkey, Lesbos (Greece) and a small area of the western Caucasus. Dark cap and rufous breast band distinctive.
  **a Male**: Neatly demarcated black forecrown, well-defined white supercilium and blackish eyestripe. Rufous 'breastplate'; remainder of underparts pale grey with chestnut undertail-coverts. **b Female**: As male but black forecrown duller and less well defined at rear, eyestripe paler, breast averages paler and more orange-rufous, lower breast washed buff. **c Juvenile**: Much dingier. Lacks black forecrown, supercilium and eyestripe poorly marked, and breast pale rufous, poorly demarcated from dirty drab-brown belly.

10a

10b

10d

10c

9a

9b

11c

11a

11b

**PLATE 6    SMALLER NUTHATCHES, CHINA & AMERICA**

## 12  Chinese Nuthatch *Sitta villosa*                    Text page 140

Dark cap and eyestripe and white supercilium distinctive within range.
  ***S. v. villosa*** Southern Ussuriland, Korea and northern China. **a Male**: Black cap and eyestripe and broad white supercilium. Cheeks and chin dirty white, grading to pale greyish-buff underparts. **b Juvenile male**: Slightly duller, wings fringed more cinnamon-grey, underparts richer and more cinnamon. **c Female**: Cap grey, only slightly darker than upperparts, eyestripe narrower and duller than male's, supercilium narrower, upperparts duller and browner, underparts slightly darker and browner. **d Female**: In worn plumage, cap becomes darker and more contrasting as blue-grey tips abrade; forehead may be blackish and cap gradually merges with blue-grey nape. ***S. v. bangsi*** Western China in central Gansu and Qinghai. **e Male**: Underparts orange-cinnamon. (From below, may resemble Chinese race of White-cheeked Nuthatch.)

## 14  Red-breasted Nuthatch *Sitta canadensis*          Text page 144

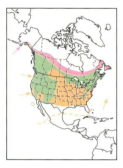

North America, extending south to Mexican border in irruptions. White supercilium diagnostic in range.
  **a Male**: Black cap and eyestripe. Underparts ochre-cinnamon (may be buffy-white on dullest males). **b Female**: In worn plumage, cap blackish-grey, forehead and eyestripe dull black (in fresh plumage, cap usually nearly concolorous with upperparts, as juvenile female, but eyestripe usually darker than cap). A dull bird, with underparts cinnamon-buff. **c Juvenile female**: Crown grey, concolorous with mantle (as many fresh adult females; juvenile male has cap dull blackish). Juveniles of both sexes may show faint dark specks on supercilium, chin and cheeks, buffish tips to greater coverts, and pale underparts.

## 13  Yunnan Nuthatch *Sitta yunnanensis*               Text page 143

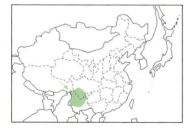

Endemic to SW China. Combination of prominent black eyestripe, expanding broadly at rear, and narrow white supercilium distinctive.
  **a Adult**: Underparts pale pinkish-buff. **b Adult**: In worn plumage, fore supercilium may be reduced to few white flecks; eyestripe broader, bridging base of bill. Upperparts duller, and underparts fade to dirty pale buffish-grey. **c Juvenile**: Supercilia faint or absent, not meeting on forehead and sometimes barely paler than crown (unlike worn adult, and eyestripe also reduced). Underparts dull, near worn adult's.

## 15  White-cheeked Nuthatch *Sitta leucopsis*          Text page 148

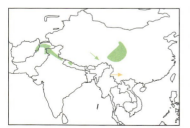

Prominent white cheek patch encompasses eye.
  ***S. l. leucopsis*** Eastern Afghanistan to western Nepal. **a Adult**: Crown and nape glossy black, upperparts dark blue-grey. Throat white, underparts washed creamy-buff, rear flanks rufous. **b Adult**: In worn plumage, cap and upperparts slightly duller, underparts paler and less buffy. **c Juvenile**: Cap duller, less clear-cut at rear, cheek patch more creamy-buff, with cheeks and underparts faintly barred darker. ***S. l. przewalskii*** Western China. **d Adult**: Cheeks washed orange-buff, underparts rich cinnamon (wearing paler and patchier).

12e

12d

12a

12c

12b

14a

14b

14c

13a

13b

13c

15c

15a

15b

15d

# PLATE 7 ROCK NUTHATCHES AND SOME TROPICAL NUTHATCHES

## 17 Western Rock Nuthatch *Sitta neumayer* Text page 155

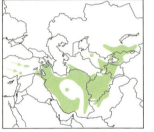

Long-billed and long-legged, often perching rather upright. Upperparts pale grey, with little or no white in tail. Cheeks, throat and breast whitish, grading to pinkish-cinnamon on rear flanks, vent and undertail-coverts.

**S. n. neumayer** SE Europe (very similar in Turkey and Levant). **a Adult**: Overall relatively dark, with rather broad black eyestripe extending onto sides of mantle, although barely encompassing eye and narrowing towards rear. **S. n. tschitscherini** West and west-central Iran. **b Adult**: Overall rather pale, with no sharp division between mantle and sides of neck, pale rear underparts, and black eyestripe much reduced, short and narrow (even absent) behind eye. **S. n. plumbea** South-central Iran (southern Kerman province). **c Adult**: Throat, breast and belly pale grey.

## 18 Eastern Rock Nuthatch *Sitta tephronota* Text page 158

Very similar to Rock Nuthatch (see text).

**S. t. dresseri** Northern Iraq, western Iran and SE Turkey. **a Adult**: As Western Rock, but larger, eyestripe rather longer and broader (often broadening behind eye), bill rather stockier, and shows contrast between the white throat and breast and pinkish-cinnamon belly and flanks, usually lacking on Western Rock. Calls and song louder, deeper and often slower. **S. t. tephronota** SE Central Asia. **b Adult**: Close to Western Rock Nuthatch (*S. n. neumayer*) in size and shape, eyestripe only slightly more prominent. **c Adult**: In flight, note lack of white spots in tail (cf. Eurasian Nuthatch).

## 22 Blue Nuthatch *Sitta azurea* Text page 168

Very distinct, although usually appears black and white.

**S. a. expectata** Malaya and Sumatra. **a Adult**: Cap black, conspicuous broad bluish-white eyering. Upperparts blackish, wing-coverts and flight feathers prominently pale blue, neatly outlined with black, with elongated 'drooping' greater coverts. Throat and breast whitish, faintly tinged buff, belly and vent blackish, with contrastingly pale blue-grey undertail-coverts. Bill, legs and feet pale blue-white. **S. a. nigriventer** West Java. **b Adult**: Upperparts violet-blue washed with grey, contrasting strongly with black cap; breast distinctly washed buff.

## 24 Beautiful Nuthatch *Sitta formosa* Text page 172

NE India, Burma and scattered records in southern China and SE Asia. Rare and little known. Large size, black upperparts with brilliant blue and white streaks, pale blue back, scapulars and rump, and cinnamon-orange underparts distinctive.

**a Adult**: Sexes similar (juvenile apparently very similar to adult). **b Adult**: In flight, white patch at base of primaries contrasts with blackish underwing-coverts.

## PLATE 8   THE VELVET-FRONTED NUTHATCH COMPLEX

## 19   Velvet-fronted Nuthatch   *Sitta frontalis*   Text page 161

Black forehead and bright red bill distinctive.

**S. f. frontalis** Indian Subcontinent, southern China and SE Asia. **a Male**: Supercilium black, upperparts violet-blue. Cheeks dull violet-blue, fading to lavender on ear-coverts and sides of neck. Chin and throat whitish, underparts dull beige with flanks, belly and vent darker, washed lavender, and undertail-coverts diffusely tipped lavender. **b Male**: In worn plumage, upperparts duller and greyer and underparts slightly duller, paler and less lilac. **c Female**: Lacks black supercilium, and underparts average more cinnamon and slightly less lilac, especially breast and belly. **d Juvenile male**: Bill blackish, upperparts slightly duller and greyer, chin and throat duller, and underparts washed cinnamon-orange or orange-buff, lacking lilac tones (slightly more orange-buff than adult female). Notably, undertail-coverts pale pinkish-buff with fine dark cinnamon-brown bars. **S. f. saturatior** Peninsular Thailand, Malaya and northern Sumatra. **e Male**: Underparts relatively dark: chin off-white, throat and underparts pinkish-buff, washed lilac. **S. f. velata** Java **f Male**: Throat extensively white (although ear-coverts still lilac), underparts pale and washed-out, more pinkish-buff, with reduced lilac and increased grey tones. **S. f. palawana** Palawan and Balabac, Philippine islands. **g Male**: Underparts slightly darker and browner, throat less extensively white.

## 20   Yellow-billed Nuthatch   *Sitta solangiae*   Text page 164

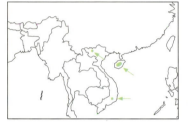

Confined to Vietnam and Hainan island (China). Yellow bill distinctive, as are pale underparts and mauve or lilac tones to head and nape.

**S. s. fortior** South-central Annam, Vietnam. **a Male**: Crown washed violet-blue, nape contrastingly pale greyish-mauve. Throat whitish, remainder of underparts pale greyish-beige, washed violet. **b Female**: Lacks black eyestripe. **S. s. solangiae** NW Tonkin, Vietnam. **c Male**: Crown paler, more lavender or violet and less blue (showing less contrast with nape), upperparts slightly paler, greyer blue, underparts more greyish-drab, lacking violet wash.

## 21   Sulphur-billed Nuthatch   *Sitta oenochlamys*   Text page 165

Endemic to the Philippines.

**S. o. isarog** Southern and central Luzon and through the Sierra Madre to extreme NE Luzon. **a Male**: Ear-coverts violet-blue; 'shawl' on nape and upper mantle only slightly greyer and more lilac than remainder of upperparts. Underparts vinaceous-buff, washed lilac. **b Juvenile male**: Underparts more cinnamon-orange. **S. o. mesoleuca** Western Cordillera mountains, NW Luzon. **c Male**: Palest race. Ear-coverts violet-blue, faint lilac tinge to 'shawl' (shawl pale pinkish-buff, washed lilac, often with very pale, even whitish, centre), underparts pale pinkish-buff with no lilac tinge. **S. o. zamboanga** Western Mindanao (Zamboanga peninsula). **d Male**: Most lilac-tinged race. Ear-coverts lilac, vinaceous-lilac 'shawl', underparts deep vinaceous, washed lilac, especially on breast, belly and flanks.

## PLATE 9   TREECREEPERS 1

### 27  Brown Creeper *Certhia americana*                   Text page 184

The only treecreeper in the Americas.

**C. a. americana** Central and eastern Canada (winters south to Texas, SE Coahuila and Florida, and west to Colorado). **a Adult**: 'Dark phase', upperparts relatively dark. **b Adult**: 'Brown phase', upperparts relatively paler and more grey-brown. **C. a. albescens** SE Arizona, SW New Mexico, and Sierra Madre Occidental of western Mexico. **c Adult**: Upperparts blackest of any race, with well-defined narrow whitish streaks and very contrasting chestnut rump. Throat white, breast and belly light grey, undertail-coverts light drab-buff. **C. a. pernigra** Chiapas, southernmost Mexico, to western Guatemala. **d Adult**: Upperparts darkest brown of any race, with very narrow cinnamon-brown streaks. Underparts less grey, often with faint darker spotting (= juveniles?).

### 28  Short-toed Treecreeper *Certhia brachydactyla*     Text page 190

A very tough identification problem. See text.

**C. b. megarhyncha** Western Europe (east to western Germany). **a Adult**: Relatively long-billed. Upperparts dull, grey-brown, contrastingly streaked paler, supercilia short, not pure white and not meeting over bill, and underparts dingy with contrastingly whiter throat. **C. b. brachydactyla** Central Europe. **b Adult**: Slightly darker and colder brown, with better-defined whitish streaking on upperparts.

### 26  Eurasian Treecreeper *Certhia familiaris*           Text page 177

**C. f. britannica** British Isles. **a Adult**: Upperparts relatively dark and rufous, underparts off-white, washed buff on flanks, belly and vent; undertail-coverts pale buff, tipped white. **b Juvenile**: Relatively dull, pale-spotted and dark-scalloped; underparts indistinctly and finely spotted darker, especially breast and flanks. **C. f. familiaris** Scandinavia, eastern Europe and western Siberia. **c Adult**: Upperparts relatively bright and pale, rufous-brown, well spotted whitish, rump contrastingly rufous; supercilium and underparts almost pure white with faint buff wash on flanks etc. **C. f. hodgsoni** Western Himalayas (to NW India). **d Adult**: Upperparts dull brown, prominently spotted whitish; rump contrastingly cinnamon-orange; underparts off-white, rear flanks etc. lightly washed dull buff. **C. f. mandellii** Central and eastern Himalayas. **e Adult**: Upperparts sooty-black, spotted and streaked cinnamon-buff; underparts whitish, rear flanks etc. drab-buff.

### 30  Rusty-flanked Treecreeper *Certhia nipalensis*      Text page 198

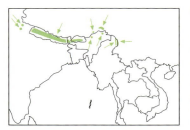

Himalayas from Nepal to west Yunnan (China) and NE Burma.

**a Adult**: Rather dark. Head and mantle blackish with fine buff streaks and spots, lower mantle and scapulars dull cinnamon-buff with dark scallops, rump contrastingly cinnamon-rufous, tail unmarked. Broad buff supercilium encircling near solidly dark ear-coverts. Throat and breast whitish, contrasting strongly with cinnamon sides of breast, flanks, belly and vent; remainder of underparts washed buff. **b Juvenile**: Rump duller and less contrasting, faint dark scalloping on underparts, and cinnamon flank patch more restricted.

27a 27b 27c 27d

28a 28b

26a

26b

26c

30a 30b 26d 26e

PLATE 10    TREECREEPERS 2, WALLCREEPER

## 29  Bar-tailed Treecreeper  *Certhia himalayana*    **Text page 195**

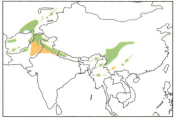

Tail with well-defined dark cross-bars.
    ***C. h. taeniura*** Central Asia and northern Afghanistan. **a Adult**: Upperparts relatively pale and grey; rump with reduced warmth (but same relative contrast with upperparts); underparts pale and grey (little buff), reduced contrast between throat and breast. ***C. h. himalayana*** Eastern Afghanistan and Himalayas. **b Adult**: Relatively darker and browner. **c Juvenile**: Upperparts slightly warmer and browner, with less well-defined pale spots (especially on crown) and dark scallops. More contrast between blotchy white throat and breast and dull drab-buff belly and vent; some very fine dark marks on underparts. ***C. h. yunnanensis*** SW China. **d Adult**: Overall darker, upperparts more blackish-brown, breast and belly smoky-buff.

## 31  Brown-throated Treecreeper  *Certhia discolor*    **Text page 200**

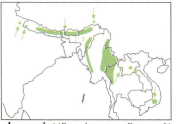

In Himalayas, separated with care from Eurasian and Rusty-flanked by dull underparts with pale brown wash on throat and breast and lack of contrasting flanks.
    ***C. d. discolor*** Himalayas, southern Tibet and Nagaland. **a Adult**: Throat and breast light drab-buff, paling to dull drab-white on rear flanks etc. **b Juvenile**: As adult, but fine dark scales on throat and breast, which are also tinged cinnamon-buff. ***C. d. manipurensis*** Southern Manipur and SW Burma. **c Adult**: Throat and breast rich cinnamon (wearing duller, and undertail-coverts cinnamon. Upperparts relatively warm, more orange-buff. ***C. d. shanensis*** NE and eastern Burma, Yunnan, Thailand, Laos and NW Vietnam. **d Adult**: Underparts rather dark and dingy; throat and breast mid-dark sooty-drab, belly dull mid grey, undertail-coverts buff or cinnamon-buff. Upperparts relatively cold and grey. ***C. d. meridionalis*** Da Lat plateau, southern Vietnam. **e Adult**: As *shanensis,* but upperparts much warmer and more rufous, underparts possibly slightly darker, purer grey.

## 25  Wallcreeper  *Tichodroma muraria*    **Text page 173**

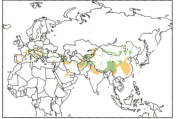

This flamboyant species is totally unique.
    ***T. m. nepalensis*** Turkmenistan and eastern Iran to China. **a Male breeding**: Face, throat and centre of breast (sometimes whole breast) dull black, grading to mid grey on ear-coverts and underparts. **b Male**: In flight conspicuous white spots in wing. **c Female breeding**: Face and sides of neck greyish with contrasting pale eyering. Chin to centre of breast white, variable dark patch on lower throat and breast (exceptionally as extensive as black of male). **d Adult non-breeding**: Crown washed pale brown. Throat and breast uniform whitish. **e Juvenile**: Underparts more uniformly grey, lacking contrast between whitish bib and dark grey belly. Bill straighter. ***T. m. muraria*** Europe east to northern and western Iran. **f Adult non-breeding**: As *nepalensis,* but upperparts paler, crown purer grey, belly paler, spots in wings and tail larger, bill averages longer.

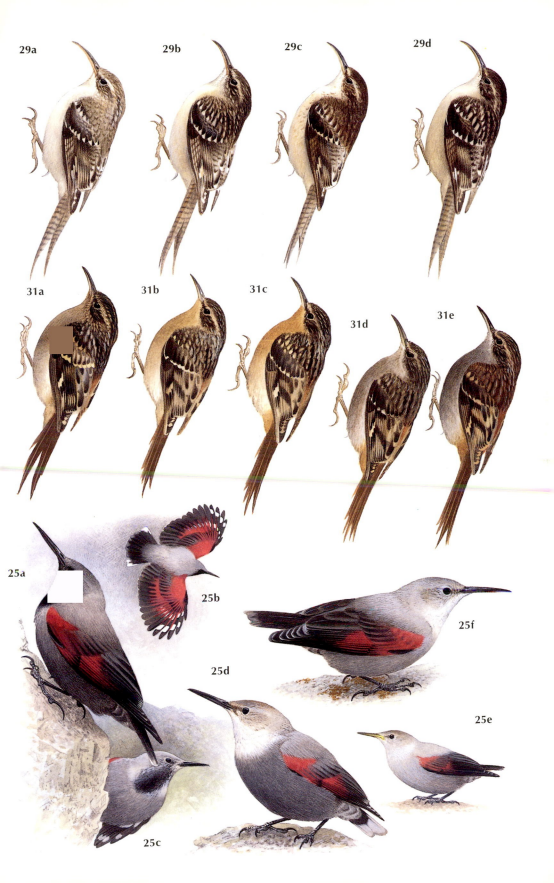

## PLATE 11    EUROPEAN AND WEST ASIAN PENDULINE TITS

## 33  European Penduline Tit *Remiz pendulinus*    Text page 205

**R. p. pendulinus** Europe and western Turkey. **a Male**: Black 'highwayman's mask', narrow chestnut band on forecrown, cap dull grey (wearing whiter). Upperparts chestnut, paler and more cinnam vinous-buff on scapulars. Throat white, grading to buffish on breast and buffy-cinnamon on flanks; sometimes shows diffuse chestnut mottling on breast. **b Female**: Mask paler and less extensive and no chestnut on forecrown. Cap dusky grey-brown (never wearing as white), breast spots reduced or absent. **c Juvenile**: Head and upperparts plain, with pale eyering and short supercilium, warmer mantle and sometimes slightly darker mask. Underparts pale buff. **d 1st-adult female**: A dull individual (resembling juvenile), dark mask heavily mottled paler and crown and nape pale brownish-grey. **R. p. caspius** SE Russia and western shores of Caspian Sea. **e Adult male**: More chestnut on forecrown, often extending to centre of crown; rear crown and nape mixed chestnut and whitish, occasionally uniform chestnut. Mantle richer chestnut, lower scapulars, back and rump paler. Broader pale fringes to tail and flight feathers, chestnut mottling on underparts averages more prominent. **f Adult male**: Variation in extent of chestnut on crown and nape. **g Adult female**: Nearer nominate *pendulinus,* but cap and upper mantle paler and greyer (contrasting more with lower mantle); may show traces of chestnut on forehead and sides of crown, underparts whiter.

## 34  Black-headed Penduline Tit *Remiz macronyx*    Text page 211

**R. m. macronyx** Central Asia. **a Male**: Hood blackish, finely peppered buffish, extending to breast. Cinnamon-buff collar, chestnut upper mantle and sides of breast, underparts buff.. **b Male**: In worn plumage, hood uniformly blackish, narrow pale collar, upperparts uniformly chestnut, bib variably dark, mottling on underparts more extensive. **c 1st-adult male**: Head pale dull buffish, whiter on forecrown, only forehead and mask dark, throat pale grey, variably mottled darker; upperparts paler than adult. **R. m. nigricans** Sistan, SE Iran. **d Male**: In worn plumage, black hood very extensive, extending to mantle and sometimes rump, tertials and breast, lower mantle dark chestnut, underparts dark chestnut.

**Hybrid Black-headed x European Penduline Tit** ('*altaicus*'), from South Caspian coast.

**e Adult**: Head dark grey, but centre of crown and nape with extensive white frosting, more obvious pale grey collar.

## 35  White-crowned Penduline Tit *Remiz coronatus*    Text page 213

**a Male**: Whitish head with black nuchal band separated from chestnut upperparts by broad white collar. Narrow black band on forehead, but never chestnut on head. **b Male**: In worn plumage, nuchal band broader (but forehead always white). Narrower band of chestnut across mantle, back and rump paler; underparts duller, more dark spotting on breast. **c Female**: Duller and paler, rear crown pale grey, mask and especially bridle paler, slightly browner, and less extensive, with little dark on forehead. Collar dull pale grey, underparts washed paler pink. **d 1st-adult female**: Uniform appearance recalls juvenile. Crown and nape cinnamon-drab, forehead whitish (no black at base of bill), mask sooty-brown, feathers tipped paler.

33a

33b

33d

33c

33e

33f

33g

34b

34a

34e

34c

34d

35a

35b

35c

35d

## PLATE 12    ASIAN PENDULINE TITS, YELLOW-BROWED TIT

## 36  Chinese Penduline Tit  *Remiz consobrinus*          Text page 216

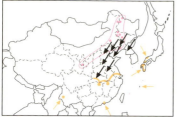

China; migrant Japan and Korea. The only penduline tit in the region.

**a Male**: Dull black mask bordered whitish above. Cap and nape pale grey, diffusely streaked darker, especially at rear. Upper mantle and mottled half-collar on sides of breast chestnut. Broad white submoustachial stripe, centre of throat pale buff, becoming buff on breast and cinnamon on flanks. **b Female**: Crown and nape duller and browner, mask smaller and browner, upperparts lack chestnut collar (although traces when worn). **c 1st-adult male**: Mask smaller and duller, finely 'peppered' buff when fresh, crown browner and more uniform, duller chestnut collar, and buff-washed submoustachial (near adult female, but mask blacker and chestnut collar more prominent). **d 1st-adult female**: Dark mask may be even less contrasting, plain head pattern recalling juvenile.

## 43  Fire-capped Tit  *Cephalopyrus flammiceps*          Text page 229

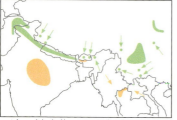

Distinctive in breeding plumage, otherwise compare with Yellow-browed Tit.

*C. f. flammiceps* Western Himalayas. **a Breeding male**: Reddish forecrown, chin and throat. **b Non-breeding female**: Throat pale grey-white (whiter than breast). (Non-breeding male averages brighter on underparts, with cleaner yellow wash to breast.) **c Breeding female**: Forecrown dull golden-olive and throat and breast dull olive-yellow, yellower than belly and vent. **d Juvenile**: As non-breeding adult, but underparts lack yellow. **e Old female?**: In late April, some show golden-yellow forecrown with odd dull orange feathers and golden-yellow chin. These may be 1st-adult males or, perhaps more likely, old females. *C. f. olivaceous* Eastern Himalayas and western China. **f Breeding male**: As *flammiceps*, but upperparts slightly darker and greener, reddish band on forehead much reduced, reddish restricted to chin and centre of throat, remainder of throat golden-yellow; breast greener, yellowish-olive, grading to dirty pale yellow on belly.

## 101  Yellow-browed Tit  *Sylviparus modestus*          Text page 415

An aberrant tit recalling a leaf-warbler (*Phylloscopus*), but note narrow yellowish eyering, stubbier bill, stocky pale blue-grey legs and feet, lack of a prominent long pale supercilium or dark eye-stripe and, when raised, short crest. Told from female and immature Fire-capped Tits by crest, much less obvious single wingbar, and lack of paler rump or distinct pale tertial fringes.

*S. m. modestus* Himalayas from Nepal eastwards, NE India, Burma, China, Laos, north Vietnam and Thailand. **a Adult**: Variable pale wingbar and contrasting yellow patch at bend of wing. Yellow supercilium revealed only when alarmed or excited, but often shows slight crest. **b Adult**: In worn plumage, overall duller, darker and greyer, wingbar paler and narrower, underparts with reduced yellow tones. *S. m. simlaensis* Western Himalayas (east to northern Uttar Pradesh). **c Adult**: As *modestus*, but brighter and yellower, with brighter fringes to tertials, flight feathers and tail. (Supercilium concealed.)

36a

36b

36c

36d

43a

43b

43c

43d

43e

43f

101a

101b

101c

**PLATE 13    AFRICAN PENDULINE TITS**

## 37  Sennar Penduline Tit *Anthoscopus punctifrons*    Text page 218

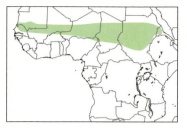

Creamy or creamy-buff underparts.
  **a Adult**: Forehead yellowish, finely spotted darker, wing feathers fringed paler. **b Juvenile**: Upperparts slightly duller and greyer, fringes to tertials and greater coverts duller.

## 39  Mouse-coloured Penduline Tit *A. musculus*    Text page 220

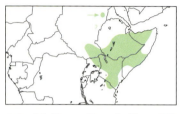

Forehead finely spotted darker, underparts whitish, tinged buff on belly and vent.
  **a Adult**: Upperparts greyish, tinged olive, short, slightly paler supercilium, wings and tail paler and purer grey. **b Adult**: Note forehead and underparts.

## 38  Yellow Penduline Tit *Anthoscopus parvulus*    Text page 219

Yellow underparts and usually obvious whitish fringes to greater coverts and tertials.
  **A. p. parvulus** Lake Chad to south Sudan and NE Zaïre. **a Adult**: Forehead bright yellow, finely dotted black. Upperparts olive-green, washed grey, rump yellower. **b Juvenile**: Forecrown duller and less contrasting, underparts paler. **A. p. senegalensis** Senegal to Nigeria and Lake Chad. **c Adult**: Upperparts more yellow-green (forehead less contrasting). **A. p. aureus** Northern Ghana. **d Adult**: Dull. Forehead olive-yellow (little contrast), with reduced spotting. Wing fringes broader. Underparts pale yellow, tinged olive on throat and upper breast.

## 41  African Penduline Tit *Anthoscopus caroli*    Text page 223

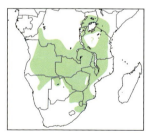

Widespread and very variable.
  **A. c. ansorgei** Angola and SW Zaïre. **a Adult**: Forehead yellowish, upperparts olive-green, sides of head and underparts off-white, breast downwards faintly washed yellow. **A. c. roccatii** Uganda, Rwanda, NE Zaïre. **b Adult**: Forehead pale yellow, upperparts greyish-olive, throat sullied grey, underparts creamy-yellow. **A. c. caroli** Northern Namibia, southern Angola, northern Botswana and southern Zambia. **c Adult**: Forehead dull pale buff-white, sometimes spotted darker, upperparts light grey (tinged olive). Sides of head dirty pale buff, throat and breast pale grey-white (tinged buff), underparts buffish. **A. c. robertsi** NE Zambia, northern Mozambique, southern Malawi, and eastern Tanzania and Kenya. **d Adult**: As *caroli*, but throat and breast whiter, washed yellowish, upperparts slightly more olive. **A. c. sylviella** ('Rungwe Penduline Tit') South-central Kenya and central Tanzania (map above). **e Adult**: Forehead dirty pale buff, upperparts clean grey, sides of head dirty buff-white, underparts cinnamon-buff.

## 42  Cape Penduline Tit *Anthoscopus minutus*    Text page 227

Blackish forehead and lores, short whitish supercilium (speckled blackish) and yellowish underparts. Map above. **A. m. damarensis** Angola, northern Namibia, Botswana, Zimbabwe, central Orange Free State and Transvaal. **a Adult**: Upperparts grey, tinged olive, rump yellower, underparts yellow. **b Juvenile**: Underparts paler yellow, sullied grey on throat and breast. **A. m. minutus** Cape province (except southeast), western Orange Free State and southern Namibia. **c Adult**: Crown and nape washed brown, upperparts greyish olive-brown, rump dull cinnamon, chin and throat washed grey, diffusely spotted, underparts dull yellow-buff. **A. m. gigi** SE Cape province (Little Karoo and southern Great Karoo). **d Adult**: Upperparts brownest (least grey), underparts buffer and less yellowish.

## PLATE 14    AFRICAN FOREST TITS

## 40  Forest Penduline Tit  *Anthoscopus flavifrons*    **Text page 222**

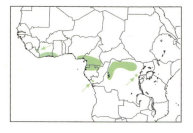

Distinct if seen well. Note stubby bill and yellowish underparts.
  *A. f. flavifrons* Lower Guinea forest (Nigeria, Cameroon, Gabon and northern Zaïre). **a Adult**: Forehead dull golden-yellow (hard to see), upperparts olive-green, and underparts dull olive-yellow, faintly mottled. **b Juvenile**: Only narrow band of dull buff on forehead. Underparts cleaner, throat slightly paler and whiter, breast lightly tinged buff, and belly slightly paler and purer yellow.
  *A. f. waldroni* Upper Guinea forest (Ghana; presumably also Ivory Coast and Liberia). **c Adult**: Upperparts slightly brighter, more yellowish-green, and underparts cleaner, paler and yellower, especially breast.

## 44  Tit-Hylia  *Pholidornis rushiae*    **Text page 232**

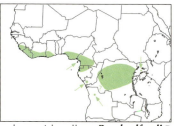

Streaked throat, yellow rump and tiny size best field marks; bright yellow legs and feet noticeable.
  *P. r. rushiae* Southern Nigeria to central Cameroon and Gabon. **a Adult**: Head streaked or mottled, mantle, scapulars and wing neatly scaled, back and rump yellowish. Throat and breast boldly streaked dark brown and off-white, grading to dull yellowish on belly and vent. **b Adult**: In worn plumage, upperparts and sides of head darker and more uniform. **c Juvenile**: Head and upperparts darker and more uniform (lacking distinct scaled pattern), throat and breast dirty light grey, only faintly streaked darker, underparts
pale greyish-yellow. *P. r. bedfordi* Fernando Po (Bioko). **d Adult**: Rump streaked, and streaking on throat and breast broad, dark and extending to flanks and belly. *P. r. denti* SE Cameroon, NW Angola, Zaïre and Uganda. **e Adult**: Rump and underparts bright orange-yellow, streaking on throat and breast quite fine and sparse. *P. r. ussheri* Sierra Leone to Ghana. **f Adult**: Mantle and scapulars lack distinct scalloped pattern, wing-coverts and flight feathers fringed olive-yellow, streaking on throat and breast very fine.

## 76  Dusky Tit  *Parus funereus*    **Text page 335**

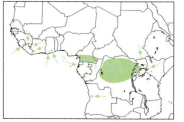

Confined to evergreen forest, where unlikely to be confused with any other tit. Voice and typically acrobatic behaviour should prevent confusion with other all-dark forest birds.
  *P. f. funereus* Liberia to Kenya, south to Zaïre and Uganda. **a Male**: Upperparts blackish, faintly glossed oily blue-green, underparts dull black, slightly greyer on flanks and faintly glossed greenish on breast. Conspicuous reddish eye. **b Male**: Head-on view. **c Female**: Head and upper mantle slightly duller and greyer, crown often faintly scaled. Underparts slightly paler, more mouse grey. **d Female**: In worn plumage, underparts dull brown, faintly
streaked greyer. **e Juvenile**: As adult male, but wing-coverts tipped white, reduced pale fringes to flight feathers and eye brown (sexes similar in juvenile plumage).

PLATE 15    MARSH AND SOMBRE TITS & ALLIES

## 46  Marsh Tit  *Parus palustris*                    Text page 237

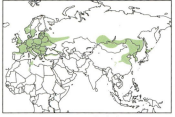

Often difficult to separate from Willow Tit (see text).
**P. p. dresseri** England and NW France. Smallest and darkest of western races. **a Adult**: Cap glossy black, upperparts warm brown, white cheek patches and bib relatively small; underparts creamy-white, flanks extensively washed pale buff-brown. **b Juvenile**: Cap dull sooty-black, bib smaller, underparts whiter. **P. p. stagnatilis** Eastern Europe and northern Turkey. **c Adult**: Largest and palest of western races. Upperparts very slightly paler and buffer, under-parts slightly whiter, flanks washed creamy-grey. **P. p. hellmayri** NE China and South Korea (cf. Black-bibbed Tit). **d Adult**: Upperparts warm drab-brown (resembling European birds), but slightly paler fringes to flight feathers, cheek patch relatively small, bib confined to chin and upper throat; underparts off-white, distinctly washed buff. **e Adult**: In worn plumage, bib more extensive, underparts whiter.

## 47  Black-bibbed Tit  *Parus hypermelaena*          Text page 242

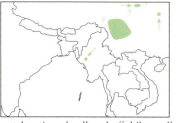

SW China and Mount Victoria, Burma. As Marsh Tit, but upper-parts distinctly tinged olive-green. May show short, ragged crest.
**a Adult** (Yunnan): Cap extensive, glossy black, no obvious pale fringes to flight feathers. White cheek patch extensive, especially at rear (may appear fluffy). Bib extends well onto breast, poorly defined at lower border, underparts heavily washed greyish olive-brown. **b Adult** (Mount Victoria): In worn plumage, cap duller, upperparts greyer (less olive), and underparts whiter, although still dingy, washed grey on breast and belly. **c Juvenile** (Mount Victoria): Cap dull and rather small, upperparts warmer (less olive), cheek patches tinged yellow-buff, bib smaller, and underparts paler, heavily washed yellow-buff.

## 48  Sombre Tit  *Parus lugubris*                    Text page 245

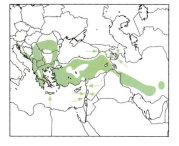

Large size and drab plumage distinctive. Cap and bib extensive, cheek patches narrow and wedge-shaped; flanks drab-grey, lacking cinnamon or buff tones.
**P. l. lugubris** SE Europe. **a Male**: Cap sooty-brown, bib sooty-black. **b Female**: Cap dark grey-brown, variably contrasting with mantle, bib brown or grey-brown. **P. l. anatoliae** Middle East (to ? NW Iran). Upperparts greyer, underparts purer white. **c Male**: Cap and bib black. **d Female**: Cap and bib blackish-brown or sooty-brown. **e Juvenile**: Rather duller. Cap drab-brown, slightly darker than upperparts, bib mid grey-brown. **P. l. dubius** Iran. Upperparts pale sandy-grey, underparts whitish. **f Male**: Well-defined black cap and bib (sexual dimorphism reduced, female rather similar).

## 49  Caspian Tit  *Parus hyrcanus*                   Text page 248

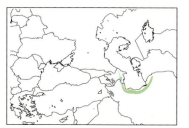

Northern Iran and SE Azerbaydzhan. Extensive dark brown cap and bib distinctive, as are pale pinkish-buff underparts in fresh plumage.
**a Adult**: Extensive sooty-brown bib (darker than cap), ill-defined at lower border. **b Adult**: In worn plumage, upperparts slightly paler and greyer, bib slightly darker, more extensive and better-defined, remainder of underparts off-white, flanks lightly washed buff. **c Juvenile**: Cap slightly duller, fringes to secondaries more cinnamon, bib averages slightly smaller; underparts as worn adult.

PLATE 16    WILLOW TIT/BLACK-CAPPED CHICKADEE COMPLEX

## 53  Black-capped Chickadee  *Parus atricapillus*    Text page 265

Much like Carolina Chickadee, but inner greater coverts broadly fringed whitish (on Carolina, greater coverts near-uniform). On both species, pale fringes form pale panel on secondaries on closed wing, but this is more strongly contrasting on Black-capped. Song usually distinctive. See text for details.

***P. a. atricapillus*** Eastern Canada and NE USA. **a Adult**: Upperparts mid olive-grey, variably washed buff. **b Adult**: In very worn plumage, upperparts greyer, pale fringes to coverts and flight feathers rather abraded, bib slightly more extensive, better defined, and underparts paler. ***P. a. nevadensis*** SW USA (Great Basin region). **c Adult**: Upperparts relatively pale and grey, pale fringes on wings and tail broader (extreme for species); underparts pale, with reduced buff on flanks. ***P. a. occidentalis*** SW British Columbia to NW California. Small and brown. **d Adult**: Upperparts brownish-olive, pale fringes on wings and tail reduced, flanks extensively washed dull cinnamon-brown. ***P. a. practicus*** Appalachian mountains. Cf. Carolina Chickadee. **e Adult**: As *atricapillus,* but upperparts average slightly darker (less buffy) and fringes on wings and tail duller and narrower, underparts slightly paler, flanks more contrasting.

## 52  Carolina Chickadee  *Parus carolinensis*    Text page 261

The southern equivalent of Black-capped Chickadee. Beware hybrids at the range interface (see text for details).

***P. c. extimus*** New Jersey west to Missouri, and south to Tennessee and North Carolina. Relatively brown. **a Adult**: Upperparts mid grey with buffy-olive cast, flanks and undertail-coverts pale drab-buff. ***P. c. atricapilloides*** Southern Kansas to west-central Texas. **b Adult**: Upperparts purer grey, underparts paler with much-reduced buff on flanks.

## 50  Willow Tit  *Parus montanus*    Text page 249

As Marsh Tit, but slightly smaller, with relatively large head and more rounded tail. Cap more extensive, never obviously glossy, cheek patches larger, bib larger and ill-defined, and usually shows contrasting pale wing panel. At all times, voice best distinction.

***P. m. kleinschmidti*** Britain. Smallest and darkest. **a Adult**: Upperparts dark drab-brown, fringes to tertials and secondaries pale buff. Cheeks washed creamy-buff, underparts washed pale cinnamon-brown, deepest on flanks. **b Adult**: In worn plumage, upperparts greyer, cheeks purer white, bib larger, underparts paler; pale fringes abraded, but wing panel, although reduced, still distinct unless heavily worn. ***P. m. borealis*** Fennoscandia and European Russia. **c Adult**: Upperparts grey, washed drab, cap very slightly glossy, fringes to tertials and secondaries whiter, cheeks and underparts white, flanks pinkish-buff. ***P. m. montanus*** Alps and Carpathians. Large and relatively short-tailed. **d Adult**: Upperparts drab-brown, underparts washed drab-grey with pinkish-buff flanks. ***P. m. baicalensis*** Eastern Siberia south to north China. **e Adult**: Upperparts greyish, fringes of flight feathers white, underparts white, flanks washed pale pinkish-grey. ***P. m. kamtschatkensis*** Kamchatka. **f Adult**: Very pale. Mantle grey-white, tertials, secondaries and outer tail feathers very broadly fringed white, underparts uniformly whitish.

## 51  Songar Tit  *Parus songarus*    Text page 257

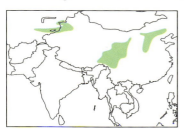

The southern counterpart of Willow Tit; their respective ranges approach each other closely. No hybrids are known.

***P. s. songarus*** Tien Shan. **a Male**: Cap dull black, tinged brown, upperparts pale cinnamon-brown with moderate wing panel. Cheek patches off-white, washed cinnamon-buff at rear. Extensive, ill-defined, dull black bib, underparts washed cinnamon. ***P. s. stoetzneri*** NE China. **b Male**: Cap mid brown, upperparts drab-brown; cinnamon-buff on underparts relatively restricted.

53a

53b

53c

53d

53e

52a

50a

52b

50b

50c

50d

50e

50f

51a

51b

## PLATE 17 SOME TITS FROM WESTERN NORTH AMERICA

### 54 Mountain Chickadee *Parus gambeli* Text page 275

Broad white supercilium unique among North American chickadees.

***P. g. gambeli*** Rocky Mountains and associated ranges from central Montana to eastern Arizona, New Mexico and Texas. **a Adult**: The brownest race in upperpart coloration. Cap, lores and eyestripe black, with forehead 'hoary'. Cheek patches extensively white, base of bill and bib black. Underparts white with flanks and undertail-coverts extensively pale drab-buff. **b Adult**: In worn plumage, white tips on forehead and sides of crown abraded (when very worn, supercilium may almost vanish). Bib better defined, underparts slightly duller and less buff. ***P. g. baileyae*** Canada and most of USA west of the Rockies. **c Adult**: Upperparts rather greyer, flanks variably duller and drabber. **d Juvenile**: Cap and bib slightly paler and less intensely black, cap rather less extensive at rear, supercilium slightly greyer and less distinct, and fringes to tertials and greater coverts tinged buff.

### 55 Mexican Chickadee *Parus sclateri* Text page 279

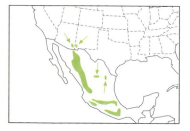

The only chickadee in its range. Note extensive black bib.

***P. s. eidos*** Arizona, New Mexico, and Sierra Madre of northern Mexico. **a Adult**: The greyest race. Cap black, cheek patches extensively white (forming a half-collar), and upperparts dull olive-grey. Bib sooty-black, extending to upper breast, underparts extensively dull smoke-grey. ***P. s. rayi*** Southern Mexico in Sierra Madre de Colima of SW Jalisco and Sierra Madre del Sur of Guerrero and western Oaxaca. **b Adult**: Upperparts and flanks slightly more olive-toned.

### 97 Bridled Titmouse *Parus wollweberi* Text page 403

Striking black and white 'bridled' face pattern with a relatively small black bib and prominent crest distinctive.

***P. w. wollweberi*** Central and southern Mexico. **a Adult**: Upperparts olive-grey (back and rump more olive), dirty white half-collar below bib, rest of underparts light grey, washed yellowish-buff on centre of breast, more intensely so on flanks, belly, vent and undertail-coverts **b Adult**: In worn plumage, cap more extensively black, upperparts duller and rather greyer, wings browner and underparts whiter. **c Juvenile**: Rather dull. Crest shorter, face pattern less well defined, bib pale and washed-out, upperparts browner. ***P. w. phillipsi*** Southern Arizona and northern Sonora and Chihuahua. **d Adult**: Upperparts a little paler and less olive, underparts slightly greyer (less yellow).

54a

54b

54c

54d

55a

55b

97a

97b

97c

97d

## PLATE 18   SOME FAR-EASTERN TITS

### 57  Père David's Tit  *Parus davidi*                     **Text page 283**

Endemic to SW China.
  **Adult**: Black cap and bib, contrastingly 'fluffy' white cheeks and bright cinnamon underparts distinctive.

### 56  White-browed Tit  *Parus superciliosus*             **Text page 282**

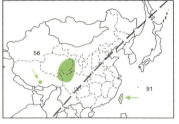

Endemic to SW China.
  **Adult**: White forehead and supercilium and pale pinkish-cinnamon underparts unique. Cap, eyestripe and bib blackish.

### 65  Yellow-bellied Tit  *Parus venustulus*              **Text page 309**

Endemic to China. Small and very short-tailed, with yellow underparts and pale cheeks. Beware juvenile Coal Tit (see Plate 21).
  **a Male**: In breeding plumage, head and bib black with white cheek and nuchal patches. Upperparts mixed grey-blue and black, rump silvery, wingbars, tips to tertials and 'flashes' at sides of tail white. **b Male**: In non-breeding plumage, yellow centre to throat. **c Female**: Cap blue-grey, small pale superciliary spot, mantle and scapulars olive-green, rump yellowish-olive, throat off-white with greyish malar. **d Juvenile male**: Cap and upperparts olive-green, small pale superciliary spot, cheek patches off-white, malar stripe poorly defined, throat pale yellow. **e Juvenile female**: Wings and tail paler, cheek patches duller, malar stripe less defined. **f Male**: In post-juvenile moult September–March, cap mottled olive-green and black.

### 95  Varied Tit  *Parus varius*                          **Text page 397**

Underparts rufous, usually with contrastingly paler forehead and cheek patches.
  ***P. v. varius*** Kurile islands, NE China, Korea, the main islands of Japan, Goto islands and Izu O-shima. **a Adult**: Forehead, lores, and cheek patches buff, bib, crown and nape black with narrow whitish nuchal-patch, chestnut collar and mid grey upperparts. Underparts rufous with buff ventral line. **b Juvenile**: Much duller. Head sooty olive-grey, with forehead and lores dull buff and cheek and nuchal patches dull yellowish; upperparts dull greyish-olive with diffuse dull rufous collar. Bib smoky-grey, underparts pale rufous with broad yellowish ventral line. ***P. v. owstoni*** Outer Izu islands. **c Adult**: Darkest race. Forecrown and cheek patches rufous, nuchal patch orange-rufous, underparts cinnamon-rufous; upperparts distinctly tinged olive. ***P. v. castaneoventris*** Taiwan. **d Adult**: Rather small. Forehead, lores and cheek patches buffy-white, underparts dark rufous with no pale median line.

### 91  Yellow Tit  *Parus holsti*                          **Text page 383**

Endemic to Taiwan. Distinctive. Map above. **a Male**: Forehead, cheek patches and underparts rich yellow, vent black. Cap and crest black, nuchal patch whitish. Upperparts dark oily green, wings and tail more iridescent blue. **b Female**: Crest slightly shorter, upperparts duller, more olive-green, and lacks black vent. **c Juvenile**: Rather paler. Upperparts, including crest, blue-grey, washed olive on nape and mantle, underparts white, only faintly washed yellow.

57

56

65a

65c

65b

65f

65e

65d

95a

95b

95c

95d

91a

91b

91c

## PLATE 19    THE SIBERIAN TIT COMPLEX

## 59  Boreal Chickadee  *Parus hudsonicus*          **Text page 288**

Combination of brownish cap and bright orange-cinnamon flanks unique.

**P. h. hudsonicus** Eastern Canada. **a Adult**: Cap pinkish-brown, fore-cheek white, grading into pale grey half-collar. Upperparts olive-grey, showing little contrast with cap; rather fine paler fringes to wing feathers. Small sooty-black bib; breast and belly off-white. **b Adult**: In worn plumage pale fringes on wings abraded, bib larger and better defined, cheek patches duller; rufous of flanks may be paler and more restricted. **c Juvenile**: Cap browner, not so pink, and showing less contrast with upperparts, which are also browner. Bib slightly smaller and paler, more brownish, fringes to wing feathers tinged dull cinnamon, and flanks and vent paler, more cinnamon-buff.

## 60  Chestnut-backed Chickadee  *Parus rufescens*          **Text page 292**

Dull chestnut upperparts with contrastingly dark grey wings and tail distinctive among North American chickadees.

**P. r. rufescens** Alaska south to central California. **a Adult**: Cap dark brown, extending well onto upper mantle; cheek patches whitish, extending onto side of nape. Bib dark brown, flanks chestnut-brown, remainder of underparts off-white. **b Juvenile**: Overall duller and less contrastingly patterned. Cap paler and less pinkish-brown, mantle paler and less rufous, cheek patch slightly duller, underparts greyer and flank patches duller and less extensive. **P. r. neglectus** SW Marin Co., central coastal California. **c Adult**: Underparts light grey, white confined to narrow ventral line, flank patches paler and much more restricted, and inner tertials finely fringed rufous. **P. r. barlowi** Southern coastal California (San Francisco Bay southwards). **d Adult**: Flanks light grey, tertial fringes always pale rufous.

## 58  Siberian Tit  *Parus cinctus*          **Text page 285**

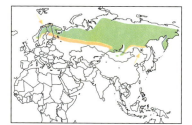

Northerly distribution and extensive brownish-grey cap unique in Eurasia, but see Boreal Chickadee in NW North America.

**P. c. lapponicus** Scandinavia and northern Europe. **a Adult**: Upperparts pale cinnamon-brown; on closed wing whitish fringes form paler panel. Long off-white cheek patches, extensive sooty-brown bib, and underparts pale rufous-cinnamon with whitish confined to centre of breast and belly. **b Adult**: In worn plumage, upperparts duller, contrasting less with cap, bib better defined, and underparts rather whiter, flanks and undertail-coverts paler and buffer. **c Juvenile**: As worn adult, but less contrast between cap and mantle (almost none when worn), less cinnamon in upperparts, narrower cheek patches, dingier underparts and paler, ill-defined bib. **P. c. cinctus** Northern Siberia. **d Adult**: Upperparts paler and greyer than *lapponicus*, less contrast between cap and mantle. Fringes to wing feathers broader and whiter, and underparts paler, with more restricted area of pinkish-buff on flanks and undertail-coverts. **P. c. lathami** Alaska and NW Mackenzie. **e Adult**: Pale and greyish as Siberian birds. Separated from Boreal Chickadee by gleaming white cheek patches extending to nape (not greyish rear ear-coverts and sides of neck) and prominent pale fringes to greater coverts and tertials.

59a

59b

59c

60a

60b

60c

60d

58a

58b

58c

58d

58e

PLATE 20   CRESTED TIT AND SOME HIMALAYAN TITS

## 61  Rufous-naped Tit  *Parus rufonuchalis*          Text page 294

Central Asia, western Himalayas. Largest and darkest of crested tits in region.
**a Adult**: Bib reaches upper belly, upperparts olive-grey, nuchal spot often tinged buff, underparts clean grey. **b Juvenile**: Cap duller, with shorter crest, upperparts and belly washed brown, bib much paler, and axillaries and under-tail-coverts pale buff.

## 62  Rufous-vented Tit  *Parus rubidiventris*          Text page 296

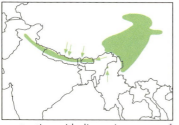

Combination of black cap, crest and bib, whitish cheek and nuchal patches, greyish upperparts (lacking pale wingbars) and underpart coloration distinctive.
   ***P. r. rubidiventris*** ('Rufous-bellied Crested Tit') Western Himalayas. **a Adult**: Upperparts tinged olive, nuchal spot washed pale rufous, cheek patch off-white, lower breast, centre of belly and vent cinnamon-rufous, flanks mid grey, washed buff. **b Juvenile**: Crest smaller, cap sooty-grey, contrasting less with upperparts (which are grey, washed olive, with some darker mottling), nuchal spot dirty buff-white, cheek patch tinged yellowish, and bib sooty-grey, contrasting with dingy cinnamon-rufous underparts. ***P. r. beavani*** ('Sikkim Black Tit') Eastern Himalayas (east from central Nepal), NE Burma, Tibet and SW China. **c Adult**: Upperparts tinged blue, cheek and nuchal patches faintly tinged buff, underparts light–mid grey washed buff (distinctly so when very fresh), especially on centre of breast and belly; cinnamon axillaries may show at bend of wing. **d Juvenile**: As *rubidiventris*, but upperparts slightly darker, washed buff, more pronounced yellow-buff tinge to cheek patches, bib usually poorly demarcated from dull greyish-drab belly and vent; undertail-coverts dull buff.

## 68  Crested Tit  *Parus cristatus*          Text page 317

Crest and black and white head markings unique among European tits.
   ***P. c. scoticus*** Scotland. **a Adult**: Upperparts dull brown, fringes to crown feathers tinged drab, and underparts dull, flanks and undertail-coverts washed brownish. **b Juvenile**: Crest shorter, cap, crest and bib duller and browner, crown spotted (not scaled). Eyestripe narrower, and no dark collar. ***P. c. abadiei*** NW France in Bretagne. **c Adult**: Buffest race. Forehead, cheeks and fringes to crown feathers washed buff, upperparts rufous-brown, flanks washed bright cinnamon. ***P. c. cristatus*** Scandinavia, Russia and eastern Europe. **d Adult**: Palest and greyest race, with whitest underparts (bird illustrated is '*bureschi*' of Balkans).

## 69  Grey-crested Tit  *Parus dichrous*          Text page 320

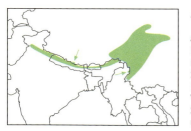

A plain tit, lacking blacks or yellows, with an erect, pointed crest.
   ***P. d. kangrae*** NW Himalayas (eastern Himalayan birds similar). **a Adult**: Upperparts dull greyish. Pale submoustachial stripe and half-collar, throat light grey-buff, contrasting with pale drab-cinnamon underparts. ***P. d. wellsi*** NE Burma and SW China in western Sichuan and NW Yunnan. **b Adult**: Underparts paler and buffer, lacking contrast between throat and breast. ***P. d. dichroides*** Western China in NE Tibet, northern Sichuan, Qinghai, Gansu and Shaanxi. **c Adult**: Grey cap and crest contrast with dark drab-grey upperparts. Underparts as *wellsi*.

## PLATE 21    COAL AND SPOT-WINGED TITS

## 64  Coal Tit  *Parus ater*                    **Text page 302**

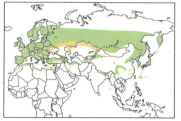

Through most of huge range, spotted double wingbars unique.

**P. a. hibernicus** Ireland. **a Male**: Upperparts greenish-olive, pale areas of plumage light yellow (wearing to whitish), flanks and vent cinnamon-buff. **P. a. britannicus** Britain. **b Male**: Cheek and nuchal patches washed creamy, upperparts greyish olive-buff, flanks and vent pale cinnamon-buff (wear to pale buff). **P. a. ater** Continental Europe and Asia to NE China. **c Male**: White nuchal and cheek patches. Upperparts blue-grey, tinged olive when fresh. Breast and belly white, flanks and vent extensively greyish-buff. **d Female**: Black areas fractionally duller; from January to about March, upperparts more greenish. **e Juvenile**: Dull. Pale areas washed yellow, nuchal patch ill-defined, upperparts duller and greener, bib small and ill-defined. **P. a. pekinensis** NE China. **f Male**: Cheek and nuchal patches washed buff and underparts pale buff, washed greyer on flanks. Sports a short crest. **P. a. atlas** North Morocco. **g Male**: Upperparts dull greyish-olive (wear greyer), bib extensive, pale areas of plumage yellow-white, flanks extensively dark smoke-grey (wearing paler). **P. a. ledouci** Northern Tunisia and NE Algeria. **h Male**: Pale areas of plumage washed yellow (even when worn), upperparts greyish-green, flanks to vent olive-grey. **P. a. cypriotes** Cyprus. **i Male**: Head extensively black, cheek and nuchal patches rather small, upperparts rich brown, median-covert tips washed rusty-buff, underparts pale pinkish-buff, flanks to vent rufous-brown. **P. a. chorassanicus** NE Iran and southern Turkmenistan. **j Male**: Upperparts sandy-brown, flanks grey-buffy. **P. a. aemodius** Eastern Himalayas, western China and northern Burma. **k Male**: Conspicuous crest. Upperparts dull and greyish, wingbars tinged buffy. A pale individual, underparts pinkish-white. **l Juvenile**: Cheek patches obviously washed yellowish; underparts pale, with contrast between dull olive-grey bib and dirty buffy-yellow breast (cf. juvenile Spot-winged Tit).

## 63  Spot-winged Tit  *Parus melanolophus*                    **Text page 299**

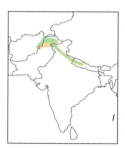

West Himalayas complex from east Afghanistan to western Nepal. Spotted double white wingbars and blue-grey underparts with rufous flanks and undertail-coverts distinctive.

**a Adult**: Head black, with long crest and white cheek and nuchal patches. Upperparts blue-grey. **b Juvenile**: Head dark brown, upperparts washed olive-brown (greyer than juvenile Coal Tit). Wingbars obviously washed rusty-buff, but cheek patches only faintly tinged yellowish. Bib hardly contrasts with dull buffy-grey underparts; upper flanks rusty-buff.

## Hybrid Coal Tit x Spot-winged Tit Frequent in west-central Nepal.

**c Spot-winged-type hybrid**: As Spot-winged, but flank patches paler rufous. **d Coal Tit-type hybrid**: As Coal, but variable amounts of grey or black on underparts, usually as irregular extensions of bib. **e Cinnamon-bellied hybrid**: Distinctive, with broad band of cinnamon-orange from bib to lower belly.

64a

64b

64c

64d

64e

64f

64g

64h

64i

64j

64k

64l

63a

63b

63c

63d

63e

## PLATE 22    ENDEMIC PHILIPPINE TITS

## 66  Elegant Tit  *Parus elegans*                    **Text page 311**

The most widespread Philippine Tit.
   ***P. e. elegans*** Central and southern Luzon, Catanduanes, Mindoro and Panay.
**a Male**: Upperparts blackish, spotted whitish and pale yellow-grey, back and
rump pale yellow-grey. **b Female**: Cap slightly duller, forehead and bib sooty-
brown, upperparts greenish-grey with few blackish spots, less white in wings and
tail, cheeks, nuchal spot and underparts paler and duller yellow. **c Juvenile male**:
Cap and upperparts greenish-grey (with odd dark feather centres or dirty white
spots), reduced white in wings and tail, nuchal patch, cheeks and underparts
dirty pale yellow, malar stripe dark greenish-grey. **d Juvenile female**: Cap paler
and nuchal spot even smaller; lacks malar stripe. ***P. e. gilliardi*** Bataan peninsula, central Luzon. **e Male**: Nuchal spot rich yellow, upperparts spotted yellow,
extensive white in wings and tail. Sexual dimorphism reduced (see text). ***P. e. albescens*** Negros,
Guimaras, Masbate and Ticao. **f Male** (Masbate): Large whitish spots on upperparts; back and rump light
olive yellowish-grey, cheeks and especially underparts pale yellow, with clean flanks. For Negros males
see text. ***P. e. mindanensis*** Mindanao, Samar, Leyte and probably Biliran. **g Male**: Upperparts profusely
spotted olive-yellow, back and rump olive-yellow. **h Female**: Cap sooty olive-brown, faintly scaled olive,
upperparts olive-green, wing and tail spots reduced, bib dark olive-green, flanks extensively washed olive-
green.

## 67  Palawan Tit  *Parus amabilis*                    **Text page 315**

Restricted to Palawan and Balabac, and to Calawit in the Calamian group.
   **a Male**: Head and breast glossy blue-black, upperparts yellow, rump blue-
grey, extensive white corners to tail, wingbars and tertials tips, and largely white
primary coverts. **b Female**: Head and especially breast paler and browner, with
pale yellow collar, mantle and scapulars greenish, back grey, rump yellow, less
white in tail, and narrower wingbars and tertial tips. **c Juvenile**: Upperparts
almost uniformly olive (cap paler than female's), no yellow collar, wingbars very
narrow, and only faint indication of bib. **d Male**: In treetops, viewed from below.

## 96  White-fronted Tit  *Parus semilarvatus*           **Text page 401**

Distinctive. The rarest Philippine Tit.
   ***P. s. semilarvatus*** Southern and central Luzon. **a Male**: Brownish-black,
glossed deep blue; forehead, lores and fore cheeks buffy-white. **b Female**:
Upperparts slightly duller and less glossy, underparts dull milk-chocolate-brown.
**c Male**: Showing underwing-coverts. ***P. s. snowi*** NE Luzon (northern Sierra
Madre). **d Female**: Small whitish spots on nape and sides of neck. **e Juvenile
male**: Upperparts duller than adult, especially scapulars, back and rump, underparts blackish-brown with little or no gloss; shows narrow whitish half-collar.
***P. s. nehrkorni*** Mindanao. **f Male**: White band across base of flight feathers.

66a

66b

66c

66d

66e

66f

66g

66h

67a

67b

67c

67d

96a

96b

96c

96d

96e

96f

# PLATE 23    AFRICAN BLACK TITS 1

## 73  Carp's Tit  *Parus carpi*                    Text page 330

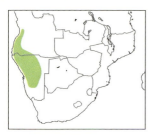

SW Angola and Namibia. On closed wing, median and inner greater coverts solidly white, dark centres visible on *c.* 5 outer greater coverts. Broad white fringes to outermost tertial and inner secondaries form solid white stripe.

**a Male**: Glossy blue-black, tail variably fringed and tipped white; undertail-coverts and thighs variably but narrowly fringed whitish. **b Female**: 'Face' and throat paler and browner. **c Juvenile**: Deep brownish-black with reduced blue gloss (especially females), less white in tail, fringes to flight feathers tinged dull buffy-yellow.

## 72  Southern Black Tit  *Parus niger*           Text page 326

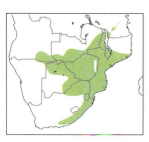

Must be carefully distinguished from Carp's and White-winged Tits, but in overlap zones shows less white in wing.

*P. n. niger* Eastern Cape province to southern Mozambique. **a Male**: Dusty dull blue-black, rather greyer on belly and vent, undertail-coverts tipped white and tail broadly fringed and tipped white. Dark centres visible on at least 6 outer greater coverts and no solid white stripe along tertials and inner secondaries. **b Female**: Upperparts slightly less glossy and underparts paler, especially belly, pale tips to undertail-coverts showing less contrast. **c Juvenile**: Upperparts dark brown, crown faintly glossed blue, with reduced white at tip of tail, fringes to flight feathers washed yellow, and 'face' and underparts pale brown, washed grey on underparts.

*P. n. ravidus* Central Mozambique, plateau of Zimbabwe and northern Transvaal. More white in wing, especially on inner greater coverts. **d Female**: Underparts paler and greyer, plain mouse-grey. *P. n. xanthostomus* NE Namibia and Angola to NW Zimbabwe, northern Mozambique and SE Tanzania. White in wing as *niger*. **e Female**: Underparts intermediate between *niger* and *ravidus*. (Note figures d and e have been reduced slightly in size.)

## 71  White-winged Tit  *Parus leucomelas*        Text page 324

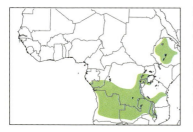

Ethiopia and south-central Africa. Fringes to wing-coverts, tertials and inner secondaries form solid white panel on closed wing. Iris dark.

*P. l. insignis* Central and southern Africa. **a Male**: Body glossed blue, narrow white rim to tail and no white in undertail-coverts. **b Female**: Underparts slightly duller and not so glossy. **c Juvenile**: Dull with no gloss, underparts dark sooty-brown. Fringes to flight feathers faintly washed yellow, outer greater coverts may show dark centres.

## 70  White-shouldered Tit  *Parus guineensis*    Text page 321

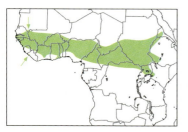

Senegal to Kenya and SW Ethiopia. Relatively small, adult with prominent pale eye. Fringes to coverts, tertials and inner secondaries form solid white panel on closed wing. No white in tail or undertail-coverts.

**a Adult**: Glossy blue-black. **b Juvenile**: Duller, fringes to flight feathers yellow, and dark centres to outer greater coverts may show on closed wing. Iris grey or brown.

## PLATE 24    AFRICAN BLACK TITS 2, SPOTTED CREEPER

## 74  White-bellied Tit  *Parus albiventris*          Text page 332

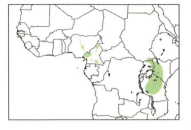

Disjunct populations in West Africa (Cameroon) and East Africa (from Sudan south to Tanzania). A 'black' tit with lower breast to undertail-coverts diagnostically white.
  **a Male**: Upperparts, bib and upper flanks faintly glossy. Tail broadly bordered and more narrowly tipped white, broad white wingbars and fringes to outer tertials and inner secondaries, and narrower pale fringes to remaining flight feathers. **b Female**: Duller. Upperparts and bib sooty coal-grey and, most noticeably, 'face' and throat obviously paler and browner. **c Juvenile**: Upperparts and bib browner than adult female, flight-feathers fringes faintly washed yellow; all except outer tail feathers lack white tips.

## 75  White-backed Tit  *Parus leuconotus*          Text page 334

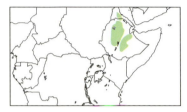

Endemic to highlands of Ethiopia and Eritrea. All-dark plumage with white back unique.
  **a Male**: Overall black, with faint blue gloss to much of plumage, tail rather narrowly rimmed white; mantle dirty creamy-white, forming a conspicuous saddle (may be a little smaller in worn plumage). Female similar, but underparts slightly duller. **b Juvenile**: Slightly duller and browner, with pale saddle tinged buff and little or no gloss to plumage.

## 32  Spotted Creeper  *Salpornis spilonotus*          Text page 202

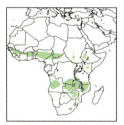

Scattered populations through Africa and in India. Unmistakable.
  ***S. s. spilonotus*** Western and central India (except range of *rajputanae*). **a Adult**: Bill long, slender and decurved. Upperparts dark brown, spotted whitish, prominently so on mantle and scapulars; wings and tail dark brown, boldly barred white. Long off-white supercilium and dark brown eyestripe; sides of head and underparts off-white (sometimes washed cinnamon), variably but finely spotted and barred brown. ***S. s. rajputanae*** Central and SE Rajasthan. **b Adult**: Upperparts slightly paler, pale spotting slightly larger and more profuse; underparts (but not throat or upper breast) washed cinnamon, dark markings reduced, especially on breast. ***S. s. emini*** Northern tropics of Africa from Senegal to NE Uganda. **c Adult**: Pale spots on upperparts slightly larger than in nominate s*pilonotus*, underparts whiter, diffuse dark markings present on throat, but dark markings on breast and belly sparser. ***S. s. erlangeri*** Ethiopia. **d Adult**: Spots on upperparts washed cinnamon-buff; underparts washed cinnamon, with bold dark markings and contrasting white spots. Bill short. ***S. s. salvadori*** Eastern Uganda, western Kenya, and Africa south of Equator. **e Adult**: Pale spots on upperparts washed buff (intermediate between *emini* and *erlangeri*). Underparts washed cinnamon-buff (whiter than *erlangeri,* with dark markings and white spotting reduced). Bill short.

PLATE 25    SOME AFRICAN TITS

## 77  Rufous-bellied Tit  *Parus rufiventris*                    Text page 337

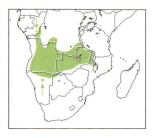

Blackish hood and rufous underparts diagnostic. Eye conspicuously yellow in adult, dark in juvenile.

**P. r. rufiventris** Angola, Zaïre and western Zambia. **a Male**: Slightly glossy on crown. Broad white wingbars, narrow white fringes to tertials and flight feathers, and variable white flash at base of primaries. Breast dark grey. **b Juvenile male**: Duller. Black replaced by dark sooty-grey, upperparts tinged brown, wingbars and fringes to flight feathers tinged yellow-buff, white border to tail much reduced, and underparts slightly paler and duller. **P. r. masukuensis** SE Zaïre, eastern Zambia and Malawi. **c Male**: Upperparts and breast paler grey, underparts paler, more pinkish-cinnamon.

## 78  Cinnamon-breasted Tit  *Parus pallidiventris*          Text page 339

As Rufous-bellied Tit, but breast grey rather than black and remainder of underparts rather paler and more washed-out. Notably, at all ages, iris brown.

**P. p. pallidiventris** Tanzania, Malawi and northern Mozambique. **a Adult**: Head and throat black, grading to grey on upper breast and upper flanks and pale pinkish-buff on remainder of underparts (washed grey on lower flanks and undertail coverts). White 'flash' at base of primaries. **b Juvenile male**: Rather duller and browner, with duller wingbars and tertial fringes, brown primary coverts (finely fringed rusty-brown), flight feathers narrowly fringed dirty yellow-white, and lower breast grey, tinged brown (juvenile female lacks this greyish collar).

## 79  Red-throated Tit  *Parus fringillinus*                    Text page 342

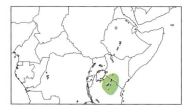

Kenya and Tanzania. Dark grey cap and pale rufous collar unique.
  **a Male**: Cap finely scaled paler, bordered by pale rufous. Two broad white wingbars. Sides of head, throat and breast cinnamon-buff, becoming greyish on flanks and drab-grey on belly and vent. **b Male**: In worn plumage, cap darker, wingbars less distinct. **c Female**: Underparts duller, throat and breast pale pinkish-buff. **d Juvenile**: Crown feathers fringed cinnamon, less white in tail, underparts slightly paler and greyer.

## 80  Stripe-breasted Tit  *Parus fasciiventer*                Text page 343

Distinctive. Lacks white cheek patches, and the only 'grey' tit in montane forest (above 1800 m).
  **P. f. fasciiventer** SW Uganda, eastern Zaïre and Rwanda. **a Male**: Head and breast blackish, with cap slightly glossy and sides of head and breast slightly browner, with blacker ventral stripe to centre of belly; flanks dirty white. Upperparts mid grey, tinged brown. Sexes very similar. **b Juvenile**: Slightly duller and browner, with nape and sides of head, throat and breast dull cinnamon-brown, contrasting more with blackish chin and short, narrow blackish ventral stripe. Yellowish tinge to fringes of flight feathers. **P. f. tanganjicae** Itombwe mountains, SE Kivu province, Zaïre. **c Male**: Near female *fasciiventer,* but head, nape and breast browner, with rather restricted black cap, underparts washed dull buff. **P. f. kaboboensis** Mount Kabobo, SE Kivu province, Zaïre. **d Adult**: Upperparts clean blue-grey, underparts washed smoke-grey.

77a

77c

77b

78a

78b

79a

79b

79c

79d

80a

80c

80b

80d

PLATE 26    AFRICAN GREY TITS

## 81  Acacia Tit  *Parus thruppi*                          Text page 345

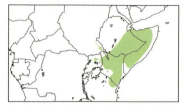

*Acacia* savanna. Pale lores and complete black surround to cheeks unique in this group.

**P. t. thruppi** Ethiopia and Somalia. **a Adult**: Large whitish nuchal patch, upperparts faintly washed drab, forehead and chin mottled paler, lores buffish, cheek patches pure white. Ventral stripe narrowly bordered off-white, grading through pale pinkish-buff to light drab-grey on flanks. **b Adult**: In worn plumage, cap duller, upperparts darker and browner, white fringes on wings abraded, forehead and chin blacker. **c Juvenile**: Overall duller and browner, no gloss on cap, bib duller and smaller, ventral line faint or absent. **P. t. barakae** SW Somalia, Kenya, Uganda and Tanzania. **d Adult**: Slightly paler, with broader, less buffy border to ventral line and slightly paler, purer grey flanks.

## 82  Miombo Tit  *Parus griseiventris*                   Text page 347

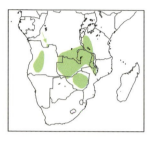

Confined to mature *Brachystegia* woodland from Tanzania to Angola and Zimbabwe (overlaps with Ashy Tit in latter, but usually separated by habitat).

**a Adult**: Cap only faintly glossy, nuchal spot small or absent, extensive white in wing, cheek patches dingy grey-white, bib and ventral line sooty-blackish, flanks light grey, remainder of underparts off-white, washed greyish-buff. Sexes very similar. **b Juvenile**: Slightly duller, flight-feather fringes faintly washed yellow-buff and less white in tail; lacks ventral line.

## 83  Ashy Tit  *Parus cinerascens*                       Text page 349

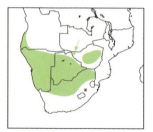

Well-developed *Acacia* savanna from SW Angola and Zimbabwe to northern Cape Province and Transvaal. Separated from Miombo Tit by darker appearance, glossier cap and bib, larger, purer white nuchal patch, and darker, mid grey underparts with only narrow pale border to ventral line.

**P. c. cinerascens** Most of range. **a Male**: Upperparts mid grey. **b Male**: In worn plumage, cap less glossy, nuchal patch smaller and upperparts duller, faintly tinged brown; pale fringes on wings much reduced. Bib sooty-brown with no gloss, and underparts slightly browner. When very worn, black may encircle cheek patches. **c Female**: As male, but overall faintly tinged drab-brown, bib slightly duller. **d Juvenile**: Cap duller, browner and more restricted, upperparts washed slightly browner, flight-feather fringes tinged dull buff, bib duller. **P. c. benguelae** SW Angola. **e Male**: Underparts slightly paler, lacking contrasting pale border to ventral line.

## 84  Southern Grey Tit  *Parus afer*                      Text page 351

Overlaps with Ashy Tit in Namibia and around the Orange river in northern Cape province, but much duller and browner.

**P. a. arens** Lesotho highlands, SW Orange Free State and the Karoo of eastern Cape Province. **a Male**: Upperparts mouse-brown, nuchal patch dull buff-white, underparts dull pale buff. **b Female**: Bib smaller, more restricted, and dull sooty-brown, cap slightly duller. **c Juvenile female**: Duller, cap and bib browner.

PLATE 27    GREAT TIT 1: *MAJOR* AND *MINOR* GROUPS

## 85   Great Tit *Parus major*                    Text page 353

**The *Major* Group** Europe and NW Africa east to Iran, Mongolia and NE Asia. White cheek patches, black bib and ventral line and yellowish underparts distinctive.

*P. m. newtoni* British Isles. **a Male**: Cap, bib and ventral line glossy black, ventral line broad and usually widening to a large patch between legs. **b Female**: Black areas duller, especially bib and ventral line, which are often dull grey-black. Black rear border to cheek patches averages narrower, and ventral line also rather narrower and sometimes broken, merely a small dark patch between legs. **c Juvenile**: Duller, paler and more washed-out. Cap dark sooty-brown, cheek patches washed yellowish, upperparts dull olive-green, wing-coverts olive-grey, bib small and poorly defined, ventral line faint or absent, and underparts pale yellow. *P. m. niethammeri* Crete. **d Male**: Upperparts duller and darker, less green and yellow, underparts very pale. *P. m. blanfordi* Northern Iraq, northern and western Iran. **e Male**: As nominate *major*, but mantle and scapulars slightly duller, more greyish and washed-out, underparts purer and rather paler yellow.

**The *Minor* Group** SE Russia and Japan south to southern Tibet and northern SE Asia. Combination of white cheek patches, single white wingbar, black bib and ventral line, whitish underparts and lack of crest unique.

*P. m. minor* Amurland and Ussuriland, Korea, NE and east-central China, also Sakhalin, the southern Kurile islands and Japan (except Nansei islands). **f Male**: Border of upper mantle olive-yellow, grading to olive on lower mantle and mid greyish-olive on scapulars and back. Underparts whitish, sides of breast and upper flanks washed pale ochre, rear flanks washed pale drab-grey. **g Female**: Differs from male as in nominate *major*, although tertial fringes washed olive. **h Juvenile**: Differs from adult as in *major* group. *P. m. tibetanus* SW China around Tibetan plateau. **i Male**: Large, with dull upperparts and extensive white in tail. *P. m. okinawae* Okinawa and Yagachi, central Nansei Shoto (Ryukyu islands). **j Male**: Green reduced to wash on upper mantle; back and rump dark. *P. m. nigriloris* Ishigaki-jima and Iriomote-jima, southern Nansei Shoto. **k Male**: Upperparts dark blue-grey with no trace of green, no pale nuchal spot, white in tail restricted to tip of T6. Lores black, small white cheek patch, underparts dark. *P. m. commixtus* Southern China and northern Vietnam. (Perhaps of hybrid origin, connecting *cinereus* and *minor* groups.) **l Male**: Green on upperparts reduced, lower mantle and scapulars grey, and underparts washed greyish pinkish-drab.

85a

85b

85c

85d

85e

85f

85g

85h

85i

85l

85j

85k

# PLATE 28   GREAT TIT 2: THE *CINEREUS* GROUP & TURKESTAN TIT

## 85  Great Tit  *Parus major*                       Text page 353

The ***Cinereus* Group** NE Iran, southern Afghanistan, Indian sub-continent, SE Asia and Indonesia. Grey upperparts, whitish cheeks and underparts and black bib and ventral line generally distinctive, but hard to separate from Turkestan Tit (see text).

***P. m. intermedius*** SW Turkmenistan and NE Iran. **m Male:** Upperparts dull light grey, tinged blue, usually with faint trace of olive on upper mantle, alula contrastingly dark, greater coverts light blue-grey; underparts off-white, washed dull creamy. **n Female:** A little duller. **o Male:** Head-on to show square-cut tail with relatively little white in undertail (cf. Turkestan Tit). ***P. m. caschmirensis*** NE Afghanistan and western Himalayas. **p Male:** Large and pale. Upperparts with no trace of olive, tail with extensive white, underparts light-pale grey, washed buffy-drab, border of bib and ventral line slightly whiter. **q Juvenile:** Upperparts tinged yellowish-olive, nuchal patch, cheeks and underparts variably pale yellow-white. ***P. m. ambiguus*** Malay peninsula and Sumatra. **r Male:** Small and dark. Lores often blackish, nuchal spot reduced, tail with reduced white, greater coverts black, fringes bluer than mantle but pale tips rather small and dull, tertials fringed pale grey, underparts light greyish-drab. ***P. m. cinereus*** Java and Lesser Sundas. **s Male:** As *ambiguus,* but underparts slightly paler, cleaner and pinker, greater-covert fringes a little duller blue but tips whitish, tertial fringes whitish. ***P. m. sarawacensis*** Borneo. **t Adult:** Upperparts dark, tail with little white, black cap extending onto nape and white nuchal patch faint or absent, lores black, uppertail-coverts black (not grey), broad black ventral stripe.

## 86  Turkestan Tit  *Parus bokharensis*              Text page 367

Central Asia from NE Iran to NW China. Near 'Grey Tit' (*P. m. intermedius*), but 20–25% longer-tailed, upperparts purer grey, and cheek patch extends further behind eye, with blackish rear border averaging slightly narrower and less distinct (on some, bib may not join cap at rear). Alula concolorous with rest of wing. See text for details.

***P. b. bokharensis*** Western Central Asia. **a Male:** Cap and bib glossy black. **b Female:** Slightly duller. Cap less glossy, upperparts faintly tinged brown, bib and especially ventral line rather duller and more restricted. **c Male:** Head-on to show graduated tail with extensive white on undertail. **d Male:** In worn plumage. nuchal patch larger, with broader black band on sides of neck, bib larger and better defined, and ventral line more regular and better-defined. **e Juvenile:** Rather duller. Cap and especially bib less extensive and duller, dark brown, ventral line poorly developed, and less white in tail. Some (perhaps mostly from southeast of range) have upperparts faintly tinged olive-green and nuchal spot, cheeks, wingbar and underparts tinged yellow.

85m

85n

85o

85q

85p

85r

85s

85t

86b

86a

86c

86d

86e

# PLATE 29  BLUE TIT AND SOME ASIAN TITS

## 88  White-naped Tit  *Parus nuchalis*

Text page 374

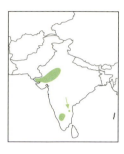

NW and southern peninsular India.
  **a Male**: In breeding plumage, upperparts glossy blue-black, bib and ventral line black, slightly glossy. Underparts creamy, tinged yellow on sides of breast and flanks. **b Female**: As male, but only cap glossy, upperparts·sooty-black, bib and ventral line sooty-brown. **c Juvenile male**: Lacks gloss. Nuchal patch smaller, and less white in wings and tail, although greater coverts tipped·white.

## 87  Green-backed Tit  *Parus monticolus*

Text page 372

Recalls Great Tit (*major* group), but note *two* white wingbars.
  ***P. m. monticolus*** Western Himalayas (very similar in eastern Himalayas, Burma and China). **a Adult**: Cap black, cheek patches white and upperparts olive-green. **b Juvenile**: Overall duller. Cap, bib and ventral line sooty-black, wingbars and tertial fringes washed yellow. ***P. m. legendrei*** Da Lat plateau, southern Vietnam. **c Adult**: Upperparts duller and greyer, slightly less white in wing; ventral stripe averages much broader, with pale dull yellow restricted to flanks.

## 92  Blue Tit *Parus caeruleus*

Text page 385

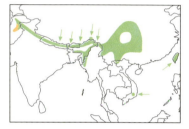

Two groups of subspecies, perhaps better treated as distinct species.
  **The *caeruleus* group** Europe. Blue cap, bordered white, white cheek patches and yellow underparts distinctive. ***P. c. obscurus*** Britain, Ireland and Channel Islands. **a Male**: Relatively dark. Cap dark blue, upperparts greyish-green (relatively green). Tail and wings fringed blue, with relatively narrow white wingbars and tips to tertials. Underparts deep dull yellow with narrow black ventral line. **b Juvenile**: Face, supercilium and nape pale dirty yellow. Cap, eyestripe and nuchal band hardly darker than upperparts. Tail and wings dull, washed green, wingbar tinged yellowish, and underparts dull yellow with much reduced bib and no ventral line. ***P. c. orientalis*** SE European Russia. **c Male**: Upperparts relatively paler, olive-grey, tinged yellow; underparts brighter and paler yellow. ***P. c. persicus*** SW Iran. **d Male**: The palest race. Upperparts bluish green-grey; underparts variable, from uniform yellow-white to richer yellow on breast, whiter on belly and vent.
  **The *teneriffae* group** North Africa and Canary Islands. Cap blackish. ***P. c. palmensis*** La Palma. **e Male**: Upperparts dark grey, sometimes tinged green, narrow white wingbar; belly extensively white. ***P. c. teneriffae*** Gomera. **f Male**: Upperparts slaty-blue, nuchal band and collar relatively broad, no wingbar; underparts rich dark yellow, ventral line much reduced. **g Juvenile**: Cap and stripes on head dark grey, relatively well defined, upperparts grey-green; face and underparts relatively bright yellow, sometimes traces of small greyish bib. ***P. c. ombriosus*** Hierro. **h Male**: Upperparts greenish, narrow greyish-white wingbar. ***P. c. degener*** Fuerteventura and Lanzarote. **i Male**: Upperparts grey, washed blue, nuchal band and collar relatively narrow, broad white wingbar; underparts clean pale yellow, belly whitish.

88a

88b

88c

87b

87a

87c

92a

92b

92d

92c

92e

92h

92f

92g

92i

# PLATE 30 AZURE AND YELLOW-BREASTED TITS

## 93 Azure Tit *Parus cyanus*                Text page 390

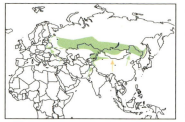

A pallid tit with white head, extensive white in wings and tail (much more than Blue Tit) and proportionally long, slightly graduated tail; often appears slightly 'fluffy'.

***P. c. cyanus*** European Russia. **a Adult**: Head white with narrow black eyestripes and dark blue nuchal band. Upperparts blue-grey, broad white wingbars, white tips to primary coverts, and extensively white tertials (forming broad white inverted 'V' on wings). Irregular blue-black ventral line. **b Juvenile**: Crown and upperparts greyer, eyestripe and nuchal band duller, wing-coverts grey (not bright blue), ventral line often absent. ***P. c. hyperrhiphaeus*** Easternmost European Russia, western Siberia and northern Kazakhstan. **c Male**: Paler than nominate *cyanus*. Upperparts light grey, tinged lavender, rump almost white. Blue of nuchal band, wings and tail duller, but more white in wings and tail. ***P. c. tianschanicus*** Central Asia. **d Adult**: Duller and slightly darker than nominate *cyanus*. Head pale grey, tinged lavender towards rear crown. **e Juvenile**: Underparts may be washed very pale yellow.

### Hybrid Azure x Blue Tit (sometimes known as 'Pleske's Tit *P. pleskii*')
**f, g** and **h** Three variants: Very variable. Cap darker than on Azure Tit, from lavender-grey to blue or even black, upperparts pale greyish, much less white in tail (but more than Blue Tit), less white in wing. Gradation of underpart patterns, from traces of dark collar, through a dark bib to a yellowish wash. Some hybrids (back-crosses?) may more closely resemble one or other parent species. Vagrants to Europe are sometimes hybrid Azure x Blue Tits.

## 94 Yellow-breasted Tit *Parus flavipectus*                Text page 394

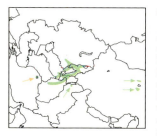

Grey or whitish head and yellow breast band distinctive.

***P. f. flavipectus*** Western Tien Shan, south to Fergana basin, northern Afghanistan and northern Pakistan. **a Male**: Head pale grey, paler nuchal spot, and upperparts blue-grey with extensive white in wings and tail. Yellow breast band, remainder of underparts whitish with faintly darker bib and prominent dark ventral line. **b Female**: Slightly duller, with paler and less blue upperparts and slightly paler yellow breast band. **c Juvenile**: Head and underparts variably washed yellow, mantle and scapulars washed greenish. ***P. f. carruthersi*** SW Tien Shan west to Samarkand and south to the Afghan border. **d Male**: As nominate *flavipectus,* but overall duller. Crown almost concolorous with upperparts, no paler nuchal spot, less white in tail; throat darker and greyer, breast darker yellow and belly dirtier white. ***P. f. berezowskii*** Qinghai, north-central China. **e Male**: As nominate *flavipectus,* but head and throat rather paler, lacking dark eyestripe, and nuchal band reduced to narrow line; upperparts slightly duller and greyer, breast slightly paler yellow.

93a

93b

93e

93c

93d

93g

93h

93f

94a

94b

94c

94d

94e

# PLATE 31    CRESTED ORIENTAL TITS

## 90  Yellow-cheeked Tit  *Parus spilonotus*      **Text page 380**

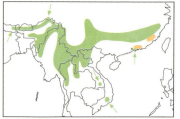

Distinctive combination of yellow cheeks and prominent crest, but needs to be carefully distinguished from Black-lored Tit in easternmost Nepal, Darjeeling and Sikkim.

**P. s. spilonotus** Eastern Himalayas, NE Burma, southern Tibet and NW Yunnan. **a Adult**: Upperparts olive-yellow, spotted or streaked black, underparts pale yellow. Sexes very similar. **b Juvenile**: Cap and bib duller, upperparts with less well-defined black spotting, wingbars and tertial fringes washed yellow, and underparts paler yellow. **P. s. rex** Southern China, NW Vietnam and NE Laos. **c Male**: Upperparts blue-grey, streaked black, bib and ventral line very extensive, remainder of underparts grey. **d Female**: Duller, upperparts washed olive with reduced dark markings, bib barely contrasting with underparts. **e Juvenile male**: Much duller. Cap sooty, sides of head and nuchal spot paler yellow, upperparts washed olive, bib sooty-brown, ventral line indistinct and underparts washed yellow-olive.

## 89  Black-lored Tit  *Parus xanthogenys*      **Text page 377**

The only crested tit in peninsular India, and combination of crest and yellow cheeks distinctive in Himalayas (but see Yellow-cheeked Tit).

**P. x. xanthogenys** Himalayas from Himachal Pradesh to Nepal, rarely to Darjeeling. **a Male**: Separated from Yellow-cheeked Tit by black forehead and lores, plain upperparts with blackish streaks confined to scapulars, and olive rump. Sexes very similar. **P. x. aplonotus** Northern and eastern peninsular India. **b Female**: The male (not illustrated) is similar to adult nominate *xanthogenys*, although slightly duller; the female is much duller, with the nuchal and cheek patches and underparts paler yellow, and bib and ventral line greyish-olive. **P. x. travancoreensis** Southern India in the Western Ghats. **c Male**: Much duller than nominate *xanthogenys* and male *aplonotus*. Upperparts olive-grey, cheeks washed-out yellow, and underparts dull pale yellow, tinged olive. **d Female**: Duller even than female *aplonotus*. Cap and crest olive-grey, uniform with upperparts, and bib and ventral line showing reduced contrast with underparts, which are only faintly tinged yellow. **e Juvenile female**: Cap sooty-brown (darker than adult female's), cheeks and sides of breast dull yellowish, and little contrast between bib and remainder of underparts.

## 102  Sultan Tit  *Melanochlora sultanea*      **Text page 418**

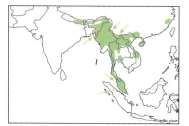

The largest tit, distinctive in all plumages.

**M. s. sultanea** Nepal, NE India, SW China and Burma. **a Male**: Upperparts and bib glossy blue-black. **b Female**: Upperparts dark oily green, wings blackish-brown with dull olive fringes to coverts and flight feathers, bib yellowish olive-green. **c Juvenile**: Crest shorter, greater coverts finely tipped whitish, dark areas of plumage duller and lacking gloss. **M. s. gayeti** Southern Laos and central Vietnam. **d Male**: Cap and crest glossy blue-black.

90a

90b

90c

90e

90d

89a

89e

89b

89c

89d

102b

102c

102a

102d

## PLATE 32   TUFTED TITMOUSE AND ALLIES

### 99  Tufted Titmouse  *Parus bicolor*     Text page 409

Eastern North America. Black forehead and conspicuous grey crest distinctive.
   **a Adult**: Crest and upperparts grey. Lores very pale buff, face and underparts whitish, with prominent large dark eye and rufous-buff flanks. **b Juvenile**: Forehead duller and browner, cap and crest sooty-grey, upperparts darker and browner. Breast washed grey and belly and vent washed buff, thus showing less contrast with buff flanks.

### 100  Black-crested Titmouse  *Parus atricristatus*     Text page 412

Texas and eastern Mexico. Buff forehead and long spiky black crest distinctive.
   **P. a. sennetti** Central and southern Texas. **a Male**: Upperparts mid grey, washed olive-brown. Face and underparts whitish, with orange-buff flanks. **b Juvenile**: Forehead drab-white (bisected by thin dark line back from bill), crown and crest brown, only slightly darker than upperparts, which are rather browner than adult's. Underparts dull, breast washed dull buff, flanks washed dull cinnamon-buff.

### Hybrid Black-crested x Tufted Titmouse
   **c Adult**: Variant A, crest only slightly darker than upperparts (owing to slightly darker feather centres).
**d Adult**: Variant B, crest sooty-black or sooty-brown with much grey.

### 98  Plain Titmouse  *Parus inornatus*     Text page 406

Western USA and Baja California. Very drab, with a short, shaggy crest.
   **P. i. inornatus** Western California (east to Sierra Nevada). **a Adult**: Overall brown. Forehead and face mottled dusty white and dull grey-brown, upperparts, including wings and tail, dull grey-brown, underparts pale buffy. **b Adult**: In worn plumage, fringes to wing and tail feathers paler and more worn, underparts duller. **P. i. affabilis** SW California and northern Baja California Norte. **c Adult**: Upperparts fractionally darker and browner than nominate *inornatus,* underparts rather duller, more heavily washed grey-brown. **P. i. ridgwayi** Interior western North America. **d Adult**: Overall much greyer. Upperparts mid grey, tinged brownish, with greyer fringes to wing and tail feathers.

99a

99b

100a

100d

100c

100b

98a

98c

98b

98d

PLATE 33    LONG-TAILED TIT

## 103  Long-tailed Tit  *Aegithalos caudatus*          **Text page 420**

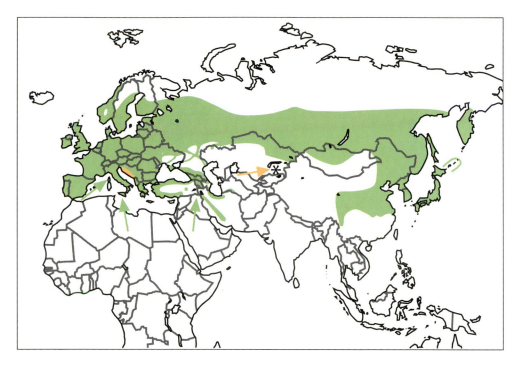

Through most of the range, the only long-tailed tit and highly distinctive. Divisible into four groups.

**The *caudatus* group** One race in northern Europe and Asia. Head, throat and underparts pure white, mantle black, variably marked with pink. ***A. c. caudatus* a Adult**: Flanks contrastingly pink, tertials and secondaries broadly fringed white. **b Juvenile**: Shorter-tailed and overall darker and browner, with cheek patches dusky, accentuating the pale (often raspberry-red) eyering; only forehead dirty brown-white. Upperparts brown, lacking pink, underparts dull off-white, belly tinged buff.

**The *europaeus* group** Nine races in southern and western Europe, NE China and Japan. Head whitish with broad blackish lateral crown stripes, mantle as *caudatus* group. ***A. c. europaeus*** France, Germany, northern Italy and Yugoslavia, east to northern Bulgaria and western Romania. **c Adult**: Rather variable, but usually bright and pale with narrow lateral crown stripes, broad pure white central crown, and clean white cheek patches. ***A. c. rosaceus*** Britain and Ireland. **d Adult**: Darker, with broader lateral crown stripes, centre of crown sullied brown and underparts tinged grey; often shows gorget of darker streaks. ***A. c. taiti*** Southern France and northern Spain and Portugal. **e Adult**: Small and dark. Broad lateral crown stripes and little pink in upperparts.

**The *alpinus* group** Seven races around Mediterranean and in SW Asia. Head as *europaeus* group, but cheek patches streaked darker and some show dark throat spot. Upperparts mainly grey, with little or no pink. ***A. c. irbii*** Southern Spain and Portugal, also Corsica. **f Adult**: Lateral crown stripes blackish, narrow black border to upper mantle. ***A. c. siculus*** Sicily. **g Adult**: Lateral crown stripes dull brownish, crown stripe washed buff, dark border to upper mantle reduced (brownish-black), upperparts virtually lacking pink; may show faint sooty-black spot on lower throat. ***A. c. tephronotus*** Turkey. **h Adult**: Lateral crown stripes black, dark border to upper mantle faint or lacking, underparts buff with neat blackish spot on throat. **i Juvenile**: Head brownish, centre of crown streaked dirty white and sides of crown slightly darker; upper mantle and rump grey, lower mantle and scapulars dull brownish. Underparts dirty white. ***A. c. passekii*** Western Iran. **j Adult**: Rather pale, especially underparts, with only faint brown wash on belly, crown stripe white; lacks gorget.

**The *glaucogularis* group** China. Head dull buffish with glossy black lateral crown stripes, upperparts grey, underparts dull buffish with dark bib. Juvenile distinctive. ***A. c. glaucogularis*** China. Separated from other long-tailed tits in region by dark eye, not encircled by lateral crown stripe, and lack of breast band. **k Adult**: Crown stripe often reduced to buff streak towards rear. Chin and submoustachial stripe off-white, throat sooty-black, finely peppered pale grey. **l Juvenile**: Throat and breast vinous-pink, contrasting with white submoustachial stripe and sides of neck, underparts washed yellow-buff.

103b

103a

103d

103c

103e

103f

103g

103i

103h

103j

103l

103k

PLATE 34    HIMALAYAN LONG-TAILED TITS

## 106  White-throated Tit  *Aegithalos niveogularis*    Text page 430

Western Himalayas from Pakistan to western Nepal. Whitish throat and fore-crown distinctive.
    **a Adult**: Crown stripe fades to cinnamon-brown at rear and lateral crown stripes also paler and ill-defined at rear. Whitish throat clearly demarcated from narrow cinnamon-brown breast band; underparts beige. **b Juvenile**: Crown stripe duller, tinged buff on forecrown, upperparts browner, sides of neck and submoustachial stripe washed buff, and throat dull pinkish, showing reduced contrast with narrow, irregular breast band.

## 107  Black-browed Tit  *Aegithalos iouschistos*    Text page 432

Extensive black sides to head, totally encompassing yellow eye.
    ***A. i. iouschistos*** Himalayas from central Nepal to SE Tibet. **a Adult**: Narrow cinnamon-buff crown stripe. Small silvery bib bordered by black chin and blackish sides to throat (forming inverted 'V'). Ear-coverts and sides of neck cinnamon-buff, submoustachial stripe and lower border of bib rich orange-rufous, underparts cinnamon-rufous, pinker on flanks and belly. **b Juvenile**: Crown stripe and underparts dull pale buff, with no contrast between throat and breast. ***A. i. bonvaloti*** NE Burma, easternmost SE Tibet and western China. **c Adult**: Crown stripe slightly paler, throat pattern more black and white, contrasting with cinnamon-rufous breast band, which is well demarcated from white lower breast and belly; lower flanks and vent pinkish-buff. ***A. i. sharpei*** Mount Victoria, SW Burma. **d Adult**: Crown stripe whitish, lateral crown stripes relatively narrow. Blackish throat pattern well defined, centre of throat and submoustachial stripe white, well demarcated from cinnamon-brown breast; underparts pale cinnamon.

## 105  Black-throated Tit  *Aegithalos concinnus*    Text page 427

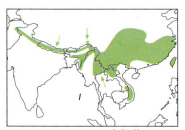

Black bib of adults separates from all long-tailed tits except west Himalayan White-cheeked, but note also white chin and rufous crown.
    ***A. c. iredalei*** Himalayas. **a Adult**: Crown rufous; broad black lateral crown stripes form 'highwayman's mask', framing pale eye, with white supercilium from eye to nape. Chin and submoustachial area white, separating mask and bib, breast rufous-buff, flanks more pinkish. **b Juvenile**: Cap slightly paler, upperparts drabber, supercilium poorly marked, throat and breast off-white, necklace of dark spots, and remainder of underparts pale cinnamon-orange. ***A. c. pulchellus*** Eastern Burma and NW Thailand. **c Adult**: Crown light drab, supercilium much reduced; breast and flanks rufous-cinnamon, separated from black bib by narrow white collar, centre of breast and belly whitish. ***A. c. talifuensis*** NE Burma and SW China (nominate *concinnus* in southern China very similar). **d Adult**: Crown orange; breast band and flanks well defined, rufous-chestnut. ***A. c. annamensis*** Southern Vietnam and southern Laos (Bolovens plateau). **e Adult**: Crown dull grey, breast band greyish-drab, underparts dirty white, flanks washed light greyish-pink. **f Juvenile**: Throat dirty buff, necklace of dark spots and underparts grey-buff, flanks washed buffy-cinnamon.

PLATE 35    VERDIN & WHITE-CHEEKED AND SOOTY TITS

## 45  Verdin  *Auriparus flaviceps*                    Text page 234

Small, with distinctively pointed, conical black bill and strong legs and feet. Builds conspicuous spherical stick nests.
  **A. f. ornatus** SE Arizona, New Mexico, Texas and Oklahoma south to northern Sonora, southern Coahuila, probably northern San Luis Potosi and central Tamaulipas **a Male**: Forecrown, ear-coverts and throat dull yellowish-olive, upperparts mouse-grey, underparts pale grey-white. **b Male**: In worn plumage, yellow of head brighter and more extensive, extending onto rear crown and upper breast; some, especially in south and west, may show chest-nut forecrown and more extensively yellow underparts. **c Male**: Lesser coverts chestnut, forming contrasting patch at shoulder, but often concealed at rest. **d Juvenile**: Duller, lacks yellow on head and chestnut lesser coverts. When recently fledged, conspicuous pinkish-orange bill. **A. f. lamprocephalus** Southern Baja California Sur. **e Male**: Upperparts very slightly paler, yellow on head brighter, often with chestnut forecrown. **A. f. sinaloae** NW Sinaloa. **f Adult**: A bird in moderately fresh plumage. Yellow on head brighter and more extensive, extending broadly onto centre of breast (lower breast and belly may be yellow when worn), upperparts faintly tinged yellow, especially rump of male; usually lacks chestnut on forecrown.

## 104  White-cheeked Tit  *Aegithalos leucogenys*                    Text page 425

NE Afghanistan to NW India. Note dull cap, lack of supercilium and black chin and throat.
  **a Adult**: Cap cinnamon-drab, bordered black (lateral crown stripes barely encompassing yellow eye, and duller and poorly defined at rear). Cheek patch white, underparts drab-grey (with indistinct greyish breast band), grading to pale pinkish-buff on flanks and vent. **b Adult**: From Baluchistan. Upperparts purer grey, crown stripe paler and more contrasting (more cinnamon-grey); underparts slightly paler and more uniform, with narrower, paler and much less obvious breast band. **c Juvenile**: Crown paler, more buffish-drab, lateral crown stripes slightly narrower but better defined at rear, and upperparts slightly duller and browner. Lacks black bib (cheeks and throat pale buff, but may show traces of narrow darker bib on chin and centre of throat), underparts pale pinkish-buff, variably streaked dark brown on upper breast.

## 108  Sooty Tit  *Aegithalos fuliginosus*                    Text page 436

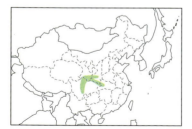

West and central China. Brownish upperparts, lack of black head markings, silver-grey cheek patches and clear-cut dark breast band distinctive among local long-tailed tits.
  **a Adult**: Upperparts dark brown with contrasting pale grey cheek patches, demarcated below by dark moustachial area. Throat grey, separated from broad brown breast band by white half-collar; belly white and flanks pinkish. **b Juvenile**: Forehead and centre of crown white, crown sides rather darker, slightly paler cheeks with blackish wedge behind eye. **c Juvenile**: Darker breast band and purer white throat and underparts than adult, lacking pinkish flanks.

45a

45b

45c

45d

45e

45f

104a

104b

104c

108a

108b

108c

PLATE 36 BUSHTIT AND PYGMY TIT

## 109 Bushtit *Psaltriparus minimus*  Text page 438

Tiny size, long tail, plain plumage and gregarious habits distinctive. All males have dark brown eyes and adult females whitish eyes; whilst juvenile females have dark eyes, these pale within a few weeks of fledging.

The ***Minimus* Group** 'Plain' or 'Common Bushtit'. The Pacific coast region from British Columbia to Baja California. Cap brown, upperparts greyish, ear-coverts dull brownish-drab. ***P. m. minimus*** Northern Oregon to California west of Cascades and Coast Ranges, south to Santa Barbara Co. **a Male**: Cap olive-brown, contrasting strongly with olive-washed upperparts. Throat whitish and rear flanks washed pinkish-drab. **b Female**: Throat and breast duller, washed drab-grey. **c Juvenile**: Cap paler and drabber, contrasting less with mantle (differences between sexes reduced). ***P. m. grindae*** Southern Baja California. **d Juvenile male**: At all ages, upperparts purer grey than on other west-coast birds.

The ***Plumbeus* Group** 'Lead-coloured Bushtit'. Interior western North America from Oregon to eastern California, southern Arizona and New Mexico, northern Sonora and western Texas. Upperparts grey with no contrast between cap and mantle, ear-coverts dull brownish-drab. ***P. m. plumbeus* e Male**: White throat and upper breast contrast with pale drab-grey underparts. **f Female**: Sexes very similar, but throat duller and less contrasting, more obvious buff tinge to belly and vent. **g Juvenile**: Slightly duller and drabber, with less contrastingly brownish ear-coverts (i.e. as worn adult, although wings and tail fresh; ear-coverts variably black on some juvenile males, especially in southern Arizona and New Mexico, where occasionally juvenile females also show black).

The ***Melanotis* Group** 'Black-eared Bushtit'. Mexico and Guatemala. Southwards, shows more contrast between cap and mantle and an increasing proportion of birds have black masks. ***P. m. dimorphicus*** Northern Mexico. **h Male**: Upperparts near *plumbeus*, but slightly more contrast between cap and mantle; underparts (especially rear flanks) tinged light vinaceous-grey, contrasting more with white throat. All males have sooty-black mask (often including chin; light drab on adult female, juvenile female dimorphic). ***P. m. iulus*** Central Mexico. **i Male**: Upperparts mid grey, washed brownish-olive, contrasting with grey cap. All males black-eared, faintly glossy on adults. Throat and sides of neck white, contrasting with rich cinnamon-buff rear flanks and vent. **j Female**: Chin washed drab, throat and sides of neck pale grey-white, grading to pale buff on rear flanks and vent. Often shows sooty-black on upper and rear ear-coverts, especially when worn. **k Juvenile female**: Less contrast between cap and mantle, and underparts duller and paler buff than adult female. Ear-coverts mixed sooty-black and drab-brown, black most frequent on upper and rear ear-coverts. ***P. m. personatus*** South-central Mexico. **l Male**: Mantle cinnamon-brown, contrasting more with cap, breast and belly washed drab. Black mask may form narrow nuchal band. **m Female**: Underparts more strongly washed buff than on *iulus*.

## 110 Pygmy Tit *Psaltria exilis*  Text page 443

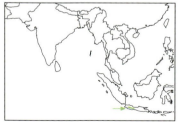

Endemic to Java.
**a, b Adults**: A tiny, plain, long-tailed tit.

109a

109b

109c

109d

109e

109f

109g

109h

109i

109j

109k

109l

109m

110a

110b

Other names: Nuthatch, Common Nuthatch

The most widespread of all the nuthatches, this noisy and acrobatic species is a familiar forest bird from Britain to Japan.

**IDENTIFICATION** Total length 140 mm (5.5 in). Medium-sized. Upperparts blue-grey, with a long, rather broad, black eyestripe. Underpart coloration variable; cheeks, throat and breast whitish to dull buffy-brown, flanks, lower belly and undertail-coverts bright chestnut to pale buff, pale centres to the undertail-coverts forming a mottled patch (see Geographical Variation). Spread tail dark grey, with white subterminal spots on the outer three pairs of feathers. Through most of the vast range, the compact outline with a short tail and long, chisel-like bill are unmistakable. In SE Europe and SW Asia, separated from the larger rock nuthatches (which may also be found on trees) by the prominent white spots in the tail, which show well on perched birds if viewed from below and are often obvious in flight; in addition, the upperparts are slightly darker and the underparts more richly coloured, with contrastingly pale centres to the undertail-coverts. In Asia Minor, distinguished from Krüper's Nuthatch by its larger size and lack of a black cap and rusty breast patch. A much more difficult problem is separation from Chestnut-vented Nuthatch in SW China. Chestnut-vented is slightly larger (although size varies with altitude), darker and bluer above, and shows less whitish below the eye and on the chin. In fresh or little-worn plumage its underparts are buffy as on Eurasian Nuthatch, although duller, browner and less cinnamon; in worn (spring) plumage Chestnut-vented is much greyer below, greyish-buff rather than the cinnamon-buff of Eurasian (see p. 114 for full details).

**SEX/AGE** The sexes differ to a variable extent and in some races are separable even as well-grown nestlings. In the *caesia* group of southern and western Europe the male has the flanks, rear vent and undertail-coverts brick red, well demarcated from the dull orange-buff of the underparts (occasionally the reddish is restricted to a few feathers), whilst the female has these areas rufous-orange, fading into the orange-buff underparts. In the *europaea* group of northern Europe and Asia, the sexes are easily distinguished in the nominate race *europaea*, the male having the flanks to undertail-coverts bright chestnut, clearly demarcated from the whitish underparts, whilst the female has the flanks to undertail-coverts rufous-buff, grading into the underparts (which are usually lightly washed buff). In the eastern subspecies *asiatica*, however, the sexes are very similar, some males having the flanks etc. chestnut, but in others they are yellow-buff, as in the female. Juveniles are very similar to adults (especially adult females). Their upperparts are slightly duller, with a faint brown cast and sometimes paler feather centres, especially on the forehead. Their eyestripe is duller, slightly browner and less well defined, and

the underparts are also slightly duller, while the fringes to the outer primaries and tips of the greater coverts may have a rufous tone. Their flight feathers are fresh when those of adults are often worn or moulting. The 1st adult is very similar to the adult, but most (90% in Europe) show moult contrasts in the median coverts, any retained outer feathers being greyish-brown with only a faint blue tinge (lost with wear), whilst the new inner 1st-adult feathers are as blue as the lesser and marginal coverts and scapulars. 1st adults may also show traces of brownish tips to retained greater coverts, and these and the retained primary coverts and flight feathers are slightly paler and less bluish than the new median coverts and scapulars, the flight feathers also being browner and more worn than those of an adult at a similar time of year.

**VOICE** Very vocal, the loud, piping and trilling calls demanding attention. The commonest call is used in excitement: an abrupt, liquid *twit* or *dwip*, given singly or sometimes in a slow sequence, but more usually in couplets (*dwip-dwip*) or groups of 3–4 notes in quick succession (*dwip-ip-ip*), but when very excited units may be given at a rate of 7 per second. Also gives a shrill, sibilant, almost trilling *sirrrr* or *tsi-si-si*, becoming a harsher *tsirrp* (recalling Long-tailed Tit) in excitement or alarm, and a cat-like *meeu-meeu* or *neu-neu*, whilst in extreme agitation gives a harsh *trah*. Contact call a high *tsit* or *seet*, often given just prior to taking flight, and other calls include a very high, thin, lisping *tsee-tsee-tsee...* Song rather variable, from 3–6 drawled, penetrating whistles, slowly repeated, *pee-pee-pee...*, *ueeh ueeh ueeh...* or *weeu weeu weeu...* (c. 2 notes per second), to a rapid tremolo of up to at least 32 units (given at a rate of as many as 19 per second), *wiwiwiwiwiwiwi...*; there are many intermediates and variants. (Partly after Cramp & Simmons 1993.)

**DISTRIBUTION AND MOVEMENTS** In **Britain** widespread in southern England and Wales, becoming more local in northern England (north to Northumberland and Durham), and an increasingly regular vagrant Scotland, with breeding first proven in 1989; absent Channel Islands, Isle of Man and Ireland. In **Morocco** occurs in the Rif and Atlas mountains (in the central High Atlas from about Midelt to about Télouet, south to Jbel Anrhomer, 31° 20' N, 7° W: Anon 1986). Found throughout mainland **Europe**, although confined to the south of **Norway** and **Sweden**, and sporadic in **Finland**. Also occurs on northern **Sicily**, but absent from all other Mediterranean islands, although found on most islands in the southern Baltic. Occurs in SW, west and northern **Turkey**, and also in extreme SE Turkey, extending into Kurdistan in northern **Iraq** and the Zagros mountains of **Iran** (southeast to Fars province). Also found in northern Iran in the Elburz and Caspian districts east to Golestan NP at *c.* 56° E and extreme NW Khorasan ('Kotaliyeckinar': Vaurie 1950b; in the Kopet Dag?). May occur in adjacent SW **Turkmenistan** (Dunajewski 1934), but this is not supported by Rustamov (1958) or Stepanyan (1990). In **Syria** found in the 'Allovit mountains above Slenfe' (= Jabal al Nusayriyah) in April 1992 and 1993, and recorded carrying nesting material, the first breeding record for the country (Baumgart & Stephan 1994). In southern **Russia** breeds in the Caucasus (extending north to the Terek and Kuban' Basins) and in **Georgia**, **Armenia** and **Azerbaydzhan**. Also across the forest belt of northern Russia and **Siberia** east to Anadyrland, north to *c.* 64° N in the Urals, 66° N in the Ob' valley, 67° 30' N on the Yenisey and 69° N on the Kolyma, south to northern **Ukraine** (Poltava, Khar'kov, and to 49° N in the valley of the Severnyi Donets), in southern Russia to 52° N between the valley of the Don and the Urals, to *c.* 54-55° N between the Urals and valley of the Irtysh, and in NE **Kazakhstan** to Kokchetav and along the Irtysh valley to the Saur and Tarbagatay mountains on the border with China. Also to the southern Altai, southern Transbaykalia, southern Yakutia, Stanovoy mountains, and Amur river. Breeds on **Sakhalin** and the **Kurile Islands** (Paramushir, Urup, Iturup, Kunashir and Shikotan). Found in west and central **Mongolia**, south to the western Mongolian Altai (east to the Mönh Hayrhan massif and south to the Bulgan river), the northern slopes of the Hangayn range (east to the Ulan Bator region) and the upper Kerulen river in the Hentiyn range, and also in the far east in the Greater Khingan range. Occurs in adjacent **NW China** in northern **Xinjiang**, in the Altai (around Altay), and presumably disjunctly in the easternmost Tien Shan (Hami). Also found in **NE, central and west-central China** from NE **Nei Mongol** (south to at least Ergun Youqi and Zalantun) and **Heilongjiang**, south to **Guizhou**, **Guangxi Zhuang**, **Hunan**, **Jiangxi** and **Fujian** and west to **Hebei**, **Shanxi**, southern **Shaanxi** (Qin Ling mountains), southern **Gansu** and central **Sichuan** (to Wanyuan and the western borders of the Red Basin at Pingwu, Barkam, Guan Xian, Ya'an, Baoxing and Emei Shan). Also **Taiwan**, but occasional records from **Hong Kong** are thought to relate to escapes from captivity. In **Japan** occurs on Hokkaido, Rishiri-to, Honshu, Shikoku and Kyushu. In **Korea** breeds in the northern and central highlands, with some southward dispersal in winter; also breeds on Cheju island. Generally very sedentary, but juveniles may disperse, usually over short distances, in the late summer and autumn. These movements may sometimes become irruptions or invasions when populations are high. In Europe the numbers involved are usually small, even in an 'irruption', and nuthatches avoid even short water crossings (although vagrants have been recorded on Heligoland in Germany, Hilbre Island in northern England and on the Isle of Man, with two unconfirmed records on Fair Isle, Scotland, in the 1930s). In cold years, some may disperse into coastal areas of Spain. Northern and eastern populations are much more prone to irrupt, considerable numbers appearing away from the breeding areas, probably owing to their dependence on the crop of cones of Siberian Stone Pine. Failed crops may result in mass emigrations from the breeding areas (e.g. in 1981 'several dozens of thousands' were noted during 4–12 August flying southwards from Mirnoye, central Siberia), and birds of the race *asiatica* may appear in northern Finland and Sweden, where thousands are sometimes noted, odd birds occasionally reaching Norway and Estonia. Such irruptions occur from August onwards, with invaders leaving by April, although some remain to breed. Others disperse to the north, regularly to 68° 40' on the Yenisey, and exceptionally to the tundra at 71° 40' N at Gol'chikha. In eastern Asia, the race *arctica* may make rather limited movements south (to *c.* 60° N) and east in the winter, whilst the race *amurensis* is a regular visitor to Korea, sometimes in large numbers; in 1980, 30,000–40,000 were recorded on 3–6 October moving southwest in groups of 40–50 along the coast of the Sea of Japan in Ussuriland (Cramp & Perrins 1993). Conversely, only a single record from Beidaihe in Hebei in NE China, and a rare migrant at Shuangtaizihekou NNR at the mouth of the Taizi river in southern Liaoning, although resident in nearby mountains. Throughout the range, montane populations may undertake rather limited altitudinal movements.

**HABITAT** In much of Europe found in deciduous and mixed forest, especially oak, usually in rather open woodland containing mature, large-trunked trees with well-spread crowns. Also found in parkland and sometimes large gardens. Similar habitats are occupied in the Russian Far East. In northern Europe and throughout much of the range in Asia, found also in coniferous woodland, even quite stunted larch forests in the forest-tundra zone. In the east, occurs in old deciduous forest in Japan, but also evergreen, mixed and coniferous forest, and favours pine forest on Taiwan. Outside the breeding season, wandering birds may occur in riverine thickets, orchards and shelterbelts in the steppe zone, and noted among Dwarf Junipers in western Mongolia, at least 50 km from the nearest woodland, and in rocky terrain in the Sayan mountains of southern Siberia. Generally found in the lowlands in the northern parts of the range, but in southern Europe extends to the treeline in Switzerland, although uncommon above 1200 m, and to 1500 m, exceptionally to near the treeline at 1800–2100 m, in Austria. Found at up to 1800 m in the Caucasus (where favours mixed forest), at least 1830 m in northern Iraq and 2225 m in SW Iran, and in Morocco in the Moyen Atlas restricted to cedar and mixed forest at *c.* 1750–1850 m. In the Altai and northern Mongolia found at up to 2200 m. In Japan primarily montane, found in central Honshu at 760–2400 m and on Shikoku at 1370–1525 m, but occurs at *c.* 300–1300 m in northern Honshu and from sea level to *c.* 915 m (Mount Daisetsu) on Hokkaido. Also montane on Taiwan, recorded at 800–3300 m, and found to at least 2000 m in NE China, but in SW China confined to low and moderate altitudes, being replaced at higher levels by Chestnut-vented Nuthatch (see also Relationships under Chestnut-vented Nuthatch, p. 116).

**POPULATION** Generally common, but densities may be lower in coniferous forest and towards the north of the range, being lowest (sometimes rare) near the treeline. In Siberia, numbers are variable and closely tied to the size of the cone crop. Local population densities peak when all the juveniles have fledged, and are then determined by food abundance (when food is scarce, nuthatches defend larger territories) and the severity of the winter. The species has spread north and west in Western Europe, in Norway and the Netherlands, and into Wales, northern England and most recently Scotland, whilst in Morocco it has spread to the Haut Atlas. Breeds irregularly in Finland (10–30 pairs) and northern Sweden, following irruptions of the race *asiatica* from the east.

**HABITS** Found singly and in pairs, and often quite tame. Monogamous and very territorial, most pairs remain together in close contact on their territory throughout the year, but they may join mixed-species foraging flocks as these pass through. Unmated 'invaders' from further north and east may also maintain winter territories. After fledging, family parties quickly break up and the juveniles are usually excluded from existing territories, occupying vacant ones, often of a lower quality, or dividing larger territories into smaller ones, although odd immature birds may be tolerated during the autumn. (Older females tend to lay slightly earlier in the season, and the first juveniles settling in a territory tend to remain there as a result of their higher social status in comparison with juveniles that appear later - even among nuthatches, possession is nine-tenths of the law!) Conflicts resume in the spring, and immatures that have not found mates or territories during the winter may disperse again, to be finally integrated into the territory system, replacing or usurping adults. Rather aggressive, territorial disputes are common and deaths resulting from fights are probably not rare. Roosts, normally singly, in holes, the female roosting on the nest. Forages on the trunks and larger branches of trees, and also, especially in the spring, on smaller branches and in clusters of twigs; and, in both spring and autumn, feeds on the ground. May remove pieces of bark to gain access to food, and the resulting loud tapping is often a clue to its presence, but unable to chisel into wood like a woodpecker unless it is rotten. May flycatch, and able to hover. Food insects etc. and, mainly in autumn and winter, also seeds, spending up to 90% of its time in winter gathering food; sometimes also feeds on sap, and readily visits birdtables in the winter. A confirmed food-hoarder, storing seeds in the autumn in bark crevices, in the ground or in wall cavities, and detailed knowledge of the territory and the location of stored food may be an important reason for the species' rather sedentary nature. This hidden food is exploited mainly when temperatures are low. In Siberia, specialises in the seeds of the Siberian Stone Pine, and following good cone

crops larders may contain enough food to last an entire year, potentially allowing the territory-holder to survive a failed crop the following winter; poor cone crops force the birds to emigrate.

**BREEDING BIOLOGY** Season April–May (occasionally late March, very exceptionally February) in Europe, the Caucasus, NW Africa and SE China; May–June in Siberia. The nest is placed in a hole in a tree, either natural or an abandoned woodpecker hole, usually 3.5–20 m above ground; also uses nestboxes and rarely wall cavities, holes in rock faces or buildings, crevices between tree roots, or even haystacks or old Common Magpie nests. If too large, the entrance hole is reduced by plastering with mud, helping to prevent intrusion by competitors or predators. The interior of the cavity is also often heavily plastered to protect the nest against wind and rain. Mud and clay are brought in pellets and hammered into shape around the entrance. This plaster occasionally incorporates animal dung (although dung may be the main building material in SW Iran), and also rootlets and moss as binding material, but saliva is not mixed into the plaster. The final choice of nest site is probably made by the female, and plastering of the hole and nest building are undertaken almost entirely by the female over a period of 2–3 weeks, although plastering continues even after the eggs hatch. The nest is a foundation of wood chips surmounted by bark flakes (usually pine), rarely incorporating leaf litter. Clutch 6–9 (4–13): eggs white, lightly speckled and blotched red, reddish-brown or reddish-purple, markings usually concentrated at the broader end; 19.5 x 14.4 mm (*S. e. caesia*). Female incubates, period 13–18 days, she also broods, but the nestlings are fed by both parents. Young fledge after 20–24 (18–28) days and are largely independent after a further 8–14 days. Single-brooded, exceptionally double-brooded.

**DESCRIPTION** *S. e. caesia* **Adult Male**: *In fresh plumage* (autumn–winter), upperparts, including lesser and median coverts and central tail feathers, dull mid blue-grey; T2–T6 blackish, tipped blue-grey (broadest on T6), T4–T6 with white subterminal spot on inner web which may extend as a bar across the outer web, especially on T6 (see figure, p. 112). Wing-coverts and tertials mid blue-grey, the inner webs dark grey. Primaries, secondaries, primary coverts and alula dark grey-brown; secondaries, inner primaries and primary coverts fringed blue-grey, widest on inner secondaries, P3–P5 fringed pale brownish-white inwards of emarginations, small feathers of alula very narrowly fringed whitish. Black eyestripe from nostril through eye, ending irregularly at sides of mantle. Chin whitish, cheeks, ear-coverts and throat white, tinged buff, merging into dull orange-buff or cinnamon-buff on remainder of underparts; flanks and rear vent deep rufous or brick-red, sides of belly and fore vent streaked chestnut. Undertail-coverts whitish, broadly fringed deep rufous and either not at all or very narrowly tipped rufous. Underwing-coverts and axillaries grey, tipped cinnamon-buff or rufous; under primary coverts black; tips, outermost feather and base of pri-

*Figure 1.1 Tail of* S. e. caesia.

maries contrastingly white. *In worn plumage* (spring–early summer), upperparts duller and not so blue, underparts slightly paler and not so rich cinnamon, more buffish. **Bare Parts**: Iris brown to blackish-brown; bill dark grey, darkest on culmen and tip, base of lower mandible bluish-white or horn-grey; legs and feet greenish-yellow, pale brown, blue-grey or dark grey, with blackish front of tarsus and upper surface of toes. **Adult Female**: As male, although upperparts may be slightly paler, eyestripe slightly browner and less well defined. Flanks, lower vent and sides of undertail-coverts rufous-orange. Under primary coverts may be dark grey, not black. **Juvenile**: Similar to adult, especially adult female. Upperparts average slightly duller and less blue, feathers with paler grey or whitish centres, especially on forehead. Eyestripe dark grey-brown (especially in females), duller and less well defined. Underparts paler (although breast may be more rufous), with a duller, greyer tone (feather bases and centres showing through). Fringes to base of outer primaries and tips to greater coverts may show some rufous. Difference between sexes as adults. Base of bill (except culmen) pale flesh-blue or pale blue; legs and feet average paler than adult. **1st Adult**: As adult (see Sex/Age). **Measurements**: Wing of male 82–92, of female 80–89; tail of male 42–48, of female 41–47; bill 18–22.7; tarsus 19.2–21.9. Weight 17–28 g.

**MOULT** Adult post-breeding complete (duration *c.* 80 days; West Palearctic and Caucasus, late May–late September, Siberia, June–mid September). Adult pre-breeding rare or absent. Post-juvenile partial, includes lesser coverts (usually all, sometimes not outermost), median coverts (usually 3–6), occasionally also innermost greater covert or rarely tertials (commencing at *c.* 8 weeks old, late May-August in West Palearctic, late June-early September in the Caucasus, late July–early September in Siberia).

**GEOGRAPHICAL VARIATION** Complex, although the subspecies can be divided into three basic groups, the buff-breasted *caesia* and *sinensis* groups, found in western Eurasia and China respectively, separated by the white-breasted *europaea* group. These groups were apparently isolated from each other until the relatively recent past and now come into contact in zones of secondary intergradation, occupied by very variable 'hybrid' populations.

**THE *CAESIA* GROUP** Western Europe, North Africa, Asia Minor, the Caucasus and Iran. Breast rich buffish, cheeks whitish. Variation slight,

except for the race *persica*. In the north and north-east, the *caesia* group is connected to the *europaea* group by a very variable hybrid population. Intermediates are found over a broad front from Denmark (Sjaelland, Lolland, Falster and Langeland), eastern Poland (east of Gdansk, Warsaw and Lublin), Lithuania, western Belarus, western Ukraine, eastern Romania and Bulgaria, to European Turkey.

***S. e. caesia*** Western Europe from Britain east to Denmark (from Jylland and Fyn), eastern Germany, western Poland, the Czech Republic, Hungary, the Carpathian mountains and western Bulgaria and NW Turkey (Thrace), south to northern Spain (the Cantabrian mountains and Pyrénées), the Alps, Yugoslavia (not Dalmatian coast), Albania and Greece. See Description.

***S. e. hispaniensis*** Portugal, central Spain and Morocco. Rather poorly marked. As *caesia*, but underparts paler, pinkish-cinnamon or pinkish-buff, the flanks more contrasting. Smaller; the bill averages slightly more slender and pointed. In Morocco, underparts average very slightly darker. Wing of male 81–91, of female 80–85; bill 18.3–21.6.

***S. e. cisalpina*** Switzerland (south of the Alps), Italy, Sicily, and coastal Yugoslavia south to SW Montenegro. Poorly marked. As *caesia*, but underparts brighter, more orange-buff or orange-cinnamon, less brownish-buff. Bill averages shorter and more slender and pointed. Wing of male 83–89, of female 80–85; bill 17.6–21.7.

***S. e. levantina*** Western Turkey (east in the south to at least the Euphrates). Poorly marked. As *hispaniensis,* but underparts more pinkish, less buff, flanks slightly paler and less contrasting. Upperparts average slightly paler grey (especially in the southeast); often shows faint white forehead. Bill slender and sharply attenuated. Size variable, small in western Turkey, larger in NW Turkey. Wing of male 83–89, of female 81–86; bill 17.5–21.5.

***S. e. persica*** The Zagros mountains of Iran; intergrades with *levantina* in northern Iraq. Distinctive. As *levantina,* but upperparts paler grey (the palest of the group, but only slightly paler than *caesia*), underparts pale, throat white, remainder of underparts pale orange-buff, wearing to creamy-buff. White forehead and supercilium always present and better marked than in *levantina* or *caucasica*. Bill relatively short, very slender and attenuated. Wing of male 82–87, of female 79–85; bill 19.5–21.5.

***S. e. caucasica*** North and NE Turkey, the Caucasus and Transcaucasia (except extreme southeast). Poorly marked. As *cisalpina*, but underparts slightly darker, bright orange-cinnamon-buff (brighter and deeper cinnamon than *caesia*, and darker than *levantina* and *persica*), chestnut flanks of male paler and less extensive, often shows a faint narrow white forehead and supercilium, and white in outer tail feathers broad and well defined. Bill short, thick and blunt. Wing of male 81–88, of female 80–88; bill 18–20.5.

***S. e. rubiginosa*** SE Transcaucasia (Talyshskiye Gory mountains and Lenkoran' area) and northern

Iran. Poorly marked. As *caucasica*, but upperparts darker (marginally the darkest and most slaty of the *caesia* group), underparts average paler orange-buff, usually lacks white forehead and supercilium, and white in tail reduced; bill slightly longer. Wing of male 83–89, of female 82–89; bill 20–25.

**THE *EUROPAEA* GROUP** Scandinavia to Japan, extending south to the eastern Tien Shan mountains and northern China. Cheeks, throat and breast white, belly varying from white to buffy-brown. The *europaea* group intergrades with the *sinensis* group in a relatively narrow zone of secondary intergradation in NE Hebei, China. The race *arctica* is very distinct, and there are records of *arctica* and *asiatica* being collected together at the same site. It may be an incipient species (it was treated as a separate species by Dunajewski 1934).

**S. e. europaea** Scandinavia and Russia east to the Volga and Vyatka Basins, south to northern Latvia, Belarus (east from around Minsk), eastern Ukraine (east of the Dnepr river), and Saratov. Underparts of male off-white or creamy with extensive deep rufous on flanks, lower vent and sides of undertail-coverts, female usually lightly washed buff with flanks etc. rufous-buff. No white on forehead (except occasionally in northern Russia). Bill stout and moderately blunt. Averages marginally larger and paler in the east. Wing of male 84–94, of female 82–92; bill 18.1–23.

**S. e. asiatica** Eastern European Russia (from Orenburg, Ufa, and the western foothills of the middle Urals), east through Siberia to the Sea of Okhotsk, Shantarskiye islands, southern Kurile islands, northern Japan (Hokkaido, Rishiri-to, and on Honshu in the Japanese Alps above 1500 m and at lower elevations in the north). North in Yakutia to *c.* 57–58° N, in the northern Sea of Okhotsk region to 61–62° N. South, between the Urals and Irtysh valley, to 54–55° N, to NE Kazakhstan and Mongolia, NE China in NE Nei Mongol and NW Heilongjiang (Nen Jiang river), and northern Amurland (south to *c.* 52° N). Intergrades with *amurensis* in the southeast. Vagrant west to Fennoscandia. As nominate *europaea* but rather smaller, with a shorter and finer, sharply pointed bill. Upperparts very slightly paler blue-grey, forehead and supercilium often white. Greater and sometimes median coverts tipped white when fresh (1st adults only?). Underparts snow-white, lower belly occasionally with a faint rufous-buff tinge, flanks etc. chestnut in male, coloration rather more restricted than nominate *europaea* and sometimes yellow-buff as female. Wing of male 72.5–85.5, of female 72–84; bill 15.3–21. Includes 'takatsukasai' of the southern Kurile islands (Urup, Iturup, Shikotan and Kunashir), with paler grey upperparts and a more pronounced white forehead and supercilium.

**S. e. seorsa** NW China in northern Xinjiang. As *asiatica*, but belly tinged rosy-buff. Wing of male 81, 82.

**S. e. arctica** NE Siberia (from *c.* 105°–106° E) from Yakutia to Anadyrland, north of *asiatica* (south in the west to *c.* 57–58° N, east of the

Verkhoyanskiy range south to 61–62° N). Vagrant west to northern Europe. Very distinct. As *asiatica*, but upperparts slightly paler grey, black eyestripe shorter, white of forehead more extensive and more white in outer two tail feathers. Also larger, bill longer and more slender, tarsus short and wings more pointed (P2 = P7 rather than P2 > P7). Wing 76–88.5, of male 76–83, of female 81.

**S. e. sakhalinensis** Sakhalin. As *asiatica* but paler, more orange-chesnut on flanks etc., wing and tarsus average shorter, bill more slender. Wing of male 74–77, of female 73–79.5; bill 15.9–18.4; tarsus 14.5–17.5.

**S. e. albifrons** Kamchatka peninsula and Paramushir in the northern Kurile islands. Poorly marked. As *arctica*, but less white in tail, more rounded wingtip, upperparts slightly paler, flanks paler, and white of forehead and supercilium may be slightly more pronounced. Wing of male 82–85.5, of female 80.5, 81.5; bill 19–21.5.

**S. e. amurensis** SE Russia in southern and eastern Amurland (north to *c.* 52° N and Komsomol'sk-na-Amure, and west to about the meridian of the Bol'shoy Khingan (= Da Hinggan Ling)), and Ussuriland; islands in Zaliv Petra Velikogo (Popova, Rikorda and Stenina), NE China in Heilongjiang, Jilin, Liaoning and NE Hebei, Korea, and central Honshu, Japan. Vagrant Sakhalin (8–10 in May 1979, (Cape Kuznetsov). Intergrades with *asiatica* in Transbaykalia, NW Amurland and eastern Heilongjiang (Nen Jiang river and Harbin). As *asiatica*, but belly and flanks variably washed pale buffy-brown; also averages slightly larger. Wing of male 77–86.5, of female 75–84.5; bill 17.5–21.5.

**S. e. roseilia** Southern Japan in SE Honshu (the Pacific coast south and west of the Izu peninsula), Shikoku and Kyushu. As *amurensis*, but upperparts darker, more slaty and bluer grey, underparts more rufous brownish-buff.

**S. e. bedfordi** Cheju island, Korea. Poorly marked. As *roseilia*, but throat and breast whiter and belly contrastingly darker orange-buff. Wing of male 80–82.5; bill 19–20.

**THE *SINENSIS* GROUP** Central and eastern China. Underpart coloration near that of the *caesia* group, but cheeks cinnamon-buff rather than white or whitish.

**S. e. sinensis** China (except the far northeast) from NE Hebei (Dongling) and Beijing southwards, generally at low and middle altitudes (replaced at higher altitudes in Fujian by Chestnut-vented Nuthatch). Also Taiwan. In fresh plumage (September), male has underparts, including throat, pale cinnamon-buff, grading to white on chin, cheeks and below eye; sides of neck slightly richer and brighter orange-buff. Rear flanks brick-red with slight orange wash, contrasting strongly with underparts. Undertail-coverts rufous with a mid-grey base and off-white shaft streak, broadening at the tip (appearing as a white inverted triangle). Female as male, but chin and cheeks lightly washed buff (not so pure white), rear flanks rufous-orange, showing little contrast with the rest of the underparts, and undertail-coverts rufous-orange (paler and showing less contrast with vent than in male). Little seasonal variation in underpart coloration, but in worn plumage slightly duller and less 'pure' (more cinnamon, even a hint of a drab-grey wash); cheeks and chin not so pure white. Some variation, with populations at higher elevations being slightly larger, with greyer underparts, and on Taiwan the underparts are very slightly brighter ('*formosana*'). Wing of male 72–82, of female 72–77; tail of male 35–47, of female 39–50; bill 14.5–19.5; tarsus 17–20. Weight 14–20 g. The relationship of Eurasian Nuthatch to Chestnut-vented Nuthatch in SW China is not clear. See p. 116 for full details.

RELATIONSHIPS Forms a superspecies with Chestnut-vented, Chestnut-bellied and Kashmir Nuthatches, which replace each other, generally without overlapping, in different areas of Europe and Asia. This situation has resulted in a variety of treatments by taxonomists, the complex being treated as anything from one to four species. Löhrl (1963) showed that the songs and especially the alarm calls of Eurasian and Chestnut-bellied Nuthatches were distinctly different, and, whilst the 'location calls' of juveniles (which Löhrl considered to be species-specific) clearly showed the relationship between the two, they also were sufficiently different to support their status as distinct species (see also p. 120).

REFERENCES Cramp & Perrins (1993), Dementiev & Gladkov (1966-70), Pravosudov (1993), Rogacheva (1992), Stepanyan (1990), Vaurie (1959), Voous & van Marle (1953).

# 2 CHESTNUT-VENTED NUTHATCH *Sitta nagaensis*                   Plate 2

Closely related to Eurasian Nuthatch, and replacing it in western China and SE Asia, Chestnut-vented's status as a distinct species is perhaps questionable.

IDENTIFICATION Length 125–140 mm (5–5.5 in). Medium-small to medium-sized. Upperparts blue-grey with a prominent black eyestripe, and underparts pale grey, variably tinged buff, with contrastingly rufous rear flanks. Undertail-coverts rufous with a line of broad white scallops down each side (but see also Geographical Variation). The range overlaps broadly with that of Chestnut-bellied Nuthatch, although the present species is generally found at higher altitudes. Most individuals are easily separated from Chestnut-bellied by having pale greyish to greyish-buff underparts with the chin, cheeks and ear-coverts concolorous with the throat (or only slightly paler, and not forming a contrasting whitish patch), and contrastingly rufous rear flanks and rufous, white-scalloped undertail-coverts. In fresh plumage, however, the buffest examples of Chestnut-vented Nuthatch may approach female, or especially immature, Chestnut-bellied (particularly of the pale race *S. c. neglecta*, found in Burma and Thailand) in underpart coloration. Chestnut-vented can then be distinguished by its slightly darker and duller blue upperparts, contrastingly rufous rear flanks, and undertail-covert pattern (the undertail-coverts appear white, very finely scalloped chestnut, in race *neglecta* of Chestnut-bellied). In the hand, Chestnut-vented usually shows a marked white panel in the centre of the outer web of the outer tail feather (T6), which is faint or absent in most Chestnut-bellied (*neglecta*). Chestnut-vented Nuthatch (*S. n. montium*) overlaps with Eurasian Nuthatch (*S. e. sinensis*) in central Sichuan and Fujian, China. Eurasian shows little seasonal variation in underpart coloration, being cinnamon-buff year-round, only slightly duller when worn. In worn plumage in spring and summer, Chestnut-vented is identified by its much paler dirty grey-buff underparts with rufous rear flanks, but in fresh autumn plumage it is buffer on the underparts, much more similar to Eurasian, although still slightly duller and less orange (dull pale buff with a slight grey wash, rather than pale cinnamon-buff), and still showing more contrast between the rufous rear flanks and the remainder of underparts. The flanks of male Eurasian are slightly paler and more orange than the brick-red of male Chestnut-vented; female Chestnut-vented's are rufous, close to male Eurasian, although still showing more contrast with the rest of the underparts, whilst in female Eurasian the flanks are rufous-orange, showing little contrast with the underparts. Also, the cheeks, fore ear-coverts and chin are only slightly paler than the underparts, while in male Eurasian they are contrastingly off-white, although in female Eurasian they are washed buff, approaching Chestnut-vented. Note that, in underpart coloration, some Eurasian, especially females, can be very similar to fresh Chestnut-vented and, despite their slightly more orange-toned underparts and less contrasting flanks, may be virtually impossible to separate in the field (in the hand, Chestnut-vented may show a distinct grey wash to the sides of the belly and vent). Chestnut-vented also has very slightly bluer and perhaps darker upperparts, and is usually larger than Eurasian Nuthatch, although size varies with altitude (see Geographical Variation). Finally, the vocalisations differ, Chestnut-vented seeming to lack the lilting *dwip, dwip* call of Eurasian. Identification is complicated by the possibility that Chestnut-vented Nuthatch intergrades with Eurasian Nuthatch in Sichuan, the race *sinensis* of the latter varying in size and coloration, becoming greyer below, darker above and larger as its populations ascend from the lowlands (although typical *S. n. montium* is greyer still and lacks the whitish chin and cheeks that are typical of Eurasian). In NE India and NW Burma, Chestnut-vented overlaps with White-tailed Nuthatch and the two are often found in similar habitats. Chestnut-vented is separated by the lack of white in the central tail feathers (although this is often difficult to see on White-tailed). Additionally, White-tailed has more orange-buff underparts, lacking contrasting rufous rear flanks, and has uniform undertail-coverts. It is also slightly darker and bluer above, with a shorter black eyestripe and stouter bill. In NE India, Burma and NW Thailand, Chestnut-vented is separated from Giant Nuthatch by its much smaller size, with the crown and nape as dark as the mantle or only slightly paler.

**SEX/AGE** Sexes marginally distinct. The rear flanks of the male are deep brick-red, deeper and less orange than the undertail-coverts, whilst the female's flanks are rufous, concolorous with the undertail-coverts; also, the underparts of the female may average marginally duller buff. The juvenile differs only slightly from the adult, the underparts averaging slightly buffer than in worn adults (but not so buff as fresh adults), with the flight feathers fresh when those of adults are worn. No information on 1st adult.

**VOICE** Calls include a slightly squeaky *sit*, often given as a couplet *sit-sit*, with varied emphasis and inflection and repeated faster and more slowly in irregular series. Also a similar but lower and 'drier' *chip* or *chit*, often run together into a trilling *chit-it-it-it...* (recalling a Winter Wren, and not so emphatic and structured as the song). In alarm and agitation gives a nasal, inquisitive or whining *quir*, *kner* or *mew* and loud, hard, emphatic and metallic *tsit* notes, which may be doubled, or run into a fast series *tsit-tsit-tsit-tsit...* (the individual units sometimes repeated very rapidly, but rather higher, thinner and less full than the song). Song a stereotyped fast, flat, monotonous stony rattle or tremolo, *chichichichichi...* or *trr-r-r-r-r-r-r-ri...*, c. 0.5–1 second per burst and sometimes slightly rising in pitch towards the end, the individual units often repeated in machine-gun fashion and so fast as to be almost indistinguishable, but sometimes rather slower, comprising shriller, better-spaced units, *chi-chi-chi-chi-chi...* (or a much slower *diu-diu-diu-diu-diu*; these 'chitters' may closely resemble one of the song variants of Eurasian Nuthatch).

**DISTRIBUTION AND MOVEMENTS** Found in **NE India** in **Arunachal Pradesh** around Kahaa in the extreme east (Singh 1994) and the Patkai range in the southeast, **Nagaland**, **Manipur**, the Cachar hills of southern **Assam** and Khasi hills of **Meghalaya**. In **Myanmar (Burma)** breeds in the west in the Chin hills south to Mount Victoria, and in the east from the Adung valley in the extreme north of Kachin south through the Bhamo hills to the Southern Shan States (to at least about Kengtung and Kalaw); presumably occurs in the upper Chindwin and NW Kachin, thus connecting west and east, but no records traced. Breeds in **SE Tibet**, where confined to the northern watershed of the Himalayas in the valleys of the Tsangpo, east to Langong Chu at *c.* 29º E, also its tributaries the Nyang Qu (to Guncang), Yi'ong Zangbo (to Yi'ong) and Po Tsangpo (to Sumzom), and the far southeast at Zayu (adjacent to Kahaa, Arunachal Pradesh). In western **China** occurs in west and SW **Sichuan**, north to Baiyü and east to Kangding,

Guan Xian, Mabian and Huidong, NW and western **Yunnan** (including the Gaoligong Shan south to Tengchong), also south (Xishuangbanna = about Mengla) and SE Yunnan, extending marginally into SW **Guizhou** around Xingyi. There is an isolated population in eastern **China** in the higher mountains of NW Fujian (Huanggang Shan). In NW **Thailand** confined to Chaiya Prakan, Mae Hong Son and Chiang Mai provinces (including Doi Ang Khang, Doi Pha Hom Pok, Doi Chiang Dao, Doi Suthep and Doi Inthanon), and there is a disjunct population in southern **Vietnam** on the Da Lat plateau (south to Mount Pantar, near Di Linh). Resident. May be some withdrawal to lower altitudes in winter, but also recorded at or near the top of the altitudinal range in the cold months.

**HABITAT** Hill evergreen forest, also pine forest (or stands of pines on the drier ridges amid hill evergreen). In NE India also recorded in mixed and light deciduous forests; in NE Burma in open oak and alder forest; in SE Tibet in Holly Oak and deciduous forest along the Tsangpo river; in Yunnan in spruce, fir and rhododendron; and in Sichuan in valley-bottom poplar and Walnut trees. Altitudinal range in NE India 1400–2600 m, occasionally to 3200 m; in eastern Burma recorded at 1220–2285 m and on Mount Victoria 1400–2600 m, occasionally to 2800 m. In SE Tibet recorded at 1980–3650 m, and in western China found in Yunnan at 1525–4570 m, in Sichuan at 1200–3960 m and in Guizhou at 1250–2480 m; while in NW Fujian occurs above 1000 m. In Thailand recorded above 1300 m, and in southern Vietnam at 915–2285 m.

**POPULATION** Generally fairly common throughout the range.

**HABITS** Found singly and in pairs, and outside the breeding season also in small, loose parties, often joining mixed-species foraging flocks. Often feeds on the ground, foraging over rocks and the sides of old cuttings as well as on trees.

**BREEDING BIOLOGY** Season in NE India March–June; eastern Burma April–early June, on Mount Victoria families with recently fledged juveniles observed 31 March; Fujian, China, April-May; Thailand, March-May (and nest-building in January); and in Vietnam nest-building recorded in January. Nest placed in a hole in a tree or stump, noted at *c.* 10 m above ground; the entrance may be reduced with 'plaster' (as in Eurasian Nuthatch). The nest itself is a pad of scraps of bark or moss, lined with fur. Clutch 2–5: eggs white, spotted with red over underlying reddish-violet spots, the markings concentrated at the larger end; 18.3 x 14 mm (*S. n. montium*).

**DESCRIPTION** *S. n. montium* **Adult Male**: *In fresh plumage* (late August–March/May), upperparts, lesser and median coverts and tertials dull mid blue-grey; odd whitish feather bases may show on nape or upper mantle. Central tail feathers as upperparts, with traces of dark shaft streaks; T2–T6 blackish-grey, tipped dull blue-grey, increasing in extent towards T6, T3 with small white spot on tip of inner web, T4–T6 with larger white spot subterminally on inner web, T6 with pronounced white panel in centre of outer web (see figure 2.1). Remainder of wing dark grey, greater coverts broadly fringed and tipped dull blue-grey, primary coverts finely fringed blue-grey, smaller feathers of alula, secondaries and inner primaries fringed dull blue-grey, P3–P5 fringed pale blue-grey inwards of emarginations (not extending to base). Blackish eyestripe from lores to sides of mantle. Chin and cheeks buff-white, ear-coverts, sides of neck and underparts dull pale buff with slight grey wash. Rear flanks deep brick-red. Undertail-coverts white, very narrowly tipped and slightly more broadly fringed rufous (slightly more orange-rufous than flanks, basal half of inner web and extreme base of outer web mid grey); concealed bases dull blue-grey (appear white with rufous 'ladders' on each side and a rufous centre). Thighs mid grey, tipped pale buff. Axillaries buff, underwing-coverts sooty-black, longer under primary coverts and base of primaries white. *In worn plumage* (c. April–August), upperparts duller, faintly tinged brown; pale feather bases may show on crown and nape as pale flecking. Wing and tail feathers bleached browner, fringes abraded. Underparts rather greyer, greyish-buff with a paler throat, but even when very worn show traces of buff. **Bare Parts**: Iris brown or dark brown; bill

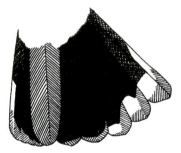

*Figure 2.1  Tail of* S. n. montium.

grey-black to blackish, base or basal half of lower mandible (and sometimes upper) slate-grey or grey-blue; legs and feet greenish-brown, reddish-brown, dark brown, dark blue-grey or black; claws horny-black. **Adult Female**: As male, but rear flanks rufous; underparts may average slightly duller buff with a reduced grey tone. **Juvenile**: As adult, but plumage 'looser', revealing more white feather bases on head, nape, chin and throat. Fresh juvenile has underparts slightly less buff than fresh adult (i.e. as moderately worn adult). **Ist Adult**: No information. **Measurements**: Wing of male 72–89, of female 71–88; tail of male 40–51, of female 37–49; bill 16.5–22; tarsus 16–20. Weight 12–22 g.

**MOULT** Post-breeding complete (late June–September; in south Vietnam May–July). Adult pre-breeding occasional?, partial (October/November). Post-juvenile partial (July, Thailand).

**GEOGRAPHICAL VARIATION** Moderate. There is a gradual reduction in the buff tones on the underparts from western China south through Burma and South-East Asia, becoming purest grey at the two southern outposts of Mount Victoria,

Burma, and the Langbian plateau, southern Vietnam. It is difficult to draw precise boundaries between the subspecies, but three races are recognised (following Vaurie 1957d, 1959).

**S. n. montium** China, eastern Burma and Thailand (includes 'nebulosa', 'kongboensis', 'tibetosinensis' and 'delacouri'). See Description. Birds from Fujian and Yunnan show a greyish cast to the sides of belly and vent, with odd rusty feather tips, whilst those from SE Tibet perhaps average slightly purer and cleaner buff on the underparts. Size varies geographically, the largest birds coming from SE Tibet and Sichuan (wing of male 77–89; tail of male 45–49, of female 45–49), the smallest from Fujian (wing 72–78.5; tail of male 40–41.5, of female 37–38), NE Burma (wing of male 77–82), and SW Burma and NW Thailand (wing 71–77). Size apparently also varies with altitude, however, obscuring the geographical trends.

**S. n. nagaensis** NE India and adjacent north Chin hills, western Burma (also the 'Kachin hills': Vaurie 1959). As *montium,* but in fresh plumage underparts, including chin, ear-coverts and sides

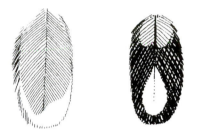

*Figure 2.2  Single undertail-covert feather of* S. n. montium *(left) and* S. n. nagaensis *(right).*

of neck very pale grey, faintly washed buff (smoky-grey), contrasting strongly with the brick-red (male) or rufous (female) rear flanks. Undertail-coverts with much broader brick-red or rufous-fringes, more extensive grey base and much more limited white subterminal spot (appear rusty or rufous with tear-shaped white spots). When very fresh, intensity of buff on the underparts as worn *montium.* In worn plumage, underparts slightly purer grey than in *montium.* Wing of male 75–81, of female 72, 75.

**S. n. grisiventris** Southern Vietnam and Mount Victoria, SW Burma (no information as to whether this population joins that of *montium* in the north Chin hills). Poorly marked. As nominate *nagaensis,* but underparts purer grey (pale to light grey); in fresh plumage (October) the male shows no trace of buff, in worn plumage underparts slightly drabber grey (less whitish). Females (sexed by flank colour) tend to have a buff wash in the centre of the belly and vent. Birds from Vietnam average slightly darker dirty blue-grey on the underparts than those from Mount Victoria. Wing of male 71–83, of female 69–80.5.

**RELATIONSHIPS** Forms a superspecies with Eurasian, Chestnut-bellied and Kashmir Nuthatches, and often considered conspecific with Eurasian Nuthatch. Thayer & Bangs (1912) proposed specific separation of *sinensis* and *montium*, and Chestnut-vented was treated as a separate species by Greenway (1967), albeit with a footnote that it was possibly conspecific with Eurasian Nuthatch, but the justification for this is unclear. It overlaps with Eurasian Nuthatch (*S. e. sinensis*) in Fujian, eastern China, where Chestnut-vented is montane and Eurasian Nuthatch a lowland form, but the mere fact of altitudinal replacement is not sufficient grounds to separate Chestnut-vented from Eurasian Nuthatch (e.g. in Japan the lowland form of Eurasian Nuthatch *S. e. amurensis* is replaced at higher altitudes on Honshu by *S. e. asiatica*). Further west, according to Voous & van Marle (1953), Vaurie (1957d, 1959) and Cheng (1987), the subspecies *montium* (which Greenway treated as a form of Chestnut-vented) intergrades in central Sichuan with the subspecies *sinensis* (which Greenway treated as a form of Eurasian Nuthatch) in the region west of Wenchuan and around Guan Xian, Ya'an and Mount Erlang, at *c.* 2135–3050 m.

Traylor (1967) reports, however, that at Guan Xian the 'lowland' *sinensis* meets the 'highland' *montium* (and does not report any intergrades). Thus in Sichuan, too, it may be a case of altitudinal replacement. There are vocal differences between the two species, but their general appearance supports the treatment of the races *grisiventris-nagaensis-montium-sinensis* as a natural grouping of subspecies of Eurasian Nuthatch. Further detailed study of the exact relationship of *montium* and *sinensis* in Fujian and the apparent zone of intergradation in Sichuan is clearly needed. Whatever its specific status, Chestnut-vented Nuthatch apparently fills a closely similar niche to that of White-tailed Nuthatch (and also of the montane race *tonkinensis* of Chestnut-bellied Nuthatch), and competitive exclusion may be the reason for the absence of Chestnut-vented from all but the easternmost Himalayas, from Laos and from most of Vietnam.

**REFERENCES** Deignan (1945), Vaurie (1957d, 1959), Voous & van Marle (1953).

## 3 KASHMIR NUTHATCH *Sitta cashmirensis* Plate 3

This enigmatic nuthatch has suffered badly at the hands of taxonomists, frequently being 'lumped' with Eurasian Nuthatch. Its vocalisations are rather different, however, and it has a curiously interrupted distribution in the NW Himalayas.

**IDENTIFICATION** Length 140 mm (5.5 in). Medium-sized. Upperparts blue-grey, with a black eyestripe extending to the nape. The male has the chin, cheeks and ear-coverts whitish, forming a conspicuous silver-grey cheek patch, and the throat buff, grading through cinnamon on the breast to uniform deep rufous on the rear flanks, vent and undertail-coverts. The female's cheek patch is washed buff and her underparts are paler, pinkish-buff on the breast and rich cinnamon on the rear flanks and undertail-coverts. In the western Himalayas Kashmir Nuthatch is usually found at higher altitudes than Chestnut-bellied, and at all times is distinguished by its uniform undertail-coverts (chestnut with white scalloping in male Chestnut-bellied, pinkish-cinnamon with buff-white markings in the female). Chestnut-bellied also has slightly paler and purer blue-grey upperparts, and males are easily identified by their white chin, cheeks and fore ear-coverts, contrasting strongly with the underparts, which are *uniformly* orange-brown from the throat to the rear flanks and vent; the female's underparts are paler and more cinnamon, but still *uniform* (not paling on the breast and lower throat). On Kashmir, the cheek patch is less well defined and the underparts *gradually* darken from the throat to the vent (although the overall tone is sometimes only slightly paler than on female Chestnut-bellied). Kashmir overlaps with White-tailed Nuthatch in northern India (from northern Himachal Pradesh eastwards) and western Nepal. The two species are rather similar, and both have uniform under-tail-coverts. White-tailed is *c.* 15% smaller and relatively shorter-billed than Kashmir, and the white in the *central* tail feathers is diagnostic when seen, although often concealed. Male Kashmir has the chin, cheeks and ear-coverts whitish, relatively well demarcated from remainder of underparts, which average slightly darker and more pinkish-cinnamon (less cinnamon-orange) than on White-tailed. White-tailed has the chin, cheeks and throat variable, off-white to pale orange-buff (although the chin is almost always white), fading more gradually into the cinnamon-orange underparts, with the rear ear-coverts usually pale orange rather than white. Female Kashmir has the cheeks, ear-coverts and chin off-white, and throat washed pinkish-buff, grading into the cinnamon underparts; there is no sharp contrast between the throat and remainder of the underparts (thus resembling White-tailed), but the ear-coverts are whiter and the underparts more pinkish-cinnamon than on White-tailed.

**SEX/AGE** Sexes reasonably distinct (even as nestlings). The female resembles the male, but has the white of the chin and cheeks lightly washed buff, thus showing less contrast with the remainder of the underparts, which are much paler and more uniform than the male's, with the rear flanks and vent rich cinnamon, only slightly darker and richer than the belly. Juveniles are very similar to adults, but may show more pale mottling on the nape (paler feather centres) and dark barring in the submoustachial area (dark grey featherbases). 1st adult as adult, and probably not separable, even in the hand (although the flight feathers may be more worn than adult's at a similar time of year).

**VOICE** Quite vocal throughout the year, foraging pairs frequently giving squeaking *tsi-tsi* contact calls. Territorial or advertising call a rapidly repeated, high-pitched squeaking whistle, usually repeated 4–5 times, *pee-pee-pee-pee-pee* (Roberts 1992). Excitement call, given in intraspecific conflicts and in alarm (often when a human is near), a repeated, loud, far-carrying, harsh, rasping *kraaaa* or *schree*, recalling a Eurasian Jay (similar to the grating calls of Corsican and Western Rock Nuthatches, and very different from any vocalisation of Eurasian Nuthatch; Löhrl 1968, Löhrl & Thielcke 1969).

**DISTRIBUTION AND MOVEMENTS** In NE **Afghanistan** found from Nuristan and Kohistan south to the Safed Koh (Konar, Laghman and Nangarhar provinces, but probably confined to regions south of the Hindu Kush watershed). Breeds in **Pakistan** from the Shinghar range (= north Sulaiman range) in Zhob, northernmost Baluchistan, and the adjacent Takht-i-Sulaiman range of southern Waziristan, north through the upper Kurram valley and the Peiwar spur of the Safed Koh, the dividing range between Dir and SE Chitral, southern and western Chitral (Kafiristan) and northern Swat to Indus Kohistan; no records from Gilgit or Baltistan. In the western Himalayas breeds in Pakistan from Hazara and the Murree hills to Azad Kashmir, northeast in the Neelum (= Kishen Ganga) valley to Gurais, and in the Pir Panjal range. In **India** occurs from Kashmir east to Kumaon (Bates & Lowther 1952, although few records away from Kashmir). Also in **NW Nepal** in Humla, Mugu, Jumla and Dolpo east to Phoksumdo Tal and south to Surkhet. Resident, with some limited seasonal altitudinal movements.

**HABITAT** In eastern Afghanistan primarily fir, spruce and Deodar (cedar) forests, occurring uncommonly at lower altitudes in adjoining degraded stands of Holm Oak, more regularly in valley-bottom Hazel scrub and poplar groves (Paludan 1959), although Löhrl & Thielcke (1969) note it as abundant in Holm Oak. In SW Pakistan found in pines, and further north in Deodar with an understorey of witch-hazel, and in Kashmir in coniferous forest. Also recorded from groves of Walnut, and in Nepal found in oak, spruce and pine forests. Apparently has some dependence on the presence of deciduous, broadleaved tree species, even in essentially coniferous habitats. In Afghanistan recorded at 1850–2600 m, with breeding proven at 2000–2400 m. In Pakistan and NW India breeds at 2100–3050 m, locally down to *c.* 1800 m in Kashmir and up to 3350 m in Chitral. In winter descends regularly to *c.* 1800 m, although recorded in December at 2500 m in deep snow in the Murree hills. In Nepal found at 2400–3505 m.

**POPULATION** Common in eastern Afghanistan, Pakistan and NW India (although scarce in the Murree hills), and fairly common in Nepal.

**HABITS** In summer found singly and in pairs, and outside the breeding season usually in mixed-species foraging flocks. Not shy. Forages on trunks and larger branches, usually at low levels, and often in the understorey or on the ground, on fallen and rotten trees and logs and moss-covered boulders. Utilises both conifers and oaks if present. Food insects, spiders and, especially in the winter, seeds and nuts; grit often found in stomach. Often occurs in same habitat as White-cheeked Nuthatch, although more likely to be found at lower altitudes and in deciduous trees. Where the two species occur together, they apparently do not associate in the same foraging flocks and Kashmir apparently occupies a different niche, foraging at lower levels on the trunks and the upperside of branches, whilst White-cheeked favours the upper branches, foraging on the underside of thick lichen-draped limbs.

**BREEDING BIOLOGY** Season May–June in Afghanistan, late April–late June in India and Pakistan. Nest placed in a tree hole, often an abandoned woodpecker hole or natural knothole, 2–9 m or more above ground (mostly over 10 m in Afghanistan). The tree selected may be in deep forest or in well-wooded open country. The entrance may be reduced with a plaster of wet mud to a diameter of *c.* 38 mm or less. Often the masonry work is not prominent, but in up to a third of nests it may take the form of a short cone, the plaster occasionally extending for some distance around the hole, smoothing over depressions in the bark (perhaps a consequence of the reuse of nests from year to year and thus a build-up of material). The mud often dries to terracotta hardness, although at times it may be quite brittle and come away easily; chipped pieces may reveal small seeds within the dried mud (see Eurasian Nuthatch). Nest a lining of bark chips, seed husks and dried leaves. The male assists in nest-building and plastering. Clutch 5–7 (–8): eggs white with reddish spots and small blotches; 19.7 x 14.4 mm. Incubation and fledging periods unknown, but both sexes feed the young and the fledged juveniles may remain with the adults for 5–6 weeks after leaving the nest.

**DESCRIPTION Adult Male:** *In fresh plumage* (September–March/April), upperparts, including wing-coverts and tertials, dull blue-grey. Central tail feathers dull blue-grey (sometimes dark shaft streak near tip); T2–T6 blackish-grey tipped mid drab-grey (more extensive on outer web), pale tips progressively wider towards T6; T4 with dull white spot on tip of inner web, T5 with dull white subterminal spot on inner web, T6 similar, but with dull white panel on outer web midway along feather. Alula and primary coverts dark brownish-grey, the latter fringed dull blue-grey. Primaries and secondaries dark brownish-grey, secondaries and P3–P10 fringed dull blue-grey (on P3–P6 inwards of emarginations only). Extreme base of bill and lores sooty-black, the eyestripe extending to the sides of the mantle, where it broadens somewhat. Cheeks and chin off-white, grading through pale buff ear-coverts to buff or pale cinnamon on upper throat and sides of neck, rich cinnamon on lower throat and breast, and cinnamon-rufous on sides of breast, fore flanks and belly. Rear flanks, vent and undertail-coverts deep rufous, undertail-coverts uniform or showing at most a trace of greyish or greyish-brown on the feather centres. Thighs dull blue-grey with darker grey feather tips. Axillaries blue-grey, finely tipped whitish. Underwing-coverts blackish-grey, tips of under primary coverts and base of flight feathers contrastingly white. *In worn plumage* (April–August), upperparts slightly duller, some whitish feather bases may show on nape and upper mantle. Flight feathers bleached and abraded browner, the blue-grey fringes slightly worn. Little seasonal variation in underpart coloration. **Bare Parts**: Iris reddish to dark brown; bill blackish-grey or blackish-brown, basal half of lower mandible whitish to horn-grey; legs and feet greyish, dark olive-brown or yellow-brown, soles dull yellow; claws dark slaty or blackish. **Adult Female**: In fresh plumage as male, but chin and cheeks with slight buff wash, lower throat and breast pinkish-buff, fore flanks, belly and vent cinnamon or rich cinnamon and rear flanks rich cinnamon. **Juvenile and 1st Adult**: As adult (but see Sex/Age). **Measurements**: Wing of male 81–87, of female 78–87; tail 40–46; bill 18.5–23.5; tarsus 16.9–19. Weight 17.2–21 g.

**MOULT** Adult post-breeding complete (late June–September). Post-juvenile partial (November).

**GEOGRAPHICAL VARIATION** No races recognised, although birds in Afghanistan and SW Pakistan (Safed Koh, Shinghar range) average slightly longer-billed and perhaps slightly darker on the underparts, and have been named *'hariabica'*.

**RELATIONSHIPS** A member of the *europaea*

superspecies, Kashmir Nuthatch is intermediate in many respects between Eurasian and Chestnut-bellied Nuthatches, although probably closer to Eurasian. It has been treated as a distinct species (e.g. Inskipp & Inskipp 1991, Sibley & Monroe 1990), as a race of Eurasian Nuthatch (Ripley 1982, Vaurie 1959), as a race of Chestnut-bellied Nuthatch (Voous 1977) or as part of a single species encompassing the entire group (Voous & van Marle 1953). Kashmir Nuthatch differs from both Eurasian and Chestnut-bellied in vocalisations and coloration, especially its uniform undertail-coverts (although female Kashmir is otherwise very similar to female Eurasian of the races *caesia* and *rubiginosa*: Vaurie 1950b). There is no good reason to treat it as a race of Chestnut-bellied Nuthatch: in Pakistan it occurs in the Murree hills within *c.* 5 km of Chestnut-bellied, but at different elevations and in different habitats; its alarm and advertising calls are also quite distinct (Roberts 1992). In plumage and habitat it resembles more closely Eurasian Nuthatch, but Kashmir is totally isolated from that species and, given the marked vocal differences (the excitement calls in particular differ strongly from those of Eurasian Nuthatch: Löhrl 1968, Lohrl & Thielcke 1969), it seems best to treat it as a distinct species. (Note that pronounced sexual dimorphism, often quoted as a distinction from Eurasian Nuthatch, is shown by both species.)

**REFERENCES** Ali & Ripley (1983), Baker (1932–33), Löhrl & Thielcke (1968), Paludan (1959), Roberts (1992).

# 4 CHESTNUT-BELLIED NUTHATCH *Sitta castanea* Plate 2

This bright nuthatch is a familiar member of bird parties in the dry forests of India and South-East Asia, and its curious mosaic of races may conceal one or more 'cryptic species'.

**IDENTIFICATION** Length 130 mm (5.25 in). Medium-sized. Upperparts blue-grey, with a narrow black eyestripe which expands very broadly onto the sides of the mantle, and sometimes also shows a faint pale supercilium behind the eye. Underparts brick-red to brownish-orange in the male, with a well-defined white cheek patch; paler pinkish-cinnamon to pale orange-drab in the female, showing much less contrast with the whitish cheeks. The undertail-coverts appear blackish, grey or white, variably scalloped with chestnut (see Geographical Variation). Over most of range, the male is easily distinguished from other nuthatches by its uniform chestnut underparts and clear-cut white patch on the chin, cheeks and ear-coverts. Away from the plains of India, however, females and juveniles require more care. In the western Himalayas (Murree hills in Pakistan to western Nepal) they must be distinguished from Kashmir Nuthatch, although that species is normally found at higher altitudes: note the better-defined white cheek patch, slightly richer cinnamon underparts and especially the whitish

undertail-coverts marked with chestnut scalloping (Kashmir has uniform undertail-coverts). Throughout the Himalayan foothills it may overlap marginally in altitudinal distribution with White-tailed Nuthatch: female Chestnut-bellied are identified by their larger size, longer black eyestripe, slightly richer cinnamon (not cinnamon-orange) underparts, and whitish undertail-coverts with chestnut scalloping (uniform on White-tailed); the white patch at the base of the *central* tail feathers on White-tailed is diagnostic, but often difficult to see. In NE India and SE Asia confusion is possible with Chestnut-vented Nuthatch, although that species, too, is normally found at higher altitudes. Note Chestnut-bellied's uniform cinnamon to pale orange-drab underparts, without contrasting darker flanks. In the hand, Chestnut-vented usually shows a white block in the centre of the outer web of T6; this is usually faint or absent on Chestnut-bellied (but may be pronounced in *neglecta*); check also the under tail-covert pattern. In much of South-East Asia, the subspecies *neglecta* of Chestnut-bellied has a reduced black eyestripe which does not expand broadly onto the sides of the mantle, a paler throat, showing less contrast with the cheek patch, and reduced sexual dimorphism, the male having the underparts paler and more orange than males of other races. Both sexes may be separated from Chestnut-vented by the features given above for females.

**SEX/AGE** Most races are strikingly sexually dimorphic (see Geographical Variation). Juveniles marginally distinct, often showing a combination of diffuse paler centres, faint darker fringes and rufous subterminal marks in the feathers of the crown, nape, mantle and scapulars, and faint darker barring on the cheek patches and chin. In underpart coloration juveniles of both sexes resemble the adult female, averaging paler and more orange than the respective adult; in particular, juvenile males have rather paler and more orange-rufous underparts than the adult male (but usually slightly darker and more rufous than the adult female), with the throat paler than the breast and showing less contrast with the white cheek patch, whilst juvenile females are slightly paler and more orange on the underparts than juvenile males and thus less distinct from the adult female. 1st adult as adult, although the retained juvenile flight feathers average browner and more worn than the adult's.

**VOICE** Rather noisy, with a varied vocabulary, flocks keeping contact with chattering and twittering. Calls include a pure, high, mouse-like *seet*, a lower and more squeaky *vit* or *nit*, and a full *chip*, *chlip* or *chup*. Frequently gives an explosive rattle in short bursts, *sitit, sidititit*, with brief and irregular gaps between each burst. This may be a contact call, but in agitation may be given in longer bouts, with even shorter gaps between each burst, sometimes even faster and given almost continuously, but occasionally it is reduced to single metallic *chit* notes (alarm also given as a loud, raucous *bzirp*; Rand & Fleming 1957). The song (?) is a single pure whistle repeated every few seconds, *wheeu, c.* 0.5 seconds in duration, and slightly inflected (although thinner towards the end). This may change to a slight tremolo (almost like a referee's whistle), and extensions from this theme are full, mellow, quavering trills, *trilililili... of c.* 1 second's duration, with the individual units barely distinguishable, slower variants with the units more separated, and even slower, flatter and less musical trills, *tutututututu...* or *titititiii....* Other calls include a sparrow-like *cheep-cheep-cheep...* given in a long series with occasional pauses, and a mellow, whistled *tui-tui* or *tui-tui-tui*, recalling Eurasian Nuthatch. Song period in Nepal January–April and August–October.

**DISTRIBUTION AND MOVEMENTS** **Pakistan**, **India**, **Nepal**, **Bhutan**, **China**, **Myanmar** (**Burma**), **Thailand**, **Laos**, **Vietnam** and **Cambodia** (see Geographical Variation for details). Resident, with no evidence of altitudinal movements. Recently confirmed as occurring in **Pakistan**. Baker (1922) included the Murree hills in the species' range and there are specimens in the Natural History Museum, Tring, labelled 'Murree', but Whistler (1930) stated that it did not occur

there. Collected at Kotli, Azad Kashmir, by Waite in 1943–47 and rediscovered at Murree by T. J. Roberts in 1983 in the Manga valley at 900 m, with breeding proved in 1986. A sight record in riverine forest in the Sukkur district of Sind in January 1905 is generally discounted, but the occurrence there of a wanderer is not impossible (Roberts 1992). Formerly resident in the Chittagong hill tracts of SE **Bangladesh**, but no recent records.

**HABITAT** Over most of range a bird of open dry deciduous forest, especially 'sal' forest (dominated by *Shorea robusta*). Also light forest, scattered trees, mango groves, bamboo clumps, orchards, village groves and roadside trees, and sometimes gardens. In NE Thailand, Cambodia and the western Himalayas found in pine forest, and in NE India (*S. c. koelzi*) and northern Laos and NW Vietnam (*S. c. tonkinensis*) found in hill evergreen forest. Over most of the range, occurs in the plains and foothills. In northern India present at up to 600 m, and in the Himalayan foothills to 1830 m, optimally 600–1500 m. South of the Brahmaputra river occurs from base of hills to 1830 m, and in peninsular India recorded at 600–1070 m. In Burma noted at 305–1525 m and in northern Thailand at 500–850 m. In central and southern Laos and southern Vietnam (South Annam) found below 500 m; but recorded only at 500-1000 m in Cambodia (Thomas 1964). The race *tonkinensis* is found in northern Vietnam and north and central Laos at 1200–2200 m, rarely under 1000 m (although collected in Tonkin at 365 m), the statement 'rarely above 1400 m' for Thailand presumably referring to this race (Lekagul & Cronin 1974).

**POPULATION** Common in India and Nepal, although rather local in the plains and peninsula, being commonest in the north, especially in Bihar, scarce in Madhya Pradesh and Andhra Pradesh and presumably rare in the Himalayan foothills west of Uttar Pradesh, and rare and local in Pakistan. Locally fairly common to common in Burma, Thailand, northern Laos and NW Vietnam, but uncommon to scarce in central Laos, Cambodia and southern Vietnam. Very rare in China.

**HABITS** Found singly, but more often in pairs or loose family parties, and frequently joins mixed-species foraging flocks. May be found in the same flocks as Velvet-fronted Nuthatch without interspecific aggression (Baker 1922; Delacour & Jabouille 1931; Roberts 1992) but Ali & Ripley (1983) state that it invariably treats Velvet-fronted as a competitor and chases it off if on the same or a nearby branch. Usually forages in the upper half of trees, on the trunk and smaller branches, but may feed on the ground on ants and termites and, especially in NE India, Burma and Indochina, frequently forages on walls, cliffs and banks. Food insects, spiders and, particularly in the winter, seeds and nuts.

**BREEDING BIOLOGY** Season: Himalayan foothills mainly April–June; northern peninsular India late February–May; Andhra Pradesh April–September; Meghalaya April–May; Burma

March–April; Thailand?–April. Nest usually placed in a natural cavity or abandoned woodpecker hole in a tree, up to 10 m above ground, but in the Khasi hills (Meghalaya) and Indochina (race *tonkinensis* only) the preferred site is a hole in a wall or steep bank. The entrance, whether in a tree or wall, is usually reduced with 'masonry' to leave an opening 30–40 mm in diameter. The masonry comprises mud, berries and tree resin and may be up to 50 mm thick, drying to a terracotta hardness. Even when the hole selected is small enough, the area around, both outside and inside, may be plastered. Any damage to the masonry is quickly repaired, and the same hole may be reused in successive years. The nest is a layer of dried leaves, wood chips, bark fragments, seed cases or moss, lined with a pad of fur or wool, although sometimes merely a bed of wood chips. Clutch 4–6 (2–7): eggs white to pale pink, finely spotted reddish, the spots often concentrated at the larger end; 17 x 16.5 mm (*S. c. castanea*). According to Baker (1932–33) both sexes incubate, but Gill (1923–25) states that only the female incubates, being fed on the nest by the male; period 11–12 days (Baker 1932–33). Both sexes feed the young. Possibly double-brooded (Baker 1922).

**DESCRIPTION** *S. c. castanea* **Adult Male**: *In fresh plumage* (September to about March), crown, nape and upper mantle light blue-grey, remainder of upperparts, lesser and median coverts, tertials and central tail feathers mid blue-grey. T2–T6 blackish-grey, broadly fringed dull blue-grey on outer web and tip of inner (widest on T6), T4 with small whitish tip to inner web, T5–T6 with off-white subterminal spot on inner web (see figure 4.1). Greater and primary coverts and alula dark grey, fringed and tipped blue-grey. Primaries and secondaries dark grey-brown, secondaries and inner primaries broadly fringed blue-grey, P6–P3 fringed light blue-grey inwards of emargination. Extreme base of bill and lores blackish, extending into black eyestripe which expands broadly on sides of mantle; may show faint paler supercilium immediately behind eye. Chin, cheeks and fore ear-coverts white, feathers very faintly tipped darker. Rear ear-coverts, sides of neck and underparts brick-red, faintly washed orange, undertail-coverts mid blue-grey (occasionally with creamy subterminal band), broadly fringed brick-red. Thigh feathers dark grey with blue-grey subterminal band and brick-red tip. Axillaries blue-grey, tipped brick-red; underwing-coverts sooty-black, longer under primary coverts and base of primaries contrastingly white. *In worn plumage* (April–August), crown to upper mantle paler and more contrasting (some pale feather bases show), remainder of upperparts duller blue-grey, flight feathers bleached and worn duller and browner, and underparts slightly paler and more orange. **Bare Parts**: Iris reddish-brown to dark brown; bill black with variable blue-grey base to culmen, cutting edges and lower mandible; legs and feet pale horn to blackish, soles paler; claws horn to slaty. **Adult Female**: In fresh plumage as male, but chin, cheeks and fore ear-coverts off-white (less well defined). Sides of neck, throat and

*Figure 4.1 Tail of* S. c. castanea.

breast dull beige, belly and vent dull pinkish-cinnamon, and rear flanks vinaceous-cinnamon. undertail-coverts mid grey, fringed pinkish-cinnamon. **Juvenile Male**: As adult, but tiny pale feather centres on forehead and forecrown, with feathers of crown and scapulars variably tipped faintly darker. Greater coverts finely tipped rufous. Feathers of cheeks and chin tipped faintly darker, and throat slightly paler, some feathers with tiny pale centres. Remainder of underparts slightly paler and more orange-brown. **Juvenile Female**: Differs from adult as in juvenile male; underparts more uniform, slightly duller, drabber and more orange (less pinkish) than adult female, with less contrast between the breast and belly. **1st Adult**: see Sex/Age. **Measurements**. Wing of male 71–83, of female 70–79; tail of male 35–43, of female 35–41.5; bill 18–21.5; tarsus 16.5–19. Weight 12–18.2 g.

**MOULT** Adult post-breeding complete (July–September in Indian subcontinent, July–October in Burma, August–September in Thailand). Post-juvenile partial, includes a variable number of greater coverts and tertials and occasionally central tail feathers (July–September in Indian subcontinent, June–July in Burma, July in Thailand).

**GEOGRAPHICAL VARIATION** Marked, with six races recognised, divisible into three groups.

**THE PLAINS GROUP** Small, with a short, slender bill. Undertail-coverts mid grey (as mantle), broadly fringed brick-red in male and pinkish-cinnamon in female, with a narrow pale subterminal band present in 54%, faintly indicated in 28% and absent in 18% (Vaurie 1950b); the effect is of chestnut scalloping with no white showing. Crown and nape generally paler than mantle. Underparts of male brick-red with slight orange tinge, slightly darker than in the foothills group and much darker than *neglecta*. Underparts of female dull beige, slightly darker pinkish-cinnamon on the belly, slightly pinker or more beige than *almorae*, with contrast between the pinkish breast and more orange belly. Well-defined white 'cheeks'. Generally a lowland form, and in northern India replaced in the hills by the large, heavy-billed forms of the foothills group, but elsewhere in central, peninsular and southern India (where the large forms do not occur) *castanea* occurs on both the high and the low ground. The ecological separation is sharp and no intermediates are found (Vaurie 1950b).

***S. c. castanea*** Northern and central India east

Figure 4.2 Single undertail-covert feather of (from left to right) the races castanea (Plains group), almorae, cinnamoventris, tonkinensis (Foothills group) and neglecta (neglecta group).

of a line from the south-central Punjab (about Ferozepore) through eastern Rajasthan to northern Maharashtra (about Nasik), in the terai (including SW Nepal) and the Gangetic plain east to Bihar (Darbhanga and the Rajmahal hills) and east-central Bengal (Nadia), and locally south to *c*. 16° N in Maharashtra and Andhra Pradesh. An apparently disjunct population in the foothills of the southern Western Ghats from southern Karnataka (Kodagu) south through the Nilgiris, Biligirirangan and Palghat hills of eastern Kerala and western Tamil Nadu. See Description. Includes 'prateri' from the Eastern Ghats in Orissa and Andhra Pradesh from *c*. 19° N south to the Godavari river, doubtfully distinct on basis of slightly longer bill (male 21–22.2, female 20–22), underparts of male paler (as *cinnamoventris*) and narrow pale buff subterminal band on undertail-coverts, but this last feature shown by *castanea* s.s. (see above).

**THE FOOTHILLS GROUP** Large, with a long, deep, broad-tipped bill. Undertail-coverts mid grey to slaty-black with broad white subterminal band and fine chestnut fringes; appear whitish with chestnut scalloping. Upperparts slightly darker than nominate *castanea*, with crown marginally, if at all, paler than mantle. Underparts of male slightly paler and less brown, more orange than *castanea*, those of female (except *koelzi*) slightly paler, more uniform and less 'pinkish'.

***S. c. almorae*** Foothills of western Himalayas from Murree hills and Azad Kashmir, Pakistan, though Himachal Pradesh, Haryana (Ambala) and Uttar Pradesh to central Nepal, with isolated record from east Nepal. Intergrades with *cinnamoventris* in east-central Nepal. Base of undertail-coverts mid grey. White feathers of cheek patch sometimes show faint pale brown tips. Underparts of male orange-brown (near *neglecta*); of female cinnamon, slightly darker on lower belly (lacking contrast between breast and belly of female nominate *castanea*). Juveniles may show subterminal rufous markings on the nape. Wing of male 81–87, of female 78–86; bill 21.5–24.7. Weight 17.4–20.9 g.

***S. c. cinnamoventris*** Foothills of eastern Himalayas from eastern Nepal to Arunachal Pradesh (including the northern portion of the plains of the Jalpaiguri district, West Bengal, but absent from the plains of northern Assam). Also Meghalaya (Garo and Khasi hills), Manipur, Mizoram, and hills of Bangladesh south to the Chittagong hill tracts (but see Distribution). Adjacent NE Burma south to around Myitkyina, and westernmost Yunnan (Yingjiang river). Intergrades with *almorae* in east-central Nepal. As *almorae*, but chestnut fringes to undertail-coverts average slightly narrower (undertail-coverts appear white with orange scalloping), underparts of male darker, more chestnut-brown (thus nearer *castanea*), those of female marginally darker; upperparts, including flight feathers and tertials, slightly darker, blue-grey fringes confined to base of P3–P6 and absent on inner primaries and secondaries. Female may show faint dark barring on the cheek patch, and juveniles subterminal chestnut and white bands on the upperparts. Wing of male 79–87, of female 76–83; bill 19–24. Weight 19.5–22.5 g.

***S. c. koelzi*** SE Arunachal Pradesh in Patkai range on the Burmese border, south through Nagaland to the Baril range in northern Cachar (Assam); presumably occurs in adjacent NW Burma. Poorly marked. As *cinnamoventris*, but underparts of female slightly darker and pinker (pinkish-cinnamon), upperparts slightly darker, feathers of cheeks and sides of throat tipped blackish, centre of undertail-coverts slaty-black.

***S. c. tonkinensis*** Southern Yunnan in the eastern Mekong drainage (Simao, Xishuangbanna (= about Mengla)); northern Vietnam (Cha Pa in NW Tonkin), northern and central Laos (west to at least around Luang Prabang and south in Annamatic chain to at least Nape); apparently isolated population in northern Thailand (Doi Hua Mot, 19° 07′ N, 99° 20′ E *c*. 50 km northeast of Chiang Mai). Male as *cinnamoventris*, but undertail-coverts black, very finely fringed chestnut, white feathers of lores and cheeks finely tipped black, appearing barred, upperparts very slightly darker, but underparts slightly paler (i.e. as *almorae*). Female as *cinnamoventris*, but note undertail-covert pattern and barred cheek patch (although the latter not so well marked as on the male). Wing of male 83–91, of female 83–90; bill 20–24.1.

**THE *NEGLECTA* GROUP** Small and thin-billed. Undertail-coverts blackish-grey, grading to dark grey with a broad whitish subterminal band and fine chestnut fringe; appear white with fine chestnut scallops. Crown as mantle. Extension of black eyestripe onto sides of mantle much reduced. Underparts paler and more orange than in other races, slightly darker on the flanks and lower belly; throat paler than breast, often pale orange-buff, thus whitish cheek patch less contrasting. Underparts of male very similar to *almorae*, but slightly more orange and thus near female *cinnamoventris;* those of female near female *almorae* or paler, pale orange-drab. Juveniles more distinctive than in other races, being more noticeably paler and more washed-out on the underparts than in the adult; pale buffy-orange in the male, and pale drab-grey, tinged buff, in the female. Wing 74–84; bill averages 20.6 in Burma, 19.4 in Thailand.

**S. c. neglecta** Burma north to *c.* 24° N (Bhamo hills), south in the west to at least Mount Victoria and in the east through the Southern Shan States and Kayah to southern Karen (Mount Mulayit at *c.* 16° N); northern Thailand (except the Mekong drainage in Chiang Rai, Phayao and Chaiya Prakan), also NE and western Thailand, south to Kanchanaburi; central and southern Laos in the lowlands, north to at least Vientiane; Cambodia (localities include Sambor, Kompong Thom, Kompong Speu and Bokor) and southern Vietnam in central Annam (Pleiku).

**RELATIONSHIPS** Forms a superspecies with Eurasian, Chestnut-vented and Kashmir Nuthatches (see Eurasian Nuthatch). Chestnut-bel-

lied overlaps with Chestnut-vented Nuthatch in parts of NE India, Burma and South-East Asia, but the two either replace each other altitudinally, with Chestnut-bellied confined to lower elevations, or geographically in the case of the montane race *tonkinensis* of Chestnut-bellied. Deignan (1945) speculates that the southern populations of Chestnut-vented Nuthatch are relicts of a period when their moister habitat was more widespread. Chestnut-bellied Nuthatches occur in the drier habitats surrounding these ecological islands, but, whenever the hills are unoccupied by Chestnut-vented, Chestnut-bellied has undergone 'ecological release' and can penetrate to higher elevations. However, the situation in NE Thailand, where *tonkinensis* occurs on Doi Hua Mot, a massif where Chestnut-vented is absent (even though it is found on neighbouring Doi Langka), with the race *neglecta* of Chestnut-bellied generally distributed in the lowlands between Doi Hua Mot and the mountains of Laos (Deignan 1945), deserves further study. Could *tonkinensis* be reproductively isolated from *neglecta*, thus meriting specific status?

**REFERENCES** Ali & Ripley (1983), Baker (1922, 1932–33), Deignan (1945), Roberts (1992), Vaurie (1950b), Voous & van Marle (1953).

# 5 WHITE-TAILED NUTHATCH *Sitta himalayensis*     Plate 3

Despite its name, the white in the tail of this Himalayan nuthatch is often hard to see. In the west of the range it must be carefully separated from Kashmir Nuthatch, whilst in the east the range is unusually fragmented, with scattered records in Burma and Indochina.

**IDENTIFICATION** Length 120 mm (4.75 in). A small, dumpy, relatively short-billed nuthatch. Upperparts dull blue-grey, with a black eyestripe extending broadly onto the sides of the mantle. May show an indistinct off-white supercilium above and behind the eye. The basal half of the central tail feathers is white. Cheeks and throat whitish, grading to cinnamon-orange on the breast and fore flanks and darker orange-cinnamon on the belly, vent and undertail-coverts. The white bases to the *central* tail feathers are diagnostic when visible, but this feature is often concealed by the wings at rest and is best seen when the tail is spread, such as when alighting. When the white tail base is not visible, White-tailed must be carefully separated from Kashmir and female Chestnut-bellied Nuthatches, and also from Chestnut-vented Nuthatch. Note that all four species show white subterminal spots on the *outer* tail feathers, prominent in flight. For separation from White-browed Nuthatch, see that species. White-tailed overlaps with Kashmir Nuthatch in the western Himalayas from western Nepal to Himachal Pradesh. Kashmir is *c.* 15% larger and relatively longer-billed, but their overall coloration is rather similar, and both species have uniform undertail-coverts. On White-tailed, the chin, cheeks and throat are white or buff-white, grading into cinnamon-orange on the sides of neck and

breast, with the ear-coverts, especially at the rear, usually also cinnamon-orange. Male Kashmir is slightly darker, more pinkish-cinnamon, on the underparts, with relatively better-defined white throat, cheeks and ear-coverts (the ear-coverts contrast with the sides of the neck and lower throat). On some White-tailed only the chin is white, whilst in others white extends to the throat and centre of the upper breast (and all are whiter in worn plumage), but even those with extensive white on the throat still lack the contrast shown by male Kashmir, and usually still have the ear-coverts washed orange. Female Kashmir has more uniform underparts than the male, lacking the marked contrast between the throat and underparts, but still has whiter ear-coverts and more pinkish-buff underparts than White-tailed. Throughout its range White-tailed may overlap marginally in altitude with Chestnut-bellied Nuthatch. Male Chestnut-bellied is distinctive, with much darker underparts and contrastingly white chin, cheeks and ear-coverts. Female and juvenile Chestnut-bellied are more similar to White-tailed, but are a little larger, with slightly richer cinnamon (not cinnamon-orange) underparts, a longer black eyestripe and, most obviously, whitish undertail-coverts with chestnut scalloping (rather than uniform orange-cinnamon). In NE India and NW Burma White-tailed overlaps with

Chestnut-vented Nuthatch, but has more uniform cinnamon-orange underparts, lacking the contrastingly rufous rear flanks of Chestnut-vented. It is also slightly darker and bluer above, with a stouter bill and shorter black eyestripe.

**SEX/AGE** Sexes similar, although the female averages slightly paler and duller on the underparts. Juvenile as adult (see Description).

**VOICE** Calls include a squeaky single *nit,* and a soft, mellow but full *chak* or *tschak* (sometimes *sthak*), given singly at irregular intervals. Harder and sharper, almost stone-clicking versions may be doubled in a couplet *chak'kak* or given in short, irregular groups, and may be combined in monotonous rattles in which up to 25 units are given at a rate of *c.* 10 per second, *chik'kak'ka'ka'ka'ka...*, these may again break into couplets. In alarm or agitation gives a similar but louder, shrill (sometimes squeaky) but full *chik,* near disyllabic *ts'lik* or an even shriller *tsik.* These notes are often given in series which are initially quite fast but slow to *c.* 3 notes per second, and in prolonged series may tail off to a maximum of *c.* 2 notes per second, the units sometimes then becoming a shriller, parakeet-like *shree* which may be repeated for minutes at a time. (These series of notes from agitated birds may be at higher and lower pitches, perhaps reflecting a difference between the sexes. Pairs (?) may duet, with higher and thinner *tsik* calls and lower but squeaky *chik* notes, in an almost sparrow-like chatter.) Also gives a high-pitched, thin, sibilant *sisirrr* or *sisisit,* a variety of fussy twitterings, and strange long, shrill, squealing or quavering notes, e.g. *kreeeeeeeeeee* or *preeeeuh;* these may rise or fall in pitch, and last almost 1.5 seconds. The 'fast' song is a crescendo of 3–10 whistles given at various tones and inflections at 5–7 notes per second, e.g. *tiu'tiu'tiu...,* *tu'tu'tu...,* *dwi-dwi-dwi...* or *pli'pli'pli....* The 'slow' song comprises 2–4 similar whistles, but given at 4 notes per second, e.g. *tui-tui-tui-tui* or *pui-pui.* Short song-phrases may be introduced by the clicking *chak'kak* couplet. Song period in Nepal February–May.

**DISTRIBUTION AND MOVEMENTS** The **Himalayas** from Chamba in NW Himachal Pradesh, **India,** east through northern Uttar Pradesh, **Nepal, Sikkim** and **Bhutan** to Arunachal Pradesh, extending north of the main range into southern **Tibet** along the valleys of the Trisuli river (Gyirong) and Sun Kosi river (Nyalam), and also recorded in the Manas valley on the border of Arunachal Pradesh and Tibet. In **NE India** found in Nagaland, Manipur, the Cachar hills of southern Assam, the Lushai hills of Mizoram, south to at least Blue Mountain, and adjacent **western Myanmar (Burma)** in the Chin hills, where recorded at Thiangin (23° 12' N, 93° 48' E), Laiva Dam (22° 51' N, 93° 32' E), once (?) in April on Mount Victoria, and at Yinkwetaung (20° 44' N, 93° 58' E) at 1675 m in January (Wood & Finn 1902; this is *c.* 50 km *south* of Mount Victoria). Possibly disjunct populations are found in **NE Burma** south to at least Kambaiti and in adjacent **SW China,** where confined to the Gaoligong Shan (Shweli-Salween divide) in western **Yunnan,** south to

Tengchong, and in northern **Vietnam** at Fan Si Pan in NW Tonkin. There are also single records from **eastern Burma,** near Kengtung in the Southern Shan States at Loi-hsam-hsum in the Salween-Mekong watershed on the Thai border, and in northern **Laos** on the Tranninh plateau (Phu Kobo, just south of Xieng Khouang: David-Beaulieu 1944); these may refer to winter visitors, as may records in SW Burma (especially Mount Victoria). Otherwise resident, with seasonal altitudinal movements.

**HABITAT** In the Himalayas and NE Burma, mid-altitude oak and rhododendron forests, with a preference for mossy forest. Also found at higher altitudes in mixed forests of fir, hemlock, rhododendron, oak and maple, although apparently avoids pure stands of conifers. (In Nepal, found in oak-rhododendron forest at 1525–2135 m and maple-hemlock forest at 2745–3050 m.) In the NE hill states of India found in broadleaf evergreen forest. Breeds in the Himalayas at 1400–3500 m, occurring at the highest altitudes in the east; optimum zone 1800–2750 m. May descend in winter, with records down to 915 m in Nepal, 945 m in Sikkim (March) and 700 m in Bhutan (October, January), but also recorded as high as 3050 m in January in Nepal and Darjeeling. In the NE hill states of India found above 1700 m, and in adjacent Burma recorded at 1675 m in the Chin hills and at *c.* 2440 m in April on Mount Victoria. In NE Burma, occurs at 1525–2900 m and recorded at 2285 m in the Southern Shan States. In western Yunnan noted at 2000–2745 m. In NW Vietnam found from 2000 m to at least 2800 m, and recorded in north-central Laos at *c.* 2000 m.

**POPULATION** Common in the Himalayas, perhaps occurring at the highest densities in the east. Variously described as rare, uncommon, and fairly common in the NE hill states of India and probably occurs there at a reduced density. Not uncommon in NE Burma, but only one record from eastern Burma and perhaps rare in adjacent western Yunnan. Common in NW Vietnam, but status in Laos unknown, the only record being of a single flock at Tranninh.

**HABITS** Found in pairs and small parties, often joining mixed-species foraging flocks. Forages on mossy branches, usually in the upper parts of trees, less frequently on the trunk and occasionally in low shrubs. Diet mainly insects, but also nuts and seeds.

**BREEDING BIOLOGY** Season in Indian subcontinent February–May, and in NE Burma observed in pairs in March and family parties in late May. The nest, placed in a tree hole 1–15 m above the ground, usually in an oak, is a pad of green (sometimes dried) moss, moss roots and rhododendron leaves. The hole may be plastered up with a mixture of mud and berries and large quantities of larvae if it is too large, the diameter reduced to 25–38 mm, the plaster setting rock-hard. Clutch 4–7: eggs white, densely covered with dark red spots and blotches, which may form an ill-defined ring at the larger end; 18.6 x 13.4 mm. Both sexes incubate and feed the young (Baker 1922).

**DESCRIPTION Adult Male**: *In fresh plumage* (September–April), crown to rump dull blue-grey, crown and especially nape and upper mantle may be slightly paler. Forehead, lores and eyestripe sooty-black, expanding broadly on the sides of the upper mantle; may show an indistinct narrow grey-white supercilium just above and behind eye. Central tail feathers dull blue-grey, slightly darker and greyer along shaft and at tip, basal half of outer web adjacent to shaft white, basal two-thirds of inner web white; T2–T6 sooty-black, T5 with large white subterminal spot on inner web, T6 with white diagonal stripe subterminally across feather (see Plate 3). Wings dark grey-brown, coverts (including primary coverts) fringed blue-grey, extensively so on outer web of greater coverts; alula fringed blue-grey on outer web; tertials mid-grey, tinged blue on outer web, secondaries broadly fringed blue-grey, primaries finely fringed light grey, pale fringes progressively restricted to base of feather towards outer wing. Cheeks, chin and throat whitish, variably washed buff, grading into cinnamon-orange on upper and rear ear-coverts, fore flanks and breast and a darker and richer orange-cinnamon on the belly, flanks, vent, thighs and undertail-coverts. Axillaries grey-buff, under wing-coverts sooty-black, base of primaries and secondaries (inner webs only) white. *In worn plumage* (April to about August), whitish feather bases may show on nape and upper mantle, and black eyestripe more extensive, especially at rear on upper mantle. Blue-grey fringes to wing feathers abraded, wings thus darker and sootier. Underparts paler and whiter, may be buff-white on breast and belly. **Bare Parts**: Iris brown (also purple: Rothschild 1921); bill black or blackish-brown, base of lower mandible bluish-white or grey; legs, feet and claws dark brown, dark greenish-brown or dark yellowish-brown, soles greyish-white. **Adult**

**Female**: As male, but ear-coverts and underparts average slightly paler and duller. **Juvenile**: As adult, but wings and tail darker and upperparts notably bluer than on worn and abraded adults at a similar time of year; underparts may average slightly paler than on fresh adult. **1st Adult**: No information. **Measurements**: Wing of male 69–79, of female 67–79; tail of male 34–42, of female 33–42; bill 15–19; tarsus 16–21. Weight 11–17 g.

**MOULT** Adult post-breeding complete (May–early September). Post-juvenile partial (August). A male, age unspecified, from Bhutan on 9 March had the tail in moult (Ali *et al.* in press); this could perhaps indicate adult pre-breeding or late post-juvenile moult.

**GEOGRAPHICAL VARIATION** Slight. A cline of decreasing size runs eastwards, with birds from Indochina averaging smallest (in NW Vietnam, wing 66–73, tail 34–38, bill 15–16). Eastern birds, as well as those from the south of the species' range (Naga hills, Manipur, Mizoram), also average very slightly richer and more extensively rufous on the underparts in fresh plumage. The following races have been named: '*australis*' from NE India, '*lushaiensis*' from the Lushai hills (Mizoram) and '*whistleri*' from NW Vietnam. The differences are, however, very slight and largely masked by individual variation, and no subspecies are recognised.

**RELATIONSHIPS** May form a superspecies with White-browed Nuthatch. Based on the common character of white in the tail, Kleinschmidt (1932–33) allied White-tailed Nuthatch with Pygmy and Brown-headed Nuthatches, whilst Voous & van Marle (1953) pointed out the similarity of the strongly developed black eyestripe and the uniform undertail-coverts to those of Yunnan Nuthatch.

**REFERENCES** Ali & Ripley (1983), Baker (1922, 1932–33), Vaurie (1957d).

## 6 WHITE-BROWED NUTHATCH *Sitta victoriae*      Plate 3

Endemic to the Mount Victoria region in SW Burma, this is perhaps the rarest nuthatch in the world and its long-term survival must be in doubt given the scale of forest destruction in tropical Asia.

**IDENTIFICATION** Length 115 mm (4.5 in). A small nuthatch. Upperparts dull blue-grey, base of central tail feathers extensively white (may be concealed at rest). Narrow black eyestripe, broadening on the sides of the upper mantle, and white forehead and narrow white supercilium, latter often extending downwards to the rear of the ear-coverts and thus broken at the rear by the dark eyestripe. Ear-coverts, sides of neck and flanks orange-rufous, becoming darker and more rufous on the rear flanks, vent and undertail-coverts. Cheeks, throat, breast and belly white. White-tailed Nuthatch also has white in the central tail feathers, but White-browed is easily separated by its white forehead and distinct white supercilium, more sharply defined black eyestripe, and more contrastingly patterned underparts, with the white

(rather than rufous) throat and breast contrasting with the orange-rufous flanks, vent and undertail-coverts. Also, the bill is rather shorter and finer.

**SEX/AGE** Sexes apparently similar. Juvenile distinct, the orange-rufous sides to the neck (and also the breast and flanks?) much fainter (Stresemann & Heinrich 1940).

**VOICE** Calls include a subdued, soft, liquid *pit* or *plit*, given at irregular intervals, and an insistent *pee, pee, pee...*, a single note recalling a 'lost chick', repeated at a rate of 2.5–3.5 per second at more or less regular intervals for prolonged periods (the latter not given by White-tailed?). The song (?) in a crescendo made up of 9–12 units given at a rate of 9 notes per second, *whi-whi-whi...* (near the 'fast' song of White-tailed Nuthatch).

## DISTRIBUTION AND MOVEMENTS
Endemic to **Myanmar** (**Burma**), where found only on Mount Victoria in the southern Chin hills, and in spring 1995 also on another ridge 22 km to the northwest (21º 24' N, 93º 47' E). Resident.

**HABITAT** Found in the alpine zone of Mount Victoria (summit 3053 m), in stunted lichen-covered oaks, avoiding pure stands of pines, from 2285–2800 m. Recorded only above 2600 m by Stresemann & Heinrich (1940) and above *c.* 2700 m in spring 1995, but Rippon collected six birds between 22 March and 30 April from 2285–2745 m (Ludlow & Kinnear 1944; Rippon 1904), so there may be a slight withdrawal from higher altitudes in the winter.

**POPULATION** Little information. Recorded for the first time since 1937 in spring 1995. Appears to occur at low density, but precise status unknown. Given its extremely limited distribution and the prevalent trend in forest destruction, despite the continued existence of extensive habitat above 2135 m, the species must be considered gravely at risk. Listed as vulnerable in BirdLife International's world checklist of threatened birds (Collar *et al.* 1994).

**HABITS** Poorly known. Forages on the smaller branches and trunks of oaks, exploring knarled bark and lichen.

**BREEDING BIOLOGY** The only information is that all birds were paired in early April, and a record of fledged young at 2600 m on 28 April.

**DESCRIPTION Adult:** *In fresh plumage* forehead and narrow supercilium (to rear of earcoverts) whitish. Crown to rump dull blue-grey; nape and upper mantle paler, with white feather bases showing as variable whitish mottling. Central tail feathers with basal half of inner web and narrow streak along shaft of outer web whitish, grading into blue-grey on distal half with a dark border to outer web and marbled with grey towards the tip, often with a triangular black spot near the tip of the shaft; T2–T6 blackish-grey, small white triangle on tip of inner web of T4, large white subterminal spot on inner web and variable white subterminal streak along shaft on outer web of T5, and large white subterminal streak diagonally across both inner and outer webs of T6 (see Plate 3). Wing dark grey-brown; coverts (including primary coverts) fringed blue-grey, outer webs of tertials extensively blue-grey, secondaries fringed blue-grey, primaries finely fringed paler at base. Narrow black eyestripe, broadening considerably on the upper mantle. Lores and cheeks whitish. Upper and rear ear-coverts variably orange-rufous (rearmost earcoverts often contrastingly white), rufous then forming a continuous line down the sides of the neck and onto the flanks, rear flanks darker and more extensively rufous, innermost rear flanks blue-grey. Chin, throat, lower ear-coverts, breast and belly white. Vent and undertail-coverts cinnamon-rufous. Thighs grey. Axillaries blue-grey; under primary coverts sooty-black, longest coverts and base of primaries contrastingly white. **Bare Parts**: Iris red-brown or dark brown; bill slate-grey, paler on culmen and lower mandible and black at tip; legs and feet dull yellowish-brown or olive-brown. **Juvenile and 1st Adult**: No information (see Sex/Age). **Measurements**: Wing of male 68–73, of female 67–69; tail 36–37.5; bill 15–16.1; tarsus 14.5–16.5. Weight: no information.

**MOULT** No information.

**GEOGRAPHICAL VARIATION** None.

**RELATIONSHIPS** Formerly considered conspecific with White-tailed Nuthatch. White-browed, however, is quite distinct from White-tailed, and both nuthatches occur on Mount Victoria. Ticehurst (*Ibis* 1941: 56, footnote) states that both species have been collected at 'about the same time in April' and at the same elevation, but the only record traced is a specimen of White-tailed Nuthatch in the Natural History Museum, Tring, collected at 1370 m on 12 April 1904. According to Ripley (1959), White-tailed Nuthatch occurs on Mount Victoria at up to 2800 m, coexisting with White-browed in mixed and alpine forest, but the source of this statement has not been traced. Vaurie (1957d) considered it possible that White-tailed may be only a visitor or straggler to Mount Victoria and that it was not proven that both occurred together, as only White-browed was definitely known to breed there; he treated White-browed as conspecific with White-tailed, although with reservations, as did Mayr (in Stanford & Mayr 1940–41). Recent field observations appear to confirm Vaurie, with only White-browed Nuthatch present on Mount Victoria in early April (although White-tailed was almost certainly resident at Laiva Dam, just 160 km to the north). Even if White-tailed is only a rare winter visitor on Mount Victoria, however, White-tailed Nuthatches from the Lushai hills (= Naga hills), including Blue Mountain, only 180 km northeast of Mount Victoria, show no trace of intergradation with White-browed Nuthatch (Vaurie 1957d). The small size, uniform undertail-coverts and prominent white supercilium of White-browed Nuthatch indicate a possible affinity with Yunnan Nuthatch, and, given the general uncertainty, it is thus best treated as specifically distinct.

**REFERENCES** D. Farrow & C. Robson (*in litt.*), Stresemann & Heinrich (1940), Vaurie (1957d).

This tiny nuthatch is a familiar bird of montane pine woods in the south and west Nearctic. Very sociable, roosts of up to 160 birds have been recorded, an adaptation to survive long, cold nights.

**IDENTIFICATION** Length 110 mm (4.25 in). Very small. Upperparts mid blue-grey, cap brownish-olive, tinged grey (slightly greyer in worn plumage and very grey in juveniles), with a dark eyestripe along the lower border in most US populations. A pale spot on the nape is visible only at close range. Chin, cheeks and ear-coverts whitish, darkening to buff on the underparts - varying from very pale to rich buff (often appearing quite brownish), generally palest in interior USA and Baja California, and becoming whiter in worn plumage. Very similar to Brown-headed Nuthatch, but identification simplified by the lack of overlap between the ranges of the two species. For distinctions see Brown-headed Nuthatch.

**SEX/AGE** Sexes similar. Juvenile similar to adult, but cap greyer, often mid-grey and tinged brown, showing little contrast with remainder of upperparts, which are relatively duller than the adult's. (Note that the cap of worn adults is slightly paler and greyer than in fresh plumage, thus showing a reduced contrast with the mantle; it still, however, has a definite brown tone.) Lores and eyestripe dark sooty-grey, not so dark as on fresh adult and less contrasting than on worn adult. Nuchal spot reduced or absent. Greater coverts fringed brownish. Underparts pale grey-white, washed buff (near worn adults, and not so clean and yellow-buff as a fresh adult). Notably, for up to three months after fledging the base of the lower mandible is pink to off-white, rather than grey to black as in adults. 1st adult as adult; in the hand, may show pale grey rather than dark grey patch on marginal and inframarginal coverts (Norris 1958), and a slight contrast between the worn primary coverts and fresh greater coverts.

**VOICE** Noisy. Call a clear, high-pitched, rapid, *kit-kit, kit-kit..., pit-pit, pit, pit-pit...* or *peep peep*, given in a variety of pitches and sequences; in flocks may be prolonged into twittering *de-de-de-de-de-de-de... pit-pi-dit, pi-dit, pi-dit...*, sometimes calls of individuals becoming so mixed with those of others as to sound like a brood of chicks. Other calls include a high-pitched *bree-ee-ee-ee-ee-eep* (given when tending young, especially by females). Song a rapid, high-pitched, staccato sequence of disyllabic piping units, *wee-bee, wee-bee, wee-bee...* or *ki-dee, ki-dee, ki-dee.* Song given February–midsummer in California, but similar calls may be heard throughout the year, and the alarm is also similar, although averages a faster repetition of more monosyllabic or irregularly disyllabic notes, sometimes just 3–4 units. Pairs may have rapid, synchronised duets, male/female uttering *poo toot/ pee tit / poo toot / pee tit.* The juvenile's call differs from that of Brown-headed, a rapid, slurred, chattering *durp-urp-urp-urp-urp...* varied with a louder *swe-swe swe-swe swe-swe swe-swe swee-swee swee-swee....* Overall, voice higher-pitched and purer than that

of Brown-headed Nuthatch. (After Norris 1958.)
**DISTRIBUTION AND MOVEMENTS** Range roughly parallels that of Ponderosa and Jeffrey Pines, although absent from much of Montana (perhaps because winter temperatures are too low). In **Canada** found in southern **British Columbia** (from about Lytton south and east to Newgate), south into the **USA**, through the Cascades and Sierra Nevada to **Baja California Norte** in **Mexico**; also the inner coastal ranges of northern **California**, and coastal California (south to San Luis Obispo Co.). The Rocky Mountains east to western **Montana**, SW **South Dakota** (the southern Black Hills), western **Nebraska** (the Pine Ridge area in Sioux and Dawes Cos.), and the scattered pine-capped desert mountains of **Utah**, **Arizona** and **New Mexico** east to western **Texas** (Davis and Guadalupe mountains). In **Mexico** found in **Baja California Norte** (Sierra de Juarez and Sierra San Pedro Martir), the Sierra Madre Occidental in eastern **Sonora** (west to the Bavispe river), **Sinaloa** and **Nayarit**, and western **Chihuahua**, **Durango** and **Zacatecas**, south to northern **Jalisco**, and the southern central plateau from southern Jalisco (Nevado de Colima), through **Michoacan**, **Mexico**, **Distrito Federal**, **Morelos** and **Puebla** to western **Veracruz**, with widely separated populations in northern **Coahuila** (Sierra del Carmen), and in SE Coahuila (southeast of Saltillo)/SW **Nuevo Leon** (Cerro Potosi). Resident, although limited seasonal altitudinal movements occur in montane populations (e.g. Wyoming, Colorado). Otherwise, little autumn and winter dispersal with remarkably few records from the plains, even from areas immediately adjacent to the breeding range (e.g. in Colorado very rarely east to Logan and Yuma Cos.), although there are irregular 'micro-irruptions' when dispersal is slightly more pronounced, perhaps associated with failure of the cone crop. Thus a rare visitor to the **Oklahoma** 'panhandle' (recorded August, December and May in NW Cimarron Co., but no evidence of breeding), and in **Texas** away from the breeding areas a rare migrant and winter visitor to El Paso and the Chisos mountains in the Trans-Pecos and to the Panhandle (Lubbock, Potter and Randall Cos.), with a single record from Dallas Co. in the northwest (December 1966). A rare and erratic visitor to the coastal lowlands of SW **California**, SW **Arizona** (adjacent to breeding areas at Phoenix, Superior, Tucson and the Babocomari river, even to Yuma in September 1902) and eastern **New Mexico**. Away from these areas, an extremely rare vagrant to SW **British Columbia** (near Vancouver and on Vancouver Island near Comrox in October 1931), **Alberta** (hypothetical list only), central and eastern **Montana** (Chouteau, Fergus and Custer Cos.), eastern **Nebraska** (Douglas Co., *c.* 1900), **Kansas** (a flock of *c.* 10 recorded Wichita,

Sedgwick Co., November 1961–January 1962, also recorded Ford, Geary, Morton and Saline Cos.), and **Iowa** (Des Moines Co., January–April 1977).

**HABITAT** A pine-forest specialist, with distribution closely paralleling that of Ponderosa and Jeffrey Pines, and in California also in Monterey and Bishop Pines; occasionally other conifer species (e.g. Lodgepole Pine in northern Colorado). Favours open, park-like woodland, and in Mexico very much a bird of high, cold pine forests. In winter, may occur in Douglas Fir and pinyon–juniper woodlands, mixed pine-oak forest, riparian woodlands and conifer plantations, but very rarely in pure deciduous forest. From below or near sea level to 1220 m in coastal California, otherwise at 550–3350 m in the USA, 1585–2745 m in Baja California and 1830–4270 m in remainder of Mexico (highest altitudes in the south, e.g. on Popocatepetl).

**POPULATION** Common in Oregon, California, Arizona, New Mexico and Baja California Norte; often abundant and one of the most numerous birds in pine forests, although numbers fluctuate with the size of the cone crop. Otherwise fairly common within the breeding range in Idaho, Nevada, Utah, Colorado and Texas, uncommon in British Columbia, Washington, Montana, Wyoming, and rare in Nebraska and South Dakota. In Mexico away from northern Baja California locally fairly common. High winter densities are found in the Spring Mountains of southern Nevada, the foothills around Spokane, Washington, the foothills of the Rocky Mountains in Colorado, and in Monterey, California. Human population growth and forestry (notably the removal of suitable nesting trees) have resulted in some local declines.

**HABITS** Highly social, active, restless and not shy. Tends to form permanent pair-bonds and maintain a year-round territory, selected by the male and comprising the nest/roost site and foraging areas; territories of pairs with 'helpers' (see Breeding Biology) average larger. There is little overlap between territories, but they are actively defended only in the breeding season, defence usually being limited to the vicinity of the nest site; possession is announced with song. After breeding, 1st adults may disperse slightly further than adults, but families tend to stay together in the autumn, sooner or later forming stable winter groups with other families which may roam over the area formerly occupied by several territories, occasionally more widely. In some areas tends to form single-species groups (usually 5–16, but up to 100 birds recorded), but in montane habitats joins mixed-species foraging flocks. Flocks break up in the spring and the surplus young are usually driven off (exclusion from the roost site may be an important factor in this process), but males may be allowed to remain as 'helpers', and some may remain as 'floaters' (neither breeding nor helping). Roosts throughout the year in tree cavities, the pair using the nest hole throughout the breeding season, but otherwise roosts socially in close body contact, in family parties or small flocks (the win-

ter group); exceptionally, over 100 birds have been recorded using a single large cavity, with a total of over 160 in the same dead stub. The remains of up to 13 mummified nuthatches have been found in similar holes; these may have been suffocated by the crush whilst in a large roost (Knorr 1957). Has also been recorded roosting in nestboxes. Communal roosting is an adaptation for this small species to survive very cold nights, and the colder it is the larger the number of birds that roost together. Roosting Pygmy Nuthatches may also enter a state of hypothermia, lowering their body temperature by at least 10° C to minimise energy expenditure. Indeed, in periods of heavy snowfall, when needle clusters, the usual foraging site, are inaccessible, they may not leave the roost at all, spending up to 40 hours in the cavity without food. Forages in pines (sometimes in other trees, such as oak, especially in the winter), high up in the top and outer branches, feeding tit-like among needle clusters, cones and young shoots; also (especially in winter) feeds on the trunks and larger limbs, flaking off pieces of bark to find insects. May flycatch or pick off insects while hovering. Also utilises broadleaved trees and shrubs and may go to ground after swarming termites, extracting seeds from fallen cones and retrieving fallen items, and has even been noted consuming a flaky layer of ice (in a very dry winter; Marshall 1957). Food pine seeds, especially in the autumn and winter, and insects and spiders, the young being fed principally on animal matter. May store pine seeds, hiding them in bark crevices.

**BREEDING BIOLOGY** Season in USA mid April–late June, possibly slightly earlier in southern Mexico. Nests in tree holes, sometimes excavates its own hole in standing dead wood or may reuse old cavities or old woodpecker holes, and recorded breeding in telephone poles and old buildings (Burleigh 1972). Excavation, which take 3–6 weeks in mid March–early June, is predominantly by the male. Several holes may be started before the final selection, and the nest may be some distance from the foraging area. Cavities 1–30 m above ground, usually above 6 m. 'Caulks' the hole more extensively than Brown-headed Nuthatch (Norris 1958). The nest is built by both sexes, from bark chips, pine-cone scales, moss etc., lined with feathers, fur, hair, wool, snakeskin and various soft plant fibres. Clutch 6–9 (4–11; averages 7): eggs white, sparsely and unevenly spotted reddish-brown; 15.4 x 12 mm. Female incubates, period 15–16 days, fed on and off the nest by the male. The young usually are fed by both sexes, the male making the most feeding visits, but only the female broods the nestlings. Fledging period 20–22 days, but juveniles are not fully independent until 45–50 days after hatching. Very occasionally double-brooded, and replacement clutches unusual. About 30% of pairs are assisted by 1–3 male 'helpers' (exceptionally four), usually a related 1st adult or sibling of the pair, and always a member of the same winter group. These secondary males do not court or copulate with the female, but assist in defending the nest and territory, in nest building and in nest sanitation, feed the female on the nest, feed the young, and at all stages of the breeding cycle roost in the nest. Pairs with helpers are less likely to lose their nest to predators or other causes of nest abandonment - a clear advantage; and the helpers may benefit by gaining entrance to the winter group, membership of which is critical for survival.

DESCRIPTION *S. p. melanotis* **Adult**: *In fresh plumage* (late August–February), crown, nape and upper mantle brownish-olive with a greyish cast, lores and eyestripe sooty-brown. Concealed or indistinct paler nuchal spot in centre of upper mantle. Remainder of upperparts, including tertials and wing-coverts, mid blue-grey; inner webs of tertials slightly darker, concealed inner webs of greater coverts dark brown. Central tail feathers mid blue-grey, with broad off-white shaft streak on basal half; T2–T6 blackish-grey, tipped brownish-olive, broadly so on T6, T5–T6 with broad off-white diagonal subterminal stripe (see figure 7.1). Alula and primary coverts blackish, smaller feathers of alula fringed blue-grey, primary coverts finely fringed mid grey. Primaries and secondaries sooty-brown, secondaries fringed mid-grey, inner primaries finely fringed light grey, P3 broadly fringed white on basal third, P4-P7 with whitish fringe around emargination; P3–P6 with white at base showing as slight flash at tips of primary coverts. Chin, cheeks and ear-coverts off-white, darkening to pale buff on sides of neck, throat and upper breast and yellow-buff on remainder of underparts (varies from very pale buff to rich buff, generally paler in the interior); flanks pale grey. Axillaries light grey; underwing-coverts dark grey, longer under primary coverts and base of primaries white. *In worn plumage* (February–August), cap slightly paler and tinged greyer (feather bases exposed), lores and eyestripe blackish, more contrasting. Off-white feather bases show on upper mantle, buffish or whitish nuchal spot exposed. Upperparts slightly duller and less blue. Flight feathers worn and bleached paler. Underparts paler and less buff, more dirty grey-white with a hint of buff. **Bare Parts**: Iris brown; upper mandible blackish, lower dusky grey with pale blue-grey base; legs and feet dark brown, greyish or greyish-black, soles often pale yellow or greenish-yellow, claws blackish. **Juvenile**: As adult, but cap mid grey, tinged brown, remainder of upperparts mid grey, showing little contrast with the cap. Nuchal spot indistinct or absent, but often some pale buff-white of feather bases shows in

*Figure 7.1  Tail of* S. p. melanotis.

centre of upper mantle. Lores and eyestripe dark sooty-grey. Greater coverts fringed brownish. Underparts pale grey-white, washed buff, flanks pale buffy-brown. Extensive pink to off-white base to lower mandible when recently fledged. **1st Adult**: See Sex/Age. **Measurements**: Wing of male 64–68 (chord 59.5–69), of female 60.5–67 (chord 57–65.5); tail of male 29–35.5, of female 33–35; bill 15–17.7; tarsus 13.3–15.8. Weight averages 9.3–11.4g.

MOULT Adult post-breeding complete (early July–early October). Adult pre-breeding limited, includes underparts, also nape? (February–May). Post-juvenile partial (late June–August).

GEOGRAPHICAL VARIATION Slight. Seven races recognised, but all depend on subtle differences in size and proportions and, to a lesser extent, coloration. Notably, all the Mexican races are very similar.

*S. p. melanotis* British Columbia, western USA (except areas occupied by *pygmaea* and *leuconucha*), northern Mexico in extreme NE Sonora (San Jose mountains) and (disjunctly) northern Coahuila. On Howell Mountain, Napa Co., California, intermediate with *pygmaea*. See Description. Average measurements of male: wing (chord) 64.3; tail 31.6; bill (nostril) 11; tarsus 14.4. Rather variable; larger and paler in southern California (approaching *leuconucha*), browner-capped in the Chiricahua mountains, SE Arizona (approaching *chihuahuae*), and underparts paler and less buffy in the interior. Includes poorly differentiated 'canescens' (Spring and Sheep mountains of southern Nevada; slightly paler).

*S. p. pygmaea* Coastal California from Mendocino to San Luis Obispo Cos. Very similar to *melanotis*, but eyestripe ill-defined, especially behind the eye, contrasting little, if at all, with the cap, which in turn averages slightly browner and less grey than in *melanotis* (brownish-olive). Relatively short wing and long tarsus, average measurements of male: wing (chord) 61.4; tarsus 14.9. Coastal birds are smaller and more richly coloured, while above 900 m in Monterey Co. they are larger, relatively pale and greyish (approaching *leuconucha*).

*S. p. leuconucha* Southernmost California (San Jacinto and Laguna mountains) and northern Baja California. Intergrades with *melanotis* north towards the San Bernardino mountains, California. Poorly marked. As *melanotis* and *pygmaea*, but upperparts paler and greyer, underparts whiter; overlaps in cap coloration with *melanotis*; darker and bill longer than in other Mexican races. Average measurements of male: wing (chord) 68; tail 33.5; bill (nostril) 12.1; tarsus 15.3.

*S. p. chihuahuae* Mexico in Sierra Madre Occidental from NE Sonora south to northern Jalisco (south to Santa Teresa and Guadalajara). Poorly marked (synonymised with *melanotis* by Phillips 1986). As *pygmaea*, but upperparts average slightly darker; wing longer, bill and tarsus relatively shorter. Differs from *melanotis* in cap coloration, slightly darker and bluer upperparts, and buffy breast but pale grey belly; also wing and bill shorter. Average measurements of male: wing (chord) 64; tail 32.1; bill (nostril) 10.5; tarsus 14.4. Averages fractionally shorter-winged and shorter-billed in the south, where cap fractionally warmer brown and underparts buffer, approaching *brunnescens* (thus thought to be well differentiated only in Durango and Zacatecas by Webster 1984).

**S. p. brunnescens** SW Mexico in southern Jalisco and Michoacan. Poorly marked. As *chihuahuae*, but cap averages slightly browner (olive-brown), nuchal spot slightly more prominent, tinged yellow-buff, and underparts buffy (as *melanotis*). Juvenile has underparts, especially belly and flanks, pinkish-cinnamon, slightly pinker than juvenile *chihuahuae*. Fairly large, bill large. Average measurements of male: wing (chord) 65.6; tail 32.5; bill (nostril) 10.8; tarsus 14.6.

**S. p. flavinucha** Two populations: (i) Western Veracruz (at Volcano Citlaltepetl (= Mount Orizaba), and Las Vigas (= Perote area); (ii) western Puebla, Morelos, and Mexico. Poorly marked. As *chihuahuae*, but cap may be fractionally less brown (although birds from Mount Toluca, Mexico, may match *brunnescens*). Nape spot only faintly tinged buffy-yellow. Norris (1958) claimed that juveniles are washed pinkish-buff on the underparts (ochraceous-buff in other Mexican races), but two juvenile *brunnescens* from Jalisco have stronger pinkish-buff wash than four juve-

nile/moulting *flavinucha* (from Cofre de Perote, Veracruz). The two populations are rather different in size and proportions: (i) is large and long-winged, average measurements of male: wing (chord) 65; bill (nostril) 9.6; tarsus 15; (ii) is medium to medium-large with a long tarsus and exceptionally short bill, average measurements of male: wing (chord) 69.1; bill (nostril) 10; tarsus 15.5. (Note: Phillips (1986) states that the Morelos population is not long-winged, being one of the smallest groups: wing (chord) of male 60.6–66.2, of female 62.1–66.2.)

**S. p. elii** Phillips (1986) SW Nuevo Leon and SE Coahuila. As *chihuahuae*, but longer wing, tail and tarsus (probably the largest race), and with upperparts paler, underparts dull and pale (as *leuconucha*), but bill smaller, and juvenile darker, except on throat and breast. Compared with *flavinucha* is larger, and juveniles lack yellow-brown fringes to the median and greater coverts and are whiter, less buffy, below. Wing (chord) of male 67–71, of female 66.5–70; tail of male 36.5–37.5, of female 36–37.5; bill (exposed culmen) 12.2–13.3.

**RELATIONSHIPS** See Brown-headed Nuthatch.
**REFERENCES** Bent (1948), Güntert *et al.* (1988), Norris (1958), Phillips (1986), Sydeman (1989), Sydeman *et al.* (1988).

# 8 BROWN-HEADED NUTHATCH *Sitta pusilla*     **Plate 4**

This tiny nuthatch is the eastern counterpart of the Pygmy Nuthatch and is the only North American bird known to be a regular tool-user.

**IDENTIFICATION** Length 105 mm (4 in). Very small. Cap warm pale brown in late summer and early autumn; mottled rather paler during the rest of the year, with a contrastingly darker eyestripe. Whitish spot on nape visible at close range. Upperparts mid blue-grey. Cheeks, ear-coverts and sides of neck whitish, darkening to buff on the remainder of underparts. Much smaller than White-breasted Nuthatch, with a brown rather than black cap. Also smaller than Red-breasted Nuthatch, and lacks its black eyestripe and white supercilium. Very similar to Pygmy Nuthatch and best separated by range. Extralimital birds must be critically examined, and the following criteria apply to adults and 1st adults (juveniles are probably not safely identifiable). The cap of Brown-headed is warm pale brown in August–November; otherwise mottled with pale buffy-grey, giving a 'frosted' effect, with a darker eyestripe. The cap of Pygmy is brownish-olive with a variable grey cast, never mottled paler and showing much less contrast with the mantle. Brown-headed has a conspicuous white nuchal spot, either indistinct or absent on Pygmy, and averages paler and less yellow-buff on the underparts in fresh plumage. In the hand, the central tail feathers are usually only slightly paler at the base on Brown-headed (the extreme base being light grey), although they may

show a narrow whitish shaft streak, whilst Pygmy shows extensive white at the base of the tail (basal half of inner web), with the extreme base of the feathers blackish. The outer two tail feathers show a broken greyish-white subterminal bar on Brown-headed and a broad white subterminal bar in Pygmy.

**SEX/AGE** Sexes similar. Juveniles marginally distinct, with much less contrast between the cap (which is generally greyer than the adult's) and the mantle (which is slightly browner than the adult's); the nuchal spot is less conspicuous, the greater coverts are fringed buffish and the tertial and secondary fringes are also washed buff. Underparts as fresh adult, but with a slight rosy flush and browner flanks. 1st adult as adult; in the hand, there may be slight moult contrasts between the old primary coverts and new greater coverts, and exceptionally 1st adults retain some juvenile inner greater coverts.

**VOICE** Rather vocal. Commonest call, given constantly while foraging, a twittering *pit, pit, pit ...*, which may be accelerated in flight into soft, slurred, rolling *de-ur-ur-ur-ur-ur....* Also gives a thin, metallic *tnee-tnee-tnee*. The searching call, also given in alarm or excitement, is an abrupt, nasal *tnzii-u, tnzii-u* or *tsziu, tsziu*. Song essentially a repetition of this call, a repeated *tze-da tze-da* or *ki-day ki-day* (variant *ki-dee-dee*, or *pri-u, de-u, de-u*) recalling a squeaky toy, given in a rapid series which may last several minutes. Juveniles (and adults) give a buzzy *sh-h-r-r-r-p, sh-h-r-r-r-p*. Voice generally slightly lower-pitched, less pure and 'reedier' than that of Pygmy Nuthatch, the song generally slower, and quite unlike those of White-breasted and Red-breasted Nuthatches. (After Norris 1958.)

**DISTRIBUTION AND MOVEMENTS** In the USA found in SE **Oklahoma** (Le Flore and McCurtain Cos.; also recorded Pushmataha Co., July 1920), eastern **Texas** (west to Harris and Anderson Cos., occasionally south in winter to the Freeport area), southern and western **Arkansas** (north to the Ouachita mountains and Arkansas valley and in the coastal plain east to Drew Co.; also reported from the Ozarks in Franklin and Van Burren Cos., and from Jackson Co. in the NE), the **Gulf States**, northern **Florida** (south to Collier Co., where relict population in Big Cypress National Preserve), SE **Tennessee** (breeds Hamilton and Bradley Cos.; also recorded Van Burren Co.), **Georgia** (although absent from most of the mountainous part of the state except southern Rabun Co. and near Lake Chatuge (bred 1983)), **South Carolina**, east and central **North Carolina** and **Virginia**, SE **Maryland** (north and west to Kent, Calvert and St Marys Cos.), and southern **Delaware**. Also **Grand Bahama**. Absent from the grassland strip along the Louisiana and Texas coasts. May have bred SE **Missouri** (a pair was collected in Shannon Co., March 1907, also recorded St Louis in May 1878). Accidental **Wisconsin** (Milwaukee, October 1971–January 1972), **New York** (Chemung Co., 24 May 1888), **Indiana** (Lake Co., April 1932) and **Pennsylvania** (not for at least 50 years). Resident, with only very limited post-breeding dispersal.

**HABITAT** Closely associated with the Loblolly Pine (also Longleaf and Shortleaf Pines), favouring mature open woodland and edge habitats with plenty of standing dead wood, such as burnt-over areas, clearings and forest edge. Also pine-oak woodland, cypress swamps, and will venture outside woodland to areas of scattered trees, seedling pines in abandoned farmland, and even fence posts and telegraph poles along roads, and may be better adapted to such edge habitats than Pygmy Nuthatch. Also occurs in oak-hickory-pine forests (which hold the highest winter densities) and swamp forests in the Mississippi valley. Shows much hostility towards White-breasted Nuthatch, and interspecific competition may influence the ranges of the two species. Found in the coastal plains and piedmont, usually below 150 m (90 m in Texas, but up to 670 m in Georgia, although a rare accidental in the mountains of the Carolinas).

**POPULATION** Common throughout most of the range, but only fairly common in Texas and Virginia, uncommon in Arkansas, Tennessee, Maryland and Delaware, and rare in Oklahoma. The highest winter concentrations are in the swamp forests of the Mississippi river near the Felsenthan National Wildlife Refuge in Louisiana. On Grand Bahama, not uncommon on the borders of the pine forest, but rare or absent in the interior of the island. Expanding its range northwards in Georgia, and first recorded SE Tennessee in 1968, with a population of 50–70 birds by 1981. In western North Carolina, recent records from Caldwell and Buncombe Cos. may indicate a westward range expansion. Conversely, may have been extirpated in Missouri, although the two records there may well have involved vagrants rather than breeding birds (despite the ravages of forestry, apparently suitable habitat remains in Missouri and is unoccupied). Has also declined in southern Florida as a result of logging.

**HABITS** Active, restless and not shy. May form permanent pair-bonds, and males probably maintain permanent territories around the nest hole, singing and chasing away other males. Those pairs with a helper male (see Breeding Biology) hold a larger territory than simple pairs, but these territories, and those of non-breeding pairs, may overlap more extensively with those of their neighbours. Families tend to remain together through the autumn and winter, and forage beyond their territorial boundaries. These small flocks may amalgamate to form single-species flocks (groups of up to 24 have been recorded) or join mixed-species foraging flocks. Generally forages in the treetops, near the tips of branches, often hanging upside-down, exploring the clusters of needles for insects or picking seeds from cones. Less frequently feeds on trunks and the larger branches, especially when alone or in single-species flocks. Food in the winter mainly pine seeds, but in summer more insects and spiders are taken, and the young are fed exclusively on animal material. May store pine seeds, pounding them with its bill into crevices in the bark of a pine; does not, however, have large caches. (Compared with Pygmy Nuthatch, spends more time on larger branches and trunks, descends to ground more often to forage and drink, and more frequently catches insects on the wing.) Prises off bark scales to reveal hidden prey and occasionally uses a scale of Longleaf Pine bark as an extension of its bill, utilising it as a wedge to pry off bark scales. Usually drops its 'tool' after removing a scale, but may remove 3–4 scales before dropping it, or may carry its tool from tree to tree. The use of tools occurs most frequently in years of poor seed crop, and may have developed from the species' habit of wedging pine seeds into cracks in the bark while it hammers them open. The female or both sexes may roost in the nest cavity during breeding, but in the late summer roosts in the open in the crowns of trees or may return to roost in cavities as a family party, and has been found roosting communally in nest-boxes.

**BREEDING BIOLOGY** Season early March–mid May (sometimes February in Florida, exceptionally mid July in Georgia). Excavates its own hole in standing, partially rotten wood, usually a stump or dead tree, sometimes a fence post, with a preference for pines. May reuse old excavations or nestboxes, occasionally natural holes (including cavities under bark) without excavation, and rarely old woodpecker holes. Often

selects sites in clearcuts, along roadsides, in wind-
breaks, over ponds, and in fields, sometimes well
away from foraging areas. Excavation, which takes
1–6 weeks in late February–early March (late
January–early May), is predominantly by the male,
and several holes may be started before he makes
the final choice. Exceptionally, two pairs may
share the same cavity (Houck & Oliver 1954).
Entrance 0.15–28 m above ground, usually below
3.5 m. The nest is 'caulked' less extensively than
that of Pygmy Nuthatch. Nest constructed by both
sexes, usually of pine seed wings, also bark chips,
grass and other vegetable fibres, lined with cotton,
feathers, wool and seed wings, although sometimes eggs are laid on the bare floor of the cavity.
Clutch 4–6 (3–7, very rarely 9): eggs white or
creamy, heavily spotted reddish-brown; 15.3 x
12.1 mm. Female incubates, period 14 days, fed
on and off the nest by the male. Female broods,
but young fed by both sexes, fledging after 18–19
(–23) days, although not fully independent until *c.*
44 days after hatching. Around 20% of pairs are
assisted by a helper male (usually a 1st adult and
related to one of the pair); the helper male does
not court or copulate with the female, or roost
with her in the nest, but does assist in nest construction and sanitation, feeds the female on the
nest and feeds the young. Rarely, two helper males
may be associated with a breeding pair. Rarely
double-brooded, and occasionally replaces lost
clutches.

**DESCRIPTION** *S. p. pusilla* **Adult**: *In fresh
plumage* (August–October), lores, crown, nape
and upper mantle warm, pale, 'milk-chocolate'
brown. Variable whitish spot in centre of upper
mantle. Upperparts, including lesser coverts, mid
blue-grey. Central tail feathers mid blue-grey,
slightly paler at base, and may show whitish along
shaft; T2–T6 sooty-black, tipped mid to light grey,
narrowly so on T2–T3, broadly so on T6, T5–T6
with broken diagonal greyish-white subterminal
bar (see figure 8.1). Lesser and median coverts mid
grey fringed blue-grey, greater coverts and tertials
mid grey, faintly washed brown, greater coverts
finely fringed light grey or blue-grey, tertials slightly darker on inner web. Alula, primary coverts,
primaries and secondaries dark brownish-grey,
primary coverts finely fringed mid grey, secondaries fringed light grey, inner primaries very finely fringed pale grey, P3–P5 narrowly fringed off-
white around emargination. Cheeks, ear-coverts
and sides of neck whitish, chin white, washed
buff, and darkening to pale buff on throat, buffish
or pale cinnamon-buff on breast (quickly wears to
pale buff) and greyish-buff on belly, vent, undertail-coverts and thighs; sides of breast and flanks
light grey. Axillaries light grey; underwing-coverts
mid grey, longer under primary coverts and base
of primaries white. *In worn plumage*
(October/November–August), cap averages rather
paler, the feather tips extensively bleached to pale
greyish-drab or whitish-buff, lores and eyestripe
contrastingly darker brown. Nuchal spot whiter
and more prominent. Upperparts slightly duller
and less blue. Flight feathers worn and bleached
paler, fringes rather worn. Underparts paler,

*Figure 8.1 Tail of* S. p. pusilla.

whitish or dirty pale grey, tinged buff. **Bare Parts**:
Iris brown; bill dark slate, lower mandible extensively pale bluish-grey at base; legs and feet dark
grey or dull brown, soles paler; claws blackish.
**Juvenile**: As adult, but cap pale brown to grey,
generally much greyer-brown than adult, always
showing reduced (sometimes no) contrast with
upperparts, which are mid brownish-grey, the
upper mantle slightly greyer. Nuchal spot reduced.
Greater coverts fringed or washed pale cinnamon-
buff, tertial and secondary fringes tinged cinnamon, primary coverts tinged drab-grey. Underparts
washed vinaceous-buff (as deep as fresh adult but
more 'rosy'), flanks and vent cinnamon-drab. **1st
Adult**: As adult, but may occasionally retain some
buff-fringed inner greater coverts. **Measurements**:
Wing of male 61–67 (chord 60–69), of female
61–67.5 (chord 62.5–67.5); tail of male 30–34.5,
of female 29.5–33; bill 14.9–17.9; tarsus 13–16.
Average weight 10.2 g.

**MOULT** Adult post-breeding complete
(July–September, occasionally from late May).
Adult pre-breeding limited (February–April). Post-
juvenile partial, includes variable number of
greater coverts, usually all but occasionally only
inner 1–2 (July–August).

**GEOGRAPHICAL VARIATION** Slight, two
subspecies recognised.

   *S. p. pusilla* USA. See Description. A slight
north-south cline of decreasing size with a 'step'
between the more or less isolated population in
Maryland (large, long-winged, deep-billed) and
that of Virginia/North Carolina. Includes '*cani-
ceps*' of peninsular Florida, which has cap marginally paler and warmer brown (when fresh) and
is also slightly smaller, with the bill relatively long
and thick; Norris (1958) considered that the
colour characters fall within the range of individual variation and did not recognise this race.

   *S. p. insularis* Grand Bahama Island. As nominate *pusilla*, but bill longer and thinner (*c.* 2.5 mm
longer than on birds from Florida) and eyestripe
darker.

**RELATIONSHIPS** Forms a superspecies with
Pygmy Nuthatch and sometimes considered conspecific. Mayr & Short (1970) found nothing in
Norris (1958) to support the specific separation of
Brown-headed and Pygmy Nuthatches, considering the described differences (crown colour and
tail pattern, wing/tail ratio, vocalisations, foraging
behaviour, breeding biology, roosting habits and
population density) to be typical of disjunct conspecific populations inhabiting somewhat differ-

ent environments; they followed Phillips *et al.* (1964) in considering the two conspecific. Notably, however, the voices of juveniles of the two species are rather different, and the location call of juveniles was the main character which led Löhrl (1960, 1961) to consider Red-breasted and Corsican Nuthatches to be distinct species. Kleinschmidt (1932–33) considered Pygmy and

Brown-headed Nuthatches to be closely related to White-tailed Nuthatch, sharing white at the base of the tail and at the base of the feathers of the nape.

**REFERENCES** Bent (1948), Norris (1958), McNair (1984), Morse (1968), Oberholser (1974), Root (1988).

# 9 CORSICAN NUTHATCH *Sitta whiteheadi*       **Plate 5**

Discovered as recently as 1883 by John Whitehead, the Corsican Nuthatch is one of just a handful of birds endemic to Europe.

**IDENTIFICATION** Length 120 mm (4.75 in). Small, but rather long-billed. Upperparts mid blue-grey, with a prominent broad white supercilium. Cap and eyestripe vary from contrastingly black in males to blue-grey, concolorous with the upperparts, in females. Outer tail feathers black with whitish subterminal spots and pale grey tips. Sides of head and throat white, grading to pale greyish-white underparts, variably washed buff on the flanks, belly and undertail-coverts. The only nuthatch on Corsica, so identification straightforward. For distinction from a vagrant Red-breasted Nuthatch, see that species.

**SEX/AGE** Sexes distinct. The male has the cap and eyestripe black, whilst the female has the crown blue-grey with concealed dark grey feather bases which may be revealed, especially on the forehead and forecrown, in worn plumage. The female's eyestripe is grey behind the eye and rather less well defined than male's. Juvenile as respective sex of adult, although slightly duller overall, with faint brown tips to the greater coverts. 1st adult as adult, but any retained juvenile greater coverts may show traces of pale tips until midwinter.

**VOICE** Contact call a soft, whistled *pu*, given singly or in groups of 5–6 notes, sometimes as a rapid trilling series, *pupupupupu...*, especially immediately prior to or during flight. Also gives a thin, sometimes lisping *tsi-tsi-tsi* and a nasal *pink*, often in an irregular series. In agitation gives a hissing *psch-psch-psch...* and a nasal, toy-trumpet-like note, becoming louder and harsher in excitement or alarm, a repeated *chay-chay-chay...* or *sch-wer sch-wer...*, recalling a distant Eurasian Jay, and given in increasing intensity as excitement heightens, when it may lose its harsh quality and become more musical. Song a series of clear, high-pitched units given in a rapid, sometimes quavering tremolo, *hididididid...* (faster than the corresponding song of Krüper's Nuthatch), also a slower variant of pure, ascending whistled units, *dew-dew-dew...* or *dui-dui-dui...*; the two may be combined, *dewdewdewdewdew-di-di-di-di-di*. Sings fairly regularly in spring (unlike Red-breasted Nuthatch), but may be quiet and inconspicuous whilst feeding young. (Partly after Cramp & Perrins 1993.)

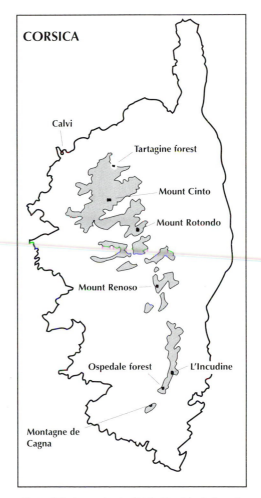

*Figure 9.1 Approximate distribution (shaded area), corresponding very closely with that of Corsican Pine, together with some localities mentioned in text. (After Brichetti & Capri 1987)*

**DISTRIBUTION AND MOVEMENTS** Endemic to **Corsica**, **France**, where it occurs on inland mountain ridges from Tartagine south to Ospedale, also perhaps Montagne de Cagna (although recorded by Jourdain (in Thibault 1983), there are no recent records from this isolated massif, from which Corsican Pine is absent). The main concentrations are around the Cinto, Rotondo, Renoso and Incudine mountains (see map, p. 133). Resident, although some dispersal in winter to slightly lower altitudes, usually by immatures and unmated birds. Such movements are most frequent following snowfalls, when recorded in the valleys of central Corsica at 300–600 m, and towards the west coast, even at sea level at Calvi in October.

**HABITAT** Primarily forests of Corsican Pine, characterised by heavy autumn and winter rainfall and rather dry summers. The best habitat is unmanaged pure stands of tall trees (some 300 years old) with abundant standing dead and rotting trunks and occasional clearings. Found April–October at 750–1800 m, with breeding recorded 760–1600 m, optimum zone 1000–1500 m. Lower densities (less than 20% of maximum density) occur in young forests, mature stands under heavy management, and where Corsican Pines are mixed with Maritime European Pine, Common Beech or Silver Fir, usually below 1000 m; densities are also low above 1500 m, where, owing to the harsh conditions, the trees are scattered and stunted. In winter, some dispersal below 1000 m into the Maritime Pine zone and occasionally further afield, although still favours pines.

**POPULATION** Estimated at *c.* 2,000 pairs in 1981–84, based on an average density of 0.85 pairs/10 ha in *c.* 24,000 ha of suitable forest. This is a marked decline from an estimated population of 3,000 pairs (in 43,750 ha of forest) in the late 1950s. The main factors limiting its abundance are fire, which may destroy the habitat for many decades, and the removal of dead and rotting trees, which are used as nesting sites. Large numbers of Great Spotted Woodpeckers may result in a high predation of chicks, but houses, power lines and traffic are readily tolerated. Almost the entire population occurs within the Natural Regional Park. Listed as near-threatened in BirdLife International's world checklist of threatened birds (Collar *et al.* 1994).

**HABITS** Highly territorial, and mated pairs remain on territory all year, often within 50 m of each other, maintaining contact with quiet calls. Not shy. Forages tit-like in needle clusters and among small branches, especially in the spring and summer, and, particularly in the winter, also on the trunks and larger branches. May hover to pick small items from cones etc., and can also fly-catch. Outside the breeding season may join mixed-species foraging flocks. Food largely insects and spiders in May–August, switching to seeds, especially those of Corsican Pine, during the rest of the year. Stores seeds, caching items behind bark or placing them on thicker branches and then covering the seed with fragments of bark or lichen. These stores are probably essential to survival, especially in the early spring when snow prevents access to pine cones.

**BREEDING BIOLOGY** Season April–May (pairs lay eggs synchronously, generally at the end of April or in the first ten days of May). The nest is usually sited in a medium to large dead or dying Corsican Pine, 1.6–30 m above ground. The majority of nests are excavated by the birds themselves, usually in dead pine stumps, 200–300 years old at the time of death, 3.5–22 m high and well rotted; occasionally, living pines with a rotting top may be used. The majority of excavations exploit holes originally started by woodpeckers, and some, in very rotten trunks, may have two entrances. Excavation is carried out by both sexes, but Corsican Nuthatches do not use mud or resin to plaster the entrance to the nest cavity. The nest itself is a foundation of pine needles, wood chips and bark pieces, lined with hair, feathers, moss, lichen or plant fibres, built by both sexes. Clutch 5–6: eggs white, speckled reddish, especially at the broader end, and sometimes with light brown or dark violet-grey markings; 17.2–13 mm. Female incubates, period unknown; she is fed on the nest by the male. The young fledge after 22–24 days. May be double-brooded, and replacement clutches certainly occur.

**DESCRIPTION Adult Male**: *In fresh plumage* (autumn), forehead, crown and nape black, cap ill-defined at rear. Upperparts, including lesser and median coverts, mid blue-grey. Central tail feathers dull blue-grey; T2–T6 sooty-black, tipped mid grey, widest on T6; T4–T6 marbled with white subterminally, especially on inner webs (see figure 9.2). Wing-coverts and flight feathers dark grey-brown, tertials washed blue-grey on outer web, greater and primary coverts, secondaries and inner primaries narrowly fringed blue-grey, P3–P6 finely fringed blue-grey inwards of emarginations; secondaries and inner primaries finely tipped white when fresh. Supercilia from nostril (not quite meeting on forehead) to sides of mantle white, faintly washed buff, and ending irregularly at rear. Eyestripe black, finely spotted with white behind eye, and less well defined to rear of ear-coverts, merging irregularly into mantle. Narrow white eyering. Cheeks, ear-coverts, chin and throat white, washed dirty buff, sides of neck and remainder of underparts pale drab-grey, variably tinged buff, especially on flanks, belly and under tail-coverts. Underwing-coverts and axillaries whitish, median under primary coverts mid grey, base of primaries white, not strongly contrasting. *In worn plumage* (summer), crown slightly less glossy, upperparts duller and less blue, flight feathers abraded and bleached paler, supercilium,

*Figure 9.2 Tail.*

throat, cheeks and ear-coverts whiter, and underparts duller, light drab-grey with little or no buff wash. **Bare Parts**: Iris dark brown; bill slate-black to grey-brown, more bluish at base of upper mandible, base of lower mandible pale grey to whitish; legs and feet dark grey-brown or slate-grey, soles sometimes yellow. **Adult Female**: As male, but crown and ear-coverts mid blue-grey (as upperparts), dark feather centres largely or totally concealed, but may show as slightly darker mottling, usually on forecrown and forehead, especially in worn plumage, when exceptionally may show dull blackish forecrown. Supercilium and underparts may show more of a grey tone, but variable and matched by some males. **Juvenile**: As respective sex of adult, but may be very slightly paler on the upper- and underparts, with a stronger grey tone to the underparts, and paler and buffer undertail-coverts, and have the greater coverts faintly tipped grey-buff or pale grey; when very young, the cap of the juvenile male may be sooty-black with no gloss, whilst the juvenile female lacks blackish feather bases on the forecrown. Pale base to lower mandible more extensive, legs paler grey. **1st Adult**: As adult (but see Sex/Age). **Measurements**: Wing of male 70–76, of female 68–75; tail of male 37–42, of female 37–40; bill 16–19.5; tarsus 16.9–18.6. Weight 11.8–14.4 g.

**MOULT** Adult post-breeding complete (summer). Post-juvenile partial, no information on its extent (mid August–late September; onset c. 8 weeks after fledging).

**GEOGRAPHICAL VARIATION** None .

**RELATIONSHIPS** A member of the *canadensis* group and closely related to both Red-breasted and Chinese Nuthatches; indeed, has in the past been considered conspecific with one or both of these species (see Red-breasted Nuthatch). Studies of the vocalisations of Corsican Nuthatches, together with those of breeding biology and behaviour, were decisive in the definitive specific separation of Corsican from Red-breasted Nuthatch. The song of Corsican Nuthatch is closer to those of Algerian and Krüper's Nuthatches than to Red-breasted, whilst the location calls (given by juveniles once they have left the nest) of the two species are distinctly different: a clear, drawn-out whistle, often combined with a deeper grating note, in Corsican, and just a squeaking nasal note in Red-breasted.

**REFERENCES** Cramp & Perrins (1993), Brichetti & Di Capi (1985, 1987), Löhrl (1960, 1961), Matthysen & Adriaensen (1989), Thibault (1983).

# 10 ALGERIAN NUTHATCH *Sitta ledanti* Plate 5

Other name: Kabylie Nuthatch

Causing a sensation when it was discovered in 1975, the Algerian Nuthatch was the first new species of bird to be found in the Palearctic Region since 1937.

**IDENTIFICATION** Length 135 mm (5.25 in). Medium-sized, with a short, slender and sharply pointed bill which often appears uptilted owing to the rather straight culmen and distinct angle at the gonys. Upperparts blue-grey with a prominent whitish supercilium, underparts cream-pink to orange-buff. Depending on age and sex, the forecrown and eyestripe vary from black, forming a small, well-defined cap, to blue-grey, concolorous with the upperparts. Identification is straightforward, as there are no other nuthatches in Algeria (although there is a remote possibility that Eurasian Nuthatch may occur there).

**SEX/AGE** Variation not fully understood. Sexes distinct. The male has a well-defined black cap on the forecrown, well-marked whitish supercilium and variable black eyestripe, the head pattern being most pronounced in the spring and summer. In fresh autumn plumage, the female has most of crown and eyestripe concolorous with the upperparts, with blackish confined to a diffuse spot on the forehead, but, when worn, the female shows a variable black cap, although generally paler, rather less extensive and less well defined than the male's. Juveniles have the cap and eyestripe concolorous with the upperparts, the supercilium very poorly marked, the upperparts paler and less blue than the adult's and the underparts also paler.

Vielliard (1976, 1978) described black-capped juveniles, but the existence of this plumage was strongly contested by subsequent observers. Nevertheless, Fosse (1992) confirms that juveniles from a single nest may show a variable head pattern: of a brood of three, one had a black forecrown and resembled the adult male, one resembled the adult female (and was thus duller than the male), and in the third the crown was grey, concolorous with the mantle. Juveniles are therefore presumably sexually dimorphic, as in Corsican and Red-breasted Nuthatches. No information on the 1st adult male, but probably resembles the adult. The 1st adult female is thought to resemble the adult female, but with broader blue-grey fringes to the feathers of the cap and eyestripe, totally concealing the black feather bases in fresh plumage, and the supercilium is mottled grey (although, unlike on the juvenile, still broad and prominent). In worn plumage, the 1st adult female shows limited black mottling on the forehead.

**VOICE** Gives a quiet, soft, nasal *kna* whilst foraging and in flight (recalling Red-breasted Nuthatch), which may become an inquisitive *quuwee* (recalling the *diuwee* note of European Greenfinch). In excitement or territorial defence gives a harsh, rasping *vschrr vschrr* or *schrr, schrr, schrr* (rather like a Eurasian Jay) and sometimes when more agitated, a louder, even 'cawing', *chwa-chwa-chwa*. Other calls include a nasal, inquisitive *du-wa, du-wa* or *qu-wa-di-wa*, and the song is a stereotyped repetition of 7–12 similar units, sometimes nasal, sometimes fluty, lasting 2–4 seconds: *quair-di, quair-di, quair-di...* or *verdi-verdi-verdi...*, which can be slightly rising in pitch. The song may be slightly faster, *du-wid-du-wid-du-wid...*, or even more accelerated, each unit almost monosyllabic and slightly higher-pitched, *vid-vid-vid....* At all times, the song is quite distinct from the mellow, tremulous trill of Corsican Nuthatch.

## DISTRIBUTION AND MOVEMENTS

Endemic to NE **Algeria**, where first discovered in 1975 on the Djebel Babor and initially thought to be confined to the summit of this isolated massif. In June 1989, however, a population was found in Guerrouch forest in the nearby Taza National Park (Jijel), and in June and July 1990 the species was discovered in Tamentout forest (Setif) and Djimla forest (Jijel). All four sites are in the Petite Kabylie region and within 5–30 km of each other, although separated by tracts of unsuitable habitat (see map below). Resident. On Djebel Babor may undertake some altitudinal movements and limited post-juvenile dispersal, but movement downslope is inhibited by the treeless zone below the breeding area; thus the nuthatches are therefore presumed to winter on Babor, despite deep snow, perhaps aided by cached food supplies (in mid April birds have been seen in the breeding area with snow still 2–3 m deep). The movements of the Guerrouch, Tamentout and Djimla populations are unknown, as is any possible interchange between these areas.

**HABITAT** On Djebel Babor, a relict stand of montane forest with many epiphytic mosses and lichens, the climate is cool and humid with an annual precipitation of 2000–2500 mm, most falling in the winter; snow up to 4 m deep may be present in November–April/May. The forest is dominated at 1200–1650 m by the deciduous Atlas Oak, although with a significant proportion of Atlas Cedar. There is an increasing percentage of cedar and Algerian Fir (endemic to Djebel Babor) from 1650 to 1800 m, and the summit area from 1800 to 2004 m is dominated by cedars, although still with a proportion of oak and fir. Nuthatches are found above 1450 m, with the highest densities in the summit forest above 1900 m (territories covering just 3.3 ha) and much lower densities in pure stands of oak or cedar. A good mixture of tree species (and thus a reliable supply of seeds) may be important for winter survival, while the size and age of trees and hence the amount of dead wood and epiphytes are also important. Guerrouch forest in Taza National Park has a rather warmer and drier climate, rarely experiencing frosts, with an annual rainfall of 1000–1400 mm. At lower altitudes the forest is dominated by Cork Oak and at higher altitudes by Algerian Chestnut-leaved Oak, with Algerian Oak also prominent. Importantly, there is a good understorey of alder, cherry, willow, ash and maple. Nuthatches have been found from 350 m to the summit at 1121 m, with densities apparently increasing with altitude. Tamentout forest lies along the line of a ridge which culminates in the peak of Tamesguida, 1626 m, while Djimla forest, just 5 km to the east, rises to 1532 m. Both are similar to Guerrouch, but nuthatches are apparently found largely above 1000 m, in Algerian Oak and Algerian Chestnut-leaved Oak, and are

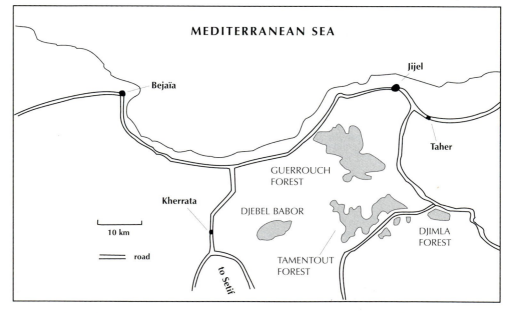

*Figure 10.1 Sketch map of the Petite Kabylie region of NE Algeria, showing location of the four known sites for the species (shaded areas). (After Bellatreche 1991)*

rarely encountered below 1000 m and in the Cork Oaks, and then only in Tamentout. The range of habitats utilised by the Algerian Nuthatch suggest that its distribution is circumscribed by the availability of forest rather than by a very specific ecological niche, and is not linked to the presence of Algerian Fir or Atlas Cedar.

**POPULATION** The forest on Djebel Babor covers c. 1300 ha, but optimum habitat extends for less than 250 ha in the summit area; there were initially thought to be just 12 pairs in 1976, but the population was estimated at c. 80 pairs in 1982. The Taza National Park (total area 3807 ha) protects the forested massif of Guerrouch; in summer 1989, surveys in Taza revealed 91 individuals in 800 ha and this was extrapolated to give a figure of 364 individuals in the 3197 ha of forest within the park (total forest cover on Gerrouch was estimated at 8577 ha in 1955, and nuthatches were also found to the southwest of the park boundary). Tamentout forest covers an area of c. 9500 ha and Djimla forest c. 1000 ha; there is no information on these populations, but, with a total area of 10, 500 ha, they may hold a summer population of around 1,200 individuals if the density is similar to that at Guerrouch. Searches elsewhere in the region have failed to find any more populations of the nuthatch. Listed as endangered in BirdLife International's world checklist of threatened birds (Collar & Stuart 1985; Collar et al. 1994). Although the area has national park status, the summit forests of Djebel Babor are threatened, but their conservation has received some attention since the discovery of the species. Nevertheless, grazing hinders regeneration, wood-cutting removes potential nest sites, and fires result in the replacement of the rich mixed forest by a poorer cedar-dominated succession. All three factors reduce the quality of the habitat and lead to a reduction in the total forest area. The Taza population is not considered threatened, as the national park is fully protected, but at Tamentout and Djimla grazing has resulted in an impoverished understorey and poor regeneration, and deforestation throughout the region is rife.

**HABITS** Strongly territorial in the breeding season, both sexes defending the territory boundaries. In the summer, forages tit-like in the twigs and outer branches of oaks, feeding on insects and spiders, with seeds perhaps assuming more importance when feeding young. Not known to flycatch. Feeds in winter on the trunks and branches of moss- or lichen-covered oaks, cedars and firs, often knocking off chips of bark to reveal morsels of food; also stores seeds in lichen-covered branches and thick moss cushions for later retrieval (even as late as the breeding season). Diet in winter largely seeds and nuts, and the four seed-producing trees on Djebel Babor appear to ensure a relatively constant supply, with fir and maple fruiting regularly and oak and cedar less predictably. Birds defend winter territories and may join mixed-species foraging flocks.

**BREEDING BIOLOGY** Season on Djebel Babor May–June, dependent on weather conditions or perhaps the abundance of food, whilst in Taza National Park the breeding season was over by late June. Nest placed in a hole in a dead or dying tree, usually in a dead branch, 3–15 m above ground. On Djebel Babor most are in firs, although also uses oaks and cedars, and often uses cavities produced by snow damage to the lower crowns of trees. May excavate its own hole, or take over abandoned woodpecker holes. The entrance is often relatively large, and, of nine nests located in 1978, one abandoned site had the entrance extensively plastered with a masonry of clay and rotten wood (although it has been suggested that this was the work of a vagrant Eurasian Nuthatch). The nest is constructed from wood chips, leaves, feathers and hog bristles. Clutch size unknown, although broods of 2–4 young have been recorded. Incubation probably by female alone, but the young are fed by both parents and probably fledge after 22–25 days. Juveniles continue to be fed for 1–2 days after fledging, but become fully independent relatively quickly, wandering into adjacent territories after just seven days. Probably single-brooded.

**DESCRIPTION** **Adult Male**: *In fresh plumage* (autumn), forecrown black, odd feathers faintly tipped grey. Remainder of upperparts, including sides of neck, tertials, wing-coverts and central tail feathers, blue-grey, wing-coverts diffusely tipped paler; T2–T6 blackish, narrowly tipped blue-grey, with subterminal white bar from outer web of T3 to T6, broadest on T6. Primaries and secondaries sooty-black, secondaries fringed blue-grey, outer primaries finely fringed pale grey at base; inner primaries and secondaries tipped white. Broad white or creamy supercilium from nostril to nape, gradually merging at rear with blue-grey upperparts; some grey flecking in front of eye. Narrow whitish eyering. Dull black eyestripe from bill to rear ear-coverts, ill-defined behind eye. Cheeks and ear-coverts white, washed buff and variably mottled blackish or dark grey, especially at rear. Underparts creamy-pink or washed pinkish-buff, some grey feather centres showing on undertail-coverts. *In worn plumage* (spring), cap pure black, supercilium purer white, eyestripe darker, also broader at rear, and encompassing the lower ear-coverts (where mottled off-white), upperparts duller and less blue, tail and flight feathers bleached slightly paler, pale tips to wing-coverts and flight feathers abraded, and underparts orange-buff to creamy, washed pinkish-buff. When heavily worn (summer), some grey feathers may be visible on forecrown. **Bare Parts**: Iris blackish-brown; bill slaty-black, base of cutting edge of upper mandible and basal half of lower mandible blue-grey; legs and feet grey or dark grey. **Adult Female**: In fresh plumage as male, but black feathers of cap and eyestripe finely fringed grey on lores and forehead, more broadly so on forecrown and behind eye so that black of forecrown and rear eyestripe largely concealed, showing only as small, diffuse black spot on forehead. In worn plumage, grey fringes abrade to reveal reduced dull black cap, poorly defined at the sides; when very worn in summer, some females may approach male in colour and extent of black cap. **Juvenile**: Crown blue-grey, as upperparts (unlike adult/1st adult, feathers lacking blackish bases?), eyestripe blue-grey or barely darker than cheeks, supercilium poorly defined, mottled grey, upperparts paler and less bluish than on adult, and underparts paler buff than on female, especially on breast and throat (?). Bill short-grown on fledging, slate-grey with greenish-grey or yellowish base to the lower mandible; legs and feet paler than adult's (see also Sex/Age). **1st Adult Male**: Probably similar to adult. **1st Adult Female**: Presumed 1st adults lack black cap and eyestripe in fresh plumage, these areas being blue-grey (blackish feather centres fully concealed by broad blue-grey fringes, 1–2 mm wide); supercilium finely mottled grey, although still broad and prominent. Bill occasionally still paler than adult's. In worn plumage, shows black mottling on forehead. **Measurements**: Wing of male 80–83, of female 77–81; tail, no information; tarsus 19–22; bill 16–17.5. Weight 16.6 g, 18 g. (After Cramp & Perrins 1993.)

**MOULT** Post-breeding complete (July–October). Post-juvenile partial, presumably as for other nuthatches (June).
**GEOGRAPHICAL VARIATION** None.
**RELATIONSHIPS** A member of the *canadensis* group (see Red-breasted Nuthatch). It differs slightly from the other members of the group, being somewhat larger and less restricted to coniferous forest. Initially thought to be a relict, 'trapped' on the ecological island of Djebel Babor. The discovery of new sites and a much broader range of habitat preferences suggests, however, a previously much wider distribution, deforestation, which has occurred in historical times rather than over geological time periods, having reduced the range to the current tiny fragments.
**REFERENCES** Bellatreche (1991), Bellatreche & Chalabi (1990), Collar & Stuart (1985), Cramp & Perrins (1993), Gatter & Mattes (1979), Jacobs *et al.* (1978), Ledant & Jacobs (1977), Ledant *et al.* (1985), Vielliard (1978).

# 11 KRÜPER'S NUTHATCH *Sitta krueperi*                                    Plate 5

Almost endemic to Turkey, this nuthatch is another 'relict' species. Its distribution is closely tied to that of the Turkish Pine, and it is just possible that there are undiscovered populations in the Middle East.

**IDENTIFICATION** Length 125 mm (5 in). A medium-small nuthatch. Upperparts mid blue-grey, with a neatly demarcated black forecrown, well-defined white supercilium and black eyestripe (rather ill-defined behind the eye). Ear-coverts and throat white, remainder of the underparts pale grey, variably washed buff, with a rufous, crescent-shaped 'breastplate'. Undertail-coverts chestnut with paler fringes, often conspicuous when viewed from below. The combination of small size, rufous breast, white supercilium and, in adults, black forecrown, is distinctive.
**SEX/AGE** The sexes differ slightly, the female having the black of the forecrown duller and less well defined at the rear, the eyestripe paler, the 'breastplate' averaging paler, and the lower breast washed buff rather than being pure grey as in the male. In worn plumage, these differences (apart from the buffish lower breast) are less obvious. Juvenile distinct, being much dingier than the adult, lacking the black forecrown, although the forehead may be marginally darker than the rest of the crown; the supercilium and eyestripe are poorly marked and the breastplate is pale rufous, poorly demarcated from the dirty drab-brown of the belly. Juveniles may be confused with worn adult females, but they lack the black forecrown, their breast patch and undertail-coverts are paler, and their flight feathers are fresh when those of the adult are worn. 1st adult as adult, but in fresh plumage some may be distinguished by traces of brownish tips on the retained juvenile greater coverts.
**VOICE** Very vocal and often most easily located by call. In excitement or alarm gives a subdued,

often rather quiet, harsh or hissing *cha* or *scharr* (recalling a distant Eurasian Jay), becoming louder and given in series as agitation mounts, and may be accelerated into an excited, scolding, churring rattle. Other calls include a soft *pwit* (like a very soft rendition of call of a spotted woodpecker) and a *doid* or *dui* (recalling a European Greenfinch or Atlantic Canary). In flight, gives a Brambling-like *jek*. Song a trill given at different speeds and with different inflections, in its basic form a shrill, rippling, often rapid repetition of simple units, *pip-pip-pip-pip...* or *veet-veet-veet...*, lasting 4–8 seconds with the individual notes delivered at a rate of 8 per second (thus not countable). In a more complex form the song comprises disyllable units repeated more slowly, although still high-pitched and yodelling, the phrase lasting 3–4 seconds and containing 15–20 units, *yu-di yu-di yu-di yu-di* or *wicka-wicka-wicka....* Sings throughout the year, although most frequently in spring. (Partly after Cramp & Perrins 1993.)
**DISTRIBUTION AND MOVEMENTS** Restricted in **Greece** to the island of Mytilene (Lesbos). In **Turkey**, fairly widespread in western Anatolia and in the Taurus mountains along the south coast, locally also in the mountains along the Black Sea and the northern edge of the central plateau. Extends marginally into **Georgia**, in the foothills of Kuzey Anadolu mountains (Bakhmaro, Abastumani, Bakuriani), and disjunctly (?) in the **Russian republic** on the northern watershed of the NW Caucasus (recorded from Pseashkho to at least as far southeast as Dombay and Teberda). Has a particular association with the Turkish Pine, the two species having near-coincident ranges.

Outlying populations of Turkish Pine in the Crimea, NW Syria, Lebanon, northern Iraq and Azarbaijan may have once held Krüper's Nuthatches, or indeed may still hold undiscovered populations. Resident, with some post-breeding dispersal in Turkey and noted at the Çamlica hills in Istanbul in the autumn, whilst in spring found on the Black Sea coast at the Kizil Irmak delta in late April. Also undertakes some seasonal altitudinal movements, perhaps largely involving 1st adults. In the Caucasus some birds descend into montane broadleaved woodland, whilst others reach the foothills and even the Black Sea coast between Loo and Adler, where found in mixed woodland and regularly in the conifer arboretum at Sochi. Many, however, remain near their high-altitude breeding grounds throughout the winter. Vagrant to mainland **Greece**, at Thessaloniki in October 1955.

**HABITAT** Forests of Turkish Pine at lower altitudes and of Caucasian Spruce, Caucasian or Cilician Firs, Black Pine, Lebanon Cedar and occasionally juniper at higher altitudes. Frequents both dense and open woodland, and sometimes found in areas of scattered trees. On Lesbos dependent on Turkish Pine, although will nest in broadleaved trees if there are pines nearby. In the Caucasus found in the spruce-fir zone, usually in old stands of Caucasian Fir, and in the NW Caucasus in pine forests, although commonly only where there is a good mixture of fir or spruce. Occurs in Turkey from sea level up to 2000 m and locally even to the treeline at 2500 m, although usually in hilly or mountainous areas and in SW Turkey optimally at 200–1200 m (although the optimum altitude is also noted as 1200–1700 m by Kumerloeve 1958); in the Caucasus, found at 1000–2000 m.

**POPULATION** Fairly common in Turkey, but not numerous in the Caucasus. On Lesbos, although commercial resin extraction has reduced the number of old trees suitable for nesting, the population is believed to be stable, at several tens of pairs.

**HABITS** Found singly and in pairs in the breeding season, when territories vigorously defended, usually by song-duels at the territory boundary, the rufous breast being expanded in threat displays. After fledging the family remains together for several days, and in the autumn found in parties of 2–5 and may join mixed-species foraging flocks. Restless and active. Often rather tame; may droop its wings and cock its tail, and in agitation sits upright, flicking its wings, or perches on a prominent snag, jinking its body from side to side. Normally forages in the treetops among the smaller branches and cones, but will utilise all levels of the vegetation, including bushes, and sometimes feeds on the ground. Food largely insects in the breeding season, sometimes taken in flight, switching to pine and other conifer seeds in the autumn and winter. The bill is inserted between the scales to pull the seeds from the cone, the seeds then being taken to bark crevices and hammered open. Will store food for future consumption and, as seeds can be extracted from the cones of Turkish Pine only when these are partly open,

when the cones temporarily close in wet weather the nuthatches may rely largely on this cached food. Territories are probably maintained through the winter to guard these hoards.

**BREEDING BIOLOGY** Season mid March–mid May in Turkey (dependent on altitude and locality), April–May in the Caucasus. The nest is placed in a hole in a tree, usually a conifer, up to 24 m above ground. (Sometimes eggs may be laid on top of a stump or even in a pile of twigs in a fork, perhaps only when holes are not available.) Excavates its own hole in dead trunks or branches, or more frequently cleans out existing cavities, the work being undertaken largely by the female. The entrance is not reduced with mud or resin. Nest a foundation of bark chips, rotten wood and cone scales lined with a pad of moss, bark fibres, hair, wool, fur and feathers, built largely by the female. Clutch 5–7: eggs creamy-white with rusty or purplish spots, often concentrated at the larger end; 17 x 13 mm. Female incubates, period *c*. 14–17 days; she is fed on and off the nest by the male. The young are also brooded by the female, although fed by both parents. Fledging period 16–19 days. Probably single-brooded.

**DESCRIPTION Adult Male**: *In fresh plumage* (autumn and winter), forecrown black with slight blue gloss, sharply demarcated from rear crown. Remainder of upperparts, including lesser and median coverts and tertials, mid blue-grey; dark centres of coverts fully concealed, tertials tipped slightly paler. Central tail feathers dark brown, tinged blue-grey, especially on outer web; T2–T5 black, tipped blue-grey, broadest on T6, often with some white subterminally on T5–T6 (see figure 11.1). Greater and primary coverts blue-grey, inner webs dark brown. Primaries, secondaries and alula dark brown-grey, smaller feathers of alula, secondaries and inner primaries fringed pale blue-grey, P3–P6 fringed blue-grey inwards of emargination. Forehead and supercilium (from nostril to rear of ear-coverts) white, occasionally mottled grey. Narrow white eyering. Black eye-stripe well defined on lores, broken and ill-defined behind eye. Cheeks, ear-coverts, sides of neck and throat white. Centre of breast deep rufous, sides of breast and flanks light blue-grey, and lower breast, belly and vent pale grey, often washed buffish-brown on sides of breast, flanks, thighs and vent. Undertail-coverts chestnut, tipped whitish. Underwing-coverts and axillaries off-white, longer under primary coverts tipped sooty-black. *In worn plumage* (summer), cap,

*Figure 11.1 Tail.*

supercilium and eyestripe duller and less well defined, cap sometimes showing grey mottling. Upperparts duller and less blue, primaries, secondaries and tertials browner, breast patch paler and less well defined, underparts darker, with a slight buff tinge, some grey mottling on belly and vent, and white tips on undertail-coverts are worn away. **Bare Parts**: Iris dark cinnamon or brown; bill dark horn-grey, cutting edge of upper mandible at base and entire base of lower mandible blue-grey; legs and feet grey-brown or dark grey. **Adult Female**: As male, but cap duller and less well defined, feathers finely tipped grey in fresh plumage. Eyestripe paler and less well defined. Breast patch and undertail-coverts average paler, more orange-rufous, lower breast and belly washed dirty buff or brown, and rear flanks and vent dull cinnamon-grey. In worn plumage, differences from male, apart from underpart coloration, less obvious. **Juvenile**: As adult, but upperparts (including whole crown, tertials and wing-coverts) mid grey with reduced blue tone, forehead very slightly darker. Greater and median coverts and tertials sometimes faintly tipped buffy-brown. Primaries and secondaries slightly browner, with narrower and less well-defined fringes. Supercilium obscure, pale grey mottled darker. Eyestripe obscure, mottled cream, buff

and grey. Throat whitish, and upper breast pale rufous, mottled slightly paler, not well demarcated from dirty drab-brown of remainder of underparts. Undertail-coverts pinkish-cinnamon. Sexes probably similar, though breast patch of juvenile male possibly darker and more rufous. Bill dark horn-brown, base of lower mandible tinged pink, gape yellow. **1st Adult**: As adult (see Sex/Age). **Measurements**: Wing of male 71–81, of female 68–74; tail of male 33–40, of female 33–38; bill 17.9–20.2; tarsus 16.9–19.3. Weight, male 10–14.3 g.

**MOULT** Adult post-breeding complete (mid May–early September). Adult pre-breeding occasional, partial, includes breast (March). Post-Juvenile partial, includes median coverts (timing unknown).

**GEOGRAPHICAL VARIATION** None.

**RELATIONSHIPS** A member of the *canadensis* group (see Red-breasted Nuthatch). The rufous breast patch of Krüper's and its significance in courtship and territorial display are, however, clear distinctions from the other members of the group, as is the relatively large difference between adults and juveniles.

**REFERENCES** Cramp & Perrins (1993), Delin & Svensson (1988), Frankis (1991), Neufeldt & Wunderlich (1984).

## 12 CHINESE NUTHATCH *Sitta villosa*      Plate 6

This nuthatch is virtually confined to the remaining areas of pine forest in northern China, but has recently been discovered in Ussuriland in the Russian Far East and remarkably, even on Sakhalin island.

**IDENTIFICATION** Length 115 mm (4.25 in). Small. Upperparts mid blue-grey, with a variably prominent white supercilium and somewhat ill-defined blackish eyestripe. The cap varies from contrastingly glossy black to dark grey, and the underparts from dull greyish-buff to orange-cinnamon, depending on sex, wear and race. Bill slender and sharply pointed, and may show a distinct uptilted effect owing to the straight culmen. Distinguished from Eurasian Nuthatch by its smaller size, white supercilium, more uniform underparts lacking a contrasting rufous patch on the flanks and undertail-coverts and, in the male, its black cap. In northern Sichuan, southern Gansu and eastern Qinghai, this species overlaps with the eastern race of White-cheeked Nuthatch, and in this region both have rich cinnamon underparts; White-cheeked is, however, easily distinguished by plain whitish sides to the head, lacking a dark eyestripe. Remarkably similar to Corsican Nuthatch, although, given the vast distance separating the two species, this is unlikely to pose an identification problem! Chinese averages brighter than Corsican on the underparts, but in worn plumage is only slightly buffer than a fresh-plumaged Corsican. Red-breasted Nuthatch, on the other hand, is usually brighter than Chinese on the underparts, with a more solidly black eyestripe.

**SEX/AGE** Sexes distinct. In the adult male, the cap is deep black with a broad white supercilium and neat blackish eyestripe. In fresh autumn plumage the female's cap is grey, only slightly darker than the mantle, although when worn it becomes a darker and more contrasting sooty-grey, especially on the forehead, and in some cases the entire crown may be sooty-black. The female differs additionally in its slightly narrower supercilium, duller and less well-defined eyestripe, duller upperparts (especially the scapulars), brown tinge to the fringes of the wing feathers, and slightly duller and darker underparts. Juvenile marginally distinct. The juvenile male has the cap duller and less glossy black than the adult (but blacker than even the darkest-crowned female), and rather darker and richer cinnamon underparts. Juveniles of the nominate race also show a cinnamon tone to the fringes of the wing feathers, but adults (especially adult females) may have a drab wash to the fringes of the flight feathers and greater coverts, making this feature difficult to use (look for the cleaner and purer grey fringes to the primary coverts on adults, compared with the juvenile's cinnamon-washed fringes). No information on juvenile female or 1st adult, but the latter presumably retains the juvenile flight feathers and perhaps greater coverts, which may still show a more distinct cinnamon tone.

**VOICE** There are three basic calls. **1** A prolonged, harsh, scolding *schraa, schraa* (recalling a Eurasian Jay, and similar to equivalent calls of Corsican, Algerian and Krüper's Nuthatches). Given, in agitation or excitement, singly or in irregular series at intervals of 0.3–1 second. **2** Various quiet, conversational, single short units, more melodic or 'piping' and repeated in series, e.g. *wip, wip wip...* or *quip-quip-quip-quip*, becoming a thin, squeaky *quit, quit...*, given in series which are very variable in duration and the number of notes (short or long, and the individual notes repeated either very rapidly or at irregular intervals. **3** Short, nasal *quir, quir* notes at varying pitches, again sometimes given in long series, either very rapidly or at irregular intervals. (A variant 'slow song' is a slow repetition of 7–11 *quir* notes.) The song is merely a repetition of *c.* 5–30 calls of type 2, increasing in volume during the first part of the series. The series of relatively pure, melodic, upward-inflected whistles is given at a rate of *c.* 7 units per second (though each unit is easily distinguishable), and lasts *c.* 1.5–2.25 seconds; it may be introduced by a higher note, *tsi-pui-pui pui-pui...*(it may recall a rock nuthatch). A variant is a much flatter, less musical and more monotonous rattle (*c.* 12 units per second), *duiduiduidui...* (recalling some song variants of Chestnut-vented Nuthatch in speed of delivery and duration, but a little mellower and lower-pitched). (Partly after Matthysen *et al.* 1991.)

**DISTRIBUTION AND MOVEMENTS** Found in **north** and **NE China** in southern **Jilin** in the Changbai Shan, southern **Liaoning** on the Liaodong peninsula, northern **Hebei** south to at least Pingquan, the mountains north of Beidaihe/Qinhuangdao (including 'Old Peak'), and the Eastern Qing Tombs, and dispersing to the lowlands, occasionally to near the coast (e.g. near Qinhuangdao), **Beijing Municipality** in the hills at Mentougou, **Shanxi** from Kelan and Pangqangou NR south to the Zhongtiao Shan, southern **Shaanxi** in the Qin Ling Shan, **Ningxia Hui** north to the Helan Shan on the border of Nei Mongol, southern and central **Gansu** west to the western Qilian Shan range and south to about Min Xian, and adjacent NE **Qinghai** in the Daban Shan range and northern **Sichuan** north of Songpan and Jiuzhaigou Panda Reserve near Nanping. Resident in northern **North Korea**, around Mount Paektu (Yanggang province, on the Chinese border in the Changbai Shan), with some dispersal into the surrounding area in autumn, and recorded from North Hamgyong in July-August, and also May–November from Mount Myohyang, North P'yongan. In **South Korea** a very rare winter visitor, records from sites including the mountains of Kyonggi (October–March, also July 1917) and North Kyongsang (November); the only recent record is from Kwangnung Experimental Forest, near Soul, Kangwon province, in March 1968 (Gore & Won 1971). In **Russia** confined to **southern Ussuriland** (Primorskiy Kray) south of 45° N, in the Chuguevskiy and Ussuriyskiy districts; the species is also regular on passage in May on Bol'shoy Pelis island in Zaliv Petra Velikogo (=

Peter the Great Bay). One record from **Sakhalin**, but status there not clear: a pair was recorded at Novoaleksandrovsk (near Yuzhno-Sakhalinsk) on 22 May 1983; the female was seen entering a tree cavity, but this contained no nest material, although the entrance had been 'plastered' (perhaps by Eurasian Nuthatch, see Breeding Biology), whilst the male was singing nearby (Leonovich & Veprintsev 1986). Resident, with some altitudinal movements and some erratic dispersal in winter (see Hebei and Korea above).

**HABITAT** Coniferous forest, probably chiefly pine but also recorded from spruce, relict larch forest in southern Ussuriland and mixed forest in Gansu. Breeds predominantly in the hills (but perhaps also in relict stands of trees around tombs and temples in the lowlands); recorded in northern Sichuan at 2100–2600 m, in the Changbai Shan, Jilin, from 780 to 2100 m with breeding noted at 780–1800 m, and breeds in the Beijing area at 1300 m. In winter also recorded at plains level.

**POPULATION** Fairly common in China, although not found at high densities, and confined to remaining areas of pine forest in the hills. Deforestation has undoubtedly reduced the population of this nuthatch throughout much of the range, for example, in west-central Shanxi, King (1987) reported near-total forest destruction away from reserves. In North Korea, common around Mount Paektu on the Chinese border but rare further south, and only a very rare winter visitor to South Korea. Rare in Ussuriland, suitable habitat covering just 30–40 km², while the remaining areas are being degraded by fire and logging; the population is unlikely to exceed 20–30 pairs and recent systematic searches have found only 2–3 pairs (Ler 1989). Listed as near-threatened in BirdLife International's world checklist of threatened birds (Collar *et al.* 1994).

**HABITS** Little information. In winter found in mixed-species foraging flocks, normally in pairs. Forages in the tops of moderately tall pines or spruces, clinging upside-down to the small cones with rapidly fluttering wings. Song is delivered from treetops, with flicking of wings and tail. Food insects, fat meat and flesh, nuts, seeds and fruits of trees (Wilder & Hubbard 1938), in summer almost exclusively insects, the young being fed entirely on animal matter.

**BREEDING BIOLOGY** Season in Jilin late April–early June. Nests in cavities in conifers, rotten stumps and old buildings; 13 nests averaged 9.4 m above ground level, another noted at *c.* 3 m. Entrance hole *c.* 35 mm in diameter (does not, apparently, daub the nest hole with mud or resin). Nest bowl-shaped, built from plant fibres, feathers and grass, by both sexes over 7–8 days. Clutch 5–6 (4–9): eggs white, marked with reddish-brown; 15–17 x 12.5–13 mm. Female incubates, period 15–17 days; she is fed on the nest by the male. The male 'brings mud to the female for repairing the inside wall of the nest hole' (Gao 1978). Young fed by both sexes. Single-brooded.

**DESCRIPTION** *S. v. villosa* **Adult Male**: *In fresh plumage* (August–midwinter), crown and nape

*Figure 12.1 Tail of* S. v. villosa.

black, slightly glossy. Upperparts mid blue-grey. Central tail feathers dull blue-grey; T2–T6 sooty-black, tipped mid grey, tips tiny on T2, extensive on outer web of T6; whitish subterminal area on outer web of T6, extending diagonally onto inner web and faintly indicated on T5, especially on tip of inner web (see figure 12.1). Wing-coverts dark brownish-grey (greater coverts washed blue-grey), fringed mid blue-grey. Primary coverts and alula dark grey, fringed mid blue-grey. Tertials and flight feathers dark brownish-grey (tertials washed blue-grey), secondaries and inner primaries fringed blue-grey, P3–P6 fringed paler and greyer (and inwards of emarginations only). Supercilium white, faintly washed buff, and flecked blackish over bill and at rear; supercilia barely meet over bill, but extend broadly onto sides of mantle. Narrow eyestripe from nostril to rear of ear-coverts, blackish with some pale grey feather tips which may largely obscure black bases. Narrow whitish eyering. Cheeks, ear-coverts, chin and upper throat white, grading to buffy-white on the lower throat and sides of neck and pale greyish-buff (or pale pinkish-buff, washed grey) on the remainder of the underparts, slightly cleaner and more cinnamon on the flanks and belly; thighs dark grey, tipped dull buff. Axillaries buffish-drab. Underwing-coverts mid-dark grey, finely tipped paler; longer under primary coverts and base of primaries white. *In worn plumage* (about February–July), upperparts duller and slightly less blue, flight feathers bleached and worn paler, but underparts little changed. **Bare Parts**: Iris brown or dark brown; bill slaty-black, base of lower mandible grey-blue; legs and feet dull blue-grey or brownish-grey. **Adult Female**: As male, but crown and nape only slightly darker than mantle, sooty-grey feather centres largely concealed, showing as a slightly darker shade, especially on forehead. Upperparts slightly duller and less blue, with a faint brownish cast, especially on scapulars. Fringes to greater and primary coverts and flight feathers slightly browner (but not cinnamon, still

showing a grey tone). Supercilium slightly narrower. Eyestripe slightly paler, sooty-blackish, more extensively invaded with pale grey. Underparts slightly darker and richer, washed drab. In worn plumage, blue-grey tips to crown feathers gradually abrade, cap becoming darker and more sooty-grey; forehead or whole crown may be sooty-black, with faint paler feather tips gradually merging at rear with blue-grey nape. **Juvenile Male**: As adult male, but cap slightly duller, less glossy and less well defined at rear, upperparts slightly greyer and less blue, more whitish feather bases revealed on upper mantle, greater coverts fringed cinnamon-brown, fringes on outer tertial, secondaries, inner primaries and primary coverts washed cinnamon, and underparts cinnamon. **Juvenile Female and 1st Adult**: No information. **Measurements**: Wing of male 63–70, of female 63–69; tail of male 34–40, of female 31–38; bill 14.5–18; tarsus 13.5–17. Weight 8–11 g; on fledging, juveniles average 11.3 g.

**MOULT**  Adult post-breeding complete (July–August). Post-juvenile no information.

**GEOGRAPHICAL VARIATION**  A cline of increasing colour saturation and increasing size runs east-west, with birds in the western part of the range being largest and darkest below, and those in the east (especially Korea) being palest. Two races recognised.

*S. v. villosa* Russia, Korea, China east to southern Gansu and Ningxia Hui. See Description. In Korea, averages very slightly paler below and slightly smaller, this population sometimes named 'corea'.

*S. v. bangsi* Central Gansu (north of the Huang Ho river?) and Qinghai. Underparts brighter, sex for sex, than in nominate *villosa*: in fresh plumage, the male is orange-cinnamon (slightly darker than the juvenile male of the nominate race), the female dull buffy-cinnamon (but both sexes may wear paler by late winter, near to nominate *villosa*?). Additionally, the fringes to the greater coverts, tertials and flight feathers are tinged cinnamon, and is larger, averaging c. 4 mm longer-winged. Wing of male, 67–75, of female 67–72; tail of male 37–41, of female 35–40.

**RELATIONSHIPS**  A member of the *canadensis* group (see Red-breasted Nuthatch), and regarded as the most primitive member of the genus *Sitta* by Vielliard (1978). It resembles Red-breasted and, especially, Corsican Nuthatches rather closely. Indeed, sometimes treated as conspecific with Red-breasted Nuthatch under the name *S. canadensis*.

**REFERENCES**  Ler (1989), Gao (1978), Matthysen et al. (1991).

Endemic to SW China, this nuthatch is rather poorly known. It has a very restricted range and is probably threatened by forest clearance.

**IDENTIFICATION** Length 120 mm (4.75 in). A small nuthatch. Upperparts mid grey-blue, with a narrow whitish supercilium and long black eyestripe, the latter expanding broadly on the sides of the mantle, sometimes also curving downwards at the rear. Underparts pale pinkish-buff, becoming dirty pale buffy-grey when worn. Bill slender and slightly upturned. The combination of small size, slender bill, prominent black eyestripe, narrow whitish supercilium and uniform underparts is diagnostic, although the supercilium is not prominent at range and is reduced or absent in worn plumage. Giant Nuthatch may be found in similar habitat, but is much larger. Chestnut-vented Nuthatch is more similar in size, but at all times shows contrasting deep rufous flanks and lacks a white supercilium.

**SEX/AGE** Sexes very similar, although the female's eyestripe averages less intensely black and her underparts slightly duller and greyer than the male's, less pure pale pinkish-buff. Juvenile duller than the adult, with the supercilia faint and not meeting on the forehead and sometimes almost lacking, being only marginally paler than the crown, and the eyestripe is similarly reduced or absent altogether; the cheek patch is dirty greywhite rather than pure white, the throat is whiter than the adult's, and the remainder of the underparts are dull greyish-cinnamon (duller and dingier than on a fresh adult, although not so pale as a worn adult). When recently fledged, the bill is rather shorter than the adult's, with an extensive pale base. No information on 1st adult.

**VOICE** Rather vocal. Calls include a nasal *nit* or *kni*, a shorter, more abrupt and higher-pitched (although still nasal) *tit*, a squeaky, abrupt *pit* and a low, nasal *toik*. All these calls are given singly, but the *nit* call is sometimes given in couplets as a full *nit-nit* or abrupt, nasal *chit-chit*, and also often in a series of 4–10 units at a rate of 5–6 notes per second, *kni-kni-kni...*, variations including a purer, thinner and more 'peevish' *kit-kit-kit...*, a clearer and more piping *pi-pi-pi...*, and a more nasal (but relatively high and weak) *niew-niew-niew...*, each unit falling slightly in pitch. Other calls include a harsh, scolding *schri-schri-schri...* (or *szi-szi-szi...*), the Eurasian Jay-like call common to all of the small Palearctic nuthatches. This may grade into a high, strident nasal *ziew-ziew-ziew...*, recalling a squeaky toy, given in series at a rate of c. 3 calls per second. The '*ziew*' calls may be quite well separated or may be run together into a cacophony of sound, and are sometimes shortened to a *zi*. Related calls include a full and explosive nasal *quit-quit-quit*, given singly or in groups of 2–3 units, a harsher and emphatic nasal *schu-schu-schu*, and thinner, upward-inflected nasal *tui-tui-tui*. The song, if there is one, is unknown.

**DISTRIBUTION AND MOVEMENTS** Endemic to **SW China**, breeding in central and western **Yunnan**, south to Lushui, Baoshan, Jinggu, Shiping and Kunming, and west to the Shweli-Salween divide (Gaoligong Shan) on the Burmese border, south to around Tengchong and west to Yingpanjie; also SW **Sichuan** at Huidong and Xichang and north along the Yalong valley to Yajiang, extreme SE **Tibet** at Zayu and 'Zhuwagen', and western **Guizhou**, where recorded from Shuicheng, with two birds at Tuoda forest, 60 km northwest of Weining, in November 1987. Resident.

**HABITAT** Open mature pine forest with little undergrowth or scrub, apparently avoiding denser stands of spruce and fir. Will occasionally forage in relatively small pines, even as low as 2–3 m tall, in open forest and among scattered trees. Found in summer at 2440–3960 m, and some movement to lower altitudes in winter, when recorded in Guizhou at 1670 m in March and c. 2750 m in November, whilst in Yunnan noted at 1200 m in the Gaoligong Shan in February and 2000 m at Shuangbai in September, but also at 2600–4000 m in November–January.

**POPULATION** Stated to be rare by Cheng (1987), but locally common in relict pine forest at Lijiang, Yunnan. Undoubtedly, forest destruction has affected the species, and with its relatively limited range its long-term survival must be in doubt. It could be dependent on mature pines, which are disappearing, but may be able to utilise degraded forest; detailed ecological studies are needed. Listed as vulnerable in BirdLife International's world checklist of threatened birds (Collar *et al.* 1994).

**HABITS** Little information. Frequently forages titlike among the foliage of pines. Food insects.

**BREEDING BIOLOGY** Apparently unknown. A female collected in Guizhou on 9 March was near to laying, and juveniles have been collected from 21 May onwards.

**DESCRIPTION Adult Male**: *In fresh plumage* (August–spring), upperparts, including tertials, wing coverts and central tail feathers, mid greyblue; some paler feather centres may show on nape and upper mantle, inner webs of tertials greyer, grey inner webs of greater coverts fully concealed. T2–T6 blackish, broadly tipped mid blue-grey (extending along fringe of outer web). Amount of white in the tail variable: on some, T4–T6 with white triangle subterminally on fringe of inner web, T6 narrowly fringed white on inner web; on others, a much larger subterminal white spot on inner web of T4–T5, and a narrow, broken diagonal subterminal bar extending across both webs of T6 (see figure 13.1). Alula, primary coverts and flight feathers dark grey-brown; smaller feathers of alula, primary coverts, inner primaries and secondaries fringed grey-blue, P3–P6 fringed pale grey-blue inwards of emargination. Forehead and narrow supercilium extending to

*Figure 13.1 Tail.*

rear of ear-coverts whitish. Narrow white eyering. Eyestripe from nostril to sides of mantle black, broad (*c.* 5 mm) at rear; may be invaded with grey to the rear of the ear-coverts. Chin, cheeks, lower ear-coverts and sides of neck white (forming a contrasting line below the eyestripe). Underparts clean pale pinkish-buff, flanks and vent washed greyer; thighs dark grey, tipped pale pinkish-buff. Axillaries light grey, underwing-coverts sooty-grey, longest under primary coverts and base of primaries contrastingly whitish. *In worn plumage* (spring–July), whitish feather tips forming supercilium abrade, and on forehead supercilium may be reduced to a few white flecks (on some, the supercilium may be entirely absent). Eyestripe broader and more prominent, bridging bill (black feather bases on forehead revealed). Odd whitish feather bases may show on crown. Upperparts duller and less blue. Wings and tail become very abraded, but grey-blue fringes persist on flight feathers until at least May. Underparts fade to dirty pale buff-grey or greyish-white, and when very worn dark feather bases show and underparts very dingy. **Bare Parts**: Iris dark brown; bill grey-black with yellowish-horn base to lower mandible (in specimens); legs and feet grey-black. **Adult Female**: As male (but see Sex/Age). **Juvenile**: As adult, but upperparts rather duller and greyer, with faint paler subterminal bands on feathers of crown, nape and upper mantle. Supercilia reduced: pale

grey, not meeting on forehead and often obvious only immediately above eye; in some cases, supercilium may be only slightly paler than the crown. Eyestripe sooty-grey, shorter, narrower and paler than on adult, and may be reduced to merely an indication of neutral grey on the ear-coverts. Cheeks dirty grey-white, throat whiter, remainder of underparts pale cinnamon-drab with much grey of feather bases visible. Undertail-coverts dull pinkish-buff with concealed mid-grey centres. Bill considerably shorter than adult's, yellowish-horn base to lower mandible more extensive. **1st Adult**: No information. **Measurements**: Wing 67–77, of male 69.5–74, of female 67–74; tail 31–43, of male 35–41, of female 36–38; bill 16.8–19.5; tarsus 14.8–19. Weight 7.5–13 g.

**MOULT** Adult post-breeding complete (July–September). Adult pre-breeding occasional (?), partial, includes breast (January or February). Post-juvenile, no information.

**GEOGRAPHICAL VARIATION** None.

**RELATIONSHIPS** Often considered a member of the *canadensis* group of species (see Red-breasted Nuthatch). Yunnan Nuthatch differs, however, from the other members of the group in having the crown of the male concolorous with the upperparts. This led Vaurie (1957d) to consider that its closest relative was probably the White-tailed Nuthatch, while Voous & van Marle (1953) thought on the one hand that it formed a connecting link between the *canadensis* group and the *europaea* group, and on the other that it was the most 'conservative' of the *canadensis* group, in terms of both range and coloration (despite the fact that they considered the black-capped *canadensis* group to be older than the grey-crowned *europaea* group). Nevertheless, recent field observations of habitat, habits and calls support Yunnan Nuthatch's affinities with the *canadensis* group.

**REFERENCES** Cheng (1987), Riley (1926, 1931), Vaurie (1957d).

# 14 RED-BREASTED NUTHATCH *Sitta canadensis*                Plate 6

One of the few nuthatches to undertake regular migrations, this species undergoes irregular irruptions closely tied to the scale of the cone crop in the breeding areas. Presumably as a consequence, it is the only nuthatch to have crossed the Atlantic.

**IDENTIFICATION** Length 115 mm (4.5 in). A small nuthatch. Upperparts mid grey-blue with a conspicuous white supercilium, the cap and eyestripe varying from black, contrasting strongly with the upperparts, to grey, uniform with the mantle. Cheeks, ear-coverts and throat whitish, underparts buffy-white to ochre-cinnamon. Easily distinguished from other North American nuthatches by the white supercilium and dark eyestripe, and usually also by the bright orange-buff underparts. In Europe, a vagrant Red-breasted Nuthatch can be distinguished from a Corsican Nuthatch by the supercilia meeting on the forehead, a longer,

broader and better-defined black eyestripe, and the outer three tail feathers having dark tips with a whitish subterminal bar (rather than merely pale grey tips). Importantly, males have more richly coloured underparts than the similarly black-capped male Corsican (cinnamon-orange rather than light drab-grey with buff wash and, although worn summer Red-breasted may be much more similar to Corsican, they still have an orange-buff wash). Female Red-breasted Nuthatches are also more richly coloured below than female Corsican, and even when very worn show an orange tone, especially to the vent and flanks.

**SEX/AGE** Sexes distinct. The male has the cap and eyestripe black, contrasting strongly with the mantle. In the female, the cap in fresh autumn plumage varies from mid grey-blue to blackish-grey, while in worn plumage the forecrown may be dull black; the eyestripe is narrower than the male's, mottled grey when fresh but usually dull black when worn, and year-round is often darker than the cap. The female's underparts average paler and duller. The juvenile is rather similar to the adult, but has a yellow base to the lower mandible (changing to white after 2–4 weeks) and paler legs for a short period after fledging; the upperparts are less bluish than on a fresh adult, some showing a few black fringes, the supercilium, chin and cheeks may show faint dark specks, the greater coverts may be faintly tipped brownish and the underparts average paler. The juvenile male has the cap dull black, duller and less well defined than the adult male, while the juvenile female has the cap and eyestripe dull grey, concolorous with the mantle (the feather bases are grey, so it does not wear darker). 1st adult as adult, but may show traces of buff tips to the retained juvenile greater coverts.

**VOICE** Commonest call a nasal, bleating or mewing *knair-knair-knair-yna-yna-yna* or *kng-kng-kng*, recalling a toy tin horn (rather more nasal, less cawing, than the equivalent call of White-breasted Nuthatch). Usually far-carrying, the call may be quiet and inconspicuous in absence of other nuthatches, and varies in pitch and inflection. It may be repeated in a rapid series (*k-k-k-k-k...*) or in a slow, regular sequence, *yaaaaa, yaaaaa, yaaaaa*. From late winter onwards, the call is given by unpaired males from tall trees and probably serves both territorial and courtship functions. When angry or annoyed, gives a variable, monotonous, fast but slightly quavering series of notes, *hnhnhnhn..., , nananana-..., biddy-biddy-biddy... ,* sometimes in a long series, essentially a rapid repetition of the call, which at high intensity recalls an electric buzzer, and in heightened excitement this becomes a trilled *thiiiiirrrrr.* The contact call is a soft, conversational *it, pit* or *het* (similar to the contact call of White-breasted Nuthatch). Other calls include *phew*, given singly or in a short series, in situations of emotional intensity (as for the *phee-oo* note of White-breasted), and sometimes elaborated into a 'song'; a *zee zee zee zee zee*, used by the male when scolding an intruder near the nest and when chasing a rival; a *purp, purp, purp...*, becoming *we-we-we* or *peep, peep, peep ... ,* given by the female when soliciting food from the male; and a variety of musical 'songs', comprised of low twitterings and medleys of notes, given at greater volume and intensity by the male when feeding the female or young, and more loudly during courtship or fights, e.g. a quavering, soft *tee-you-you-you* and *wee-wur-tee-tee-too-too-wee-rr.* (After Kilham 1973.)

**DISTRIBUTION AND MOVEMENTS** Breeds in the boreal-forest zone from the south coast of **Alaska** (irregularly west to the Kenai peninsula and Kodiak Island, also rarely central Alaska) east through **Canada**, north to southern **Yukon**, SW **Mackenzie** (Fort Simpson, Tazin river), NW **Saskatchewan** (Lake Athabasca, southern Reindeer Lake), central **Manitoba** and **Ontario** (Moosonee and Big Trout Lake), south-central **Quebec** and southern **Labrador** (Goose Bay and Makkovik) to **Newfoundland**. Breeds on Queen Charlotte, Vancouver, Prince Edward and Anticosti islands; also Miquelon and St Pierre (to France). In the **western USA** breeds south through the **Rocky Mountains**, east to western **South Dakota** (Harding Co. and the Black Hills), and irregularly to SW **North Dakota**, northern **Nebraska** (the Pine Ridge area and central Niobrara valley), central **Colorado** (and has bred Denver and Jefferson Co.), SW **New Mexico** (probably east to Sierra Grande) and SE **Arizona** (south to the Chiricahua and probably also Huachuca mountains). Also breeds south through the **Cascades** to the northern inner Coast Ranges of **California** (south to Alameda Co.; absent coastal fog belt north of Sonoma Co.) and through the **Sierra Nevada** to the San Jacinto mountains, Riverside Co., California (exceptionally to Mount Palomar, San Diego Co., and since 1964 in plantations at Point Loma); has bred Guadalupe island, **Baja California Norte**, and occurs irregularly, possibly breeding, on Santa Cruz Island, California. In the **eastern USA**, breeds south to southern **Minnesota** (Minneapolis), northern **Wisconsin** (Polk, Shawano and Door Cos., rarely to Sauk Co.), **Michigan** (including Isle Royale, but rare in south and absent extreme south), northern and western **Ohio** (regularly Lucas, Fulton and Portage Cos., otherwise rare, exceptionally south to Hamilton Co.), northern **Pennsylvania, New York** (occasionally including Long Island), and northern **Connecticut** (also once New Haven Co.), ranging south sparingly in the **Appalachians** through eastern **West Virginia** and western **Virginia** to eastern **Tennessee** and western **North Carolina**. The southern boundary of the breeding range is variable, with greater numbers breeding on the southern periphery in years following good cone crops in these areas. Irregular in summer NW **Indiana** (south to Vigo Co.), southern **New Jersey**, **Connecticut** and **Rhode Island**. Extremely rare breeder **Iowa** (Des Moines Co.), **Kansas** (Geary, Sedgwick and Cowley Cos.), **Missouri** (Kansas City), **Illinois** (Whiteside Co.) and **Maryland**; recorded **Kentucky** (Nelson and Harlan Cos., but no proof of local breeding). Has spread in recent years to SW **California** coast, northern **Nebraska** and the piedmont of **North Carolina** (Rockingham Co.) and **Tennessee**. Occasionally recorded north of breeding range to western and central **Alaska** and the coastal tundra of northern **Manitoba**. An irruptive migrant, the winter distribution and abundance are dependent on the crop of spruce, fir and pine seeds, and generally has a two-year cycle, although invasions are sometimes paired. In years with a good cone crop in the north, the centre of gravity of the population moves southwards only slightly, with records north to SE and south coastal **Alaska** (rare; also casually in central Alaska), northern-central **Alberta** (Fort McMurrey), central **Saskatchewan**, southern **Ontario** (rarely north to Thunder Bay and Manitouwadge), southern **Quebec** and **Nova Scotia**. Also, montane populations remain at higher altitudes (see Habitat). In years of cone crop failure, however, there is a variable exodus from the breeding areas and birds may reach southernmost **California**, the lowlands of southern **Arizona** and southern **New Mexico**, southern **Texas** (occasionally as far south as the Rio Grande delta), the Gulf Coast and northern **Florida**. The degree to which birds penetrate the southern USA is variable, with large numbers reaching the Gulf Coast (where otherwise uncommon) every 5–10 years. Largely absent from the Great Plains, however, and a rare winter visitor to northern **Mexico**, in **Baja California Norte** (two records, September and April) and irregularly south to southern **Sonora**, **Sinaloa** and NE **Nuevo Leon**. The timing of these southward movements is variable. Typically, migration begins in late July or August and may continue until November, the first birds penetrating south of the breeding range from late September. Major invasions may be initiated somewhat earlier, with large numbers on the eastern seaboard and southern marches of the breeding range from mid August or even July. Recorded in the southern states from late September or October to mid April, exceptionally late August–early May. In big 'flights', there may be impressive passages of nuthatches, with several hundreds moving south in a few hours. Northward passage in spring occurs March–May, and is always less impressive than the autumn movement. Casual in autumn in SW and west **Alaska**. Vagrant Isla Socorro, **Mexico** (March 1957), **Bermuda** (three recent records, Octobers of 1975 and 1977 and March 1978), **Iceland** (adult male Vestmannaeyjar/Westman Islands, May 1970) and **England** (adult male Holkham, Norfolk, October 1989–May 1990).

**HABITAT** Breeding habitat coniferous forest, especially spruce and fir, less frequently pine and hemlock; also found in mixed woodland with a strong coniferous element and more rarely in deciduous woodland such as American Aspen. Standing dead wood is required for nest sites. In the southern parts of range in the USA, suitable habitat is usually montane or submontane: thus, in California breeds Sierra Nevada at 760–3075 m, although recorded in summer in northern Coast Range as low as 275 m; breeds North Carolina above 900 m, Tennessee above 1060 m, and on Isla Guadalupe, Baja California, at c. 1200 m. Winters in the same habitat, but away from breeding areas also utilises a much wider range of habitats, including deciduous forest, orchards, scrub, riparian woodland, and parks, shade trees and gardens in suburban areas, although shows a distinct preference for conifers where available. Montane breeders may descend to lower altitudes in winter, but, depending on food supply, they may remain in montane coniferous forests throughout the season, e.g. recorded midwinter in Idaho at 1830 m and above. On migration may be found in a very wide range of wooded habitats, even shrubs and isolated riparian woodlands in desert areas, and may sometimes be found away from trees, foraging on rocks, cliffs and roofs or in weeds and long grass.

**POPULATION** As a breeding bird generally fairly common, with the highest densities from British Columbia south to California, Idaho, Montana and Wyoming, and in Manitoba, Ontario, New Hampshire, Maine and Nova Scotia, and lower densities in Newfoundland, Yukon and Alaska (where uncommon to rare). Formerly bred on Isla Guadalupe, Baja California Norte, but last recorded in 1971 and not located in 1984/85 despite searches (Ruiz-Campos & Quintana-Barrios 1991). The species has spread southwards in the 20th century, especially in the east, e.g. to NW Indiana, northern Ohio (since 1980s), southern Ontario, and lowland areas of New York (including Long and Staten Islands) and Pennsylvania, with the colonisation of mature spruce and fir plantations and ornamental conifers. The winter abundance is very variable, but areas which consistently hold high numbers are the dense forests of the NE USA, the Michigan–Wisconsin border, and in NE Washington.

**HABITS** Can be very tame, but active and restless, and often rather inconspicuous, as typically feeds high in the trees. In summer usually found in pairs, which may stay together on territory throughout the winter if food resources are adequate, remaining mated for more than one season. Otherwise migrants, juveniles and non-breeding birds may be found singly or in small flocks, and both migrants and residents may join mixed-species foraging flocks. Forages in the canopy, in the dense crowns of conifers, but may feed much lower on the trees, on trunks, in dense herbaceous plants or on the ground, especially in autumn, searching for fallen seeds. Winter diet largely conifer seeds, extracted from cones with the bill. May store food such as seeds in bark crevices or in disused sapsucker holes, covering the stored item with a scrap of bark, and has been noted stuffing seeds into rock cracks on the granite wall hundreds of feet above the valley floor in Yosemite NP, California (Gaines 1988). Often attracted to feeders, a good place to find the species where wintering densities in natural forest are low (e.g. southern USA). In summer diet mainly insects, and the young may be fed exclusively on animal matter; may flycatch.

**BREEDING BIOLOGY** Season late April–June. Excavates a hole, usually in standing dead wood, in a rotten stump, branch or post; favours conifers, although will use deciduous trees. Occasionally takes over an abandoned woodpecker hole, and may use nestboxes. Pairs prospect for nest sites together, starting several excavations before the female makes the final choice and undertakes the initial excavation; work takes 1–8 weeks. The entrance hole is usually 2–12 m (0.6–37 m) above ground. Regularly (invariably?) smears the entrance and the trunk around it with pitch - the sticky resin from Balsam Fir, spruce or pine - and fresh globules of pitch are brought by both sexes until the young fledge. The layer of pitch may be thick enough to flow down the trunk, and this may be an anti-predator device, to discourage squirrels etc. or insects; the nuthatches avoid the pitch by flying straight into the nest, but a female has been found dead, stuck to the resin. The nest, which is built by the female with some help from the male, is a bed of bark chips, grass or rootlets, often lined with hair, fur or feathers. Clutch 5–6 (4–7, and 8 recorded by Jewett et al. 1953): eggs white, sometimes pinkish-white, variably spotted reddish-brown; 15.2 x 11.9 mm. Female incubates, period 12 days. Young fed by both sexes, fledge at 18–21 days (14 days is also sometimes quoted). Single-brooded (?).

**DESCRIPTION Adult Male**: *In fresh plumage* (August–January), crown and nape black, faintly glossed blue. Upperparts, including lesser and median coverts and central tail feathers, mid grey-blue, some white feather centres often showing on nape; T2–T6 black, T3–T6 tipped blue-grey, T4–T6 with diagonal white subterminal bar, largest on T6 (see figure 14.1). Greater coverts and tertials dark brown-grey, broadly fringed mid grey-blue. Primaries, secondaries, primary coverts and alula dark grey-brown, all but outer primaries narrowly fringed grey-blue; P3–P6 fringed pale grey inwards of emargination. Forehead and supercilium whitish, extending to sides of upper mantle. Extreme base of bill and eyestripe black, extending to sides of upper mantle; black may be very broad at rear, connecting with the rear crown, although narrower on others, with white mottling on the lower border and sides of neck. Narrow white eye-ring. Chin, cheeks, ear-coverts and sides of neck pale buff to whitish, darkening to cinnamon-orange on breast and rufous-cinnamon on sides of breast, flanks, belly, vent and undertail-coverts (underparts, however, very variable, from buffy-white to ochre-cinnamon). Underwing-coverts and axillaries whitish, washed cinnamon, median under primary coverts dark grey, base of primaries whitish. *In worn plumage* (January–August), cap duller, loses gloss (feather tips abraded), upperparts duller and less blue, with more white mottling on nape, flight feathers bleached paler and browner, and underparts paler and less richly coloured, dirty pale orange-buff. **Bare Parts**: Iris brown; upper mandible black, lower pale blue-grey, darker towards the tip; legs and feet dusky. **Adult Female**: As male, but crown and eyestripe may be mid grey-blue as upperparts, although usually slightly darker, blackish-grey; sooty-black feather bases show to variable extent, especially on forecrown, which may wear to dull black (and in worn plumage whole cap averages darker). Feathers of eyestripe blackish, fringed grey; black may show on some birds when fresh, especially behind eye, and on most when worn, though eyestripe never as wide or black as on male. White supercilium less contrasting, and underparts average paler and not so richly coloured, cinnamon-buff. **Juvenile Male**: As adult, but black on head duller and less well defined, upperparts may show a few faint black fringes, supercilium, chin and cheeks may show faint dark specks, and underparts paler, washed grey (pinkish-buff, darkening to pale cinnamon on the undertail-coverts). Greater coverts may be faintly tipped rufous or

buff. Upper mandible horn-brown with flesh-grey base, lower more extensively blue-grey than on adult, tinged pink at base and with yellow gape; feet pinkish-buff, darkening with age. **Juvenile Female**: As adult, but head markings duller and less well defined, and never showing blackish, even with wear. White feather bases may show to greater extent on upper mantle and almost unite supercilia in a 'bridle'. Differences from adult otherwise as for male. **1st Adult**: As adult. **Measurements**: Wing of male, 65–71 (chord 64–73), of female 63–70 (chord 60–70); tail of male 34.5–42.5, of female 33–38; bill 14.8–17.1; tarsus 14.2–17. Weight 10.3–11.8 g, autumn migrants in New Jersey 8–12.7 g.

**MOULT** Adult post-breeding complete (mid June–October, primarily in breeding area). Adult pre-breeding limited, occasionally absent, includes cheeks, throat and variable area of underparts, occasionally also a few upperpart feathers (mid March–mid May). Post-juvenile partial, includes median coverts (July–September, primarily in breeding area, starts about six weeks after fledging) First pre-breeding absent or limited (March–April).

*Figure 14.1 Tail.*

**GEOGRAPHICAL VARIATION** None.

**RELATIONSHIPS** Gives its name to the *canadensis* group of small nuthatches (which includes Chinese, Yunnan, Krüper's, Corsican and Algerian Nuthatches), which usually excavate their own nest hole and are sometimes considered to form a superspecies (e.g. Sibley & Monroe 1990). The similarity of the members of the group in terms of their plumage, voice and habitat indicates a close relationship, and the usual assumption is that they are relict populations of a once widespread ancestral species. An analysis of their morphology (e.g. Vaurie 1957d) suggests, however, that many of the similarities may be superficial, and some members of the complex, especially Yunnan and Krüper's Nuthatches, are rather distinct. Notably Red-breasted lacks the harsh, jay-like scream of Corsican, Algerian, Krüper's and Chinese Nuthatches, indicating that it may not be so closely related to these smaller Old World species as it seems. Red-breasted has been treated as conspecific with one, two or all three of Chinese, Krüper's and Corsican Nuthatches under the name *canadensis*. Löhrl (1960, 1961, 1963) found behavioural similarities as well as differences between Corsican and Red-breasted Nuthatches, tending to bear out the view that they are closely related but specifically distinct. In particular, the location calls of juveniles of Red-breasted, Krüper's and Corsican Nuthatches (which are used in the period after fledging to announce their location to their parents, and which are innate, rather than learned), differ greatly, indicating a more extensive differentiation than would be expected in view of their similar appearance. The rather different vocal repertoire of the adults may develop from these notes. The relict distribution of the *canadensis* group and its colonisation of North America (presumably during a Pleistocene period of low sea level) are considered to indicate a more ancient origin than that of the *europaea* complex (Voous & van Marle 1953). **REFERENCES** AOU (1983), Bent (1948), Cramp & Perrins (1993), Bock & Lepthien (1972), Godfrey (1986), Kilham (1973), Phillips (1986), Root (1988).

# 15 WHITE-CHEEKED NUTHATCH *Sitta leucopsis*      Plate 6
Other name: Przevalski's Nuthatch

In vocalisations and appearance this species strongly recalls White-breasted Nuthatch of North America, but it prefers montane coniferous forests and has a curiously interrupted distribution at the western and eastern ends of the Himalayan chain.

**IDENTIFICATION** Length 130 mm (5 in). A medium-sized nuthatch. Crown and nape black, with the remainder of the upperparts dark grey-blue, contrasting with the extensive whitish cheek patch surrounding the eye, and the whitish throat. In the western Himalayas the remainder of underparts are white, washed creamy-buff, with the rear flanks and undertail-coverts rufous, whilst in western China the cheeks are washed orange-buff and the entire underparts are rich cinnamon. Easily identified by the combination of a black cap and whitish sides to the head, lacking a black eyestripe. In western China the range overlaps with that of Chinese Nuthatch in NE Qinghai (the Daban Shan), southern Gansu and northern Sichuan, and the local subspecies of Chinese Nuthatch has similarly rich cinnamon underparts. Confusion is possible, especially given the difficulty of obtaining good views in the treetops, but the black eyestripe and white supercilium of Chinese Nuthatch are immediate distinctions when seen.

**SEX/AGE** Sexes similar. Juvenile marginally distinct, being duller overall, especially on the cap and underparts (see Description). No information on 1st adult.

**VOICE** Contact call, given constantly while foraging (although may be very quiet during latter stages of breeding season), a low, muffled, nasal or bleating note, often given in couplets, *kner-kner* (or *quair-quair* or *ni-nit*), with slight variations. This may be repeated 10–12 times without pause. In excitement or alarm may give a continuous series of similar, but single, notes, and when excited continues to call long after the danger has passed. Song an elaboration of this call, a continuous and rapid repetition of wailing squeaks, given all day in the summer; whilst a loud, clear *ti-tüi ti-tüi ti-tüi...*, with the stress on the second syllable, may also be the song (P. Alström, *in litt.*). (After Roberts 1992.)

**DISTRIBUTION AND MOVEMENTS** Two disjunct populations, at the western and eastern ends of the Himalayan chain. The western population occurs in NE **Afghanistan** from Nuristan south to the northern slopes of the Safed Koh and the Gardez forest (in at least Konar, Nangarhar and Paktia provinces, and probably confined to areas in the southern watershed of the Hindu Kush). Also northern **Pakistan** from the Kurram valley in the North West Frontier Provinces north to Swat and Chitral, locally also Gilgit and Astor, and in the **western Himalayas** in Indus Kohistan (including the Kagan valley) and Azad Kashmir in the Neelum valley (= Kishen Ganga), south to the Murree hills. Breeds in **NW India** in Kashmir, northern Himachal Pradesh (including Simla and the Great Himalayan NP) and northern Uttar Pradesh southeast to at least Mount Dunagiri and Nanda Devi NP in Kumaon/Garhwal. Occurs in NW **Nepal** in the Langu valley, Rara Lake NP and Dolpo, east to Tarakot. The eastern population is found in **western China** in eastern **Qinghai** from the Daban Shan (north to about Menyuan) south to the Amdo plateau (c. 35° N, 101° E) and upper Hwang Ho (around Xinghai), also southern Qinghai at 'Dza Chu' (= Nangqen; Vaurie 1972). In SW **Gansu** recorded in the region southwest of Xiahe and Min Xian, and also in adjacent northern **Sichuan** in the Songpan region (including Jiuzhaigou Panda Reserve), in central Sichuan in the Qionglai Shan at Wolong Te Qu (near Barkam: G.M. Kirwan *in litt.*) and western Sichuan around Litang. In NE **Tibet** (Xizang) found northeast of Qamdo, and in SE Tibet recorded in Kongbo in the Tsangpo valley (at Tse in December and at Dzeng in April, both localities near Qabnag at the confluence of the Tsangpo and Nyang Qu rivers). Its status in SE Tibet is uncertain; may only be a winter visitor, with the bird at Dzeng being in atypical habitat; the December female from Tse, however, had the underparts 'a good deal paler' than in typical *przewalskii* (as did the itinerant April female, Ludlow 1951), indicating some introgression with nominate *leucopsis*, and thus that they may be of a local origin. Discovered in central **Yunnan** at Kunming in December 1986, when parties of three and four were recorded; status in this region unknown, but presumably a winter visitor (Stott 1993). Resident with some altitudinal movements, although recorded as high as 2400 m in Pakistan in winter, and may not be unduly inconvenienced even with deep-lying snow.

**HABITAT** In the western Himalayas inhabits coniferous forest, occasionally mixed deciduous-coniferous forest. In Afghanistan, recorded together with Kashmir Nuthatch in pine, fir, spruce and Deodar (cedar). In Pakistan, found in the inner, colder mountain valleys in the dry coniferous zone and also in moist temperate forest with a richer mixture of broadleaved and coniferous trees. In Chitral found in Deodar forests, and in Gilgit confined to the few areas of Blue Pine and spruce. In China, recorded from spruce and fir forest, also more open 'parkland' (Schäfer 1938), whilst Ludlow (1951) records a bird in SE Tibet in April in a willow tree at Dzeng far from any coniferous forest, possibly a migrant or wanderer. Altitudinal range generally extends to near the treeline. In eastern Afghanistan, recorded from 2135 m in the Safed Koh to 3000–3200 m in Nuristan, where found to the limit of coniferous forest (although not extending up into the juniper zone). In Pakistan and NW India, summers at c. 2100–3000 m, even as high as 3660 m in Chitral (and an undated record at 3500 m in Nanda Devi NP, Uttar Pradesh), optimum zone 2440–3000 m. Descends in winter locally to 1800 m. In western Nepal recorded at 2745–4575 m. In China, recorded at 4270m in Sichuan in August and c. 2250 m in June, in Tibet at 3500–4000 m in the northeast and 2895–3050 m in the southeast, and in Qinghai at 2590–2895 m.

**POPULATION** Rather scarce in Nuristan, NE Afghanistan, although common in the Safed Koh. Also common throughout the range in Pakistan and fairly common in the NW Himalayas and western Nepal, but rare in China and SE Tibet.

**HABITS** Usually found in pairs in spring and summer, otherwise may join mixed-species foraging flocks. Sometimes rather shy. Forages in the upper canopy of tall trees, on the trunk or the small branches, favouring the underside of thick, lichen-draped branches; less frequently forages lower down on the main trunk. Thus, can be difficult to see, and often most easily located by call. The male may perch on the top of a tall fir, jerking his body from side to side and flicking his wings, calling all the while, in an apparent territorial display. Food insects and seeds (of various species of conifer), and noted flycatching in the summer, but few details of diet.

**BREEDING BIOLOGY** Season in western Himalayas late April–early July. Nest placed in a hole or crevice in a conifer, often a crack in the trunk of a lightning-struck tree, from 5.5–30 m above ground, and usually above 9 m; may use abandoned woodpecker excavations, and has been recorded using a hole in the ground below a root. Does not use mud or resin to reduce the size of the entrance hole (although Baker 1932–33 refers to a single description of a nest 'closed up with mud etc.'). Nest variable, may be simply a pad of grass and dead leaves, or a more elaborate construction of moss lined with fur and hair. Clutch 6–8 (4–8): eggs pinkish-white, with numerous reddish and purple-grey spots concentrated at one end; 18.1 x 13.8 mm. Female incubates, period unknown, and both sexes feed the young. Single-brooded (?).

**DESCRIPTION** *S. l. leucopsis* **Adult:** *In fresh plumage* (August–January/March), crown, nape, sides of mantle and sides of neck glossy black. Upperparts, including tertials, wing-coverts and central tail feathers, mid to dark grey-blue, median and greater coverts centred dark grey; T2–T6 blackish-grey, tipped mid grey, tips progressively broader towards outer feathers; T5 with small subterminal white spot on inner web, T6 with oblique white bar subterminally on inner web and narrow white fringe centrally on outer web (see figure 15.1). Primary coverts and alula dark grey. Primaries and secondaries dark grey-brown, inner primaries and secondaries fringed grey-blue, P3–P5 fringed grey-blue inwards of emargination and very narrowly whitish distally of emargination. Lores, supercilium, ear-coverts and throat white, faintly tinged buff. Breast, fore flanks, belly and centre of vent white, washed creamy-buff; rear flanks and sides of vent rufous, undertail-coverts slightly paler and more orange; thighs greyish-rufous. Axillaries pale grey; underwing-coverts sooty-black, longest under primary coverts and base of primaries white. *In worn plumage* (about March–August), cap slightly less glossy, upperparts duller and greyer (when very worn, subterminal grey marks on feathers may show as faint barring on lower mantle and back). Flight feathers worn and bleached slightly paler, remaining fringes paler. Underparts paler, whiter, and rather less buffy, especially on breast and centre of belly, a dirty creamy, washed grey (greyish feather bases shining through). **Bare Parts:** Iris hazel-brown to dark brown; bill blackish, base of lower mandible pale grey; legs and feet yellowish-brown, greenish-brown or dark brown. **Juvenile:** As adult, but cap duller and not so glossy, also less extensive, often being invaded by grey-blue in centre of nape. Flight feathers slightly paler and browner, fringes paler and greyer, primaries with slightly paler tips. Supercilium, cheeks and ear-coverts washed slightly creamy-buff, feathers of this area and of throat, sides of neck and upper breast with faint darker tips, which extend onto breast and belly to form very faint bars. Underparts as fresh adult (thus rather buffer than worn adult at similar time of year). Bill base extensively yellowish. **1st Adult:** No information. **Measurements:** Wing of male 74–81, of female 70–81; tail of male 39–45, of female 37–44; bill of adult 19.8–22.7, of juvenile 18–20.5; tarsus 17.5–19. Weight 13.5–15.9 g.

*Figure 15.1 Tail of* S. l. leucopsis.

**MOULT** Adult post-breeding complete (late June–October). Adult pre-breeding occasional (?), partial, includes throat, breast and nape (April). Post-juvenile, no information.

**GEOGRAPHICAL VARIATION** Two well-marked subspecies.

*S. l. leucopsis* NW Himalayas. See Description.

*S. l. przewalskii* Western China. In fresh plumage, cheeks washed orange-buff, breast, belly and centre of vent washed rich cinnamon, sides of breast darker cinnamon-orange; flanks and under-tail-coverts as nominate *leucopsis*. In worn plumage, underparts paler and 'patchier'. Averages slightly smaller (wing c. 4 mm shorter). Bill shorter, thinner, and weaker (averages c. 17 mm, compared with 21 mm in nominate *leucopsis*). Wing of male 72–77, of female 69–74; bill 17–17.6.

**RELATIONSHIPS** Considered to be closely related to White-breasted Nuthatch of North America (indeed, they were treated as conspecific by Meinertzhagen 1928 and Kleinschmidt 1932–33), the two possibly representing an 'old' group (Voous & van Marle 1953). Notably, the contact call is rather similar to, although slightly deeper than, the equivalent note of White-breasted Nuthatch. White-cheeked Nuthatch has also been allied with the *canadensis* group (and has even been treated as conspecific with this group). Given the close similarity of all the medium-small nuthatches, however, the precise relationship of White-cheeked Nuthatch is still obscure.

**REFERENCES** Ali & Ripley (1983), Roberts (1992), Wunderlich (1988a).

# 16 WHITE-BREASTED NUTHATCH *Sitta carolinensis*  Plate 4

A familiar bird in much of North America, its habits and ecology closely resemble those of Eurasian Nuthatch, although many aspects of its biology remain unknown.

**IDENTIFICATION** Length 155 mm (6 in). Medium-large, with bill long and straight or slightly upturned. Cap and band on upper mantle black, upperparts pale blue-grey, and wing-coverts and flight feathers blackish, fringed paler, the tertials often conspicuously marked with pale grey and black, and with a slight paler wingbar on the greater coverts. Outer tail feathers black, with a broad diagonal white band across the outer three (sometimes visible in flight or display). Face and underparts white (white completely surrounding the eye), with belly and vent buff. Females and juveniles a little duller, especially on the cap. Easily distinguished from the other North American nuthatches by its blackish cap and unmarked white face, lacking the blackish eye-stripe of Red-breasted Nuthatch.

**SEX/AGE** Sexes differ slightly. In fresh plumage, males have a glossy black cap and clean blue-grey upperparts, whilst females have a duller cap, a narrower blackish band on the border of the upper mantle, paler and duller grey upperparts, variably tinged brown, a brownish or greenish wash to the fringes of the wing feathers, and a duller face and underparts, variably washed buff. The tone of the female's cap varies, however, from dull black to light grey, averaging palest in the NE USA and on the west coast, with many intermediate mixtures. Birds may be individually recognisable by cap coloration, but sexing in the field can be difficult and unreliable, with a minimum of 10% of females appearing black-capped, even in the NE USA; and, in Florida and Georgia, the Rocky Mountains, Great Basin and Mexico, the female's cap is usually blackish-grey (a minimum of 40–80% of females appearing black-capped), and thus the cap is of little value in the field for sexing nuthatches. In the hand, however, females probably always show some grey tips, especially on the forehead and nape, and their cap is never solidly glossy black. Juveniles are rather similar to adults, but a little paler and duller. On juvenile males, the cap is dull black (resembling many adult females in coloration); in the hand, they can sometimes be distinguished from adult females by the less extensive buff fringes to the wing feathers, subtly barred upperparts, and 'looser' plumage. Juvenile females have a dark grey cap (as adult females in interior and Mexican populations, but in the northeast and on the west coast sometimes darker than the adult female, lacking the extensive pale blue-grey tips); they have a stronger buff wash to the cheeks and underparts than the adult female, especially on the breast and belly, and often less extensive buff fringes to the wing feathers. In ideal conditions, juvenile females can be separated from juvenile males by their duller cap and more extensive drab wash to the fringes of the wing feathers. 1st adults are probably impossible to age, unless they show obvious moult contrasts.

**VOICE** Contact call a soft, thin, relatively high-pitched and slightly squeaky *nit* or *hit*, varying in tone and emphasis, and sometimes repeated at the rate of 30 calls per minute, or combined/alternated with a louder and more emphatic *chuck* or *tuk* as a conversational *hit-tuk, hit-tuk*. These calls are given all year, but especially in autumn and winter. A single *tchup* indicates mild excitement; but perhaps the most characteristic call is a rather nasal *kri*, often rendered 'kun', ka-un' or 'quank'; its variations indicate various levels of excitement. A single shrill and rather nasal *kri* or *qui* ('quank') is given in mild excitement, heightened excitement is indicated by an irregular series of shrill *kri, kri kri...* notes, and even greater agitation by the repetition of two *kri* calls in quick succession, *kri-kri, kri-kri*. Significant agitation or excitement (notably in territorial defence or conflicts) is also indicated by a rapid series of 4–8 (4–21) *kri*-type units (the more units, the greater the excitement, up to speed of 8–10 notes per second), given at varying pitches, *kri-kri-kri-kri-kri, kri-kri-kri-kri-kri-kri...* (averaging higher-pitched and often in rapid series in the Great Basin and Rocky Mountains (*S. c. tenuissima*)). Alternatively, may give slower and quieter series of conversational, nasal *krit, krit, krit-krit, krit...* notes. All of these *kri* (or '*quank*') calls may be given in a rather harsher, rougher and even more nasal form (the units characterised by rapid frequency modulation), given in couplets or long series at varying speeds, from strident *krrr-krrr, krrr-krrr* couplets through *krr-krr-krr* triplets, to longer series of notes, and also chattering *krrr'krr'krrr'krr* phrases. (In general, these calls are stronger, more cawing or crow-like and less nasal than those of Red-breasted Nuthatch.) A low, harsh, trilling *brr-aa* is given in aggressive encounters. In display flights, males give a quiet, long, high-pitched whistled *phee-oo* note, with a rising and then falling inflection, as do females when soliciting copulation. During courtship feeding, females give high *chrr* or *k'duck, k'duck* notes (as do begging nestlings). The song, given only by the male, comes in two varieties. 'Slow' song is a rapid series of 6–11 *que* or '*hah*' units, nasal and quite high-pitched, delivered at a rate of *c.* 6 per second: *qui-qui-qui-qui-qui-qui*, each unit sounding slightly inflected and often starting relatively quietly but quickly building in volume (similar to, but higher, thinner and less nasal than, the '*quank*' note). Variants include phrases made up of more distinctly upward-inflected units, *tui-tui-tui-tui-tui*. The 'fast' song is given in heightened states of excitement, and packs 16–26 notes into roughly the same timespan (i.e. *c.* 10–12 units per second; it is rather similar to the more rapid series of *kri* notes, although averaging faster). Song is given January–May in the NE USA, *after* the establishment of territory and pair formation, only sporadically at other times, most regularly shortly after dawn, from the top of a tall tree, the male stretching vertically upwards and bowing with each note (also occasionally given in flight). Shorter and less intense versions, as well as chattering *krrr'krr'krrr'krr* phrases, are given at other times. (Partly after Kilham 1972a, Ritchison 1983.)

## DISTRIBUTION AND MOVEMENTS

In **Canada** found on Cape Breton and Prince Edward Islands and **Nova Scotia**, and in **New Brunswick**, southern **Quebec**, including Quebec and Montreal (and recorded in April north to Arvida but no evidence of breeding), SE **Ontario** north to Ottawa, Algonquin Park, the French River and Timagani, and including Manitoulin island, and SW Ontario at Rainy River, Kenora and Thunder Bay, and recorded north to Red Lake; also southern **Manitoba** north to Winnipeg and Swan River, SE **Saskatchewan**, north and west to Prince Albert, southern **Alberta** from Lethbridge north to Lesser Slave Lake, east to the Frog Lake region and west to Calgary, Rocky Mountain House and Grande Prairie, and southern **British Columbia** from the Kootenay river north and west to Lillooet. In the **USA** found from the Canadian border south to central **Florida** (formerly to Lake Okeechobee, but now a rare winter visitor in the south), the **Gulf Coast** (although largely absent from coastal regions) and the **Mexican border**. Absent from most of Great Plains, from NE **Montana** and western **North Dakota** (where largely confined to the Missouri and Little Missouri valleys), western **South Dakota** (common only in the Black Hills), most of **Nebraska** (breeds uncommonly in the Pine Ridge area), western **Kansas** (breeds sporadically west to Decatur, Russell and Summer Cos.), western **Oklahoma** (breeds west to Osage, Lincoln, Cleveland and Comanche Cos., infrequently to Alfalfa and Dewey Cos., and rarely to Texas Co; may be spreading westwards), and from eastern **Colorado** (east of Larimer, Huerfano and Las Animas Cos.), eastern **New Mexico**, and central **Texas** (in the east, breeds south and west to Wichita, Tarrant, Brazos and Walker Cos., in the west only in the Trans-Pecos.; formerly bred on the Edwards Plateau in Tom Green and Kerr Cos.?). Also absent from central **Washington** and central **Oregon**, much of the Great Basin, the deserts of SW **Arizona**, the Mojave desert of SE **California**, coastal California south of Los Angeles Co., and the Sacramento and San Joaquin valleys of central California. In **Mexico** found in northern and southernmost **Baja California**, in the Sierra Madre Occidental and associated ranges in eastern **Sonora** (west in the north to about Nogales and Moctezuma), **Sinaloa** and **Nayarit** (west to about Tepic), northern **Jalisco**, **Aguascalientes**, and western **Chihuahua** (east to at least Lac Bustillos), **Durango** (east to about Durango), and **Zacatecas**; also the southern and eastern parts of the Central Plateau in **Jalisco**, **Michoacan**, **Guanajuato**, **Mexico**, **Morelos**, **Puebla**, **Tlaxcala**, **Hidalgo**, and west-central **Veracruz** (Jalapa, Mount Citlaltepetl). In the east, breeds in the Sierra Madre Oriental and associated ranges in **Coahuila** (Sierra del Carmen southwards), western **Nuevo Leon**, SW **Tamaulipas** (east to about Ciudad Victoria), and eastern **San Luis Potosi**, and in the south in the Sierra Madre del Sur in **Guerrero** and **Oaxaca** (east to La Parada and Rio Molino). Generally sedentary, and a familiar bird on Christmas Bird Counts, but some retreat from the northernmost parts of the range and from high altitudes (notably in the west) in winter, and some birds may return to the same wintering territory in successive years. There is also some irregular and localised dispersal in spring and autumn. These movements are usually short-distance, but may be found away from breeding areas in the Great Plains and the deserts of the southwest, in riverine forests, on isolated wooded desert massifs, and in suburban parks and gardens. Frequent in Lower Sonoran zone of Arizona, but a scarce or even rather rare winter visitor outside the breeding range in Florida, Texas (not the south) and California, August–early April. Does not undertake the irregular large-scale eruptions of Red-breasted Nuthatch, although undoubtedly commoner in some years than others away from breeding areas. Vagrant Vancouver Island, **British Columbia** (Comox, Victoria), Sable Island, **Nova Scotia**, **Californian** islands (Santa Cruz, April 1920 and winter 1972/73), SW **Sonora** (January), and

**Bermuda** (September 1931). One came aboard the RMS *Queen Mary* sailing westwards six hours out of New York on 1 October 1963 (Durand 1972).

**HABITAT** In the east, primarily a bird of mature open deciduous forest, also mixed forest (in the north, maple-hemlock-pine), orchards, woodlots, shade trees, parks, gardens and cemeteries in suburban areas, but generally absent from spruce-fir forests, e.g. the Adirondacks in New York, and from the boreal forests of the north; also absent from bottomlands in Arkansas, but in the southeast does breed in pine and oak-pine forests. Penetrates the Great Plains in riparian woodland and scattered stands of Ponderosa Pine. In the west, found in open montane pine forest (also Douglas Fir in western Washington), pinyon-juniper, American Aspen, and in the Pacific lowlands pine-oak and evergreen oak. In Mexico found in montane pine-oak, and also pine forests in northern Baja California. An essential requirement is mature or rotten trees with holes suitable for breeding, and in the east the presence of oak, beech and hickory and their fruits may be important. Favours clearings and other edge habitats. Generally a lowland species in the east, but found at up to 1675 m in Tennessee. In the west largely montane, and found at up to 2590 m in Idaho, 3200 m in Nevada, 2600 m in Arizona, at 2135–2440 m in New Mexico (dispersing to both higher (3050 m) and lower elevations (1525 m), and also in riparian woodlands in the Santa Cruz valley), up to 2590 m in the Davis mountains in SW Texas, and in California breeds at up to 3230 m, dispersing as high as 3350 m in late summer; in Yosemite NP, common below 915 m (probably the race *aculeata*), scarce at middle elevations (915–2440 m) but more numerous again above 2440 m (probably the race *tenuissima*), and often remains in winter up to at least 2600 m. In northern Baja California (Sierra San Pedro Martir) recorded 1830–2600 m, in Sinaloa 1585–1950 m, in northern Coahuila (Sierra del Carmen) 1980–2440 m; in Nayarit at 915 m, Chihuahua at 1525–3050 m, Durango at 2440 m, Mexico at 3350 m, and in Oaxaca from 1890 m to at least 2745 m.

**POPULATION** In the USA, common from Minnesota, Iowa and Missouri east to New York and Pennsylvania, also in Massachusetts and Connecticut. Otherwise fairly common, although uncommon in British Columbia, Alberta, Saskatchewan, Prince Edward Island, Nova Scotia, Montana, North Dakota, Nebraska, Kansas, Oklahoma and Texas. Additionally, scarce or rare on the northernmost perimeter of the range and necessarily local in much of the Great Plains, Great Basin and the south. In Mexico, common in SW Jalisco (Volcanes de Colima) and northern Coahuila (Sierra del Carmen), fairly common in Baja California and uncommon in Sonora and Oaxaca. Thought to have decreased in the early 20th century in the whole of the SE USA, from Texas to Florida (and close to extinction in peninsular Florida), but conversely may be extending its range in the northern Great Plains and into SE

Washington, and has increased recently in Alberta, whilst in the NE USA has expanded its distribution since the early 1900s with the regrowth of forests.

**HABITS** Not very gregarious, and usually found singly or in pairs, although in late summer (and sometimes through the winter) also in family parties, and will join mixed-species foraging flocks as these pass through its territory. Apparently pairs for life, and pair-bonds are certainly maintained from year to year, being renewed in the late winter, but members of the pair may not be together all the time, the male being more wide-ranging, especially in winter, contact being maintained vocally. Most or all pairs maintain a territory year-round, although some individuals may have separate summer and winter territories, and they may temporarily leave their territory to visit a rich food source (such as a garden feeder). Territories are relatively large and encounters with neighbours are infrequent. Once independent, all juveniles leave the territory where they were raised, and then either establish their own territory (often after pairing) or become 'floaters'. Floaters are probably all immatures without territories (and perhaps largely those involved in the irregular dispersals, see Distribution and Movements), and will replace any member of an established pair that dies or disappears. Although noisy and conspicuous from the late summer to early spring, very quiet and inconspicuous during the breeding season. An unusual and unexplained behaviour is the practice of 'bill-sweeping', whereby the bill is swept back and forwards in an arc over bark near the nest hole, sometimes for several minutes. The inside of the nest cavity may also be 'swept', and an insect is usually held in the bill during sweeping, although sometimes fur or vegetation is used, and sometimes the bill alone is used. The presence of squirrels may precipitate sweeping, and the purpose may be to use the odours from the objects being swept to confuse squirrels, which are potential predators and competitors for nest holes. Distraction displays in the face of predators include a moth-like pose with the body and bill vertical and wings and tail fully spread, the bird swaying slowly from side to side and also fluffing out the white ear-coverts, which then appear to be huge eyes when the bird is viewed from behind. Roosts singly (except in very cold weather; an astonishing record concerns 29 roosting together, see Bent 1948) in tree holes, often in stubs, and also behind loose bark. Notably, roosting birds remove their faeces from the hole when emerging in the morning. Forages on the trunk and larger branches of trees, gleaning from the bark, and also feeds among the thinner outer twigs, in shrubs and occasionally on the ground, searching leaf litter for fallen mast; can flycatch. Food in summer largely insects and spiders, and the young may be fed entirely on animal material. In the autumn and winter largely vegetarian, with a diet of nuts, seeds and berries. Stores food in large amounts, dispersing single items throughout the territory in sites such as bark crevices in the trunks and larger branches of trees (occasionally covering them with bark flakes or lichen), and also around habitations in cracks in poles, under loose shingle etc. In the spring, stores food both inside and immediately outside the nest hole and may store items such as Sugar Maple buds and soil pellets which are not eaten. Visits birdtables (feeders), where, as elsewhere, males are always dominant over females, and removes some items to store nearby. Can be very tame (even feeding from the hand).

**BREEDING BIOLOGY** Season usually rather early, e.g. Ontario, late April–May; New York, Ohio and North Dakota, mid April–May; Oklahoma, late February–March; Texas, late March–April; California, late March–June; Oaxaca, March. Nest placed in a cavity in a tree, usually a natural hole in a dead deciduous tree or decaying stump, often a rotted-out knothole; less frequently uses an abandoned woodpecker excavation, occasionally a nestbox or even a space under the eaves of a house. May enlarge the entrance of an existing cavity, but does not excavate its own hole, and prefers holes with an entrance 30–40 mm in diameter. Has been noted smearing the vicinity of the cavity entrance with dirt, but this may relate to nest sanitation rather than vestigial walling-up behaviour (Duyck *et al.* 1991). The female selects the nest site, and may even usurp a male from his roost hole in the early spring and take this for nesting. The chosen site is usually 3–12 m (0.5–21 m) above ground. The nest is a foundation of wood chips, bark strips, twigs, grass, leaves and fur (used to fill out the cavity as necessary), lined with fur, hair, wool and feathers, and built by the female (supplied with materials by male?). Clutch 5–9 (3–10): eggs white (sometimes tinged pink), spotted reddish-brown, often concentrated at the larger end, with some lavender markings; 19.3 x 14.5 mm. Female incubates, period 12–14 days; she is fed on and off the nest by the male. The young are fed by both parents, although largely by the male in the first few days after hatching, the female spending much time brooding the young; and fledge after 18–26 days (Ritchison 1981), but continue to be fed by the adults for another 14 days. Single-brooded, although replaces lost clutches (and these may be responsible for records of late-fledging broods).

**DESCRIPTION** *S. c. carolinensis* **Adult Male**: *In fresh plumage* (approximately August–March) crown, nape and upper mantle black, faintly glossed greenish-blue (may show off-white feathers at base of bill), the black narrowing at the sides of the upper mantle. Remainder of upperparts, including central tail feathers, light grey, tinged blue; T2–T6 black, T2–T3 narrowly tipped light grey, with a small whitish spot at the tip of the shaft, T4–T6 with broad diagonal white subterminal band (extending to base of outer web on T6 and tip of inner web on T4, see figure 16.1). Wing-coverts blackish-grey, fringed and tipped light grey, greater coverts variably tipped whiter, especially on inner feathers. Alula blackish, fringed white, primary coverts blackish, narrowly fringed pale grey. Inner web of inner two tertials blackish, outer web and streak along shaft of inner web of

*Figure 16.1 Tail of* S. c. carolinensis.

central tertial pale grey; inner web of outermost tertial pale grey, fringed blackish on distal half (more broadly so at tip), outer web blackish, fringed and very broadly tipped pale grey. Secondaries blackish-grey, fringed and narrowly tipped pale grey. Primaries sooty-black, inner primaries narrowly fringed grey-white and more broadly tipped pale grey, P3–P6 with broad white fringe around emargination and pale grey tip. Lores, supercilium, sides of head and underparts whitish (may show very faint dark barring on sides of neck), lower breast and belly faintly tinged buff, vent warmer buff, and rear flanks pale grey. Undertail-coverts pale grey with broad triangular white tips and broadly fringed orange-rufous at base. Thighs pale grey, tipped orange-rufous. Axillaries whitish; underwing-coverts sooty-black, longer under primary coverts and base of primaries white. *In worn plumage* (about March/April–August), flight feathers slightly browner, primary tips abraded, and underparts slightly duller, variably tinged buffish-drab. **Bare Parts**: Iris dark brown; bill grey-black or black, basal two-thirds of lower mandible paler and greyer, cutting edges off-white; legs and feet dark brown or dark grey-brown; claws blackish. **Adult Female**: In fresh plumage as male, but cap blackish-grey, feathers variably tipped mid grey (may appear uniformly grey or may be almost uniformly blackish-grey, but always shows some grey feather tips). Black band on upper mantle averages much less extensive. Upperparts slightly paler with reduced blue tinge, rather faint buff/brown tone to grey; rear scapulars may show faint buff or rufous tips. Flight feathers and coverts paler and browner, with light grey fringes washed drab, especially on tertials, secondaries and fringes (not tips) of greater coverts. Cheeks and underparts with more pronounced buff wash, flanks and vent beige or cinnamon-drab. In worn plumage, paler tips to cap and upper mantle abrade, so cap darker and more uniformly grey, band on upper mantle broader and blacker (often contrasting with cap). **Juvenile Male**: As adult male, but cap duller, blackish-grey with no gloss. Upperparts slightly paler; feathers of mantle may have fine darker tips and the scapulars may have paler tips (thus upperparts very subtly barred). Fringes at base of outer secondaries variably washed orange-buff. Underparts rather duller than on fresh adult, all except chin washed buff (near worn adult). When recently fledged, bill and feet dusky pinkish-buff.

**Juvenile Female**: As juvenile male, but cap duller grey (dark grey), and more extensive drab-buff wash on fringes of secondaries and greater coverts (especially inner feathers); greater coverts may have narrow subterminal white line. Underparts average buffer. **1st Adult**: As adult. **Measurements**: Wing of male 83.5–92, of female 82–91 (chord of male 86–97, of female 85–92.5); tail of male 44–50.5, of female 42–49.5; bill 19.8–23.2 (exposed culmen 15.5–19.5); tarsus 17–20. Weight 19.6–22.9 g.

**MOULT** Adult post-breeding complete (June–September). Adult pre-breeding rare or absent (February–March). Post-juvenile partial, includes a variable number of greater coverts (July–August).

**GEOGRAPHICAL VARIATION** Relatively slight and largely clinal. The upperparts average darkest in the Rocky Mountains and Mexico, becoming paler towards the west and, especially, the east coasts. Northeastern and mid-west populations average palest on the underparts, which become darker in Mexico and to a rather lesser degree on the west coast. Overall size and bill dimensions vary in a more complex fashion. Nine races recognised, but several are rather poorly marked.

**S. c. carolinensis** NE North America west to Saskatchewan (also Alberta: Godfrey 1986), North and South Dakota, Nebraska, Kansas, Oklahoma and eastern Texas. See Description. The palest race in cap (often grey on females) and mantle coloration, showing the greatest contrasts in the tertials. The proportion of females showing a dark cap varies, being lowest in the NE USA and Canada (c. 10%, this population sometimes named 'cookei') and highest in the SE USA, especially Georgia and Florida (with up to 83% in peninsular Florida; Wood 1992). Bill also averages longer in the north than in the south.

**S. c. nelsoni** The Rocky Mountains, from northern Montana through Wyoming, eastern Nevada, Utah, Colorado, Arizona, New Mexico, western-most Oklahoma (few records Cimarron Co.), western Texas (Davis and Guadalupe mountains), Sonora (south to c. 30° N) and extreme NW Chihuahua. As nominate carolinensis, but upperparts darker (dark grey, male with a more distinct blue tone, female with a variable rufous-brown tone to the mantle). Cap of male with more distinct and greener gloss, cap of female often nearly as dark as male's, although not so clean and glossy (shows reduced contrast with mantle). Reduced contrast in the wings, dark feather centres duller and slightly browner, fringes darker grey, tertials finely fringed rufous, central tertial with more black at base of outer web, longest with more black at base of inner web. Underparts of male cleaner and whiter, flanks and belly more extensively light grey, vent tinged buff; female perhaps slightly less buff on underparts than female nominate carolinensis. Bill longer and more slender. Wing (chord) of male, 87–95.5, of female 86–94; bill usually <23 (exposed culmen 17–21).

**S. c. tenuissima** British Columbia, the Cascades of eastern Washington and Oregon, western Montana, western Wyoming, Idaho, central and western Nevada, and eastern California (generally east of the Sierra Nevada, south to Inyo Co.). Poorly marked. As nelsoni, but upperparts fractionally paler (although still significantly darker than nominate carolinensis). Also smaller, but bill rather more slender and sharply pointed. Wing (chord) of male 83.5–94, of female 82–93; bill 23.6–24.8 (exposed culmen 18.5–23.5).

**S. c. aculeata** Western Washington, Oregon, California and northernmost Baja California (Sierra de Juarez, where approaches alexandrae), in the Pacific lowlands west of the Cascades and the crest of the Sierra Nevada and the mountains of southern California (although largely absent from the humid coastal strip). As tenuissima, but upperparts average slightly paler (distinctly paler than nelsoni, but distinctly darker than nominate carolinensis); upperparts of female slightly more olive-brown than in tenuissima (thus significantly browner than eastern races). Underparts of male average slightly buffer, less grey-toned; female slightly buffer (much buffer than female nelsoni), vent darker and more cinnamon-brown. Also smaller, and bill shorter (as nelsoni), weak and more slender. Wing (chord) of male, 80–90, of female 80.5–86; bill (exposed culmen) 16–19.

**S. c. alexandrae** Northern Baja California Norte, in the Sierra San Pedro Martir. As aculeata, but upperparts marginally darker. Also larger, and the longest-billed race. Wing (chord) of male 86.5–94, of female 84.5–91; bill 25.4–25.9 (exposed culmen 18.4–23).

**S. c. lagunae** Southernmost Baja California in the Sierra de la Lazaro (disjunct by over 960 km/600 miles from alexandrae). As alexandrae, but upperparts slightly darker; underparts of male darker with increased buff wash, upper flanks mid grey, rear flanks more cinnamon-rufous. Also smaller, and bill relatively stout (although more slender than in other Mexican races). Wing (chord) of male 86.5–88, of female 84–86; bill (exposed culmen) 17–19.

**S. c. oberholseri** SW Texas (Chisos mountains), and eastern Mexico in the northern Sierra Madre Oriental in Coahuila, western Nuevo Leon and probably interior SW Tamaulipas (La Joya de Salas). Poorly marked (and often synonomised with nelsoni). Medium-sized and dark-backed. As nelsoni, but upperparts slightly darker (especially on female), underparts slightly darker and greyer (rear flanks and vent of female especially so). Wing (chord) of male, 85.5–92, of female 83.5–88.5; bill (exposed culmen) 17–19.

**S. c. mexicana** Western Mexico in the Sierra Madre Occidental from SE Sonora and central Chihuahua (south of c. 30° N), southern and eastern parts of the Central Plateau, and the southern Sierra Madre Oriental from central Nuevo Leon (Gulf Slope) and SE Coahuila southwards. As oberholseri, but upperparts marginally duller, female with more intense olive-brown wash and fringes of greater coverts and flight feathers variably but usually strongly tinged rusty-buff (especially tertials and greater coverts, but not the tips of the latter). Underparts rather duller and sullied buff (less grey, and rather duller than in nelsoni), flanks darker and duller grey in male, and with much drab in female, pinkish-drab extending onto the belly (darker overall than female *aculeata*). Also, bill shorter and relatively stout. Wing (chord) of male 87.5–93.5, of female 86, 89; bill (exposed culmen) 15.5–17.5. Includes *'umbrosa'* of the Sierra Madre Occidental south to central-western Zacatecas and NE Nayarit, perhaps darker above, underparts slightly paler and less brownish, slightly larger, and with longer, heavier bill in male (?) Wing (chord) of male 89–96, of female 90–91.5; bill (exposed culmen) 15–19.

**S. c. kinneari** Guerrero and Oaxaca (north to central or perhaps NW Oaxaca). (Phillips 1986 allies birds from near Tepic, Nayarit, with this race; this is untenable on geographical grounds.)

As *mexicana*, but underparts of female average slightly more orange-buff, this extending onto the throat and breast. Also smaller (the smallest race, but approaches *mexicana* in size in Oaxaca), with bill short and stout. Wing (chord) of male, 82–89.5, of female 77.5–85.2; bill (exposed culmen) 14.6–16.

**RELATIONSHIPS** Uncertain. Bears a superficial resemblance to White-cheeked Nuthatch, and the two are placed in a superspecies by Sibley & Monroe (1990), although some authors, such as Mayr & Short (1970), are not so sure of such a close relationship. See also White-cheeked Nuthatch.

**REFERENCES** Aldrich (1944), Bent (1948), Godfrey (1986), Hawbecker (1948), Kilham (1968, 1972a), Oberholser (1974), Phillips (1986),

# 17 WESTERN ROCK NUTHATCH *Sitta neumayer*       Plate 7
Other name: Rock Nuthatch

The two rock nuthatches are rather similar, and it was not until 1911 that it was discovered that two species were involved (when two forms were found to overlap, apparently without interbreeding, in the Zagros mountains of SW Iran: Hellmayr 1911), and not until 1923 was it discovered to which species each of the forms belonged (von Jordans 1923). Further study has revealed this to be the classic case of 'character displacement', whereby two closely related species have evolved marked differences in the area where they overlap, allowing them to coexist without competing.

**IDENTIFICATION** Length 130–135 mm (5.25 –5.5 in). Medium-sized. Upperparts pale grey, with a broad black eyestripe extending onto the sides of the mantle (the eyestripe is reduced or absent behind the eye in some Iranian populations). The outer tail feathers are only slightly darker than the upperparts, with, at most, just slightly paler spots at the tips of outer two pairs; these are concealed at rest, but may be visible in flight. Cheeks, throat and breast whitish, grading to pinkish-cinnamon on the rear flanks, vent and undertail-coverts. Generally separated from Eurasian Nuthatch by its terrestrial, rock-loving habits, although it will feed on trees and even occasionally enter woodland; conversely, Eurasian Nuthatch may forage among rocks. Through most of the range, Western Rock Nuthatch is larger than Eurasian, proportionally longer-legged and longer-billed, and often adopts a more upright stance. It is rather paler, with a more conspicuous black eyestripe that forms a 'highwayman's mask', visible both from the front and from behind; the underparts are paler, with the breast whitish (cinnamon or orange-buff in southern races of Eurasian), and no rich rufous tones to the flanks. Most importantly, in flight Western Rock Nuthatch lacks white spots in the outer tail feathers. In SW Iran, Western Rock Nuthatch is small and pale, with a much-reduced eyestripe; here, the pale underparts and lack of a black line behind the eye are distinctive. Compared with Eurasian, the vocalisations of Western Rock Nuthatch tend to be louder, more ringing or penetrating, and more trilling and less piping. Western Rock Nuthatch overlaps with Eastern Rock Nuthatch in parts of SE

and eastern Turkey, in northern and western Iran, and in Armenia and SW Azerbaydzhan in southern Transcaucasia. Within the overlap area, the differences between the two species are more marked than elsewhere (indeed, away from this area the two species are very similar). The key identification features are the eyestripe, bill dimensions, overall size and voice. Western Rock has a narrower and often shorter eyestripe, which barely encompasses the eye and narrows towards the rear, is also smaller, with a more slender bill, and has quieter, faster and higher-pitched calls. For full details see Eastern Rock Nuthatch (p. 158).

**SEX/AGE** Sexes similar. Juveniles are very similar to the adults, although slightly duller, with a duller eyestripe, narrow rufous tips to the greater coverts, and less contrast between the breast and belly. 1st adults resemble adults and are usually indistinguishable, but in the hand may show faint brownish tips to the retained juvenile greater coverts.

**VOICE** Very vocal, with a wide repertoire of loud, often trilling, notes. Contact call a variable *pit, tsik* or *chik*, which may be given in flight, and at the slightest excitement run together to form a trill or rattle, either rapidly slowing and falling in pitch or accelerating and then decelerating (these trills resemble the song). In aggressive and sexual encounters gives a harsh *charr* or screeching *creea*, which may be subdued (recalling a Common Whitethroat's scold) or harsh (as from a Eurasian Jay). Song a loud trill, typically descending in pitch, sometimes silvery, sometimes more melodic. The individual units are usually whistles of 1–2 syllables (occasionally three), which may rise (*tui, dui* or *dwip*) or fall (*cheu* or *piu*) in pitch.

The trill is often preceded by a falling *ititit*, thus *ititit tuit-tuit-tiut-tuit-tuit....* (The song trill is typically higher-pitched and shorter than that of Eastern Rock Nuthatch.) Each male may have a repertoire of four or more different song types. Females may sing early in the season, although their song is much less variable. The pair may also engage in antiphonal duetting in the spring and autumn, at least in eastern parts of the range. (Partly after Cramp & Perrins 1993.)

**DISTRIBUTION AND MOVEMENTS** Breeds in the west of former **Yugoslavia** southeastwards from Crikvenica, also southern and SE Yugoslavia, northern **Albania**, SE **Bulgaria**, **Greece**, including Corfu, Zakinthos and Lesbos, **Turkey** (apart from Thrace, the Black Sea coastal region and the southern lowlands between the Firat and Tigris rivers), NW **Syria** south to the Damascus region, the mountains of **Lebanon**, northern **Israel** (Mount Hermon only), northern and NW **Iraq**, the Transcaucasus region of the former USSR north to the southern foothills of the Great Caucasus in southern **Georgia** (north to Abastumani and Tbilisi), **Armenia** and SW **Azerbaydzhan** (also Shemakha in the eastern foothills of the Caucasus). Also northern and western **Iran**. Resident, but some post-breeding dispersal to higher altitudes and also altitudinal movements in winter, when the species has occurred just south of the breeding range in **Israel** in NW Golan and northern Galilee.

**HABITAT** Anywhere with areas of bare rocks, typically rocky slopes, cliffs and gorges in dry or arid regions, usually on limestone. May occur in barren regions or areas with low shrubs, herbs and grasses, and a typical species of rocky maquis; occasionally found in woodland with scattered rocks. Frequently found on stone walls, old buildings and ancient ruins. Generally found in hilly and mountainous areas from near sea level up to the alpine zone. In Turkey, occurs at up to 2100 m in the Taurus mountains and to 2650 m (rarely 3300 m) on Karanfil Dagi in Anatolia. In northern Iran found as high as 3350 m and generally above 1525 m, although sometimes as low as 915 m (in contrast, Eastern Rock Nuthatch is usually found at 915–1525 m). In northern Israel recorded at 400–2200 m (largely above 1000 m), and in the Transcaucasus up to 2000 m. Those at higher altitude may descend to the foothills and valleys in winter in response to snowfall, although odd birds remain above the snowline, on rocks and in snow-free areas.

**POPULATION** Quite common, although local, throughout its range, except for the isolated population of the Kerman massif in south-central Iran, which is apparently quite scarce (Vaurie 1950b). Not uncommon in the mountains of Lebanon, and the population on the Israeli-occupied portion of Mount Hermon is *c.* 20–50 pairs.

**HABITS** Usually found singly or in pairs, and established pairs maintain a territory all year, moving around together, following one another, calling, in flight. Both sexes defend the nesting territory (i.e. immediate vicinity of the nest), and sometimes also a larger foraging territory, and territorial disputes are common at the boundaries, although there may be some overlap of feeding territories. Males sing from the top of a conspicuous rock or small tree, assuming a very upright posture. Following the breeding season, family parties are formed which persist until the post-juvenile moult, and in the autumn and winter may form larger flocks, perhaps largely of immature birds or those displaced from higher altitudes by inclement weather. Restless and active; regularly flicks its wings and 'bobs' in agitation. Generally wary, one member of the pair keeps a periodic lookout for predators, often from a high vantage point, and when alarmed by a raptor may freeze, and may hide behind a rock from intruding humans. In the autumn, the nest is refurbished and the pair roosts in it through the winter. Typically forages on rocks and the ground, hopping and jumping, taking food from cracks and crevices, although will sometimes feed in trees and shrubs. Wedges larger prey items in cracks before smashing them with its bill; may flycatch. Food in summer largely insects and spiders (and young fed entirely on animal matter); in winter mostly seeds, although snails are also important. Stores and buries food.

**BREEDING BIOLOGY** Season: Greece late April–mid May (rarely from mid March); Albania, from mid April; Israel, mid March–mid July; Transcaucasus, late March onwards; Iran, early April onwards. Nest a remarkable flask-shaped structure, sometimes rather large, with an entrance tunnel up to 100 mm long, internal diameter 30–35 mm (the tunnel usually projecting outwards), built of mud, animal dung, hair, feathers, beetle wings, etc. The nest is sited on a rock face, usually under a slight overhang, and as low as 2 m above ground, or uses an existing crevice or cave, sealing the entrance with mud; may also be placed on buildings or other man-made structures. The chamber is lined with hair, wool, feathers, grass etc., which may fill all the available space. The structure is built over 10–18 days, largely by the male, the female occasionally contributing lining material. Nests are regularly reused, sometimes for many years in succession, or a new nest may be built onto an older structure. May decorate the vicinity of the nest with a variety of objects, natural and man-made, which are wedged and stuffed into adjacent cracks and crevices. Clutch 4–10 (–13; larger recorded 'clutches' may include old eggs from previous years): eggs white, usually sparsely speckled and blotched yellowish-brown to purple-brown; 20.9 x 15.2 mm (*S. n. neumayer*). Female incubates, period 13–18 days, the male sometimes feeding her on the nest. The entrance to the nest may be blocked with a plug of lining material. Young fed by both parents, fledging after 23–30 days, but probably dependent on the parents for some time after fledging. May be double-brooded.

**DESCRIPTION** *S. n. neumayer* Adult: *In fresh plumage* (autumn-winter), upperparts, including wing-coverts and tail, light to pale grey with a faint blue tone; inner webs of tail feathers often darker, T3–T6 tipped slightly paler, T5–T6 with pale buff or whitish spot at tip of inner web. Primary coverts and tertials mid grey with slightly paler fringes. Primaries, secondaries and alula dark grey-brown, secondaries indistinctly fringed and tipped pale grey, P3–P10 indistinctly fringed paler, on P3–P6 inwards of emarginations only. Black eyestripe from nostril to sides of upper mantle (c. 3 mm broad), ending irregularly. Cheeks, ear-coverts, sides of neck and throat whitish, centre of breast and belly creamier, sides of breast and belly, flanks, vent, thighs and undertail-coverts pinkish-cinnamon. Underwing-coverts and axillaries pale greyish-buff, base of underside of primaries and secondaries whitish, under primary coverts black. *In worn plumage* (spring-summer), upperparts duller and greyer, eyestripe slightly more distinct, flight feathers bleached paler and browner, and underparts, especially flanks, paler. **Bare Parts**: Iris dark brown; bill dark grey or black, base of lower mandible pale bluish or bluish-flesh; legs and feet greenish-grey to dark grey, soles sometimes slightly yellower. **Juvenile**: As adult, but upperparts duller, with eyestripe slightly shorter, narrower, duller and less well defined. Primaries and secondaries fresh when those of adult worn; greater coverts narrowly tipped rufous. Underparts faintly washed buff. Base of lower mandible more extensively pale bluish. **1st Adult**: See Sex/Age. **Measurements**: Wing of male 78–85, of female 75–83; tail of male 43–51, of female 42–48; bill 23–27.5; tarsus 22.5–25.7. Weight 29–35.5 g.

*Figure 17.1  Tail of* S. n. neumayer.

**MOULT** Adult post-breeding complete (mid June–early November, sometimes late December?, although this may be early pre-breeding moult). Adult pre-breeding occasional, partial, includes some body feathers (January–February). Post-juvenile partial, occasionally includes a variable number of greater coverts, tertials, or central tail feathers (April–mid November). First pre-breeding occasional, partial (late April).

**GEOGRAPHICAL VARIATION** Moderate. Size decreases towards the eastern end of the species' range, but coloration shows little variation apart from the races *tschitscherini* and *plumbea* in SW Iran, which have a much-reduced eyestripe. Five races recognised.

*S. n. neumayer* SE Europe. See Description. The largest race, with a relatively heavy bill.

*S. n. syriaca* West and central Turkey, Syria, Lebanon and Israel. Poorly marked. As nominate *neumayer* but upperparts fractionally (if at all) paler, underparts slightly paler, especially on flanks (or usually buffer, less white, on throat and breast: Shirihai in press); averages slightly smaller. Wing of male 74–84, of female 75–82; bill

21.8–25.2. (In most of the range, wing of male, 79–84, of female 76–82, but averages smaller in western Turkey (east to at least Eregli and Ankara), where wing of male 74–82, of female 75–79, these latter sometimes named *'zarudnyi'.)*

*S. n. rupicola* Extreme eastern Turkey (north and east of Van Gölü), Armenia and Azerbaydzhan, northern Iraq and northern Iran from Azarbaijan eastwards through the Elburz mountains to around Gorgan, Mazandaran province (and presumably this race east to Bojnurd: Erard & Etchécopar 1970), and south to Mahabad, Qom and Kavir. Probably intergrades with *tschitscherini* roughly along a line from Mahabad to Kermanshah. Intergrades with *syriaca* in eastern Turkey and Georgia. Poorly marked. As *syriaca*, but upperparts faintly paler or bluer (palest in Azarbaijan, NW Iran), underparts slightly paler, bill slightly more slender. Wing of male 75–85, of female 78–80; weight 22.9–31 g.

*S. n. tschitscherini* Western Iran in the Zagros mountains from Kermanshah southeast to about Neyriz, Fars province, and west-central Iran (south of Qom), southeast to the Anarak massif. As *rupicola*, but upperparts slightly paler and purer grey (may be 'almost whitish-grey': Vaurie 1950b); whitish sides of neck fade into the grey mantle. Flanks, belly and undertail-coverts pinkish-buff, paler and lacking the cinnamon tones of western races. Black eyestripe reduced (2–3 mm broad), may be virtually absent, extending less than 10 mm behind eye (rather than 20–28 mm as in other races), where very narrow. Small: wing of male 74–82, of female c. 71–82; weight 20.2–22.1 g.

*S. n. plumbea* South-central Iran in the mountains of southern Kerman province (range discontinuous?). As *tschitscherini*, but upperparts slightly darker (as *rupicola*, although duller and less blue), and throat, breast and belly pale grey rather than whitish. Wing of male 76–78, of female c. 71–79.

**RELATIONSHIPS** The rock nuthatches are considered an offshoot of the Eurasian Nuthatch group by Voous (1977) and Voous & van Marle (1953). Western and Eastern Rock Nuthatches are clearly closely related, and following analysis by Vaurie (1951) are regarded as the classic case of 'character displacement'. Where the two species overlap they differ markedly in size, bill length and the prominence of the dark eyestripe, but in the areas where just one species is present they are very similar. The suggestion was that competition between them had intensified the differences in the area of overlap, thus allowing them to coexist. A detailed analysis by Grant (1975) showed that the situation was not so clear-cut, and that variation in some characters, rather than demonstrating 'displacement', could represent merely a continuation of trends shown outside the zones of overlap (e.g. bill size). Grant concluded, however, that the body size and notably the size of the eyestripe of the two species had undergone mutually divergent character displacement where they overlapped. The exaggerated differences in body size may result in different food resources being utilised and, although bill size has not been 'displaced', where they overlap they exploit seeds of different sizes, thus reducing competition. Importantly, the differences in the eyestripe help in species recognition. Thus, in many displays, the eyestripe (made more conspicuous by raising the feathers) conveys information on the bird's species, whilst bobbing is thought to give information on the bird's size, and the type of display (vertical posture in male, crouching in female) gives information on its sex. Where their eyestripes do differ markedly, the two species are able to coexist, with their home ranges overlapping and birds feeding within a few metres of one another without conflict. In addition, differences in song may also be important in species recognition, as the songs, although similar, are given at higher and lower frequencies (although the distinctions are far from clear-cut). These mechanisms of character displacement do not, however, appear to be fully developed in every region where the two species overlap. Notably, in northern Iran, the differences in the eyestripe dimensions are reduced and the two species appear unable to coexist, Western Rock being found at higher altitudes than Eastern Rock, despite the fact that there are marked differences in bill size. Here, the possibility of 'reproductive confusion' seems to keep the two species apart, despite a lack of ecological competition. Further study is required, both in Iran and in SE Turkey, where overlap has only recently been discovered

**REFERENCES** Cramp & Perrins (1993), Grant (1975), Vaurie (1950b), Wunderlich (1991).

# 18 EASTERN ROCK NUTHATCH *Sitta tephronota*          Plate 7
Other name: Great Rock Nuthatch

The eastern equivalent of Western Rock Nuthatch, breeding from SE Turkey to Pakistan, this large nuthatch builds similarly extravagant nests and has songs and calls which are even louder and more far-carrying.

**IDENTIFICATION** Size 150–160 mm (6–6.5 in). Medium-large to large, with a long, heavy bill. Upperparts light grey, most individuals showing faint paler spots at the tips of the outer two tail feathers. A broad black eyestripe extends well onto the sides of the mantle, exceptionally even meeting the other at the rear. Sides of head, throat and breast whitish, flanks, belly and vent pinkish-cinnamon, undertail-coverts more rufous-cinnamon. Confusion is possible with Eurasian Nuthatch; for distinctions see under Western Rock (p. 155). Overlaps with Western Rock Nuthatch in SE Turkey (from Gaziantep east to Hakkari and north to Siirt), and also in NE Turkey around the Aras valley (north of Mount Ararat), NW Iraq, northern Iran (east in the Elburz mountains to Gorgan), western Iran (south to Kerman), and in southern Transcaucasia. In the overlap zone, the key identification features are the eyestripe, bill dimensions, overall size and voice. * **Eyestripe** Rather longer and broader on Eastern Rock, encompassing the eye and usually of uniform width or broadening behind the eye. On Western Rock, the eyestripe barely surrounds the eye and narrows to the rear (and is even narrower and very short in the Zagros mountains of SW Iran). * **Bill** Longer on Eastern Rock, but the length relative to the body size is similar in both species; the bill of Eastern Rock is, however, noticeably stockier. * **Overall size** The larger size of Eastern Rock is usually obvious, but while Eastern Rock still looks 'large', even without direct comparison, lone Western Rock Nuthatches may not look 'small'. Eastern Rock may be comparatively sluggish, with slower wingbeats, and less frequently flicks its wings and tail. * **Voice** Perhaps the most obvious difference. In the zone of overlap, the calls of Eastern Rock are louder and deeper, with longer intervals between the notes (although in the east of the range, where Eastern Rock is smaller, the calls may be much more similar to those of Western Rock, being only fractionally slower and deeper). A subsidiary feature is the underpart coloration, Eastern Rock often showing a greater contrast between the whitish breast and fore flanks and the darker and more extensive pinkish-cinnamon of the rear flanks, belly and vent. There is individual variation, however, and some juvenile Western Rock are similarly rufous on the rear underparts, whilst juvenile Eastern Rock show less contrast than the adults. The legs of Eastern Rock may also average paler. Otherwise, the two species are similar, although the upperparts of Western Rock are paler in SW Iran (race *tschitscherini*). Despite the marked differences in size and in prominence of eyestripe in the areas where the two species overlap, outside this zone they are much more similar, and it may be impossible to identify a bird, even in the hand, without knowledge of its provenance.

**SEX/AGE** Sexes similar. Juveniles are very similar to adults, although the feathers of their upperparts are faintly tipped paler, the eyestripe is duller and less well defined, greater coverts finely fringed buff, and the underparts paler, showing less contrast between the pale buff-white breast and pale pinkish-buff flanks, belly and vent. 1st adult as adult, but may show traces of rufous fringes on retained greater coverts, and worn brown primaries and secondaries rather than the fresher and greyer flight feathers of adults (until early winter only); a few birds replace some outer primaries, thus showing moult contrast in the flight feathers.

**VOICE** Very vocal, with loud, far-carrying and often trilling calls given throughout the year, although perhaps least frequently in autumn and winter. General pattern very similar to that of Western Rock Nuthatch, but the equivalent calls are generally louder, deeper, mellower and more slowly repeated. The harsh, Eurasian Jay-like *kneuw*, given in excitement, is apparently less frequently used, but also gives a *ch-ch-ch...* in agitation. Song very like that of Western Rock Nuthatch, although slightly lower-pitched, and most descriptions could apply to both species. The male sings from a conspicuous rock or cliff, usually near the nest, and each male has a repertoire of at least four different songs, repeating each several times before switching to a different phrase. The female has a more stereotyped song, given in a duet with the male, coming in before the male has finished his phrase. Song period March through incubation. (Partly after Cramp & Perrins 1993.)

## DISTRIBUTION AND MOVEMENTS

In **Turkey** found locally in the southeast from Gaziantep east to Hakkari and north to Siirt, and also in NE Turkey in the Aras valley along the Armenian/Iranian border (the presence of the species in Turkey was long disputed, despite the occurrence there of the largest race of Eastern Rock). Also occurs locally in NW **Iraq** in Kurdistan. In northern and western **Iran** breeds in the Zagros mountains southeast to the Jebal Barez, with an isolated (?) population on the Anarak massif, also in northern Iran in the Elburz mountains, in NE Iran, and south in eastern Iran to about Iranshahr (Chandgan, Ghasreghand). In the former USSR, occurs in the southern Transcaucasus in southern **Armenia** (north to the Vedichay basin and northern watershed of the Araks) and **Azerbaydzhan**, in the southwest in the Zangezurskiy range (east to 47° E), and in the southeast in the western foothills of the Talyshskiye range (north to c. 39° N), and including Nakhichevan'. Found in southern **Turkmenistan**, from the Bol'shoy Balkhan mountains east through the Malyy and Kyurendag ranges and the northern foothills of the Kopet Dag to the Karabil' plateau, also SE Turkmenistan in the Kugitangtau mountains. In Central Asia also found in the western Pamirs (east to 73° E) and the west and central Tien Shan and Alay systems (southern **Uzbekistan**, **Tadzhikistan**, and SE **Kazakhstan**), from Nurata and the Karatau range east through the Zerav'shanskiy mountains to the western Zailiyskiy range (east to Chemolganskoe gorge), Gul'cha, Ferganskiy range, mountains west of lake Issyk-Kul' and Chu-Iliyskiye range, and also on isolated mountains of the central Kyzylkum desert in Uzbekistan (north to 43° N), and the western marches of the Dzhungarskiy Alatau in SE Kazakhstan (Kapal and Kalkany; may also occur in adjacent parts of Chinese Turkestan?). Occurs throughout most of **Afghanistan**, except the lowlands of the north, the fertile valleys of Nuristan and the Wakhan corridor. In **Pakistan** breeds throughout northern Baluchistan, south to the Ras Koh and the Kacha range in Chagai, the Harboi hills, Zhob (although largely absent Ziarat) and the Shinghar range, extending marginally into the southernmost NWFP in the Takht-i-Sulaiman in southern Waziristan. Does not occur south into the Sulaiman range (*contra* Ali & Ripley 1983; see Roberts 1992). Resident, although perhaps some post-breeding dispersal from about August

onwards, and in late autumn and winter may descend to lower altitudes, although this seems to be very dependent on local conditions. In Central Asia, those breeding at higher altitudes or in more northerly areas may descend from September onwards, although some may remain at breeding altitudes, especially on south-facing slopes. Those from lower altitudes move only in the harshest weather, when recorded down to the foothills of the Kopet Dag, with a wanderer recorded in the Karakum desert. In Pakistan, little evidence of altitudinal movements, but may descend to the lower slopes and valleys and even to plains level at c. 300 m.

**HABITAT** Rocky mountain slopes and valleys, cliffs, ravines and gorges. May have a predilection for the vicinity of streams, and the distribution is closely correlated with one vegetation type, an *Astragalus-Artemesia*-Rosaceae association (including almonds and pistachios). More arboreal than Western Rock Nuthatch and often found in more wooded country: in Pakistan, areas with scattered junipers and wormwood, although not in extensive tracts of juniper forest; in Iran, recorded breeding in rocky oak woods. Areas of exposed bare rock are generally necessary, whatever the density of local vegetation, although in southern Iran also found in dry pistachio forest on stony ground, where no rocky habitat is available; in this habitat they also nest in tree holes (Desfayes & Praz 1978). May feed in dry streambeds and on roads, and in winter in Central Asia descends from mountain slopes to forests and orchards. In Central Asia, found at up to c. 2600 m (up to 2000 m in the Tien Shan, 1500 m in the Karatau and 800–1000 m in the Dzhungarskiy Alatau), in northern and central Baluchistan (Pakistan) at 1800–2100 m and in southern Baluchistan up to 2750 m, in Afghanistan at 915–3300 m and in Turkey up to at least 2100 m. In Ziarat (Pakistan), descends to the plains in winter. In the areas of overlap, generally found at lower altitudes than Western Rock Nuthatch, and in the Elburz mountains of northern Iran the two species may even be separated by altitude, Eastern Rock being found at 915–1525 m (but in southern Iran Eastern Rock occurs up to 3000 m).

**POPULATION** Generally fairly common in suitable habitat, although apparently scarce in Armenia.

**HABITS** Usually found singly or in pairs, the male and female moving about together and following one another in flight. Established pairs probably remain together on territory all year, roosting together in the nest through the winter. Rather territorial, disputes being common at the boundaries, but after breeding often found in parties of 2–3, with up to 16 birds recorded together. May be relatively fearless, and even inquisitive, but sometimes shy; a bird 'on guard' sits motionless on the top of a prominent rock, occasionally turning its head, and when agitated bobs and wing-flicks. Forages on rock faces, boulders and on the ground, moving with jerky hops, its stance often quite upright. Bushes and sometimes trees are used for posturing and singing, more so than with Western Rock Nuthatch, but perhaps not for foraging. Seeds and snails may be wedged in cracks and crevices and smashed open with the bill. May flycatch, and recorded taking fruits in pistachio orchards. Food in summer largely insects and snails; from autumn to early spring mainly seeds, such as apricot, cherry and wild almond. From late summer onwards stores snails and seeds in cracks and crevices, which may be covered with small stones, and similar caches may be hidden under stones, behind loose bark or pressed into the ground and covered with soil. These may be an important resource in the winter months.

**BREEDING BIOLOGY** Season late February–June in southern parts of the former USSR (the later dates probably refer to second clutches); March in Iran; March–May in Afghanistan; late February–May in Pakistan. Pair formation probably occurs in early spring. The black eyestripe is conspicuous in displays, when the feathers are raised. The nest is a flask-shaped structure, usually built over a crack, cavity or hole in a rock face, tree (especially in Iran and Afghanistan?), river bank or building. The hole may be natural, may have been excavated by the birds themselves, or may be the abandoned hole of a bee-eater, roller or woodpecker; exceptionally, recorded nesting in a tree fork. Nests have been found as low as 1 m above ground. The entrance to the cavity is walled up with plaster, leaving a small hole (35–50 mm diameter) or a short conical entrance tunnel 45–150 mm long (tunnels are less frequent, and shorter, than in nests of Western Rock). The 'plaster' is a mixture of mud, saliva, excrement, resin, feathers, hair, cloth, insect fragments, and even sweet wrappers. The exterior of the nest, as well as adjacent cracks in the rock or tree, is sometimes decorated with feathers and bright objects. The interior of tree-hollows is often lined with mud. Nests may be small (c. 300 mm in diameter), but in some cases are very elaborate structures (e.g. a hollow tree with every hole plastered over, leaving a conical entrance tunnel), with several incomplete nests alongside the one in use; nests have been recorded weighing up to 32 kg. Built by both sexes, the same nest may be reused for several years running. The eggs are placed in a mud cup, sometimes lined with grass, feathers, fibres or hair. Clutch 5–7 (4–9): eggs white, usually sparsely speckled and blotched ochre and black, rarely purple-grey, the markings sometimes concentrated at the larger end; 21.1 x 16.1 mm. Female incubates, period 12–14 days; she is fed on the nest by the male. The young are fed by both parents, although mainly by the male in the first week, when the female spends much time brooding, and later mainly by the female. One adult may roost in the nest with the young, blocking the entrance with a plug of lining material. The young fledge at 24–26 days, and after fledging birds stay in family parties for a long period, these not breaking up until mid August or September. May be double-brooded, especially at lower altitudes.

**DESCRIPTION** *S. t. dresseri* **Adult**: *In fresh plumage* (September–February/March), upperparts,

including tertials, wing-coverts and tail, light grey; tail feathers finely tipped pale buff, T5–T6 with indistinct buff spot on tip of inner web, T6 fringed buff on basal half. Alula mid grey, smaller feathers fringed light grey on outer web. Primary coverts light grey, faintly washed brown. Primaries and secondaries light grey, darker towards tip and distally of emarginations on outer web of P3–P4, inner primaries washed brown on outer web. Broad black eyestripe from nostril to side of mantle (where stripes sometimes meet), c. 5 mm broad and encompassing eye. Cheeks, ear-coverts and throat whitish; sides of neck whitish, faintly tinged buff. Breast creamy-white, sides of breast washed buff, grading into pinkish-cinnamon on flanks, belly and vent and rufous-cinnamon on thighs and undertail-coverts; longer undertail-coverts centred light grey. Axillaries whitish to pale grey, underwing-coverts light-mid grey, under primary coverts dark sooty-grey, longer under primary coverts and base of flight feathers whitish. In worn plumage (March–August), upperparts duller and browner, especially on mantle and scapulars. Flight feathers bleached paler and browner. Lower breast and belly whiter, remainder of underparts slightly paler. **Bare Parts**: Iris dark brown; bill black or dark slate, base of lower mandible pale blue-grey; legs and feet grey or blue-grey. **Juvenile**: Very similar to adult. Feathers of upperparts, especially crown and scapulars, faintly tipped pale brown to grey-white (may have faintly darker subterminal markings giving very faint cross-barring). Eyestripe duller and less well defined (odd feathers tipped grey). Greater coverts finely fringed buff. Tertials and secondaries washed brownish-buff; flight feathers fresh when those of adult worn. Throat and breast washed dull pale buff, flanks, belly and vent pale pinkish-buff. Base of lower mandible more extensively pale bluish-flesh. **1st Adult**: As adult and often indistinguishable (see Sex/Age). **Measurements**: Wing 87–101, of male 90–98, of female 87–95; tail of male 47–55, of female 45–52; bill 24.6–31; tarsus 25.3–29.9. Weight 42.7–55 g.

*Figure 18.1 Tail of* S. t. dresseri.

**MOULT** Adult post-breeding complete (June (former USSR) or July (Iran, Afghanistan) to September, occasionally early December). Adult pre-breeding probably absent. Post-juvenile partial, rarely includes central tail feathers (starts shortly after fledging, date thus variable; mid July–late October). Some evidence that early-fledged juveniles may show partial primary moult, replacing outer six primaries.

**GEOGRAPHICAL VARIATION** Marked and rather complex, involving mainly body size and bill size and shape, the prominence of the eye-stripe, and to a rather lesser extent upperpart and underpart coloration. Four races recognised.

**S. t. dresseri** Iraq, western Iran (Zagros mountains from Mahabad southeast to Neyriz, Fars province, and east to Hamadan and Esfahan), probably this race SE Turkey. Intergrades with *obscura* in Iranian Azarbaijan. See Description. Largest and palest race (upperpart coloration near race *tschitscherini* of Western Rock), with bill long and heavy. A cline of decreasing saturation runs NW–SE: birds in the southern Zagros palest below, and those from northern Iraq average largest and deepest rufous on flanks and belly.

**S. t. obscura** Southern Transcaucasia, northern Iran (northern Azarbaijan through the Elburz mountains to about Gorgan, Mazandaran), presumably this race NE Iran and perhaps this race in the mountains of west-central Iran on the western marches of the Zagros mountains (Qom, Anarak massif and Yazd to Kerman), southern Sistan and Baluchistan. Intergrades with *dresseri* in Iranian Azarbaijan and with nominate *tephronota* in NE Iran (Khorasan) and SE Iran (northern Sistan). As *dresseri*, but upperparts darker, dull mid grey, eyestripe prominent (although showing slightly less contrast with rest of the upperparts). Smaller. Wing 83–97; bill 25.9–30; weight 37–44 g. Some variation in underpart coloration: as *dresseri* in Elburz mountains, but rather paler in Armenia (even paler than nominate *tephronota*). Birds from Qom to Kerman usually included in *obscura*, and upperparts even darker and duller grey, but size and underpart coloration as *dresseri*; birds from northern Sistan and Iranian Baluchistan average paler (near nominate *tephronota*).

**S. t. tephronota** SE central Asia, from extreme eastern Turkmenistan through the western and central Tien Shan mountains east to the Dzhungarskiy Alatau, and south through the Pamirs to Afghanistan and Pakistan, also NE Iran from Mashhad, Khorasan province, to Bandanin in northern Afghanistan. As *dresseri*, but upperparts slightly darker (mid grey, but paler and less bluish than *obscura*), eyestripe less prominent, narrower and barely encompassing eye (but as long), belly and flanks paler (pale pinkish-buff) and contrasting less with creamy throat and breast (though still clearly demarcated), and spots on tail distinct, sometimes forming bars, T6 with large subterminal white spot on outer web. Rather smaller than *dresseri*, close to some *obscura* from northern Iran and Transcaucasia; bill less massive and more compressed laterally. Wing 80–94; bill 23.7–30.2; weight 30–39 g. In eastern Iran (southern Khorasan), southern Afghanistan and NW Pakistan, bill averages slightly longer and heavier, upperparts slightly darker (although not so dark as *obscura* from Kerman and southern Sistan in southern Iran), eyestripe shorter (averages *c.* 26.5 mm behind eye rather than 29–31 mm) and flanks and belly slightly darker and more extensively rufous.

**S. t. iranica** SW central Asia in southern Turkmenistan (and probably neighbouring Khorasan in Iran) east to the Karabil' plateau (where intermediate with nominate *tephronota*); also isolated mountains in the central Kyzylkum desert of Uzbekistan. As nominate *tephronota*, but upperparts paler grey (near *dresseri*), eyestripe shorter, underparts paler (near race *syriaca* of Western Rock) and bill more slender. Smallest race; wing 77–88. Smallest birds (in Kyurendag mountains) barely larger than Western Rock; may intergrade with *obscura* in eastern Elburz mountains. (Introgression with race *rupicola* of Western Rock not impossible, as the two are very close in size and coloration.)

**RELATIONSHIPS** See Western Rock Nuthatch.

**REFERENCES** Cramp & Perrins (1993), Grant (1975), Loskot *et al.* (1991), Roberts (1992), Stepanyan (1990), Vaurie (1950b).

# 19 VELVET-FRONTED NUTHATCH *Sitta frontalis*          Plate 8

This brightly coloured tropical nuthatch is widespread in India and South-East Asia, where it is a familiar member of foraging parties in many types of forest.

**IDENTIFICATION** Length 125 mm (5 in). A medium-small nuthatch. Forehead black, with the remainder of the upperparts violet-blue. The underparts vary from dull beige to pinkish-buff, but generally show a distinct lilac or lavender tone. Bill bright red (blackish in juveniles), iris yellow, eyering pale yellow to orange-red. A very distinctive nuthatch. In Vietnam overlaps with rather similar Yellow-billed Nuthatch, although generally occurs at lower altitudes. In all plumages, easily distinguished by bill coloration (yellow in both adult and juvenile Yellow-billed). The range does not overlap with that of the Sulphur-billed Nuthatch of the Philippines.

**SEX/AGE** Sexes distinct. In all races, the male has a black supercilium behind the eye, lacking in the female. Additionally, the female's underparts average slightly less lilac, more cinnamon or cinnamon-buff (especially on the breast and belly). Juvenile relatively distinct, with the upperparts slightly duller and greyer than the adult's, especially on the crown, nape and rump, the chin and throat duller, and the underparts washed cinnamon-orange or orange-buff, lacking lilac tones (rather different from the adult male, and slightly more orange-buff than the adult female). Notably, the juvenile's undertail-coverts are pale pinkish-buff with fine dark cinnamon-brown bars (the adult has merely diffuse lilac fringes), and its bill blackish. 1st adult as adult.

**VOICE** Noisy. Common calls a single full, hard and slightly 'stony' *chat, chit, chlit* or *chip* and a much thinner and more sibilant *sip, sit* or *tsit* (with many intermediate notes), the former often doubled in a rapid couplet, *chit-chit*, or given in a short rattling series, *chit-chit-chit* or *chit-it-it-it*...; the two notes may be mixed, thus a typical phrase is *chip, chip, sit-sit-sit-sit-sit-sit-sit*, and both variants may be given in flight. The song is a series of *sit* units, 1.5–2 seconds in duration, with the individual notes usually still distinguishable, *sit-sit-sit-sit*...; this may become a fast, hard rattle. Whistler (1949) also mentions a 'short little warble'.

**DISTRIBUTION AND MOVEMENTS** Found in **peninsular India** southeast of a line from Dehra Dun (Uttar Pradesh) to Navsari (Gujarat), especially in the Western and Eastern Ghats and other peninsular hills, but absent from large areas (e.g. the Gangetic Plain and Deccan plateau). Also the **Himalayan foothills** from Kumaon east through **Nepal**, **Sikkim**, **Bhutan** (where first recorded April 1993 in Manas NP: Inskipp & Inskipp 1993b) and **Assam**, and **NE India** in Meghalaya, Nagaland, Manipur and Mizoram. In **Bangladesh** recorded in the northeast, southern and central areas, and resident in **Sri Lanka**. In **SW China**, breeds in western, southern and SE **Yunnan** (south to Xishuangbanna (= near Mengla)), central and southern **Guizhou** and SW **Guangxi**. Found in SW **Guangdong** at Ding Hu Shan (near Gaohe) in October 1992, and first recorded in **Hong Kong** in April 1989 and noted there with increasing regularity since, especially in Tai Po Kau, breeding in 1993. These records in Guangdong and Hong Kong may relate to birds of captive origin (Leven 1993). Widespread in **Myanmar** (**Burma**), **Thailand** (but absent from the central plains and much of northeast), **Laos** and **Vietnam**, but in **Cambodia** recorded only from Bokor and Kirirom. In **Malaysia** breeds south in the **Malay peninsula** to Johore, including Phuket (Thailand) and Penang islands (but absent **Singapore**). Occurs throughout **Borneo**, including the Maratua islands, and in **Indonesia** also on **Java**, **Sumatra**, the Lingga archipelago, Bangka and Simeulue. In the **Philippines**, confined to Palawan and Balabac. Resident, with few indications of altitudinal movements.

**HABITAT** A wide variety of forest types, including tropical rainforest, swamp forest, semi-evergreen, hill evergreen, mixed deciduous, dry dipterocarp, and pine and mixed pine-oak (especially in Burma and Thailand), and in Sumatra noted in pine plantations. In the Western Ghats of SW India, found almost exclusively in evergreen forest. Also mixed bamboo jungle, overgrown rubber plantations and other cultivation with tall trees, shade trees in tea, coffee and cardamom plantations, mangroves and coastal casuarina trees. Optimum habitat the more open evergreen types and 'moist-deciduous'/'mixed deciduous' forest Generally found at low altitudes. In Indian subcontinent, from the plains to c. 1500 m in the Himalayan foothills and the hills of the peninsula and Sri Lanka, occasionally to c. 2200 m (and recorded in Sikkim as high as 1980 m in winter). In Burma found at up to 1830 m, but in the north at 610–915 m only, and in Thailand up to 1800 m, although in the north commonest above 830 m. In

southern China, noted at 340–680 m in Guizhou, 1170 m in SE Yunnan and 1500 m in western Yunnan (and reported to occur at up to 1825 m by Meyer de Schauensee 1984). In Vietnam and Laos found at 180–1350 m, and recorded at Da Lat in southern Vietnam at 930–1350 m. In the Malay peninsula breeds at up to 975 m (and also noted at 1220–1525 m on Gunong Tahan by Hartert 1902), and on Borneo, Sumatra and Java found at up to c. 1500 m.

**POPULATION** Generally common in Indian subcontinent and SE Asia, and may be abundant in optimum habitat, although local in Bangladesh and scarce in Tonkin, Vietnam. Rather less abundant in the Malay peninsula, Sumatra, Java, Borneo and Palawan, although still fairly common; e.g. in Borneo fairly common near the coast and in submontane areas, such as on Mount Kinabalu and in the Kelabit uplands, but scarcer in the intervening lowlands, and common in central Kalimantan. Rare in China (Cheng 1987, but Rothschild 1926 gives ten records for Yunnan, and Wu et al. 1986 list 11 records for Guizhou).

**HABITS** Very active. Found in pairs and small parties (with up to 20 recorded together), and often joins mixed-species foraging flocks. Feeds both on tree trunks and on branches, generally in the upper and middle storeys of tall forest trees, although also feeds in undergrowth and on fallen logs; apparently does not visit the ground. Price (1979) commonly noted vigorous wing-flapping, apparently designed to flush insects from the face of tree trunks. Food insects and spiders.

**BREEDING BIOLOGY** Season April–June in northern India, January–May in the south and Sri Lanka; March–April in northern Burma, February–March in southern Burma, May–June in China, March in northern Thailand, April–August in West Java; nests found mid March in central Annam (Vietnam), February and May in Borneo. No breeding data for Sumatra or the Malay peninsula. Nest placed in a hole in a dead branch or a tree trunk, 1–12 m above ground, although usually below 7 m; may use abandoned woodpecker or barbet holes. The hole selected is usually small and indeed, is often enlarged by the birds themselves, but occasionally a large hole will be reduced or finished with 'masonry' (presumably mud). Nest a pad of moss (often mixed with feathers), lined with fur and feathers. Clutch 4–5 in northern India, 3–4 in southern India and Java, 3–6 in Burma; a clutch of 3 recorded in Borneo. Eggs white, variably but usually rather heavily spotted and blotched brick-red and occasionally purple; 17.2 x 13.2 mm (*S. f. frontalis*). Precise incubation period apparently unknown (Ali 1979 gives 13–14 days, but this may be inference from that of other nuthatches). Both sexes 'partake in parental duties' (Ali 1979) and both sexes recorded feeding young (Nash & Nash 1988).

**DESCRIPTION** *S. f. frontalis* **Adult Male**: *In fresh plumage* (July to about January), lores, forecrown and narrow eyestripe black. Upperparts and lesser and median coverts violet-blue, brighter and paler blue immediately adjacent to the black forecrown. Central tail feathers grey-blue, fringed

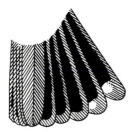

Figure 19.1 Tail of S. f. frontalis.

violet-blue; T2–T6 black, tipped grey-blue and fringed on the outer web violet-blue (T6 fringed grey-blue), T4–T6 with slightly paler subterminal spot on inner web (see figure 19.1). Greater coverts blue-grey with diffuse violet-blue fringes. Alula and primary coverts blackish, smaller feathers of alula and distal two-thirds of primary coverts fringed violet-blue. Tertials grey-blue, bluer on outer web, with concealed blackish stripe along shaft of longest tertial. Secondaries and inner primaries greyish-black, grading to grey-blue submarginally and with fine brighter blue fringes; outer primaries blackish, P3–P4 fringed pale blue inwards of emarginations, P5–P7 fringed pale blue around emarginations. Cheeks dull violet-blue, fading to lavender on ear-coverts and sides of neck. Chin and throat whitish. Breast dull beige, flanks, belly, vent and thighs darker and drabber, although washed lavender; undertail-coverts dull beige, diffusely tipped lavender. Axillaries whitish, fore feathers tipped dull violet-blue; underwing-coverts black, longer under primary coverts and base of primaries whitish. In worn plumage (January–July in southern India), upperparts duller, grey feather bases showing, especially on nape and upper mantle. Flight feathers bleached slightly paler, fringes abraded (but still pale blue fringes on primaries). Underparts slightly duller, paler and less lilac, pale grey-white washed dull buff; when very worn virtually no lilac tones, as feather tips abrade. **Bare Parts**: Iris yellow; eyering dull pale yellow to orange-red; bill red or orange-red, tip of upper mandible brown or blackish; legs and feet dark brown or brown, tinged pinkish or orange, or deep reddish, soles orange-yellow; claws horny-brown. **Adult Female**: As male, but lacks black supercilium, underparts washed cinnamon-buff, lilac tones reduced. **Juvenile**: As adult, but black forecrown slightly duller and more restricted, feathers faintly tipped grey. Upperparts slightly duller, feathers of crown, nape, back and rump mid grey, tipped blue, mantle and scapulars similar but tips broader (thus appear bluer). Ear-coverts washed brownish or greyish. Underparts washed orange-buff, especially on breast and belly; undertail-coverts mid grey, fringed pale pinkish-buff and narrowly tipped cinnamon-brown. Eyestripe as respective sex of adult. Iris brown or vinaceous-grey; bill black, pink at gape and nostrils (may become reddish before post-juvenile moult?). **1st Adult**: As adult. **Measurements**: Wing of male 68.5–83.5, of female 65–83.5; tail of male 36–46, of female 34–46; bill 14.5–18.3; tarsus 14–18.

Weight 8.5–17 g.
**MOULT** Adult post-breeding complete (July–November in Sri Lanka; January, May and June in southern India, late June–September in northern India; late July–early December in northern Thailand). Adult pre-breeding occasional (?), partial, includes at least mantle (April in Tenasserim, whilst a bird collected late January in southern India shows light moult on the upper mantle and is moulting tail feathers; this is presumed pre-breeding). Post-juvenile partial (October in southern India, June–early September in northern Thailand).
**GEOGRAPHICAL VARIATION** Moderate, with five subspecies recognised (note that the form *chienfengensis* from Hainan island is detailed under Yellow-billed Nuthatch, p. 164).

*S. f. frontalis* Continental Asia south in peninsular Thailand to the Isthmus of Kra, central and southern Sumatra, the Lingga archipelago and Bangka (but the inclusion of Sumatra and associated islands is untenable on biogeographic grounds, and these populations may be better placed with *saturatior*). See Description. A slight variation in size, averaging largest in southern India and Sri Lanka, smallest in northern Burma.

*S. f. saturatior* Peninsular Thailand south of the Isthmus of Kra, Malaya, northern Sumatra and Simeulue. Intergrades with nominate *frontalis* in southern Tenasserim. As nominate *frontalis*, but underparts darker and more lilac: chin off-white, throat and remainder of underparts pinkish-buff, washed lilac, in male, cinnamon-buff, washed lilac, in female (slightly less pure lilac than male). Legs and feet brown. Juvenile as juvenile *frontalis*, underparts washed orange-buff. Birds from Simeulue average slightly larger (as some nominate *frontalis* from Sri Lanka; Mees 1986). Wing of male 74–80, of female 71–76; tail of male 37–42, of female 35–39; bill 15–18.2. (Synonymised with nominate *frontalis* by Mees 1986.)

*S. f. corallipes* Borneo and the Maratua islands. As *saturatior*, but legs and feet bright orange-red. Wing of male 70–76, of female 68–75; tail of male 37.5–41, of female 35–38; bill 15.6–18.

*S. f. palawana* Palawan and Balabac, Philippine islands. As nominate *frontalis*, but sex-for-sex the underparts average slightly darker and browner, throat rather less extensively white. Sexes rather similar in underpart coloration: male pinkish-buff, washed lilac (near female nominate *frontalis*), female cinnamon-orange, wearing buffer as lilac feather tips abrade. Legs and feet light brown. Wing of male 74–77, of female 72–75; tail of male 37–40, of female 34–39; bill 15.5–17.7.

*S. f. velata* Temminck (1821). Java. As nominate *frontalis*, but throat more extensively white (although ear-coverts still lilac), underparts of male paler and more washed-out, more pinkish-buff, with reduced lilac and increased grey tones. Female as nominate *frontalis*? Averages c. 2.5 mm shorter-winged. Wing of male 73–79, of female 70–74; tail of male 35–40, of female 35–38; bill 16–17.1.
**RELATIONSHIPS** A distinct tropical nuthatch, with no obvious affinities with any of the temper-

ate groups, except perhaps Beautiful Nuthatch. Shows some similarities to Blue Nuthatch, especially in its bright blue upperparts and colourful orbital skin. For relationships with Yellow-billed and Sulphur-billed Nuthatches, see those species.

**REFERENCES** Ali & Ripley (1983), Leven (1993), Mees (1986).

# 20 YELLOW-BILLED NUTHATCH *Sitta solangiae*                     Plate 8

Although often described as endemic to Vietnam, Chinese ornithologists discovered Yellow-billed Nuthatches breeding on Hainan island in 1963. The relationship between this species and Sulphur-billed Nuthatch of the Philippines has yet to be elucidated.

**IDENTIFICATION** Length 125–135 mm (5–5.5 in). A medium-small to medium-sized nuthatch. Forecrown black, upperparts violet-blue, the nape, ear-coverts and sides of neck contrastingly pale greyish-mauve (as also is the crown in NW Vietnam). Throat off-white; remainder of underparts variably pale greyish-beige, tinged violet in southern Vietnam. Bill, eye and eyering yellow. Similar to Velvet-fronted Nuthatch, but at all times bill yellow. In NW Vietnam crown and nape contrastingly paler and more lilac; in southern Vietnam crown tinged violet-blue with the nape and sides of neck paler and more lilac, forming a pale collar. Overall, the upperparts are contrastingly dark compared with the underparts, Velvet-fronted showing less of a contrast.

**SEX/AGE** Sexes distinct, the male having a broad black eyestripe which is lacking in the female. Little information on the juvenile. The bill is reported to be dull yellow in recently fledged birds on Hainan, although, as with Velvet-fronted, the change from a blackish bill on fledging to adult soft-part coloration may be rapid. 1st adult presumably as adult.

**VOICE** Very similar to that of Velvet-fronted Nuthatch. Calls include *chit*, often doubled or given in a series, *chit-it* or *chit-it-it-it-it-...*. Also *sit*, and the song is a fast *sit-ti-ti-ti-ti-ti-...*, 1–2.5 seconds in duration, slower and slightly lower in pitch towards the end (perhaps faster and more 'whinnying' than the song of Velvet-fronted).

**DISTRIBUTION AND MOVEMENTS** Northern **Vietnam** in the Fan Si Pan range of NW Tonkin, where recorded around Cha Pa; and south Vietnam in south-central Annam on the Da Lat plateau (= 'Langbian Plateau'), where recorded from Mount Bi Doup, Mount Lang Bian, Cong Troi and near Da Lat. Also southern **Hainan island**, **China**, where recorded from Diaoluoshan, Wuzhishan, Bawangling (19° 05' N, 109° 05' E) and Jiangfengling (Chienfengling). There is an unconfirmed report from Vu Quang Nature Reserve in northern Annam, Vietnam (c. 18° 15'N, 105° 20' E; Collar *et al.* 1994). Resident.

**HABITAT** Hill evergreen forest, including relatively open, partially logged areas. In NW Tonkin recorded at c. 1550–2500 m, and in South Annam on the Da Lat plateau at 1450–2100 m. On Hainan, found at 700–900 m at Jiangfengling and 1100 m at Bawangling.

**POPULATION** Apparently rare in NW Vietnam, as the race *solangiae* is known only from the type,

collected at 2500 m at the pass of Loquiho, near Cha Pa, in November 1929 (Delacour & Jabouille 1930), and four birds collected at Cha Pa in January 1939 (Delacour & Greenway 1940). Rather commoner on the Da Lat plateau, South Annam, where small numbers recorded in surveys since 1990. Discovered on Hainan island as recently as 1963 and, although described as rare (Cheng 1987), found to be fairly common in the remaining areas of forest. Observed in April 1988 at Bawangling, a 2100-ha forest reserve, altitude 500–1400 m, in west-central Hainan, comprising good primary forest. In January–February 1989 1–2 were seen on most days at Jiangfengling and 2–6 almost daily at Bawangling (Hornskov 1989). The forests on Hainan are threatened, however, and in 1981 only 2420 km² remained (7.2% of the total land area), although most remaining forest is likely to be at higher altitudes and thus suitable for Yellow-billed Nuthatch. Despite this apparently large area, forest cover declined by 72% between 1949 and 1981, and its future on Hainan is far from secure. Listed as vulnerable in BirdLife International's world checklist of threatened birds (Collar *et al.* 1994).

**HABITS** Similar to that of Velvet-fronted Nuthatch. Found singly or in small groups on Hainan, and in Vietnam in groups of up to five in mixed-species foraging flocks. Food insects.

**BREEDING BIOLOGY** Unknown. On Hainan, observed on 22 April with recently fledged juveniles (active on tree trunks but still being fed by adults).

**DESCRIPTION** *S. s. fortior* **Adult Male**: *In fresh plumage*, lores, forecrown and broad eyestripe (through eye) velvet-black. Crown, nape and upper mantle light greyish-mauve, tips of crown feathers washed violet-blue and whiter feather bases showing, especially in centre of upper mantle. Remainder of upperparts dull violet-blue, with longer uppertail-coverts blackish-grey, tipped violet-blue. Central tail feathers dull violet-blue with a blackish shaft streak; T2–T6 black, T2–T5 fringed violet-blue on outer web, fringes broadening towards base, and tipped dull blue-grey, T6 similarly fringed and tipped dark grey, tips progressively broader towards T6, with a subterminal white spot on inner web, tiny on T2 and moderately well marked on T6 (see figure 20.1). Lesser and median coverts blackish-grey, fringed violet-blue, greater coverts black, broadly fringed violet-blue (dark centres concealed). Alula and primary coverts black, narrowly fringed violet-blue. Tertials dull violet-blue, greyish-black base to inner webs concealed; secondaries and inner primaries black fringed violet-blue, P6–P7 narrowly fringed pale blue around emargination, P3–P5 broadly fringed pale blue inwards of emargination. Cheeks, ear-coverts and sides of neck light greyish-mauve; chin and throat off-white, remainder of underparts pale greyish-beige with a faint violet cast, especially to flanks. Axillaries pale greyish-beige; underwing-coverts sooty-black, base of primaries whitish. *In worn plumage*, underparts presumably duller, whitish feather bases may show, especially on crown and nape (?), flight feathers worn and bleached paler. **Bare Parts**: Iris pale yellow; eyering yellow; bill lemon-yellow or golden-yellow with a small black tip to upper mandible; legs and feet grey. **Adult Female**: As male, but lacks black supercilium (a faint black line may be present behind eye). **Juvenile and 1st Adult**: No information. **Measurements**: Wing of male 81.5, 83, of female 81; tail of male 41, 45; bill 16–17; tarsus 17–18. Weight 14-16 g *(S. f. chienfengensis)*.

Figure 20.1  Tail of S. s. fortior.

**MOULT** Post-breeding complete (a bird from southern Vietnam completing primary moult in early May). Post-juvenile, no information.
**GEOGRAPHICAL VARIATION** Moderate, with three races described.
*S. s. solangiae* NW Tonkin, Vietnam. As *fortior,* but crown paler, more lavender or violet and less blue, showing less contrast with the nape (whitish feather bases not revealed on the nape?), upperparts slightly paler, a greyer blue, underparts more greyish-drab, lacking a violet wash. Rather smaller: wing of male 74, of female 78; tail 47; bill 17, 17; tarsus 19.
*S. s. fortior* South Annam, Vietnam. See Description.
*S. s. chienfengensis* Hainan island. As *fortior,* but underparts lack violet suffusion, and also smaller. As nominate *solangiae,* but upperparts

more greyish-blue (upperparts grey-blue, crown and nape washed purple, mantle tinged lilac-rufous, ear-coverts and sides of neck lilac-rufous), underparts also much paler (lower cheek, chin and throat white; underparts below breast fulvous-rufous, somewhat deepening posteriorly), and white terminal spots on tail feathers less prominent, confined to T4–T6. More extensive dark tip to bill, distal third of upper mandible blackish-brown. Bill longer. Wing of male 70–80, of female 74–79 (juvenile female 66.5); tail of male 40–47, of female 39–45 (juvenile female 34.5); bill ('culmen') 13–17, juvenile 12; tarsus 15.5–19 (Cheng *et al.* 1964).

**RELATIONSHIPS** Sometimes considered conspecific with Velvet-fronted Nuthatch (Delacour 1951 treated it as an altitudinal subspecies of Velvet-fronted, allied with the yellow-billed Philippine forms). Yellow-billed Nuthatch is, however, sympatric with Velvet-fronted in Vietnam, the two species overlapping in range but being altitudinally segregated. In the Fan Si Pan range of NW Tonkin, Yellow-billed has been recorded at 1500–2500 m, and although Velvet-fronted is not known from this locality it has been recorded at up to 1220 m at nearby Pakha (on the eastern shore of the Red River). In South Annam, the two forms occur within a few kilometres of each other on the Da Lat plateau, but at different altitudes, Yellow-billed at 1450–2100 m and Velvet-fronted up to 1350 m in hill evergreen forest on the adjacent Di Linh plateau and slopes leading up to the Da Lat plateau. Apart from the differences in coloration, Yellow-billed may be relatively shorter-winged, longer-billed and longer-tailed than Velvet-fronted. Given the relatively large differences between the two, it seems reasonable to assume that they are reproductively isolated, and thus Yellow-billed Nuthatch deserves full specific status. (An interesting parallel in the Himalayas is the red-billed Blue Magpie, which is replaced at higher altitudes by the very similar Gold-billed Magpie.) The relationship of this species with Sulphur-billed Nuthatch of the Philippines is unclear. Cheng *et al.* (1964) considered that the form *chienfengensis* from Hainan formed a link between the yellow-billed groups of Vietnam and the Philippines, and the most economic treatment may be to unite all the yellow-billed forms in one species, under the oldest available name, *Sitta oenochlamys*.
**REFERENCES** Cheng *et al.* (1964), Delacour & Greenway (1939), Delacour & Jabouille (1930), Harrap (1991), King & Liao Wei-ping (1989), Robson *et al.* (1993a, b).

## 21 SULPHUR-BILLED NUTHATCH *Sitta oenochlamys*  Plate 8

Often treated as subspecies of Velvet-fronted Nuthatch, the yellow-billed Philippine birds may, in fact, be more closely related to Yellow-billed Nuthatch of Vietnam and Hainan island.

**IDENTIFICATION** Length 125 mm (5 in). A medium-small nuthatch. Forecrown black, upper-

parts violet-blue, variably tinged lilac, and in some areas with a paler patch on the nape and sometimes also the upper mantle. Throat off-white, with remainder of the underparts pale buff, variably washed lilac. Overall rather similar to Velvet-fronted Nuthatch, but has a yellow, rather than reddish, bill (although the rather small, pale bill is often difficult to see at any distance), a white spot on the lores and, in most races, a lilac shawl or collar on the nape and upper mantle. Identification is straightforward, as the ranges of the two species do not overlap.

**SEX/AGE** Sexes distinct. Males have a long, thin black supercilium behind the eye, lacking in the female (although the latter have faintly darker sides to the crown), and in all races the female averages slightly more orange-toned on the underparts, with a reduced lilac wash. Juvenile as adult, but underparts more orange, cinnamon-orange or salmon-coloured, and juveniles may lack the pale patch on the nape/upper mantle (?). The bill coloration of recently fledged juveniles is apparently as in the adult (but in specimens, the bill of the juvenile appears dark, with a pale basal quarter to both mandibles and a paler culmen and cutting edges; as in Velvet-fronted, the change to adult soft-part coloration may be rapid). No information on 1st adult.

**VOICE** Very similar to that of Velvet-fronted Nuthatch, and includes a full *chit* and thinner, ringing *sit*, often given in series, *sit-sit-sit-sit...* (these two notes may be more similar to each other than in the corresponding calls of Velvet-fronted, and their delivery in series may average faster). Notably, also has a distinctive high, thin and squeaky *snii* or *sneer* (a 'squeaky toy' call), and a very fast winding rattle, *t-r-r-r-r-r-it* (often combined with *sit-sit-sit-sit-sit* calls), both apparently absent from Velvet-fronted's vocabulary (but recalling Blue Nuthatch).

**DISTRIBUTION AND MOVEMENTS** Endemic to the **Philippines**, where found on the islands of Luzon, Samar, Leyte, Biliran, Cebu, Negros, Guimaras, Panay, Mindanao, Basilan and East Bolod (replaced on Palawan and Balabac by Velvet-fronted Nuthatch). Resident.

**HABITAT** Pine and evergreen forests and forest edge, also clearings, relict patches of forest and secondary growth. Found at up to c. 2600 m.

**POPULATION** Fairly common to common in suitable habitat. Although the rampant forest destruction in the Philippines must have greatly reduced the overall population, this species has a wide habitat tolerance and remains fairly secure, although it may depend upon the presence of mature trees to provide nest sites.

**HABITS** Very active, generally foraging in the upper stratum and canopy of forest trees, investigating loose bark, moss and epiphytes. Found singly, in pairs or in small groups, and often joins mixed-species foraging flocks. Food insects.

**BREEDING BIOLOGY** Little information. Breeding recorded from Cebu in mid June (most Philippine passerines breed in the period April–June). The nest is built 'in hollow trees' (Gonzales & Rees 1988).

**DESCRIPTION** *S. o. apo* **Adult Male:** *In fresh plumage,* forehead and forecrown velvet-black,

*Figure 21. 1 Tail of* S. o. apo

extending behind eye as thin black eyestripe, and crown violet-blue, tinged mauve. Nape and upper mantle deep vinaceous, tinged lilac, lower mantle, scapulars, back and rump violet-blue, tinged grey. Central tail feathers dull violet-blue with dark grey shaft streak; T2–T6 sooty-black, fringed violet-blue and broadly tipped dull violet-blue, the tips progressively broader towards T6, where distal third of feather dull violet-blue; the sooty-black is fully concealed when tail closed (see figure 21.1). Wing-coverts violet-blue, inner webs of greater coverts black, not extending to tip and largely concealed at rest. Alula black, smaller feathers fringed and tipped violet-blue. Primary coverts black, outer web and tip violet-blue. Tertials violet-blue, tinged grey, with extensive black streak along shaft and inner web of longer two feathers, largely concealed at rest. Secondaries greyish-black with broad violet-blue fringes and greyer tips. Primaries sooty-black, inner primaries finely fringed lilac-blue on distal portion, quickly broadening into duller grey-blue outer webs and tips; outer primaries variably fringed violet-blue on basal half. Lores and fore cheeks pale buff, grading to pale lilac on ear-coverts and sides of neck (which merges at rear into the upper mantle to form a pale collar). Chin and throat off-white to pale fleshy, merging into vinaceous-buff underparts, strongly tinged lilac on belly, vent and flanks; thighs as belly. Axillaries vinaceous-buff, underwing-coverts sooty-black, base of primaries white. *In worn plumage,* no information; presumably loses lilac wash on underparts, and pale feather bases may show on nape and upper mantle. **Bare Parts:** Iris bright greenish-yellow to orange-yellow; orbital skin chrome-yellow or greenish-yellow; bill greenish-yellow; legs, feet and claws olive-green to brown. **Adult Female:** As male, but lacks black eyestripe, although sides of crown slightly darker and bluer behind eye, giving faint darker eyestripe (sooty, and most clear-cut, at rear). **Juvenile and 1st Adult:** See Sex/Age. **Measurements:** Wing of male 77–80, of female 75–77; tail 38–42; bill 17.3–19.1; tarsus 15–16. Weight 16.3 g, 16.4 g (*S. o. isarog*).

**MOULT** Adult post-breeding complete (August on Leyte). Post-juvenile partial, includes median coverts, but probably not greater coverts, tertials and tail? (August on Leyte).

**GEOGRAPHICAL VARIATION** Moderate, with six races currently recognised, with a cline of

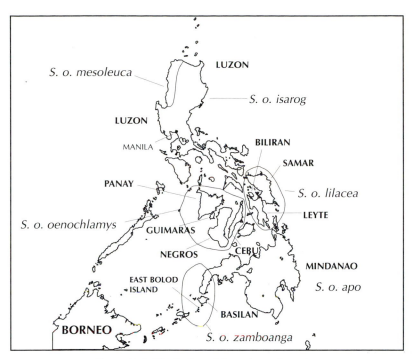

*Figure 21.2 Distribution of the various subspecies.*

increasing colour saturation and dominance of lilac tones in the plumage running north to south through the islands.

**S. o. mesoleuca** NW Luzon (western Cordillera mountains). The palest subspecies. As *apo*, but ear-coverts violet-blue; lilac shawl on nape and upper mantle fainter, pale pinkish-buff, washed lilac, often with a very pale, even whitish, centre; underparts much paler and whiter, pale pinkish-buff with no lilac tinge. Wing of male 72.5–79, of female 69–78; tail 38–41; bill 17.5–18.6.

**S. o. isarog** Southern and central Luzon north to the Manila area and through the Sierra Madre to extreme NE Luzon. As *apo*, but ear-coverts violet-blue; lilac shawl much reduced, nape and upper mantle merely slightly greyer with a faint lilac wash. Underparts of male near *apo*, vinaceous-buff and washed lilac (*contra* Rand & Rabor 1967), much darker and more lilac-tinged than *mesoleuca*; also, pale markings on nape and upper neck reduced and more pinkish compared with *mesoleuca*. Wing of male 74–79, of female 75; tail 38.5–41; bill 18–19.5.

**S. o. oenochlamys** Cebu, Guimaras, Panay, Negros. Male as *apo* but ear-coverts violet-blue, shawl paler and more extensive but slightly less lilac-toned (pale buff feather bases more extensively revealed, although lacks whitish centre to nape of *mesoleuca*), underparts more orange-tinged, pale cinnamon-orange, lightly washed lilac, with chin and centre of throat paler and whiter (similarly much more orange-toned than *isarog*, but wearing paler and thus closer to *mesoleuca*). Wing of male 73–79, of female 69–77; tail 39–44; bill 16.6–19.1.

**S. o. lilacea** Samar, Leyte, Biliran. As *apo*, but ear-coverts lilac-blue, upperparts average slightly darker, with more extensive greyish-lilac wash, underparts average slightly darker and more cinnamon and more distinctly washed lilac (as *zamboanga*, but perhaps averages slightly more cinnamon and less lilac). Slightly shorter-winged than *apo*. Wing of male 72–78, of female 70–72; tail 37–41; bill 17.7–18.9.

**S. o. apo** Mindanao (except Zamboanga peninsula). See Description.

**S. o. zamboanga** Western Mindanao on Zamboanga peninsula, Basilan, East Bolod island. Poorly marked. As *apo*, but averages slightly darker; upperparts marginally darker, with similar vinaceous-lilac shawl, underparts average darker and more lilac (deep vinaceous, washed lilac, especially on breast, belly and flanks; marginally the darkest race). Very similar to *lilacea*, but underparts marginally darker and more lilac, ear-coverts lilac (not blue), and is slightly longer-winged. Wing of male 72–82, of female 70–75; tail 39–42; bill 15–18.3.

**RELATIONSHIPS** Often treated as conspecific with Velvet-fronted Nuthatch, most recently by Dickinson *et al.* (1991). The yellow-billed birds of the Philippines may, however, be more closely related to the Yellow-billed Nuthatch of Hainan and Vietnam (a biogeographic connection between Hainan and the island of Mindoro in the Philippines has already been established: see Tan *et al.* 1988). The Philippine birds are thus treated here as a separate species pending a full investigation of the relationships of the various red- and yellow-billed members of the Velvet-fronted Nuthatch complex, following Gonzales & Rees (1988) and Sibley & Monroe (1990).

**REFERENCES** Dickinson *et al.* (1991), McGregor (1909–1910), Parkes (1973), Rand & Rabor (1960, 1967).

# 22 BLUE NUTHATCH *Sitta azurea*                                       Plate 7

This bright tropical nuthatch is confined to Malaya, Sumatra and Java, and is the only member of the family to have a distribution centred on the Sunda Shelf.

**IDENTIFICATION** Length 135 mm (5.25 in). Medium-sized. Cap black, with a conspicuous broad bluish-white eyering. Upperparts violet-blue in Java, but rather duller in Malaya and Sumatra, where blackish with merely a tinge of violet-blue. Wing-coverts and flight feathers pale blue, neatly outlined with black, the greater coverts rather elongated and 'drooping'. Throat and breast whitish, variably washed buff, belly and vent blackish, with the undertail-coverts conspicuously pale blue-grey. Bill, legs and feet pale blue-white. A very distinctive nuthatch, although in all but the best conditions it appears blackish with a white throat and breast. The eyering and pale blue markings on the wing-coverts and flight feathers are, however, always prominent.

**VOICE** Rather varied, and similar to that of Velvet-fronted and especially Sulphur-billed Nuthatches. Common calls are a mellow *tup* or *tip*, an abrupt *whit*, a thin, sibilant *sit* and a fuller, harder and more emphatic *chit*. When excited, the *sit* and *chit* notes are often given in short, rapid repetitions, *chi-chit, chit-chit-chit* or *chir-ri-rit*; this may become extended into a fast series, accelerating into a staccato trilling *tititititititik*, or even become a winding rattle *tr-r-r-r-r-r-t*. Also gives thin, squeaking *zhe* and *zhe-zhe* and a nasal *snieu* or *kneu* (a 'squeaky toy' call).

**SEX/AGE** Sexes similar, although Kuroda (1936) states that the female has fractionally duller upperparts. Juvenile marginally distinct, very similar to the adult, but with the crown and ear-coverts slightly duller, tinged brown, the belly dull blackish and the undertail-coverts irregularly fringed and tipped creamy-white (Kuroda 1936; Robinson 1928). More importantly, the juvenile's bill is blackish, with a variable fleshy-pink base. No information on 1st adult.

**DISTRIBUTION AND MOVEMENTS** In Malaysia found in the **Malay peninsula** in the Larut Hills (Perak), the Main Range south to Ulu Langat (Selangor), on the isolated massifs of Gunong Benom (Pahang), Gunong Rabong (Kelantan) and Gunong Tahan (Kelantan/Pahang) and in the East Coast Range on Gunong Padang. In **Indonesia** breeds in **Sumatra** throughout the Bukit Barisan (central mountain range), from the Gayo and Batak Highlands (Aceh and Utara provinces) in the north to Mount Dempu (Selatan province) in the south. Found in both East and West **Java**. Resident.

**HABITAT** Lower montane forest. In Malaya recorded from *c.* 1070 m to the summits (i.e. a

maximum of 2186 m), in Sumatra at 900–2400 m, and in Java at 915–2745 m, although noted as also occurring rarely in the lowlands of Java by MacKinnon (1988).

**POPULATION** Fairly common in Malaya and Java, and common in Sumatra, being very common on Kerinci Peak (Robinson & Kloss 1918).

**HABITS** Restless and rather tame, the species is often found in small parties, and very frequently associates with mixed-species foraging flocks. Feeds in the middle and upper storeys of tall forest, although sometimes also in smaller trees. Food insects.

**BREEDING BIOLOGY** Poorly known. Season in West Java April–July. Few breeding data from the Malay peninsula, although recently fledged juveniles observed in late June. A record of an adult feeding juveniles on 9 May in Sumatra. The nest is placed in a small hole in a tree. Clutch 3–4: eggs dirty white or pale fleshy, heavily speckled with rufous-brown with greyish-lavender underlying markings; *c.* 19.3 x 13.4 mm.

**DESCRIPTION** *S. a. expectata* **Adult**: *In fresh plumage* (about August–April), crown, nape and ear-coverts black, feathers of nape thick and velvety. Mantle, scapulars and back blackish-grey, tinged deep violet-blue, palest and most violet on upper border of mantle; rump more intensely violet. Uppertail-coverts cobalt-blue. Central tail feathers sky-blue with black shafts and narrow sooty-black tips; T2–T6 sooty-black with sky-blue fringes and tips, broadest on T6 (approximately a third of the feather), and extreme tip black on T6 (see figure 22.1). Lesser coverts dull violet-blue, fringed blackish. Median coverts elongated, sky-blue and tinged violet, with blue-black fringes and bluer tips. Greater coverts greatly elongated, sky-blue, fringed and tipped black. Alula black, primary coverts black with irregular dark sky-blue subterminal markings. Innermost tertial black with

*Figure 22.1 Tail of* S. a. expectata.

168

sky-blue shaft streak, central tertial sky-blue with broad black fringes (except basal half of outer web), outermost tertial sky-blue with narrow black tip to outer web and concealed broad black shaft streak on inner web. Secondaries black, very broadly fringed sky-blue (except at tip). Primaries sooty-black, P6–P10 fringed sky-blue on distal part of outer web, with subterminal sky-blue patch on inner web of P6–P8; P5 fringed sky-blue distally of emargination, P4 fringed sky-blue around emargination, P3 fringed sky-blue inwards of emargination (P4–P3 with iridescent pale blue fringes near tip). Chin, throat, sides of neck and belly white, tinged buff. Lower belly, vent and rear flanks sooty-black with faint violet tinge. Undertail-coverts dull sky-blue. Thighs sooty-black. Axillaries sooty-black, tipped whitish; underwing-coverts sooty-black with contrasting white patch at base of primaries. *In worn plumage* (May–August), underparts whiter, blackish feather bases may show. **Bare Parts:** Iris white to greenish-yellow; orbital skin bluish grey-white to greenish-white; bill pale lavender, tinged green, black at tip; legs and feet pale lavender, tinged green; claws slaty or black. **Juvenile:** See Sex/Age. **1st Adult:** No information. **Measurements:** Wing of male 75–83, of female 75–80; tail of male 41–45, of female 39.5–46; bill 16.1–17.6; tarsus 15–18. Weight: no information.
**MOULT** Adult post-breeding complete (March–April in Java, August in Malaya; a bird

from Sumatra in body moult on 6 June may be a 1st adult). Adult pre-breeding incomplete, includes throat, breast and mantle (*expectata* February–March, *azurea* March–April; Banks 1978). No information on the post-juvenile moult.
**GEOGRAPHICAL VARIATION** Moderately well marked, with variation in the colour of the upperparts, breast and vent. Birds from Java are distinctly bluer on the upperparts than those from Malaya or Sumatra. Three races recognised.
    *S. a. expectata* Malay peninsula and Sumatra. See Description.
    *S. a. azurea* East Java. As *expectata*, but upperparts bluer (violet-blue, washed with grey), contrasting strongly with the black cap; vent, rear flanks and thighs with distinct violet tinge. Wing 77–80; bill 15.3–17.2.
    *S. a. nigriventer* West Java. As *azurea*, but breast variably but usually distinctly washed buff in fresh plumage (February), paler when worn (about April, when as *expectata/azurea*), vent faintly washed violet (as *expectata*). Wing 77–85; bill 16–17.7.
**RELATIONSHIPS** A member of a tropical group of nuthatches which also includes Velvet-fronted, Yellow-billed and Sulphur-billed, but the relationship of Blue Nuthatch to this group, and to the various Holarctic nuthatches, is unclear.
**REFERENCES** Kuroda (1936), Medway & Wells (1976), Robinson (1928).

# 23 GIANT NUTHATCH *Sitta magna*                  Plate 3

The largest of the nuthatches, this striking species is a pine-forest specialist in South-East Asia and southern China, where it is endangered by forest destruction.

**IDENTIFICATION** Length 195 mm (7.75 in). Very large and comparatively long-tailed. Crown, nape and upper mantle light grey, variably streaked black and enclosed by broad black eye-stripes which extend to the sides of the mantle; in profile, birds may even appear to have a black hood. The remainder of the upperparts are contrastingly darker bluish-grey. Cheeks and throat off-white, underparts pale grey, variably washed cinnamon, undertail-coverts rufous with large whitish spots or scallops. Large size distinctive, but, when this is not obvious, confusion possible with Chestnut-vented Nuthatch. Giant has much broader black eyestripes, encompassing the crown, nape and upper mantle, which are considerably paler than the remainder of the upperparts, while the underparts lack contrasting rufous rear flanks.
**SEX/AGE** Sexes differ. The male has a deep black eyestripe (faintly glossed blue) and off-white cheeks and throat, with the remainder of underparts pale to light grey with a slight buff tinge on the centre of the belly and vent. The female has a duller eyestripe, the nape and upper mantle faintly washed buff, the lower mantle paler, greyer and less blue (thus showing slightly less contrast with

the nape) and, most obviously, buffer underparts, with the flanks, belly and vent washed cinnamon. Note that both sexes can show blackish streaking of variable intensity on the forehead and crown. Juveniles resemble adult females, but have the crown mealy, the upperparts greyer and less blue, a duller eyestripe, warm brown fringes to the tertials and greater coverts, and the flight feathers fresh when those of adult are worn or moulting. Juveniles with short-grown bills appear rather blunt-billed.
**VOICE** Commonest call, repeated frequently whilst foraging, a distinctive chuntering motif comprising three harsh notes rapidly repeated, and variously transcribed *gd-da-da*, *dig-er-up* or even *get-it-up*, distinctly corvine in character and strongly recalling the chatter of a Common Magpie. It may be elaborated into a slightly more melodic and more structured (less chattering) motif, *kid-der-ku* or *ge-de-ku*, with the last note louder, more ringing and less harsh, or become a harsh, repeated *gu-drr, gu-drr, gu-drr* (recalling a gamebird). Also gives a *naa*, like a toy trumpet, while a single, clear, piping or bell-like *kip*, or *keep* note, repeated at irregular intervals (and reminiscent of a loud tree frog), may be the song.

**DISTRIBUTION AND MOVEMENTS** Breeds in SE **Myanmar** (**Burma**) from the Mogok hills south through the Shan States (west to the Menetaung range (near Myinkyado) and Kalaw, and east to Loi Mwe and the Mekong valley), to Mount Nattaung in northern Karen. In **SW China** found in southernmost **Sichuan**, southern and western **Yunnan** (north to Lijiang and the Yulongxue Shan, Dali, Shuangbai and Mile, and south to Longpeng and Xishuangbanna (= near Mengla); presumably also adjacent northern Laos), and also southwesternmost **Guizhou** (Xingyi, near Qianxinan). In **Thailand** confined to the northwest, where recorded localities include Doi Ang Khang, Doi Pha Hom Pok, Doi Chiang Dao, Doi Khun Tan, Lum Nam Pai, Mae Hong Son and Doi Inthanon(but see also Population). Resident, with no evidence of altitudinal movements.

**HABITAT** Closely associated with pines. In NW Thailand, found in open hill evergreen forest of oak-chestnut where stands of tall mature Khasi Pine are frequent, usually on the drier ridgetops. It may forage in relatively open country, moving from one small tree to the next. Generally found at moderate to high elevations. In Thailand recorded at 1200–1800 m, in Burma at 1220 m to at least 1830 m in the Shan States and at 1680 m in Karen. For China, Cheng (1987) gives 1000–2000 m and Meyer de Schauensee (1984) 1350 m plus, but all records traced for Yunnan fall between 2500 m (August) and 3350 m (May); recorded in Guizhou at 1250 m.

**POPULATION** Described as not rare in the Southern Shan States by Bingham (1903) and not uncommon in eastern Burma by Smythies (1986), but information on its current status in Burma is lacking. Rare in China, with recent records only from Lijiang, Yunnan. Local and uncommon in northern Thailand, where the favoured habitat of open hill evergreen forest with stands of pine has been largely destroyed by shifting cultivators ('hill

*Figure 23.1  Distribution of Giant Nuthatch, with a selection of specific localities. The species is closely associ-ated with pines and a region that has suffered dramatic deforestation, and is listed as vulnerable in Collar et al. (1994).*

tribes'); the remaining areas of undisturbed forest are found above 1800 m, that is *above* the altitudinal limit there of Giant Nuthatch. In addition, pines may be selectively cut for firewood. It has apparently disappeared from at least one protected area (Doi Suthep-Pui NP, where present in the 1960s), although the reasons for this are unclear. Similar threats undoubtedly exist in both Burma and China, and the species is listed as vulnerable in BirdLife International's world checklist of threatened birds (Collar *et al.* 1994).

**HABITS** Usually found singly or in pairs. A conspicuous species, with loud call notes. Flight over short distances level and straight, with whirring wingbeats, the broad butterfly-like wings conspicuous as it drops from one branch to another. Over longer distances, flight dipping and woodpecker-like. Generally not so restless as the smaller nuthatches, but behaviour otherwise similar, and frequently adopts the characteristic head-down pose. Tail may be half-cocked. Forages largely in pines, and also recorded feeding actively on insects on the limbs of trees, rather than on the trunk (Wickham 1929). No other information on diet.

**BREEDING BIOLOGY** Poorly known. In the Southern Shan States, Burma, a nest found on 4 April contained three 'half-fledged' young: it was sited in a natural hole in a tree trunk *c.* 2 m above ground; barely large enough to admit the adult birds, the entrance hole had been 'rounded off slightly by the parent bird ... and opened skywards'; there was no mud plastering, and the nest was a pad of material similar to that used by other nuthatches (Livesey 1933). A nest found on 8 April in NW Thailand contained three young, and was sited in a hollow oak about 8 m tall, with the entrance about 3 m above the ground where the trunk diameter was 25 cm (Round 1983).

**DESCRIPTION** *S. m. magna* **Adult Male**: In fresh plumage (May to about January), forehead black, variably streaked light grey, crown light grey, variably streaked black; on some individuals, forehead and crown may be almost solidly black. Nape and upper mantle (enclosed by eyestripes) light to pale grey, often paler than crown, sharply demarcated at rear from mid blue-grey lower mantle, back and scapulars; rump mid grey, uppertail-coverts mid to pale grey. Central tail feathers grey-brown with a blue cast; T2–T3 blackish-grey, tipped dark blue-grey, T4–T5 similar but pale tips broader and subterminal white spot on inner web, inner web of T6 blackish-grey with subterminal white spot and dark grey tip, outer web white, tipped mid grey (see figure 23.2). Lesser and median coverts dark grey, fringed blue-grey, broadest on lesser coverts. Alula and primary coverts blackish-grey, fringed blue-grey, outer web of largest feather of alula whitish. Greater coverts and flight feathers blackish grey-brown, outer webs of tertials and inner greater coverts dull blue-grey, outer greater coverts fringed blue-grey and tipped pale grey, secondaries fringed and tipped mid grey, inner primaries fringed mid grey and tipped pale grey, outer primaries fringed paler on basal half (near-whitish on P3-P4) and tipped

*Figure 23.2 Tail of* S. m. magna

whitish. Broad eyestripe from nostrils to sides of mantle deep black, slightly glossy. Cheeks, ear-coverts, chin and throat off-white, sides of neck and remainder of underparts pale to light grey, with slight buff tinge on centre of belly and vent. Undertail-coverts rufous, broadly tipped white; thighs cinnamon. Axillaries pale grey underwing-coverts black, longest under primary coverts and diagonal stripe on base of primaries contrastingly whitish. *In worn plumage* (January–May), whitish feather bases show on nape and upper mantle, pale fringes on wings abrade, underparts very slightly buffer. **Bare Parts**: Iris brown or hazel-brown; bill black, basal half of lower mandible paler, bluish-white to bluish-lilac; legs and feet dull greenish-slaty, greenish-brown or pale yellowish-brown; claws dark horn, dark brown or dull greenish-slaty. **Adult Female**: As male, but nape and upper mantle faintly washed buff, lower mantle slightly paler, greyer and less bluish (the upper and lower mantle therefore showing slightly less contrast). Eyestripe blackish-grey, averaging paler, especially in front of the eye, and generally glossy only at rear. Throat slightly buffer, not so pure white, underparts washed cinnamon, especially on flanks, centre of belly and vent. **Juvenile**: As female, but crown mid grey with pale drab-grey feather centres and narrow dark fringes. Upperparts greyer and less blue, eyestripe duller, dark grey. Tertials and greater coverts fringed warm brown. Bill shorter (*c.* 27 mm). **Measurements**: Wing of male 115–121.5, of female 115–119; tail of male 58–64, of female 58–63; bill of male 29.1–33.1, of female 29.5–32.5; tarsus 19–22. Weight 36–47 g (*S. m. ligea*).

**MOULT** Adult post-breeding complete (in advanced primary moult in early May). Adult pre-breeding occasional (?), incomplete, includes throat and nape (November–December). Post-juvenile, no information.

**GEOGRAPHICAL VARIATION** Slight, two races recognised.

*S. m. magna* Burma and NW Thailand (perhaps also SW Yunnan?, and presumably intergrades with *ligea*). See Description.

*S. m. ligea* SW China. As nominate *magna*, but bill averages *c.* 4 mm shorter and laterally more slender. Wing of male 111–117, of female 109–117; bill of male 25.9–29.2, of female *c.* 23–28.2.

**RELATIONSHIPS** Unclear. Sibley & Monroe (1990) place it between Blue and Beautiful

Nuthatches, but its affinities seem to be with the Palearctic Eurasian Nuthatch group, rather than with these brightly coloured, predominantly tropical species.

**REFERENCES** Deignan (1938), Livesey (1933), Round (1983, 1988).

## 24 BEAUTIFUL NUTHATCH *Sitta formosa*    Plate 7

Aptly named, this stunning nuthatch is rare and little known. Almost the entire range is in politically sensitive and largely inaccessible areas and, given the scale of forest destruction in NE India and Burma (especially at middle altitudes), its long-term survival must be cause for special concern.

**IDENTIFICATION** Length 165 mm (6.5 in). A large nuthatch. Crown and mantle black, streaked pale blue-white, scapulars, back and rump pale blue. Median and greater coverts black, tipped white to form narrow wingbars. Flight feathers black, variably fringed pale blue. Supercilium, cheeks and throat buff-white with an irregular dark eyestripe behind the eye, remainder of underparts cinnamon-orange. Large size, black upperparts with brilliant blue and white streaks and cinnamon-orange underparts distinctive. In flight, the white patch at the base of the primaries, contrasting with the blackish underwing, is conspicuous.
**SEX/AGE** Sexes similar. Juvenile similar to adult (see Description).
**VOICE** Almost unknown. Low and sweet in tone (Baker 1922). A typical nuthatch call, though less harsh than that of Eurasian Nuthatch (Meinertzhagen 1927).
**DISTRIBUTION AND MOVEMENTS** Found in **NE India** in **Darjeeling** (West Bengal), old localities including Rangiroon and Tiger hill, but no recent records, **Sikkim** (Rangpo), **Bhutan** (one recent record: Collar *et al.* 1994), **Arunachal Pradesh** in the 'Bhutia foothills' on the borders of Bhutan, around the Bhareli valley in Eagles Nest WS (Sesni) and Pakhui WS (Sessa) (Singh 1994), the Dafla hills, Subansiri district, Abor and Mishmi hills (including the Etalin-Malinye track, Singh 1994), and Namdapha NP in Tirap (Anon. 1994), **Nagaland**, **Manipur**, **Meghalaya** in the Khasi hills, and **Assam** in the North Cachar hills (Haflong and Barail range). Recorded in **Myanmar** (**Burma**) in the Upper Chindwin (once on Mount Sarameti), northern Chin hills (although occurrence here possibly doubtful according to Ticehurst 1939b), and apparently absent central Chin hills, including Mount Victoria), Arakan Yoma (several records from the border between Thayetmyo and Minbu districts), Kachin (the Nmai Hka drainage from Launggyaung and The Triangle north to the Tamai valley), and the Southern Shan States (one record Salween-Mekong watershed, east of Mong Hang). Although stated to occur in the Chittagong region by Ali & Ripley (1983), there are no definite records for **Bangladesh** (Thompson *et al.* 1993). In **Laos** found once in the north at Phu Kobo, just south of Xieng-Khouang, Tranninh, in February, and in central Laos 'good numbers' were recorded in 1994 from Nakai-Nam Theun reserve southeast of Nape (Poole 1994). One record from **China**, in April in the Ailao Shan in SE Yunnan (Meyer de Schauensee 1984 states that it has been recorded in NW Yunnan, north of 28° N and west of the Salween, i.e. adjacent to Nmai Hka drainage of NE Burma, but no records can be traced from this area). Single records also from northern **Thailand** (Doi Pha Hom Pok, January 1986) and northern **Vietnam**, where two were collected in February at Cha Pa in NW Tonkin; may be a rare winter visitor in these areas, but possibly resident, although rare and overlooked (e.g. recorded in February 1901 from eastern Burma 'east of Mong Hang', on the same massif as Doi Pha Hom Pok in Thailand). Resident, with some seasonal altitudinal movements.
**HABITAT** Dense evergreen, semi-evergreen and hill evergreen forest, although in northern Burma recorded in open country with scattered trees (Smythies 1949). In NE India, said to summer in the range 1500–2100 m, perhaps to 2400 m (Ali & Ripley 1983), and reported to breed in North Cachar and the Khasi hills at c. 1525–1890 m (Baker 1907, 1932). May move to lower altitudes in winter, when recorded at 335–2135 m: thus noted at 335 m at Rangpo in Sikkim and 1950 m at Rangiroon, Darjeeling (both December), and in Arunachal Pradesh at 460 m in the Bhutia foothills in August, at 1300 m in Eagles Nest WS in April, 1525 m in the Dafla hills in April, 1675 m in the Mishmi hills (December/January), and c. 600–800 m in Tirap in February, with an undated record at 2135 m at Subansiri. In Burma, recorded from 975–1830 m: in the southwest in the Arakan Yoma at c. 1525 m; on Mount Sarameti at 1580 m in December; in the northeast in Kachin at 975 m, 1370 m (April: breeding?) and 1030 m (December); in 'Upper Burma' at 975 m (January), and in the Southern Shan States at 2135 m. For China, Meyer de Schauensee (1984) gives a range of 1350–1975 m (but see Distribution and Movements above), and in Laos recorded at c. 2000 m in Tranninh and at 950–1700 m in Nakai-Nam Theun reserve, whilst the single record for Thailand was at 2290 m.
**POPULATION** Very rare and local throughout its range. The species has undoubtedly been affected by forest destruction: for example, in Darjeeling most historical localities are now deforested or severely degraded. However, it has always been considered rare, and the reasons for this 'natural' scarcity are obscure; it may have very specialised habitat needs. Listed in Birdlife International's world checklist of threatened birds (Collar *et al.* 1994).
**HABITS** Little known. Found singly, in pairs or in

parties of 4–5, often in association with mixed-species foraging flocks. Usually forages high in tall trees draped in mosses, lichens, orchids and other epiphytes. Variously described as the shyest and most elusive of all the nuthatches (Baker 1922–30; Smythies 1986) and not shy (Ali 1962). Actions typical of a nuthatch, although slower and more deliberate. Flight fast.

**BREEDING BIOLOGY** Poorly known. Season in NE India (Khasi and north Cachar hills) April–May. Nest placed in a hole in a tree 2–8 m above the ground; recorded from oaks and live and dead rhododendrons, as well as 'tall forest trees'. The nest itself a base of leaves and bark chips lined with a pad of fur (especially that of the Bamboo Rat). Entrance hole reduced with clay masonry when too large. Clutch 4–6: eggs white with small dark red specks and spots; 20.8 x 15.3 mm.

**DESCRIPTION** **Adult**: *In fresh plumage* (September to about March), upperparts from forehead to mantle black, feathers of forehead finely tipped off-white, feathers of crown, nape and upper mantle tipped lilac-white, violet-blue or cornflower-blue (often white on nape and upper mantle), forming streaks. Scapulars, back, rump and uppertail-coverts sky-blue, longest uppertail-coverts sometimes tipped white; black centres and grey feather bases may show as grey mottling and the odd black spot. Central tail feathers sky-blue, washed grey, with a black central stripe (not reaching tip); T2–T6 black, tipped grey-blue and fringed flaxflower-blue, tips broader towards T6 but fringes reduced towards outer tail feathers, very narrow and restricted to distal half of feather on T5; T4–T6 with white subterminal spot on inner web (see figure 24.1). Lesser coverts flaxflower-blue, median coverts black, basally mid grey, fringed white (fringes tinged blue on outer web). Greater coverts black, basally sky-blue with grey wash, tipped white with very fine blue fringe. Alula black. Primary coverts black, fringed violet-blue. Flight feathers black, tertials broadly fringed and tipped dull grey-blue, extreme fringe on inner two white; secondaries fringed sky-blue; primaries fringed violet-blue (confined to basal half on outer primaries). Lores and supercilium off-white, variably washed cinnamon-orange and with some

*Figure 24.1 Tail.*

black streaking; irregular dark eyestripe behind eye. Chin, throat and ear-coverts off-white, sides of neck and remainder of underparts cinnamon-orange, deepest on vent and flanks, paler and buffer on under tail-coverts. Thighs sooty-brown. Axillaries dark grey, narrowly fringed grey-buff; underwing-coverts black, with contrasting diagonal white stripe at base of primaries. *In worn plumage*, little different. Streaking on head slightly less clear-cut, underparts slightly paler (?). **Bare Parts**: Iris reddish-brown to dark brown; bill black, whitish at base of lower mandible; legs and feet yellowish-brown, olive-brown or greenish-horn. **Juvenile**: Poorly known. Tentative differences from adult include streaks on mantle usually blue rather than white, primary coverts more narrowly fringed blue, and underparts rather paler and whiter, especially on breast. **1st Adult**: No information. **Measurements**: Wing of male 98–109, of female 97–100; tail of male 48–60, of female 52–56; bill 20–24.9; tarsus 19–22. Weight: no information.

**MOULT** Adult post-breeding complete (one bird just completing in December). Post-juvenile partial, includes variable number of tail feathers (August–November).

**GEOGRAPHICAL VARIATION** None.

**RELATIONSHIPS** Obscure. The lustrous blue coloration may hint at an affinity with Velvet-fronted and Blue Nuthatches, but the east Himalayan centre of distribution and the unique plumage pattern militate against this.

**REFERENCES** Ali & Ripley (1983), Baker (1922, 1932–34), Smythies (1949, 1986).

# 25 WALLCREEPER *Tichodroma muraria*         **Plate 10**

One of the most spectacular birds in the world, this species is aptly named the 'rock flower' in Chinese. Often nesting in inaccessible mountain retreats, it is a 'Red Letter' bird whenever seen, but the details of its distribution remain to be worked out, especially in the east.

**IDENTIFICATION** Total length 165 mm (6.5 in). Bill long, slender and decurved. Upperparts mid grey, tail black, tipped grey, with whiter subterminal spots at the corners. Most of wing-coverts and base of secondaries and inner primaries red, with large white spots on the outer primaries. Throat extensively black, and underparts grey on breeding males, but underparts otherwise whitish.

Unmistakable. Foraging birds constantly flick their wings open to reveal the red patches, and in the desultory, fluttering, jerky flight the markings are fully revealed on its long, broad, butterfly-like wings. Wallcreepers may sometimes be seen flying high across mountain valleys or over passes, either on migration or when moving from one precipice to another distant cliff. Rather agile in flight around cliffs and pinnacles, whilst its jerky, hopping gait on rock faces recalls that of a nuthatch, and unlike treecreepers it does not use its tail for support.

**SEX/AGE** Sexes seasonally distinct. In breeding plumage, the male has a large black bib, whilst the female has a variable dusky spot on the lower throat, occasionally as extensive as the male's bib, but sometimes absent. The sexes are similar in non-breeding plumage, with a whitish throat and breast. Juvenile distinct, similar to the non-breeding adult, but with the underparts more uniformly grey, lacking contrast between the bib and belly, and a straighter bill. 1st adult non-breeding very similar to adult non-breeding, showing at best only slight moult contrasts; the crown and bib may be tinged with buff and the lores paler, but 1st adults are not identifiable in the field.

**VOICE** During the breeding season, contact call a short, quiet, chirping whistled *tseeoo, tschö* or *tschju* (recalling Eurasian Tree Sparrow), given by foraging birds and also by the male when offering food to the female or by adults to nestlings. Also gives a short, thin, chirruping whistle, *tuee* or *tuweehtt*. Year-round, in aggressive encounters, uses *chuit dweeoo* and other whistles, rising or falling in pitch. The male's full song, given May–July, is an ascending series of 4–5 clear, piping whistled units in a gradually slowing sequence, the individual notes sometimes slightly rising in pitch, *zee-zee-zee-zee-zwee*, followed by a prolonged (c. 1 second), lower-pitched and very quiet note, given only in full song. The whole phrase lasts c. 3.5–4 seconds, but often delivers incomplete versions, quieter and frequently missing the last note or comprising 3–4 whistles, *ziziz-itui, ti tiu treeh* or *tiu-tueh-tee-ü* (such versions may be given in flight and are used outside the breeding season). Sometimes weak, and in the distance or against loud background noise such as rushing water only the highest note of the song may be audible. At other times, the mountain acoustics help the song to sound loud and powerful. The female's song is similar, although a little shorter, less emphatic and sometimes faster. Other 'songs' comprise a short, very quiet introductory note and then prolonged rising and falling whistles, *pu wheeer teeu, pu wheeer teeu...*(or *tu ruuee zeeeeeu*, the last two notes recalling a Common Starling in tone). A variety of other phrases have been noted, e.g. high, clear, ringing, partly trilled notes, uttered singly or in twos and threes; *toy; toy-tsee; toi-tsee-tweeeu; chick-err-tsee-woy* (Keith & Gooders 1980); and throaty, whistling *chewee cheweeooo, wee woo weeoo* and *pu pu piu*, a shorter, weaker and squeaky *ticky-teu sip* and whistling *wooo* and *wiwooo* notes separated by throaty, Common Starling-like noises (Rabbitts & Vinicombe 1978). These may all be 'warm-up' songs, given in early spring and often characterised by chattering 'r' sounds as from a Common Starling. May sing in winter (to establish a feeding territory), as well as in spring, but variations in the song are apparently complex and not well understood. (Largely after Cramp & Perrins 1993.)

**DISTRIBUTION AND MOVEMENTS** Breeds in Europe, in northern **Spain** in the Cordillera Cantabrica and Pyrénées, in SE **France** in the Jura and Alps, also **Corsica** (Thibault 1983), and in the Alps in **Switzerland**, **Austria** and **Italy**, in the Appennines, and very locally in southern **Germany** in the Bayerische Alps (also bred Schwäbische Alb mountains 1989). Small numbers breed in the Tatra mountains of **Poland/Slovakia**, and also found in the Carpathian mountains of SW **Ukraine** and **Romania**, the Muntii Apuseni of Romania, and locally in **Bulgaria**, especially in the Stara and Rodopi ranges. Found in the higher mountains of former **Yugoslavia**, **Albania** and **Greece** (where bred Pelopónnisos 1989). In SW Asia breeds locally in southern **Turkey** in the Taurus mountains (Bolkar Daglari, Toros Dagi and Ala Daglari ranges and Erciyas Dagi), the eastern Black Sea coast ranges (Anadolu Daglari), and also the extreme southeast in Hakkâri province (probably occurs much more widely, especially in the east, on all suitable precipitous peaks). Also found in the Caucasus and Transcaucasus in southern **Russia**, **Georgia**, **Armenia** and **Azerbaydzhan**, NW and northern **Iran** in the Elburz mountains east to about Gorgan and Khorasan and western Iran in the Zagros mountains south to Luristan (also Kerman?), and SW **Turkmenistan** in the Kopet Dag. In Central Asia, occurs widely in SE **Kazakhstan**, **Kyrgyzstan**, SE **Uzbekistan** and **Tadzhikistan** in the Pamir-Alai system, Tien Shan, Dzhungarskiy Alatau and Tarbagatay ranges. Also adjacent **Xinjiang**, **NW China**, in the Dzhungarskiy Alatau, central Tien Shan, and the Altun Shan and Kun Lun ranges on the northern border of the Tibetan Plateau. In **Mongolia** found in the SE Mongolian Altai (east of the Jargalant massif and Üyönch Gol valley) and Govialtay ranges, southeast to the Ih Bogd Uul and Gurvan Sayhan Uul mountains (and probably to the Chinese border at c. 106° 30′ E); also a winter record from region of the Ih-Hayrhaan range, and unconfirmed reports from the southern parts of the Hangayn mountains. In **Afghanistan** found in summer and presumed to breed in Badakhshan and the northern Hindu Kush, and probably also the Paropamisus. Breeding proven in the Safed Koh on the border with Pakistan, and in northern **Pakistan** in the Kagan valley, and presumably also breeds in Chitral, Gilgit, Hunza and Baltistan. In NW **India** breeds in Ladakh, and found in the Himalayas from Kashmir through Himachal Pradesh and northern Uttar Pradesh to **Nepal**, **Sikkim**, **Bhutan** and possibly **Arunachal Pradesh** (but few breeding reports from the Himalayas). In adjacent **Tibet** (Xizang) found in the southwest at Zanda and Burang, in the south at Gamba, the Chumbi valley, Gyangze, region of Nam Co, Lhunzhub and Lhasa (where often seen in summer on the Potala and Chagpori, and in the neighbouring hills: Ludlow 1950), and in the southeast in the Yi'ong Zangbo and Po Tsangpo valleys, around Baxoi and Qamdo. In **China** found in eastern and SE **Qinghai**, the Qaidam Basin (west to about Golmud) and south-central Qinghai around Zhidoi, Qumarleb, Nangqen and Yushu, in western **Sichuan** east to Songpan, the Qionglai Shan,

Ya'an and Miyi, and south in the east to Batang, SW **Gansu** (south and west of Lanzhou, including the Min Shan), NW **Ningxia** in the Helan Shan, central-southern **Nei Mongol** at Baotou (March), southern **Shaanxi** in the Qin Ling Shan, northern **Hebei** at Dongling, and western **Liaoning**. In much of the range, especially in the east, few breeding records, and most sightings relate to migrant or wintering birds. In particular, the extent of the true breeding distribution in Tibet and NE China is unknown. In the immediate post-breeding period, late July–August/September, many move upslope, but with the onset of winter they descend again to a variable (and largely unknown) extent. Although some birds (especially juveniles) are probably sedentary, remaining at higher altitudes through the winter, in all areas an altitudinal migrant, and some may undertake longer and more regular movements, even returning to the same wintering site from year to year. In the period October–April, part of the population moves to 'secondary uplands' near the core breeding areas, including the Vosges and Alpilles in southern **France**, **Corsica** (probably some immigration from Italy, and regular on cliffs on the west coast and at Cap Corse), the Schwarzwald in SW **Germany**, the **Swiss** Jura, Bükk mountains of NE **Hungary**, coastal mountains of the **former Yugoslavia**, **Cyprus** (fairly common and widespread; regular on the southern cliffs at Episkopi), the foothills of the **Caucasus**, mountains around Samarkand and the Gissar valley in SE **Uzbekistan**, the Tehran region of **Iran** (with a record from Shiraz in the southern Elburz), **Afghanistan** from Balkh to Bala Morghab and Kushka in the north, Herat in the west and Farah and Kandahar in the south (and more rarely to Sistan), and the **Himalayan foothills**, including the Vale of Kashmir, Kathmandu valley, and the fringe of the hills in Jalpaiguri district (West Bengal) and northern Assam, east to at least the Subansiri river. Rather smaller numbers move to lowland areas further afield, e.g. to the Camargue in southern **France** (only exceptionally), south to c. 45° S in **Italy**, coastal **Yugoslavia** (e.g. Split, Dubrovnik), the Mediterranean coast of **Turkey**, northern **Iraq**, **Syria**, northern **Israel** (mid November–mid April, mainly late December–late February, usually fewer than five annually, southernmost records Massada and near Bet Shemesh), **Lebanon** (may have bred?), SE **Kazakhstan**, the plains of **Xinjiang**, **NW China**, south to Kashi and Wushi, the plains of northern **Pakistan** in the northern Punjab from Mianwali and Kalabagh on the Indus east through the Salt Range to Faisalabad and Lahore, and in small numbers also to northern Baluchistan (Quetta), the plains of northern **India** south to Delhi, and to Uttar Pradesh at Fatehpur Sikri, Etawah and Ghazipur, also Rajasthan?, the terai of **Nepal** (where uncommon in winter at Chitwan NP), and in eastern **China** in the eastern plains of **Hebei** (including the Eastern Tombs), southern **Shaanxi**, **Jiangsu**, **Anhui**, **Henan**, **Hubei**, **Jiangxi**, central and NW **Fujian**, and also in the southwest in **Sichuan** and in **Yunnan**, where recorded from the Gaoligong Shan, Lijiang, Dali and Kunming,

and possibly also **Guangdong**. In the spring, returns to the breeding areas in April–May, and may have to linger on south-facing slopes near the breeding cliffs until snow clears, whilst late snowfalls may force birds to move downslope temporarily. Alternatively, some may 'overshoot' the breeding zone and move higher up the mountains (thus recorded in Switzerland at 4500 m in April). Vagrants have been recorded in northern and western **France**, **England** (ten records since 1792, September–early June, including a bird at Cheddar, Somerset, November–April 1976/77 and 1977/78), **Jersey**, **Channel Islands** (March 1972), **Portugal** (two records, including winter 1975/76), **Gibraltar** (two recent records), **Netherlands** (one wintered Amsterdam November–April 1989/90 and 1990/91), **Belgium** (six records in 20th century, all but one since 1985 and including a returning individual in a stone pit near Liège in March 1986, winter 1986/87 and December 1987), NE **Germany**, **Malta** (November 1904, November 1972), **Balearic Islands**, **Sardinia**, **Morocco**, **Algeria** and **Jordan** (two at Wadi al Mujib, spring 1897).

**HABITAT** Breeds in mountain regions, in areas with steep cliffs, rock faces and precipitous boulder-strewn slopes (limestone being the preferred substrate), often near tunnels, caves, scree slopes or moraine, and typically near water (especially waterfalls). Very often found in gorges, will also use quarries, and the availability of suitable nest sites may be an important limiting factor. Although associated with high mountains, the lower altitudinal limit may depend on the availability of suitable rock faces. Breeds in Switzerland at 1000–2000 m (350–2700 m), in Austria at 700–2000 m (430–2700 m), in Bulgaria to c. 2135 m, in Corsica probably at 1800–2500 m, in Turkey c. 2450–3000 m, in the Caucasus to 3100 m and in the western Tien Shan at 2500–4000 m. Noted at 2900–4100 m in NE Afghanistan, in Pakistan breeds at 3600–4600 m, in Kashmir breeds at 3350 m (and breeding proven at 6400 m in Ladakh: Meinertzhagen 1927) and in the Himalayas in general probably breeds largely above 3600 m. In Tibet noted at c. 3660–5100 m in summer, and in China at 3050–4000 m in Gansu and c. 3415–4785 m in Sichuan. After the breeding season (up to mid September), recorded in Nepal at 3800–5000 m in an upslope dispersal. In the winter, as well as around rock faces (including sea cliffs), may also be found in rocky riverbeds, including those of rather large rivers, earth and clay banks and cliffs, newly built road-cuttings, quarries, buildings (such as castles, cathedrals and churches, even in urban areas), bridges and ruins. Occupies a very wide altitudinal range in winter, occurring down to sea level in southern Turkey, to the plains of northern India and Pakistan, to 245 m in Nepal and 305 m in Sikkim. Also winters at considerable altitudes, e.g. 1800–3200 m in Switzerland, 1200–2400 m in the northern valleys of Pakistan, 4000 m in Ladakh (January), up to 5730 m in Nepal, 3600 m in Sikkim, usually above 1000 m in Bhutan, and in China at 1400–2500 m in Sichuan and at 2925 m in Yunnan (February).

**POPULATION** Generally rather uncommon and local in Europe and western Asia, pairs being 1–2 km apart even in areas of continuous suitable habitat. Very few in southern Germany (c. 20 pairs) and c. 8–12 pairs in the Tatra mountains of Poland/Slovakia, with a few in the Pieniny mountains. In the Caucasus, Transcaucasus and Turkmenistan not common (locally even rare), but much commoner in the Tien Shan, Altai and associated ranges in Central Asia and Mongolia, and locally common (especially in winter) in Afghanistan and the Himalayas, although somewhat scarce in southern Tibet and uncommon and sporadic in China. Formerly bred in Sudety mountains of Poland, and the range in Romania has contracted since c. 1920.

**HABITS** Sometimes tame (especially vagrants?), but more often indifferent to man or will hide if it becomes aware that it is being watched. Characteristically flicks its wings half-open, to reveal the red and white markings. This habit is invariable, and adopted by juveniles as soon as they fledge. The wings are flicked faster and to a greater extent when excited, but freezes, sometimes with head and bill pointing upwards, in the face of a threat from an aerial predator. Solitary in winter, both male and female vigorously defending a feeding territory, although loose groups of 2–6 have also been recorded, and, very exceptionally, flocks of up to 50 birds have been seen in late autumn. Territorial disputes may be prolonged and involve aerial fights. Pairs are formed in the spring, although some birds fail to establish a territory and become summer 'floaters', wandering away from the breeding grounds. May form family parties in late summer, but juveniles are normally solitary following their dispersal in October. Roost singly, in a small hole or rock crevice. Forages on cliffs and rock faces, but sometimes in wet weather along streams or among pebbles and rocks below cliffs, and very occasionally on tree trunks. In the winter, frequently feeds along river- and streambeds, earthen banks and even roadsides. May flycatch, and often disappears into deep holes and crevices. Food insects, spiders and other invertebrates.

**BREEDING BIOLOGY** Season: Europe, late April–mid June (dependent on altitude); Caucasus, June; Kazakhstan, late May–June; Pakistan (Safed Koh), mid May; Himalayas, May–July. The nest is placed in a secure rock cavity, such as a crevice in a rock face, behind a rock, in scree or in a boulder pile. It may be at the base of a rock wall or up to 100 m high, and is often placed very close to a waterfall. Artificial sites may also be used, in the walls of buildings, ventilation holes or pipes. There are typically two entrances to the cavity. The nest itself is built by the female over a period of c. 5 days and is a foundation of moss with the addition of lichen, pine needles, grass and roots, lined with hair, feathers, wool and rootlets. Clutch 4–5 (3–5): eggs white, finely and sparsely speckled dark red to black, speckles often concentrated at broader end; 20.7 x 15 mm. Female incubates, period 18.5–20 days; she is fed by the male. The female also broods, but both sexes feed the young,

which fledge after 28.5–30 days and are independent after a further 5–6 days. Single-brooded.

**DESCRIPTION** *T. m. muraria* **Adult Male Breeding**: *In fresh plumage* (March–May), crown and ear-coverts mid grey, nape and sides of neck slightly paler, grading into pale french grey on mantle and scapulars; longer scapulars and back slightly darker. Rump mid grey, grading to dark grey or blackish-grey on uppertail-coverts. Tail black, T1–T3 broadly tipped dull mid grey, T4–T5 tipped grey with white subterminal patch or bar (mainly on inner web), T6 with broad white subterminal band (8–17 mm deep) and narrow grey tip (see figure 25.1). Lesser and median coverts pale grey, broadly tipped geranium-red, may show white at base and centre. Innermost greater coverts mid grey; central greater coverts with grey inner web and duller reddish outer web, poorly demarcated from black tip; outer greater coverts black on inner web, narrowly tipped geranium-red, outer web geranium-red, blackish at base. Shorter feathers of alula and primary coverts as outermost greater coverts. Largest feather of alula dull black, vaguely fringed grey; tertials similar, but pale red-pink at base of outer web with some white at shaft. Flight feathers black, inner primaries and secondaries tipped pale grey to off-white, large white subterminal spot on P2–P5 (P2–P6), largest on P2, and another large white spot near base of inner web; basal half to two-thirds of secondaries and P3–P10 bright reddish-pink. Lores, cheeks, throat and centre of breast (sometimes whole breast) dull black, shading into mid grey of ear-coverts; sometimes a white stripe on lower ear-coverts. Rest of underparts mid grey, sometimes slightly darker on undertail-coverts, which are tipped white. Underwing-coverts and axillaries pale red-pink, dark grey often showing at base of longer feathers; under primary coverts dark grey or blackish-grey. *In worn breeding plumage* (May–August), crown paler grey, mantle paler and whiter; grey fringes to tertials and pale tips to flight feathers abraded; more white shows at centre of lesser and median coverts; breast, flanks and belly duller and less uniformly grey. **Bare Parts**: Iris dark brown to black-brown; bill black or greyish-black, sometimes paler slate-grey around nostril and base of lower mandible; legs and feet brown-black to black. **Adult Female Breeding**: As male, but lores mid grey, ear-coverts and sides of neck light grey to greyish-white, with a contrasting creamy to white eyering. Chin to

*Figure 25.1  Tail of adult male* T. m. muraria.

centre of breast white, usually with a variable dark grey or grey-black mottled patch on lower throat and breast (exceptionally as extensive as black throat of male). **Adult Male and Female Non-breeding**: *In fresh plumage* (September to about February), as adult female breeding, but throat and centre of breast uniform whitish. Crown light mid grey (as nape, thus lacking contrast shown by breeding adult), but variably, although faintly, washed buff. Wing-coverts, flight feathers and tail fresh. **Juvenile**: As adult non-breeding, but crown and nape dull mid grey, mantle and scapulars only slightly paler, cheeks, sides of neck, throat and centre of breast pale grey, merging into mid grey of remainder of underparts. Wings and tail as adult, but black tips to greater and primary coverts less sharply defined. Underwing-coverts paler grey than adult, red-pink tips more restricted. When fresh, may show faint red-pink tips to feathers of upperparts, sides of head, throat and breast. Bill of recently fledged juveniles dull slate with slight flesh tinge, some whitish-yellow at gape; legs and feet dull slate with slight flesh tinge. **1st Adult Non-breeding**: As adult non-breeding, but retained wing and tail feathers may be slightly browner and more abraded. Forehead and crown often show more pronounced buff-brown tinge (cf. *nepalensis* below), lores often paler grey (less contrasting), throat and centre of breast with faint buff tinge. **Measurements**: Wing of male 94–105, of female 94–106; tail of male 51–57, of female 48–58; bill 25.5–38.8; tarsus 21.3–23.9. Weight 13–19.6 g; summer average 19.3 g, winter average 17.3 g.
**MOULT** Adult post-breeding complete (July–mid September). Adult pre-breeding partial, includes head, throat, centre of breast and sometimes a few feathers of sides of breast and mantle; odd non-breeding feathers frequently retained (February–April, occasionally from late December). Post-juvenile partial, includes median coverts (late July–September, occasionally early November). First pre-breeding as adult, but may be less extensive in some.
**GEOGRAPHICAL VARIATION** Rather slight, and species often considered monotypic. Two races recognised.

*T. m. muraria* Europe and SW Asia east to northern and western Iran. See Description. Averages slightly shorter-billed than European birds in the Caucasus and Iran.

*T. m. nepalensis* From Turkmenistan in southern Central Asia and eastern Iran (Kerman and Khorasan) east to China. As nominate *muraria,* but upperparts slightly darker and more blue-grey, crown often washed pale drab or brown in winter, belly sometimes darker grey or blackish, pale spots on tail and primaries average larger, pink tinge on base of tail feathers more frequent, and centres of lesser coverts pale grey (not white). Wing averages longer, but bill averages shorter. Wing of male 98–115, of female 95–105 (92: Rand & Fleming 1957); bill 27–42. Intergrades broadly with nominate *muraria* across western Asia. Birds from Central Asia approach nominate *muraria* in coloration, but dimensions as *nepalensis.*
**RELATIONSHIPS** Long debated. Formerly often considered to be a member of the treecreepers Certhiidae, but anatomical and behavioural evidence was used to argue for a closer relationship with the nuthatches Sittidae, and DNA-DNA hybridisation data have confirmed this latter alliance (Sibley & Ahlquist 1985). Placed in the subfamily Tichodrominae by Sibley & Monroe (1990), but in its own family, the Tichodromadidae, by Voous (1977), as 'The extraordinary adaptations to extreme mountain conditions... might not immediately have justified the recognition of a family of its own, but they surely mark the arrival at a new structural and ecological level with promising possibilities'.
**REFERENCES** Cramp & Perrins (1993), Vaurie (1950b, 1957d).

## 26 EURASIAN TREECREEPER *Certhia familiaris* Plate 9

Other names: Treecreeper, Northern Treecreeper, Common Treecreeper

The most widespread of the treecreepers, breeding from Ireland to Japan and south to the Mediterranean, Himalayas and China. Its inconspicuous habits result in its being widely overlooked.

**IDENTIFICATION** Length 125 mm (5 in). Upperparts warm brown, variably streaked and spotted buff to whitish, rump more rufous, and flight feathers intricately barred. Tail plain brown and rather long, with the individual feathers stiff and pointed. Supercilium and underparts whitish, the belly, flanks and vent variably tinged dull buff. The characteristic jerky movements make it very difficult to note fine plumage details accurately. Treecreepers are distinctive, with cryptically marked upperparts, a relatively long, slender, decurved bill, and the invariable habit of feeding, woodpecker-like, on the trunks and larger boughs of trees. They use their tail for support and often climb along the underside of branches, but unlike nuthatches are largely unable to move head-first downwards. Distribution overlaps with that of Short-toed Treecreeper in Europe and Turkey, and specific identification is difficult (sometimes impossible). Eurasian has more distinct supercilia, especially in front of the eye (they may even meet at the base of the bill), cleaner and paler underparts (prominently so in northern birds), warmer, paler and more spotted or scalloped (less streaked) upperparts, and a slightly shorter bill. The best distinction is, however, voice. Eurasian's vocabulary

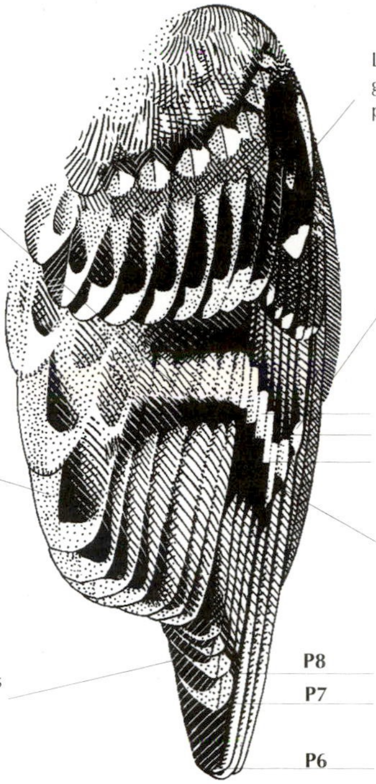

Note: Primaries numbered asdendantly, ie from
the outside of the wing towards the body.
P4=P5,with P6 slightly shorter.
(Based on Daunicht, 1991, figure 15).

Largest feather of alula
generally lacks *complete*
pale fringe to outer web

Blackish bar on outer
four secondaries often
becomes narrower on
outermost

Inner web of longest
tertial averages
relatively pale, often
obviously contrasting
with blackish
subterminal area on
outer web, but not
obviously paler than
tip of outer web

Pale bar near base of
P4 always prominent

Pale bars on P7 and P8
generally overlap more
than those on P7 and P6

Distal edge of pale bars on outer
webs of P6 to P8 generally straight or
rounded ('stepped'), but sometimes
shallowly pointed

Pale spots at tips of inner primaries
duller, slightly more diffuse and
extensive, and more
cresent-shaped (extending further
onto inner web)

P8
P7
P6

Distance between tips of
P6 and P7 often obviously
greater than distance
between tips of P7 and P8

*Figure 26.1  Wing of* C. f. britannica.

is rather limited, and its song is much more stereo-typed and is usually twice as long as that of Short-toed, with three times as many notes and a wider range of pitch; it is also less far-carrying. See Voice, and also Short-toed Treecreeper (p. 190) for full discussion of this tricky identification problem. Overlaps in range with Bar-tailed, Brown-throated and Rusty-flanked Treecreepers in Central Asia, the Himalayas and western China. Easily separated from Bar-tailed by its plain, unbarred tail, and from Brown-throated by its white (not brown) throat and breast and dull brown tail. Separation from Rusty-flanked not quite so straightforward, but generally found at higher altitudes where the two species overlap, and Eurasian has dull white underparts, washed drab-buff on the rear flanks and vent, and appearing rather uniformly pale, lacking the extensive and strongly contrasting cinnamon flanks and vent of Rusty-flanked (see also p. 198).

**SEX/AGE** Sexes similar. Juvenile as adult, but upperparts duller, with larger whitish feather centres, appearing pale-spotted and dark-scalloped; underparts duller, indistinctly and finely spotted darker, especially on the breast and flanks. 1st adult as adult.

**VOICE** Contact call a very quiet, thin and high-pitched *sit* or *tsit*. The most distinctive call is a shrill, high-pitched, but characteristically emphatic and penetrating, *srrih* or *tsree*, with a percepti-ble rolling or vibrato quality. It is often given in a regular slow series, *tsree-tsree-tsree-tsree*, and although usually used as a contact call may also be given in aggressive encounters or by begging females (it is higher and thinner than the '*tsree*' call occasionally given by Short-toed). Also gives a pure, plain *tee*, or *teeeh*, sometimes repeated in slow series (recalling Coal Tit and possibly confusable with the *tyt* of Short-toed, but finer, and, when repeated in series, always slower). In heightened excitement, gives a slightly higher-pitched, thin, sharp and almost hissing *tsee* or *ziih*, slightly falling in pitch; this, too, may be given in fast series when challenging an intruding treecreeper, or in slower series in alarm. Flight call a short, thin, high-pitched *si* or *sit*, often given in series *sit, sit, sit...* (slightly fuller and louder than the contact call). Only the male sings, a thin, high-pitched, silvery phrase up to 3 seconds in duration, falling progressively in pitch. Thin and tremulous to start with, it gains in power and volume and terminates with a sibilant flourish (the overall rhythm recalls the song of a Common Chaffinch or Willow Warbler). It comprises a block of 2–3 *srrih* units, followed by 3–7 thin and tremulous twittering notes falling in pitch in a descending trill (recalling Goldcrest), and, after a characteristic 'hiccup', 5–14 units (starting at a higher pitch than the end of the second block) in a fine, descending ripple (softer versions recalling a Blue Tit), the terminal note being a clear falling then rising whistle (*suih*): thus, *tsee-tsee-tsi-tsi-si-si-si-si-sisisisisi-tsee* (or *tsee-tsu-wizzizu-izzizu-ee* or *tsee-tsee-tsee-wiz-zizu-ee*). Song given throughout the year, but especially in late winter and spring, and males may perform song-duels. Subsong a faint halting repetition of 5–6 notes, without the plaintiveness and the *ee* sound of the full song. (Partly after Cramp & Perrins 1993, Witherby *et al.* 1944.) 'Mixed' singers regularly occur in Continental Europe, in which Eurasian imitates Short-toed's song and vice-versa or, more frequently, part of one song is 'dubbed' or mixed into the other. It was once thought that all mixed singers were Eurasian, but Short-toed, too, may become mixed singers, especially on the edge of their range (and, in general, the mixed singers in a given area should be the less numerous of the sibling pair). Each species has learnt the 'wrong' song from its neighbours, be they of the other species or existing mixed singers. The imitations are perfect, but, although Eurasian are the better mimics, only a few are able to give the multiple song types of Short-toed. Some geographical variation also exists in Eurasian's song. Possibly thinner and more delicate in Scandinavia, it is shorter in Corsica, often lacking the final ripple. Song in the Himalayas (subspecies *mandellii*) distinctive, described as a high-pitched, rising then descending *tzee, tzee, tze-tzizitzi* (Fleming *et al.* 1984).

## DISTRIBUTION AND MOVEMENTS

**NORTHERN RACES**: Breeds in **Britain** (including the Isle of Man; but very local Outer Hebrides in Stornoway woods and absent Isles of Scilly, Orkney and Shetland) and **Ireland** (absent far west). Locally in northern **Spain** in the Cordillera Cantabrica, Sierra Gebollera and Pyrénées, and very local in western **France**, although more widespread in the south and east (including the Pyrénées, Massif Central, Jura, Vosges and Alps); also **Corsica**. Breeds in **Luxembourg**, SE **Belgium** (Ardennes) and the extreme SE **Netherlands** (near Vaals and Epen, Zuid-Limburg), and then across central and eastern Europe, south to **Italy** in the Alps and also locally in the Appennines south to Abruzzese, the mountains of former **Yugoslavia**, **Albania**, **Greece** (south to Parnassos and possibly the Peloponnisos, also Mount Olympus) and **Bulgaria** in the Stara, Rila and Rodopi ranges. Also south to **Moldavia**, the central **Ukraine**, at Slobodka, *c.* 47° N in the Dnepr basin, Dnepropetrovsk and Voroshilovgrad, and in **southern Russia** to Voronezh, Penza and Kuybyshev, and to Kuvandyk at the southern end of the Urals. In Europe, breeds north to northern **Norway** (Tromso), **Sweden** and **Finland**, and in **northern Russia** to Kandalakshskaya Bay and the Solovetskiye islands in the White Sea, Arkhangel'sk, and to *c.* 65° N on the Mezen' and Pechora rivers and in the Ural mountains. The range extends east through southern **Siberia** to Amurland, Ussuriland, the Shantar islands, Sakhalin and Urup, Iturup and Shikotan in the southern Kurile islands. In **Japan**, breeds on Hokkaido and northern and central Honshu, and much more locally in SW Honshu, Shikoku and

Kyushu. Breeds north to *c.* 61° N in western **Siberia** (including the Tym river in the Ob' valley, *c.* 60° N on the Yenisey (exceptionally to Komsa) and Chadobets on the Angara river), and to *c.* 59° N from the Yenisey eastwards (including Kirensk and the Stanovoy and Tukuringra ranges), and south to *c.* 56° N between the Urals and the Irtysh basin and to NE **Kazakhstan** in the Irtysh valley to the Tarbagatay and Saur mountains. In northern **Mongolia** found in the NW Mongolia Altai, Turgen Uul massif, Great Lakes depression, Tesiyn valley, the Hangayn mountains south to the northern slopes of the main range and upper reaches of the Orhon river, and the Hentiyn range south to the Bogdo Uul massif (near Ulan Bator), upper Kerulen river and east to the upper Onon river. Also recorded in winter in the outliers of the Greater Khingan range (the Halh'n Gol basin). In eastern Russia breeds south to the Greater Khingan range. In NE China breeds in **Heilongjiang**, in the Xiao Hinggan range and Harbin region, southern **Jilin** in the Changbai Shan, **Liaoning** at Caohekou, Chaoyang and the Liaodong peninsula, northern **Hebei** at Weichang, Dongling, the Eastern Tombs, and the hills north of Qinhuangdao and Shanhaiguan, and **Beijing** (Ming Tombs, winter only?). Presumably breeds in northern **North Korea** (summer records from Hamgyong-Pukdo and Pyongan-Pukdo). Two marginally isolated populations are found to the south of the main range. The first is in the **Crimea**, locally in western and NE **Turkey** (south in the east to Karakurt; distribution probably continuous with populations of Greece), the **Caucasus** northwest to Slavyansk-na-Kubani and southeast to Ismailly in **Azerbaydzhan**, also the Talysh mountains, **Georgia** and **Armenia** in Transcaucasia, and northern **Iran** in the Elburz mountains east to Gonbad-e-Kavus. The second population is in the central and eastern Tien Shan in SE **Kazakhstan** and **Kyrgyzstan**, west to the Kyrgyzskiy Alatau and Terskey Alatau ranges, Naryn and At-Bashi, and the Kokshaal Tau (and presumably to the eastern Alay system in the eastern Zaalayskiy and Alayskiy mountains). In adjacent **Xinjiang**, **NW China**, found east to Turpan (Ala Gour river) and Hami (the Koshmak valley, late March, perhaps a migrant), south to Aksu; also the Dzhungarskiy Alatau (recorded at Panfilov, SE Kazakhstan, in winter, and at Kapal), Borohoro Shan (north of Yining), and mountains north of Ebinur Hu (and thus presumably contiguous with the populations of the Tarbagatay mountains and southern Siberia). Western and southern populations are largely resident (e.g. most British birds move less than 20 km), but birds from more northerly areas tend to move southwards in winter, although numbers and distances vary in an irregular pattern (but may be only a summer visitor on the northern marches of the range?). Dispersal takes place mid September–mid November (from mid August in 'irruption' years), with return movements mid March–early May. Local resident populations tend to 'mask' the presence of such migrants, but wanderers of the northern nominate race have reached **England** (including - this race? - the Isles of Scilly, nine records), **Scotland** (where a very rare migrant Orkney, Fair Isle, where all five records nominate *familiaris*, and Shetland), the **Netherlands**, **Denmark**, western **Germany**, southern **Turkey** (?), SE **Russia** (including Saratov), the Caspian Sea and Sea of Azov. Apparently very reluctant to cross water, however, and little evidence of immigration in Britain apart from the few records of vagrant *C. f. familiaris*. There is also some northward post-breeding dispersal. In the east, an uncommon passage migrant in southern **North Korea** and migrant and winter visitor in **South Korea**, whilst in NE **China** a few occur away from the breeding areas, e.g. at Beidaihe, coastal Hebei, in late autumn (Williams *et al.* 1991) and recorded in Shandong at Qingdao, February–March. Additionally, upland populations may undertake some altitudinal movements (e.g. in Japan, the Tien Shan from late September onwards, western Ukraine, and the Caucasus October–early March), but in Scotland treecreepers may remain through the winter in upland area. Vagrant **Netherlands** (first December 1971 and near-annual since, with a maximum of 53 in autumn 1973, especially on Waddensea islands; breeds Zuid-Limburg), **Mallorca** (Spain), **Channel Islands** (UK, three records) and **Faeroe** islands (July 1986: Anon 1993a).

**SINO-HIMALAYAN RACES** Breeds in the Himalayas of **Pakistan**, where found in Hazara (Kagan valley), Indus Kohistan (Kandia valley) and Gilgit (Chilas, Nanga Parbat and Astor; also a single doubtful breeding record from the Murree hills, see Roberts 1992), and NW **India** in Kashmir (Gulmarg, Sonamarg and the Liddar valley), Himachal Pradesh and northern Uttar Pradesh, **Nepal**, **Sikkim**, **Bhutan** and Arunachal Pradesh (Manas valley adjacent to Bhutan at Mago and Tawang, Subansiri district in the Talley valley, and in the far east around Kahaa: Singh 1994). Extends north of the main range into adjacent southern **Tibet** (Xizang) along the Sun Kosi valley to Nyalam, the Arun Kosi to Sakyetang, in the Chumbi valley, and in the Tsangpo valley west to *c.* 94° E (and on the Nyang river to Güncang and, in the east, on the Yi'ang Zangbo and Nagang Chu (to Bomi)). Also found in Tibet, south of the main range in the Subansiri drainage, in the extreme southeast on the Burmese border (area of Hkakabo Razi) and in NE Tibet in the Qamdo region. Also found in extreme northern **Myanmar** (**Burma**), where recorded once in the Adung valley in June. In **western China** found in NW **Yunnan** in the Lijiang range and the Nu Shan (Salween-Mekong divide; replaced in the Gaoligong Shan by Rusty-flanked Treecreeper), through eastern **Sichuan** east to Songpan, Pingwu, Dayi, Emei Shan, Muli, Mabian and Meigu, eastern **Qinghai** in the eastern Qilian Shan mountains and Menyuan, in the valley of the Huang He (Xunhua west to about Xinghai) and also in southernmost Qinghai around the Nangqen in the Mekong basin and the Mekong-Yangtse divide (Yushu), SW and southern **Gansu**, including the Min Shan range and Lanzhou region, southern **Shaanxi** in the Qin Ling range, and west-central **Shanxi** in the Luliang Shan (Pangquanguo reserve, King 1987). (Said to have

occurred in Meghalaya and Nagaland in NE India, but its occurrence south of the Brahmaputra is very doubtful.) Resident, but undertakes some altitudinal movements.

**HABITAT** Forest and woodland, generally requiring well-grown trees with many cracks and crevices in the bark suitable for foraging, roosting and nesting.

**NORTHERN RACES** In western and central Europe (especially in areas where the range overlaps that of Short-toed Treecreeper), *tends* to be found in beech and coniferous woodland (especially spruce and fir, and to a lesser extent pine), often favouring higher altitudes, but also frequents mixed and deciduous woodland, including riverine woodland, at least locally. In the British Isles (where Short-toed Treecreeper is absent), found in deciduous broadleaved and mixed woodland, less often in coniferous forests, also well-wooded farmland, parkland, orchards and occasionally large gardens, even in urban areas. Similarly, in European Russia (where Short-toed is also absent) shows a strong preference for mature broadleaved and mixed forest rather than conifers, in the Caucasus found in mature hardwood forest and alder forests in marshy localities, and in Iran exclusively in broadleaved forests, but in Siberia found in coniferous forests of larch, pine, fir and spruce, as well as mixed and riverine broadleaved woodland in the lowlands. Similarly in Japan, found in mixed and coniferous woodland. In all areas, may disperse into almost any wooded habitat outside the breeding season. In the north of the range breeds down to sea level, but largely montane in the south; in the Pyrénées occurs above 1370 m, and in the Appennines of Italy (Abruzzo province) above 1160 m, whilst breeds at up to 2230 m in Switzerland, 1800 m (occasionally 2000 m) in Austria, 1800 m in Corsica, *c.* 3000 m in Turkey/Iran and the Caucasus, 1500 m in the Altai, to the treeline on the Sayan mountains and at least 2440 m in the Tien Shan in Central Asia. In the east, occurs from near sea level up to 915 m on Hokkaido, but further south in Japan at 1065–2135 m (or to the treeline, exceptionally down to 730 m), and in NE China also montane (e.g. occurs at *c.* 400–2100 m in the Changbai Shan in Jilin) and only a rare winter visitor to the coastal plains.

**SINO-HIMALAYAN RACES** Perhaps primarily high-altitude forest of conifers such as Blue Pine, hemlock, Deodar, fir and juniper with an admixture of birch, less optimally conifers mixed with rhododendron or oak, but also pure stands of conifers or birch. In winter, may descend into mixed oak-rhododendron. In Pakistan found in summer above 3000 m, and in Kashmir, NW India, from 3000 m to at least 3660 m, descending in autumn and winter to 2135 m, whilst in northern Uttar Pradesh recorded at 2590–3960 m. In the central and eastern Himalayas breeds from *c.* 2700 m to the timberline, although mostly above 3300 m: in more detail, in Nepal summers at *c.* 2800–4200 m and recorded in winter at 2000–3800 m; in Sikkim and Darjeeling generally found at 2440–3660 m, sometimes to 4115 m, and in winter down to c. 1675 m. In Bhutan noted up to 3965 m in summer and at 2440–4150 m in September–February. In SE Tibet found at 2925–4115 m in summer, moving down to 2285 m in winter. In Burma recorded at 3960 m in June, and in Yunnan recorded at 2745 m to at least 3660 m, and still found in winter above 3050 m. In Sichuan breeds at c. 2900–3960 m, moving down to 1600 m in winter (although found at Wolong at 2440–3050 m throughout the winter), and in Qinghai noted at 3350 m in May. Generally found at higher altitudes than Rusty-flanked Treecreeper, but there is some overlap, at least in winter.

**POPULATION** Overall fairly common, if unobtrusive, but very uncommon to rare and becoming local or even sporadic towards the northern boundary of the range (including northern Japan), also local and uncommon in Turkey, scarce in Iran and Xinjiang, NW China (although fairly common in the Tien Shan of the former USSR), and rare in southern Japan, western Transcaucasia and the Crimea (although fairly common in the Caucasus). In the Himalayas, rare and erratic in Pakistan and apparently very rare in Kashmir, but not uncommon from northern Uttar Pradesh east to Bhutan and the commonest treecreeper in SE Tibet. Uncommon in SW China. Vulnerable to hard winters, especially extended periods of glazed frost or freezing rain, whilst northern and eastern populations tend to fluctuate in an irregular pattern, possibly tied to varying crops of spruce seeds (Rogacheva 1992). Some increase in Britain, and first bred Outer Hebrides (Scotland) in 1962, also a northward spread in Norway since c. 1970. First bred in the Netherlands in 1993, with a population of at least 13 pairs in Zuid-Limburg in an area where there was none in 1982.

**HABITS** Often tame and, indeed, indifferent to man, although it has the annoying habit of moving to the side of the tree trunk invisible to the observer, and altogether inconspicuous and unassuming, neither plumage nor voice demanding attention in the way of most tits and nuthatches. Typically found singly in winter, sometimes in pairs (the pair-bond apparently sometimes persists outside the breeding season, or in some regions pairs may be established in the autumn), and very often joining mixed-species foraging flocks. The breeding pair occupies a home range, and the area around the nest is apparently defended by the male as a nesting territory, usually with song (mixed singers will defend their territory against both Eurasian and Short-toed Treecreepers). After fledging, forms family parties (the family staying together for c. 14 days, although this is dependent on the occurrence of second clutches, the young sometimes being divided between the pair), and on independence the young, too, join mixed flocks. Roosts in a variety of crevices or behind bark flaps, and where sites available will excavate suitable cavities in decayed stumps or hemispherical hollows in the soft bark of ornamental redwoods (including Giant Sequoia). Also roosts under ivy, and sometimes in buildings. Both solitary and communal roosting are known, the birds either using separate holes in the same tree, or sleeping in close physi-

cal contact huddled together in a hollow or in the open on a trunk (up to 13–14 together). Such huddling is probably regular for fledglings, otherwise occurring only on cold nights. The female roosts in the nest once it is completed. Forages mouse-like on the trunks and larger boughs of trees, sometimes among the outer foliage, extracting prey from cracks and crevices with its fine bill. The usual method of progression is to fly to the bottom of a tree, work upwards in jerky hops, spiralling around the trunk, and then fly to the bottom of another tree. Occasionally also feeds on walls, buildings, fences and bare grassy ground or among fallen needles, and may flycatch. Food insects, spiders and, in winter, also some seeds (especially pine and spruce).

**BREEDING BIOLOGY** Season in West Palearctic, late March–June; in Japan, May–July. The nest is placed behind a flap of loose bark or in a crevice on a tree trunk, sometimes on or in buildings or stone walls, occasionally hidden among or behind vegetation (especially ivy), in masses of dead leaves accumulated in trees, and very rarely on the ground. Will use specially designed nestboxes or artificial nest flaps, especially in coniferous woodland. Nests may be as high as 16 m above ground. A foundation of twigs, conifer needles, bark fibres, grass, moss, lichen, wood chips etc. is lined with feathers, hair, wool, lichen, spiders' webs, eggs and cocoons etc., and in conifer woods usually also moss. Both sexes build the base over a period of 4–9 (–20) days, but only the female adds the lining. Clutch 5–6 (3–9) in West Palearctic, 3–5 (3–9) in Japan: eggs white, very finely marked with pink to reddish-brown speckles, usually confined to the broader end in a ring or cap; 15.5 x 12.1 mm (C. f. britannica). Female incubates, period 13–16 (12–20) days. The young are fed by both sexes, although tended only by the female, and fledge after 13–18.5 days (up to 23 days when fed by female alone); they make the first attempts to feed themselves c. 7 days after fledging. Juveniles return to the nest to roost for the first few nights after fledging, and family parties show marked cohesion, even huddling together for concealment. An unusual anti-predator response is to freeze in an upright bittern-like posture. About 20% of pairs are double-brooded, especially in the south and west of the range, and overlapping broods are not unusual, the male building a new nest and the female even laying the second clutch whilst still feeding the first brood. Serial polygyny occasionally recorded, the male mating with a second female and feeding her young rather than, or in addition to, the young of the primary female.

**SINO-HIMALAYAN RACES** Breeding biology poorly known, as few nests have been found. The details available suggest that it is similar to that of northern populations. Season in Himalayas, May–June (April?). Clutch 4–6: eggs pale pinkish-white, heavily spotted and speckled with reddish-brown, more densely at the broad end; 15.8 x 11.9 mm (C. f. hodgsoni).

**DESCRIPTION** C. f. britannica **Adult:** In fresh plumage (September onwards), crown and nape rufous-brown, feathers fringed black with a narrow whitish shaft streak. Mantle and scapulars similar but slightly warmer brown, feathers only tipped black and shaft-streaks broader, forming slightly spotted (whitish centre) and scalloped (dark tip) pattern. Back, rump and uppertail-coverts cinnamon-orange, feathers with concealed whitish bases and vague paler shaft streaks. Tail pale brown, darker adjacent to shaft; shaft pale buff. Wing-coverts dark brown: lesser coverts with broad rufous-buff centres and darker tips; median coverts tipped whitish and broadly fringed rufous-buff; greater coverts broadly tipped off-white on outer web and fringed at base rufous-buff, may show fine white shaft streak. Alula dark brown, broadly tipped off-white. Primary coverts dark brown, tipped buff on outer web. Inner webs of tertials pale grey-brown, outer webs brown, becoming black towards tip, fringed and broadly tipped pale buff. Primaries and secondaries mid brown, P4–P10 and secondaries with broad buff band across feather (outer web only on P4), bordered on each side by a black-brown band, fringed pale buff distally of these bands and broadly tipped off-white (fringes and tips less distinct on outer primaries). Lores blackish; long white supercilium from base of upper mandible to nape, may be indistinct over lores. Cheeks and ear-coverts mottled black, white and rufous-brown. Sides of neck and underparts off-white, washed pale buff or rufous on flanks, belly and vent. Undertail-coverts pale buff, tipped white. Underwing-coverts and axillaries whitish. *In worn plumage* (c. spring onwards), dark fringes to feathers of upperparts abrade, thus pale streaks on crown and nape better defined and upperparts slightly colder and less rufous. **Bare Parts**: Iris brown; upper mandible dark brown to blackish, cutting edges paler brown, lower mandible pale brown to pinkish or whitish, tipped dark brown; legs, feet and claws pale brown to dark brown. **Juvenile**: As adult, but upperparts (especially rump) less rufous, with larger whitish feather centres. Underparts dull whitish, indistinctly and finely spotted darker, especially on breast and flanks; belly and undertail-coverts pale buff. **1st Adult**: As adult. **Measurements**: Wing of male 61–67, of female 60–64; tail of male 57.5–67, of female 56–61; bill of male 14.3–19.1, of female 15.1–18.6; tarsus 14.2–16.8; hindclaw 7.9–9.7. Weight 7–12.9 g (*C. f. familiaris*).

**MOULT** Adult post-breeding complete (mid June–early September, rarely early October, in West Palearctic, duration c. 75 days). Post-juvenile partial, includes tertials and greater coverts (July–October).

**GEOGRAPHICAL VARIATION** Two groups of subspecies: the northern *familiaris* group in the Palearctic from the British Isles to Japan, with southern outliers in Asia Minor/the Caucasus/Iran and the Tien Shan in Central Asia (once thought to be isolated, these populations are almost certainly well connected with the northern populations); and the rather distinct Sino-Himalayan group. The relationship of the two groups has not been well studied, but some (perhaps significant) differences have been documented.

**THE NORTHERN *FAMILIARIS* GROUP** Variation rather slight. A cline of decreasing colour saturation runs eastwards from northern Europe, the upperparts becoming paler and greyer (less rufous) and the white streaking better defined, but this cline is reversed in Amurland, NE China and Japan. The populations along this cline are relatively pale and variation is slight. In Europe, a cline of increasing colour saturation runs south/west, *familiaris-macrodactyla*, with British birds (*britannica*), although isolated, representing an extension of this cline. The isolated population of Corsica is rather distinct but appears to be related to *macrodactyla*, whilst the isolated southern races *persica* and *tianschanica* closely resemble nominate *familiaris*.

*C. f. britannica* Britain and Ireland. See Description. Irish birds average very slightly darker and are sometimes separated as 'meinertzhageni'.

*C. f. macrodactyla* Western Europe east to the Oder river (Germany/Poland, where intergrades with nominate *familiaris*), Slovakia, central Hungary, and the northwest of former Yugoslavia. As *britannica*, but upperparts slightly paler (less extensive dark fringes and broader whitish feather centres); averages less rufous, especially on rump; underparts whiter (purer white on breast, with reduced buff wash on flanks, belly and undertail-coverts). Wing of male 58–69, of female 55–67; bill of male 14.7–20.2, of female 14.4–20; hindclaw 7.7–11. Note: birds from Vosges (France) almost lack white on upperparts, with largest amount of buff or rufous wash on underparts (Cramp & Perrins 1993); bill longer.

*C. f. corsa* Corsica. Relatively distinct. As *macrodactyla*, but upperparts more sharply streaked white, outer primaries fringed brighter rufous-buff; entire underparts tinged buff (less dusky on breast and belly), and when fresh show brownish fringes to feathers of lower breast, belly and flanks (although faint, more prominent than in other races); also larger. Wing of male 65–71, of female 64–67; bill of male 17.8–22, of female 17.3–20.7; hindclaw 8–10.

*C. f. familiaris* Fennoscandia, eastern Europe from Poland, eastern Hungary, Romania, Bulgaria, Makedonia (former Yugoslavia) and Greece east through European Russia, northern Ukraine and western Siberia to the Yenisey basin (where intergrades with *daurica*). Mainly resident, but has reached England, Scotland, the Netherlands, Denmark, western Germany, SE Russia (including Saratov), the Caspian Sea and Sea of Azov, also irregularly north to Lapland and the White Sea (Arkhangel'sk and Mezen'). As *macrodactyla*, but upperparts slightly paler (brighter and paler, more rufous-brown), with more extensive and purer white feather centres giving a more 'spotted' appearance; rump more contrastingly rufous (with more white in centre of feathers of rump and uppertail-coverts); supercilium and underparts cleaner white (almost pure white), with only faint buff wash on flanks, vent and undertail-coverts. A cline of decreasing saturation runs eastwards, and towards northern Scandinavia and Siberia upperparts gradually paler and greyer, rump more rufous, with reduced browns and better-defined white streaks, and underparts gradually purer white; birds from eastern Russia and western Siberia ('rossica') thus slightly paler and greyer, approaching *daurica*. Wing of male 60–69, of female 59–68; bill of male 15.3–20.8, of female 14.3–18.1; hindclaw 8.2–11.6.

**C. f. daurica** Siberia from the Yenisey basin to the Sea of Okhotsk, south to the Saur mountains, northern Mongolia, *c.* 51° N on the Amur (?), and Heilongjiang in NE China. Poorly marked. As nominate *familiaris*, but upperparts appear paler and greyer, with more extensive whitish feather centres (almost whole feather, and the extensive whitish centres on the rump and uppertail-coverts reduce their contrast with the mantle). Wing of male 60.5–67, of female 63–68.

**C. f. orientalis** Amurland (presumably south of *c.* 51°–52° N), Ussuriland, NE China from Jilin to Hebei (and migrants recorded in Shandong), Kurile islands, Sakhalin, and Hokkaido in northern Japan; breeds (?) North Korea, passage migrant and winter visitor south to at least Kyonggi-do in South Korea (Austin & Kuroda 1953). Very poorly marked. As *daurica*, but upperparts not so grey (close to nominate *familiaris*, but not quite so rufous-toned, and streaks relatively well defined as in *daurica*). Wing 60.5–68, of male 60.5–65, of female 61–63.5.

**C. f. japonica** Honshu, Shikoku and Kyushu, southern Japan; passage migrant and winter visitor South Korea (Austin & Kuroda 1953). As *orientalis*, but upperparts darker and distinctly more rufous (white spotting smaller; very near nominate *familiaris*). Also smaller? Wing 61–67.

**C. f. persica** Crimea, Turkey, Caucasus, Transcaucasus and northern Iran. May intergrade with nominate *familiaris*, as distribution probably nearly continuous through northern Turkey. As nominate *familiaris*, but upperparts slightly duller and darker, less rufous, whitish streaks slightly better defined; bill averages slightly longer (Vaurie 1959). Wing of male 60.5–69, of female 58–62; bill 16–20. Averages paler, approaching nominate *familiaris*, in the Caucasus and Crimea.

**C. f. tianschanica** The central and eastern Tien Shan, Tarbagatay (presumably?; Stepanyan 1990), Dzhungarskiy Alatau and Borohoro Shan in the former USSR and NW China. As nominate *familiaris*, but upperparts slightly paler and more rufous, fringes to primaries slightly richer (as *corsa*), lower flanks and undertail-coverts darker, washed dull pale buff. Large: wing of male 64–72, of female 62–66; bill 18–22.

**THE SINO-HIMALAYAN GROUP** Upperparts dark to very dark. Variation relatively pronounced. A cline of increasing colour saturation runs from Shaanxi south and west to the Himalayas, but is reversed in the western Himalayas.

**C. f. bianchii** Eastern Qinghai, Gansu, Shaanxi and (this race?) Shanxi. Close to nominate *familiaris*, but upperparts darker and duller (feather centres pale grey or grey-buff, not whitish), rump

slightly more orange-buff with paler and more whitish centres; belly, flanks and undertail-coverts duller, washed dull buff. Wing of female 64, 65.

**C. f. khamensis** Southern Gansu (where probably intergrades with *bianchii*) south to southern Tibet (northern watershed of Himalayas only?) and Yunnan (including southernmost Qinghai), also NE Burma and Bhutan (the race occurring in Arunachal Pradesh is not known). As *bianchii*, but rather darker and more rufous. Crown and nape black-brown, with narrow off-white to pale buff shaft streaks; mantle and scapulars slightly paler, feather centres more extensively cinnamon-buff with paler tips; rump richer cinnamon-orange, also more uniform. Belly cleaner white, but rear flanks, vent and undertail-coverts darker and duller, drab-grey. Juvenile greyer than adult, less rusty, especially on the rump. Wing of male 64–72, of female 62; bill 17–18.5.

**C. f. mandellii** Himalayas from Himachal Pradesh (Kulu) to extreme western Arunachal Pradesh (Tawang). Intergrades with *hodgsoni* in the west, but eastern boundary obscure: Ripley (1982) states that this form occurs in Bhutan and is replaced above *c.* 3500 m there by *khamensis*; Ali *et al.* (in press) dispute its occurrence in Bhutan, but specimens examined from Bhutan appear indeed to be *mandellii*. Poorly marked. As *khamensis*, but feather centres on upperparts (especially lower mantle and scapulars) richer and distinctly more rufous (cinnamon-buff). Rear flanks, vent and undertail-coverts average slightly warmer and buffer. Wing of male 63–71, of female 63–69; bill 16–18.5.

**C. f. hodgsoni** Western Himalayas east to Himachal Pradesh (Lahul), where intergrades with *mandellii*. As *mandellii*, but rather paler, greyer and less rufous, feathers of upperparts dull brown, centres larger, paler and more whitish (thus more 'spotted'); rump paler, cinnamon-orange; rear flanks, vent and undertail-coverts paler. Closer to nominate *familiaris* than *mandellii*, but underparts not so pure white, belly, rear flanks and vent lightly washed dull buff. Wing of male 63–70, of female 63–63.5; bill 16–21.

**RELATIONSHIPS** Forms a superspecies with Brown Creeper of North America. Indeed, they are often treated as conspecific (e.g. Voous 1977), but some workers consider that Brown Creeper is closer to Short-toed Treecreeper. Notably, Brown Creeper's song is overall more variable in the sequence of units than Eurasian's, and with 4–8 notes is closer to that of Short-toed, but is so different from both Eurasian's and Short-toed's that mutual recognition would be doubtful. Given the uncertainty over its relationships, Brown Creeper is best separated as a distinct species. Overlaps widely in range with Short-toed Treecreeper in the Western Palearctic, and individuals of the two species often fight, Eurasian being dominant.

**REFERENCES** Cramp & Perrins (1993), Portenko & Stübs (1977), Stepanyan (1990), Vaurie (1957e, 1959).

Other name: American Treecreeper

The only representative of the family in the New World, this species occupies a vast range, stretching from Alaska to Nicaragua. Although often united with Eurasian Treecreeper, its relationship with the Old World treecreepers is far from clear.

**IDENTIFICATION** Length 130 mm (5.25 in). Upperparts dark brown to blackish, streaked whitish on the crown, nape and upper mantle and more broadly spotted pale grey or buff on the lower mantle and scapulars. Rump and uppertail-coverts cinnamon-orange, mottled whitish, tail mid grey-brown. Greater and primary coverts dark brown, tipped buff or whitish, tips forming spotted wingbars. Tertials light grey-brown, broadly tipped and fringed off-white, flight feathers dark brown, crossed by two broad, diagonal buff bands. Supercilium off-white to buffy, lores and ear-coverts dark brown, mottled paler towards the rear. Sides of neck and underparts whitish, variably washed pale grey on the breast and dull pale buff on the flanks, belly and vent. Distinctive, as no other North American bird combines mottled brownish upperparts, whitish underparts, a moderately long, decurved bill and tree-creeping habits. In Central America, however, this species may be confused with a woodcreeper (see appendix), but Brown Creeper is smaller and more heav-

ily marked than any woodcreeper.

A vagrant Brown Creeper in Europe would be doubtfully distinguishable from Eurasian Treecreeper. Their calls are rather similar, and song is unlikely to be heard from a migrant. Comparing birds from NE North America (nominate *americana*) with the race *britannica* of Eurasian, Brown has slightly more prominently streaked upperparts (appearing less spotted), with the streaks whiter on the mantle and scapulars; 'dark-phase' Brown Creepers are also slightly colder and darker (thus closer to Short-toed Treecreeper). In the hand, Brown Creeper combines characters of both Eurasian and Short-toed Treecreepers (see Table 1, p.185, for summary).

**SEX/AGE** Sexes similar. Juvenile marginally distinct, being relatively buffer, with larger buff spots on upperparts (especially noticeable on the crown) and faint dark spotting on the throat and scaling on the breast; some also show buffy fringes to the wing-coverts. 1st adult as adult.

**VOICE** Little studied in comparison with

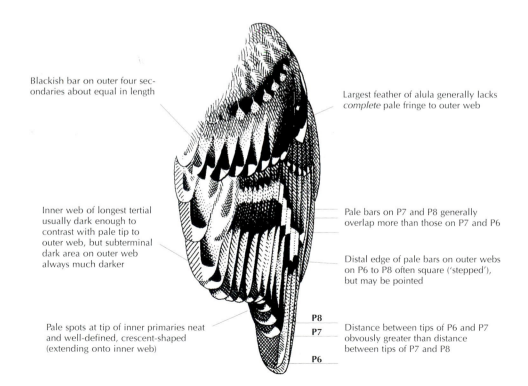

Blackish bar on outer four secondaries about equal in length

Largest feather of alula generally lacks *complete* pale fringe to outer web

Inner web of longest tertial usually dark enough to contrast with pale tip to outer web, but subterminal dark area on outer web always much darker

Pale bars on P7 and P8 generally overlap more than those on P7 and P6

Distal edge of pale bars on outer webs on P6 to P8 often square ('stepped'), but may be pointed

Pale spots at tip of inner primaries neat and well-defined, crescent-shaped (extending onto inner web)

P8
P7
P6

Distance between tips of P6 and P7 obviously greater than distance between tips of P7 and P8

*Figure 27.1  Wing of* C. a. americana.

**Table 1. Summary of features in the wing of Brown Creeper compared with Eurasian Treecreeper**

| | | |
|---|---|---|
| Largest feather of alula | generally lacks complete pale fringe to outer web | i.e. as Eurasian |
| Outer blackish bar on outer 4 secondaries | about equal in width across all feathers | i.e. as Short-toed |
| Flight feathers | relatively dark, with neat, well-defined pale tips 'hooking back' onto inner webs, forming crescents | pale tips average slightly better defined than on Eurasian, but shape similar, and not diamond-shaped as on Short-toed |
| Pattern of pale bar on P6–P8 | pale bars on P7 and P8 generally overlap more than those on P7 and P6 (forming a step) | i.e. as Eurasian |
| Shape of distal edge of pale spot on outer web of P8–P6 | often square-cut (i.e. stepped), but may be pointed | i.e. usually as Eurasian |
| Wing formula | distance between tips of P6 and P7 obviously greater than between P7 and P8 | i.e. as Eurasian |
| Colour contrast on longest tertial | inner web variable, usually dark enough to contrast with whitish tip to outer web, but dark on outer web always much darker, contrasting strongly (beware angle of light) | intermediate, but perhaps closer to Short-toed |
| Shafts of central tail feathers | paler than vane | i.e. as Eurasian |

European treecreepers. Calls include a soft but penetrating, high-pitched, drawn-out, sibilant *seee* or *trsee*, a pure, tinkling or bell-like *ti* or *tyt* and an incisive *tsit*, sometimes repeated, *tsit, tsit, tsit*; flight call a brief *chip* or *sit*. Fledged juveniles gives a high, sibilant *tsssi* or *ts-tssi* location call, and when begging *chee*. Song a short, weak warble (although audible at up to 120 m), comprising 4–8 thin, high-pitched and sometimes sibilant whistled units, and often introduced by the *tsree* note, e.g. *tsee-tuti-sedu-wee* or *tsee-trrrr-sit-tu-tee* (or in California *tsee, sisi'suisi*); the phrase lasts *c.* 1 second and is repeated several times. Only males sing, and each gives a stereotyped song, although there is some variation, with odd notes (especially the terminal note) being dropped or units slurred, and some birds may give double or triple song phrases in which the standard phrase is repeated to make a very long song. There is also some geographical variation, with distinct regional dialects: in California, the 'northern song' is introduced with a buzzing note, whilst 'southern songs' terminate in a buzz (and the isolated population on Angel Island in San Francisco Bay gives a song of simpler structure but greater individual variability). Song is given from prominent song-posts in early spring, and more sporadically once territories are established, ceasing once the young have fledged. (Partly after Baptista & Johnson 1982, Bent 1948, Cramp & Perrins 1993, C.M. Davis 1978.)

**DISTRIBUTION AND MOVEMENTS** The breeding range encompasses much of North and Middle America, but its northern border in Alaska and Canada is imperfectly known. In **Alaska** found in the south and southeast (including the Alexander archipelago), west to the Skwentna river, Kenai peninsula and Kodiak island, and more rarely in central Alaska north to at least Mount McKinley and Fairbanks. Breeds in **Canada** in western and southern **British Columbia**, north in the west to the Stikine river and Dease Lake; also breeds on Queen Charlotte and Vancouver islands. In central **Alberta** found south to Calgary and Edmonton, north to around the Wapiti river and Fort McMurray, and also in the Rockies, with confirmed breeding in the extreme southwest. Breeds in a band across central **Saskatchewan** (with summer records north to Wollaston Lake) and central and southern **Manitoba,** and through most of **Ontario** north to Big Trout Lake and Moosonee, with an isolated (?) population in the

Sutton Ridges; absent Hudson Bay lowlands and rare in the extreme southwest. Also breeds in southern **Quebec**, north to Lac Mistassini and Natashquan, and including Anticosti Island. The range extends east to **New Brunswick**, **Nova Scotia**, **Newfoundland** and **Prince Edward Island**. In the Lower 48 of the **USA** breeds in the west in **Washington** (absent from the Columbia river basin), **Oregon**, **Idaho**, western **Montana** and western **Wyoming**, and in **California** found in the coast ranges south to Morro Bay, San Luis Obispo Co., in the Sierra Nevada south to Kern Co. and also the White mountains (and recorded in summer, but no evidence of breeding, in the Clark mountains), and in the mountains of SW California from Mount Pinos in northern Ventura Co. south to San Diego Co. The range extends to **Nevada**, **Utah**, western **Colorado**, eastern and central **Arizona** west to the Kaibab Plateau and Bradshaw, Santa Rita and Huachuca mountains (and has occurred in the Hualapai mountains in midsummer), **New Mexico** south to the Animas and Peloncillo mountains, and to SW **Texas** in the Guadalupe mountains in Culberson Co. (and possibly other montane areas in the Trans-Pecos). There is an isolated breeding population in the Black Hills of **South Dakota** (formerly also Clay Co., with continuing summer records from the eastern counties), and present in the breeding season in the Pine Ridge of adjacent NW **Nebraska**, and also in **North Dakota**, where breeding presumed but not proven. In the Great Lakes region in north-central **Minnesota** recorded breeding in Clearwater and Hubbard Cos., and in **Wisconsin** in the north and east, south to Burnett, Taylor, Shawano and Ozaukee Cos., also along the Mississippi and Wisconsin rivers, with scattered summer records from elsewhere in the state. Occurs throughout **Michigan**, although absent from the southern tier of counties, except Berrien Co. In the Mississippi basin, sporadic nesting occurs to the south of the usual breeding range, largely in floodplain forest and relict cypress swamps. Nesting has been recorded in eastern **Nebraska** along the Missouri and lower Niobrara rivers, in **Iowa** (mostly in the north and east), and in **Missouri**, where formerly regular in cypress swamps in the Mississippi lowlands, with continuing summer records from the Mississippi valley with breeding proven at Big Oak Tree SP. In **Illinois** breeding proven in Mercer Co., probable in Williams Co. and scattered summer records south to Alexander Co., in **Indiana** breeding recorded from Steuben and Posey Cos., probably also Porter Co. and perhaps elsewhere in the north and around Indianapolis, in **Kentucky** breeding proven in the extreme west in Ballard Co., in western **Tennessee** has bred Dyer Co. and singing males recorded in summer in Lake, Shelby, Fayette, Madison and Henry Cos., and in NE and central **Ohio** has recently bred in small numbers south to Hamilton, Clark, Delaware, Wayne and Columbiana Cos. Has also been recorded very rarely in midsummer in **Arkansas** in Craighead, Izard and Hempstead Cos., in **Georgia** in Rabun Co., and in **Delaware** and the **District of Columbia**. In the NE USA, breeds throughout **New England** (although very scarce near the coast in **Connecticut**), **Pennsylvania** (absent only from the extreme southwest), **New York** (including, since 1947, Long Island), **New Jersey**, **Maryland** and recently in the lowlands of northernmost **Virginia**. Also in the southern Appalachians in northern and eastern **West Virginia**, SW **Virginia**, eastern **Tennessee** in the Great Smoky Mountains NP north to Sullivan and Carter Cos., and western **North Carolina**, including Mount Mitchell and the Great Smoky Mountains. In **Mexico** breeds throughout the highlands: in the Sierra Madre Occidental in NE **Sonora** (west to the Pajaritos mountains) and western **Chihuahua**, south through eastern **Sinaloa**, western **Durango** and eastern **Nayarit** to **Jalisco** (Nevado de Colima) and NW **Zacatecas**; in the central highlands from **Jalisco** through **Michoacan**, **Mexico**, **Distrito Federal**, **Morelos**, **Hidalgo** and **Puebla** to western **Veracruz** (Cofre de Perote) and northern **Oaxaca**; in the Sierra Madre Oriental from northern **Hidalgo** north through **San Luis Potosi** to SW **Coahuila**, **Nuevo Leon** and westernmost **Tamaulipas**; also the Sierra Madre del Sur in **Guerrero** and (perhaps disjunctly) in southern **Oaxaca**, and east of the Isthmus of Tehuantepec in **Chiapas**. A rare resident or winter visitor in **Baja California Norte**, with February and May records from the Sierra San Pedro Mártir. In northern Central America found in the highlands from **Guatemala** through **Honduras** (and **El Salvador?**, Sibley & Monroe 1990) to north-central **Nicaragua** (to at least San Rafael del Norte). Winters north to the coast of southern Alaska, southern Canada (occasionally to NE British Columbia, central Alberta and Newfoundland) and the coasts of the Maritime Provinces. There is, however, a partial withdrawal from the north of the range (e.g. less common during the winter at Banff and Jasper NPs in the Rocky Mountains of SW Alberta), and some northern breeders winter irregularly south throughout the eastern USA to central **Florida** (and rarely to southern Florida, where recorded Everglades, Corkscrew Swamp, Coconut Grove and Collier Co.), the **Gulf Coast**, **Texas**, and NE Mexico in **Coahuila** and central **Nuevo Leon** (casually to central Tamaulipas). In the west, an uncommon winter visitor to riverine woodland in southern **Arizona**, especially around Camp Verde and Tucson, rarely west to the lower Colorado river (Arizonan breeding birds are apparently resident, migrants coming from further afield). Also occasional records from NW **Sonora**, and casually to central Sonora. In southern **California**, a rare autumn and winter visitor to the coastal lowlands and Channel Islands, and also rare in the desert (primarily in the autumn). Migrants penetrate south of the breeding range from late August onwards, with the main passage period September–mid November; does not usually occur in any numbers until mid September in the northeast and October–November in Florida, the Gulf States, Texas and Arizona. Return passage northwards is in March–mid May, most birds having left southern areas by early-mid April and the northeast by May. In Mexico, the extreme dates for northern migrants are 9 November–18 April. Vagrant southern **Yukon**, with summer records at Dezadeash and Tagish Lakes, and **Bermuda**, where three or four in November 1870, at least seven in October 1970 and a singleton in November 1987.

**HABITAT** Breeds in coniferous or mixed woodland, also deciduous forests. Prefers more extensive areas of mature old growth, especially dense, well-shaded stands, e.g. Incense Cedar, Lodgepole Pine, fir, hemlock and spruce, and maple-hemlock-pine and maple-elm associations. Also favours wet areas, such as forested floodplains, swamps and bogs, often with large dead trees (prolonged flooding may kill trees and produce the large peeling flakes of bark suitable for nesting; the presence of suitable nest sites may be the critical limiting factor in its breeding distribution). Drier upland forests, however, are also frequented. In Mexico and Central America, breeds in pine or pine-oak woodland. In autumn and winter found in a wider variety of wooded habitats, more regularly including deciduous woodland, and also riparian cottonwoods, scrub, well-wooded suburban areas, parks and cemeteries, and exceptionally will even forage on walls. Northern populations are found from sea level upwards (e.g. in New York, and in Vermont generally *below* 915 m), but primarily a montane species in the south of the range, occurring only locally in the lowlands. Thus, found at up to 2070 m in Washington, at least 2745 m in Idaho, to 3350 m in Colorado, and further south in the Sierra Nevada of California at 915–2440 m, less commonly to 3050 m (but down to 150 m in the inner coast ranges and to near sea level in coastal California); at 2135–3355 m in New Mexico (dispersing upwards to 3660 m), 2440–2590 m in SW Texas and generally above 1200 m in eastern Tennessee. In Mexico, occurs at 1525–3050 m in Chihuahua, above 1525 m in Sinaloa, to 3960 m in Jalisco, at 1890 m to at least 2955 m in Oaxaca, and from at least 2225 m to 3900 m in Chiapas. In Guatemala occurs at 1550-3350 m.

**POPULATION** Fairly common in summer in most of the breeding range, but only uncommon in Alaska, Alberta, Saskatchewan, Newfoundland, New Brunswick, Prince Edward Island, Montana, South Dakota, Wisconsin, Michigan, the eastern seaboard from Massachusetts to Maryland, Pennsylvania, the southern Appalachians and Texas. On the southern marches of the range in the NE USA, breeding is sporadic or very local. Thus, rare in summer in North Dakota, Nebraska, Iowa, Missouri, Illinois, Ohio and Indiana. Generally fairly common to common in Mexico, although uncommon in Oaxaca, and common in Guatemala. In some parts of the east and northeast more abundant on migration, especially in the autumn, than at other times of year. Thus, common on passage in Ontario, Minnesota, Iowa, Missouri, Wisconsin, Michigan, Illinois, Indiana, Ohio, Massachusetts, Connecticut, New York, Pennsylvania and New Jersey, and fairly common on Rhode Island. The centre of gravity of the population shifts southwards in winter, with some withdrawal from the north of the range, especially away from the ameliorating effects of the coast. Is therefore uncommon in winter in Ontario, Quebec, North and South Dakota, Minnesota, Wisconsin, Michigan, Maine, New Hampshire, Vermont, Massachusetts, Rhode Island, and in the far south in Florida, in Texas south of c. 29° N and in SW Texas, and rare in winter in Saskatchewan, Manitoba and Newfoundland. Otherwise, fairly common throughout the range in winter. There has been some recent expansion of the range in the NE USA, spreading into SW and SE Pennsylvania, with a southward spread down the east coast since the 1960s. Also, numbers have increased in New England, probably as a result of the regrowth of forests, and the widespread mortality of American elms from Dutch elm disease may also have temporarily helped the species. Additionally, breeding south of the main range has apparently become more regular in the Mississippi basin, perhaps owing to better coverage or to the maturation of relict swamp forests.

**HABITS** Unobtrusive and rather easily overlooked, but not shy. Usually found singly or in pairs, but forms family parties for about three weeks after the young fledge, and sometimes occurs in small, loose monospecific flocks on migration (rarely, up to 20 individuals together). May join mixed-species foraging flocks. Beautifully camouflaged, when threatened will freeze for several minutes, relying on its cryptic coloration for protection against aerial predators. Following fledging, family parties of juveniles (not adults) roost together in the open, forming a tight circle with all heads facing inwards (as in Short-toed Treecreeper; see figure 28.2, p. 193); different sites are used each night. Up to 11 birds have also been recorded roosting in April in a cavity in a beam in a barn. Otherwise presumably solitary at the roost, and in winter may roost on or even inside buildings. Foraging behaviour typical of treecreepers, feeding almost exclusively on the bark of trees and stubs, delicately picking items from cracks and crevices with its fine, tweezers-like bill. Food insects and spiders, and sometimes in the winter small quantities of seeds or nuts (e.g. acorns and corn). Will occasionally visit feeders to take suet and chopped peanuts.

**BREEDING BIOLOGY** Season: Washington, late March–mid July; Ontario, late April–mid July; Nova Scotia, May; Michigan, May–June; New York, May–mid July; Vermont, June; Oaxaca, March–April?; Durango, Puebla and Chiapas, March. The nest is usually well concealed between the trunk and a loose flap of bark on a large tree or stump, usually dead or dying, 0.6–7 m (–18 m) above ground. Both deciduous and coniferous trees are utilised, but nest sites are frequently (or always) within c. 60 m of standing or running water (C.M. Davis 1978). Less commonly, the nest is placed in a natural cavity such as a knothole or abandoned woodpecker excavation, even in fence posts, behind loose shingles on buildings, or under a piece of tin on an outhouse roof (Peck & James 1987). Will use specially designed artificial nest

187

sites. The foundation of twigs and wood and bark chips is often crescent-shaped, with the 'horns' higher than the cup, and sometimes bound with spiders' webs and egg cases. This supports a cup of finer bark shreds, moss, plant down and sometimes hair or feathers. The female builds, although the male may bring materials to the site, and construction takes 6–30 days. Clutch 5–6 (4–9): eggs white, variably but usually sparsely spotted reddish-brown, the larger markings sometimes concentrated at the larger end; 15.1 x 11.8 mm (C. a. americana). Female incubates, period 14–17 days; she is fed at the nest by the male. The female also broods the young, which are fed by both sexes and fledge after (13–) 14–16 days, remaining with, and dependent on, the adults for up to at least 17 days. Single-brooded (but may lay replacement clutches).

**DESCRIPTION** C. a. americana **Adult**: *In fresh plumage* (September–March/April), crown and nape blackish-brown, feathers with light grey shaft streaks that are bordered warmer brown. Mantle and scapulars similar, but pale centres much larger, with blacker-brown fringes around tip (the 'brown phase' - see below - has the light grey feather centres larger, more diffuse and lightly washed drab, with broader, dull cinnamon-brown borders and the blackish-brown areas around the feather fringes reduced or absent). Back, rump and uppertail-coverts cinnamon-orange, with faint whiter shaft streaks and whiter feather bases. Tail mid grey-brown, feathers darker along shaft; shaft buffy. Lesser coverts mid brown-buff with large white centres and darker fringes. Median coverts dark brown, shaft and tip pale buff. Greater coverts dark brown, outer web tipped and fringed off-white, fringes broader and whiter on inner feathers. Primary coverts dark brown, outer webs finely tipped pale buff-white. Alula dark brown, tipped whitish. Tertials light grey-brown, outer webs becoming dark brown towards tip, broadly tipped and fringed off-white on distal half. Primaries and secondaries mid-dark brown, P5–P10 and secondaries with broad buff-white band across the feathers near base, broad buff-white slot subterminally on outer web and small white tip to outer web; primaries slightly paler at extreme base. Supercilium off-white (buffy in brown phase). Lores and upper ear-coverts dark brown, cheeks and lower ear-coverts mottled pale grey and dark brown. Sides of neck off-white. Underparts white, breast washed pale grey, flanks, belly, vent, and thighs washed pale drab-buff, undertail-coverts washed buff and tipped white. Axillaries and underwing-coverts white. *In worn plumage* (April–August), darker fringes and especially tips to upperpart feathers abrade, so pale centres reach tips, producing a more streaked, less spotted, effect. Underparts slightly duller. **Bare Parts**: Iris brown; bill black, base of lower mandible dull pale yellow or pale flesh; legs and feet dark brown, claws slightly darker. **Juvenile**: As adult, but feathers of upperparts with larger buff-white centres giving a buff-spotted appearance (the crown especially being more spotted). Fine dark tips to feathers of underparts, giving faint

speckling on throat and scaling on breast. **1st Adult**: As adult. **Measurements**: Wing of male 64–68 (chord 61–70), of female 58–68 (chord 60–67); tail of male (49) 60–67, of female 55–65; bill of male 16–19.9, of female 14.8–18.2; tarsus 13–16. Weight 8–9.9 g; autumn migrants in coastal New Jersey 6.5–9.8 g (Murray & Jehl 1964).

**MOULT** Adult post-breeding complete (August–September, in breeding areas). Post-juvenile incomplete, includes the tail (August–September, in breeding areas).

**GEOGRAPHICAL VARIATION** Slight and largely clinal, although there is a marked difference between northern and Mexican birds. Twelve races recognised (largely following Webster 1986).

***C. a. americana*** Canada from northern Saskatchewan east to Newfoundland (populations comprising intergrades with *nigrescens* breed in the NE USA from Minnesota eastwards, south to Pennsylvania and West Virginia); winters south to Texas, SE Coahuila and Florida and west to Colorado. See Description. Bill relatively short, wing relatively long. Upperparts moderately brown to greyish-brown: virtually dimorphic in upperpart coloration, with a paler phase, usually a paler and greyer brown, and a darker, blacker phase (as well as intermediates). The 'brown phase' is commonest in the Maritime Provinces and dominant in Newfoundland ('*anticostiensis*'); the populations in the NE USA intermediate with *nigrescens* lack the brown phase and average rustier on the upperparts.

***C. a. nigrescens*** Great Smoky Mountains of Tennessee and North Carolina; recorded in winter in Texas and Kansas. As nominate *americana*, but upperparts rustier (darker than in extreme reddish nominate *americana*); pale streaks more brown-tinged than in all but Middle American and Pacific coast races.

***C. a. idahoensis*** Webster 1986. Northernmost Idaho (Bonner Co.) and NW Montana north to central Alberta (Fort Assiniboine); winters south to Arizona, west to British Columbia and east to New York. (Synonymised with *montana* by Browning 1990.) As nominate *americana*, but upperparts darker and redder, reddish-brown streaked pale grey (pale streaks greyer); as *montana*, but upperparts rustier with whiter streaks, bill shorter (male 14.2-17.3). Underparts white, may be variably washed buff; undertail-coverts dull pale buff to orange-buff, this colour often extending to the flanks.

***C. a. montana*** Interior British Columbia, central-north Idaho (Latah and Clearwater Cos.) and western South Dakota (Black Hills), south to southern Arizona (Santa Catalina mountains) and extreme western Texas (Guadalupe mountains) and west to the eastern flanks of the Coast Range of British Columbia, the Cascades of Washington and Oregon (Wheeler and Harney Cos.) and eastern Nevada, intergrading with *albescens* in Arizona, western New Mexico and Texas; winters at lower altitudes and also south to northern Coahuila, west to the Pacific coast and east to

Wisconsin and Louisiana. Essentially dimorphic. Grey phase has whitish supercilium and is near *alascensis*, but even the greyest birds have the white streaks on the crown sparser and narrower; brown phase slightly darker, with reduced reddish-brown tones, than nominate *americana* (but close to 'dark phase'?) and *idahoensis*, with pale streaks better defined and greyer, rump duller and reduced buff on flanks. Underparts white, rarely with slight buff wash on breast, undertail-coverts dull pale buff to buffy-grey (rarely more orange-buff, this colour extending onto flanks). Bill long, male 14–20; wing (chord) of male 58–69. Includes '*leucosticta*' of southern Nevada and western Utah (perhaps south to central Arizona, winter only?), with larger pale feather centres on the upperparts and a paler, more buffy-orange rump.

**C. a. alascensis** Webster 1986. South-central Alaska, Intergrading with *occidentalis* (or *montana*: Browning 1990) in south coastal Alaska; winters Idaho to SE Arizona and SW New Mexico. As *montana*, but upperparts paler and greyer, with white streaks broader and more numerous, especially on crown; bill shorter, male 13.5–17.5.

**C. a. occidentalis** Pacific coast from SE Alaska south to California (Monterey Co.), east to coastal slopes of Coast Range in SE Alaska and British Columbia, western slope of Cascades in Washington, and Cascades in Oregon (west to Crook Co.); some may move south within range in winter, also east to central-south British Columbia and west-central California. Upperparts rather buffer and browner than in *montana*, especially the pale streaks (although slightly darker than brown-phase nominate *americana*), also much browner than *alascensis*, and bill longer (male 13.7–18.8); breast washed buff, undertail-coverts orange-buff, this colour usually extending onto flanks. Wing (chord) of male 58–66.

**C. a. stewarti** Webster 1986. Queen Charlotte Island, British Columbia (possibly also northern Vancouver Island). As *occidentalis*, but upperparts brighter orange (most orange of all races). Wing (chord) of male 59-66.

**C. a. zelotes** Southern Oregon (eastern Douglas to Lake Cos.) south through the Sierra Nevada to southern California (Riverside Co.; west to Los Angeles, Santa Barbara and Ventura Cos.) and east to Nevada (Washoe Co.), also the Coast Range of northern California (east of coastal counties and south to Napa Co.); winters at lower elevations, also recorded Arizona and New Mexico. Upperparts browner than in *montana* and darker, duller and more reddish-brown than in *occidentalis* (less orange-brown), with pale streaks pale smoke-grey; rump dark reddish-tawny, darker and duller than *montana* and duller than *occidentalis*. Underparts white, may be slightly washed buff on breast; undertail-coverts orange-buff, this colour often extending onto the flanks. Wing (chord) of male 57–68; bill of male 15–20.3.

**C. a. albescens** SE Arizona (Santa Rita, Huachuca and Chiricahua mountains) and SW New Mexico (San Luis Mountains) south in NW Mexico in the Sierra Madre Occidental to NE Nayarit (Santa Teresa), NW Jalisco (Bolanos) and

western Zacatecas. Resident, with little altitudinal movement. Upperparts very dark, sooty-black (blackest, least brownish), with well-defined whitish streaks (narrower and whiter than in adjacent races) and very contrasting rump (darker and more chestnut than in northern races). Throat white, breast and belly light grey with slight drab wash, undertail-coverts light drab-buff. Bill shorter than in *montana* (male 13.9–17.8). Wing (chord) of male 58–67.

**C. a. alticola** Southern Mexico in Transvolcanic range, Sierra Madre del Sur, and Sierra Madre Oriental from Jalisco east to Oaxaca and Veracruz, north to Coahuila, Nuevo Leon and Tamaulipas; an isolated population from the Sierra Madre Oriental (SE Coahuila, Tamaulipas, Nuevo Leon and northern Hidalgo) is intermediate with *albescens*. As *albescens*, but upperparts browner (less black), pale streaks washed olive-drab; rump paler, more orange and less rufous; underparts less grey, more drab or buffy, especially undertail-coverts. Wing (chord) of male 57–67; bill of male 13.5–17.3. (Includes '*jaliscensis*' of southern Jalisco, Michoacan and western Mexico, with the upperparts variably paler and browner; '*guerrerensis*' of Guerrero, with the upperpart streaks darker and redder and the rump more chestnut; and '*molinensis*' of Oaxaca, with the upperparts slightly browner, but not so reddish as Guerrero birds.)

**C. a. pernigra** Chiapas, southernmost Mexico (from San Cristóbel de La Casas south to Volcán Tacaná) to Volcán de Fuego, Guatemala. Upperparts darkest brown of any race (rather than sooty-black as *albescens*, and browner than in *alticola*), with narrower pale streaks than in all races except *extima* (narrower and more cinnamon-brown than in *alticola*). Underparts as *alticola*; often faint darker tips to feathers of underparts (= juveniles?). Bill of male 14.8–17.2.

**C. a. extima** Eastern Guatemala (Sierra de las Minas), Honduras, and NW Nicaragua. As *pernigra*, but crown and upperparts slightly less brownish, more black, with slightly broader and whiter streaks, rump darker (more rufous, less orange), and underparts paler and a purer grey (pale grey rather than light drab-grey); bill longer. Compared with *alticola*, upperparts blacker, less brownish, pale streaks finer and underparts paler and purer grey. Wing (chord) of male 57–65; bill of male 15.3–18.8.

**RELATIONSHIPS** Often considered conspecific with Eurasian Treecreeper of Europe and Asia. However, the song of Brown Creeper is more variable than the rather stereotyped song of Eurasian Treecreeper and, although similarly more variable than that of Short-toed Treecreeper, is closer to that species in having 4–8 units per song. Thielcke (1962) showed in field experiments that Eurasian Treecreepers were able to discriminate between their own vocalisations and those of Brown Creeper, and showed little response to the latter's vocalisations. The introductory *tsree* note of Brown Creeper's song is similar to the *tsree* note of Eurasian (and Short-toed), and the similarity of this single note was thought to be responsible for eliciting the limited response from both Eurasian and Short-toed Treecreepers. These playback experiments, as well as analysis of sonagrams, support the treatment of Brown Creeper as a separate species (as in AOU 1983, Sibley & Monroe 1990). REFERENCES Baptista & Johnson (1982), Bent (1948), C.M. Davis (1978), DeSante & Pyle (1986), Webster (1986).

## 28 SHORT-TOED TREECREEPER *Certhia brachydactyla*        Plate 9

Endemic to the Western Palearctic, this species has to be critically distinguished from the Eurasian Treecreeper, with which it overlaps widely.

**IDENTIFICATION** Length 125 mm (5 in). Overall very similar in appearance to Eurasian Treecreeper, and separation of the two species is often difficult and can be impossible. The key character in the field is voice. * **Voice** Both species have a variety of similar calls, but Short-toed has a constantly louder, more emphatic and more varied vocabulary, including a diagnostic shrill, explosive, monosyllabic *tyt* or *tut* (recalling a Coal Tit). This is typically given in a short, slightly accelerating series, *tyt...tyt, tyt-tyt,* sometimes with a slight fall in pitch at the end ('as clear as silver drops'). The usual call of Eurasian Treecreeper is a high-pitched, shrill, penetrating *srrih* or *tsree,* with a distinct vibrato quality, often given in a deliberate slow series; Short-toed has a similar call, but uses it relatively rarely, thus this call is *highly suggestive* of Eurasian Treecreeper. The songs are also dis-

tinctively different, although occasionally one species may give a perfect imitation of the other. Short-toed's full song is *tyt, tyt, siriti-toi-see,* shorter (half the length, with only a third the number of notes), lower-pitched, louder and more emphatic than Eurasian's sibilant cadence (see Voice for details). * **Supercilium** The most important plumage feature. Greyish-white to creamy-white, shorter, narrower and less prominent than on the majority of Eurasian, and often inconspicuous in front of the eye (the supercilia never join above the base of the bill, and juveniles may lack any indication of a supercilium in front of the eye), but sometimes broad and well defined behind the eye. On Eurasian, the supercilia are often pure white (usually so in nominate *familiaris*), more contrasting and may join above the base of the bill (often so in nominate *familiaris*). * **Crown** Forehead often

Note: primaries numbered asdendantly, ie from the outside of the wing towards the body. Wingpoint P4=P5, with P6 slightly shorter. Based on Daunicht 1991, figure 15.)

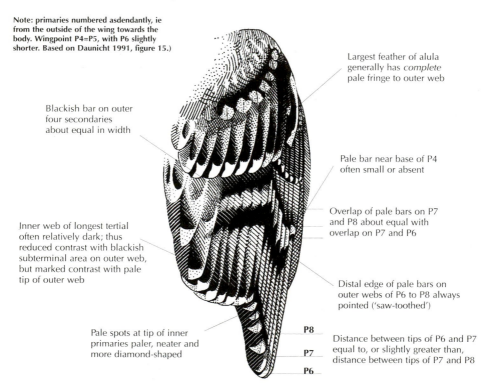

Largest feather of alula generally has *complete* pale fringe to outer web

Blackish bar on outer four secondaries about equal in width

Pale bar near base of P4 often small or absent

Overlap of pale bars on P7 and P8 about equal with overlap on P7 and P6

Inner web of longest tertial often relatively dark; thus reduced contrast with blackish subterminal area on outer web, but marked contrast with pale tip of outer web

Distal edge of pale bars on outer webs of P6 to P8 always pointed ('saw-toothed')

P8

Pale spots at tip of inner primaries paler, neater and more diamond-shaped

P7

Distance between tips of P6 and P7 equal to, or slightly greater than, distance between tips of P7 and P8

P6

*Wing of* C. b. megarhyncha.

rather uniformly brown, lacking marked whitish streaks, but always streaked whitish on Eurasian.
* **Upperparts** Differences in the markings on the upperparts are difficult to define, owing to the complexity of the pattern. Compared with Eurasian Treecreepers of the races *britannica* and *macrodactyla* of western and southern Europe, Short-toed's upperparts average a little colder and darker, with narrower and better-defined pale streaking, especially on the nape and upper mantle (the race *megarhyncha* of Short-toed from western parts of Europe has slightly warmer brown upperparts with slightly less well-defined pale streaks than nominate *brachydactyla* from further east). Compared with Eurasian Treecreepers from Scandinavia and eastern Europe (nominate *familiaris*) Short-toed is rather darker, and lacks the pale-spotted appearance. Note: in worn plumage (i.e. spring and summer) the dark fringes on the upperparts are abraded, and on Eurasian the pale streaks on the crown and nape are consequently better defined and the overall tone of the upperparts slightly colder and less rufous. Also, juveniles of both species have more spotted, less streaked, upperparts. Additional slight differences are that on Eurasian the ground colour of the crown and nape is colder and darker than the mantle, whereas it is virtually uniform with the mantle on Short-toed. Also, on Short-toed the lower scapulars are long, pointed and prominent, with *long* pale shaft streaks and dark fringes on the inner webs, whilst on Eurasian the lower rear scapulars tend not to be obviously long and lanceolate, appearing scaled rather than streaked and lacking the dark fringe to the inner web. * **Rump** The rump is slightly less orange-rufous on Short-toed than on Eurasian, but there may be *more* contrast between the rump and mantle. * **Underparts** More sullied with dirty buff on the breast and flanks than Eurasian; on some Short-toed, only the throat is pure white. The underparts are usually silky-white on Eurasian, only faintly washed buff on the vent and undertail-coverts; some Eurasian Treecreepers from southern England, however, are dull (possibly from soot or other discoloration) and closely approach Short-toed in this feature, and there is also overlap in many other areas of Europe. * **Bill** Typically longer and more decurved or abruptly bent than on Eurasian, but there is much overlap (and averages as short as Eurasian's in northern France) and the length of the bill is difficult to assess critically in the field, whilst juvenile Short-toed may show shorter bill than adult Eurasian. Bill colour is of no use in separation from Eurasian Treecreeper; either may show an all-dark upper mandible, completely cloaking the tip of the lower and thus producing a dark-tipped bill, or a pale cutting edge to the upper mandible with only the culmen ridge dark, giving an extensively pale-sided bill with a pale tip.
* **Geographical variation** The birds which resemble each other most are British Eurasian Treecreepers and Short-toed from the near Continent, and to overcome the variation in both species a combination of most, if not all, the features outlined above must be used. Although a Short-toed Treecreeper may stand out in general appearance, convincing identification of lone birds will often be difficult. A long-billed treecreeper with dull, dark, well-streaked upperparts, short supercilia (not pure white and not meeting over the bill) and dingy underparts with a contrastingly whiter throat may well be a Short-toed. Details of voice should always be sought, however, as supporting evidence. See Table 1, p. 192, for summary.

**IDENTIFICATION IN THE HAND** Far from straightforward. * **Biometrics** Careful measurements of bill and hindclaw are required. Two discriminant functions have been advocated: In some north and central European and Iberian populations, hindclaw < 0.456 x bill = Short-toed. In western Europe, hindclaw < 0.14 x bill + 5.6 = Short-toed. However, neither is infallible and at best will allow 95% of birds to be identified correctly, so attention to plumage and vocalisations is essential even with trapped birds. Note that juveniles may still be growing their bills for three months, and also their claws, and measurements in June–August may be of little help.

**PLUMAGE FEATURES** There are several plumage features of practicable use only in the hand (or on close inspection of photographs). All are 'percentage' characters or subjective in their assessment, and should be used in combination (see figure 28.1, p. 190). * **Alula** The largest feather of the alula generally has a complete or near-complete pale fringe on Short-toed. This is lacking or broken on most Eurasian, which usually have only a pale tip to the feather or a broken pale fringe. However, there is some overlap in this character and it is a guide only. * **Primaries a.** Pale bar near base of P4 often small or even absent (always prominent on Eurasian). **b.** Overlap of pale bars on P7 and P8 about equal with overlap on P7 and P6; on Eurasian, light bars on P7 and P8 generally overlap more extensively than those on P7 and P6. **c.** Distal border of pale spot on centre of outer webs of P6–P8 always pointed (giving a more 'saw-toothed' appearance); on Eurasian, often more or less straight or rounded, although sometimes shallowly pointed (giving a more 'stepped' appearance). **d.** Primaries darker and tips on inner primaries whiter, better defined and more diamond-shaped; on Eurasian, primaries slightly paler (mid brown), and pale tips duller, slightly more diffuse and more extensive, extending well onto the inner web, and thus pale tips more crescent-shaped. * **Secondaries** The blackish bar across the outer 4 secondaries is about even in width on Short-toed; on Eurasian, it often becomes narrower on the outermost secondaries. * **Tertials** The longest tertial is often dark on the inner web, showing little contrast with the dark subterminal area on the outer web, but generally showing an obvious contrast with the pale tip to the outer web. On some birds, however, the inner web may be just as pale as on Eurasian, on which the inner web is generally relatively pale, often contrasting with black subterminal area on the outer web, but showing little obvious contrast in tone with the pale tip to the outer web (although there is a slight

**Table 1. Summary of differences in plumage and bare parts between Eurasian and Short-toed Treecreepers**

| | EURASIAN | SHORT-TOED |
|---|---|---|
| Forehead (adults only) | prominent and relatively contrasting pale streaks | streaks poorly marked or lacking |
| Supercilium | often pure white, well defined between bill and eye | off-white, usually not reaching base of bill or ill-defined at that point |
| Upperparts | average paler and warmer, more scaled | average colder and greyer-brown, more streaked |
| Rump | cinnamon-orange, brighter than Short-toed but showing less contrast with mantle | cinnamon-rufous, usually slightly less rufous than Eurasian but may show more contrast with mantle |
| Underparts (except flanks) | pure white to whitish | greyish-white to pale grey, variably washed rufous-brown on breast and belly; throat white |
| Flanks | white to pale buff or pale rufous | washed rufous-brown to brown |
| Shaft of central tail feathers | usually clearly paler than vane | usually concolorous with vane or only slightly paler |
| Bill | relatively short | relatively long |
| Hindclaw | relatively long | relatively short |

**Table 2. Summary of details of the wing of Eurasian and Short-toed Treecreepers**

| | EURASIAN | SHORT-TOED |
|---|---|---|
| Largest feather of alula | generally lacks complete pale fringe to outer web | generally has complete pale fringe to outer web |
| Outer blackish bar on outer 4 secondaries | often becomes narrower on outermost | about uniform in width |
| Spots on tips of inner primaries | duller, more diffuse, and more crescent-shaped (extend further onto inner web) | paler, neater and more diamond-shaped |
| Pattern of pale bar on P6–P8 | pale bars on P7 and P8 generally overlap more than those on P7 and P6 | overlap of pale bars on P7 and P8 about equal to overlap of P7 and P6 |
| Shape of distal edge of pale spot on outer web of P8-P6 | generally straight, rounded or shallowly pointed | more or less clearly pointed |
| Wing formula | distance between tips of P6 and P7 often obviously greater than between P7 and P8 | distances between tips of P6 and P7 equal to, or slightly greater than, between P7 and P8 |
| Colour contrast on longest tertial | inner web averages relatively pale; often obvious contrast with blackish subterminal area of outer web, but not obviously paler than tip | inner web averages relatively dark; reduced contrast with dark subterminal area of outer web, but marked contrast with pale tip of outer web |

On both species wingpoint P4=P5, with P6 slightly shorter.

colour contrast, with the inner web being browner and the pale tip to the outer web greyer). * **Wing formula** The distance between the tips of P8 and P7 is about equal to that between tips of P7 and P6 (or P6–P7 slightly greater than P7–P8, and always <2x); on Eurasian, the distance between P6–P7 is often obviously greater than P7–P8, and usually >2x. (On both species wingpoint P4=P5, with P6 slightly shorter.) * **Tail** The shafts of the inner tail feathers (especially T1) are dark grey-brown, concolorous with the vane or only slightly paler. On Eurasian, the shafts are pale brown, clearly paler than vane (this character is probably of practicable use only when direct comparison is possible). See Table 2 for summary.

**VOICE** Calls include the 'excitement call', a diagnostic, clear, explosive *tyt* or *tut* (also transcribed as 'teeut', 'zeet', 'tseep' or 'sit', and likened in quality to a call of Coal Tit). It is given singly, in a slow series at well-spaced intervals, in a fast series (almost trills) or in a characteristic short phrase with a 'dripping' rhythm, which accelerates and falls slightly in pitch (tyt...tyt, tyt tyt-tyt); some series may be prolonged. It is used in alarm or aggressive encounters, as well as in flight. May also occasionally give a loud, penetrating *tsree* or *srieh* (rather similar to the *tsree* call of Eurasian, although fractionally lower-pitched, less pure and 'looser', and sometimes louder and more emphatic). Given singly and in series at varying speeds, this is used as a contact call, and also in intraspecific disputes and by begging females; helpfully for identification purposes, the *tyt* call may be combined with the *tsree* call. Other flight calls include a quiet, thin, high-pitched *si, sit* or *tsup* (again, only subtly different from Eurasian's flight call). Full song a stereotyped phrase rising in pitch towards the end, comprising 6 (4–9) loud, clear, whistled notes, evenly spaced, but with a slightly 'jolting' rhythm, rapidly and energetically delivered, it begins with *tyt* calls and terminates with *tsree* units: *tyt, tyt, siriti-toi-see* (also rendered *teet-teet-teet-e-roi-i—tiit, teet, teet, teeteroititt; sit, sit, sittere-uitt; or dizwi-dizwidi*), c. 1.1–1.5 seconds in duration. Some songs are abbreviated to 3–4 units (notably in Denmark). Each male has 1–3 song types and there are also regional dialects within Europe, but these variations are generally distinguishable only on sonagrams. The North African population has a different, lower-pitched song, not recognised as conspecific by European birds, whilst the song on Cyprus is very short and simple, comprising 3–6 units, and again producing little response from European birds. Short-toed can mimic Eurasian Treecreeper, although the latter is the more frequent mimic (see under that species for details). Sings throughout the year, but especially March–July. (Largely after Cramp & Perrins 1993, Bruun *et al.* 1986.)

**SEX/AGE** Sexes similar. Juveniles have more spotted (less streaked) upperparts, and some small brownish or grey spots on the underparts (usually more extensive and obvious than on juvenile Eurasian). 1st adult as adult.

**DISTRIBUTION AND MOVEMENTS** Endemic to the Western Palearctic. Breeds on Jersey, Guernsey, Sark and Alderney in the Channel Islands (**UK**), and in Continental Europe from **Portugal** and **Spain** north and east to southern **Denmark** (Jutland), **Poland** (northeast to Suwalki), the western **Ukraine** (L'vov region, Carpathians and Transcarpathia, east to c. 26° E; rare straggler to the Kiev region and Uman), **Slovakia**, **Hungary**, locally in **Bulgaria** and **Romania** (southeast to Tulcea), and south to **Italy** and Sicily, **Greece**, Crete, **Cyprus**, European **Turkey** (Thrace), and western Turkey (Western Anatolia, the Black Sea coastlands east to at least the Kizil Irmak delta, locally on the central plateau in the Ankara region and at Kizilcahamam, and the southern coastlands east to Pozanti and the Sultan Marshes). There are apparently isolated populations at the foot of the western Caucasus on the Black Sea coast from Novorossiysk in **Russia** southeast to at least Sukhumi in the **Abkhazian Republic** (and perhaps to the Turkish border). The eastern boundary in the Caucasus is poorly known, but extends to Svenetia and Kolkhida in western **Georgia**, and may extend to Kislovodsk in the northern Caucasus. (Also recorded from the Talysh range in SE Azerbaydzhan in January-February 1964, but according to Stepanyan 1990 the treecreepers of the Talysh range and adjacent lowlands are Eurasian Treecreepers.) In North Africa, found in **Morocco** (south to Moyen and Haut Atlas), **Algeria** (south to Atlas Saharien and Aures range) and NW **Tunisia**. Resident and rather strictly sedentary, with very limited post-breeding dispersal and few ringing recoveries beyond 10 km, but a few may perhaps move slightly longer

*Figure 28.2  Roosting Short-toed Treecreepers.*

distances in September–October and March–June. Recorded September 1966 at Rybachiy (= Rossitten) on the Kurische Wehrung, **Kaliningrad** region, **Russia**. Vagrant NW **Belarus** (recorded 'not uncommonly' May–October 1918 northeast of Grodno (east to Tsubrovo), and a pair March 1931 on the upper Shchara river east of Slonim), southern **Lithuania** (M. Zalakevicius *in litt.*), **Sweden** (11 records up to 1994, all but one at Falsterbo), **England** (17 records up to 1993, April–May and September–early November; 14 of these from Kent, especially Dungeness, and all but one trapped). Also vagrant (?) **Corsica**, January 1908. Tape recordings made in April 1969 of three singing birds near Piana in SW Corsica were identified as this species, giving the song of the North African race; they were presumably of North African origin, and may represent a recently established population, but there have been no subsequent records.

**HABITAT** Mixed and broadleaved deciduous woodland, particularly oak, favouring edge habitats, as well as pine forest (especially in the south), riverine willows and poplars, copses, orchards and parks, usually with a dense understorey, well-wooded farmland and suburban areas, and sometimes plantations of rough-barked exotic conifers (but generally avoids pure stands of fir, spruce and beech). In southern Spain, prefers open forests of Cork Oaks or Stone Pines with some shrubby undergrowth, and groves of European Wild Olives. Overall, the essential requirement is for stands of mature, rough-barked trees, and the presence or absence of this species may affect the local occurrence of Eurasian Treecreeper. In Europe usually found in the lowlands, but in Germany occurs at up to 900 m, in SE France (Alpes-Maritimes) up to 1800 m, in southern Switzerland to *c.* 1400 m, but to only 1000 m in central Switzerland, in Austria usually nests below 500 m, exceptionally found up to 1050 m, and in Bulgaria to c. 1070 m. In Turkey, however, found at up to considerable altitudes, and in North Africa in montane forests of Aleppo Pine, Atlas Cedar, juniper, and Cork and Holm Oaks.

**POPULATION** Generally fairly common, but rare in the Caucasus. In the Channel Islands, common on Jersey and Guernsey, uncommon on Sark and very few on Alderney. Has spread north into Denmark (first bred 1946, expansion continues and now *c.* 300 pairs).

**HABITS** Not shy, but unassuming and inconspicuous. Usually solitary in winter, remaining on or near the breeding territory, occasionally also found in pairs (and will gather at favoured roosts). Often joins mixed-species foraging flocks, sometimes together with Eurasian Treecreeper. Territorial during the breeding season, although territories may overlap, and boundaries may be poorly defined and poorly defended (less pugnacious than Eurasian Treecreeper, and territories may overlap with those of Eurasian with little or no conflict). May roost communally, with up to 20 birds together in a dense huddle in cold weather, usually on buildings, the birds clinging to the wall under the eaves in a star formation, and some indi-

viduals may be totally hidden (see figure 28.2). Otherwise roosts in trees, choosing very similar sites to those used by Eurasian Treecreeper (see p. 181). Once the bond has formed, the pair will roost close together, but the female roosts in the nest from the onset of laying. Foraging behaviour very much like that of Eurasian Treecreeper, and similarly will feed on walls and buildings, but a little slower and less agile, making more spirals and hops. Food mainly insects and spiders, but also some seeds.

**BREEDING BIOLOGY** Season April–mid June, occasionally from late March. The nest is placed behind a bark flap or in a crack or crevice (including abandoned woodpecker holes), as well as in cavities in buildings (wooden or stone) or woodpiles, sometimes behind ivy, in the base of a raptor's nest or squirrel's drey, and exceptionally in a tangle of twigs close to a tree trunk; will use specially designed nestboxes. In Morocco, breeds in holes or a narrow fork of the trunk, but not behind bark flaps. Most nests are sited 0.5–4 m above ground, only a few above 10 m. The nest is a foundation of twigs, conifer needles, grass, bark, plants fibres, cloth, paper etc. (often large and untidy, filling the cavity), lined with feathers, hair, down, rootlets, moss and lichen. Usually the male builds 2–3 foundations and the female selects one to complete, the process taking up to 32 days. Clutch 5–7 (4–9): eggs white, spotted and blotched with reddish-purple and reddish-brown (sometimes very faint) concentrated at the broader end; 15.6 x 12.2 mm (*C. b. megarhyncha*). Female incubates, period 13–15 days, and only the female broods the young, although they are fed by both sexes, fledging after 15–18 days. The young probably disperse rather quickly. Usually double-brooded, and broods may overlap, the male starting a new nest whilst the female is still feeding the first brood. When the young are 10–12 days old, the male takes over feeding them while the female completes the second nest, sometimes laying the second clutch before young from the first have fledged. Apparently occasionally polygynous, and simultaneous bigamy has been recorded, two females incubating eggs and feeding young at the same time in the same nestbox.

**DESCRIPTION** *C. b. megarhyncha* **Adult**: *In fresh plumage* (autumn–winter), feathers of crown and nape brown, fringed blackish, with narrow off-white shaft streaks. Mantle and scapulars similar, but only feather tips blackish and off-white centres broader. Rump and uppertail-coverts cinnamon-rufous, feather centres whitish (and may reach tip of shaft), concealed base blackish, concealed subbasal area whitish. Tail feathers pale brown, slightly darker around shaft, which is pale rufous-brown. Lesser coverts brown, tipped orange-buff. Median and greater coverts black-brown, median coverts tipped orange-buff and centred whitish, greater coverts fringed and broadly tipped pale buff to rufous-brown, sometimes with a pale shaft streak. Alula and primary coverts black-brown, tipped pale buff, largest feather of alula often with complete pale fringe on outer web. Inner web of tertials mid-light brown, outer web dark brown, black from centre towards tip, with narrow buff-white fringe and broad white tip. Primaries and secondaries mid brown, P4/P5–P10 and secondaries with broad pale buff band across feather (only on outer web P4/P5), bordered on each side by a blackish-brown band, fringed orange-buff distally of these bands (especially on the secondaries) and tipped off-white. Supercilium greyish-white to brownish-white, usually indistinct or absent in front of eye. Lores blackish. Ear-coverts mottled white, black and brown. Underparts greyish-white to pale grey, breast and belly usually variably washed rufous-brown or brown, flanks washed rufous-brown; undertail-coverts pale rufous-brown, tipped whitish; thighs pale grey. Underwing-coverts and axillaries white. **Bare parts**: Iris brown; upper mandible dark brown, cutting edges paler, lower mandible pale brown, tipped dark brown; legs and feet pale brown. **Juvenile**: As adult, but feather centres on upperparts larger, underparts whitish or greyish-white, some feathers with small brownish or grey spots; belly may be uniformly buffish. **1st Adult**: As adult. **Measurements**: Wing of male 58.5–67, of female 56–65; tail of male 53.5–64, of female 56–64; bill of male 15.5–19.9, of female 15.4–20.3; tarsus 14.1–16.6; hindclaw 6.7–8.9. Weight 7.5–11 g.

**MOULT** Adult post-breeding complete (late June–mid September). Post-juvenile partial, probably includes tertials and greater coverts (late June–mid October).

**GEOGRAPHICAL VARIATION** Slight and largely clinal, involving minor differences in size and coloration. Five poorly marked races recognised.

*C. b. megarhyncha* Western Europe in Portugal, NW Spain, the western Pyrénées (east to Cauterets), Channel Islands, western and northern France, Belgium, the Netherlands and western Germany. Intergrades with nominate *brachydactyla* in the central Pyrénées, western and southern Spain and southern Portugal. See Description. Averages slightly paler and more rufous in the westernmost parts of the range (Brittany).

*C. b. brachydactyla* Continental Europe, east of *megarhyncha*, from Spain (except NW), eastern and SE France (eastern Pyrénées), central Germany and Denmark eastwards, including Sicily and Crete. As *megarhyncha*, but averages slightly darker and colder brown, with better-defined whitish streaking on upperparts. Wing of male, 58–67, of female 58–67, bill 15.8–23 of male 16.3–20, of female 15.8–18; hindclaw 6–8.6.

*C. b. mauritanica* North Africa. Poorly marked. As nominate *brachydactyla*, but upperparts slightly darker and colder, pale streaks on crown average narrower and less conspicuous, underparts less whitish, breast and flanks more extensively washed dull buff. Longest wing and bill: wing, of male 60–70; bill of male 17–22.

*C. b. dorotheae* Cyprus. Poorly marked. As nominate *brachydactyla*, but upperparts slightly greyer and more 'floury' (especially the rump), underparts purer white, with a paler and greyer wash on the flanks; bill much longer than that of its nearest neighbours (Mead 1975). Wing 58–65, of male 61–65; bill of male 18–21.5.

*C. b. harterti* Asia Minor and the Caucasus. As *megarhyncha*, but upperparts duller rufous, especially the rump (although very slightly more rufous than nominate *brachydactyla*).

**RELATIONSHIPS** A sibling species of Eurasian Treecreeper, and may form a superspecies with Brown Creeper (see p. 189).

**REFERENCES** Cramp & Perrins (1993), Daunicht (1991), Harrap (1992), Hirschfeld (1985), Mead & Wallace (1976), Svensson (1992).

# 29 BAR-TAILED TREECREEPER *Certhia himalayana*          Plate 10
Other name: Himalayan Treecreeper

A hardy species able to survive at high altitudes, this treecreeper has a curiously interrupted distribution at each end of the Himalayan chain, recalling that of White-cheeked Nuthatch.

**IDENTIFICATION** Length 140 mm (5.5 in). Crown, nape and upper mantle mottled blackish-brown and mid brown and finely streaked paler, lower mantle and scapulars paler and more mealy, marked with dark scallops. Back and rump only slightly warmer, indistinctly mottled dull cinnamon-orange. Wings intricately marked (and tertials and primaries barred dark brown), and tail mid grey-brown with well-defined dark brown cross-bars. Long, thin creamy supercilium, with lores and ear-coverts dark brown. Throat and centre of breast creamy-white, grading to greyish-buff on the lower flanks, vent and undertail-coverts. Distinguished from Eurasian, Brown-throated and Rusty-flanked Treecreepers by the thin blackish bars on the tail, easily visible at close range.

**SEX/AGE** Sexes alike, although males average *c.* 1.7 mm longer-billed. Juvenile marginally distinct, with the upperparts slightly warmer and browner than the adult's, with less well-defined pale spots (especially on the crown) and dark scallops; more contrast on the underparts between the blotchy white throat and breast and the dull drab-buff belly and vent, with scattered very fine dark spots and scallops (note that adults, when very fresh, may show faint dark scallops on the breast and belly). 1st adult as adult.

**VOICE** Calls include a thin, descending *tsiu* (a little like a whining dog), sometimes given in a slow descending series, a thin *tsee* or *see*, which may become a slightly rising *tseeet* or have a slight rolling or vibrato quality (cf. Eurasian Treecreeper), an even higher-pitched and thinner *tsee* (even more Goldcrest-like), a relatively full *chit* (cf. Brown-throated Treecreeper), and a sharp, thin *psit* or *tsit*, given with variable power and emphasis. The song is a trill of 10–12 (7–16) full, slightly disyllabic, relatively high-pitched, whistled units given at a rate of c. 6–7 per second (sometimes as fast as 12 per second). On about the same pitch, the phrase is introduced by a short, sweet *tsee* note, e.g. *tsee-tsui'tsui'tsui'tsui'tsui'tsui'tsui'tsui'tsui'tsui'tsuip* or sometimes a more slurred *si-liu-liu-liu-liu-liu-liu....* The exact structure of the units is quite variable, but they are generally sweet and musical (or occasionally a little hollow or 'wooden'); the song is slower, more musical and less rattling than that of Brown-throated Treecreeper, and rather longer than Rusty-flanked's short accelerating trill. Shorter and more tinkling songs are sometimes given, comprising c. 8 units given at a rate of c. 10 units per second. These short songs often fall and then rise in pitch in tripping, lilting rhythm (almost laughing), e.g. *tsee'tsu-tsu'tsut'tut'tut'ti'tee*, or *ti, ti'tu-du-du-du-du*.

**DISTRIBUTION AND MOVEMENTS** Two discrete and widely separated populations. In the west, breeds through the western Tien Shan in the Chatkal'skiy, Kuraminskiy and Ferganskiy ranges, and in the Alay system in the Alayskiy, Turkestanskiy, Zerav'shanskiy and Gissarskiy ranges, Baysuntau, Kugitangtau, Babatag and Aktau ranges, and south to western Badakhshanskaya (Shugnan), in western **Kyrgyzstan**, eastern **Uzbekistan**, western **Tadzhikistan** and extreme SE **Turkmenistan**. Reported from southern **Kazakhstan**, in the Karatau range (Vaurie 1959) and in the Alma-Ata region (Portenko & Wunderlich 1980), but Dolgushin *et al.* (1972) state that the only confirmed record for Kazakhstan is from the Ugam river in February; possibly also breeds in the upper Aksu river in the Talasskiy Alatau, but sight records in this area may refer to wintering Eurasian Treecreepers. Scattered records from **Afghanistan**, in the northwest in the Paropamisus range, in the north in the northern foothills of the Hindu Kush, in the south at Kandahar, and in the northeast in Nuristan, Laghman, Nangarhar and the Safed Koh. In **Pakistan** breeds in central and northern Baluchistan (south to at least the Ziarat region), north to the Shinghar range in Zhob and Takht-i-Sulaiman range in southern Waziristan; also northern Pakistan in Swat, Dir and Chitral, the western Himalayas in Hazara (including the Kagan valley), the Neelum valley (= Kishen Ganga valley) in Azad Kashmir and the Murree hills, and also north of the main range of the Himalayas in the upper Indus and associated valleys in Gilgit, Hunza, Skardu, Astor and Baltistan (including the Shigar valley, January). In adjacent **NW India** recorded from Ladakh (but three records only: Dras, April; Khalatse, November; and Leh, February, possibly a winter visitor only). Also breeds in **Kashmir** from the Pir Panjal range east-wards, in **Himachal Pradesh** (including the Simla region), northern **Uttar Pradesh** and western **Nepal**, where regularly seen east to the upper Kali Gandaki valley (occasionally a little further east, to Ghorepani, and once Pisang). Said to have been collected further east in the Himalayas, in Darjeeling and Bhutan, but there are no authenticated records from this region and its occurrence there is unlikely (although note the records from extreme SE Tibet, below). A partial migrant in Pakistan, NW India and western Nepal, some birds moving south to the foothills and plains in late October–early April (from September around Kohat), although others remain at high altitude through the winter. In Pakistan occurs south to Mianwali, the Salt Range, Jhelum and Lahore, and sometimes to Jhang and the southern Punjab in Multan and Bahawalpur districts (including Chachran and Bhong near Sadiqabad), and in India recorded in the northern Punjab (Shahabad), northern Haryana (including Ambala) and NW Uttar Pradesh (Saharanpur). Although locally quite plentiful in Pakistan, apparently rather scarcer in winter at low altitudes in India and only occasional in NW Nepal. In the east, breeds in western **China** in southern **Shaanxi** in the Qin Ling mountains, SW **Gansu** in the Min Shan region, western **Sichuan** from Songpan and Pingwu south and west through Guan Xian, Barkam, Ya'an, Emei Shan, Dawu and Kangding to Baiyü, Batang and Muli, in SW **Guizhou**, and in NW and western **Yunnan**, including the Lijiang range and the Gaoligong Shan south to the Tengchong region, and rarely also Kunming, the latter two localities perhaps in winter only? Also adjacent SE **Tibet** (Xizang) at Zayü and in extreme eastern **Arunachal Pradesh**, **India**, around Kahaa in September (Singh 1994), and a record from northern **Myanmar** (**Burma**) at the Panwa Pass (above Sinhkung, Kachin state) in February. Also breeds in SW Burma, on Mount Victoria in the southern Chin hills. Largely resident in the east, but most populations move altitudinally in winter.

**HABITAT** Forest, especially coniferous forest. In Central Asia, northern Afghanistan and SW Pakistan, favours mature juniper forest, whilst in eastern Afghanistan, northern Pakistan, the western Himalayas and western China occurs in forests of pine, spruce, Deodar (cedar) and fir, as well as rhododendron, juniper and birch at high altitudes, occurring even in the more arid treeless regions of the trans-Himalayas of northern Pakistan. Also recorded from mixed forest, but generally avoids stands of oak and other deciduous trees (although Fleming *et al.* 1984 note the habitat in Nepal as oak forests). In eastern Afghanistan, Paludan (1959) notes that it favours tree trunks still remaining in areas where forest has been destroyed by fire; a straggler in Ladakh was noted at 3050 m in April in stunted willows. In SW Burma, found on Mount Victoria exclusively in mature pine forest. In winter, on the plains of Pakistan and NW India, may be found in olive groves (e.g. in the Salt Range) and in sparsely wooded country in riverine woodland, orchards, village trees, gardens and roadside avenues, even when these are isolated amid treeless semi-desert tracts; particularly fond of Shisham trees. In Central Asia breeds at up to c. 2500 m, and in eastern Afghanistan up to 3000 m, whilst on the Safed Koh on the border with Pakistan breeds at 2135–2745 m. In SW Pakistan recorded in summer in Baluchistan around Quetta at 2590–2745 m, and in northern Pakistan up to at least 3350 m, and found on the Murree hills at 1830–2745 m, whilst in NW India noted at 1980–3500 m (especially 2440–2745 m in Kashmir), and in Nepal breeds at c. 2740–3660 m. Most populations move to lower altitudes in winter. Recorded at 1100 m in March in Nuristan, eastern Afghanistan, whilst western Himalayan populations winter below 1800 m in the west and 1400 m in the east (occasionally up to c. 2400 m). In Nepal, however, sometimes found in winter down to 1800 m, occasionally to 305 m and exceptionally to 75 m (Tikapur in the southwest). In SW China, found in Shaanxi at c. 1300–2800 m and in Sichuan at c. 2600–3400 m (and to 3965 m according to Riley 1931 and Thayer & Bangs 1912), descending in winter to at least 650 m. In Yunnan recorded at 2135–3660 m (and at 3660–3965 m in August according to Riley 1931), down to 1200 m in winter, and in Guizhou noted at 1100 m, also in winter. In eastern Arunachal Pradesh, India, recorded at 1300 m in September. On Mount Victoria, Burma, found at 2500–3000 m, and the single record from NE Burma was at 2135 m.

**POPULATION** Not uncommon in Central Asia, northern Afghanistan and SW and northern Pakistan (although scarcer in the more arid regions of the trans-Himalayas) and fairly common in the western Himalayas. Uncommon in western China (but locally common in western Sichuan), and distinctly rarer than Brown-throated Treecreeper on Mount Victoria.

**HABITS** Found singly or in pairs, and in small family parties after the breeding season, but later in the winter usually singly, although such individuals often join mixed-species foraging flocks. Foraging behaviour typical of the family, but sometimes flycatches and occasionally also seen foraging on the ground and, in winter at least, on stone walls. Food insects, spiders and other small invertebrates, occasionally also seeds.

**BREEDING BIOLOGY** Season early April–June (sometimes from late March), generally towards latter end of this period in the NW Himalayas and Central Asia. Fledged young noted on Mount Victoria in early May. The nest is sited from near ground level to c. 15 m high, although usually at low levels, behind the loose bark of a large dead or dying tree, sometimes in the angle between the trunk and a branch, in a crack or crevice (even among exposed roots) or occasionally in old woodpecker excavations. A loose construction of bark fragments, twigs, dry grass, moss etc. is lined with fur, hair and feathers; as the cavity may be large, twigs are dropped in until some are wedged in to form a base, and thus a variable but sometimes considerable accumulation of material may result. Both sexes build the nest over a period of c. 14 days. Clutch 4–6: eggs white with reddish-

brown freckles which form an indistinct zone around the larger end; 15.8 x 12.2 mm (*C. h. himalayana*). Apparently only the female incubates, period 13–14 days; she is fed on the nest by the male. Care of young by both sexes, fledging period c. 21 days. Apparently single-brooded.

**DESCRIPTION** *C. h. himalayana* **Adult**: *In fresh plumage* (September–February), crown, nape and centre of upper mantle dark drab with slightly paler shaft streaks (especially on nape) and blackish-brown fringes, giving a mottled effect. Feathers of lower mantle and scapulars with drab-white centres, fine warm brown subterminal markings and fine blackish-brown fringes, giving a mealy, dark-scalloped appearance on a paler ground. Feathers of back and rump dull cinnamon-orange subterminally with light drab tips. Uppertail-coverts light drab, faintly barred darker. Tail mid drab with neat dark brown cross-bars; shafts pale rufous-brown. Lesser and median coverts dark brown, tipped buff-white. Greater coverts dark brown, inner feathers tipped dull buff-white, with pale buff shafts. Alula and primary coverts dark brown, feathers of alula tipped dirty white on outer web. Tertials mid drab, barred dark brown, outer webs with subterminal dark brown spot and drab-white tip. Secondaries drab-brown, slightly warmer on outer feathers, with dark subterminal band and dirty white tip; central portion and base dark brown, separated by pale orange-buff band. Primaries mid brown, drab-brown on distal part of outer webs; P3–P4 barred dark brown inwards of emarginations, P5–P10 dark brown at base and in centre, separated by pale orange-buff band as on secondaries. Lores, cheeks and ear-coverts dark brown; supercilium buff-white, extended onto sides of mantle by very pale (drab-white) feather centres. Chin, throat and centre of upper breast creamy-white, sides of neck and breast washed pale buff, lower breast, upper flanks and belly very pale drab-buff, rear flanks, vent, thighs and under tail-coverts pale drab. When very fresh, may show fine dark fringes to feathers of breast and belly, giving a faint scalloped effect. Axillaries and underwing-coverts pale buff. *In worn plumage* (March–August), underparts paler and whiter; when more heavily worn, underparts dingy pale grey, crown and nape with a more distinctly streaked appearance, and loses warm tones on mantle and scapulars. **Bare Parts**: Iris brown or dark brown; upper mandible dark horn-brown to blackish, lower mandible pale fleshy, tipped brown; legs and feet brown to fleshy, claws slightly darker. **Juvenile**: As adult, but feather centres of forehead, crown and nape larger, browner and less distinct, giving a more mottled appearance; upperparts slightly warmer and browner, more blotched (less scalloped). Throat and breast whiter (but blotchy, grey feather bases showing), more sharply contrasted with drab-buff lower belly, vent and undertail-coverts, feathers with fine dark fringes, forming scattered faint dark spots or scallops. **1st Adult**: As adult. **Measurements**: Wing of male 67–75, of female 64–72; tail of male 56–72, of female 57–71; bill of male 21–25, of female 18–23.2; tarsus 15–18. Weight 7.8–10.3 g.

**MOULT** Adult post-breeding complete (late June–mid September). Post-juvenile partial, includes median coverts (late June–late October) (Vaurie 1950b).

**GEOGRAPHICAL VARIATION** Clinal, despite the discontinuity in the range, with western birds being palest, with a longer bill, and eastern birds darker and shorter-billed (but the cline is apparently reversed at the easternmost parts of the range in China (NE Sichuan), where the population is slightly paler again). Note that marked local individual variation tends to mask the geographical variation.

*C. h. taeniura* Central Asia and Afghanistan north of the Hindu Kush, also recorded from Ladakh in April (Meinertzhagen 1927). As nominate *himalayana*, but paler and greyer; feather centres of upperparts greyer (less warm brown subterminally), fringes narrower and paler (pale brown rather than black-brown); ground colour of rump and tail paler grey (rump with reduced warmth but same relative contrast with upperparts); underparts paler and greyer, with little or no buff wash even when fresh (except on lower belly and vent), and less contrast between throat and breast. Bill longer. Wing of male 69–74, of female 64–70; bill 22–26.

*C. h. himalayana* Eastern Afghanistan (south of Hindu Kush), northern Pakistan and Himalayas east to central Nepal. See Description. A cline of increasing saturation runs eastwards, and three populations have been named: '*limes*' (eastern Afghanistan, Pakistan and eastern Kashmir), *himalayana* (eastern Kashmir to Kumaun, northern Uttar Pradesh) and '*infima*' (Nepal). '*Limes*' is closer to nominate *himalayana* in coloration (brown rather than grey) than to *taeniura*, and has the same short bill, whilst '*infima*' is generally slightly more rufous, with more contrasting whitish streaking and blackish tail bars and with darker underparts. All three are stages in the cline, however, and do not warrant recognition; *himalayana*, as the oldest name, is applied to all three.

*C. h. yunnanensis* SW China and, presumably this race, Burma. As nominate *himalayana*, but upperparts darker, feathers blackish-brown, breast and belly darker, smoky-buff. Averages larger. Wing of male 64.5–77, of female 65–69.5; tail of male 55–67, of female 56–67; bill 20–27; weight 7–11 g. Slightly paler in NE Sichuan.

*C. h. ripponi* Mount Victoria, western Burma. As *yunnanensis*, but upperparts slightly warmer and paler brown (although still darker than nominate *himalayana*), with more obvious rufous tinge to lower back and rump. Slightly smaller. Wing of male 65–73, of female 65; tail 55–72; bill 17–19.

**RELATIONSHIPS** No obvious affinities among the treecreepers, although its song is surprisingly similar to that of Brown-throated Treecreeper.

**REFERENCES** Ali & Ripley (1983), Baker (1932–33), Dementiev & Gladkov (1966-70), Portenko & Wunderlich (1980), Roberts (1992), Stepanyan (1990).

# 30 RUSTY-FLANKED TREECREEPER *Certhia nipalensis*     Plate 9

Other names: Nepal Treecreeper, Stoliczka's Treecreeper

The most localised of the treecreepers, this species is found around the central and eastern Himalayas, but is probably overlooked owing to the ongoing problems with treecreeper identification in this region.

**IDENTIFICATION** Length 140 mm (5.5 in). A rather dark treecreeper. Head and mantle blackish with fine buff streaks and spots, lower mantle and scapulars dull cinnamon-buff with dark scallops, rump contrastingly cinnamon-rufous. Throat and breast white, washed buff, and contrasting strongly with the brownish-cinnamon sides of the breast and the cinnamon flanks, belly and vent. Easily distinguished from Bar-tailed Treecreeper by its plain, unmarked tail, and from Brown-throated Treecreeper by its rather paler, buff-white throat and breast. Separation from Eurasian Treecreeper (of the Himalayan subspecies *mandellii*) is also normally straightforward. On Rusty-flanked, the sides of the breast, flanks, belly and vent are richly coloured, extensively so in fresh plumage, whilst the remainder of the underparts are washed buff; in worn plumage, the throat and centre of the breast and belly are whitish, contrasting strongly with the more restricted flank patch. On Eurasian, the underparts are dull white, washed drab-buff on the rear flanks and vent, and thus appearing much more uniform. Rusty-flanked also shows a broad buff supercilium encircling the almost solidly dark ear-coverts. Eurasian shows a broad whitish supercilium, which may encircle the ear-coverts to fade out into the whitish sides to the neck, but the ear-covert patch is rather paler and smaller. Additionally, Rusty-flanked shows a more scalloped appearance to the scapulars and lower mantle, this area appearing mottled on Eurasian.

**VOICE** Generally rather quiet and unobtrusive. Call a thin *sit*. Song a high-pitched, short, rapid, accelerating trill introduced by three clear, silvery and more distinctly enunciated high-pitched *si* or *see* notes, *si-si-sit'st't't't*, the whole phrase lasting *c.* 0.75 seconds (the terminal trill is more penetrating, and may be all that is audible at a distance).

**SEX/AGE** Sexes similar. Juvenile as adult, but rump duller and less contrasting, faint dark scalloping on underparts, and cinnamon flank patch more restricted. 1st adult as adult.

**DISTRIBUTION AND MOVEMENTS** Breeds in the Himalayas in NW **India**, from Garhwal, northern **Uttar Pradesh** (Rajaji NP, Pandey *et al.*

1994; and Kedarnath Sanctuary, Chamoli district, Green 1986), east through **Nepal**, **Darjeeling**, **Sikkim** and **Bhutan**; also **Arunachal Pradesh** at Anini (= about Hupu) and the Talley valley in Subansiri district (Singh 1994; Ali & Ripley 1983 give Ludlow 1944 as authority for its occurrence in Arunachal Pradesh, but, of Ludlow's four localities, three are in Bhutan and one (Lo La) is in SE Tibet). Penetrates north of the main range into SE **Tibet** (Xizang) along the valleys of Sun Kosi river (Nyalam), and in the 'gorge country' along the Nagong Chu (= Po Tsangpo river, at Trulung, Tangmai and Bomi) and Yi'ong Zangbo river (at Yi'ong). Also collected at the southern foot of the Lo La pass near the border with India (28º 58' N, 93º 58' E), but not recorded from the Tsangpo valley itself. Also occurs in SW **China** in extreme western **Yunnan**, west of the Salween river in the Gaoligong Shan (Gongshan and Lushui) and in adjacent NE **Myanmar** (**Burma**) around the Chimili pass (near Pawahku) and Nyetmaw and Hpare passes in SE Kachin state. Reported to occur in winter in the north Cachar hills, Assam, at 1525–1830 m (Baker 1922), but there are no specimens from this area (Ali & Ripley 1983), and also possibly found in the Naga hills and Manipur (Ali 1962; Baker 1932–33; Oates 1889). Given the past confusion over the nomenclature of Indian treecreepers, and the possibility of misidentification, the occurrence of any species other than Brown-throated south of the Brahmaputra river is doubtful. Resident, but moves altitudinally.

**HABITAT** Breeds in the subalpine and upper temperate zones in forests of oak or mixed oak, rhododendron, fir and hemlock, often with many epiphytes and an understorey of dwarf bamboo, descending in winter into broadleaved forests in the lower temperate zone. Recorded at 3050–3140 m in northern Uttar Pradesh and summers at 2550–3660 m in Nepal, Sikkim and Bhutan; recorded in winter down to 1830 m in Nepal, 1585 in Sikkim and 1525 m in Bhutan, although also remaining at high altitudes, up to at least 3505 m in Nepal and 3600 m in Sikkim (S. C. Madge pers. comm.). In Arunachal Pradesh noted at 1500–2500 m, in SE Tibet recorded at 1980–3500 m, in NE Burma at 2285–3050 m and in SW Yunnan at 1500 m. Generally found at higher altitudes than Brown-throated Treecreeper, although lower than Bar-tailed and Eurasian Treecreepers, but there is some overlap with all three species, and seasonal altitudinal movements further obscure any altitudinal separation.

**POPULATION** Fairly common in the Himalayas and not uncommon in NE Burma, but noted as rare in China (although probably owing to the lack of observations in its limited range there). As with all treecreepers, easy to overlook. The distribution as currently understood is strangely restricted, and the species may be vulnerable, especially in view of the widespread deterioration of forests at mid altitudes.

**HABITS** Occurs singly or in loose pairs, and may join mixed-species foraging flocks, although apparently less prone to do so than other treecreepers. Also more silent, slower, and more deliberate in its movements (Meinertzhagen 1927). Forages among epiphytes such as moss and ferns, keeping largely to the lower branches and tree trunks; seldom found high up in the branches. Food insects.

**BREEDING BIOLOGY** Poorly known. The only documented records come from Nepal and are as follows: a nest found on 4 May at 3400 m at Dhorpatan; feeding young on 21 May at 3505 m in Helambu; repeatedly flying to a crevice c. 12 m above ground in the main trunk of an oak (and presumed feeding young) on 30 April in the upper Langtang valley; specimens collected 'in breeding condition' at Ting Sang (3000–3400 m) on 7 May and 2 June (Inskipp & Inskipp 1991).

**DESCRIPTION** Adult: *In fresh plumage* (September–March), feathers of forehead buff, fringed dark brown. Crown, nape and upper mantle sooty-brown, buff shaft streaks broadening towards the feather tips (becoming broadest and palest on the upper mantle, which appears spotted). Lower mantle and scapulars dull cinnamon-buff with slightly paler shaft streaks and sooty-brown fringes (appear scalloped). Back, rump and uppertail-coverts rich cinnamon-rufous, feathers faintly tipped darker. Tail mid grey-brown, feathers darker adjacent to the shaft; shafts rufous-buff. Wing-coverts sooty-brown, lesser and median with buff spot near tip, greater coverts with outer webs tipped rich buff and narrowly fringed orange-buff. Alula sooty-brown, broadly tipped buff; 80% lack a pale fringe, the remainder having alula indistinctly fringed paler and buffer towards base. Primary coverts sooty-brown. Tertials pale grey-brown, becoming blackish-brown towards tips, shaft pale buff and outer web with pale buff fringe and tip and subterminal buff notch or band. Primaries and secondaries dark brown, outer webs of P3–P4 slightly paler, P5–P10 and secondaries with a broad pale band across the feather (restricted to outer web on P5), buff on outer web and contrastingly white on concealed inner web; P5–P6 paler towards base and tip, P7–P10 and secondaries with dull buff slot near tip of outer web and dull paler tip. Lores blackish, cheeks mottled buff and dark brown, ear-coverts sooty-black with a few fine buff streaks. Supercilium pale buff, narrow and poorly marked in front of eye, connecting with pale buff sides to neck. Chin whitish; throat, breast and centre of belly white, washed buff. Sides of breast brownish-cinnamon (may extend to form a broken breast band, with faint darker feather tips when very fresh). Flanks, belly, vent and thighs cinnamon, becoming rufous-cinnamon on rear thighs, undertail-coverts tipped slightly paler. Axillaries pale buff, underwing-coverts white. *In worn plumage* (April–August), upperparts slightly duller, and underparts whiter (chin to centre of belly very white, contrasting strongly with the more restricted cinnamon of the flanks etc.). **Bare Parts**: Iris red-brown to brown; bill pale horny-brown to black, cutting edges and base of lower mandible pale horny to pinkish-white; legs and feet pale fleshy-horn to brown. **Juvenile**: As adult, but streaks on crown and nape narrower and buffer,

feathers of lower back, rump and uppertail-coverts duller with dark brown subterminal band (thus rump patch not so contrastingly rufous). Underparts duller, feathers of sides of throat, breast, belly and flanks fringed darker in an irregular scaled pattern; contrasting colour of flanks etc. more restricted, obvious only on rear flanks. **1st Adult**: As adult. **Measurements**: Wing of male 66–76, of female, 65–71 (–78: Rand & Fleming 1957); tail of male 73–84 (–90: Academica Sinica 1980), of female 69–76; bill 14–17.9; tarsus 15–20; hindclaw mean 9.8. Weight 8–12 g.
**MOULT** Adult post-breeding complete (August). Post-juvenile, no information.
**GEOGRAPHICAL VARIATION** Negligible. Birds from the west of the range may average slightly richer in coloration (Rand & Fleming 1957), but no subspecies are recognised.
**RELATIONSHIPS** Considered a race of Eurasian Treecreeper by Dementiev & Gladkov (1966–70), an opinion supported by Mead (1975), because *nipalensis* conformed to the general pattern of increasing dimensions (wing and bill, although it has a relatively long claw) from west to east in the Himalayan races of Eurasian Treecreeper. However, its vocalisations are rather different (Martens 1981), and it is sympatric with the subspecies *mandelli* of Eurasian Treecreeper, so specific separation is fully justified.
**REFERENCES** Martens (1981), Mead (1985), Meinerthagen (1927).

# 31 BROWN-THROATED TREECREEPER *Certhia discolor*    Plate 10
Other name: Sikkim Treecreeper

The only treecreeper truly to penetrate the Oriental Region, this species has a curiously disjunct distribution, with scattered populations in South-East Asia.

**IDENTIFICATION** Length 140 mm (5.5 in). Upperparts mottled warm brown and blackish and streaked pale buff, lower mantle and scapulars browner, with more scaly dark markings. Rump orange-rufous, tail plain dull cinnamon. Wings intricately barred. Supercilium pale buff, better marked behind the eye and contrasting with the dark brown cheeks and ear-coverts. In the Himalayas the throat and breast are light drab-buff, paling to dull drab-white on the rear flanks, belly and vent; in western Burma the throat and breast are rich cinnamon, paling to drab-buff on the belly etc.; and in eastern Burma and South-East Asia the throat and breast are sooty-drab-grey, paling to dull mid grey on the belly etc. (in the field the underparts appear whitish, lightly washed brown on the throat, flanks and undertail-coverts). In the Himalayas, its distribution overlaps that of Eurasian, Bar-tailed and Rusty-flanked Treecreepers, although Brown-throated is largely separated altitudinally from first two during breeding season (see Habitat). Distinguished from Bar-tailed Treecreeper by its plain, unbarred tail, and separated with care from Eurasian and Rusty-flanked by its dull underparts, with a pale brown wash to the throat and breast, and lack of contrastingly cinnamon flanks.
**SEX/AGE** Sexes similar. Juvenile as adult, but with fine dark scales on the throat and breast, which are also tinged cinnamon-buff (especially noticeable in the grey-breasted southern forms). 1st adult as adult.
**VOICE** Call a full, explosive *chit* or *tchip*, almost 'wooden' in tone, and lower and more powerful than most treecreeper calls. Also gives a higher, thinner and softer *tsit* or *seep*. In antagonistic situations, gives bursts of 4–5 *chit*-type notes in a short, explosive, rattling phrase, *chi'r'r'it*, lasting c. 0.25 seconds and too fast for the individual notes to be readily distinguished. In the Himalayas the song is a longer monotonous rattle comprising 6–37 *chit*-type notes, given at a rate of 12–17 per second, the phrase thus lasting from 0.5 to 3 seconds, *chit-it-it-it-it-it-it-it-it-it* or *tchi-chi-chi-chi-chi-chi-chip*. The individual notes are all about the same pitch and are either rather well spaced and easily distinguishable or faster and more trilling (and sometimes higher-pitched, cricket-like trills of 5–8 units). The phrase may increase in volume and then diminish again towards the end, or waver at random. Sometimes it is introduced by c. 5 fuller *si* notes. The song is much fuller, deeper and less sibilant, and usually rather longer than that of Rusty-flanked Treecreeper, and fuller, lower-pitched, less musical and more rattling than that of Bar-tailed Treecreeper. There is some geographical variation, and in SW Burma, Thailand and southern Vietnam the units are paired, giving the phrase a halting or 'trotting' rhythm, e.g. *tchi-tchi, tchi-chi, tchi-chi, tchi-chi, tchichip*. Song period in Nepal early February–May, in NW Thailand March–June.
**DISTRIBUTION AND MOVEMENTS** In the Himalayas, recorded in NW **India** in Kumaun, northern **Uttar Pradesh** (at 'Bona' in June 1948: Vaurie 1950b) and **Nepal**, where found regularly west to the Dhaulagiri massif, with one record in the far west, at Badalmachi (near Dhangarhi) in March (possibly a straggler); also **Darjeeling** (West Bengal), **Sikkim** and **Bhutan**, and **Arunachal Pradesh** in the Dafla hills, Subansiri area, and Abor hills. Extends north of the main range into southern **Tibet** in the Chumbi valley (recorded Yadong, June) and Tsangpo valley (Tangmai, March: Robson 1986). South of the Brahmaputra river, found in NE India in **Nagaland** and **Manipur** (and probably also the Khasi hills of Meghalaya and Cachar hills of southern Assam), from where

there are sight records of treecreepers thought to be this species, but there are no specimens to support the identification, although no other treecreeper is known to occur south of the Brahmaputra. Breeds in western **Myanmar** (**Burma**) in the Chin hills south to Mount Victoria and the Arakan Yoma, and in NE Burma from Kachin (Kambaiti, Bhamo and around Pawahku) south to the Shan States (southeast to the Mekong valley, to at least area of Mong Yawng) and the Karenni (to at least Nattaung), also Tenasserim (?). The range extends marginally into SW **China** in **Yunnan** in the Gaoligong Shan (Shweli-Salween divide) south to Tengchong. In South-East Asia, found in NW **Thailand** (including Doi Inthanon NP), north-central **Laos** on the Tranninh plateau (around Xieng Khouang), and in NW **Vietnam** in northern Tonkin on the Fansipan massif and southern Vietnam on the Da Lat plateau. Resident, but undertakes some altitudinal movements and perhaps also some dispersal in winter.

**HABITAT** In the Himalayas, mature broadleaved forest, both deciduous and evergreen, especially mossy oak forest, less frequently rhododendrons. In NE India, Burma and South-East Asia, hill evergreen forest (especially the denser and damper stands) and locally also pine forest, especially when in association with stands of broadleaved trees. Occupies the subtropical zone, the lowest altitudinal belt of the four species of treecreeper found in the Himalayas and associated ranges, normally overlapping in the breeding season only with Rusty-flanked Treecreeper; in winter however, this separation is obscured by altitudinal movements. In Himalayas, found in the breeding season at 1440–2750 m, but usually above 1800 m and occasionally to 3050 m. Specifically, in Nepal 2000–2750 m, occasionally to 3030 m, wintering at 1800–3050 m, exceptionally to 305 m in December. Winters in Sikkim at 700–1830 m, although also recorded there at 2760–3630 m in late December (Meinertzhagen 1927; perhaps doubtful?), and in Bhutan recorded at 600–3200 m. In Arunachal Pradesh recorded at 1100–2400 m, and in southern Tibet at 2800 m in June and 2130 m in late March. In Nagaland and Manipur found at c. 800–2300 m, and in the northern Chin hills of western Burma breeding proven at 1830 m, whilst further south, on Mount Victoria, noted at 1400–3000 m, most frequently at the lower altitudes. In NE Burma noted at 2135–2195 m, and in SE Burma 1465–2285 m. In Yunnan recorded at 2000–3050 m, in NW Thailand found from 1370 m to at least 2440 m, and in NW Vietnam recorded above 2000 m, and in southern Vietnam at 1000–2500 m.

**POPULATION** Fairly common in suitable habitat in the Himalayas, especially in eastern areas, and, although uncommon in Nepal, fairly common on Phulchowki in the Kathmandu valley. In NE India apparently very rare in the Khasi and Cachar hills, but not uncommon in Burma (and common in the southeast). Uncommon in Thailand, and now absent or very rare at Doi Suthep-Pui NP, a locality where it was formerly not uncommon. Very rare in NW Vietnam. As with all treecreepers, easy to overlook.

**HABITS** Typical of the genus, creeping jerkily on moss- and lichen-covered trunks and boughs. Not shy. Found singly or in pairs, often in mixed-species foraging flocks. Food insects and spiders.

**BREEDING BIOLOGY** Poorly known. Season: Himalayas March–May (circumstantial); Nagaland, Manipur and North Chin hills, April–May; Mount Victoria, fledged young seen on 31 March; NW Thailand, a pair at the nest on 6 February, with a juvenile recorded in early May; southern Vietnam, about January–July. The nest is placed behind bark flaps or in crevices and other holes in trees and stumps, noted at 2.4–9 m above ground. The pad of fibres, moss, rootlets and a few feathers is lined thickly with fur. Clutch 3–5: eggs white, blotched and freckled with pale reddish or reddish-brown, markings sometimes concentrated towards the broader end; 16.3 x 12.5 mm (*C. d. discolor*). Incubation and division of labour in the care of the young unknown.

**DESCRIPTION** *C. d. discolor* **Adult**: *In fresh plumage* (September–late winter), feathers of upperparts from forehead to mantle cinnamon-brown with paler buff shafts and dark brown fringes, forming on the crown and upper mantle a neat pattern of pale buff spots, on the lower mantle and scapulars a more scaled appearance. Lower back, rump and uppertail-coverts orange-rufous. Tail dull cinnamon, shafts pale rufous. Lesser coverts as mantle; median coverts blackish-brown, tipped cinnamon-buff. Greater coverts dark brown, inner with buff tip, shaft streak and fringe to outer web; outer tipped buff. Alula and primary coverts dark brown, alula tipped pale buff, largest feather also fringed pale buff. Tertials dull buff, inner web washed brown, outer web with dark brown subterminal band adjacent to shaft on distal half, separated from the dark brown basal half by a buff band. Secondaries dark brown, tipped pale buff, with buff notch on distal quarter of outer web and pale band across base (buffy-white on outer web and white on concealed inner web). Primaries dark brown, P3–P4 pale brown on outer web, P5–P10 with pale notch on distal quarter of outer web and crossed by pale band at base (continuous with band on secondaries); P6–P10 tipped pale grey. Lores dark brown; supercilium flecked pale buff with odd whitish feathers, not well demarcated from crown, although broader and whiter behind eye. Cheeks and ear-coverts dark brown, feathers of ear-coverts tipped buff. Throat and breast light drab-buff, paling to dull drab-white on rear flanks, belly and vent; when very fresh, may show faint darker tips on chin, throat and sides of neck. Thighs light drab-buff, undertail-coverts warm buff. Underwing-coverts and axillaries clean white. *In worn plumage* (spring–summer), underparts average slightly duller, dingier and less buffy, belly slightly darker and duller. When very worn, pale streaks on crown and nape narrower and better defined. **Bare Parts**: Iris reddish-brown to dark brown; upper mandible horn-brown to dark brown, almost black on culmen, lower mandible pale horn to whitish, darker at tip; legs, feet and claws pale fleshy-brown to dark brown. **Juvenile**: As adult, but feathers of chin, throat and breast slightly more cinnamon-buff, with distinct fine dark fringes forming dark scallops; odd dark tips on pale grey of belly and vent, especially at sides. Lower back and rump with reduced area of orange-rufous? (feathers of back and rump fringed darker). **1st Adult**: As adult. **Measurements**: Wing of male 65–76, of female 64–72; tail of male 68–84, of female 68–80; bill of male 17–20.5, of female 16–18; tarsus 15.5–20. Weight 8–12.5 g.

**MOULT** Adult post-breeding complete (eastern Himalayas, July–August; Thailand, September). Post-juvenile, no information on extent (Thailand, April–May).

**GEOGRAPHICAL VARIATION** Well marked, populations becoming rich cinnamon on the underparts in the southwest, but greyer to the south and east. Five races recognised.

  *C. d. discolor* Himalayas, southern Tibet, Nagaland and northern Manipur. See Description.

  *C. d. manipurensis* Southern Manipur (Aimol) and SW Burma in the Chin Hills and (?) Arakan Yoma. As nominate *discolor,* but throat and breast rich cinnamon or cinnamon-orange (wearing duller), belly and vent duller and paler, pale drab-cinnamon or drab-buff; undertail-coverts as throat. Upperparts warmer, more orange-buff, with slightly blacker-brown feather fringes (especially on crown). Wing of male 67–73, of female 64–69, tail 65–68, bill 18.2–20.9. May be richest and most cinnamon in southern Chin hills ('*victoriae*').

  *C. d. shanensis* NE and eastern Burma, Yunnan, Thailand and NW Vietnam (also 'upper Laos': Vaurie 1959). As nominate *discolor,* but underparts rather darker, dingier and less buff, throat and breast mid-dark sooty-drab, belly dull mid grey, undertail-coverts buff or cinnamon-buff. Feathers of upperparts fringed slightly blacker-brown (as *manipurensis*), centres colder and greyer, especially on crown and nape. Wing of male 66–73, of female 64–67.

  *C. d. meridionalis* Da Lat plateau, southern Vietnam. As *shanensis,* but upperparts much warmer, feathers essentially rufous with finer dark fringes, especially on mantle, back and scapulars, and only slightly paler shaft streaks; and back and rump slightly richer and more rufous (upperparts overall more rufous and less spotted than in nominate *discolor*). Crown and nape slightly paler and buffer (thus nearer nominate *discolor*); underparts may average darker and purer grey. Wing of male 66–71, of female 67–71; tail of male 79, of female 83.

  *C. d. laotiana* Tranninh plateau, Laos. As *meridionalis,* but upperparts less rufous and much more strongly marked black and bright tawny; undertail-coverts and tail slightly brighter rufous. Wing 68–72. (No specimens seen.)

**RELATIONSHIPS** Unclear, with no obvious affinity with any other treecreeper.

**REFERENCES** Ali & Ripley (1983), Baker (1922), Hopwood & Mackenzie (1917), Martens (1981).

# 32 SPOTTED CREEPER *Salpornis spilonotus*     Plate 24

Other name: Spotted Grey Creeper

The sole member of its genus, this species has an oddly disjunct distribution in India and Africa, and presumably once occurred in the intervening areas.

**IDENTIFICATION** Length 150 mm (6 in). Bill long, slender and decurved. Upperparts dark brown, spotted whitish, prominently so on the mantle and scapulars. Wings and tail dark brown, boldly barred white. Long off-white supercilium and dark brown eyestripe; sides of head and underparts off-white (sometimes washed cinnamon), variably but finely spotted and barred with brown. Very distinctive. The spotted plumage and tree-creeping habits are matched by no other species in Africa or India. Behaviour rather nuthatch-like; the tail is slightly rounded and, unlike treecreepers, this species does not use it for support.

**SEX/AGE** Sexes similar. Juveniles are similar to adults, but tend to have the pale spotting on the upperparts slightly duller and less well defined, and the dark markings on the underparts much more diffuse and less contrasting, with the ground colour duller and greyer. No information on the 1st adult.

**VOICE** Calls include 5–6 high, even croaking notes, *kek-kek-kek-kek-kek* (recalling a coot:

Vincent 1933, 1935), a faint *see-ee,* repeated 3–4 times, with the emphasis on the first syllable (Benson 1946), and a single, tit-like *tseee* (Williams & Arlott 1980). Song a very high-pitched, almost lisping phrase, *tsit'tsit-tsui, tsit'tsit-tsui, tsiu-tsiu-tsiu-tsiu, tsit'tsit-tsui, tsit'tsit-tsui, tsiu-tsiu...,* the phrase lasting 3–4 seconds and repeated several times in succession (often transcribed as '*sweepy-swee-seepy*' or '*sweepy-swip-swip-swip*'); also gives *tswiu, tsuu, tsuu* phrase of a similar tone.

**DISTRIBUTION AND MOVEMENTS** One of the few passerines to occur in both India and Africa, where there are several scattered and apparently disjunct populations. In central **India** found from **Rajasthan** (west to Sambhar, Ajmer, the Aravalli hills and Mount Abu), eastern **Gujarat** (west to Rajpiplaand Disa) and presumably northern **Maharashtra**, through southern **Haryana** (Gurgaon) and **Uttar Pradesh** (to Gonda, near the Nepalese border) to northern **Bihar** (the 'Bihar terai' east to Manbhum) and SE **Madhya Pradesh** in the Bastar district, and south to eastern

**Maharashtra** at Sironcha. Resident. In Africa in the northern tropics, occurs irregularly in a relatively narrow band. In **Senegal** recorded at Niokolo-Koba NP in April1969, in **Guinea-Bissau** near Binar, and in NW **Guinea** old records from the north of the Fouta-Djallon massif. In NW **Sierra Leone** frequent March–May in Kilimi, Bombali district, and in northern **Ivory Coast** found from Odienné and Tingrela to Komoé NP. Also recorded from northern **Ghana**, where regular in Mole NP and recorded south to Wenchi, Ejura and Kete. Listed for **Burkina Faso** (**Upper Volta**). In **Nigeria** found from Shaki, Enugu and Serti north to Zaria and Kari (and frequent near Obudu), and in northern **Cameroon** recorded from the Adoumaoua plateau and the southern Bénoué plain. Also recorded from southern **Chad**, and in the northern **Central African Republic** from Manovo-Gounda-Saint Floris NP. In NE Africa, found in the southern **Sudan** in southernmost Western and Eastern Equatoria, from Tambura to Kajo Kaji, and in adjacent **NE Zaïre** in Haut-Uele in Dungu and Faradje districts (including Garamba NP), and in NW **Uganda** in West Nile. A small population is found in extreme eastern **Uganda** on the northwest slopes of Mount Elgon, and in the adjacent highlands of western **Kenya** from Londiani and Elgeyu to Kaimosi, Kapenguria and Kitale. In **Ethiopia** found in the western highlands from Kefa north to at least Dangila and in the southeast highlands south to at least Alghe. In the southern tropics of Africa, found in **Angola** on the central plateau from northern Huila north to Cuanza Sul, western Malanje and central Moxico (Lac Cameia). In SE **Zaïre** recorded in SW Shaba north to Kasaji, Upemba NP, and Marungu, and found in most of **Zambia**, in Eastern Province south to Chadiza (but largely absent from the Luangwa and Middle Zambezi valleys), in Central Province to Chilanga, in Southern Province to about Choma and Kalomo, and in Western Province south to Kaoma and Mongu (and largely absent west of the Zambezi river, with one record from Zambezi). In SW **Tanzania** found north to Kipili and Mpanda, and in southern Tanzania north to Songea and Liwale; also occurs throughout **Malawi**, and in northern **Mozambique** recorded south to the Zambezi river. In **Zimbabwe** found on the central plateau in northern Matabeleland and Mashonaland, east to Rusape and Inyazura, west to Chirisa GR, the Mafungabusi plateau and Sengwa river, north to the Zambezi Escarpment, and south to Shurugwi, around Sabi, Great Zimbabwe and probably Bikita. Also occurs in immediately adjacent **Mozambique** on the Manica platform in Manica e Sofala district (south to the Save river). African populations are largely resident, but some seasonal movements are thought to take place. Vagrant **Gambia**, with three records (near Bondali in March 1963, two at Keneba in May 1976, and one at Abuko NR in December 1977), and **South Africa**, where one was seen in April 1959 or 1960 in the Bangu Gorge, Kruger NP, Transvaal (Tarboton *et al.* 1987).

**HABITAT** In India, found in fairly open decidu-ous forest of *Acacia*, teak etc., and also well-wooded country and mango groves. Favours mature trees with deep-fissured bark. Found in the plains and hills. In Africa, occupies two distinct habitats. In the northern tropics from Senegal to western Kenya, found in the Guinea Savanna Zone in mature open *Acacia* woodland (in the Central African Republic occasional also in T*erminalia macroptera–Pseudocedrela kotschyi* savanna woodland: Carroll 1988). Recorded in Sierra Leone to at least 760 m, in Nigeria to at least 1350 m and in Kenya at 1000–2300 m. In Ethiopia, probably found in any mature forest or woodland above 1500 m (e.g. *Acacia* at Awasa). In the southern tropics, largely confined to mature miombo (*Brachystegia*) woodlands, favouring well-developed stands with a canopy of 10–15 m. Also found in *Mavunda* forest in Zambia, *Terminalia* woodland in Malawi (exceptionally also in riparian evergreen forest) and gallery woodland in Angola. In Malawi, occurs at 915–1525 m (occasionally 305–1675 m).

**POPULATION** In India rather scarce and patchily distributed, but not uncommon locally. In the northern tropics of Africa scarce and local, thus uncommon in Ghana and Nigeria, but frequent in NW Sierra Leone, probably fairly common in northern Ivory Coast and uncommon to locally frequent in Ethiopia. Scarce or rare and local, however, in southern Sudan, NE Zaïre, Uganda and Kenya. In Kenya, there have been very few records in recent years owing to habitat loss, but recorded at Kapenguria in January and June 1990. Rather commoner in the southern tropics, where common in Angola in northern Huila (although rare in the Zaïre basin), quite common in Zambia (although scarcer in drier woodland), not uncommon in Malawi west of the Rift Valley (scarcer elsewhere) and locally common in Tanzania; but, again, in Zimbabwe sparse and local. Easily overlooked, and may be commoner in areas of suitable habitat than records suggest.

**HABITS** Usually found singly or in pairs, but may join mixed-species foraging parties, and Baker (1922) notes that small flocks may be formed in the winter in India. The cryptic plumage provides excellent camouflage and the species is also often shy, keeping the tree trunk between itself and a would-be observer. Sitting birds may, however, be very tame and confiding. Forages on the trunks and larger branches of trees, starting near the base and working upwards, then moving to the base of the next tree. May also forage on horizontal branches. The tail is held away from the bark as the bird moves (thus resembling a nuthatch), and may cling to branches upside-down. Flight undulating and woodpecker-like. Food insects and spiders.

**BREEDING BIOLOGY** Season: India, February–May; Ghana, January; Ethiopia, April and possibly March; Kenya/Uganda May, December; Tanzania, November; NE Zaïre, October–December; southern Zaïre, August–October, February–March; Zambia, July–September; Malawi, September–October; Zimbabwe, August–October, peak in September.

*Figure 32.1 Spotted Creeper on nest.*

The nest is placed in a tree fork, often where a horizontal branch joins the main trunk and where there is a knot or other protuberance to break up the nest's outline. Nests may be sited 3–12 m above ground. A neat, deep cup is constructed from leaf stalks, rootlets and bark chips, cemented on the outside with spiders' webs, insect cocoons, caterpillars' excreta and vegetable down, covered with lichen, and lined with spiders' egg sacs. It is superbly camouflaged and extremely hard to find. Exterior diameter *c.* 70 mm, interior diameter *c.* 45 mm, thickness of wall *c.* 12 mm, depth of cup *c.* 45 mm. Clutch 1–3 (usually 2 in India, 3 in southern Africa): eggs in India pale grey or greenish-grey with dark brown specks and paler secondary blotches, especially at the larger end, *c.* 19 x 13 mm (Ali & Ripley 1983); in Africa pale turquoise-blue, bluish-green or pale green, with grey or lavender undermarkings and irregular black and brown spots, often concentrated at the broader end, 17.9 x 13.4 mm (Maclean 1993). Female incubates, period unknown. She often sits with her bill pointing up into the air and gives a high-pitched, twittering call to maintain contact with the male, which is usually feeding nearby. The female is fed by the male.

**DESCRIPTION** *S. s. spilonotus* **Adult**: *In fresh plumage* (about October onwards), forehead drab-brown, upperparts very dark brown; crown and nape with buff-white shaft streaks, feathers of remainder of upperparts tipped white, extreme tips narrowly margined brown (white feather bases fully concealed). Tail dark brown, boldly barred white, T1 with extensive pale drab-grey areas along shaft and at tip. Lesser coverts pale drab-grey with a dark brown subterminal bar, median and greater coverts dark brown with white spots at the tip and at the base of the shaft. Alula mid drab-brown, slightly paler at tip. Primary coverts drab-brown with off-white fringes at tip and a white notch centrally on outer web. Flight feathers dark brown, tertials drab-brown on basal portion of inner web, with off-white notches along the fringe of the outer web and white tips; secondaries and P3–P10 similar, but white tips much reduced on primaries and P3–P5 unmarked distally of the emarginations (flight feathers with concealed white bars on inner webs). Long, broad, off-white supercilium; lores and upper ear-coverts dark brown, cheeks and sides of neck off-white with some dark brown fringes on sides of neck. Chin and throat white, poorly demarcated from remainder of underparts, where feathers white with bold brown bars and narrow cinnamon-brown margins to the white tips (appearing variably spotted and barred brown and white); variable cinnamon fringes to feathers may give a cinnamon wash to the whole underparts. Axillaries and underwing-coverts similar. *In worn plumage* (May onwards), white spotting on upperparts slightly reduced (white tips abraded), and white spotting on wings reduced as white notches abraded. **Bare Parts**: Iris dark brown; bill blackish- or brownish-horn, lower mandible and cutting edge of upper mandible fleshy or pale horn; legs and feet greyish or purplish-grey to blue-black. **Juvenile**: As adult, but pale markings on upperparts slightly more diffuse and less well defined (pale spots washed pale grey). Dark markings on underparts much more diffuse, merely ill-defined dark bars/scallops, with a greyish wash to pale areas (loose feather texture revealing grey underdown). (Juvenile nominate *spilonotus* not seen; description based on juvenile *emini*.) **1st Adult**: No information. **Measurements**: Wing of male 88.5–93, of female 87–93; tail of male 50–55, of female 48–56; bill 24–28; tarsus 14–17.5. Weight 14 g (16 g recorded for *S. s. salvadori*).

**MOULT** Adult post-breeding complete (India, June–October; Sierra Leone, March; Guinea-Bissau, July; Angola, February; SE Zaïre, January). Post-juvenile, no information.

**GEOGRAPHICAL VARIATION** Relatively slight, involving the colour and intensity of the markings on both the upperparts and the underparts. Six races recognised.

*S. s. spilonotus* Central and western India (except range of *rajputanae*). See Description.

*S. s. rajputanae* Central and SE Rajasthan from Sambhar to Mount Abu. As nominate *spilonotus*, but ground colour of upperparts slightly paler and browner; pale spotting may average slightly larger and more profuse. Breast plainer with much-reduced dark markings; remainder of underparts washed cinnamon-buff (broad cinnamon-buff fringes), with dark markings averaging smaller.

*S. s. emini* Northern Afrotropics from Senegal to NE Zaïre and NW Uganda. As nominate *spilonotus*, but pale spots on upperparts slightly larger and perhaps less well defined and more profuse (i.e. near *rajputanae*), and underparts slightly paler and whiter (drab-white), the cinnamon-buff wash slightly reduced. Diffuse dark markings present on chin and throat, but on remainder of underparts dark markings averaging slightly smaller and sparser. Wing 85–96 of male 88–95, of female 87–93; bill 24.1–26.7.

*S. s. erlangeri* Ethiopia. As *emini*, but pale spots on upperparts variably washed cinnamon-buff (especially on crown, mantle, scapulars and pri-

maries). Underparts strongly marked with cinnamon, with contrasting white spotting; dark markings on underparts variable, from spots to scallops. Bill also shorter. Wing of male 91.5–93.5, of female 89–95; bill 20.9–23.5.

*S. s. salvadori* Extreme eastern Uganda (Mount Elgon) and western Kenya, also the southern Afrotropics (except Zimbabwe and adjacent Mozambique). As *emini*, but pale spots on upperparts variably washed buff (i.e. intermediate between *emini* and *erlangeri*) and may average larger. Underparts washed cinnamon-buff (near *erlangeri* but paler, more buffy-white and more uniform, less white-spotted and dark markings reduced, feathers with rather narrower dark bars and tips, sometimes to merely fine irregular dark bars); bill also shorter. Wing 87–102, of male 90–98, of female 87–98.5; tail 50–60; bill 20.9–24.2.

*S. s. xylodromus* Zimbabwe and adjacent Mozambique. As *salvadori*, but starkly black and white. Mantle and wings sooty-black (not dark brown), pale subterminal barring whiter (buff wash reduced), terminal spots purer white, tail more sharply black and white. Throat whiter, remainder of underparts paler buff. Wing of male 89–100, of female 87–98.5; tail 50–60; bill 23.

**RELATIONSHIPS** The Spotted Creeper resembles the treecreepers in build and general coloration, and has frequently been placed in the Certhiidae (e.g. 'Peters', Short *et al.* 1990). However, it lacks the stiffened tail feathers of the Certhiidae and because of this has been treated as a subfamily of the nuthatches (Sittidae). Sibley & Monroe (1990), based on DNA-DNA hybridisation data, place it in the tribe Salpornithini, distinct from the typical treecreepers, in the family Certhiidae.

**REFERENCES** Ali & Ripley (1983), Baker (1922), Bannerman (1930–51), Ginn *et al.* (1989).

# 33 EUROPEAN PENDULINE TIT *Remiz pendulinus*       Plate 11
Other names: Penduline Tit, Eurasian Penduline Tit

This species is named after its elaborate pendulous hanging nests, which until recently were used in central Europe as children's slippers. It has an extraordinarily complex mating system, and is rather gregarious, even on migration. These may be adaptations to exploit transient habitats, and, indeed, the species has undergone a dramatic range extension in recent decades.

**IDENTIFICATION** Length 110 mm (4.75 in). A small, compact tit with a relatively long tail and a distinctive short, conical black bill with a straight culmen and finely pointed tip. Narrow band on forehead, lores and ear-coverts black, forming a 'highwayman's mask', surmounted by a variable but usually narrow chestnut band on the fore-crown (see Geographical Variation). Remainder of head dull grey (wearing whiter). Upperparts chestnut, becoming paler and buffer on the rump. Greater coverts chestnut, tipped paler, forming an indistinct wingbar. Tail and flight feathers blackish, tertials and secondaries broadly fringed pale buff.

Throat white, grading to buffish on the breast and buffy-cinnamon on the flanks, and sometimes showing diffuse darker chestnut spotting on the breast. Juvenile rather plainer and duller. Adults are distinctive with their pale head, black 'bandit' mask and chestnut upperparts (although adults resemble a miniature male Red-backed Shrike). The rather nondescript juveniles could be confused, in a brief view, with many small passerines, notably juvenile female Bearded Tit, which, however, has extensive white fringes to the primaries and primary coverts and a longer, graduated tail. In SW Asia, overlaps in range with both Black-headed and White-crowned Penduline Tits. Black-headed is easily distinguished by its wholly black head, including the throat and often also the upper breast. White-crowned is more similar, although in most plumages it shows a dark 'bridle' extending from the mask around the back of the head and joining on the nape, and separated from the chestnut upperparts by a broad pale collar; this may be faint or absent at times, but White-crowned never shows any chestnut on the forecrown. Juveniles of the three species are very similar and probably not safely identifiable.

**SEX/AGE** Sexes reasonably distinct. Most importantly, the male has a solidly black mask which bridges the bill across the forehead and is surmounted there by a variable, but usually narrow, band of chestnut. The female's mask is less extensive, especially towards the rear, and in all but very worn plumage is finely speckled buff; it does not usually bridge the bill, and she almost always lacks chestnut on the forehead, this area being grey-buff and white (see Geographical Variation). Her head is duller and drabber, dusky grey-brown, never wearing quite so white. The upperparts are slightly paler, the fringes to the wing-coverts narrower and duller, and the chestnut spotting on the breast reduced or absent. Juvenile distinct, with the head and upperparts almost uniform plain pale grey-buff, underparts pale buff and bill yellowish. 1st adult as adult but, depending on the extent of the post-juvenile moult, may be identified with caution in the hand. Some undergo a complete moult, and are indistinguishable from the respective adult sex (although some 1st-adult males perhaps resemble an adult female, as below). Most 1st adults retain a variable number of juvenile flight feathers, primary coverts and greater coverts, with browner centres and paler and more worn fringes and tips than the adjacent new feathers. Head, body and lesser and median coverts may be as respective sex of adult, but 1st-adult males may show a reduced black mask, duller, grey-brown crown and nape, paler chestnut on mantle and greater coverts, and reduced spotting on the breast (thus approaching an adult female - look for moult contrasts in the wing), whilst 1st-adult females may be even duller, the mask very dull, heavily mottled grey-buff or even lacking (i.e. completely buff), the crown and nape pale brownish-grey, with the mantle only slightly warmer and more cinnamon (thus near a juvenile). 1st adults are, however, sometimes difficult to sex. See also Hybrids.

**VOICE** Commonest call a high-pitched, soft and thin but penetrating, slightly lisping whistle, rendered tseee, pseee, seeo or ziih, of variable length and thinner, often apparently falling in pitch, towards the end. Confusion possible with calls of Red-throated Pipit, European Robin and Common Reed Bunting, which may share similar wetland habitats, but European Penduline Tit's call is higher-pitched, longer and fuller, with a less abrupt ending. It varies, however, among individuals and in different contexts, territorial males giving a longer and stronger call than the more delicate note of the female. Other calls include tseeze-tseeze-tseeze, while a shorter variant, given in a fast, twittering series, may be used as a contact call, swi-swi-swi... or tsi-tsi-tsi..., sometimes slightly nasal or hoarse. In alarm a variant of the sooee call is used, but sharper, more evenly pitched, and trilled. Song rather finch-like, with canary-like trilling, it incorporates the seeoo call, each phrase consisting of a variety of motifs and lasting up to 4 seconds, e.g. suwi-wi-wi-wi, suwi-wi-wi-wi, suwi-swee-o, suwi-swee-o, s-r-r-r-r-r, pseeoo, pseeoo, tseee etc. Other variants include see su-ree su-ree su-ree su-ri and zeeu-seewut zeeu-seewut zeeu-seewu, on the 'tea-cher' theme and not so elaborate as the finch-like song. Each male has a repertoire of several different song types. When given by the male trying to attract a female to the nest, the song is relatively loud and powerful. More subdued brief twittering subsongs are also given in early spring whilst foraging or collecting nest materials. (Partly after Cramp & Perrins 1993.)

**DISTRIBUTION AND MOVEMENTS** Breeds through much of mainland **Europe** (although absent from most of **France** and **Switzerland**), north to southern **Sweden**, SW **Finland**, **Estonia**, and about Rostov in **European Russia**, and extends into SW **Siberia**, east to the Ob' valley, north in the eastern Urals to the Tuva river and further east to c. 57° N, and south through the Urals to the Mugodzhary plateau (NW **Kazakhstan**, also to the upper Irgiz river?), to 49° N and to the upper Ob' and Irtysh valleys at the foot of the NW Altai (to at least Semipalatinsk). Breeds south in SE Europe along the Volga and Ural rivers to the Caspian Sea, along the western shores of the Caspian Sea to the Caucasus, and into western Asia, in **Turkey** (where widespread but rather local), **Iraq** (first bred 1966), the **Transcaucasus** and NW **Iran** in the Zagros mountains southeast to the Dez and Karub rivers (and possibly Fars province?). Northern and eastern populations are migratory, those further south and west progressively less so, and southern birds are resident (and individuals occasionally remain to winter in the north of the range). Birds from southern Scandinavia and central Europe move west and south to Iberia (has wintered annually in **Portugal** since 1975), the Atlantic coast of **France**, and the Mediterranean basin east to **Italy**, although small numbers remain around the Neusiedler See in eastern **Austria**. On passage, recorded to the west of the current breeding range (e.g. **Belgium**, with c. 60 in October 1991). Those from eastern Turkey, the former USSR and NW Iran winter in western **Turkey**, **Iraq**, central and southern **Iran** (commonly reaching the Persian Gulf, Baluchistan and the Pakistan border in the extreme southeast, occasionally also Sistan; D.A. Scott pers. comm.), and southern **Turkmenistan**, **Uzbekistan** and **Tadzhikistan** on the Syrdar'ya (southeast to about Tashkent), Amudar'ya (south to Pyandzh on the Afghan border?), Angren and Zeravshan rivers. Occurs widely on passage in Central Asia, mixing with locally breeding Black-headed and White-crowned Penduline Tits, around the Aral Sea, Amudar'ya and Syrdar'ya rivers, and Lake Balkhash and Sasykkol'. Reported (by Zarudny, see Vaurie 1957c) to breed around

Leninabad on the Syrdar'ya in NW Tadzhikistan and around Dzhililkul' in SW Tadzhikistan, and thus within the breeding range of Black-headed and White-crowned Penduline Tits, but this has not been confirmed by subsequent observations. Juveniles begin to disperse from mid July onwards (some moving northwards), adults move south in September–October (movements continuing to mid December in Israel). Return northward passage is in February–mid May depending on latitude, with the main arrival on breeding grounds in April. Additionally, birds may move considerable distances between breeding attempts, breeding early in one area and then moving several tens of kilometres for a second attempt (hence breeding population reaches Neusiedler See in eastern Austria in May or early June, having already bred in riverine forest 60 km distant). Apparently avoids sea-crossings, and a rare migrant and winter visitor **Corsica** (first recorded 1965), a rare migrant **Malta** (first recorded 1972, but wintering in increasing numbers since the mid 1980s), and a scarce to fairly common winter visitor **Cyprus** (may have bred 1982). In the east, a fairly common passage migrant and winter visitor in **Israel** early October–early April (–early May); recent abundance on passage suggests that numbers winter somewhere to the south; also juveniles recorded in northern Israel in the Hula valley in June. Winters in NE **Egypt**, where first recorded 1976 in NE Sinai; still a rare and local winter visitor late November–late March, although now regular in small parties Suez (southernmost record Bir Beida, c. 26° N on the Red Sea coast). In **Jordan** small numbers winter in the Jordan valley (especially along the Jordan river) and, since 1979, at Azraq, where passage is also noted in April (Andrews 1995). Rare in **Lebanon** (recorded Anjar in December 1974 and Ammiq in February 1977), and **Syria**, where recorded from the Euphrates and Asi rivers and breeding reported in 1934 (three clutches collected June 1934 on the Asi river in NW Homs: Kumerloeve 1967); also recorded February 1977 at Lake Mzayrib, Deraa, in the far south. In **Iraq** winters in the Tigris-Euphrates basin, and a scarce or rare winter visitor to Arabia late October–early April. First recorded **Kuwait** November 1977, and since then up to 25 have wintered annually. In **Bahrain**, up to seven noted December 1970 and March–April 1971, also recorded April 1990 and November 1992. In NW **Saudi Arabia** recorded regularly in small numbers at Tabuk, in the Central province single records of small parties from Al Jawf and Riyadh, and in the eastern Province occasional records from Ad Dammam, Al Aba, Buqayq and Al Jubayl. Winters SW and southern **Iran** in Khuzestan, Fars and Kerman (southeast to at least Bam); may winter in eastern Iran, but, as in Arabia and the Gulf States, the situation is clouded by the occurrence of White-crowned Penduline Tit, not always distinguished (either in the field or in the literature). One record in winter from SW **Afghanistan** (a few small parties found in March 1949 around the estuary of the Farah Rud river in Seistan). Although migration thought to be mainly nocturnal, diurnal

migration also recorded (e.g. low-flying groups of up to 35 birds reported moving east, especially in the early morning, along the coast of southern Turkey at Cukurova in mid October: van den Berk 1991). Vagrant **Norway** (first record 1989; seven by 1993, when bred Slevdalsvann, Vest-Agder: Anon. 1993b) and **Britain**, where first recorded 1966, second in 1979 but then 73 records to 1993, mainly in autumn, but including overwintering birds and a male which built two nests in spring but failed to attract a mate (one ringed in East Sussex in October 1988 was recovered in Sweden in May 1989). Also the Channel Islands (UK, first 1975), **Morocco** (six records between 1976/77 and 1993), and **Tunisia**.

**HABITAT** Favours a mosaic of reeds, bulrush and other rank vegetation with patches of willow, poplar, alders, tamarisk and similar bushes and small trees, in deltas and estuaries, and by lakes, rivers, canals and marshes (both fresh and brackish); also waterside trees and damp woodland and carr with marshy pools. Occasionally breeds well away from water (nesting high in tall trees), and in eastern Turkey and NW Iran breeds in orchards and poplar groves along upland river valleys. In Austria, breeds up to a maximum of 650 m in some of the larger alpine river valleys.

**POPULATION** Locally fairly common, and in regions with much suitable habitat may be very common (e.g. Volga and Ural deltas). Generally scarce or rare, however, towards the northern borders of the range. Winter distribution poorly known, especially in the east, and scarce in southern Iran (and apparently also southern Iraq) in winter and scarce or rare in Central Asia. The range has expanded westwards. The border of the range advanced c. 300 km during 1930–1965, reaching Switzerland (first bred 1952, although still rare), Slovakia and the Czech Republic, Poland, Estonia (first bred 1960), Latvia (recorded breeding in 18th century, recolonised in 20th, spreading from 1960s, and 25 pairs at one site in 1989), western Germany, Denmark (first bred 1964), and southern Sweden (first bred 1964, and an explosive increase 1988–89, with breeding in six southern provinces; autumn population perhaps 1,000 birds). After a short hiatus, again moved rapidly c. 250 km west and 200 km north in 1975–85, reaching the Netherlands (first bred 1968, main colonisation from 1981, over 150 pairs by 1992), Belgium (first breeding attempt 1982, confirmed breeding 1993), Finland (confirmed breeding 1985) and Norway (bred 1993). In the southwest, there has been a marked expansion in Spain (west and south; first nest in Cádiz, southernmost province, 1990), but, conversely, some withdrawl from southern France since about 1950, and also from Greece.

**HABITS** Found singly and in pairs, but generally rather gregarious. In the winter and spring may be found in loose-knit flocks of up to 15 birds, whilst in the late summer and autumn flocks of up to 60 have been recorded, predominantly juveniles. Its gregarious nature is emphasised on migration, when often encountered in parties of 3–10 (rarely, as many as 40), and juveniles from the same brood may travel together. Even vagrants are often recorded as pairs or small parties, but this species only occasionally joins mixed-species foraging flocks. Usually rather tame but sometimes skulking, and also erratic and 'flighty', birds suddenly taking off and flying long distances for no apparent reason. Often returns to the breeding grounds in small flocks, and it is reported that some birds are already paired at this stage; conversely, males are said to arrive ahead of females. If the weather is fine, males start nest-building within a few days, older males arriving earlier and acquiring the best sites (even breeding before 1st-adult males appear on the scene). Males select a site and begin by twining plant fibres around the base of a twig fork, using both bill and feet. Once the nest has reached the 'basket' stage, he will advertise it for up to three weeks before giving up if a female is not attracted, although the nest is by now near completion. If a female does show interest, much calling, singing, tail-pulling and chasing precede copulation, and pair formation is completed with the pair nest-building together. Pair-bonds are typically short-lived and last 5–10 days, the duration of joint nest-building operations; after nest-building and copulation, the female may become increasingly aggressive towards the male when they meet near the nest. The territory comprises the nest and its immediate area, and the male is very aggressive towards other males during the breeding season. Nevertheless, the conspicuous nest is usually visited by other penduline tits in the area, both males and females. Intruding males approach cautiously and, if the owner is not present, may call and sing on or near the nest. The intruder may be driven off by the resident male (occasionally by the female), but he may be persistent, and nests (and the paired female) can be usurped by strange males. Alternatively, in the later stages of breeding, males may allow strange females and juveniles to approach and even to enter the nest. May be semi-colonial, with a number of nests in a small area. The mating system is very complex, involving monogamy and also serial polygyny (in which the male pairs with more than one female during the season) and serial polyandry (the female pairs with more than one male). Polygamous males attempt to mate with a number of females, building a nest to the basket stage, attracting a female, continuing to build and mating, and then leaving the female to complete the nest and lay whilst they start another nest and try to attract another female. Males may also incubate and feed one of the resultant clutches themselves. Correspondingly, 10–30% of females may be polyandrous, pairing with 2–4 males in rapid succession and raising the last clutch themselves. Exceptionally, some females may pair with up to six males, laying six clutches and up to 20 eggs in a season. Around 10–30% of clutches are deserted by both mates. Roosts singly or in groups, in willow thickets or reedbeds, and during the breeding season in the nest, even during the early stages of construction. Also recorded roosting in a hole in a wall. The fledged brood roosts with the parent for a short while in a nest (not necessarily its own; the young

are strongly attracted to any nest, and those from different broods may roost together), or sometimes in reeds. No information on wild birds during the winter, but captives have been noted roosting in a tight huddle (as with Long-tailed Tit). Food insects and spiders; also plant material, notably reed seeds, outside the breeding season. Forages in reedbeds, and in trees and bushes, in the outermost twigs and branches or among seed heads and flowers. Also explores crevices in the bark of the trunk and larger branches of trees. Picks food items from the surface, although will open cocoons and cases, and in the winter pecks at reed stems to extract insects hidden inside. As *Parus* tits, holds prey items down with its feet.

**BREEDING BIOLOGY** Season in central and northern Europe late April–early July (c. 1–2 months later in populations in reedbeds of Austria; these have probably already bred elsewhere, and reeds are unable to support nests before June). The nest is placed in a tree or bush, frequently a willow or birch, suspended in a fork in the outermost twigs (often over water), usually less than 7.5 m above ground/water level. Alternatively, it may be slung between 2–3 reed or bulrush stems, c. 1 m above water. The nest itself is a large, free-hanging globular pouch, with an entrance tube projecting downwards near the top; c. 25 cm tall (including the 'sling') x 10 cm in diameter. Constructed from plant fibres and down (notably bulrush seed down), animal hair and grass, woven and compacted to form a dense felt, it is lined with plant down, occasionally also feathers. Exceptionally, there may be two entrance tubes, or two nests may be attached (the male building the second whilst the female is still incubating in the first). Males may build a selection of incomplete nests (usually

*Figure 33.1  Nest of European Penduline Tit.*

3–4, sometimes up to 7, they may be close together, even in the same tree, or as much as 45 km apart). The female assists in completion, usually building the entrance tube and lining the nest; both sexes may work on the nest simultaneously, one inside, one outside. Building takes 15–24 days, although only 6–7 days for second or third nests, and work may continue until the young fledge. A nest from the previous season may be repaired and reused, or abandoned half-built nests may be taken over, but the species is rather capricious, and partially built nests may be deserted, the male (or pair) starting a new one. Clutch 2–7 (1–10), average *c.* 5 when incubated by female, 2–5 when incubated by male, and largest reported clutches may result from two females laying in the same nest: eggs white; 16.2 x 10.7 mm (*R. p. pendulinus*). Incubation period 13–14 (–21) days, by female (*c.* 55%) or male (*c.* 14%) but not by both, and *c.* 32% of clutches are deserted. Earlier clutches are usually incubated by the female, later ones by the male. Similarly, the young are fed and cared for by either sex, but seldom by both. Fledging after 22 (18–26) days, the young may be fed for another 10–14 days. Second clutch after successful first brood not uncommon, usually overlapping, but often deserted, and second broods successful only in long favourable seasons.

**DESCRIPTION** *R. p. pendulinus* **Adult Male**: *In fresh plumage* (autumn–winter), lores to ear-coverts black, forming a mask which surrounds eye and narrowly bridges bill. Narrow chestnut band on forehead, 3–5 mm deep, remainder of crown, nape, upper mantle and sides of neck light grey, feathers tipped drab in centre of crown and on nape. Mantle chestnut, grading into cinnamon on scapulars and back and cinnamon-buff on rump; uppertail-coverts dark brown, broadly fringed light drab-grey. Tail brownish-black, T1 fringed pale buffy-grey, T2–T6 finely fringed pale grey on outer webs and tips and broadly fringed off-white on inner webs. Lesser and median coverts dark grey, broadly fringed cinnamon-rufous, greater coverts blackish, broadly fringed chestnut and tipped cinnamon. Primary coverts blackish, finely fringed and tipped cinnamon-buff. Alula blackish, finely fringed chestnut. Flight feathers dark grey-brown, tertials broadly fringed pale buff (dark centre almost reduced to a shaft streak on innermost), secondaries fringed pale buff, whiter towards tips, P3–P10 narrowly fringed whitish (not distally of emargination on P3–P6). Throat white, remainder of underparts buffish, grading into buffish-cinnamon on flanks and thighs; chestnut feather centres on lower throat and breast shine through to give a vinous-pink tinge and may show as darker spots. Underwing-coverts and axillaries buff, marginal coverts cinnamon-rufous. *In worn plumage* (spring–summer), chestnut forehead variably mixed with white (may be all white), crown and nape whiter, chestnut of mantle paler and less extensive, scapulars, back and rump paler and buffer. Fringes to tail and flight feathers bleached whiter, wing-coverts abraded and revealing more of dark centres. Chestnut feather centres on breast variably revealed, and underparts paler buff, centre of belly and undertail-coverts almost white. **Bare Parts**: Iris brown to dark brown; bill horn-black or grey with black cul-

men and base and pinkish to whitish cutting edges; legs and feet dark blue-grey to blue-glossed black. **Adult Female**: In fresh plumage as adult male, but black mask less extensive, especially on ear-coverts, and finely speckled dull buff (unless heavily worn), with black and chestnut on forehead restricted or absent, replaced by grey-buff and white. Crown, nape, border of upper mantle and sides of neck darker grey with more extensive drab tips and less white at base of feathers (thus not so white when worn). Upper mantle rufous, lower mantle to rump slightly duller and buffer. Fringes of lesser and median coverts average paler and buffer, fringes to greater coverts average duller and less extensive, revealing blackish centres. Dark feather centres on underparts paler and more cinnamon, may be almost absent. **Juvenile**: Upperparts and sides of neck light greyish-buff, forehead and vague supercilium above eye often slightly paler, and mantle and scapulars slightly warmer cinnamon-buff. Tail as adult, but feathers slightly paler, fringes slightly buffer and tips more pointed. Lesser and median coverts dark grey, tipped dull cinnamon. Greater coverts blackish-brown, fringed rufous and more broadly tipped cinnamon. Flight feathers and primary coverts as adult, but fringes paler and less well defined. Lores and ear-coverts as upperparts, but feathers may be tipped slightly darker, forming faint mask. Narrow creamy broken eyering. Throat creamy-white, remainder of underparts pale buff. Underwing-coverts and axillaries creamy. In worn plumage, upperparts sandy-buff, tail and flight feathers sepia-brown, fringed off-white, and greater coverts blackish-brown with traces of cinnamon-buff fringes and off-white tips. Bill yellowish or pale grey with black culmen ridge and gonys. **1st Adult**: See Sex/Age. **Measurements**: Wing of male 54–59, of female 53–59; tail of male 43–49, of female 42–47; bill 10.1–12.5; tarsus 14.3–15.9. Weight 8–12.5 g.

**MOULT** Adult post-breeding complete (July–September). Adult pre-breeding apparently absent (although a female collected on 9 March in SW Afghanistan was moulting the tail and some body feathers, and Dementiev & Gladkov 1966–70 report a partial spring moult, involving only the head and neck, in December–January). Post-juvenile partial in northern populations of *pendulinus*, includes a variable number of greater coverts (sometimes all), tertials, and central or all tail feathers; apparently sometimes complete in some individuals in southern populations, such as in Spain and Iran (July–September).

**GEOGRAPHICAL VARIATION** Pronounced, although the situation is complicated by variation with age and sex, individual variation (especially in areas where different races meet or where this species hybridises with Black-headed Penduline Tit) and by the migration of northern populations into the breeding range of the southern subspecies. See also Hybrids.

*R. p. pendulinus* Europe east to the Ural mountains and middle Volga (south to Tambov), the northern foothills of western Greater Caucasus, and western Turkey. Some southward movements in winter (see Distribution and Movements), when recorded east to Israel; also this race wintering Cyprus and Egypt? See Description.

**R. p. menzbieri** Southern and eastern Turkey, Armenia and Azerbaydzhan (south from the foothills of the Greater Caucasus), and NW Iran; also this race breeding Syria? Winters in Israel, southern Iraq, and SW and southern Iran in Khuzestan and Kerman; also this race wintering Cyprus and Egypt? Poorly marked. As nominate *pendulinus*, but chestnut band on forehead usually faint or absent (but occasionally wider), mantle paler, back and rump slightly paler and whiter, contrasting more with mantle, and lesser coverts rather paler. Smaller, with a thinner bill. Wing of male 50.5–55, of female 50.5–57; tail of male 41–46, of female 38–45; bill 10–11.5.

**R. p. caspius** SE Russia and NW Kazakhstan in the Volga-Ural plains south from Kuybyshev (Volga valley) and Orenburg (Ural valley) and along the western shore of the Caspian Sea, south to the lower Kuma and Terek rivers in the northern foothills of the eastern Greater Caucasus, also Mangyshlak peninsula on the NE Caspian Sea. Winters around the Caspian Sea and in southern Iraq, and recorded in winter in Uzbekistan and SW Afghanistan (Seistan). Male as nominate *pendulinus*, but chestnut band on forehead wider, often extending to centre of crown, rear crown and nape mixed chestnut and whitish, occasionally uniform chestnut (although often still a narrow whitish nuchal band); mantle richer chestnut, lower scapulars, back and rump creamy-buff, uppertail-coverts off-white with dark brown shaft streaks. Pale fringes to tail and flight feathers broader (inner tertial may be almost uniformly whitish), lesser coverts may be paler, and chestnut spotting on underparts more prominent. Female and 1st adult nearer nominate *pendulinus*, but female has crown, nape and upper mantle paler and greyer (contrasting more with the rufous lower mantle) and may show traces of chestnut on the forehead and sides of the crown, wings and tail fringed whiter and underparts average whiter. 1st adult with narrow chestnut band on forehead, often extending back in narrow band above black mask, crown often with some chestnut admixture, and upperparts paler (near adult female, but crown whiter with more chestnut on front and sides, more chestnut spotting on breast, especially when worn, and even whiter underparts). Juvenile has paler and more washed-out head and upperparts than nominate *pendulinus*. Wing of male 55–59, of female 52–57; tail of male 43–50, of female 42.5–47; bill 10–12. A March migrant weighed only 6 g.

**R. p. jaxarticus** The eastern watershed of Urals and Mugodzhary plateau in NW Kazakhstan, east through western Siberia and northern Kazakhstan. Poorly marked. As nominate *pendulinus* but paler, mantle and lesser coverts cinnamon (not chestnut). 1st adult has a duller and less well-defined black mask, whitish forehead surmounted by a chestnut band (absent in race *stoliczkae* of White-crowned Penduline Tit), and the mantle either reddish-brown or buff. Smaller than nominate *pen-*

*dulinus*, with a finer bill and more slender feet and claws. Wing of male 52–57, of female 53; tail 41–46; bill 8.5–12.

**HYBRIDS** Hybridisation occurs between Black-headed and European Penduline Tits along the northern and southwestern shores of the Caspian Sea. In the north, at the mouth of the Ural river, the nominate race of Black-headed hybridises with the race *caspius*, the resultant variable population sometimes named '*bostanjogli*'. In SE Azerbaydzhan (between the lower Kura river and Lenkoran), the race *menzbieri* of European hybridises with the subspecies *neglectus* of Black-headed, the resultant hybrid population sometimes named '*loudoni*' or '*altaicus*', with the coloration of European and the large bill and feet of Black-headed; '*altaicus*' is treated by Stepanyan (1990) as a race of Black-headed. Similar hybrids have also been collected in winter on the 'Potemkin Peninsula' at the southeast corner of the Caspian Sea and recorded in winter from Israel (where apparently rare but regular winter visitors in the north and east). Also, birds resembling European Penduline Tit (hybrids?) have been recorded, together with Black-headed, around the southeast corner of the Caspian Sea during the breeding season (D.A. Scott *in litt.*), and apparent hybrids have also been collected around the Iranian/Turkmenistan border (black throat and white crown, but lacking a chestnut forehead) and southern Caspian (black throat and crown, though centre of crown white; Vaurie 1952).

**RELATIONSHIPS** Complex and confused. The four forms treated here as distinct species (European, Black-headed, White-crowned and Chinese Penduline Tits) are often lumped into just one species (*R. pendulinus*, the Penduline Tit). Other alternatives are to treat them as two species, splitting Black-headed from the European-White-crowned-Chinese complex, e.g. Stepanyan (1990); or as three, European, Black-headed and White-crowned/Chinese, e.g. as recommended by Cramp & Perrins (1993 p. 395), or European/Black-headed, White-crowned and Chinese, as in Sibley & Monroe (1992). Some uncertainty exists, however, as to the precise distributions of all four groups, especially in the crucial areas of Central Asia. Populations of hybrids between European and Black-headed Penduline Tits are found around the southwest corner of the Caspian Sea, and also perhaps around Lakes Balkhash, Sasykkol' and Alakol' (although the latter are treated here as a race of Black-headed *R. p. ssaposhnikowi*); the two may be a variant on the classic 'ring' species, the two halves of the ring meeting in these hybrid zones. Given the very distinctive appearance and structure of the Black-headed forms and their specialised ecology, it seems best to elevate them to the status of a full species, pending detailed field studies. The breeding range of European Penduline Tit does not, apparently, overlap with that of White-crowned Penduline Tit in Central Asia. (Records of 'breeding' European Penduline Tits from the delta of the Amudar'ya, and also possibly around Leninabad on the Syrdar'ya and at Dzhilikul near the

Amudar'ya in southernmost Tadzhikistan, proba- bly refer to migrants.) Their respective ranges cer- tainly abut however, around the foothills of the NW Altai, but no hybrids have been reported between European and White-crowned in this area, although according to Hartert (1903–10) in the east of its range the race *jaxarticus* of European 'tends' towards the northeastern race of White- crowned *R. c. stoliczkae* in size and plumage (but previous records of 'hybrids' did not take into account the variation with age, sex and wear of White-crowned Penduline Tit). Given the lack of hybridisation, and some differences in habitat, it seems best to treat them as distinct species. The breeding range of White-crowned overlaps with that of Black-headed Penduline Tit in much of

Central Asia, although the two are separated eco- logically, Black-headed being confined to reedbeds and White-crowned breeding in riverine forest and scrub and on bushy hillsides. White- crowned is also largely migratory, unlike Black- headed. No hybrids have been reported. Chinese Penduline Tit does not apparently overlap at any stage with any of the other forms (although note the occurrence of White-crowned in Ningxia in central China). It is widely separated from European Penduline Tit by White-crowned Penduline Tit and is perhaps best treated as a fourth distinct species.

**REFERENCES** Cramp & Perrins (1993), Dementiev & Gladkov (1966–70), Stepanyan (1990), Vaurie (1950a, 1957c, 1959).

# 34 BLACK-HEADED PENDULINE TIT *Remiz macronyx*     Plate 11

Often considered conspecific with European Penduline Tit, this elusive tit is confined to reedbeds in Iran and Central Asia and appears to be rather scarce in many areas.

**IDENTIFICATION** Length 110 mm (4.5 in). A small tit, rather similar to European Penduline Tit in proportions, but bill long and relatively thick, although still showing the distinctive conical pointed shape characteristic of the genus; legs, toes and claws generally large. Head, neck and throat blackish, finely peppered cinnamon-buff in fresh plumage; bib poorly defined and extending irregularly onto the breast. Upperparts chestnut, grading to cinnamon on the back and buff on the uppertail-coverts, and separated from the blackish head by a cinnamon-buff collar (although blackish may extend well onto the upperparts, even to the rump, with the pale collar absent). Greater coverts blackish, broadly fringed chestnut and tipped cin- namon-buff, forming a diffuse wingbar. Flight feathers blackish, fringed buffish. Sides of breast chestnut, and underparts buff, variably spotted chestnut. Distinctive and unlikely to be mistaken, although the rather nondescript juveniles could be confused in a brief view with many small passer- ines, in particular juvenile female Bearded Tit, which, however, has extensive white fringes to the primaries and primary coverts and a longer, grad- uated tail. 1st adults have a paler head, lacking the blackish hood, and are closer to European Penduline Tit in appearance, but their mask is slightly more extensive and their throat blackish- grey. Notably, juveniles are very similar to juvenile European and White-crowned Penduline Tits, and probably not safely identifiable.

**SEX/AGE** Sexes rather similar, although the female's throat may average paler, with broader dull buff feather tips in fresh plumage. Juvenile distinct, with the head and upperparts pale grey- buff with a darker and greyer crown and warmer and browner mantle; wings and tail as adult but paler, with the feather fringes paler and less well defined and underparts pale buff. Bill yellowish? 1st adult as adult, but crown, nape and sides of neck pale dull cinnamon-buff, whiter on fore-

crown, forehead and mask sooty-black with buff- ish feather tips, and throat pale grey, mottled dark- er (darker feather bases revealed to a variable extent); upper mantle and scapulars cinnamon, grading into cinnamon-buff on back, rump and lower scapulars (upperparts paler than adult), less- er and median coverts cinnamon-buff (bases grey; thus also paler than adult), and breast pale grey- buff, grading to buff on remainder of underparts.

**VOICE** Presumably as that of European Penduline Tit, but said to be louder and somewhat coarser; in spring, males give a brief, quiet trill (Dementiev & Gladkov 1966–70).

**DISTRIBUTION AND MOVEMENTS** In SE **Iran** found along the lower Helmand river in Sistan (and presumably adjacent SW Afghanistan, but see Population). Also northern Iran along the southern shores of the Caspian Sea from the Atrek river west to at least Rasht (replaced further west in Azerbaydzhan from Lenkoran' to the Kura delta by a hybrid population x European Penduline Tit), adjacent SW **Turkmenistan** along the Atrek river, and SE Turkmenistan along the Tedzhen valley and in the Murgab river north to Mary. **Uzbekistan** and southern **Kazakhstan** on the eastern shores of the Aral Sea and islands close to the shore (formerly?), between the deltas of the Syrdar'ya and Amudar'ya rivers, and along the Amudar'ya river to Pyandzh and Dzhilikul on the Vakhsh river in SW **Tadzhikistan** (and thus presumably also north- ern Afghanistan, as the river forms the border for several hundred kilometres); also the Zeravshan river to Samarkand, along the Syrdar'ya river to the western foothills of the Tien Shan (to at least Leninabad in Tadzhikistan), lower Keles river, the Fergana region and the Chirchik and Angren rivers. Also southern **Kazakhstan** on the lower Emba river (NE Caspian), and central Kazakhstan along the Sarysu river, on the lower Ili river, and around Lakes Balkhash, Sasykkol' and Alakol'. Resident in Iran, and found throughout the year in southern Kazakhstan, although numbers in winter are fairly low and some areas are apparently vacated, the winter quarters lying in southern **Turkmenistan** and northern **Iran** on the southern shores of the Caspian Sea, with migrants noted around Tashkent in late March–early April and late September–early winter (Dementiev & Gladkov 1966–70). Rare winter visitor (this species?) **Israel** (see Geographical Variation). Vagrant **Oman**? (a penduline tit at Azaiba, near Muscat, in March 1971 had a 'black head').

**HABITAT** Breeds exclusively in reedbeds and bulrush, favouring the edges and avoiding dense reedbeds.

**POPULATION** Common in northern Iran, and along the Atrek river on the border of Turkmenistan, nests were reported to be spaced at 250-m intervals. In SE Iran, however, scarce or rare. In 1971/72 and again in the mid–late 1980s, regional droughts resulted in the Sistan marshes drying out on the Iranian side; the penduline tits may, however, retreat in such circumstances to more permanent wetlands in Afghanistan, recolonising once the correct conditions are re-established. Presumably occurs in SW Afghanistan in Sistan, although no records have been traced (thus not found by Paludan 1959, although he failed to locate suitable reedbed habitats). In Central Asia, with the introduction of intensive agriculture based on irrigation, and the consequent desiccation of the Aral Sea, numbers have probably fallen considerably; recent visits to the area have usually failed to locate the species.

**HABITS** Forages among reeds, moving rapidly and adroitly. Food insects, spiders and seeds.

**BREEDING BIOLOGY** Season late May–early June; begins nest-building in the period following the spring floods, when the reed stems have grown sufficiently to support the weight of a structure. Also, according to Dementiev & Gladkov (1966–70), occasionally nests in trees. Nest more or less that of European Penduline Tit, an elongated, oval bag, with the entrance a short thickened tube. It is constructed from fibres stripped from green reed leaves, bound together with cobwebs, vegetable down and reed flowers, and woven between two reed stems. Invariably placed above water, up to 5 m high. The reeds may be woven together below the nest to protect it from strong winds. Clutch 6–7: eggs white; c. 16.7 x 10.6 mm.

**DESCRIPTION** *R. m. macronyx* **Adult Male**: *In fresh plumage* (October onwards), forehead, crown and nape sooty-black or dark mahogany-brown, feathers variably, although usually finely, tipped cinnamon-buff. Border of upper mantle cinnamon-buff, forming a pale collar. Upper scapulars and mantle chestnut, feathers finely tipped cinnamon, especially on scapulars; lower scapulars and back cinnamon, rump cinnamon-buff, uppertail-coverts buff or dull white with grey shaft streaks. Tail blackish, all feathers fringed off-white, narrowly so on T6. Lesser and median coverts chestnut, fringed cinnamon (extreme bases mid grey). Greater coverts blackish, fringed chestnut and tipped cinnamon-buff. Alula black, nar-

rowly fringed cinnamon. Primary coverts blackish, fringed cinnamon. Flight feathers dark brownish-grey, fringed pale buff, broadly so on tertials (where more cinnamon at base), narrowly so on P2 and distally of emarginations on P3–P5. Lores and sides of head and neck sooty-black, throat and upper breast sooty-black or very dark mahogany-brown, feathers finely tipped buff, sides of breast chestnut, fringed buff. Remainder of underparts pale buff, concealed feather bases chestnut, blackish extending variably onto the lower breast and bib poorly demarcated. *In worn plumage* (summer), crown, nape and sides of head nearly uniform sooty-black, narrow off-white or very pale drab collar on border of upper mantle, mantle and scapulars uniformly chestnut, bib variably dark (throat may be light grey and breast sooty-black), chestnut bases to underpart feathers revealed to a variable extent. **Adult Female**: As male, though throat may average paler, with broader dull buff feather tips. **Juvenile**: As juvenile White-crowned Penduline Tit. **1st Adult**: As adult (see Sex/Age). **Measurements**: Wing of male 53.5–60, of female 57; tail of male 46–50, of female 47; bill 10.5–12.5; tarsus 14–15. Weight 9.3–10.5 g.

**MOULT** No information.

**GEOGRAPHICAL VARIATION** Relatively pronounced, although the situation is complicated by variation with age and sex and individual variation (especially problematic where this species hybridises with European Penduline Tit). Four races recognised, although one (*ssaposhnikowi*) is probably of hybrid origin and should, perhaps, not be recognised.

*R. m. macronyx* SW Kazakhstan, Uzbekistan, Tadzhikistan and northern and SE Turkmenistan. Hybridises with the race *caspius* of European Penduline Tit at the mouth of the Ural river. See Description.

*R. m. neglectus* SW Turkmenistan and northern Iran in the Atrak and Gorgan valleys; replaced in the southwest corner of the Caspian by a hybrid population *neglectus* x *menzbieri* (a race of European Penduline Tit; this hybrid population is sometimes named '*altaicus*', and treated by Stepanyan 1990 as a race of Black-headed; '*altaicus*' has been recorded in Israel (Paz 1987), and is thought to be a rare but regular winter visitor there in the north and east (Shirihai in press). Poorly marked. As *macronyx*, but smaller. Wing 50–56, of male 51–55, of female 52, 53; tail of male 43; bill 12.5. Synonymised with *macronyx* by Vaurie (1959).

*R. m. nigricans* SE Iran. As *macronyx*, but black of head more extensive, extending to mantle and sometimes rump, tertials and breast (thus no pale collar), with lower mantle and lesser coverts otherwise dark chestnut and breast and rump extensively chestnut; when worn, underparts dark chestnut (extensive feather bases fully revealed), coverts black. Smaller (as *neglectus*). Wing 54–58, of male 56–58, of female 55; tail of male 45.7–50, of female 50; bill 12–13.

*R. m. ssaposhnikowi* SE Kazakhstan around Lakes Balkhash, Sasykkol' and Alakol'. Rather variable in colour: head pattern mainly as *R. p. caspius* (a race of Eurpean Penduline Tit), although may be close to *macronyx*, and on some black of head replaced by chestnut or white on crown and nape and by white on throat. Size near *macronyx*. Synonymised with *macronyx* by Stepanyan (1990), while treated as hybrid swarm *jaxarticus* x *macronyx* and placed with *macronyx* by Vaurie

(1957c), although range now disjunct from both of these.

**HYBRIDS** See European Penduline Tit.

**RELATIONSHIPS** Frequently treated as conspecific with European Penduline Tit (see that species).

**REFERENCES** Dementiev & Gladkov (1966–70), Stepanyan (1990), Vaurie (1950a, 1957c, 1959).

# 35 WHITE-CROWNED PENDULINE TIT *Remiz coronatus*   Plate 11

This poorly known tit is superficially similar to European Penduline Tit, although it apparently shuns reedbeds and prefers to breed and forage in trees, and can sometimes be seen flitting from bush to bush on open hillsides. There is one record for Europe.

**IDENTIFICATION** Length 100 mm (4 in). Bill typical for the genus, but compared with that of European Penduline Tit relatively small and thin; the legs, toes and claws are also rather small and weak. The male has a white head with a narrow black band on the forehead and black 'highwayman's mask' which joins at the rear with a variable black nuchal band (the female's head pattern is more diffuse). A broad white collar separates the nuchal band from a relatively narrow band of chestnut on the lower mantle and scapulars, while the back and rump are paler, more buffish-grey. Wing-coverts cinnamon, becoming richer and more chestnut on the greater coverts, which are also tipped paler, forming a diffuse wingbar. Tail and flight feathers blackish, neatly fringed off-white. Underparts whitish, tinged pinkish on the breast and buff on the rear flanks, with odd chestnut spots on the breast. In worn plumage, the nuchal band becomes progressively broader (as the white feather tips on the crown are abraded), and may extend forwards to cover most of the crown, although the forecrown is always white. Rather similar to European Penduline Tit (and their ranges may overlap in southern Siberia and the NW Altai, as well as more extensively in winter in Central Asia and Iran), but overall paler, and never shows any chestnut on the crown. Adults also differ in their pale grey or white crown and distinctive dark 'bridle' around the nape (although this may not be obvious at a distance), separated from the upperparts by a broad pale collar. Juveniles are very similar to juvenile European Penduline Tits (and probably not identifiable), although they may average slightly greyer (and thus identical to juvenile Black-headed Penduline Tit).

**SEX/AGE** Sexes differ slightly, the female being overall duller and paler, with the cap pale grey rather than white (especially obvious towards the rear, contrasting with the more restricted white forecrown), and the mask and especially the bridle paler, browner and less extensive, with little dark on the forehead and blackish not extending so far onto the crown in worn plumage; the pale collar is dull pale grey rather than white, the upperparts are slightly paler, and the pinkish wash on the underparts is paler. Juveniles are very distinct, being dirty grey on the head and upperparts,

tinged cinnamon on the scapulars, back and rump, with the fringes to the tail and flight feathers paler and more diffuse than those of the adult, the wing-coverts more washed-out, and the underparts uniformly pale buff. 1st-adult males resemble adult females, but have a richer and more chestnut mantle, whilst 1st-adult females are close to juveniles in appearance, but have a washed out dark mask (see Description).

**VOICE** Calls include a thin *pseee* (as European Penduline Tit, but perhaps slightly shorter and fuller, not 'trailing off' so much at the end), a *swee-swee* phrase and shorter, high-pitched, plaintive *see* or *tsi* notes; in flight, *ti-ti-ti-ti-ti*.

**DISTRIBUTION AND MOVEMENTS** Breeds in southern **Turkmenistan** in the Murgab valley (north to Mary) and the Tedzhen valley and perhaps also adjacent Khorasan in NE **Iran** and NW **Afghanistan**, where recorded in April at Tirpul on the Hari Rud (= Tedzhen). Also breeds in the valley of the Amudar'ya in **Uzbekistan** and Turkmenistan from the Aral Sea south to **Tadzhikistan** and the foothills of the Alai and southern Tien Shan, extending into Badakhshan in NE **Afghanistan**. In southern **Kazakhstan** breeds along the Syrdar'ya from the Aral Sea southeast to the Fergana basin in Uzbekistan, and in the foothills of the Tien Shan from the northern foothills of the Zailiyskiy Alatau to the upper Chu valley, Talasskiy Alatau, and Karatau. Also SE Kazakhstan in the Dzhungarskiy Alatau, around Lake Alakol', in the foothills of the Tarbagatay, the Zaysan basin and valley of the 'Chernyi' Irtysh, and the western foothills of the Altai. Found in **SE Russia** in southern Siberia in the foothills of the Altai, the Minusinsk steppe and headwaters of the Yenisey, Tuvinskaya district, and southern Transbaykalia east to at least Chita. In western and central **Mongolia** found in the Bulgan valley in the far southwest, the western Altai (and recorded east to the eastern outliers of the Gobian Altai at *c.* 104° E, but these are presumably migrants). Also the Hovd Gol valley from the Achit Nuur to the Har Us Nuur, the Hangayn-Hentiyn mountains (including the Orhon-Selenge Mörön drainage on the northern watershed, east to Bayandelger on the Kerulen river), and the Halhin Gol valley on the border of Nei Mongol. In **NW China** occurs in

213

**Xinjiang** in the northern Junggar basin, the foothills of the Tien Shan east to Urümqi, the Yarkant valley from Kashi to at least Bachu, and the southern rim of the Tarim Basin in the Kun Lun and Altun Shan (Astin Tagh), east to Lop Nur, also northern **Ningxia** (on the border of Nei Mongol) in the Helan Shan (Ala Shan). In NW **India** recorded in the Chang Chenmo valley in NE Ladakh (at 4500 m in June 1925), where a male was collected and another seen, and breeding was considered probable (Meinertzhagen 1927): the specimen is, however, in very fresh plumage and seems unlikely to have been collected on this date; some sort of mistake cannot be ruled out, and confirmation of its occurrence in Ladakh is required. Migratory to a variable extent. A summer visitor to Mongolia (late May or early June–September), southern Siberia and Kazakhstan, departing entirely from the latter by mid October, but in Tadzhikistan and Uzbekistan some remain at lower levels in mild winters. Status in NW China not clear; recorded in small parties at Bachu in Xinjiang in late March, and possibly only a migrant in this region (not recorded around the northern rim of the Tarim basin, including Bosten Hu, in a midsummer visit: Grimmett & Taylor 1992). Recorded on passage in SW Turkmenistan on the Uzboy river, and winters in eastern **Iran**, south to southern Khorasan and Sistan (November–February, recorded south to Jalq on the border of Pakistani Baluchistan, but the only recent field observation comes from Doruneh in western Khorasan in April: D.A. Scott *in litt.*), in SW **Afghanistan** in Seistan (Quala-i-Kang, November), and in **Pakistan** (December–late March, sometimes as early as late September) in the major river systems of the Punjab and northern Sind, occasionally south to lower Sind. Occurs along the Indus north to the Kohat region, with spring passage noted mid March–mid April in the nearby Kurram valley, but scarce or rare from Sukkur southwards. Also in the Jhelum valley north to Lahore, the southern Punjab and Jhelum district, and along the Sutlej northeast to Bahalwalnagar. Listed by Abdulali & Unnithan (1992) for Harunabad, this presumably being Shahabad in northern Haryana, NW **India**. Records from northern Afghanistan in late autumn, at Maymaneh (October) and Pol-e Khomri (November), may indicate either passage or wintering birds. Vagrant **Austria** (Neusiedler See, 1 August 1987).

**HABITAT** Breeds in riverine forest and thickets, both in the lowlands and in mountains. Thus, along the Syrdar'ya found in willow scrub along the river banks and on islands, in floodmeadows and along adjacent tributaries and irrigation canals (sometimes in solitary trees). May breed locally in town and village gardens. In the Kyzylkum desert, breeds in Turanga Trees amid stands of saxaul. At higher latitudes, in the foothills of the Tien Shan, breeds in riverine stands of birch-willow-poplar, less commonly in scattered bushes on adjacent mountain slopes. Also valley-bottom walnut groves. In the Talasskiy Alatau (western Tien Shan) breeds at up to 2400

m, but only to 1500–1700 m in the Zailiyskiy Alatau. Apparently dependent on the presence of willow and poplar, which are essential sources of nesting material. On migration may occur in gardens, woods and orchards, low montane scrub and creeping juniper, saxaul, tamarisk, Salt Trees, rank weeds and tall grass and reedbeds. Winters in Pakistan in reedbeds, and in *Acacia*, tamarisk and Shisham trees alongside waterways, on flood-protection embankments and around reservoirs, and in irrigated forest plantations.

**POPULATION** Neither rare nor numerous in Central Asia, but scarce to rare in the Krasnoyarsk region of SE Russia, and reported to have been extirpated in the Minusinsk depression as a result of intensive economic development (Rogacheva 1992). A scarce winter visitor to Pakistan (rare in lower Sind).

**HABITS** Similar to those of European Penduline Tit. Gregarious, and flocks of up to 50 have been reported in the autumn, comprising mainly juveniles, with up to 40 noted on spring passage. Food insects and spiders and, in winter, seeds, including bulrush; willow seeds are reported to be the main food item in northern Mongolia during the breeding season (Kozlova 1932–33). Spring migrants in Pakistan noted as usually feeding in the tree canopy.

**BREEDING BIOLOGY** Season: Mongolia and Transbaykalia, June; Central Asia, May–June. The nest resembles that of European Penduline Tit, and is built from vegetable down, especially from poplars and willows. It is apparently always sited in trees, usually 6–8 m high at the end of a horizontal branch (the entrance opening to the south or southeast); some nests are placed high above the ground in large trees some distance from water. A fresh nest is built each year, often in the vicinity of the old nest. Both sexes build, the female laying as soon as the purse is ready, the male completing the nest. The female is fed on the nest by the male, who roosts in the nest, together with the female (Kozlova 1932–33, Dementiev & Gladkov 1966–70). Clutch 3–9: eggs as those of European Penduline Tit?; c. 14.9 x 10.4 mm (*R. c. coronatus*).

**DESCRIPTION** *R. c. coronatus* **Adult Male**: *In fresh plumage* (August–c. March), forehead, crown, nape, lores, cheeks and ear-coverts black, feathers of forecrown broadly tipped white (concealing black bases), tips progressively narrower towards hindcrown, variably revealing black feather bases towards rear; always a dark nuchal band, forehead always white. Upper mantle and sides of neck off-white, forming a complete collar and well demarcated from nuchal band. Lower mantle and scapulars chestnut, scapulars broadly tipped cinnamon. Back, rump and uppertail-coverts light buffish-cinnamon-drab, feathers diffusely tipped slightly paler (thus slightly mottled). Tail blackish, T1 broadly fringed and tipped off-white, T2–T6 narrowly fringed white on outer web, broadly so on inner web. Wing-coverts dark grey, lesser coverts broadly tipped cinnamon, median coverts tipped cinnamon-rufous, extreme tips slightly paler, greater coverts broadly tipped cinnamon-buff, outer web largely chestnut. Alula blackish, very finely fringed pale grey. Primary coverts blackish, finely fringed cinnamon-rufous and tipped paler. Tertials dark grey, paler on inner webs and broadly fringed buffy-white. Primaries and secondaries blackish, secondaries and inner primaries broadly fringed buffy-white, whiter towards tips, fringes narrower and off-white on P2 and distally of emarginations on P3–P6. Throat, breast and upper flanks off-white, chestnut feather bases to breast feathers shining through to give a vinous-pink hue and odd centres fully revealed; flanks tinged buff, especially at rear. Belly to undertail-coverts, axillaries and underwing-coverts buffy-white; thighs dark grey, tipped cinnamon. *In worn plumage* (April–August), white tips to crown feathers progressively abraded (when very worn, white confined to forecrown), chestnut of mantle slightly paler and more restricted, forming a narrower cinnamon-rufous band, back and rump bleached paler, dark centres to greater coverts revealed, tips to flight feathers abraded; underparts duller, dark grey and orange-rufous feather bases progressively revealed on breast; belly and vent buffer. **Bare Parts**: Iris deep red to dark brown; bill dark brown to dark blue-grey with paler cutting edges; legs and feet dark slate or blackish-grey. **Adult Female**: In fresh plumage as male, but feathers of crown and nape more broadly tipped light to mid grey, with a narrow whitish band on the forecrown, dark feather bases smaller and browner and mask thus duller and browner, blackish band on forehead much reduced and only odd dark centres revealed on nape. Upper mantle light drab, lower mantle cinnamon (forming a narrower and paler band than on male), back and rump duller and grey, less drab. Underparts as male, but much-reduced rufous bases to breast feathers (thus much paler pink wash). **Juvenile**: Entire upperparts and sides of head pale drab-grey, becoming more cinnamon-drab on scapulars, back and rump. Tail as adult, but pale fringes average broader and less well defined. Wings as adult, but lesser coverts light grey, fringed cinnamon-drab, greater coverts fringed cinnamon (not chestnut), and pale fringes to tertials and secondaries broader (tertials buff with darker shaft streaks). Underparts uniformly pale buff. **1st-Adult Male**: As adult male, but crown feathers tipped light drab-grey (duller and less grey than female), mask browner, blackish forehead band reduced, nape and upper mantle light drab-grey (thus no white collar), lower mantle and scapulars rich chestnut (darker and richer than female). **1st-Adult Female**:

As adult female, but crown and nape cinnamon-drab, poorly demarcated from upperparts, forehead whitish (no black at base of bill). Lores, cheeks and ear-coverts sooty-brown, feathers tipped paler. Underparts buffer. **Measurements**: Wing of male 49–55, of female 50–54; tail of male 38–44, of female 38–43; bill 10–12; tarsus 12–14. Weight 5.2–7.8 g.

**MOULT** Adult post-breeding complete (July–August). Post-juvenile poorly known, includes at least greater coverts but may be incomplete (or even complete) (early July–early September).

**GEOGRAPHICAL VARIATION** Rather slight, with two races recognised.

*R. p. coronatus* Central Asia in Turkmenistan, Uzbekistan, Tadzhikistan, Kirgizia and SE Kazakhstan, extending marginally into NW Xinjiang, China, along the Ili valley; also NE Afghanistan, probably NE Iran and NW Afghanistan, possibly NW India (Ladakh). Winters also in eastern Iran, SW Afghanistan and Pakistan. See Description.

*R. p. stoliczkae* Southern Siberia from the Altai east to southern Transbaykalia, Mongolia and NW China (except for range of nominate *coronatus*). Intergrades with nominate *coronatus* in the Zaysan basin/'Chernyi' Irtysh valley of SE Kazakhstan. Resident and migratory (but no clues as to where winter range may be; possibly the recent increase in eastern China and Japan of Chinese Penduline Tit may involve some birds of this species). Poorly marked. As nominate *coronatus*, but upperparts paler and buffer, nuchal band less prominent (usually sooty or blackish, not so deep and uniformly black), lesser coverts uniform cinnamon-buff; bill averages 1.5 mm shorter, also thinner and more needle-like. Wing of male 53–55, of female 54–55; tail of male 38–45, of female 39–45; bill 8–10.5; weight 7–10 g.

**RELATIONSHIPS** Often considered conspecific with European Penduline Tit, but their ranges do not appear to overlap and where they abut they are separated ecologically: White-crowned breeds in riverine forest and thickets, both in the lowlands and in the hills, European in reedbeds. 'The present evidence suggests that *coronatus* has probably reached species level, though this cannot be decided without field studies' (Vaurie 1957c). See European Penduline Tit.

**REFERENCES** Cramp & Perrins (1993), Dementiev & Gladkov (1966–70), Dolgushin *et al.* (1972), Roberts (1992), Stepanyan (1990), Vaurie (1950a, 1957c, 1959).

Very much the eastern counterpart of European Penduline Tit, this species has similarly undergone a major population explosion in recent years, and is now regular in both Japan and Hong Kong in winter; the source of these birds is, however, a mystery.

**IDENTIFICATION** Length 105 mm (4.25 in). A small tit, in shape and jizz very similar to European Penduline Tit, with the conical pointed bill characteristic of the genus. Dull black 'highwayman's mask' from the bill through the eye, narrowly bordered above by whitish, with remainder of cap and nape pale grey, diffusely streaked or mottled darker, especially at the rear (where the streaks coalesce). Upper mantle chestnut in the male, extending as a mottled half-collar onto the sides of the breast and grading to rich buff on the rump, which is diffusely streaked darker. Tail blackish, all feathers broadly fringed and tipped buff. Wing-coverts cinnamon, richer and more chestnut on the greater coverts, which also have diffuse paler tips. Flight feathers dark grey, tertials and secondaries broadly fringed buffish. Dark mask bordered below by a broad white submoustachial stripe, and centre of throat pale buff, becoming buff on the breast and cinnamon on the flanks. In worn plumage overall paler, with the cap more uniform. The range is well separated from that of the European Penduline Tit, but White-crowned Penduline Tit occurs in northern Ningxia in central China (Chinese breeding in southern Ningxia), and it should not be assumed that any penduline tit in China is Chinese. In most plumages, White-crowned has a white cap and variable black 'bridle' around the nape (extending well onto the crown in worn plumage), joining with its black mask, and separated from the chestnut upper mantle by a broad pale collar. Seen well, it is quite distinct from the rather mealy head of Chinese, which never shows black on the rear crown or nape. Juveniles of the two species are, however, probably indistinguishable. White-crowned also favours more wooded habitats, often at higher altitudes, than Chinese.

**SEX/AGE** The sexes differ slightly. Female as male, but crown and nape duller and browner, mask dark brown with a reduced extension onto the forehead, and upperparts uniform buffish-drab, lacking any trace of a chestnut collar except when worn. Juveniles apparently more or less uniform buffish-drab on head and upperparts. 1st-adult males are near adults, but have a smaller and duller mask, finely 'peppered' buff in fresh plumage, a browner and more uniform crown, reduced and less contrasting chestnut collar, and buff-washed submoustachial stripe; they are close to adult females, but usually separable by a blacker mask and more prominent chestnut collar. 1st-adult females resemble adult females, but their mask may be even less contrasting and their plain head pattern thus near that of a juvenile. In the hand, 1st adults may be aged after the partial post-juvenile moult by moult contrasts in the wings, with up to five juvenile outer greater coverts retained, these being paler, with the fringes and

especially tips worn and bleached paler than the adjacent new feathers; they may also show contrasts in the tail and secondaries (?).

**VOICE** Very similar to that of European Penduline Tit. Call a high-pitched, soft and thin but penetrating whistle, *tseee* or *pseee* etc. Also a fuller *piu* and a faster series of notes, *siu-siu-siu-siu*. Song also similar, including *si-si-tiu, si-si-tiu...* phrases on an elaborated 'tea-cher' theme.

**DISTRIBUTION AND MOVEMENTS** Breeds China (presumably also the Russian Far East), and migrant and winter visitor North and South Korea and Japan. Breeds in **NE China** in eastern **Nei Mongol** (Linxi, and Zalantun in the Nen Jiang basin), adjacent **Heilongjiang** (Nenjiang on the Nenjiang river, also Aihui (= Heihe) on the Amur river), NW **Jilin** (Baicheng, Xiang Hai marshes, Changchun and Siping; present mid April–late September) and southernmost **Ningxia** (Jingyuan). Probably breeds in southern **Liaoning**, where recorded in late April and May and an old nest of presumed local origin seen at Shuangtaizihekou NNR at the mouth of the Taizi river (Brazil 1992). Status in **Hebei** unclear: Shaw (1936) stated that it was resident in the plains (listing records for March, April and December), and Meyer de Schauensee (1984) also states that it breeds in Hebei, but La Touche (1920, 1925) and Cheng (1987) consider it a migrant in NE Hebei in spring and autumn (recorded in May and October), although not common. Further south, Li *et al.* (1982) state that it breeds in the **Shanghai** area, but noted only as a winter visitor, November–April, by Wang (1986). Presumably breeds in the **Russian Far East**, as recorded along the Chinese side of the Amur river, which forms the border with China (although not known in Russia). Recorded on passage in **eastern China** in an apparently narrow corridor in SE **Nei Mongol** (Chifeng), **Jilin** (Siping), western **Liaoning** (Chaoyang, also Niuzhuang in February: La Touche 1925), **Hebei** (recorded at Qinhuangdao, and at Beidaihe in late April–May and late September–late November), **Henan** and **Shandong** (Anqiu, April). A fairly common spring migrant April–May in **North Korea**. Irregular passage migrant and winter visitor October–May **South Korea**. Winters in the middle and lower reaches of the River Yangtze (eastwards from **Hubei**, including the Poyang lakes in **Jiangxi**), and in western **Yunnan** along the Nu Jiang (= Salween), where localities include Tengchong at *c.* 1800 m (with the suggestion, probably incorrect, that it is found in the high valleys in the summer: Ménégaux & Didier 1913), and recently also **Hong Kong**. Winter visitor to **Japan**, mainly **Kyushu** and western **Honshu**, but also north on Honshu to Toyama prefecture and east to Chiba and Ibaraki prefectures; recorded Okinawa in March 1987.

**HABITAT** Throughout the year favours a mixture of reedbeds and bushes, both in fresh- and saltwater habitats, and also poplar plantations and apple orchards some distance from water (although still in the vicinity of wetland areas) in Jilin, and on migration may be found in a wider variety of bushy habitats and rank vegetation, especially near the coast.

**POPULATION** Uncommon in China, and the breeding population in Jilin is thought to be relatively small and should be protected (Wildlife Conservation Society of Jilin Province 1987), although noted as common in NW Jilin by Zhao *et al.* (no date). However, marked increases in migrant and wintering numbers have been noted in Japan, eastern China and Hong Kong, and the source of these birds is a mystery. At Beidaihe, coastal Hebei, only a handful of migrants recorded in the 1920s and 1940s, but now abundant, with up to 1,103 bird-days in spring (1989) and 4,187 in autumn (1988, when 2,715 birds moved south in a single day) (Williams & Dorner 1991; Williams *et al.* 1992). In Japan, formerly a vagrant, with just six records in the period 1877–99, but there was a marked increase in the 1970s and the species is now an uncommon or locally common winter visitor to western Japan, especially Kyushu and western Honshu, and is recorded in large flocks at some locations in the southwest. In Hong Kong, first recorded at Mai Po in April 1980, and recorded in Hong Kong in four subsequent springs, followed by an invasion in December 1989–May 1990, during which 69 individuals were trapped. Common again at Mai Po in subsequent winters, November–mid April, *c.* 250 passing over on 24 November 1991. Intriguingly, up to the end of 1992 a total of 132 was trapped at Mai Po, and the complete absence of retraps indicates either a large population or a very fast turnover of migrants, or perhaps both. (*Hong Kong Bird Report* 1991; Melville & Galsworthy 1991.)

**HABITS** Apparently very similar to those of European Penduline Tit. In winter found in flocks, sometimes in large flocks. Frequently forages in reed heads. Food insects and seeds.

**BREEDING BIOLOGY** Nest hung from the tips of slender reeds and bushes, made of vegetable fibres and down, oval, with the entrance at the upper end. A nest in Jilin was sited *c.* 4 m up in a poplar tree (on the edge of a plantation) several hundred metres from open water. Clutch 5–10: eggs white; 15.5 x 10.5 mm (Wilder & Hubbard 1938).

**DESCRIPTION Adult Male**: *In fresh plumage* (about September–April), lores to ear-coverts sooty-black, forming a mask which surrounds the eye and narrowly bridges bill. Crown, nape and sides of neck light grey, feathers fringed pale grey and tipped cinnamon-drab, tips broadest on nape and side of neck, where almost uniformly drab-grey; border of forehead and mask off-white. Border of upper mantle chestnut, feathers tipped cinnamon, grading to cinnamon on lower mantle and scapulars, with dark feather bases showing on some scapulars. Back, rump and uppertail-coverts buffish-cinnamon, darker feather bases giving a slight mottled effect. Tail blackish-brown, all feath-

ers broadly fringed and tipped buff. Wings dark grey, lesser coverts broadly fringed cinnamon (blackish bases fully concealed); median coverts broadly tipped cinnamon, extreme tips slightly paler and buffer; greater coverts fringed chestnut and tipped cinnamon-buff, extreme tips pale buff; alula and primary coverts narrowly fringed buffish-cinnamon; tertials very broadly fringed buffish (becoming chestnut at base of outer webs; dark centres almost reduced to shaft streaks on inner two) and tipped pale buff to white; secondaries fringed buffish-cinnamon, paler and buffer towards tips; primaries fringed buff, narrowly so on P2 and distally of emargination on P3–P6. Sides of throat white, forming broad white sub-moustachial area, sides of breast cinnamon and chestnut, forming extension of collar; chin and centre of throat pale buff, grading to buff on remainder of underparts, flanks washed cinnamon, longer undertail-coverts centred pale buff. Axillaries and underwing-coverts pale buff. *In worn plumage* (about May–August), crown more uniformly mid drab-grey with narrow white border to forehead and mask, upperparts bleached paler and buffer, chestnut collar slightly reduced although showing greater contrast, pale fringes to median and greater coverts and flight feathers heavily worn to reveal dark centres of coverts (sometimes even of lesser coverts), and underparts slightly paler. **Bare Parts**: Iris dark brown; bill grey or greyish-black, culmen blackish; legs and feet leaden-blue. **Adult Female**: In fresh plumage as male, but crown, nape and upper mantle light greyish-drab, forehead slightly paler and sides whitish. Mask from lores to ear-coverts dark brown or dull chestnut, barely bridging bill, some feathers tipped cinnamon. Upperparts uniform buffish-drab with diffuse paler fringes, giving a slightly mottled effect, darker collar absent or much reduced, chestnut feather bases largely concealed, sides of breast cinnamon with no dark half-collar. In worn plumage, dark feather bases may show on upper mantle and at sides of breast. **Juvenile**: No information (but see Sex/Age). **1st-Adult Male**: As adult male, but mask duller, dark brown with fine cinnamon feather tips, also more restricted, especially at rear. Crown more uniformly light drab-grey or light drab (feathers fringed buff rather than pale grey), greyer on the forecrown and nape, with narrow whitish band on forehead and above eye. Chestnut collar on upper mantle more broadly fringed cinnamon (thus less contrasting), sub-moustachial tinged buff. **1st-Adult Female**: As adult female, but mask may be rather less contrasting, and thus close to juvenile. See also Sex/Age. **Measurements**: Wing of male 53–59, of female 52–56.5; tail of male 40–47, of female 39–46; bill 9–12.5; tarsus 13.5–15. Weight 7.5–11.9 g.

**MOULT** Adult post-breeding complete (no data on timing). Adult pre-breeding occasional, partial, includes head and/or body (February–March). Post-juvenile partial, includes a variable number of greater coverts (up to five juvenile greater coverts retained). First pre-breeding occasional, partial (as adult) (March–April).

**GEOGRAPHICAL VARIATION** None.
**RELATIONSHIPS** See European Penduline Tit.

**REFERENCES** Cheng (1987), Melville & Galsworthy (1991).

## 37 SENNAR PENDULINE TIT *Anthoscopus punctifrons*    Plate 13
Other name: Sudan Penduline Tit

Despite a range extending across northern Africa from the Atlantic to the Red Sea, this tit is perhaps the least-known member of the genus.

**IDENTIFICATION** Length 85 mm (3.25 in). A tiny tit with the short tail and triangular, sharply pointed bill characteristic of the genus. Upperparts clean yellowish-olive, tinged grey, with the forehead brighter and more yellowish, finely spotted darker, and the rump slightly brighter and buffer. Tail and wings dark brown, the feathers finely fringed paler, especially the greater coverts, tertials and secondaries. Face off-white, underparts creamy or creamy-buff. Easily distinguished from Yellow Penduline Tit by its creamy rather than bright yellow underparts. The blackish spots on the forehead are difficult to see except at very close range, and, like all members of the genus, this species is easily overlooked.

**SEX/AGE** Sexes similar. Juvenile as adult, but upperparts, especially crown and nape, slightly duller and greyer, fringes to tertials and greater coverts duller and not so olive, and tail feathers slightly narrower and more pointed. No information on 1st adult.

**VOICE** A short *tsit*, a high, thin, plaintive t*sui-tsui-tsui-tsui...* and an even thinner *tsee-tsee-tsee....* Also a very fast grating rattle *tzrrrrrrrrrrrrrr*, often introduced by a squeaky *tuzi* (recalling a child's squeaky toy), and a rhythmic, mechanical, buzzing *bizur, bizur, bizur, bizur....*

**DISTRIBUTION AND MOVEMENTS** Found in northern and eastern **Senegal** (east of Richard Toll and north of 14° N), and in adjacent **Mauritania** occurs locally from the Senegal river to 17° N, also around Tagant (near Garaouel at 17° 30′ N). In **Mali** found between c. 14° and 17° 30′ N, and in **Niger** recorded at Takoukout, Farak and Mts Bagzans, but apparently no records since 1922. Found in extreme NE **Nigeria** in the Sahel zone, mostly close to Lake Chad, and in northernmost **Cameroon** south to Waza. Apparently widespread in a broad band across central **Chad** south to at least Kenem, including the Ouadi Rime-Ouadi Achim Faunal Reserve. In central **Sudan** widely distributed in a belt between 9° N and 19° N, with records concentrated along the White Nile. Recorded in northern **Eritrea** (north of 15° N), but although listed for Ethiopia by Dowsett (1993) apparently unknown there (J.S. Ash *in litt.*). Resident.

**HABITAT** Confined to a relatively narrow band of semi-desert in the Sahel zone on the southern fringes of the Sahara, in *Acacia* savanna, thorn scrub and gallery forest. In more arid areas favours wadis and other relatively well-vegetated areas, and sometimes plentiful near watercourses and wells, and where animals congregate to drink.

Generally found at lower altitudes, and usually below 1050 m in Eritrea.

**POPULATION** Generally fairly common to common, at least locally, although uncommon in Nigeria and Eritrea.

**HABITS** Poorly known. Unobtrusive, but tame and very active. Often found in parties of three, keeping contact with constant calling. Forages among the leaves and flowers of *Acacia* trees. Food insects.

**BREEDING BIOLOGY** Poorly known. Season: Mauritania, June–September; Senegal, June–August; Mali, July–August; Nigeria, July; Chad, July–September (wet season); Sudan, February–March and September; and possibly May in Eritrea. The nest is described as being typical of the genus, but large for the bird. One found in Chad on 23 September contained two juveniles near to fledging (Mackworth-Praed & Grant 1973; Salvan 1967–69).

**DESCRIPTION** Adult: *In fresh plumage*, forehead olive-yellow, variably spotted darker (chocolate-brown feather centres). Upperparts from crown to uppertail-coverts greyish yellow-olive (scapulars may be slightly greyer), rump and uppertail-coverts slightly brighter, tinged buff. Tail dark brown, feathers tipped off-white and fringed buffish olive-yellow. Wings dark brown, lesser and median coverts fringed greyish yellow-olive; greater coverts submarginally pale grey and finely fringed buffish-olive-yellow; alula and primary coverts very finely fringed pale grey; tertials and secondaries broadly tipped pale grey and fringed buffish olive-yellow; P3–P10 fringed pale grey, tinged buffish-yellow on inner primaries (fringes present only inwards of emarginations on P3–P6). Lores, cheeks, ear-coverts, sides of neck and throat off-white, remainder of underparts creamy or creamy-buff. Axillaries creamy, underwing-coverts whitish. In worn plumage, upperparts duller and greyer, wings and tail bleached paler and browner, olive-yellow fringes abraded. **Bare Parts**: Iris light hazel to brownish-black; bill slate to black, cutting edges and base of lower mandible pale grey or whitish; legs, feet and claws bluish-slate or bright blue-grey. **Juvenile**: As adult, but upperparts, especially crown and nape, slightly duller and greyer, fringes to tertials and greater coverts duller and not so olive, and tail feathers slightly narrower and more pointed. **1st Adult**: No information. **Measurements**: Wing of male 49–56, of female 48–53; tail of male 27–30, of female 27–30.5; bill 9–11.3; tarsus 11–15. Weight: no information.

**MOULT** Adult post-breeding complete (late .

November–May, perhaps early July). Post-juvenile presumably incomplete, and thusincluding greater coverts and a variable number of tertials, secondaries and alula and tail feathers, possibly also some inner primaries, as in other *Anthoscopus* (November–December, June).

**GEOGRAPHICAL VARIATION** None.
**RELATIONSHIPS** A member of the *caroli* super-species.
**REFERENCES** Bannerman (1930–51), Mackworth- Praed & Grant (1973).

# 38 YELLOW PENDULINE TIT *Anthoscopus parvulus*　　　Plate 13
Other name: West African Penduline Tit

This brightly coloured tit is strangely scarce over much of its range, and many aspects of its biology remain poorly known.

**IDENTIFICATION** Length 80 mm (3 in). A tiny, neat, brightly coloured tit with a short tail and the triangular, sharply pointed bill characteristic of *Anthoscopus*. Upperparts greenish with a brighter and yellower rump and a contrastingly yellow forehead marked with tiny black dots. Tail and wings dark brown, the greater coverts and tertials neatly and prominently fringed whitish. Face and underparts yellow (see also Geographical Variation). Often surprisingly conspicuous, perhaps owing to its bright coloration, this species is unlikely to be confused with Sennar Penduline Tit, being distinguished by yellow underparts, rather than creamy or creamy-buff, and very obvious pale fringes to the wing feathers.

**SEX/AGE** Sexes similar. Juvenile as adult, but forecrown duller yellow, contrasting less with the crown, and underparts a paler and more washed-out yellow. No information on 1st adult.

**VOICE** Poorly known. Calls include a thin, quiet contact call, *si, sli-li-lii* (vaguely reminiscent of Long-tailed Tit), a high-pitched, but full and slightly hoarse *bzee-bzee-bzee-bzee*, and a deep, buzzing, rhythmical phrase, *chura-chura-chura...* or *duza-duza-duza...*, comprising 3–8 units (recalling African, Cape and Sennar Penduline Tits). Also a short *ch, ch, ch.*

**DISTRIBUTION AND MOVEMENTS** Recorded from southern **Mauritania** in the Senegal valley and southern Guidimaka, with scattered records throughout **Senegal**, and also occurs throughout the **Gambia** (recorded from Brufut, Yundum, Keneba, Mansakonko and Bansang). Found in southern **Mali** from the south of Bamako to *c*. 15° N, including the Mopti region and the Boucle du Baoulé Biosphere Reserve. In the **Ivory Coast** found locally in dry woodland north of 9° N, and in **Ghana** found in the northern savanna, where regular at Tumu and Mole, with a recent record from the coast near Lome on the **Ghana/Togo** border. Recorded from **Burkina** (Upper Volta), including the Fada-N'Gourma region and de L'Arly NP, and also the adjacent Pendjari NP in northern **Benin**. Occurs in northern **Nigeria** from Sokoto to Potiskum and Lake Chad, south to the Kainji Lake NP, Zaria and Falgore GR. In **Cameroon** recorded from Benoue NP, and probably widespread in central Cameroon. In the **Central African Republic** known from the

Bamamgui river and Bozoum, and in central and southern **Chad** occurs north to at least Chari-Baguirmi prefecture and Abeche. In southern **Sudan** there are scattered records east to the White Nile, north to Southern Kordofan, but in northern **Zaïre** known only from NE Haut-Zaïre (Dungu and also Mahagi near the Ugandan border). Listed for **Guinea-Bissau** by Serle & Morel (1977), but no further details; presumably occurs in **Guinea**, and may be expected to occur in extreme NE **Uganda**, as recorded from adjacent Sudan and Zaïre. Resident, but some evidence of seasonal movements; in northern Ghana numbers may fall in some years at Mole at the end of the dry season.

**HABITAT** Essentially a species of the semi-arid Sudan Savanna zone, extending marginally into the Sahel region to the north and the Guinea Savanna to the south. Favours open woodland with large trees and *Acacia*, as well as more degraded areas with scattered low *Acacia* and rank grass, riparian woodland and the vicinity of human habitations.

**POPULATION** Generally considered local and uncommon or even rare, the species may be overlooked, although, unlike Mouse-coloured Penduline Tit, this brightly coloured bird is unlikely to be misidentified. In some areas, however, such as Ghana and locally in Nigeria, not uncommon, and considered common on the Benin/Burkina border.

**HABITS** Found singly or in parties of 3–25, and may join mixed-species foraging flocks. Restless and active; forages in the canopy, flitting from branch to branch. Flight dipping. Food insects.

**BREEDING BIOLOGY** Poorly known. Season: Mauritania, February–March; Gambia, March; Ghana, December–January, also nest-building in April; Mali, February–March; Nigeria, June. The nest is a thin-walled elliptical pouch or purse of felted vegetable down, very strong and tough, *c*. 115 mm high and 65 mm in diameter. The opening is near the top of the pouch, and resembles a short flat tube *c*. 40 mm long composed of an upper and a lower flap which are self-closing and have to be separated by the bird as it enters or leaves. The nest is suspended from a bough or twig, and has been recorded at 5.5 m above ground level. Clutch 2: eggs dull white; *c*. 13.1 x 9.4 mm.

**DESCRIPTION** *A. p. senegalensis* **Adult**: *In fresh plumage,* forehead bright yellow, fading to yellowish olive-green on crown; feathers of forehead and forecrown with dark brown subterminal spots, largest and most diffuse on forecrown. Nape to back as crown; rump and uppertail-coverts brighter and yellower (yellow, tinged olive). Tail dark brown, feathers with narrow submarginal off-white band and very finely fringed olive-yellow on T1–T5; tips fringed off-white. Wings dark brown, lesser and median coverts fringed yellowish-olive-green; greater coverts and tertials with narrow submarginal off-white band and very fine olive-yellow fringes; alula finely fringed olive-yellow; primary coverts, primaries and secondaries finely fringed off-white (fringes absent on P1–P2 and present only inwards of emarginations on P4–P6). Sides of neck olive-yellow, lores, cheeks, ear-coverts and underparts rich yellow, faintly tinged olive. Axillaries yellowish; underwing-coverts white, tipped yellowish, especially on leading edge of wing. *In worn plumage,* wings bleached paler and browner, olive-yellow fringes abraded (least so on greater coverts and tertials), underparts duller and dirtier yellow. **Bare Parts**: Iris brown to dark brown; bill blackish-brown or blackish-horn, lower mandible and cutting edges whitish or bluish; legs and feet blue-grey to dark slaty-blue. **Juvenile**: As adult, but forecrown duller yellow, pale fringes on tertials more diffuse, underparts a paler and more washed-out yellow. **1st Adult**: No information. **Measurements**: Wing of male 48, of female 47–51; tail of male 29, of female 26–29; bill 9.4–11.1; tarsus 10–13. Weight: no information.

**MOULT**    Adult    post-breeding    complete

(December, Mali; June, Nigeria; May, Sudan). Post-juvenile, no information (presumably incomplete, see Cape Penduline Tit; April–May in Sudan).

**GEOGRAPHICAL VARIATION** Rather slight. Four races have been described, but on the basis of a rather small number of birds, and not taking into account variation with age and wear. All four are synonymised with nominate *parvulus* in 'Peters'.

*A. p. senegalensis* Senegal to Nigeria and the Lake Chad region. Intergrades with nominate *parvulus* to the east and with *citrinus* to the southeast. See Description.

*A. p. aureus* Northern Ghana. A dull race. As *senegalensis*, but forehead olive-yellow, showing little contrast with the crown and with only a few fine dark spots, greater coverts and tertials more broadly fringed off-white, and underparts a slightly more washed-out yellow, tinged olive on the throat and upper breast. Wing 50; tail 28.

*A. p. citrinus* Central African Republic (and presumably this race in northern Cameroon). Poorly marked. As *senegalensis*, but overall slightly brighter yellow. Wing 49–54; tail 30.

*A. p. parvulus* Lake Chad to southern Sudan and NE Zaïre. As *senegalensis*, but upperparts duller and more olive-green, washed grey (thus yellow forehead shows more contrast), and underparts very slightly paler and duller yellow. Wing 50–52; tail 27–28.

**RELATIONSHIPS** A member of the *caroli* superspecies, and considered the ecological representative of African Penduline Tit in the northern woodlands by Hall & Moreau (1970).

**REFERENCES** Bannerman (1948).

# 39 MOUSE-COLOURED PENDULINE TIT *Anthoscopus musculus*
## Plate 13

Once described as a 'denizen of the utter wilderness' (Archer & Godman 1961), this species is inconspicuous and widely overlooked, although a relatively common bird in the dry-country scrub of the more arid parts of East Africa.

**IDENTIFICATION** Length 80 mm (3 in). A tiny, drab tit with a short tail, the triangular, sharply pointed bill characteristic of the genus, and stocky legs and feet. The upperparts are medium drab-grey or olive-grey, with the forehead finely peppered darker and the wings and tail a paler and purer grey (although the coverts and flight feathers always seem to appear slightly dishevelled and irregular). The lores are dark brown, the face dull buff with faint darker mottling and a slightly paler supercilium from the eye to the bill, and the underparts off-white, tinged buff on the belly and vent. Bill blackish with a paler base; legs and feet slaty-blue. Overlaps with African Penduline Tit (of the *sylviella* group) in southern Kenya and NE Tanzania, but easily distinguished by its grey (rather than pale buff) forehead and its whitish underparts, only faintly tinged buff (not pale cinnamon-buff); Mouse-coloured Penduline Tit may

overlap with African Penduline Tits of the *caroli* group in interior eastern Tanzania and interior eastern Kenya, but differs as above, although the buff of the forehead and underparts is tinged yellow in the *caroli* group. The range also overlaps with that of Yellow and Sennar Penduline Tits in Sudan, but Yellow Penduline Tit has bright yellow underparts and Sennar has yellow-green upperparts with a more obviously speckled forehead. This species is more likely to be confused with some small, nondescript warblers found in the same habitat (probably resulting in its being widely overlooked). Yellow-vented Eremomela is a similarly small, short-tailed grey-and-white bird, but has a longer tail (although still short for a warbler), and longer and stockier legs, showing more of the tibia (yellow is confined to its vent and undertail-coverts and is often invisible at any distance). Yellow-bellied Eremomela is similar, but with more yellow on the belly, whilst Buff-bellied Warbler is also nondescript, but has pale greyish-olive upperparts and pale creamy-yellow underparts, with a narrow white rim and tip to the tail, as well as reddish eyes and a pink bill and legs. In addition, when seen well, the characteristic conical bill shape should always distinguish the penduline tit.

**SEX/AGE** Sexes similar. Juvenile and 1st adult as adult (but see Description).

**VOICE** Contact and flight call *tit, tit,...* or *stit, stit...*, also an abrupt, nasal *tzee* or *bzeeu*. Song phrases include a sibilant trill, *chu-wi-wi-wi-wi-wi-...*, a very fast, monotonous rattling trill, *tizizizizi...* (recalling a tinny machine-gun), and a rapid repetition of a ringing couplet, *chu-we-cha–we-cha-we-cha-we-cha...* in the 'tea-cher' pattern (but very fast).

**DISTRIBUTION AND MOVEMENTS** Known from SE **Sudan**, west to Lado and Tombe on the upper White Nile, with an isolated record in the northeast in the Kassala region. In **Ethiopia** widespread in the Rift Valley, as well as to the south and east of it (north to *c.* 10° 30′ N, including Nechisar and other NPs), and scattered records in **Somalia**, in the northwest (north of 8° N and west of 49° 30′ E) and in the south from 2° to 4° 30′ N. Extends marginally into extreme NE **Uganda**, from Kidepo NP south to Moroto, and also recorded from Serere (Teso). Widespread in northern and western **Kenya** from the Ugandan border and Lake Turkana basin, east through the Huri hills, Marsabit and Wajir to the Somali border, south (east of the highlands and west of the coastal lowlands) to the Lake Bogoria region and through Isiolo to Lake Magadi, Kajiado and the northern part of Tsavo East NP. The distribution within these areas may not be continuous, and there are few records from the arid east and northeast of Kenya or from Somalia south of 2° N; this may merely reflect the lack of coverage in these areas, or reveal a genuine aversion to the driest areas (i.e. annual rainfall below 250 mm). In extreme NE **Tanzania** occurs in the region southeast of Mount Kilimanjaro to the North Pare foothills, and north of Arusha. Resident.

**HABITAT** Dry *Acacia* bush, woodland and short-grass savanna, usually in arid or semi-arid country (annual rainfall below 1000 mm). Rarely found above 1500 m in Ethiopia, and in Kenya recorded at 400–1600 m, while in NE Tanzania found at up to 900 m.

**POPULATION** Generally considered rather uncommon and local (although in Ethiopia noted as 'fairly common' by Benson 1946 and 'frequent?' by Urban & Brown 1971), but probably rather commoner than records indicate, as this tiny bird is easily overlooked; at certain well-watched localities, such as Samburu in central Kenya, has been found to be relatively common.

**HABITS** Found in pairs or small parties, often joining mixed-species foraging flocks. Usually very tame. Forages in the canopy of small *Acacia* trees or in low scrub, and rather acrobatic, often perching quite upright.

**BREEDING BIOLOGY** Season: Sudan, December; Ethiopia, February–March and September–October; southern Somalia, November. Few nests have been found. One was sited about 2 m above ground in a thorn bush, with no attempt at concealment. Constructed from plant fibres, it was very similar to that of African Penduline Tit, and contained four pure white eggs, average dimensions 13.2 x 9.6 mm. The sitting female came to the entrance several times to view the intruder before closing it. Later, the nest was collected with the female still inside (Benson 1946). Also in Ethiopia, nests have been found at *c.* 1.5, 4.5 and 6 m above ground in *Acacia* trees, one apparently constructed from dead white *Acacia* flowers, a spectacular structure (J.S. Ash *in litt.*). In Kenya, a nest at Marsabit contained two newly hatched fledglings in May.

**DESCRIPTION** Adult: In fresh plumage, upperparts from forehead to uppertail-coverts mid drab-grey or olive-grey, small feathers of forehead centred darker and browner. Tail dark grey-brown, feathers narrowly fringed light grey-drab. Wings dark grey-brown, lesser and median coverts broadly fringed mid drab-grey, greater coverts, tertials and flight feathers fringed and tipped light grey-drab, secondaries and inner primaries narrowly so (fringes absent on P1–2 and distally of emarginations on P3–P7). Lores dark brown; supercilium, cheeks and ear-coverts dull buff, feathers tipped slightly darker; may show slightly paler supercilium from eye to bill. Underparts, axillaries and underwing-coverts whitish, washed pale buff on belly, vent and undertail-coverts. In worn plumage, pale fringes on wings and tail abraded. **Bare Parts**: Iris brown; bill blackish, base and cutting edges pale bluish or yellow-horn; legs and feet slate-blue, soles pale grey. **Juvenile**: As adult, but upperparts and fringes to flight feathers may average slightly warmer and browner. **1st Adult**: As adult, but apparently retains juvenile primaries, which contrast with the new secondaries and greater coverts. **Measurements**: Wing of male 46.5–51, of female 46.5–52; tail of male 25–28, of female 26–28; bill 8.7–11.2; tarsus 12–16. Weight: no information.

**MOULT** Adult post-breeding complete (January–April, August and possibly October in Kenya; June–August in Ethiopia). Post-juvenile presumably incomplete (thus including greater coverts, tertials, most or all secondaries, and tail, as in African and Cape Penduline Tits).

**GEOGRAPHICAL VARIATION** Slight or absent. Two races have been described, nominate *musculus* over much of the north of the range and *A. m. guasso*, with greyer upperparts, in northern, central and eastern Kenya as far north as Marsabit, and southern Somalia and NE Tanzania. The difference, however, must be slight and *guasso* is not usually recognised.

**RELATIONSHIPS** A member of the *caroli* superspecies.

**REFERENCES** J.S. Ash (*in litt.*), Ash & Miskell (1983), Austin (1978b), Benson (1946), Lewis & Pomeroy (1989), Mackworth-Praed & Grant (1960).

Other name: Yellow-fronted Penduline Tit

The largest of the African penduline tits, this species is apparently rare over much of its range. Although the bird itself was seldom seen, its durable felted nests were once sold as curios to European explorers and naturalists.

**IDENTIFICATION** Length 90 mm (3.5 in). A typical penduline tit, with a relatively heavy, conical bill (which appears slightly downcurved). Forehead dull golden-yellow, with the remainder of the upperparts olive-green. Lores dusky, and may appear to have a short whitish supercilium. Sides of head dusky olive, finely streaked yellow-olive, cheeks and chin slightly paler and whiter. Throat and upper breast dull olive-yellow, faintly barred or mottled; remainder of underparts dull yellow, washed olive, slightly mottled, with the belly yellowest. Quite distinct *if seen well*, but the yellowish forehead is very difficult to see and it usually appears to be a tiny, short-tailed, dull and featureless bird, which on a poor view may be dismissed as a sunbird. None of the similarly sized non-metallic sunbirds, however, has such bright yellow underparts, and its short stubby bill is a useful feature. The range may abut that of the olive-and-yellow/white forms of African Penduline Tit, but the underparts of Forest Penduline Tit are olive-yellow rather than creamy-white.

**SEX/AGE** Sexes apparently similar. Juvenile as adult, but with only a narrow band of dull buff on the forehead, the throat slightly paler and whiter, with reduced mottling, the breast lightly tinged buff (not so dark or olive as the adult), and the belly slightly paler and purer yellow. No information on the 1st adult.

**VOICE** Rather silent (?). Vocalisations include an emphatic *phsit*, high-pitched and almost cricket-like (hence easily overlooked), and a clearer *tsi*, accelerating into a shrill, trilling *tsi-si-si-si-si-si....*

**DISTRIBUTION AND MOVEMENTS** Probably confined to evergreen rainforest, and, given its scarcity and elusiveness, likely to be more widespread than records suggest (indeed, some records in the literature relate to old nests, rather than birds seen). In the Upper Guinea forest block, recorded from Mount Nimba in **Liberia** (and presumably also adjacent areas of the mountain in **Guinea** and the Ivory Coast). Also known from Tai NP, Fresco and Yapo forest in the **Ivory Coast** and, in **Ghana**, from Goaso and Kakum Forest Reserve. In the Lower Guinea forest block found in **Nigeria**, although noted only at Umuagwu, Itu and possibly also near Lagos. In **Cameroon** found throughout the forest zone, and widespread in northern **Gabon**, where noted from the Makokou region, Belinga, and the Mondah river. In SW **Congo** noted at Goumina and Bena in the Kouilou basin. In **Zaïre** known from Equateur (Lake Tumba, Mbandaka, Ingende, Gemena, Lisala and Bumba) and Haut-Zaïre (Buta, Banalia and Paulis in Uele and Mambasa in Ituri), and also SE Kivu province (see Geographical Variation); there is a surprising lack of records from the south-ern edge of the Congo forest block. Unconfirmed reports only from **Equatorial Guinea** (Mbini).

**HABITAT** Primary lowland evergreen forest, perhaps especially forest edge, clearings, treefall gaps and also well-grown secondary forest and overgrown plantations; may favour flowering silk cotton trees.

**POPULATION** Generally considered uncommon or rare, although probably more widespread than records suggest, its small size, dull coloration and inconspicuous habits (usually keeping high in the canopy) making it easy to miss.

**HABITS** Very active and found in pairs or parties of 3–5, which may forage over a wide area. Sometimes joins mixed-species foraging flocks, especially with sunbirds, and a flock of 30 birds was disturbed when feeding on debris from old red-ant nests (Grimes 1987). May use the nest as a roost outside the breeding season, and allopreening has been noted (L. Fishpool *in litt.*). Forages in the canopy and the lower storey of forest trees, and may favour clumps of parasitic mistletoe. Easily overlooked. Food insects, also fruit, and has been noted systematically excavating the nests of social spiders.

**BREEDING BIOLOGY** Poorly known. Season: NW Zaïre, July (nest and young); NE Zaïre, October (nest-building); SE Zaïre, September; and apparently fresh nests have been found in December in Cameroon and in October in Gabon, whilst an adult in breeding condition was collected in November in Nigeria. The nest itself is typical of the genus, a pouch of densely felted vegetable down, usually brown and resembling a large cocoon, although cotton fibres may be used when available. The entrance tube opens into the top (rather than the side), the lips of the opening remaining closed in a horizontal slit until the bird opens them with one foot as it clings to the side of the nest below the entrance. Nests have been noted at 5–10 m above ground. They may be extremely durable, and old nests are often the only evidence of the species' presence. Eggs apparently undescribed. May be a cooperative breeder, as three adult males have been captured at the same nest in the space of a few hours, and 3–4 adults have been observed attending a nest; also a party of three noted descending to the edge of the forest, chasing each other over a piece of downy nest material (Brosset & Erard 1986; Dowsett & Dowsett-Lemaire 1991).

**DESCRIPTION** *A. f. flavifrons* **Adult**: *In fresh plumage*, extreme base of bill dusky, forehead dull golden-yellow (sometimes with small faint blackish feather tips), remainder of upperparts olive-green, feather bases darker and duller. Tail blackish-grey, outer webs fringed olive-green. Wings blackish-grey, all feathers fringed olive-green apart from alula, P1–P2, and P3–P6 distally of emarginations; fringes slightly paler and yellower on primaries and secondaries. Lores, ear-coverts and sides of neck dusky olive, finely streaked yellow-olive. Cheeks and chin slightly paler and whiter; throat and upper breast dull olive-yellow, faintly barred or mottled (feather tips slightly yellower, bases greyer). Remainder of underparts dull yellow, washed olive, slightly mottled, the belly yellowest (feather tips yellower and bases more olive, extreme bases grey). Axillaries and underwing-coverts off-white, washed pale yellow. In worn plumage, upperparts slightly darker and duller, fringes on wings abraded, especially on greater coverts, underparts dingier. **Bare Parts**: Iris brown to blackish; bill black, cutting edges and base of lower mandible light grey or bluish-white; legs and feet slate-grey to blue-grey. **Juvenile**: As adult, but forehead band dull buff and narrower, and remainder of upperparts, especially crown, average slightly duller and greyer. Throat slightly paler and whiter, less barred/mottled, breast lightly tinged buff, and belly slightly paler and purer yellow. **1st Adult**: No information; presumably as adult. **Measurements**: Wing of male 54–59, of female 54.5–58; tail of male 26–30, of female 26.5–28; bill 10.6–12.6; tarsus 14–15. Weight: no information.

**MOULT** Adult post-breeding complete (December, Cameroon). Post-juvenile partial, may include tertials and alula (July, Nigeria).

**GEOGRAPHICAL VARIATION** Poorly understood, with *waldroni* known from just a single specimen. Three races recognised.

*A. f. waldroni* Upper Guinea forest in Ghana (and presumably this race also in the Ivory Coast and Liberia). As nominate *flavifrons*, but upperparts and wing-coverts slightly brighter, more yellowish-green, and underparts paler and yellower, especially breast, lacking olive tones or mottling. Male: wing 55, tail 28.

*A. f. flavifrons* Lower Guinea forest, in Nigeria, Cameroon, Gabon and northern Zaïre. See Description.

*A. f. ruthae* SE Zaïre, where known from the single type specimen collected in SE Kivu province (Nyamiringe, 1º 39′ S, 28º 06′ E, near Mutiko, at 640 m), and from sightings at 850 m at Bungakiri (2º 10′ S, 28º 34′ E; I. S. Robertson pers. comm.). As nominate *flavifrons*, but forehead buffy-rufous with prominent black spots at tips of feathers, cheeks cinnamon, throat cinnamon-buff (paler in centre), and remainder of underparts dirty white, lightly washed pale yellowish-buff, more intensely so on the lower belly and undertail-coverts, with diffuse brownish patches at the sides of the breast. Wing 55; tail 27; bill 10.5; tarsus 14.5 (female, type; Chapin 1958).

**RELATIONSHIPS** Treated as a member of the *caroli* superspecies by Hall & Moreau (1970).

**REFERENCES** Bannerman (1948), Chapin (1954), Schouteden (1956).

# 41 AFRICAN PENDULINE TIT *Anthoscopus caroli*      Plate 13

Other name: Grey Penduline Tit

The most widespread of the Afrotropical penduline tits, ranging from Kenya to South Africa. It shows marked geographical variation, with as many as 11 subspecies recognised, reflecting a diversity of colour, pattern and ecology.

**IDENTIFICATION** Length 90 mm (3.5 in). Very small, short-tailed and rather warbler-like. Bill triangular and sharply pointed. Among the plainest of the African penduline tits, and likely to be dismissed as a warbler (especially an *Eremomela* warbler), but note the distinctive bill shape. In southern and much of eastern Africa (north to southern Angola, Zambia, NE Tanzania and eastern Kenya), the upperparts are grey, variably tinged green, the forehead and ear-coverts pale yellow or buff, the throat and breast whitish and the belly variably buff. In northern Namibia, eastern Botswana, southern Angola, SW Zimbabwe and NE South Africa, this species overlaps with Cape Penduline Tit, but in these areas is generally much plainer and greyer than Cape Penduline, with a uniform pale buff forehead and 'face' and unmarked lores and throat (whereas Cape Penduline has blackish speckles on the forehead and variably also on the throat, and blackish lores); in addition, the throat and breast are off-white, becoming buff on the belly and vent (overall pale yellow in Cape Penduline). Note that in eastern Zimbabwe some populations of African Penduline Tit have dark slate-grey upperparts and whitish underparts, with only the lower belly and flanks pinkish-buff. In parts of southern Kenya and northernmost Tanzania, African Penduline Tit may overlap with Mouse-coloured Penduline Tit, and both species are rather plain and grey. African Penduline has a pale buff forehead (rather than grey, uniform with the rest of the upperparts), an olive tinge to the upperparts (especially to the wings and tail), and its belly and vent are distinctly yellowish-buff, rather than being whitish with just a hint of pale buff. There is also an atypical population of African Penduline Tit, the *sylviella* group, in southern Kenya and central Tanzania (sometimes treated as a distinct species) which has the upperparts plain grey and the underparts uniform pale cinnamon-buff, the latter feature immediately distinguishing it from Mouse-coloured

Penduline Tit, as does its dull pale buff forehead. In the more humid areas of central Africa, in Angola, Zaïre, NE Zambia, western Tanzania and Uganda, the upperparts of African Penduline Tit are distinctly greenish, the forehead yellower, ear-coverts whiter, and underparts paler and more uniformly off-white (variably but rather faintly washed yellow or buff); the green and yellow tones immediately distinguish it from Mouse-coloured Penduline Tit. Yellow Penduline Tit (whose range approaches that of African in NE Zaïre) has bright yellow underparts and a conspicuous black-spotted yellow forehead. Forest Penduline Tit (a rainforest species) also approaches the range of African in parts of Zaïre, but has dull olive-yellow underparts.

**SEX/AGE** Sexes similar. The juvenile plumage is identical to the adult, although the underparts may average slightly paler and more washed-out (and noted as having yellowish underparts in Zambia: Benson *et al.* 1971).

**VOICE** A very harsh, deep, rasping mechanical *chizizee, chizizee, chizizee, chizizee* or *chizee, chizee, chizee* (like gravel being swirled around in a sieve), also a slightly sweeter and more musical *chachazi, chachazi, chachazi...* or a slow *chew cheweez, chew cheweez*, and a sweet, more tit-like and plaintive *tswee, tswee, tswee*. A soft *chissick* or *tseeeep* is also noted (Sinclair 1987). Song a squeaky disyllabic whistled motif, the first syllable highest, repeated rapidly 5–6 times, *tshwee, tshwhee...*; this is also the location call given by 'lost' individuals separated from the flock (Vincent 1933, 1935), and also uses a high-pitched, sibilant trill, *see-see-see...*, gradually dying away (Ulfstrand 1960).

**DISTRIBUTION AND MOVEMENTS** In central Africa found in SW and southern **Zaïre**, north in the west to the Bolobo region, also NE Zaïre in north Kivu (see Geographical Variation), southern and central **Uganda**, north to Lango (about Lira) and Mount Elgon, eastern **Rwanda** around the Kagera and Akanyaru rivers, and eastern **Burundi** (including the Ruvuba and Kumoso basins). In SW and southern **Kenya** found locally north to Kongelai and Kakamega in the west, and east of the Rift Valley, from Amboseli and Simba north to Kitui and Thika (see also Population). In **Tanzania** found east to Naberera, Korogwe (and perhaps the Pangani river, although may have disappeared from the coastal lowlands), Kidugallo, Liwale and Nachingwea, south to the Nandembo-Kilimarondo area and Songea, and west to Usambiro (south of Lake Victoria), Longido, Dodoma and Mbeya, also the Ufipa (Fip) plateau in the southwest, Kigoma in the central-west, and in the extreme northwest in Ziwa Magharibi, south to Nyarumbugu and Muhange (*c.* 3° S). In southern Africa, found in central and eastern **Angola**, west to Quilengues in the south, and north (in the west) to at least southern Cuanza Sul and western Malanje (and presumably to the Zaïre border). Occurs throughout **Zambia**, except for the Luangwa and much of the Middle Zambezi valleys, and throughout **Malawi** and most of **Mozambique** (although absent from some lowland

areas?). In northern **Namibia** breeds in Ovamboland, Kavango and the Caprivi Strip, with isolated records south to Windhoek, and also found in eastern **Botswana** and in the north in the Okavango delta region. Occurs throughout most of **Zimbabwe**, although absent from the eastern highlands and perhaps only a dry-season visitor to the Middle Zambezi valley. Breeds in NE **South Africa** in northern Natal (extending south and west to Estcourt and Ladysmith), Swaziland and the central and eastern Transvaal (south and west to about Rustenburg). Largely resident, but may be a seasonal visitor to the middle Zambezi valley in Zimbabwe, and an uncommon and occasional non-breeding visitor, March–May and October–November, at semi-arid Baringo in Kenya (where Mouse-coloured Penduline Tit is a common breeding resident; Lewis & Pomeroy 1989).

**HABITAT** A variety of woodland, including *Brachystegia* (miombo) and other dry evergreen types, such as *Mutemwa* woodland in Zambia, also broadleaved and mixed-deciduous woodland, typically in medium-rainfall areas (e.g. most Kenyan records are in areas with more than 500 mm of rain per annum, although the species is scarce in the humid areas of the highlands and the west). Additionally, found in drier *Acacia* woodland, but may be excluded from this habitat where the range abuts/overlaps that of Cape or Mouse-coloured Penduline Tits. Also wooded grassland and savanna, riverine forest and riparian *Acacia*, forest edge and occasionally forest interiors. Generally occurs at middle altitudes, 1000–2200 m in East Africa and 750–1525 m in Malawi (although locally down to 75 m in Malawi, 180 m in Zimbabwe and to coastal areas of southern Mozambique).

**POPULATION** Fairly common in southern Africa, including Malawi and southern Mozambique, although uncommon in Botswana and scarce in the Transvaal, and also uncommon and local in East Africa. As with all the African penduline tits, however, easily overlooked. The range in SE Kenya has apparently contracted in recent years and the species is now absent from the coastal lowlands. Noted by Britton (1980) and Short *et al.* (1990) as occurring north to the lower Tana river, also at Voi, Samburu and Taru in the southeast, and the race '*taruensis*' was described from coastal southern Kenya and NE Tanzania. There have, however, been no recent records from these areas (see also White-bellied Tit; Lewis & Pomeroy 1989).

**HABITS** Found in pairs or family parties of 3–7 birds, maintaining contact with frequent calling, and may join mixed-species foraging flocks. When disturbed, members of the group fly in a loose procession, follow-my-leader fashion, to the next tree or bush, resembling fluffy little balls in flight. Although found for most of the year in small parties, in southern Africa they pair off at the beginning of the austral summer for nesting. May roost in old weavers' nests, as well as collectively in its own nest. Movements very rapid, foraging in trees and bushes, often in flower clusters and among budding leaves, and also in fruit trees (attracted to insects rather than fruit?). In miombo woodland feeds largely in the canopy, but has been seen foraging in low scrubby growth almost at ground level. Food insects, also fruit.

**BREEDING BIOLOGY** Season: southern Africa, August–April (mainly during the rainy season); Zambia, September–November; Malawi, October–November; Zaïre, March–September (thus mainly in the dry season); East Africa, February, April–June and September–December (mainly in the rains, but some records from dry months). Nest ball- or pear-shaped, constructed from densely felted vegetable fibres, wild cotton, wool, etc. Usually greyish-white and rather conspicuous, that is placed in, or suspended from the end of, a bough of a bush or low tree. In *Acacia* savanna, nests may be 1–3 m above ground in a thick thorn bush, but in miombo woodlands they are usually placed high in the canopy. The well-made entrance tube is sited at the side near the top, and is barely large enough for the bird to pass through. The entrance is generally 'zipped up' by the bird hooking the top and bottom of the tube together with the bill as it leaves (unless it is to be absent for less than five minutes). Under the entrance tube there is often a little platform or 'porch' (which is exposed and appears as a pocket, forming a 'false entrance' when the tube is closed). On its return, the bird grips the nest with one foot and uses the other to 'unzip' the entrance by pulling down the lower lip (and thus covering the 'false' entrance; see figure below). Because the nest frays, it needs constant attention during the breeding season so that it does not come apart; when not feeding the young, the adults spend considerable time on repairs. Both sexes build. Clutch 4–6 (2–8), although larger clutches are possibly the result of more than one female laying in the same nest (up to three different adults have been seen attending nests with eggs or young, so may be a cooperative breeder): eggs white; 14.2 x 9.5 mm (southern Africa). Incubation and fledging periods unknown. Both sexes feed the young.

**DESCRIPTION** *A. c. caroli* **Adult**: *In fresh plumage*, forehead and short supercilium (extending to just above the eye) dull pale buff-white, sometimes showing dark feather centres. Upperparts light grey, faintly washed olive (especially when very fresh), buffer on sides of crown and nape. Uppertail-coverts dull buff or buffish-grey. Tail dark grey-brown, feathers finely fringed off-white. Wings dark grey-brown, lesser and median coverts fringed light buffish-grey (dark centres fully concealed), remainder of wing feathers fringed and tipped pale grey, fringes broadest and lightly washed brown or buff on tertials and secondaries, and variably whiter on tips of greater coverts, forming a diffuse wingbar (pale fringes absent on P1–2 and present only inwards of emarginations on P3–P6). Lores grey-brown, cheeks and ear-coverts dirty pale buff. Sides of neck, throat and breast pale grey-white, faintly washed buff, lower flanks, belly, vent, thighs and undertail-coverts buff or pinkish-buff, richest on rear flanks. Axillaries and underwing-coverts off-white. *In worn plumage*, fringes to coverts and flight feathers abraded and bleached paler. **Bare Parts**: Iris brown to black; bill dark blue-grey with paler cutting edges, especially on lower mandible; legs and feet dark blue-grey to blackish. **Juvenile**: As adult, although may average slightly paler buff on underparts. **1st Adult**: As adult. **Measurements**: Wing of male 53–55, of female 52–56; tail of male 29–32.5, of female 27–31; bill 9.5–11.8; tarsus 11–14. Weight 6–6.9 g.

**MOULT** Adult post-breeding complete (February–June, Tanzania; January–July, Zimbabwe; November–June, Zambia, although light body moult may occur at all times of year; February–March, Kenya; May–July, Uganda; January–March, Mozambique; December, Malawi). Post-juvenile incomplete, includes greater coverts, tertials, secondaries and tail (averages later than adult post-breeding, starting as most adults near completion; July, Zambia).

**GEOGRAPHICAL VARIATION** Rather pronounced, with 11 races divisible into five groups. The *caroli* group occurs in the drier parts of the range in the south and east, and the *roccatii* and *ansorgei* groups westwards and northwards into regions of higher rainfall in Angola, Zambia, Zaïre, Uganda and Tanzania. Within this broad range of variation two atypical populations are found, both of which occur close to typical birds, apparently without intergrading: the *sylviella* group from southern Kenya and central Tanzania, and the *rankinei* group of eastern Zimbabwe.

**THE *CAROLI* GROUP** Predominantly grey-and-white races from southern and eastern Africa, with

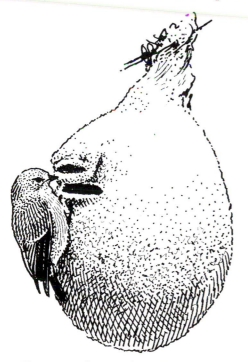

*Figure 41.1  African Penduline Tit at nest (note 'false' entrance).*

225

the forehead and ear-coverts pale buff or yellow and a variable buff wash to the flanks, belly and vent.

**A. c. caroli** Namibia, south and SW Angola (central and southern Huila and Cubango), Botswana and SW Zambia (Barotse, Southern and Central provinces north to Kalabo in the west and Kabwe in the east). See Description.

**A. c. hellmayri** South Africa, southern Mozambique (north to the Limpopo river and, inland, to about the Save river and SW Manica Sofala) and Zimbabwe. Poorly marked. As nominate *caroli*, but throat, breast and upper belly lightly washed buff, and buff of rear flanks and vent averages darker. Wing of male 52.5–57, of female 53.5–57; tail of male 27.5–33, of female 27.5–31.5.

**A. c. robertsi** Mozambique (north of the Inhambane district and, in the lowlands, north of about Coguno and the Limpopo river), Malawi, SE Zambia (west to at least Chipata and probably much of the Eastern province plateau), and interior eastern Tanzania (east of *sylviella*) north to Korogwe and Naberera; formerly coastal Kenya. Poorly marked. As nominate *caroli*, but throat and breast whiter, washed yellowish (not washed buff as in *hellmayri*), flanks and vent average paler and more yellowish-buff; also upperparts slightly more distinctly washed olive, wings and tail feathers fringed olive. Wing of male 50–54, of female 48–53; tail of male 26–30.5, of female 27.5–29. Includes 'taruensis' of coastal southern Kenya north to the Tana river and west to Taru (but see Population), also NE Tanzania south and east to the southern Masai district and Kilosa (and perhaps the Ruaha river), which averages slightly smaller: wing 49–51.

**A. c. winterbottomi** NW Zambia in North-Western and Copperbelt provinces, south to c. 14° S; also adjacent southern Zaïre in southern Shaba (Dilolo and the Lubumbashi region). Poorly marked. More or less intermediate between nominate *caroli* and *rhodesiae*, and near *robertsi* although upperparts average slightly more olive. Intergrades with *rhodesiae* over a short distance in central Zambia (west of the Muchinga escarpment at about Mpika and Serenje). Wing 48–57.

**THE *ROCCATII* GROUP** An isolated olive-and-yellow race from the Albertine Rift region of East Africa.

**A. c. roccatii** Uganda, Rwanda, NE Zaïre (Butembo in north Kivu) and extreme NW Tanzania. Forehead pale yellow, upperparts greyish-olive, throat sullied grey (grey feather bases shining through), remainder of underparts pale creamy-yellow, slightly richer and buffer on vent and undertail-coverts. Overall very dull and nondescript. Wing of male 53–56, of female 51–53.

**THE *ANSORGEI* GROUP** Predominantly green-and-yellow races from the more humid areas of central Africa. This group was formerly treated as specifically distinct.

**A. c. ansorgei** Angola (except extreme south) and SW Zaïre (north to Bolobo in NW Bandundu, to Luebo and Kananga (= Luluabourg) in southern Kasai Occidental and Mwene Ditu in SW Kasai

Oriental). Very distinctive. Forehead yellow, tinged olive, upperparts olive-green. Tail and wings dark grey, wing-coverts and tail fringed olive-green, greater coverts tipped yellow-white, tertials and flight feathers fringed olive-grey. Sides of head and underparts off-white, breast to undertail-coverts faintly washed yellow. Wing 54–60. Intergrades with *rhodesiae* in SW Shaba.

**A. c. rhodesiae** SW Tanzania on Ufipa plateau, NE Zambia (south to Luwingu and Kasama and probably Kawambwa, and east to Mbala), and SE Zaïre in SE Shaba (from the Lubumbashi region north to the Marungu mountains and Tembwe, and including Upemba NP). Forehead pale yellow, upperparts dull olive, washed grey (much duller than *ansorgei*, but slightly more olive than *roccatii*). Greater coverts, tertials, secondaries and tail feathers fringed pale yellow-olive. Underparts off-white, tinged grey on the throat and breast and lightly washed buff on the belly, flanks and vent; juveniles have yellowish underparts. Wing 48–57, of male 52.5–55, of female 53–56. Intergrades with *winterbottomi* in southern Zaïre (northeast of Lubumbashi), and possibly with *robertsi* in extreme NW Malawi.

**A. c. pallescens** Kigoma, Kungwe-Mahali peninsula, central-west Tanzania. Forehead pale yellowish-grey, upperparts greenish-grey (paler green than *rhodesiae*), rump greener, underparts greyish, slightly washed yellow and faintly tinged buff on undertail-coverts. Wing of male 53, 57; tail of male 34, 34.

**THE *SYLVIELLA* GROUP** Sometimes considered a separate species, A. *sylviella*, Rungwe Penduline Tit (e.g. 'Peters', Sibley & Monroe 1990), owing to its distinctive coloration and because it approaches *robertsi* closely in eastern Tanzania without apparently interbreeding. Largely a highland form, and confined to miombo woodland in the south of the range.

**A. c. sylviella** South-central Kenya, east of the rift, from Kajiado north to Murang'a and Simba north to Kitui, with old records from Voi (see Population), and in central Tanzania from Longido south to Dodoma, Iringa and Mbeya. Forehead dirty pale buff, upperparts mid grey (as nominate *caroli*, with olive tones faint or absent), uppertail-coverts tinged buff. Greater coverts and flight feathers fringed pale grey. Ear-coverts, sides of neck and throat dirty white, washed buff, underparts uniform pale cinnamon-buff. (Near *robertsi*, but forehead buff rather than yellow-buff, upperparts purer grey, and underparts uniformly buff (more cinnamon-buff, not so yellow-buff)). Wing 51–58. Includes 'rothschildi' of Simba and Kitui areas, Kenya, with pale ochre-yellow underparts: Wing 51–54.

**A. c. sharpei** SW Kenya, east and south of Lake Victoria, from Kakamega, south Nyanza and Loita to Usambiro in NW Tanzania. Poorly marked. As *sylviella*, but forehead dull cinnamon and underparts darker and more cinnamon.

**THE *RANKINEI* GROUP** This grey-backed race may also merit full specific status. It is very distinct from the surrounding races *hellmayri/robertsi*, which have the upperparts washed olive and which occur in close proximity. Indeed, both olive- and grey-backed birds have been collected at the same locality, further strengthening the case for treatment as a full species.

**A. c. rankinei** Eastern borders of Zimbabwe, where known only from the north, in the middle Zambezi valley (Kapsuku hills on the south bank of river opposite Luangwa), at Mafuto on the lower Mazoe river on the border with Mozambique, and in the east at Humani Ranch, near Birchenough Bridge on the Sabi river (where found alongside *hellmayri*). Upperparts dark slate-grey (greyer than *sylviella* and considerably greyer than Mouse-coloured Penduline Tit), forehead, cheeks and ear-coverts dull whitish, underparts off-white, lower belly and flanks pinkish-buff (near nominate *caroli*, and distinctly different from the yellowish-buff of *robertsi*). Wing of male, 52, of female 49.5, tail of male 27, of female 29. Recorded at 365–410 m in riparian *Acacia*, whilst *hellmayri* is confined to miombo on the surrounding plateau. This may be due to competitive exclusion, as elsewhere the olive-backed races occupy a very similar habitat to that of *rankinei*.

**RELATIONSHIPS** Forms a superspecies with the other African penduline tits.

**REFERENCES** Austin (1978b), Ginn *et al.* (1989), Irwin (1963), Lawson (1961).

# 42 CAPE PENDULINE TIT *Anthoscopus minutus* Plate 13

A bird of arid SW Africa, this tit builds an intricate, often conspicuous, globular nest of felted fibres with a 'false entrance', perhaps an adaptation to mislead predators.

**IDENTIFICATION** Length 90 mm (3.5 in ). A tiny tit with a short, pointed bill that has a virtually straight culmen and keel. Forehead and lores blackish, surmounted by a short whitish supercilium that is marked with some blackish speckles. The upperparts vary from mid grey to grey-brown and are tinged olive, with a yellower or more cinnamon rump. Chin, cheeks and fore ear-coverts whitish, with a diffuse paler crescent below the eye. The underparts vary from yellow to dull yellow-buff, with some diffuse spotting on the throat. The range overlaps with that of African Penduline Tit in northern Namibia, southern Angola, NE Botswana, SW Zimbabwe and the northern Transvaal, and the two species may sometimes be found in the same flock. Cape Penduline Tit is separated by its black lores, black and white forehead (uniform pale buff in African Penduline Tit), and pale yellowish underparts (off-white on the throat and breast and buff on the flanks, belly and vent in African Penduline), with the throat faintly spotted darker on some birds. Like all the African penduline tits, the species superficially has a rather warbler-like appearance, but can be distinguished from eremomelas (the most similar group of warblers) by its tiny size, conical bill, rotund body and very short tail, whilst the blackish speckled forehead is also distinctive.

**SEX/AGE** Sexes similar. Juvenile marginally distinct, with paler and patchier yellow underparts, sullied grey on the throat and breast. Worn adults may appear similarly blotchy, but in the hand juveniles show fresh wing and tail feathers, whilst on worn adults these feathers are bleached and abraded.

**VOICE** A series of high, sweet, slightly plaintive notes, *tswee, tswee, tsweep, tswee...*, also an abrupt *tsik*, coupled with a disyllabic *tissik, tissik*, and a distinctive nasal *zuwi-zuwi-zuwi...* or *tzui-tzui-tzui...* given in a series which rises slightly in pitch. These transcriptions may overlap with the following vocabulary detailed by Skead (1959): Contact call a quiet, single bell-like *tillink* or *tillilink*, begging fledglings giving a similar, but higher-pitched *zittery-zittery....* The 'assembly call', given as a bird moves off to entice others to follow, is a loud, raspy *zizzit*, whilst a louder, high-pitched and slightly plaintive note, *tswee, tswee..., chawee, chawee...* or *tsi-wizza, tsi-wizza...*, repeated 6–8 times, is given in excitement or as an advertisement during the breeding season, and also to assemble the flock when dispersed and in pre-roost gatherings. In courtship flight gives an abrupt *zwayt*, and when displaying at the nest a quiet, rapid, stuttering *ch, ch, ch....*

**DISTRIBUTION AND MOVEMENTS** Confined in **Angola** to the arid coastal strip between Huxe and Benguela town, but widely distributed in **Namibia**, except in the north and the Caprivi Strip, and also found throughout **Botswana**, except in the Okavango delta and the extreme east. In **Zimbabwe** found in a limited area of the western central plateau from the Matopo hills north to Nkayi, and also the Sibanani Pan in the Hwange NP. In **South Africa** found throughout Cape Province, western, central and northern Orange Free State and the west and central Transvaal (east to Messina and Burgersfort and, very locally, the western Highveld). Resident, although probably rather nomadic.

**HABITAT** Generally dry or semi-desert areas, in *Acacia* woodland and savanna, secondary thornbrush, fynbos and karoo scrub, and found in the central Kalahari where there may be only isolated trees and thorn bushes. In the eastern parts of the range restricted to *Acacia* woodlands, and replaced in broadleaved woodlands by African Penduline Tit (the two species do overlap in some areas, e.g. NE Botswana and Zimbabwe, where African Penduline Tits may be found in the typical *Acacia* habitat of Cape Penduline but not vice versa).

**POPULATION** Generally fairly common, although local and nowhere very common in Zimbabwe, uncommon in SW Cape Province and uncommon to rare in the Orange Free State.

**HABITS** Sociable and gregarious; usually found in pairs and, except in the period between nest-building and the fledging of the first brood, in parties of up to eight and occasionally as many as 20 birds. May join mixed-species foraging flocks. Tame and often restless and active, moving in 'follow-my-leader' fashion from one bush to the next with a bouncing flight. Attracts attention with constant calling. Up to six adults may roost together with the eggs or nestlings in the nest, and after the breeding season up to 18 birds may roost together in the nest (see below); also roosts in old weavers' nests. Forages in the canopy of trees, in bushes, or among flowers and shrubs, gleaning from leaves, twigs and bark, and often investigating webs and galls. Food insects and berries.

**BREEDING BIOLOGY** Season: Namibia, January–February; Zimbabwe, October–February; Kalahari, August–March; Cape Province, June–January; Transvaal, October–January; probably largely opportunistic after rain in arid areas. The nest is an oval bag of soft felted plant and animal fibres, including sheep's wool and cotton, bound together with cobwebs; usually off-white, it may be blackish in areas where Karakul sheep are present. Slung at the end of a thin branch or attached at the sides between thin upright twigs, 2–3 m (0.3–5.5 m) above ground, it is often conspicuous, but usually inaccessible. Outside dimensions c. 140 mm high x 75 mm wide, interior chamber c. 90 mm x 55 mm. The entrance tunnel is to the side and facing slightly downwards, c. 25 mm diameter x 20–60 mm long, thin-walled, soft and collapsible. A curved ledge below the tube, c. 30 mm wide, is used as perch by the incoming tit as it opens the entrance with one foot. Otherwise, the entrance tube closes automatically, forming a roof over the ledge and producing a 'false entrance'. Both sexes build, the first egg being laid after c. 3 weeks, but material is added throughout incubation. Clutch 3–6 (2–12, but more than one female may use the same nest and clutches of more than 5 eggs may have been laid by two females): eggs white; 14.1 x 9.8 mm. Both sexes incubate, period 13–15 days. The young are also fed by both sexes and fledge after 22–24 days. Probably a cooperative breeder in some instances, as the young may be fed by helpers. Normally double-brooded, the same nest is usually used for the second brood and, despite the presence of eggs and later young, the fledged juveniles from the first brood roost in the nest with the parents (and, in their turn, juveniles from the second brood may roost together in the nest with the first brood). Probably raises several broods in a year.

**DESCRIPTION** *A. m. damarensis* **Adult:** *In fresh plumage,* lores and forehead dull black, feathers broadly fringed whitish, especially on the upper border, forming a short supercilium. Crown and nape mid grey, remainder of upperparts mid olive-grey, rump and uppertail-coverts olive-yellow. Tail dark grey-brown, feathers narrowly fringed drab-grey. Wings dark grey-brown, lesser and median coverts broadly fringed mid grey (dark centres

fully concealed), greater and primary coverts and alula fringed and tipped pale drab-grey; flight feathers and tertials fringed and tipped paler grey or whitish, tinged buff on tertials and inner secondaries, fringes broadest on the tertials and secondaries (absent on P1–P2 and present only inwards of emarginations on P3–P7). Chin, cheeks and fore ear-coverts off-white, paler immediately below eye, forming diffuse broken eyering (some dark grey feather centres may be revealed), rear ear-coverts and sides of neck mid grey. Throat and sides of breast pale yellow, remainder of underparts yellow. Thighs, axillaries and underwing-coverts pale creamy buff-white. *In worn plumage,* black and white markings on forehead more conspicuous, wings and tail bleached paler and browner, underparts paler and more blotchy, with more whitish admixture. **Bare Parts**: Iris yellowish-brown to blackish-brown; bill black, horn, grey or blue-grey, cutting edges paler; legs and feet black, dark cobalt-blue, dark greenish-grey, blue-grey or grey. **Juvenile**: As adult, but underparts slightly paler and duller yellow, especially on throat and breast (greyish feather bases shining through), with less contrast between the chin and throat/breast. Fringes to tail feathers faintly washed yellow, fringes to greater coverts, tertials and inner secondaries faintly washed yellow-buff. **1st Adult**: As adult. **Measurements**: Wing of male 48–53, of female 44–53.5; tail of male 31–36, of female 28–37; bill 8.8–12; tarsus 13–15. Weight: no information.

**MOULT** Adult post-breeding complete (October–June). Post-juvenile incomplete, includes greater coverts, tertials, secondaries and tail (averages later than post-breeding moult).

**GEOGRAPHICAL VARIATION** Slight, with northern populations being purer grey above and cleaner yellow below. Three races recognised.

*A. m. damarensis* Angola, northern Namibia, Botswana, Zimbabwe, central Orange Free State and Transvaal. See Description.

*A. m. minutus* Cape Province (except southeast), western Orange Free State and Namibia, north to about Windhoek, where intergrades with *damarensis*. As *damarensis*, but upperparts slightly browner (crown and nape washed brown, contrasting less with the greyish drab-olive mantle), with rump and uppertail-coverts dull cinnamon; may show some dark brown feather centres on forecrown. Chin and throat duller, washed grey, dark feather centres more conspicuous (thus diffusely spotted); remainder of underparts dull yellow-buff, flanks slightly buffer, undertail-coverts and underwing-coverts washed buff. Wing of male 47–51, of female 48–50.

*A. m. gigi* SE Cape Province in the Little Karoo (Oudtshoorn) and southern Great Karoo (Graaff-Reinet), east to Queenstown. The brownest race. As nominate *minutus*, but upperparts average browner and less grey, with the underparts buffer and less yellow.

**RELATIONSHIPS** A member of the *caroli* superspecies, which includes all the African penduline tits (although the slight overlap in range with African Penduline Tit means that, strictly, the 'superspecies' concept does not apply and the collective should be treated as a species group).

**REFERENCES** Austin (1978b), Clancey (1980), Maclean (1993), Skead (1959).

## 43 FIRE-CAPPED TIT *Cephalopyrus flammiceps* Plate 12

This aptly named tit has a scattered distribution from Pakistan to central China, and is nowhere really common. Unlike all other penduline tits, it lays its blue-green eggs in tree cavities.

**IDENTIFICATION** Length 100 mm (4 in). A small, dumpy, short-tailed tit, with bill rather spike-like, elongated, slender and conical with a sharply pointed tip. In non-breeding plumage, upperparts yellowish-olive with a yellower rump. Wings and tail dark olive-brown, the tail feathers finely tipped off-white, and the wing-coverts, flight feathers and especially tertials fringed dull yellowish, the tips of the wing-covers paler, forming two dull pale wingbars. Underparts off-white or pale grey, washed yellowish or yellowish-olive on the breast and belly. In breeding plumage, assumed February–July, the male has a reddish-orange forecrown, golden-yellow lores and short yellow supercilium, and a reddish chin and throat, grading to golden-yellow on the breast and pale yellow on the belly. Breeding females have a dull golden-olive forecrown, dull yellow throat and breast, and yellow rump. Breeding male distinctive, otherwise confusion possible with Yellow-browed Tit. In breeding plumage, female Fire-capped is yellower on the throat and breast than Yellow-browed, with a yellow forecrown. Non-breeding adults of both sexes are rather more similar, but show bold yellowish fringes to the median and greater coverts and tertials, often forming two wingbars, cleaner and paler underparts than Yellow-browed, with a more distinct yellow tinge, yellow-washed undertail-coverts extending well down the tail, and often a paler and yellower, although ill-defined, rump patch. Juveniles are even more similar to Yellow-browed Tits, lacking the yellowish tinge to the underparts and rump of the adults, but note the contrasting pale fringes to the coverts and tertials and the lack of a crest. Distinguished from Green Shrike-babbler by its daintier build and much more slender bill; from flowerpeckers by its wingbars, from *Phylloscopus* warblers by its lack of pale supercilia and stockier, more conical bill, and from Goldcrest by the yellow-washed underparts, bill shape and, on males, more extensive red on cap, face and throat.

**SEX/AGE** Sexes variably distinct. In breeding plumage, the male has a reddish forecrown, chin and throat, while the female has the forecrown dull yellowish and the throat and breast dull olive-yellow, yellower than the belly and vent (in non-breeding plumage, the throat is pale grey-white in both sexes, whiter than the breast). Out of breeding plumage, the sexes are much more similar, although the female averages slightly greyer on the upperparts and duller on the underparts, tinged buffish, with a duller and more olive-yellow wash to the breast (which is pale lemon-yellow in the

male). Juveniles as non-breeding adults, but underparts lack any trace of yellow. No information on 1st adult. Some birds dated late April show a golden-yellow forecrown with odd dull orange feathers and a golden-yellow chin; these may be 1st-adult males in breeding plumage or, perhaps more likely, old females.

**VOICE** Calls include a high-pitched, but full and abrupt *tsit*, given at irregular intervals (c. 0.5 seconds) for prolonged periods, e.g. *tsit, tsit, tsit-tsit, tsit....* Perhaps different is a loud *si-si-si* (Löhrl 1967). Roberts (1992) also notes the contact call as a soft and weak, disyllabic and rather tit-like, *whitoo-whitoo*, although much softer, and single rather chirruping notes, recalling a sparrow but much softer. The song is composed of rather thin, high-pitched motifs, repeated 1–7 times (often twice) in each song phrase. Motifs are given at a rate of 3–6 per second, the faster phrases thus almost trills, and with various emphasis, sometimes slurred, sometimes a little harsh, and sometimes very pure and ringing (often they are reminiscent in tone of a European Penduline Tit). Most are distinctly disyllabic, on the 'tea-cher' theme, e.g. *pit-si, pis-su, psoo't* or *tsi't*, but some are nearly monosyllabic, e.g. *tink* or *psii*. After the repetition of several phrases the male switches to a new motif, and tapes of a single bird reveal a repertoire of at least nine song types. Thus typical song phrases are a deliberate *pit'su-pit'su...*, hurried *pis-su-psi'su-pis'su-pis'su...*, very thin *tink-tink-tink-tink*, ringing *psing-psing-psing...*, and sweet but plaintive *tsui, tsui-tsui...* (rather Coal Tit-like). Song is repeated for long periods from conspicuous perches in the tops of tall trees, and occasionally given in a brief, fluttery song flight.

**DISTRIBUTION AND MOVEMENTS** In the western Himalayas, found in summer in northern **Pakistan** in the Murree hills, the Neelum valley (= Kishen Ganga) in Azad Kashmir, the Kagan valley in Hazara, and in Gilgit, Skardu, and Baltistan. In **NW India** breeds in Ladakh from Kargil to at least Rangdum in the Suru valley, Kashmir (including the Sind and Lidar valleys and Pir Panjal range), and Himachal Pradesh (including Simla and the Great Himalayan NP, and noted at Mani and Dankhar in the Spiti valley in late September, these latter perhaps migrants or stragglers?); also in northern Uttar Pradesh in Garhwal and Kumaun (including Dehra Dun, Nanda Devi NP and occasionally Naini Tal). Recorded from adjacent SW **Tibet** on the Shiquan (Indus) river and at Burang. Occurs throughout Nepal, but status uncertain: breeding proved at Khaptad NP, near Silgarhi-

Doti, in the far west, otherwise an uncommon and erratic visitor, although observations are increasing, notably in the upper Kali Gandaki valley in March–April and occasionally also the Kathmandu valley in January–March; an influx in February–May 1982 involved parties of up to 12 birds. Some, at least, of the western population are migratory, wintering mid October–March (once May) in the better-wooded parts of the plains of northern and central **India**, from western Rajasthan (Bharatpur, where recorded in January) and southern Uttar Pradesh (Etawah and Kanpur) south through central Madhya Pradesh (Sehore and Raipur) to NW Maharashtra (Nagpur); a December record from Ambala in northern Haryana presumably involved migrants. Passage through the foothills takes place largely mid March–mid April, and birds arrive on the breeding grounds from April. The autumn migration is, however, undocumented. There are few records from the **eastern Himalayas**. Noted as probably breeding in **Darjeeling** district, although rare (Matthews & Edwards 1944), in **Sikkim** recorded November–May at Rongphu in the Tista valley and at Dentam in the southwest, and in **Bhutan** recorded from Gomchu and the lower Nyam Jang Chu at Changpu (the Manas drainage on the border with Arunachal Pradesh; the latter locality is presumably the record listed by Cheng 1987 for Zhangpu in southern Tibet); in central Bhutan a flock of c. 100 noted in March 1994 at Pele La (Robson 1994). In western **Arunachal Pradesh** recorded at Bomdila in August (Singh 1994). The east Himalayan populations undergo seasonal altitudinal movements, but apparently there is little or no dispersal away from foothills, and recorded in winter from the Jalpaiguri duars (**West Bengal**), Goalpara in **Assam** and also the 'Buxa duars' in SW Bhutan. Breeds in western **China**, in the Qin Ling mountains of southern **Shaanxi**, the Liupan mountains of southernmost **Ningxia** and adjacent parts of SE **Gansu**. Also found in central-southern **Sichuan**, from Guan Xian south through Emei Shan to Mabian (Dafengding Panda Reserve), Xichang and Meigu, in extreme SE **Tibet** on the southern slope of the Mekong-Yangtze watershed (Ningjing Shan), and in **Yunnan** recorded in the southwest at Tengchong, the northwest at Lijiang, the northeast at Ludian and in the southeast (at about Gejiu?), with parties of 10 and 12 observed at Kunming in central Yunnan in June. Also recorded around Weining in western **Guizhou**. Noted at Nanchong in the Red Basin of eastern Sichuan, but this presumably refers to migrant or wintering birds, as may the records from SW and SE Yunnan. Rare winter visitor to NW **Thailand**, localities including Doi Pha Hom Pok and Doi Pui (with 10 recorded near the summit of Doi Pui in January 1992). Vagrant or rare winter visitor to **Myanmar** (**Burma**), where a flock of c. 10 was seen in March 1972 in the Southern Shan States at Taung-gyi (King et al. 1973), and to NW **Laos**, where a small flock recorded at Lo-tiao near Luang Prabang, on the upper Mekong, in January 1939 (Delacour & Greenway 1940). (Listed in error as a vagrant to **Afghanistan** by Ali & Ripley 1983.)

**HABITAT** Forest, woodland and areas of scattered trees, favouring moist-temperate mixed or deciduous forest of oak, Hazel, elm and walnut (just below the coniferous zone), also broadleaved evergreen forest (winter only?) and wanders to higher altitudes, when found in Bird Cherry and willow scrub with scattered trees and, in Kashmir and Ladakh (including the Suru valley), breeds in high-altitude scrub. Also orchards and stands of poplars, and has a particular association with maple (which may account for its capricious distribution), whilst in China also recorded in spruce and fir forests and rhododendrons (Meyer de Schauensee 1984), and in NW Thailand favours hill evergreen forest. In the west, breeds in Pakistan at 1800–2600 m, in NW India recorded at 1800–3500 m (in Ladakh, breeding confirmed at 3050 m and noted up to c. 4000 m in September), and in SW Tibet found at 3800–4300 m in August. In Nepal recorded at 2135–3000 m. The western populations winter in the plains of central India. In the eastern Himalayas, recorded in southern Sikkim November–May at 305–1370 m, whilst in Bhutan recorded at 1980–3355 m in March. Matthews & Edwards (1944) considered that it probably breeds in Darjeeling at c. 1220 m, moving lower in winter, when recorded in the nearby Jalpaiguri and Buxa duars at up to 600 m. In western China recorded March–October at 800–3660 m, mostly 1525–2300 m; no breeding data, and records at lower altitudes probably represent migrants (e.g. a flock of 10 at Mabian, Sichuan, at 1800–2000 m in late April). In Thailand, wintering birds noted from 1400 m to at least 2135 m, with one record from riverine scrub on the plains, and winter vagrants found at 1800 m in Burma.

**POPULATION** Generally rather scarce or uncommon, and even rare in Gilgit and Baltistan, but locally common in Himachal Pradesh (e.g. Kulu). Away from the breeding areas apparently rather rare, with just a handful of records in South-East Asia, and even in Thailand, from where the bulk of winter records emanate, considered rare. Some evidence of local population changes, with a decrease noted in the Murree hills in Pakistan but an increase in the number of records from Nepal.

**HABITS** Not shy, but active and restless, flicking its wings in a manner recalling a leaf-warbler, and its jizz may also recall Yellow-browed Tit. In winter and on migration generally found in small parties, with flocks of up to 100 recorded on passage. May join mixed-species foraging flocks, even in summer, but often seen in single-species flocks, and may regularly alternate feeding grounds, flying in small flocks high across bare hillsides. Flight strong, recalling finches, as may flocks when loafing in bare trees. Forages in the crowns of tall trees, but also occasionally in bushes near ground level. Generally rather agile, and will both hang upside-down and climb along the underside of branches, but movements also often slow and deliberate when feeding, moving along branches with a sliding, parrot-like gait. Rolled leaves are pried open with the bill, which is inserted and opened in a starling-like manner, and with typical dexterity it pulls leaves in with the bill and then holds these firmly with the foot. Food largely insects, also leaf and flower buds and possibly pollen and sap. Prey items are held, tit-like, under its feet whilst being dealt with by the bill, and larger insects are opened and the contents extracted, the empty husk then being discarded (as in *Parus*, but apparently never breaks the whole object into bits as the true tits do).

**BREEDING BIOLOGY** Season early April–mid June, although noted feeding juvenile on 31 August in Ladakh (Holmes 1986). The nest is placed in a hole in a tree, in the trunk or larger branches, and favours cavities with a protruding rim. Uses natural holes or the abandoned excavations of woodpeckers and barbets, and will occasionally enlarge and clean out a hole in a rotten branch. The small entrance to the nest is hard to spot, usually being 6–12 m (1–15 m) above the ground. The nest is a cup of dry grass and rootlets, sometimes also a few feathers, lined with finer grass and a variable quantity of feathers, built by the female, but with the male in close attendance, often singing. Clutch 4 (3–5): eggs dull blue-green; 14.6 x 11 mm. Incubation period unknown. Female sits very tight, and if disturbed 'puffs' or hisses at intruders (cf. tits *Parus*). Whether male shares incubation unknown. Young fed by both sexes; nest sanitation apparently by female only.

**DESCRIPTION** *C. f. flammiceps* **Adult Male**: *In fresh plumage* (September to about January), crown feathers dark olive-brown, fringed yellowish olive-green, upperparts to scapulars yellowish olive-green, back yellowish-olive, rump olive-yellow to golden olive-yellow (variably contrasting). Uppertail-coverts yellowish-olive, longer feathers dark drab-grey and fringed yellowish-olive (uppertail-coverts rather long, cloaking about three-quarters of the tail). Tail dark olive-brown, all feathers tipped off-white, T1–T5 narrowly fringed yellowish-olive. Wings dark olive-brown, coverts fringed yellowish olive-green, median coverts tipped yellower, greater coverts tipped slightly paler and whiter; primary coverts narrowly fringed dull yellowish-olive; tertials broadly fringed pale olive-yellow; secondaries and P3–P10 narrowly fringed yellowish-olive, fringes finer and whiter distally of emargination on P3–P5, secondaries tipped paler and whiter, P10–P4 neatly tipped off-white. Lores and throat off-white, breast, belly and flanks lemon-yellow, thighs, vent, and undertail-coverts pale grey. Marginal wing-coverts pale yellow. Axillaries pale yellow; underwing-coverts white, tipped yellow, mid grey feather bases revealed on under primary coverts. *In breeding plumage* (February–July), forehead and forecrown chrome-orange/orange-scarlet, feather bases yellow (width of red cap 7–12 mm: Vaurie 1950a); feathers slightly stiff and 'tufty'. White tips to tail feathers abraded, fringes to tertials narrower and abraded, pale grey to pale yellow. Lores and supercilium to just behind eye golden-yellow, variably washed scarlet, cheeks, ear-coverts and sides of neck yellowish-olive. Chin and upper throat chrome-orange, grading into golden-yellow on the breast;

sides of breast and upper flanks yellow-olive, rear flanks and belly pale yellow. *In worn breeding plumage* (c. May–July), tips of greater coverts abraded (thus wingbars faint or lacking), wings and tail abraded, especially tertial and secondary fringes and primary tips. **Bare Parts**: Iris brown to dark brown; bill dark blue-grey, culmen darker; legs and feet dark blue-grey. **Adult Female**: In fresh plumage as male, but upperparts from crown to mantle (including supercilium, cheeks, ear-coverts and sides of neck) greyish olive-green, forehead slightly greener; may show odd dull orange-brown feathers in forehead. Back and rump yellowish-olive. Wing-coverts dark olive-brown, lesser coverts fringed greyish olive-green, median and greater coverts fringed yellowish-olive or olive-yellow, greater coverts tipped slightly paler (wingbar not so distinct as on male). Lores pale grey, chin and throat grey-white, grading to pale drab-grey on remainder of underparts; breast washed yellowish-olive or olive-yellow, upper flanks and belly washed pale yellow. Axillaries pale grey; underwing coverts pale grey, feather bases mid to dark grey and tips dull yellow. *In breeding plumage*, forecrown dull golden-olive, rump brighter and paler yellow, and chin, throat and breast dull olive-yellow, contrasting with the paler and whiter belly and vent. **Juvenile**: As autumn female, but rump duller and more olive, feather fringes tinged yellow-olive on rump and uppertail-coverts, and underparts pale grey with no trace of yellow. **1st Adult**: Little information. 1st-adult male in breeding plumage as adult, but darker and with scarlet confined to the forehead (Baker 1922); see also Sex/Age. 1st-adult female in breeding plumage may be as adult female non-breeding. **Measurements**: Wing of male 58–64, of female 58.5–64; tail of male 30–34, of female 29–35; bill 9–11; tarsus 13–16. Weight 7 g.

**MOULT** Adult post-breeding complete (June–September). Adult pre-breeding partial, includes crown, sides of head, throat and breast (November–early March; one in body moult on 15 May may be 1st adult?). Post-juvenile partial, includes at least some coverts (August to at least November; note that Vaurie 1950a described the post-juvenile moult as complete, but the specimens to which he referred are almost certainly adult males in post-breeding moult).

**GEOGRAPHICAL VARIATION** Slight, apparently clinal, with eastern birds being generally smaller and darker.

*C. f. flammiceps* Western Himalayas east to Garhwal (probably also to Nepal). See Description.

*C. f. olivaceus* Eastern Himalayas from at least eastern Nepal to Bhutan (the location of the boundary between the races in Nepal is unknown); western China. As nominate *flammiceps*, but upperparts slightly darker and greener,. Male in breeding plumage (January–March) duller, reddish band on forehead much reduced (c. 4 mm deep), reddish on underparts reduced, restricted to chin and centre of throat, remainder of throat golden-yellow, breast greener, yellowish-olive, grading to dirty pale yellow on belly. Underparts of female slightly duller and duskier than in nominate *flammiceps*, and juvenile duller and greyer, upperparts dark drab olive-grey. Wing of male 57–61, of female 55.5–60.5; tail of male 30–35, of female 35–36. Weight 6–8 g.

**RELATIONSHIPS** Problematic. Usually placed in the Remizidae, but diverges from the penduline tits in its breeding biology (nesting in tree cavities rather than building a felted purse-shaped nest)

and egg colour (soft blue-green, rather than white as in *Remiz*, *Anthoscopus* and Tit-Hylia, although the eggs of Verdin are similarly blue-green). Löhrl (1967) considered that its feeding techniques placed it close to the Remizidae, and this is followed here, with reservations. DNA data may help to resolve the problem.

**REFERENCES** Ali & Ripley (1983), Baker (1922, 1932–33), Löhrl (1967), Wunderlich (1991c).

## 44 TIT-HYLIA *Pholidornis rushiae*             **Plate 14**
Other name: Tiny Tit-weaver

Probably the smallest bird in Africa (so small that it has been found entangled in a spider's web), the family relationships of this species have long caused confusion.

**IDENTIFICATION** Length 75 mm (3 in). A tiny tit with a slender, pointed, slightly decurved bill and rather short tail. Crown and nape very finely streaked or mottled dark brown and dirty white. Mantle and scapulars brown, feathers neatly fringed pale buffy-grey or olive and oddly large, sometimes giving a scaled appearance. Back and rump dull yellow. Wings brown, finely fringed pale buffy-grey, giving a delicate lace-like effect. Throat and breast boldly streaked dark brown and off-white, grading into dull yellowish on the belly and vent. Unmistakable when seen well: the streaked throat, yellow rump and tiny size are the best field marks, and the bright yellow legs and feet are always very noticeable.

**SEX/AGE** Sexes almost alike. Males have orange, orange-brown or red eyes and females a creamy, grey or brown iris. Juvenile as adult, but with the crown and nape dark brown, only finely streaked paler, the upperparts darker and more uniform, lacking a distinct scaled pattern, the throat and breast dirty light grey, faintly spotted or very finely streaked darker, and the remainder of underparts dull pale yellow, washed grey and much duller than adult; eye grey or brown.

**VOICE** Adults give a brief *ptu* or *ptiu*, also a shrill *psii* (recalling the anxiety call of Tree Pipit), whilst begging juveniles give a shrill, rapid *tsi-tsi-tsi...* (Brosset & Erard 1986). The advertising song is reasonably loud, far-carrying and stereotyped, and consists of a rapid trill (the individual units barely distinguishable), introduced by c. 3 clear whistled notes, *pui-pui-pui-tjitjitjitjitjitj-u*, flatter and falling in pitch on the last note of the trill, and the whole phrase lasting c. 1.5 seconds; it is sometimes preceded by two grating notes, *ruirui*, and then lasts nearly 2 seconds. The birds keep on the move whilst singing (Dowsett & Dowsett-Lemaire 1991, who consider that the relatively loud, far-carrying and stereotyped nature of the song recalls a warbler Sylviidae rather than a Remizidae, but both European Penduline and Fire-capped Tits have clear trilling elements to their songs, and Tit-Hylia recalls the tone of these species, although its voice is a little more emphatic). Song period in SW Congo September–October, with reduced song

November–December.

**DISTRIBUTION AND MOVEMENTS** Distribution imperfectly known owing to its elusive habits. Confined to evergreen forest, and in the Upper Guinea forest block extends from southern **Sierra Leone** (including the Gola forest region), SW **Guinea** on the Mount Nimba massif and SE Guinea around Macenta, through **Liberia** (including Mount Nimba), southern **Ivory Coast** and throughout the forest zone of southern **Ghana** (although only occasional on the Cape Coast). In the Lower Guinea forest zone, found in southern **Nigeria** from Lagos to Calabar and throughout the forest zone in southern **Cameroon**, but in **Gabon** noted only at M'Passa, near Makokou (January 1975 and March 1985) and from the 'Moonda River' (= Mondah river, the type locality of the species). Noted in May 1978 in the extreme south of **Central African Republic** at Botambi (near Bimbo; Germain & Cornet 1994). Found on the island of **Fernando Po** (**Bioko**) in the Gulf of Guinea. In **Congo**, widespread in the Mayombe forest of the Kouilou basin (Goumina, Kakamoeka to Dimonika and Mount Bamba). Scattered reports throughout much of northern and eastern **Zaïre**, in SW Equateur (Mbandaka, Ingende), NE Haut-Zaïre (Bambesa, Wamba, Mambasa and Bunia), southern Kivu (east to Ituri forest and Kamituga), southern Kasai Occidental (Tshikapa and Kananga) and NW Bandundu (Keseki, Kunungu and Bokalakala); not recorded from Mayombe forest, Zaïre, but considered certain to occur in the lower Congo region as collected in NW Angola (Chapin 1954). In **Uganda** known from two birds collected at Mabira forest, east of Kampala in north Buganda, with more recent records from the nearby Kifu forest and from Budongo forest (near Masindi), and in NW **Angola** known only in northern Cuanza Norte at Quiculungo and coffee estates near Salazar. No information on occurrence in **Togo**, **Benin** or **Equatorial Guinea**, and unconfirmed reports only from **Equatorial Guinea** (Mbini). Mapped range tentative, especially in Zaïre.

**HABITAT** Evergreen forest, with a preference for edge habitats such as clearings, and for secondary forest; also plantations, and in the Ivory Coast even in very degraded scrub and cassava plantations (Demey & Fishpool 1991) and the gardens around the buildings at Adiopod-Oumé, while in Congo found in isolated big trees left in gardens. Found in both lowland and montane forest; on Mount Nimba, Liberia, recorded at up to 1200 m, and in Guinea up to 1000 m.

**POPULATION** Probably generally fairly common, although frequently overlooked and considered 'rare'. Thus, not uncommon, at least locally, in the Ivory Coast (e.g. Yapo forest), Ghana and Nigeria, and common in the Mayombe region of the Kouilou basin in SW Congo, with densities of 5–10 territories per square km in the Goumina area (Dowsett & Dowsett-Lemaire 1991).

**HABITS** In primary forest, an elusive, difficult-to-see bird which spends all the time in the forest canopy. Tape playback from the ground will not bring singers down into easy view, and only occasionally descends to the middle storey, although nests may be comparatively low. Forages among the leaf and flower buds in the tops of tall forest trees, often those in clearings, and favours flowering silk cotton tress or clumps of mistletoe. In forest edge and garden habitats, however, will forage much lower, in vine tangles and undergrowth. Occurs in pairs or parties of 3–8, occasionally together with sunbirds in flowering trees, and may join mixed parties of small insectivores. Active, moving rapidly through the foliage and smaller branches, often hammering at twigs, woodpecker- or crombec-like, hanging upside-down and flicking its wings, and also noted flycatching. Foraging birds have been observed poking underneath leaves and along the bark of twigs. Food insects, perhaps especially scale-insects (Coccidae), and also some seeds. Roosts in its nest, 4–5 birds together, even during nest-building, although once incubation begins the female roosts alone.

**BREEDING BIOLOGY** Season apparently very variable, and probably dependent on local conditions. The nest is domed and rounded, c. 150 mm in diameter (large for the size of the bird), and made from plant down which forms a thick felted fabric, with the narrow entrance hole opening downwards to one side. It may be pendent and rather weaver-like, suspended from a bough, vine or creeper, or wedged among the smaller branches of a tree or attached to a bramble or tangle of hanging vines, 3–12 m above ground. A third variety of nest site, inside an old weaver's nest, has also been described. Clutch 2: eggs white; c. 13 x 10.3 mm. May well be a cooperative breeder, as fledged juveniles have been recorded being fed in quick succession by at least four adults, begging with quivering wings and a low sibilant note (Vernon & Dean 1975).

**DESCRIPTION** *P. r. rushiae* **Adult**: *In fresh plumage*, forehead, crown and nape dark brown, feathers fringed and very finely tipped pale drab-grey (feathers unusually 'spiky' in texture); sides of forehead tinged cinnamon. Mantle and scapulars mid-dark brown, feathers very finely fringed pale buff-grey (fringes not reaching tips on longer scapulars and lower mantle). Back, rump and uppertail-coverts yellow, faintly tinged olive, with some diffuse brown feather centres, especially on back and longer uppertail-coverts. Tail blackish-brown. Wing-coverts and flight feathers mid-dark brown, very finely fringed pale buffy-grey (fringes absent on P1–P2 and distally of emarginations on P3–P6). Lores and eyering cinnamon. Chin, throat and breast light drab-grey, feathers with rather broad dark brown shaft streaks; dark centres progressively broader and fringes narrower on cheeks, ear-coverts and sides of neck to merge with crown. Flanks, belly and undertail-coverts dirty yellow, tinged olive, with diffuse mid brown shaft streaks; vent dirty yellow, tinged olive. Thighs light drab grey with dark grey feather centres and dull yellow fringes. Axillaries and underwing-coverts creamy, feathers tipped pale yellow. *In worn plumage*, pale fringes on upperparts abraded, thus crown rather darker and blacker, mantle and scapulars browner and sides of head darker. **Bare Parts**: Iris of male dark orange, red, reddish-brown or orange-brown, of female creamy, light or dark grey to grey-brown; bill blackish, base of lower mandible yellowish; legs and feet bright yellow; claws yellow or grey. **Juvenile**: As adult, but forehead, crown and nape dark brown, feathers finely fringed dirty pale grey. Mantle and scapulars mid brown, feathers diffusely fringed olive-brown. Wing-coverts and flight feathers mid brown, feathers diffusely fringed pale brownish-olive or dull olive-yellow. Lores and eyering dull cinnamon; cheeks, ear-coverts and sides of neck dark brown, faintly streaked pale drab-grey. Chin, throat and breast dull light grey or grey-white, faintly tinged yellow, and small dark brown feather centres show as faint spotting or very fine shaft streaks (sometimes concentrated in malar region, or extending diffusely onto the breast). Remainder of underparts dull pale yellow, washed grey on the flanks, belly and vent; base of lower mandible extensively yellow. **1st Adult**: Presumably as adult. **Measurements**: Wing of male 42.5–51, of female 42–49; tail of male 23–25, of female 25–26; bill 9.2–11.4; tarsus 11–13. Weight (*P. r. ussheri*) 4.6–5.9 g.

**MOULT** Adult post-breeding complete (June–September in Liberia, February–July in Cameroon). Post-juvenile partial?, may not include tail (January–April in Liberia).

**GEOGRAPHICAL VARIATION** Relatively well marked.

*P. r. ussheri* Sierra Leone to Ghana. As nominate *rushiae*, but fringes on mantle and scapulars slightly more olive and diffuse (hence no scalloped pattern), wing-coverts and flight feathers fringed olive-yellow, streaking on throat and breast rather finer. Wing of male 41–47, of female 41.5–47.

*P. r. rushiae* Southern Nigeria to west and central Cameroon and Gabon. See Description.

*P. r. bedfordi* Fernando Po (Bioko). As nominate *rushiae*, but rump feathers centred brown, streaking on throat and breast broad and darker, almost blackish-brown, and more extensive, extending to the flanks and belly. Larger? Wing of male 45.5, of female 46; tail of male 30, of female 25.

**P. r. denti** SE Cameroon (Yokadouma), Central African Republic, NW Angola, Zaïre and Uganda. As nominate *rushiae*, but rump and underparts brighter and more orange-yellow, breast and throat slightly creamier, streaking on underparts finer and rather sparser (although not so fine as in *ussheri*), and paler fringes on primaries and secondaries reduced. Wing of male 51.5, of female 49, 49.5.

**RELATIONSHIPS** Uncertain and confused, and sometimes left as *genus incertae sedis*. The species has been placed in no fewer than seven different families: the warblers Sylviidae; tits Paridae; sunbirds Nectariniidae; flowerpeckers Dicaeidae; estrildid finches Estrildidae; together with the aberrant warbler, the Green Hylia, in a family of its own (Hyliidae); or even with the Australian honeyeaters Meliphagidae. Hall & Moreau (1970) did not even place it in a family and, 'purely for convenience' listed it between the nuthatches and the sunbirds. Vernon & Dean (1975), however, argued that it is closely similar to the penduline tits *Anthoscopus* in calls, social behaviour, flight, feeding behaviour, size, juvenile plumage, nest structure and roosting and breeding behaviour; they suggested either that it be treated as a member of the Remizidae, or that it is a remarkable case of convergence with that family. Dowsett & Forbes-Watson (1993) have reservations, however, noting its Sylviidae-type song. Further investigation, especially DNA analysis, is required.

**REFERENCES** Bannerman (1953), Chapin (1954), Dowsett & Dowsett-Lemaire (1991), Serle (1965), Vernon & Dean (1975).

# 45 VERDIN *Auriparus flaviceps* Plate 35

Characteristic of the deserts of SW USA and Mexico, the affinities of this 'penduline tit' are still debated. One of the most active nest-builders in North America, its bulky breeding nests are more conspicuous than the bird itself, and it also builds separate nests to roost in.

**IDENTIFICATION** Length 100–110 mm (4–4.5 in). A small tit with a distinctively heavy, pointed conical black bill and strong legs and feet. Forecrown, ear-coverts and throat dull yellowish-olive, the yellow tones becoming brighter and more extensive in spring and summer, extending onto the rear crown and upper breast; some, especially in the south and west, may show a chestnut forehead and more extensively yellow underparts. Upperparts, including wings and tail, mouse-grey, the outer tail feathers rather narrowly fringed and tipped whitish. Lesser coverts variably chestnut, showing as a contrasting patch at the shoulder, although often concealed. Underparts pale grey-white. Juveniles duller, lacking the yellow head and chestnut lesser coverts. Adults are distinctive, but juvenile Verdins are singularly drab and easily confused with juvenile Bushtits, which they resemble in size and proportions, although they have a shorter tail (43–50 mm when fully grown, compared with 46–62 mm in Bushtit, but beware recently fledged birds with short-grown tails). Not so gregarious, Verdins are best separated by their large, conical bill, pale-based in juveniles, and quite different from Bushtit's rather insignificant instrument. They also have a very plain heads (although they quickly begin to show some yellowish as they moult into 1st-adult plumage), lacking the brown-washed cap or dark ear-coverts of a young Bushtit. Their very loud vocalisations are distinctive. Juveniles can also be separated from the superficially similar Northern Beardless-Tyrannulet by their lack of dark lores, rounded crown (rather than slightly bushy-crested profile), more conical bill and different 'jizz' (tyrannulets perch rather upright and frequently wag their tail).

**SEX/AGE** Sexes very similar. In the hand, males average slightly brighter yellow on the head, with the lesser coverts chestnut-red (inner webs reddish or broadly tipped reddish). Females are duller yellow on the head and throat, washed brownish in fresh plumage, with the lesser coverts pale chestnut or tawny (inner webs grey or narrowly tipped reddish). These characters are rather subtle, however, and probably unreliable for many intermediate birds, especially without direct comparison. Juveniles distinct, lacking yellow on the head, with the lesser coverts olive to olive-red-brown on males and grey on females; bill bright pinkish-orange with a darker culmen, but soon darkening. Following the incomplete juvenile moult, 1st adults have the retained juvenile primary coverts and inner 2–5 primaries brownish and faded, contrasting with the greyer and fresher greater coverts and secondaries, the primary coverts being rounded and tipped pale brown. Adults have the coverts, primaries and secondaries uniformly grey, but many intermediates may be difficult or impossible to age: compare also the intensity of yellow on the head, as 1st adults average duller yellow than adults, sex-for-sex.

**VOICE** Vocalisations generally rather loud. The most frequent call comprises sharp *tschep*, *tschik* or *chip* notes (almost like ball-bearings knocking together), repeated in a chattering, staccato series, *tschik-tschik-tschik...*, the number of notes and the speed of delivery being very variable (and sometimes interspersed with slightly squeaky *tsieu*, *tsieu* notes); in alarm or excitement, the pitch and rapidity of the chatter may increase, and chatters may be given for over 60 seconds without pause, but the pace of delivery may slow towards the end of a series, the notes becoming well spaced. Other notes include a rather sparrow-like *cheep*, *tseet* or *tsuu*, given in slow, well-spaced series as a contact call and as an advertising call by the male in spring, and a lisping, twittering, rapidly repeated series of weak notes (the 'tweedle call'). The aerial-predator alarm is a churring *gee-gee-gee-gee....* Begging females and nestlings give a high-pitched, repeated *tseee*. Song, given in spring and summer, is a whistled *chee-chee-chee*, the number of units variable but all on the same pitch, or a slow, measured series of clearer, full but rather 'sad' whistled units, each phrase repeated 2–3 times and then the unit varied, variously transcribed as *tseet* notes followed by 1–3 (usually 1–2) *tsoor* notes, thus *tseet-tsoor-tsoor, tsee-tu-tu, tsee-tu-tee,* or as *ti-du-pud-di, ti-du-pu-di, tu-du-ti, tu-du-ti, ti-du, ti-du* etc.; it is vaguely on the 'tea-cher' theme. Also a more complex phrase, composed of *c.* 2 mellow, whistled units and a trill, *pheet, pheet, tsitsitsitsisi-sisi, pheet, pheet, tsitsitsitsisisisi.* (Largely after Taylor 1971.)

**DISTRIBUTION AND MOVEMENTS** In the USA breeds in SE **California** in the Colorado and Mohave deserts north and west to eastern Kern Co. and the Amargosa river, Inyo Co. (formerly to extreme SW San Diego Co. in the Tijuana valley, and vagrant north on the coast to Chula Vista and San Elijo Lagoon). Resident in southern **Nevada**, SW **Utah** in the Virgin river valley and associated tributaries (especially Beaver Dam Wash), most of western and southern **Arizona**, in the Lower Sonoran Zone (except the bottom of the Grand Canyon), north to the Virgin river valley in the extreme northwest and Yavapai, Gila and Greenlee Cos. Breeds in southern **New Mexico**, north to at least Grant, Socorro and Chaves Cos., and in SW and north-central **Texas** (west to Nueces, Gonzales, Travis, Burnet, San Saba, Erath and Clay Cos., possibly to Aransas and Bastrop Cos., and north to Martin, Borden, Knox and Wilbarger Cos., with isolated winter records from Lubbock, Potter and? Chambers Cos.). In SW **Oklahoma** found in Harmon and Jackson Cos.. In **Mexico** breeds throughout **Baja California** (although apparently absent from the extreme northwest), including the islands of Angel de la Guarda, San Lorenzo, Tortuga, Carmen, San Jose, San Francisco, Espíritu Santo and Cerralvo in the Gulf of California and Santa Magdalena and Santa Margarita islands on the Pacific coast. Also **Sonora** (not SE, but including San Sebastian and Tiburon islands), NW and central **Sinaloa** (south to El Molino), **Chihuahua** (not SW), **Coahuila**, **Nuevo Leon**, northern and western **Tamaulipas** (in the Sierra Madre Oriental, east to Soto la Marina and, in the south, to at least Jaumave), eastern **Durango**, **Zacatecas** (south to at least Fresnillo; not extreme south), central and western **San Luis Potosi**, **Aguascalientes**, NE **Jalisco** (southwest to at least Lagos de Moreno), northern and central **Guanajuato**, northern **Queretaro** (southwest to at least Tolimán) and central **Hidalgo**. Resident.

**HABITAT** Deserts, where favours the better-vegetated areas along washes and watercourses, with thorny shrubs such as paloverde, mesquite, salt cedar (tamarisk), *Acacia*, Catclaw Acacia and cholla, also desert flats dominated by Creosote Bushes, and brush, riverine poplars and willows, and evergreen oaks. Generally found at low elevations, although recorded at up to 915 m in California, 1220 m in Arizona, 1675 m in New Mexico, 1830 m in Texas, 1460 m in Coahuila (Sierra del Carmen), 1370 m in San Luis Potosi, and 2135 m in Aguascalientes.

**POPULATION** In US portion of range fairly common, with the highest densities in Arizona (where common), but scarcer on the edge of the range, thus uncommon in Utah and rare in Oklahoma and peripheral areas in northern Texas. Numbers in Arizona are said to have increased with the spread of mesquite. In Mexico, common in Baja California and Sonora.

**HABITS** Generally rather solitary, but also found in pairs, family parties or sometimes in small loose flocks, usually around a favoured food source. Also joins mixed-species foraging flocks. Restless and very active, the actions are tit-like, but drastically curtails its activity as the temperature tops 35° C and, not surprisingly, prefers to loaf in deep shade when it is very hot (45° C plus). Shy and retiring during the breeding season until the eggs hatch, and, although more approachable at other times, may be elusive in thick habitats and more often heard than seen, as they keep in contact with their loud calls. Shows little territorial behaviour, although breeding birds occupy discrete home ranges and the immediate vicinity of the nest is defended by both sexes; other disputes between males may be related to 'mate-guarding'. Male and female in the pair apparently separate at the end of the breeding season and, like the year's young, disperse quite widely. Verdins are apparently territorial in winter, however, and join foraging flocks only as these pass through their territory. Going to roost early, and emerging late, Verdins are notable for building roosting nests. Each individual usually constructs several such nests (unaided by the opposite sex) during the year, but males build more than females. Roosting nests differ from breeding nests (see below) in being placed in forks rather than among more slender twigs, and in having less lining material, a more centrally placed entrance, and a shallower cup. Smaller nests are built by adults and immatures in late summer, with little or no lining and virtually no cup, and larger ones, more similar to breeding nests, in autumn and winter (if in good repair, these may be used by the male through the breeding season). Abandoned and even dilapidated breeding nests may also be used for roosting, and the female roosts in the active breeding nest. Adults never roost together, although juveniles roost communally in the breeding nest for the first few days after fledging, sometimes with one of the adults. Later, the male's roosting nest or, indeed, any available nest may be used by the brood, until they become independent of the adult and disperse. Fledged juveniles may also, with persistence, usurp an adult from its roosting nest. Overall, the use of these roosts is an important factor in allowing Verdins to survive the harsh desert environment, and their overnight energy expenditure is substantially reduced. Food insects, spiders and, especially in autumn and winter, fruit and berries (pulp, but not seeds). Forages among the foliage and flowers of desert shrubs (never on the ground), examining the twigs and bark, and one of the few birds to forage on the Creosote Bush, pecking minute objects from the bark of twigs. Uses its feet to grasp branches and pull these towards itself, allowing a close inspection of the leaves. Insects and spider cocoons are held under the toes and torn apart with the bill, being completely consumed (as with *Parus* tits, and unlike Fire-capped Tit). As another adaptation to the desert, does not, apparently, need to drink.

**BREEDING BIOLOGY** Season March–June (although exceptionally from late February, and occasionally as late as August in Mexico and Arizona and September in Texas). The elaborate nest is built over 4–6 days by both sexes, the male taking a more active role in the early stages, the female dominating in the latter stages, especially in completion of the lining. It is a large globular structure (up to 20 cm external diameter) constructed from as many as 2,000 thorny twigs woven around the plant's limbs, the spiny ends sticking outwards to deter predators. Nests are usually placed at or near the end of a low limb of a thorny tree or shrub, up to 3 m (0.6–9 m) above ground. The nest is composed of three layers, an outer layer of interlaced dry twigs, both thorny and thornless, mixed with variable amounts of spiders' webs, feathers, fur, wool, leaves and seed pods. Initially a horizontal platform is constructed from such material, bound to the supporting branches with cobwebs, followed by a complete domed shell. To this the middle layer is added, comprising shorter thornless twigs with a similar mix of webs, fur, leaves etc., and also moss and lichen. The third layer comprises the lining, mostly feathers but also sometimes fur and wool, and lining material continues to be added right through to fledging. Very exceptionally nests are constructed largely from cobwebs and plant down, reinforced with a few twigs and stems, and in Baja California spineless twigs are used in favour of spiny thorns. Material may be taken from old nests or from roosting nests, or may be stolen from other Verdins. The entrance is to the side, c. 25 mm in diameter, usually facing outwards, and well concealed, especially by a 'roof' of outward projecting sticks 25–65 mm deep. Early-season nests are oriented so that the entrance is protected from the prevailing winds (to avoid chilling), late-season nests are oriented to face the wind (to aid cooling). In addition, well-used nests, both breeding and roosting, may have a mass of dried faecal material adhering to the lower rim of the entrance, and evaporation from faecal sacs may help to cool the nest later in the season. Being durable and conspicuous, and lasting several seasons, the nests may give the impression of a greater abundance of Verdins than is actually the case. Clutch, USA 4 (often 3 later in season and in repeat clutches; up to 6 recorded), Mexico 3 (2–4): eggs blue-green to greenish-white, finely spotted reddish-brown, sometimes chiefly at the larger end to form a cap; 15.3 x 11.1 mm. Female incubates, period 14–17 days. Both sexes feed the young (in first week largely the female), which fledge after 17–19 days but continue to be fed by both parents for c. 18 days; this may be largely undertaken by the male,

while the female begins a second clutch. Second broods are not uncommon, and up to four nesting attempts have been recorded in a season resulting in, two successful broods.

**DESCRIPTION** *A. f. ornatus* **Adult Male**: *In fresh plumage* (September to about March), forehead, crown and sometimes nape yellowish olive-green (yellow feather bases show over base of bill and on forehead, otherwise concealed by olive-green tips). Nape to uppertail-coverts dull mid grey, washed drab; occasionally shows odd yellowish feather bases on back or rump. Tail dark grey-brown, inner feathers fringed as upperparts, T4–T5 fringed whitish distally, T6 narrowly fringed and tipped whitish. Lesser coverts chestnut-red. Median and greater coverts dark grey-brown, fringed as upperparts. Alula sooty-brown, smaller feathers narrowly fringed pale grey. Primary coverts dark grey-brown, very finely fringed as upperparts. Flight feathers dark grey-brown, fringed as upperparts on tertials, secondaries and basal half of primaries (not P1–P2), fringes narrower and whiter on P4-P6; all flight feathers finely tipped paler. Lores dark grey-brown. Cheeks, ear-coverts and chin olive-yellow, feathers of rear ear-coverts tipped as upperparts; throat more washed-out olive-yellow, feathers of lower throat tipped light grey. Sides of neck and breast light grey, fading into soft grey-white on remainder of underparts. Axillaries and underwing-coverts whitish. *In worn plumage* (about April–August), dull tips to feathers of crown, ear-coverts and throat abraded and yellow on head more intense; forehead yellow, forecrown dull olive-yellow, rear crown, nape and ear-coverts yellowish olive-green, chin and throat (extending onto upper breast) dull yellow. Some may have small reddish-chestnut spot on the forecrown (rufous feather bases revealed). Fringes to flight feathers and tail abraded and bleached paler; alula contrastingly dark. **Bare Parts**: Iris dark brown; bill black or dark blue-grey; legs and feet dark blue-grey. **Adult Female**: As male (but see Sex/Age). **Juvenile**: As adult, but upperparts, including head, lesser coverts and fringes to median and greater coverts, rather browner, a uniform grey-fawn. Uppertail-coverts and fringes to tail feathers and tertials slightly more cinnamon-drab. Secondaries and primaries fringed off-white (including P2). Lores and ear-coverts washed grey-fawn, chin to under tail-coverts soft grey-white. Bill bright pinkish-orange with a darker culmen. Sexes very similar (see Sex/Age). **1st Adult**: As adult (but see Sex/Age). **Measurements**: Wing of male 51–55 (chord 52–55.5), of female 52–53.5 (chord 49.5–54); tail 39–51.5, of male 46–51.5, of female 44.5–49; bill 9.5–11.6; tarsus 14.5–16. Weight 6–8.2 g (*A. f. acaciarum*).

**MOULT** Adult post-breeding complete (late May–October). Post-juvenile incomplete, usually includes tail feathers and all flight feathers except the *inner 2–5 primaries* (and the primary coverts) (June–September, begins with appearance of yellow feathers on the head).

**GEOGRAPHICAL VARIATION** Slight, largely clinal, and poorly understood. Northern and eastern races (acaciarum, ornatus) are slightly larger and duller, while southern and western birds are smaller and tend to be a richer yellow on the head (sometimes with a chestnut forehead) and more extensively yellow on the underparts. Six races recognised (largely following Phillips 1986).

**A. f. acaciarum** California, Nevada, Utah, and the Colorado valley of western Arizona (Yuma, La Paz and Mohave Cos.) (Phillips 1986 extends range east to SW New Mexico), south to southern Baja California Norte (c. 29° N), NW and central Sonora (south to at least Puerto Libertad), Chihuahua, central Durango (?) and central Coahuila. Intergrades with ornatus in central Arizona (Middle Gila drainage). Poorly marked. As ornatus, but upperparts average slightly paler (near lamprocephalus), especially back and rump, and washed buffish on upperparts and flanks. Averages slightly smaller? Wing (chord) of male 52.5–54; tail of male 46–50.5.

**A. f. ornatus** SE Arizona, New Mexico, Texas and Oklahoma south to extreme NE, central and north-central Sonora (south and west to c. 29° N and 111° E; replaced in the Yaqui basin by nominate flaviceps), southern Coahuila, central-south Tamaulipas (San Fernando, Xicohtencatl), and northern San Luis Potosi. See Description.

**A. f. flaviceps** Central Baja California south of acaciarum and north of lamprocephalus, NE and southern Sonora, north in the west to Isla Tiburon and in the east to c. 30° 30' N in the Yaqui basin; also Isla San Esteban (= Isla San Sebastian) and northern Sinaloa. As ornatus, but crown and throat average brighter chrome-yellow; also smaller and shorter-tailed. Wing (chord) of male averages 51, tail 43. Includes 'fraterculus' of central-west (and NE?) Sonora to north Sinaloa, with upperparts perhaps paler and throat duller.

**A. f. lamprocephalus** Oberholser (1897). Baja California Sur, south of c. 24° 35' N on Pacific slope and c. 25° N on Gulf coast, including at least San Jose and San Francisco islands. As flaviceps, but upperparts paler (near acaciarum). Male with crown and throat brighter (tending slightly towards sinaloae), throat clear yellow (less chrome); most males have chestnut forecrown (more extensive chestnut at base of forehead feathers). Juveniles as other races, with higher percentage tending to have faintly yellowish-tinged rump. Smaller than northern races, and particularly short-tailed. Wing (chord) of male, 48.5–52, of female 47–51; tail of male 39.5–44, of female 39–44.

**A. f. sinaloae** Phillips (1986). NW Sinaloa from about Culiacán north to Guamuchil. The yellowest race. As lamprocephalus, but yellow tones slightly richer, deeper (especially on throat, which is marginally richer than lamprocephalus) and more extensive. In fresh plumage, olive-grey feather tips on crown less extensive (thus crown brighter), or if tips extensive these are more yellowish olive-green; upperparts faintly tinged yellow, especially rump of male. Yellow extends broadly onto the centre of breast, and in worn plumage the extensive yellow feather bases on the lower breast, belly and undertail-coverts may be revealed (otherwise these areas dirty pale grey to whitish), brightest in male. Males usually lack chestnut on the forecrown of most male lamprocephalus (with only a faint indication of a golden patch at the base of the forehead feathers); female darker than lamprocephalus? Wing (chord) of male 49–50; tail of male 43.5–46.

**A. f. hidalgensis** Phillips (1986). Aguascalientes, NE Jalisco, south-central Guanajuato and southern San Luis Potosi south to central-east Hidalgo. At all ages, the darkest race on upper- and underparts (adult often the brownest on the flanks, juvenile often the brownest), crown and throat deep, dull yellow. Large? Wing (chord) of male 53, 53.5; tail of male 49.5, 49.5.

**RELATIONSHIPS** The affinities of the Verdin have been much debated. Originally placed in the true tits Paridae (e.g. Bent 1948), it was moved to the penduline tits Remizidae (e.g. Snow 1967), but this has been disputed, as Verdin differs from Remiz and Anthoscopus in its structure (with the bill broader and not so fine at the tip, the tail rounded rather than attenuated, and P1 much larger), its blue-green rather than white eggs, and certain aspects of its breeding biology and behaviour. It was placed in the bananaquits Coerebidae by Taylor (1970a), on the grounds of distribution and behaviour, and in the subfamily Polioptilinae (gnatwrens, gnatcatchers) of the Certhiidae (which includes wrens and treecreepers) by Sibley & Ahlquist (1990), on the basis of biochemical evidence. Doubtless the debate will continue, but the structure (especially bill shape), moult (especially incomplete post-juvenile moult) and nest are all similar to those of the other penduline tits.

**REFERENCES** Austin (1977), Austin & Rea (1971), Bent (1948), Oberholser (1974), Phillips (1986), Taylor (1970a, b, 1971).

# 46 MARSH TIT Parus palustris Plate 15

Despite its name, this species has no association with marshes (or even with damp woodland). With a curiously disjunct distribution in Europe and eastern Asia, in parts of the range it provides one of the toughest field-identification problems.

**IDENTIFICATION** Length 115 mm (4.5 in). A medium-sized tit with a stocky bill. Cap glossy black, upperparts dull brown, cheek patches white, a rather small blackish bib, remainder of underparts off-white with a variable buff or brown wash on the flanks. Distinguished from most tits by the lack of a pale nuchal spot, lack of pale wingbars, and absence of yellow in the plumage, but often rather difficult to separate from Willow Tit. By far the best distinction is voice, but some notes are rather similar to those of Willow, especially to the inexperienced ear. Marsh has a characteristic sneezing *pitchuu* or *psip-tchiu*, never given by Willow, but both species have a nasal *dzee* or *tchay*-type note, although that of Marsh Tit averages higher-pitched, is rather shorter and raspier, is more often given in long series, and is more hurriedly repeated, lacking the deliberate, deep, sonorous quality of Willow Tit. Marsh often combines the *psip-tchiu* and *chay* calls, whilst Willow combines the nasal motif with a thinner and higher-pitched *si-si* or sharp *chick*. Generally, where the two species occur together, both in northern and eastern Europe and in eastern Asia, Willow Tit is paler and greyer. In some areas, however, notably Britain, their general coloration is very similar, and silent birds must be identified by shape and subtle plumage features; even then, some (especially juveniles) must be left unidentified. Compared to Willow Tit, Marsh is a little bigger but with a relatively smaller, more evenly proportioned head. It does not appear 'bull-necked' and shows a less extensive black cap. Marsh is also usually somewhat neater and sleeker and has a more square-cut tail. Adults have a glossy black cap (matt black in Willow Tit and in juveniles of both species), a smaller and neater black bib, and less extensive white cheeks (the ear-coverts are washed buff at the rear), lacking the 'swept-back' appearance of Willow Tit's cheek patches. In very fresh plumage Marsh Tits may show a slight wing panel formed by pale drab-brown fringes to the secondaries and tertials, but generally it lacks the prominent pale fringes to the flight feathers which form a conspicuous wing panel on all but rather worn Willow Tits. An additional character in Britain and western Europe is the paler flanks of Marsh Tit, but the extent of white in the outer tail feathers is not a useful feature (see also Willow Tit, p. 249). In central China, may overlap with the closely similar Black-bibbed Tit, but has a paler, warmer brown mantle, much paler creamy or buffy underparts and a less extensive black bib, and never shows the slight crest of Black-bibbed. See p. 242 for a full discussion.

**SEX/AGE** Sexes very similar. Males have a blacker and glossier cap than that of females (which may occasionally approach the sooty-black of Willow Tit), and their bib is larger and darker (beware, however, juvenile males, which are duller than adults). Also, in at least nominate *palustris* in fresh plumage, females have a slightly warmer and more extensive pale buffish- or pinkish-drab-brown wash on the sides of breast, belly and flanks. Juvenile similar to the adult, but cap dull sooty-black, bib smaller and underparts whiter. 1st adult as adult, but retains the juvenile flight feathers, tertials, primary coverts, and occasionally a few outer greater coverts or tail feathers: ageing is possible in the hand, as the primary coverts and tail feathers are narrower and more pointed than an adult's, and relatively more worn until about February; in addition, some 1st adults retain some juvenile outer greater coverts, or

replace some tail feathers, and then show moult contrasts in these areas.

**VOICE** A noisy tit, with a very varied vocabulary. Contact call a high-pitched, thin *tip*, and also gives a high, thin, slightly sibilant *see* or *see-see-see* and a sharp but liquid *psit* or *stip*, repeatedly so in flight, *stip, stip, stip*.... The species has a 'chick-a-dee' call system (see Black-capped Chickadee, p. 267), but this is relatively poorly known and the 'rules' of syntax for the system are unstudied (it is apparently more variable than in Black-capped Chickadee, and A, B, C and D are not analogous to the chickadee's notes and are not necessarily given in that order; a bout of Ds may be followed by other notes). Components include a thin, sometimes sibilant *pssip* (= A), a sharp *psip* or *psit* (= B; also an almost metallic *tip*, thus B here probably encompasses more than one note type), a sneezing, explosive *psiup* or *tchiu* (= C), and a nasal *dee* or *zee* (= D). In this system A, B, C, and D may be given once, repeated several times or omitted altogether, but Marsh Tit relatively seldom gives 'D' notes alone (unlike Willow Tit). The most characteristic call is an abrupt, 'sneezing' *pitchuu*, *pssi'tchiu* or *stip'tchiu*. This is either an AC combination, that is a thin, sibilant *pssip* combined with the abrupt *psiup* or *tchiu*, or a BC combination, an abrupt *psip* (sometimes the metallic *stip* or *tip*) combined with *psiup* or *tchiu*. A, B and C may also be given alone, and there can be more complex combinations such as ABC, AAC etc. The full-blown 'chick-a-dee' incorporates at least one D, e.g. *psip-dzaa, psiup-ze-ze-ze*, and often includes a relatively large number of rapidly repeated Ds (up to at least 21), e.g. *tip'tip'psiup'zee-zee-zee-zee-zee-zee-zeezee-zeezee*. Compared with Willow Tit, the D notes tend to be rather shorter (0.05–0.2 seconds in duration, compared with 0.25–0.5 seconds in Willow). Other calls include a chattering scold, *chrrrrrrr*..., which is rather sparrow-like (or may recall a Blue Tit) and comprises 8–33 units given at a rate of 14–16 per second (far too quickly to distinguish the individual notes); in longer series the notes are initially given even more rapidly, and such scolds may last up to 2 seconds. Also thin, squeaky *pzee* notes (when begging?), a shrill *pitz* or *pitz-itz-itz* as the hawk-alarm, and females disturbed on the nest give an explosive hiss. Song loud and full, but very variable. The commonest and simplest variant is the 'rattle song', 8–19 rapidly repeated monosyllabic units (c. 7–10 units per second, the individual notes nevertheless easily distinguishable, and similar to the C call), e.g. a sharp *tchip'chip'chip'chip*... or *chi'chi'chi*.... Similarly simple songs comprise 3–9 apparently monosyllabic units (but probably usually two notes 'stuttered' into each other), given rather more slowly, c. 4–6 units per second, e.g. *s'chip's'chip's'chip*..., *swi-sweet'weet'weet*... and a rather sweet and very Willow-Tit-like *tsiu-tiu-tiu-tiu*.... These slower songs tend, however, to be made up of clearly disyllabic motifs given at a rate of c. 2.75–5 per second and often introduced by a single sharper monosyllabic note, e.g. *puu, sp'puu-u'sp'puu'sp'puu*..., *ts'chirup'chirup'chirup*..., *psiup-tupee-tupee-tupee...*, or *chip-wichu-wichu-wichu...*; some may recall a Coal Tit in their sweet, plaintive tone, e.g. *spi-du-pidu-pidu...* or *spi'tchu-spi'tchu-spi'tchu....* Rather scarcer song variants are composed from more complicated motifs, e.g. *chip'pi'we-chip'pi'we-chip'pi'we* or *pitchaweeo-pitchaweeo-pitchawee*. Each male may have a repertoire of up to 19 song variants, giving a bout of one song type before switching to another (and at the transition a mixture of units may be sung). The female may also sing, but her song is softer and less stereotyped, and only one phrase is given at a time. The subsong is a soft, jumbled version of the song combined with whispering and twittering notes. Perhaps serving some of the functions of a song (and associated with aggressive encounters), occasionally gives 'gargles', conglomerations of more or less musical notes rapidly repeated in a short phrase that tends to drop in pitch; gargles may be repeated up to at least four times. (Perhaps there may be some intergradation between the more complex songs and gargles?) The voice of the Caucasus race is reported to be a loud trill (Flint *et al.* 1984), but otherwise there is apparently little geographical variation in song or calls across the vast range. (Partly after Cramp & Perrins 1993.)

## DISTRIBUTION AND MOVEMENTS Two widely separated groups.

**WEST PALEARCTIC POPULATIONS** Breeds in **England** (absent Isle of Man) and **Wales**, but very local in **Scotland** (first record 1921, breeding first proved 1945) and confined to the southeast (breeds Borders, and recent records of wanderers from Lothian and Dumfries & Galloway). In Continental Europe breeds north to central **Norway**, southern **Sweden** (and sporadically north to northern Sweden), **Estonia**, and in **Russia** north to the southern parts of the St Petersburg region, Smolensk, Tula, Ul'yanovsk, and east to Ufa in Bashkirskaya. The range extends south to the Pyrénées and Cantabrian mountains in northern **Spain**, **Italy**, NE **Sicily**, **Greece**, the Rhodope mountains of southern **Bulgaria**, the central **Ukraine** at Ivano-Frankovsk, Kamenèts-Podol'skiy, Vinnitsa, Kirovograd, Dneprodzerzhinsk and Khar'kov, and in **Russia** found south to Voronezh, Tambov and Penza. Also found in Thrace and northern **Turkey** in NW Anatolia and the Black Sea coastlands, with a possibly disjunct population in **SW Russia** and NW **Georgia** in the NW Greater Caucasus (north to the Kuban' valley and northern foothills, east to at least the area of Ordzhonikidze, and south to the southern foothills). Resident and generally *highly* sedentary, with rather limited post-breeding dispersal; less than 1% of British Marsh Tits move more than 50 km. Birds from northern populations may, however, wander during late August–March, often to the south, but this species does not participate in 'irruptions'. Recorded in the steppe zone of the southern **Ukraine** and **SE Russia**, south to the Sea of Azov (and the Crimea?). Also two records in winter in the Karatau range in southern **Kazakhstan**, and vagrant **Corsica** (one old record; Thibault 1983), **Ireland** (Bray, Co. Wicklow,

December 1990), and **Finland** (*c.* 8 records, the most recent in Helsinki, October 1993, but the identification of some may be in doubt).

**EASTERN POPULATIONS** Breeds in **Russia** in SE **Siberia** from the Altai and Sayan ranges, Minusinsk, the Krasnoyarsk region and Kansk east through the Baykal region (north to Irkutsk) to Amurland and Ussuriland (north in the Amur basin to 53° N, and including Askold island), also **Sakhalin** (north to Tymorvskoye), the southern **Kurile islands** on Iturup, Kunashir and Shikotan (also Urup according to 'Peters') and, in northern **Japan**, Hokkaido and adjacent Rishiri-to. In northern **Mongolia** found in the Hangayn and Hentiyn massifs, from the Tesiyn Gol valley and Haanhöhiy Uul range in the west to the upper Uuldza Gol valley in the east, and south to the northern slopes of the Hangayn range, Bogdo Uul massif (near Ulan Bator), Tuul Gol valley, upper Kerulen valley and southern tributaries of the Onon Gol. Also **North** and **South Korea** (in the highlands south to at least Kyonggi-Do) and **NE** and **eastern China** in NE **Nei Mongol** (Zalantun and the Da Hinggan range), **Heilongjiang** (Nenjiang, Xian Hinggan range), **Jilin** (Changbai Shan), **Liaoning** (Shenyang, Qiano Shan range), **Hebei** (including the Eastern Qing Tombs and Qinhuangdao), **Shanxi**, **Shaanxi** (including 'Ma Hsien' (= Mei Xian) and 'Hsu-hsien' (= Hu Xian) on the northern marches of the Qin Ling mountains, although Qin Ling birds are placed with Black-bibbed Tit by Cheng 1987; see p. 242 for details), **Sichuan** (where Marsh Tit has been collected at 'Chin-chien-san', presumably in the lowlands of the east or centre, or perhaps Emei Shan (see gazetteer in Traylor 1967), and perhaps a winter visitor only), **Henan**, **Shandong** and **Jiangsu** (Zhenjiang on the Yangtze). Occasional records from **Hong Kong** are thought to relate to escapes from captivity. Resident, although those from more northerly populations may wander in late August–March.

**HABITAT** Primarily mature deciduous woodland, typically of oak or beech, usually where found in reasonably extensive stands. Also breeds in mixed forest, riverine woodland, alder carr, well-wooded farmland, orchards, sometimes parks and occasionally overgrown gardens and even reedy marshes in Japan, but seldom found in urban areas. In the taiga of southern Siberia and Sakhalin, favours riverine stands of poplar, birch, willow and Bird Cherry, and avoids conifers. In some areas, however, may occur in conifers, usually where Willow Tit is absent, e.g. locally in Britain, and in Denmark, Austria, the Caucasus, Mongolia and Korea. Old or decaying trees suitable for nesting are an essential requirement. Outside the breeding season favours a slightly broader range of habitats, more often including conifers, and often visits garden birdtables where these can be found close to woodland. In Europe essentially a lowland species, although occasionally occurs up to *c.* 1300 m in the Alps, and found at up to *c.* 1000-1200 m in the Altai and Sayan mountains in SW Siberia. Similarly, on Hokkaido in northern Japan, found from the lowlands to near the treeline at *c.* 1400 m, but in Korea and NE China primarily montane, and recorded in the Changbai Shan (Jilin) from 650 m to at least 2100 m, descending to the plains in winter.

**POPULATION** Generally fairly common to common, although often local and somewhat sporadic in occurrence, and scarcer towards the northern boundaries of the range and scarce in the Caucasus and Sayan mountains. On the other hand, abundant in Ussuriland. Not especially susceptible to hard winters, but there is evidence for a slow decline in Britain.

**HABITS** Tame and often inquisitive, but generally less sociable than other tits. Found singly but normally in pairs, which stay close together, maintaining contact with frequent calling. Territories are established by the male and maintained all year. Pair formation is dependent on the possession of a territory by the male; most new pairs are formed in February–March, and birds may mate for life. Juveniles and unpaired 1st adults may join mixed-species foraging flocks, as do established pairs outside the breeding season as the flock passes through their territory, dropping out as the flock reaches the edge of the territory. Sometimes forms small single-species flocks in the autumn and winter, with up to 20 noted together. Roosts singly, in sprays of foliage, tree holes or sometimes rodent holes in the ground, and the female roosts in the nest until the young are *c.* 13 days old. Sings most commonly mid January–late May, with a peak of activity around dawn. Rival males may engage in song-duels, sometimes at a considerable distance. Forages at all levels of the vegetation, from the canopy downwards, but has a preference for shrubs and the lower branches of trees and, especially in winter, the ground. Food largely insects and spiders in the spring and summer, adding seeds, nuts (especially beechmast) and berries (seeds rather than pulp) in the autumn and winter. Commonly stores food such as seeds and nuts, especially in the autumn, in bark crevices, under moss or lichen, among the leaf litter, and in and on the ground.

**BREEDING BIOLOGY** Season mid April–May in West Palearctic, April–May in southern Siberia, late April–June in NE China, May–June in Japan. The nest site is a hole in a tree or stump up to 10 m above ground (although generally rather low), among roots, or occasionally in a cavity in a wall or the ground. Seldom uses nestboxes. Does not excavate its own hole, but may widen and deepen existing cavities or take over the old excavations of Willow Tit, which it may enlarge. The final selection of the nest site is probably made by the female. The nest is a deep pad of moss, occasionally mixed with other vegetable material, lined with fur and sometimes a few feathers. It is built by the female, although both sexes may perform some initial chipping of the cavity entrance. Clutch 7–10 (3–12) in West Palearctic (in the former USSR first clutch 7–10, second clutches 6–9), 5–8 in Japan: eggs white, usually finely and sparsely spotted with reddish-brown, especially at the broader end, with some violet-grey undermarkings; 15.8 x 12.3 mm (*P. p. dresseri*, England).

Female incubates, period 13–17 days; she is fed both on and off the nest by the male. Both sexes feed the young, although only the female broods them; they fledge after 16–20 days and are fed by the parents for a further 7 days or so, dispersing *c.* 14 days after fledging. Second broods rare, except in the former USSR.

**DESCRIPTION** *P. p. palustris* **Adult**: *In fresh plumage* (August–February), crown and nape black with glossy blue feather tips, especially on crown. Upperparts cold drab-brown, sometimes slightly warmer buff-brown on rump. Tail dark brownish-grey, feathers vaguely fringed drab-grey or olive-grey, T6 narrowly fringed pale grey on outer web. Wing-coverts as upperparts; alula and primary coverts dark brownish-grey, vaguely fringed and tipped drab-brown. Flight feathers dark brownish-grey, innermost tertial largely drab-brown, remainder broadly fringed drab-brown, secondaries sharply fringed drab-grey, primaries faintly fringed dirty white. Cheek patch dirty white, tinged grey-drab at rear. Small black bib on chin and upper throat. Breast white, sides of breast, flanks and vent pale grey-drab tinged pale pinkish-brown when very fresh; remainder of underparts, underwing-coverts and axillaries dirty white. *In worn plumage* (March–July), upperparts slightly paler and greyer, fringes to wing and tail feathers paler and greyer, but still no paler than upperparts. Cheeks and underparts dirty white, with pale drab-grey wash restricted to sides of breast and flanks. Bib slightly larger. **Bare Parts**: Iris dark brown to blackish-brown; bill horn-black to black with paler grey cutting edges; legs and feet blue-grey to dark slate-grey. **Juvenile**: As adult, but cap sooty-black, occasionally slightly tinged brown, with little or no gloss. Upperparts slightly greyer and paler, fringes to wing and tail feathers sometimes slightly washed rusty. Cheek patch whiter, with little or no drab wash at rear. Bib smaller and paler (dark grey or blackish-grey); on some birds, whitish tips partly obscure bib. Underparts purer white, with buff-grey or drab wash either absent or restricted to flanks and vent. **1st Adult**: See Sex/Age. **Measurements**: Wing of male 62.5–70, of female 60–65; tail of male 50–57, of female 48–55; bill 9.2–11; tarsus 15.9–17.5. Weight 8.9–15.0 g.

**MOULT** Adult post-breeding complete (mid May–mid September, duration *c.* 80 days). Post-juvenile partial, usually includes all greater coverts, occasionally a tertial and variable number of tail feathers (June–November). First pre-breeding partial?; some may replace the tail in late winter and spring.

**GEOGRAPHICAL VARIATION** Slight, with three groups of subspecies, differing mainly in proportions. The *palustris* group is found in Europe and the Caucasus, the *brevirostris* group in eastern Asia, and the *hellmayri* group in NE China. (Note that Black-bibbed Tit *P. hypermelaena* of China and Burma is often considered conspecific with Marsh Tit, forming a fourth group.)

**THE *PALUSTRIS* GROUP** West Palearctic. Distribution largely continuous and variation mainly clinal, with cline of decreasing size and increasing colour saturation running east to west. Another less well-marked cline of decreasing size and increasing colour saturation runs from central Europe south through Italy to Sicily. Many races have been described, based on tiny differences in colour and size, but only five are recognised here, the ends of the clines and the central, rather variable race, nominate *palustris*, but it may be preferable to recognise none at all (e.g. *stagnatilis* and *kabardensis* are included in nominate *palustris* by Stepanyan 1990).

**P. p. dresseri** England north to Lancashire and Yorkshire, and NW France (Bretagne, Anjou and Poitou). Intergrades with nominate *palustris* in Normandie, Touraine and the western border of the Massif Central. Relatively well marked. The smallest and darkest race in this group. Upperparts warm brown, slightly darker and less grey than nominate *palustris*, underparts slightly duller, creamy white or with slight buff wash, and sides of neck and breast, flanks and side of belly extensively washed pale buff-brown; averages slightly smaller. Wing of male 60–67.5, of female 59–63; tail of male 49–53, of female 46–52.

**P. p. palustris** Northern England, southern Scotland and Continental Europe east to central Poland, western Slovakia, western Hungary, the mountains of the south and east of former Yugoslavia, Bulgaria and Greece, south to central France and the Swiss and Austrian Alps. See Description.

**P. p. stagnatilis** Northern Turkey, European Russia, the plains of northern and eastern Yugoslavia and Bulgaria, and eastern Europe, east of nominate *palustris*. Possibly intergrades with *kabardensis* in NE Turkey or western Caucasus. Rather poorly marked. The largest and palest race in this group. As nominate *palustris*, but upperparts very slightly paler and buffer, and underparts slightly whiter with paler and less extensive cream-grey wash on sides of breast and flanks. Wing of male 65–70, of female 63–67; tail of male 51–56, of female 49–53.

**P. p. italicus** French Alps and Italy. Poorly marked. Upperparts intermediate between *dresseri* and nominate *palustris*, underparts also intermediate; in the south, both upper- and underparts have slight rufous tinge. Wing of male 59–67, of female 59–64; tail of male 51–55.

**P. p. kabardensis** ('*brandtii*') Northern Caucasus (range may be contiguous with populations in NE Turkey). Rather poorly marked. As nominate *palustris*, but upperparts slightly paler and greyer and cheeks and underparts whiter, with buff of flanks very restricted or absent; averages smaller. Coloration and relatively long tail close to *brevirostris* group, but also, apart from shorter wing, very close to *stagnatilis* of northern Asia Minor. Wing of male 62–66, of female 59–62.5; tail of male 54.5–57, of female 53–54.

**THE BREVIROSTRIS GROUP** East Palearctic. Relatively long-tailed.

**P. p. brevirostris** Siberia east through Mongolia to Amurland and Ussuriland, NE China south to

Liaoning, and Korea north of *c*. 40° N. As nominate *palustris*, but upperparts distinctly paler and greyer, little or no buff on underparts, and pale fringes on wing and tail feathers slightly more prominent (forming a slight pale panel on the closed wing). Wing 63–69; tail 60–67.5. Includes '*altaicus*' of the Krasnoyarsk region, Altai and western Sayan mountains, which is very slightly darker, as is '*crassirostris*' of eastern Amurland, Ussuriland, Korea, and NE China: wing 63–71; tail 57–69.

**P. p. ernsti** Sakhalin. As *brevirostris* but overall paler (upperparts ash-grey, lightly washed brown, rather than 'pale sandy-grey'), bib rather large, tail shorter (near *hensoni*). Wing of male 64–68, of female 60–65; tail of male 57–63, of female 55–60.

**P. p. hensoni** Southern Kurile islands and Hokkaido. Poorly marked. As *brevirostris* ('*crassirostris*'), but slightly paler on the upper- and underparts (i.e. as typical *brevirostris*?); also shorter-tailed (as *ernsti*, but darker). Wing 61–70; tail 53–65.

**THE HELLMAYRI GROUP** Recognised by Eck (1980a). Upperparts browner than in *brevirostris* group, underparts darker and buffer; bib tends to be smaller.

**P. p. hellmayri** NE China from Hebei south and west to Sichuan, and Korea south of *c*. 40° N. As *brevirostris*, but upperparts slightly darker and browner (drab-brown or sandy-brown, resembling nominate *palustris*), and underparts slightly buffer (off-white distinctly washed buff in fresh plumage; belly, vent and flanks buffer than nominate *palustris*, but quite whitish when worn); bib averages smaller. Relatively small (especially in the south). Those in Shanxi, Shaanxi and Sichuan differ slightly from the populations of NE China and Korea in being more heavily washed buff on the underparts and in having a slightly more extensive black bib. Wing of male 57–65, of female 55–63; tail of male 49–59, of female 45–58 (excluding '*jeholicus*'); weight 7–14 g. Includes '*jeholicus*' of northern Hebei (Chengde), which is slightly paler and larger: wing 60–67.5, of male 62–66.5, of female 60–64; tail 56.5–67, of male 63–67, of female 62–65 (Cramp & Perrins 1993; Hartert & Steinbacher 1933).

**HYBRIDS** A mixed pair of male Willow x female Marsh Tits was noted in Belgium in two successive years, in an area where Marsh Tit is rare but Willow Tit regular. It fledged five young in the first year, and the nest and young resembled those of Marsh Tit (Dhondt & Hublé 1969). A presumed Marsh x Great Tit hybrid was recorded in France in 1993 (Duquet 1995).

**RELATIONSHIPS** A member of the subgenus *Poecile*, and forms a superspecies with Black-bibbed Tit of eastern Asia; indeed, the two are so closely similar that they are often considered conspecific (see p. 244 for details).

**REFERENCES** Cramp & Perrins (1993), J. R. King (1990), Stepanyan (1990), Vaurie (1959), Witherby *et al.* (1938).

Closely related to Marsh Tit, this enigmatic bird has caused confusion ever since it was first described, having been associated with the crested tits and with Willow Tit, before eventually coming to rest in the Marsh Tit superspecies.

**IDENTIFICATION** Length 115 mm (4.5 in). Cap glossy black, extending onto the centre of the upper mantle, with the feathers of the nape elongated to form a shaggy peak to the hindcrown. Upperparts brownish-olive, slightly more ochre on the rump. Wings and tail dark brownish-grey, with no obvious pale fringes to the flight feathers. Cheek patch dirty whitish, bib sooty-black, extending onto the upper breast (even in fresh plumage) and poorly defined along the lower border, with the remainder of the underparts dirty white, heavily washed greyish olive-brown. In worn summer plumage, the cap is duller and the underparts whiter, although still dingy, washed grey on the breast and belly. In Burma, this is the only black-capped tit lacking wingbars, a pale nuchal patch or rufous or buff on the underparts, making identification straightforward. In much of western China, however, it needs to be carefully distinguished from Songar and Marsh Tits, especially in view of the considerable uncertainties regarding its precise distribution and specific status. In size and shape very similar to Marsh Tit, although proportionally shorter-tailed. In fresh plumage the upperparts are rather duller, with a distinct greenish-olive tone, rather than a warm drab-brown or sandy-brown wash; worn adult Black-bibbed are, however, greyer brown, lacking the olive tones, and juveniles are warmer brown on the upperparts. Sometimes shows a short, rather ragged crest, although this may be inconspicuous, and the cap is more extensive than in Marsh Tit, extending further onto the mantle. The cheek patch is more extensive at the rear, being 'fluffy' and 'swept up' onto the sides of the nape. Importantly, the bib is much more extensive, reaching onto the upper breast; in extent it resembles a Coal Tit's and, even in fresh plumage, is not confined to the chin and upper throat as on fresh Marsh Tits (the cheek patches therefore appear more 'enclosed' than on Marsh). In worn plumage, however, Marsh Tit's bib is more extensive, and may even approach Black-bibbed's in size when very worn in the summer. The underparts are much duller, extensively washed a deep greyish olive-brown rather than light drab or buff, and although both species wear whiter on the underparts Black-bibbed remains dingier, and the dull underparts make the whitish cheeks more prominent (juvenile Black-bibbed are, however, rather buff on the underparts). The wings and tail are rather plain, lacking pale fringes to the flight feathers or outer tail feathers; even in worn plumage, Marsh Tits show clearly paler fringes to the flight feathers and a distinct pale grey outer web to the outer tail feather, although juvenile Black-bibbed, too, shows a fine whitish fringe to the outer tail feathers. In the hand, the wing and tail measurements are a valuable identification feature, Black-bibbed being relatively short-tailed compared with Marsh Tit, with a tail/wing ratio of 76–82%, compared with 80–90% in Marsh Tits (*P. p. hellmayri*; birds with heavily worn tails should be treated with caution). The tail is also square-ended, T6 being no more than 1.5 mm shorter than T1 (Dresser & Delmar Morgan 1899). Separated from Songar Tit by the glossy blue-black cap (rather than dark olive-brown or dull brownish-black), brownish-olive upperparts (rather than cinnamon-brown or drab-brown), slightly blacker bib and greyish olive-brown wash to the underparts (rather than cinnamon-brown), and square-ended, not rounded, tail; also averages slightly smaller.

**SEX/AGE** Sexes similar. Juvenile distinct, with the cap sooty-brown and much more restricted, the upperparts warmer brown (less olive), the cheek patches tinged yellow-buff, the bib smaller and the underparts paler, heavily washed yellow-buff. 1st adult as adult, but retains juvenile wing and tail feathers, the latter narrower and more pointed than the adults', and relatively worn compared with an adult at a similar time of year (see Marsh Tit).

**VOICE** Very poorly known. Calls include a high, thin *stip*, thin *si-si* and explosive *psiup*, the latter often combined in a rapid 'pitchuu' phrase, *si-si psiup* (similar to Marsh Tit). Also gives a chattering *chrrrrr* and scolding *chay*.

**DISTRIBUTION AND MOVEMENTS** Breeds in western **China** in southern **Gansu**, NW **Hubei**, and in SW **Sichuan** north to Batang, Litang and Kangding, northeast to Emei Shan and south to Muli. Vaurie (1959) states that it probably occurs in NW Sichuan, connecting the population of Gansu with those of SW Sichuan, Yunnan and SE Tibet. Found in extreme western **Guizhou** in the Wumeng Shan (west and southwest of Weining), and in Tuoda forest (60 km northwest of Weining; Zhikang *et al.* 1994). In **Yunnan** occurs from Deqen and Lijiang south to about Xiaguan. Status in **China** otherwise problematic. The species was described from **Shaanxi**, near the borders with Gansu and Sichuan (Dresser & Delmar Morgan 1899), and Cheng (1973, 1987) lists it for the Qin Ling mountains of southern Shaanxi, although Vaurie (1959) specifically states that it does not occur further east than the Shaanxi/Gansu border, being replaced in the Qin Ling by Marsh Tit (and, indeed, birds examined from Mei Xian and Hu Xian on the northern borders of the Qin Ling Shan are Marsh Tits). The occurrence of the species in the Qin Ling Shan needs confirmation. For SE **Tibet** Zheng *et al.* (1983) list records from Zayu (August), Jomda (August) and Markam (September), and this is presumably the basis for the inclusion of these localities in Cheng (1987); available measurements suggest, however, that

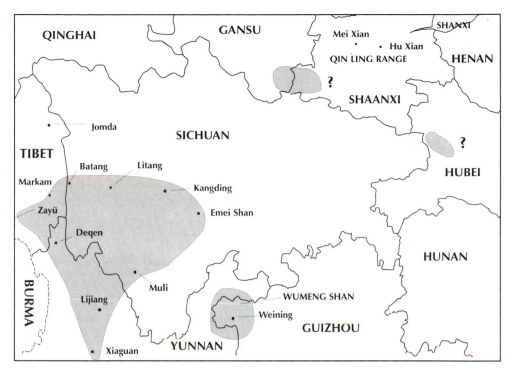

*Figure 47.1 Approximate distribution of Black-bibbed Tit in west and central China, together with some localities mentioned in text. (Note that the species also occurs in SW Burma.)*

none of these are referable to Black-bibbed Tit (tail/wing ratio *c.* 84%, 92% and 91%). Also, a worn adult male was reported to have been collected at 3960 m in July in the Yigrong range, Kongbo, at Penam Chu, with the comment that it was possibly Black-bibbed, although the bill seems large and the head lacks lustre, although the seemingly large bill and glossless head may be due to featherwear (Ludlow 1951); examination of this bird shows it to be a Songar Tit. In **Myanmar (Burma)** known only from the north Chin hills (Smythies 1986) and Mount Victoria. May occur in NE Burma, as Baker (1922) gives a record of a bird from near Maymyo 'in the Kachin Hills'. Wickham (1929), however, states that, 'to correct the Fauna, Maymyo is in the Shan Hills, not Kachin Hills, but I cannot find the record and Maymyo should perhaps be read as Bhamo'. Yet again, a mystery. Resident.

**HABITAT** In SW China found in conifers, usually rather dry pine forest, specifically in Yunnan in open forest of regenerating pines with an evergreen shrub layer (although Greenway 1933 notes birds from spruce, fir and rhododendron in NW Yunnan); at Batang, Sichuan found only in the deep Yangtze gorge, not ascending into mixed forest at higher altitudes (Dolan 1938), and recorded on the high plateau with conifers. In the Qin Ling mountains of southern Shaanxi found in summer in broadleaved forest in the foothills, usually near streams or paths, dispersing to the plains in winter (but see above)(Cheng 1973). Recorded in Yunnan at 2750–4270 m, in NW Hubei at 1525–2135 m in

the winter and spring, in Sichuan at 2600–3960 m, in Guizhou at 2200–2500 m (breeding recorded at 2350 m), and in SE Tibet at 3000 m (but see above on the identity of these birds). On Mount Victoria, SW Burma, confined to pine forest in the alpine zone from 2200 m to the summit at *c.* 3000 m.

**POPULATION** Rare in Sichuan, but locally fairly common in Yunnan. Common in the north Chin hills, Burma (Smythies 1986).

**HABITS** Poorly known. Found singly or in flocks of 3–5. Forages in the mid storey and canopy of regenerating pine forest in Yunnan, also low down in scrubs and saplings. Food insects and berries.

**BREEDING BIOLOGY** On Mount Victoria, a nest was found at the edge of pine forest in a young tree that was broken off 8 m above the ground; the trunk was hollow and the upper part of the cavity formed the nest chamber, the entrance being at the point of fracture. The young were almost fledged on 19 April. Further north in the Chin hills, a record of fledglings being fed in April. A nest found in Guizhou (on 29 May), in a wall, was constructed from rootlets and hair and contained 6 eggs, white with purplish specks, *c.* 17.9 x 13.1 mm (Wu *et al.* 1986).

**DESCRIPTION** **Adult**: *In fresh plumage* (October onwards), crown (down to middle of eye) and nape black with a slight blue gloss, feathers of nape slightly elongated to form a short crest. Centre of upper mantle black, lower mantle, scapulars and back brownish-olive, rump slightly more ochre. Tail dark brownish-grey, T1–T5 finely fringed brownish-olive. Wing-coverts dark brown-

243

ish-grey, fringed brownish-olive. Alula and primary coverts blackish-grey, primary coverts finely fringed brownish-olive. Flight feathers dark brownish-grey, tertials and secondaries fringed brownish-olive, rather narrowly so on the tertials, inner primaries more narrowly fringed paler greyish-olive, only inwards of emarginations on P3–P6. Cheeks, ear-coverts and sides of neck dull whitish, longer feathers at rear tipped brownish-olive. Chin, throat and upper breast sooty-black, extending onto upper flanks, feathers of lower border tipped whitish (thus lower border of bib ill-defined); remainder of underparts dirty white, heavily washed greyish olive-brown, especially on flanks, belly, vent and undertail-coverts. Axillaries buff-white, underwing-coverts whitish. *In worn plumage,* cap duller and very slightly browner, lacking blue gloss, upperparts slightly greyer and less olive, brownish-olive fringes on wings and tail abraded, bib slightly duller, greyer and less extensive (not extending onto sides of breast), and underparts whiter, but dingy and rather greyish on breast and belly. **Bare parts**: Iris brown to dark brown; bill black with paler cutting edges; legs and feet lead-grey to black. **Juvenile**: Cap dark brownish-olive, lacking any gloss and not extending onto upper mantle. Upperparts greyish cinnamon-brown, rump slightly warmer and paler with no olive tinge. Tail as adult, but T1–T5 fringed olive, more broadly and less well defined than on adult, and T6 finely fringed off-white. Wings as adult, but fringes olive (as upperparts but slightly more olive). Cheeks white, tinged yellow-buff, curving up at rear of cap to form half-collar. Chin and throat mid grey, tinged brown. Underparts whitish, heavily washed yellow-buff. **1st Adult**: See Sex/Age. **Measurements**: Wing 55–71, of male 57–68.5, of female 55–64.3; tail of male 42.5–60, of female 44.5–53; bill 9–11; tarsus 14–16.5. Weight 9–11.5 g.

**MOULT** No information.

**GEOGRAPHICAL VARIATION** Poorly understood, but slight or absent and no subspecies are recognised. The original description of *hypermelaena* was based on a bird from southern Shaanxi, and Cheng (1987) gives the range of this form as southern Gansu, southern Shaanxi and Hubei, separating it from *P. h. dejeani* of Sichuan, Guizhou, Yunnan and SE Tibet. According to Hartert (1903–10), *dejeani* is barely distinguishable, being slightly larger, with the flanks somewhat more rusty and the upperparts also apparently slightly more olive-brownish, but his material was limited. Cheng (1973) and Zheng *et al.* (1983) report that birds from southern Shaanxi have a

glossy black cap, compared with the duller, greyer and more blackish-brown crown of *dejeani* from Yunnan and SE Tibet, and those in SE Tibet also have a larger bib. The disjunct population in SW Burma may represent another subspecies. Compared with birds from Sichuan and northern Yunnan, the crown feathers of Mount Victoria birds are reported to be somewhat shorter, and thus the black of the crown more restricted (Stresemann & Heinrich 1940; Vaurie 1957b). The Mount Victoria specimens, however, were in worn plumage and of five adults examined, all worn, four have the black of the crown as extensive as three adults from Yunnan (the fifth is missing feathers from the nape). The upperpart coloration is the same, but the bib may average slightly smaller, with much more extensive whitish tips, especially on the lower border and at the sides.

**RELATIONSHIPS** Often considered conspecific with Marsh Tit (as *P. palustris hypermelaena*), but in view of the general similarity of all races of Marsh Tit to one another (despite a disjunct distribution ranging from England to Japan), and the dissimilarity of the Black-bibbed Tit, it seems best to separate it (as done, for example, by Stresemann & Heinrich 1940). In western China no intermediates appear to have been recorded, although in Shaanxi Marsh Tit *P. p. hellmayri* has been collected at Hsu-hsien (= Hu Xian), *c.* 160 km from where the type of *hypermelaena* was collected (Snow 1957). Marsh Tits examined from Shaanxi are typical in having warm brown upperparts and a tail/wing ratio of 83–89%, although differing slightly from the populations of NE China and Korea in being more heavily washed buff on the underparts and in having a slightly more exten-sive black bib. This may indicate some intergradation with Black-bibbed Tit, or alternatively the presence of both species so close together may indicate that they overlap without hybridising (resulting in the confusion over the range in Shaanxi: see Distribution and Movements), a point that can be elucidated only by field studies. In Sichuan, Marsh Tit (*P. p. hellmayri*) has been collected at Chin-chien-san (presumably in the lowlands of the east or centre) and Black-bibbed has been collected in the west of the province (Snow 1957). Thus, again, the two may be reproductively isolated, and Black-bibbed may replace Marsh at higher altitudes. Pending further investigation, I prefer to separate them as distinct species (although they are 'lumped' by Sibley & Monroe 1990).

**REFERENCES** Dresser & Delmar Morgan (1899), Stresemann (1940), Zhikang *et al.* (1986).

This dull tit is confined to SE Europe and SW Asia, and, unusually for a tit, it may be shy, retiring and unsociable.

**IDENTIFICATION** Length 140 mm (5.5 in). A large, strong-billed tit. The cap and bib vary from grey-brown to black, encompassing rather narrow pure white cheek patches. The upperparts range from cinnamon-brown to pale sandy-grey, often showing a slightly paler wing panel, and the underparts are white, washed drab-grey on the flanks. The plumage varies geographically, with the most contrast between the cap and upperparts in Iranian birds and the least in European populations. The large size and drab plumage, together with habitat and distribution, are distinctive. Confusion is possible with Marsh and Willow Tits, but Sombre Tit is rather larger, with a heavy, powerful bill, more extensive and usually duller dark cap (which extends marginally below the eye), large dark bib, narrower and more wedge-shaped cheek patches, and drab-grey flanks, lacking any cinnamon or buff tones. Juveniles are duller than adults and may resemble dull juvenile Great Tits, but can be easily distinguished by their lack of a dark ventral stripe. For separation from Caspian Tit, see that species.

**SEX/AGE** Sexes rather similar, differing in the colour of the cap, which in Europe is sooty-brown in the male and variable in the female, sometimes dark grey-brown, barely contrasting with the mantle, but at other times blackish-brown and almost as dark as the male's. The female's bib is similarly brown or grey-brown, rather than sooty-black. In Asia Minor and the Levant, the cap is blackish in the male and sooty-brown in the female, while in Iran the sexes are less distinct, both having a black cap, although the female's may be faintly tinged brown. Juveniles are variably distinct, differing from adults in the colour of the cap and bib. In Europe, the cap is only slightly browner than the adult female's, but the bib is small, pale and ill-defined. In Turkey and the Levant, juveniles are very different from the adult female, with a rather browner cap and a much paler, less extensive and poorly demarcated bib. In Iran, juveniles have a more restricted and browner cap than the adults' and a browner bib, and their upperparts are rather darker (but compared with juveniles from Turkey their cap and bib are darker and better defined, the bib also being slightly more extensive). The 1st adult resembles the adult, but cap and bib are slightly duller and retains the juvenile flight feathers, tertials, primary coverts, a variable number of tail feathers and occasionally the outer greater coverts. Ageing is possible in the hand during the autumn and winter, when adults are either completing the post-breeding moult or in fresh plumage, with glossy, dark grey flight feathers. On 1st adults, the retained juvenile feathers are slightly browner and less glossy, becoming worn dull brown-grey from October onwards; additionally, the tips of the primary coverts and tail feathers are narrower and more pointed than on the adult, and

are abraded from October onwards (the adult's remain fresh until about March).

**VOICE** The contact call is a thin, silvery *si* or *zee*, given singly or in groups of up to seven notes, the series characteristically falling in pitch in a delicate cadence, *si-si-si-si-si-si* (it may recall Long-tailed Tit). Sometimes, such series terminate in a short chatter, e.g. *tsi'si'si'si'si'si'si'trrrr* (the chatter as described below but generally a little quieter; this phrase may recall Blue Tit's scold). Also gives a harder *sit* or *chit* note in rattling, machine-gun-like bursts of 4–6 units, *chit'cht'cht'cht'cht'cht*, and such phrases are often introduced by one or more thinner, silvery *si* notes, e.g. *tis's'sit'cht'cht'cht'cht'cht*. Other calls include *tsi-tsi-tsi-zee* (the *zee* being a 'Broken D': see Black-capped Chickadee, p. 268), of unknown function. At low levels of excitement gives a single sharp *chip* or *chit*, and in greater alarm or agitation gives a characteristic loud, deep, chattering and rather sparrow-like *trrrrrrrr* or *chrrrrrrr*, comprising a *chit*-type call repeated initially very rapidly and then settling at a rate of 10–12 per second (the individual units are indistinguishable). The chatter contains 7–34 units, and is thus sometimes prolonged, lasting *c.* 3 seconds. It is usually preceded by a higher-pitched, buzzing, insect-like phrase of 3–8 units, *tiz'ze'ze'ze...* (recalling a grasshopper or even a River Warbler's song), thus *tiz'ze'ze'ze'ze'ze'ze-trrrrrrr* or *tsit'zit'zit-chrrrrrrr*. This grasshopper-like phrase may also be given alone, *tzi-zi-zi-zi-zit*. (Further study may reveal that the *si*, *chip* and *tiz* notes are components of a 'chick-a-dee' system.) The song is constructed from motifs comprising 1–3 syllables, repeated 2–7 (2–13) times, after which the motif may be changed. This pattern recalls the 'tea-cher' song of Great Tit, and the song is perhaps equally variable, but Sombre Tit's motifs are characteristically low-pitched (they may even recall a bulbul), strident, and often slightly hoarse, grating, buzzing or 'gruff': e.g. *chiz-ze*, *chiz-ze*, *ribit-ribit-ribit*, *chuvi-chuvi...*, or *choi-choi-choi-choi*. The motifs may be more metallic, e.g. *tszuu-zuu-zuu*; hissing, e.g. *wuisst-wuisst...*; buzzing, e.g. *chizit-dzu*, *chizit-dzu*; or slightly more complex, with the introductory motif a little different from those that follow, e.g. *wuchit-chudi'chudi'chudi'chudi* or *chuvi-vi-vi-vi-vi-vi*. Sometimes, motifs may be rapidly switched in a complex burst of song in which several motifs may be combined, e.g. *chiz-za chiz-za*, *zurrr-ribit*, *chreep*, *zurrr-ribit*, *chut-zi-tu*, *zurrr-ribit*, *chizit-dzu chizit-dzu chizit-dzu*.

**DISTRIBUTION AND MOVEMENTS** In Europe, found in south-central **Romania** in the Carpathians, SW and southern **Bulgaria**, with scattered records from eastern Bulgaria, the south and west of former **Yugoslavia** (north in the west to the Italian border), **Greece**, including the Peloponnisos peninsula, Evvoia, Thasos, **Crete**

and Lesbos, and **European Turkey**. In Asiatic **Turkey** widespread in western Anatolia and the south coast region, extending more locally across the remainder of the country, although apparently absent from much of the arid lowlands of the southeast (between Birecik and Sirnak, and north to about Bingöl), from most of the central plateau and from the high mountains of the east; in much of eastern Turkey may be confined to the river valleys, e.g. the Coruh valley, and presumably extends along these valleys into **Georgia**, where recorded from the Black Sea coast around Batumi, and also in southernmost **Armenia** around Megri and in extreme SW **Azerbaydzhan** at Zangelan (Wunderlich 1982). To the south, recorded sparsely in western **Syria**, where 'not uncommon' in pine forests below Saraya in May 1945 (Kumerloeve 1967–69) and recorded from the Qatana region (Macfarlane 1978). Also breeds in the **Lebanon** and on Mount Hermon in northern **Israel**. Found in western **Iran** in the Zagros mountains from around Saqqez south to Neyriz in Fars province, with a disjunct population in southern Iran in the mountains of Kerman province, south of Kerman and the Kuh-e-Jebal Barez; also breeds very locally in northern Iranian Azarbaijan in the Kaleybar (Kalibar) mountains. Recorded in NE **Iraq** in the foothills of the Zagros mountains (Dahuk, Rawandiz, Diyala lake), and presumably breeds in these areas, although possibly only a winter visitor. (Although frequently mapped for **Hungary**, no authenticated records for that country.) Accidental northern **Italy** (six records). Resident and strictly sedentary, although there is some evidence of altitudinal movements in the Zagros mountains and Israel, and may wander in autumn and winter to central Turkey. In Israel, apparently commoner in winter than in summer on Mount Hermon, suggesting some immigration, and also recorded from Mount Golan in winter 1988/89, Jerusalem in winter 1944 and Sarid in April 1945 (Hovel 1987).

**HABITAT** Essentially a bird of maquis-type habitats of scattered trees and bushes, especially olive and other fruit trees, scrub oak (especially relict woodland of Downy Oak), cedars and pines, on dry, rocky, boulder-strewn slopes, often intermixed with scattered areas of cultivation. Also open forest of oak, beech, cedar and pine, olive groves, riverside willows and poplars, orchards, vineyards and parks, and in southern Iran Almond-pistachio woodlands. Occurs at 700–2000 m in the Peloponnisos of southern Greece, up to 2100 m (sometimes 2300 m) in Turkey, at 800–1000 m in NW Iran, at 1250–2400 m in the Zagros mountains and 1900–2800 m in Kerman province, and at 750–1700 m (down to 600–900 m in winter) on Mount Hermon in northern Israel. There may be some dispersal into rocky, treeless areas at higher altitudes.

**POPULATION** Generally uncommon and local, although fairly common in western Turkey and common in the Zagros mountains and Kerman, Iran. Common but local in northern Israel, with an estimated 50–80 pairs on Mount Hermon in the 1970s–80s. Rather scarce in NW Iran, rare and sporadic in western Georgia and the Transcaucasus in Armenia and Azerbaydzhan, and scarce or rare in the Lebanon. Evidence of a substantial decline in Bulgaria, where noted as common and widespread in the 19th century (Mountfort & Ferguson-Lees 1961). Conversely, may have recently spread north in Transylvania, Romania.

**HABITS** Less gregarious than many tits; usually found in pairs and sometimes solitary in winter, although also gathers in loosely associated groups in the autumn and winter, occasionally with other tits. May be shy. Forages largely on the lower branches of trees and in the shrub layer, and sometimes on the ground, but always returns to the nearest branch with items of food. Also feeds on the seed heads of herbs, among buds, on thick branches, and climbs tree trunks like a nuthatch; may also flycatch. Generally, however, less volatile and acrobatic than other tits. Food insects and seeds, and will store food items.

**BREEDING BIOLOGY** Season March–July, depending on latitude, and towards the end of this period at higher altitudes. The nest is placed in a hole in a tree, often a fruit tree, in rotton wood; observations scanty, but no clear evidence that the species excavates its own nest hole. Less frequently, nests are placed among rocks or on rocky banks, up to at least 7 m above ground; will use nestboxes. The cup of wool and plant material is lined with feathers. Clutch 5–7 (4–10): eggs white, finely speckled reddish; 17 x 13.5 mm. Female incubates, period 12–14 days, and both sexes feed the young, which fledge after 22 (17–22) days. In some years, up to c. 20% of pairs may be double-brooded (and two broods frequent in Israel).

**DESCRIPTION** *P. l. lugubris* **Adult Male**: *In fresh plumage* (late August–March), crown (to lower border of eye) and nape sooty-brown, poorly demarcated from the remainder of the upperparts, which are dark drab-brown, tinged cinnamon. Tail dark grey-brown, outer webs fringed pale olive-grey, fringes narrower and almost white on T6. Wing-coverts as upperparts, greater coverts fringed pale grey-brown to off-white. Alula dark grey-brown. Tertials dark grey-brown, broadly fringed and tipped pale olive-grey to off-white. Primary coverts, primaries and secondaries dark grey, inner secondaries fringed pale drab-grey, becoming paler and narrower towards inner primaries and almost white (and inwards of emarginations only) on P3–P7. Cheeks, ear-coverts and sides of neck white, longest ear-coverts tipped cinnamon-drab. Chin, throat and lower cheeks sooty-black, feathers tipped whitish, especially on lower cheek and lower throat (border of bib ill-defined). Underparts whitish, lightly washed grey, sides of breast cinnamon-drab, merging with paler drab-grey flanks. Underwing-coverts and axillaries whitish. *In worn plumage* (April–July), cap slightly duller and browner, upperparts duller and greyer, pale fringes on tail and flight feathers partly abraded, bib grey-brown, sharply defined at rear, underparts paler, more dirty white, and flanks paler. **Bare Parts**: Iris brown to dark brown; bill dark horn-grey to blackish-horn, cutting edges pale blue-grey or whitish; legs and feet dark grey to bluish slate-grey. **Adult Female**: As male, but cap varies from dark grey-brown, sometimes barely contrasting with the mantle, to blackish-brown, almost as dark as male's. Bib brown or grey-brown rather than blackish, underparts with more pronounced pale drab-grey wash. In worn plumage, cap sometimes sepia-brown, bib paler grey-brown, underparts dirty-white. **Juvenile**: Close to adult female, but cap dark brown or dark grey-brown, not contrasting with dark cinnamon-brown upperparts. Innermost greater coverts fringed greyish-pink, all greater coverts tipped dirty white on outer web. Cheek patch white, extensively washed brown on sides of neck. Bib smaller than on adult, grey-brown with grey-buff (not white) feather tips when fresh; underparts washed pinkish-buff or creamy-buff, vent dirty white, some dark grey feather bases shining through. In worn plumage (at *c.* 2–3 months), cap grey-brown or sepia-brown, mantle and scapulars greyish-drab-brown, cheek patch and underparts whiter, bib grey-brown. **1st Adult**: As adult (but see Sex/Age). Sexes similar in autumn, but by spring the female's cap is browner than the male's. **Measurements**: Wing of male 68–80, of female 69–75; tail of male 58–68, of female 55–63; bill 11.4–13.5; tarsus 19.1–21.2. Weight 16–19 g.

**MOULT** Adult post-breeding complete (late May–early September). Post-juvenile partial, usually includes all greater coverts and a variable number of tail feathers (late June–September).

**GEOGRAPHICAL VARIATION** Moderate. Two groups of subspecies, differing in tail/wing ratio: the western *lugubris* group with the wing relatively short and the tail long, and the *dubius* group in Iran. Four subspecies recognised (note that the form *hyrcanus*, sometimes treated as a race of Sombre Tit, is here considered a separate species, Caspian Tit).

### THE *LUGUBRIS* GROUP

**P. l. lugubris** Europe south to Greece, and presumably this race on Crete. Intergrades with *anatoliae* in NE Greece and European Turkey. See Description. Three clines are detectable in Europe: (i) decreasing size from north to south; (ii) cap and bib become paler from north/east to south; (iii) upperparts become paler from west to east. In addition, most populations are rather variable in coloration. Three races are sometimes recognised in Europe: '*lugubris*' in Yugoslavia, Albania and NW Greece; '*splendens*' in eastern Romania and eastern Bulgaria; and '*lugens*' in southern Greece (Mount Olimbos to Peloponnisos). The extremes, '*lugens*' (small, cap and bib of male dark sooty brown-grey, of female paler dark grey-brown) and '*splendens*' (large, greyer upperparts and whiter underparts) are readily separable from each other, but neither is easy to separate from '*lugubris*' (intermediate size, cap of male blackish-brown or dark sooty-brown, of female slightly greyer black-brown or dark chocolate-brown).

**P. l. anatoliae** Lesbos (Greece), Turkey, western Georgia, southern Armenia and SW Azerbaydzhan, the Levant, northern Iraq and NW Iran. Probably intergrades with *dubius* around the extreme NW Zagros and into NE Iraq and SE Turkey. As nominate *lugubris,* but the mantle and scapulars average slightly greyer and less cinnamon, dark drab-grey when fresh, dark grey when worn, and the underparts are whiter, with the flanks washed cinnamon when fresh. The cap and bib average darker and better defined: black in the male, only occasionally tinged brown; and black-brown or sooty-brown in the female, often no darker than in male *lugubris* but still better defined. Juvenile has cap drab-brown, slightly darker than mantle and scapulars, bib mid grey-brown; cap and bib poorly defined. Wing of male 68–75, of female 68–73; tail of male 57–64; bill 11.3–12.8.

### THE *DUBIUS* GROUP

**P. l. dubius** Western Iran in the Zagros mountains; recorded in winter in NE Iraq in the Zagros foothills. Male with cap and bib sharply defined, velvet-black, female with cap very slightly tinged brown (still slightly blacker than in *anatoliae*). Upperparts pale drab-grey or pale sandy-grey, much paler than *anatoliae*, underparts whitish with slight creamy wash. Bill long and slender, not so heavy as in other races. Juvenile has upperparts rather darker than adult; cap not so extensive, dark brown (not black), as bib. Compared with juvenile *anatoliae*, cap and bib darker and better defined and bib slightly more extensive, otherwise similar (thus quite similar to adult female *lugubris* in bib and cap coloration, but upperparts slightly paler and rather greyer). Wing of male 69–78, of female 71–74; tail of male 54–63, of female 57–60; bill 12–14.

**P. l. kirmanensis** Southern Iran in the isolated mountain ranges of Kerman province. Poorly marked. As *dubius*, but upperparts average slightly darker and browner. Large: wing of male 75–78, of female 71–76; tail of male 57–64, of female 57–61; bill 12.5–14.

**RELATIONSHIPS** A member of the large *Poecile* subgenus. Placed in the same species as Père David's Tit of SW China, largely on the basis of proportions, by Eck (1980a, 1988). Eck also separates Sombre Tit into three further 'Complexes', the *lugubris* group and the *dubius* group, together with the *hyrcanus* group, which I treat as a distinct species, Caspian Tit (see p. 249).

**REFERENCES** Cramp & Perrins (1993), Vaurie (1950a, 1959), Wunderlich (1982).

Other name: Hyrcanian Tit

Often treated as a race of Sombre Tit, work by Russian ornithologists has shown that this tit from the montane forests of northern Iran is a distinct species, perhaps more closely allied to Willow and Songar Tits.

**IDENTIFICATION** Length 125 mm (5 in). Cap dark brown, extending broadly onto the upper mantle; remainder of upperparts dull cinnamon-brown, with the outer tail feathers narrowly fringed whitish and the flight feathers fringed pale grey. Large white cheek patches and a large sooty-brown bib (darker than the cap), ill-defined on the lower border. Underparts pale pinkish-buff. In worn plumage, the fringes to the greater coverts and tertials are bleached paler, the bib is better defined, and the underparts are off-white. Resembles a small, heavy-billed and proportionally short-tailed Sombre Tit, but easily distinguished from the Iranian races of the latter, which have a black cap and bib, by the rather more extensive brown cap and less well-defined sooty-brown bib. Additionally, the upperparts are darker and browner, lacking pale fringes to the tertials and, in fresh plumage, the underparts have a pronounced pinkish-buff wash. Juvenile Sombre Tits are rather more similar in appearance, but Caspian Tit has a more extensive cap, slightly darker upperparts and a darker but less-defined bib. Caspian Tit is closer in appearance to the race *anatoliae* of Sombre Tit, which occurs in Armenia, SW Azerbaydzhan, and also in NW Iran, although not in the same areas as Caspian Tit (but the ranges are separated by only *c.* 140 km). The two have similar upperpart coloration, and the cap of Caspian Tit is only slightly browner than on some female *anatoliae*, although still more extensive, whilst the bib is slightly browner, with a less well-defined lower border. The underparts, when fresh, differ as above. Juveniles are even closer to juvenile *anatoliae*, but note the more extensive cap and rather darker and less 'ghostly' bib.

**SEX/AGE** Sexes similar, although the cap and the bib of the female are slightly paler. Juvenile distinct, with a duller brown cap, broad cinnamon-buff fringes to the secondaries (rather than narrow grey-white fringes), a slightly smaller bib and, most noticeably, only a faint buff wash to the off-white underparts, but note that worn adults have similarly pale underparts, although the fresh fringes to the juvenile's greater coverts and tertials are cinnamon, rather than bleached pale grey-brown or off-white as in such worn adults. In the hand, the juvenile's tail feathers are narrower and more pointed. No information on 1st adults.

**VOICE** Generally rather silent. Calls include a thin *tsi* or *tsit*, and the alarm call is a full, abrupt and rather short, nasal *chev* or *tshet*, repeated several times in an irregular rhythm, *chev-chev, chev-chev-chev...*, sometimes for prolonged periods (sonagraphic analysis reveals that this is a 'Broken D': see Black-capped Chickadee, p. 268). Song a clear, sonorous and slightly attenuated *tiu*, repeated 3–5 times, with pauses of 5–7 seconds between songs (very similar to the songs of Willow and Songar Tits). Song is given from the top of a tree or bush, but males seldom sing, typically for just 1–2 minutes per hour, and song ceases once the female begins to incubate (Loskot 1982, 1987).

**DISTRIBUTION AND MOVEMENTS** Northern **Iran** on the northern slopes of the Elburz mountains in Gilan and Mazandaran provinces, east to Golestan NP (near Tangar) and presumably further east, to the limits of the Caspian forest (*c.* 40 km north of Dasht). Extends marginally into SE **Azerbaydzhan** (former USSR), in the Talyshskiye Gory range of Lenkoran district. Largely sedentary, but some evidence of post-breeding dispersal, with a juvenile recorded in the 'Diabar Basin', far from any forest (Loskot 1987), and some withdrawal to lower altitudes in winter. Exceptionally recorded away from the Elburz, with four birds in December in a tiny, isolated patch of forest at Dasht-e Naz Wildlife Park (12 m below sea level in the SE Caspian littoral, Mazandaran), and a single bird in gardens in Tehran in January (D. Scott pers. comm.).

**HABITAT** Well-watered deciduous montane forest. In Elburz mountains of Iran recorded at 400–2200 m, whilst in Azerbaydzhan found in 'middle' montane forest at 550–1100 m and 'higher' montane forest at 1100–1500 m (and absent from lower levels, which even wandering juveniles shun). In middle montane forest favours open woodland of Hornbeam, oak and maple, with a rich shrub layer, and within this habitat favours forest edge, clearings and the breaks along paths and roads. In higher montane forest found in areas of open, partially degraded woodland where extensive bushy thickets and grazed clearings form a mosaic with sparse stunted trees, largely beech, Hornbeam and oak, which have been lopped for firewood.

**POPULATION** Quite scarce and hard to find in Iran, and occurs at low densities in the middle montane forests of Azerbaydzhan, with pairs irregularly distributed 0.3–2 km apart. Relatively numerous in the upper montane forest, however, with four pairs recorded from 20 ha, with nests 90 m, 140 m and 230 m apart.

**HABITS** Usually found in pairs. Generally remains in the vicinity of the nest during the breeding season and territorial conflicts are rare, with little 'trespassing'. During the breeding season, the female roosts on the nest. Forages among the crowns of trees and also in shrubs on the forest edge, carefully investigating the thinner branches and twigs, rather than the trunks and branches, and readily descends to the ground (although less frequently than Sombre Tit). Food insects, also small molluscs and seeds.

**BREEDING BIOLOGY** In SE Azerbaydzhan,

nest-building begins in mid March at lower elevations and at the end of April at higher altitudes. All 11 nests found by Loskot had been excavated by the birds themselves, both sexes working in regular shifts, debris being carried 7–25 m from the hole and crumbled, leaving no traces. Nest a base of bark chips, hair, wool and plant fibres, lined with a cup of hairs and fibres, occasionally a few feathers; built by the female. Clutch 5–7 (4–7): eggs white, sometimes faintly spotted and blotched rufous-brown, especially at the larger end; 16.9 x 12.8 mm. Female incubates, period 13–14 days, and is fed on the nest by the male. The young are fed by both sexes (Loskot 1987).

**DESCRIPTION Adult**: *In fresh plumage* (autumn and winter) crown (to lower border of eye), nape and upper mantle dark brown, faintly tinged pink. Remainder of upperparts drab-brown, tinged cinnamon. Tail dark grey-brown, outer webs fringed pale olive-grey, fringes narrower and almost white on T5–T6. Wings dark grey-brown, lesser and median coverts fringed drab-brown, greater coverts and tertials broadly fringed pale pinkish-cinnamon, primary coverts finely fringed dark drab, secondaries and inner primaries fringed grey-white, more narrowly so distally of emarginations on P3–P7. Cheeks, ear-coverts and sides of neck white. Chin, lower cheeks, throat and border of upper breast sooty-brown (darker than cap), feathers of lower cheeks and upper breast tipped white, thus sides and especially lower border of bib ill-defined. Remainder of underparts pale pinkish-buff, paler on the belly. Underwing-coverts pale buff-white. *In worn plumage* (about April–July), upperparts slightly paler and greyer, pale fringes on greater coverts, tertials and flight feathers (especially primaries) bleached and abraded. Bib slightly darker and blacker, also more extensive and better defined, sides of breast and upper flanks olive-drab (pale feather tips abraded). Remainder of underparts off-white, flanks lightly washed buff. **Bare Parts**: No information. **Juvenile**: As adult, but cap averages slightly duller brown, fringes to greater coverts and tertials slightly richer and more cinnamon, and secondaries fringed cinnamon-buff. Bib averages slightly smaller, with broader white feather tips, especially at sides and on lower border; remainder of underparts off-white, faintly tinged buff. **1st Adult**: No information. **Measurements**: Wing of male 66–73, of female 67–71; tail of male 53–58, of female 53, 56; bill 11.5–13; tarsus 15.5–17.5. Weight: no information.

**MOULT** Adult post-breeding complete (July). Post-juvenile partial, includes greater coverts (onset of moult recorded late July).

**GEOGRAPHICAL VARIATION** None.

**RELATIONSHIPS** Problematic. Until recently, this tit, with a restricted distribution around the southern shores of the Caspian Sea, was treated as a subspecies of Sombre Tit. Field studies have shown, however, that its voice and breeding biology more closely resemble those of the Willow-Songar Tit complex. Specific status is supported by the apparent lack of intergradation with adjacent populations of Sombre Tit and by differences in habitat (Loskot 1987). Eck (1980a) considered, however, that some characteristics of Caspian Tit may not be so species-specific as claimed. Structurally, it is similar to the Iranian races of Sombre Tit (and is similarly short-tailed compared with the western *lugubris* group of Sombre Tit: tail/wing index 73.6–82.6, against 78.2–84 for Iranian races of Sombre Tit and 82.6–89.2 in the *lugubris* group). The pinkish-buff tinge to the flanks may be shown by very fresh Sombre Tits of the races *anatoliae* and *kirmanensis* (although it quickly abrades). Nevertheless, the song of Caspian Tit is clearly distinct, although details of its full vocal repertoire, documented with tapes and sonagrams, are desirable. On balance, specific separation seems fully justified.

**REFERENCES** Cramp & Perrins (1993), Eck (1980a), Loskot (1982, 1987).

# 50 WILLOW TIT *Parus montanus*                                 Plate 16

Closely similar to Marsh Tit, this is one of the toughest identification challenges among the titmice. Indeed, not until 1900 was it realised that this species occurred in Britain (when an endemic subspecies was described from specimens collected near Finchley in London in 1897). Recent research has shown that its song varies markedly across its range, but the taxonomic consequences of this have yet to be fully elucidated.

**IDENTIFICATION** Length 110 mm (4.25 in). A bulky but relatively slender-billed tit. Cap matt black, upperparts dark drab-brown to drab-grey, paler fringes to the tertials and secondaries forming a variably conspicuous pale panel on the closed wing. Cheek patches whitish, bib dull black, rather small and ill-defined, and remainder of underparts white, variably washed cinnamon-brown. In the north, the range overlaps broadly with that of Siberian Tit, but Willow is easily identified by its black cap (brownish-grey on Siberian Tit) and, in these northern populations, its grey- and-white plumage (pale brownish in Siberian Tits). For separation from Songar Tit, see p. 257. Willow is rather similar to Marsh Tit and often difficult to distinguish. The following criteria may be useful: * **Voice** At all times, the most reliable distinction, although Willow Tits are relatively silent and may go for long periods without calling. Both species have a nasal *dzee* or *tchay* call, but those of Willow are much longer, fuller and more sonorous and, on average, lower-pitched. They are delivered more slowly and deliberately, and usually in shorter series, but nevertheless, when subdued or distant, the *dzee* notes of the two species can be confused. Willow Tit's *dzee* is often given alone or is introduced by a thin *si-si* phrase (too quiet to be heard at a distance), less often by a loud, sharp *tzit* or *tzit-tzit*, whilst Marsh Tit's is often introduced by a bright, explosive *'pitchuu'*, a call which Willow Tit never gives, either alone or in combination with the nasal *tchay* The songs of the two species are variable, and are occasionally rather similar (see the respective Voice accounts).

* **Structure** Slightly smaller, but relatively big-headed and more bull-necked or 'neckless' than Marsh Tit (exaggerated by its looser, longer and denser plumage on the head and body). Tail slightly more rounded at the tip, the outer tail feather *c.* 4–8 (1–10) mm shorter than the remainder on Willow compared with *c.* 2 mm on Marsh (0–5 mm in Marsh). * **Cap**. In all races, more extensive, reaching onto the upper mantle, and always dull black or even very slightly brownish-black, never glossy as on adult Marsh. The apparent gloss on the cap can vary with the light conditions, however, and juvenile and occasionally female Marsh Tits have relatively dull caps; thus, while a bird showing an obvious glossy cap is a Marsh, a dull cap is not always diagnostic of Willow. * **Cheek patches** Larger and more 'swept back', extending well onto the sides of the neck (lightly washed buff in southern races). * **Bib** Larger, extending further onto the lower throat, and rather poorly defined (but its size and shape are strongly dependent upon degree of abrasion and posture). * **Wing panel** The most useful plumage feature. When fresh, Willow shows a contrasting pale panel formed by pale fringes to the secondaries and longest tertial, whitish in northern and eastern races, but in Britain and western Europe buffish (wearing to off-white) and thus not so strongly contrasting, especially if worn. The centres of the greater coverts, tertials, primaries, secondaries and tail feathers are blacker on Willow, heightening the contrast with the pale fringes, especially on tertials, coverts and tail. Note that fresh-plumaged Marsh Tits may show a slight wing panel (pale drab-brown, paler and more obvious in eastern Europe), but never as well marked as that of Willow. Conversely, in very worn plumage in mid-summer, the pale wing panel of Willow may be absent, and it is much reduced on juveniles. * **Tail** Shows slightly more obvious white at the sides of the tail, with a white outer web to T6, often apparent in the field whether viewed from above or below (on Marsh Tit, T6 is very narrowly fringed whitish and this is seldom visible in the field). * **Coloration** Differences depend on locality. In Britain and western Europe, the underparts of Willow Tit are more extensively and deeper buff than on Marsh, especially in fresh plumage, and the cheeks more creamy-buff. In Scandinavia, however, Willow Tit is overall rather greyer, with paler and whiter underparts and cheeks than Marsh Tit, while in eastern Europe (east from eastern Poland) the underparts are equally pale. In the Alps and Carpathians, the flanks of Willow Tit are pinkish-buff, compared with greyish-buff on Marsh Tit. * **Juveniles** Some cannot be reliably dis-

tinguished from juvenile Marsh on plumage criteria, although they usually show paler buff tertial fringes and deeper pinkish-buff flanks.

**SEX/AGE** Sexes very similar, but in fresh plumage females average slightly darker and browner on the mantle and scapulars, less pure white on the cheeks, and slightly deeper and more extensively brownish-buff on the underparts. Juvenile as adult, but when recently fledged the cap is slightly duller and browner and the upperparts colder; also, the cheeks are tinged creamy, the bib smaller and paler (dark grey, partly concealed at the margins by broad white feather tips) and the underparts paler (cream, with rather extensive pinkish-buff on the flanks and undertail-coverts). The tips of the primary coverts and tail feathers also average more pointed than on the adult, and are more abraded at the same time of year. 1st adult as adult, but retains the juvenile primaries, primary coverts, secondaries, 1–3 tertials and usually some greater coverts, and the primary coverts and especially the tail feathers still differ from the adult's in shape and the degree of wear.

**VOICE** Generally rather quiet, and uses a rather limited vocabulary. Contact calls include a very high-pitched, thin, and rather kinglet-like *tsit* or *see*, and a lower, fuller, and sharper *tsit-tsit-tsit*. In common with other chickadees in the subgenus *Poecile*, has a 'chick-a-dee' call system, but unlike that of its close relative the Black-capped Chickadee (which see p. 267) this has not been intensively studied, and the 'rules' of syntax have yet to be worked out. 'Chick-a-dees' are given in a variety of contexts, e.g. as contact calls and in excitement or alarm. They presumably comprise a combination of at least four note types, A, B, C and D, in which each note may be given singly, repeated several times, or omitted altogether. A and B are thin and rather quiet *si*, *sit* or *tsit* notes (sometimes rather high and thin). C is a loud, sharp, stony *chik*, *chit* or *tzit* or a slightly lower-pitched, softer and more sibilant *psit* or *pseet*. D is a loud, deep, sonorous, nasal *dzee*, *tchaaa* or *tchay*, given with varying emphasis, and perhaps averaging deeper and more nasal from males than from females. The D note is often given on its own in groups of up to six notes, perhaps most frequently two at a time (and in longer series the Ds may be noticeably 'paired'), e.g. *dzee-dzee* or *dzee-dzee*, *dzee-dzee*. This is Willow Tit's most characteristic call, and unlike that of Marsh Tit is never preceded by an explosive *pitchuu* (although the B note, a hard *chit*, may approach the *'pitch'* call of Marsh). Otherwise, the commonest combinations are AD, e.g. *tsi-si tchay tchay*, *si-si tchay-tchay-tchay* (and the A components may be so quiet as to be inaudible at a distance). CD combinations are used principally when alarmed or agitated, e.g. *chik-dzee-dzee* or *psee-dzee*, and in CD combinations the C is sometimes slurred into the D, e.g. *szerr* or *ts'dzee-dzee*, or in a series of CD notes, e.g. *ziu-ziew-ziew-ziew* (and this CD combination may also sound as if only D notes are being given, strengthening the impression that Willow Tit's principal call is a simple nasal *dzee*). Call C may be given alone, in a short sparrow-like

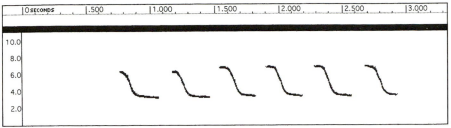

tsiu-tsiu-tsiu-tsiu-tsiu-tsiu

*Figure 50.1 'Lowland Song' of Willow Tit (Norfolk, England; Simon Harrap). Each note is pure and ringing, and shows pronounced drop in pitch.*

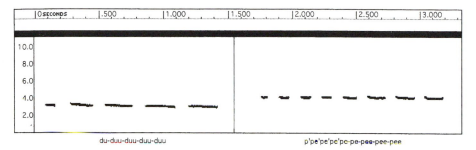

du-duu-duu-duu-duu          p'pe'pe'pe'pe-pe-pee-pee-pee

*Figure 50.2 'Alpine Song' of Willow Tit (Roché 1990). Two examples. Individual notes show little or no fall in pitch, but songs may be given at a lower pitch, sounding soft, almost 'melancholy' (left), and a higher pitch, being more shrill and ringing (right); in both cases, the song slows with notes lengthening towards the end.*

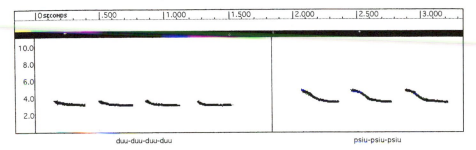

duu-duu-duu-duu          psiu-psiu-psiu

*Figure 50.3 'Siberian Song' of Willow Tit (Novosibirsk; Mild 1987). Two songs from the same bird. Left, the 'flat' and melancholy 'modified' Alpine Song, with a slight initial drop in pitch; right, the shriller and more ringing 'Lowland-type song (but note the rather small drop in pitch in Siberia compared with full-blown Lowland Song from western Europe, as in figure 50.1).*

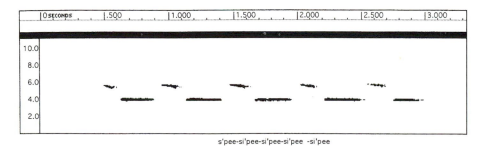

s'pee-si'pee-si'pee-si'pee  -si'pee

*Figure 50.4 'Sino-Japanese Song' of Willow Tit (Kabaya 1990). Two (sometimes three) notes alternate in length and pitch, producing a ringing 'tea-cher'-type song more reminiscent of Great Tit than of Willow Tits from Europe or nothern Asia.*

series, *chik'ik'ik'ik*, in heightened alarm (often introduced by 1–2 thin, high-pitched A-type notes), or in very rapid series of 11–22 notes at *c.* 16–18 units per second (too fast for the individual notes to be distinguished) as a scolding, almost sparrow-like chatter, *chrrrrrrr...* (which may recall Marsh, Great or Blue Tits). The hawk-alarm is a very high *sisisisi*. A high-pitched, rather squeaky but nasal *zeh* or *zeh-ze* (a 'Broken D') probably relates to begging females, and begging juveniles give a series of 2–5 similar notes, but characteristically descending the scale, e.g. *d'dze'dze'dzah*, or sometimes on a more even pitch, *zeeh-ze-ze*. There is marked geographical variation in the song. In Britain and NW, SE and central Europe, the 'Lowland Song' is a repetition of 2–7 whistled motifs, given at a rate of *c.* 3 per second. Often pure and ringing but sometimes more sibilant, each whistle falls in pitch, e.g. *tsiu-tsiu-tsiu...* or *piu-piu-piu....* Successive notes may fall slightly more sharply in pitch and perhaps become a little shorter, but the whole phrase is either at a constant pitch or with the first motif a little lower than the rest (see figure 50.1). This song type may recall a Wood Warbler, and is quite closely matched by one of the less common variants of Marsh Tit's song. Individual males may have a repertoire of 1–3 song types, but the differences are subtle and difficult to appreciate. Song-duels are common. Song is given throughout the year in Britain, although most frequently in late winter and early spring and again in late summer, but in central Europe only from late winter until May. In the Alps and associated ranges (see Geographical Variation and Relationships), birds of the *montanus* group give the rather different 'Alpine Song'. This comprises 5–10 monosyllabic whistles, piercing but soft and sometimes almost melancholy in tone. The individual units are on an even pitch (or only slightly downward-inflected) and average shorter than in the Lowland Song, but they tend to lengthen as the phrase progresses (and the song also decelerates towards the end as the individual units lengthen). Although individual song phrases are at a constant frequency or fall very slightly in pitch, songs vary in pitch and speed, higher-pitched songs being delivered more rapidly. Examples are a slower and lower-pitched *du-duu-duu-duu-duu* and a faster and higher-pitched *p'pe'pe'pe'pe-pe-pee-pee-pee* (see figure 50.2). In some areas on the borders of the Alps (e.g. the eastern foothills), intergrades with the lowland race give an intermediate or 'modified' Alpine Song, with a slight fall in pitch (see Relationships) In Scandinavia, Finland, Poland (at least locally), Siberia, Ussuriland and Sakhalin, gives the 'Siberian Song', in which males may have a repertoire of up to 6–7 song types, and can give Alpine, 'modified' Alpine and Lowland Songs (although some males may only give one type?). Birds may switch from phrases of one type to those of the other during a bout of singing. Songs comprise 2–9 whistles, and sometimes the notes within a phrase of the Lowland type may change as the song progresses, showing a variable fall in pitch, and in Ussuriland both pure Alpine and Lowland-type notes may be given within the same song phrase. Notably, however, the Lowland Song in Siberia never shows the pronounced fall in pitch exhibited in western Europe, although in Ussuriland Lowland-type notes closer to those in western Europe have been recorded (see figure 50.3). Rogacheva (1992) notes two variants in central Siberia, *tiu-tiu-tiu...*, descending in pitch, and *lui-li-lui-li-lui-li...*, ascending in pitch, the latter variant given more frequently; and also a 'gurgling' song, *pirluir-lirliurliurliu* (presumably a 'gargle'; see below). In Hokkaido in northern Japan, the song is of the Alpine type. Further south in Japan, the song is a ringing disyllabic or trisyllabic motif comprising 2–3 pure whistles with a variable change of frequency between the units in a 'step', each motif repeated 4–5 times, e.g. *s'pee-si'pee-si'pee-si'pee-si'pee*, in tone suggesting a squeaky gate, and very much in the 'tea-cher' pattern (the 'Sino-Japanese Song'; see figure 50.4). Japanese Willow Tits also occasionally give songs of the Alpine type (i.e. at a constant pitch), but in an unusual rhythm, alternating long and short units in each phrase (as in the variant song of Black-capped Chickadees from Alaska). At higher altitudes in the eastern Altai mountains of southern Siberian also gives Sino-Japanese Song (a trisyllabic *duh-diduh...*), as well as variations on Alpine and Lowland Songs, in varying proportions (Ernst 1991; J. Martens pers. comm.), although in nearby Mongolia only the Lowland type was given, but material from here is scanty. Presumably throughout the range, Willow Tits occasionally give 'gargles' which serve some of the functions of 'song'. These are rapid jumbles of wheezing and short, more or less musical mellow notes, often incorporating trills and rattles (at any stage in the gargle; terminal rattles may be prolonged), e.g. *tusip'tsleep'peetu* or *chewip-che-wee-chip'ip'ip'ip'ip'ip'ip'ip*. Gargles may be incorporated in the whistled song, and are sometimes termed the 'aggressive song'. The 'nightingale-like song', deep, rich, melodious *chu-chu-chu* notes mingled with soft, sweet, musical warblings, uttered in fairly brief snatches and not far-carrying (even recalling an Atlantic Canary), is thus presumably a gargle. The subsong is a weak warbling. (Partly after Martens & Nazarenko 1993.)

**DISTRIBUTION AND MOVEMENTS** Breeds in **England** (absent most of Lake District and much of the southwest), **Wales** and locally in SW and parts of SE **Scotland**, then across **western** and **central Europe** from **France** (where absent from the south and west), north to the treeline in **Norway** and **Russia** (to the northern part of the Kola peninsula and, further east, to *c.* 68° N), although absent most of **Denmark** and the Baltic islands), and south to extreme northern **Italy**, **Austria**, **Slovakia**, parts of northern **Hungary** (including the Zemplen hills), the northern **Ukraine** (south to the Carpathians, Kiev, Poltava and Khar'kov, and wandering south to Dnepropetrovsk), and in SE European **Russia** south to Voronezh, Penza, Saratov, Kuybyshev, Orenburg and the Bashkirskaya region. Also extends south in mountain regions in the former **Yugoslavia**, **Albania**,

Greece, Romania (Carpathians, Muntii Apuseni) and Bulgaria (Stara and Rodopi ranges), with a disjunct population in southern Abruzzo in the central Appennines in Italy. In Siberia breeds east to the Kamchatka peninsula, Sea of Okhotsk, Shantarskiye islands and Sakhalin (and presumably the northern Kurile islands, but southern limits of distribution there not known certainly absent from Iturup southwards), and north to 65° N on the Yenisey (more rarely to 68° N and the Putorana mountains), between the Yenisey and the Verkhoyansk mountains north to 66° N, and to the northern limit of the Anadyr' basin. In the south extends to northern Kazakhstan, to 52° N in the northern Kyrgyz steppes, Karkaralinsk area, Semipalatinsk and the Tarbagatay and Saur ranges, and to NW China in northern Xinjiang in the eastern foothills of the Tarbagatay range and foothills of the Altai (additionally, the Junggar basin?). Also western and north-central Mongolia, in the Turgen Uul range, Uvs Nuur region, Tesin Gol valley and Great Lakes depression, northern watershed of the Hangayn range (including the upper Orhon and Tuul Gol valleys), Bogdo Uul range (just south of Ulan Bator), and the Hentiyn range, also the NW Mongolian Altai (east to Mönh Hayrhan Uul) and, in the east, the Halhin Gol valley. In adjacent NE China breeds in NE Nei Mongol (Da Hinggan Ling mountains, Hailar), Heilongjiang (Dailing (= about Langxiang), Harbin), Jilin (Changbai Shan) and Liaoning (Dandong). In Japan breeds on Hokkaido, Honshu, Shikoku and Kyushu, and also recorded Tobi-shima, Awa-shima and Sado. Breeds locally in northern North Korea, in Yanggang and North Hamgyong provinces, and a rare winter visitor further south and to South Korea, where most frequent at Kwangnung (near Soul in Kyonggi province), and in the far south at Mount Chiri-san (Kyongsang province). Vagrant Corsica (one 19th-century record; Thibault 1983), and one record Fair Isle, Scotland (November 1935). In western Europe highly sedentary, generally moving less than 5 km (and rarely more than 50 km). Some northern populations, mainly from Finland and further east, have regular dispersive movements from late July onwards, continuing into the winter, and also undergo periodic irregular 'eruptions', involving large numbers of birds (perhaps mainly juveniles). These may be triggered by a poor cone crop, especially if it follows a season with an above-average crop. In such cases, heavy movements may be noted in central Siberia from August onwards ('dozens of thousands' may pass south in a single day at migration bottlenecks such as major rivers, and in central Siberia there is also a regular, unrelated northwards movement, peaking in mid September, and exceptionally recorded north to c. 71° N at Kresty in the southern Tymyr peninsula). In irruption years, immigration into Sweden and to a lesser extent southern Norway may be apparent during late August–early November. Much smaller movements may be evident in the spring, in late April–May (even to mid June in late springs in Siberia), perhaps largely involving 1st-adult birds that had not established territories the previous autumn. Avoids water-

crossings, and in Siberia even crossing the River Yenisey poses a problem; many tits, sometimes several hundreds, gather in one tree at strategic crossing points before attempting a passage (and even then many abort their first attempt). Consequently, few records of 'Northern' Willow Tits in Britain.

HABITAT In Scandinavia, eastern Europe and Siberia found in coniferous forest, in stands of pine, larch and especially spruce and Siberian Stone Pine, often near *Sphagnum* bogs, also mixed woodland and montane and boreal birch forest, in eastern Siberia in riverine thickets, and in NW Mongolia occasionally Osier beds. Breeds to the treeline (in the Altai to 2000–2300 m). In west and central Europe, favours stands of willow, alder, birch, and woody shrubs such as elder, usually in damp areas (coniferous trees, if present, are peripheral to requirements, although will use conifer plantations). In Britain, copses, riverside woodland and the scrub around gravel pits and reservoirs all fall into this category, although areas such as heathland and hedgerows are also used in the winter. Infrequently found in mature deciduous woodland. In southern Europe montane, recorded up to the treeline (at least 1525 m in Bulgaria, 1800–2000 m (occasionally 2100 m) in the Austrian Alps and 1830 m in Switzerland (and to 2000 m plus in January), and thus altitudinally separated from Marsh Tit). Breeds here in conifer forest where interspersed with open areas and damp stands of willow or alder and containing a supply of rotten stumps. In NE China, recorded in secondary broadleaved, mixed and coniferous forest; in Jilin found in the Changbai Shan range at 1100–1800 m (800–1800 m). On Hokkaido and northern Honshu in Japan found both in the lowlands and at lower elevations in the mountains, but to the south, in central Honshu, breeds at 800–2400 m in deciduous, mixed and coniferous forests, descending to the lowlands, even occasionally to suburban gardens, in winter.

POPULATION In Britain and western Europe locally not uncommon, but in southern parts of the range generally much more local and often uncommon. Conversely, in northern Europe, Siberia and Mongolia found at much higher densities and generally common (even near the northern boundaries of the range), and the most numerous tit in central Siberia, indeed, the most numerous bird species in the southern parts of the Yenisey taiga, although population levels are apparently tied to the level of the previous year's crop of Siberian Stone Pine seeds (Rogacheva 1992). Range expansions have been reported from many parts of northern and central Europe. First recorded (breeding proven) in Denmark in 1977 and now established as a sparse breeder in South Jutland. In Scotland, however, there has been a notable contraction since 1950. In the Far East the situation is reversed, and rather uncommon on Hokkaido in northern Japan, but common on Kyushu, Shikoku and Honshu in southern Japan.

HABITS Not so tame or inquisitive as Marsh Tit, generally rather sedate and sometimes even skulking, being first detected by call. Generally less gregarious than other tits. Found singly and in pairs, established pairs remaining together on territory throughout the year. In northern Europe, territories are occupied in the winter by flocks of 4–6 birds: an adult pair and 1–2 pairs of 1st-year birds. These form in late summer and autumn following the post-fledging dispersal, and the adults and young in the flock are not related, the adults having bred in that territory and the young moving in from elsewhere, forming provisional juvenile pairs in the late summer. The flock may join roving tit parties. Some juveniles do not join up with adult pairs, and remain solitary through the winter. These flocks break up in the spring, the 'adult' pair (with any replacement partner - on the death of one of the adults, the widow chooses a new partner from the group) remaining to breed in the winter territory, the others dispersing. In more southerly parts of the range, the adult pair is not joined by juveniles during the winter, and, although they may join mixed-species foraging flocks as these pass through their territory, they spend much of their time foraging alone. Roosts largely in rodent burrows and in crevices among tree roots, sometimes in tree holes, squirrel dreys or in snow holes; can dig a 20-cm tunnel in snow in 10–15 seconds and may use the same burrow for extended periods in winter, digging itself out after fresh snowfalls. In northern populations, roosting birds enter a state of hypothermia, lowering their body temperature by 5° C. During laying, the female roosts on the nest. Forages largely by sight (does not hammer and tear at lichen and bark so much as Marsh Tit), favouring the herb and shrub layers and the lower branches and foliage of trees, although does not usually feed on the ground. Sometimes flycatches, but seldom visits birdtables. Food insects, spiders and other invertebrates, especially during the breeding season, whilst seeds and berries assume greater importance during the winter. The young may be fed on conifer seeds as well as animal matter. Hoards food for winter use in lichen and bark crevices, largely spiders and insects in the autumn, these usually being killed prior to storage, and generally switches to seeds in the spring. In NW Russia, up to 200 items per day may be stored in the winter and up to 4,700 per day in the spring, with an annual total of c. 460,000 items, sufficient to provide 2–3 times the winter energy requirement. Juveniles are, however, unable to build up sufficient stores by their first winter and must rely on other resources.

**BREEDING BIOLOGY** Season: in West Palearctic, April–early June (rarely July); European Russia, May–June; Siberia, late May–early June; northern Mongolia, late May onwards; Japan May–July. The nest is placed in a hole in a rotten tree trunk or stump, sometimes a rotten post, as little as 7–8 cm in diameter. The entrance is generally below 3 m above the ground, exceptionally up to 10 m. The nest hole is usually excavated by the birds themselves, although an existing hole may be enlarged. Nestboxes may also be used if there is no alternative, and nests have also been found in a squirrel's drey and in old bird nests (is unable to peck through birch bark, so in this tree species natural cracks or woodpecker excavations must be used). Both sexes excavate (the female taking the larger share), at first working on several holes and then concentrating on one, completing the cavity over a period of up to 25 days. The nest itself is built by the female alone and is a simple pad of bark strips, grass and plant down (seldom any moss, unlike Marsh Tit), lined with wood chippings, hair, fur, plant fibres and maybe a few feathers. Clutch 6–9 (4–12, perhaps 13): eggs white, variably speckled and spotted reddish-brown, often concentrated at the broader end, with pale reddish-violet undermarkings; 15.8 x 12.3 mm (*P. m. kleinschmidti*). Female incubates, period 13–15 days (11–19, very long periods due to a gap between laying of last egg and start of incubation). The young are fed by both sexes, although brooded only by the female, and fledge after 17–20 days. The juveniles remain dependent on the adult for 12–15 days, dispersing after 15–20 days. Single-brooded.

**DESCRIPTION** *P. m. kleinschmidti* **Adult**: *In fresh plumage* (August–March), cap from forehead to centre of upper mantle dull black, remainder of upperparts, including lesser coverts, dark drab-brown. Tail greyish-black, feathers fringed pale buff on outer webs. Median and greater coverts dark grey, broadly fringed dark drab-brown. Primary coverts dark grey-brown, alula blackish-brown. Primaries greyish-black, finely fringed pale buff, secondaries similar but pale fringes broader, tertials as secondaries but tinged brown on inner webs. Cheeks white, washed creamy-buff, deepest on sides of neck. Chin and throat dull black, feathers of sides and lower border of bib tipped whitish, thus bib ill-defined. Remainder of underparts white, washed pale cinnamon-brown, centre of breast and belly slightly paler, flanks more olive-brown. Underwing-coverts and axillaries grey-buff to pink-buff. *In worn plumage* (April–July), cap duller, upperparts greyer (not so brown), cheeks purer white, bib larger (but not sharply defined), breast to vent dirty whitish, warmer buff restricted to flanks and undertail-coverts, and pale fringes to wing and tail feathers abraded, but still distinct on secondaries and tertials unless heavily worn. **Bare Parts**: Iris brown to dark brown; bill blue-black to black with paler cutting edges; legs and feet dark grey-blue. **Juvenile**: As adult, but cap dull brownish-black, upperparts colder brown, cheeks pale creamy-buff (wearing to dirty white), bib smaller and paler (dark brown-grey, sides and lower edge partially concealed by broad white feather tips), and remainder of underparts paler and whiter with buff wash restricted to flanks and undertail-coverts. Bill brownish-black with yellow cutting edges. **1st Adult**: As adult, although retains juvenile wing and tail feathers (see Sex/Age). **Measurements**: Wing of male 56–62, of female 56–62; tail of male 46–53; bill 9.5–11.5; tarsus 15.5–17.2. Weight 8–15 g (races combined).

**MOULT** Adult post-breeding complete (mid May–October, sometimes early November, duration c. 70–77 days). Post-juvenile partial, includes a variable number of greater coverts, frequently 1–3 tertials and rarely T1 (June–mid October).

**GEOGRAPHICAL VARIATION** Three groups of subspecies: the *salicarius* group in northern Eurasia, the *kamtschatkensis* group around the Pacific rim in eastern Asia, and the *montanus* group in the mountains of central Europe. (Note that Songar Tit of Central Asia, here considered a separate species, is often treated as a form of Willow Tit, forming a fourth group of subspecies).

**THE *SALICARIUS* GROUP** Distributed almost continuously across northern Europe and Asia, and variation largely clinal. From Scandinavia to eastern Siberia (*borealis-uralensis-baicalensis*), birds become slightly larger, longer-tailed and distinctly paler both above and below, with more prominent pale fringes to the wing and tail feathers; the cheek patches also tend to extend farther back. In the west, from northern Fennoscandia southwest to France and Britain (*borealis-salicarius-rhenanus-kleinschmidti*), birds become darker, with browner upperparts, buffer underparts and duller white cheek patches (in response to a more humid oceanic climate); they are also smaller. Six races recognised, all continental races intergrading across a wide region.

**P. m. kleinschmidti** Britain. The smallest and darkest race. See Description.

**P. m. rhenanus** Western Europe east to westernmost Germany and northern Switzerland. As *kleinschmidti*, but upperparts drab-brown, very slightly paler and greyer (less cinnamon), cheeks whiter, tinged cream or pale greyish-buff, centre of breast and belly whiter with variable pale grey-buff wash, and remainder of underparts extensively tinged cinnamon-buff. Wing of male 56.5–63, of female 56–61.5.

**P. m. salicarius** Central Europe (east of *rhenanus*) east to western Poland and the Czech Republic and south to northern and eastern Austria and SW Germany. Intergrades with nominate *montanus* in NE Switzerland, SW Germany and NW Austria. Poorly marked. As *rhenanus*, but upperparts drab-brown, not so warm, cheeks white with a reduced creamy wash, and underparts creamy-white with a reduced buff or greyish-buff wash on the flanks. Wing of male 59.5–67, of female 58–64.

**P. m. borealis** Fennoscandia, Denmark, the Baltic States, and European Russia, south to northern foothills of the Carpathian mountains in the Ukraine and to Penza in SE European Russia. Rather greyer than preceding races, thus basically grey rather than basically brown. Upperparts mid grey, distinctly washed drab, cheeks white, bib slightly smaller, breast, centre of belly and vent creamy-white (wearing to pure white), flanks and undertail-coverts pale pinkish-buff; cap and centres of remiges and rectrices slightly deeper black (cap sometimes faintly glossy), with contrasting whitish or pale buff fringes, greater coverts fringed paler (as tertials and secondaries). Wing of male 59–70, of female 57–67; tail of male 52–64, of female 53–58. Those from western Norway ('*colletti*') are slightly drabber overall, those from northern Scandinavia and NW Russia ('*loennbergi*') a little paler. Northern populations partly migratory, and vagrant Britain (about seven records,

September–May: Limbert 1984) and probably also the Netherlands (van Marle *et al.* 1973). Note very white cheek patches, greyer upperparts, more prominent and cleaner white wing panel, and purer white underparts of vagrants.

**P. m. uralensis** SE Russia, southern Urals, SW Siberia and northern Kazakhstan. Boundaries poorly defined, as intergrades with surrounding races. Poorly marked. As *borealis*, but upperparts greyer, drab tinge faint or absent, fringes of primaries, secondaries and tertials white; underparts white, washed pale pinkish-grey on flanks. Wing of male 62.5–69, of female 61.5.

**P. m. baicalensis** Eastern Siberia from the Yenisey basin and Altai east to the Kolyma highlands and west coast of the Sea of Okhotsk, south to NW China, Mongolia, Ussuriland and NE China. Rare winter visitor (?) Korea. Poorly marked. As *uralensis*, but tail longer. Wing of male 60.5–72, of female 58–68; tail of male 58–68. It is not known which race inhabits northern European Russia and neighbouring NW Siberia, north of *borealis* and *uralensis*, east of '*loennbergi*' (i.e. = *borealis* in northern Scandinavia) and west of *baicalensis*.

**THE *KAMTSCHATKENSIS* GROUP** Identified by Eck (1980) on the basis of morphology (especially wing/tail proportions); gives Sino-Japanese, Alpine and Siberian song types, depending on locality (see Voice). A cline runs from Kamchatka south to Japan (*kamtschatkensis-sachalinensis-restrictus*), the populations becoming smaller and darker, with Japanese birds being very similar to those in Scandinavia.

**P. m. anadyrensis** NE Siberia from the Kolyma highlands east to the Anadyr' basin, south to the north coast of Sea of Okhotsk (Gizhiga). Presumed to intergrade with *baicalensis* in the Kolyma highlands. Poorly marked. Intermediate between *baicalensis* and *kamtschatkensis*.

**P. m. kamtschatkensis** Kamchatka peninsula. Very pale. Mantle grey-white with faint drab wash, crown black (blacker than in any race except *borealis*), greater coverts, tertials and secondaries very broadly fringed white, tail feathers broadly fringed white (outer web of T6 white), and underparts (including flanks) white with faint creamy wash. Wing of male 62–65, of female 63–64.5.

**P. m. sachalinensis** Sakhalin island; possibly vagrant Hokkaido. Poorly marked. As *restrictus*, but slightly paler and greyer, especially on underparts.

**P. m. restrictus** Japan. Much darker than *kamtschatkensis*. As *borealis*, but crown very slightly duller and browner, mantle slightly duller and more sandy grey-brown, underparts with a slightly stronger drab-buff wash. Wing of male 62–67; tail of male 50–55.

**THE *MONTANUS* GROUP** Compared with the *salicarius* group, larger, with a relatively short tail, duller black cap and more pinkish-buff flanks (less brownish-buff), resembling in these respects Songar Tit. Compared with *P. m. salicarius*, upperparts slightly paler and greyer (drab-brown, close to *borealis*), underparts more extensively washed drab-grey to pinkish-buff (and thus much more sullied than *borealis*). Importantly, the song of most or all populations is rather different (see Voice). Much local variation, with up to 12 races named; many populations are more or less isolated in mountain valleys, the different micro habitats being reflected in tiny plumage differences, but only one race recognised here.

**P. m. montanus** Central Europe in the Jura and the Alps and their foothills in France, Switzerland, southern Germany, Austria, northern Yugoslavia and northern Italy; also the central Appennines in Italy, Yugoslavia, Tatry mountains of Slovakia, Carpathian mountains, Carpatii Meridionali Muntii (Transylvanian Alps) and Muntii Apuseni in Bulgaria, Stara and Rodopi ranges in Bulgaria, and locally in Greece. Vagrant Corsica. Wing of male 63–71, of female 60.5–67; tail of male 54–60, of female 52–58; bill 10.4–11.8; tarsus 16.7–17.7. Of the numerous named races, 'transsylvanicus' of Carpathians and Transylvanian Alps perhaps worthy of recognition, having slightly paler and browner (less grey) upperparts and the pale pinkish-drab of the underparts paler but more extensive, and also 'rhodopeus' of Bulgaria (and probably SE Yugoslavia and Greece), apparently rather small and brown (Eck 1980a). It is not certain that all populations have been correctly placed. Alpine Song has been recorded from the Alps (usually above 1000 m, but sometimes as low as 570 m), from Savoie and the French Alps east to Steiermark in Austria and in the north of former Yugoslavia, the Carpathian mountains and Transylvanian Alps in Romania, north (presumably through the eastern Ukraine) to the Tatry mountains on the Slovakia/Poland border. Alpine Song has, however, only rarely been recorded in the Jura (and also in the Böhmer Wald in the SW Czech Republic), and Lowland Song has been heard from birds near Sarajevo in former Yugoslavia and the Rhodope mountains of Bulgaria (Eck 1990; thus 'rhodopeus' may be better placed with the salicarius group). Birds of the salicarius group do not respond to Alpine Song and those of the montanus group do not respond to the Lowland Song. In some areas, especially the western Alps, the division between the song types is very sharp and the two groups appear fully isolated in physical characteristics, ecology and song. This appears to be the situation in most of Switzerland (although 'mixed singers' are occasionally found, e.g. in the St Gallen region, which give and react to both song types), whilst in the Tatry mountains (Slovakia/Poland border) birds of the salicarius group are found at lower altitudes than those of the montanus group. In other areas, however, on the northern flanks of the Austrian-Bavarian Alps (Bayerische Alpen, from about Munich to Salzburg), birds may give both song types as well as intermediates, and be intermediate in appearance between the montanus and the salicarius groups. Thus, as separation has not occurred everywhere, the montanus group is, at best, treated as an incipient species.

**HYBRIDS** Willow x Siberian Tits are not rare (see p. 288). In Japan, hybrids have also been recorded with Varied Tit (at least six instances), being intermediate in plumage but having the voice of Varied Tit, although 'finer' (Mishima 1969). In Finland, an obvious hybrid with Coal Tit has been found, broadly intermediate in appearance, showing vestigial wingbars and a small nuchal spot, but with the underparts and especially the undertail-coverts closer to those of Willow (Hildén 1983). In Belgium, a nesting mixed pair of male Willow x female Marsh Tits was noted in two successive years, fledging five young in the first year; the nest and young resembled those of Marsh Tit (Dhondt & Hublé 1969). Finally, presumed hybrids with Crested Tit have also been noted (Gray 1958).

**RELATIONSHIPS** A member of the atricapillus group of tits, which includes the widespread salicarius group in northern Eurasia, the kamtschatkensis group in eastern Asia, and various more or less isolated southern populations: the montanus group in central Europe, Songar Tit in Central Asia, and Black-capped and Carolina Chickadees in North America. The relationships between the various groups, however, are not well understood. They are often treated as comprising a single superspecies and, indeed, all are sometimes combined as a single species, taking the oldest name, atricapillus (most recently by Eck 1988 and Martens & Nazarenko 1993). The conspecificity of Willow Tit and Black-capped Chickadee was initially proposed by Hartert (1903–10), but later disputed by Mayr (1956), Snow (1956) and Vaurie (1957b), especially in view of the marked differences in voice between Black-capped Chickadee and the Willow Tits of NW Europe. Subsequent research showed that Willow Tits in the Alps sang a different song, a little closer to Black-capped Chickadee, and that across the range into eastern Asia there was even more variability, with birds in Japan having a variant which is close to one of the songs of Alaskan Black-capped Chickadees (but the prevalence of this song in Alaska is apparently unknown) (Martens & Nazarenko 1993). Investigating protein relationships, Gill et al. (1989) found that Willow Tit did not appear to be closely related genetically to Black-capped Chickadee, but Sheldon et al. (1992) considered the two to be too closely related for the technique of DNA hybridisation to resolve their status. In view of the marked difference in song between all documented populations of Willow Tit and almost all Black-capped Chickadees, and the differences in biochemistry and appearance, I continue to treat them as specifically distinct. Perhaps the best interpretation is that tits are, in evolutionary terms rather conservative in their vocalisations, with many clearly distinct species having somewhat similar voices. Thus, whilst distinctive vocalisations hint strongly at specific status, similar (or even apparently identical) songs and calls require a more cautious approach. Populations may have diverged markedly in morphology, and perhaps also in ecology, yet share similar vocalisations. Study of calls and songs can, however, throw much light on their ancestry. The Alpine and Lowland song types are thought to have derived from the older and more complex Siberian song type when populations of ancestral Willow Tits, isolated during periods of glaciation in Pleistocene refuges in the southern Alps and the Balkans, 'lost' the Lowland and Alpine Songs respectively. The 'mixed singers' in Scandinavia sing (primary) Siberian Song, as they brought their complex repertoire with them in the post-glacial immigration from Siberia, whilst the mixed singers in the contact zones around the Alps sing a 'secondary' Siberian Song, combining Lowland and Alpine Songs. (Martens & Nazarenko 1993.)

**REFERENCES** Cramp & Perrins (1993), Eck (1980a), Martens & Nazarenko (1993), Rogacheva (1992), Stepanyan (1990), Thönen (1962), Witherby et al. (1938).

## 51 SONGAR TIT *Parus songarus*                    Plate 16

Often treated as a member of the Willow Tit complex, this species is confined to Central Asia and China, and in some ways recalls Siberian Tit.

**IDENTIFICATION** Length 130 mm (5.25 in). Overall, coloration reminiscent of west European Willow Tits and quite distinct from the generally grey-and-white Asian races of Willow. The cap is brown or dull black, the upperparts vary from grey-brown to very dark brown or bright ochre, and the underparts are variably washed cinnamon-brown. There are three distinct populations. In the Tien Shan in Central Asia and NW China (nominate *songarus*), the cap is dull black with a brown tinge, extending well onto the upper mantle. Upperparts pale cinnamon-brown, with the primaries and secondaries fringed pale drab-grey, forming a moderately obvious pale panel on the closed wing. Cheek patches off-white, washed cinnamon-buff at the rear. Extensive, but ill-defined, dull black bib. Flanks pale cinnamon-brown, becoming off-white and tinged buff on the breast and centre of the belly and slightly paler pinkish-cinnamon on the vent and undertail-coverts. Willow Tits (of the northern race *baicalensis*) occur a little to the north, in the Tarbagatay mountains. The two species are, however, very different. On Songar Tit, the cap is slightly more restricted and rather browner (not black), the upperparts much warmer and browner (not mid grey, tinged olive-brown), with a less prominent pale wing panel, and the underparts are duller, extensively washed cinnamon (not off-white, tinged drab grey, with the flanks only slightly buffer).The population in north-central China (NE Qinghai to Ningxia Hui, *P. s. affinis*) is close to nominate *songarus*, but the cap is a little paler and browner and the bib browner (dark brown). In SW China (Yunnan north to SE Qinghai, *P. s. weigoldicus*), the cap is darker brown or brownish-black, the upperparts are darker and duller brown, and the underparts dingier. In SE Tibet and SW China, Songar Tit must be carefully separated from Black-bibbed Tit. Its cap is paler and browner (distinctly so in *affinis*), compared with glossy black on Black-bibbed, and Songar Tit *never* shows any hint of a crest. Its upperparts are distinctly tinged cinnamon (rather than olive), its bib is browner and often less extensive and less well defined, and its underparts are darker but brighter, more obviously washed buff (less greyish-olive). Juvenile Black-bibbed is rather closer in appearance to Songar Tit: it has the cap brown (as *affinis*!), the upperparts tinged cinnamon, and the bib paler (mid grey, washed brown) and more restrict-

ed than the adult's, but its underparts are distinctly washed yellow-buff, rather than the pinkish-cinnamon of Songar Tit. The race of Songar Tit in NE China (*P. s. stoetzneri*) is similar to *affinis*, but paler, especially on the underparts, with restricted cinnamon-buff on the flanks. It is easily separated from Willow Tit (again of the northern race *baicalensis*) by its distinctly browner and more restricted cap, rather warmer brown upperparts and dingier underparts, washed cinnamon-buff on the flanks. (Vaurie (1957b) states, however, that the upperparts are greyish-brown and the flanks buffy-white, the colour of the cap being the main difference from Willow Tit). In much of its range in China (from eastern Sichuan to Manchuria), Songar Tit must be separated from Marsh Tit. Its cap is brown, rather than glossy black as on Marsh, its upperparts are slightly darker, richer and more cinnamon, and the bib is browner and usually much more extensive, with the underparts darker and more extensively washed cinnamon-brown than on Marsh. Another possible source of confusion is with Siberian Tit, which *may* have been recorded in Nei Mongol and the mountains of northern Hebei (see p. 286 for details). The two species are rather similar, although Siberian Tit is larger. The cap of Songar Tit is darker and browner (not brownish-grey), better defined at the rear and not extending so far onto the mantle. Its upperparts are slightly warmer and more cinnamon (Siberian is a little greyer) and, notably, Songar Tit lacks contrasting whitish fringes to the greater coverts and flight feathers (although its pale wing panel is quite obvious, it is rather buffer, and the greater-covert fringes are much more cinnamon-buff). Its cheeks are washed buff (whiter on Siberian) and, although the two have bibs very similar in coloration, the breast and centre of the belly are buffer on Songar Tit (cleaner and whiter on Siberian).

**SEX/AGE** Sexes very similar, although the female may average more extensively pale cinnamon-brown on the underparts (less pinkish-cinnamon, with only the centre of the breast and the sides of the throat whitish; remainder of underparts pale cinnamon-brown). No difference in cap or upperpart coloration is detectable. Juvenile marginally distinct. As adult, but cap a little browner and less extensive, not extending onto the upper mantle (except in the centre), rear cheeks and upper side of neck paler and whiter, extending into a half-col-

257

lar at the rear of the cap, and bib slightly paler and greyer-brown (not so deep black), not extending onto upper breast until rather worn (1st adult?), when as extensive as on adult, although still slightly paler; underparts slightly dingier, especially on breast. Tail feathers narrower and more pointed. 1st adult as adult, but retains the juvenile wing and tail feathers, which are distinctly more worn than adult's at similar time of year (until late winter?).

**VOICE** Similar to that of Willow Tit, but apparently rather more varied, with some calls that may be absent from Willow Tit's vocabulary (conversely, the 'chick-a-dee' call may be less varied than in Willow Tit, with the exception of the race *stoetzneri*). Notably, the nasal *'tchay'* call is often harsher and less structured than in Willow, sounding more rasping or hoarse (recalling the 'scream' of a Eurasian Jay; again, excepting at times *stoetzneri*). The four disjunct subspecies are discussed separately. In the Tien Shan (**P. s. songarus**), gives a 'chick-a-dee' call (see Black-capped Chickadee, p. 267), *psit-dzee-dzee*, *'psit'* being a 'noisy' C-type call, with the nasal *dzee* (D) prolonged as in Willow Tit, and a *psit-zer* in which the D is rather shortened. Also gives a strange nasal *chiur* (a combination of a sharp *chit* and short nasal *zer* with the individual units indistinguishable) in rapid bouts of 2–9 calls, often tagged on to the end of a *psit-zer* motif (the compound *chiur* phrase thus used as a D in the 'chick-a-dee', and apparently very different from any vocalisation of Willow Tit). The song comprises 3–7 variable pure whistles in a mixture of motifs equivalent to the 'Siberian Song' of Willow Tit (see p. 250), although with some modifications. Some phrases have the indi-vidual notes falling only slightly in pitch (much less so than in the similar motifs of Willow Tit, figure 50.1), e.g. *piu-piu-piu...* (see figure 51.1), and some have the notes more ringing and clearly falling in tone, e.g. *psiu-psiu-psiu...* (see figure 51.2). Also gives 'gargles', which often terminate in rattles. In SW China (**P. s. weigoldicus**), the calls include a 'chick-a-dee' with a nasal, scolding *dzee* often combined with a thin *sisi* or sharp *psit* (= A-type), e.g. *psit-dzee*, and the sharp introductory note is often slurred into the first D note, e.g. *tszee* or *t'zee*, and this combination may be shortened to *tsuiz*. There is no information on the song. In north-central China (**P. s. affinis**), calls include a thin *see* or *sip*, sometimes repeated in groups of 2–6, and has the usual 'chick-a-dee' call system, with the D note prolonged as in Willow Tit (but see below). C is a short, quiet, nasal *tup* or *nip*, grading into a louder, rattling *chip*, and A is a sibilant *tsip*. The commonest combinations are CD and AD (B-type notes and BD combinations being seldom used?), and A is often slurred into a very short D note, thus *tsiur*; such combined AD notes are given alone or as introduction to a series of normal D notes, e.g. *tsiur-dzeer-dzeer*. The rattling 'chip' version of C may also be given in a short, chattering series, *chip'ip'ip'ip* (recalling a Great Tit's scold). In addition, gives 5–13 short D-type nasal notes in a fast series, *zizizizizizi...* at *c.* 8 calls per second, the rapid repetition and short duration of the individual notes (*c.* 0.1 second) being closer to Marsh than to Willow Tit. The song is made up of 3–8 whistled units, each on a constant pitch or falling very slightly (especially towards the end of the series), with the entire phrase sometimes subtly

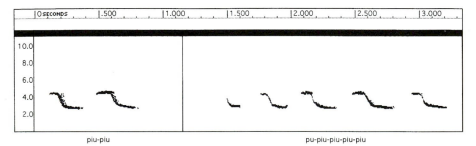

piu-piu       pu-piu-piu-piu-piu

*Figure 51.1 Example of 'Lowland Song' of Songar Tit, subspecies* songarus *(Tien Shan; Per Alström). Relatively loud and ringing, but with the individual notes showing a rather limited drop in pitch.*

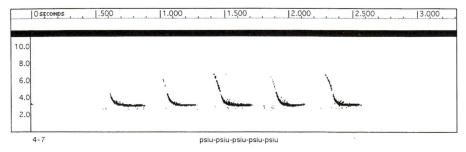

4-7       psiu-psiu-psiu-psiu-psiu

*Figure 51.2 'Lowland Song' of Songar Tit, subspecies* songarus *(Alma Ata, Kazakhstan; Nicolai Formosov/National Sound Archive). This example with a more pronounced fall in pitch.*

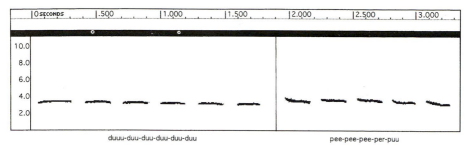

Figure 51.3 'Alpine-type' song of Songar Tit, subspecies affinis (Xining, Qinghai; Paul Holt). Two examples from two different males. Left, the notes are almost constant in pitch (although the whole phrase descends the scale very slightly), and the tone thin and 'wistful'; right, the individual notes fall slightly in pitch towards the end of the phrase, and are more piercing in tone.

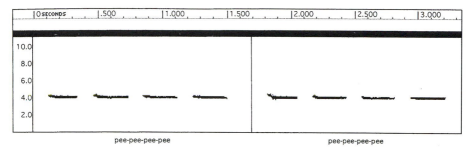

Figure 51.4 'Alpine-type' song of Songar Tit, subspecies weigoldicus (Badaling, Hebei; Per Alström). Two examples from the same male. Both the individual notes and the whole phrase are at a constant pitch.

descending the scale. In tone it is sometimes thin and slightly 'wistful', e.g. *duuu-duu-duu-duu-duu-duu*, and sometimes more piercing, e.g. *pee-pee-pee-per-puu*. It is similar to the 'Alpine Song' of Willow Tit, but the individual notes may become slightly shorter towards the end of the series, rather than longer (see figure 51.3). Notably, in some songs short and long whistles are alternated (as in song variants of Willow Tit from Japan and Black-capped Chickadee from Alaska). Sometimes gives a fast, 'wooden' rattle of 7–13 units delivered at a rate of *c.* 18 per second, *tilililililililili...*, occasionally introduced by A-type notes; this may be an abbreviated 'gargle'. In NE China (**P. s. stoetzneri**), gives a thin *sip* contact call, and the 'chick-a-dee' call system includes at least three note types. A is a high, thin *sip* or *tsip*, and C is a sharp, stony *tship* or *chip*. Recorded combinations include a slurred AD motif, *ps'zur* or *tsiur* (as in *weigoldicus* and *affinis*), which may be doubled; AAD combinations, e.g. *tsi'stip'dzah*; CD combinations, e.g. *tchip-dzee-dzee*; and deep, prolonged D notes given in bouts of 1–3 calls, e.g. *dzeeh-dzeeh-dzee* (thus it may have a more diverse vocabulary than other races). The song is of the 'Alpine Type', 2–5 plaintive whistled units, *pee-pee-pee...*, with both the individual notes and the whole phrase at a remarkably constant pitch (see figure 51.4).

**DISTRIBUTION AND MOVEMENTS** Three populations. In the west found in the northern **Tien Shan**, where in the former USSR breeds in SE **Kazakhstan** and **Kyrgyzstan**, from the Karatau range in the northwestern foothills of the Tien Shan (Vaurie 1959) east through the Kirgizskiy range, Zailiyskiy and Kungey Alatau, and south of lake Issyk Kul in the Terskey Alatau to the upper Naryn valley, Naryntau, Atbashitau and Kokshaaltau. Also recorded in the Ketmen' range and Dzhungarskiy Alatau. In extreme NW **Xinjiang** in NW **China** recorded on the northern watershed of the Tien Shan around the Tekes valley (and east in the Tien Shan to 85–86º E: Stepanyan 1990), in the Borohoro Shan and the environs of the Sayram Hu on the southern watershed of the Dzhungarskiy Alatau. The second population is found in **northern China**, from the Alxa and the Helan Shan range on the borders of NW **Ningxia Hui** and **Nei Mongol**, west through SW and southern **Gansu** (north to Wushan, Xiahe and the southern Qilian Shan north to *c.* 37º N) to NE **Qinghai**, east to the Qinghai Hui and around Xinghai and Qamalung, also SE Qinghai, north to Yushu and on the Tongtian He river to Dy Chu at *c.* 33º 45' N, 95º 55' E, and to Ngangqian (= Nangqen). Breeds in west and central **Sichuan**, east to Pingwu, Songpan, Barkam, Kangding and Muli, eastern **Tibet** in the Qamdo region, west to *c.* 97º E; also noted at Rawu (Robson 1986) and collected further west in southern Tibet, in the Yigrong range in Kongbo at 'Penam Chu' (near Xoka; identified as Black-bibbed Tit, see p. 243). Also occurs in NW **Yunnan**, along the Lancang Jiang (Mekong) valley, at 'Tehtsin' (*c.* 28º N, just north of Tzeku). The third population occurs in **NE China**, in SE **Nei Mongol**, where recorded from the Ural mountains and Chifeng, northern **Hebei** (Chengde), western **Beijing Municipality**, where the species breeds in the Baihua Shan (around Mentougou; perhaps only a winter visitor to the Ming Tombs and Beijing), **Shanxi**, and NE **Henan**. This population may be separated from that of Ningxia, Gansu etc., as there are no records from the Qin Ling Shan of Shaanxi. Resident, but in at least the Tien Shan undertakes some altitudinal movements.

**HABITAT** In the Tien Shan, found in montane coniferous forests, especially spruce, and recorded at 1830–2745 m on the northern watershed of the eastern Tien Shan in Xinjiang. In SW China, similarly found in coniferous forest, mainly spruce but also fir, pine and perhaps juniper (although perhaps favouring non-coniferous trees within these associations), mixed forests at lower altitudes and valley-bottom willow thickets. Also found in low shrubs above the treeline. Noted at 2200–4275 m in Sichuan (breeding confirmed at c. 2400 m at Wolong in central Sichuan, and generally found in the lower part of this altitudinal range in northern Sichuan and? during the winter), and in Qinghai at c. 3350–4000 m. Recorded in southern Tibet at 3960 m in July and at 3840 in dry hill scrub in March. In NE China found in mixed forest, in western Beijing Municipality largely at 1200–1500 m (breeding noted at 1500 m), and recorded at 1220 m in midwinter in Shanxi.

**POPULATION** Locally common in the Tien Shan and in SW China, being quite common in Sichuan and locally very common in NE Qinghai. Apparently uncommon or even rare, however, in NE China, with rather few records, although reported to be common at Pangquanguo Reserve in the Luliang Shan in Shanxi (King 1987).

**HABITS** Tame. Found in small parties, occasionally joining mixed-species foraging flocks (perhaps rather infrequently compared with other tits). Recorded as feeding largely on willow catkins in April in Xinjiang (Ludlow & Kinnear 1933–34).

**BREEDING BIOLOGY** In the Tien Shan, nests are placed in rotten spruce stumps, the entrance being as low as 0.6 m above ground level, or in the trunks of spruce trees, the hole being 1.1–2 m high. Natural cavities, abandoned woodpecker holes or nestboxes are used, up to 12 m high, but apparently usually excavates its own nest hole. The nest is built by both sexes from bark fibre, moss, dry grass, plant down and feathers, but the dominant material is wool, fur and hair. Only the female adds the lining. Clutch 5–6 (4–6): eggs white with small reddish-rust spots and speckles, concentrated at the broader end; 16.3–17.5 x 12.4–13.2 mm. Female incubates, period 13–15 days. The young fledge after 22 days. In Sichuan, China, noted excavating a nest hole in a rotten birch at Jiuzhaigou (C. Robson *in litt.*), and two adults carrying food to a nest in a tree stump c. 2 m above ground at Wolong (G. M. Kirwan *in litt.*).

**DESCRIPTION** *P. s. songarus* **Adult Male**: *In fresh plumage* (late August to about February), cap from forehead to central upper mantle dark chocolate-brown (dull black with a faint brown tinge). Mantle, scapulars, back and rump pale cinnamon-brown. Tail dark grey-brown, all feathers

narrowly fringed pale brown on outer web, becoming slightly paler and greyer on T5 and T6; tail slightly rounded, T5 and especially T6 shorter than longest feathers (latter by c. 6 mm). Lesser coverts as upperparts; median and greater coverts dark grey, broadly fringed pale cinnamon-brown, primary coverts similar but fringes narrower. Alula blackish-brown. Flight feathers dark grey-brown, tertials fringed pale cinnamon-brown, paler at tips, secondaries fringed paler brown, primaries narrowly fringed pale grey (pale wing panel as prominent as on British race of Willow Tit). Cheeks, ear-coverts and sides of neck white, washed cinnamon-buff, especially at rear. Chin and throat dull black, feathers at sides and lower border broadly tipped buffish-white (bib rather ill-defined). Lower sides of neck and flanks pale cinnamon-brown, sides of belly, vent and undertail-coverts slightly paler pinkish-cinnamon, breast and centre of belly off-white tinged buff. Thighs, axillaries and underwing-coverts pale cinnamon-brown. *In worn plumage*, pale fringes on wings and tail abraded and bleached paler, pale fringes on bib abraded and bib more extensive (although still irregularly defined), and breast and centre of belly marginally paler, a dirtier white. **Bare Parts**: Iris brown or dark brown; bill grey-black to black; legs and feet blue-grey to dark slate. **Adult Female**: As male (but see Sex/Age). **Juvenile and 1st Adult**: See Sex/Age. Legs and feet of juvenile pale slaty. **Measurements**: Wing of male 67.5–73, of female 67–72; tail of male 57–62, of female 56–60; bill 12.8–14.6; tarsus 16–19. Weight: no information (but see *P. s. stoetzneri* below).

**MOULT** Adult post-breeding complete (late June–September). Post-juvenile presumably partial (July–August).

**GEOGRAPHICAL VARIATION** Slight and largely clinal. In the eastern populations, there is a cline of increasing colour saturation from east to west (*stoetzneri-affinis-weigoldicus*), the cap becoming blacker and the body a darker, more cinnamon brown. The western population (nominate *songarus*), although separated from eastern birds by a large gap in distribution, forms a logical continuation of this trend, having the blackest cap and the richest and most cinnamon-brown body (although a paler brown). This suggests that the separation of the various populations is relatively recent.

*P. s. songarus* Tien Shan. See Description. Wing and especially bill average long, bill at least 2 mm longer than in any other subspecies (and longer than that of Willow Tit; Vaurie 1957b).

*P. s. weigoldicus* SW China in Sichuan, extreme SE Qinghai, eastern Tibet and NW Yunnan. Presumably intergrades with *affinis* in eastern Qinghai. As nominate *songarus*, but cap slightly browner (brownish-black), upperparts rather darker and duller brown, flanks darker and browner (although underparts may wear duller but paler?); also smaller. Wing of male 66–69, of female 66–69.5; tail 54–57; bill 10.5–12.6.

*P. s. affinis* North-central China from Ningxia Hui west through southern Gansu to NE Qinghai. As *weigoldicus*, but cap slightly paler and browner (mid brown with a slight pinkish cast), bib browner (dark brown), upperparts paler (dark drab-brown, as nominate *songarus* but slightly darker), flanks slightly paler (as nominate *songarus*). Size as *weigoldicus*. Wing 63–68.5; tail 55–65.5; bill 10.2–11.5.

**P. s. stoetzneri** NE China from SE Nei Mongol, through Hebei and Shanxi to Henan. Poorly marked? As *affinis* (with a brown cap and blackish-brown bib), but overall slightly paler: upperparts slightly paler and greyer (dark drab), underparts paler, with the breast and centre of belly dull greyish-white and the cinnamon-buff of the flanks rather more restricted and notably less pinkish-cinnamon. Small. Wing of male 59–66, of female 58–65; tail of male 57–66, of female 53–65; bill 10.5–11.3; tarsus 15–17.5; weight 8–12 g.

**RELATIONSHIPS** Forms a superspecies with Willow Tit, with which it is often considered conspecific. In the west, the population in the Tien Shan/Dzhungarskiy Alatau is separated by just *c.* 250 km of perhaps unsuitable habitat from the Tarbagatay mountains, which are inhabited by Willow Tits (of the northern race *baicalensis*). Morphologically, the two are rather different. Furthermore, in NE China, Willow Tits (*P. m. baicalensis*) range south to Liaoning and Songar Tits north and east to northern Hebei, with apparently little or no ecological barrier between them, although their ranges may not quite meet. In this region, the differences between the two species are striking, the race *stoetzneri* of Songar Tit having a brown cap, as against Willow Tit's black crown. Given their marked differences in appearance, the two are treated as distinct species, following Cramp & Perrins (1993) and Stepanyan (1990).

**REFERENCES** Kovshar' (1976), Stepanyan (1990), Vaurie (1959).

# 52 CAROLINA CHICKADEE *Parus carolinensis* Plate 16

It was not until 1834 that Audubon realised that there were two species of chickadee in eastern North America, a century after 'the' chickadee had been discovered by Europeans. The exact relationship of Carolina and Black-capped Chickadees remains enigmatic, despite much research.

**IDENTIFICATION** Length 120 mm (4.75 in). Cap black; upperparts grey, in fresh plumage variably tinged buff and olive. Tail dark grey, outer feathers narrowly fringed grey-white. Greater coverts and flight feathers dark grey-brown, inner greater coverts fringed light buffy-grey, longest tertial, secondaries and primaries finely fringed pale greyish. Cheek patches whitish, bib sooty-black, sides of breast olive-grey, flanks and undertail-coverts variably pale buff to creamy, and centre of breast and belly white, washed buff. One of a group of three closely similar North American chickadees, its range is well separated from that of Mexican Chickadee, leaving Black-capped Chickadee the only confusion species. Easily distinguished from all other North American tits by its small size, neat black cap, whitish cheeks and greyish upperparts. The breeding ranges of Carolina and Black-capped Chickadees approach each other closely (but do not overlap) along a line from southern Kansas, through central Missouri and Illinois, northern Indiana and Ohio and southern Pennsylvania to central New Jersey, and Black-capped replaces Carolina locally at higher altitudes in the Appalachians south to North Carolina. In the autumn and winter, however, small numbers of Black-capped move south into the northern marches of Carolina's range. On Carolina, the fringes to the longest tertials and secondaries are rather narrower and duller than on Black-capped Chickadee (on which they are rather broader and whiter), but the pale fringes nevertheless usually form a paler panel on the closed wing, although this is never so conspicuous as on Black-capped. More importantly, Carolina lacks the broad white fringes to the inner greater coverts, the fringes being only a little paler than the rest of the feather, and the greater coverts therefore appear *uniform* or at most form a very slightly paler patch; the uniform greater coverts thus contrast with the paler panel on the tertials and secondaries. Similarly, Carolina has narrower and duller pale margins to the outer tail feathers. Subsidiary differences are Carolina's smaller size and proportionally shorter tail and its slightly smaller and neater bib, with the lower border usually better defined; also, its flanks are washed pale buff or pale drab-buff (slightly paler and less cinnamon than on Black-capped), contrasting less with the remainder of the underparts. Identification is often relatively straightforward in autumn and winter, when birds are in fresh plumage. In summer, however, worn Black-capped Chickadees may be more similar to Carolina, showing a reduced contrast between the flanks and belly, and, when very worn, may lack pale fringes on the wing feathers. Voice is often a good distinction, especially the whistled song, typically a two-note *fee-bee* or *fee-bee'ee* (with second note 'stuttered') in Black-capped, with the first note slightly higher-pitched, and a four-note *see-bee-see-bay* in Carolina, with the first and third notes much higher in pitch. Both species, however, may also give three-note variants (although Black-capped rarely so), and in areas where their ranges abut each may mimic the song of the other. Hybrids also occur, and these, too, may give both songs, as well as intermediates. Thus, paradoxically, in the regions where identification is a real issue, voice is often *not* a reliable feature. For further details, and for separation in the hand, see Black-capped Chickadee.

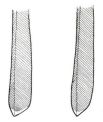

Figure 52.1 Outer tail feathers (T6) of adult (left), juvenile (right): note shape and distribution of white.

**SEX/AGE** Sexes similar. Juvenile as adult, but the cap and bib are slightly duller and browner, and the underparts more uniform, with less contrast between the breast and flanks. Also distinguished in the hand by the shape and pattern of the outer tail feather (T6), which is narrower and more pointed than the adult's, with white confined to the extreme tip (adults have the white fringe extending slightly more broadly around the tip; see figure 52.1). 1st adult as adult, but birds from more northerly populations retain the juvenile tail feathers, which differ from those of adults as above. In more southerly populations, all the tail feathers may be replaced in the post-juvenile moult, and it may not be possible to age birds after September.

**VOICE** In general, very similar to that of Black-capped Chickadee, and studied in detail by S.T. Smith (1972). The contact call is a thin *tsit*, whilst the 'flight call' is a loud, abrupt but liquid *psit*; this is given most frequently, and sometimes in series, when the pair or flock is about to move off. Also gives a very high, thin *seet*, usually in irregular series as a fussy, mouse-like twitter, e.g. *sisisisisi* (the 'variable see', this is often followed by a 'gargle' and is slightly fuller than the equivalent call of Black-capped Chickadee; it is given by both sexes during the breeding season, including as a prelude to copulation). The alarm is a high-pitched clicking *see* or *zee*, usually given in a series of 2–6 or more notes, and when disturbed on the nest incubating birds give a snake-like hiss. Peevish, nasal *zee-zee-zee* calls ('broken dees') are given by females during the breeding season, usually to solicit food from the male, and a similar call is given by begging fledglings. The 'chick-a-dee' call is broadly similar to that of Black-capped

Chickadee (which see), a *chick-a-dee-dee-dee-dee*, although usually higher-pitched and faster, with the 'dee' note hoarser and more rasping than Black-capped's rather sonorous, nasal *dee-dee-dee*. The phrase is of the same combination of four components, A, B, C and D, although these differ slightly from those of Black-capped Chickadee, notably in that types A and B intergrade (but they can presumably be used in the same array of combinations). Always given in the order ABCD, the individual units can be given once, repeated, or omitted altogether. In particular, the D unit is often given alone in a scolding series, sometimes quite prolonged, *dee-dee-dee-dee-dee-dee-dee*, and sometimes preceded by extended harsh *chr'r'r'r'r* phrases, e.g. *chr'r'r'r'r'r'dee'dee'dee*. Softer versions of the D note are also given, often together with lisping *tssleet* notes, in a soft version of the 'chick-a-dee' call. The typical song comprises a combination of mellow whistles, pure in tone, and recalling a squeaking gate in timbre, at higher ('fee') and lower pitches ('bee' and 'bay'). The individual notes are about equal in duration, but the first note tends to be slurred, and the low *bee* notes are softer and less far-carrying. Songs usually start with a high 'fee' note, and the 'typical' song is a four-note phrase, *fee-bee-fee-bay* or *sufee-subee*, with the first and third notes of the phrase much higher-pitched than the second and fourth. There are three-note variants, *see-bee-bee*, with the first note also rather higher-pitched, and songs comprising 2–8 (1–12) notes have been recorded, each male having a repertoire of song types. Some regional differences exist, with variations in the number of notes, a shift from the regular alternation in pitch, or a slurred tone (e.g. a slightly lisping *tsee-bee-tsebay*); and also 'song variants', in which the high ('H') and low ('L') notes may not be alternated (e.g. HHLL, HHLLL, HLLH, LLL). Quieter and softer versions of the song, often missing the terminal unit, are given by the male when approaching the nest. Song period from January onwards. The other 'song' is a 'gargle' phrase used in aggressive encounters. Gargles sound like apparently random collections of short musical notes jumbled together in rapid succession, tending to fall in pitch towards the end and often ending in a trill or nasal *dee* note; they are conversational and almost 'fussy', one rendition being *spee-deedle-dee-deedle-dee*. Gargles and

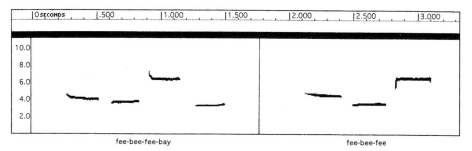

Figure 52.2  Carolina Chickadee (National Geographic Society/Cornell Laboratory of Ornithology 1986). Left, a four-note song, with the third note much higher in pitch than the rest. The song is variable (probably more so than Black-capped) Chickadee, and on the right is a three-note variant.

'chick-a-dee' calls may be run together, and there may also be intermediate calls. (Partly after Hailman 1989, S.T. Smith 1972.)

**DISTRIBUTION AND MOVEMENTS** Breeds in the SE **USA** north to southern **Kansas** (the southern tier of counties west to Seward Co., north in the east to Greenwood Co.), central **Missouri** (Barton, Henry, Osage and St Luis Cos.), **Illinois** (Madison, Fayette, Shelby, Champaign, Ford and Kankakee Cos.), **Indiana** (Grant Co.), **Ohio** (Paulding, Wyandot and southern Mahoning Cos.), **Pennsylvania** (only the extreme southwest north to Beaver Co. and east to SW Westmorland, and the southeast west to Fulton/Franklin Cos.) and northern **New Jersey** (to about the southern Raritan river). The range extends west to **Kansas**, **Oklahoma** (Beaver Co., exceptionally to Texas Co.) and central **Texas** (west in the panhandle to about Hutchinson Co. and locally Oldham Co., and to Hardeman, Callahan, Kerr, Real, Edwards, Atascosa and San Patricio Cos. and south to the Aransas river), and south to the Gulf Coast and central **Florida** (about Tampa Bay). Absent from higher elevations in the Appalachian mountains in **West Virginia**, eastern **Tennessee** and western **Maryland**, **Virginia** and **North Carolina**. (Note that the precise northern boundary of the range has still to be defined in some areas, and confusion with Black-capped Chickadees or hybrids may be responsible for some northern records.) Generally highly sedentary (more so than Black-capped Chickadee), but has wandered north to central Kansas (Ellis and Douglas Cos.) and northern Illinois. Vagrant **Ontario**, **Canada**, where collected at Long Point in May 1983 (*P. c. extimus*), with sight records from Toronto in April 1914 and Rondeau Provincial Park in July 1960; and SE

**Michigan** and **Nebraska** (also Iowa?: there is a specimen of this species from Keokuk collected in May 1888, but it is only 'hypothetical' on the state checklist).

**HABITAT** Broadleaved woodland, especially along streams and watercourses and favouring edge habitats, including clearings and a mixture of large trees and second growth. Also swamp forest, scrub and second growth, parks, well-wooded suburban areas and, in Florida, cypress swamps and the fringes of open pine woodland. In the more arid parts of the range in the southwest generally confined to riverine woodland, but also found in stands of juniper. (May be more confined to extensive areas of woodland than Black-capped Chickadee, but similarly occurs in a wider variety of habitats in winter.) A lowland species, found at up to *c*. 850 m in Texas. In the Appalachians, generally encountered at lower elevations than Black-capped Chickadee, in the valleys and foothills, but occurs at up to 1400 m in Pennsylvania, 1525 m in the Blue Ridge Mountains of Virginia (although locally not above 915 m, as in e.g. Giles Co.), 850 m in Tennessee (locally to 1200 m in the absence of Black-capped Chickadee), and 1380 m in North Carolina (locally 1800 m where Black-capped is absent).

**POPULATION** Common throughout the range. There has been some contraction of the range northwards in Florida.

**HABITS** Found in pairs, most being formed (or reaffirmed) in early spring, and usually pairs for life. In the late summer, the resident 'alpha' pair is often joined by several juvenile or 1st-adult individuals (probably not their own offspring) to form a small 'winter' flock of 2–7 birds which occupies a larger home range than the breeding territory.

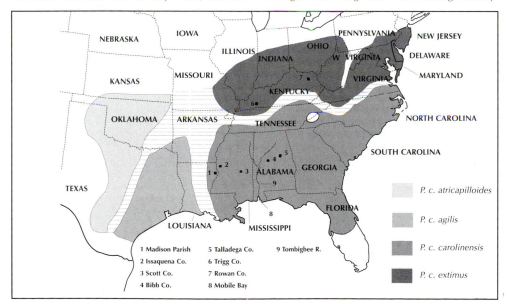

*Figure 52.3 Approximate ranges of the four subspecies of Carolina Chickadee (largely from Phillips 1986). The hatched area indicates zones of intergradation. Gill* et al. *(1993) found that the species was split genetically into two distinct eastern and western components, probably dividing around the Tombigbee drainage (see text).*

Initially at least (before the winter takes its toll), flocks are probably made up largely of paired birds. These flocks often join mixed-species foraging flocks. The winter home ranges are well defined and defended, usually by the male of the alpha pair. Each flock has a well-defined hierarchy, often linear, with the male of the alpha pair being the dominant bird in the flock (although the hierarchy is somewhat more flexible, especially among the lower ranks, than in Black-capped Chickadee). In the early spring, the flocks break up and territory is re-established by the alpha pair within the home range used during the winter, and some of the other flock members (the highest-ranking subordinates) may also pair and establish territory nearby (also within the winter range). The lowest-ranking birds in the flock are forced to move further afield, perhaps into more marginal habitats. Territory boundaries are vigorously defended, usually vocally, by the male. In late summer forms family parties, but when fully independent juveniles from several broods may form (temporary?) loose roaming flocks. Roosts in the winter singly in cavities located within the flock's home range, sometimes among dense vines. In harsh weather, enters the roost earlier and leaves later than in milder periods, and in midwinter may spend as much as 15 hours per day roosting. Roosting birds can enter a state of regulated hypothermia, lowering their body temperature to make significant energy savings. Feeds in trees and thickets, foraging among twigs and smaller branches and inspecting bark surfaces, but seldom descends to the ground. Regularly visits birdtables (feeders). Food insects, spiders, and also seeds. Stores food in bark crevices, rotten logs, clusters of conifer needles, or in hollow plant stems.

**BREEDING BIOLOGY** Season: Texas, late March–late April (mid February–early June); Florida, late March–late April; New Jersey, mid April–mid June. Nests are placed 1.5–4.5 m (0.3–12 m) above ground, usually in holes excavated by the birds themselves in decayed wood, often in stubs 1.65–2 m high and 110–130 mm in diameter, but also in trees and sometimes in fence-posts. Will also use natural cavities, old woodpecker excavations and even pipes, and noted using an old American Cliff Swallow nest (Sutton 1967). Even if not excavated in full, the hole may be 'cleaned out' by the pair. Will use nestboxes (especially if filled with sawdust) and bluebird houses. A variety of sites may be inspected, and excavation and even nest-building begun at several before the final selection is made. Both sexes excavate, over a period of c. 14 days. The nest is a foundation of moss, bark strips, grass and feathers, lined with plant down, fur and hair, built by the female. Lining material continues to be added through the laying period, forming a flap which is used to cover the eggs when the female is off the nest. Clutch 5–6 (3–9); eggs white, finely spotted reddish-brown, the markings often concentrated at the larger end; 14.9 x 11.7 mm (*P. c. agilis*). Female incubates, period 11–14 days; she is fed on and off the nest by the male. The young are fed by both sexes, although predominantly by the male during the first few days, and fledge after 16 (13–17) days. They remain on or near the breeding territory, becoming fully independent after another 14–21 days. Single-brooded.

**DESCRIPTION** *P. c. extimus* **Adult**: *In fresh plumage* (autumn–winter), crown (down to eye), nape and centre of upper mantle dull black. Mantle, back and scapulars mid grey with slight olive tinge and faintly washed buff, especially on upper mantle, scapulars and rump. Uppertail-coverts slightly paler and buffer. Tail dark grey, feathers narrowly fringed light grey; on T6 fringes rather narrower and paler, more grey-white, and tip whiter. Lesser and median coverts as upperparts, median coverts with small dark grey centres. Greater coverts mid-dark grey, outer 3–4 narrowly fringed light-mid grey, inner more broadly fringed light buffy-grey. Alula blackish-grey, very finely fringed mid grey, primary coverts dark grey, very finely fringed mid grey. Flight feathers dark grey-brown, longest tertial fringed very pale buff-grey or pale grey (tt1 and tt2 generally only very faintly fringed paler), secondaries finely fringed pale grey, primaries very finely fringed pale greyish-white, broadest inwards of emarginations. Cheeks whitish. Chin and throat sooty-black, feathers of lower border tipped white, giving slightly irregular margin. Sides of breast pale olive-grey, flanks and undertail-coverts pale buff, variably tinged drab, centre of breast and belly white, faintly washed drab-buff. Thighs pale greyish-buff. Axillaries and underwing-coverts pale buff. *In worn plumage* (summer), upperparts greyer, lacking any hint of buff, pale fringes on wings duller and narrower, lower border to bib more sharply defined, and underparts slightly paler and less buffy, with sides of breast greyer, less olive, flanks paler buff, breast and belly dingy grey-white. **Bare Parts**: Iris dark brown; bill bluish-black to black; legs and feet blue-grey. **Juvenile**: As adult, but cap duller and slightly browner, more restricted (not extending onto upper mantle), bib slightly duller and browner, and underparts slightly more uniform, generally pale buff, with less contrast between breast and flanks. **1st Adult**: As adult (see Sex/Age). **Measurements**: Wing of male 60–65.5 (chord 59.5–67), of female 59–64 (chord 57–65); tail of male 52–62, of female 48.5–58; bill 8.7–10.3; tarsus 14.5–17. Weight 9–12 g.

**MOULT** Adult post-breeding complete (July–August). Post-juvenile partial, may include tertials and some or all of the tail feathers in southern populations (July–September).

**GEOGRAPHICAL VARIATION** Slight and largely clinal. Size decreases from north to south, and birds become paler and greyer (less brownish) above and paler on the flanks in a cline running from east to west (with a steep 'step' in the cline in the Mississippi valley area). Thus, palest in the southwest of the range (*agilis*), with those in the southeast (nominate *carolinensis*) being smallest and darkest. There is also a gradual reduction in the prominence of the pale fringes to the wing feathers from north to south. Gill *et al.* (1993) studied mtDNA and found that Carolina Chickadee could be split into genetically distinct eastern and western components which have apparently been separated from each other for at least one million years (and have diverged genetically by c. 3%, that is about half the distance of recognised chickadee species, and as much as that of two well-marked, geographically isolated subspecies of Mountain Chickadee). Both genetic types have been collected in central Mississippi (Scott Co.) and in SW Kentucky (Trigg Co.), with the 'split' between the components probably roughly following the Mississippi/Alabama state line along the Tombigbee river system south to Mobile Bay (an established biogeographical divide): only eastern types were collected in Bibb and Talladega Cos., Alabama, and Rowan Co., eastern Kentucky, and only western types in Madison Parish, Louisiana, and Issaquena Co., western Mississippi (on opposite sides of the Mississippi river); see figure 52.3. (Gill *et al.* note that this division does not correspond to that of the recognised subspecies, but there is substantial disagreement and confusion regarding the range of the subspecies.) Although they are not known to differ in terms of appearance or vocalisations, the western component, 'Cajun Chickadee', may merit full specific status. Four races recognised, largely following Phillips (1986).

***P. c. extimus*** The northeast portion of the range, west to central Missouri (to about the Mississippi valley, where intergrades with *atricapilloides*) and south to western Tennessee and central North Carolina (where intergrades with nominate *carolinensis*). Relatively poorly differentiated from nominate *carolinensis*. Large and brown. See Description.

***P. c. carolinensis*** SE USA, north to northern Arkansas, SE Kentucky, central North Carolina and SE Virginia, west to eastern Louisiana. Intergrades with *extimus* in the north and with *agilis* in the west. The smallest and darkest race. As *extimus*, but upperparts slightly darker and browner (but

brownish feather tips lost with wear), pale fringes to wing and tail feathers slightly duller, tertials fringed slightly duller, not so white (pale smoky-grey); buff of flanks averages paler and cleaner. Wing (chord) of male 56.5–65, of female 56.5–62; tail of male 48–54.5, of female 46.5–52.5.

***P. c. atricapilloides*** The northwest portion of the range, from southern Kansas through Oklahoma to west-central Texas (Panhandle, Blacklands to Fanin and Navarro Cos., and the Edwards Plateau). Intergrades with *extimus* in western Arkansas and SW Missouri and with *agilis* over a broad zone in the southeast. Large and grey. As *extimus*, but overall paler, upperparts purer grey, mid-light grey, underparts paler with much-reduced buff on the flanks (lightly washed clean creamy-buff when fresh, may be almost white when worn). Also larger (the largest race). Wing (chord) of male 62–69, of female 59–66; tail of male 54–63.5, of female 51–62.

***P. c. agilis*** SW USA in eastern and SE Texas (north and west to about Bexar and Red River Cos.), Louisiana and southern Arkansas. Intergrades with *atricapilloides* to the north and with nominate *carolinensis* to the east. Small and grey. As *atricapilloides*, but slightly reduced buff wash on flanks and pale fringes to flight feathers slightly less conspicuous. Also rather smaller. Wing (chord) of male 58.5–66, of female 56–62; tail of male 47.5–56.5, of female 47–55.5.

**HYBRIDS** Hybridises regularly with Black-capped Chickadee along the northern edge of the range (see p. 272 for details).

**RELATIONSHIPS** A member of the *Poecile* subgenus, and usually placed in a superspecies with Black-capped Chickadee, Songar and Willow Tits of the Old World, and possibly also Mexican Chickadee. See Black-capped Chickadee for details (p. 274).

**REFERENCES** Bent (1946), Brewer (1961), Dixon (1963), Lunk (1952), S.T. Smith (1972).

---

# 53 BLACK-CAPPED CHICKADEE *Parus atricapillus*    Plate 16

A familiar backyard bird through most of Canada and the northern USA, this chickadee shares with Great Tit the distinction of being one of the most intensively studied birds in the world. Its complex vocalisations are thought to approach human language in terms of the quality of information that they can convey.

**IDENTIFICATION** Length 130 mm (5 in). Cap sooty-black, extending onto the centre of the upper mantle. Upperparts mid olive-grey, sometimes with a slight buff tinge, tail blackish-grey, the outer two feathers broadly fringed off-white. Greater coverts, tertials and flight feathers blackish-grey, the longest tertial and most of the greater coverts broadly fringed off-white, with the secondaries more narrowly fringed whitish, forming a pale panel on the closed wing. Cheek patches whitish, faintly tinged drab-buff, extending well onto the sides of the neck. Bib sooty-black, extending onto the upper breast, but rather ragged on the lower border. Underparts whitish, with the sides of the breast variably olive-buff and the

flanks, vent and undertail-coverts variably pale cinnamon-buff. Plumage soft and loose. Easily distinguished from most North American tits by its small size, neat black cap, lack of a supercilium and olive-grey upperparts. There are, however, two closely similar chickadees, Mexican and Carolina. Black-capped's range is widely separated from that of Mexican Chickadee, leaving the main confusion species as Carolina Chickadee. These two species replace each other abruptly along a line from southern Kansas, through central Missouri and Illinois, northern Indiana and Ohio and southern Pennsylvania to central New Jersey, and Black-capped also largely replaces Carolina at higher altitudes in the Appalachians south to

North Carolina. Their breeding ranges do not overlap, but they approach each other very closely (although there is sometimes a small gap), and in autumn and winter Black-capped may wander a little further south, into the range of Carolina (the two species may even be found in the same mixed flocks). Thus, although any individual well north of this line can be assumed to be Black-capped, and any bird significantly to the south a Carolina, in these states range is *not* a reliable guide and particular care should be taken over identifications (see also Hybrids). Although slightly larger and relatively long-tailed, Black-capped is very similar to Carolina Chickadee. The most important difference is found in the inner greater coverts, which on Black-capped are broadly fringed whitish, contrasting with the dark grey feather centres (and with the dark centres to the tertials); on Carolina Chickadee, the fringes to the greater coverts are only a little paler than the centres. On both species, the tertials, secondaries and primaries are fringed paler, but these fringes are broader and whiter on Black-capped, forming a strongly contrasting pale panel on the secondaries on the closed wing. On Carolina they are a little narrower and duller, being dull pale grey. With wear, the pale fringes on the wing feathers are reduced, and although the differences between the two species are obvious in autumn and winter they may be very subdued in summer. An additional feature is the lower border of the bib, uneven on Black-capped (owing to white tips to the black feathers), rather than the neat, well-defined demarcation shown by Carolina; this feature, however, is at best indicative, and is of less use in worn plumage. Another minor character is underpart coloration, Black-capped having slightly richer and more cinnamon-buff flanks which show more contrast with the whitish breast and belly. Finally, the fringes to the outer tail feathers are broader and whiter on Black-capped. Note that Carolina Chickadees in the north of the range (thus nearest to Black-capped Chickadee) average largest, approaching the smaller populations of Black-capped in size (notably *P. a. practicus*) and also slightly in proportions, being proportionally slightly longer-tailed than southern populations. Northern Carolina Chickadees also have the most pronounced pale fringes to the wing feathers (especially compared with their swarthy southern cousins). Voice is often the best feature by which to separate the two species. The nasal 'dee' component of the 'chick-a-dee' call of Black-capped *tends* to be lower-pitched, fuller, and repeated in slower and more deliberate series than that of Carolina Chickadee, but these calls are very variable and the differences would be apparent only to a trained ear. The whistled song provides a better clue: a two-note *fee-bee* or *fee-bee'ee* from Black-capped (the second note may be 'stuttered'), with the first note a little higher-pitched, and a four-note *see-bee-see-bay* from Carolina, with the first and third notes much higher in pitch. Black-capped may rarely give a three-note variant, *fee-bee-bee*, or a one-note song, and Carolina may also give a three-note song, *see-bee-bee*, with

only the first note higher, but Carolina's introductory note is still *much* higher-pitched than in Black-capped, and a Black-capped giving a one- or three-note variant should eventually give the typical two-note song. In general, the song of Carolina is much more variable in terms of the number of notes than the rather stereotyped two-note song of Black-capped. In the areas where the ranges of Black-capped and Carolina Chickadees meet, either species may sing the other's song and hybrids (see below) may also sing either song, as well as intermediates. Thus, for sure identification of a particular bird in the hybrid zone (or of extralimital birds), the typical voice of one species should be consistently noted, as well as *all* the plumage features. In the hand, Black-capped is best separated from Carolina Chickadee by a combination of plumage features and measurements. The most useful in the region of the hybrid zone is tail length: 57–67 mm in Black-capped, and 48–58 mm in Carolina. Problematic birds may be separated by tail/wing ratio (wing measured as chord): 0.886–1.032 for Black-capped, 0.819–0.922 (most ≤ 0.9) for Carolina (Pyle *et al.* 1987). A few individuals, however, may not be identifiable, even in the hand, and beware also hybrids. Black-capped Chickadee is a potential vagrant to Europe, and would have to be carefully distinguished from Marsh Tit and especially from Willow Tit. At all times, Black-capped is noticeably longer-tailed than Willow Tit. Its cap is more restricted at the rear, with broad expansion of the cheek patches onto the sides of neck and nape. In fresh autumn plumage (nominate *atricapillus*, compared with Willow of the British race *P. m. kleinschmidti*), the upperparts are slightly greyer and less brown and the cap slightly purer black. The greater coverts, tertials and secondaries are fringed whitish (rather than pale buff) and the bib is much more extensive (even in worn plumage), extending to the lower cheeks and upper breast, and rather better defined at the sides and on the lower border, with far fewer whitish feather tips. The cheek patches, breast and centre of the belly are purer white, but the flanks and vent are similarly washed pale cinnamon-brown. Black-capped Chickadee more closely resembles Willow Tit of the northern race (*P. m. borealis*) in the colour of the upperparts and cap, although Black-capped's upperparts may average slightly darker and more olive, with less of a drab wash to the grey. The wing feathers of northern Willow Tits are similarly fringed whitish, and its cheek patches are as pure white. However, Black-capped's tail is longer, its cap more restricted, with the white cheeks broader at the rear, its bib is larger and better defined (all as above), and its underparts are much buffer, especially on the flanks, belly and undertail-coverts (northern Willow has just a pale pinkish-buff wash on the flanks and undertail-coverts).

**SEX/AGE** Sexes similar. Juvenile very similar to the adult, but with the cap and bib more restricted and not so intensely black and the outer tail feathers narrower and more pointed, with white confined to the fringe of the outer web and extreme tip of the inner web (on adults, the white fringes

*Figure 53.1 Outer tail feathers (T6) of adult (left), juvenile (right): note shape and distribution of white.*

usually extend well around the tip of the inner web; see figure 53.1). 1st adult as adult, but the retained juvenile wing and tail feathers are relatively worn compared with the adult's at the same time of year; compare also the shape and pattern of the retained juvenile tail feathers.

**VOICE** Intensively studied, with at least 15 distinct classes of vocalisation. The contact call is a quiet, thin *tsit*, usually given constantly but singly at irregular intervals. This may become a louder and much fuller, sharp *tsit*, *psit* or *tsleet* (the 'flight note'), clicking but liquid in tone, which is given at a greater frequency when the pair or flock is about to move off, sometimes in a short, staccato, almost rattling series of up to c. 10 units (the notes tending to be paired), e.g. *tsleet'slit'slit'slit'sui*. Another call (the 'variable see') is made up of very thin, rather high-pitched, mouse-like *seet* units,

usually given in a short series of 10 or more notes (it may last 6 seconds), *seet-seet-seet...* or *sisisisisi...*, often with a slightly irregular rhythm, as a fussy, rodent-like twitter. It is often followed by a 'gargle' (see below), and is given by both sexes during the breeding season, especially as a prelude to, and during, copulation. Throughout the year, but especially outside the breeding season, both sexes give a characteristic *chick-a-dee-dee-dee*. This is a complex vocalisation, serving several functions. Each phrase is made up of four different note types, dubbed A, B, C and D (see figure 53.2): 'chick' = A, 'k' = B (both high-frequency notes), 'ka' = C (at a lower frequency), and the nasal, buzzing 'dee' = D (A, B, & C are rather similar, and are close to the *tsleet* call). Whatever the combination used, the four are almost always given in a fixed sequence, ABCD, and each note type may be omitted, given once, or repeated a variable number of times. Phrases comprising just A and D combinations are commonest, and D especially may be repeated, with scolding birds giving prolonged series of nasal *dee-dee-dee-dee-dee-dee-dee-dee...* units. With an unlimited number of possible call types, 'chick-a-dee' can be used to convey much information, and is the only known system of combinatorial animal communication apart from human language. Notably, chick-a-dees may convey both individual and flock identity (the precise structure of the 'dee' note rapidly converging among flock members).

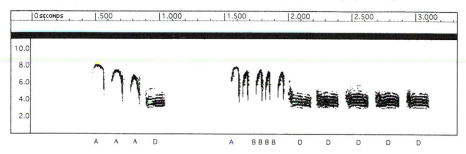

*Figure 53.2 Black-capped Chickadee (left, Brigham 1994; right, J.C. Roché/National Sound Archive). Two 'chick-a-dees', which are combinations of three high-frequency notes 'A', 'B' and 'C', and a low-frequency note, 'D', characterised on sonagrams by a banded appearance, and sounding buzzing or nasal. A is very variable but with a short arm, B has the arms near equal in length, and C is similar to B but lower-pitched and 'noisy' (M.S. Ficken in litt.). The phrase on the left could be written tis's'sle'dee, and that on the right tis's'si'li'i'dee-dee-dee-dee-dee.*

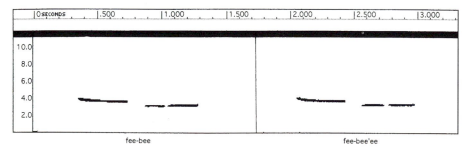

*Figure 53.3 Black-capped Chickadee song (left, Cornell Laboratory of Ornithology/Interactive Audio 1990; right, Brigham 1994). Two examples of the whistled 'fee-bee' song. Characterstically there are just two notes, the 'bee' a little lower-pitched than the 'fee'. Left, the 'bee' is split, but the gap is not perceptible to human ears, and the note sounds as a continuous bee; right, the gap is greater, hence the 'bee' sounds distinctly stuttered, bee'ee.*

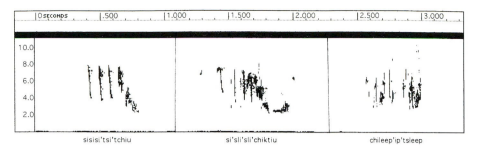

Figure 53.4 Black-capped Chickadee (left and centre, Cornell Laboratory of Ornithology/Interactive Audio 1990; right, Cornell Laboratory of Ornithology/Interactive Audio 1992). Three examples of 'gargles', which are made up of very short musical notes jumbled together in rapid succession, sounding conversational and almost 'fussy'. The phrase often falls in pitch towards the end.

Common functions may be as a contact call, to alert other chickadees to 'come here', to convey agitation, and to give the 'all clear'. In alarm gives a high-pitched *zee* (higher-pitched and longer as the alarm increases, and causing other chickadees to freeze until a *chick-a-dee* call signals the 'all clear'), and when surprised on the nest a loud hiss *haaah* in the typical *Parus* 'snake display'. Peevish, thin but nasal *zee-zee-zee* calls ('broken dees') are given in series of 1–7 notes by females during the breeding season, usually to solicit food from the male, and begging fledglings give a rather similar series of notes but descending the scale, *zee-zee-zizizi-ziu* (the 'begging dee'), whilst recently fledged young also give a very faint, long and sometimes musical 'subsong'. There are two types of 'song', that is vocalisations that are used to advertise territories and/or repel rivals. The first is a stereotyped phrase made up of two clear, whistled units, each note on an even pitch, but with the first note characteristically a little higher than the following unit; it is often verbalised as *fee-bee* (or sometimes *phoebe*). In fact, the second unit may be composed of two 'bee' notes separated by a very short interval (a mere stutter), and then the second 'bee' may be *very slightly* higher-pitched; this may be written *fee-bee'ee*. Songs with three *well-separated* notes are rare, as are variants with just one note (see figure 53.3). In tone, this song sounds very much like a slowly moving unoiled swing, or a squeaking gate. Although given primarily by males from mid December to early summer (especially April–July), it may be heard occasionally throughout the year and is sometimes given by females (and thus has other functions than 'song', serving to lead flocks and being used in individual recognition). 'Fee-bees' are, however, given less frequently than is song in many other Passerine birds, even during the breeding season. They serve to summon males to their territorial boundary, and a whistled imitation of the song will attract male chickadees ('quickest summons in the bird world'). Much quieter, 'faint' *fee-bee* phrases are given by both sexes as a contact call during the breeding season, but especially by males when feeding females, or by adults to fledged young. Each male may have a repertoire of two or more song types, but they differ only in pitch (the less frequently given 'frequency-shifted' songs at a lower pitch being a more aggressive signal). Otherwise, there is little variation across the range, but in SW Washington and similarly in Alaska there may be no change in pitch, *duu-duu-duu-duu-duu*, and the units may alternate with much shorter pulses (recalling a variant Willow Tit song from Japan), whilst presumably similar monotonal 2–3-note variants are recorded from Martha's Vineyard (Massachusetts), Ontario and the Gaspé peninsula of Quebec (Brewer 1961). The second song is the 'gargle', a complex phrase given largely by males during the autumn and winter. Gargles sound like apparently random collections of very short musical notes jumbled together in rapid succession, often falling in pitch towards the end of the phrase and terminating with a trill or nasal 'dee'-type unit; they are conversational and almost 'fussy'. There are endless variations, but phrases such as *sisisi'tsi'tchiu*, *si'sli'sli'chiktiu*, or *ch'dl'i-ch'dl'u* give a general impression. They comprise a combination of 2–13 units (or 'syllables'), each male having a repertoire of at least 13 syllables to choose from in constructing a gargle, with 23 different syllable types documented for the species. Males can produce at least 15 different types of gargle, although most are rather infrequent (but the number of *possible* combinations of 15 syllables is astronomical). Notably, there is considerable microgeographic variation in gargles, and each local repertoire may change from year to year. Gargles are used in aggressive and sexual encounters, and probably have other functions, too (see figure 53.4). (Partly after Smith 1993.)

**DISTRIBUTION AND MOVEMENTS** Breeds north to the treeline, in the **USA** to central and southern **Alaska** (west to the Alaska peninsula and north to Kotzebue Sound, and including Kodiak Island and the Shumagin islands; has wandered to Nunivak Island) and in **Canada** to southern **Yukon** (north to the southern Ogilvie range, Burwash Landing and Dezadeash Lake), SW **Mackenzie** (to Nahanni NP, Fort Simpson and the Great Slave Lake), northern **Saskatchewan** (to Lake Athabasca and Stony Rapids), central **Manitoba** (Thicket Portage), central **Ontario** (to Big Trout Lake and Moosonee, and rarely to Little Sachigo Lake and locally along the shores of James Bay to Attawapiskat), central **Quebec** (to the southern parts of James Bay, Lake Mistassini and the northern shore of the St Lawrence estuary, and including Anticosti Island and Iles de la Madeleine), the **Maritimes**, and **Newfoundland**, including Prince Edward Island. The range extends south to NW **California** (western Siskiyou, north and west Humboldt and Del Norte Cos.), southern **Oregon**, NE **Nevada** (perhaps winter only), southern **Utah**, northern **New Mexico** (San Juan river and Sangre de Cristo range), southern **Kansas** (absent southern tier of counties), central **Missouri** (south to Barton, Henry, Osage and St Luis Cos.), **Illinois** (to Madison, Fayette, Shelby, Champaign, Ford and Kankakee Cos.), **Indiana** (to Kosciusko and Noble Cos., dubiously (?) to Madison Co.; Mumford & Keller 1984) and **Ohio** (to Paulding, Wyandot and Columbiana Cos.), **Pennsylvania** (absent extreme southwest and southeast, east of York Co.) and northern **New Jersey** (to about the north Raritan river), and also the Appalachian mountains in eastern **West Virginia**, western **Maryland** and (very locally?) western **Virginia** (including Giles Co.), with apparently isolated populations in the southern Appalachians in the Great Smoky mountains of eastern **Tennessee** and western **North Carolina**, also the Great and Plott Balsam mountains and formerly Mount Mitchell (the Black mountains) of western North Carolina, and occasionally other sites in the eastern mountains of Tennessee. Absent Vancouver Island and the northern coastal regions of British Columbia. The distribution is necessarily rather local in the Great Plains region. Largely resident, but in years of poor food supply, especially failure of the northern seed crop, 'irruptions' may occur in which large numbers, predominantly of 1st-adult birds, move south during mid September–mid November. Although usually not penetrating beyond the southern limits of the range, a small number of individuals do move to areas away from the breeding range (but these may be largely juveniles from local populations engaged in the normal random post-fledging dispersal, rather than migrants from further north). Unusually for a Passerine, is largely a diurnal migrant, and significant passages may be noted at migration bottlenecks; chickadees are loath to cross open water, and 36,000 moved along the lakeshore near Rochester, New York, in October 1961 (Smith 1993). Return passage may be noted in early March–mid May. Additionally, some montane populations undertake altitudinal movements (as with the north-south movements, these involve largely or almost exclusively 1st-adult birds). In winter occurs irregularly, but fairly commonly, in **Delaware**, and also in the Piedmont of **Maryland** and **Virginia** (although uncommonly so in Virginia), and an irregular and rare winter visitor to the **District of Columbia**. Accidental in winter in southern **Missouri**, in the Ozarks and Mississippi lowlands. Vagrant **Arizona** (the extreme north at Teec Nos Pos and at Navajo and Pipe Spring National Monuments, October–February), western **Oklahoma** (Cimarron Co., December 1985–January 1986; a bird collected Harper Co.

in April 1956 may be a hybrid), **Texas** (19th-century specimens probably best discounted, but well-documented sight records, although not on official state checklist) and **Kentucky** (including Cumberland Gap National Historical Park, January 1969). Occasionally, individuals may also wander north of the breeding range (e.g. to Point Barrow, Alaska).

**HABITAT** Deciduous and mixed forest, especially stands of birch and alder, and favours edge habitats. Locally also in coniferous woodland (e.g. spruce-fir forest in the Adirondacks in New York and near the northern boundary of the range, and pinyon-juniper in Colorado), riverine willows, alders and cottonwoods (especially in the boreal zone and in the more arid mid-west), well-wooded farmland, parks, cemeteries and wooded suburban areas. The presence of suitable nest sites may be an important limiting factor. In the winter and on migration may be found in a wider variety of bushy habitats, including urban areas, and more frequently in conifers. Generally a lowland species, e.g. in NW California recorded at up to 915 m, in Idaho up to 1920 m and in New York up to 1220 m. In the southeastern parts of the range, however, largely or exclusively montane. Thus, in Tennessee breeds above 1200 m, descending in winter to 600 m (occasionally lingering as late as May at low elevations), and in North Carolina breeds above 1200 m in spruce-fir forests. Overall, in the Appalachians generally found at higher elevations than Carolina Chickadee, although replaced by the latter species on some mountaintops on the Great Smoky Mountains of Tennessee/North Carolina. In the southwest, found at up to 2775 m in Colorado and at 2285–c. 3200 m in New Mexico.

**POPULATION** Overall common, but only fairly common in Mackenzie (becoming uncommon there in winter), New Mexico, Tennessee and North Carolina, and uncommon in California and Nevada. Undergoes periodic fluctuations in numbers, especially in the southern parts of the range, peaking every 2–3 years, and there has been a general upward trend in numbers in the eastern parts of the range.

**HABITS** Often tame and confiding, and may quickly learn to feed from the hand, but relatively quiet and secretive from egg-laying to fledging. Found singly, in pairs or in small parties. Pair formation may take place at any time of year, but predominantly in late summer/early autumn, at the same time as the formation of winter flocks, and again in winter and early spring, usually as a result of winter fatalities among established pairs. Most individuals probably pair for life. Following the break-up of family parties in the late summer, each young chickadee disperses independently from its natal area, often moving several kilometres. Temporary and rather unstable flocks of juveniles are sometimes formed in July–August (–September), but these quickly disperse. True 'winter flocks', also formed in late summer, comprise 6–12 (2–18) birds, generally being largest in areas where food is supplemented by bird feeders (or around other 'honey-pots') and where compound flocks are formed by temporary amalgamations of two or more flocks, and possibly averaging smallest in southern populations. These flocks of chickadees often form the nucleus of mixed-species foraging parties (most commonly in areas away from feeders and in hard weather). The winter flock is maintained during about September–February and occupies a distinct (and relatively small) home range, which may be defended against intrusion by members of other flocks (and hence more properly be termed a 'territory', i.e. a defended area), although in other cases flock home ranges may overlap, especially where there are particularly rich food sources. Birds may also intrude into neighbouring home ranges when food is scarce. The winter flock is made up of local breeders and 1st adults from more distant broods. Initially at least (before the winter takes its toll), it probably consists largely of pairs. The flock has a stable membership and contains well-established linear dominance hierarchies, with males usually dominating over females and adults ranking above 1st adults (although the pecking order between the *pairs*, rather than individuals, may be most important). A chickadee's rank within the flock will significantly affect its behaviour and its chances of survival (higher-rank individuals may forage in the safest and/or most food-rich parts of the habitat). Some older, high-ranking individuals or pairs ('dominant wanderers') may wander more widely than the rest of the flock, covering an area encompassing up to five flock territories, although they return to their own home range to roost with their flock at night. Some lone unpaired 1st adults ('winter floaters') are not regular members of a particular flock, switching instead among 3–6 flocks, but have an established low-ranking position in the hierarchy of each. When moving between flocks, they are silent and furtive. Should a high-ranking flock member disappear, a floater may insert itself into the flock, taking over the widow(er) and rank of the dead bird. These substitutions occur, however, only when the density of floaters is high enough; at low floater densities, the gaps in the flock structure will remain unfilled until the spring break-up. Migrant chickadees from further north or higher latitudes may also be outside the winter-flock system, having their own individual home range which overlaps several flock ranges, and be largely solitary; they have relatively high rank (unlike winter floaters), are vocal and conspicuous, and do not attempt to join local flocks, even when opportunities exist. The winter flocks break up in early spring and territories are established, the high-ranking pair within the flock usually occupying a territory within the winter home range, other pairs dispersing to areas outwith the home range, especially when population densities are high. At this time, pair formation may take place within the flock, filling the gaps left by the winter's fatalities (if they have not already been filled by winter floaters). Some birds may stay and become 'summer floaters' and remain unpaired. These occasionally try to associate with an established pair, but are generally solitary, ranging over a 'home

range' that encompasses several occupied breeding territories. If a member of a territory-holding breeding pair dies, it may be replaced by a summer floater. Roosts singly, primarily in thick vegetation (especially dense conifers), and on mild nights members of the winter flock usually roost within a few metres of each other. Otherwise, especially on colder nights, roosts in holes, the females roost in the nest from the initial stages of construction until the young are at least 12 days old. Occasionally, will use abandoned birds' nests. Very hardy, the species occurs in areas where the temperature may drop to -52° C, and in Alaska there may be just 3 hours and 38 minutes of daylight in which to forage in midwinter; can survive the extreme cold of midwinter in the Brooks Range, feeding among willow branches blown clear of snow, miles to the north of the summer breeding habitat in the forest (Vaughan 1991). Roosting chickadees can enter a state of regulated hypothermia, lowering their body temperature to 10–12° C below the daytime norm of 42° C, and thus making significant energy savings; notably, however, chickadees are able to fly (and thus escape predators) when still in a state of hypothermia. (Unlike other studies, Grossman & West 1977 found no evidence of marked hypothermia in roosting birds in Alaska, with a drop in body temperature of just 3° C; this anomaly has yet to be explained.) Forages in trees and bushes, exploring the bark from the trunk to the thinnest twigs. In summer also feeds among foliage, and in winter in low herbs and on the ground (although the latter behaviour is relatively infrequent); in cold and windy weather, will feed in low dense shrubs which offer some shelter. Occasionally flycatches. Regularly visits feeders (birdtables). Food in summer largely insects (especially caterpillars), spiders and other invertebrates, but also seeds (especially hemlock) and berries (e.g. Poison Ivy, bayberry). Vegetable items comprise c. 50% of the autumn and winter diet. May also feed on the sap of Sugar Maple, the fat of animal carcasses, and even on dead fish. Often carries food, especially larger items, to cover before eating it. Stores food, mostly seeds but also insects and spiders, often removing the heads prior to caching. Food is stored largely in the autumn, and more frequently by northern birds. Items to be cached are placed separately ('scatter-hoarded') in bark crevices and knotholes, among clusters of conifer needles and dead leaves, and even in earth or snow. The species has an exceptional spatial memory, being able to retrieve items up to a month later, and these food supplies are probably important for winter survival, especially in northern populations. (Largely after Smith 1991.)

**BREEDING BIOLOGY** Season: Oregon, mid April–late June; Kansas, late March–mid June; Illinois, late April–mid June; Michigan, mid April–early July; Massachusetts and Vermont, May–mid July; Ontario, late April–mid July; Nova Scotia, late May–early June. The nest is placed in a tree cavity, usually in dead snags (especially birch and American Aspen), but sometimes in knotholes or rotting branches, and occasionally in a fence post; some are in abandoned old woodpecker excavations. Cavities are 1.5–7 m above ground (0–20 m, rarely *in* the ground). The birds (both sexes) excavate the hole themselves, often starting several holes before the final selection is made (frequently by the female). The chippings are carried away and scattered. Will use nestboxes if natural cavities are scarce, especially if half-filled with dead-wood chippings or sawdust which the birds can then excavate. Seldom reuses old nest sites. The nest, built by the female alone over a period of 3–5 (2–14) days, is a foundation of moss, bark, pine needles, grass and vegetable fibres, lined with fur, hair, wool, spiders' cocoons and sometimes feathers. Rarely, the eggs may be laid on the cavity floor. Clutch 6–8 (1–13): eggs white, finely speckled with reddish-brown, often concentrated at the larger end; 15.2 x 12.2 mm (*P. a. atricapillus*). Female incubates, period 12–13 (11–14) days; she is fed on the nest by the male. Only the female broods the young, but they are fed by both sexes and fledge after 16 days (as early as 12 days if disturbed). They remain with both parents and are fed for a further 21–28 (14–28) days, although they are able to find some of their own food from seven days after fledging. Second broods are rare.

**DESCRIPTION** *P. a. atricapillus* **Adult**: *In fresh plumage* (autumn–winter), forehead, crown (to below eye) and centre of upper mantle sooty-black. Upperparts mid olive-grey with a variable buffy tinge, especially to upper mantle and uppertail-coverts. Tail blackish-grey, outer webs fringed off-white, broadly so on T5 and T6; tail slightly rounded, outer feathers *c.* 7 mm shorter than longest. Lesser and median coverts as upperparts, median with small dark grey centres; greater coverts blackish-grey, outer two narrowly fringed mid grey, remainder broadly fringed off-white. Alula blackish-grey, very narrowly fringed pale grey, primary coverts similar but more broadly fringed mid grey. Flight feathers blackish-grey, longest tertial broadly fringed whitish and tipped pale grey (tt2 very narrowly fringed pale drab-grey), secondaries more narrowly fringed and tipped pale grey to whitish, primaries very finely fringed whitish, more broadly so inwards of emargination. Cheeks and sides of neck whitish, faintly tinged drab-buff. Chin, throat, sides of cheeks and upper breast sooty-black, feathers of lower bib and sides of breast broadly fringed whitish, giving irregular border to bib. Sides of breast olive-buff, flanks cinnamon-buff, vent and undertail-coverts slightly paler; centre of breast and belly whitish, lightly washed buff on breast. Thighs pale drab-grey. Underwing-coverts pale cinnamon-buff. *In worn plumage* (spring–summer), upperparts duller and slightly greyer (less olive/buff). Pale fringes on greater coverts and flight feathers variably worn; may still be prominent in April, or may be rather abraded by March. Whitish fringes to lower border of bib abraded, thus bib averages slightly more extensive and better defined. Underparts paler, breast and belly dirty greyish-white, flanks slightly paler cinnamon-buff. **Bare Parts**: Iris dark brown to black; bill brownish-black to black; legs and feet blue-grey. **Juvenile**: As adult, but cap very slightly browner and more restricted, upperparts slightly darker, duller and more brownish, and bib slightly browner with slightly more extensive pale grey tips, especially at sides; bill paler at base. **1st Adult**: See Sex/Age. **Measurements**: Wing of male 63.5–69 (chord 60–70), of female 63–66.5 (chord 60–67); tail of male 56–73, of female 53–64; bill 9.5–11.2; tarsus 15–18.5. Weight 9.2–14 g.

**MOULT** Adult post-breeding complete (June–October). Post-juvenile partial, sometimes includes tertials and occasionally the innermost secondary (?) (July–October).

**GEOGRAPHICAL VARIATION** Rather slight, with variations in size more pronounced than differences in coloration. Nine subspecies are recognised, but more thorough investigations are needed to confirm the validity of some (hardly any authors agree on the distribution of the various races, and I largely follow Phillips 1986). All races intergrade at their common boundaries. Despite the vast range, the species is remarkably homogeneous in its genetic make-up, the mtDNA varying little among the various populations (only *P. a. bartletti* being identifiable genetically). This suggests a relatively recent and rapid expansion to the current limits (since the retreat of the Wisconsin ice shield, i.e. within the last 10,000 years, with the genetically distinct population on Newfoundland corresponding to an ice-free refugium where chickadee populations may have survived through the last ice age).

*P. a. bartletti* Newfoundland and Miquelon island. As nominate *atricapillus*, but upperparts darker and browner (brownish-olive), pale fringes to wing and tail feathers narrower and duller, lightly washed grey, and flanks and vent washed a slightly darker colour, more cinnamon-buff. Also larger. Very similar to *occidentalis*, but larger and marginally paler and greyer. Wing (chord) of male 65–68, of female 61–64.5; tail of male 59–64, of female 57.5–61.5.

*P. a. atricapillus* Eastern Canada and NE USA, west to around the Ontario/Manitoba border, SE Manitoba, Minnesota, Iowa and eastern Kansas, and south in the east to central Pennsylvania and New Jersey. See Description. Includes 'anamesus' of northern Ontario, with paler flanks.

*P. a. practicus* Appalachian mountains north to south-central Pennsylvania (State College south to Franklin and Adams Cos.) and? eastern Ohio. Poorly marked. As nominate *atricapillus*, but upperparts average slightly darker and less buffy (also less buffy than *septentrionalis*, but not so pure grey as *turneri* or *nevadensis*), pale fringes on wing and tail feathers slightly duller and narrower, and underparts slightly paler with more contrast between the white breast/centre of belly and the duller buff flanks (i.e. as *septentrionalis*). Also slightly smaller. Wing (chord) of male 61.5–67, of female 59.5; tail of male 57–61.5, of female 57–60.5.

*P. a. septentrionalis* Western Canada and the central USA, west of nominate *atricapillus*, west to Yukon, northern British Columbia (south to Vanderhoof and Hazelton), and about central

Montana, Wyoming and NE Colorado. As nominate *atricapillus*, but upperparts slightly paler and greyer, fringes on tail and wings slightly whiter, and underparts whiter with buff wash on belly and flanks slightly paler and more restricted. Also slightly larger. Wing (chord) of male 64.5–73, of female 63.5–68.5; tail of male 63–72.5, of female 61–67.

*P. a. turneri* Alaska. Large and pale. As nominate *atricapillus*, but upperparts purer olive-grey (light grey with distinct olive cast, the palest of any race), with only a faint buff wash, fringes to wing and tail feathers purer white and slightly more extensive, and underparts much whiter, with belly, vent and flanks washed pale buff, sides of breast lightly washed light drab, and more extensive white tips to feathers of lower border of bib. As *septentrionalis*, but averages greyer, upperparts with much-reduced buff tone, fringes to wing and tail feathers marginally broader and whiter, underparts whiter. Also smaller. Wing (chord) of male 61–68, of female 61–66.5; tail of male 62–70.5, of female 61–66.

*P. a. occidentalis* Extreme SW British Columbia (Vancouver, Chilliwack), Washington and Oregon west of the Cascades, and NW California. Distinctive, the smallest and brownest race. As nominate *atricapillus*, but upperparts darker (brownish-olive with a buff cast), pale fringes to wing and tail feathers reduced, underparts duller and darker, flanks more extensively washed dull cinnamon-brown, sides of breast and upper flanks average more extensively olive-brown, and breast and belly washed drab-grey. Also smaller. As *bartletti*, but slightly darker, browner and smaller. Wing (chord) of male 57.5–64, of female 57.5–63.5; tail of male 53.5–60.5, of female 53–59.5.

*P. a. fortuitus* Southern interior British Columbia (north to Lillooet and Revelstoke, east to the Flathead valley?), Washington and Oregon (east of the Cascade mountains), NW Montana and NW Idaho. As *septentrionalis*, but slightly buffer (overall very similar to nominate *atricapillus,* but a little paler and fringes to wing and tail feathers paler and broader). Wing (chord) of male 60–67, of female 59–67; tail of male 57.5–67, of female 57–65.

*P. a garrinus* Rocky Mountains from south-central Montana and SE Idaho (Lemhi Co. southeastwards) south through Wyoming, eastern Utah and Colorado to New Mexico. Poorly marked. As *fortuitus*, but slightly paler, rump more buffy and contrasting more with mantle, more white in wing and tail feathers. Also larger. Wing (chord) of male 64.5–70.5, of female 63.5–76.5; tail of male 61.5–70, of female 63–70.

*P. a. nevadensis* SW USA in the Great Basin region, in eastern Oregon, SW and south-central Idaho (north to Blaine Co.), Nevada and western Utah (northeast to the Wasatch Plateau). Pale and grey. As *septentrionalis*, but upperparts rather less buffy, pale fringes to wing and tail feathers broader, underparts rather paler. As *turneri*, but upperparts not quite so pure grey, fringes on wing and tail feathers slightly broader (the extreme for the

species), all tail feathers fringed white on outer web, and underparts slightly paler; also larger. Wing (chord) of male 64–72, of female 63.5–70.5; tail of male 64–71.5, of female 63.5–70.5.

**HYBRIDS** The ranges of Black-capped and Carolina Chickadees abut in the breeding season and overlap only very locally, if at all, but the southward dispersal of a few Black-capped in winter can result in a more widespread, but nevertheless narrow, zone of overlap. There is often even a narrow gap between the breeding ranges, an area occupied by neither species (e.g. in northern Indiana and the Appalachians). They hybridise to a variable extent within a very narrow zone along the common boundary. Detailed studies have been conducted at various points along the range interface, producing a variety of conclusions as to their relationship. In southern **Kansas** the ranges abut, and hybridisation is strongly suspected there, with 23% of birds in the contact zone being 'hybrids' (this figure may be an underestimate, since the local population may have been diluted by immigrants as the study was undertaken in the winter months). A single apparent mixed pair was also recorded (Rising 1968). In **Missouri** the ranges abut, and there is a hybrid zone c. 15 km wide in the southwest, in which almost every individual is a hybrid. The zone parallels the ecotone between the forested Ozark Plateau in the south and the largely treeless Great Plains to the north, but is displaced a few kilometres north onto the plains. This may reflect a greater 'pressure' from Carolina Chickadee, which is considerably commoner (Robbins *et al.* 1986). Apparent hybrids have also been recorded from the eastern part of the state (Brewer 1963). In south-central **Illinois** the ranges abut, and many birds appear to be hybrids (Brewer 1961, 1963, who also recorded an apparently mixed pair; the population in the hybrid zone was thought to be less successful in producing fledged young). In eastern Illinois (east from Fayette Co.) there is apparently a narrow gap of c. 25 km between the two species (Brewer 1963). In western **Indiana** there is a region c. 65 km wide in which chickadees are extremely scarce or absent, and in NE Indiana there is a gap of c. 30 km between the breeding ranges, although the winter ranges overlap by c. 25 km owing to a southward dispersal by Black-capped Chickadees. Hybridisation may occur, but if so to a very restricted extent (less than 5%), with limited and inconclusive evidence (Merritt 1978, 1981). In **Ohio** anecdotal evidence exists of a gap between the breeding ranges, but there have been no detailed studies, and the authors of a recent breeding-bird atlas emphasise caution in its use to produce a precise definition of the respective boundaries of the two species (Peterjohn & Rice 1991). In **Pennsylvania** the ranges overlap in the southwest, where in Beaver Co. both species occur along the Ohio river, and also in the southeast, where the hybrid zone is a band c. 20 km wide through eastern Lancaster, southern Berks, northern Chester and northern Montgomery Cos. (records of 'hybrids' based on song; Gill in Brauning 1992, Ward & Ward 1974). In **New**

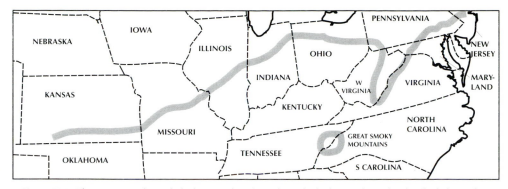

*Figure 53.5 The range interface of Black-capped and Carolina Chickadees is shown by the shaded grey line. Black-capped breeds to the north, Carolina to the south. In the Appalachians the boundary is less definite. At some points along the interface there is a narrow hybrid zone, whilst at others there is a small gap (c. 25 km) between their ranges, unoccupied by chickadees.*

**Jersey** hybridisation occurs, with two old records of mixed pairs. As well as a north-south division running from Kansas to New Jersey, Black-capped and Carolina Chickadees are also separated altitudinally in the Appalachians. In western **Maryland** and western **Virginia** Black-capped replaces Carolina Chickadee at higher elevations, and in Virginia there is a hybrid population in the Mountain Lake Region of Giles Co. (Johnston 1971). In the Great Smoky mountains of **Tennessee** and **North Carolina** Black-capped breeds above 1200 m (occasionally down to 1035 m). On the peaks where both species are present (e.g. Mount LeConte) Carolina Chickadee breeds at lower altitudes, up to 850 m, and there is thus usually a gap of 185 m in altitude where no chickadees are present; both Black-capped and Carolina Chickadees become scarce as this altitudinal gap is approached. In winter Black-capped withdraws to lower levels, sometimes down to *c.* 600 m, whilst Carolina Chickadee may occasionally wander upslope to 1675 m. Notably, paired Black-capped Chickadees (1st-adults?) may remain down to *c.* 915 m until early May and sing, but they apparently then move upslope to breed. They may give aberrant songs or be 'mixed' singers, but on plumage and measurements are typical Black-capped. On some peaks in the Great Smoky mountains (e.g. Cove mountain) Black-capped Chickadee is absent from the higher elevations, perhaps because the area of suitable habitat on these lower peaks is too small? Carolina Chickadee then breeds up to *c.* 1220 m and winters up to at least 1130 m (Tanner 1952). Similarly, in North Carolina in the northern Great Balsam mountains, Carolina Chickadee is replaced at higher altitudes by Black-capped with no evidence of hybridisation, but in the Plott Balsam range, although Black-capped are 'pure' above 1500 m, there is some evidence, from measurements, of hybridisation at lower elevations (perhaps because this is a very small population of Black-capped surrounded by Carolinas?). Black-capped Chickadee is absent from the mountains away from the Great Smokies, and although

Carolina Chickadee is scarce above 1380 m it may then occur up to 1800 m (Potter *et al.* 1980). Throughout, hybrids have been recognised as such on the basis of plumage characters, measurements and song. Birds that are intermediate between the two species in the coloration of the fringes of the greater coverts, tertials/secondaries and outer tail feathers are treated as hybrids, and occasionally also the degree of white encroachment onto the bib is used as an indicator. Wing, tail, tarsus and bill lengths are measured, and sometimes also weight (!), with an intermediate tail/wing ratio being considered one of the best indicators. The more sophisticated researchers have used multivariate analyses that incorporate plumage and mensural characters (e.g. Rising 1968) and also song (Robbins *et al.* 1986). Clearly, given the close similarity of Black-capped and Carolina Chickadees, the identification of individuals as hybrids requires the most careful examination of birds in the hand. 'Hybrids' have also been identified on the basis of song. Some birds may give both typical Black-capped and typical Carolina songs, and react aggressively to playback of either song. Such bilingual individuals have been recorded from Missouri, northern Indiana, western Virginia, the Great Smoky Mountains and, more commonly, SE Pennsylvania. 'Hybrids' may also give a wide variety of intermediate vocalisations. These include anomalous songs, closer to Carolina Chickadee (i.e four or more units) but anomalous in some way, e.g. higher-pitched and given with greater intensity than is usual among chickadees. Intermediate songs have been recorded from Kansas, Missouri, Illinois, Indiana, SE Pennsylvania and western Virginia. Arguments used to indicate that intermediate songs are given by 'hybrids' are that they are found most frequently in or near the contact zone, and are far outside the normal range of variation of the two parent species. Song is nevertheless even more problematic than plumage and measurements as an indicator of a hybrid origin. First, the range of normal variation in both Black-capped and Carolina Chickadees is overlooked. Thus, 'intermediate' songs are given by Carolina Chickadees far from the contact zone (S.T. Smith 1972). Secondly, among chickadees song is at least partly learnt, and so cannot be used as evidence either of mixed parentage or of genetic similarity: birds in the contact zone may learn the other species' song in addition to their own, and may even develop intermediate songs as a means of maintaining a territory in the presence of both species, using whichever song is most effective in repelling rivals. Notably, the concentration of intermediate songs in the hybrid zone (with little 'introgression' of such songs into the surrounding populations), and the fact that playback experiments demonstrate little or no response to the 'wrong' song from birds just a few kilometres from the zone (Robbins et al. 1986), suggest that intermediate songs and the recognition of, and response to, both types of pure song are functional only in the hybrid zone, as this is the only area where competition exists. (Note also the parallel with the 'mixed singers' found among both Short-toed and European Treecreepers in Europe.) In short, without much more study, song should be discounted as evidence of hybridisation. Black-capped Chickadee is also reported to hybridise with Mountain Chickadee, albeit rarely. This is doubted by Phillips (1986), and one reported hybrid, showing traces of a white supercilium, has been reidentified as an aberrant Black-capped (and both Black-capped and Carolina Chickadees may occasionally show traces of white feather fringes at the sides of the crown; Banks 1970a). The two species are nevertheless reported to hybridise along the Rio Grande in New Mexico (Braun & Robbins 1986).

**RELATIONSHIPS** A member of the subgenus Poecile, and part of the atricapillus superspecies, which includes Willow and Songar Tits as well as Carolina and perhaps Mexican Chickadees. Until fairly recently Black-capped Chickadee was considered conspecific with Willow Tit, and there continue to be doubts about their specific separation (e.g. Thönen 1962, Martens & Nazarenko 1993). Plumage, voice, behaviour and genetic studies all, however, tend to support their separation (e.g. Gill et al. 1989 consider that the North American members of the subgenus Poecile are more closely related to each other than any is to Willow or Marsh Tit, and Black-capped Chickadee and Willow Tit may not even be 'sister-taxa' (but see below); see p. 256 for details). The relationship between Black-capped and Carolina Chickadees is even more problematic, as they meet and hybridise along a long common boundary (see Hybrids). The hybrid zone can be viewed, however, as a dynamic event that changes over time. It came into being when two rather similar but separate populations of ancestral chickadees came together. After this, there are three possibilities. The populations could merge, with a substantial gene-flow across the zone, which consequently expands and dilutes until it disappears (in this event, the two populations are clearly of the same species). On the other hand, the populations may remain more or less separate (with gene-flow seriously impaired) and behavioural mechanisms

develop to hinder hybridisation; the hybrid zone will shrink and vanish, and two clearly separate species emerge. The third possibility is stasis, an equilibrium in which a narrow hybrid zone is maintained, but it does not expand or contract, although it may shift north or south as ecological or climatic conditions change. The hybrid zone between Black-capped and Carolina Chickadees is very narrow and apparently very stable, suggesting that an equilibrium may have been reached. There is little evidence of 'introgression' whereby the zone is expanding into the parental populations. (The boundary between the species has moved, however: e.g. in Illinois it is thought to have moved north, with Carolina replacing Black-capped Chickadee, Brewer 1963; in western Virginia it has moved downslope, with Black-capped replacing Carolina, Johnston 1971; and on Mount Mitchell in North Carolina, Carolina Chickadee has replaced Black-capped at higher altitudes, probably as a result of habitat changes, Tanner 1952.) To understand its dynamics further, attention has centred on the ecological and genetic relationships between the two species in this zone. Black-capped and Carolina Chickadees are clearly competing species, limiting each other's distribution. The best evidence for this comes from the southern Appalachians, where Black-capped has a patchy distribution on the higher mountains: where Black-capped occurs, Carolina is confined to lower altitudes (below Black-capped), but, in its absence, Carolina undergoes 'ecological release' and breeds up to much higher altitudes. More curious is the gap between the ranges in some areas (e.g. eastern Illinois and Indiana, and the Great Smoky Mountains of the southern Appalachians). This has been interpreted in two ways: (i) First, as competitive exclusion between two species, chickadees withdrawing from the contested area in the breeding season to avoid the possible adverse effects of competition on their reproductive success, either through direct competition for resources or from the reduced 'fitness' of any hybrid offspring. There is some evidence that mixed pairs may sometimes produce infertile or unfit eggs (Brewer 1961), and the narrowness of the hybrid zone suggests that hybrids are at a selective disadvantage (and that the hybrid zone is maintained only by constant immigration of the parent forms; both parent forms were thought to occur in the hybrid zone in both Illinois and Virginia; Johnston 1971) or that hybrids can compete successfully only in very particular ecological conditions. (ii) Secondly, the gap between their ranges may merely reflect a lack of suitable habitat. Thus, although in Indiana the gap is occupied in winter, it could still be marginal breeding habitat. In the southern Appalachians, however, apparently suitable breeding habitat does exist in the gap. As the abundance of each species (especially Carolina Chickadee) rises sharply from the boundary, its seems that they are excluding each other from their respective ranges, even in winter (thus supporting the notion of competitive exclusion). Moreover, at the common boundary of the ranges there is some limited interspecific recognition of, and response to, song, and some birds give both songs, as well as intermediates. This has also been interpreted as evidence of interspecific competition, whereby the birds defend territories against each other and imitate the other species' song in order more successfully to repel a competing bird (Ward & Ward 1974). Set against the existence of a hybrid zone, there are many important differences between the two species. The pre-copulatory vocalisations of both males and females are very different: Black-capped give 'variable sees', the male sometimes also a special gargle call, whilst in Carolina the male initiates events with the four-note whistled song, the female responding with 'broken dees' (these differences may reduce the chances of hybridisation). Further, whilst Black-capped Chickadees place more importance on the relative pitch of the notes in the whistled *fee-bee* song, in Carolina Chickadee the absolute pitch may be crucial. The organisation of winter flocks also differs between the two (Smith 1991). The biochemical evidence is partly contradictory, but on balance suggests that Black-capped and Carolina Chickadees are sufficiently distinct to be treated as separate species. Braun & Robbins (1986) analysed proteins that correspond to about 35 genes and found the difference between pure populations of Black-capped and Carolina Chickadees to be *less* than that between most subspecies, although they noted that 'extreme protein similarity cannot by itself be taken as strong evidence for conspecifici-

ty of bird populations'. Studies of mitochondrial DNA by Mack *et al.* (1986) showed, however, that Black-capped and Carolina Chickadees were well separated genetically: their mtDNA patterns show a divergence of *c.* 4%, indicating a separation of 1–2 million years and that they are closely related, but separate species. Gill *et al.* (1989), examining protein relationships, found that Black-capped's closest relatives were Mountain and Mexican Chickadees, with Carolina Chickadee being somewhat more distant and not necessarily a 'sister-taxon' (more distant, in fact, than Boreal and Chestnut-backed Chickadees!). Gill *et al.* (1993) again examined mtDNA and found no introgression of Carolina Chickadee mtDNA into populations of Black-capped Chickadee or vice versa, except in the hybrid zone itself. Their determination of the genetic distance at 4–5% suggests a separation of *c.* 2 million years. They, too, considered that these two chickadees are not sister-species, rather that Mountain and Black-capped Chickadees are sister-species, and that Marsh and Willow Tits are closer to this complex, being a 'sister-group', than is Carolina Chickadee. The existence of a hybrid zone is merely further evidence that such zones may involve species which are less closely related than had been supposed and whose similarity is a product of the retention of ancestral features.

**REFERENCES** Bent (1946), Duvall (1945), Ficken *et al.* (1978), Kaufman (1990), Phillips (1986), Smith (1991, 1993).

## 54 MOUNTAIN CHICKADEE *Parus gambeli* Plate 17

A characteristic bird of the coniferous forests of western North America, this hardy tit is often the only species to be met with in winter in the 'silent' forests, where temperatures routinely fall below freezing and the trees are often covered with a layer of impenetrable glazed snow.

**IDENTIFICATION** Length 135 mm (5.25 in). Forehead hoary, joining the variable but usually broad white supercilia, which terminate rather abruptly over the rear ear-coverts. Cap, lores and eyestripe black (not quite reaching the bill). Cheek patches and sides of neck extensively white, forming a half-collar; base of bill and bib black. Upperparts variably greyish, fringes to flight feathers paler and greyer. Breast and centre of belly off-white, flanks and undertail-coverts extensively pale buff to drab-grey. The lack of a crest and combination of black cap and white forehead and supercilia are unique among North American titmice. In worn plumage in mid-late summer, however, the white feather tips which form the white forehead and supercilia become abraded, and when very worn the supercilia may almost disappear. Confusion is then possible with Black-capped or Mexican Chickadees, and such abraded late-summer Mountains are probably responsible for most reports of extralimital Mexican Chickadees. Conversely, Black-capped Chickadees may *very* occasionally show traces of a white supercilium. Compared with Black-

capped, however, Mountain has a longer bill and gives a hoarser 'chick-a-dee' call.

**SEX/AGE** Sexes similar. Juvenile similar to the adult, but its cap and bib are slightly paler and less intensely black, the cap rather less extensive at the rear, and its supercilia are slightly greyer and less distinct, and the fringes to the tertials and greater coverts are tinged buff; also, the tail feathers are also more pointed than the adult's (see figure 53.1 under Black-capped Chickadee, p. 267; the shape is similar, but shows less white in the tail at all ages). 1st adult as adult, but in the hand the retained juvenile outer tail feathers still differ in shape from the adult's.

**VOICE** Contact calls include a full *stip* or *tip* and a very thin, high-pitched *seeh* or *seep*, and may give very high-pitched, whispering sibilant calls. Other calls include a 'gargle', a fussy, rambling warble, an example of which may be verbalised as *tsiddleou, tsiddleou*; gargles are frequently used in aggressive encounters. The hawk-alarm is very high-pitched, and if disturbed on the nest the female may give an explosive snake-like hiss and lunge at the intruder. In common with other chickadees, frequently uses a 'chick-a-dee' call. This has not be studied in detail, but a preliminary analysis indicates that as in Black-capped Chickadee it comprises at least four different note types, A, B, C and D (with C and D at least analogous to the notes in the Black-capped Chickadee system). A is a thin, high-pitched, sometimes sibilant *tsi* or *psit*. B is a high, thin *tsleep* or *tsip* (sometimes nasal or 'noisy'; perhaps more than one note type?), C is a loud, hoarse, 'noisy' *chit*, *chri* or *chrit*, and D is low, harsh *dzee* or *zuur*, sometimes very hoarse and 'breathy'. All four components may be given singly or in combination with others, but not always in the order ABCD. Some variants of the 'chick-a-dee' omit the D note and are thus not obviously 'chick-a-dees', but these nevertheless fit into the system. Examples are a single nasal *chrit* (=C), *tsip-tsi* (=BA), *chri-tsip-tsip* (=CBB), *chrit-tsi-tsi* (=CAA), *tsi'st'st'st'st'st* (=AAAAAA), and some long, noisy scolds are apparently made up largely of C notes. The full-blown 'chick-a-dee' is a combination of A, B, C and D notes, in which the A notes descend the scale in a short cadence and often the last A is slurred into the first D, e.g. *tsi-si'si'si'si'siur-zeee* (=AAAAA'DD) or *chri't-si'tsi'tstzur-zur* (=CAAA'DD). The introductory 'chick-a' component is often quite prolonged, but there are relatively few Ds (usually 1–5). Compared with Black-capped Chickadee, the phrase usually contains fewer Ds, and they are longer, more slowly repeated and harsher (although less nasal and 'bleating'), and the 'chick-a' is often more sibilant, longer and is slurred into the Ds. The song is made up of pure whistled units, on a higher (*fee*) and a slightly lower pitch (*bee*), although some songs are composed only of 'fees' and are thus on the same pitch. Plaintive and almost sad in tone, it strongly recalls the song of Black-capped Chickadee. It is more variable, however, with probably both regional dialects and individual repertoires. The song may be made up of two, three or four notes, e.g. *fee-fee*, *fee-bee* (very like Black-capped Chickadee's typical song, although very slightly flatter), *fee-fee-fee*, *fee-bee-bee* or *fee-bee-fee-bee*, and characteristically the first 1–2 notes are often 'stuttered', e.g. f'*fee-bee*, f'fi'*fee-bee*, fe'*fee-fee-fee*, and f'*fee-bee-bee*. Sometimes there are three notes at successively lower pitches, *fee-bee-bay* (the cadence then recalling 'three blind mice'). Song may be interspersed with gargles.

**DISTRIBUTION AND MOVEMENTS** Occurs in **Canada** from southernmost **Yukon** at Dezadeash Lake and Whitehorse (breeds?), through western **British Columbia** from Atlin southwards, west to the Vancouver area and Kleena Kleene, and east to at least Topley, Vanderhoof and the Rocky Mountains; also adjacent SW **Alberta** east to Jasper, Banff and Waterton Lakes NPs. In the **USA** found from **Washington** and **Oregon**, mainly east of the Cascade watershed (and absent from the valley of the Columbia river) south to **California**, where in the northwest occurs west to the Siskiyou and Trinity mountains and high Inner Coast Ranges (south to Mendocino and Colusa Cos.) and in the

east found in the Sierra Nevada and from the White mountains south to the Clark and New York mountains in San Bernardino Co. (and summer records from the Granite mountains); also breeds in coastal California in the Santa Lucia mountains, Monterey Co., and to the west of the deserts in southern California in all the major ranges from Santa Barbara Co. south to San Diego Co. (also reported breeding locally in 1980s in riparian woodland at Victorville, San Bernardino Co.). Breeds in **Idaho**, west and central **Montana**, east to at least Phillips, Fergus and Carbon Cos., **Wyoming** (absent from the Great Plains region in the extreme east), **Colorado**, east to Boulder, El Paso, Las Animas and Baca Cos., **Utah** and **Nevada**. The range extends south to central and SE **Arizona**, where found in the mountains south to Mazatzal and Pinal peaks, the Pinaleno and Santa Catalina mountains and Rincon peak, but only occasionally recorded in the Hualapai mountains and Huachuca range and otherwise absent from the Mexican border ranges, such as the Chiricahua mountains (excluded by the Mexican Chickadee?). Also breeds south to central and SE **New Mexico**, south to Pinos Altos, Magdalena and the Capitan and Guadalupe mountains; reported breeding locally in 1980s in riparian woodland on the Rio Grande, and to western **Texas**, where confined to the Davis and Guadalupe mountains in the Trans-Pecos region. In northern **Mexico** found in **Baja California Norte** in the Sierra Juárez and Sierra San Pedro Mártir. Generally rather sedentary, but undertakes some limited altitudinal movements in autumn and winter (from early September), the centre of gravity of the population moving to lower altitudes, with some dispersal to adjacent foothills and valleys, even occasionally to nearby plains regions. (There may also be some late-summer dispersal upslope to above the treeline.) These movements involve primarily 1st adults and are irregular, rarely occurring on a large scale. Birds begin to return to higher altitudes from February. Thus has rarely wandered eastwards in **Alberta** to Edmonton, Elk Island NP, Calgary and Lethbridge, and rare in SW **Kansas**, where found most regularly in Morton Co., but recorded north and east to Finney Co. (October–May). Uncommon in autumn and rare in winter in **Oklahoma** in the western panhandle in NW Cimarron Co. (October–mid April, extremes late September–May), in **Texas** rarely strays to El Paso Co. and the high plains of the western panhandle, and in central-west and southern **Arizona** wanders to Phoenix, Tucson and rarely the Colorado river. Occasionally wanders to the coastal regions of western **Washington** (including Bellingham, Seattle, Tacoma and Olympia) and to NW **Oregon** (Tillamook Co.), and a rare but regular visitor to the coastal lowlands of **California** (extreme dates August–late May), and rarely and irregularly in autumn and winter also to the desert regions of the south, primarily from the Mohave desert northwards, especially to ranges such as the Providence mountains and Little San Bernardino mountains. In **Baja California Norte** recorded downslope to Valladares and Valle de La Trinidad. Vagrant SE **Alaska**, with records throughout the year, including Juneau and Warm Pass valley (may breed?), SW **Saskatchewan**, where noted in winter 1966–67 at Piapot and Maple Creek (although not on official state checklist), **South Dakota** in the Black Hills, with at least three records Rapid City mid November–mid April, and western **Nebraska**. A record of 14 individuals in northern North Dakota in J. Clark Salyer National Wildlife Refuge in winter 1971 (Root 1988) is not accepted.

**HABITAT** Primarily a bird of montane coniferous woodland, where found in a wide variety of associations, both open and dense (but favouring more open areas?), including spruce-fir, hemlock, a selection of pines, and juniper. Also marginally in pinyon-juniper, pine-oak, and stands of deciduous trees in the mountains (usually, but not always, adjacent to coniferous forests, such as American Aspens, oaks, willows, cottonwoods and mountain mahogany, even montane chaparral with scattered trees and snags (e.g. in the Sierra Nevada of SW California). In Baja California Norte occurs in pines. In winter also found at lower altitudes in shrublands, foothills chaparral, scrubby oaks on mesas, pine or spruce plantations, riparian willows, Hackberries and cottonwoods, and also in urban and suburban areas with good stands of planted conifers, and rarely even in mesquite and treeless sagebrush scrub. Almost exclusively montane, generally breeding at c. 1830–3350 m in the Rocky Mountains, also 915–3505 m in eastern California (maximum 3780 m), above 730 m in NW California, and at 915–3230 m in SW California, at 2135–3660 m in New Mexico (descending in winter to 1525 m), and at c. 2135–2590 m in Texas. In Baja California Norte, altitudinal range 1500–3000 m (lower in winter). In winter still primarily montane, usually remaining above 1525 m in the eastern foothills of the Rocky Mountains and seldom below 915 m in the west, although occurs down to 585 m in Baja California, and stragglers do reach plains level.

**POPULATION** Common in Baja California Norte, British Columbia and through most of the range in the USA, although in Texas only fairly common in the Guadalupe mountains and scarce in the Davis mountains, fairly common in Alberta, and rare in Yukon. Dense populations occur in Oregon in the Cascades near Upper Klamath Lake, in Colorado and Wyoming in the Front Range of the Rocky Mountains, and in southern California and Nevada in the San Bernardino mountains, Spring mountains and surrounding areas.

**HABITS** In autumn and winter, found in scattered pairs or forms flocks of 3–6 (3–20) birds, amalgamations of the surviving members of neighbouring pairs (i.e. adults), the flock's winter range encompassing their territories. Within the winter flocks, pairs probably remain together and dominance hierarchies are formed, males outranking females, and established members of the flock dominating newcomers. Access to food may be governed by an individual's position within the hierarchy, and status can therefore have important consequences for survival. Rarely, 1st-adult birds find a place within these flocks, but most 1st adults move downslope in autumn, to winter below the montane conifer zone either singly or in small flocks. Mountain Chickadees may join mixed-species foraging flocks. Flocks break up in the spring and breeding territories are established, surviving adults tending to reoccupy the same territory (which had formed part of their winter range). Usually (?) mates for life. Depending on the population density, 1st adults are then incorporated into the territory system, pairing with widowed adults or occupying territories where both adults have perished during the winter. Roosts through the winter singly in cavities, but any physiological adaptations to survival (e.g. controlled hypothermia) have yet to be studied. During the breeding season, females roost in the nest chamber. Forages 2–15 m above ground among the smaller branches (including dead twigs) and foliage, tending to be highest in summer, sometimes probing among needle clusters at the tip of branches. Occasionally also feeds on the lower branches, trunks and on the ground. (Generally forages at higher levels and in taller trees than Black-capped Chickadee, more often in the crown, and more likely to be found in conifers.) Food mainly insects, also spiders and, in autumn and winter, a variable proportion of conifer seeds and berries. Will visit bird feeders. When a surplus of food is available, both seeds and dead invertebrates are 'scatter-hoarded'. These food caches are important for winter survival.

**BREEDING BIOLOGY** Season: Washington, May–June; Oregon, late May–mid June; California, May–early July; Colorado, April–June; New Mexico, May. The nest is placed in a cavity in a tree or stump, usually an old woodpecker excavation, or sometimes a Black-capped Chickadee's hole or a natural cavity; may nest in the ground, e.g. in old rodent holes. Cavities may be reused from season to season, and both coniferous and deciduous trees (especially American Aspens) are used. Nests are usually placed 1–3 m (0.15–24.5 m) above ground, and are often sited in clearings or on forest edges. Will use nestboxes and even holes in buildings or drain pipes, and has been noted nesting under rocks and below ground in a squirrel hole under a dead pine stub (Bent 1946). Occasionally excavates its own hole (definite proof lacking?). The female cleans out the cavity, but both sexes build the nest, which is a lining of soft material, e.g. moss, fur, feathers, plant fibres, shredded bark. Clutch 5–9 (5–12); eggs white, sometimes variably spotted reddish-brown; 15.6 x 12.3 mm (*P. g. gambeli*). Female incubates, period 14 days; she is fed by the male. The young are fed by both sexes, although the male initially collects the majority of food for the young, the female spending more time attending them at the nest. Fledging period 20–21 days. Occasionally double-brooded? The fledglings are dependent on the parents for up to 21 days after leaving the nest, and then disperse.

**DESCRIPTION** *P. g. gambeli* **Adult**: *In fresh plumage* (August–March), forehead feathers black, broadly tipped white. Crown (to below and just forward of eye), nape and centre of upper mantle black, feathers at sides of crown broadly tipped white, producing a whitish supercilium. Upperparts smoke-grey or dull fawn-grey (i.e. grey with a distinctly brown wash). Tail grey-brown, T1–T4 fringed smoke-grey, fringes narrower and paler grey on T5–T6. Lesser coverts smoke-grey. Remainder of wing grey-brown, median coverts broadly and greater coverts narrowly fringed smoke-grey, primary coverts finely fringed light grey, tertials fringed (not tipped) smoke-grey or dull buff, fringes on secondaries paler and greyer, P3–P10 narrowly fringed pale grey-white, almost white inwards of emarginations on P3–P7. Cheeks, ear-coverts and sides of neck whitish. Extreme base of bill, chin, throat and upper breast black, a few feathers at the sides of chin and sides of the upper breast tipped white (thus border of bib irregular at base of bill and at lower corners). Breast and centre of belly off-white, flanks, sides of belly and undertail-coverts pale drab-buff. Thighs pale-mid grey. Underwing-coverts and axillaries white, washed drab-buff. *In worn plumage* (April–July), white tips to feathers of forehead and sides of crown abraded, and when very worn supercilium may be almost absent. Bib better defined (pale tips abraded), pale fringes on wings, especially coverts, and tail abraded. Underparts slightly duller and less buff, with less pure white on breast and centre of belly (dark feather bases shining through). **Bare Parts**: Iris dark reddish-brown or purple-brown to blackish; bill black; legs and feet leaden-grey to blackish. **Juvenile**: As adult, but cap and bib paler and less intensely black (blackish-grey), cap not extending onto upper mantle. Supercilium less distinct, feathers tipped light grey, not white. Fringes to greater coverts and tertials tinged buff. **1st Adult**: As adult (see Sex/Age). **Measurements**: Wing of male 68–74 (chord 66–75), of female 68.5–70 (chord 64.5–75.5); tail of male 58–67, of female 56.5–67.5; bill 11.5–13.6; tarsus 16.5–18.5. Weight 10–13.5 g.

**MOULT** Adult post-breeding complete (July–September). Post-Juvenile partial, may include the tertials and occasionally the innermost secondary (July–August).

**GEOGRAPHICAL VARIATION** Rather slight, with western birds averaging greyer, both on the upperparts and flanks, than Rocky Mountain populations. In the west, a slight cline of increasing colour saturation runs north-south. There is much individual and seasonal variation, however, obscuring the trends. Nevertheless, biochemical studies show that nominate *gambeli* from Arizona and *baileyi* from coastal California differ significantly in their mtDNA (by *c.* 3%: Gill *et al.* 1993). Five intergrading races recognised, largely following Phillips (1986).

*P. g. gambeli* The Rocky Mountains and associated ranges in central Montana, Wyoming, Colorado, SE Utah, eastern Arizona, New Mexico and Texas. Intergrades with *baileyae* in western Montana and with *wasatchensis* in central-east Idaho, SW Wyoming and SE Utah. The brownest race in upperpart coloration; bill relatively short and stubby. See Description. Some variation, with birds paler in some areas (notably on southeast borders of Rockies), but the variation is mosaic in nature. Also averages smaller in the Davis mountains of SW Texas: wing (chord) of male 65.5–67.5, of female 66; tail of male 57.5–60, of female 58 (this population may deserve recognition as a distinct subspecies: Phillips 1986).

*P. g. wasatchensis* Southern Idaho and Utah. Intergrades with *inyoensis* in SW Idaho and westernmost Utah. Synonymised with nominate *gambeli* by Phillips (1986), and with *inyoensis* in 'Peters' (and perhaps closer to the latter). Poorly marked. As *inyoensis*, but upperparts slightly darker (washed more olive, less greyish-pink), tail averages slightly longer. Compared with nominate *gambeli*, upperparts very slightly greyer, flanks slightly cleaner buff, bill longer and thinner. Wing (chord) of male 67.5–73.5, of female 64.5–69; tail of male 59–68.5, of female 58–66.

*P. g. inyoensis* The Great Basin region from SE Oregon and SW Idaho south through Nevada and western Utah to central-eastern California (White, Inyo, Panamint, New York and Clark mountains), and NW Arizona (from Williams westwards). The palest race. As nominate *gambeli*, but averages paler; in fresh plumage upperparts tinged pale buff (not brown; wears greyer), supercilium broader, flanks average slightly paler buff; bill longer and relatively thin. Wing (chord) of male 64.5–75, of female 62.5–70.5; tail of male 54–69.5, of female 54.5–66.

*P. g. baileyae* Canada, western Montana, northern Idaho, Washington, Oregon (not southeast), western Nevada and mountains of California south to San Diego Co. (replaced in central-eastern California by *inyoensis*). As nominate *gambeli*, but upperparts rather greyer, flanks variably duller and drabber; bill heavy and moderately long, tail short. Includes 'grinnelli' of Canada, eastern Washington, Idaho and Montana. Upperparts relatively dark, lightly tinged olive, flanks slightly cleaner and buffer, bill relatively small (closer to nominate *gambeli*). Wing (chord) of male 62–70.5, of female 60.5–70; tail of male 54.5–65, of female 54–61. Also 'abbreviatus' of the Cascade and Siskiyou mountains of western Washington and Oregon, Nevada and northern California. Relatively pale (especially underparts, but upperparts darker and greyer than *inyoensis*) and pure grey. Wing (chord) of male 63.5–74, of female 62–70.5; tail of male 53–65.5, of female 52–70. Also *baileyae* (s.s.) of mountains of southern California (Santa Lucia mountains, Mount Pinos, and the San Bernardino, San Jacinto and Laguna mountains). Flanks darker and more extensively drab-grey, bill relatively heavy. Wing (chord) of male 60–73, of female 63.5–68.5; tail of male 54–63.5, of female 54–60.5.

*P. g. atratus* Baja California Norte. As *baileyae*, but slightly darker, upperparts and flanks (also centres of flight feathers) average sootier and supercilium narrower; tail averages slightly longer. Wing (chord) of male 66–72.5, of female 63–68.5; tail of male 54.5–62.5.

**HYBRIDS** Reported to hybridise rarely with Black-capped Chickadee, but what is apparently the only existing specimen of a 'hybrid' proved to be an aberrant Black-capped Chickadee (Banks 1970a).

**RELATIONSHIPS** A member of the subgenus *Poecile*, but relationships within this group of closely related chickadees are disputed. Mountain Chickadee is sometimes placed in a superspecies with Mexican Chickadee (e.g. Sibley & Monroe 1990), with which its range does not overlap. Investigation of protein relationships (Gill *et al.* 1989) suggests that the two are very closely related, supporting this treatment. On the other hand, Mexican Chickadee is sometimes placed in a superspecies, together with Black-capped and Carolina Chickadees and Willow and Songar Tits. Mountain Chickadee, which overlaps broadly with Black-capped Chickadee, cannot be a member of this super-species (which by definition cannot include species whose ranges overlap substantially), even though biochemical evidence supports a close relationship with Black-capped Chickadee (Gill *et al.* 1989, 1993, who found Mountain and Black-capped Chickadees to be sister-species). Another treatment is that of Eck (1980a, 1988), who places Mountain Chickadee in a species group ('komplex')with White-browed Tit of western China, despite some rather gross differences in ecology and vocalisations. Further research is clearly needed.

**REFERENCES** Behle (1956), Bent (1946), Dixon (1985), Phillips (1986).

# 55 MEXICAN CHICKADEE *Parus sclateri*      Plate 17
Other name: Gray-sided Chickadee

Almost endemic to Mexico, this species just creeps into the southern USA in the 'sky islands' of southern Arizona and New Mexico. It has an unusually complex song for a tit and exhibits some unique behaviours, such as daubing the outside of its nest hole with insects, probably to deter predators.

**IDENTIFICATION** Length 130 mm (5 in). Rather dull, but otherwise a typical chickadee in appearance. Cap black, faintly glossy, upperparts mid olive-grey and tail dark grey. Cheek patches white, broad at the rear and forming a half-collar. Bib sooty-black, extending to the upper breast, where bordered dirty white, with remainder of underparts light-mid smoke-grey. The only breeding chickadee in its range, but approaches Mountain Chickadee in the north. Normally easily distinguished by the absence of a white supercilium, but some worn, late-summer Mountain may lack a supercilium and such birds probably account for most or all reports of out-of-range Mexican Chickadees. These worn Mountain Chickadees have the dull greyish flanks of Mexican, but lack its large black bib (extending well onto the upper breast on Mexican).

**SEX/AGE** Sexes similar. Juvenile as adult, but the cap and bib are slightly duller, the cap averaging slightly more restricted at the rear, and the tail feathers are narrower and more pointed. 1st adult as adult, but the retained juvenile tail feathers still differ subtly in shape from an adult's (see figure below).

*Figure 55.1 Outer tail feathers (T6) of adult (left), and juvenile (right): note shape.*

**VOICE** Rather varied. Calls include a full *tip, tsip* or *tseet*, and the contact call is a thinner, higher-pitched *sip*, grading into a more buzzing *szip*, given singly, in couplets or in series at irregular intervals. In common with other members of the *Poecile* subgenus, has a 'chick-a-dee' call, made up of a combination of four note types, dubbed A, B, C and D, always given in the order ABCD, in which any note may be omitted, given singly or repeated a variable number of times. Compared with other chickadees, the 'chick-a' usually has a buzzing quality and, although the individual notes average longer, the number of units in the call is usually shorter (a maximum of 14 notes recorded in a single call, compared with 24 for Black-capped Chickadee). Call A is a buzzing *szree* (closely related to the *szip* contact call, but longer, louder, even more buzzing and almost cricket-like), call B is a sharp *spik*, and call C is an abrupt, stony *chit*, usually given in rapid series. Call D is a deep, harsh *char, schaa* or *dzaa*, sometimes almost hissing, or rather 'breathy' and hoarse; it may recall the harsh scream of a Eurasian Jay or the smaller nuthatches of Europe and Asia, and indeed it is sometimes almost 'white noise'. Call A is one of Mexican Chickadee's commonest calls, often given on its own, either singly (often combined with a shorter and fainter *szip* contact call), in grasshopper-like couplets, *szree-szree*, or in bouts of 2–4 units, with the last two notes in the series often running into each other, thus *szree-zee'e, szree-szree'ep* or *szree-zee'ep zeep* (even when there are just two units, there is a tendency to 'stutter' into the beginning of a third). Call D is also commonly given alone in groups of 1–4 units (or with an initial A so abbreviated and slurred into the first D as to be nearly inaudible), e.g. *schaa-schaa-schaa*. Call C may also be given on its own, usually in rapid bursts of calling as a short rattle or scold (the individual units paired), e.g. *chit'it'it'it'it'it* or *chrrrrrit*; such bursts of C notes are given in mild alarm and in flight. Call B is rarely used, either alone or in combination. The commonest combination is AD (always in that sequence), with the A component often slurred into the nasal D, e.g. *sri'dzee*, *sri'dzee-dzee*. Such AD combinations are given by undisturbed flocking chickadees. Other calls include a variable, snake-like hiss, similar to the call given by females of many tit species when disturbed on the nest, but in Mexican Chickadee also used away from the nest, often in circumstances of slight agitation or fear. The hiss sounds rather similar to the D note, but is more variable in pitch and duration, usually given singly and never in conjunction with other notes. The hawk-alarm is a high-pitched *zee-zee*, becoming higher-pitched with heightened alarm (on hearing this call, all the chickadees in a flock will freeze, as will other species). An even higher-pitched *see-see-see*... is uttered by both male and female when in close contact in the autumn (during pair formation?) and in interactions at the nest. In disputes, males give 'gargles', complex phrases made up of 2–20 units selected from a vocabulary of *c*. 14–20 different note types. Although there are almost limitless possible combinations and permutations using such a wide vocabulary, the number of combinations actually used by a given population of chickadees is quite limited, and in the range of 3–10. There is also only limited individual variation in the note types. Gargles are short but quite full and warbling phrases, often falling in average pitch towards the end of the phrase, with a relatively deep tone (which may recall a bulbul), or fussy and twittering, and they often terminate in trills or rattles, or in D-type notes, e.g. *siup-trrr'rip breee*, *tsit-tsree-tsip-pu-tsip-pu* or *sipi'chirup'siu'zhee-zherrr*. Gargles may be repeated at intervals, and in territorial encounters a particular gargle may be doubled, tripled or even quadrupled, to produce a phrase lasting more than two seconds; they are also given in several other contexts, including sexual encounters. Two vocalisations have some of the functions of 'song'. The first is a simple two-note whistle, a loud, rapid, vigorous *si-cha*, *si-cha*... or *peeta-peeta*... repeated about three times (although quite stereotyped, the number of notes varies, with a single high-pitched unit followed by 1–5 lower-pitched units). Abrupt, rather flat and unmusical, it recalls Plain Titmouse rather than the sweet, high-pitched musical whistles of Carolina and Black-capped Chickadees. It is given in autumn and early spring (when dawn singing may be common). A more complex song is also given in spring, although infrequently and in short bouts, probably to proclaim territory ownership. This 'complex song' is made up of several different types of notes in different combinations, and each male has a vocabulary of numerous different song types, based around variations in the note types and differing combinations. (Partly after Ficken & Nocedal 1992, Ficken *et al.* 1994.)

**DISTRIBUTION AND MOVEMENTS** In the **USA** breeds in two discrete areas, both separated from the main range in Mexico: in extreme SE **Arizona** found in the Chiricahua mountains in Cochise Co., and in SW **New Mexico** in the Animas range in Hidalgo Co. In **Mexico** the range is continuous in the Sierra Madre Occidental from extreme NE **Sonora** (San Luis mountains) and NW **Chihuahua** south through western **Durango**, SW **Zacatecas**, NE **Nayarit** and SE **Sinaloa** to northern **Jalisco**. Also the highlands of southern Mexico from SW **Jalisco** (Sierra Madre de Colima) and **Colima** through SW **Michoacan** and southeast (continuously?) through the Sierra Madre del Sur of **Guerrero** and **Oaxaca** (southeast to about Valle Nacional and Rio Molino); and through north-central Oaxaca to the Sierra Volcánica Transversal of eastern **Puebla**, west-central **Veracruz** (Cofre de Perote), southern **Hidalgo**, **Mexico**, **Distrito Federal**, and northern **Morelos** to northern **Michoacan**. There are two disjunct populations on minor mountain ranges in the Mexican plateau, in SW **Coahuila** (Sierra Encarnación and Sierra Guadalupe) and in SE Coahuila/central-west **Nuevo Leon** (around Saltillo). Although some limited altitudinal movements occur on the breeding ranges from August onwards, there is very little evidence of more distant dispersal. In **Arizona** there is a sight record in January 1924 from the Swisshelm mountains (southwest of the Chiricahua range), but records from the Santa Catalina mountains have not been confirmed and probably refer to worn Mountain Chickadees. In **New Mexico**, the species has wandered to the Peloncillo mountains (Clanton Canyon, July 1963).

**HABITAT** Montane coniferous forest, breeding in Arizona and New Mexico in open, park-like stands of Ponderosa Pine above *c*. 2000 m and Engelmann Spruce–Douglas Fir above 2600 m. In Mexico, the species is less restricted to conifers and in the Sierra Madre usually breeds above 2200 m. Thus, in Durango, occurs in oak woodland (with some pine or juniper) at 1900–2500 m (presumably only below 2200 m outside the breeding season), and breeds in pine and fir forests at higher altitudes. Further south, in the Valley of Mexico, occurs in dry oak woodland above 2300 m, humid fir forest at 2900 m and also in pine and pine-alder forests. In central Mexico breeds at up to 4115 m, and in the Sierra Madre del Sur of southern Mexico found at 2130–3510 m (2225-3030 m in Oaxaca). Throughout the range densities are highest in pine-alder and especially fir forest, and in some areas may be only a non-breeding visitor to pure oak. In the late summer, from August onwards, there is some dispersal to a wider variety of habitats, regularly to oak-pine and stands of Arizona Cypress; some move downslope, and recorded down to 1525 m in Arizona (April) and *c*. 1850 m in the Sierra Madre. Lower altitudinal limit in Mexico is about 1500 m.

**POPULATION** In the USA, common in Arizona and uncommon in New Mexico. There is some evidence of a decline in recent years in Arizona, and the New Mexico population, estimated at 200–300 pairs, may not be large enough to ensure its long-term survival. Common to locally abundant in Mexico, although uncommon in the far south in Oaxaca. Local declines may be caused by logging and grazing, and fir forest, the optimum habitat, is patchily distributed in the volcanic belt of central Mexico.

**HABITS** Individuals occupy the same home range in summer and winter, the pair remaining together throughout the year, but the flock structure is not well understood. From late summer onwards forms flocks, usually comprising 4–6 birds in Arizona but larger, with 3–13 birds, in Mexico. These range over rather large areas, and usually join mixed-species foraging flocks, of which chickadees are core species. These may total 30–100 individual birds and include 8–16 chickadees and sometimes also Bridled Titmice. Although not very pugnacious, Mexican Chickadees may raise the feathers of the nape in agitation. A unique habit, recorded for no other tit, is that the female often applies crushed beetles to the outside of the nest hole with a sweeping motion of the bill, perhaps using noxious chemicals released by the insects to deter predators (cf. White-breasted Nuthatch, p. 152). Forages among leaves and twigs and investigates open pine cones, from c. 2 m upwards (but generally higher in the trees, more often above 5 m, in winter). Can hover and occasionally flycatches. Food insects. Recorded storing food in captivity.

**BREEDING BIOLOGY** Poorly known. Season early April–mid June. Nest placed in a cavity, usually in a dead tree or stub (both in pines and in oaks), 0.15–18 m above ground; also noted behind a slab of bark or on the underside of large dead limbs some distance from the trunk. The cavity is probably often excavated by the birds themselves, but this has not been directly observed. Will use nestboxes placed 4–5 m up, with sawdust on the floor. The nest cavity is lined with a cup of moss, plant down, catkins, fur, hair or other soft material by the female, with the male in close attendance. Clutch 5–9; eggs dull white, finely spotted reddish-brown, mainly at the larger end; 15.4 x 11.9 mm (*P. s. eidos*). The female incubates and is fed near the nest by the male; both sexes feed the young. Incubation and fledging periods unknown. Probably single-brooded. May be a cooperative breeder at times, as a 'couple with youngster' were observed several times during the nest-building period in April by Brandt (1951).

**DESCRIPTION** *P. s. sclateri* **Adult**: *In fresh plumage* (August–March), crown (to below eye), nape and centre of upper mantle black, faintly glossed blue (glossy blue feather tips). Upperparts and lesser coverts mid olive-grey, rump slightly paler and more olive. Tail dark grey, fringed dull olive-grey. Wings dark grey (alula slightly darker); median coverts broadly fringed olive-grey, greater coverts fringed and tipped olive-grey, primary coverts very finely fringed olive-grey, tertials fringed (not tipped) olive-grey or slightly paler, secondaries more narrowly fringed olive-grey, primary fringes narrower and paler, especially

inwards of emarginations on P3–P5. Cheeks, ear-coverts and sides of neck white. Chin, throat and upper breast sooty-black, feathers of lower bib fringed paler, thus lower border of bib slightly irregular. Upper breast bordering bib dirty white, remainder of underparts mid-light smoke-grey. Thighs pale grey-brown. Axillaries and under-wing-coverts whitish, washed drab-grey. *In worn plumage* (April–August), bib slightly more extensive, lower border neater; pale fringes on flight feathers and tail abraded. **Bare Parts**: Iris brown; bill greyish-black or black; legs and feet blue-grey. **Juvenile**: As adult, but cap more restricted at rear (not extending onto upper mantle), slightly duller, paler and less intensely black with no gloss; bib slightly paler. **1st Adult**: As adult (see Sex/Age). **Measurements**: Wing of male 65–74, of female 62–69 (both sexes, chord, 63–70); tail 50–64, of male 56–64, of female 55–60; bill 10.1–12.1; tarsus 14.2–18.5. Weight 7.5–11 g.

**MOULT** Adult post-breeding complete (July–August; probably later in more southerly populations, extending to October). Post-juvenile partial, may include some tertials, especially in more southerly populations, and also in Mexico some tail feathers (July–September, to early December in Mexico).

**GEOGRAPHICAL VARIATION** Rather slight and largely clinal, averaging slightly larger and paler in the north. Four poorly marked races recognised, following Phillips (1986).

*P. s. eidos* Arizona, New Mexico, and the Sierra Madre south to western Durango (south to at least El Salto) and probably also Zacatecas; also disjunctly in SW Coahuila. As nominate *sclateri*, but upperparts and flanks slightly paler and greyer (less olive). Averages slightly larger. Wing of male 64–73 (chord 65–74), of female 67 (chord 63–71).

*P. s. garzai* Phillips 1986. A disjunct population in SE Coahuila/Nuevo Leon. The purest grey, least buffy, on the mantle and flanks (mantle cold mid grey, flanks light grey, faintly tinged olive). Paler than the occasional grey extremes of *eidos*. Wing (chord) 64–68.

*P. s. sclateri* The southern Sierra Madre in central and north-central Jalisco, intergrading with *eidos* in the region of SE Sinaloa and NE Nayarit; boundary between races poorly known. Also northern Michoacan east to Morelos, Puebla and possibly western Veracruz (where intergrades with *rayi*). See Description.

*P. s. rayi* Southern Jalisco south through SW Michoacan, the Sierra Madre del Sur and adjacent ranges in Guerrero and Oaxaca, and then north to central Veracruz (where intergrades with nominate *sclateri*, boundary imperfectly known; Binford 1989 considers all Oaxaca birds to be nominate *sclateri*). As nominate *sclateri*, but upperparts and especially flanks slightly more olive (noticeably so compared with *eidos*), rump faintly tinged brownish-drab and breast tinged yellowish. Smaller than *eidos*? Wing of male 67–73 (chord 64.5–72), of female 67.5–68 (chord 64.5–67).

**RELATIONSHIPS** Problematic. Sometimes placed in a superspecies (or even a single species;

Eck 1979, 1980a) together with Black-capped and Carolina Chickadees and Willow and Songar Tits. Electrophoretic analysis strongly suggests, however, that Mexican Chickadee's closest relative is Mountain Chickadee (Gill *et al.* 1989), whilst vocalisations, especially the song, indicate that Mexican Chickadee is not close to Black-capped Chickadee. The ranges of Mexican and Mountain Chickadees do not overlap and, indeed, are separated by mountain ranges with suitable habitat where neither occurs, and they may be too close ecologically to coexist. Accordingly, placed in a superspecies with Mountain Chickadee by Sibley & Monroe (1990). Gill *et al.* (1993) examined mtDNA, however, and found that Mexican Chickadee was not a sister-species of Mountain Chickadee; rather, it clustered with Chestnut-backed and Boreal Chickadees. Notably, all three differ from other North American chickadees (subgenus *Poecile*) in lacking a whistled song, and less significantly in the 'nasal' tone of their chick-a-dee calls. Further study may show that they are primitive members of the subgenus.

**REFERENCES** Bent (1946), Dixon & Martin (1979), Ficken (1990a, b), Ficken & Nocedal (1992), Monson & Phillips (1981), Phillips (1986).

## 56 WHITE-BROWED TIT *Parus superciliosus*                    Plate 18

Endemic to China, this species bears an uncanny resemblance to Mountain Chickadee of North America, yet is confined to high-altitude scrub around the Tibetan plateau. It has a variety of loud whistling and rattling calls.

**IDENTIFICATION** Length 135 mm (5.25 in). A stocky, relatively long-tailed tit with a large, conical bill. Forehead and supercilium white, cap and broad eyestripe blackish. Upperparts dark grey, washed olive; tail dark grey-brown, outer feathers narrowly bordered white. Ear-coverts dirty cinnamon, paler on the lower border and forming a slightly paler moustachial line. Bib sooty-black, remainder of underparts pale pinkish-cinnamon. The dull pinkish underparts, black bib and obvious white supercilium are diagnostic. The only possible confusion is with Père David's Tit, but White-browed is 10–15% larger and relatively longer-tailed, with drabber pink underparts, and, notably, lacks white cheek patches. The two species are also found in very different habitats.

**SEX/AGE** Sexes very similar, although the cap and bib of the female average duller black, the bib is smaller, supercilium a little narrower, and the upperparts are slightly buffer (less olive). The juvenile is very similar to the adult, but may have a broader and whiter rim and tip to the tail. No information on 1st adult, but may retain the juvenile tail feathers.

**VOICE** Rather noisy, the vocalisations are very distinctive, combining loud, clear, ringing whistled notes with rattles and trills. Calls include a very thin *si-si* and an even higher and thinner *see-see*, given in series of 2–8 calls, and also an abrupt, thin *tip* or *stip*. An unusual call type for a tit is a winding, dry, insect-like rattle, *trrrrrp* or *tsirrrr*, which may be given on its own or combined with other calls (it may recall the call of certain redstarts). In excitement in territorial or sexual encounters and in alarm gives a series of 1–15 *si*, *sip*, *sit* or *tchip* notes, variably soft and silvery or hard and clicking depending on distance and emphasis. The series initially descends the scale in a cadence (which may recall a rock nuthatch), e.g. *tsi-sit-sit-sit-sit-sit-sit-sip*. These phrases may be preceded by a quiet, nasal *te* or (during courtship feeding) a single *tsi* note may be preceded by a disyllabic *tnu-te*, or the cadence may be followed by a low, rattled or churring *trrrrrr* (perhaps equivalent to the D in a 'chick-a-dee' call system). The song is very variable, being a combination of various distinct and relatively stereotyped whistled or rattled elements into motifs which are then repeated. Songs may incorporate one or two of the following: **1** a whistled *tsee-tsee-tsee*, given in bouts of 3–6 calls; **2** a lower-pitched, pure, ringing whistled *pee*, given in bouts of 1–4 notes or combined into a couplet, *pwi-pee*; **3** an even lower-pitched, mellow, whistled *tu-tuuu*; **4** a loud, clicking *tchip-tchip*; **5** 3–9 whistled *peta-peta-peta...* notes given in a rapid series (at *c.* 3 notes per second), recalling a 'tea-cher' song, the tone bringing to mind an unoiled gate; **6** a winding, insect-like rattled *tsirrrr* (as above); **7** a lower-pitched rattled *tsirr'r'r'r'r* (not so 'dry' as 7); **8** an even lower-pitched, less insect-like and more 'wooden' rattle of 9–21 elements (given at a rate of *c.* 15 per second, hence these rattles may be prolonged, lasting well over a second), *tir'ir'ir'ir'ir'ir'ir....* Examples of song phrases include *tsee-tsee-tsee-pwi-peee*; *tchip-tchip-pwi-pee*; *tsirrrr-pwi-pee*; *tsee-tsee-tsee-tse-tir'ir'ir'ir'ir'ir'ir'ir'ir'ir'ir'ir* (the initial *tsee* note may sometimes be prolonged); *tsir'r'r'r'r-pee-pee-pee*; *tsirrrr-tu-tuuu*; and *peta-peta-peta-peta-peta*. Also perhaps a song is a phrase comprising very thin *si-si-si* notes which descend the scale to merge into the dry, insect-like rattle, and which may then be followed by the *tu-tuu* motif, thus *si-si-si-r'r'r'r'r'tu-tuuu*.

**DISTRIBUTION AND MOVEMENTS** Endemic to western **China**, the distribution being centred around the eastern parts of the Tibetan plateau. Central and eastern **Qinghai** (west in the north to *c.* 98° 30' E in the 'South Koko Nor range' and the eastern Qaidam basin, and west in the south to Yushu), the Qilian Shan range of the border of Qinghai and Gansu (eastern parts only?) east to west-central **Gansu** (to Wuwei, Lanzhou, and south to the Min Shan), NW **Sichuan** (south to Kangding in the Daxue Shan range and to Litang in the Shaluli Shan range, and east to Songpan), and adjacent eastern **Tibet** (Xizang) in the Qamdo region. Also recorded in southern Tibet from the Lhasa region and Lhunzhub. Resident.

**HABITAT** Dwarf scrub of deciduous shrubs such as willow, barberry, buckthorn and honeysuckle, 1–2 m tall, in the alpine zone, favouring the better-vegetated areas along watercourses. In autumn and winter moves into taller shrubby thickets and rhododendron, occasionally into more open areas of forest at the upper limit of the spruce zone, and presumably undertakes altitudinal movements in response to hard weather, when it may possibly withdraw into forest at lower altitudes (thus noted in poplar groves and spruce forests in southern Gansu: Bangs & Peters 1928). Recorded in summer and early autumn at 3350 m in western Gansu, c. 3200–3400 m in Qinghai, 3700–4235 m in Sichuan, and 3000 m in Tibet. (Vaurie 1959 gives the altitudinal range as 4000–5000 m and Meyer de Schauensee (1984) as 3800–4880 m, but substantiating details have not been traced.)

**POPULATION** Generally uncommon, but may be locally common in areas of suitable habitat.

**HABITS** Rather shy, but behaviour typically tit-like. Found in pairs during the breeding season, occasionally three birds together, and apparently territorial. Otherwise found in parties of 2–4 (sometimes up to 10–12 birds), frequently with Severtzov's Tit-warbler. Forages among the stems and twigs, well down in the shrubs where sheltered from the wind, occasionally coming to the top of the vegetation, calling and then flying off for some distance.

**BREEDING BIOLOGY** Poorly known (until recently widely held to be the sole member of the genus *Parus* to build a free-standing grass nest, despite reports to the contrary dating back to 1890; see Martens & Gebauer 1993). Season May(?)–June. The nest is placed in old vole burrows in vertical earth banks or in holes among rocks and roots. The female is fed in and around the nest by the male.

**DESCRIPTION Adult Male**: *In fresh plumage* (October–March), base of bill blackish, forehead white, crown dull black, the cap extending onto the central nape and centre of the upper mantle; feathers at sides of crown tipped white, forming rather broad, white-flecked 'supercilia', which join on the forehead and taper and often curve downwards towards the rear. Upperparts dark grey, heavily washed olive. Tail dark brownish-grey, each feather finely fringed grey-brown (paler and greyer than upperparts) and tipped drab-white; outer web of T6 largely pale drab-white. Wings dark grey-brown, greater and median coverts and tertials narrowly fringed as upperparts, secondaries with wider, paler and greyer fringes and narrow grey-white tips, primaries narrowly and indistinctly fringed paler. Superciliary area, lores and a broad eyestripe black. Upper ear-coverts pale greyish-cinnamon, cheeks and lower ear-coverts dirty pale cinnamon, tinged grey (extending to the bill in a pale moustachial line), sides of neck and nape light grey. Chin and throat sooty-black, remainder of underparts, including sides of neck, axillaries and underwing-coverts pale pinkish-cinnamon. *In worn plumage* (about April–August?), upperparts slightly greyer, pale fringes to wing and tail feathers abrade, fringe to T6 wearing whiter, and underparts slightly darker and richer pink. **Bare Parts**: Iris colour unknown; bill black; legs and feet black. **Adult Female**: As male, but cap slightly duller, not so glossy black, supercilium slightly narrower, and upperparts mid smoke-grey, tinged buff; bib averages slightly smaller and duller, more sooty-black. **Juvenile**: As adult, but pale tips to tail feathers broader and whiter, T6 fringed whiter; tail feathers narrower and more pointed? **1st Adult**. No information. **Measurements**: Wing of male 61–69, of female 60–67; tail 61–69, of male 67–69, of female 65–67 (tail well graduated, with T6 c. 9 mm shorter than T1); bill 10.3–12; tarsus 16.5–18.5. Weight 10.1–12.4 g.

**MOULT** No information.

**GEOGRAPHICAL VARIATION** No subspecies described. Birds from NW Sichuan and southern Qinghai are reported to average less pure grey on the upperparts (more brownish-grey or olive-grey), and darker, richer, more brick-brown on the breast and belly, than those from Gansu (Schäfer & Meyer de Schauensee 1938).

**RELATIONSHIPS** Generally treated as a member of a superspecies together with the Mountain Chickadee of North America, on the basis of similar plumage features, and the two were even treated as conspecific by Eck (1980a). Apart from the great difference in habitat, White-browed Tit has rather different vocalisations and, notably, apparently lacks a 'chick-a-dee' call. It may not, therefore, be appropriate to place it in a superspecies with Mountain Chickadee. Biochemical data may help to resolve the issue.

**REFERENCES** McCallum *et al.* (in prep.), Martens & Gebauer (1993).

# 57 PÈRE DAVID'S TIT *Parus davidi*                 Plate 18
Other name: Red-bellied Tit.

Named after Père Armand David, the greatest name in Chinese ornithology and pioneer explorer of the forests of western China, this poorly known tit is endemic to China and shares its montane forest home with Giant Pandas.

**IDENTIFICATION** Length 120 mm (4.75 in).

Cap black; upperparts dark olive-brown, with a

cinnamon half-collar extending to sides of nape, and the primaries finely fringed paler. Cheek patch white (may appear 'fluffy'), bib dull black, and underparts bright cinnamon, slightly paler in the centre of the belly. Distinctive. The brightly coloured underparts are unique among the bibbed tits, although Songar Tit has the breast and centre of the belly pale buffy-white, flanks pale cinnamon-brown and remainder of the underparts dull pinkish-cinnamon. Songar, however, is rather duller than Père David's Tit, with a duller and browner cap and bib.

**SEX/AGE** Sexes similar. Juvenile as adult, but cap and bib duller black, flight feathers with a faint olive-brown panel in the wing formed by paler fringes to the inner secondaries (adults at similar

thin, sibilant *tis*, and a harder and slightly lower-pitched *sit* or *ssit*. The D note is a nasal *dzee* or *zee*, typically rather short and relatively high-pitched, and sometimes given alone in extended series. Chick-a-dee phrases are short and simple, usually terminating with just one or occasionally two Ds, and are delivered relatively rapidly, sometimes in extended series. The initial high-pitched notes are often 'stuttered' or slurred together (as they are when given without Ds, e.g. *t'sip*), and typical combinations are *t'sip-zee*, *t'sip't-zee* and *t'sip-zee-zee*. There is no whistled song, rather the species sings at the nest with the 'chick-a-dee' call (McCallum *et al.* 1994).

**DISTRIBUTION AND MOVEMENTS** Endemic to western **China** in the mountains bor-

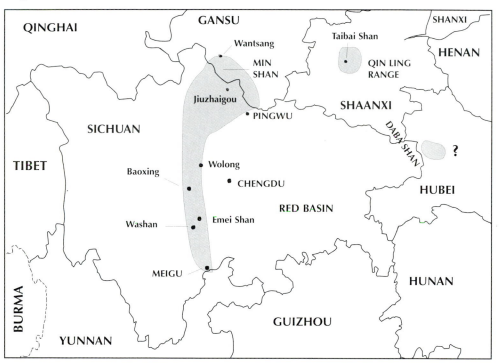

*Figure 57.1 Approximate range in west and central China, with some known localities. With an altitudinal range of c. 2135–3350 m, this highly restricted species is especially vulnerable to deforestation.*

time of year are worn, lacking a pale wing panel); cheek patches more buffish, underparts duller, pale brownish-buff or pale rufous (not so orange-cinnamon), bill orange-yellow with basal three-quarters of culmen darker. No information on 1st adult.

**VOICE** Has a relatively limited vocabulary of *c.* 12 distinct note types, perhaps the most primitive among the subgenus *Poecile*. Calls include a full *sip* or *tsip* and a more sibilant *psit*. Also gives a full, hard *chit*, which may be run into a short, chattering series, *chit'it'it*. In common with other *Poecile*, has a 'chick-a-dee' call system (see Black-capped Chickadee, p. 267), which combines thin, high-pitched calls with low, nasal D notes. The higher-pitched components include the full *tsip*, a

dering the Red Basin in western **Hubei** (eastern parts of Daba Shan?; no details of distribution available), southern **Shaanxi** on Taibai Shan in the northern Qin Ling mountains, southern **Gansu** in at least the Min Shan, and in **Sichuan** south to Meigu, including Wanglang NR (Pingwu), Emei Shan, and Wolong and Jiuzhaigou Panda Reserves. Resident, with some altitudinal movements.

**HABITAT** Mature mixed forest at mid elevations in the upper temperate zone, of spruce, fir, pine, birch, poplar, willow, alder and oak, with bamboo undergrowth and scattered clearings. Especially fond of large, red-barked birches. Altitudinal range *c.* 2135–3350 m; noted in southern Shaanxi at 2135–2745 m, in southern Gansu at 2440–2590 m, and in Sichuan at 2200–3200 m (especially at 2300–2800 m). No information on any seasonal altitudinal movements, but noted in Sichuan at Wolong through the winter at 2440–3050 m, and at Wanglang at 2200–2600 m in autumn.

**POPULATION** Although listed as very rare by Cheng (1987), not uncommon in some areas of suitable habitat (e.g. jiuzhaigou), but very local. With a very limited range and preference for fast-disappearing forest, the long-term survival of this species must, however, be in doubt.

**HABITS** Outside the breeding season (from late June onwards) occurs in parties of 5–10 birds. Very agile and active; usually forages in the canopy of tall trees, moving acrobatically among catkins, removing buds etc., and also in the middle storey and shrub layer.

**BREEDING BIOLOGY** Poorly known. Season May: in Sichuan, nest-building observed in mid May, a male singing (using the 'chick-a-dee' call) for 20 minutes at dawn outside a nest hole in mid May (laying?), a male feeding an incubating (?) female on the nest in mid May, and agitated birds around a nest hole in mid June. The nest is placed in cavities in rotten trees or stumps, c. 4–10 m above ground level. Nest material includes lichen.

**DESCRIPTION Adult:** *In fresh plumage* (autumn–winter), forehead, crown (to lower border of eye) and nape black, very slightly glossy; remainder of upperparts dark drab, tinged olive. Tail and wings dark grey-brown (alula and primary coverts a little darker), the tail feathers fringed olive-drab, wing-coverts fringed dark drab, tertials and secondaries fringed drab-buff, and primaries finely fringed pale drab-white, palest at tips. Cheeks, ear-coverts and rear lower border of cap white. Throat and upper breast dull sooty-black.

Sides of neck cinnamon, extending onto sides of nape in a half-collar (interrupted by black cap extending onto upper mantle) and forming a cinnamon border to the upper mantle. Remainder of underparts and axillaries cinnamon, slightly paler in centre of belly. Underwing-coverts pale buff. *In worn plumage* (summer), upperparts slightly less brown, pale fringes to wing feathers abraded. **Bare Parts:** Iris dark brown; bill black; legs and feet lead-grey to black. **Juvenile:** As adult, but ear-coverts lightly washed yellow-buff, especially at the rear, underparts very slightly paler and more yellowish-cinnamon, tail feathers slightly narrower and more pointed than those of adults. (See also Sex/Age for information on field observations.) **1st Adult:** No information. **Measurements:** Wing of male 65–68, of female 64–67, unsexed 68.5, 71; tail 47–54; bill 9.5–11.1; tarsus 14–18. Weight 12–12.5 g; and three birds from Sichuan averaged 10.3 g.

**MOULT** Little known. A bird dated October is at the end of a complete post-breeding moult, whilst one dated 14 November is at the end of the post-juvenile moult, but retains the juvenile tail feathers.

**GEOGRAPHICAL VARIATION** None.

**RELATIONSHIPS** Obscure. Although considered conspecific with Sombre Tit of SE Europe and western Asia by Eck (1980a), largely on the basis of proportions, this draws no support from field observations. Possibly more closely allied with White-browed Tit, the two being sister-species.

**REFERENCES** M.A.S. Beaman pers. comm., Dresser & Delmar Morgan (1899), Kleinschmidt & Weigolds (1922), McCallum *et al.* (in prep.), R.P. Martins pers. comm.

## 58 SIBERIAN TIT *Parus cinctus*                    Plate 19
Other name: Gray-headed Chickadee

This is the only tit to occur in both the Old and the New World, and displays amazing adaptations to survive the Arctic winter. An apparently recent colonist of Alaska and NW Canada, it is one of the most elusive of all North American breeding birds.

**IDENTIFICATION** Length 135 mm (5.25 in). A medium-large tit with a relatively long tail and often rather fluffy plumage. Cap brownish-grey, extending well onto the nape, remainder of upperparts pale brownish, with prominent pale fringes to the greater coverts and flight feathers (on the closed wing, these form a paler panel on the inner secondaries and tertials). Long off-white cheek patches, extensive sooty-brown bib, and whitish underparts with the sides of the breast, flanks, vent and undertail-coverts contrastingly pale rufous-cinnamon. When worn, the upperparts are duller and the underparts rather whiter. In Europe and Siberia, the large size, dull brown cap, showing little contrast with the upperparts, and often rather extensive and ragged bib are distinctive. The only possible confusion is with Willow Tit, which has a

black cap and is neatly grey and white in the northern races. Siberian Tits have been reported in NE China, and could certainly wander to the Tien Shan of Central Asia, and in both areas would have to be distinguished from the similarly brown-capped Songar Tit; see p. 257 for details. In Alaska and NW Canada, Siberian Tit must be very carefully distinguished from Boreal Chickadee. Siberian Tit has a much more extensive and cleaner, pure white cheek patch, extending to the nape (thus its cheek patches are similar in extent to those of Black-capped Chickadee), whilst on Boreal Chickadee only the cheeks and fore ear-coverts are white, the rear ear-coverts and sides of the neck being greyish. Siberian Tit also has prominent pale fringes to the greater coverts and tertials, lacking on Boreal Chickadee. Minor differences are the slightly greyer cap, paler flanks and relatively longer tail of Siberian Tit, but these should always be considered merely as supporting characters (in worn plumage both species have rather paler flanks, and juvenile Boreal Chickadees resemble Siberian Tits in cap and flank coloration). The 'dee' portions of the 'chick-a-dee' calls of Siberian Tit average deeper and more sonorous and powerful than in Boreal Chickadee.

**SEX/AGE** Sexes similar. Juvenile marginally distinct, resembling a worn summer adult; most noticeably, the bib is slightly paler and rather more extensive and ill-defined. Additionally, juveniles show even less contrast between the cap and mantle (and almost none when worn), little cinnamon coloration on the upperparts except on the lower mantle and scapulars, and narrower cheek patches; the flanks and undertail-coverts are pale buffish or buff-white (paler and buffer than on a fresh adult, becoming almost uniform dirty white when worn), with the remainder of the underparts dingy white. 1st adult as adult, and sometimes difficult to age even in the hand, especially in spring; retains juvenile tail feathers, primaries, secondaries, tertials and greater and primary coverts. In the autumn, the retained juvenile wing and tail feathers are duller, browner and rather worn compared with the fresh and glossy feathers of an adult; the tail feathers and primary coverts are also narrower and occasionally more pointed, and the greater coverts have broader and whiter tips. Occasionally, 1st adults also show moult contrasts in the tail.

**VOICE** Apparently very variable, but there have been no systematic studies and the various accounts are difficult to reconcile. Calls include *tsit*, a thin disyllabic *chit'sit* or higher, faster and more rodent-like *si-si*, a much fuller, sharp *chik* (almost like knocking stones together, and to some ears recalling a crossbill's call) which may be given in closely linked groups of 2–3 notes (*chik-chik-chik*) or as part of a 'chick-a-dee' call (see below), and a sharp and slightly hoarse *psiup*, which may be given as a triplet, *psiup-psiup-psiup*. Other calls are a harsh, jay-like *schaar*, and a squeaky *ziew* or *kniew* (a 'broken D' call, probably used by begging females or juveniles). During courtship and preceding copulations, gives a high *sisisi...* or *pi-pi-pip pip pip...* (Cramp & Perrins 1993). As other members of the *Poecile* subgenus, commonly uses a 'chick-a-dee' call, strongly recalling Willow Tit. As with the American chickadees (see Black-capped, p. 267), this is a combination of various high-frequency introductory 'chick-a' notes (A, B, C, etc; the exact number is unknown, but there appear to be at least three note types, possibly rather more) and a low-pitched, nasal D note. The 'chick-a' component may be very thin high-pitched *tsi-tsi* notes (e.g. *tsi-tsi ziew*, *tsi-tsi-zieuuw-ziew*), a longer and fussier, but still high-pitched phrase (e.g. *sisit-sisit-tsee dza-dza-dza-dza-dza-dza*), or the sharp *chik* note (e.g. *chick-zee*, *chick-zee-zee*). The D notes are quite variable, sometimes higher and more nasal, sometimes lower and more sonorous; occasionally they are a very deep and hoarse *char-char-*

*char....* 'D's may be given alone in bouts of 2–7 calls, e.g. *dee-dee-dee* or *zschee-zschee-zschee*, often quite slowly; this is one of the commonest calls. (Overall, the Ds are more powerful, deeper, and not so shrill and nasal as those of Boreal Chickadee.) There is some question as to what is the song of Siberian Tit. There is apparently no stereotyped whistled song (unlike, for example, Willow Tit or Black-capped Chickadee). What may be a song comprising rather shrill notes, e.g. *shrii-shrii...*, *tschi-tschi...* or *chi-chi...*, given in groups of 3–4 (2–6) units, which may run into a rather mellow, bulbul-like phrase, e.g. *chi-chi-chi chi-diddle-wi*. Other 'songs' are repetitions of strange, vibrant and almost insect-like phrases, e.g. *prrreee-prrreee-prrreee*, and in Norway the 'song' is described as short, low-pitched and variable, e.g. *ptri-pyy* or rising *ptri-poi* (Haftorn 1973). Perhaps having some of the functions of song, Siberian Tits use a 'gargle' in aggressive territorial situations (cf. Black-capped Chickadee). This is a short but very complex burst of musical notes in an almost 'fussy' phrase, which is very variable but may be roughly transcribed as *tisisiddlewee* or *seeseeditwuy*. Gargles may be introduced by the *psiup* call or 1–2 sharp *chiks*, and may end either in a sweet pure note, in a harsher and more nasal unit, in an almost cicada-like rising *preee*, or in a bulbul-like chattering *breeee*, and gargles are occasionally prolonged.

**DISTRIBUTION AND MOVEMENTS** Found in northern **Norway** and **Sweden** from 64°–69°/70° N, with an isolated population in the mountains of southern Norway, and through northern **Finland** and the taiga of northern **Russia** from the southern Kola peninsula (north to *c.* 69°/70° N), east across Siberia to the Anadyr' basin, Bering Sea, Kamchatka peninsula and Sea of Okhotsk. Occurs north to the limits of the taiga and the forest-tundra zone, to 67° N in European Russia, *c.* 72° N on the Taymyr peninsula, *c.* 70° N in the Lena, Yana and Indigirka valleys, to the lower Kolyma, and northern Anadyr' basin. The range extends south in European Russia and the Urals to 60° N, and in Siberia in the Irtysh and Ob' valleys to 58° N, to the Tomsk area, the Altai and Sayan mountains and Krasnoyarsk. In eastern Siberia, found south to the Khamar-Daban range, around Lake Baykal, the Yablonovyy and Stanovoy ranges, and the mouth of the Uda river on the Sea of Okhotsk. Also NW **Mongolia** south to the Hövsgöl area and Hangayn mountains, and NE Mongolia in the Hentiyn range. In the **USA** found in central **Alaska**, principally in the upper and central Yukon river drainage (west to Kaltag, the Seaward peninsula and the Noatak river) and the foothills of the Brooks range (especially in the northeast); occurs in McKinley NP, although very sparingly. In NW **Canada** found in northern Yukon and NW Mackenzie, in the Inuvik Region east to about the Anderson river. Status in **China** uncertain. David & Oustalet (1877) stated that Siberian Tit bred and seemed to be resident in the mountains of Nei Mongol, while Shaw (1936) records the species as resident in the mountains of northern Hebei (at the Eastern Tombs and Hsiao-wu-tai-shan). These localities are far distant from the known distribution of the species, and its occurrence in China requires confirmation. It may be merely an erratic winter visitor (note the record from the middle Amur, below), or more likely the records could be the result of confusion with Songar Tit (and this is strongly suggested by the measurements in Shaw 1936: wing of male 60–65.5, of female 59–62; weight 9–13 g). Largely sedentary, but some juveniles move up to 200 km south of the breeding range during late August–late March (with northward migration continuing well into May), and has reached as far south as Lake Vänern in Sweden, and in Russia south to St Petersburg, Moscow (in 1870s and 1880s), Nizhniy Novgorod (= Gor'kiy) and Kazan' in the Volga region, Sverdlovsk in the southern Urals, and c. 54° N in western Siberia and the northern Kulunda steppe, whilst recorded in August in the Amur region at 'Lesser Khingan' (Dementiev & Gladkov 1966–70). There are also occasionally 'irruptions' in late June–October when larger numbers move south, reaching the Baltic coast (but apparently avoiding sea-crossings). Three records in **Estonia**, all from Kabli (October 1977, 1983 and 1986). Montane populations in southern Siberia undertake limited altitudinal movements.

**HABITAT** Coniferous forests of larch, pine and especially spruce, also montane birch forest. Prefers virgin old growth, although not a closed canopy, but where forests are managed favours closed stands of conifers with mature and dead trees and some birch (and moves to areas with more birch once the young fledge). Also found in broadleaved riverine forest where this runs through the conifer zone, and sometimes aspen woods. Occurs mainly in river bottoms and basins in the north of the range in Eurasia, but favours montane coniferous forests in southern Siberia, NW Mongolia and Kamchatka, and will wander north of the limits of the forest into stunted waterside willows and low alpine heaths. In Alaska and NW Canada has a strong association with willows: found near the treeline at the interface of forest and tundra in stands of mature willows (c. 4.5–6 m high) along watercourses and on riverside sand bars, both in the spruce zone and in tongues of spruce and willow along rivers and creeks extending into the tundra; but, despite the apparent association with willows, also found within spruce forest and, in winter, in alder and Aspen.

**POPULATION** Generally rather uncommon in the west of the range, with 0.2–7 pairs per km2 in suitable habitat (and occurring more patchily at 0.5 pairs per km² in heavily managed forests, rising to 1.5 pairs with the provision of nestboxes), but commoner in Siberia and at higher altitudes in the Sayan mountains (although again locally scarce near the northern limits of the forest). A recent sharp decline and contraction of the range in Finland, with a withdrawal from southern areas, is perhaps due to climatic change, but also to modern forestry practices - clear-felling and heavy thinning in managed areas. In North America, rather, rare.

**HABITS** Often very tame and, indeed, indifferent to man. Found in pairs or small parties, and pairs for life. Adults are strictly sedentary, remaining on territory all year (frequently two pairs may share a territory). Sometimes joins mixed-species foraging flocks, especially with Willow Tits. Following fledging and dispersal, some juveniles may move considerable distances. Others settle in adult territories, and Siberian Tits are sometimes found in parties of up to nine birds from late summer onwards. During the breeding season, the female roosts on the nest and the male in a nearby tree. In the winter in the northern Siberian taiga, temperatures of -60° C are encountered, and only 4–5 hours of daylight are available to find the 7–8 g of frozen insects and larch seeds necessary to survive the night. Thus, to save energy whilst roosting in tree holes, Siberian Tits pull in their legs and head and fluff out the plumage, which is specially adapted with over 100 barbs and barbules per cubic mm. On very cold nights, they can also lower their body temperature by 5–10° C and pass the night in semi-hibernation (taking a considerable time to wake up if disturbed). Regularly roosts in snow holes. Forages at all levels of the vegetation and, especially in early spring and autumn, on the ground, but perhaps most frequently in the shrub layer and on the trunks and larger branches. Works very methodically, searching every tree thoroughly before moving on. Food insects, snails, spiders and seeds, and in winter will visit refuse tips and birdtables, and has been seen eating fat from a frozen caribou carcass. Stores food profusely throughout the year (up to 500,000 items per individual per year), in clumps of needles, bark crevices and lichen clusters. These stores are exploited during the winter, but hardly at all at other times.

**BREEDING BIOLOGY** Season May–June. The nest is placed in a hole in a tree, often a decaying stump or abandoned woodpecker excavation, 0.3–5 m above ground. The hole is often cleaned out, rotten wood being removed. May use nestboxes. The nest is built by the female alone, and is usually a base of decayed wood covered by moss and grass and lined with a thick cup of hair or fur. Clutch 6–10 (4–11): eggs white, sparingly spotted with rust-brown with olive-brown and pale violet-grey undermarkings; c. 16.6 x 12.9 mm. Female incubates, period 15–18 days. The nestlings are fed by both sexes, but brooded by the female. Fledging after 19–20 days, the young disperse 7–13 days later. Single-brooded, with some replacement clutches if eggs preyed on, although in southern Siberia (Altai mountains) may be double-brooded.

**DESCRIPTION** P. c. lapponicus **Adult**: In fresh plumage (August/September to about April), crown, nape and upper mantle brownish-grey, sides of cap darker from lores to just behind eye. Lower mantle and scapulars pale cinnamon-brown, back, rump and uppertail-coverts similar or slightly paler buff-brown. Tail grey-black, outer webs vaguely fringed paler. Wings grey-black (tertials paler on inner webs), lesser and median coverts finely fringed brownish-grey, greater coverts and tertials fringed pale cinnamon-drab, primary coverts and secondaries finely fringed and tipped pale greyish, P10–P2 finely fringed pale grey (only inwards of emarginations on P3–P6). Cheeks, ear-coverts and sides of neck off-white. Chin and throat sooty-brown, feathers along cheeks and lower throat tipped white, bib there thus poorly demarcated. Centre of breast and belly white, faintly washed buff. Sides of breast, flanks, vent and undertail-coverts pale rufous-cinnamon. Axillaries and underwing-coverts grey-buff to off-white, with dark grey bases to shorter feathers. *In worn plumage* (April/May onwards), mantle and scapulars slightly greyer, showing slightly less contrast with cap, pale fringes to wings bleached whiter and abraded (least so on inner secondaries and tertials), bib better demarcated as white tips to peripheral feathers largely abraded, breast and belly more extensively white (but when very worn grey feather bases may show), and flanks and undertail-coverts rather paler and buffer. **Bare Parts**: Iris dark brown; bill brown-black or black; legs and feet blue-grey to dark grey. **Juvenile**: As adult, but cap paler, upperparts drabber, greyer and less cinnamon (drab-grey), bib larger, paler (mid-dark brown) and less well defined, flanks and undertail-coverts paler and buffer. In worn plumage, upperparts (including cap) virtually uniform brown-grey, white cheek patch rather narrow, bib more contrasting, underparts dirty whitish (little buff on flanks) with grey feather bases visible. **1st Adult**: As adult, but retains juvenile wing and tail feathers (see Sex/Age). **Measurements**: Wing of male 65–71, of female 62–69; tail of male 57–65, of female 60–64; bill 10.3–12.4; tarsus 16.6–18.2. Weight 11–14 g.

**MOULT** Adult post-breeding complete (mid June–early September). Post-juvenile partial, sometimes includes central tail feathers (late July–September).

**GEOGRAPHICAL VARIATION** Slight and largely clinal, with the boundaries between the races difficult to define; the general trend is towards paler plumage in eastern Asia, with the head and upperparts paler grey, the contrast between cap and scapulars gradually reduced, and flanks to vent gradually paler rufous, but this cline is reversed in the Far East. There is also a cline in central Siberia towards paler plumage in the north. Four races are recognised.

*P. c. lapponicus* Fennoscandia, the southern Kola peninsula and northern European Russia (east to Dvina and Mezen' valleys). Intergrades with nominate *cinctus* in NE European Russia (Pechora basin), southern Urals and SW Siberia (between Urals and Irtysh valley). See Description.

*P. c. cinctus* Russia from the northern Urals (north of 60° N) east to the Bering Sea, also NE Mongolia. As *lapponicus*, but upperparts paler, drab-grey, with reduced cinnamon tones to the mantle and scapulars and thus less contrast between the cap and upperparts; fringes to greater coverts and tertials broader and whiter. Underparts paler, flanks and undertail-coverts with a more restricted area of pinkish-buff. Bib narrower in fresh plumage, with broader white tips to peripheral feathers (thus cheek patch broader). Wing of male 62–74, of female 62.5–71. Palest and greyest on Taymyr peninsula and in the valley of lower Lena, darker and browner in NE Siberia and southeast of Lake Baykal (approaching *lapponicus*, but cap duller drab-grey, remainder of upperparts more buffish-drab, flanks to undertail-coverts extensively but pale pink-cinnamon).

*P. c. sayanus* Minusinsk taiga, the Altai, Sayan and Tannu-Ola mountains, south to NW Mongolia. Coloration falls within variation of nominate *cinctus*, but wing and especially bill larger. Wing of male 69.5–75.5, of female 68.5–73; bill 12.5.

*P. c. lathami* Alaska and NW Canada. Poorly marked, coloration falling within variation of nominate *cinctus*, although the upperparts average slightly greyer and underparts more extensively washed darker pinkish-cinnamon. Bill 9.2–11.3, only marginally smaller than in nominate *cinctus* (incorrectly reported to be conspicuously shorter and thinner). Wing of male 67–72, of female 65.5–70; tail of male 65–68, of female 61.5–69.

**HYBRIDS** Mixed pairs with Willow Tit are perhaps not infrequent (but usually unsuccessful), the scattered nature of suitable habitat and low population density perhaps leading to lone isolated individuals being faced with little choice. Although hybridisation (as opposed to adoption or egg-dumping) has not been proven in most cases, 'hybrids' are intermediate in appearance or resemble one or other of the parents (Järvinen 1987, 1989; Järvinen et al. 1985).

**RELATIONSHIPS** A member of the *hudsonicus* superspecies, together with Boreal and Chestnut-backed Chickadees of North America. Notably, Boreal Chickadee is closely similar to the race *lapponicus* of Siberian Tit, and Siberian Tit could easily be considered a race of the chickadee. Both species are found in Alaska, however, with no evidence of hybridisation or intergradation, and are thus treated as distinct species.

**REFERENCES** Balch (1980), Cramp & Perrins (1993), Vaurie (1957b, 1959), Virkkala (1990), Virkkala & Liehu (1990).

# 59 BOREAL CHICKADEE *Parus hudsonicus*　　　　Plate 19

This aptly named tit inhabits the boreal forests of North America. Very hardy, it uses stored food supplies to survive the winter and is generally seldom seen south of its breeding range.

**IDENTIFICATION** Length 140 mm (5.5 in). Cap pinkish-brown, extending well onto the upper mantle. Cheek patches white, grading into a pale grey half-collar. Upperparts olive-grey, showing little contrast with the cap (being more or less the same tone). Wings and tail dark grey, with the coverts and flight feathers rather finely fringed paler. Bib sooty-black and relatively small, breast and belly off-white and flanks strikingly bright orange-cinnamon. Distinguished from Black-capped Chickadee by the mid brown rather than black cap (hardly contrasting with the mantle), more restricted white cheeks and contrastingly bright orange-cinnamon flanks. Note also its smaller bib and lack of prominent pale fringes to the greater coverts, tertials and secondaries. In Alaska and NW Mackenzie, Boreal Chickadee overlaps with the much rarer Siberian Tit. The two are quite similar in appearance, but Boreal has a rather small area of white on the cheeks, the rear ear-coverts being grey, and lacks prominent pale fringes to the greater coverts and tertials. In addition, its cap is slightly browner, its flanks richer and more orange-cinnamon, it has a shorter tail, and the 'dee' component of its 'chick-a-dee' call averages shriller and more nasal than Siberian's deep, sonorous call. Note, however, that in late summer wear and bleaching greatly reduce the differences in cap and flank coloration, and that juvenile Boreal Chickadees have hoarser calls than adults and also a duller and browner cap and paler flanks (approaching Siberian Tit). The extent of the white on the cheeks and in the wing remain, however, valid identification features. Easily separated from Chestnut-backed Chickadee by its olive-grey rather than dull chestnut upperparts.

**SEX/AGE** Sexes similar. Juveniles are similar to adults, but their cap and upperparts are browner (showing even less contrast with the upperparts), their bib slightly smaller, paler and more brownish, the fringes to the wing feathers are tinged dull cinnamon, and their flanks and vent are paler. In the field in late summer, the cheeks of juveniles may appear clean white compared with the dingy, unmoulted adults. In the hand, juveniles also show narrower and more pointed outer tail feathers (see figure below). 1st adults are very close to adults in appearance, but retain the juvenile tail feathers and may show moult contrasts in the wing.

*Figure 59.1 Outer tail feathers (T6) of adult (left) and juvenile (right): note shape.*

**VOICE** Rather silent except during the early spring, and has a rather limited vocabulary. Contact call a sweet *seep* or *siup*, given in series in territorial disputes, usually in association with the 'chick-a-dee' call. A sequence of up to five similar but shriller calls is given as a hawk-alarm, and on hearing this call other members of the flock, if exposed, will fly to cover and then freeze. Another common call is a sharp, tongue-clicking *chit* or *chik*, often used in situations of mild arousal. Begging females and juveniles give a very hoarse and breathless *zer*, and other calls include high, 'breathy' *tseeh* notes, sometimes given in series. When disturbed on the nest, sitting females give a snake-like hiss. The 'chick-a-dee' call is a combination of 4–5 note types which comprise the 'chick-a', and low, nasal *char* or *zer* notes. These are analogous to the A, B, C & D components of the Black-capped Chickadee's call (see p. 267), but the precise structure of the various elements has yet to be studied (but the *chit* and *seep* calls may be incorporated into the 'chick-a-dee'). Characteristically, the 'chick-a-dee' call is rather short, with only 1–2 repetitions of the nasal D unit, and often slurred, with the 'chick-a' notes running straight into the D. The D note itself may be either higher, or lower, fuller and hoarser. Examples include *pi-s'zer-zerr*, *sisi-siu'zer-zer*, *chick-chick-char-char* and *tsi-ts'zer zer*, or, with the 'chick-a' and D motif separated, *pit-siup char*, *siup chur chur* or *chi'chik char*. D notes may be given alone, but again generally singly or in pairs, e.g. a slightly hoarse *zerr-zer*. Variations include an abbreviated 'chick-a-dee' in which both the 'chick-a' and the 'dee' portions of the call are truncated. 'Chick-a-dee' calls are given by perched birds as a contact and location call, and very soft versions are also given by the male when calling the female off the nest. As in other chickadees, however, this call probably has several functions. The D portion of the 'chick-a-dee' is nasal and drawling (sometimes almost whining), thinner, weaker and given more slowly than that of Black-capped Chickadee, and often higher-pitched and more nasal. Compared with that of Chestnut-backed Chickadee, it is lower and often more nasal and 'drawled', whilst Siberian Tit gives less nasal but deeper and more powerful *dzee-dzee-dzee* calls. There is apparently no whistled song, but the vocabulary includes gargles (cf. Black-capped Chickadee). These are fussy, sweet, warbling, musical phrases, e.g. *wissipawiddlee*, often followed by a staccato trill. Gargles are used by males in territorial situations, most commonly in early spring, just as the winter flock breaks up, and again when the young fledge. There is also a closely related 'musical' call (perhaps just a variation on the gargle), a repeated sequence of 2–8 near-identical musical motifs, each motif made up of c. 4 high-pitched units, progressively descending in pitch. (Partly after McClaren 1976).

**DISTRIBUTION AND MOVEMENTS** In the **USA** and **Canada** breeds north to the treeline in SW, central and western **Alaska** (west to the Kobuk valley, Kotzebue Sound and the base of the Alaskan peninsula, being commonest in central Alaska, rare on the south coast and only accidental in the southeast; reported Kodiak Island), northern **Yukon** (north to the middle Firth river), NW and south-central **Mackenzie** (to the Mackenzie delta, Great Bear Lake and Great Slave Lake), northern **Saskatchewan** (to Lakes Athabasca and Newham), northern **Manitoba** (to Churchill), northern **Ontario**, northern **Quebec** (to Koroc river, George river and Kuujjuaq), **Labrador** (to Okak) and **Newfoundland**. The range extends south to the limits of the boreal forest zone, including its southerly extensions in the mountains of the NE and NW USA. Thus, breeds through **British Columbia** (east of the coast ranges), to extreme north-central **Washington** (the northern Cascades in northern Okanogan Co.), northern **Idaho** in the northern panhandle (very few records, but breeding confirmed: Stephens & Sturts 1991) and NW **Montana** (south to the Teton river). Also breeds south to SW and central **Alberta** (to Banff and about Cold Lake), central **Saskatchewan** (Flotten Lake, Prince Albert and Nipawin), southern **Manitoba** (Clear Lake and Sprague), northern **Minnesota** (southwest to Clearwater Co.), northern **Wisconsin** (south to a line from Gordon, Douglas Co., to Antigo, Langlade Co., then north to Florence Co.), northern **Michigan** in the upper peninsula (largely absent southern tier of counties, but present Isle Royale), **Ontario** (south to Sudbury and the Algonquin highlands), **Quebec** (to Campbell's Bay, absent extreme southwest, but breeds Anticosti island and Iles de la Madeleine), NE **New York** in the Adirondacks, NE **Vermont** (south and west to Washington Co.), northern **New Hampshire** (south to the White mountains), **Maine** (absent southwest), **New Brunswick**, **Prince Edward Island** and **Nova Scotia**. Resident, wintering mainly within breeding range, north at least locally to its northern limits. There are also irruptive movements southwards in autumn and winter every 2–3 years (sometimes skipping a turn), when small numbers occur a little to the south of the breeding range, with slightly larger-scale irruptions every 6–8 years. In such irruptions occurs uncommonly south to **Massachusetts** (including Plymouth Co.), southern **New York** and extreme southern **Ontario** (to Point Pelee), and rarely to **North Dakota**, central and southern **Wisconsin** (just 1–5 birds south of breeding range, even in irruptions), **Michigan** (south to Kalamazoo and Monroe Cos.), southern **Vermont**, **Rhode Island** (fewer than five records in total), **Connecticut**, **Pennsylvania** (including the Pocono mountains), northern **New Jersey** and Long Island. Irruptions are probably synchronised with fluctuations in conifer seed crops, and take place at the same time as those of other irruptive boreal species. Birds may be present outside the breeding range during October–mid April (late September–early May), and such winter wanderers are often attracted to feeders. Local concentrations of migrants have been recorded, e.g. at Whitefish Point, Michigan, in April–May, with peaks of over 100 birds (Brewer *et al.* 1991). Montane populations may undertake seasonal altitudinal movements. Rare vagrant **Ohio**. Extremely rare vagrant **Wyoming** (June 1977), **South Dakota** (Deuel and Brookings Cos., November 1972), **Nebraska** (1972), **Iowa** (Des Moines Co., November 1976–March 1977, Mitchell Co., November 1978), **Illinois** (several old records; also Whiteside Co., November 1961, and Lee Co., February 1963), **Indiana** (several in Lake and Porter Cos.,

winter 1951/52, Allen Co., May–June 1976, and also reported there in January 1977 and in Monroe Co. in October 1976), **West Virginia**, **Delaware**, **Maryland** (Allegany, Baltimore, Montgomery and Anne Arundel Cos.) and **Virginia**.

**HABITAT** The preferred habitat is dense boreal coniferous forest, primarily where dominated by Black Spruce-Balsam Fir, but will also frequent mixed woodland with a limited deciduous component (especially American Aspen, birch and waterside willow thickets). Often breeds near bogs or muskeg. Winter wanderers occur in a wider variety of habitats, but still favour coniferous trees. In New York breeds at 460–1130 m, and recorded at up to 2070 m in Washington and at least 1525 m in British Columbia.

**POPULATION** Generally common in the breeding range, but only fairly common in Alberta, Manitoba, Ontario (where irregularly common in winter), Quebec, Prince Edward Island, Nova Scotia, Minnesota and New York; uncommon in British Columbia, Washington, Montana, Michigan, New Hampshire and Vermont, and rare in Idaho and Wisconsin. Erskine (1977) found densities of 2–11 per km$^2$ in various parts of Canada, typically 4–5, with populations peaking during spruce-budworm outbreaks. Its northerly distribution and its preference for forests of limited economic value have resulted in relatively little habitat loss through clearance for agriculture and, despite some losses to logging, its range and abundance have probably changed little.

**HABITS** Sometimes tame, but sometimes shy, and often inconspicuous (less vocal than Black-capped Chickadee). Found singly and in pairs and, from late summer onwards, forms small flocks (family parties?). There may be larger flocks in winter, with up to 25 recorded together. May join mixed-species foraging flocks. Pair-bonds are gradually formed as the flocks break up in spring, and probably mates for life, the pair reoccupying their territory of the previous season. Territories are apparently not advertised using 'song', but are defended vocally if the male comes across a trespasser. Forages largely among the foliage and the tips of branches in the upper part of trees (often in the interior); may extract seeds from cones, but only occasionally gleans from the bark. Sometimes also feeds on the ground, especially in early spring when melting snow has revealed material dropped from the trees over the winter. Will visit birdtables. Food insects and spiders, also fruit and conifer and birch seeds. Stores food in deep bark crevices (above winter snow, but below branches that will be exposed to the blizzards).

**BREEDING BIOLOGY** Season: Alaska, June; Alberta, mid May–mid June; Ontario, late May–mid June; Nova Scotia, mid May–early June; New York, June–mid July. The nest is placed in a tree or stub at heights of 0.15–4.6 m above ground. The nest hole is excavated in soft heartwood (with a hard outer layer), the female starting the work and apparently taking the major share, the male participating after a few days. The wood chippings are initially dropped, but later are carried away and often wedged among conifer needles. Excavation may last 1–10 days. Unusually, the entrance hole often faces upwards (cf. Mexican Chickadee). Natural cavities or abandoned woodpecker excavations are also sometimes used, and occasionally nestboxes. The nest is a pad of moss, lichen, fur, feathers, plant down, bark shreds and other soft materials, built by the female. Clutch 6–7 (4–9): eggs white, finely marked with reddish-brown; 16 x 12.2 mm (*P. h. littoralis*). Female incubates, period 15 days (11–16 days); she is fed on and off the nest by the male. The young are fed by both sexes, although predominantly by the male in the period immediately following hatching. They fledge after 18 days (occasionally as early as 15 days, but the juveniles cannot fly until 18 days old), and continue to be fed by the adults, becoming fully independent and leaving the parents' territory only after a further 14–21 days. Single-brooded.

**DESCRIPTION** *P. h. hudsonicus* **Adult**: *In fresh plumage* (September–March), crown (to below eye), nape and centre of upper mantle pinkish-brown or fawn-brown. Remainder of upperparts mid grey, washed olive, rump and uppertail-coverts slightly warmer and browner. Tail dark grey, all feathers fringed light grey. Wing dark grey, lesser and median coverts finely fringed as upperparts, greater coverts fringed light grey and tipped slightly paler and whiter; alula and primary coverts finely fringed mid grey; tertials, secondaries and inner primaries fringed light grey, P2–P5 whiter around and distally of emarginations. Cheeks and fore ear-coverts off-white, becoming pure light grey on rear ear-coverts and sides of neck and sides of upper mantle (forming a half-collar). Lores dark brown; chin and throat sooty-black, bib extending marginally onto upper breast with feathers at sides and lower border fringed whitish, thus border indistinct. Breast and belly off-white, sides of breast and upper flanks light grey, flanks orange-cinnamon to rufous-brown, vent slightly duller and browner. Undertail-coverts drab, with paler feather tips. Underwing-coverts and axillaries whitish. *In worn plumage* (April–August), pale fringes on wings abrade; bib larger and better defined; dusky bases to feathers of cheeks may show; rufous of flanks may be paler and more restricted. **Bare Parts**: Iris brown; bill black, blue-grey at base of lower mandible; legs and feet grey-blue to slaty-black. **Juvenile**: As adult, but cap slightly browner and less pinkish, upperparts slightly browner and less olive (mid grey-brown), hence less contrast between cap and mantle. Bib slightly paler and browner, also less extensive, not extending onto the upper breast. Fringes to greater coverts, tertials and inner secondaries tinged cinnamon-drab (although tips of greater coverts paler, as on adult). Flanks and vent paler, more cinnamon-buff. **1st Adult**: As adult (see Sex/Age). **Measurements**: Wing of male 62–67.5 (chord 63–66), of female 60–66 (chord 58.5–64); tail of male 57–66, of female 55–63; bill 10.2–11.7; tarsus 16–18. Weight: no information.

**MOULT** Adult post-breeding complete (duration c. 77 days, June–August). Post-juvenile partial,

includes wing-coverts (August–September).

**GEOGRAPHICAL VARIATION** Rather slight and difficult to appreciate owing to marked seasonal and individual variation. Despite the vast range, the species is remarkably homogeneous in its genetic make-up, the mtDNA varying little among the various populations (only the populations on Newfoundland and Nova Scotia being identifiable genetically). This indicates a recent and rapid expansion to the current limits (since the retreat of the Wisconsin ice shield, i.e. within the last 10,000 years, with the genetically distinct population on Newfoundland and Nova Scotia corresponding to an ice-free coastal refugium where chickadees may have survived through the last ice age; Gill *et al.* 1993). Five races recognised, following Phillips (1986).

*P. h. littoralis* Southern Quebec (south of the St Lawrence river, with the exception of the Gaspé peninsula, west to at least Compton and Stanstead Cos.), Nova Scotia, Prince Edward Island and NE USA west to New York. As *hudsonicus*, but upperparts slightly warmer and more rufous-brown; also smaller and shorter-billed. Wing (chord) of male 58–64, of female 51–61; tail of male 56–61.5, of female 53–58.5.

*P. h. hudsonicus* Central Alaska and Yukon, northern Mackenzie (also the southwest?), eastern Manitoba (to c. 95° W) and Minnesota to northern and central Quebec (south to around Lake Saint-Jean, the north shore of the Gulf of St Lawrence and Anticosti island; apparently also the Gaspé peninsula), Labrador and Newfoundland. See Description.

*P. h. farleyi* NE British Columbia and Alberta (west to the foothills of the Rockies), southern Mackenzie, Saskatchewan and west and central Manitoba. Poorly marked. As nominate *hudsonicus*, but upperparts slightly paler and browner, sides of neck average paler grey; also slightly larger. Wing (chord) of male 65–70, of female 61.5–65.5; tail of male 62.5–67, of female 58.5–64.

*P. h. stoneyi* Northern Alaska, northern Yukon and NW Mackenzie. As nominate *hudsonicus*, but upperparts slightly paler and greyer (the palest race), and bill averages shorter. (Similar to *farleyi*, but pale and grey, not pale and brown, and lacks pale grey at sides of neck.)

*P. h. columbianus* Southern Alaska (west to the Kenai peninsula), southern Yukon, British Columbia east to the Rocky Mountains, SW Alberta, Montana and Washington. As nominate *hudsonicus*, but upperparts slightly darker and less brown. Includes 'cascadensis' of Washington and southern British Columbia, with the cap supposedly darker and sootier.

**RELATIONSHIPS** A member of the *hudsonicus* superspecies, to which it gives its name, together with Siberian Tit and Chestnut-backed Chickadee. They are treated as a single species by Eck (1980a). Boreal Chickadee overlaps widely with Siberian Tit in Alaska, and with Chestnut-backed Chickadee in SW British Columbia and northern Washington, Idaho and Montana. No hybrids or intergrades are known, and treatment as three distinct species is thus wholly appropriate, and even the use of the superspecies concept is open to doubt with such broadly overlapping ranges. Biochemical data show that Boreal and Chestnut-backed Chickadees are sister-species and that, of North American tits, they are most closely related to Black-capped Chickadee (Gill *et al.* 1989), but Gill *et al.* (1993) linked Boreal and Chestnut-backed Chickadees with Mexican Chickadee (see p. 282 for details).

**REFERENCES** Bent (1946), Godfrey (1951), McClaren (1975, 1976).

## 60 CHESTNUT-BACKED CHICKADEE *Parus rufescens*     Plate 19

Characteristic of the American North-West, this is one of the commonest birds of the fog-bound conifer forests of the Pacific coast.

**IDENTIFICATION** Length 115 mm (4.5 in). Cap dark brown (tinged pinkish-grey), extending well onto upper mantle, remainder of upperparts, including median coverts, dull chestnut. Wings and tail contrastingly dark grey, greater coverts tipped paler, forming a faint wingbar, flight feathers fringed pale grey. Large whitish cheek patches, extending well back onto the sides of the nape. Bib dark brown, flanks dull chestnut (paler on juveniles, and much greyer on the coast of central California); remainder of underparts off-white. The combination of dark brown cap and bib, chestnut upperparts and flanks, and large white cheek patches is distinctive. Juveniles have duller flanks and from below may be confused with juvenile Boreal Chickadees, both species having similarly coloured underparts, but juvenile Chestnut-backed has cinnamon-brown upperparts and a dark cap, rather than olive brown upperparts with a barely contrasting cap.

**SEX/AGE** Sexes similar. Juvenile as adult, but cap slightly paler and not so pink, also more restricted at rear, and upperparts cinnamon-brown, paler and much less rufous than on the adult; cheek patch slightly duller, flank patches paler and much less extensive than the adult's, and underparts slightly duller and greyer. In the hand, the tail feathers are slightly narrower and more pointed (see figure below). 1st adult as adult, but retains the juvenile greater and primary coverts, flight feathers and tail feathers; the last especially may differ subtly in shape and the extent of wear from those of an adult at the same time of year.

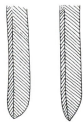

*Figure 60.1  Outer tail feathers (T6) of adult (left) and juvenile (right): note shape.*

**VOICE** Varied. Contact call a high, thin, *seet*, sometimes repeated 2–4 times and strongly recalling a kinglet. Also gives a high, thin, metallic or squeaky 'chirruping' *tsi'lip* or thinner *tsit*, some-times doubled, *tsui-tip*. More complex phrases include a sparrow-like *chis-li*, a similar but longer tinkling *chlee'sit-chsleet-tsleet*, a full, explosive and clicking *chlit-chit*, thin, sweet *swi-swi-swit*, short, scolding *chid'it'it*, and an almost canary-like, sweet, musical *siu'swee*. These may be combined into complex phrases, such as a rapid *chlit-chit-sisi-ziew* (with the 'ziew' unit sounding rather like a toy trumpet), and more standard 'chick-a-dee' phrases (composed of discrete units given in various combinations) include *chis-li-zee, chi-sli-slit zee-zee, chi-chli-slitit zee-zee*, and fuller *chlit-chlit-zee-zee*. In 'chick-a-dee' combinations, the nasal 'dee' is typically a rather high, thin and weak *zee*, given just once or twice. Also uses a lower and deeper *dee-dee-dee-dee...* on its own in more prolonged bouts of calling (this call may be used in territorial disputes, Root 1964; and is also used in 'chick-a-dee' combinations). Other calls include squeaky, nasal *dzui* and *sizi* notes given in combination, e.g. *sizi-dzui-sizi, sizi-dzui-sizi-dzui*, or together with a thin, almost peevish *dzee*, e.g. *sizi-dzee-dzee-dzee, dzee-si-dzee* (a 'broken dee', perhaps a begging call?, and also used in 'chick-a-dee' combinations). Has a 'gargle' phrase (see Black-capped Chickadee, p. 267) which may serve some of the functions of 'song', but apparently lacks a whistled 'fee-bee'-type song. Dixon (1954), however, records, as a 'song' a series of notes on one pitch, accelerating progressively until the last note, *chip-chip-chi-chi-chi-chi-chip*, often given in aggressive encounters with other birds. The notes in this phrase may be disyllabic, *chulip-chulip-chulip...*, 'like the snipping of a barber's shears', and this 'song' recalls that of Chipping Sparrow (Bent 1946). In anxiety near the nest, gives a weak, squeaking *peep* (Bowles 1909).

**DISTRIBUTION AND MOVEMENTS** In the **USA** breeds in **Alaska**, from the southeast along the south coast west to Prince William Sound and Resurrection Bay on the Kenai peninsula, and also on all major and many minor inshore islands west to Montague island. In **Canada** found in western **British Columbia**, east to Hazelton and the Fraser river, recorded in summer in the Okanagan valley, and in SW British Columbia probably breeds locally in Wells Gray and Mount Revelstoke Parks and recorded Glacier NP and West Kootenay (see also Montana), also breeds Vancouver Island and the Queen Charlotte islands, and in the extreme northwest probably breeds in the Klehini valley.

Found throughout **Washington** (although sparse east of the Cascades), in northern **Idaho** (east to Clearwater Co. and south to Idaho Co.), and NW **Montana** (west of the continental divide in the Clark Fork valley, Sanders Co. and the Lewis range of Glacier NP, Flathead Co.). In **Oregon** found east to the Blue Mountains and Klamath Co. In **California** breeds in the Klamath and Siskiyou mountains and the Coast Range south to San Luis Obispo Co. and the Santa Ynez river in extreme western Santa Barbara Co. (confined to the narrow coastal belt south of Marin Co.), and also inland on the Pacific slopes of the Cascades and Sierra Nevada south to Mariposa Co. (and reported south to Bakersfield, Kern Co.: Root 1988). Resident, but some limited altitudinal movements, and prone to wander in autumn and winter (about November–March), when recorded in southern and eastern Idaho, in south-central Oregon (Adel), and in California just south of the breeding range in Santa Barbara, Santa Barbara Co. and in Santa Paula, Ventura Co. Vagrant **Alberta** (including Seebe and Waterton Lake in the extreme southwest, contiguous with the Lewis range of Montana).

**HABITAT** Coniferous forest, particularly the dense forests of the Pacific coastal regions, in firs, spruces, cedars, hemlocks and tamaracks (larches) and, in California, redwoods. Also pines, conifer plantations, live oak and pine-oak, riparian alder and willow thickets, scrub and even ornamental and exotic trees such as eucalyptus and cypress, and burnt-over areas. Favours edge habitats and watercourses. May be found in well-wooded suburban areas, especially in the autumn and winter. Generally lives at low to medium altitudes, usually below 915 m, although in the Sierra Nevada of NW California found at 610–1525 m and occasionally seen as high as 1830 m, and found up to at least 1830 m in Idaho.

**POPULATION** Generally common, although local in southern California and uncommon in the Sierra Nevada of NW California and in Idaho and Montana. The range has apparently expanded eastwards into the Sierra Nevada of NW California since c. 1939, thus discovered in Yosemite NP (a well-watched locality) as recently as 1958; this expansion is probably the result of an increase in the proportion of Douglas Fir in the Sierran forests following logging early in the 20th century. The species has also spread into south-central California, into the region east of San Francisco Bay (Alameda and Contra Costa Cos.), exploiting the maturing areas of orchards and shade trees: in this region, however, Chestnut-backed Chickadee occurs at lower densities and occupies more marginal areas, appearing to be excluded from some of the prime habitat by Plain Titmouse (which, until c. 1940, was the only tit in the area).

**HABITS** Inquisitive and not shy; responds well to 'squeaking'. Forms flocks of 4–20 birds outside the breeding season (June–February in southern California), sometimes joining mixed-species foraging flocks. Territorial during the breeding period, although sometimes nests in loose 'colonies' (with seven nests found in close proximity in Washington: Bowles 1909). Once the young have fledged, the family may remain on territory, or may move to more optimal habitat. Forages acrobatically among the foliage, often high in tall conifers, and to a lesser extent on branches and trunks and in tangled undergrowth, but seldom on the ground, although noted feeding on rotting logs, boulders and rocks, and even on boats in dry dock (Bent 1946). May flycatch. Will visit bird-tables. Food insects, spiders and, especially in autumn and winter, fruit pulp and seeds.

**BREEDING BIOLOGY** Poorly known. Season: Alaska, May; Washington, April–mid June; California, mid March–early June. The nest is placed in a cavity in a dead tree or stub (or dead part of living tree), either coniferous or deciduous, 0.5–4.5 m (–25 m) above ground. The hole may be excavated by the chickadees themselves (often choosing a site where a piece of bark or wood has been split away, or where a wood-boring insect has already broken the surface), or maybe an old woodpecker hole or natural cavity. Sometimes uses artificial locations, such as pipes and buildings, and recorded using an American Cliff Swallow nest by Dixon (1954). In California the site is usually in deep shade, but further north may be in sunny glades. The nest is a foundation of green moss, lined with soft materials such as hair, fur, plant down and feathers. Clutch 6–8 (5–9): eggs white, lightly spotted with reddish-brown or light red; 12 x 15.3 mm. When disturbed on the nest, the incubating bird hisses and flutters its wings. Incubation and fledging periods and the division of labour in the care of the young unknown.

**DESCRIPTION** *P. r. rufescens* **Adult**: *In fresh plumage* (August–early spring), crown (to below eye), nape and upper mantle chocolate-brown, tinged pinkish-grey, slightly darker at sides of crown. Lower mantle, scapulars, back and rump dull chestnut; uppertail-coverts dark olive-brown. Tail dark grey, outer webs tinged olive-drab, all feathers faintly tipped paler. Wing-coverts mid grey, median coverts fringed chestnut-brown, greater coverts finely fringed pale grey and tipped whitish (tinged chestnut on inner greater coverts). Alula dark grey-brown, smaller feathers fringed light grey; primary coverts dark grey-brown, very finely fringed mid grey. Tertials and secondaries mid grey-brown, fringed pale grey, broadly so on outer tertial and more narrowly on outer secondaries; primaries dark grey, P10–P7 very finely fringed light grey, P6–P3 more broadly fringed white around emarginations. Lower lores, cheeks, ear-coverts and sides of neck off-white, faintly washed buff. Chin, throat, upper and sides of breast dark brown. Flanks dull chestnut or rufous-chestnut (forming a variably broad band), breast and centre of belly white, washed pale buffy-grey, undertail-coverts white, washed dirty buff; thighs mid grey. Axillaries and underwing-coverts whitish. *In worn plumage* (March–July), pale fringes to wing feathers abraded. **Bare Parts**: Iris brown; bill blackish, cutting edges and extreme base paler and more fleshy-pink; legs and feet purplish-grey. **Juvenile**: As adult, but cap slightly

paler, more neutral mid brown, not extending onto upper mantle. Upperparts cinnamon-brown, cheek patch off-white, and bib mid-dark brown (darker than cap). Upper flanks cinnamon (much less extensive than on adult), underparts slightly duller and greyer (more feather bases showing). **1st Adult**: As adult (but see Sex/Age). **Measurements**: Wing of male 57.5–65 (chord 60–64.5), of female 59.5–64 (chord 55–67); tail of male 44–52.5, of female 44–49; bill 10–11.3; tarsus 14.5–16.5. Weight averages 9.5 g.
**MOULT** Adult post-breeding complete (August–September). Post-juvenile partial, does not include tail or median and greater coverts (Gabrielson & Lincoln 1959) (August–September).
**GEOGRAPHICAL VARIATION** Relatively well marked, with the colour of the flanks paling abruptly in California (owing to reduced relative humidity?). Three races recognised.

*P. r. rufescens* Alaska south to Sebastopol, Sonoma Co., central coastal California, and also the Sierra Nevada of NW California. See Description.

*P. r. neglectus* SW Marin Co., coastal California. Intergrades to the north with nominate *rufescens*. As nominate *rufescens*, but flank patch paler (more rufous) and much more restricted, remainder of underparts pale grey with the centre of the

breast and belly white, bib slightly paler; inner two tertials finely fringed rufous, outer tertial fringe narrower and duller (not so white). Wing (chord) of male 58–60, of female 56–58; tail of male 47–49, of female 46–50.

*P. r. barlowi* Coastal southern California from San Francisco Bay southwards. As *neglectus*, but flanks light grey, narrowly washed pinkish-buff (largely concealed at rest), all tertials fringed pale rufous, uppertail-coverts slightly paler. Wing (chord) of male 59–63, of female 56–62; tail of male 49–54, of female 48.
**RELATIONSHIPS** A member of the *hudsonicus* superspecies, together with Siberian Tit and Boreal Chickadee, and genetically rather close to Boreal Chickadee (Gill *et al.* 1989). The ranges of Chestnut-backed and Boreal Chickadees overlap or abut in southern Alaska, western British Columbia and northernmost Idaho (and thus they are not, strictly, members of the same superspecies). As there is no evidence of hybridisation or intergradation, there is little doubt that they are distinct species. Gill *et al.* (1993) linked Boreal and Chestnut-backed with Mexican Chickadee (see p. 282 for details).
**REFERENCES** Bent (1946), Crase (1976), Gabrielson & Lincoln (1959), Godfrey (1986), Grinnell (1904).

# 61 RUFOUS-NAPED TIT *Parus rufonuchalis* Plate 20
Other names: Black Tit, Simla Black Tit, Black Crested Tit

This robust tit penetrates north of the Himalayan massif into the Pamirs, Tien Shan and Alai mountains of southern Central Asia and China, and until recently was considered conspecific with Rufous-vented Tit.

**IDENTIFICATION** Length 130 mm (5 in). Cap and spiky, upright crest black, lozenge-shaped cheek patch dirty white, nuchal spot white, often tinged cinnamon-buff on the lower border, and remainder of upperparts olive-grey. Bib black, extending broadly onto the upper belly; remainder of underparts mid grey, with a small cinnamon flank patch and cinnamon undertail-coverts. Juvenile rather duller. The largest and darkest of a group of grey-and-black, crested tits in southern Asia and the Himalayas. Distinguished by its large size and very extensive black bib, covering the whole breast and extending onto the upper belly. Rather similar to the eastern race of Rufous-vented Tit ('Sikkim Black Tit'), but larger, with a buff tinge to the nuchal spot, paler, more olive-washed upperparts, purer white cheek patches, a more extensive black bib, and cleaner grey underparts. Importantly, the geographical ranges of the two species are widely separated. Distinguished from Spot-winged Tit by the lack of wingbars, more extensive black bib, and less extensive cinnamon flank patches (see p. 299 for further details).
**SEX/AGE** Sexes very similar, females tending to have a slightly less extensive and duller black bib and a less glossy crown. Juvenile distinct, immedi-

ately distinguishable from the adult by its much paler bib, contrasting less with the rest of the underparts; in addition, the juvenile's cap is duller and the crest shorter, the rufous tinge is almost absent from the nuchal patch, the upperparts and belly are washed with brown, and the axillaries and undertail-coverts are paler and buffer, thus less contrasting. 1st adult as adult, but the cap and bib are slightly duller, the crest marginally shorter and bib slightly less extensive, and the greater coverts and flight feathers slightly browner. In the hand, moult contrasts may be apparent in the tertials and sometimes the greater coverts, and retains the juvenile tail and flight feathers, the latter averaging slightly more pointed than an adult's.
**VOICE** Rather vocal. Calls include a plaintive, chick-like *cheep* or *peep* and a short *sip*, which may become an abrupt *siup* or *tchiup*. These and similar calls may be given in simple combinations, e.g. *sip'sip'sip, pee-sip, sih-pee, pu-sih-pu, tu-si-si* etc. Also gives a lower *chut* or *chut-chut* (recalling a crossbill) and short, squeaky, low-pitched conversational phrases, e.g. *trip'ip'ip, trip'ip'ip'ip* and *chip'pu'pip*. Begging young give a low-pitched, plaintive, wheezy *zwee-zwee-zweeh* (Roberts 1992). Alarm call a rapid chattering *trrr*, recalling

Great Tit (Ali & Ripley 1983). Has two song types, the trilling song used for 'territory-marking' and a whistle song used in 'territory defence'. The trilling song is very variable, but typically comprises 2–6 whistled notes followed by a rapid 'wooden' trill or buzz, and sometimes concluding with 1–2 whistles; a typical example is *tip'tip-pee-trrrrrrrr*. The whistle song is similarly variable, and comprises whistled motifs (similar to those introducing the trilling song), but without the trill, e.g. *si-si-si-pu* (similarly, Roberts 1992 notes a three-note motif, comprising two high, metallic whistles followed by a downward-inflected whistle, *tsi-tsi-peeduw*, given in series of 4–5 motifs every few seconds, and Fleming *et al.* 1984 a rather thrush-like *leu-ti-tee-de*). Some whistle songs may recall the 'tea-cher' motif of Coal Tit, e.g. *whi-whee, pitch-u*, a loud, cheery *gypsie-bee* or *tju-tju-hee*, but these are slower and deeper in tone than those of Coal Tit. A soft, bubbling, twittering subsong is given during courtship. (Partly after Martens 1975.)

**DISTRIBUTION AND MOVEMENTS** South-central Asia in **Uzbekistan**, **Tadzhikistan** and **Kyrgyzstan**, in the Tien Shan mountains from the Kirgizskiy and Ferganskiy ranges west to the Pskemskiy, Chatkal'skiy (Chimgan) and Kuraminskiy ranges; also the western Pamirs west to the lower Bartang river and Vanch, and the Alai mountains from the Alayskiy and Zaalayskiy ranges west to the Turkestanskiy and Gissarskiy ranges and also the Kugitangtau on the border with Turkmenistan. Extends into NW China in **Xinjiang**, in the Tien Shan mountains and eastern Pamirs (around Kongur Shan, southwest of Kashi; Ludlow & Kinnear 1933). In **Afghanistan** recorded in the northwest from the the Sauzak Kotal (north-east of Herat) and Bend-i-Turkestan range, and in eastern Afghanistan from north of Salang, and from Nuristan south to the Safed Koh (Nangarhar) and Gardez, with a January record from Kabul. Found in **Pakistan** from north-central Baluchistan (Zargun, Wam, Ziarat, Loralai, occasionally descending to Quetta in the winter), north through Zhob (the Shinghar range) to the Takht-i-Sulaiman range on the border with NWFP, although no specimens from the NWFP and confirmation is required of its occurrence there (Roberts 1992, *contra* Ali & Ripley 1983); also lower Chitral (Dir), Swot Kohistan (from Bahrain to the Utrot and Ushu valleys), Gilgit (Naltar valley), Astor, Hunza, Baltistan (Skardu), and south through Hazara, the Neelum valley and Murree hills. Then east through **NW India** in the western Himalayas through Kashmir, Himachal Pradesh and northern Uttar Pradesh and east more locally to central **Nepal**, where occasionally found on the eastern flanks of Dhaulagiri in the upper Kali Gandaki valley. Recorded in Ladakh in NW India in January, in remote side valleys along the Zanskar gorge, at 3800 m in juniper and mixed willow and birch, perhaps a relict population from a time when area had more trees (Mallon 1987). Resident, with rather limited seasonal altitudinal movements, and this robust tit is apparently able to remain at high altitudes during the winter.

**HABITAT** Essentially a bird of coniferous forests, usually spruce, fir and Deodar (cedar) at high altitudes and sometimes also pines at lower elevations. May favour more open forest. In the drier western portions of the range in Central Asia, NW Afghanistan, and Gilgit and Baluchistan in Pakistan, closely associated with junipers, and in NW India and Nepal also sometimes found in rhododendrons, birch and mixed oak and spruce, in Nepal inhabiting the drier areas towards the rain-shadow region of the inner Himalayas. The species is not confined to forest, however, and will utilise scattered scrub and conifers on open hill-sides, and in Baltistan, NW Pakistan, where forest is absent, it occurs in poplars, willows, and mulberries around cultivation, while elsewhere valley-bottom Hazel scrub and birches are also frequented. In Central Asia breeds at 1800–3000 m, descending in the autumn to spruce forests and wintering at 1200–1500 m. In NW China recorded at *c.* 2900–3500 m, in NW Afghanistan at 2400–2500 m, and in eastern Afghanistan at about 2000–3050 m. Breeds in Pakistan and India at 2200–3700 m, with limited altitudinal movements; in Baluchistan winters above 2440 m, and in Gilgit recorded at 2100 m in December, although sometimes descends to 1450 m. Exceptionally found in the foothills in winter, e.g. in the Murree hills in dry scrub at Margalla at 760 m, and at Rawalpindi and Sang-jani. In Nepal summers from 2600 to 4000 m; winter range poorly known, although no marked altitudinal movements.

**POPULATION** Uncommon in NW China, although noted 'in large numbers' in the eastern Pamirs (Ludlow & Kinnear 1933), locally common in Central Asia, Afghanistan, Pakistan and India, and fairly common in Nepal.

**HABITS** Found singly, in pairs and in small parties, and frequently joins mixed-species feeding parties. Forages in the canopy, shrub layer and on the ground, food insects, seeds and berries, the young being fed largely or wholly on insects. Has regular 'anvils' on branches, where it wedges hard-shelled seeds and nuts in cracks in the bark and hammers them open. Often found with Spot-winged Tit, although forages more frequently on the ground, has a heavier bill (and is thus presumably able to exploit slightly different food sources), and seems better adapted to cold conditions and high altitudes (Roberts 1992).

**BREEDING BIOLOGY** Season throughout the range May–June, although from late April in Afghanistan and reportedly from early April in Ziarat, Pakistan (Meinertzhagen 1920). Nest placed in a hole or crevice in the ground, a steep bank or stone wall, under large stones or the roots of a large tree, and also sometimes a cleft or hollow in a trunk or stump up to 1 m above ground level. The nest is usually placed deep in the cavity, and is a pad of moss lined with feathers, hair and wool; both sexes build, and the male continues to add material after the eggs have been laid. Clutch 4–6: eggs white, lightly speckled with reddish-brown; 17.7 x 12.9 mm. Incubation and fledging periods unknown. Both sexes feed the young.

**DESCRIPTION Adult**: *In fresh plumage* (August to about March, occasionally to May), forehead, crown and crest black, faintly glossed blue. Whitish patch on nape, lower border buff or cinnamon-buff. Upperparts, including rump and uppertail-coverts, mid-dark grey, washed olive-grey. Tail dark grey, feathers finely fringed mid blue-grey. Wing-coverts dark grey, fringed mid blue-grey, alula dark grey, primary coverts, tertials, secondaries and primaries dark grey fringed mid blue-grey, primaries finely so and only inwards of emarginations on P3–P7 (fringes absent on P1–P2); outer primaries faintly tipped white when very fresh. Cheeks white, faintly washed buff. Chin, throat, sides of neck, breast and upper belly dull black, usually clearly demarcated from the mid grey of rest of underparts. Thighs grey, undertail-coverts cinnamon. Axillaries and upper flanks cinnamon-buff to cinnamon-rufous (largely concealed by wing). Under primary coverts sooty, broadly fringed whitish, under secondary coverts whitish. Sexes similar (but see Sex/Age). *In worn plumage* (April–July), cap and bib less glossy, nuchal patch reduced (with buff absent from lower border), upperparts purer grey, wing and tail feathers worn. **Bare Parts**: Iris brown; bill black; legs and feet lead-grey or blackish. **Juvenile**: Forehead, crown and much-reduced crest sooty-grey. Nuchal patch reduced, dull whitish. Upperparts dull brownish-grey. Tail and wings as adult. Cheeks whitish with faint rusty-buff wash. Chin, throat and breast sooty-grey (slightly paler than crown), often slightly mottled dull brownish-grey when very fresh (fine feather tips). Axillaries and upper flanks pale greyish-buff, remainder of underparts dull brownish-grey; undertail-coverts pale buff. **1st Adult**: As adult (but see Sex/Age).

**Measurements**: Wing of male 71–80, of female 69–76; tail of male 49–58, of female 48–56; bill 12–15; tarsus 18–20.5. Weight 11.4–14.7 g.

**MOULT** Adult post-breeding complete (June–September). Adult pre-breeding partial?, some may undertake a partial spring moult (a bird dated 19 May from Astor is replacing a central tail feather, and some May individuals have very fresh body plumage). Post-juvenile partial, includes a variable number of wing-coverts and tertials (June–October).

**GEOGRAPHICAL VARIATION** Birds from eastern Afghanistan, Fergana and Gilgit have been named '*blanchardi*', with a more extensive black throat and purer grey mantle, while those from the drier areas of Pakistan (Baluchistan, Chitral and Swat) tend to have a purer white nuchal spot, lacking a buff tinge to the lower border, and paler and more buffy undertail-coverts than those from more humid areas. These characters are rather poorly marked, however, and no subspecies are currently recognised.

**RELATIONSHIPS** Sometimes treated as conspecific with Rufous-vented Tit as *P. rubidiventris rufonuchalis*. The ranges of the two species, however, overlap from Kashmir east to central Nepal, with no evidence of interbreeding. In addition, the songs of the two species are very different, and tapes of the song of Rufous-vented Tit elicit no response from this species. Given such strong evidence of reproductive isolation, treatment of Rufous-naped Tit as a full species is fully justified (Martens 1971).

**REFERENCES** Ali & Ripley (1983), Dementiev & Gladkov (1966–70), Martens (1971), Paludan (1959), Roberts (1992), Stepanyan (1990), Vaurie (1950a).

# 62 RUFOUS-VENTED TIT *Parus rubidiventris*　　　　　　Plate 20

Other names: Rufous-breasted Black Tit, Rufous-bellied Crested Tit, Sikkim Black Tit

This hardy tit is found at high altitudes in the Himalayas and western China, and is divided into two strikingly different populations, at the eastern and western ends of the range.

**IDENTIFICATION** Length 120 mm (4.75 in). Black cap, bib and conspicuous spiky crest, with whitish cheek and nuchal patches. Two distinct populations. In the western Himalayas, the nominate race (sometimes known as 'Rufous-bellied Crested Tit') has the nuchal spot washed pale rufous, the cheek patch white, the upperparts dark grey, tinged olive, and the underparts from the bib down cinnamon-rufous with buffy-grey flanks. In the eastern Himalayas, NE Burma and China, the race *beavani* (sometimes known as 'Sikkim Black Tit') has the nuchal spot white (only faintly tinged buff), the cheek patch tinged buff, the upperparts dark grey tinged blue, and the underparts below the bib mid grey, variably washed buff, cinnamon being confined to the undertail-coverts and axillaries (and sometimes visible at the bend of the wing). One of a group of four grey and black tits

found in the Himalayas and western China, the Rufous-vented Tit is distinguished from Coal and Spot-winged Tits by its lack of wingbars, larger size and darker overall coloration. The rufous-bellied form (Rufous-bellied Crested Tit), found from Kashmir to east-central Nepal, differs from Spot-winged Tit additionally in its cinnamon-rufous, not greyish, underparts. Rufous-vented Tit also overlaps with Rufous-naped Tit in the same region, but is again distinguished by its cinnamon-rufous underparts, as well as its smaller size, cleaner grey upperparts and much less extensive black bib. The eastern race *beavani* (Sikkim Black Tit) has greyish underparts and is thus more similar to Rufous-naped Tit. Their ranges do not overlap, however, making identification straightforward, although, in Nepal, out-of-range birds of either species should be critically examined. Sikkim Black Tit is rather smaller than Rufous-naped, with clean blue-grey upperparts, a duller and less extensive black bib and a distinct buff wash to the grey of the underparts. It differs from Coal Tit in its greyish rather than rufous-buff underparts, with a contrasting rufous patch at the bend of the wing.

**SEX/AGE** Sexes similar, although males may average slightly darker and more intensely black on the bib. Juveniles distinct, with a smaller crest and duller cap than the adult, showing less contrast with the similarly dingy upperparts, and a much duller bib, which in the eastern race *beavani* sometimes barely contrasts with the dull, buff-washed underparts, although in the nominate western races still standing out against the dingy cinnamon-rufous underparts. 1st adult as adult, but in the hand may show moult contrasts in the tertials or greater coverts; the shape of the tail feathers is not a reliable ageing character.

**VOICE** Has a wide variety of calls, although most are generally thin and high-pitched. Calls include a very high and thin *seet*, a high, thin, almost sibilant *psset*, a more definite *seep*, a sharp *psit*, a full but plaintive, 'lost-chick'-like *pee* or *piu*, a sharp, clicking *chip*, a full *tip* or *tiu*, a mellow *pwit* or *whip*, and a sharp *chit*, which may be given in rapid bouts of 1–4 notes in a querulous scold, *chit'it'it'it*. These simple calls may be combined to form more complex phrases, e.g. *seep-seep, seep-'seep'sip-ti, pseet-seep, tip-pee, tip-piu-sweep, tip-piu-chip*, whilst more complex combinations include *ch'ch'ch'ch'pseep'sweep* and *pssep'ch'ch'ch'tiu*. The song varies geographically. The western form (*P. r. rufiventris*, 'Rufous-bellied Crested Tit') gives a 'rattle song', a repetition of identical units or motifs on an even pitch but at variable speeds. The exact make-up of the individual units is very variable, but they are all constructed from a few simple elements. The rattle song may be a true rattle, a fast, vigorous rattling of 13–34 units delivered at c. 10 notes per second (the individual notes thus still easily distinguishable), e.g. a rather 'stony' or 'wooden' *chi-chi-chi-chi...* or *chip-chip-chip-chip-chip-chip...* (this is presumably what Smythies 1986 notes as 'a most characteristic call, a vibrating note something like the twanging of a low-pitched guitar string'; it may strongly recall the song of Brown-throated Treecreeper, and can be very similar to the rattle song of Marsh Tit, see p. 238). Some songs are, however, delivered much more slowly, with 3–6 units given at c. 4–5 units per second. The eastern form (*P. r. beavani*, 'Sikkim Black Tit') gives the 'rattle song' exactly as above, but it also gives less structured whistled songs, combining pure notes and slurred whistles at varying pitches, which resemble the 'whistle song' of Rufous-naped Tit. These phrases, however, are inserted into sequences of the rattle song only if the bird has been disturbed or is agitated, and are not apparently given spontaneously. Notably, *beavani* will also occasionally give phrases which resemble the trilling song of Rufous-naped Tit. Song period in Nepal mid March–mid June. (Partly after Martens 1975.)

**DISTRIBUTION AND MOVEMENTS** The Himalayas from Kashmir in **NW India** (west to the Overa Wildlife Sanctuary near Pahlgam: Jamdar & Price 1990), through Himachal Pradesh (recorded Simla, Great Himalayan NP), northern Uttar Pradesh (including Kedarnath Sanctuary, Chamoli district), **Nepal**, **Sikkim** and **Bhutan** and in extreme western **Arunachal Pradesh** in the Manas drainage at Thingbu-Mago (Ludlow 1937; Singh 1994) and presumably further east, although apparently no definite records. Recorded north of the main range in southern **Tibet** in the valleys of the Sun Kosi (Nyalam), Arun, Chumbi (Yadong), Tsangpo, Nyang Qu, Po Tsangpo and Zayu rivers, and is also found in eastern Tibet in the Salween valley (Baxoi) and in NE Tibet in the Salween watershed north and west to about Sog Xian. Occurs in **western China** in eastern **Qinghai** north to Menyuan and west to about Tianjun in the Qinghai Nanshan range, and in the south, west to about Ngangqian (= Nagqen?), and in SW **Gansu** in the Min Shan (but not NW Gansu, *contra* Cheng 1987; locality given, 'Tiangtang Temple' = T'ien-t'ang Ssu of Vaurie 1972, is in Qinghai). Also southern **Shaanxi** on Taibai Shan in the Qin Ling range, western **Sichuan**, east to Pingwu, Dayi, Emei Shan and Muli, and NW and western **Yunnan**, including Lijiang in the northwest and the Gaoligong and Nu Shan mountains south to about Caojian in the west. Listed for **Nagaland**, **NE India**, by Ali & Ripley (1983) but apparently on the basis of two birds collected in upper Chindwin, **Myanmar** (**Burma**), on Mount Sarameti, which straddles the Indian-Burmese border. Also found in extreme NE Burma from the Hpimaw and Chimili passes north to the Adung valley. Resident, with some seasonal altitudinal movements.

**HABITAT** A variety of forest, from oak and mixed broadleaved woodland at lower altitudes, through mixed stands of pine, fir, hemlock, cypress, rhododendron and, at higher altitudes, birch, pure fir or rhododendron, and also juniper and dwarf willow and rhododendron scrub above the treeline (but perhaps not breeding). Prefers more open stands and edge habitats. Recorded from pine forests in Yunnan. Outside the breeding season, may descend to temperate oak forest. Generally found at high altitudes in the upper temperate and subalpine zones. In the breeding season, in the western Himalayas at 3000–4100 m, in Nepal at 2700 m (breeding proven) to 4250 m (especially 3100–3700 m, and once 4575 m), and in the eastern Himalayas at 2745–4270 m. Some limited altitudinal movements, and recorded in winter down to c. 2400 m in the western Himalayas, 2135 m in Nepal, and 2200 m in the eastern Himalayas, but generally rather hardy and noted as high as 4270 m in February in Nepal. Elsewhere, altitudinal movements are less well known. Recorded on Mount Sarameti at c. 3200 m, NE Burma at 2745–3660 m, SE Tibet at 2130–3660 m, and in SW China in Shaanxi above 2000 m, in NE Qinghai above 2500 m, in Sichuan at 2100–4575 m (wintering to at least 2440–3050 m), and in Yunnan at 2440–4000 m.

**POPULATION** Common in the Himalayas (although rather scarcer in the western Himalayas,

297

in the range of nominate *rubidiventris*), and fairly common in NE Burma, but the lack of records from Kashmir and Himachal Pradesh suggests that the species must be uncommon, if not rare, in those regions. Noted as uncommon in China by Cheng (1987), but common in SE Tibet, SW Sichuan and NE Qinghai.

**HABITS** Found in pairs and, more frequently, in small parties of 10–20, even during the breeding season. Often joins mixed-species foraging flocks. Feeds largely in the canopy, although also descends to the shrub layer. Food insects and seeds.

**BREEDING BIOLOGY** Poorly known. Season in Himalayas April–May. The nest site is a tree hole 0.5-6 m up, though also recorded using a cavity among tree roots on a sloping mossy bank, and the nest is a pad of fur and moss, sometimes just hair. Clutch 2–3 (perhaps even 1?): eggs white, spotted reddish; c. 18.7 x 13.9 mm.

**DESCRIPTION** *P. r. beavani* **Adult**: *In fresh plumage* (August–March), crown, crest and border of upper mantle black, faintly glossed blue; nuchal patch off-white, tinged buff. Remainder of upperparts dark grey, tinged blue, uppertail-coverts washed buff. Tail dark grey, feathers fringed blue-grey. Wings dark grey, coverts grey, fringed blue-grey, alula, primary coverts, tertials and flight feathers fringed and tipped blue-grey, fringes narrower and paler on inner primaries, P3–P6 fringed inwards of emarginations only, and fringes absent on P1–P2. Cheeks and ear-coverts white, tinged buff. Throat, sides of neck and upper breast sooty-black. Remainder of underparts light-mid grey, washed buff, distinctly so when very fresh, especially on the centre of the breast and belly. Thighs grey, undertail-coverts buff to rufous. Axillaries cinnamon, largely concealed by wing at rest. Marginal coverts white, under primary coverts dark grey, narrowly fringed buff-white, under secondary coverts cinnamon-buff. In worn plumage (April–August), cap not so glossy, upperparts darker and less blue, underparts duller and drabber. **Bare Parts**: Iris blackish-brown, brown or reddish-brown; bill black; legs and feet blue-grey, claws horny-brown. **Juvenile**: As adult, but crown and much-reduced crest sooty-grey, nuchal spot dull dirty buff-white. Upperparts dark grey, washed buff, some feathers broadly tipped grey-black, uppertail-coverts faintly tinged buff. Cheeks and ear-coverts pale buffy-yellow. Throat and upper breast variably sooty-grey, on some so pale as to show little contrast with remainder of underparts, and usually not well demarcated from dull greyish-drab belly and vent; undertail-coverts dull buff. **1st Adult**: As adult, but retains juvenile flight feathers and greater coverts and a variable number of tail feathers and tertials. **Measurements**: Wing of male 67–75, of female 67–72.5; tail of male 45–52, of female 46–50; bill 10.5–12; tarsus 16–21. Weight 7–13.1 g.

**MOULT** Adult post-breeding complete (July–November). Post-juvenile partial, includes median coverts, occasionally T1 and T6, also sometimes 1–2 tertials? (August–September).

**GEOGRAPHICAL VARIATION** Marked, with

three distinct subspecies recognised. Nominate *rubidiventris* and *beavani* do not overlap, although their respective ranges abut in Nepal, and odd birds of one form have wandered into the range of the other. Their songs are identical and in playback experiments nominate *rubidiventris* reacts fully to the song of *beavani* (Martens 1971), but no 'hybrids' are known. They are treated as specifically distinct by Haffer (1989) and Wolters (1980), but more information from the contact zone is needed before this 'split' can be endorsed, and the relationship of the apparently isolated *saramatii* would also have to be clarified.

*P. r. rubidiventris* NW India east to central Nepal (east to the Bhote Kosi, with a single record from near Jiri in east Nepal). As *beavani*, but upperparts washed olive, nuchal spot tinged pale rufous, cheek patch off-white, lower breast, centre of belly and vent cinnamon-rufous, and flanks and sides of belly mid grey washed buff. Juvenile as juvenile *beavani*, but upperparts slightly paler and less sooty, with a more pronounced olive wash, a reduced yellow-buff tinge to the cheeks, and bib sooty-grey, contrasting with dingy cinnamon-rufous underparts. Averages slightly larger. Wing of male 67–74; of female 66–70; tail of male 45–49.5, of female 43–49.

*P. r. beavani* Central Nepal (from the Bhote Kosi eastwards, although also recorded slightly further west in the upper Langtang valley) to Arunachal Pradesh, NE Burma, Tibet and SW China. See Description. Birds from NE Qinghai have been named 'whistleri' and average very slightly paler on the mantle and uppertail-coverts, with a paler and more rufous belly.

*P. r. saramatii* NW Burma at Mount Sarameti in the Naga hills; presumably also adjacent Nagaland in NE India. Upperparts greyish buffy-olive, the grey with a faint isabelline cast, more pronounced on rump; underparts deep olive-grey, washed drab, especially on centre of the belly and undertail-coverts. Wing of male 66.5, of female 65; tail of male 48, of female 46.5; bill 10 (Ripley 1961).

**RELATIONSHIPS** Complex. Until recently, the race *beavani* (Sikkim Black Tit) and Rufous-naped Tit were treated as conspecific (as *P. rufonuchalis beavani* and *P. r. rufonuchalis*), and distinct from Rufous-bellied Crested Tit *P. rubidiventris*, which occupies a range between the two grey-bellied birds. Once the similarities between Rufous-bellied Crested Tit and Sikkim Black Tit were appreciated, however, all three were treated as conspecific, taking the oldest name, *P. rubidiventris*. The three forms were believed to be allopatric, but recent field work has shown that the ranges of Rufous-naped Tit and Rufous-bellied Crested Tit overlap widely in NW India and Nepal. Martens (1971) and Jamdar & Price (1990) found no evidence of intergradation or hybridisation. In the zone of overlap, Rufous-vented Tit is usually found at higher altitudes (close to the treeline in spring), Rufous-vented having a rather broader and lower altitudinal range. The treatment of Rufous-naped and Rufous-vented Tits (the latter combining both *beavani* and *rubidiventris*) as distinct species is therefore fully justified. Martens (1975) showed that *beavani* and *rubidiventris* have identical songs (the 'rattle song') that are very different from the 'trilling' and 'whistle' songs given by Rufous-naped Tit, confirming the close relationship of 'Rufous-bellied Crested Tit' and 'Sikkim Black Tit', and their separation from Rufous-naped Tit. Notably, however, whilst Rufous-bellied Crested Tit (which overlaps with Rufous-naped Tit in the west-central Himalayas) gives only the rattle song, Sikkim Black Tit may give whistle song and even occasionally trilling song (although not, apparently, as part of its spontaneous song repertoire). Thus the 'whistle' and 'trilling' song types are considered to be of ancient origin, and have been 'lost' entirely by the Rufous-bellied form, which will not react to playback of the whistle song. Presumably, this enhances reproductive isolation between the Rufous-bellied form and Rufous-naped Tit in the area of overlap. Sikkim Black Tit on the other hand, which does not overlap with Rufous-naped Tit, has had no need to develop isolating mechanisms and has thus not totally lost these song types from its repertoire; notably, it will respond to playback of the whistle song of Rufous-naped Tit. Both Rufous-vented and Rufous-naped Tits are placed in a species group (subgenus *Periparus*) together with Coal and Spot-winged Tits.

**REFERENCES** Ali & Ripley (1983), Baker (1932–33), Cheng (1987), Jamdar & Price (1990), Martens (1971), Martens & Eck (in press.).

## 63 SPOT-WINGED TIT *Parus melanolophus*                    Plate 21
Other names: Crested Black Tit, Spot-winged Black Tit

Endemic to the complex of mountains around the western Himalayas, this close relative of the Coal Tit ranges east to central Nepal, where a confusing variety of hybrids with Coal Tit has been recorded.

**IDENTIFICATION** Length 110 mm (4.5 in). Head, throat and upper breast black, with a long bushy and spiky crest, roughly square white cheek patches and small but conspicuous white nuchal patch. Upperparts mid blue-grey; underparts similar, with cinnamon-rufous flanks and cinnamon undertail-coverts. Pale tips to greater and median coverts form two spotted wingbars, buffy on the median coverts and buff-white to white on the greater coverts. Throughout its range overlaps with Rufous-naped Tit, but easily distinguished by its double wingbars, although these may be difficult to see at long range. Differs additionally in its longer crest, purer blue-grey upperparts, pure white nuchal patch, less extensive black bib, slightly smaller size and slimmer build. Juveniles of the two species are rather more similar, but juvenile Spot-wing has two wingbars and a less well-defined bib. In NW India and western Nepal, separated from Rufous-vented Tit by the same features, and also by basically grey (rather than rufous) underparts. Spot-winged Tit differs from Coal Tit, which has similar spotted wingbars, in its dark grey breast and belly, small rufous patch on the flanks and rufous undertail-coverts. Compared with juvenile Coal Tit, juvenile Spot-winged averages purer grey on the upperparts, with a reduced olive wash, and has purer white cheek patches (obviously washed yellow on Coal), but its wing spots are usually more obviously tinged rusty-buff; its underparts are much more uniform, with little contrast between the olive-grey-brown bib and the drab-grey breast and belly, although there is a rusty-buff patch at the side of the breast. On Coal Tit the underparts are much paler, with an obvious contrast between the dull olive-grey bib and dirty buffy-yellow breast. The ranges of Spot-winged and Coal Tits do not, apparently, overlap in Nepal. There is a narrow zone of introgression in west-central Nepal (see Hybrids) where only hybrids between the two species have been recorded. Some hybrids resemble one or other of the parent species, Spot-winged Tit-type hybrids differing only in their paler and less extensive rufous flank patches, whilst Coal Tit-type hybrids have variable amounts of grey or black on the underparts, usually as irregular extensions of the bib. Some hybrids, however, differ strikingly from both parent species in having a broad band of cinnamon-orange extending from the bib down the centre of the underparts to the lower belly.

**SEX/AGE** Sexes similar. Juvenile distinct, with the cap and crest dark brown and the cap more restricted than the adult's, not extending onto the upper mantle. The upperparts are washed olive-brown and the wingbars are buff and often continuous, rather than being discrete pale spots; the cheeks are faintly washed yellowish and the bib is pale olive-grey-brown, poorly demarcated from the buffy-drab-grey of the remainder of the underparts. 1st adult as adult, but retains the juvenile greater and median coverts, flight feathers and tail, which average paler, browner and more abraded than those of the adults; also, the retained tail feathers are marginally narrower and more pointed (see figure below).

*Figure 63.1  Outer tail feathers (T6) of adult (left), juvenile (right): note shape.*

**VOICE** Very vocal, and many (or most?) vocalisations rather similar to those of Coal Tit. Calls include a thin *stit*, which may become a fuller and more emphatic *psip* or *pip* (recalling Marsh Tit), and this is often combined with an explosive, squeaky *chziou*, *psiu* or *ziu* in an irregular series, *pip-sziu*, *pip*, *pip-sziu*.... Also has a more plaintive, lower-pitched three-note phrase, *tsi-tsu-whichooh*, *tsi-tsu-whichooh*... (Roberts 1992). Gives a high, thin *si* or *sih*, repeated as *sisisi*, and may give a squeaky, conversational jumble of notes, interspersed with *psip* notes. Alarm a high squeak, of a similar quality to the song (in extreme agitation, caged birds have been recorded using harsh churring notes). The incubating female has been recorded giving a powerful snake-like hissing or spitting noise, presumably to discourage intruders. Song a repeated *psip-iu* ..., *chip-wi* ... or *te-pi* ... in the 'tea-cher' pattern, very similar to that of Coal Tit although perhaps averaging slightly fuller and more measured. There may be slight local variations or dialects, especially between populations north and south of the main range of the Himalayas (such variation is apparently not shown by Himalayan Coal Tits; Martens & Eck in press.). Whistler (1949) also notes the song as a 'whirring, reeling trill of the grasshopper type'.

**DISTRIBUTION AND MOVEMENTS** Breeds in eastern **Afghanistan** from Usman Khel (Gardez) north through the Safed Koh (Nangarhar) to Nuristan. Also **Pakistan** in the Safed Koh (Kurram) and north through Dir to lower Chitral, then east through Swat Kohistan, Gilgit, Astor and Baltistan, and south of the main range of the Himalayas through Indus Kohistan and Hazara (Kagan valley), to the Murree hills. In **NW India** found in Kashmir, Himachal Pradesh (including Lahul Spiti) and northern Uttar Pradesh (Simla, Garhwal, Kumaon), and in western **Nepal** occurs east to the Namlang and Langu valleys and Ringmo. See also Hybrids. Resident, with limited seasonal altitudinal movements.

**HABITAT** Primarily a bird of coniferous forest, of pine, Deodar (cedar), fir, spruce and juniper, often mixed with rhododendron, and with birch at higher altitudes, whilst extends into oak at lower altitudes. In eastern Afghanistan also recorded from valley-bottom Hazel groves and on mountain slopes with grass, scrub and a few isolated conifers, and in Kashmir in winter in valley-bottom willows. Breeds in Afghanistan at 1500–3000 m, and in Pakistan at 1800–3200 m (to 3660 m in Chitral: Baker 1932–33); in NW India at 1525–3355 m, up to 3700 m in the east; and in western Nepal at 2800–4000 m (optimally 3000–3700 m, down to at least 2135 m in winter). Some limited dispersal to lower altitudes in winter, sometimes as low as c. 600 m, although in Pakistan recorded in winter in deep snow at 2400 m, and in Kashmir at 2955 m in April with snow still lying. Occurs down to 1000 m in Nuristan, NE Afghanistan, in late February and March. In Pakistan, some dispersal to the lower foothills (e.g. at Attock, in the Margalla hills of the Murree foothills, in January at 370 m, and in gardens in Islamabad and Rawalpindi) and odd records from the adjacent plains (e.g. recorded at Kohat in December and even in the Multan district on the plains of the Indus in February). Little information on winter distribution in Nepal.

**POPULATION** Generally common to abundant, and the most abundant tit in the Murree hills, Pakistan, Kashmir and west Nepal, although uncommon in Gilgit.

**HABITS** Active, not shy and rather gregarious. Usually occurs in pairs or small parties, and found in mixed-species foraging flocks, even in summer, although breeding pairs join flocks only for brief periods, if at all. In autumn, up to 70–80 Spot-winged Tits have been recorded in a single mixed flock, whilst groups of up to 50 are noted in winter, with 30–40 still together in April. In November, a flock of c. 65 was noted going to roost, with groups of up to 25 perched in the crowns of tall Deodars (Gaston 1979). May forage on the trunks of larger trees, especially in the autumn, whilst in spring works the canopy of deciduous trees. Otherwise, most frequently found feeding in the needles of conifers (mostly up to c. 15 m above ground) and may hover around the very tips of the branches. Also feeds on banks, walls, in the shrub layer and occasionally on the forest floor. Food insects, also berries, fruits and seeds, and will visit gardens to take sunflower seeds etc.

**BREEDING BIOLOGY** Season: Afghanistan, May–June; Pakistan, April–June; NW India, mid April–June, occasionally early July; Nepal, late April–early May. Nest placed in a natural hole in a tree or stump, occasionally in a stone wall (even the walls of human habitations) or bank, rarely in the ground at the base of a tree. The cavity entrance is usually below 3 m high, although recorded up to 12–15 m. The nest is constructed from moss, lined with fur, wool and hair; in small cavities, the moss foundation may be dispensed with. Both sexes carry nesting material to the hole. Clutch 5–6 (4–10): eggs white, variably spotted with reddish-brown (often concentrated in a ring at the larger end); 15.7 x 11.7 mm. Female incubates, sitting very tight, period c. 14–15 days; she is occasionally fed on the nest by the male. Both sexes feed the young, which fledge after c. 21 days. Apparently single-brooded (Roberts 1992), although reported to be double-brooded, at least at lower elevations (Baker 1922, 1932–33).

**DESCRIPTION** Adult: *In fresh plumage* (September–March), crown, crest, nape and upper mantle black, feather fringes glossed blue. White patch in centre of nape and upper mantle. Upperparts mid blue-grey. Tail dark brownish-grey, feathers fringed mid blue-grey. Wing-coverts blackish-grey, lesser coverts broadly fringed mid blue-grey; median and greater coverts with discrete whitish spot at tip of shaft, distal portion of spot buff on median and outer greater coverts. Alula blackish, smaller feathers fringed blue-grey and finely tipped white. Primary coverts blackish-grey, fringed blue-grey. Flight feathers dark brownish-grey, tertials fringed blue grey and finely tipped white, secondaries and P6–P10 fringed blue-grey, P3–P5 fringed whiter basally of emarginations;

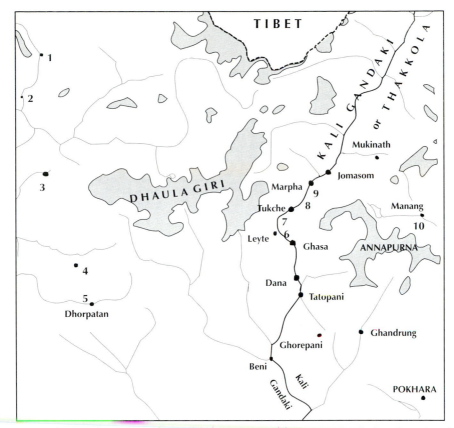

Figure 63.2 The area of central Nepal around the Dhaulagiri and Annapurna massifs where Spot-winged Tit in the west meets Coal Tit in the east. The shaded area indicates areas above 6000 m. (After Martens 1972, 1975)

Key to numbered localities:
**Spot-winged Tit**
1 Ringmo/Phoksumdo Tal
**'Spot-winged-type' hybrids**
2 Suli-Gad-Tal
3 Tarakot
4 Thankur
5 Dhorpatan
**Cinnamon-bellied hybrids**
5 Dhorpatan

**'Coal-type' hybrids**
6 Chaziou-Khola (near Leyte)
7 below Nabrikot
8 Thaksang (above Tukche)
9 above Dhumpha and old Marpha (= Burano Marpha)
**Coal Tit**
10 Manang

when very fresh, primaries and secondaries very finely tipped white, especially on inner secondaries. Lores and supercilium black, sides of neck, throat and upper breast blackish. Cheeks and ear-coverts white. Lower breast, belly and vent mid grey, tinged blue. Upper flanks cinnamon-rufous, and narrow cinnamon band on lower flanks. Undertail-coverts cinnamon (disjunct from rear flanks); thighs mid grey, fringed dark drab. Axillaries cinnamon, underwing-coverts dark grey, tipped cinnamon. *In worn plumage* (April–July), crown duller and not so glossy, crest slightly shorter; upperparts duller and not so blue. Tips to greater coverts may be heavily abraded, pale spots reduced; tips to median and greater coverts abraded and bleached whiter. Fringes and tips of tertials

and flight feathers worn and abraded. Bib duller and a sootier black, underparts duller and slightly drabber. **Bare Parts**: Iris brown; bill black; legs and feet lead-grey or dark bluish-grey. **Juvenile**: Crown, crest and nape dark brownish (cap not extending onto upper mantle); nuchal patch off-white, feathers very finely fringed brownish. Upperparts mid grey, faintly washed olive-brown. Tail as adult. Wing-coverts as adult but slightly paler, fringes as upperparts; tips of greater and median coverts extensively buff (often forming solid, rather than spotted, wingbars). Flight feathers as adult, but inner tertial tipped buffish, all feathers finely tipped white when very fresh. Lores and chin dark brownish, becoming grey-tinged olive-brown on sides of neck, throat and breast, and drab-grey on

301

remainder of underparts (including undertail-coverts), variably tinged buff, especially at rear. Upper flanks as adult. Cheek patch lightly washed yellow. **1st Adult**: As adult (see Sex/Age). **Measurements**: Wing of male 59–68, of female 58–66; tail of male 39–48, of female 39–46.5; bill 11–12; tarsus 16–17.8. Weight 7–9.8 g.

**MOULT** Adult post-breeding complete (mid June–October). Post-juvenile partial, includes lesser coverts (mid June–mid October).

**GEOGRAPHICAL VARIATION** No subspecies have been named. Birds from the western end of the range in Afghanistan and the Safed Koh (Afghanistan/Pakistan border) average slightly larger and slightly darker on the upperparts, and may merit a subspecific name (Paynter 1962).

**HYBRIDS** In central Nepal, there is a narrow zone of introgression with Coal Tit centred around the Dhaulagiri massif. Birds showing slight introgression with Coal Tit ('Spot-winged-type' hybrids) have been collected at Suli-Gad-Tal (near Ringmo), Tarakot, Thankur and Dhorpatan; cinnamon-bellied hybrids from Dhorpatan; and birds close to Coal Tit ('Coal-type' hybrids) from various localities in the upper Kali Gandaki (Thakkola) valley, east of Dhaulagiri. Note that the aberrant features in the coloration of the respective 'hybrids' are not shown by the other, neighbouring, species; it is hypothesised that they represent the genetic effects of hybridisation (and experimental crossings of Spot-winged Tits with European Coal Tits produce a reddening of the underparts, one of the features of some of the hybrids). Sight records of Spot-winged Tits (and hybrids) from the eastern marches of the range (to Ghorepani and the upper Kali Gandaki valley, see map, p. 301) require confirmation, and any tit seen in this area should be very carefully examined. Although there are no records of mixed pairs or even of Coal and Spot-winged Tits occurring together during the breeding season, there is probably a very narrow hybrid zone. Martens & Eck (in press.) suggest, however, another possibility. The Spot-winged-type hybrids (with paler and less extensive rufous flank patches) are merely normal variants in Spot-winged Tit, and a bird with traces of cinnamon on the underparts has been collected in NW India, far from the 'hybrid' zone. The cinnamon-bellied 'hybrids', which are found only in the Dhorpatan valley, within the range of Spot-winged, represent an unrecognised form of Spot-winged with a very restricted range (perhaps to the east of Dhorpatan?); they have a more constant and uniform appearance than might be expected from hybrids. Finally, the Coal-type hybrids (with varying amounts of grey or black on the underparts) are Coal Tits from a small and very variable population confined to the upper Kali Gandaki valley (which merits subspecific status).

**RELATIONSHIPS** A member of the *Periparus* subgenus together with Coal, Rufous-naped and Rufous-vented Tits. Very closely related to Coal Tit, but, despite the presumed hybridisation between the two species in a narrow zone of secondary contact in western Nepal, their similar territorial songs, and no obvious differences in their ecology, Spot-winged Tit is treated as a separate species, following Sibley & Monroe (1990) and Voous (1977). Similarly, Martens (1975) and Diesselhorst & Martens (1972) consider them 'semispecies' within the polytypic superspecies *P. ater*. There are apparently partial isolating mechanisms between the two in the rather narrow zone of hybridisation. Moreover, hybrids between Spot-winged and Coal Tits not only appear similar to both parent species, but may also be strikingly different, having extensive cinnamon on the underparts, which may indicate a marked genetic divergence between the two. If, on the other hand, there is no hybrid zone (see above) and the ranges of Spot-winged and Coal Tits meet without any hybridisation, the case for specific status for Spot-winged is actually strengthened.

**REFERENCES** Baker (1922, 1932–33), Bates & Lowther (1952), Diesselhorst & Martens (1972), Martens (1975), Martens & Eck (in press.), Paludan (1959), Roberts (1992), Vaurie (1950a).

# 64 COAL TIT *Parus ater* Plate 21

This small tit occupies a vast range across Europe and Asia from Britain to Japan, and the tendency of all populations towards the disportment of a crest reaches its fullest and most flamboyant expression in the Himalayas.

**IDENTIFICATION** Length 110 mm (4 in). A small, slender-billed, relatively large-headed tit with a short, narrow tail. Often appears very slightly crested in western populations, whilst those in southern and eastern China and the Himalayas have a long floppy crest. Cap and upper mantle black, with a large white nuchal spot. Upperparts blue-grey to olive-buff or brownish with two prominent spotted wingbars, whilst the tertials are often tipped off-white. Cheek patches white, bordered by an extensive black bib which connects at the rear with the black of the nape. Underparts white or buffy-white, flanks, belly and vent extensively buffish or brownish. Over most of the range, the combination of small size, prominent white nuchal patch, white cheeks, spotted white wingbars and very extensive black bib is distinctive. In the central Himalayas, however, should be carefully distinguished from Spot-winged Tit (for full details, see p. 299). In the eastern Himalayas and China, separated from Rufous-vented Tit by the double white wingbars and pinkish-buff underparts (not mid buffy-grey with cinnamon on the flanks). In the Tien Shan and Pamirs of Central Asia and NW China, distinguished from Rufous-naped Tit also by its double white wing-bars, less extensive black bib, and buffy underpart coloration (mid grey with a small cinnamon flank patch and cinnamon undertail-coverts on Rufous-naped).

**SEX/AGE** Sexes very similar, although the female's (and 1st adult's) cap and bib average fractionally duller, more brownish and less blue and glossy. The bib also differs in shape and extent (at least in *P. a. britannicus*, but this distinction is much reduced in *P. a. hibernicus* and unstudied in other races), the male's being broader and more triangular, frequently extending to the wing carpals, the female's being shorter, narrower and less triangular (Gosler & King 1989, King & Griffiths 1994; see figure below). The female's upperparts tend to be more olive; thus, in Europe, some birds may be sexed in January–March by the dark blue-grey upperparts of the male compared with the distinct greenish-olive tinge shown by females. In addition, in the male the lesser and marginal coverts are black, fringed blue-grey, while in the female they are dark grey, fringed dull lead-grey. Individual variation and differences in the extent of wear however, can make sexing almost impossible, even in the hand. Juvenile distinct, duller than the adult, variably tinged yellow. The black on the head is sootier, nuchal patch ill-defined and washed yellowish, upperparts dull greyish-olive, wing spots duller and washed yellowish, wing and tail feathers fringed greenish-grey or olive-green, cheek patches pale yellow, bib small and ill-defined (mid grey, washed yellow), and the underparts washed yellowish. 1st adult as adult, but retains the juvenile primaries, secondaries and primary coverts and, in northern and central Europe, the alula and tertials, some outer greater coverts and usually all the tail feath-

*Figure 64.1 Difference in bib shape of male (left) and female (right) P. a. britannicus.*

ers. 1st adults may then be aged by moult contrasts in the greater coverts between the new, inner coverts (dark, fringed blue-grey) and the old outer feathers (paler and fringed duller blue-, green- or buffish-grey), although some juveniles, especially from second broods, retain all the greater coverts, thus lacking moult contrasts in this tract (but the old greater coverts then contrast with the new median coverts). Conversely, in northern Europe all the greater coverts are occasionally replaced, and in the Mediterranean basin replacement of all greater coverts, tertials, alula and some tail feathers is relatively common. Look then for a contrast in wear and coloration between the new greater coverts and the retained primary coverts/alula, or moult contrasts in the tertials and/or alula; ageing is, however, sometimes difficult or impossible. By spring all coverts are worn, with the fringes bleached to grey, and ageing is impossible.

**VOICE** Quite varied, but almost all vocalisations are high-pitched and rather pure and sweet. Commonest call a variable but usually plaintive *pui, pwi*, or *tsuee*, with many variants, such as a cheerful *tsueet*; also gives a related flat but emphatic *sui, chuu* or slightly breathless and piping *sih* (usually in early spring during courtship display). These notes may be repeated in a slow series, and are often combined with a very slightly hoarse or buzzing *pi* or *pih* in a characteristic disyllabic *swee-pi, sui-pi or pui-ti*, or followed by an explosive twitter. Other calls include a full *pipi* or *pipipi*, and a thin *sisisi* (very like that of a Goldcrest), whilst a rapid *chit, chipipip* (cf. Blue and Great Tits) is given by at least the Central Asian population. Also gives a rambling, formless series of sibilant squeaks and churrs, and when disturbed on the nest females give a drawn-out hiss. In anxiety gives a steady series of emphatic *pwee* or *pih* notes (near to a Common Chaffinch's 'pink'), and in alarm these become more ringing and are combined with a hoarse *szee* or *eez* and given in irregular series, *szee-pih, szee-pih-szee....* NW African populations have a distinctive churring or dull trilling alarm call (a low-frequency scolding; such notes are otherwise almost entirely absent from the Coal Tit's vocabulary, being used rarely when very excited). The male's song, given from January onwards, is a 2- or 3-syllable motif repeated 2–8 times with a wide variety of speeds, tones and inflections e.g. *tu-wa-chi, tu-wa-chi...*, an emphatic *ti-t'wa, ti-t'wa...*, rapid *chi-chi-chi...* or *pe-twi, pe-twi...*, and rolling, slurred and almost jangling *sit'tui-sit'tui-sit'tui....* The most characteristic is, however, a thin, plaintive *chip-pe, chip-pe...* or *peechoo-peechoo-peechoo....* There are many variants, and each male may have a repertoire of up to 16 song types. Males often change the song each time they switch perches, and song-duels between males are common, each one switching its songs to match its neighbour's when countersinging. There is little variation in the song across the vast range (e.g. rather similar in Central Asia, the Himalayas and Taiwan), although on Cyprus it is slightly slower and lower-pitched. Overall, the song recalls the 'tea-cher' note of Great Tit but is usually faster and rather sweeter, but thinner, less ringing and more plaintive. The female's song is similar to the male's, although quieter, with only 1–2 motifs given at a time. (Partly after Cramp & Perrins 1993.)

**DISTRIBUTION AND MOVEMENTS** Breeds from **Britain** and **Ireland** (including Channel Islands and Inner Hebrides, but sporadic Outer Hebrides and absent Orkney and Shetland), across **Europe** and **Russia** to the Sea of Okhotsk and Kamchatka peninsula. Occurs north to central **Norway**, northern **Sweden** and central **Finland**, to 67° N on the Kola peninsula, *c.* 65° N in European Russia, 64° N on the Ob' river, 63° N on the Yenisey river, 62° N in central Siberia, to the

Verkhoyanskiy range in Yakutia and Magadan on the Sea of Okhotsk, and c. 59° N on the Kamchatka peninsula. Found south to **Spain**, **Portugal**, **Italy**, **Greece**, the Stara and Rodopi mountains of **Bulgaria**, Carpathian mountains of **Romania**, central **Ukraine** (Zhitomir and Kiev), SE **European Russia** (Kaluga, Tula and Ryazan', Ul'yanovsk on the Volga, and probably the southern Urals), and also **Corsica**, **Sardinia**, **Sicily**, **Crete** and **Cyprus**. In Asia, breeds south to the limit of the forest in the northern Kyrgyz Steppes (probably to 55° N in western Siberia), Semipalatinsk in NE **Kazakhstan**, the Kuznetskiy Alatau, Salairskiy, Altai, Tannu Ola and Sayan mountains, Mongolia and NE China. In winter may disperse to the steppes of the Ukraine, lower Ural basin, southern Kyrgyz Steppes and Lake Zaysan region. In northern **Mongolia** found in the Tesiyn Gol and Tuul Gol valleys, Bogdo Uul massif (near Ulan Bator), Hentiyn mountains, and (winter only?) the Hangayn mountains; also the western Mongolian Altai. In NE **China** found in **Heilongjiang** in the basins of the Amur (Heilong Jiang) and Ussuri (Wusuli Jiang) rivers, south through **Liaoning** and northern **Hebei** (winter visitor Beijing and Eastern Tombs) to northern and western (Luliang Shan) **Shanxi**, also eastern **Shandong** (Qingdao, where recorded in November, and Yantai; a migrant only?). Presumably breeds in both **North** and **South Korea** (south in summer to at least Chungchong Pukdo), including Cheju island. Found on **Sakhalin** and Moneron, and in the southern **Kurile islands**, on Urup, Iturup, Kunashir and Shikotan, and throughout **Japan**, from Hokkaido south to Yakushima, including Rishiri-to, Honshu, Sado, Shikoku, Kyushu and Tsushima, also Oshima in the Izu islands, and reported from the Nansei Shoto archipelago. There are several disjunct southern populations. In **North Africa** breeds in northern **Morocco** in the Haut and Moyen Atlas and Rif, in northern **Tunisia** in the Massif de l'Ouarsenis and Atlas Saharien, and in NE **Algeria**. In the **Middle East** found in much of **Turkey** (absent from the central plateau and the southeast), and the mountains of **Lebanon**, and presumably breeds in western **Syria** (e.g. ten recorded Jabal al Nusayriyah in April: Baumgart & Stephan 1994). Also western **Iran** in the Zagros mountains (recorded around Shiraz: see *P. a. phaeonotus* in Geographical Variation) and northern Iran in the Elburz mountains and NE Khorasan, and in the adjacent Kopet Dag mountains of SW **Turkmenistan** (east to about Ashkhabad). In southern **Ukraine** found in the Krymskiye mountains of the southern **Crimea**, and also in the **Caucasus** (north to the basin of the Kuban' river) and **Transcaucasus** (see Geographical Variation). Disperses in winter to the plains of the Transcaucasus. Very rare **Israel**, where recorded in 1942 (two, January and March), winter 1945/46 (three) and 1976 (three, February). In **Central Asia** breeds in SE **Kazakhstan** in the Dzhungarskiy Alatau, Ketmen' range and Zailiyskiy Alatau, and in adjacent **Kyrgyzstan** in the Tien Shan complex eastwards from the eastern Kirgizskiy mountains

(west to 74–75° E), south to the Kokshaal-tau, and also the Alay system in the eastern Alayskiy and Zaalayskiy ranges. In NW **China** occurs in **Xinjiang** in the Tien Shan, Borohoro Shan, Bogda Shan and related ranges (through Kashi, Aksu, the Tekes valley and Hejing east to Hami). Disperses in winter onto the adjacent plains. In the **eastern Himalayas** breeds from the Kali Gandaki valley in central **Nepal** (see also Hybrids), east through **Sikkim** to at least **Bhutan**. Also NE **Myanmar** (**Burma**) from the Adung valley south through the Irrawaddy-Salween divide to about Pawahku. In adjacent SW **China** occurs in southern **Tibet** (penetrating north of the Himalayas in the valley of the Sun Kosi to Nyalam, the Chumbi valley, and in the Subansiri drainage to Lung and Bimbi La (just north of the border with Arunachal Pradesh), and SE Tibet in the Tsangpo valley west to the Nyang Qu (to Güncang) and east to Pome and the Po Tsangpo valley (east to Sumzom). Also NW **Yunnan** (Gaoligong Shan, Lijiang, Yangtze-Mekong watershed and Zhongdian, and recorded Kunming), western **Guizhou** (Weining), the mountains bordering the western and northern marches of the Red Basin of **Sichuan** (Muli, Mabian, Emei Shan, Baoxing, Guan Xian and Wanyuan), western **Hubei** (Yichang region), southern **Gansu** and southern **Shaanxi** (Qin Ling and Daba Shan ranges). Breeds disjunctly in SE **China** in the Huang Shan mountains of SE **Anhui**, Taishun, southern **Zhejiang** (King & Zheng 1988), and Guadun/Huanggang Shan in NW **Fujian**. Also **Taiwan**. Some recent records from **Hong Kong** are thought to involve individuals of captive origin. Largely sedentary in the south and west of the range, with British birds rarely moving more than 50 km and southern European populations undertaking no more than a slight dispersal or altitudinal movements; most movements away from the home range are in response to food shortages. Some northern and eastern populations, however, regularly move south for variable distances in the autumn and winter. When seeds crops are poor these movements sometimes become large-scale 'irruptions' usually involving almost exclusively juveniles, when thousands of birds may be recorded at migration bottlenecks in late August–early November/December (e.g. 35,000 at Hanko Bird Observatory, southern Finland, in Autumn 1991, coinciding with influxes of Willow and Long-tailed Tits), with return passage northwards in spring. Passage may be diurnal, but, even during irruptions, tends to avoid water-crossings, and Continental birds are scarce or rare in Britain (except during major influxes such as those of 1957 and 1959; vagrant Fair Isle, with just three records). In the autumn, there may also be some northward dispersal into the northern taiga, to Lapland, 69° N in the Obskaya Guba, 66° 25' N on the Yenisey, the Putorana mountains and even the shores of the Arctic Ocean on the Taymyr peninsula, where Coal Tits came aboard the schooner *Zarya* as it manoeuvred among ice floes at 75° N in October 1900 (Rogacheva 1992). In the south, occurs as a rare winter straggler to the Tehran area in Iran. In the Eastern Palearctic the pattern is similar, and a regular migrant in NE China: e.g. at Beidaihe, coastal Hebei, 223 bird-days in October–November 1991 (higher numbers than normal, perhaps indicating an irruption; Williams *et al.* 1991). In Japan some seasonal altitudinal movements, and some withdrawal southwards from Hokkaido in the winter. May be partially migratory in Korea, and is certainly an altitudinal migrant there.

**HABITAT**  Essentially coniferous forest. In the northern parts of the range favours spruce, although also found in mixed forest and in pine and larch in Siberia. Further south, tolerates a broader range of coniferous species and more often found in mixed woodland, and on the southern margins of the range in southern Europe, North Africa, the Caucasus and Iran, where largely montane, found additionally in beech and oak forest. In Iran also occurs in high-altitude juniper woodland in the Kopet Dag, and in northern and western Britain found in Sessile Oak and birch. In the mountains of Central Asia, the Himalayas and China, largely confined to coniferous forests of spruce, fir and hemlock, also pines (especially in southern and eastern China), birch-fir and dwarf junipers above the treeline, and, as in the West Palearctic, occurs locally also in mixed forest, especially in southern parts of the range, such as Japan. In disturbed environments found in conifer plantations and urban and suburban areas where there are at least a few conifers, and in irruptions and during the winter favours a wider variety of habitats, including deciduous woodland, parks and gardens. In West Palearctic breeds from sea level up to the treeline, thus recorded to 1800 m (exceptionally 2050 m) in Austria, but only above 450 m in the Caucasus and at 1220–1830 m in SW Bulgaria. Found at 1220–2135 m in northern Iran and at 2135 m in SW Iran. In NE China and Korea breeds in the foothills and mountains (e.g. 800–1800 m in the Changbai Shan of southern Jilin), and in southern Japan found from 600–2500 m to the treeline, but on Hokkaido in northern Japan also in the lowlands. In Central Asia present in Xinjiang, NW China, at 1220–2745 m. In the eastern Himalayas found in the upper temperate and subalpine zones. Breeds in Nepal at 2600–4000 m (and occasionally seen in summer in the range 2440–4250 m) and winters at 2500–3050 m (occasionally noted at 1830–4270 m), and in Sikkim and Bhutan summers at 2745–3940 m, wintering at 2135–3660 m. Hardy, and may be the only species in snow-clad conifer forests in winter. In NE Burma recorded at 2745–3500 m in winter, and in SE Tibet occurs at 2775–3810, down to 2285 m in winter. In SW China recorded in summer at 2100–4570 m in Yunnan and Sichuan, wintering up to at least 2440–3050 m at Wolong in Sichuan, and noted in Hubei at 1670 m in December. In SE China, found in Fujian at 1370–1830 m (breeding above 1500 m only?) and noted in Zhejiang at 1200–1300 m in April. On Taiwan, resident at 2000–3500 m and does not descend to lower altitudes in winter.

**POPULATION**  Generally fairly common to common, although rare in Turkmenistan and uncommon in Mongolia and Zhejiang, SE China. In SW Iran, the local race in the Zagros mountains is apparently very rare, and may not have been seen since its description in 1873. Throughout the range, large annual fluctuations in the population are commonplace. Has spread north and west in the 20th century; breeds irregularly Outer Hebrides, has expanded into western France and western Ireland, and first bred in the Channel Islands in 1968 and in the Isles of Scilly in 1975. Population increases have been reported from Britain and Belgium, generally a result of the increase in commercial conifer plantations.

**HABITS**  Active and restless, sometimes tame and confiding, sometimes shy. Found singly and in pairs, and in resident populations probably pairs for life. Gregarious outside the breeding season, forming flocks, sometimes of as many as 50 (several hundreds or even several thousands together have been recorded: Dementiev & Gladkov 1966–70). Joins mixed-species foraging parties, within which resident pairs may associate together. Roosts singly, often under drooping branches, in old nests, in clumps of ivy and in holes and crevices, sometimes excavating roost holes in rotten wood. The female roosts on the nest during incubation and until the chicks are about nine days old. Forages in the crown of conifers, gleaning insects or extracting seeds from among the cones and needles with great agility, its narrow bill being ideal for picking food items from between the needles. May also investigate the thicker branches and trunks, especially of deciduous trees. Regularly feeds on the ground, especially in the winter; this is apparently much commoner in Britain, where the normal lack of snow cover gives access to the fallen fruits of chestnut, beech and oak. Also able to feed on the underside of snow-bound branches. Regularly visits birdtables. Food insects and spiders, also seeds in the autumn and winter (although spruce seeds, the favoured food items, are often unavailable for several years). Much food is stored, especially in June–December and April. Both seeds and insects are cached, depending on availability, usually in the upper parts of trees in empty buds and clumps of needles, but also in lichen and bark crevices, and on the ground amongst soil. These caches help to tide the tits over during periods of food shortage and compensate for its inability to store large reserves of body fat (owing to its very small size). Notably, in Britain, Coal Tit populations are less affected by hard weather than other small birds.

**BREEDING BIOLOGY**  Season: West Palearctic, April–late July; Himalayas, April–June? The nest is placed in a hole in a tree or tree stump, an abandoned rodent hole, or in cracks and crevices in rocks, walls, under stones or among tree roots; may use nestboxes. Both sexes prospect for potential holes, but the final selection is probably made by the female. The nest hole may be enlarged if it is in a rotting tree or the ground. The nest itself is a cup of moss lined with hair, wool and sometimes a few feathers, built by the female alone in a period of up to 26 days (although the first egg may be laid on the moss base and the lining added subsequently). Clutch 8–11 (5–13) in most of Europe, 4–7 in the western Mediterranean (and second broods average slightly smaller), 5–8 (–13) in Japan: eggs white, finely spotted and speckled reddish-brown, occasionally unmarked; 15 x 11.6 mm (*P. a. britannicus*). Female incubates, period 14–16 days (–18 days in Japan). The young are fed by both sexes, but only the female broods. Fledging after 18–22 days (16 days in Japan), the juveniles remain together in thick cover for several days, calling to attract the parents' attention (unlike other tits, where the young follow the adults from tree to tree). Regularly double-brooded, and occasionally three broods are raised.

**DESCRIPTION** *P. a. ater* **Adult Male**: *In fresh plumage* (September–November), crown and nape black, slightly glossed blue. Large whitish nuchal patch. Upper border of mantle blackish, remainder of mantle, scapulars and back dark blue-grey, feathers variably, although usually faintly, tipped greenish-olive or olive-brown (rarely, tips may largely conceal bases). Rump and uppertail-coverts olive-brown or buff-brown, longer coverts mid olive-grey. Tail dark grey-brown, T1–T5 fringed mid olive-grey, T6 faintly fringed pale grey. Lesser and marginal coverts black, fringed blue-grey, median and greater coverts blackish-grey, fringed blue-grey and broadly tipped white (largely on outer web). Primary coverts and alula blackish-grey, primary coverts very finely fringed blue-grey, second largest feather of alula fringed grey and tipped white. Flight feathers dark grey-brown, outer webs of tertials tinged blue-grey, fringed olive-grey at base and pale grey or whitish towards tip, often ending in a white spot; secondaries fringed olive-grey, P1–P8 finely fringed grey, fringes whiter and present only inwards of emarginations on P3–P6. Cheeks and ear-coverts white. Lores, chin, throat and rear sides of neck black, connecting with black of nape and extending onto sides of breast. Flanks, sides of belly, vent and undertail-coverts greyish-buff to pale cinnamon-buff; breast and centre of belly white, black feather bases often visible on breast, belly sometimes washed buff. Underwing-coverts and axillaries pale buffy-white; dark grey feather bases may be visible, especially on leading edge of wing. *In worn plumage* (March onwards; sometimes from December), nuchal patch less clearcut, some dark feather bases visible, mantle and scapulars uniform dark blue-grey with olive-brown wash to lower rump only; pale fringes on wing-coverts abraded and white tips partly abraded (by May–June fully abraded), pale fringes on wing and tail feathers bleached paler and greyer, those on primaries and sometimes tertials and tail may be completely abraded; cheeks dirty white, flanks and vent with restricted amount of greyish-drab (lacking any warm buff), breast and belly extensively dirty white (occasionally pale drab-grey). **Bare Parts**: Iris brown to blackish-brown; bill black with pale grey cutting edges; legs and feet leaden-blue to slate-grey. **Adult Female**: As male, but mantle and scapulars average slightly more greenish-olive. Cap less glossy and bib aver-

ages slightly duller, more brownish-black; some may have bib less extensive. Lesser and marginal coverts dark grey, fringed dull lead-grey. Flanks and vent average slightly darker and more extensively greyish-buff. In lightly worn plumage (December–March, sometimes to May), mantle and scapulars distinctly more greenish-olive than on male (which has worn to dark blue-grey); when more worn, upperparts of female as male. **Juvenile**: Forehead and crown dark sooty-grey, nape dark grey (sometimes tinged olive). Nuchal patch ill-defined, yellowish-white. Upperparts and lesser coverts dark grey, washed dull greenish-olive. Median and greater coverts dark grey, fringed greenish-olive and tipped dirty white (the white spot often finely fringed grey). Primary coverts and alula grey-black, fringed greenish-olive. Flight feathers and tail as adult, although fringed greenish-grey or olive-green (less blue-grey). Cheek patch pale yellow, whiter at rear. Bib small and ill-defined, mid grey washed yellow. Underparts yellowish-white, flanks, vent and undertail-coverts pale buff. Yellow wash on nuchal and cheek patches and underparts rapidly bleached. Bill horn-black up to *c*. 2 months old. **1st Adult**: As adult (see Sex/Age). **Measurements**: Wing of male 58–70, of female 57–66; tail of male 43–53, of female 41–50; bill 10–12.1; tarsus 15.7–18.3. Weight 7.6–12 g.

**MOULT** Adult post-breeding complete (late May–early September, sometimes early October; may migrate whilst still in moult). Post-juvenile partial, includes a variable number of greater coverts (usually 6–8, rarely none and seldom all), rarely 1–3 tertials and sometimes the alula (and then at least six greater coverts moulted), occasionally some tail feathers (especially T1); moult tends to be more extensive in first brood than in second-brood young, and more extensive in southern Europe, see Sex/Age (commences at 4–6 weeks of age, June–August, occasionally late September).

**GEOGRAPHICAL VARIATION** Marked and complex, with much local and individual variation even within the named races. Broadly, a cline of decreasing colour saturation runs across Europe to Central Asia, with the opposite trend further east (with Britain, Ireland, Corsica and Sardinia forming the western ends and Japan the eastern end of the cline, despite these being isolated island populations). Twenty subspecies are recognised, divisible into six groups: the *ater* group across northern Europe and Asia from the British Isles to Japan and NE China; the *atlas* group in NW Africa; the *cypriotes* group on Cyprus; the Caucasus group in SW Asia; the *aemodius* group in the Tien Shan, eastern Himalayas and SW China; and the *ptilosus* group in SE China and Taiwan. In all races, the variation in juveniles parallels that of adults, but the yellow of the cheeks and underparts is brightest and most extensive in *hibernicus* and *ledouci* and dullest in nominate *ater* from eastern Europe and western Siberia.

**THE *ATER* GROUP** Small, with a short tarsus and slender bill. Variation largely clinal, with birds in eastern Asia and Japan being smallest, those in central Europe larger with a longer tarsus.

*P. a. hibernicus* Ireland (except Co. Down in extreme northeast). As *britannicus*, but whole plumage suffused yellow. Upperparts dull greenish-olive (less buff than *britannicus*), cheeks, nuchal patch and underparts pale yellow, flanks and undertail-coverts warm cinnamon-buff. Also, on males, the bib averages smaller, paler and browner (on females, bib averages larger and darker than on female *britannicus*, hence sexual dimorphism in bib coloration much reduced). In worn plumage, yellows variably bleached whiter. Wing of male 57–63, of female 57–61.

*P. a. britannicus* Britain and NE Ireland (where intergrades with *hibernicus*). As nominate *ater*, but, when fresh, cheek and nuchal patches washed cream or pale yellow, upperparts greyish-olive-buff (less blue-grey than *ater*, but wearing to dark grey with traces of olive), fringes on wing and tail feathers olive, black bib may be more restricted, flanks, vent and undertail-coverts pale cinnamon-buff (less olive-grey than nominate *ater*, wearing to a pale buff rather than grey). Includes 'pinicolus' of Scotland, with upperparts more olive-grey (less buff), flanks to undertail-coverts browner-buff (less cinnamon). Wing of male 57–63, of female 57–62.

*P. a. ater* Continental Europe and Asia, east to Sakhalin and south to France, Sicily, western Turkey, Lebanon, Ukraine, the Altai mountains, Mongolia, and NE China in Heilongjiang and eastern Liaoning (Dandong, Xiongyue); also breeds Isles of Scilly (England). Recorded in winter in Britain, Ireland, Corsica and Sardinia. See Description. Some slight variation, with Fennoscandian and western Russian birds (south to NE Poland and the northern Carpathians) having cheek and nuchal patches, underparts and wing spots pure white, upperparts with only slight olive-green tinge even in fresh plumage, flanks to undertail-coverts grey-buff. When fresh, birds from central and western Europe have, on average, more extensive greenish-olive fringes to the upperpart feathers and a more extensive area of darker grey-buff on the flanks to undertail-coverts (i.e. as in Description; extremes approach *britannicus*, but flanks greyer); these are sometimes named 'abietum'. Birds from Italy and Sicily average more cinnamon (less grey) on the flanks, and those in the Balkans and western Turkey have a paler and more restricted area of grey-buff on the flanks (as northern birds); they also have a very short crest (a ragged angle at the back of the head). From Moscow east to at least Lake Baykal, the upperparts average paler blue-grey than in Scandinavia, the breast and belly more extensively pure white and flanks to undertail-coverts pale buff-drab; these populations are sometimes separated as 'rossosibiricus'. Those in the Amur and Ussuri valleys, on Sakhalin and on the southeast coast of the Sea of Okhotsk have the underparts slightly darker and show traces of a crest; they are sometimes named 'amurensis'.

*P. a. vieirae* Iberia. Intergrades with nominate *ater* in the Pyrénées. As nominate *ater* but upperparts washed olive-brown, flanks buffy-brown.

Very similar to *britannicus*, but in fresh plumage upperparts darker and less buffy and flanks average darker and more rufous-buff; juveniles may also show a more extensive sooty bib. Wing of male 54–65.

*P. a. sardus* Corsica and Sardinia. As nominate *ater*, but upperparts washed olive-brown when fresh (more extensive and less greenish than 'abietum', not so pale and buff as *britannicus*); flanks to undertail-coverts washed pale buff-brown. As *vieirae*, but upperparts average slightly less olive-brown and is larger, especially in tarsus and bill. In worn plumage, as nominate *ater* ('abietum') from central Europe. Wing of male 56–65, of female 58–63.

*P. a. pekinensis* NE China from southernmost Liaoning (Lushun) southwest to Shanxi (including this race? the Luliang Shan), also eastern Shandong, where perhaps a migrant only. Intergrades with nominate *ater* in Liaoning, Korea and the Amur/Ussuri region. As nominate *ater*, but feathers of hindcrown elongated, forming a short crest, cheek patches and to a lesser extent nuchal patch washed buff, mantle faintly washed olive, and underparts rather buffer, pale buff or pale horn, washed greyer on flanks. Sexes apparently similar. Wing of male 56.5–63.5, of female 55–62.

*P. a. insularis* Southern Kurile islands, Japan and Cheju island (Korea). Recorded in NE China in western Liaoning (Chaoyang) and NE Hebei (Qinhuangdao, April and October–November); these are presumably migrants. Poorly marked. As nominate *ater*, but underparts creamier or buffer (this colour extending to the belly) and tips of median coverts faintly washed buff; averages slightly smaller. Wing of male 57–62, of female 56.5–60.5.

**THE *ATLAS* GROUP** North Africa. Alarm call distinctive: see Voice.

*P. a. atlas* Morocco. As nominate *ater*, but upperparts dull greyish-olive (wears greyer), bib extends onto upper breast, cheek and nuchal patches, breast and centre of belly yellow-white, flanks extensively dark smoke-grey (wearing paler, brownish-grey). Wing of male 65–74, of female 63–70.

*P. a. ledouci* Tunisia and Algeria, intergrading with *atlas* in Atlas Saharien. As *atlas*, but whole plumage washed yellow; upperparts green, washed greyish-olive (not so dull and greyish), cheek and nuchal patches, lower breast and centre of belly washed pale yellow (even when worn), flanks to vent olive-grey; also smaller. Sexes similar, but female slightly duller and greyer on upperparts, with duller and less intensely black bib? Wing of male 58–71, of female 59–66.

**THE *CYPRIOTES* GROUP** Cyprus. Rather brown.

*P. a. cypriotes* Mount Troodos, Cyprus. Black on head extends onto upper mantle and upper breast, cheek and nuchal patches rather narrow, upperparts rich mid brown, fringes to wing and tail feathers washed brownish, tips to median coverts washed rusty-buff, breast and centre of belly pale pinkish-buff, flanks to undertail-coverts rufous-brown. Wing of male 58–64, of female 58–63.

**THE *CAUCASUS* GROUP** Crimea and NE Turkey to SW Turkmenistan. Large, with a relatively thick bill; coloration generally rather similar to that of *ater* group. Some races poorly defined, and much individual variation.

**P. a. moltchanovi** Crimea. As *ater,* but mantle slightly paler (although still blue-grey), underparts paler, belly, flanks, and undertail-coverts whitish rather than buff or olive-grey; bill larger. Juvenile very pale, especially on crown. Wing of male 67–70; bill 12–12.5.

**P. a. derjugini** Mountains in NE Turkey, western Georgia on southern slopes of western Greater Caucasus, and probably northwest to Novorossiysk on the Black Sea coast of Russia. Intergrades with nominate *ater* in northern Turkey and with *michalowskii* east of Artvin and Sarikamis in NE Turkey. Poorly marked. As nominate *ater,* but mantle slightly browner (grey with faint olive tinge), flanks to undertail-coverts sepia or greyish (colour close to nominate *ater* ('*abietum*') and *sardus,* but perhaps paler and greyer); also longer-winged and bill longer, deeper and attenuated (although not so thick as that of *michalowskii*). Wing of male 65–70; bill 13.2, 14.

**P. a. michalowskii** Northern and eastern Greater Caucasus and Transcaucasus, northwest to the Kuban' and Laba valleys, except area occupied by *derjugini*. As nominate *ater* but mantle and scapulars pale olive-brown, flanks to undertail-coverts washed pale buff. Wing of male 65–71, of female 64–66.

**P. a. gaddi** Talysh region of SE Azerbaydzhan and northern Iran (east to Gorgan). As *michalowskii,* but mantle and scapulars richer and darker brown (less olive, near *cypriotes*), flanks to undertail-coverts extensively washed a darker buff-brown. Wing of male 65–70, of female 63–70.

**P. a. chorassanicus** NE Iran and SW Turkmenistan. As *gaddi* but paler, mantle slightly paler, greyer and more sandy, and bill marginally slighter; as *michalowski,* but upperparts rather browner and flanks slightly paler and greyer, less buff. Wing of male 66–70.

**P. a. phaeonotus** Zagros mountains of SW Iran. Poorly marked. The brownest of the Caucasus group. As *gaddi,* but upperparts slightly more cinnamon-brown and underparts paler: mantle and scapulars dull cinnamon-brown, underparts off-white, flanks, vent and undertail-coverts buff. Wing of male *c.* 67–70. Three birds were collected in June 1870 at 1525–2135 m in oak forest west of Shiraz (Blanford 1873), but this form has not been recorded since, despite extensive fieldwork in the region (L. Cornwallis & D. Scott pers. comm.).

**THE *AEMODIUS* GROUP** Tien Shan, Himalayas and SW China. Crested (juveniles lack crest).

**P. a. rufipectus** Tien Shan and associated ranges in the former USSR and Xinjiang, NW China. As nominate *ater,* but feathers of hindcrown elongated to form a short crest, mantle slightly duller and greyer (less blue), tips of median coverts buffy or yellow, of greater coverts pale buffy-white. Underparts darker: in fresh plumage, breast and centre of belly pale pinkish-buff, flanks to undertail-coverts buffy-cinnamon (showing little contrast with belly); in worn plumage, underparts paler and whiter. Relatively long-tailed. Wing of male 60–67, of female 61, 63.

**P. a. aemodius** Eastern Himalayas, NE Myanmar (Burma), Tibet and SW China (north and east to Shaanxi). As *rufipectus,* but crest longer (*c.* 16–20 mm) and underparts average paler and purer pink (some fresh birds paler and whiter; all paler when worn); averages slightly smaller. Bill rather fine. Wing of male 55.5–64, of female 55–61.

**THE *PTILOSUS* GROUP** SE China and Taiwan. Crested.

**P. a. kuatunensis** SE China in Anhui, Fujian and, presumably this race, Zhejiang. Crest well developed. As *pekinensis,* but mantle blue-grey with faint olive tinge to back, underparts creamy-buff, flanks greyish, cheeks pale buff, and nuchal spot paler, nearly white. Wing of male 52.5–58.5, of female 52.5–57.5.

**P. a. ptilosus** Taiwan. As *kuatunensis,* but crest longer, upperparts slightly darker and underparts less buff. Wing 56–59.5.

**HYBRIDS** Recorded hybridising rarely with Crested and Great Tits, and a single documented case with Willow Tit. An obvious Coal x Willow Tit was captured on migration in Finland in September 1981: it was broadly intermediate in appearance, showing vestigial wingbars and a small nuchal spot, but with the underparts, especially the undertail-coverts, closer to those of Willow (Hildén 1983). In central Nepal, from the Kali Gandaki valley westwards, Coal regularly hybridises with Spot-winged Tit (see p. 302 for details).

**RELATIONSHIPS** A member of the *Periparus* subgenus, together with Spot-winged Tit of the NW Himalayas (with which it forms a super-species), Rufous-vented Tit of the eastern Himalayas and western China, and Rufous-naped Tit of Central Asia and western Himalayas. See also Spot-winged Tit.

**REFERENCES** Cramp & Perrins (1993), Jenni & Winkler (1994), Snow (1955), Stepanyan (1990), Vaurie (1959).

Endemic to China, this is one of the few tits to show pronounced differences between the sexes and to have distinct breeding and non-breeding plumages. Although widespread and with broad habitat preferences, the breeding range is now rather fragmented as a result of deforestation.

**IDENTIFICATION** Length 100 mm (4 in). A relatively small, big-headed and very short-tailed tit. The male has a black head with narrow white cheek patches and a long, narrow white nuchal patch. The upperparts are grey-blue, variably mixed with black and becoming more silvery on the rump. Tail black, with a white 'flash' at the sides. Wings black with two spotted white wingbars, white tips to the tertials and yellowish-olive fringes to the inner flight feathers (forming a paler panel on the closed wing). In breeding plumage the bib is black, but the centre of the throat becomes variably yellow in non-breeding plumage (acquired in the late autumn). Underparts yellow, extensively washed olive on the flanks. The female and juvenile are duller, with the black of the head replaced by mid blue-grey or olive-grey and the bib lacking, there being merely darker malar stripes. The small size, black cap and bib and yellow underparts are distinctive in the male. Females and immatures could be confused with juvenile Coal Tits, which frequently show a yellow wash to the plumage, but Coal Tits' underparts are never as bright and rich yellow as on a Yellow-bellied and they also lack white 'flashes' in the outer tail feathers.

**SEX/AGE** Sexes distinct. The female has the cap dull blue-grey rather than black, the mantle and scapulars olive-green rather than mid grey-blue and black, the rump largely yellowish-olive rather than silvery blue-grey, and the throat off-white with greyish malar stripes. The juvenile resembles the female, but has the cap and upperparts uniformly olive-green (lacking blue-grey on the cap, back and rump), nuchal stripe fainter and yellower, cheek patches duller (off-white to dirty pale yellow), malar stripes less well defined, and throat pale yellow. The juvenile male has the wings and tail darker than the juvenile female, with the white markings crisper and purer white. The sexes become very distinct as the post-juvenile moult (which is protracted) progresses. Ageing of 1st adults often rather difficult. The 1st-adult male resembles the adult male, but has a slightly duller black bib and may also show moult contrasts in the greater coverts, any retained juvenile feathers being browner with more obvious olive-green fringes. 1st adults may also show a contrast between the retained primary coverts and alula and new greater coverts, whilst the fringes to the retained flight feathers average paler and greyer than the adults' (through wear and bleaching, adults typically having brighter yellow-olive fringes). 1st adults probably retain the juvenile tail, but this is very similar to that of the adults.

**VOICE** Rather varied. Calls include a nasal *dzee, dzee, dzee...*, and *sip-eeh, sip, zee-zee-zeh* (a 'chick-a-dee' call). Also a quiet, thin *sit-oo*, and Viney & Phillipps (1983) note a rapid, high-pitched *si-si-si-si-si*. The song is a mono- or disyllabic motif repeated 2–5 times. Always shrill, it is sometimes metallic, sometimes lisping or buzzing, e.g. *swi-swi-swi, suwi-suwi-suwi, sipu-sipu-sipu...* or *swhich-i swhich-i swhich-ist* (on the 'tea-cher' theme, and recalling Coal Tit, but often fuller and more powerful). Sometimes the motif is more complex, e.g. *spid-i-chu-spid-i-chu..., wee-wa-chi, wee-wa-chi, wee-wa-chi..., psi-wed-i, psi-wed-i, psi-wed-i...*, or the phrase is slower, more sonorous and more ringing, e.g. *sper-di, sper-di, sper....*

**DISTRIBUTION AND MOVEMENTS** Endemic to **China**. Recorded from central and NE **Hebei** (Eastern Qing Tombs, Shanhaiguan), **Beijing Municipality** (where first noted breeding in 1974 in the Baihua Shan (in the west near Mentougou); a winter visitor to the Summer Palace), southern **Shanxi**, southern **Shaanxi** (at least the Qin Ling mountains), southernmost **Ningxia Hui** (Liupan Shan mountains), southern **Gansu**, central and eastern **Sichuan** on the eastern, northern and western borders of the Red Basin (Wanxian, Wanyuan, Pingwu, Dayi, Baoxing, Tianquan, Emei Shan and Xichang), NE **Yunnan** (where commonly recorded at Kunming: Stott 1993), western **Henan** (Funiu Shan mountains), western **Hubei**, southern **Anhui** (Huang Shan mountains), central and eastern **Guizhou** (from the Chishui river south to Huishui and Leishan), central **Hunan** (Changde, Xinhua), northern **Jiangxi** (Mufu Shan mountains), NW **Guangxi**, northern **Guangdong**, and NW **Fujian**. Perhaps absent from the region between the lower Huang He and Yangtze rivers (Shandong, southern Jiangsu, northern Anhui, Henan east of the Funiu Shan mountains and eastern Hubei, although may occur here as an irregular winter visitor). Mapped range tentative. Presumably resident throughout much of the range, but status obscure. As a breeding bird largely confined to montane areas (and a summer visitor to many such upland areas, e.g. the Beijing hills), but suitable forested habitat is now almost totally absent in intervening lowlands and the species may have formerly bred more widely. Some wander in autumn and winter, in a somewhat irruptive pattern, dispersing over the plains of eastern China, when recorded in **Jiangxi** (Poyang Hu), and south and east to coastal areas in southern **Jiangsu** (Nanjing), **Zhejiang** (Ningbo), **Fujian** (Fuzhou) and **Guangdong**. A sporadic winter visitor to **Hong Kong** in November–early April (first recorded 1969), with occasional influxes interspersed by years with no records. A regular migrant at Beidaihe, coastal **Hebei**, in late April-May and late September–late November, with up to 377 bird-days in an autumn season. The large numbers and regular occurrences at Beidaihe suggest the possibility of a range expansion, with a migratory population now breeding to the north of the known range (Williams *et al.* 1992).

**HABITAT** Open broadleaved forest (both deciduous and subtropical evergreen), mixed and tall coniferous forest, bamboo, willow groves, larch plantations and scattered village trees around cultivation (but perhaps confined to more heavily wooded areas for breeding). In winter may be found in almost any patch of trees, however small. Generally montane during the breeding season. In Beijing Municipality recorded in summer at 1200–1500 m, in southern Shaanxi from 500 m to at least 2500 m, in Sichuan and western Hubei at 600–2700 m, and in Guizhou at 600–1500 m (extreme range 350–1600 m); recorded at up to 3050 m in June in southern Gansu, and in NW Fujian breeds at *c.* 1070 m. Descends in winter to lower altitudes, usually below 1000 m, and down to 100 m in the west, and has been recorded at coastal localities.

**POPULATION** Locally common, but with massive deforestation in China it must have declined. Thus, reported to be common in mountains of NW Fujian by La Touche (1925), but not found there on a brief visit in summer 1986 (Viney 1986), and rare in NE China even in the 1930s owing to the lack of forested mountains (Wilder & Hubbard 1938). Uncommon in the Mufu Shan, NW Jiangxi, in one of the few remaining areas of extensive forest in the province (King 1987). Conversely, some evidence of an increase in numbers in NE China, and a regular migrant at Beidaihe in recent years, despite the fact that it was not recorded in the 1940s (Hemmingsen 1951; Hemmingsen & Guildal 1968). In irruption years, may be locally common in wooded areas in Hong Kong.

**HABITS** Found in pairs, groups of 2–3 or family parties, and outside the breeding season usually in flocks of up to 10, sometimes as many as 30 together; may join mixed-species foraging flocks. Usually forages at low to medium levels in the vegetation. Food insects and berries, and stores food items.

**BREEDING BIOLOGY** Poorly known. Season May–June. The nest is placed in a natural cavity in a tree or in a crevice among rocks, and probably also in earth banks. The deep cup of green moss and leaf skeletons is lined with soft material such as wool, plant fibres and, especially, hair. Clutch 5–7: eggs white, variably but usually extensively spotted red and brown with indistinct lavender undermarkings; 16.4 x 12.5 mm. Incubation by female alone?, period 12 days. Both sexes feed the young, which fledge after 16–17 days and are relatively independent and able to find their own food after a further three days.

**DESCRIPTION** Adult Male: *In fresh plumage* (autumn to about January), crown black, glossed blue, sometimes with a very short, narrow yellow supercilium above and behind eye. Lores, fore cheeks, forehead, eyestripe, nape and sides of upper mantle black, feathers of central nape tipped white (forming a very variable nuchal patch), feathers of sides of upper mantle with progressively larger mid grey-blue tips (thus grading into lower mantle). Centre of upper mantle light grey-blue with white spots in feather centres (a

*Fogure 65.1 Tail of adult male.*

variable and irregular continuation of the nuchal patch). Scapulars mid grey-blue, fringed olive-green, lower mantle and back mid grey-blue; rump light silvery grey-blue, longer feathers tipped olive-green. Uppertail-coverts black, 1–2 finely tipped olive-green. Tail blackish-grey, all feathers rather finely tipped white (largest on T6), T2–T6 narrowly fringed pale grey (fringes may be tinged olive towards tip), T4–T6 with a long inverted triangle of white on distal parts of outer web (see figure above). Lesser coverts black, finely fringed glossy blue; longer feathers may be tipped pale blue-grey. Greater and median coverts black, tipped white (extreme tip olive or olive-yellow); greater coverts may be finely fringed dark olive-green, especially outer 1–2 feathers. Remainder of wing brownish-black, primary coverts narrowly fringed olive-green, outer web of small feather of alula variably white, fringed yellowish, larger feather sometimes tipped white. Tertials and secondaries fringed yellowish-olive and tipped off-white (narrowly so on secondaries), P10–P7 fringed olive-green, P6–P3 fringed olive-grey basally with narrower white fringes distally of emarginations (coloration of flight-feather fringes variable, yellowish-white to olive-grey, occasionally light blue-grey). Rear cheeks and ear-coverts white, chin, throat and sides of upper breast black, feathers of centre of throat broadly tipped yellow or occasionally white, thus centre of throat yellow or mottled yellow and black. Remainder of underparts yellow, slightly paler on the undertail-coverts, flanks extensively washed olive. Axillaries and underwing-coverts white, tinged yellow. Following the *partial pre-breeding moult* (about January–late summer), the throat, upper breast and sides of neck are sooty-black. In worn plumage little different, but white feather tips may abrade on centre of nape and upper mantle, nuchal patch reduced, and blue-grey tips to feathers at side of mantle abraded, mantle becoming blacker (on some, black with just scattered grey-blue tips), contrasting more with the silvery grey-blue rump. **Bare Parts**: Iris brown or dark brown; bill blackish or blue-black; legs, feet and claws lead-grey. **Adult Female**: In fresh plumage, crown dull blue-grey, slightly darker feather centres giving a mottled or scaled effect, slightly paler supercilium above and behind eye, sides of crown slightly darker and greyer. Nape, mantle and scapulars olive-green with a narrow pale yellow and white nuchal stripe on centre of nape and upper mantle. Back greyish-olive (mid blue-grey feather bases revealed), upper rump blue-grey, feathers tipped yellowish-olive, lower rump yellowish-olive, shorter uppertail-coverts mid grey, longer black, tipped blue-grey. Tail as that of male. Lesser coverts mid grey, fringed olive-green, remainder of wing as male but rather paler and browner, tips of median coverts washed yellow, greater coverts fringed olive-green and fringes to flight feathers slightly greener. Lores and fore cheeks light grey, rear cheeks and ear-coverts off-white, submoustachial and malar regions dull light grey, throat off-white, remainder of underparts as male. In worn plumage, cap duller and more olive, upperparts duller, throat duller, not so white, and underparts paler and patchier yellow. **Juvenile Male**: Crown and upper-parts olive-green, cap with variably greyer feather bases, small off-white superciliary spot just above and behind eye, irregular narrow pale yellow patch on nape and upper mantle, back variably tinged blue-grey, and longer uppertail-coverts sooty-brown. Tail as adult, but T2–T6 narrowly fringed olive on distal half. Wing-coverts dark grey-brown, lesser coverts finely fringed olive-green, median coverts fringed olive-green and tipped pale yellow-white (margins yellower), greater coverts similar but tips largely confined to outer web. Alula, primary coverts and flight feathers dark brown, tertials and secondaries fringed olive-yellow and finely fringed white at tip (inner two tertials tipped pale yellow-olive), P10–P7 similar, but white tips smaller, and P6–P3 fringed olive-yellow, narrower and whiter distally of emarginations. Lores olive-grey, broad yellowish eye-ring, upper ear-coverts dusky olive-green, lower ear-coverts and sides of neck off-white, malar region variably darker (but malar stripe usually poorly defined). Throat pale yellow to dull pale yellow-white, remainder of underparts yellow; underwing-coverts off-white, tipped yellow.

**Juvenile Female**: As juvenile male, but wings and tail paler, especially tertials and T1–T2, and white markings duller, more yellow-tinged (e.g. cheek patches dirty yellow-white), also malar stripe not so well defined; underparts duller and paler yellow? **1st Adult**: As adult (see Sex/Age). In the post-juvenile moult, at least some 1st-adult males assume a solidly black throat, whilst others have yellow tips to the centre of the throat, as non-breeding adult; this dependent on the timing of the post-juvenile moult? **Measurements**: Wing of male 61–68, of female 59.5–65.5; tail of male 31–42, of female 31.5–41; bill 9.3–11.8; tarsus 14.2–18. Weight 9–12.5 g.

**MOULT** Adult post-breeding complete (late July to about October). Adult pre-breeding partial, in males includes throat, cheeks and cap, especially forecrown (November–March). Post-juvenile partial, usually includes all median coverts, a variable number of greater coverts (occasionally none, sometimes all) and rarely tertials, but apparently not tail (September–March, unusually protracted, with some birds in almost full 1st-adult plumage in December, others still largely in juvenile plumage in March). 1st pre-breeding as adult pre-breeding? (January–March, as a continuation of the post-juvenile moult?).

**GEOGRAPHICAL VARIATION** None.

**RELATIONSHIPS** Generally considered to be closely related to Coal Tit, but placed in the sub-genus *Pardaliparus* (together with Elegant and Palawan Tits), while Löhrl (1988) noted similarities with Yellow-browed Tit, especially in the juvenile and female plumages, Note also that male Yellow-bellied Tits may have a tiny yellow supercilium (usually concealed at rest?).

**REFERENCES** Caldwell & Caldwell (1931), La Touche (1925), Löhrl (1988).

# 66 ELEGANT TIT *Parus elegans* Plate 22

This colourful tit is endemic to the Philippines, where, given the tendency of the genus *Parus* towards geographical variation, it is not surprising that it has radiated into a wide variety of races.

**IDENTIFICATION** Length 115 mm (4.5 in). The male has the cap glossy black with a long yellow nuchal patch, the mantle and scapulars blackish, variably spotted paler, the back and rump pale greyish, variably tinged yellow or green, and the wings blackish with two spotted wingbars. The cheeks and underparts are yellow and the bib glossy black. The female is similar but duller, especially on the bib. Juveniles are even duller, with a dark greenish or brownish cap and a yellowish throat with merely a 'ghost' bib. The range does not overlap with that of the superficially similar Palawan Tit, and Elegant Tit is very different from White-fronted Tit, the only other tit in the Philippines.

**SEX/AGE** Sexes variably distinct. In northern races the female has a black cap, similar to the male's although less glossy, whilst on Panay, Negros and Mindanao the female's cap is sooty olive-brown. On all females, the nuchal spot is slightly paler and duller yellow than the male's, the lower mantle and scapulars more greenish-grey, the white tips to the tail feathers smaller and faintly margined yellow, the white spots in the side of the tail reduced, the tips of the median and greater coverts and tertials smaller and finely margined pale yellow, and the tertials, secondaries and primaries duller black, fringed olive-grey rather than whitish. The forehead and bib average paler and more sooty-brown (not black), and the cheek patches and underparts are also paler and duller yellow, sometimes washed grey. Juvenile distinct, generally much duller than the adult. The cap is dark greenish-grey or dark brown (not black), and the upperparts nearly uniform olive-grey, although they may show odd dark feather centres or dirty white spots. The tail feathers are narrower and more pointed, with smaller pale tips, and the wing spots are smaller and duller, margined yellow. The cheek patch and underparts are dirty pale yellow, lacking a darker bib, although the juvenile male has a broad dark malar stripe. In some respects, juveniles resemble adult females from Panay, Negros and Mindanao, but their cap is almost concolorous with the upperparts, the mantle more uniform (lacking dull olive-brown bases, especially prominent on the upper mantle on adult females), and they lack a bib. Several aspects of adult sexual dimorphism are present in juveniles, especially in the details of the wing and tail feathers. 1st adults are marginally distinct from adults, and can be aged with care in the hand. They retain the juvenile alula, primary coverts, primaries and secondaries, which average paler and browner than the new tertials and greater coverts. In the male, the retained flight feathers and coverts also differ in detail from those of the adult, with all-dark primary coverts and primaries P2–P10 narrowly fringed whitish on the distal half. Some adult males have white tips to the primary coverts in the northern races (although only narrow olive fringes in the southern group), sometimes a small white tip to the outermost primary and a white fringe to P2, and always white tips to the secondaries and P8–P10, with P3–P6 broadly fringed yellow-white distally of the emarginations, and P7–P9 with yellowish fringes to the central portion. 1st adults may also show moult contrasts in the greater coverts, and in the 1st-adult female any retained juvenile greater coverts are fringed olive (rather than darker and blacker as in the adult on the northern races). Tail feathers new, as adult.

**VOICE** Very varied. Calls include an abrupt *sit* or *sit-sit* (given both at rest and in flight), a thin *sisisi* and a light, rippling, silvery trill, *silililili*, of variable length (may be prolonged) and falling slightly in pitch towards the end. Also commonly gives a nasal *chay* (recalling Willow Tit). More complex vocalisations include *si-si-si-tzee* or *si-si-si-tzee-tzee*, and in excitement or alarm gives a scolding *tchrrrr* (recalling Blue Tit) and a variety of loud trills. Rather different are mellow, whistled calls on an even pitch, *twi-wi-wi-wi-wi-wi, tui-tui-tui-tui-tui*. The song (?) is a very Coal Tit-like *pi-tu, pi-tu, pi-tu* and variants (on the 'tea-cher' theme), with more complex combinations such as *pi-pi-tu, si-si pi-pi-tu, pi-pi-tu, si-si-si pi-pi-tu* or *tu-tu sipi sipi tu-tu*. Also has a warbling, canary-like song, with many muffled and buzzy trills.

**DISTRIBUTION AND MOVEMENTS**
Endemic to the **Philippines**, where recorded from the islands of Luzon, Catanduanes, Mindoro, Panay, Guimaras, Negros, Cebu, Masbate, Ticao, Samar, Leyte, Biliran, Mindanao, in the Babuyan group on Calayan and Camiguin Norte, and in the Sulu archipelago on Jolo, Tawitawi, Sanga Sanga and Bongao. Absent Palawan. Resident.

**HABITAT** Forest, generally dense primary evergreen forest, mossy forest and pine forest, but also forest edge, second growth, and scattered trees in cultivation. Occurs at all elevations (up to at least 2470 m).

**POPULATION** Fairly common. Of all the forest-

dependent birds in the Philippines, the Elegant Tit is found in one of the broadest ranges of habitats and is apparently able to thrive in many marginal areas.

**HABITS** Very active. Occurs in pairs or in flocks of 4–8, often joining mixed-species foraging flocks. Generally feeds in the middle stratum of the forest or in the canopy of smaller trees. Like most Philippine passerines, Elegant Tits totally ignore both 'pishing' and 'squeaking' Food insects, spiders, fruit and seeds.

**BREEDING BIOLOGY** Very poorly known. Breeding noted in June from Cebu, a fledgling recorded from southern Luzon in April, birds carrying nest material noted in March–April in northern Luzon, and juveniles recorded during March–November on Luzon and in October on Mindanao (most Philippine passerines breed in the period April–June). Nests in hollow trees; nest material includes moss.

**DESCRIPTION** *P. e. elegans* **Adult Male:** *In fresh plumage* (November–March), crown (to lower border of eye), nape, mantle and scapulars black, glossed blue. Irregular long pale yellow nuchal patch, scattered large white spots on mantle, inner scapulars irregularly tipped light yellowish-grey, and longest scapulars with terminal half of feather white. Back and rump light yellowish-grey, lower rump slightly paler and yellower, uppertail-coverts black. Tail black, all feathers with large triangular white spot at tip of shaft, T4–T6 with mid portion of outer web entirely white and a corresponding small white patch on T3 (see figure below). Wings black, terminal half of median coverts white, large triangular white spot at tip of outer web of greater coverts (extending marginally onto inner web); elongated white spot at tips of outer webs of feathers of alula; primary coverts sometimes tipped white, inner two tertials with large white spot at tip, outer tertial, secondaries and P7–10 tipped white on outer web, tiny on outer secondaries and inner primaries, P1 sometimes tipped white; P7–P9 finely fringed pale yellow around centre, P3–P6 fringed yellow-white distally of emargination and P2 sometimes finely fringed white. Base of bill, lores, chin, throat and upper breast black, feathers of lower border of bib tipped yellow. Cheeks and ear-coverts pale yellow, sides of neck (extending onto sides of mantle) and underparts rich yellow, rear flanks pale greyish lime-green. Thighs sooty, tipped pale yellow. Axillaries pale yellow; underwing-coverts white, fringed pale yellow. *In worn plumage* (about April–August), crown slightly less glossy, nuchal patch reduced,

*Figure 66.1 Tail of adult male* P. e. elegans.

*Figure 66.2 Tail of adult male* P. e. gilliardi.

pale spots on upperparts bleached and abraded paler and whiter, rump greyer, tips to tail feathers and greater coverts abraded, tips and fringes on flight feathers abraded, bib slightly duller. When heavily worn, from June onwards, white spots in wings may be absent, yellows very bleached and mantle and flight feathers very abraded. **Bare Parts**: Iris reddish-brown to black; bill black, may be blue at base; legs, feet and claws pale blue-grey to slaty-black. **Adult Female**: In fresh plumage, crown, nape and upper mantle black, less glossy than male, especially sides of crown and nape, nuchal spot slightly paler and duller yellow. Upper mantle blackish, lower mantle, scapulars, back and rump greenish-grey with blackish feather centres, especially on mantle, and may show a few yellow-white spots on mantle. uppertail-coverts black, faintly tipped yellow when fresh. Tail black, tipped and fringed white as on male, although tips

smaller (especially on T5–T6) and faintly margined yellow, spots on centre of T3–T6 reduced, not covering entire outer web. Wings dark blackish-brown, lesser coverts finely tipped greenish-grey, median and greater coverts and tertials tipped white, although tips smaller than on male and finely margined pale yellow, feathers fringed darker and blacker; longest tertial and inner secondaries finely tipped white on outer web; tertials, secondaries and P3–P10 fringed olive-grey, not reaching tips of primaries, and whiter distally of emarginations on P3–P6; smaller feathers of alula finely fringed greenish-grey. Forehead, lores, base of bill and throat sooty-brown. Cheeks, ear-coverts and sides of neck dull pale yellow (paler and duller than on male). Underparts pale yellow, washed olive-grey, especially on flanks. **Juvenile Male**: Lores, forehead, crown (to below eye) and nape dark grey with extensive dull greenish-grey fringes (appears dark greenish-grey); dirty pale yellow nuchal patch, feathers tipped greenish-grey. Upperparts greenish-grey, odd dark grey feather centres visible on mantle and scapulars, and may show one or two dirty white spots on mantle; back and rump tinged light grey, uppertail-coverts blackish, finely tipped greenish-olive. Tail as adult male. Wings as adult male, but overall slightly less intensely black (especially coverts), lesser coverts fringed greenish-grey, pale spots on coverts and inner two tertials smaller and duller, narrowly fringed pale yellow, and P2–P10 fringed yellow-

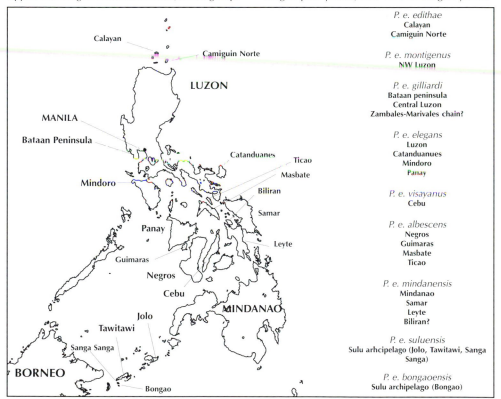

*Figure 66.3 Distribution of the various subspecies.*

313

white on distal half (white distally of emargination on P3–P6). Cheeks, ear-coverts and sides of neck dirty pale yellow. Broad dark greenish-grey malar stripe. Throat and upper breast dirty pale yellow-white, lower breast and undertail-coverts dirty pale yellow, belly and vent pale yellow, flanks washed light greenish-grey. Bill yellow with dark grey culmen and gonys; iris dark grey. **Juvenile Female**: As juvenile male, but crown and nape dark greenish-grey, feathers with only slightly darker and browner centres, nuchal patch smaller and duller. Tail and wings as adult female, but outer greater coverts narrowly fringed greenish-grey, primary coverts sometimes narrowly fringed olive-green. Cheeks and ear-coverts dirty pale yellow, throat and upper breast pale greyish-yellow with faint hint of darker malar stripe, remainder of underparts dull yellow. **1st-Adult Male and Female**: See Sex/Age. **Measurements**: Wing of male 63–72, of female 60–65; tail 37–45.5; bill 11.1–13 (8–9 from anterior edge of nostril); tarsus 16–18.5. Weight 12–15 g (*P. e. albescens*).

**MOULT** Adult post-breeding complete (August–December). Post-juvenile partial to incomplete, includes tertials, some or all greater coverts, some or all tail feathers (just beginning, 6 September, Luzon; near completion, 26 December, Guimaras).

**GEOGRAPHICAL VARIATION** Marked and complex, with nine races recognised. Variation, both individual and according to age and sex, has served to complicate any understanding of geographical forms, and it is likely that other acceptable races could be described. Overall size decreases slightly from north to south, and there is also variation in the degree of sexual dimorphism. In the northern group (*edithae* to *visayanus*), males have the outer primaries fringed white and females have a black cap. In the southern group (*mindanensis*, also *suluensis* and *bongaoensis*?), males have yellowish fringes to the flight feathers and females a sooty olive-brown cap, whilst *albescens* is somewhat intermediate between the two groups.

*P. e. edithae* Calayan and Camiguin Norte, Babuyan group. As nominate *elegans*, but yellows pale and dull. Male has mantle black with little white spotting, back and rump dark greenish-grey, reduced wing spots, and cheeks and nuchal spot creamy-white. Large; bill and probably also wings longest of all races. Wing of male 70, of female 68; bill 9–10 (from nostril).

*P. e. montigenus* NW Luzon. As nominate *elegans*, but nuchal spot often extends onto central mantle; white spots on wing may average smaller. Male with reduced pale spots on mantle (although not on back or scapulars) and underparts and especially cheeks slightly paler yellow. Female with mantle more extensively greenish-grey with fewer dark grey feather centres showing, and back greyer (less yellowish-green). Wing of male 62–72, of female 61.5–66; bill 7.5–9 (from nostril).

*P. e. gilliardi* Bataan peninsula, central Luzon (may occur in the entire Zambales-Mariveles chain); presumably intergrades with nominate *elegans*. As nominate *elegans*, but male has nuchal spot richer yellow, upperparts spotted dull pale yellow; wing spots average larger, finely margined yellow; more white in tertials (appear almost white on closed wing); tail spots larger and finely margined yellow (white in outer web of T2–T5, extensive on T4–T5 with distal two-thirds of T6 all white: see figure, 66.2, p. 313). Females differ from nominate *elegans* in slightly larger nuchal patch, with mantle and back slightly more yellow-ochre, cheeks and underparts slightly richer yellow, wing spots margined yellow, primary fringes slightly greener, tail with slightly more extensive white tips. Reduced sexual dimorphism, with bib and wings of female nearly as dark as on male. Wing of male 67–70, of female 62–67; bill 8-9 (from nostril).

*P. e. elegans* Central and southern Luzon from Manila area southwards, Catanduanes, Mindoro and Panay. See Description. Allocation of Panay birds to this race is anomalous on zoogeographical grounds; a female from Panay resembles female *albescens* from Negros rather than female *elegans* from Luzon, and Panay birds may be better separated as *panayensis* Mearns 1916.

*P. e. visayanus* Cebu. Close to nominate *elegans*, male with slightly more white on the mantle, rump bluish or greyish with no green or yellow tinge, less white at tip of tail, wing spots slightly smaller, cheek patch and underparts paler yellow, and flanks greyer, less greenish; female very similar to nominate *elegans*, but flanks greyer and slightly less spotting on wings. 1st-adult male has yellowish fringes to distal half of P2–P6. Wing of male 62–66.5, of female 62.5.

*P. e. albescens* Negros, Guimaras, Masbate and Ticao. As nominate *elegans*, but male has extensive pale grey-white tips to mantle and scapulars, back and rump uniform light grey, washed olive-yellow, white tips to tertials, secondaries and wing-coverts average slightly larger, and cheeks and especially underparts slightly paler yellow with no darkening on flanks. Female as nominate *elegans*, but mantle, scapulars and back with more extensive yellow spotting, wing spots slightly larger, underparts slightly richer yellow. Birds from Negros slightly different: some males have a pronounced yellow wash to the back spots and rump, whilst females have the cap slightly paler than female nominate *elegans* (less glossy blue-black, more sooty-black-brown), centres to mantle feathers sooty black-brown (not blackish), greater coverts finely fringed olive-green (not blackish), reduced white tips to coverts and tertials, flight feathers fringed yellow-olive, and bib slightly paler and less black, thus close to female *mindanensis* but bib darker and browner, wing and tail spots and tips to the tail feathers purer white. Wing of male 63.5–69, of female 63–66.5; bill 7.5–9 (from nostril).

*P. e. mindanensis* Mindanao (highlands only?), Samar, Leyte and probably also Biliran. As nominate *elegans*, but numerous olive-yellow spots on mantle and scapulars, back and rump olive-yellow, tail spots margined yellow, wing spots broadly margined and washed yellow; primary coverts faintly tipped olive; P10–P3, secondaries and tertials fringed olive-yellow, whiter distally of emarginations on P3–P5, P2 fringed off-white. Female as female *elegans*, but cap sooty olive-brown, extending broadly onto sides of mantle, feathers very finely fringed greenish (giving a faintly scaled appearance), mantle feathers with sooty-olive-brown bases (not blackish), back and rump olive-green with no dark centres, rather small white tips to tail feathers, tail spots margined olive-yellow, wing spots small, margined olive-yellow, greater coverts fringed olive-green, and flight feathers paler and browner, tertials, secondaries and P10–P3 fringed olive-green (only inwards of emarginations on P3–P6); bib dark olive-green, underparts extensively washed olive-green on flanks. Juvenile (probably female) as juvenile *elegans*, but cap and mantle browner (less grey-green), tiny yellow-white tips to tail feathers, and coverts and flight feathers much browner, wing spots much smaller, margined yellow, tertials and flight feathers fringed olive-green. Males from the lowlands of Mindanao differ from those on Mount Apo in their deeper yellow cheeks and underparts and reduced yellow margins to the wing and tail spots, whilst a single female differs in having a glossier and blacker crown, blacker bib, more black on the mantle and reduced yellow margins to the wing and tail spots; these may be separable as an as yet unnamed race (Parkes 1958). Wing of male 62–66, of female 60–62.5; bill 7–8.5 (from nostril).

**P. e. suluensis** Sulu archipelago on Jolo, Tawitawi and Sanga Sanga. Poorly marked. Near *mindanensis,* but male has reduced white spotting on mantle and white tips to greater coverts and tertials. Sexual dimorphism reduced, males with rather greenish upperparts, scapulars grey-green, with a few yellowish ('white') spots on the mantle (lacking on females), slightly blacker crown and bib, and slightly richer yellow underparts. Parkes (1958) states that this race is pale in respect of its yellows, the nuchal spot being almost white, but a male from Tawitawi has rich yellow underparts, nuchal spot and mantle spots. Small. Wing of male 59–62; bill 7–8 (from nostril).

**P. e. bongaoensis** Sulu archipelago on Bongao. The smallest and darkest race. As *suluensis,* but male has mantle much blacker, back blackish with reduced green fringes (darker than any other race). Tail spots much reduced, wing spots slightly smaller, yellow margins reduced or absent, flight feathers fringed more greenish (less yellowish). Female dark, with reduced white markings. Juvenile female as *suluensis,* but upperparts much blacker, wing spots much reduced; centre of belly deeper yellow, contrasting with olivaceous flanks. Wing of male 56, 62.5, of female 58.5; bill 7–7.5 (from nostril).

**RELATIONSHIPS** Considered to be closely related to Palawan Tit, and also to Yellow-bellied Tit of mainland China. These three species were once placed in the genus *Pardaliparus* (now subgenus) and are sometimes considered to form a superspecies; all three are thought to derive from the Coal Tit (Parkes 1958).

**REFERENCES** Dickinson *et al.* (1991), Mearns (1916), Parkes (1958, 1963).

# 67 PALAWAN TIT *Parus amabilis*

Plate 22

Endemic to Palawan and associated islands in the Philippines, this brightly coloured tit shows strong sexual dimorphism and attracts attention with its ringing calls.

**IDENTIFICATION** Length 120 mm (4.75 in). The male has the head and breast glossy blue-black, upperparts and underparts yellow, rump blue-grey, tail black with extensive white corners, and black wings with two very broad white wingbars, white tips to the tertials and largely white primary coverts (when very worn, the upperparts are dirty white and the white wingbars and tertial tips may be absent). Females and juveniles are rather duller. A distinctive species and the only tit on Palawan, the range thus not overlapping with that of the superficially similar Elegant Tit. When viewed from below in tall forest trees, the dark head, yellow underparts and white sides to the tail are distinctive.

**SEX/AGE** Sexes distinct. The female is rather duller than the male, with the head and especially the breast paler and browner, a pale yellow collar, greenish mantle and scapulars, grey back, yellow rump, less white in the sides of the tail, and narrower whitish wingbars and tertial tips. Juvenile distinct, with the upperparts almost uniformly olive (darker and duller than the female, with a paler cap and no yellow collar), very narrow pale wingbars, and the whole underparts pale yellow, with only a faint indication of a bib. No information on the 1st adult (in the hand, 1st-year birds may show retained juvenile feathers in the tail and wing, but information on the post-juvenile moult is incomplete).

**VOICE** Very vocal, and heard more often than seen. Calls include a rapid, rather harsh, stereotyped repetition of a disyllabic motif, *chuwi-chuwi-chuwi-chuwi...,* *wichi-wichi-wichi-wichi...,* or *wicha-wicha-wicha-wicha...,* and simpler accelerating rattles composed of repeated monosyllables, *wich-chi-chi-chi-chi-chi....* Also a more typically tit-like, musical *tui-tui-tui-tui-tui-...,* a thin *sit, sisisi* and a silvery descending trill, *srilililili* (recalling Elegant Tit). Song (?) a very Coal Tit-like *ti-da, ti-da, ti-da....*

**HABITAT** Forest, forest edge, the wooded fringes of swamps, and second growth, reportedly at all elevations (although rising to 2085 m, the upland areas of Palawan comprise a rather different habitat from that found in the tropical lowlands and the occurrence of this species at higher elevations needs to be confirmed).

**DISTRIBUTION AND MOVEMENTS** The **Philippines**, where restricted to Palawan and Balabac, and also the tiny island of Calawit in the Calamian group.

**POPULATION** Generally uncommon. The extent of the Palawan Tit's dependence upon primary forest is unknown. Although persistent malaria has, until recently, ensured a low human population on Palawan, and the generally steep terrain has deterred loggers, the rate of deforestation on the island has now increased and the long-term survival of all forest-dependent species must raise cause for concern.

**HABITS** Usually seen singly or in pairs, though may occur in groups and joins mixed-species foraging flocks. Very active and volatile; generally forages in the canopy and middle storey of the forest, although may descend to the shrub layer.

**BREEDING BIOLOGY** No information.

**DESCRIPTION Adult Male**: *In fresh plumage*, head and breast black, all except lores glossed deep indigo-blue. Mantle and scapulars sulphur-yellow to pale yellow, rump mid blue-grey, longest feathers with slightly paler tips, uppertail-coverts black, glossed deep indigo-blue. Tail black, T1–T2 tipped white, T3–T6 with distal two-thirds of outer web white (see figure 67.1). Lesser coverts black, glossed deep indigo-blue, median coverts white, greater coverts black basally, but distal half white with faint yellow wash to fringes. Primary coverts black, tipped white for entire visible portion, alula black with small white tip. Flight feathers brownish-black, innermost tertial extensively tipped white (widest on outer web), central tertial tipped white (white extending along outer web), outer tertial with smallest white tip but near-complete white fringe, all tertial fringes (but not tips) washed yellow; secondaries finely tipped white and narrowly fringed pale grey on distal two-thirds, tips progressively smaller towards outermost; primaries finely tipped white, tips smallest on outermost. Sides of breast and remainder of underparts rich sulphur-yellow, palest on undertail-coverts, flanks lightly washed olive. Thighs yellow, mottled olive-brown. Axillaries yellow-white; underwing-coverts black, tipped white. *In worn plumage*, mantle fades to dirty yellow-white, white tips to flight feathers and central tail feathers fully abraded. **Bare Parts**: Iris brown; bill black; legs and feet grey. **Adult Female**: In fresh plumage, crown, nape, sides of neck and ear-coverts dark sepia-brown with a slight gloss (cap glossier in old females?) Chin, throat and breast paler, brownish-olive. Upper mantle pale yellow, forming narrow collar, remainder of mantle and scapulars olive-green, back mid grey, rump sulphur-yellow, uppertail-coverts blackish. Tail brownish-black, white fringes to basal half of tail only (widest on T6), all feathers tipped white; on some (old females?) pattern more as male, with white in outer web extending to tips of T3–T6 (see figure 67.1). Lesser coverts pale sepia-brown, tipped pale grey, median coverts whitish. Remainder of wing dark

*Figure 67.1 Tail of adult male.*

brown, greater coverts tipped pale yellow-white, primary coverts may show whitish subterminal spots; tertials tipped white (less extensive than on male) and narrowly fringed yellow-white; secondaries tipped whitish and fringed pale grey; primaries finely tipped whitish. Underparts from belly to undertail-coverts sulphur-yellow, palest on undertail-coverts, flanks washed olive. Axillaries pale yellow; underwing-coverts yellow-white, brownish feather bases showing on longer under primary coverts. **Juvenile Male**: Forehead, crown, nape and ear-coverts olive-brown. Upperparts to rump dull olive, slightly paler than head, with a variable, usually faint or narrow, yellowish border to upper mantle. Uppertail-coverts sooty-brown. Tail as female, although the pale tips average smaller, T4–T6 fringed mid grey on distal half. Wings dark brown, lesser coverts fringed olive, median and greater coverts fringed olive-green with yellow-white tips; primary coverts faintly fringed olive and may show paler subterminal spots; tertials and secondaries fringed pale olive-grey, tertials finely tipped yellow-white and innermost secondaries tipped off-white, primaries narrowly fringed olive on basal half of P3–P10. Underparts from chin to undertail-coverts pale sulphur-yellow, tinged olive on throat. Bill paler than that of adult, yellowish-orange around cutting edges and at base and tip of lower mandible. **Juvenile Female**: As juvenile male, but tail paler and browner, whitish fringes less extensive and tinged yellow, white tips narrower and not so pure white; secondaries fringed more yellow-green. **1st Adult**: No information. **Measurements**: Wing of male 70–76, of female 65–70; tail of male 44–47, of female 40–43; bill 9.1–11.7; tarsus 15–17.5. Weight: no information.

**MOULT** Adult post-breeding complete (June–September). Post-juvenile partial, includes greater coverts, tertials, perhaps also central tail feathers and alula and possibly primary coverts (January, April).

**GEOGRAPHICAL VARIATION** None.

**RELATIONSHIPS** Closely related to Elegant Tit and to Yellow-bellied Tit of mainland China, with which it is sometimes considered to form a super-species. Interestingly, Dickinson *et al.* (1991) suggest that Palawan Tit could be an older derivative of Yellow-bellied Tit (and hence the descendant of an earlier colonist of the Philippines), rather than an offshoot of Elegant Tit (see also Elegant Tit).

**REFERENCES** Dickinson *et al.* (1991).

This distinctive tit is endemic to Europe, breeding west to Britain. It has a curiously restricted distribution there, being confined to the highlands of Scotland.

**IDENTIFICATION** Length 115 mm (4.5 in). Cap and crest blackish, neatly scaled and streaked with white. Nape and sides of head whitish, with a black eyestripe and rear border to the ear-coverts and a narrow black collar from the upper mantle to the bib. Upperparts brownish, underparts whitish, variably washed buff on the flanks. The crest is raised in excitement or agitation, and when singing. Distinctive, the conspicuous crest and black and white head markings being unique among European tits.

**SEX/AGE** Sexes very similar and not distinguishable in the field, although females have, on average, a slightly shorter crest, narrower black stripes on the side of the head, a buff wash to the pale fringes to the crest feathers, and slightly richer and more extensive buff on the flanks. Juvenile similar to adult, but crest shorter and cap, crest and bib duller and browner, with the crown spotted, not scaled; the eyestripe is narrower and the black of the throat does not extend in a collar onto the sides of the neck, while the blackish border to the upper mantle is reduced or lacking. The 1st adult is very similar to the adult. In the hand, moult contrasts may be apparent in the greater coverts and occasionally also the tail, and the retained juvenile primary coverts and especially tail feathers are narrower and more pointed than those of the adults, and abrade earlier in the season (late autumn or early winter onwards). Adults have a reddish-brown iris, whilst the eye of 1st adults is grey-brown to mid brown until about February, gradually becoming brick-red at the start of the breeding season (Svensson 1992).

**VOICE** Characteristic call a low scolding or purring 'tremolo', *burrurrlt, burrurrlt* or *brrrrrr, t'brrrrrr...* (recalling a deeper version of Blue Tit's scold), often preceded by variably thin, weaker high-pitched notes, *tsee-tsee-tsee...* or *zizizi....* Other calls that may be combined with the scold include a silvery *si-si-si-sisisisisi* (falling in pitch towards the end) and ringing *sizi-za, sizi-za, sizi-za* (approaching a 'tea-cher' motif). Other notes include a thin, piercing *see*, often given in series, *see-see-see...*, a bell-like *tink* (recalling Short-toed Treecreeper), a squeaky, conversational *sith, sith, sililililili*, and squeaky, nasal *sniu-zhih* (recalling a squeaky toy). Song merely a louder version of the scold, alternating with a high-pitched motif, the phrase repeated rapidly and persistently: *seeh-i-i-burrurrlt-seeh-i-i-burrurrlt-....* (Partly after Cramp & Perrins 1993.)

**DISTRIBUTION AND MOVEMENTS** Endemic to the Western Palearctic. Breeds in **Scotland**, where confined to the Moray basin catchment, in Highland (Easter Ross and central and eastern Inverness, locally also Nairn and sporadically SE Sutherland) and Grampian (Moray and locally northern Banff, and records in 1970s in Deeside in Aberdeenshire, where breeding may have taken place). Found in much of **Continental Europe** north to central **Norway** (65° N), **Sweden** (north to about the Arctic Circle), central **Finland**, and northern **Russia** north to Arkhangel'sk, Mezen', Syktyvkar, Ust'Kulom, Okhansk and Sverdlovsk, and east to the Urals. The range extends south to **Portugal** and **Spain**, southern **France**, northern **Italy**, western and northern **Hungary**, the mountains of former **Yugoslavia** and western **Greece** (south to Mounts Olimbos and Parnassos), the Rodopi mountains of **Bulgaria**, and the Carpathians and Muntii Apuseni (Transylvanian Alps) of **Romania**. Further east, extends south to the southern **Ukraine** at Kamenets-Podol'skiy, Zhitomir, Cherkassy, Novomoskovsk and Izyum, and in southern **Russia** south to Voronezh, Morshansk, Penza, Kuybyshev, Ufa, and the area of Beloretsk, and in the southern Urals to *c.* 53° N. May breed in the Crimea, but status there requires clarification. Generally extremely sedentary, with only very limited post-breeding dispersal, and rarely recorded at migration watchpoints. Exceptionally, winter wanderings may take birds up to 100 km further afield. In the eastern parts of range, however, occasionally recorded well away from breeding areas in the autumn and winter, e.g. north in Russia to Lapland (the southern Kola peninsula, where recorded south of Lake Imandra) and to the River Sula near the mouth of the Pechora, and also in the south, where a rare winter visitor in **Moldavia** and the southern Ukraine (including Odessa) and recorded in southern Russia at Orenburg. Vagrant **England**, with about ten records, mostly in the 19th century in the south and east (including North Yorkshire, Norfolk, Suffolk, Berkshire, Surrey, Hampshire, Isle of Wight, Wiltshire, Devon and the Isles of Scilly), involving both nominate *cristatus* and *P. c. mitratus* from Continental Europe; also vagrant in Scotland away from the breeding range, to Angus and Perth (Tayside), Stirling (Central) and Lanark (Strathclyde). Vagrant to northern **Morocco**, **Transcaucasia**, central **Siberia** (Komsa on the River Yenisey in August 1986: Rogacheva 1992), and SE **Kazakhstan** ('Semireche': Dementiev & Gladkov 1966–70). May have occurred in **Corsica** (April 1980: Thibault 1983), but no authenticated records from Turkey. Range expansions are thought to be the product of the opportunistic breeding of such vagrants, but the species' sedentary nature makes colonisation of new areas a very slow process.

**HABITAT** Rather limited. In northern Europe, usually in pure stands of conifers, especially pine and spruce, although also mixed woodland or even parks if enough conifers are present. In Scotland, confined to old open stands of Scots Pine and also plantations of Scots Pine at least 20 years old, although will accept an admixture of birch and alder. In the southern parts of the range exhibits a wider habitat choice and found in mixed forest, in the Pyrénées in beech and in southern Spain in Cork Oak. Prefers rather open woodland with a well-developed shrub layer, and low rotten stumps (or nestboxes) are essential for breeding. Outside the breeding season, will often forage in adjacent areas of shrubby heather or juniper, sometimes away from mature trees; in Scotland, long bushy heather is important as it allows ground feeding during snowy periods. Will visit nearby gardens and birdtables, and in the southern Ukraine may also wander to orchards and parks. Breeds up to the treeline, in Scotland to c. 615 m and in the Austrian Alps to c. 1800 m, and largely montane in the southern parts of the range.

POPULATION Generally fairly common. There have been some local increases following the spread of conifer plantations (e.g. in Belgium and the Netherlands), and the range has expanded northwards in Finland and Denmark and westwards in the Netherlands and central and southern France. On the other hand, modern forestry practices have led to declines (e.g. in Finland, where a 50% decrease during 1955–85: Anon 1986). The range in Scotland contracted owing to the destruction of the native Caledonian pine forest in the 18th century, but there has been some recovery since about 1920; now uncommon, with c. 900 pairs. Numbers fluctuate markedly as the species is rather vulnerable to hard weather.

HABITS Sometimes aloof, sometimes confiding and inquisitive, but always restless, often flicking the wings and tail. Responds well to 'squeaking'. Found singly and in pairs, and generally quiet and unobtrusive. In areas with a reasonable population density, occurs outside the breeding season in groups of 2–6 birds which maintain a common territory; these territories overlap slightly, and disputes are common at the borders. The flock typically comprises the resident pair (which is mated for life) and young birds (not their offspring), which may form subordinate 'pre-pairs' from July onwards and then disperse in the early spring. The remaining pair will maintain the territory and breed there (and territories are rather stable from year to year); alternatively, when widowed, the survivor will pair with one of the subadults. In Russia (also Switzerland, D.A. Christie pers comm.), larger flocks are sometimes found in October–February, occasionally involving several dozen birds. On the other hand, in areas where the population density is low (e.g. Scotland) birds may be largely solitary during the winter, flocks being the product of chance encounters and changing in composition from day to day, and territorial boundaries are loose and poorly defended. Often joins mixed-species foraging flocks, but established pairs abandon these when they approach the territory boundary. Roosting habits poorly known, but the female roosts on the nest until the young are 10–13 days old. Forages in the canopy among the twigs and needles, especially during the summer, but also on larger branches and trunks and, particularly in the winter, descends to the shrub layer, saplings and the ground. Will visit birdtables. Food insects and spiders, with conifer seeds important outside the breeding season. Commonly caches food items throughout the year, although most actively stores insect larvae in the autumn (for winter consumption) and conifer seeds in the spring. Insects and spiders may be decapitated or otherwise paralysed and remain alive in storage for up to a week. Other items may be cached for several months. Food is placed in cracks and crevices in the bark, usually around the middle part of the tree, and in tufts of lichen on trees, where they are wedged into place, or stuck with saliva, body fluids or spiders' webs.

BREEDING BIOLOGY Season March–early May (second clutch in June in the Ukraine). The nest is placed in a rotting stump at least 15 cm in diameter, a hole in a dead tree or a fork in a living tree (typically where there is some local decay), usually below 4 m, occasionally up to 13 m above ground. Will use nestboxes, and occasionally fence posts, abandoned woodpecker excavations, a hole in the ground, an old crow's or raptor's nest or a squirrel's drey. The hole is usually excavated or at least substantially enlarged, the work being undertaken by the female. The nest itself is a cup of moss, occasionally also lichen, lined with hair, wool and sometimes feathers or cobwebs, also built by the female. Clutch 5–8 (3–11, averaging smallest in the north): eggs white, spotted and blotched rust-red or violet-red, markings usually concentrated at the broader end; c. 16.5 x 12.7 mm (nominate cristatus). Female incubates, period 13–18 days. The young are fed by both sexes and fledge after 17–18 days (16–22), but are dependent on the adults for a further 23 days or so after leaving the nest. Occasionally double-brooded in the south of the range.

DESCRIPTION P. c. mitratus Adult Male: In fresh plumage (September to about March), forehead, crown and crest dull black, feathers fringed and tipped whitish (forecrown scaled, hindcrown and crest more streaked). Centre of nape and upper border of mantle dull black. Upperparts cinnamon-brown, rump and uppertail-coverts slightly warmer and pinker. Tail brownish-grey, feathers finely fringed cinnamon-brown, narrower and whiter on T6. Tertials, secondaries and wing-coverts brownish-grey, fringed cinnamon-brown. Remainder of wing dark brownish-grey, inner primaries narrowly fringed grey-brown, paler and whiter distally of emarginations on P3–P6, primary coverts very narrowly fringed cinnamon-brown. Lores, supercilium, cheeks and ear-coverts off-white, feathers finely tipped mid grey (fine speckling and mottling). Eyestripe black, narrow in front of eye and not reaching bill, rear border of ear-coverts black. Submoustachial stripe, sides of throat and sides of neck (connecting with supercilium) off-white. Chin, throat and upper breast dull black, connecting with blackish border to upper mantle. Remainder of underparts off-white, breast and upper belly washed buff, flanks, lower belly, thighs, vent and undertail-coverts washed brownish-cinnamon. Axillaries and underwing coverts off-white. In worn plumage (March

–August), crown blacker, crest shorter, sides of head whiter as grey tips abraded (although dull grey feather bases may show), wings and tail duller and browner, fringes abraded, cinnamon-buff of flanks and vent paler and more restricted, and remainder of underparts dirty white (some greyish feather bases may be revealed). **Bare Parts**: Iris light brown to brick-red; bill black; legs and feet olive-grey to blue-grey. **Adult Female**: See Sex/Age. **Juvenile**: As adult, but crest feathers rather shorter, tips rounded, cap dark brown with a variable number of off-white feather tips (thus forehead and crown spotted, not scaled). Upperparts slightly duller, paler and less cinnamon, with diffuse dark border to centre of upper mantle. White of sides of head sometimes washed buff, dark feather tips more extensive, thus more heavily speckled black, but eyestripe and rear border of ear-coverts average narrower, browner and less well defined. Bib dark brown, some feathers tipped off-white, especially on lower border; not joining sides of neck. Flanks, vent and undertail-coverts paler and more pinkish-buff, 'looser' feathering revealing sooty feather bases. Iris grey on fledging, quickly becoming grey-brown or mid brown. **1st Adult**: As adult, but retains juvenile tail, flight feathers, primary coverts and greater coverts; see Sex/Age. **Measurements**: Wing of male 61–70, of female 61–66; tail of male 47–53, of female 46–55; bill 9.5–11.9; tarsus 17.5–19.8. Weight 10–12.5 g (9.7–15.8 g in other races).

**MOULT** Adult post-breeding complete (mid June–October). Post-juvenile partial, includes most or all greater coverts, sometimes one or more tertials, occasionally central tail feathers (July–September).

**GEOGRAPHICAL VARIATION** Slight and largely clinal, with the smallest and darkest birds on the western seaboard of Europe and the palest populations in the east. The upperparts vary from rufous-brown in the west, through buff-brown in central Europe to brownish-grey in the eastern and southeastern portions of the range. Moving west-east, the underparts also vary from extensively cinnamon-buff to white with restricted buff on flanks. Wear, bleaching and the variation between the sexes all combine, however, to obscure the racial characters. Five races recognised.

*P. c. scoticus* Scotland. As *mitratus,* but slightly darker, upperparts rather duller, browner and less cinnamon, fringes to crown feathers tinged drab and underparts duller, with flanks and undertail-coverts washed darker and browner, less buffy; also smaller. Wing of male 60–66, of female 58–65.

*P. c. weigoldi* Portugal, western Spain in Sierra de Gredos and southern Spain. Intergrades with *mitratus* in NW Spain (southern Galicia), SE Spain (Murcia area) and perhaps Sierra de Gredos. Poorly marked. Very similar to *scoticus,* but pale fringes on forehead and crown slightly broader and whiter (although sometimes creamy-buff on females), upperparts very slightly paler and greyer (less olive), underparts slightly whiter. Small, size as *abadiei* and *scoticus.* Wing of male 60–65.5, of female 57.5.

*P. c. abadiei* NW France in Bretagne, intergrading with *mitratus* in west-central France. As *mitratus,* but forehead, cheeks and fringes to crown feathers washed buff, upperparts slightly richer and more rufous, rump more orange-cinnamon, and flanks brighter, washed purer cinnamon. Small, size as *scoticus,* but overall more rufous.

*P. c. mitratus* Central and western Europe from France (except Bretagne), south to NW and central Spain, the Pyrénées and Alps, east to eastern Germany, Bohemia (Czech Republic), western Hungary, Montenegro and western Serbia (former Yugoslavia); vagrant England (Isle of Wight, prior to 1844). Intergrades with nominate *cristatus* over wide area from the Baltic States (Pskov to Kaliningrad) and Poland, through Slovakia, probably northern Hungary, the mountains of the Carpathian basin and Muntii Apuseni, to eastern Serbia; in this zone apparently dimorphic, with both greyer and browner individuals (perhaps indicating relatively recent contact in a zone of secondary intergradation?). See Description. In NE, central and southern France averages overall buffer, tending towards *abadiei;* in the Alps and Pyrénées greyer on upperparts and whiter on face and underparts, near nominate *cristatus.*

*P. c. cristatus* Fennoscandia, Russia, eastern Carpathians of Romania, southern Yugoslavia (Kosovo and Makedonija), southern Bulgaria, Albania and Greece; vagrant England (North Yorkshire, March 1872). As *mitratus,* but upperparts colder and greyer, greyish-brown, wing-coverts and fringes of tail and flight feathers greyer, sides of head and fringes to crown feathers purer white, underparts whiter, sides of breast, flanks and undertail-coverts washed buffish-grey. Wing of male 61–68, of female 59–64.5; tail of male 47–52, of female 45–51. Includes 'baschkirikus' of the southern Urals (south from Sverdlovsk) and Bashkirskaya, with the upperparts paler and greyer and the flanks only faintly tinged buff; and '*bureschi*' of Yugoslavia, Bulgaria, Albania and Greece, also very slightly paler and greyer, with the upperparts slightly duller (but darker than '*baschkirikus*'), and the flanks yellower.

**HYBRIDS** Presumed hybrids with Coal Tit have been noted (Gray 1958).

**RELATIONSHIPS** Placed in the subgenus *Lophophanes,* together with Grey-Crested Tit, but the precise relationships of these two species are unclear. The Bridled Titmouse of North America was formerly thought to be very closely related to Crested Tit, on the basis of morphology and distribution (e.g. Eck 1988, Thielcke 1968), but biochemical evidence has recently shown that this is far from the case, Bridled Titmouse being close to the Tufted/Black-crested/Plain Titmouse group, subgenus *Baeolophus.*

**REFERENCES** Cramp & Perrins (1993) Dementiev & Gladkov (1966–70), Mauersberger & Stephan (1967), Vaurie (1959).

# 69 GREY-CRESTED TIT *Parus dichrous*                    Plate 20
Other name: Brown Crested Tit

A rather drab tit of high altitudes in the Himalayas and China, in many ways this species is the equivalent of the Crested Tit, but its exact relationships are unclear.

**IDENTIFICATION** Length 120 mm (4.75 in). Upperparts, including cap and the erect, pointed crest, dull greyish (upperparts browner than cap in western China). Submoustachial stripe and sides of neck whitish or buffy, forming a conspicuous pale half-collar. Throat light grey-buff, remainder of underparts dull pale cinnamon (entire underparts more uniformly pale cinnamon in western China). A rather plain tit, but this itself is distinctive, as all other crested tits in the region have conspicuous areas of black or yellow in the plumage. Yellow-browed Tit is similarly nondescript, but has olive-green upperparts, greyish-yellow-olive underparts, a much smaller and less conspicuous crest, and lacks the pale half-collar. When the family identity is not clear, Grey-crested Tit could be confused with Whiskered Yuhina or even Stripe-throated Yuhina, but note the small size, acrobatic behaviour and lack of a dark moustachial stripe or dark throat streaks.
**SEX/AGE** Sexes similar. The juvenile is similar to the adult, but has a shorter crest, with faintly dark-tipped feathers, and paler and less uniform underparts with slightly darker mottling on a cinnamon-buff ground. 1st adult as adult, but retains the juvenile tail feathers, tertials and greater coverts, and in the hand the tail feathers are narrower and more pointed than the adult's.
**VOICE** Rather quiet. Calls include a characteristic, high-pitched, thin *zai* (Ali & Ripley 1983); also a rapid, stuttering *ti-di* or *ti-ti-ti-ti*, a conversational *sip-pi-pi*, a plaintive *pee-di* or *pi-dui*, and lisping *sip, sip, sip....* Alarm a rapid, medium-pitched *cheea, cheea*. Song *whee-whee-tz-tz-tz* (Fleming *et al.* 1984), a combination of various notes (including some of the calls), notably trills (Martens & Eck in press.).
**DISTRIBUTION AND MOVEMENTS** The **Himalayas** of northern **India** from southern Kashmir through Himachal Pradesh to northern Uttar Pradesh, also **Nepal**, **Sikkim**, **Bhutan**, Arunachal Pradesh, and adjacent NE **Burma** (**Myanmar**) in the Chimili Pass area. Extends north of the main range of the Himalayas into southern Tibet along the Sun Kosi valley to Nyalam and into the Tsangpo Bend area, where noted at Dongjug, Güncang in the Nyang Qu valley and Bomi in the Po Tsangpo valley; also found in NE Tibet in the eastern Tanggula Shan (Penam Chu; Vaurie 1972), east to the region north of Qamdo, and at Baxoi in the Salween valley. In SW **China** found in NW **Yunnan**, including Lijiang and Zhongdian, the Mekong-Salween and Mekong-Yangtze divides, and west of the Salween in the Gaoligong Shan (south to about Tengchong), and in western **Sichuan**, east to Pingwu and Ebian on the border of the Red Basin, eastern and southern **Qinghai**, west to Yushu and north to 'Tiangtang Temple' (=

T'ien-t'ang Ssu of Vaurie 1972, not NW Gansu, *contra* Cheng 1987), SW **Gansu** in the Min Shan range, and the Taibai Shan in the Qin Ling range of southern **Shaanxi**.
**HABITAT** A forest bird, breeding in the Himalayas in a wide variety of forest types, from broadleaved forests of oak and rhododendron at lower altitudes, through mixed fir, hemlock, oak and rhododendron, to pine, spruce, birch and rhododendron at higher levels. In NE Burma recorded from mixed fir, hemlock, bamboo and hydrangea, and in western China favours coniferous forest, especially spruce-fir. Found at high altitudes in the upper temperate and subalpine zones, breeding in NW India at 2400–3300 m and in Nepal at 2720 to around 3800 m (occasionally 4200 m in Khumbu). Recorded in Sikkim at 2440–3960 m, in Bhutan at 2745–4240 m, in Arunachal Pradesh at 3000–3800 m, in NE Burma at 2745–3200 m, in SE Tibet at 2775–3900 m, and in western China in Yunnan at 2750–3960 m, Sichuan at 2300–4570 m and Shaanxi at 3000 m. Some movement within these ranges in winter, with birds descending to lower altitudes; recorded in Nepal in winter at 2000–3660 m, but also as high as 4270 m in February, and through the winter at 2440–3050 m at Wolong in Sichuan. Generally rather hardy.
**POPULATION** Fairly common in the eastern Himalayas, but uncommon in the western Himalayas, SE Tibet and SW China, although noted as very numerous in northern Sichuan (Bangs & Peters 1928).
**HABITS** Often shy, quiet and unobtrusive. Found in pairs and occasionally small parties, frequently joining mixed-species feeding flocks. Forages in the lower and middle storeys of trees, hopping along the tops of limbs, in bushes and also on the ground, especially in the winter, when the species has been recorded feeding amongst snow between dwarf rhododendron and birch scrub (Stevens 1923–25). Food largely insects.
**BREEDING BIOLOGY** Season April–June in western Himalayas. The nest is placed in holes in trees and stumps (probably at least sometimes excavated by the birds themselves), *c.* 3–7 m above ground level. The pad of moss is lined with fur, hair and feathers. Clutch 4–5: eggs white, densely spotted reddish; 17.1 x 12.8 mm (Himalayas). Incubation period unknown. Both sexes feed the young.
**DESCRIPTION** *P. d. kangrae* **Adult**: *In fresh plumage* (September–February/March), forehead pale grey, grading to mid grey on crown and crest; upperparts mid grey, washed buffy-brown. Tail feathers dark brownish-grey, diffusely fringed mid buffy-grey. Wings dark brownish-grey, all feathers diffusely fringed pale drab-grey, very finely so on

primary coverts and only inwards of emarginations on P3–P6; P1–P2 and alula all dark. Lores and cheeks mottled mid grey and buff-white; ear-coverts very pale buff, feathers neatly fringed and tipped dark grey, rear border slightly darker. Submoustachial region and sides of neck whitish, forming a narrow half-collar which is backed by a grey extension of the upper mantle. Throat light grey-buff, variably but often well demarcated from remainder of underparts, which are pale-mid drab-cinnamon, the palest individuals showing a whitish centre to the belly, breast and vent (although only slightly darker in tone, the throat contrasts in colour with the remainder of the underparts). Thighs pale grey-cinnamon. Axillaries and underwing-coverts pale buff. *In worn plumage* (about April–August), upperparts slightly darker and purer grey, throat paler and purer grey, remainder of underparts paler, more drab-buff (showing more tonal contrast with the throat).
**Bare Parts**: Iris orange-brown or reddish-brown to crimson; bill black or dark grey; legs and feet bright blue-grey or dark grey, claws darker, horny-brown. **Juvenile**: As adult, but crest shorter, feathers of crest and upperparts faintly tipped darker, rump often tinged buff. Tail feathers distinctly pointed. Ear-coverts whiter, mottled dark grey, feathers of sides of neck tipped dark drab. Throat paler grey, underparts paler cinnamon, grading to buff on belly, feathers usually tipped light-mid grey (thus underparts mottled grey and cinnamon, showing much reduced contrast with throat). **1st Adult**: As adult (see Sex/Age). **Measurements**: Wing of male 68–73, of female 65–67; tail of male 44–46.5, of female 43–46; bill 11–12; tarsus 17.5–19.2. Weight 11.2–14 g (*P. d. dichrous*).

**MOULT** Adult post-breeding complete (July–October). Post-juvenile partial, includes median coverts, occasionally 1–2 tertials, also occasionally inner greater coverts? (August–September).

**GEOGRAPHICAL VARIATION** Slight, with four subspecies recognised:

*P. d. kangrae* NW Himalayas from Kashmir east to northern Uttar Pradesh. Poorly marked. See Description.

*P. d. dichrous* Central and eastern Himalayas from western Nepal to Arunachal Pradesh and adjacent southern Tibet (Nyalam, Bomi and Baxoi). As *kangrae*, but darker. Upperparts marginally darker and purer grey, half-collar slightly duller, throat duller and browner, showing rather less contrast with the breast, which is also slightly duller and drabber cinnamon. Wing of male 65–76, of female 62–70; tail of male 43–54, of female 42–50; bill 10–11; tarsus 18–21. Includes '*izzardi*' of eastern Nepal, averaging slightly larger (wing of male 71–75) than birds from central Nepal (wing of male 65.5–69).

*P. d. wellsi* NE Burma and SW China in western Sichuan and NW Yunnan. Intergrades with nominate *dichrous* to the west, and with *dichroides* in NW Sichuan (Songpan region). As nominate *dichrous* but upperparts average slightly darker and purer grey and underparts paler, lacking contrast between throat and breast (throat dull pale buff, paler and less grey than *dichrous*, breast and centre of belly as throat, vent and flanks richer and more cinnamon). Wing of male 67–77, of female 65–75; tail of male 51–58, of female 47–50.

*P. d. dichroides* SW China in NE Tibet (northern part of Qamdo region), northern Sichuan (Songpan, Pingwu, and the Min Shan on the border with Gansu), Qinghai, Gansu and Shaanxi. Well marked. Underparts as *wellsi*, with no contrast between the throat and breast, but unlike all other races shows a marked contrast between the grey cap and crest and dark drab-grey upperparts (rather than upperparts uniformly greyish). One male, wing 64, tail 52.

**RELATIONSHIPS** Placed with Crested Tit and Bridled Titmouse in the subgenus *Lophophanes* by Thielcke (1968), on the basis of morphology and distribution, whilst Eck (1988) placed all three in a 'species group', further emphasising their close relationship. Sheldon *et al.* (1992) found, however, that DNA-DNA hybridisation indicated that Bridled Titmouse was not closely related to Grey-crested Tit, but their data did not address the relationship of Crested and Grey-crested Tits. Thus, the relationships of this species remain enigmatic.
**REFERENCES** Ali (1979), Ali & Ripley (1983), Baker (1932–33), Stevens (1923–25).

# 70 WHITE-SHOULDERED TIT *Parus guineensis*      Plate 23
Other name: White-shouldered Black Tit

The northern and western counterpart of White-winged Tit, this species is unique among the African black tits in having a pale eye.

**IDENTIFICATION** Length 140 mm (5.5 in). Generally glossy black with a prominent yellowish iris. May show a slight crest, giving a rather ragged appearance to the nape. White fringes to the greater and median coverts, tertials and inner secondaries form a solid white panel on the closed wing and are noticeable in flight. Juvenile duller, with a grey eye. Easily separated from White-bellied Tit by the lack of a white belly. In SW Ethiopia, Uganda, Rwanda, Burundi, eastern Zaïre and NW Tanzania, may overlap with the very similar White-winged Tit. The present species is some 10% smaller, usually lacks any white in the tail, and adults have a yellow or whitish eye. In the hand, shows a distinct purple tone to the blue gloss on the upperparts (White-winged Tits show an oily green tone to the blue gloss, although the Ethiopian race shows the same purple tinge as White-shouldered).

**SEX/AGE** Sexes similar. Juvenile distinct, duller than the adult, with little or no gloss to the plumage; the fringes to the flight feathers are washed yellow, there are no white fringes to the primary coverts, and the broader dark centres to the greater coverts may show on the closed wing, especially on the outer 2–3 feathers. Notably, the juvenile's iris is grey or brown. 1st adult as adult, but retains the juvenile primary coverts, inner 2–3 primaries and most or all of the secondaries (and sometimes some tail feathers), and may be aged in the hand by the contrast between these old feathers, which are abraded and bleached paler, and the new tertials and greater coverts (note that in both adults and juveniles the primaries and secondaries are distinctly browner than the tertials and greater coverts). 1st adults may also retain 2–3 juvenile outer greater coverts, which are bleached and well abraded, showing dark centres.

**VOICE** Very varied. Many calls are harsh and buzzing, but the song is sweet and clear. Any differences from White-winged Tit have yet to be described. The usual call is a loud, harsh, sibilant *churr*, frequently preceded by 2–3 softer, non-sibilant *chip* notes (Greig-Smith 1978). Other calls include a nasal, finch-like rising *dzwee, dzwee, dzwiu...* or *ziu, dziu, dziu...*, repeated at irregular intervals, and in excitement (?) becoming a higher-pitched and more rapid crescendo *dwi-zwi-zwi-zwi-zwi...* (this is probably the call described by Bannerman 1948 as a rather harsh *twe-a*). Also a harsh, grating *chut, chut*, and a very thin, silvery *sisisi-pee* (the last note louder and fuller, more bell-like), followed by a lower-pitched, slightly grating *ruwi-uwi*. Serle & Morel (1977) also note a rather harsh *teer-teer-zeet*. The song is a ringing, pleasant, whistled *sree, tip-tu-wip, tu-wip, tu-wip, tu-wip...*, with more complex variants such as *swip-pedu-wip, pe-du-wip* etc. Also gives a rather harsh, more warbling jumble of notes. The song is also described as clear and simple, a thrush- or bell-like reiterated *chu-wee*; the male is reported to shoot up into the air as he utters the pretty song (Bannerman 1948; Chapin 1954).

**DISTRIBUTION AND MOVEMENTS** In **West Africa** widely but locally distributed in the lower and middle river regions of the **Gambia**, and widespread in Senegal south of c. 14º N. Occurs in **Guinea-Bissau**, in **Guinea** noted from the Fouta Djallon massif and from just north of Siguiri, and recorded from northern and NE **Sierra Leone**. In the **Ivory Coast** widespread in the Guinea zone, including a southward extension to Lamto at c. 6º N, and similarly found in northern **Ghana**, south through the Volta region to Ho in the far southeast and to the wooded inselbergs on the coastal plains around Accra (although no records from the coastal thicket zone). In **Togo** recorded from around Mo and Aledjo, and in adjacent **Benin** noted north of Kilibo, and in Pendjari/Arli NPs, Benin/**Burkina Faso** (ex Upper Volta). In **Nigeria** found in the Guinea and Sudan savannas south to Ilorin, Enugu and Obudu, and north to at least

Gaya, but shuns areas degraded by farming. Recorded in **Liberia** in gardens in Monrovia in April 1988, but status unknown, perhaps merely a vagrant? (Gore 1994). In the **Sahel** and **NE Africa** an irregular migrant in the rainy season (July–October) to southern **Mauritania**, to the Senegal valley in southern Guidimaka. In **Mali** recorded south of 14º 30′ N at Mopti, Bouclé de Baoulé NP, and the Monts Mandingues in the far southwest. In SW **Niger** found along the river Niger in Park W and at Tillaberi, and also at Sabongari. In southern **Chad** occurs north to Logone, Zakouma NP and the Azoum river. Widely distributed in southern **Sudan** south of 13º N, extending into SW **Ethiopia** in Ilubabor, Kafa and Gamo Gofa provinces (although the boundary between this species and White-winged Tit is poorly known; the two may even overlap), and into NW Ethiopia from Gallabat on the Sudanese border north to c. 16º N in NW **Eritrea**. In **central and eastern Africa** found in the savanna zone of **Cameroon**, including the Adamawa massif, Benue plain and grasslands of the Montane district, from about Galim, Didango, Bafia and Nachtigal north to Yagoua. In **Central African Republic** recorded from Bamingui-Bangoran NP, Manovo-Gounda-Saint Floris NP and Vakaga and Lobaye prefectures. In NE **Zaïre** found in northern Equateur (Businga) and northern Haut-Zaïre, south to Buta, Poko and Mahagi (the Lendu plateau west of Lake Albert). May occur in easternmost Kivu, **Rwanda** and **Burundi**, but these records of '*purpurascens*' probably relate to White-winged Tit (see that species). Widespread in central and northern **Uganda**, south and west to Bunyoro district (Hoima), Mubende, and Masaka, and found in SW **Kenya** west of Rift Valley from Mount Elgon and Kapenguria south to at least the Nyando valley east of Kisumu (noted in NW **Tanzania** in Ziwa Magharibi (Nyarumbugu) by Britton 1980, but this requires confirmation). Claimed to occur in **Equatorial Guinea** (this species rather than White-winged Tit?), but this, too, requires confirmation.

**HABITAT** Open woodland and *Acacia* savanna in the Guinea Savanna Zone, in bushed and wooded grassland, cultivated country with trees, clearings and woodland edge. Extends into the forest-savanna mosaic on the northern marches of the rainforest zone, and found in well-wooded country and forest in southern Uganda, while in the north, found in the dry Sudan Savanna Zone in gallery forest along watercourses. Fond of trees with fairly open foliage. Recorded up to at least 1220 m in Cameroon, and in Kenya found above 1000 m.

**POPULATION** Generally fairly common to common, and the most frequent species in mixed-species foraging flocks in parts of Cross River State, Nigeria. Scarce to rare, however, on the extremities of the range in Mauritania, Gambia, Liberia, Chad, the dry northeast of Uganda and western Kenya (one near Mumias in December 1989 was the first in Kenya for many years); uncommon in NE Central African Republic and in Uganda around Kampala, and not very common in Mali and in Sudan east of the Nile. Status uncertain in Ethiopia.

**HABITS** Found in pairs or in parties of 3–6, and often joins mixed-species foraging flocks; noted as the key 'nuclear' species in such parties in Ghana. Restless and possibly shyer than other African tits, keeping to taller trees. Flight undulating and indirect, the birds maintaining contact with frequent calling. Forages in crevices and cracks in the bark of boughs and branches in the middle stratum, perhaps in preference to gleaning from the foliage, and may take insects on the wing. Food insects, also fruit.

**BREEDING BIOLOGY** Poorly known. Season: West Africa about January–June; NE Zaïre, March–April; Uganda, October/November (?), March (?) and May–July; Sudan, April–May; also feeding young in the nest in western Ethiopia in June. Nest placed in a hole in a tree, noted at 1 m above ground.

**DESCRIPTION** Adult: In fresh plumage, upperparts black, crown to uppertail-coverts glossed blue (with a hint of purple). Tail sooty-black, outer webs fringed glossy blue-black, a few birds having T6 narrowly fringed white and T5 narrowly tipped white. Marginal coverts black, tipped white. Lesser coverts black, longer tipped white, lower all white. Median coverts white (dark bases fully concealed). Greater coverts white with dark streak along shaft, largely on inner web (fully concealed at rest; inner web of innermost covert sooty-black). Alula, tertials and primary coverts black, alula very finely tipped white, primary coverts finely fringed white, tertials with glossier blue fringes, outermost fringed (not tipped) white. Primaries and secondaries blackish-brown, secondaries broadly fringed white, the fringes on the inner 4–5 forming a solid white panel on closed wing (fringes may be slightly duller and buffer on outer secondaries), P3–P10 narrowly fringed off-white (only inwards of emarginations on P3–P7). Lores, sides of head and sides of neck black, slightly glossed blue. Underparts black, glossed bluish, least so on flanks, vent and undertail-coverts. Axillaries sooty-black, underwing-coverts white (may show some black admixture). In worn plumage, overall a little duller, when very worn fringes to outer webs of outer greater coverts may abrade to show dark centres and the pale fringes on the secondaries become fragmented and abraded. **Bare Parts**: Iris pale ochre, yellow, creamy-white or white; bill black; legs and feet dark brown or bluish-grey to black. **Juvenile**: Upperparts brownish-black, tail sooty-black, amount of white in T5–T6 as adult. Wing-coverts as adult, but white areas slightly sullied and with broader sooty-brown centres to greater coverts (dark centres may show on outer 2–3 greater coverts, outermost almost all dark). Remainder of wing sooty-black, alula and primary coverts faintly fringed paler, outer tertial fringed yellowish-white on basal two-thirds; secondaries fringed yellowish-white, fringes broadest and whitest on inner 3–4 secondaries, primaries narrowly fringed yellow-white, whitest at base of P3–P5. Lores, sides of head and neck and underparts dull dark sooty-brown. Underwing-coverts and axillaries as adult. Iris grey, grey-green or brown; bill black with light greenish cutting edges

and yellow-white gape flanges; legs and feet slate or purplish-grey, claws black. **1st Adult**: See Sex/Age. **Measurements**: Wing of male 72–84, of female 70–81.5; tail of male 52–68, of female 51–66 (see also 'purpurascens' below); bill 11–14; tarsus 17–20. Weight 12.9–17.9 g (Ethiopia, J.S. Ash in litt.), 21 g (Cameroon, Louette & Prévost 1987).

**MOULT** Adult post-breeding complete (July, Ghana; June–September, Nigeria; June–September, January, Uganda; September, Kenya; May–July, Ethiopia). Post-juvenile incomplete, includes P1–P7/P8, often inner secondary (sometimes inner two and/or outermost), tertials, alula, and most or all greater coverts and tail feathers, rarely some outer primary coverts (June–August, Nigeria; December, Mali; August Uganda; April, Sudan; June, August, January, Ethiopia).

**GEOGRAPHICAL VARIATION** Slight, with some upland populations averaging a little larger, including 'purpurascens' in SW Ethiopia, central and SE Uganda (north to about Lira, Soroti, and Mount Elgon) and probably also easternmost Haut-Zaïre (on the Lendu plateau south to at least Bogoro): wing of male 80–90, of female 78–85; tail of male 60–70, of female 60–67. The population in the highlands of Cameroon also averages larger: wing of male 78–87, of female 78–80; tail of male 60–69, of female 60–65.

**RELATIONSHIPS** A member of the *niger* superspecies and usually treated, although with reservations, as conspecific with White-winged Tit. Eye colour may, however, play an important role in species recognition, and the relationship between the small and conspicuously pale-eyed White-shouldered Tit and the larger, dark-eyed White-winged Tit has not been carefully investigated. In Ethiopia, White-winged Tit appears to be separated by both altitude and ecology from White-shouldered Tit in the areas where their ranges adjoin. It is possible that the biometrically larger population in SW Ethiopia ('purpurascens') represents intergradation with White-winged Tit, but there are no data on eye coloration from this area. There appears to be no good evidence that the ranges of the two species overlap in Uganda (despite statements to the contrary). White-winged Tit is confined to the far southwest of Uganda, in Ankole, Kigezi and Toro district (north to about the Ruwenzoris, Fort Portal and Masaka, and perhaps the Kampala region, although Carswell 1986 noted only pale-eyed birds in the Kampala area). White-shouldered Tit is found north from Hoima and Entebbe, and, although Hall (1960) notes that 'Colonel Meinertzhagen has a record of a mixed flock seen at Sango Bay near the mouth of the Kagera River', this record is open to doubt. It is sometimes stated that the population in Uganda is 'mixed' and unstable, showing variable eye coloration, and the name *purpurascens*, type locality Entebbe, has sometimes been applied to this 'mixed' population. The only brown-eyed 'purpurascens' seen, however, proved to be a juvenile White-shouldered Tit and, as the type description makes clear, 'purpurascens', if used at all, is properly applied to a form of *P. guineensis*. The two species may overlap in the far northwest of Tanzania and possibly in eastern Kivu, Zaïre, and in Rwanda-Burundi, but data area lacking. Benson (1946) notes that a bird from northern Turkana (SW Ethiopia) is less purple, more green-glossed than southern Ethiopian specimens, and that 'Turkwell' birds (presumably in fact SW Ethiopia, as not recorded from the Turkwell region of Kenya by Britton 1980) are probably intergrades between White-winged and White-shouldered Tits, but specimens from near Lake Turkana appear to be typical White-shoul-dered (although too often data on eye colour are lacking). Given the difference in size and eye colour, White-shouldered Tit is treated as specifically distinct, following Sibley & Monroe (1990). This treatment is disputed by Dowsett & Dowsett-Lemaire (1993), since White (1963) pointed out that intergrades between *guineensis* and nominate *leucomelas* occur in SW Uganda (where 'eye colour is not constant'). As noted above, however, evidence for this is lacking.

**REFERENCES** Chapin (1954), Hall (1960).

## 71 WHITE-WINGED TIT *Parus leucomelas*                    Plate 23
Other names: Black Tit, White-winged Black Tit

This robust tit is widespread in south-central Africa, although avoiding true forest, with an isolated population in Ethiopia.

**IDENTIFICATION** Length 160 mm (6.25 in). A heavy-billed black tit with a slight greenish-blue gloss, narrow white margins to the tail and a dark eye. May show a slight crest, giving a ragged appearance to the nape. White fringes to the median and greater coverts, tertials and inner secondaries form a solid white panel on the closed wing and are noticeable in flight. Easily separated from White-bellied Tit by its lack of a white belly. In SW Ethiopia, eastern Zaïre, southern Uganda, Rwanda, Burundi and NW Tanzania, this species needs to be carefully distinguished from White-shouldered Tit, which is smaller, lacks white fringes to the outer tail feathers, and, in adults, shows a prominent pale eye. White-winged overlaps with Southern Black Tit in Zambia, Malawi and northern Mozambique, although the two species are largely distinguished by altitude and habitat, White-winged Tit in scattered bushes in open country at higher altitudes, Southern Black Tit in mopane and other dry woodland. Adults are separated from male Southern Black Tits (of the northern subspecies *xanthostomus*) by their darker underparts (especially the belly and vent), with a noticeable gloss (some female White-winged, however are less glossy), and uniform blue-black undertail-coverts. They also have much less white in the tail than Southern Black, just a narrow white fringe and tip (the whole of the outer web of T6 is white on Southern Black; see figure 71.1, p. 326 and 72.1, p. 329). On the closed wing, the greater coverts are uniformly white (Southern Black shows dark centres to about six outer greater coverts), and the broader white fringes to the outermost tertial and the secondaries form a solid white panel on the closed wing (this is much narrower on Southern Black, and confined to the outermost tertial and innermost secondaries). (Note that the race *ravidus* of Southern Black Tit from Zimbabwe shows more white in the wing, but the outer greater coverts still show dark centres at rest.) Female Southern Black Tit is much paler ashy-brown on the underparts than adult White-winged (and rather paler even than juvenile White-winged), hence the white tips to undertail-coverts are less obvious, showing reduced contrast with the grey feather bases. Juvenile White-winged Tit is only slightly paler below than the adult female (dark sooty-brown without any gloss), and has a slight yellow wash on the fringes to the secondaries (this is always shown by juvenile Southern Black). It is much darker than juvenile Southern Black, lacking a pale vent, and with little white in the tail, no white in the undertail-coverts (i.e. as the adult) and more white in the greater coverts (although dark centres may show on outer 2–3 feathers). For separation from Carp's Tit, see p. 330.

**SEX/AGE** Sexes very similar, the degree of difference varying geographically. In Ethiopia nominate *leucomelas* shows no differences between the sexes (although in southern Ethiopia females may be very slightly duller), whilst in the southern race *insignis* the female is always slightly duller and rather less glossy on the underparts. Juvenile distinct, duller than the adult, lacking gloss and with the underparts dark sooty-brown; the fringes to the flight feathers are often washed yellow-buff, although only faintly, while the broader dark centres to the greater coverts may show on the closed wing, especially on the outer 2–3 feathers. Iris brown, as in the adult. 1st adult as adult, but retains the juvenile primary coverts, primaries, secondaries and sometimes the alula, and may be aged in the hand by the contrast between these old feathers, which are abraded and bleached paler, and the new tertials and greater coverts.

**VOICE** Calls include a shrill, explosive *chut* or *chit*, often combined with more buzzing calls as an introductory note, thus a characteristic *chit-zzzzz-r*, or *chut-drrrrrr-du*, and a strange, low, grating phrase, *chik-zworrrr, chik-zworrrrr*. Also gives more complex and musical phrases, such as *tszee-tuwu, tszee-tuwu* (in the 'tea-cher' pattern, but rather slow), and the song is a complex, rather sad whistled phrase, *ter-si, du, l-l-l-l-l-tuwi* (recalling a lark or chat and not at all tit-like, it is perhaps more mournful than the song of White-winged and Southern Black Tits). Reported to be vocally quite dissimilar to Southern Black Tit (Benson *et al.* 1971; Dowsett & Forbes-Watson 1993), and probably lacks Southern Black's stereotyped nasal, buzzing *tsi-tsi-chacha* on the 'chick-a-dee' pattern, but both species, in common with all tits, have a wide vocabulary. (Note that, following Vincent (1933, 1935), many texts described the calls as '*twiddy-zeet-zeet-zeet*, a shrill note followed by three rasping syllables and a strange and shrill buzzing twitter followed by a shriller note *zeu-zeu-zeu-twit*'. These transcriptions may have been based on observations of Southern Black Tit and, indeed, identical renditions are used for that species in many field guides.)

**DISTRIBUTION AND MOVEMENTS** Two disjunct populations. The **northern population** is found in **Ethiopia** in the southeastern highlands (south to Yabelo in Sidamo province), in central and eastern parts of southern Ethiopia and in the northeast (above 300 m), north to Tigray province. (Note that Hall & Moreau 1970 map 'brown-eyed' birds for central-eastern Sudan, north of *c.* 10° N and east of 34° E, and in Ethiopia in the western highlands north to Eritrea, apparently on the basis of a brown-eyed individual from Roseires on the Blue Nile in Sudan, but all those examined from these areas appear to be White-shouldered Tits, although data on eye colour are lacking, and the boundary between the two species is poorly known). In **central Africa** occurs in southernmost **Gabon** north to at least Tchibanga, and the southern **Congo** north to at least Djambala. Also south and SE **Zaïre**, south of the Equatorial forest block, north to Bolobo on the Zaïre river (NW Bandundu), Kwango, southern Kasai Occidental (north to Port-Francqui, Luluabourg and Sentery), and NE Katanga (Tanganika district), and north in eastern Kivu to the Virungas, Lake Edward, Beni and the Semliki valley and the Ruwenzori region. Presumably occurs in adjacent **Rwanda** and **Burundi** (recorded from the Kagera river by Chapin 1954, whilst the '*purpurascens*' noted for western Rwanda (east to Butare) and the Ruzizi valley and Ngozi in northern Burundi by Schouteden 1966a, b presumably refer to this species rather than White-shouldered Tit; see also p. 323). Found in SW **Uganda** in Ankole, Kigezi and Toro, north to about the Ruwenzoris, Fort Portal and the Kampala area (Entebbe, although only White-shouldered Tits were noted around Kampala by Carswell 1986), and in NW **Tanzania** recorded in Ngara and about Lake Victoria at Mwanza, and also in the southwestern highlands from Njombe north to the Ufipa plateau and the Uzungwe mountains, with scattered records elsewhere, including Kidugallo and Bagamoyo (Britton 1980). In **southern Africa** occurs in the plateau woodlands of northern and central **Angola** from Capelongo in central Huila north to Cabinda, Cuanza Norte and Malanje, west in the south to Caconda, Calulo and Duque de Braganca, and east to the Zaïre-Zambian border; also found in the coastal lowlands below the escarpment from Camabatela to at least *c.* 13° 30' S on the Cubal river. Found throughout northern

**Zambia**, in Eastern province south to Chadiza, in Southern province to Mazabuka and Chunga, and in Western province to Kaoma, Kalabo and the south Luete river (replaced below 915 m throughout the Luangwa valley by Southern Black Tit); also reported from Cameron Bay on Lake Tanganyika. In **Malawi** recorded west of the Rift Valley from Dzonze and Dedza northwards, including the Viphya mountains, and in adjacent **Mozambique** recorded in NE Tete province at Ulongue (Vincent 1933, 1935), occurring also in northern Mozambique in the Niassa district (Clancey 1972).

**HABITAT** The northern population in Ethiopia frequents the drier highland forests of juniper, olive and podocarp at up to 2750 m, as well as lowland subtropical and riverine forest, thorn bush and *Acacia* savanna. In central Africa, the favoured habitat is variable and apparently influenced by competition with other tits (e.g. Southern Black and Rufous-bellied Tits in Zambia and Malawi), but overall favours light woodland and edge habitats, avoiding evergreen forest (both montane and lowland) and arid areas. The typical population favours the edges and clearings in miombo (*Brachystegia*) woodland in Angola and southern Zaïre, occasionally occurring in *Acacia*. In Gabon, the Congo, Tanzanian highlands, Zambia, Malawi and Mozambique, found in thickets and bushes in open ground, grasslands and savanna, as well as the edge of miombo and occasionally secondary *Brachystegia* (apparently replaced in miombo woodland by Rufous-bellied Tit). In SE Zaïre and SW Uganda, a smaller population is found in *Acacia* woodland, and in savanna with scattered trees and bushes, and in western Angola another small population is found in mist-belt woodland below the escarpment (inland and north of the arid coastal strip). The typical population in Angola, southern Zaïre, Zambia and Malawi is found above 915 m (although noted at 760 m near Lake Tanganyika in Zambia and at 570 m in Tete province, Mozambique), up to at least 1860 m in Zaïre, 1710 m in the Viphya mountains of Malawi, 2040 m on the Nyika plateau of Zambia and 2000 m in East Africa; recorded at 730 m in southern Gabon.

**POPULATION** Generally frequent to common, and noted as the commonest tit in southern Uganda (although this may refer also to White-shouldered Tit) and commoner than Miombo and Rufous-bellied Tits in Zambia (White 1945, 1946). Perhaps rare, however, in Ethiopia (e.g. in riverine woodland in Nechisar NP).

**HABITS** Found in pairs or small parties, and often joins mixed-species foraging flocks. Possibly shyer than other African tits and keeping to taller trees. Food insects, and searches for prey in crevices of bark and may take insects on the wing.

**BREEDING BIOLOGY** Season: Ethiopia, August, December and possibly March; Tanzania highlands, September–December; southern Africa, late August–November; Uganda, March, June (and probably this species May and July); southern Zaïre, May, July, and September–November, near the Equator breeding dates much less regular. The nest is placed in a hole in a tree or stump 0.3–4 m above ground, occasionally in buildings, and is a pad of soft materials, such as grass and lichens. Clutch (2?) 3–5: eggs white to pinkish-white, spotted brown or rufous with grey undermarkings; *c.* 19.7 x 14.1 mm. The young fledge after at least 26 days.

**DESCRIPTION** *P. l. insignis* **Adult Male**: *In fresh plumage*, forehead black, crown to uppertail-coverts black, glossed blue (with a distinct green tinge, slightly 'oily' and tending towards bottle-green). Tail black, outer webs fringed glossy blue-black, T6 narrowly fringed and tipped white, T2–T5 with narrow white tip, extending finely onto distal quarter of outer web on T4–T5 (see figure below). Wings black, marginal coverts tipped white, median coverts white (dark bases fully concealed), greater coverts broadly fringed and tipped white, outer webs largely white on inner 6 feathers, dark centres may show on outer 1–2; alula faintly tipped white, primary coverts finely fringed white; tertials with glossier blue fringes, outermost fringed (not tipped) white; secondaries broadly fringed white, inner 4–5 forming a solid white panel on closed wing (fringes may be slightly duller and buffer on outer secondaries); primaries P3–P10 narrowly fringed off-white (only inwards of emarginations on P3–P7). Lores, sides of head and sides of neck black with slight blue gloss. Underparts black, glossed blue (tinged green as the upperparts, only more so), least glossy on flanks, vent and undertail-coverts. Axillaries sooty-black, underwing-coverts white. *In worn plumage*, less glossy, fringes to flight feathers may be heavily abraded, and dark centres to outer two greater coverts may be more conspicuous. **Bare Parts**: Iris grey or brown; bill black; legs and feet black to dark bluish-grey or dark brown, claws black. **Adult Female**: As male, but underparts average a sootier black, with blue gloss much reduced.

*Figure 71.1  Tail of adult male* P. l. insignis.

**Juvenile**: Upperparts from forehead to uppertail-coverts blackish-brown. Tail sooty-black, T5–T6 narrowly fringed white on distal half (very finely so on T5). Wing-coverts as adult, but larger sooty-brown centres to greater coverts. Alula and primary coverts sooty-black, faintly fringed paler. Flight feathers sooty-black, outer tertial broadly fringed white on basal two-thirds, secondaries and primaries fringed white (fringes broadest on inner 3–4 secondaries and at base of P3–P5); on most individuals, the fringes to the outer 4 secondaries and the primaries are tinged yellow-buff, as sometimes is the fringe to the outer tertial. Lores, sides of head and neck and underparts dark sooty-brown with no gloss. Underwing-coverts and axillaries as adult. **1st Adult**: See Sex/Age. **Measurements**: Wing of male 86–97, of female 84–93; tail of male 67–80.5, of female 65–76 (see also below); bill 12.5–15; tarsus 17–21. Weight 21–24 g (*P. l. leucomelas*; J.S. Ash *in litt.*).

**MOULT** Adult post-breeding complete (January, Zaïre; June, July, September, Uganda; April, Malawi). Post-Juvenile partial, includes tertials, greater coverts, a variable number of tail feathers, often the alula and occasionally the innermost secondary (May, September, Uganda; December, Tanzania; May, Malawi).

**GEOGRAPHICAL VARIATION** Two disjunct populations, but variation slight, involving the exact tone of the gloss and the amount of white in the tail and underwing-coverts.

*P. l. leucomelas* Ethiopia. As *insignis,* but the body glossed blue, tinged purple, with little or no white in the tail (T6 may be faintly fringed and tipped paler). Underwing-coverts sooty-black, tipped white. Wing of male 83–92, of female 80–94; tail of male 63–70, of female 61–67.

*P. l. insignis* Central and southern Africa. See Description. Smaller populations in NW Angola (below the escarpment), Congo and southern Gabon measure wing of male 81–88, of female 82–86; tail of male 69–73, of female 65–70. Another slightly smaller population in SW in Uganda and NE Zaïre (the Lake Edward region) has wing of male 83–89, of female 82–84; tail of male 63–68, of female 60–63.

**RELATIONSHIPS** Part of the *niger* superspecies. For relationships with White-shouldered Tit, see that species (p. 323).

**REFERENCES** Hall (1960).

# 72 SOUTHERN BLACK TIT *Parus niger*                     Plate 23

This large dusty-black tit is the best-known of the African tits and the first to be found to have a cooperative breeding system.

**IDENTIFICATION** Length 160 mm (6.25 in). A large, rather drab, black tit. Overall dull blue-black, greyer on the belly and vent, with white tips to the undertail-coverts and the tail fringed and tipped white. Wing extensively white, with solid white median coverts and neat fringes to the greater coverts and flight feathers. The female is variably greyer on the face and underparts (see Geographical Variation). Confusion is possible with White-winged Tit, as their ranges abut over a broad area, overlapping in parts of Zambia and possibly also Malawi. They are partially separated by habitat, White-winged Tit occurring in drier and more open areas such as *Acacia* savanna and woodland edge. Notably, the vocalisations of the two species are relatively dissimilar (see Voice). In all plumages, Southern Black is distinguished from White-winged by white fringes to the undertail-coverts, broad white fringes to the outer tail feathers and dark centres to at least the six outer greater coverts, clearly visible at rest (but note that worn 1st-adult White-winged may show dark centres to 1–2 outer greater coverts). On the closed wing dark centres also show over most of the secondaries, and thus Southern Black lacks White-winged's uniform white secondary panel. Additionally, male Southern Black has paler underparts, especially the belly and vent, lacking blue gloss, whilst female Southern Black has much paler ashy-brown underparts (paler even than juvenile White-winged Tit). Juveniles of both species have distinctly yellow-white fringes to the flight feathers (although these may be pure white on some White-winged), but juvenile Southern Black has rather paler underparts. In NE Namibia (and southern Angola?), the range of Southern Black approaches that of Carp's Tit. Male Southern Black is rather similar to both sexes of Carp's, but has a rather heavier bill, paler vent and narrower white fringes to the wing feathers, which do not form solid white patches. Notably, dark centres are visible at rest on all the greater coverts. Southern Black also shows prominent white fringes to the undertail-coverts (although Carp's may show whitish fringes, they are invariably narrow). Southern Black also has rather more white in the tail, and when fresh the white tip is broad and obvious. Female Southern Black are rather paler than Carp's, especially on the underparts, sooty-brown rather than glossy blue-black, and differ as above in the extent of white in the wing and tail. Juvenile Carp's is paler than the adult, but its underparts are still not so pale as on a female Southern Black, especially on the vent; note that the upperparts of juvenile Carp's are dark sooty-brown, lacking the blue gloss of an adult female Southern Black. Juvenile Southern Black is much paler ashy-brown on the underparts than any plumage of Carp's.

**SEX/AGE** Sexes moderately distinct, the female being slightly paler and greyer than the male on the face and underparts, with the breast dusky grey and belly pale grey; the upperparts are also less glossy (but see Geographical Variation). Juveniles resemble the female, but have the underparts paler and faintly washed buffy-brown, little white on the tip of the tail, and the whitish fringes to the primaries and secondaries washed yellow. 1st adult as adult, but retains a variable number of juvenile tail feathers and shows moult contrasts in the wings between the faded brown retained juvenile primaries and secondaries (which are fringed yellowish), alula and primary coverts, and the new median coverts and any new tertials or greater coverts (which are black, fringed white).

**VOICE** Noisy, maintaining continual conversational calling among members of the group. Commonest contact call a stereotyped nasal, buzzing *tsi-tsi-chacha* or *tit-si-chachacha* (on the 'chick-a-dee' theme and recalling Southern Grey Tit, although slower) and a harsh, chattering *chrrr-chrrr-chrrr*, whilst the female and young give a rasping begging call. Other calls include a whining *chew-ri*, *chew-ri*, *chew-ri* and a much mellower *cheru-cheru-cheru*, *cheru-cheru-cheru* (recalling certain bee-eaters). Also a musical *phee-cher-phee-cher* (Sinclair *et al.* 1993). The song, given relatively infrequently, is a combination of various shrill, ringing motifs, such as *chip-we*, *chip-we*, *chip-we*, *pi-cher*, *pi-cher*, *pi-cher*, *tiroo*, *tiroo*, *tiroo*, *peetit-woo*, *peetit-woo*, *peetit-woo*, *pee-wirrit*, *pee-wirrit*, *pee-wirrit*..., interspersed with harsh grating notes, and is very thrush-like. Voice reported to be distinct from that of White-winged Tit (Benson *et al.* 1971; Dowsett & Dowsett-Lemaire 1993), and that species appears to lack the stereotyped 'chick-a-dee' contact call. Both species, however, share pleasant, warbling songs, but that of Southern Black may be rather more strident, more repetitious and less mournful.

**DISTRIBUTION AND MOVEMENTS** Breeds in eastern **South Africa** in the Transvaal (although absent from the highveld areas of the south), Swaziland, Natal, Transkei and SE Cape Province (west to the Sundays and Gamtoos rivers and Algoa Bay). Also northern and eastern **Botswana** from the Tsodilo and Aha hills through the Okavango delta region and in the east north to Kasane in Chobe district and south through Lake Xau to Kanye. In NE **Namibia** confined to the valley of the Okavango river (from Andara west to Makamba) and the Caprivi Strip. Found throughout most of **Zimbabwe**, although absent from the eastern highlands, especially the moister eastern slopes (from Inyangani southwards to the Vumba, Banti, and Chimanimani mountains, but present Melsetter, Chipinga highlands and Mutare). In **Mozambique** recorded north to Tete province and Mirrote on the Lurio river (Vincent 1933, 1935), and in **Malawi** found in the Shire valley north in the east to Makanjila, and in the west to about Kasache, and in the northwest from Kasuni to Katumbi. Occurs in much of southern and SE **Zambia**, in Western province north to Senanga, Nangweshi, and Lupuka on the Mashi river, throughout Southern province, in Central province north to Chunga and Chilanga, and in Eastern province to Maweni and the Luangwa valley north to 10º 45' N. Occurs locally in SE **Tanzania** ('*fülleborni*', described from Songea, was shown by Eck 1988 to be a synonym of *xanthostomus*), and presumably occurs in SE **Angola** (Cuando-Cubango) adjacent to Botswana and the Caprivi Strip (see map in Hall & Moreau 1970), but not mentioned by Traylor (1963, although the reference to Cubango under *P. n. carpi* presumably refers to this form). Resident.

**HABITAT** Generally rather adaptable and found in a wide variety of woodland and wooded savanna, although generally prefers drier broadleaved woodland (including mopane and idigbo woodland), mixed deciduous woodland; thornveld (especially Camelthorn) and, in Zambia, the thinner, drier types of miombo (Benson *et al.* 1971, but see below). Also found in exotic plantations and large suburban gardens, but sparse and local in the highland grassland regions of South Africa, and absent from evergreen forests in the mist-belt of the Drakensberg and the coastal forests of Natal (although may be found on the edge of the forest). Usually below *c.* 1070 m. Habitat preferences seem to be partly dictated by the presence or absence of other tits. Thus, Southern Black Tit is usually found in less arid areas than the grey tits, although in Zimbabwe it occurs in dry miombo woodland alongside Miombo Tit, but is largely replaced by Cinnamon-breasted Tit in the richer, taller miombo woodland found in parts of northern and eastern Zimbabwe, the two species being hardly ever found in exactly the same areas (Benson *et al.* 1971; Irwin 1981). In Zambia, however, Southern Black was observed only once in miombo woodland, on the edge of a forest clearing, and was not considered a regular inhabitant of miombo. It was, however, the only tit to be regularly found in *Acacia*-dominated woodland (where its density was similar to the combined densities of Rufous-bellied and Miombo Tits in miombo woodland); its feeding niche is broadly similar to that of Rufous-bellied Tit, so it is to be expected that the two species are mutually exclusive (Alerstam & Ulfstrand 1977).

**POPULATION** Generally common, notably so in the Okavango woodland of NE Namibia (Winterbottom 1966a). In Malawi, however, never plentiful except in mopane woodland or *Acacia* savanna (Benson & Benson 1977), and not common on the northern periphery of the range in Zambia (Benson *et al.* 1971), while in central Mozambique markedly less numerous in the lowland forest-savanna woodland mosaic north of Beira, although again common in the more open habitats of the Manica Platform and in Tete district (Clancey 1971).

**HABITS** Found in pairs and in parties of up to six individuals, and may join mixed-species foraging flocks in the non-breeding season. Restless; flocks may travel up to 10 km per day whilst foraging. Birds keep contact with constant calling, and may also draw attention to themselves by tapping on dry tree pods, dropping the discarded husks to the ground. Groups defend a permanent territory (25–30 ha for a pair, 36–48 ha for 3–4 adults), the boundaries of which may outlive the individual occupants. Males are generally loyal to the territory, but females and juveniles may switch groups and territories, dependent young often switching in the mix-ups following territorial disputes. Disputes occur between groups on the territory boundaries, most frequently in winter (April–July), when flocks happen to arrive at the common boundary simultaneously, or come within vocal range. Most disputes involve chasing and physical fighting, though some do not progress beyond excited calling. Trespassing occurs occasionally if a flock is not challenged at the boundary of its territory, but in their neighbours' territory they will behave furtively (being silent rather than giving the normal contact calls), and if challenged will flee without offering resistance. Roosts in tree holes.

Generally forages in the middle and upper storeys of trees and bushes, 5–10 m above ground, on branches, under bark and in the foliage, at times on the trunk, sometimes tearing off pieces of bark or lichen. In summer the staple diet is Lepidoptera larvae, but in winter food items are smaller and birds may take up to eight times as many prey items to consume an equivalent weight. Although many caterpillars have evolved elaborate patterns and cryptic colours to escape detection, the tits are adept at finding them, apparently looking for indirect clues, such as leaf damage, to locate food. Other species of Lepidoptera have evolved toxic hairs to deter predators, but these, too, are eaten. In winter, searches the pods of certain trees for larvae and pupae.

**BREEDING BIOLOGY** Has a cooperative breeding system, which is generally encountered among tropical or subtropical, sedentary, long-lived species which occur at saturated densities in their preferred habitats, often defending permanent territories which are occupied by successive generations within the group. About 60% of breeding units are not simple pairs, but consist of an adult female, a dominant or 'alpha' male (which is paired with the female during breeding), up to three male 'helpers', and the young reared by the pair during the most recent breeding season (which may remain with the group for up to nine months before dispersing). Territories are defended for their food resources, especially critical in winter, and pairs with helpers rear more young, perhaps because groups are able to defend larger territories, with access to more, and possibly a greater diversity of, food. How do the helpers benefit? Only males have been recorded as helpers in Southern Black Tit, and there is a skewed sex ratio, with 40% of males unable to find mates. They have a choice between remaining as a helper in a favourable territory where they have the chance of succeeding the alpha male, or occupying a marginal territory immediately. The helper's choice is influenced by a low turnover in the population, and the fact that the preferred habitat is occupied to capacity (Tarboton 1981). Season throughout the range September–November (August–January), i.e. the austral spring. Display involves courtship feeding, and in groups with more than one male the alpha male will attempt to prevent the helpers from feeding the female by chasing them away, although with two or more helpers the alpha male cannot 'guard' the female all the time, one helper feeding the female while he chases the other(s) away. Once egg-laying is completed, the alpha male stops trying to prevent feeding the female and all males feed her during incubation and the early nestling period. Nest usually placed in a natural hole in a tree trunk, less frequently in an old woodpecker or barbet excavation, and will occasionally use hollow fence posts; reuse of the same hole is not usual. Sites are usually 2–5 m above ground. The nest, built by the female, is a soft pad of fine plant material (e.g. lichen and grasses) and hair. Clutch 4–5 (2–6, with 2–3 recorded only from Malawi): eggs white, finely speckled reddish, brown and grey; *c.* 13.9 x 18 mm. Female incubates, period 15 days, and when disturbed the sitting female may hiss and suddenly recoil the head, giving the impression of a snake striking. Fledging period 24 days, only the female brooding the young in the early stages and feeding them with food provided by the group. In the later stages, the female leaves the young for progressively longer periods and they are then fed directly by the males. Recently fledged juveniles are dependent on adults for food (their begging behaviour and calls being indistinguishable from the female's during courtship). Juveniles begin to forage about seven days after leaving the nest, becoming fully independent after *c.* 50 days. Single-brooded.

**DESCRIPTION** *P. n. niger* **Adult Male:** *In fresh plumage* (winter–spring), forehead black, upperparts from crown to uppertail-coverts black, glossed blue. Tail blackish, T1–T5 glossed blue on fringes to outer webs and tipped white, broadest on T5; T6 broadly fringed white on outer web, widest towards tip, and also tipped white (see figure below). Wing-coverts dark sooty-brown, longer lesser coverts tipped white, median coverts white (dark bases fully concealed), greater coverts tipped and fringed white (rather narrowly so on outermost, but outer web may be almost entirely white on inner three, sometimes inner five). Alula and primary coverts blackish, outer web of alula fringed white, primary coverts finely fringed (not tipped) white. Flight feathers dark sooty-brown, outermost tertial broadly fringed white on outer web, secondaries narrowly fringed and tipped white (fringes broader on inner secondaries), P10–P3 narrowly fringed white, only inwards of emarginations on P3–P6. Lores, sides of face and sides of neck dark sooty-brown. Chin, throat and breast sooty-brown with blue-black bloom. Rear flanks, belly and vent dull brown, washed grey, with paler grey-brown tips to some feathers. Undertail-coverts sooty-brown, tipped whitish. Thighs sooty-brown, feathers tipped whitish. Axillaries sooty-brown, marginal wing-coverts sooty-brown, tipped white, underwing-coverts blackish, broadly tipped white. *In worn plumage* (summer), white tips to tail feathers abrade, especially on T1, and pale fringes to greater coverts and tertials may be virtually absent. **Bare Parts:** Iris brown; bill black; legs and feet dark slate-grey, blue-grey or grey. **Adult Female:** As male, but upperparts slightly less glossy, chin and throat slightly paler (mid ash-grey), breast and especially belly rather paler (light grey, darker on sides of breast). Undertail-coverts grey, tipped whitish (as

male, but less contrast). **Juvenile:** Upperparts from forehead to uppertail-coverts dark brown, crown faintly glossed blue. Tail dark brown, T5 very finely fringed and tipped pale brown, T6 broadly fringed white on outer web and tipped white on inner. Wing-coverts dark brown, extent of white as adult. Alula dark brown, fringed white on outer web, primary coverts dark brown, very finely fringed buff. Flight feathers dark brown, outer tertial fringed whitish, secondaries and P10–P3 narrowly fringed whitish with distinct yellow wash, very fine on P3–P6 except inwards of emargination. Lores, sides of head and neck pale brown. Underparts pale brown with distinct grey wash, paler on belly and vent, undertail-coverts and thighs with faintly paler tips. **1st Adult:** See Sex/Age. **Measurements:** Wing of male 82–89, of female 76.5–81; tail of male 69–73.5, of female 64.5–71; bill 11.5–13; tarsus 17–21. Weight 19.9–26 g.

**MOULT** Adult post-breeding complete (late January–late May, Transvaal; January–May, Zambia; June, Mozambique). Post-juvenile partial-incomplete, includes tertials, a variable number of tail feathers and greater coverts (usually all greater coverts?), sometimes the alula and up to at least three inner secondaries (at *c.* 4 months old; March–April, Transvaal; March, Natal; January, Zambia; July–August, Malawi; February–March, June, August, Mozambique).

**GEOGRAPHICAL VARIATION** Slight, with three intergrading races recognised: *xanthostomus* in the north and west and nominate *niger* from the southeastern coastal strip, both with relatively little white in the wing, and *ravidus* with rather more white in the wing (as Carp's Tit). Subspecific boundaries imperfectly understood (compare Clancey 1964a, 1972 and 1980); ranges given based on Clancey *in litt.* (1990).

**P. n. niger** Eastern Cape Province, Natal, Zululand, SE Swaziland and southern Mozambique (north to the Limpopo river mouth). Intergrades with *ravidus* in eastern Swaziland and southern Mozambique. See Description.

**P. n. ravidus** Central Mozambique (from the Limpopo north to the Zambezi), the plateau of Zimbabwe and northern Transvaal. Poorly marked. As nominate *niger*, but white in greater coverts more extensive (almost as white as Carp's Tit, forming a solid white panel on inner 3–4 greater coverts), white fringes to primaries and secondaries slightly broader. Female with underparts rather paler and greyer (and slightly paler than *xanthostomus*), plain mouse-grey (Clancey *in litt.* 1990). Eastern lowland populations smaller, but on plateau of Zimbabwe as large as *xanthostomus*. Wing of male 82–88, of female 80–82, tail, of male 70–75, of female 70.5–75, bill 11.5–13.5.

**P. n. xanthostomus** Namibia, Angola, Botswana, Zambia, NW and northern (?) Zimbabwe, Malawi, northern Mozambique and SE Tanzania. As nominate *niger*, but male with very slightly paler underparts, especially sides of breast and flanks, female with underparts slightly paler (compared with *ravidus*, underparts slightly darker and much invaded with black). Larger than

*Figure 72.1 Tail of adult male* P. n. niger.

nominate *niger.* Wing of male 81–90, of female 80–86; tail of male 72–78, of female 67–77; bill 11–13.

**RELATIONSHIPS** Part of the *niger* superspecies, in which Hall & Moreau (1970) included all the African black tits (i.e. White-backed, White-bellied, White-shouldered, White-winged, Southern Black and Carp's). Short *et al.* (1990), however, excluded White-backed Tit from the superspecies, and it is restricted by Sibley & Monroe (1990) to just White-shouldered, White-winged and Southern Black/Carp's Tits. Southern Black was formerly considered conspecific with White-winged Tit, but the two are rather distinct and overlap in Zambia in Western and Southern provinces (Mazabuka, Chilanga and Chunga; in the Kafue basin the overlap zone is at least 100 km wide) and probably also on the Eastern province plateau. There is also reported to be an overlap in Malawi (Hall & Moreau 1970), but, although Southern Black Tit *may* be present in western Dedza district (Lilongwe to the upper Bua river), only White-winged Tit has actually been recorded in this area, and thus overlap between the two species has not been proven (Benson & Benson 1977). Nevertheless, the overlap in Zambia, apparently without hybridisation or intergradation, confirms their specific separation, and the two species also have quite distinct vocalisations (Benson *et al.* 1971; Dowsett & Dowsett-Lemaire 1993). For relationship to Carp's Tit, see that species.

**REFERENCES** Clancey (1972), Ginn *et al.* (1989), Maclean (1993), Tarboton (1981).

## 73 CARP'S TIT *Parus carpi*                                      Plate 23
Other name: Carp's Black Tit

Sometimes treated as a race of Southern Black Tit, in many ways Carp's is closer to White-winged Tit. It overlaps, however, with the latter species in southern Angola and is thus treated as a distinct species.

**IDENTIFICATION** Length 150 mm (6 in). A relatively small, neat all-black tit, rather 'square-headed' with a full nape. Upperparts glossy blue-black with the tail narrowly fringed and tipped white. Much white in the wing, with the median coverts all white, the greater coverts appearing as a solid white patch with dark centres visible only on the outer 4–5 feathers, and the outermost tertial and the secondaries broadly fringed white, forming a wide white line on the closed wing. Face and underparts deep brownish-black, glossed blue, with the undertail-coverts and thighs variably but always narrowly fringed whitish. The range of Carp's Tit abuts that of Southern Black Tit in NE Namibia (where Southern Black is confined to the Okavango valley and Caprivi Strip). Carp's is distinguished from male Southern Black Tit by its smaller size, relatively shorter tail and smaller bill, with glossier, deeper black body plumage, especially on the underparts, lacking a noticeably paler belly and vent. There is usually rather less white in the tail of Carp's Tit, and it often lacks white fringes to the undertail-coverts (although some Carp's may show as much white as Southern Black). In addition, compared with the western subspecies of Southern Black Tit, Carp's has broader white fringes to the greater coverts, and on the closed wing the inner 4–5 greater coverts are solidly white, whereas Southern Black usually shows dark centres to all the greater coverts. Carp's also has broader white fringes to the outer tertial and inner secondaries which form a more uniformly solid white panel. (Note that Carp's wing pattern is nearly identical to that of the *eastern* subspecies of Southern Black Tit.) Female Carp's differs from the male only in its dark brown face and throat, but female Southern Black is rather paler, with sooty-brown underparts.

Juvenile Carp's has paler underparts than the adult, but is still not so pale as female Southern Black, especially on the vent, although the extent of white in the wing may be similar. Juvenile Carp's, however, has dark sooty-brown upperparts, lacking the blue gloss of adults, but is *much* darker below than juvenile Southern Black, which has ashy-brown underparts. The range overlaps that of White-winged Tit in SW Angola. Compared with White-winged (of the race *insignis*), Carp's is smaller, with a relatively smaller bill. On the closed wing, dark centres are visible on the outer 4–5 greater coverts, whereas in White-winged greater coverts are usually uniformly white. In addition, the outer tail feathers have slightly broader white fringes and tips. The undertail-coverts of Carp's are variable: some are uniformly blackish (as on White-winged), most show vestigial pale fringes, visible in the field, while others are broadly fringed white (as on Southern Black). Sexual dimorphism is slight in both species, although female Carp's has the face and throat marginally paler and browner than the male. Juveniles of both species are rather similar, but compared with White-winged juvenile Carp's has narrower white fringes and tips to the greater coverts and duller and narrower pale fringes to the flight feathers (off-white to pale buff-brown), not forming an extensive white panel on the closed wing.

**SEX/AGE** The sexes differ only slightly, the female having the throat and sides of the head paler and browner, with slightly less white in the wing than the male. Juvenile duller than the adult, with deep brownish-black upperparts with a reduced gloss (especially faint in females), similarly dull underparts, less white in the tail, and the fringes to the primaries and secondaries (and, in the female, the greater coverts) duller, tinged buffy-yellow. 1st adults can be aged in the hand by moult contrasts: the tertials, greater coverts and a variable number of secondaries are replaced and the retained juvenile flight feathers are contrastingly browner, with the pale fringes relatively more abraded.

**VOICE** Overall rather similar to that of Southern Black Tit. Calls include a rather bulbul-like *churia-churia-churia*, a squeaky, slurred *si-u, si-u, si-u*, clear, whistled *piu-piu-piu-piu-piu...*, *witch-a witch-a witch-a...*, and a harsh, rasping, nasal *tsi-tsi, tsi-cha-cha-cha-cha...*, the last a 'chick-a-dee' call close to the commonest call of Southern Black Tit.

**DISTRIBUTION AND MOVEMENTS** Southern Africa, in **Angola** south along the coastal strip from Sumbe (Novo Redondo) in Guanza Sul through Benguela to Namibe (Mocamedes), extending inland into Namib above the escarpment to Quilengues and Sa da Bandeira, and south and west of the escarpment in southern and western Huila. In **Namibia** found in the highlands and Namib edge (absent from the Namib desert), from the Angola border south through Ovamboland, Etosha NP (east to Halali camp), Otavi, the Waterberg plateau and the Damaraland highlands, to Hardap Dam and Mariental in northern Great Namaqualand; extends west to the Kaokoveld and the lower Cunene river, but absent from the Kalahari sandveld and Okavango woodlands of NE Namibia (extent of range in NE Namibia problematic; Hall & Moreau 1970 map '*P. niger*' from much of NE Namibia, but made no distinction between Southern Black Tit and Carp's Tit). Resident.

**HABITAT** Endemic to the South West Arid Zone of southern Africa, where found in *Acacia* woodland and scrub, often in the better-developed stands along watercourses, and also in dry mopane woodland. Has a preference for rugged, hilly country, especially adjacent to escarpments and koppies, and in SW Angola found in the tangled thickets of the coastal grasslands (Hall 1960). Recorded in Angola at 1220–1830 m, and in Namibia at 1220 m.

**POPULATION** Uncommon and rather local, the species may have rather precise habitat requirements which are not yet fully understood.

**HABITS** Found singly, in pairs or in parties of up to six birds, and occasionally joins mixed-species foraging flocks in the dry winter months. Active and acrobatic, forages in smaller trees and bushes, moving quickly from tree to tree with a dipping flight. Food insects, but also at times mainly seeds; to obtain larvae or seeds pecks at pods or insect galls, woodpecker-like, to extract the contents.

**BREEDING BIOLOGY** Season October–January. The nest is placed in a natural tree hole, sometimes an old barbet or woodpecker excavation; one near Windhoek in Namibia was in an iron pole 50 mm in diameter supporting a road sign, the nest probably being at ground level 2 m below the entrance hole. The nest is simply a pad of vegetable down or animal hair. Clutch 3 (3–5): eggs white, variably tinged pink, and densely spotted with reddish-brown and grey; 20.5 x

14.5 mm. Incubation and fledging periods unknown. Presumably a cooperative breeder, with breeding pairs assisted in feeding the young by one, possibly two, adult 'helpers' (C.F. Clinning *in litt.* 1991).

**DESCRIPTION Adult Male:** *In fresh plumage* (about April–September), crown to uppertail-coverts glossy blue-black. Tail deep brownish-black, fringes glossy blue-black; variably fringed and tipped white (at the most extensive, T3–T5 finely tipped white, T5 narrowly fringed white on distal half of outer web and T6 broadly fringed and tipped white; at least extensive T5 finely tipped white on outer web and T6 tipped and fringed white on distal half of outer web) (see figure below). Marginal coverts blackish, tipped white. Wing-coverts and flight feathers deep brownish-black; lesser coverts tipped white, medi-

*Figure 73.1 Tail of adult male.*

an coverts white (dark bases fully concealed), greater coverts fringed and more broadly tipped white, outer webs largely white on inner greaters (on closed wing, dark centres visible on about five outer coverts, inner coverts appearing solidly white); alula fringed (and on outer web tipped) white, primary coverts with variable narrow whitish fringes to outer webs; inner two tertials narrowly fringed glossy blue-black, outermost tertial fringed white; outer web of secondaries fringed and tipped white, broadly so on inner 2–3 (on the closed wing forming a solid white line); primaries narrowly fringed white (extending around tips on inner primaries), only inwards of emarginations on P4–P5, P2–P4 faintly tipped white. Lores, cheeks and ear-coverts deep brownish-black, faintly glossed blue, underparts (including thighs) similar but blue gloss more prominent; undertail-coverts and thighs variably but narrowly fringed whitish. Underwing-coverts and axillaries black, broadly tipped white. *In worn plumage* (about September–April), overall duller and less glossy, pale fringes to greater and primary coverts and flight feathers abraded, and outer 4–5 greater coverts may appear solidly dark. **Bare Parts:** Iris brown to dark brown; bill black with paler cutting edges; legs and feet grey, blue-grey, dark slate-blue or black. **Adult Female:** In fresh plumage as male, but lores, cheeks, ear-coverts and throat paler and browner, white fringes on greater coverts, secondaries and primaries average slightly narrower. **Juvenile Male:** Upperparts deep brownish-black, glossed dull blue on cap, mantle and scapulars. Underparts similar, glossed blue on breast. Tail as adult, but fringes to T6 narrow, and no white tips. Wings slightly browner than on adult, lacking blue gloss to fringes of inner tertials. Extent of white in coverts, tertials and inner secondaries similar to adult, fringes to primaries and secondaries duller,tinged dull buffy-yellow. Primary coverts lack white fringes. **Juvenile Female**: As juvenile male, but cap, mantle, scapulars and breast only faintly glossed blue, fringes (not tips) of greater coverts buffy-brown. **1st Adult**: As adult (see Sex/Age). **Measurements**: Wing of male 75–83, of female 74.5–82; tail of male 61–70 (once 75 Hall 1960), of female 61–70, bill 11–13; tarsus 17.5–19. Weight: no information.

**MOULT**   Adult post-breeding complete (January–April; a bird moulting the tail in September could perhaps be in pre-breeding moult?). Post-juvenile partial-incomplete, includes greater coverts, alula, tertials and a variable number of secondaries and tail feathers (April–May).

**GEOGRAPHICAL VARIATION** None.

**HYBRIDS** Two males from 'Elephant Vlei' (in the Kavango valley, c. 18° S, 18° E; Winterbottom 1966a) were considered by Hall (1960) to be intermediate between Carp's and Southern Black Tits.They have the belly and vent matt black, with some white in the undertail-coverts and thighs, broad white fringes to the inner two greater coverts only, and possibly a fine white tip to T6 (although their tails are quite worn). Measurements: wing 82, 87; tail 69, 72; bill 13.1, 12.8. They are from the region where the ranges of Carp's and Southern Black Tits approach one another, and these birds may be hybrids between two species, intergrades between two subspecies, or perhaps just normal variants of Southern Black Tit (or possibly Carp's Tit). More information is required to resolve the issue.

**RELATIONSHIPS** A member of the *niger* super-species, and originally described as *P. niger carpi*, i.e. as a subspecies of Southern Black Tit, largely because of similarities in habitat rather than in appearance. Clancey (1964a, 1972), however, demonstrated that Carp's is closer to White-winged Tit, with deep glossy black plumage, reduced sexual dimorphism, and little or no white in the undertail-coverts, a relationship supported by Eck (1988). The range of Carp's Tit does not overlap with that of Southern Black Tit (although the situation in NE Namibia is far from clear), while in southern Angola it apparently overlaps slightly with White-winged Tit (which occurs largely to the northeast of Carp's Tit in miombo woodland: see map in Hall & Moreau 1970). There is no intergradation in Angola between Carp's and the much larger White-winged Tit, supporting the treatment by Clancey (1972, 1985) of Carp's as a full species. Specific status is, however, disputed by Dowsett & Forbes-Watson (1993) on the grounds that Carp's Tit resembles Southern Black Tit in appearance (lacking the very extensive white in the wing of White-winged Tit), and more importantly that its vocalisations are typical of Southern Black Tit (and very different from White-winged). Sibley & Monroe (1990) list Carp's Tit as a race of Southern Black, but Sibley & Monroe (1993) amend this to list it as a race of White-winged Tit (citing Clancey 1972 and Eck 1988). Given the acknowledged vocal differences between Carp's and White-winged Tits, and the differences in appearance from Southern Black, it seems best to follow Southern African authors and treat it as a distinct species, pending further investigation.

**REFERENCES** Clancey (1972, 1985), Maclean (1993).

## 74 WHITE-BELLIED TIT *Parus albiventris*                Plate 24
Other name: White-breasted Tit

The most distinctive of the African black tits, this species has a curiously disjunct distribution, with the populations in East and West Africa separated by about 1500 km.

**IDENTIFICATION** Length 150 mm (6 in). A large, stocky, long-tailed, black and white tit. Head, upperparts, bib and upper flanks black, faintly glossy (duller and greyer in the female), and lower breast to undertail-coverts white. Tail black, broadly bordered and more narrowly tipped white; wings black with two broad white wingbars (especially prominent on the median coverts), broad white fringes to the outer tertials and inner secondaries, and narrower pale fringes to the remaining flight feathers. Immediately identified as a 'black' tit, and the white lower breast, belly and undertail-coverts are diagnostic. From behind, separated from White-shouldered Tit by the white rim and tip to the tail (almost lacking on White-shouldered).

**SEX/AGE** Sexes distinct. Female duller than the male, with sootier, coal-grey upperparts and bib and a browner 'face' and throat; in the field, there may be little obvious difference in upperpart coloration from the male's, but the 'face' and bib are often clearly paler and browner (and in the hand the female may show a distinct contrast between the brown throat and greyer breast). Juvenile marginally distinct; as the adult female, but with the upperparts and bib browner and the white fringes to the flight feathers faintly washed yellow; in addition, all except the outer tail feathers lack white tips (and the rectrices are also slightly narrower and more pointed than the adult's). 1st adult as the respective adult sex, but retains the juvenile primaries and secondaries, which are more abraded than the adult's at a similar time of year, although the yellow tone to their fringes is faint or absent owing to bleaching and wear: look for moult contrasts in the wing, either within the greater coverts, or between the new greater coverts and tertials and the old flight feathers, primary coverts and sometimes alula, and also for moult contrasts in the tail, where any new feathers are fresher, blacker, and show fine white tips (absent on all but the outermost juvenile tail feathers).

**VOICE** Calls include a hoarse buzzing note, introduced by a stuttering, thin, sweet couplet, in a 'chick-a-dee' pattern: *pt'tsi-tsi cher-cher-cher-cher*. Sharp *tss, tsee* or *tss, tss, tss tee* phrases may also be given, and the song is a soft, repeated, warbling *pee-pee-purr* (Mackworth-Praed & Grant 1960; Williams & Arlott 1980).

**DISTRIBUTION AND MOVEMENTS** Two disjunct populations. In West Africa found in the montane district of western **Cameroon** (localities include Bamenda and Kumbo), although also recorded from the forest-savanna mosaic and on the Adamawa plateau. Two records from SE **Nigeria**, around the Obudu plateau (April 1977 and April 1981). In East Africa occurs in southern **Sudan** in the highlands of southern Eastern Equatoria (Didinga highlands, Dongotona mountains, Mount Kinyeti/Imatong mountains), and in NE **Uganda** in Karamoja and the Elgon region. Found in the highlands and peripheral lowlands of western **Kenya**, throughout the southwestern plateau, north to Mount Elgon and the forested islands of Mount Nyiru and Mount Kulal, and east to Mount Kenya, the western Tsavo region and (formerly) Tsavo East, Sagala and Samburu in SE Kenya and perhaps the coastal strip from Lamu south to Vanga. Also interior central and northern **Tanzania**, west to Mwanza, Tabora, Rukwa and the Fip (= Ufipa) plateau, south to Mount Rungwe and east to Kilosa, southern Masailand, and southern Arusha (Kijunguu). Resident.

**HABITAT** In Cameroon, found in highland savanna at 1070–2135 m. In East Africa, habitat essentially light woodland and forest edge, in bushland, *Acacia* savanna, cultivation, gardens and riverine woods, and sometimes forests; perhaps formerly coastal scrub (see below). In East Africa occurs at up to 3400 m, mostly above 1000 m, in areas with comparatively good rainfall (above 500 mm p.a.). Found above 1600 m in SE Sudan.

**POPULATION** In East Africa and Sudan locally common, but there is some evidence of a retraction of the range from the lowest altitudes. The species has recently disappeared from one formerly regular haunt in Tsavo East NP, and Jackson (1938) cited records from Sagala and Samburu in SE Kenya, arid areas that are also now abandoned. He also mentioned this species for the coastal strip from Lamu to Vanga, but gave no actual localities. Apart from error, this may indicate that a range contraction was well under way in Jackson's time (Lewis & Pomeroy 1989).

**HABITS** Found singly, in pairs or in parties (quite large flocks have been recorded). May join mixed-species foraging flocks, and sometimes a key 'nuclear' species in such flocks (e.g. in dry montane forest near Nairobi in Kenya). Restless, noisy and active. Roosts in holes in trees. Usually forages in the middle storey and canopy of trees, but may also be found near ground level, gleaning among foliage and along branches, investigating nooks and crannies in the bark. Food insects and especially spiders, and may visit flowers, presumably for insects.

**BREEDING BIOLOGY** Poorly known. Season: Kenya highlands, mainly December–June, but with records throughout the year; Tanzania, October–January (thus breeding in both countries mainly in the rains, with scattered records at other times); Sudan, January. The nest is placed in decaying stumps, holes, or crevices behind bark, usually at some height from the ground (recorded up to c. 8 m). The nest itself is a cup of hair, bark fibre and vegetable down. Clutch 3–5: eggs white, with sparse maroon spotting concentrated at the larger end.

**DESCRIPTION** **Adult Male**: *In fresh plumage*, upperparts black, faintly glossed blue. Tail black, all feathers tipped white, narrowly so on T1, more broadly towards T6; T4 variably but narrowly fringed white on distal two-thirds of outer web, T5 variably but broadly fringed white on outer web and very finely fringed white on distal half of inner web, T6 often all white on outer web and finely fringed white on inner web. Median coverts white, remainder of wing black, longer feathers of lesser coverts tipped white; greater coverts fringed and broadly tipped white (fringes broader on the inner coverts, and outer web of inner two may be entirely white); alula fringed and tipped white; primary coverts finely fringed faintly paler and browner; outer web of longest tertial broadly fringed white, outer web of central tertial variably fringed white; secondaries narrowly fringed and tipped white, more broadly so on innermost; P3–P10 narrowly fringed white, only inwards of emarginations on P3–P7 (when very fresh, primaries may be faintly tipped paler). Lores, ear-coverts and sides of neck black. Throat and upper breast black, glossed blue, the bib extending irregularly onto blackish upper flanks; feathers of lower border of bib tipped whitish, especially at the sides. Lower breast, lower flanks, belly, vent and undertail-coverts white, thighs sooty-black, feathers tipped whitish. Axillaries blackish, underwing-coverts white. *In worn plumage*, face, throat and breast slightly browner, white tips to tail feathers abraded, white fringes on flight feathers abraded, especially on secondaries. Some birds may be rather greyer (Bannerman 1948). **Bare Parts**: Iris dark brown or black; bill black; legs and feet blue-grey to black. **Adult Female**: As male, but upperparts and sides of neck slightly greyer, duller and a sootier black, lacking gloss; when very fresh, feathers of upperparts tipped brownish. Lores, supercilium, cheeks and ear-coverts sooty-brown, often also chin and throat; remainder of bib either as upperparts or slightly paler and greyer. Flight feathers very slightly paler and browner. **Juvenile**: Both sexes as adult female, but upperparts slightly browner (more sooty-brown, less grey), T1–T5 lack white tips, white fringes on primaries and secondaries washed yellowish, throat slightly paler and browner. **1st Adult**: As respective sex of adult (see Sex/Age). **Measurements**: Wing 73–88, of male 76–88, of female 76–86; tail of male 58–70, of female 58–67; bill 11.5–14.5; tarsus 16–21.5. Weight: no information.

**MOULT** Adult post-breeding complete (February–October in East Africa). Post-juvenile partial, includes median coverts, a variable number of greater coverts (sometimes all), tertials, a variable number of tail feathers and sometimes alula (October–November and March in East Africa).

**GEOGRAPHICAL VARIATION** None, despite the great distance separating the Cameroon population from East African birds (suggesting that the two populations were in contact until relatively recently).

**RELATIONSHIPS** Part of the *niger* superspecies, and the range does not overlap with those of White-winged and Southern Black Tits. Almost allopatric with White-shouldered Tit, the ranges overlapping in Cameroon and marginally in western Kenya and SE Sudan (and inclusion of this species in the *niger* superspecies is disputed by Sibley & Monroe 1990, on the basis of an 'extensive' overlap in range). In these areas White-bellied Tit is separated altitudinally from White-shouldered, occurring at higher elevations, but away from these limited areas of overlap White-bellied Tit appears to undergo an 'ecological release', and is not restricted by altitude. The strangely disjunct distribution, with widely separated populations in West and East Africa, may be a product of this relationship with White-shouldered Tit.

**REFERENCES** Lewis & Pomeroy (1989), Mackworth-Praed & Grant (1960).

# 75 WHITE-BACKED TIT  *Parus leuconotus*  Plate 24

This distinctive but poorly known tit is restricted to the highlands of Ethiopia and Eritrea, and is one of 28 species endemic to those two countries.

**IDENTIFICATION** Length 135 mm (5.5 in). Bill relatively small. Overall black with a faint blue gloss to much of the plumage, tail rather narrowly rimmed white. Mantle dirty brown-white, forming a conspicuous 'saddle'. At all times, the blackish plumage and buffish-white mantle are distinctive.

**SEX/AGE** Sexes very similar, the female averaging a little duller on the underparts. Juvenile rather similar to adult, but duller, very slightly browner and less glossy, with the pale saddle tinged buff. 1st adult as adult, but the retained juvenile primaries, secondaries, primary coverts and outer greater coverts are contrastingly duller and browner than the adjacent tertials and inner greater coverts; may also show moult contrasts in the tail.

**VOICE** Vocabulary poorly known but evidently complex. Calls include a rather sparrow-like *tchu*, often given as a triplet, *tchu-chu-chu*, a clicking but liquid *plit* or *quit*, a harder *pik* and a thin *tsit*; the *plit* note may be given in duet with a mellower (and bulbul-like) *tchiu-p'du*, thus *plit, tchiu-p'du, plit, tchiu-p'du*.... Also gives a variety of 'chick-a-dee'-type calls, including a harsh *tzzet-tzee-tzee, tzzet-tzee-tzee-tzzet...* and a thinner and faster *tsi-za-za-za*. Song consists of rather loud stereotyped phrases which may recall a bulbul in tone, e.g. *tchu, plit'kli chu-eee'u, tchu, plit'kli chu-eee'u* (incorporating the '*plit*' and the rather sparrow-like '*tchu*' calls). Vocalisations also include a loud *tit-teet-toraykeet, jit-jit*, and *geeb-geeb-geeb* (J.S. Ash *in litt.*).

**DISTRIBUTION AND MOVEMENTS** Endemic to northern and central Ethiopia in the western and southeastern highlands south to about Jima and Ginir and c. 7° 30' N; also Eritrea.

**HABITAT** Woodlands, thickets and forests, especially in the valleys of small streams. More specifically *Hagenia* forests, highland bamboo (*Arundinaria*), and juniper-podocarp-olive forest at 1800–3200 m, and giant heath forest and *Hypericum*-bamboo at higher altitudes (3200–3500 m). Generally found above 1800 m, although also recorded at 1370 m near Jima.

**POPULATION** Locally frequent to common except in Eritrea, where it is uncommon. No evidence of any recent decline in abundance (Ash & Gullick 1989).

**HABITS** Occurs in pairs or small parties.

**BREEDING BIOLOGY** Season in Ethiopia May and August (J.S. Ash *in litt.*), and possibly also January. Otherwise unknown.

**DESCRIPTION Adult Male**: *In fresh plumage* (November to about June), forehead blackish, crown and nape black with feather tips glossed deep blue. Mantle dirty creamy-white; grey-black feather bases show patchily, especially on upper border of mantle. Scapulars, back, rump and uppertail-coverts sooty-black, faintly glossed deep blue. Tail sooty-black, fringes of T1–T5 slightly glossier blue-black; faint white tips to T4–T5, T6 very finely fringed and tipped white, Wings sooty-black, finely fringed deep glossy blue (very finely and faintly on secondaries and primaries, and only inwards of the emarginations on P3–P7, fringes absent P1–P2; occasionally shows white tips to one or more tertials or secondaries and fine white fringes or tips to P3–P5). Lores, supercilium, cheeks and ear-coverts sooty-black. Chin, throat, sides of neck and breast blackish with faint deep blue gloss. Flanks, belly, vent, thighs and undertail-coverts sooty-black, undertail-coverts may show whitish tips. Axillaries and underwing-coverts sooty-black. *In worn plumage* (about June–October) may show more blackish on upper mantle as brown-white feather tips abrade, flight feathers and tail duller and browner, underparts slightly duller, paler and less glossy. When very worn, brown-white patch on mantle may be restricted to V-shaped 'saddle'. **Bare Parts**: Iris brown; bill black; legs and feet dark slate to black. **Adult Female**: Underparts average a sootier brown and less glossy. **Juvenile**: As adult, but overall slightly duller and browner, lacking the blue gloss, and with little or no gloss to the fringes of the greater coverts, tertials or flight feathers, although may show fine white tips to greater coverts. Pale 'saddle' slightly duller and tinged buff (looser plumage may also reveal more of dark feather centres); little or no white in tail. **1st Adult**: See Sex/Age. **Measurements**: Wing 71–81, of male 73–81, of female 73–81; tail of male 54–62, of female 53–61; bill 10.5–13.6; tarsus 17–21.

Weight 16.6 g, 16.8 g (J.S. Ash *in litt.*).
**MOULT** Adult post-breeding complete (October–June). Post-juvenile partial, includes tertials, a variable number of inner greater coverts, and some or all of the tail feathers (October–June).
**GEOGRAPHICAL VARIATION** None.
**RELATIONSHIPS** Placed in the *niger* superspecies by Hall & Moreau (1970), and, although specifically excluded from the superspecies by Short *et al.* (1990) and Sibley & Monroe (1990), it is clearly closely related to the other African black tits.
**REFERENCES** Urban (1980), Urban & Brown (1971).

## 76 DUSKY TIT *Parus funereus* Plate 14

Confined to evergreen forest, this unusually drab tit has a curiously local and sporadic distribution, but may have been widely overlooked.

**IDENTIFICATION** Length 145 mm (5.75 in). A uniformly dark tit with a short, rather broad-based bill. Upperparts blackish, faintly glossed dull, oily blue-green. Underparts dull black in the male, slightly paler and greyer in the female. The reddish eyes are surprisingly conspicuous in the field. Distinctive. No other tit occurs in its forest habitat, and confusion is more likely with other uniformly dark forest birds (e.g. Maxwell's Black Weaver, Square-tailed Drongo or Western Black Flycatcher), but Dusky Tit is smaller and shorter-tailed than the various confusion species, with typical tit-like actions and calls.
**SEX/AGE** Sexes distinct. In the male, the underparts are blackish with slightly greyer flanks, and in very fresh plumage there may be a grey bloom to the entire underparts. In the female, the underparts are pale mouse-grey, wearing to dull brown with faintly greyer streaking. Thus, males in fresh plumage may be close to females, but have a greenish-blue gloss to the breast whilst females have a distinct brownish tone to the underparts. Additionally, females have slightly duller and greyer upperparts, especially the head and upper mantle, with a reduced gloss; the crown may appear faintly scaled owing to grey feather fringes. Females have been reported to have orange eyes, compared with red in the male (e.g. Mackworth-Praed & Grant 1973), but five females from Mount Nimba, Liberia, all had red eyes. Juveniles of both sexes are almost as dark as the adult male, but have reduced pale fringes to the flight feathers and large white spots on the tips of the median and greater coverts, forming spotted wingbars. Juveniles' eyes are brown, but apparently quickly change to red, before the post-juvenile moult (both red and brown eyes are noted for juveniles collected on Mount Nimba). No information on the 1st adult, although females moult from a blackish juvenile plumage into a greyer 1st-adult plumage.

**VOICE** Noisy, with very varied vocalisations. Most calls are short whistled or metallic single-syllable notes, the alarm note churring (Chapin 1954; Mackworth-Praed & Grant 1973). They include a harsh, metallic and typically tit-like *chut-chut*, *tzi-tzi-tzi* (a 'chick-a-dee'-like call), a clearer and more whistled *tsi-tsi-tsi-tu*, a slow, deliberate series of harsh, slightly trilled motifs, *tirrru, tirrru, tirrru, turee, tirrru...*, and a sparrow-like chattering. Dowsett (1990) noted the song as a pot-pourri of various calls and churrs, with occasional imitations of other birds; it is a rather jumbled medley of harsh and whistled notes (recalling an *Acrocephalus* warbler or perhaps a drongo). Another 'song' is a slow, ringing, metallic *tsi-piu, tsi-piu, tsi-piu* or *tsi-pupu, tsi-pu, tsi-pupu, tsitsi-pu...* (on the 'tea-cher' theme, and presumably equivalent to a far-carrying squeaky whistle, *fui-tsiu*, noted by Dowsett 1990); also a repeated '*zi-zizi-huititi-tihui-tihui*' (Mackworth-Praed & Grant 1973).
**DISTRIBUTION AND MOVEMENTS** A rather fragmented distribution in west and central Africa, extending marginally into east and southern Africa. In **Sierra Leone** recorded from Mogbai in the northern Gola forest (Kenema district, Eastern province), and in **Liberia** recorded only from Mount Nimba (and presumably occurs on adjacent areas of the Nimba massif in both Guinea and the Ivory Coast). In SE **Guinea** noted on the Ziama massif, Macenta, and in the **Ivory Coast** recorded from La Téné and Tai NP in the extreme southwest. In **Ghana** recorded from the Eastern region at Worobong and Atewa Forest Reserves, with an old specimen record from near Elmina on the coast. In **Cameroon** recorded from few localities, but thought to be widespread and found in extreme SW **Central African Republic** in Sangha-Mbaere prefecture. Hall & Moreau (1970) note that old records from 'Gaboon' have not subsequently been confirmed, but this species has been

found commonly from 1976 onwards in NE **Gabon** in Ogooué-Ivindo province, and there may have been a recent range extension (Brosset & Erard 1986). Found in much of northern and central **Zaïre** east to the mountains of the Albertine Rift, north to northern Equateur (Kungu, Businga) and northern Haut-Zaïre (Aketi, Buta, Poko, Niangara, Watsa and Djugu) and south to the Kwa river, central Kasai (Luebo, Lusambo) and to the Itombwe massif in Kivu province; apparently absent from the Mayombe region of NW Zaïre (records are widely scattered and the mapped range is tentative). Occurs in western **Rwanda** in the western part of the Nyungwe forest and the Cyamudongo forest, near Nyakabuye (a western relict of the Nyungwe). Also southern and western **Uganda** from Budongo, Bugoma and Itwara forests to the Kasyoha, Lutoto, Kalinzu, Maramagambo and Impenetrable (Bwindi) forests, east to the Sezibwa river and Mabira (i.e. the Victoria Nile). Isolated populations are found in the relict Kakamega and Nandi forests of western **Kenya** and in SE **Sudan**, where confined to the foothills of the Imatong mountains in Eastern Equatoria. Also perhaps disjunct is the population in **Angola** around Gabela, on the escarpment of the central plateau in Cuanza Sul. Reported from **Equatorial Guinea** (**Mbini**), but confirmation required.

**HABITAT** Confined to primary and secondary evergreen forest and (as in northern Zaïre and Uganda) thicker areas of gallery forest, and perhaps most often seen along forest edges, tracks and in clearings. In Gabon recorded from old plantations, in Angola found in tall trees amid coffee plantations and noted once in Liberia in forest-grassland mosaic. Found at low and middle altitudes, in Liberia at 550–800 m on Mount Nimba, in Guinea above 800 m, in the Congo basin up to 1500 m, and in Kivu in SE Zaïre recorded at up to 2200 m (Lippens & Wille 1976), in the Nyungwe forest of Rwanda up to 2500 m (Uwinka), but more abundant below 2100 m, and recorded at 900–1700 m in Uganda and western Kenya (up to 2130 m in the Impenetrable forest of SW Uganda) and up to 2000 m in Sudan.

**POPULATION** Although noted as fairly common in Cameroon by Traylor (1961), generally considered uncommon (e.g. Guinea, Sudan and the Central African Republic) or rare (e.g. Ivory Coast, Ghana). In well-watched localities, however, such as Kakamega forest in western Kenya, it is reasonably common, and the species may be best regarded as locally common. In NE Gabon, a density of 25–30 individuals per square km was estimated by Brosset & Erard (1986). In Angola, the species is confined to a small area of evergreen forest, much of which is now replaced with coffee plantations.

**HABITS** Usually in pairs or noisy flocks of up to 15 individuals, although mostly in family parties of 3–6 birds, and larger flocks are apparently a combination of family parties. Often joins mixed-species foraging flocks and, indeed, in Liberia almost invariably a conspicuous component of such flocks. In NE Gabon, flocks occupied territories of 12–15 ha, the 'leader' giving song in terri-

torial defence, especially when two groups met (Brosset & Erard 1986). Usually forages in the canopy of tall forest trees, mostly above 20 m above ground, and easily overlooked, although favours tall leafless trees (gleaning food from cracks and crevices in the bark) and attracts attention with frequent calling. Food includes insects and fruit.

**BREEDING BIOLOGY** Poorly known. Season very variable, apparently dependent on local conditions. Nest placed in a hole in a dead tree, lined with soft material. Clutch three: eggs white, irregularly spotted red; c. 17.5 x 14.5 mm.

**DESCRIPTION** *P. f. funereus* **Adult Male**: *In fresh plumage*, upperparts blackish, feather tips from crown to uppertail-coverts glossed dull oily blue-green. Tail and wing-coverts sooty-black, fringes of lesser and median coverts glossed dull blue-green, greater coverts finely fringed pale grey-blue; when very fresh, outer greater coverts may have a tiny whitish spot on tip of outer web. Alula blackish, fringes of smaller feathers glossy. Primary coverts sooty-black, very finely fringed glossy dull blue-green. Flight feathers sooty-black, fringes of tertials and secondaries narrowly glossed dull oily blue-green, primaries faintly fringed paler and greyer, P3–P5 finely fringed off-white around emargination, becoming pale grey at base, P6–P7 narrowly fringed mid grey on basal two-thirds. Lores, supercilium, sides of head and underparts dull blackish, lower breast and flanks bloomed dark grey; vent, thighs and undertail-coverts dark grey (when very fresh, may show a grey bloom over the entire underparts). Axillaries dark sooty-grey; underwing-coverts sooty-grey, narrowly fringed pale grey. *In worn plumage*, flight feathers paler and browner, pale fringes abraded. **Bare Parts**: Iris bright red, occasionally orange-red; bill black; legs and feet bluish or grey-blue to black. **Adult Female**: In fresh plumage, upperparts blackish-grey, feathers of forehead, crown and nape fringed mid brownish-grey (showing as quite coarse scaling on crown, but fine peppering on forehead), feathers of mantle to uppertail-coverts diffusely fringed mid to dark grey-blue (slightly paler, more blue-grey and less greenish than male). Tail sooty-black faintly fringed paler and greyer-brown. Lesser and median coverts blackish-grey finely fringed dark blue-grey. Remainder of wing sooty-black, greater coverts and alula finely fringed grey-brown, primary coverts and tertials finely fringed blue-grey, secondaries finely fringed greyer, primaries as male. Lores, supercilium, and sides of head and neck pale dusty grey-drab, throat and upper breast brownish. Remainder of underparts mid to light drab-grey or mouse-grey (feather tips greyer than bases). Axillaries and underwing-coverts light grey, underwing-coverts fringed pale grey. In worn plumage, pale fringes on crown and nape largely abraded (though forehead still 'peppered'). Lores, supercilium, sides of head and neck, throat and upper breast paler and browner; remainder of underparts less 'dusty' grey, with browner feather bases revealed, especially in centre of belly and vent, giving vague striated effect. Iris red (also orange or orange-red?). **Juvenile**: As adult male, but pale fringes to flight feathers reduced (tertials and secondaries with very fine paler fringes, P3–P5 faintly fringed whitish inwards of emarginations), greater coverts lack paler fringes but have large white triangular spots on tips of inner 4–7 feathers, median coverts with brownish-white triangle at tip of shaft. Underwing-coverts mid grey, variably tipped whitish. Iris brown or reddish-brown; legs and feet as adult, but the soles of one moulting juvenile noted as lemon-yellow. Sexes similar. **1st Adult**: See Sex/Age. **Measurements**: Wing of male 82–92.5, of female 80–87; tail of male 54–63, of female 51–56; bill 11.7–13.4; tarsus 16.5–19. Weight 22.2–29 g.

**MOULT** Adult post-breeding complete (mid March–mid August in Liberia, with single records mid August in Cameroon and October in Sudan). Post-juvenile partial, includes a variable number of tertials and greater coverts (August in Zaïre, December in Sudan).

**GEOGRAPHICAL VARIATION** Slight, with two races recognised.

*P. f. funereus* Liberia east to Kenya and south to Zaïre and Uganda. See Description.

*P. f. gabela* Central-west Angola. Known only from Gabela. As nominate *funereus*, but male paler, throat and breast dull blackish-slate (rather than black with a greenish gloss); the female averages paler and more bluish-slate on the underparts. Slightly smaller. Wing of male 86, 86, of female 77, 84; tail 60; tarsus 20. (Traylor 1961)

**RELATIONSHIPS** Not clear. Separated ecologically from all other African tits, with no obvious affinities, although thought by Hall & Moreau (1970) probably to be closest to the black tits, and similarly placed in the *niger* species-group by Eck (1988). The superficial similarity to White-fronted Tit of the Philippines is presumably due to convergence.

**REFERENCES** Brosset & Erard (1986), Chapin (1954), Mackworth-Praed & Grant (1973), Schouteden (1960), Traylor (1961).

# 77 RUFOUS-BELLIED TIT *Parus rufiventris*　　　　Plate 25
Other name: Rufous Tit

Broadly endemic to miombo woodland in southern Africa, this attractive tit is poorly known. The significance of the pale iris (dark in the closely related Cinnamon-breasted Tit) in courtship or species recognition is unknown.

**IDENTIFICATION** Length 150 mm (6 in). Head and throat black, slightly glossy on the crown, breast dark grey, remainder of underparts dull rufous. Upperparts mid grey; wings black with two broad white wingbars, narrow white fringes to the tertials and flight feathers, and a variable white flash at the base of the primaries. Tail black, bordered white. Eye conspicuously yellow in adults, although brown in juveniles. Distinctive. The blackish hood, lack of white cheek patches, pale eye and rich rufous underparts are diagnostic. Possibly overlaps with Cinnamon-breasted Tit in SE Zaïre, eastern Zambia, Malawi and NW Mozambique, and careful attention should be paid in these areas to the colour of the underparts and eyes; hybrids may occur, and should be fully documented.

**SEX/AGE** Sexes similar, although the underparts of males may average a slightly richer rufous. Juvenile distinct, being duller than the adult, with a dark sooty-grey cap showing reduced contrast with the upperparts, which are tinged brown, wings and tail dark sooty-brown, wingbars and fringes to flight feathers tinged yellow-buff, primary coverts finely fringed greyish, and the white border to the tail much reduced; chin and throat grey (rather than blackish), with the remainder of the underparts slightly paler and duller than the adult's. Notably, the juvenile has a dark iris. 1st adult as adult, but retains the juvenile inner primaries (P7/P8–P10) and most or all of the juvenile secondaries and primary coverts, which contrast with the adjacent new 1st-adult wing feathers, although there is often only a slight contrast within the primaries (look for wear at the tips); the contrast between the old primary coverts and new primaries, however, is often marked.

**VOICE** Calls include a thin *sit*, *sit* and (in alarm or agitation?) a harsh, rasping, deep *chrrr-chrrr-chrrr-chrrchrr* or *zar-zar-zar-zaza*, often introduced by a slightly less harsh *szit*; also *si-ch* or *si-cha-cha*, and a rolling, buzzing *whit-cherr, whit-cherr, whit-cherr*.... Also gives sweeter, but slightly squeaky (or sometimes 'throaty' or buzzing), rapidly repeated motifs such as *pet-tipio, pet-tipio, pet-tipio* or *peor-ti, peor-ti, peor-ti*, and rapid repetitions of a ringing bi- or trisyllabic motif (recalling Coal or Great Tit), such as *peetada, peetada, peetada..., pet-tida, pet-tida, pet-tida...* (presumably the song, often verbalised as a repeated *chick-wee, chick-wee*; Chapin 1954).

**DISTRIBUTION AND MOVEMENTS** In the **Congo** first noted in December 1990 in savanna bush north of Brazzaville (Dowsett-Lemaire *et al.* 1993). In western **Zaïre** known from various localities around Kinshasa and north along the Zaïre river to the Bolobo region in NW Bandundu (presumably contiguous with populations in NW Angola), and in southern Zaïre in southern Kasai Occidental (Luebo and Tshikapa; again, presumably contiguous with populations in NE Angola), also southern Shaba in Lualaba, Haut-Luapula and SE Tanganika districts, northeast to the Marungu region, and including Upemba NP. Occurs in most of central and eastern **Angola**, north from at least Huila and southern Cuando-Cubango to western Malanje; apparently avoids higher elevations in Huambo. In northern **Namibia** found in northern Ovamboland, Kavango and the western Caprivi Strip around the Okavaango river, with a few records from the same river in adjacent extreme NW **Botswana**. Widespread in **Zambia**, including the Eastern province plateau, but absent from the Luangwa and Middle Zambezi valleys and most of Southern province (the southernmost records are from 32 km south of Ngoma in Namwala district and Kafue Gorge), also absent from the extreme southwest of Western province. In central and northern **Malawi** found west of Lake Nyasa and the Rift Valley, south to the Mozambique border in Dedza district, and also in SW Malawi in Mwanza district at Zobue on the Mozambique border and in adjacent NE Tete province, **Mozambique** (Zobue birds were recorded by Vincent 1933, 1935 and Benson & Benson 1977 as Cinnamon-breasted Tit *P. pallidiventris*, but the single bird examined is a juvenile *P. r. masukuensis*). Resident, although Mackworth-Praed & Grant (1973) suggest that it may be locally migratory.

**HABITAT** Broadly endemic to miombo woodland (moist *Brachystegia* woodland savanna), although may be found in other similar habitats; in Zambia may occur in dry evergreen forest and in Western province perhaps regular even in drier mutemwa woodland and *Burkea* savanna (Benson *et al.* 1971), whilst in NE Namibia found in open mopane woodland. Habitat preferences may be determined in part by the presence of other tits. Rufous-bellied Tit is found with Miombo Tit in well-developed miombo woodland, the two species filling sufficiently different foraging niches to coexist in the same habitat, and to exclude Southern Black and White-winged Tits (which are generally found in drier woodland, including the thinner, drier stands of miombo, and more open bushy areas, respectively; Southern Black Tit fills a broad foraging niche equalling Miombo and Rufous-bellied Tits combined and is perhaps better adapted to areas away from well-developed miombo). Rufous-bellied Tit is not such a *Brachystegia* specialist as Miombo Tit, however, being found in other similar woodland types, and in the absence of Miombo Tit the available habitat may then be divided between Rufous-bellied and Southern Black Tits, such as in the dry woodlands of NE Namibia. Recorded in Zaïre at 600–1725 m, and most frequent in the south at 1200–1500 m; in the Mafinga mountains of NE Zambia found at up to 1950 m; in Malawi occurs largely at 760–1525 m, although noted down to the Lake Nyasa littoral and at *c.* 2000 m on the Nyika plateau.

**POPULATION** Fairly common to common in the northern parts of the range in Zaïre and Zambia, but uncommon in the south (although not uncommon in Kalahari woodland in NE Namibia), and rare (status not established) in Botswana. A density of 2.1 individuals per 10 ha recorded in miombo woodland in Zambia (Alerstam &

Ulfstrand 1977).

**HABITS** Found in pairs or small parties, and sometimes joins mixed-species foraging flocks. Occurs alongside Miombo Tits in the middle and upper strata of miombo woodland, but forages mainly among the twigs and leaves in the peripheral parts of the trees, picking insects from the foliage and often hanging in the outermost twigs (Miombo Tits concentrate on the thicker branches and trunks, gleaning from crevices in the bark, and sometimes tearing off pieces of bark and lichen). Notably, the feeding niches of Rufous-bellied Tit in miombo and Southern Black Tit in *Acacia* were found to be similar (Alerstam & Ulfstrand 1977). Food insects, especially caterpillars.

**BREEDING BIOLOGY** Poorly known. Season: SE Zaïre, September–October, sometimes from June onwards; Zambia, September–November; Malawi, October; Angola, recently fledged young recorded November. The nest is placed in a hole in a tree or stump, usually 1–3 m (–8 m) above ground; may use old woodpecker or barbet holes. The nest itself is a shallow cup or pad of grass, bark fibres, hair and other felt-like soft material. Clutch 3–4 (2–4): eggs creamy-white, speckled chestnut and pinkish-brown, usually with some dark grey markings at the larger end; *c.* 17.5 x 13.5 mm. Incubation and fledging periods unknown. May be a cooperative breeder; a group of four birds noted prospecting for nest sites in Angola in a patch of mixed miombo and *Monotes*; a number of natural holes were inspected, the final choice being *c.* 2 m above ground in a miombo tree (Dean in Ginn *et al.* 1989).

**DESCRIPTION** *P. r. rufiventris* **Adult**: *In fresh plumage,* forehead, crown and nape black, slightly glossed blue and sharply demarcated from the dark grey mantle and scapulars; back slightly paler, mid grey, rump feathers blackish-grey, fringed dark grey, uppertail-coverts blackish-grey. Tail black, T3–T6 narrowly tipped light grey, outer webs of T5–T6 fringed white, narrowly so on T5. Lesser coverts blackish-grey, diffusely fringed dark grey. Tertials blackish, narrowly tipped and fringed pale grey-white. Remainder of wing black: median coverts broadly tipped white (extending onto the fringe); greater coverts tipped and more narrowly fringed white; alula finely fringed white; primary coverts finely fringed pale grey and tipped white; secondaries finely fringed and tipped white; P1 finely fringed white at tip, P2 finely fringed white, P3–P10 fringed white, P3–P6 more broadly so around emargination and with broad white fringe at base (forming a flash adjacent to the tips of the primary coverts). Lores, supercilium, cheeks, ear-coverts, sides of neck, chin, throat and centre of upper breast black, sides of upper breast and lower breast dark grey (reasonably well demarcated from the black bib). Belly, vent and undertail-coverts dull rufous, thighs off-white, upper flanks and axillaries light grey, underwing-coverts white. *In worn plumage,* pale fringes to median, greater and primary coverts and tertials abraded, pale fringes on primaries and outer secondaries abraded, flight feathers bleached slightly paler brown, bib slightly duller and browner. **Bare**

**Parts**: Iris sulphur-yellow, pale yellow or cream-coloured; bill black; legs and feet grey, blue-grey or light blue with paler soles. **Juvenile**: As adult, but crown dark sooty-grey, upperparts mid-dark grey, faintly tinged brown. Tail dark sooty-brown, feathers only faintly tipped paler, T6 narrowly fringed and tipped brownish-white. Wing-coverts and flight feathers dark sooty-brown, fringes to greater and median coverts tinged buff, with the fringes to the greater coverts slightly narrower than the adult's, primary coverts very finely fringed mid grey, fringes to the tertials, secondaries and inner primaries tinged yellow-buff (P3–P6 fringed off-white, especially inwards of the emarginations; P1–P2 lack pale fringes); pale tips to secondaries indistinct. Chin, sides of head and breast mid grey (with no contrasts), reasonably well demarcated from rufous underparts, which are slightly duller and paler than the adult's. Iris grey, brownish-grey, dark olive-grey or black (may remain dark until at least the post-juvenile moult, and perhaps becomes yellow from the centre outwards). **1st Adult**: See Sex/Age. **Measurements**: Wing of male 79–89, of female 78–86; tail of male 61.5–69, of female 58–66.5; bill 12.7–13.8; tarsus 18–21. Weight: no information.

**MOULT**    Adult   post-breeding   complete (December, Angola; February, March, November, Zaïre; December and February, Zambia; January, Malawi). Post-juvenile incomplete, includes P1–P6/P7, a variable number of secondaries (usually just innermost), tertials, greater coverts, alula, a variable number of tail feathers, and sometimes 1–2 outer primary coverts (March, Zaïre; January, July Zambia; May Malawi; April, Mozambique).

**GEOGRAPHICAL VARIATION**   Slight, with three intergrading races recognised.

*P. r. diligens* Clancey 1979. NE Namibia, NW Botswana, southern Angola in southern Huila (perhaps as far north as Caconda, northern Huila) and southern Cuando-Cubango, and probably also SW Zambia (Western province, where specimens from as far northwest as Kalabo district approach *diligens* in wing and tail measurements). Intergrades with nominate *rufiventris* in southern Angola and SW Zambia. As nominate *rufiventris*,

but male with head duller, less glossy blue-black, grading into the blue-grey mantle (not sharply demarcated), and the chin and fore throat similarly grade into the grey of the breast (rather than being well demarcated). On females the hood is dull, being hardly darker than the mantle, and there is no black on the chin and upper throat, this area being grey. (The type description, which details two females, notes that they have juvenile tail feathers with abraded tips. In this species the tail is usually replaced in the post-juvenile moult, so the differences described for females must be based on juveniles or at best 1st-adult birds, and must be regarded as tentative.) Larger than nominate *rufiventris*, and tail longer. Wing of male 86.5–91, of female 82, 82; tail of male 70–73.

*P. r. rufiventris* Central and northern Angola, western (and southern?) Zaïre, and western and central Zambia (east to the Copperbelt Province in the north and at least 28° E in the south; Clancey 1979, *contra* Benson *et al.* 1971). Intergrades with *masukuensis* in southern Zaïre (perhaps in the region east of Lubumbashi in southern Shaba, but boundary poorly defined) and central Zambia. See Description.

*P. r. masukuensis* Extreme SE Zaïre (Marungu region, possibly also southern Shaba province), Zambia east of nominate *rufiventris*, Malawi and Mozambique. As nominate *rufiventris*, but upperparts paler (mid rather than dark grey), breast paler grey (mid to light grey, rather than dark grey), better demarcated from the blackish throat, remainder of underparts distinctly paler, more pinkish-cinnamon (and perhaps paler still in the Eastern province plateau of Zambia). Size differences between the sexes also better marked. Wing of male 83–87, of female 77.5–83.5; tail of male 61–67.5, of female 59–65.

**HYBRIDS** See Cinnamon-breasted Tit.

**RELATIONSHIPS** Forms a superspecies with Red-throated Tit and usually treated as conspecific with Cinnamon-breasted Tit, but separated here following Sibley & Monroe (1990). See that species for discussion and details of 'hybrids'.

**REFERENCES** Alerstam & Ulfstrand (1977), Benson *et al.* (1971), Clancey (1979).

---

# 78 CINNAMON-BREASTED TIT *Parus pallidiventris*    Plate 25

This poorly known tit is endemic to miombo woodland in East Africa, with an isolated population in Zimbabwe. It is usually treated as conspecific with Rufous-bellied Tit.

**IDENTIFICATION** Length 150 mm (6 in). Head and throat black, grading to mid grey on the upper breast and upper flanks and pale pinkish-buff on the remainder of the underparts (washed grey on the lower flanks and undertail-coverts). Upperparts grey, tail black, bordered and tipped white and wings black with two broad white wing-bars, whitish fringes to the tertials and secondaries and a white flash at the base of the primaries. In worn plumage, the amount of white in the wings and tail is reduced. The plumage pattern is rather

similar to that of Rufous-bellied Tit, although the breast is mid grey rather than black and the remainder of the underparts rather paler and more washed out. Notably, at all ages the eye is brown. Red-throated Tit is superficially similar in having cinnamon-buff underparts, but lacks the black hood; the ranges of the two species do not overlap, although they abut each other in central Tanzania.

**SEX/AGE** Sexes very similar, the female's bib averaging slightly browner. Juvenile distinct, being overall rather duller, with the upperparts washed brown, the wings and tail browner with duller wingbars, brown primary coverts finely fringed rusty-brown, the tertials narrowly fringed pale brown-white, and the secondaries and inner primaries narrowly fringed dirty yellow-white; the head is sooty brown-black (slightly paler on juvenile females), with the throat and upper breast slightly paler, sooty-brown. On juvenile males the lower breast is grey, tinged brown, grading to dull pale pinkish-buff on the belly, whilst on females the lower breast is dull pale pinkish-buff (thus lacking the greyish collar). 1st adult as adult, but retains the juvenile primary coverts, which are slightly browner than the adjacent fresh primaries and greater coverts, lacking pale fringes. A variable number of inner primaries and most or all of the secondaries are also retained; again, these are slightly paler, browner and more abraded (especially at the tip) than the adjacent new flight feathers, and with narrower pale fringes that are washed yellowish-buff. No variation in eye colour with age.

**VOICE** Presumably similar to that of Rufous-bellied Tit, but no details.

**DISTRIBUTION AND MOVEMENTS** Found in central and southern **Tanzania** (inland from the coast) north to Kibondo, Tabora, Mpwapwa and most of Morogoro (east to Soga), and east to Utete and Nandembo. Also NW and central **Mozambique** south to about Quelimane (and perhaps to the Save river), and western Manica province adjacent to the eastern highlands of Zimbabwe. Found throughout SE **Malawi** east of the Rift Valley, south to Thyolo and Mulanje districts, and also just west of the Rift Valley in the Phirilongwe area (SW Mangochi district; for records from Zobue, see Rufous-bellied Tit). Breeds in eastern **Zimbabwe** in the Honde and Nyamkwarara valleys and the Chimanimani range from Vumba south to the Makurupini river (apparently absent from the Chipinge Uplands); also the Mashonaland plateau from Mount Mwenji (Odzi) north to the Shamva and Salisbury areas (perhaps contiguous with the population centred around the eastern highlands). May occur in eastern **Zambia**, but data on the identification of Zambian birds are scant and perhaps incorrect. Hall & Moreau (1970) map pale-bellied birds from the northern part of the Muchinga escarpment, but no more details are available, and their identification as Cinnamon-breasted Tits has not been confirmed. Resident, although local migrations are suggested by Mackworth-Praed & Grant (1960).

**HABITAT** Broadly endemic to miombo woodland (moist *Brachystegia* woodland savanna), although may be found in other similar habitats; thus, in Tanzania is present uncommonly in other wooded and bushed habitats, especially in the east, and in Zimbabwe found frequently in mahobohobo woodland, which occurs at low to mid altitudes in the eastern highlands in a rich association with miombo. Habitat preferences may be determined in part by the presence of other tits. Cinnamon-breasted Tit coexists with Miombo Tit in miombo woodland, but appears to

fill too similar a niche to Southern Black Tit for the two species to occupy the same habitat, and in some otherwise suitable areas may be replaced by that species (e.g. in parts of the central plateau of Zimbabwe, where the two species are largely allopatric; Irwin 1981). This apparent 'competitive exclusion' may, however, be due rather to the unsuitability of the habitat, much of western and southern Zimbabwe being too dry for Cinnamon-breasted Tit, hence giving Southern Black an advantage (Clancey 1989). Noted in Tanzania at 490–670 m, recorded in Malawi at 760–1525 m, in Mozambique at 275–840 and up to 1400 m on Mount Namuli, and found in the eastern highlands of Zimbabwe at 500–1600 m.

**POPULATION** Locally fairly common in northern parts of range in Tanzania and Malawi, but apparently uncommon in Zimbabwe, being especially local on the Mashonaland plateau.

**HABITS** Found in pairs or in parties of 3–4, sometimes joins mixed-species foraging flocks, and occurs alongside Miombo Tits in miombo woodland. Forages largely in the canopy (unlike Miombo Tit). Food insects.

**BREEDING BIOLOGY** Poorly known. Season: Tanzania, November; Malawi, October; Zimbabwe, September–December. Nest, placed in a hole in a tree, is a cup or pad of fine grass, fibre or felt-like material. Clutch 4: eggs whitish, extensively freckled rufous; c. 18 x 14 mm. Incubation and fledging periods unknown.

**DESCRIPTION** *P. p. pallidiventris* **Adult Male:** *In fresh plumage,* crown and nape black, very slightly glossy. Mantle and scapulars mid-dark grey, back and rump slightly paler; uppertail-coverts dark grey with broad blackish-grey shaft streaks. Tail black, all feathers tipped white, narrowest on T1; T4–T6 fringed white on outer web, very narrowly so on T4–T5, T5–T6 also finely fringed white on inner web. Lesser coverts mid grey with diffuse darker shaft streaks. Median, greater and primary coverts and alula black, median coverts narrowly fringed and very broadly tipped white, greater coverts and alula fringed and more broadly tipped white, and primary coverts finely fringed and tipped light grey. Tertials and secondaries blackish-grey (tertials slightly paler on inner webs), fringed and tipped whitish, narrowly so on secondaries; fringes tinged pinkish or cream on outer tertials and secondaries. Primaries blackish-grey, finely fringed white distally, more broadly so inwards of emarginations on P3–P6; base of outer webs of P3–P7 entirely off-white (forming contrasting patch at tip of primary coverts). Lores, cheeks, ear-coverts, sides of neck and throat black, grading to mid grey on upper breast and sides of breast and upper flanks; lower breast to undertail-coverts pale pinkish-buff, washed grey, especially on flanks and undertail-coverts. Thighs grey-white. Axillaries mid grey, tipped white, underwing-coverts white. *In worn plumage,* fringes to greater and median coverts and tips to tail feathers abrade. **Bare Parts:** Iris sepia or pale burnt umber; bill black; legs and feet light blue to blue-grey or bluish-slate. **Adult Female:** As male, but bib averages slightly browner. **Juvenile Male:** Crown, nape, lores, cheeks and ear-coverts sooty-brown-black; throat, sides of neck and upper breast slightly paler, sooty brown. Upperparts mid-dark grey, washed brown. Tail dark brown, T1–T4 faintly tipped and fringed slightly paler, T5–T6 tipped and fringed off-white, fringe very fine on T5. Lesser coverts mid grey, tipped brown. Median coverts dark brown, broadly tipped off-white. Remainder of wing brown, greater coverts and alula tipped and more narrowly fringed off-white; primary coverts finely fringed rusty-brown; tertials narrowly fringed pale brown-white, secondaries and inner primaries narrowly fringed dirty yellow-white; outer primaries narrowly fringed off-white (not P1), P3–P5 with broader, whiter fringes inwards of the emarginations (broadest at emargination), P3–P7 with base of outer web entirely off-white, forming contrasting patch at tip of primary coverts. Upper flanks light dirty grey, lower breast and sides of breast mid grey, tinged brown, remainder of underparts dull pale pinkish-buff, poorly demarcated from bib. Iris sepia or dark sepia. When very worn, pale fringes to median and greater coverts may be completely abraded. **Juvenile Female**: As male, but head and bib slightly paler and browner, head sooty-brown, throat and breast dark grey-brown, tinged rusty, lower breast dull pale pinkish-buff (thus lacking greyish collar). **1st Adult**: As adult, but retains juvenile primary coverts, inner primaries, a variable number of secondaries and often the outermost tail feathers. Iris sepia or dark sepia. **Measurements**: Wing of male 77–84, of female 76–78; tail of male 60–67.5, of female 56–61; bill 10.8–13.6; tarsus 18–20. Weight: no information.

**MOULT** Adult post-breeding complete (July, Tanzania; April–May, Mozambique). Post-juvenile incomplete, includes greater coverts, alula, tertials, P1–P6/P8, most or all of the tail feathers, sometimes inner 1–2 secondaries and occasionally outermost secondary, 1–2 primary coverts, or smaller feathers of alula (January–May, Mozambique; July, Tanzania).

**GEOGRAPHICAL VARIATION** Slight, with two intergrading races.

*P. p. pallidiventris* Tanzania, Mozambique and Malawi (also Zambia?). See Description. Tanzanian birds average greyest (least cinnamon) on the underparts.

*P. p. stenotopicus* Zimbabwe and the Manica district of west-central Mozambique. As nominate *pallidiventris*, but black of throat sharply defined (not grading into the grey of the breast), wing-coverts more broadly fringed and tipped white, flight feathers more broadly fringed white, and white flash at base of primaries extending 7–9 mm

beyond tip of primary coverts (3–6 mm in *pallidiventris*). In addition, mantle slightly paler grey, head and throat duller and less jet-black, sides of lower breast paler grey, centre of belly paler grey-vinaceous (colour of underparts apparently somewhat variable, pinkish-buff to pale vinaceous; Irwin 1981). Eye brown or light brown. Averages slightly larger. Wing of male 80–87; of female 82; tail of male 60–72.

**HYBRIDS** 'Intermediates' with Rufous-bellied Tit have been recorded from the Kota-Kota district of central-eastern Malawi, the Dedza district of SW Malawi and the Chipata (= Fort Jameson) area of SE Zambia (Mackworth-Praed & Grant 1963). Two specimens have been traced from Kota-Kota, both adults, one with the eye colour noted as 'pale yellow', the other as 'pale brown', but both have the underparts dull dingy pale cinnamon (as the race *masukuensis* of Rufous-bellied Tit). Those from the Dedza district may be the intermediates noted by Hall & Moreau (1970) from Fort Jameson, near the Malawi border in SE Zambia. Again, two specimens have been traced, one an adult with the eye colour noted as 'black', the other a juvenile with the eye 'yellow' (although stained, they appear to match in underpart coloration a 1st-adult Rufous-bellied Tit from Fort Hill in northern Malawi which has the eye colour noted as 'brown'). Hall & Moreau (1970) also mention intermediates from Harare in Zimbabwe, with eye colour light brown (but see *stenotopicus* above). In all the 'intermediates' seen from Malawi or eastern Zambia, the underpart colouration is close to or identical to that of the paler Rufous-bellied Tits found in eastern Zambia, and their status as hybrids appears to rest on eye coloration. As this has clearly been incorrectly noted in some cases, the existence of any hybrids is still to be proven. It may well be that Cinnamon-breasted Tit is confined to Malawi east of the Rift Valley, with only Rufous-bellied Tit found in western Malawi and Zambia.

**RELATIONSHIPS** Forms a superspecies with Red-throated Tit, and usually considered conspecific with Rufous-bellied Tit. Cinnamon-breasted Tit is rather distinct in appearance, however, having brown rather than yellow eyes, a difference which may be of significance in species recognition. Although reported to hybridise with Rufous-bellied Tit in Zimbabwe and Zambia (but see above), Sibley & Monroe (1990) consider treatment as allospecies appropriate. This course is followed here with reservations, in the hope that the necessary information to make a more informed decision will be forthcoming.

**REFERENCES** Clancey (1989), Mackworth-Praed & Grant (1960).

This subtly attractive tit has a very restricted range in East Africa, but may be encountered in many of the famous game parks of Kenya and Tanzania.

**IDENTIFICATION** Length 120 mm (4.75 in). Cap dark grey, finely scaled paler and bordered by pale rufous on the forehead, lores, supercilium and nape (the grey cap may be difficult to see as it offers little tonal contrast). Upperparts dingy mid grey, tail black, broadly fringed and tipped white, and wings dark grey-brown with two broad white wingbars and white fringes to the tertials. Sides of head, throat and breast cinnamon-buff, grading to greyish on the flanks and drab-grey on the belly and vent. In worn plumage, the cap is darker and the wingbars less distinct. Closest in appearance to Cinnamon-breasted Tit, but their distributions do not overlap (although they abut in central Tanzania). Red-throated is smaller, with a relatively longer bill, and a dark grey cap and pale rufous collar, rather than the blackish hood of Cinnamon-breasted.

**SEX/AGE** Sexes very similar, the female having slightly duller underparts, with the throat and breast pale pinkish-buff rather than cinnamon-buff. Juvenile rather like the adult, but with the crown feathers variably fringed cinnamon, less white in the tail, and slightly paler and greyer underparts. 1st adult as adult, but retains most of the juvenile tail feathers (T1 sometimes replaced), thus still showing less white than the adult, and also retains the juvenile flight feathers, which contrast with the new tertials and greater coverts; even when worn, 1st adults may show moult contrasts within the greater coverts between the new inner feathers and the retained juvenile outermost coverts.

**VOICE** Rather vocal. Calls include an explosive, sometimes squeaky, sometimes flat and wooden, *chick* or *plick*, becoming a more subdued, conversational *chick-chick, chick-chick-chick, chick-chick-chick...* or *plik-plik-plik...*, which may be given in a long series. Also a deep, scolding *chrrrr* of variable length, often combined with a thin *si* or more emphatic *sit* and sometimes becoming a more elaborate *chachawi-chachawi-chachawi*, and a buzzing *bzee-zee-zee*. Mackworth-Praed & Grant (1960) also note a 'chick-a-dee'-type call, a resonant *prttt-tchay-tchay-tchay*, reminiscent of Willow Tit.

**DISTRIBUTION AND MOVEMENTS** Endemic to East Africa, in interior southern **Kenya** from Narok, the Naivasha area, Nairobi NP (where frequently seen in the Athi River Hippo Pool area), Machakos, Kiu and Amboseli south to the Tanzania border. Also interior northern **Tanzania** south to Mwanza, Mount Hanang, Dodoma, Mpwapwa, the southern Masai Steppe at Kibaya and the Lossogonoi plateau. Resident.

**HABITAT** Bushed and wooded grassland, open *Acacia* woodland and riverine woodland (typically groves of *Acacia xanthophloea*), in areas of medium rainfall. Optimum elevation 1000–1600 m, but recorded as high as 2000 m.

**POPULATION** Rather local and usually uncommon, although fairly common in the Masai Mara of southern Kenya and in Serengeti and Arusha NPs in northern Tanzania. Listed as near-threatened in BirdLife International's world checklist of threatened birds (Collar *et al.* 1994).

**HABITS** Found singly, in pairs or in small parties. Rather vocal and conspicuous, birds move slowly through the vegetation, foraging on leaves, twigs and bark.

**BREEDING BIOLOGY** Poorly known. Season shows no clear pattern, with breeding records in January, February, April, August and September. One nest described, in a cavity behind the bark of a tree, lined with down and fibres. Clutch 3: eggs white, spotted and freckled with pale reddish; 17 x 13.5 mm (Mackworth-Praed & Grant 1960).

**DESCRIPTION** **Adult Male:** *In fresh plumage*, forehead cinnamon-rufous, crown dark grey, feathers fringed light grey-brown. Nape cinnamon. Upperparts from mantle to uppertail-coverts mid grey, tinged drab, longer uppertail-coverts blackish. Tail black, T6–T5 fringed and tipped white, T5 narrowly so, T4–T2 tipped whitish. Wing-coverts, alula, primary coverts and tertials dark grey-brown, lesser coverts fringed as upperparts, median coverts broadly tipped whitish, greater coverts broadly fringed and tipped whitish, alula and primary coverts finely fringed off-white, and tertials broadly fringed and tipped white. Flight feathers grey-brown, secondaries narrowly fringed white (also tipped white on outer webs), primaries narrowly fringed dull white on P3–P10, purer white around and inward of emarginations on P3–P7. Lores and supercilium cinnamon, cheeks, ear-coverts, sides of neck, chin, throat and breast cinnamon-buff, sides of breast buffy-grey. Flanks grey with slight buff wash. Belly and vent drab-grey, washed buff. Undertail-coverts drab-grey, broadly tipped whitish. Thighs pale buff-white. Axillaries and underwing-coverts pale grey. *In worn plumage*, crown darker (pale fringes abraded), whitish fringes and tips to tail feathers may be fully abraded, wingbars narrower, pale fringes (not tips) to greater coverts may be almost absent. Tertial and secondary fringes abraded. Breast more pinkish-cinnamon. **Bare Parts:** Iris greenish-brown to dark brown; bill grey or blue-grey to blackish with paler cutting edges and a darker tip to the upper mandible; legs and feet blue or grey to black. **Adult Female:** As male, but throat and breast pale pinkish-buff, not so richly cinnamon. **Juvenile:** As adult, but crown mid grey, feathers variably fringed cinnamon. Tail shows less white, T6 rather narrowly fringed white, T5–T2 narrowly, if at all, tipped white. More contrast in the wing between the dark centres of the tertials and greater coverts and the remainder of the wing, pale fringes on primaries and secondaries narrower. Underparts as those of female or slightly grey-

er. **1st Adult**: See Sex/Age. **Measurements**: Wing 68–75, of male 70–75, of female 70–71.5; tail of male 46–49, of female 44–48; bill 12.2–13.2; tarsus 17.5–21.5. Weight: no information.
**MOULT** Adult post-breeding complete (May). Post-juvenile partial, includes tertials, greater coverts (usually not outermost) and sometimes central tail feathers (March, June).

**GEOGRAPHICAL VARIATION** None.

**RELATIONSHIPS** A member of the *rufiventris* superspecies, together with Cinnamon-breasted and Rufous-bellied Tits.

**REFERENCES** Mackworth-Praed & Grant (1960), Turner (1977).

# 80 STRIPE-BREASTED TIT *Parus fasciiventer*       Plate 25

Confined to montane forest, this species has a very limited distribution in the mountains around the Albertine Rift in east-central Africa. Despite being common, it is rather poorly known.

**IDENTIFICATION** Length 140 mm (5.5 in). Head and breast blackish with the cap slightly glossy and the sides of throat and breast variably browner, and with a dull black ventral stripe from the chin to the centre of the belly. Flanks dirty white. Upperparts greyish, tail black with white sides and a narrow white tip. Wings black, with two broad white wingbars, pale brownish-grey fringes to the tertials and secondaries and a contrasting pale flash at the base of the primaries. The combination of a blackish head and breast (lacking white cheek patches), greyish upperparts and dark ventral stripe is distinctive; the only vaguely similar species are Cinnamon-breasted and Red-throated Tits, which are both found in a very different habitat.

**SEX/AGE** In the nominate race the sexes are very similar, but females average slightly more extensively brown on the sides of throat and breast, contrasting a little more with the narrower black central stripe (but not showing so much contrast as a juvenile). Juveniles are rather similar to adults, but are overall slightly duller and browner, with a slightly duller and more restricted blackish cap; the nape and sides of the head, throat and breast are dull cinnamon-brown, contrasting with the blackish chin and a narrow blackish band in the centre of the throat and upper breast (but the continuation of this blackish ventral stripe to the belly is narrower and less obvious); wings as adult, but with a faint yellowish wash to the fringes of the flight feathers. 1st adult as adult, but retains the juvenile flight feathers (and sometimes alula), which are browner than the adjacent new tertials and greater coverts, with a faint yellowish tinge to the fringes. 1st adults are also slightly more extensively brown on the sides of the breast. (No information on variation with sex or age in other races.)

**VOICE** Calls include a sharp, abrupt *tit* or *chit*, usually combined with 1–3 nasal *char* units, with a ringing *pseet* often interposed within the *char* sequence, thus *chit-chit-char-char'pseeet'char-char*, *chit-chit-char*, *chit-chit-char-char...* (a 'chick-a-dee'-type vocalisation recalling both black and grey tits, this and similar variations being the main contact call, and used also in territorial defence; Dowsett 1990). Also gives a sharp but full *chrit* note, singly or in a series of 2–3 notes, and this may become a stuttering *chrit'it'it'it'it'it* (recalling a Blue or Great Tit's scold), and these phrases are also combined with a frog-like *crud-y* note (almost 'ribbit'!), e.g. *chrit-chit-chit crud-y-crud-y, chrit'it'it'it'it'it crud-y-crud*. Other calls are a rapid, thin, clicking *chit'lilit*, and a very deep, powerful, full *chur-chur-chur-chur*. The song is a 'tea-cher' motif, recalling Great Tit (Schottler & Henning 1993).

**DISTRIBUTION AND MOVEMENTS** A restricted range in the central African highlands around the Albertine Rift, from the Ruwenzori mountains of SW **Uganda**/NE Kivu province, eastern **Zaïre**, south through eastern Kivu province from the mountains northwest of Lake Edward to the mountains northwest of Lake Tanganyika (Itombwe forest and Mount Kabobo), also the highlands of SW Uganda, western **Rwanda** from the Virungas on the Kivu/Uganda/Rwanda border south to the Nyungwe forest, and NW **Burundi** (Rwegura and Teza). (See figure 80.1, p. 344, and also Geographical Variation.)

**HABITAT** Montane forest, bamboo and forest undergrowth, extending into the montane tree-heath zone. Recorded altitudes are from 1800–4100 m. In the Ruwenzori mountains of SW Uganda found at 1800–2745 m, occasionally to 3400 m in the tree-heath zone, and noted in bamboo at 2200–3000 m in the Ruwenzoris in Zaïre. Further south, in the Bwindi (Impenetrable) forest of SW Uganda, noted at c. 2130–2440 m, and in the forests west of Lake Edward recorded at 2170–2610 m. In the Virungas and Kivu volcanoes (Zaïre/Rwanda) extends upwards into the tree-heath zone and *Hagenia* woodland (where common at 3355 m), exceptionally to 4100 m on Mount Karisimbi. In the Nyungwe forest of SW Rwanda, widespread from c. 2100 m to at least 2800 m and common above 2300 m (exceptionally noted at 1900 m at Kamiranzovu); in Burundi, noted at 2030–2080 m. In eastern Kivu, recorded at 2000–2800 m on the Itombwe mountains and 2080–2480 m on Mount Kabobo.

**POPULATION** Generally common, even locally abundant (as in SW Uganda). The species has a very limited distribution, however, and forest destruction must pose a long-term threat to its survival.

**HABITS** Usually found in family parties of 3–15, often in mixed-species foraging flocks. Usually tame, and rather silent. Probes foliage, vegetation debris and bark in the canopy, smaller trees in

343

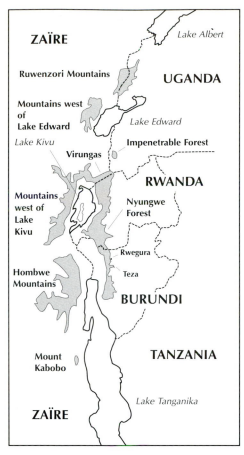

ZAÏRE

Lake Albert

UGANDA

Ruwenzori Mountains

Mountains west of Lake Edward

Lake Edward

Lake Kivu

Impenetrable Forest

Virungas

RWANDA

Mountains west of Lake Kivu

Nyungwe Forest

Rwegura

Hombwe Mountains

Teza

BURUNDI

Mount Kabobo

TANZANIA

Lake Tanganika

ZAÏRE

*Figure 80.1 The Albertine Rift region of central Africa. The shaded area shows regions above 2000 m that approximate to the range of Stripe-breasted Tit, together with some localities mentioned in the text.*

clearings and on the forest edge, down to 1–2 m above ground, but does not penetrate the understorey of closed forest (Dowsett 1990).

**BREEDING BIOLOGY** Almost unknown. The only information is that in Zaïre males in breeding condition were collected in west Ruwenzori on 30 November, and on the Ugandan side a nestling was taken in the Ruwenzoris in December, whilst in eastern Kivu birds have been collected in breeding condition in April–July (notably at Mount Karisimbi on the Rwandan border, where an adult was noted visiting an old woodpecker hole in a tree stump in mid June). Family parties with dependent fledglings in October in the Nyungwe forest of Rwanda indicate laying in August, and a group with 2–3 dependent young also included two independent immatures, suggesting that the species could be multi-brooded (Dowsett 1990).

**DESCRIPTION** *P. f. fasciiventer* **Adult Male**: In fresh plumage, forehead, crown and nape black, feather tips on crown and nape faintly glossed blue. Narrow band on upper mantle sooty-brown, remainder of upperparts mid grey, washed drab; longest uppertail-coverts blackish. Tail black, T6

broadly fringed and tipped white, T5 finely fringed and tipped white, T4–T2 finely tipped white. Lesser coverts sooty-black, fringed as upperparts, primary coverts blackish, narrowly fringed pale drab-grey; remainder of wing black, median coverts broadly fringed white, greater coverts fringed and more broadly tipped white, alula narrowly fringed white, tertials (and sub-scapulars) broadly fringed and tipped pale drab-grey on both webs, secondaries more narrowly fringed paler, primaries faintly fringed paler, fringes broader and whiter around emarginations on P3–P5/P6 (and fringes may be broader and whiter at bases of primaries, forming a pale panel adjacent to the tips of the primary coverts). Lores, supercilium, cheeks, ear-coverts, sides of head, throat, breast and centre of belly sooty brownish-black, throat and centre of breast blacker with faint blue gloss. Flanks, vent, thighs and undertail-coverts dirty white, tinged brownish at sides of breast. Axillaries and underwing-coverts white. **Bare Parts**: Iris reddish-brown through hazel to dark brown; bill black; legs and feet bluish, grey, slate-grey or olive-green. **Adult Female**: As male, but nape, sides of head and sides of breast average slightly browner. **Juvenile**: As adult, but crown slightly duller and less glossy, nape, sides of neck, ear-coverts, cheeks, lores and sides of throat and breast drab. Chin and narrow band in centre of throat and upper breast blackish, black median stripe on centre of lower breast and belly narrower and less obvious, remainder of underparts tinged yellow-buff. Narrow blackish band on upper mantle, remainder of upperparts mid greyish-drab. White in tail slightly duller, with slightly less extensive white tips to T2–T5. Faint yellow-buff wash to fringes of greater and median coverts, secondaries and primaries (inward of emarginations). **1st Adult**: See Sex/Age. **Measurements**: Wing 73–83, of male 77–81.5, of female 76–83; tail of male 57–63, of female 55.5–61; bill 11.3–12.5; tarsus 16–19.5. Weight: no information.

**MOULT** Adult post-breeding complete (October, Mount Kabobo; April, Itombwe Mountains). Post-juvenile partial, includes tertials, greater coverts, and sometimes the alula and a variable number of secondaries (January, Ruwenzori mountains).

**GEOGRAPHICAL VARIATION** Three races, listed north-south; nominate *fasciiventer* and *tanganjicae* intergrade in SW Rwanda (Nyungwe forest), but *kaboboensis* is isolated on a southern outlier of the main Albertine Rift massifs.

*P. f. fasciiventer* The Ruwenzori mountains of SW Uganda and NE Kivu, the Impenetrable (Bwindi) forest of the highlands of Kigezi district (Kabale) of SW Uganda, the Virungas of eastern Zaïre and Rwanda, and the mountains east of Lake Kivu in Rwanda south to the Nyungwe forest (Rugege forest); Burundi, and eastern Zaïre in the mountains west of Lake Edward and highlands west of Lake Kivu. See Description. A bird from the Nyungwe forest appears to be an intergrade with *tanganjicae*.

*P. f. tanganjicae* Itombwe mountains, SE Kivu province, eastern Zaïre (i.e. the range west of Uvira). Well marked. As nominate *fasciiventer*, but male has brown head and breast with a more restricted black cap. Nape (forming a narrow collar), cheeks, ear-coverts, superciliary region, sides of neck, throat and breast mid brown with a slight pinkish cast, centre of the throat and breast mottled blackish-grey (darker feather bases), centre of belly blackish-grey, and remainder of underparts washed dull buff (face, throat and breast paler and browner than female nominate *fasciiventer*, contrasting more with the glossy black cap, underparts more intensely washed buff). Wing of male 77, tail of male 51.

**P. f. kaboboensis** Mount Kabobo, southeastern most Kivu province, eastern Zaïre (29° 03' E, 5° 08' S). As *tanganjicae* (i.e. bib of male as in female nominate *fasciiventer*), but mantle slightly purer grey (clean mid-dark blue-grey with faint brown

wash), underparts much duller, breast more extensively mottled black, belly and flanks darker, washed smoke-grey; female differs as male, but breast paler.

**RELATIONSHIPS** Treated by Hall & Moreau (1970) as a member of the *afer* superspecies, but in some ways anomalous, lacking pale cheek and nuchal patches and being slightly larger than any grey tit, although with a small bill like Miombo Tit. Considered by Short *et al.* (1990) to be morphologically too divergent to be included in the *afer* superspecies, but to be more closely related to the grey tits than to either the *rufiventris* superspecies or Dusky Tit.

**REFERENCES** Chapin (1954), Dowsett (1990), Prigogine (1957).

# 81 ACACIA TIT *Parus thruppi*          Plate 26
Other names: Grey Tit, Northern Grey Tit

Often treated as conspecific with Southern Grey Tit, this species of the arid northeast of Africa has a distinctive appearance but, like most African tits, is poorly known.

**IDENTIFICATION** Length 115 mm (4.5 in). The smallest of the African grey tits. Cap glossy blue-black, with large off-white nuchal patch, and upperparts mid grey, only faintly washed drab. Tail black, fringed and tipped white. Wings blackish, with conspicuous white fringes to the tertials, secondaries and median and greater coverts (the greater coverts appearing 'slatted'). Forehead and chin blackish, feathers tipped drab-grey or buffish, lores buffish, cheek patch white but sides of neck black, connecting the cap to the black bib. Broad but irregular black ventral line, narrowly bordered off-white, grading through a narrow band of pale pinkish-buff to light drab-grey on the flanks. The range is well separated from that of Miombo Tit in Tanzania, but stray grey tits in the intervening areas should be carefully scrutinised. The most obvious distinction is Acacia Tit's black line on the sides of the neck which connects the cap and bib, completely encircling the white cheeks. Additionally, the bill is proportionally longer and deeper, the nuchal spot larger, the lores and forehead buffish (not black) and the cheek patches whiter. The plumage is overall slightly browner, with the upperparts lightly washed drab (not pure grey), the underparts rather buffer, with a contrasting whitish border to the ventral line (rather than being uniformly very pale greyish-buff), and the flanks are light grey, washed drab (not pure grey, but see also Geographical Variation, as Tanzanian birds have cleaner and whiter underparts, thus approaching Miombo Tit).

**SEX/AGE** Sexes similar, although the female's bib averages very slightly duller and less extensive, and there are narrower and duller pale fringes to the primary coverts. Juvenile relatively distinct, with the upperparts duller and browner, no gloss on the crown, the wings and tail duller and

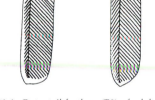

*Figure 81.1 Outer tail feathers (T6) of adult (left) and juvenile (right): note pattern of white.*

browner, bib duller, browner, and smaller, with little or no extension into a ventral line, and the underparts duller and browner. 1st adult as adult and separated in the hand by moult contrasts in the wing-coverts, tertials, secondaries and sometimes also the primaries and primary coverts: when all coverts replaced, the retained juvenile flight feathers, primary coverts and alula contrast with the new coverts and tertials more in wear than in coloration (adults also have darker and blacker tertials and greater coverts than flight feathers); some or all of the juvenile tail feathers are retained and, if present, juvenile T6 differs in pattern from that of the adult (see figure above).

**VOICE** Generally rather silent and inconspicuous, calls quiet and deep. Contact call a quiet, hoarse *chet, chet, chet...* or *chut, chut, chut...*; also *tsi-tsa-char* and when more agitated gives an explosive *tsi-tsi chay-chay-chay* or *tsi-tsi de-de-de-de-de* (in the 'chick-a-dee' pattern, with the scolding notes harsh and rather deep, but perhaps not so deep as those of Miombo Tit), also an explosive *si-ta tcharrr* and *tsia-tsia, tsia-tsia* (the high-pitched introductory note may be stuttered or slightly lisping, *tis'si'si* etc.). Other calls include a nasal, buzzing *dzrrr-ti, dzrrr-ti*, and when agitated may give scolding, rambling jumble of notes. Song described as a pleasant little warbling (Mackworth-Praed & Grant 1960), also *see-u...* repeated about six times, and *thee-chee, thee-chee* (Benson 1945–48).

**DISTRIBUTION AND MOVEMENTS** In **Ethiopia** resident in the south, southeast of the Rift Valley, and found in northern **Somalia** north of 8° N and west of 49° E, and in the south below 5° N. In northern **Kenya** occurs from the Turkwell region east along the northern border to Somalia, in the northwest (east to Marsabit and south to Kongelai, Lake Baringo and Isiolo) and in central Kenya south to the Tanzanian border (east to Garissa and south to Simba and Tsavo East); absent southeast and coast. Extends marginally into NE **Uganda** in southern Karamoja (around Moroto), and into NE **Tanzania** in the lowlands southeast of Mount Kilimanjaro.

**HABITAT** Arid or semi-arid wooded and bushed grassland, primarily in *Acacia* and favouring stands of trees along watercourses. Avoids the most arid areas, however, and in Kenya, for example, just one old record from the extreme northwest west of Lake Turkana, and occurs mainly in thicker habitats in the north of Tsavo East NP. In Ethiopia recorded up to at least 1400 m and probably to *c.* 2000 m, in Somalia at 915–2100 m, in Kenya up to 1000 m, locally to 1600 m in the northern parts of the west and central highlands, and in Tanzania to 1500 m.

**POPULATION** Generally rather uncommon, although locally common in areas of particularly suitable habitat such as riparian woodland, and frequent in southern Ethiopia.

**HABITS** Found in pairs or small parties, often joining mixed-species foraging flocks.

**BREEDING BIOLOGY** Poorly known. Season in Ethiopia probably February–April (a female with an egg in April, two records of young in the nest in mid April), in Somalia March, June. Nest holes noted in trees at *c.* 7 m and 2.5 m above ground. A nest found in a dead tree had been preyed on by a snake; the remaining egg was white, minutely and uniformly speckled and heavily blotched at the 'upper' end with rich red-brown (Archer & Godman 1961).

**DESCRIPTION** *P. t. thruppi* **Adult**: *In fresh plumage* (August–March), crown (to below eye) and nape black, glossed blue; may show pale tips to feathers of rear crown. Large off-white spot on lower nape and border of upper mantle, sometimes tinged drab, longest uppertail-coverts black, remainder of upperparts mid grey, faintly washed drab. Tail black, all feathers except sometimes T1 finely tipped white; T3–T6 fringed white, finely on T3 and broadly on T6. Lesser coverts sooty-brown, broadly fringed mid grey, median coverts sooty-black, broadly tipped white. Greater coverts, alula and tertials blackish, greater coverts and alula broadly tipped and fringed white, tertials broadly fringed white on outer web. Primary coverts sooty-black, narrowly fringed and more broadly tipped white. Primaries and secondaries brownish-black,

secondaries and P3–P10 finely fringed white, only inwards of emarginations on P3–P6. Lores drab-grey to drab-buff, cheeks and ear-coverts white, sides of neck blackish. Forehead and chin blackish, feathers tipped drab-grey or buffish, upper throat black with fine whitish feather tips, especially at the sides of the bib. Remainder of throat, centre of upper breast and irregular ventral line (extending to the centre of the vent) black, feathers of the lower edge of the bib and ventral line tipped whitish. Narrow off-white border to bib and ventral line, grading to a narrow line of pale pinkish-buff or pale horn (including thighs), remainder of underparts light grey, washed drab; undertail-coverts dark grey, broadly fringed off-white. Axillaries light grey, underwing-coverts off-white. *In worn plumage* (April–October), cap less glossy, upperparts darker and not so pure grey. White tips to tail feathers quickly abraded. White fringes on wing feathers abraded, may be absent on tertials, primaries and outer secondaries. Forehead and chin blacker, lores buffy. **Bare Parts**: Iris brown to dark brown or reddish-brown; bill dark slate or black; legs and feet grey to black, soles pale grey. **Juvenile**: As adult, but crown sooty-brown without gloss, upperparts more heavily washed drab. Tail slightly paler and a browner black, all feathers lacking white tips, reduced white fringes to outer feathers (very fine on T5 and narrower than adult on T6). Wing-coverts and tertials paler and browner. Bib sooty-brown, confined to throat and upper breast with little or no extension into a ventral line. Underparts duller, more intensely washed drab. **1st Adult**: As adult (see Sex/Age). **Measurements**: Wing of male 64–69.5, of female 61–68; tail of male 44–53, of female 42–51; bill 9.7–12.5; tarsus 17–20. Weight 12 g (one bird from Uganda).

**MOULT** Adult post-breeding complete (July–early January, Somalia; July–November, Ethiopia; January–February, Kenya). Post-juvenile rather variable, partial to incomplete, includes a variable number of greater coverts, tertials, tail feathers (often T1 and T6) and secondaries, larger feathers of alula and sometimes inner 1–2 primaries and primary coverts (June–February, Somalia; November–February, Ethiopia; January–March, Kenya;).

**GEOGRAPHICAL VARIATION** Rather slight, with two races recognised.

*P. t. thruppi* Somalia and Ethiopia, intergrading with *barakae* in northern Kenya. See Description.

*P. t. barakae* SW Somalia (Gedo), interior Kenya, Uganda, Tanzania. Poorly marked. As nominate *thruppi*, but upperparts may average slightly paler, nuchal spot smaller or absent, a broader pale border to the ventral stripe, off-white, washed grey-buff (less buffy), and slightly paler and purer grey flanks, pale grey with faint drab wash (palest in Tanzania, where close to Miombo Tit in flank coloration). Wing of male 62–70, of female 60–65.

**RELATIONSHIPS** A member of the *afer* species group with Miombo, Ashy and Southern Grey Tits, and probably forms a superspecies with Southern Grey Tit. The members of this group are superficially similar in appearance and are sometimes combined into just two species; Hall & Moreau (1970) and Lewis & Pomeroy (1989) placed Acacia Tit in a single species together with Ashy Tit and Southern Grey Tit (the 'thorn-bush group'). At other times, Acacia Tit is treated as conspecific with Southern Grey Tit, distinct from Ashy and Miombo Tits. The relationship between these two birds is problematic, as with any geographically separated forms, but the rather distinct differences in size and plumage (especially the complete black border to the cheeks in Acacia Tit, lacking in Southern Grey), and the large gap between the two ranges, support their separation as two species

(as done by Short *et al.* 1990, Sibley & Monroe 1990, and Wolters 1980, although contested by Dowsett & Dowsett-Lemaire 1993). The *afer* species group is usually thought to be closely related to the Great Tit (indeed, Meinertzhagen 1951 treated all the African grey tits as conspecific with Great Tit), the various species perhaps being a consequence of different invasions from the Palearctic. Short *et al.* (1990) consider, however, that the Afrotropical species of *Parus* are not directly related to the Great Tit, from which they differ both in behaviour and vocally.

**REFERENCES** Archer & Godman (1961), Lewis & Pomeroy (1989).

## 82 MIOMBO TIT *Parus griseiventris*                    Plate 26
Other names: Northern Grey Tit, Miombo Grey Tit

This is one of three species of tit broadly endemic to just one type of woodland, *Brachystegia* or 'miombo', found in a broad swathe across south-central Africa.

**IDENTIFICATION** Length 140 mm (5.5 in). Cap black, only faintly glossed blue, but extending onto the upper mantle, with a variable small dirty white nuchal spot; remainder of upperparts mid grey. Tail black, fringed and tipped white, and wings black with a broad white bar on the median coverts and white fringes and tips to the greater coverts forming a 'lattice'; tertials and flight feathers fringed white. Cheek patches pale grey-white, extending onto the sides of the neck; bib and ventral line sooty-blackish, flanks light grey, and remainder of underparts off-white, washed greyish-buff. Bill relatively short and slender. Overlaps with Ashy Tit in Zimbabwe, although usually separated by habitat, Ashy in *Acacia* steppe and Miombo Tit in *Brachystegia* woodland. Overall rather paler than Ashy Tit, with a duller blackish cap and bib, rather smaller and duller pale nuchal patch (sometimes absent), larger but duller pale cheek patches, broader white fringes to the wing feathers, especially the median coverts (where the white tips form a distinct bar), and much paler underparts (not uniformly mid grey with only a narrow paler border to the ventral line). The range is widely separated from that of Acacia Tit in Tanzania, but any grey tits seen in the intervening areas should be carefully examined. Compared with Acacia Tit, the lores and forehead are black (not buffish), the nuchal spot is rather smaller and duller (rather than an extensive white border between the nape and upper mantle), the upperparts are purer grey, the cheek patches duller and, importantly, there is no black line around the rear cheeks (thus the bib and cap are not connected at the rear as on Acacia Tit). Additionally, the bib is narrower and more elongated (lower border well rounded on Acacia), and the underparts paler and whiter, with pure light grey confined to the flanks (rather than pinkish-buff with drab-grey flanks and a contrasting narrow white border to the bib and ventral line).

**SEX/AGE** Sexes marginally distinct, the female having a slightly duller cap and bib. The juvenile resembles a dull female, but shows less white in the tail, has the fringes to the flight feathers faintly washed yellow-buff, and lacks the dark ventral line. The 1st adult retains the juvenile flight feathers and may show moult contrasts in the wing and tail.

**VOICE** A very harsh and deep *chrrr-chrrr-chrrr-chrrr*, often introduced by a thin *si* or *sisi*, and a squeakier *tit-tieu*. Other calls recorded include a *chissick* often followed by three notes and a more elaborate song-call, *see-oo*, repeated with variations (Mackworth-Praed & Grant 1960); a scolding *tjou-tjou-tjou-tjou* (Sinclair *et al.* 1993); rolling *swip-ji-ji-ji-ji* (Maclean 1993); and a fine, frequently repeated *tjitji*, sometimes coupled with a strident *chip* (Lippens & Wille 1976). The distinctions (if any) from Ashy and Southern Grey Tits have not been studied; the voice is similar in general to that of Ashy Tit, but it may lack the trilling song.

**DISTRIBUTION AND MOVEMENTS** In eastern **Tanzania**, scattered records from around Kibondo south to the Zambian border and east to the Tabora region. In SE **Zaïre** breeds in SE Shaba (=Katanga), in Lualaba, Haut-Luapula (Lubumbashi) and Tanganika districts, north to Marungu, and including Upemba NP, and also in south Kwilu (Lippens & Wille 1976). In **Malawi** occurs west of the Shire river south to Malawi Hill, Nsanje, and found throughout most of **Zambia**, south to the Luanga, Zambezi and south Luete rivers, reaching the lip of the Zambezi escarpment and Livingstone near the Zimbabwe border (although possibly absent from the extreme southwest in the Sesheke and Senanga districts). Found in NW **Mozambique** in NE Tete province around Furancungo and Xavier (Vincent 1933, 1935). In **Angola** recorded in the east from near the Zambian border, and in central and southern

Angola there is an apparently disjunct population on the high plateau from central Huila north to Huambo and Quela, Malanje (one record from extreme southern Huila). Another apparently isolated population in **Zimbabwe**, largely confined to the central plateau, north to the Zambezi escarpment, west to the Charama plateau, south to about Mberengwa and then east to the eastern highlands from Inyanga south to the Chimanimani and Chipinge mountains; also at Victoria Falls and Nampini Ranch in the far west (contiguous with the Zambian population). Resident.

**HABITAT** Essentially endemic to open climax miombo woodland (*Brachystegia*). In Zimbabwe, never seen away from well-developed *Brachystegia* and even absent from most of the poorer formations where a distinct canopy does not exist (Irwin 1959), but in Zambia also recorded from mavunda forest, and to some extent also in mutemwa and *Isoberlinia* woodlands. Found above 915 m in Zimbabwe on the central plateau, and at 500–1600 m in the eastern highlands. Recorded in Malawi at 915–1705 m, with an unconfirmed record from *c.* 400 m, and at *c.* 1220–1900 m in Zaïre, 975–1950 m in Zambia and noted at *c.* 2450 m in Tanzania.

**POPULATION** Usually fairly common to common, although in Tanzania rather local and sporadic, being fairly common only in the southwest around Mount Rungwe. Densities of 14 birds per 100 ha have been recorded in miombo woodland in Zambia (Alerstam & Ulfstrand 1977). Owing to its specific habitat requirements, however, the species is vulnerable to habitat destruction; with the removal of miombo woodland, it may be replaced in the resultant secondary thorn bush by Ashy Tit.

**HABITS** Occurs in pairs and small parties, keeping contact with scolding and chattering calls. Often joins mixed-species foraging parties and, although separated by habitat from Ashy Tit, in areas where their ranges overlap the two species are sometimes found in the same parties where their respective habitats adjoin. Coexists in miombo woodland with Rufous-bellied Tit, but the two species appear to occupy different niches within this habitat. Miombo Tit forages largely on the trunks, larger branches and dead boughs, 5–10 m above ground, whereas Rufous-bellied Tits forage mainly among the twigs, leaves and thinner branches of the canopy.

**BREEDING BIOLOGY** Season: Zimbabwe, August–December (mainly September); Zambia, August–September; SE Zaïre and Malawi, September–October; Angola, juvenile collected early November. The nest is a thick pad or cup of plant fibres, hair, feathers etc., placed in a natural tree hole, old woodpecker or barbet cavity, bank or ant hill, and sometimes uses cavities in man-made artefacts such as walls, fence posts and pipes. Clutch 3–5: eggs white, speckled reddish-brown with violet-grey undermarkings; *c.* 18 x 14 mm. Incubation and fledging periods unknown. Reputed to be frequently parasitised by the Lesser Honeyguide (Mackworth-Praed & Grant 1960).

**DESCRIPTION** Adult Male: *In fresh plumage* (February–August), crown (to lower rim of eye) and nape black, faintly glossed blue; small to faint/absent dirty white to grey-white nuchal spot. Upper mantle sooty-black, feathers broadly fringed mid grey, longer uppertail-coverts black, remainder of upperparts and lesser coverts mid grey. Tail blackish, T4–T5 very finely fringed pale grey on outer web, outer web of T6 pale grey; all feathers tipped pale grey, broadly so on T6. Median and greater coverts, alula and tertials blackish, distal half of median coverts white, greater coverts broadly tipped and fringed white, alula narrowly fringed white, and tertials broadly fringed white on outer web, more narrowly and diffusely so on inner web. Primary coverts and flight feathers brownish-black, primary coverts finely fringed grey, secondaries and P10–P3 fringed white, faintly so distally on emarginations on P3–P6. Lores black, cheeks, ear-coverts and sides of neck pale buff-grey. Throat and upper breast sooty-black, extending in variable diffuse blackish-grey ventral line to centre of belly; flanks light-pale grey, remainder of underparts off-white, washed greyish-buff. Undertail-coverts mid-dark grey, broadly tipped white. Axillaries light grey, underwing-coverts off-white. *In worn plumage* (September–January), cap less glossy, upperparts slightly darker, faintly tinged brown. **Bare Parts**: Iris grey, brown, dark brown or black; bill black; legs and feet grey to black, soles sometimes paler, dull yellow. **Adult Female**: As male, but cap averages slightly less glossy, bib averages slightly paler, blackish-grey. **Juvenile**: As female, but fringes to primaries and secondaries faintly washed yellow-buff, T1–T5 faintly and very narrowly fringed paler, T6 diffusely fringed white on outer web; no pale tips to tail feathers. Cheek patches duller, bib duller and less extensive with no dark ventral line. **1st Adult**: As adult, but retains juvenile primaries and secondaries, fringes tinged yellow-buff, also alula and primary coverts, which contrast in colour (less so in wear) with new tertials and greater coverts; may also show moult contrasts in the tail. **Measurements**: Wing of male 77–85, of female 74–82; tail of male 51–54, of female 50–54; bill 11–13.1; tarsus 18–20. Weight: no information.

**MOULT** Adult post-breeding complete (February–May). Post-juvenile partial, includes tertials and greater coverts, a variable number of tail feathers and occasionally inner secondaries (April).

**GEOGRAPHICAL VARIATION** Slight. There is a slight decrease in average wing length from west to east, while in underpart coloration there are two pale populations, one in SE Zaïre-eastern Zambia-Tanzania and the other in far western Zambia-northern Angola. These are separated by a darker population in central Zambia, with a second dark population in central and southern Angola. A white nape appears occasionally on Zambian and Angolan birds (Hall & Traylor 1959). Two subspecies are sometimes recognised: '*parvirostris*' from Zimbabwe and Mozambique, with the nuchal spot usually better marked; and '*lundarum*' from Zambia, with paler and purer grey upperparts, the nuchal spot well defined, median coverts more broadly tipped white, and creamy-white underparts with a slight brownish-grey wash on the sides of the breast and flanks. Hall & Traylor (1959), however, considered that it was not possible satisfactorily to define any races, and the species is usually treated as monotypic.

**RELATIONSHIPS** A member of the *afer* species group, together with Acacia, Ashy and Southern Grey Tits. Until relatively recently all four species in this group were considered conspecific. However, since Miombo and Ashy Tits occur close to each other in western Angola without interbreeding (Ashy in coastal semi-desert thorn scrub, Miombo in woods on top of the escarpment inland), and coexist in Zimbabwe in their respective habitats, they must be regarded as distinct species. Miombo Tit is more widely separated from Acacia and Southern Grey Tits, but the well-marked differences in plumage, bill size and habitat support their treatment as distinct species.

**REFERENCES** Alerstam & Ulfstrand (1977), Irwin (1959, 1981), Maclean (1993).

# 83 ASHY TIT *Parus cinerascens*                    Plate 26
Other names: Ashy Grey Tit, Acacia Grey Tit

This robust tit is found in the *Acacia* savannas of southwest Africa, and is very much the equivalent of Acacia Tit, found in similar areas around the horn of Africa.

**IDENTIFICATION** Length 145 mm (5.75 in). A large tit. Cap glossy blue-black, nuchal spot white, and upperparts mid grey. Tail black, rimmed and tipped with white, and wing-coverts and flight feathers blackish, conspicuously fringed and tipped white. Cheek patches and sides of neck white, bib and ventral line black, narrowly bordered off-white, and remainder of underparts mid grey. Overlaps with Miombo Tit in Zimbabwe, although usually segregated by habitat, Ashy Tit in thorn scrub and Miombo Tit in *Brachystegia* woodland. Ashy Tit is distinguished by its overall rather darker coloration, with a glossier cap and bib, larger and purer white nuchal patch, slightly narrower but purer white cheek patches, narrower white fringes to the wing feathers, especially the median coverts, and darker, mid grey underparts, with only a narrow pale border to the ventral line (rather than off-white underparts, washed greyish-buff, with light grey confined to the flanks; see, however, Geographical Variation). Overlaps with Southern Grey Tit in central Namibia and perhaps northern Cape Province in South Africa. Ecological separation between the two is not clear-cut, although Southern Grey Tit favours dry bush with scattered trees and Ashy Tit frequents better-developed trees and bushes. Ashy Tit is much greyer, both above and below (not mouse-brown above with a dull buff or whitish nuchal spot, dull fringes to the wing feathers and uniformly dull pale buff underparts), and its tail is also proportionally longer. Male, female and juvenile Ashy Tits are all rather similar, whilst female Southern Grey Tit is even duller than the male, and juveniles are decidedly brown.

**SEX/AGE** Sexes very similar, the female faintly tinged drab-brown overall and with a slightly duller bib. Juvenile slightly duller than the adult, with the cap duller, browner and more restricted, the upperparts washed slightly browner, the fringes to the flight feathers tinged dull buff, and the bib duller and not so intensely black. 1st adult as adult, but retains the juvenile tail, tertials, flight feathers and a variable number of greater coverts; these are duller and not so black as the fresh inner greater coverts, and are fringed buff-drab rather than white.

**VOICE** Often clearly distinguishable from that of Southern Grey Tit, the alarm call being the most stable and species-specific vocalisation; in Ashy Tit, it is a series of prolonged nasal rattles, also a harsh *chrrrrrr* or *tschrr tschrr tschrr*. Other calls include a thin, sibilant *si-si-si* of variable length and *sisisisi-cha-cha-cha* or *psi-psi-cha-cha*, also *psi-psi-chrrrrr* (this last phrase similar to one of Southern Grey Tit's, but with the final note flatter and rather more 'muffled'). Song usually a characteristic series of units rapidly repeated at the same pitch as a mellow trill, *tu-tu-tu-tu-tu*, *chi-chi-chi-chi-chi*, *tri-tri-tri-tri-tri*, sometimes slower phrases such as a full *toi-toi-toi-toi*, and squeakier variants such as *speeu-speeu-speeu-speeu*; may, however, give thrush-like couplets more reminiscent of Southern Grey Tit in pattern.

**DISTRIBUTION AND MOVEMENTS** Endemic to Southern Africa. In SW **Angola** occurs north in the arid coastal strip to Benguela, and found throughout most of **Namibia** except the far north, the Caprivi Strip and perhaps the arid southwest, and, although rather local south of about Rehoboth owing to the unsuitable habitat, has been recorded as far south as Keetmanshoop and Klein Karas. In **South Africa** breeds in northern Cape Province, in the west south to Bushman Land and south of the Orange river to at least Kenhardt and Hopetown; apparently obtained by Vieillot at Graaff Reinet in the SE Cape, well within the range of Southern Grey Tit (Clancey 1958a). Also the central, northern and NW Orange Free State and western and central Transvaal, with a few scattered records from the escarpment and lowveld regions in the eastern Transvaal, but status in these areas uncertain; absent from the SE Transvaal. Status in Lesotho also uncertain. Although noted as occurring in the 'lowlands' of northern Lesotho by Clancey (1966, 1980), there are no confirmed records (Bonde 1993); and, although apparently recorded from the Lesotho/Natal border and Orange Free State/Natal border, recorded in Natal only in winter (Sibudeni in Zululand, and Ladysmith; Clancey 1964b), with no records during the field work for the Natal atlas (Cyrus & Robson 1980). Found throughout **Botswana** except in the far north and northeast, and perhaps disjunctly on the central plateau of **Zimbabwe** from Gwaai, Plumtree and around Kezi north and east to Harare and Inyanga and south to Masvingo; also disjunctly in extreme NW Zimbabwe at Nampini Ranch, west of Victoria Falls, and may occur in suitable habitat on the Zambian side of the Zambezi river. Resident, though some evidence of winter dispersal (see above), and in Zimbabwe may wander into *Brachystegia* near suitable areas of thorn bush.

**HABITAT** Primarily a species of dry thorn bush, especially *Acacia* savanna, also Kalahari scrub and riverine woodland. Favours trees and taller bushes, but also second growth and desolate country so long as there is some cover; sometimes found in *Combretum* and other broadleaved woodland. Usually strictly separated from Miombo Tit by habitat: in SW Angola, Ashy Tit is found in the coastal semi-desert thorn country, while just inland Miombo Tit occurs in the woods on top of the escarpment. Recorded in Namibia at 275–1220 m, in South Africa at 915–1370 m, in Botswana at 915 m and in Zimbabwe largely above 1200 m, although noted down to 900 m the south and up to 1880 m in the Inyanga highlands (in an *Acacia* association adjacent to montane evergreen forest).

**POPULATION** Generally fairly common to common, and in the Transvaal a density of c. 1 pair/50 ha has been recorded in *Acacia* thornveld (Tarboton *et al.* 1987). Often rather local, with the distribution determined by the availability of suitable habitats; in the central Orange Free State largely confined to watercourses, and scarce and local on the Mashonaland plateau of Zimbabwe. In Zimbabwe, habitat changes, especially the removal of *Brachystegia*, may favour Ashy Tit at the expense of Miombo Tit.

**HABITS** Found singly or in pairs, and frequently joins mixed-species foraging parties (in the zone of overlap rarely found in the same parties as Miombo Tit, and has been recorded in the same party as Southern Black Tit, although in broadleaved woodland, an atypical habitat; Ginn *et al.* 1989). Generally forages in the middle storey. Food insects. Noted roosting in weavers' nests and also in an abandoned martins' nest in a sandbank.

**BREEDING BIOLOGY** Season: South Africa, October–December; Namibia, November–January; Zimbabwe, September–November; perhaps opportunistic in the more arid areas. The nest, placed in a tree hole or hole in the ground, is a pad or cup of soft material such as hair, feathers or plant fibres. Clutch 3–6: eggs white, spotted reddish, purple and grey; 18.8 x 13.9 mm. Incubation and fledging periods unknown. Appears to have a cooperative breeding system,

where several adults attend the nest.

**DESCRIPTION** *P. c. cinerascens* **Adult Male**: *In fresh plumage* (June to about November), crown (to below eye), nape and upper mantle black, glossed blue, with white nuchal spot in centre of upper mantle. Remainder of upperparts mid grey, longer uppertail-coverts blackish. Tail black, all feathers tipped white, although sometimes marginally so on T1, outer web of T6 narrowly fringed white. Wing-coverts blackish-grey, lesser coverts broadly fringed mid grey, median and greater coverts broadly fringed and tipped off-white, primary coverts narrowly fringed off-white. Alula blackish, narrowly fringed white. Tertials and secondaries blackish-grey, fringed and more narrowly tipped pale drab grey-white, on secondaries fringes duller and tips whiter. Primaries dark grey, P7–P10 very finely fringed and tipped white, P3–P6 fringed whitish inwards of emargination. Lores blackish, cheeks, ear-coverts and sides of neck white. Throat and upper breast black, faintly glossed blue, with ventral line extending to belly; bib and ventral line narrowly bordered light drab-grey to whitish. Remainder of underparts mid grey. Undertail-coverts blackish, broadly fringed and tipped pale drab-grey to whitish, with diffuse paler spot at tip. Axillaries mid grey, tipped paler, underwing-coverts dark grey, tipped white. *In worn plumage* (about December–May), cap fractionally less glossy and more restricted on nape, nuchal patch rather smaller and upperparts slightly duller, faintly tinged brown. Pale fringes and tips to tail feathers may be very heavily abraded (although still present), may be almost absent on wing-coverts and flight feathers. Bib duller, sooty-brown, with no gloss, and underparts slightly duller and browner; white tips to feathers of sides of neck may abrade so that, when very worn, black completely encircles the white cheek patch. **Bare Parts**: Iris brown to dark brown; bill black; legs and feet blue-grey or dark grey to black. **Adult Female**: As male, but upperparts faintly tinged brown, tail slightly browner (sooty-black), centres to wing-coverts and flight feathers slightly paler and browner, bib very slightly duller and less glossy (sooty), underparts very slightly tinged drab. **Juvenile**: As female, but cap more restricted, slightly duller and browner, with little gloss; upperparts may be more heavily tinged drab; tips to tail feathers rather narrower and duller, tinged drab (may show virtually no pale tips to T1–T3, and tips of T1–T4 quickly abrade); fringes to tertials and secondaries duller, light drab-grey or drab-buff (as wide as adult); bib paler and duller, dark grey. Sexes similar. **1st Adult**: See Sex/Age. **Measurements**: Wing of male 76–84, of female 72–84; tail 52–64, of male 54, of female 52–59; bill 13.2–15.6; tarsus 17–20. Weight 18.5–20.1 g.

**MOULT** Adult post-breeding complete (January–June). Post-juvenile partial, includes variable number of tail feathers, tertials and inner greater coverts, sometimes also alula (March–June).

**GEOGRAPHICAL VARIATION** Slight, with two subspecies recognised.

*P. c. cinerascens* Namibia, Botswana, South

Africa and Zimbabwe. See Description. Note that Clancey (1958a) concluded that there is a greyer population with purer white cheek and nuchal patches in the east of the range (east of the Vaal river in Orange Free State, and in eastern Transvaal and Zimbabwe), naming this 'orphnus', and a more buffy population in the west, in Namibia, Botswana, Cape Province, western Transvaal and Zimbabwe (retained as nominate *cinerascens*). Hall & Traylor (1959), however, considered that the grey birds were in fresh plumage and the buffer birds in worn plumage (or were old specimens), and give evidence to show that this variation is not linked to locality.

*P. c. benguelae* SW Angola, in coastal Namibe and Benguela, perhaps extending into the Kaoko Veld of NW Namibia. As nominate *cinerascens*, but underparts slightly paler, lacking the contrast-ing pale division between the black ventral line and grey flanks; smaller than nominate *cinerascens*. Wing of male 72–78, of female 71, 73; bill 14.5–15.5.

**RELATIONSHIPS** Part of the *afer* species group, and often considered conspecific with Acacia Tit *P. thruppi* (under the name *P. cinerascens*); less frequently, both these species considered conspecific with Southern Grey Tit *P. afer* (under *P. afer*, the oldest name). Overlaps with Miombo Tit in Zimbabwe and occurs close to that species in western Angola with no evidence of interbreeding, confirming the separation of these two as full species. For relationship with Southern Grey Tit, see that species.

**REFERENCES** Clancey (1964b), Ginn *et al.* (1989), Irwin (1959), Maclean (1993), Tarboton *et al.* (1987).

# 84 SOUTHERN GREY TIT *Parus afer* Plate 26
Other name: Grey Tit

Formerly thought to be virtually endemic to South Africa, this rather drab tit has recently been found to occur in central Namibia, although the details of its occurrence there are obscure.

**IDENTIFICATION** Length 130 mm (5.25 in). A large tit with a relatively long and deep bill and relatively short tail. Glossy blue-black cap and large dull buff-white or pinkish-buff nuchal patch, Ashy Tit), and dull pale buff underparts (not mid grey). The tail is also proportionally shorter.

**SEX/AGE** Sexes similar, although the cap and especially the bib of the female are slightly duller

*Figure 84.1 Bib shape. From left to right: fresh adult male; worn adult male; adult female; juvenile male.*

with remainder of upperparts grey-brown. Tail black, rimmed and tipped dull white. Wings dark grey-brown, with light drab-grey fringes to the coverts, tertials and, more narrowly, the primaries and secondaries (not forming distinct wingbars). Rather narrow, triangular white cheek patches, extending onto the sides of the upper breast, bib blackish, extending to the vent in a broad ventral line, and remainder of underparts dull pale buff or pinkish-buff. At a distance may appear rather dark overall, apart from the contrastingly white cheek patches. Superficially similar to Ashy Tit, and the ranges of the two species overlap around the Orange river in northern Cape Province and in Namibia. Southern Grey is much duller and browner, with a less clean-cut appearance. It can be separated by its brownish-grey or mouse-brown upperparts (not mid grey), dull buff-white nuchal spot, wearing to whitish (always whitish on and less glossy, and the bib and ventral line are also slightly less extensive. Juvenile marginally distinct: as adult female, but cap slightly browner and fringes and tips of tail feathers duller and not so white. The sexes differ slightly even in juvenile

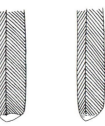

*Figure 84.2 Outer tail feathers (T6) of adult (left) and juvenile (right): note duller pale fringe and tip on juvenile.*

plumage, and the juvenile male is barely distinct from the adult female, with the juvenile female rather duller, but all juveniles are in fresh plumage when the adults are worn and abraded. 1st adult as adult, but ageing is usually possible in the hand using the contrast between the new tertials and greater coverts and the old, retained juvenile flight feathers, primary coverts and alula, and there may also be moult contrasts in the tail.

**VOICE** Common call a series of harsh grating notes introduced by thinner, more sibilant notes (in the 'chick-a-dee' pattern): *tsi-cha-cha-cha* or *tsisisi-cha-cha-cha-cha* (faster than the corresponding call of Southern Black Tit). Alarm a harsh *chrrr*. Song loud and penetrating, but melodic and almost thrush-like, each motif repeated two or three times (sometimes more), thus a cheery *klee-klee-klee*, *cheree-cheree*, *pee-peeoo pee-peeoo pee-peeoo*, *piet-jou-jou*, *piet-tjou-tjou*, *tudi-tudi-tudi-tudit* and variations; apparently lacks the rapid mellow trills of Ashy Tit (and voice noted as rather different from that of Ashy by Macdonald 1957).

**DISTRIBUTION AND MOVEMENTS** A southern African endemic. Breeds in western **South Africa** in Cape Province, east to the highlands of Lesotho (Marakabei, near Maseru, east to Sani Pass) and Port Elizabeth, and north to about the Orange river and the far south and west of the Orange Free State. Also SW **Namibia**, where recorded in Great Namaqualand north to about Lüderitz and Witputz, also central Namibia from Rehoboth about north to near Etosha and east to the Botswana border (and may occur in the extreme west of Botswana). Resident.

**HABITAT** Essentially a bird of arid low scrub in Karoo-type habitats, as well as sparse woodland, dry thornveld and fynbos, often around rocky hills and gorges; also remnant patches of scrub in agricultural areas. Compared with Ashy Tit, favours stunted scrub in preference to trees and bushes. In Namibia recorded at 1220–1320 m and in Little Namaqualand in NW Cape Province at 400–945 m, whilst in Lesotho noted in the mountains at up to 2745 m (with no records from the lowlands).

**POPULATION** Generally uncommon, and scarce in the Orange Free State, but with the northward expansion of the Karoo the range may also spread northwards.

**HABITS** Usually found in pairs or in family parties of 3–6, maintaining contact with frequent calling, and sometimes joins mixed-species foraging flocks. Restless; the flight is bouncing with quick bursts of wingbeats. Forages in smaller trees and bushes; in open scrub south of Kimberley, concentrated on bark, thick branches and twigs, a large proportion of prey being acquired by repeated pecking at the food item or into bark crevices. *Acacia* pods, especially those of Camelthorn, are treated in the same way as Southern Black Tit attacks *Combretum* pods (Ginn *et al.* 1989). Food insects.

**BREEDING BIOLOGY** Season August–March (in the SW Cape, July–October). Nest a cup or thick pad of grass, hair, wool, feathers etc. placed in a hole; in typical habitat tree holes are scarce,

and the species often uses cavities in rocks, culverts or banks, and also man-made artefacts such as pipes, fence posts and old buildings. Clutch 3–4 (2–5): eggs white, spotted reddish, purple and slate-grey; *c.* 19.2 x 14.6 mm. Incubation period *c.* 14 days. Some evidence of cooperative breeding, as the young are fed by up to four adults. Fledging period unknown.

**DESCRIPTION** *P. a. arens* **Adult Male**: *In fresh plumage* (March–August, sometimes December), forehead, crown (to below eye), nape and sides of upper mantle black, glossed blue. Large patch on lower nape and upper mantle white, variably washed drab-grey. Upperparts greyish-drab, longer uppertail-coverts sooty-black. Tail sooty-black, all feathers tipped pale drab-white, although sometimes only a small spot at the tip of T1–T2; outer web of T6 broadly fringed pale drab-white. Wing-coverts and alula dark grey-brown, fringed light drab-grey, fringes broadest on greater coverts and narrowest on alula. Primary coverts grey-brown, fringed light drab-grey. Flight feathers grey-brown, tertials broadly fringed light drab-grey, secondaries fringed and tipped light drab-grey, P3–P10 fringed and faintly tipped light drab-grey, only inwards of emarginations on P3–P6. Lores black, cheeks, ear-coverts and sides of neck off-white. Throat, upper breast and line on centre of lower breast, belly and vent blackish, faintly glossed blue on throat and breast, feathers at sides of line on breast tipped pale drab. Sides of breast off white, washed drab-grey; flanks, sides of belly and vent, and thighs and axillaries light drab. Undertail-coverts blackish, broadly fringed and tipped light drab, extreme tips slightly paler. Underwing-coverts sooty, broadly tipped light drab. *In worn plumage* (September–February), cap less glossy, upperparts slightly darker and less grey, nuchal patch, cheeks and sides of breast whiter; pale tips to tail feathers may be completely abraded, fringes to wing-coverts and flight feathers abraded, especially on tertials, tips to greater coverts and fringes at base of outer primaries bleached to off-white. Bib duller, sootier and less glossy, underparts slightly less grey and more buff. **Bare Parts**: Iris dark brown to black; bill black; legs and feet black or grey to blue-grey. **Adult Female**: Very similar to male, but bib sooty-brown, lacking gloss, and averages slightly smaller and more restricted (lower border semicircular rather than wedge-shaped), with a narrower ventral line. Cap averages slightly less glossy and slightly less deep black. **Juvenile Male**: As adult female, but cap slightly browner, with no gloss, pale tips to tail feathers rather narrower and duller, light drab, T6 more broadly fringed and tipped light drab; bib as adult female's in shape and colour. **Juvenile Female**: As juvenile male, but cap even browner and bib marginally paler and browner. **1st Adult**: See Sex/Age. **Measurements**: Wing 68–81.5, of male 71–79, of female 68–74; tail 53–60; bill 13–15.5; tarsus 17–22. Weight 17.3–22.4 g.

**MOULT** Adult post-breeding complete (December–April). Post-juvenile partial to incomplete, includes greater coverts and variable number of tertials and tail feathers, probably sometimes inner secondaries, larger feather of alula and even primary coverts (December, May).

**GEOGRAPHICAL VARIATION** Slight. Western and northwestern populations are paler than those from the more humid southern, central and eastern districts, and two poorly marked subspecies are sometimes recognised.

*P. a. arens* Lesotho, SW Orange Free State and the Karoo of the eastern Cape, south to the coast at Port Elizabeth. See Description.

*P. a. afer* Namibia and the western Cape, east to about the valley of the Great Fish river. As *arens*, but mantle and rump average slightly paler and greyer, drab-buff tones reduced, sides of breast and belly rather paler, whitish, washed yellow, and the flanks much paler, washed pale buff. Averages slightly smaller. Wing 72.5–77.

**RELATIONSHIPS** Forms a species group together with Ashy, Miombo and Acacia Tits. Long considered conspecific with Ashy Tit, as the ranges of the two species were thought not to overlap, and Macdonald (1957) reported indications of intergradation in Southern Grey Tits from Witputz in SW Namibia and in Ashy Tits from the Keetmanshoop and Klein Karas region in SE Namibia. Hall & Traylor (1959) suggested that ecological segregation between the two may not be complete where their respective habitats, the Karoo scrub and thornveld, merge. However, it is now known that the two species overlap widely in Namibia, and also in NE Cape Province at Hopetown (Clancey 1963). The voices of Ashy and Southern Grey Tits are clearly distinguishable, especially the alarm calls (the most stable and species-specific vocalisation). The status of the two as distinct species is beyond doubt, and, indeed, they cannot even be treated as members of the same superspecies given the very broad overlap in range.

**REFERENCES** Clancey (1963), Ginn *et al.* (1989), Hall & Traylor (1959), Maclean (1993).

## 85 GREAT TIT *Parus major*                    Plates 27 & 28
Other name: Grey Tit

The most widespread of the tits, its distinctive plumage, close association with man and loud and very varied vocabulary ensure that this is one of the most familiar birds in Europe. It is also perhaps the most intensively studied bird in the world.

**IDENTIFICATION** Length 140 mm (5.5 in). A rather large, bulky tit with a stout bill. Divisible into three very distinct groups.

The *major* group of Europe, NW Africa, and northern Asia east to the Pacific and south to Israel, northern Iran, Mongolia and northern China. Cap and nape glossy blue-black, connecting at the rear with the glossy blue-black bib and completely encircling the more or less triangular white cheek patches. Mantle green; rump and wing-coverts grey-blue, with a broad white wing-bar on the tips of the greater coverts. Flight feathers blackish-grey, tertials tipped white, primaries and secondaries fringed grey-blue towards the base. Tail dark blue-grey, broadly bordered white. Underparts yellow, divided by a variable black ventral line from the bib to the vent. Distinctive: the white cheek patches, lack of a white nuchal patch (although there may be a small poorly defined pale patch), and yellow underparts with a black bib and ventral line are unique.

The *cinereus* group of NE Iran, southern Afghanistan, the Indian subcontinent, SE Asia and Indonesia. Often known as 'Grey Tit'. Resembles the *major* group, but has the upperparts blue-grey and the underparts whitish. Juveniles, however, usually show a green tinge on the upperparts and faint yellow wash on the underparts. The white cheek patches, black bib and ventral line and grey upperparts are distinctive. Note that, in the Himalayas, China and Vietnam, Great Tit is replaced at higher altitudes by Green-backed Tit, which rather resembles Great Tits of the green-and-yellow *major* group (see p. 372 for details). 'Grey Tit' overlaps with Turkestan Tit in the far northeast of Iran at Sarakhs and on the northern slopes of the Kopet Dag in SW Turkmenistan and also, very locally, northern Iran (and the two may also overlap in northern Afghanistan). They are very similar and great care should be taken with identifications (see Turkestan Tit, p. 367, for full details).

The *minor* group of SE Russia and Japan south to southern Tibet and northern South-East Asia. As the *major* group, with the upperparts green (or usually showing some traces of green), but the underparts are whitish. Similarly distinctive, although in northern Xinjiang, NW China, and extreme SW Mongolia the range abuts that of Turkestan Tit. Great Tit is usually found in the mountains, Turkestan Tit in the lowlands, but the two species may hybridise in these areas, and any observations should be fully documented.

**SEX/AGE**

The *major* group Sexes only slightly distinct, but in good conditions it is possible to sex birds in the field. The male has the crown and throat glossy black and the black ventral line broad and usually glossy, widening to become a large patch on the belly which extends to the thighs. The female has the black areas duller, especially the bib and ventral line, which are only faintly glossy and often dull grey-black (although the cap may be rather black and glossy); the black rear border to the cheek patches averages narrower and the ventral line is also rather narrower and sometimes broken, becoming a *small* dark patch between the legs (vent white with some black feather bases showing, and white also more extensive on the thighs and undertail-coverts than in the male). Juvenile distinct: duller, paler and more washed-out than the adult, with the cap dark sooty-brown, cheek patches washed yellowish, upperparts dull olive-green, wing-coverts olive-grey, primary coverts dark grey and diffusely fringed greyish, bib small and poorly defined, ventral line faint or absent, and underparts pale yellow. Juveniles can be difficult to sex, but, with practice, some may even be sexed as nestlings. Females may have the dark band on the side of the neck and the ventral line faint or absent and the tail and primary coverts slightly browner and less bluish than the male, but the best character is the pale fringes to the primary coverts, which are narrow and poorly defined, brownish, greenish or pale grey in the female, better defined and bluer in the male. 1st adults can be aged in the hand by moult contrasts in the wing. In NW Europe at least, the juvenile flight feathers are retained, with rather greener fringes (especially on the secondaries) than the adult's. Notably, the juvenile primary coverts are also almost always retained. These have more worn and pointed tips than the adult's at the same time of year, and their dull greyish fringes are sometimes washed greenish (bluest, being mid grey, fringed blue-green, on 1st-adult males, but still showing a slight green cast; brown-grey fringed greenish/greyish on females). Importantly, the lesser and median coverts (and most or all of the greater coverts) are always replaced with fresh grey-blue feathers, and these always show at least a slight colour contrast with the retained primary coverts; on adults they are concolorous. There may also be moult contrasts in the greater coverts, tail and alula (which may be moulted on one wing only), with any retained juvenile feathers being greyer (less bluish), narrower and more worn than the adjacent new feathers. (In general, it is better to sex birds first, and then try to age them.)

**The *cinereus* group** The sexes differ as in the *major* group, notably differing in the extent of the ventral line; the female's underparts are also a little duller. Juveniles differ from adults much as in the *major* group, being duller, but also show more yellowish in the plumage, with a pale yellow wash on the underparts and an olive cast to the mantle and lower back, although the yellow coloration on the underparts fades or is moulted within a few weeks of fledging.

**The *minor* group** The female differs from the male as in nominate *major*, although additionally her tertial fringes are washed olive. Juveniles also differ from adults as in nominate *major*.

**VOICE** Very vocal, especially males, with an extraordinarily complex and varied vocabulary. An average male might have 32 distinct utterances, and up to 40 have been recorded. Most calls are noticeably full and loud, often with a distinctive metallic or ringing quality, but occasionally even the most experienced birdwatcher may be confused as to the identity of the vocalist. In the *major* group the territorial song of the male is a

repeated motif, perhaps most characteristically comprising two syllables, but on more detailed analysis frequently 1–4 notes (and sometimes up to 6 and occasionally as many as 10 notes). The motif is repeated up to ten times in each song phrase, and each phrase is then repeated several times. The song is loud and often sharp and rather metallic or bell-like, e.g. *teechuwee teechuwee...*, *tsi-tsi-daa, tsi-tsi-daa...*, and often transcribed as 'tea-cher, tea-cher, tea-cher...'. Each male has a repertoire of 3–7 (–18) song types, classified according to the number of notes in a phrase, the manner in which frequency and amplitude change, and the time taken to repeat a phrase. A single population may have as many as 40 song types in any one year, the song types gradually changing over time. Territorial males countersing, matching their neighbour's song phrase in song-duels. Females apparently sing very rarely. The song is very uniform across the vast range, with European Great Tits responding fully to playback of song from Siberian males. The subsong is a continuous flow of low, whispered notes. A common and characteristic call is a ringing, metallic *tink* or *pink* (often very similar to a call of the Common Chaffinch), repeated several times (*pink-pink-pink*) and used almost exclusively by the male, often when asserting territorial rights. The *tink* call is usually given in periods when there is little song and may serve similar functions to the song. Contact calls include a sibilant, thin, high-pitched *tsee*, given in rapid series, each note falling in pitch, and a lower-pitched *pee* or *tui*, also falling slightly in pitch; a *tsee-tsui* anxiety call may be slowly repeated many times. A variety of quiet, monosyllabic, unmusical notes is given whilst foraging (or during fights), *pit, chit, spick* or *squink*. A nasal *tcha-tcha-tcha* recalls Marsh Tit (especially when combined with an explosive *psiu*). Also characteristic is a wide variety of scolding 'churring' calls, such as a rapid, low, hard *chich-ich-ich-ich-ich* (recalling a Blue Tit, but louder and fuller, with the individual notes better separated) and *chur-r-r-rihihi*, given in alarm (e.g. in response to a mammalian predator) or excitement; at low levels of alarm, it is often combined with *pee, pit* and *tink* notes. The hawk-alarm is a high-pitched, trilling *seeee*. During the laying period, the female solicits food from the male with a squeaky *zeedle-zeedle-zeedle-zee*, a call also given by males during copulation. Begging juveniles give a high-pitched series of notes, *tsee-tsee-tsee-tsee-tsee*, usually rising in pitch (unlike Blue Tit, in which the phrase ends in one or more falling notes). The juvenile location call, given when temporarily isolated from parents or companions, is three rather plaintive reedy notes on the same pitch, *pee-pee-pee*. Juveniles also give a very quiet warble (recalling the adult's subsong). Incubating females disturbed at the nest give an explosive hiss (see below). (After Cramp & Perrins 1993, Gompertz 1961, Gosler 1993.) In the **cinereus group** the song sounds superficially similar to that of the *major* group. It is composed of combinations of 2–4 whistled units repeated in the 'tea-cher' pattern, e.g. a rapidly repeated *chew-a-*

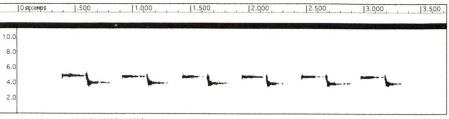

spi-tink spi-tink spi-tink...

Figure 85.1  *A single song phrase of Great Tit, subspecies* newtoni *(of the* major *group) (Norfolk, England; Simon Harrap). Although very variable, the song is typically a ringing bisyllabic motif on the 'tea-cher' pattern, in this case* spi-tink spi-tink spi-tink....*The sonagram shows the individual notes to be quite simple in structure and of roughly constant frequency.*

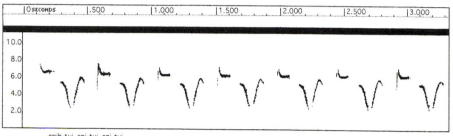

spih-tui spi-tui spi-tui...

Figure 85.2  *A single song phrase of Great Tit, subspecies* mahrattarum *(of the* cinereus *group or 'Grey Tit') (Sri Lanka; Simon Harrap). The songs of the grey-and-white* cinereus *group sound to human ears very similar to the ringing 'tea-cher' of the* major *group, although perhaps sometimes thinner; they are similarly variable. Sonagrams show, however, that the notes are very different in structure, being pronounced chevrons produced by steep frequency ascents and descents. Intriguingly, playback experiments show that there is only limited response by birds of one group to the songs of the other.*

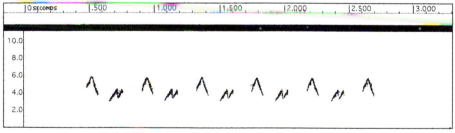

si-pwi  si-pwi  si-pwi...

Figure 85.3  *Single song phrase of Great Tit, subspecies* minor *(Hebei, NE China; Paul Holt). As in the* cinereus *group, the song sounds very like the 'tea-cher' of the* major *group, but sonagrams reveal the individual notes to be chevrons. Notably, the song of the* cinereus *group elicits full territorial response from birds of the* minor *group.*

ti, chew-a-ti, chew-a-ti..., swee-pepe-ti, swee-pepe-ti..., wheat-ear, wheat-ear... etc. There are subtle differences from the *major* group, and it tends to sound thinner and may recall Coal Tit; in both Pakistan and Afghanistan, the species lacks the metallic, saw-sharpening song (Roberts 1993, Paludan 1959). There is little geographical variation, and songs from Afghanistan, India and Nepal are remarkably similar. Detailed analysis using sonagrams reveals, however, that the individual units of the *cinereus* song are rather different in structure from those of the *major* group, and playback experiments show that there is only limited recognition of the 'wrong' song. In experiments by

Gompertz (1968), there was a complete lack of mutual recognition between a captive female of the *cinereus* group and wild birds of the *major* group; they behaved as two distinct species. In the *cinereus* song each motif is characterised by steep frequency ascents and descents, rather than being composed of simple notes of roughly constant frequency as in the *major* group. Songs of the *cinereus* group show on sonagrams as upstrokes and downstrokes combined in V-shaped chevrons, pointing either upwards or downwards, compared with the rather flat traces produced by the *major* group (see figure 85.1 and 85.2). Calls used in aggressive and assertive situations are also distinctive (especially the *cinereus* group's equivalent of 'pink' and 'pit-churring'). Most other calls are very similar, although perhaps a little weaker, and the location call, used by recently fledged juveniles, is very close in the two groups. The vocabulary of the *minor* group includes a 'tea-cher'-type song, although perhaps shriller and less pure, more rasping, than is normal in the *major* group (and thus closer to the *cinereus* group; sonagrams reveal that the structure of the syllables is similar to that of the *cinereus* group and the song of the *cinereus* group elicits full territorial response from birds of the *minor* group in Amurland; Martens & Eck in press.). The Japanese name for the species is 'Shiju kara', which, although literally meaning 'forty titmouse', is onomatopoeic of the song, shi-ju, shi-ju (Austin 1948).

## DISTRIBUTION AND MOVEMENTS

The *major* group breeds in **Ireland**, **Britain** (including Isles of Scilly, but local in Outer Hebrides and absent Orkney and Shetland), and throughout mainland **Europe**, apart from some mountainous areas in arctic Scandinavia, the Alps and Greece. Also breeds in the **Channel Islands** (UK), Baltic islands, **Balearic Islands**, **Corsica**, **Sardinia**, **Sicily**, **Crete**, the Aegean islands and **Cyprus**. In **NW Africa** widespread in **Morocco** in the Atlas mountains and the coastal districts to the north and west, and in northern **Algeria** and NW **Tunisia**. Found throughout **Turkey** except for parts of the central plateau and the southeast. In **Syria** recorded in the northwest, southwest (east to Damascus and the Yarmuk valley east to about Dar'a) and northeast (Tall Tamir, winter only?). Also **Lebanon**, western **Jordan** and northern and central **Israel**, extending marginally into NE **Egypt** (NE Sinai, between El Arish and Rafah). Recorded in northern and NE **Iraq**, and widespread in **Iran**, in the north from Azarbaijan east through the Elburz mountains, in the west, south and east in the Zagros mountains to Neyriz and (possibly disjunctly) to the Kerman highlands, and southwest into riverine forest in Khuzestan. In **Russia** found north to Arkhangel'sk and *c.* 61° N on the Yenisey. In SW Siberia, breeds south in the Ural valley to *c.* 51° N, and further east to the Altai and Sayan mountains. In northern **Kazakhstan** found south to *c.* 51° N, and in eastern Kazakhstan to Semipalatinsk, Zaysan Nor, the Tarbagatay and Saur ranges and northern slopes of the Dzhungarskiy Alatau. In Central Asia in the northern Tien Shan of eastern **Uzbekistan**, SE **Kazakhstan** and NE **Kyrgyzstan**, there are scattered records from the hills near Samarkand, through the Lake Issyk-Kul basin, east to about Charyn in the Ili valley (see Population). In **NW China** found in NW **Xinjiang** in the Dzhungarskiy Alatau and Tarbagatay mountains (on the border of Kazakhstan), and in northern **Mongolia** found south to *c.* 46° N, to the northern foothills of the Mongolian Altai, Hangayn and Hentiyn mountains, and the Kerulen river. In the **Russian Far East** found east to the Sea of Okhotsk (north to the Uda river, and recently to Magadan: pers. obs.), and in **Amurland** to the Bureiskiy Khrebet range and *c.* 131° E on the 'middle course' of the Amur river,

but southern and eastern limits unclear (and mapped range tentative). In **NE China** occurs in NE **Nei Mongol** (see Geographical Variation). Rare migrant **Malta** (mainly October). Vagrant **Iceland** (autumn 1959), and vagrant Great Tits have been reported in Central Asia from the Syrdar'ya river and Aral Sea. Resident in most of the southern and central parts of the range (e.g. 80% of British ringing recoveries involve movements of less than 10 km), but those breeding at higher elevations may undertake some limited altitudinal movements. Northern and eastern populations are eruptive migrants, moving in highly variable numbers depending on the food supply, movements sometimes involving huge numbers in years when the beech crop fails. Water-crossings are still uncommon, but less so than with other tits, and frequently but irregularly crosses the North Sea to Britain and occasionally Ireland (e.g. October 1957); occasional records from Orkney, Fair Isle and Shetland presumably all refer to birds of Continental origin. The axis of eruptive movements is west or southwest, and most invaders are 1st adults. The sex ratio is also uneven, with females predominating (males being more faithful to their territory). Some invading birds remain to breed in the wintering areas. There is good evidence that a proportion of the irruptive migrants survive to return to their natal areas the following spring. In western Siberia, some Great Tits winter in taiga forest areas, even to the north of the breeding range, but many move southwards.

The *cinereus* group breeds in SW **Turkmenistan** from the 'lower and middle' Atrek river and its tributaries (Vaurie 1959) east in the western Kopet Dag mountains to about Ashkhabad. In adjacent NE **Iran** found from Sarakhs in the extreme northeast, west around the southern watershed of the Kopet Dag to *c.* 57° E, in the Atrek valley north of Ashkhaneh (D. Scott pers. comm.) and to *c.* 56° E at Moraveh Tappeh (= 'Marave'; Vaurie 1950a), and also south to *c.* 33° N (Gesik; Vaurie 1950a). Also occurs in southern and eastern **Afghanistan** (replaced in Afghan Turkestan and Badakhshan by Turkestan Tit). In **Pakistan** breeds in northern Baluchistan (from the Harboi hills north through Ziarat to the Shinghar range and Takht-i-Sulaiman), the Safed Koh mountains (NWFP), and in southern Chitral, Dir, Swat (from the main vale up to Swat Kohistan and the Utrot and Ushu valleys), the Gilgit and Hunza valleys, Baltistan, Azad Kashmir (including the Kagan valley), Hazara, and south to the Murree hills. Breeds in northern **India** in Kashmir, Ladakh, Himachal Pradesh, northern Uttar Pradesh, Bihar, West Bengal (but not recorded Darjeeling district or Sikkim), **Bhutan**, **Bangladesh**, Assam (east to the Mishmi and Patkai hills), Nagaland, Manipur and Meghalaya, also **Nepal** and central and western **Myanmar** (**Burma**). Occurs disjunctly in central and peninsular India south of a line from central Rajasthan (Jodhpur and Sambhar Lake) and Gujarat (including the Kathiawar peninsula, although absent Kutch) east through Madhya Pradesh to Orissa, and also in **Sri Lanka**. There are other apparently disjunct populations of 'Grey Tits' on **Hainan** island, in SE Asia in southern **Laos** (south of *c.* 16° N), southern **Vietnam** (south Annam around Pleiku, and in upper Cochinchina) and adjacent NE **Thailand** (Phetchabun and Ubon provinces), and in the Malay peninsula in Thailand south of the Isthmus of Kra (in Phuket, Trang and Pattani provinces), coastal districts of extreme southern Tenasserim, **Burma**, and the west coast of **Malaya** south to Selangor, including Penang island. In the Greater Sundas occurs in **Sumatra**, **Java** and **Bali** (**Indonesia**), but status in **Borneo** not clear. Smythies (1957) dubbed it 'The mystery bird of Borneo'. First collected in the 1880s around the Bengo range, due south of Bau, on the Sarawak/Kalimantan border, it was then not recorded until 1956, when one or two were seen in mangroves at Pending, near Kuching, **Sarawak**, from where there are several subsequent records. It has also been noted at Binsulok, Kuala Penyu and on the Kinabatangan river in **Sabah**, and in **Kalimantan** at Lupak Dalam on the Kapuas river (Kalimantan Barat) and around Banjarmasin (Kalimantan Selatan), and may be thinly distributed in many coastal areas. In the Lesser Sundas of **Indonesia** found on **Lombok**, **Sumbawa**, **Komodo**, **Rinca**, **Flores**, **Paloe**, **Sumba** and **Alor**, and possibly also **Timor** (no records published since 1885; may be rare and local, but occurrence needs confirmation). In the northern part of the Indian subcontinent, there is some winter dispersal to the foothills and plains of northern Pakistan south to the Peshawar region, Kohat, Bannu, Mianwali, the Salt Range, Jhang, Sargodha, and the Punjab, mid October–March, and in Baluchistan descends to the Quetta valley and Chiltan hills. Also winters in northern India in the Punjab and western Uttar Pradesh. Rather sedentary, however, with many birds remaining at high altitudes in the valleys of Gilgit, Baltistan and Ladakh. In peninsular India, some dispersal to the plains.

The *minor* group breeds in eastern **Russia** in **Ussuriland** and **Amurland** from the Amur-Zeya plateau (to at least Pashkovo, and perhaps west to Dzhalinda) east to the lower Amur river (and the lower reaches of its 'left-bank' tributaries), Khabarovsk, and the coast of the Sea of Japan (although the northern limits of the range to the east of Khabarovsk are unclear, as are the western limits and the degree of any overlap with the *major* group; mapped range tentative); also throughout **Korea**, including Cheju-do and Ullung-do islands. Found in NE, central and southern **China**, west to **Heilongjiang** (Xiao Hinggan Ling range and Harbin), **Jilin** (Changbai Shan range), **Liaoning** (Shenyang), **Hebei**, **Shanxi**, southern **Shaanxi** (Qin Ling mountains), southern **Gansu** (Lanzhou southwards), eastern and SE **Qinghai**, **Sichuan**, SE **Tibet** and **Yunnan**. Also recorded in NE **Nei Mongol**, in the Da Hinggan Ling range around Yakeshi (non-breeding only?). Also breeds in eastern **Burma**, NW **Thailand** (Chaiya Prakan and Chiang Mai provinces), northern **Laos** (south to the Tranninh plateau and Xieng Khouang), and northern **Vietnam**. Off eastern Russia, found on **Sakhalin** island (north to the delta of the Tym river), Moneron island (off SW

Sakhalin), the **Kurile** islands on Urup, Iturup, Kunashir, Shikotan, and islands in Peter the Great Bay. Has recently spread to the **Kamchatka peninsula**, around Petropavlovsk-Kamchatskiy and Elizovo (see Population). In **Japan** breeds on Hokkaido, Rebun, Rishiri, Honshu, Sado, Oki, Shikoku, Kyushu, Tsushima, Iki (breeds?), the Goto Islands (breeds?), the Seven Islands of Izu (Oshima, Toshima, Niijima, Shikine, Kozu, Miyake, Mikura), Hachijo and Yakushima. Occurs on the Nansei (Ryukyu) islands of southern Japan on Amami-oshima, Tokunoshima, Okinawa, Yagachi, Ishigaki and Iriomote. Resident, but in the Vladivostok region of the Russian Far East most are migratory, moving south in September–October and returning March–April, and in Japan many move from Hokkaido south to Honshu in winter. There is some altitudinal movement in Japan, and also in Korea, when found in gardens in Soul in winter. Vagrant **Taiwan** (Puli Nantou, January 1920) and recorded once in northern **Sikkim** (Lachan at 3660 m, March 1952; specimen in Natural History Museum, Tring, but not from Bhutan (*contra* 'Peters').

## HABITAT

The *major* group Open mixed and deciduous forest, but only the fringes of very dense woodland. Also olive groves, orchards (especially in the Middle East), scattered trees and hedgerows in cultivated areas, cemeteries, parks and gardens; and (at low densities) coniferous forest and plantations, and in Siberia occasionally in spruce-fir forests, but found there primarily in birch, willow and mixed woodland, often along rivers and around cultivation and settlements. In more arid areas of the Middle East and Mongolia, also found in riverine woodland and thickets, in isolated trees and around human settlements, and in Mongolia also in montane forest, and migrants and wanderers have been recorded there in treeless steppe. Although essentially a lowland species, may occur up to the treeline. In Scotland seldom found above 500 m, in Switzerland exceptionally to 1900 m, in Austria to 1400 m and locally and rarely to 1950 m, on Corsica up to 1700 m, in NW Africa to 1850 m, in Lebanon to *c.* 1800 m, in northern Israel up to 1650 m, in SW Iran up to *c.* 3000 m, and in the Tien Shan up to at least 2100 m.

The *cinereus* group In NE Afghanistan occurs in oak forest and scrub, only exceptionally in pines. In Baluchistan breeds in juniper and pine forest, in the NWFP and southern Chitral in Holly Oak, and in northern Pakistan, northern Indian and Nepal in light forest of oak or Indian Horse Chestnut, pine and sometimes Deodar (but usually avoiding dense coniferous woodland), and in sal forest, groves of *Acacia*, open areas and cultivation with scattered trees, whilst in the trans-Himalayas found in orchards and stands of willow and poplars. In NE India occurs in wet deciduous and sal forests and in cultivation. (Throughout the range in the Himalayas, may be replaced in dense forest by Green-backed Tit.) In peninsular India found in dry deciduous forest, scattered trees and groves, mostly in hilly areas, generally avoiding evergreen forest. In Sri Lanka breeds in all zones.

In winter in Pakistan, wanders to the lower valleys and plains, in roadside and waterside trees, orchards, scrub forest etc. In NE Afghanistan recorded at 1000–2600 m, and around the Safed Koh on the Afghanistan-Pakistan border at c. 1500–2285 m. Found in a broad altitudinal range in the Indian subcontinent, although generally in the hills: in Baluchistan breeds above 2100 m, whilst in northern Pakistan and NW India breeds at 1200–2440 m, but in Chitral and Ladakh to as high as 3660 m; in northern India breeds up to c. 1800 m, and in Nepal to 1600 m, occasionally 1800 m (and rarely to 3050 m), but in NE India generally occurs at lower altitudes, in West Bengal below 150 m, in Assam at 150–600 m, locally to 900 m, and in Arunachal Pradesh at 150–1500 m; in the Eastern Ghats of peninsular India noted at 610–915 m, and in Kerala breeds c. 120–2285 m, most commonly at c. 1000 m. In Sri Lanka found up to at least 1770 m, and generally common above 600 m, being less common and more local in the lowlands. In western Burma found in light dry forest, especially teak, bamboo, and 'indiang', largely in the plains and foothills (recorded at c. 500–1100 m on Mount Victoria); also tidal forest at the mouth of the Rangoon river. In Thailand occurs in stands of pines in dry deciduous forest, but in peninsular Thailand, Malaya and Borneo confined to mangroves and stands of casuarina and other forest on the coast. In Sumatra, Java, Bali and the Lesser Sundas found in a wide variety of habitats, from coastal casuarina and mangroves through second growth, coniferous and montane forest and even arid tall grass up to the montane heath zone, as high as 3200 m on Sumatra and 2000 m on Java.

**The *minor* group** In far-eastern Siberia found in relatively open natural woodland, and away from areas where it overlaps with the *major* group also in and around settlements (including urban areas). In China found in light forest, wooded cultivation and gardens, also pine and occasionally spruce forest, but avoids dense broadleaved evergreen forest, in western China and Tibet preferring riverine woodland and thickets, arid river gorges, agricultural areas, and the vicinity of human habitations. Primarily a montane bird in eastern and central China (e.g. recorded at 650–1100 m in Changbai Shan, Jilin; 300–1650 m in Guizhou), perhaps owing to the total deforestation of the lowlands and extreme persecution of all birds. In western China around the rim of the Tibetan plateau found at high altitudes, up to 4040 m in SE Tibet, 4420 m in Sichuan and 3660 m in Yunnan (perhaps to 4175 m,: Voous 1960), although also found as low as 750 m (defending territories) in the Qingcheng Shan of Sichuan (McCallum *et al.* in prep.). In Burma noted in open oak and pine forest at 1220–2135 m. In NW Thailand found almost exclusively in stands of pines in hill evergreen forest, at c. 800–1675 m. In Japan occurs in open deciduous, mixed or coniferous forest, forest edge and also city parks and gardens (especially in winter), breeding at up to 1800 m, occasionally 2200 m.

**POPULATION** Generally common or very com-mon throughout the range, and the most abundant forest bird in Korea and Japan. Noted, however, as sparse and local in Gujarat, NW India, local in Bangladesh and Thailand, uncommon in Qinghai, Zhejiang and Shanxi in China, and as rather scarce and local, even rare, in the Hangayn and Hentiyn ranges in Mongolia and in northern Burma, southern Vietnam, southern Laos and Malaya. Although common in Java (even in gardens in Jakarta) and the highlands of northern Sumatra (e.g. Brestagi and Prapat), rather rare in southern Sumatra and northern Borneo (see Distribution), although recently found on the desolate south coast of Kalimantan, where locally abundant around Banjarmasin. Populations in some parts of western Europe have increased, owing in part to the provision of nestboxes and winter feeding. As with Siberian Tit and Tufted Titmouse, the provision of food and nest sites, whether deliberately or accidentally, by humans has been important in facilitating over-winter survival and range expansion in the north. Birds of the *major* group have spread north in Norway, Finland and Scotland (since c. 1900; has bred Outer Hebrides since 1962), also to the Isles of Scilly (Britain) from the 1920s onwards. European populations experience a two-year population cycle synchronised with seed-crop cycles (notably that of the Common Beech). Similarly, has spread southwards in the 1950s–80s in Israel and NE Sinai, Egypt, following the expansion of human settlement. In Central Asia formerly a winter visitor (only?) to the Dzhungarskiy Alatau of SE Kazakhstan, but spread naturally to the region as a breeding species from 1907, slowly expanding westwards along the northern watershed of the range to reach Taldy-Kurgan by 1963. Additionally, in the early 1960s hundreds of Great Tits from SW Siberia and northern Kazakhstan were released at Alma Ata, Talgar and Bishkek (Frunze) and now widespread in the northern Tien Shan, and very common in the Lake Issyk Kul basin (Formozov *et al.* 1993; J. Martens *in litt.*). In the Russian Far East, Great Tit has spread since the late 1980s to the northern shores of the Sea of Okhotsk at Magadan, and also relatively recently into Amurland in SE Siberia, following the expansion of cultivation, and it is still associated there exclusively with human habitations. The *minor* group has recently spread to Kamchatka, where first recorded in March 1978 in Petropavlovsk-Kamchatskiy and Elizovo, and now resident around these towns and in nearby deciduous forest, with breeding proven. This is thought to be a natural range expansion (Lobkov 1986). In SE Tibet, however, has declined or disappeared following the removal of trees and thickets.

**HABITS** Intensively studied in western Europe. The account below refers to the *major* group, with some material also from the *minor* group in Japan (more southerly populations have, as yet, been little studied). Bold, demonstrative and not shy. Found singly, in pairs, and in flocks. At the end of the breeding season adults stay on or near the territory, but, although they may expand their foraging range a little, they are inconspicuous and display little territorial activity. Shortly after fledging, however (sometimes within a week), juveniles begin to band together with the offspring from other nests to form flocks, and often join mixed-species foraging flocks. The composition of these juvenile flocks is very volatile, partly because of the numerous aggressive encounters among their members, and they apparently roam at random, although it is known that dispersal is short-distance and there is a net immigration into the better feeding areas. Mortality is high, and the young from second broods have a rather lower chance of survival than those from first broods, probably because they have to compete for food and space with older and more experienced juveniles. Such early-fledged young tend to be dominant, and are less likely to emigrate. Indeed, by late autumn the number of juveniles has halved through death and emigration. Note that variations in the size of the population are largely determined by the rate of juvenile survival. By the autumn, the composition of the flock has settled down a bit and it has taken up residence in the area where it will winter. Most or all of the 1st-adult males attempt to establish territories, this in turn producing an upsurge in territorial activity among adult males, but, depending on the locality, even such territory-holding males may spend some time with the winter flocks. Adult males remain on territory all year if the local environment and food supply permit this, emigrating only if forced to do so by harsh winters or inadequate food. Thus, in Israel, where there are mild, equitable winters with plentiful daylight, most adults remain paired and on territory year-round (and do not form flocks). In Sweden, where the very short days of midwinter may make it impossible to find enough food, many birds migrate and join flocks in milder areas to the south and west. Between these two extremes, in Britain, social organisation is rather unstable, with birds responding to a somewhat unpredictable environment. As the winter progresses, territorial birds tend to spend more time with the flocks, and in years (and in more marginal habitats) when the population density is relatively low (and hence there is likely to be less competition for territories the following spring) the tits tend to remain in flocks through the winter. There is probably a trade-off between holding a territory, which may put the birds in an advantageous position in the coming breeding season, and joining a flock, which may be a more efficient foraging strategy and hence to be preferred when conditions are poor. (Note that, unlike most other tits, Great Tits do not store food, so do not need to hold a territory through the winter in order to defend their caches.) The winter flock occupies an ill-defined range and comprises 2–50 individuals, usually forming part of a mixed-species foraging flock. Flocks are well integrated, moving together, especially in the mornings and during November–January. Established pairs may break up during the winter to join the flock, and/or flocks may be formed by the addition of an adult pair to a band of juveniles as the latter pass through the adults' territory. Small groups may join together to form larger flocks, and there may also be aggregations of birds at locally abundant food supplies, such as a good crop of beech mast, territorial adults travelling some distance to join concentrations of 1st adults. Indeed, several hundred birds may gather in one spot. Well-defined dominance hierarchies exist within all flocks. Adults are always dominant over young birds within each sex, and males over females within each age category; but, all things being equal, dominance is also strongly influenced by the location of the flock in relation to an individual's territory or home range (the closer to home, the more assertive the individual). Body size is also important in establishing dominance, which in turn is related to mortality, with, for example, males more likely to survive than females. In late winter there is a revival of territorial activity, boundaries being proclaimed and enforced by singing, and most breeding territories are established by January, within the range of the winter flock. About half the breeding adults die each year, but pairs usually re-form if both adults are still alive. Surviving 1st-adult males establish territories *around* the retained territorial boundaries of the surviving adult males, who may have maintained their territories through the winter or have re-established the previous year's territory. A cold snap may, however, see the temporary abandonment of territorial activity and a resurgence of flocking, but territories are quickly re-established as the weather improves and in any event their boundaries are well defined by the end of March. Pair formation itself may take place *in* the winter flock, *after* the flocks break up (but before territory is established) or, especially in the case of migratory populations, *after* the territory is established. In the various types of display, the white cheek patches and black ventral stripe are prominent. Territories are maintained by song, the male often singing from the highest available perch; neighbours respect each other's boundaries once tested. The mere occupation of the area by the territory-holder is the most significant factor in his maintenance of a claim (possession is indeed nine-tenths of the law). Nevertheless, incursions, especially by 1st-adult males, must be discouraged and physical combat occasionally results. Territory size also expands during the female's fertile period, and the male spends much time guarding his mate during this period, especially in the early mornings, when most copulations occur (he does not want to be cuckolded by another Great Tit). Once the eggs have been laid, territoriality wanes, and pairs may forage outside their boundaries, although in some habitats a well-established territory remains important for successful breeding. Few non-territorial pairs breed successfully, but in some areas of optimum habitat with an excess of nest sites not all breeding pairs are territorial; such 'guest pairs' may be tolerated by territory-holders, but they behave inconspicuously and do not sing. Roosts singly, in the winter usually in holes and crevices in trees, in nestboxes and other man-made structures, but also in the open, even in snow holes (regularly so in Siberia), where mortality is higher.

In very cold climates, if food is short, Great Tits are able to lower their body temperature overnight, from the usual 41.8° C to as low as 32° C, to reduce energy expenditure (see also Siberian Tit, p. 285). Competition for roost sites may be intense, with the more dominant males purloining the safest sites; this is perhaps a factor in the lower survival rates of females. Great Tits also use such sites, but to a lesser extent, during the late-summer moult, and the female roosts in the nest hole during the laying period and for 1–2 weeks after the hatch, and sometimes also for several days or weeks before nest-building begins. Otherwise, in the summer usually roosts in dense foliage. Food insects and spiders and, especially among northern populations during the winter, seeds and fruit, notably of Common Beech and Hazel. Food items, both invertebrates and seeds, are clamped to a twig with one (mostly insects) or both (mostly seeds) feet and hammered with the bill, producing a hole in seeds through which the contents are extracted. Larger seeds may be wedged in a crack or crevice in the bark to give better purchase. In the spring and summer generally forages in the shrub layer, but also in the canopy and on medium to large branches and the trunks or boles of trees, gleaning insects from the surface of twigs and leaves. In winter forages largely below 7 m, in the middle and lower storeys, and, as the season progresses, increasingly on the ground (although not in complete snow cover), where moves by hopping. Seeds are rarely processed on the ground, however, but rather are taken off to cover. In winter a greater proportion of the socially dominant males feed on the ground, leaving females to exploit the less productive shrub layer and bare canopy. A frequent visitor to birdtables, from where Great Tits similarly carry off food to eat in cover. In Ulan Bator in Mongolia, Great Tits have been noted foraging on house fronts, apparently stealing food put out on window ledges and balconies to keep cool in the summer heat (Mey 1988). Perhaps because of their larger size and weight, Great Tits are less adept at aerial gymnastics than other tits, hence spending more time foraging on the ground. Intelligent and adaptable, they follow food-hoarders, such as Coal and Marsh Tits, to steal from their caches. Significantly, a Great Tit has been noted using a conifer needle to extract larvae from their holes, the needle being held in the bill; the use of tools by birds is rather rare. (Largely after Gosler 1993.)

## BREEDING BIOLOGY

The *major* group Perhaps better known than any other species of bird. Season March–July (some from late January in Israel, some third clutches in the north not until early August). The nest is placed in a hole in a tree, sometimes in a wall or other human artefact, occasionally in a rock crevice; takes very readily to nestboxes. Rarely, disused squirrel dreys, old bird nests or dense tangles of twigs may be used. The nest itself is a foundation of moss, together with dry grass etc., lined with hair, wool and occasionally feathers. The nest site is chosen by the female from a selection presented by the male, and the nest is built by the female alone over a period of up to 20 days, although, especially later in the season, a nest can be built in just one day. Clutch 5–12 (3–18), in most habitats second clutches averaging 1.5–2.5 eggs smaller: eggs white, variably speckled and spotted pale-dark red, markings usually concentrated at the larger end (rarely unmarked); 18 x 13.6 mm (*P. m. newtoni*). Second broods not uncommon, especially in coniferous woodland, but less so in deciduous woodland owing to early peak in food supply (e.g. in less than 5% of British pairs in this habitat); third clutches rare. Exceptionally, in Israel following the post-breeding moult, some pairs produce a clutch in October–December (Shirihai in press). Female incubates, period 12–15 days, although incubation may not start for one or two and exceptionally as many as eight days after the last egg is laid; alternatively, incubation may begin up to three days before the clutch is complete, resulting in asynchronous hatching. The female is fed on the nest by the male. If disturbed on the nest, the female gives a distinctive threat display in which she spreads the tail, flicks the wings against the sides of the nest cavity, puffs out her white cheek patches and gives a loud hissing call (snapping the bill shut at the end of the call), often simultaneously flicking the wings sharply down, striking the side of the hole to make a booming sound. This 'hiss display' may also be given by hole-roosting Great Tits, and, in various modified forms, by other tits in Asia, Africa and North America. It may, in a dark cavity, sufficiently resemble a snake to deter predators. Alternatively, incubating birds may sit tight and even allow themselves to be gently pushed aside for inspection of the clutch. Young cared for and fed by both sexes, although brooded only by the female; fledging period 16–22 days. The young are fully dependent for another 6–8 days; first broods may be cared for by the adults for up to 25 days after fledging and second broods for double this period.

The *cinereus* group Season: Afghanistan and Pakistan, April–June; northern India, March–July; NE India and Bangladesh, March–August; peninsular India, February–August (–November); Sri Lanka, January–June, also September–November; Burma, February–April; Indochina, March; Malaysia, mid May–mid July; Java, year-round but especially April–June; Sumatra, February. Nests may be more commonly placed in cavities in human artefacts, in stone walls, natural fissures and crevices, and in rodent and kingfisher burrows, tree holes being less frequently used than in the *major* group. Clutch 3 in Afghanistan, 4–6 (–7 in Kashmir, rarely –9) in the northern Indian subcontinent and 3–5 (–6) in the south, 3–4 (–7) in Burma, 3–4 (–6) in Java: eggs 17.2 x 13.4 mm (*P. m. cashmirensis*). Double-brooded in India, especially in the south.

The *minor* group Season: China, late February–July; Korea, May; Japan, March–August. Clutch 6–10 (3–14) in China, 6–10 in Japan. May use holes in old bamboo, and often uses cavities in walls, buildings, banks and the ground. Double-brooded in China, and may raise several broods in Japan.

*Figure 85.4  Tail of adult P. m. major.*

**DESCRIPTION** *P. m. major* **Adult Male**: *In fresh plumage* (autumn and winter), crown, upper nape, sides of neck, throat and centre of breast glossy blue-black, encircling white cheeks and ear-coverts. Narrow band on lower nape dirty white, grading into greenish-yellow on border of upper mantle; remainder of mantle and scapulars green, tinged grey or olive on scapulars. Back, rump and uppertail-coverts light blue-grey, faintly washed green on rump. Longer uppertail-coverts and tail dark blue-grey, T1 with blackish shaft streak, T2–T6 with blackish inner web, T5 tipped white, T6 with outer web and wedge at tip of inner web white (see figure above). Wing-coverts grey-blue, lesser and median coverts with slightly duller centres, greater coverts with concealed blackish-grey centres to inner webs and extensive white tips (c. 5 mm deep), primary coverts with dark grey inner webs largely concealed. Alula black, narrowly fringed white. Flight feathers blackish-grey, tertials broadly fringed pale greenish-yellow, becoming off-white towards tips; secondaries and P3–P10 narrowly fringed pale grey-blue, fringes narrower and whiter distally of emarginations on P3–P7, secondaries narrowly tipped white, P7–P10 faintly tipped white. Irregular black ventral line, broadening on vent. Sides of breast and belly lemon-yellow, flanks lightly washed grey-green. Thighs black with white inner surfaces, undertail-coverts white, inner webs of longest feathers black. Underwing-coverts and axillaries whitish. *In worn plumage* (about April onwards, sometimes from winter), black of head duller and less glossy, mantle and scapulars duller green, blue of tail and wings slightly greyer, ventral line more extensive, underparts paler yellow and flanks greyer. **Bare Parts**: Iris rich reddish-brown to blackish-brown; bill horny-black to black, cutting edges paler; legs and feet blue-grey to slate-grey. **Adult Female**: In fresh plumage as adult male, but black of head averages duller and less glossy, especially bib, which is only faintly glossy, often sooty blackish-brown. Black band on sides of neck narrower and sometimes broken at sides of throat. Mantle and scapulars slightly duller and darker green, less yellowish. Blue of wings and tail averages slightly duller, fringes to greater coverts and secondaries more greenish-grey. Ventral line averages narrower and duller, more brownish, often broken and replaced by white towards rear, vent white with some black feather bases exposed. White more extensive on thighs and undertail-coverts. **Juvenile**: Cap dark brownish-olive, sometimes extending down sides of neck. Faint dirty-white or yellow nuchal spot, remainder of upperparts dull olive-green, greyer on rump and uppertail-coverts. Tail as adult but overall duller (dark grey), black areas duller, white on T6 less well defined. Wing as adult, but lesser and median coverts dull mid grey, fringed olive, and greater coverts dull mid grey, washed olive, tipped pale yellow or whitish. Primary coverts dark grey, fringed dull mid grey. Flight feathers and alula a little paler (dark grey), secondary fringes grey-green, primary fringes pale grey. Small, poorly defined sooty-grey bib, extending onto centre of upper breast, and sometimes traces of dark grey ventral line extending to belly; undertail-coverts whitish. Cheeks, ear-coverts, sides of neck and remainder of underparts variably pale yellow, washed grey on flanks. Iris greyer than adult; bill more horn-coloured, cutting edges yellow. Sexing difficult (see Sex/Age). **1st-Adult Male**: As adult, but retains juvenile flight feathers, primary coverts and sometimes a few juvenile outer greater coverts, tail feathers, or feathers of alula (see Sex/Age and Moult). Also, underparts may be slightly paler yellow, wings and tail slightly less bright grey-blue, vent sometimes less uniformly black, some feathers tipped white. Some may approach bright adult females, but note moult contrasts. **1st-Adult Female**: Differs from adult female as in 1st-adult male, but moult contrasts may be more obvious. In addition, primaries usually fringed pale greenish-grey (blue-grey on adult), tail averages duller grey, with less contrasting black shaft streak on T1, bib averages slightly paler, dull black or greyish black (not so glossy or dark as 1st-adult male), and underparts paler yellow. **Measurements**: Wing of male 71–82, of female 68.5–80.5; tail of male 59–66, of female 55–63; bill 11.6–13.5; tarsus 18.7–21.7. Weight 14–22.1 g.

**MOULT** Adult post-breeding complete: *major* group, duration c. 68–100 days, mid May–October; *cinereus* group August–November (southern India and Sri Lanka), March (peninsular Thailand), July (Malaya); *minor* group June–September (west China). Post-juvenile partial: in *major* group, includes 7–10 greater coverts (70–97% of birds replace all 10), a variable number of tail feathers (65–90% replace all), tertials (c. 70% replace all), and feathers of alula (often 1–3 feathers, but more variable), and exceptionally some inner secondaries or primary coverts (July–September; starting at age 60–105 days, duration c. 40 days, late-fledged birds start earlier and may moult more rapidly, but to lesser extent, than earlier broods; extent also differs with sex, population and season); in *cinereus* group, the post-juvenile moult may be more extensive, including inner secondaries and occasionally inner primaries (to November in India); in the *minor* group, extent as *major* group?, (July (west China), October–November (south China), August (northern Thailand)).

**GEOGRAPHICAL VARIATION** Pronounced, with variation in the amount of yellow pigment (lipochromes) in the plumage, extent of white in the tail, size and bill shape. A total of 33 races is recognised, divisible into three groups, each of which is sometimes treated as a separate species (e.g. Stepanyan 1990). Although there is some intergradation or hybridisation where the groups meet, with more investigation the best treatment may be to consider them as three species. Within each group, variation is rather slight and usually clinal.

THE *MAJOR* GROUP Eleven races, in Europe and NW Africa east to Iran, Mongolia and NE Asia. Upperparts green, underparts yellow. A slight north-south cline of reduced size (although extreme difference in average wing length only 7 mm, and masked by variation with age and sex). A similar slight north-south reduction is found in the intensity of yellow pigments, but the extent of the white wedge on the inner web of the outer tail feather (T6) varies in a more complex manner, with a reduction north-south in Europe through Spain to NW Africa, the extreme being shown by Tunisian birds, but, whilst birds from the Caspian coast have reduced white, those from the Levant, Iraq and SW Iran have increased white.

**P. m. major** Continental Europe, south to central Spain, central Italy, the former Yugoslavia, Bulgaria, Asia Minor, Transcaucasus and NW Iran (Azarbaijan), and also Siberia east to Lake Baykal and south to the Altai and Sayan mountains. Irregular migrant Britain. See Description. Extent of white on inner web of T6: male 7–34 mm, female 4–34 mm. Includes 'karelini' of SE Transcaucasus (Lenkoran region) and northern Iran (lowlands north of Elburz mountains, in Gilan and Mazandaran), with coloration (especially on underparts) tending towards *blanfordi*, also less white on T6 (0–23 mm) and averaging slightly smaller: wing of male 68.5–78, of female 67–73.

**P. m. kapustini** NW China in NW Xinjiang, Mongolia, eastern Siberia from Transbaykalia eastwards, Amurland, and NE China in NE Nei Mongol (Hulun Nor and Da Hinggan Ling range). Intergrades/hybridises with *minor* of the *minor* group along the middle Amur (see below) and (?) in Nei Mongol (where both recorded from Da Hinggan Ling range). Poorly marked (?). As nominate *major*, but upperparts paler, duller and tinged greyish-blue (as *minor*), underparts rather paler yellow.

**P. m. newtoni** British Isles. Intergrades with nominate *major* in SE England, NW France, Belgium and Netherlands. Poorly marked. As nominate *major* but, on average, mantle slightly greener, less white on T6 (male 2–27 mm, female 2–24 mm), bill longer and wider, with a straighter culmen. Wing of male 71–79, of female 69–80; tail of male 58–65, of female 55–61; bill 11–16.

**P. m. corsus** Portugal, southern Spain and Corsica. Intergrades with nominate *major* in northern Portugal and central Spain. As nominate *major*, but upperparts slightly duller and darker, more greyish-olive, nape less yellowish, underparts purer and paler yellow (less greenish), flanks extensively washed greyish (not greenish); white on T6 reduced (male 0–25 mm, female 0–16 mm). Wing of male 69–78, of female 66.5–75.

**P. m. mallorcae** Balearic Islands. Poorly marked.

As nominate *major*, but yellow pigments slightly reduced, upperparts more grey-blue (less green), underparts paler yellow (may be largely greyish-white); slightly less white on T6 (4–30 mm). Wing of male 69.5–76, of female 67–74.

**P. m. ecki** Von Jordans 1970. Sardinia. As *corsus*, but averages slightly paler (especially underparts), upperparts with more of a blue cast; white on T6 2–16 mm. Wing of male 70–78, of female 69–75.

**P. m. excelsus** NW Africa. As nominate *major*, but upperparts slightly brighter olive-green and underparts purer yellow (less greenish, although not so pale as *corsus* and *mallorcae*); white on T6 reduced or absent (0–11 mm (–29 mm)). Wing of male 74–84, of female 72–77.

**P. m. aphrodite** Southern Italy, Sicily, southern Greece (including islands north to Samothraki, east to Lesbos, Samos and perhaps Kos), and Cyprus. Intergrades with nominate *major* in Makhedonia (northern Greece), Albania, and south and SW former Yugoslavia. As nominate *major*, but upperparts darker and more olive-grey (near *corsus* and *ecki*, but not so grey as *mallorcae*), underparts variable, yellow as nominate *major* to light cream; white on T6 6–26 mm. Wing of male 70–78, of female 67–77. In mainland Italy, Sicily, southern Yugoslavia, Albania, NW Greece, Bulgaria, eastern Romania, and Asia Minor, upperparts as nominate *major* but underparts rather pure light yellow (less greenish), flanks greyish (less olive-green). Following Cramp & Perrins (1993), birds from Sicily and Italy included in *aphrodite* because of small size; larger birds from elsewhere in nominate *major*, although these could be separated as 'sulfureus'.

**P. m. niethammeri** Von Jordans 1970. Crete. As *aphrodite*, but upperparts slightly duller and darker, less green and yellow, underparts very pale (as *mallorcae* or even paler, but less greyish: palest of group); less white on T6. Wing of male 68–75, of female 67–71.

**P. m. terraesanctae** NW Syria, Lebanon, Israel and Jordan, also presumably this race NE Sinai (Egypt). Poorly marked. Size as *aphrodite*, coloration as *blanfordi* or upperparts slightly more washed-out; white on T6 18–29 mm. Wing of male 69–76, of female 67–72.

**P. m. blanfordi** Northern Iraq, Iran in the Zagros mountains and on the southern watershed of the Elburz mountains, also the eastern Elburz around Gorgan and east to the eastern outliers of the Caspian forests southeast of Moraveh Tappeh (D. Scott pers. comm.). As nominate *major*, but mantle and scapulars slightly duller, more greyish and washed-out, underparts purer and rather paler yellow; white on T6 averages more extensive (18–41 mm). Wing of male 73–81, of female 68–74; tail of male 57–69, of female 56. Averages darker in the eastern Elburz, along the southern watershed of the Elburz and west to northern Iraq, paling southwards through the Zagros mountains to Kerman and Fars. Apparent hybrids with *P. m. intermedius* have been seen south of the eastern end of the Elburz mountains, in gardens at Emamrud; they resembled 'Grey Tits', but were washed yellow (D. Scott pers. comm.). Hybrids have also been recorded from near Bojnurd (Vaurie 1950a); and in SW Turkmenistan, in the western Kopet Dag, Formozov *et al.* (1993) note a 'hybrid' population of *'karelini'* x *intermedius*, with many birds being intermediate or having the green-and yellow *major*-type coloration (such individuals being recorded as far east as Ashkhabad).

**THE *CINEREUS* GROUP** Thirteen races, in NE Iran, southern Afghanistan, the Indian subcontinent, SE Asia and Indonesia. Upperparts blue-grey, underparts whitish. Juveniles usually show a green tinge on the upperparts and faint yellow wash on the underparts (may be very faint, especially in southern Thailand and Java). See table, p. 366, for summary of characters.

***P. m. intermedius*** SW Turkmenistan and NE Iran. Intergrades with *ziaratensis* to the east. Possibly of hybrid origin, connecting the *major* and *cinereus* groups (see *P. m. blanfordi* above), but much closer to the latter. As *caschmirensis*, but usually a faint trace of olive on the upper mantle, central tail feathers paler (inner web of T1 usually concolorous with outer web or only slightly darker), much less white in tail (T5 with small whitish tip to inner web and sometimes also outer web, inner web of T6 usually fringed dark), outer webs of greater coverts light blue-grey with blackish confined to a dark wedge along the shaft at the extreme base, tertial fringes more diffuse, and underparts paler and whiter, pale grey-white, washed dull creamy (variably tinged yellow in juveniles, and sides of breast may be faintly tinged yellow in 1st adults). Note alula pattern compared with Turkestan Tit (larger feather dark grey, typically neatly fringed white on outer web, and sometimes also paling to mid grey towards fringe, central feather extensively mid grey). Large. Wing of male 73–81, of female 70–75; tail of male 58–71, of female 58–61.

***P. m. ziaratensis*** Southern Afghanistan (south of the Paropamisus and Hindu Kush from Herat to Kandahar) and Baluchistan, Pakistan. Marginally the palest race. As *caschmirensis*, but upperparts slightly paler (dull pale-light grey, tinged blue; averages slightly paler and less blue in Kandahar), tertial fringes broader and purer white, underparts slightly paler and whiter. An 'immature' from Herat shows a slight trace of green on the upper mantle (Paludan 1959). Large. Wing of male 67–78, of female 66.5–71.5; tail 54–72.

***P. m. decolorans*** SE Afghanistan, east of Kabul and south of the Hindu Kush. As *caschmirensis*,

*Figre 85.5  Tail of adult* P. m. caschmirensis.

but more black on T5 and underparts darker, with flanks especially darker, greyer and more 'smoky' (but wearing a little paler). Large. Wing of male 71–78, of female 70–72; tail of male 63–68.

***P. m. caschmirensis*** NE Afghanistan (Nuristan), and the Himalayas of northern Pakistan and India, east to northern Uttar Pradesh (where intergrades with *nipalensis* in Garhwal); some dispersal in winter to adjacent foothills and plains. Large and pale. As nominate *major*, but upperparts dull mid-light grey, tinged blue, longer uppertail-coverts dark blue-grey. Tail blackish-grey, T1–T4 very broadly fringed mid-dark blue-grey on outer web (leaving a narrow dark band adjacent to shaft), T4 tipped white on outer web, T5 with long white wedge at tip of inner web (20–45 mm deep, mostly >30 mm), dark shaft and white outer web, T6 white, fringed dark grey on basal half of inner web (see figure 85.5). Greater coverts blackish-grey, broadly fringed pale-light blue-grey (dark only along shaft and fully concealed at rest) and tipped whitish, tinged pinkish-drab (4–5 mm deep). Tertials blackish, broadly fringed and tipped dull pale grey-white. Underparts light-pale grey, washed buffy-drab, border of bib and of ventral line slightly whiter, flanks pale-light grey. Female differs as in nominate *major* (but underparts also slightly duller and drabber); juvenile differs from adult as in nominate *major* (but upperparts greener than adult, mid-light grey, tinged yellowish-olive, nuchal patch, cheeks and underparts variably pale yellow-white). Large. Wing of male 68–81.5, of female 67–77; tail of male 60–73, of female 54–66; bill 11.5–13; tarsus 17–20.5. Weight 12.5–17 g.

***P. m. nipalensis*** Foothills and adjacent plains of the Himalayas in northern India (from Kumaon eastwards), Nepal, Bhutan and NE India (except range of *vauriei*), also West Bengal, Bangladesh, and central and western Burma (north to Myitkyina, east to Sinbo, Bhamo, and the western border of the Shan plateau (below *c*. 1000 m) and south to southern Arakan, Pegu and Thaton). As *caschmirensis*, but upperparts slightly cleaner and darker (clean light-mid grey, tinged blue), T1 mid blue-grey with variably blackish shaft streak, white wedge on inner web of T5 12–38 mm (usually 25–35 mm), outer web white, variably fringed black (may comprise most of web), wingbar narrower and whiter, tertial fringes whiter, and underparts paler and whiter (pale grey-white, lightly washed buffy-drab, flanks light-mid grey). Small. Wing of male 63–71, of female 59–69; tail of male 50–61, of female 51–60.

***P. m. vauriei*** Eastern Assam (Lakhimpur district) and eastern Arunachal Pradesh (Mishmi and Patkai hills), to *c*. 900 m. As *nipalensis*, but white on inner web of T5 usually >10 mm deep, flanks darker and smokier; as *decolorans*, but smaller. Wing of male 59–65, of female 60; tail of male 53.5–58, of female 52.

***P. m. stupae*** Central and peninsular India (except range of *mahrattarum*); disjunct from *nipalensis* to the north? Poorly marked, near *mahrattarum*. As *caschmirensis*, but upperparts slightly darker, cleaner and bluer (clean light-mid grey, tinged clean blue), T1 black, fringed mid-dark blue-grey on outer web, white wedge on inner web of T5 usually 20–28 mm, shaft blackish, outer web white, T6 white, greater coverts narrowly fringed light blue-grey (appearing largely blackish on closed wing), tertials fringed cleaner white, and underparts average paler, clean pale grey, tinged pale pinkish-buff (strongest on females), flanks light grey. Small. Wing of male 60–73, of female 60–69; tail of male 47–61, of female 48–58.

***P. m. mahrattarum*** Sri Lanka and Kerala, SW India. As *stupae*, but upperparts average slightly darker and bluer, less white on T5, white wedge on inner web 16.5–34 mm (usually >25 mm), outer web may be broadly fringed black, and underparts duller (closer to *caschmirensis*). Large. Wing of male 68–75, of female 66–69; tail of male 57–65, of female 56–58.

***P. m. templorum*** NE Thailand, southern Laos and southern Vietnam. As *nipalensis*, but centre of greater coverts more extensively black (as *cinereus*), black shaft streak on T1 averages less extensive, white wedge on inner web of T5 usually 26–35 mm. Small. Wing of male 64–68.5, of female 61.5–65; tail of male 58–63, female 54–58.

***P. m. hainanus*** Hainan island. As *caschmirensis*, but upperparts slightly darker (mid grey, tinged blue), may show faint olive wash on mantle, T1 mid-dark blue-grey (as upperparts), T3 tipped white, T5 with long white wedge on inner web (12–35 mm), outer web white (may be fringed darker, sometimes very extensively so, thus outer web blackish with white tip), greater coverts black, very narrowly fringed blue-grey (appearing almost black at rest), tips clean off-white, tertials fringed whitish, underparts paler (pale grey-white, washed dull creamy, flanks pale grey-white, i.e. near *nipalensis*). As *templorum*, but upperparts darker, nuchal spot less conspicuous, and tail shorter. NB: very close to the grey *commixtus* of Vietnam (*minor* group), but bill averages rather stouter. Small. Wing of male 59–67, of female 58–63; tail of male 55–60.5, of female 52–58.

***P. m. ambiguus*** The Malay peninsula in Burma (extreme southern Tenasserim), peninsular Thailand and Malaya, also Sumatra. As *caschmirensis*, but upperparts slightly darker (mid grey, tinged blue), nuchal spot reduced, lores often blackish, T1 dark blue-grey with variable blackish shaft streak, T5 with white reduced to a small spot at the tip, inner web of T6 blackish with variable white wedge at tip (up to 35 mm deep), greater coverts black, narrowly fringed bright blue-grey (bluer than mantle and showing more contrast than other races; appear largely black at rest) and relatively narrowly tipped pale grey-white, tinged pinkish-buff, tertials finely but diffusely fringed pale grey, and underparts slightly darker (light greyish-drab, flanks light–mid grey). Small. Wing of male 64–67, of female 61–63; tail of male 55.5–61, of female 54–56.

***P. m. cinereus*** Java and the Lesser Sundas. As *caschmirensis*, but upperparts slightly darker (mid grey, tinged blue), T1 dark blue-grey with variable

blackish shaft streak, T4 tipped white, T5 blackish, tipped white, more broadly so on inner web (forming a wedge 3–13 mm deep), greater coverts black, neatly and narrowly fringed blue-grey (dark centres show on closed wing) and with tips whitish, tertials fringed whitish, and underparts cleaner and pinker. Rather paler and brighter than *ambiguus*. Small. Wing of male 63–70, of female 61–65; tail of male 50–57, of female 50–57.

***P. m. sarawacensis*** Borneo. As *cinereus*, but upperparts darker, black cap extending onto nape and white nuchal patch faint or absent, lores black, uppertail-coverts black (not grey), tail feathers black, narrowly fringed grey, T6 white, base of inner web black, no white on T5, and broad black ventral stripe. Wing 68; tail 55.

**THE *MINOR* GROUP** Nine races, in SE Russia and Japan south to southern Tibet and northern South-East Asia. Upperparts green or showing some traces of green (except *nigriloris*, or occasionally when in worn plumage). Underparts whitish. A striking cline of increasing colour saturation runs from north to south through the Japanese archipelago and the islands of the Nansei Shoto (Ryukyu islands), the cline also involving the reduction and eventual loss of green pigment on the mantle.

***P. m. minor*** SE Russia in Amurland and Ussuriland, Korea (including Cheju-do), NE and east-central China, south to the River Yangtze and Zhejiang, and west to eastern Qinghai (east to Datong, about Qinghai Hu and T'ien-t'ang Ssu) and NE and central Sichuan; also Sakhalin, Moneron island and the southern Kurile islands, and Japan (except Nansei Shoto). Recorded in NE Nei Mongol in Da Hinggan Ling range, where may overlap or hybridise with race *kapustini* of *major* group. Adult male as nominate *major*, but border of upper mantle olive-yellow, grading to olive on lower mantle and mid greyish-olive on scapulars and back. Amount of white in tail as nominate *major* (T5 tipped white, 3–27 mm deep, T6 with outer web and wedge up to 33 mm deep on tip of inner web white, see figure 85.6). Underparts whitish, sides of breast and upper flanks faintly washed dull pinkish-buff, rear flanks washed pale drab-grey. In worn plumage, the olive tones on the upperparts may be much reduced. Female differs from male as in nominate *major*, although tertial fringes washed olive; juvenile as nominate *major*. Wing of male 64–77, of female 60–77; tail of male 56–72.5, of female 54–68 (averages largest in the north of the range); tarsus 16–20. Weight 11–17 g. Includes '*artatus*' of

*Figure 85.6 Tail of adult* P. m. minor.

China and 'kagoshimae' of southernmost Kyushu and Goto islands (flanks darker). In far-eastern Siberia, in the middle Amur region around Pashkovo (Formozov *et al*. 1993), Blagoveshchensk and 'Kumari' (Vaurie 1959 = Kumara?), hybridises with *kapustini* of the *major* group (despite the profound differences in the structure of their song), hybrids being found around villages where their respective habitats meet (in the zone of overlap, *minor* prefers more natural habitats and *major* is confined to the vicinity of human habitations). Hybrids have the mantle light grey-green and the underparts pale yellow and give song verses with a typical *major* note structure, a typical *minor* note structure, and verses in which typical *major* and *minor* notes are combined (Martens in press).

**P. m. tibetanus** SW China on the Tibetan plateau in southern Qinghai (Yushu and Anmuda (Amdo) plateau south of Qinghai Hui), NW Sichuan (south to Maowen, Barkam, Dawu and Batang), and SE Tibet (from Qamdo, Riwoqe and Bomi south to Markam and west to Yangbajain, Lhasa, Xigaze, and the Chumbi valley); one record Sikkim. Large, with extensive white in the tail. As *minor*, but upperparts rather duller (border of upper mantle not so yellow-olive, lower mantle more greyish-olive, with less contrast between mantle/scapulars/back and rump/uppertail-coverts), T1 blackish, broadly fringed dark blue-grey on outer web, much larger white wedge on inner web of T5 (28–51 mm). When worn, may show little olive on upperparts, which are mid-dark dirty grey, and female even duller and less olive than male. Larger (a very abrupt change in size in some areas of Sichuan). Wing of male 71–82, of female 68–77; tail of male 62–70, of female 58–68. Weight 14–20 g.

**P. m. subtibetanus** SW China in SW Sichuan (south and west of Emei Shan and Kangding), western Guizhou, Yunnan, and SE Tibet (Nang Xian in the Tsangpo valley); possibly also NE Burma? (sight record from the Panwa Pass, east of Myitkyina). Very poorly marked (and often 'lumped' with *tibetanus*). Extent of white on inner web of T5 (18–37 mm), upperpart coloration and size intermediate between *tibetanus* and *minor*. Wing of male 61–76, of female 58–73; tail of male 62–71, of female 57–67.

**P. m. nubicolus** SE Burma in SE Kachin (south and east of Bhamo), the Shan States (and extending west to Maymyo), Kayah and northern Karen (Nattaung); also northern Thailand, northern Laos, and Vietnam in extreme western Tonkin. Poorly marked. As *subtibetanus*, but upper mantle slightly yellower, white on T5 slightly more extensive (26–40 mm), and smaller: wing of male 62–71, of female 63–67; tail of male 54–62, of female 53–61.

P. m. intermedius     P. m. ziaratensis     P. m. caschmirensis

P. m. nipalensis     P. m. vauriei     P. m. stupae

P. m. mahrattarum     P. m. hainanus     P. m. ambiguus

P. m. cinereus

*Figure 85.7  Tails of adults of* cinereus *group of subspecies.*

## Characters of the *cinereus* group of subspecies of Great Tit

| Subspecies | Size | (wing length) | Upperpart coloration (males) | Underpart coloration (males) | Greater coverts (outer webs) | Tertial fringes |
|---|---|---|---|---|---|---|
| *intermedius* | male<br>female | 73.0–81.0<br>70.0–75.0 | dull light grey tinged blue, with hint of olive on upper mantle | pale grey-white, washed dull creamy; flanks light grey | light blue-grey, with dark grey wedge at extreme base (concealed); tips pure white | diffuse, pale grey-white |
| *ziaratensis* | male<br>female | 67.0–78.0<br>66.5–71.5 | marginally the palest race, dull pale-light grey, tinged blue | pale grey, lightly washed buff-drab; flanks light grey | pale-light blue-grey, blackish only in narrow wedge along shaft; tips broad, whitish, tinged pinkish-drab | broad and well defined off-white |
| *decolorans* | male<br>female | 71.0–78.0<br>70.0–72.0 | as *caschmirensis*? | 'darker, greyer and more smoky than *caschmirensis*, especially flanks' | as *caschmirensis*? | as *caschmirensis*? |
| *caschmirensis* | male<br>female | 68.0–81.5<br>67.0–77.0 | dull mid-light grey, tinged blue | light-pale grey, washed buff-drab; flanks pale-light grey | pale-light blue-grey, blackish wedge along shaft (concealed); tips whitish, tinged pinkish-drab | well defined, dull pale grey-white |
| *nipalensis* | male<br>female | 63.0–71.0<br>59.0–69.0 | clean light-mid grey, tinged blue | pale grey-white, lightly washed buff-drab; flanks light-mid grey | pale-light blue-grey, blackish wedge along shaft; tips narrow, clean off-white | well defined, whitish |
| *vauriei* | male<br>female | 59.0–65.0<br>60.0 | as *nipalensis* | as *nipalensis* but flanks washed dark and smoky-grey | as *nipalensis* | as *nipalensis* |
| *stupae* | male<br>female | 60.0–73.0<br>60.0–69.0 | clean light-mid grey, tinged clean blue | clean pale grey, tinged pinkish-buff; flanks light grey | black, relatively narrowly fringed light blue-grey (dark centres show); tips whitish, tinged pinkish-drab | well defined, whitish |
| *mahrattarum* | male<br>female | 68.0–75.0<br>66.0–69.0 | clean mid grey tinged blue | pale grey tinged dull pinkish-buff flanks light grey | black, narrowly fringed blue-grey (dark centres show) tips whitish tinged pinkish-drab | well defined, whitish |
| *templorum* | male<br>female | 64.0–68.5<br>61.5–65.0 | as *nipalensis*? | as *nipalensis*? | centres extensively black, narrowly fringed blue-grey | as *nipalensis*? |
| *hainanus* | male<br>female | 59.0–67.0<br>58.0–63.0 | mid grey, tinged blue; may show faint olive tone on mantle | pale grey-white, washed dull creamy; flanks pale grey-white | black, very narrowly fringed blue-grey (dark centres show); tips clean off-white | well defined, whitish |
| *ambiguus* | male<br>female | 64.0–67.0<br>61.0–63.0 | mid grey, tinged blue | light greyish-drab; flanks light-mid grey | black, narrowly fringed bright blue-grey (dark centres show); tips relatively narrow, pale grey-white, tinged pinkish-buff | slightly diffuse, pale grey |
| *cinereus* | male<br>female | 63.0–70.0<br>61.0–65.0 | mid grey, tinged blue | pale-light grey, washed pinkish-drab; flanks light grey | black, neatly fringed bright blue-grey (dark centres show); tips whitish | well defined, whitish |
| *sarawacensis* | sex? | 68.0 | rather dark | | | |

(Note: palest grey tone is 'pale grey', progressing through light, mid and dark grey to blackish-grey.)

**P. m. dageletensis** Ullung-do (= Dagelet island; South Korea). As *minor*, but green of mantle more restricted, and underparts whiter, with narrower black ventral line.

**P. m. amamiensis** Amami-oshima and Tokunoshima, northern Nansei Shoto. As *minor*, but green tones confined to upper mantle, with lower back and rump darker grey. Wing of male 65–67.5.

**P. m. okinawae** Okinawa and Yagachi, central Nansei Shoto. As *amamiensis*, but green reduced to a wash on the upper mantle, and back and rump darker, mid-dark blue-grey. Wing of male 60–70.

**P. m. nigriloris** Ishigaki-jima and Iriomote-jima, southern Nansei Shoto. As *okinawae*, but much darker, with no trace of green. Upper mantle glossy blue-black (no pale nuchal spot), remainder of upperparts dark blue-grey. Tail blackish-grey, white limited to the tip of T6. Lores black. Broad black band across sides of neck and extensive blue-black bib, thus white cheek patch rather small. Underparts dark, with narrow whitish-grey border to bib and median line, flanks extensively mid grey. Wing of male 64–68.5.

**P. m. commixtus** Southern China, south of the Yangtze river and east of Yunnan, Hong Kong, northern Vietnam in eastern Tonkin (east to Bac Can, Cho Ra and, perhaps this form, Muong Boum) and coastal (?) Annam south to Hue and Da Nang. Perhaps of hybrid origin, connecting the *cinereus* and *minor* groups. As *minor*, but greenish occasionally much reduced on upperparts, almost absent on lower mantle and scapulars (usually very grey with no trace of green in Vietnam, resembling *cinereus*, but tail greyer, black confined to the shaft of T1), underparts slightly darker, more strongly washed pale greyish pinkish-drab, and more white in tail, T5 rather variable, white wedge on inner web 5–24 mm, outer web whitish to almost all dark. Wing of male 60–71, of female 61–67; tail of male 52–62, of female 50–62.

**HYBRIDS** Hybridises with Turkestan Tit; see that species for detail. Otherwise hybrids are very rare, but have been recorded with Blue, Coal and probably Marsh Tits (see p. 241).

**RELATIONSHIPS** Forms a superspecies with Turkestan Tit, and forms a species group with White-naped and Green-backed Tits of southern Asia and with the grey tit complex of Africa (although this last relationship is sometimes disputed, e.g. Short *et al.* 1990).

**REFERENCES** Ali & Ripley (1983), Cramp & Perrins (1993), Delacour & Vaurie (1950), Gosler (1993), Jenni & Winkler (1994), Vaurie (1950a, 1957b, 1959).

## 86 TURKESTAN TIT *Parus bokharensis*                    Plate 28

Closely related to Great Tit, this pallid tit is found in the oases and forests of Central Asia, and presents one of the toughest identification challenges in the family.

**IDENTIFICATION** Length 150 mm (6 in). Cap, sides of neck, bib and ventral line black, encompassing white cheek patches. Upperparts clean pale grey, variably tinged blue, with a diffuse whitish nuchal spot on the border of the upper mantle. Tail broadly fringed and tipped white, and wings with a broad white wingbar on the tips of the greater coverts and white fringes and tips to the tertials. Underparts creamy-white with light grey rear flanks. Juvenile duller, apparently occasionally showing a slight olive tinge to the upperparts and faint yellow wash to the cheeks, wingbar and underparts. In most of the range there are no confusion species, the large size and grey and white coloration being distinctive, but in **SW Asia**, where the range approaches, abuts or overlaps with that of Great Tit, great care should be taken in identifying Turkestan Tit. Great Tits of the grey-and-white *cinereus* group of races ('Grey Tits') are found in SW Turkmenistan on the northern flanks of the western Kopet Dag (occasionally at least east to Ashkhabad), and in NE Iran from about Moraveh Tappeh in extreme eastern Mazandaran east to Sarakhs in NE Khorasan (*P. m. intermedius*), and also in the Paropamisus mountains of NW Afghanistan (*P. m. ziaratensis*). Turkestan Tits are found in the lower foothills of the Kopet Dag and on the plains of Turkmenistan to the north, and in northern Afghanistan. In these regions the two may be largely separated during the breeding season by habitat, Great Tits favouring deciduous woodland on the higher mountain slopes, and Turkestan Tits riverine tamarisks and poplars (often mixed with reeds) in the lowlands (in the Kopet Dag, generally below 300 m). These habitat distinctions may be blurred in the autumn and winter, however, and the two species have been recorded in the same areas of northern Iran (Lotfabad and Sarakhs) and around Ashkhabad in Turkmenistan. The following points may be helpful. * **Size and structure** Compared with 'Grey Tit', Turkestan Tit is slightly smaller, but this is unlikely to be apparent in the field. It is also a little blunter-winged with a slightly shorter primary projection. Turkestan Tit is proportionally 20–25% longer-tailed than Great Tit. The long tail is sometimes obvious (and is probably emphasised by the slightly blunter wings); but, perhaps most notably, Turkestan Tit also shows a graduated tip to the tail, with the outer feather (T6) *c.* 10 (8–19) mm shorter than the central pair, whilst 'Grey Tit' shows a square-cut tail, with just 2–5 mm difference in *intermedius* between the longest and shortest feathers (and in the *major* group of Great Tit the difference is no greater than 9 mm). * **Upperpart coloration** Extremely similar in both species, and females of both are slightly duller and drabber than males. 'Grey Tits' are mid blue-grey, but at very close range most birds of the race *P. m. intermedius* show a faint trace of olive on the upper mantle (this is not shown by *P. m. ziaratensis* of Afghanistan). Turkestan Tit is a shade paler grey, and adults never show a greenish tinge. * **Cheek patch** Larger on Turkestan Tit, extending further behind the eye, and forming a more neatly triangular patch than on 'Grey Tit' (*P. m. intermedius*); given the effects of posture and wear, however, this can be only a supporting character. In addition, the blackish rear border averages slightly narrower and less distinct on Turkestan Tit, and the bib may not join the cap at the rear, especially on females (and perhaps more often also on birds from the eastern part of the range in NW China). * **Ventral line** In fresh plumage, rather broader and more obvious on male 'Grey Tits', but females of both species are much more similar, and male Turkestan Tits have rather broader and better-defined ventral lines when worn than in fresh plumage. Thus, the width of the ventral line is a positive character for male 'Grey Tits' only in autumn and winter, and the underpart coloration of the two species is otherwise practically identical, both showing a creamy wash. * **Fringes to flight feathers** Turkestan Tit shows slightly broader, paler and more powder-blue fringes to the primaries and secondaries. The wingbar on the tips of the greater coverts is similar in both species. * **Alula** On adults and most (or all?) 1st adults, pale-light grey with a variable darker shaft streak (usually concealed) and neat white fringe to the outer web of the largest feather. At rest, the alula is usually no darker than the rest of the wing. On 'Grey Tits' (*P. m. intermedius*), the alula is dark grey with a neat white fringe to the larger feather, contrasting with the rest of the wing. Note that the alula of juvenile Turkestan Tit resembles that of Great Tit, and the marginal coverts, which may occasionally show, are blackish on adult Turkestan Tits. * **Central tail feathers** On Turkestan Tit, mid grey with a variable, but always narrow, dark streak along the shaft (the inner web may be darker, especially in the race *ferghanensis*). The inner webs of T1 on 'Grey Tits' (*P. m. intermedius*) average darker and blacker, but some are identical to Turkestan Tit. * **Outer tail feathers** Perhaps the most useful plumage feature in the field is the amount of white in the outer tail feathers. Typically, on Turkestan Tit the whole of the outermost feather (T6) is white, with dark only on the fringe at the base of the inner web; the outer web of the penultimate pair (T5) is also white, fringed blackish on some, and the inner web has a large white triangular spot at the tip; T4 and sometimes T3 are also tipped white to a variable extent. On 'Grey Tits' of the race *intermedius,* there is only a small white tip to the outer web of T4, and T5 also *typically has just a small white spot at the tip of the outer web*, whilst the outermost feather (T6) shows a white outer web and narrow triangular white spot at the tip of the inner. The difference in pattern may be visible when the tail is spread in flight, but is best appreciated on the closed tail when viewed from below. Note that Great Tits of the *major* group show a similarly reduced amount of white in the tail, but some members of the *minor* group have the white as extensive as on

Turkestan Tit. * **Juveniles** May be more difficult to identify, but Turkestan Tits seldom show the yellow wash to the underparts obvious on most juvenile 'Grey Tits'.* **In the hand** The graduated tail and alula pattern should be distinctive, and the tail/wing index may be useful. On Turkestan Tit it is 96–116% in males and 96–106% in females, rather than 76–89% in male *P. m. intermedius* and 80–89% in male *P. m. ziaratensis* (and 79–90% in males of the *major* group and 78–86% in females). In addition, the tarsus of Turkestan Tit is slightly thicker and longer, averaging 20.5 mm (compared with 17.5 mm in Great Tits with a similar wing length). In **NE Asia**, the range of Turkestan Tit overlaps or approaches closely that of Great Tit of the green-backed *major* group of subspecies in SW Mongolia, NW China (the Ulungur He area of Xinjiang) and eastern Kazakhstan (around the Zaysan basin and Dzhungarskiy Alatau), and Great Tits have also been recently introduced in the northern Tien Shan, in eastern Uzbekistan, SE Kazakhstan and NE Kyrgyzstan, where they overlap locally with (and now sometimes outnumber) Turkestan Tit. Turkestan differs distinctly from these populations of Great Tit in having grey upperparts (rather than green, tinged blue-grey) and white underparts (not pale yellow). In SW Mongolia and SE Kazakhstan, however, hybrids have been reported, and particular care should be taken in identifications (see Hybrids).

**SEX/AGE** Sexes similar, although females average slightly duller, with the cap less glossy, the upperparts less bluish and with a faint tinge of brown, the bib and ventral line rather duller and more restricted, and the underparts faintly sullied, not so pure white; the difference in the width of the dark ventral line is easily appreciated in the field. Juvenile rather duller than the adult, with the cap and especially the bib less extensive and duller, dark brown, less white in the tail, and the dark ventral line poorly developed; on some, at least (perhaps mostly from the southeastern parts of the range, race *ferghanensis*), the upperparts are faintly tinged olive-green and the nuchal spot, cheeks, wingbar and underparts are tinged yellow.

**VOICE** Similar to that of Great Tit, the song is on the familiar 'tea-cher' theme, e.g. *pid-du, pid-du, pid-du,* although sometimes thinner and more plaintive than Great Tit (more or less recalling Coal Tit). Sonagraphic analysis shows that the fine structure of the song phrase is closest to that of Great Tits of the green-and-yellow *major* group, composed of notes on a more or less even pitch (showing as straight or slightly curved horizontal lines on a sonagram, see figure 86.1, p. 369). The similarity of these two songs has been confirmed in playback experiments (Martens in press). Its structure is thus rather different from that of the grey-and-white *cinereus* group of Great Tits. Calls include scolding 'churring' notes given in alarm or agitation, e.g. *chrrr-ich-ich-ich,* very like Great Tit and similarly combined with *pee* or *tink* notes, but also with variable, rather nuthatch-like trills: sometimes a mellow *whi-whi-whi-whi...* (recalling European Greenfinch) or a faster, rippling *pipipipi...* (even approaching Corsican Nuthatch),

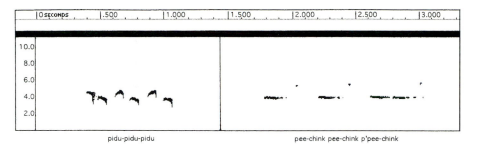

pidu-pidu-pidu       pee-chink pee-chink p'pee-chink

*Figure 86.1 Two sample song phrases of Turkestan Tit (left, Chokpak Pass, SE Kazakhstan; Paul Holt; right, Ashkhabad, Tukmenistan; Simon Harrap). Both are made up from whistled 'tea-cher' motifs and sound similar to Great Tit. Sonagrams show the structure of individual motifs to be similar to that of Great Tit of the major group (see figure 85.1), being on a more or less even pitch, but very different from the pronounced chevrons shown in sonagrams of the song of 'Grey Tit' (the grey-and-white cinereus group, see figure 85.2).*

and sometimes a little more harsh and strident, *chi-chi-chi-chi...*; such trills may be absent from Great Tit's vocabulary.

## DISTRIBUTION AND MOVEMENTS
Recorded in northern **Iran** (on the border with Turkmenistan) on the northern watershed of the Kopet Dag at Lotfabad and in the far northeast around Sarakhs in the valley of the Hari Rud (see also Relationships). In **Afghanistan** found in the northern foothills (?) of the Paropamisus range and north of the Hindu Kush in the lowlands of Afghan Turkestan and Badakhshan. In **Central Asia** found in **Turkmenistan**, **Uzbekistan**, **Tadzhikistan**, **Kyrgyzstan** and **Kazakhstan** from the eastern shore of the Aral Sea, the delta of the Amudar'ya and western Uzboy valley, north to the northeast corner of the Aral Sea, lower Syrdar'ya, Karatau range, Chu valley, southern shore of Lake Balkhash and northwestern part of the Lake Alakol' depression, south to the northern slopes of the Kopet Dag (west to at least around Ashkhabad), Tedzhen, the Afghan border, and the lower reaches of the Bartang river in Badakhshanskaya. Also found in the foothills of the Pamir-Alay system (e.g. Aman Kutan at Samarkand, the northern slopes of the Alayskiy mountains, and Dushanbe), the Fergana basin, Tashkent region and, east of 74° E, the range extends east to the northern foothills of the Tien Shan, the Ili valley (and presumably along the Ili into China), and the northern foothills of the Dzhungarskiy Alatau, including the basins of the Karatal, Aksu, Lepsa and lower Tentek. In **NW China** found in Dzungaria in northern **Xinjiang**, in the Ulungur He valley (east to at least 89° E and presumably to the Mongolian border, and presumably west to lakes Ulungur Hu and Jili Hu, and perhaps also into the southern foothills of the Altai) and on the Manas river (from Manas Hu and around Karamay south to the northern foothills of the Tien Shan). Status in **Mongolia** uncertain, but may breed in the far southwest in the Bulgan Gol valley in the headwaters of the Ulungur He; although only Turkestan-type individuals have been seen in this region, and the green-and-yellow populations of Great Tit breed well to the north (in the northern foothills of the Mongolian Altai), all six birds collected in this area are hybrid Turkestan x Great Tits (Eck & Piechocki 1977), and the occurrence of pure Turkestan Tits in Mongolia may be doubtful.

## HABITAT
In the plains, deserts and semi-desert areas found in riverine thickets of willows, poplars and tamarisks, sometimes with an understorey of reeds, and saxaul forests. Also gardens, orchards and town parks. In more mountainous regions found in woodland, sometimes well developed (coniferous, deciduous or mixed), as well as in more open areas with scattered trees and bushes (Turkestan Tit may be excluded from such habitats in the Kopet Dag of SW Turkmenistan by the presence there of Great Tits). Although generally considered a lowland bird, recorded up to at least 1550 m in NE Afghanistan, to *c.* 2000 m in the western Tien Shan and to 2135 m in the Tien Shan in NW China.

## POPULATION
Generally locally common, although noted as uncommon in Chinese Turkestan and rare in NE Iran.

## HABITS
Rather similar to those of Great Tit, although can be rather shyer and more skulking. In the autumn may form flocks, sometimes containing as many as 100 individuals. Food insects and, to a lesser extent, seeds.

## BREEDING BIOLOGY
Appears on the breeding grounds in late February, season April–late June. The nest is placed in a hole in a tree, wall or building, a burrow in a steep bank, even in a camel's skull in the Kyzylkum desert. The nest is lined with fur. Eggs white, copiously marked with reddish-cinnamon spots and dots, sometimes concentrated at the blunt end; *c.* 17.8 x 13 mm. Often (?) double-brooded.

## DESCRIPTION
*P. b. bokharensis* **Adult Male**: *In fresh plumage* (September–January), crown, nape and upper mantle black, glossed blue, border of upper mantle off-white, remainder of upperparts clean light grey with faint blue cast, longest uppertail coverts mid grey. Central tail feathers mid grey with a variable narrow dark shaft streak (may also be darker on inner web), T2–T4 mid grey with dark grey inner web, T3–T4 variably tipped white, sometimes broadly so on T4, T5 with outer web white (may be fringed darker grey), inner web dark grey with white wedge *c.* 10–30 mm long at tip, T6 white, fringed dark grey on inner web (not

*Figure 86.2  Tail of adult male P. b. bokharensis.*

extreme tip; see figure above). Marginal coverts blackish, finely tipped grey or whitish. Lesser and median coverts light grey with diffuse darker centres, faintly tipped darker when very fresh. Greater coverts light blue-grey with darker shaft streaks and broad white tips (c. 6 mm deep on outer, 4 mm on inner). Alula pale to light grey with a dark grey shaft streak of variable width (although usually very narrow) and neat broad white fringe to the outer web of the largest feather. Primary coverts mid grey, dark grey inner webs showing towards tips; extreme tips slightly paler and whiter. Tertials dull mid-dark grey, tinged brown (with darker brown shaft streaks), broadly fringed and tipped white. Primaries and secondaries dark grey, secondaries broadly fringed light blue-grey and tipped grey-white, P3–P10 fringed light blue-grey, narrower and whiter distally of emarginations on P3–P6, and faintly tipped whiter. Cheeks and ear-coverts white, sides of neck black, connecting cap and bib. Lores blackish, chin, throat and upper breast black, slightly glossed blue, black continuing as irregular ventral line to largely sooty-black belly, feathers of lower border of bib and margins of ventral line tipped white. Remainder of underparts white, washed creamy at border of ventral line, rear flanks extensively light grey, longest undertail-coverts dark grey, narrowly fringed and tipped white. Thighs blackish, white on inner surfaces. Axillaries and underwing-coverts white, marginal and longer under primary coverts blackish. *In worn plumage* (about February–July), nuchal patch larger, tail and flight feathers abraded, broader black band on sides of neck, bib larger and better defined, and ventral line more regular and better defined. **Bare Parts**: Iris dark brown; bill black; legs and feet slate-grey. **Adult Female**: As male, but cap slightly duller and less glossy, upperparts not so pure grey (faintly tinged drab), bib rather duller sooty-black and not extending so far onto upper breast, ventral line duller and narrower. Underparts faintly sullied, not so pure white. In worn plumage, bib even browner and underparts sullied dull creamy or buff. **Juvenile**: As adult, but cap dark brownish-olive with no gloss, not extending onto upper mantle. Mantle and scapulars variably but usually faintly tinged olive-green. Pale spot on upper mantle, tips of greater coverts, cheek patch and underparts faintly tinged yellow, especially at sides of breast; no grey wash to rear flanks. Less white in the tail than adult, T2–T5 with outer webs blue-grey, inner webs dark grey, T5 with small white tip to outer web, T6 with outer web white, inner web with inverted white

triangle at tip. Wings as adult, but white tertial fringes narrower and better defined. Bib rather narrow and restricted (dark border to rear of cheek patch may be absent), colour as cap but slightly paler and dustier, extending as irregular ventral line to belly. **1st Adult**: No information. **Measurements**: Wing of male 63–72.5, of female 62–71.5; tail of male 64–75, of female 74–74.5; bill 11.8–14; tarsus 17.5–21. Weight 16.9–18 g (subspecies unknown).

**MOULT** Adult post-breeding complete (late May–October). Pre-breeding partial? (one bird from Fergana is moulting the head and throat and replacing the central tail feathers on 6 March). Post-juvenile partial, includes a variable number of feathers in the tail, tertials and alula (July–September).

**GEOGRAPHICAL VARIATION** Slight, involving the tone of the upperparts, overall size and bill dimensions. Three races recognised, following Stepanyan (1990).

*P. b. bokharensis* The western and north-central sector of the range in western Central Asia east to the Chu valley, Karatau mountains, western foothills of the Tien Shan and Alayskiy system and the Paropamisus in NW Afghanistan. Intergrades in the east with *ferghanensis*. See Description. The smallest and palest race, with a well-developed bluish flush to the upperparts. There is a slight cline of decreasing size running north-south, with largest birds in the northern part of the Kyzylkum desert and the region around the lower reaches of the Syrdar'ya, whilst 'panderi' from the oases of the Transcaspian deserts has slightly paler upperparts (less bluish and more sandy).

*P. b. ferghanensis* The south-central portion of the range in the southern slopes of the Kirgizskiy mountains, western foothills of the Tien Shan and Alayskiy system (east to 74° E), the Kugitangtau mountains, Fergana basin, and the northern parts of the western Pamirs (east to 72° E and south to the Bartang valley). Also Afghan Turkestan and Badakhshan. Intergrades with nominate *bokharensis* in the west. As nominate *bokharensis* but upperparts slightly darker, more greyish-blue, flanks washed slightly darker grey. Juveniles may more frequently show yellow or olive tones. Larger. Wing of male 66–79.5, of female 65–72; tail of male 66–81, of female 70; bill 11.8–14.3.

*P. b. turkestanicus* The eastern parts of the range from the SW end of Lake Balkhash eastwards, south to the Ili valley and north to the Alakol' depression, east to Xinjiang in Chinese Turkestan and SW Mongolia. As nominate *bokharensis* but upperparts darker (although paler than *ferghanensis*). Bill heavy. Wing of male 68–77, of female 68–77; tail of male 72–84; bill 12.5–14.8.

**HYBRIDS** Hybridises to a limited extent with Great Tit in SW Mongolia, SE Kazakhstan, perhaps in SW Turkmenistan, and possibly elsewhere. In extreme SW Mongolia, in the Bulgan river region of the headwaters of the Ulungur He, a small number of hybrids between Turkestan Tits and Great Tits of the *major* group have been reported. These show a variety of characters, some resembling pale green-and-yellow Great Tits, whilst others are superficially similar to Turkestan Tit, with just a faint trace of green on the mantle. Between these two extremes are birds with a variable olive tone to the mantle and a yellow wash to the sides of the breast. Hybrids also show a variable reduction in the amount of white in the tail, and an intermediate primary projection and tail/wing ratio (Eck & Piechocki 1977). There is thus apparently a narrow contact zone between the two species in the limited areas of suitable habitat along the rivers in this arid region, although neither 'pure' Turkestan Tits nor pure Great have been recorded there (Great Tits being found on the northern watershed of the Mongolian Altai, where they are scarce or even rare, and Turkestan further west along the Ulungur He in NW China, although Great Tits *may* have spread to SW Mongolia along the Ulungur He from the Zaysan depression, 'swamping' the once pure populations of Turkestan Tit as they went). This hybridisation may be very recent, following human alterations of the environment, or may follow periodic winter influxes of Great Tits into the range of Turkestan Tit (cf. Black-crested and Tufted Titmice, p. 414). Field studies may reveal the pairing preference of birds in this area, and hence the dynamics of the hybrid zone, which may be very limited in extent, with little effect on the surrounding parent populations. Turkestan Tit also comes into contact with Great Tits of the *major* group in SE Kazakhstan in the Dzhungarskiy Alatau range (perhaps as a result both of the introduction of Great Tits into the northern Tien Shan in the 1960s, these spreading north to the Dzhungarskiy range, and of a natural spread southwards from NE Kazakhstan). Hybrids have been recorded from Ushtobe in the western outliers of the range, where they greatly outnumber both pure Turkestan and pure Great Tits. They are intermediate between the two species in the amount of olive on the upperparts and yellow on the underparts, and also in the amount of white in the tail. Preliminary evidence indicates random pair formation, but the song of the hybrids is close to or identical to that of Turkestan Tit (but this, in turn, is close to that of the *major* group). 'Obvious' hybrids have also been noted in winter near Chilik (on a tributary of the Ili), and a hybrid has been trapped west of Alma Ata (Formozov *et al.* 1993, who consider that the eastern populations of Turkestan Tit may be 'lost' in the future through this interbreeding and consequent genetic swamping). This hybridisation, clearly a very recent phenomenon, may, however, be temporary, as the isolating mechanisms sort themselves out, and in other parts of Central Asia where Great Tits have been introduced the two species seem to maintain their integrity, at least locally (in 1993, in the Charyn valley, eastern Tien Shan, only 'pure' pairs of Great or Turkestan Tits were found, even where the two overlapped, and no hybrids were collected: J. Martens *in litt.*). In SW Turkmenistan, Turkestan Tit comes into contact with Great Tit (of

the race *intermedius*) on the northern watershed of the Kopet Dag range, but whether or not they hybridise in this area is unclear. Formozov *et al.* (1993) note that in the western Kopet Dag there is apparently a 'hybrid' population, but this is of hybrid Great Tits of the *major* and *cinereus* groups and apparently not Great x Turkestan Tits (the race *intermedius* of Great Tit, a member of the *cinereus* group, is sometimes regarded as a mixed population resulting from the combination of two or more of the *major*, *cinereus* and *bokharensis* groups). In NE Iran, the ranges of the Turkestan and 'Grey Tits' may just overlap, but specimens from this area show no signs of intergradation (Vaurie 1950a). At Sarakhs in extreme NE Khorasan, a 1st-winter female Turkestan Tit was collected in August and there have also been field observations of Turkestan Tit (D. Scott pers. comm.). At the same locality, three adult 'Grey Tits' (*P. m. intermedius*) were collected in March (Vaurie 1950a). These may, however, have been winter wanderers, as the habitat is unsuitable for breeding Great Tits. At Germab (*c.* 70 km northeast of Bojnurd at 600–900 m 'on the northern side of the Achal Tekke'), an adult Turkestan Tit was collected from within the range of *intermedius* in late July (Vaurie 1950a), and at Lotfabad in northern Iran Turkestan Tit has been found below 300 m, with Great Tits in nearby montane woodland (D. Scott pers. comm.). In the Pamirs and NE Afghanistan, Turkestan Tit may overlap with 'Grey Tits' (*P. m. decolorans* and *P. m. caschmirensis*), although on given distributions this does not occur. Vaurie (1950a) stated that in the Pamirs Turkestan Tit's range may be contiguous with *cashmirensis*, and found that two out of eight 1st-adult birds had very slight traces on yellow on the mantle, perhaps signs of intergradation (but see *ferghanensis* in Geographical Variation).

**RELATIONSHIPS** Closely related to the Great Tit and, indeed, sometimes treated as a subspecies group within the Great Tit complex. Turkestan Tit resembles the *cinereus* group of races of Great Tit in plumage pattern, with grey upperparts and whitish underparts, lacking olives and yellows in the plumage; it differs markedly, however, in proportions, with a longer tail and heavier legs, and also has much more white in the tail. In addition the songs of Turkestan Tit and Great Tits of the *cinereus* group ('Grey Tit') are quite dissimilar in their fine structure. The relationship of Turkestan and Great Tits can be resolved only when the situations in the areas where their ranges abut or overlap are fully understood. As detailed above, hybridisation occurs locally, but it may be a very recent phenomenon which has yet to resolve itself. It seems best, therefore, to maintain Turkestan Tit as a separate species and to monitor the situation closely.

**REFERENCES** Delacour & Vaurie (1950), Dementiev & Gladkov (1966–70), Stepanyan (1990), Vaurie (1950a, 1957b).

So similar to Great Tit in voice, actions and plumage, this Oriental species has a complex and poorly understood ecological relationship with its larger cousin.

**IDENTIFICATION** Length 125 mm (5 in). A large tit with a glossy black cap, white cheek patches and a small whitish nuchal patch. Upperparts olive-green, rump light grey and tail black, fringed and tipped white. Wings dull black with two broad white wingbars, white fringes and tips to the tertials and blue-grey fringes to the flight feathers. Bib and ventral line black, joining the cap at the lores and sides of the neck, the remainder of the underparts being yellow (in southern Vietnam, the underparts are largely black). The black cap, lack of a crest, white cheeks, olive-green upperparts, double white wingbars and yellow underparts are distinctive. Green-backed Tit is, however, rather close in size and shape to Great Tit, which it also resembles in voice and actions. It is easily distinguished from Great Tits of the grey-and-white *cinereus* group, the 'Grey Tits', which are the common lowland form in the Indian subcontinent and South-East Asia, by its olive upperparts, yellow underparts and double white wingbars. Green-backed Tit is more similar to Great Tits of the montane, green-and-white *minor* group of the eastern Himalayas and China, but can still be distinguished by its yellow underparts and double, rather than single, wingbars, this latter feature especially important as juvenile Great Tits have yellow-washed underparts.

**SEX/AGE** Sexes similar, although on females the white tertial fringes are faintly washed olive-yellow and the fringes to the greater coverts, primaries and secondaries average slightly duller and paler blue (although males show duller fringes when worn, their tertials are still fringed pure white); also, the female's bib and ventral stripe are less extensive and slightly browner, usually lacking any gloss. The juvenile resembles the adult, but the glossy black of the cap, bib and ventral line is replaced by sooty-black, the white fringes to the greater coverts and tertials are washed yellow, and the mantle is slightly duller. 1st adults as adult and difficult to age, even in the hand, although but may show moult contrasts in the greater coverts, tertials or tail, or contrast between the new tertials and slightly older and more worn flight feathers and primary coverts. If retained the fringes to the juvenile tertials and greater coverts are rather yellower on a 1st-adult female than an adult female, and, whilst 1st-adult males have the glossy cap and bib of an adult male, their retained juvenile flight feathers have slightly duller and greyer fringes than the adult's.

**VOICE** Rather vocal. Calls similar to those of Great Tit, and similarly varied, but louder, clearer and shriller. They include a rapid, thin *si-si-si-si-si-li* and a harsh *shick-shick-shick* (perhaps the alarm call), while the flight and contact call is a three-note phrases, *te-te-whee*. Other calls include a musical *pling pling pling* followed by *tee-eurp*. The song is very variable. Common song types include the repetition of disyllabic motifs, each typically consisting of a shorter and a longer note, one rising in pitch, the other falling, e.g. *seta-seta-seta* (recalling Coal Tit) or *teeye-teeye-teeye*. Similarly, Roberts (1992) describes a loud, two-note whistle, the first note shorter, the second higher-pitched and more emphatic, and repeated in bouts of 4–6 phrases, with pauses between each bout: *tu-weeh, tu-weeh...*, *whit-ee, whit-ee...* etc. Variations include three- and four-note motifs, such as *whichy-whichy...*, *ti-ti-tee-ti...* (third syllable much prolonged), *tsing-tsing pi-diu...*, *psit-psit tutu...* or *psi-tu-tchi....* A scarcer song type consists of a series of identical pure whistled units, either rising or falling in pitch (e.g. *piu-piu...*), or on a level pitch (e.g. *tee-tee-tee...* or *pli-pli-pli-pli-pli*). Typically, the units or motifs within the song are well spaced, giving it a rather deliberate tempo. (Largely after Martens & Eck in press). Song period February–May in Nepal and from mid April onwards in Pakistan. On Taiwan, gives a strange, mechanical *heeeb t-t-tk, heeeb t-t-tk, heeeb t-t-tk...* repeated rapidly, the initial note like a squeaky gate.

**DISTRIBUTION AND MOVEMENTS** In **Pakistan** occurs from Swat Kohistan, through Hazara (the Kagan valley) to Azad Kashmir (the Neelum/Kishen Ganga valley) and south to the Murree hills. Thence east through the Himalayas in **India**, **Nepal** and **Bhutan** from the Pir Panjal range of Kashmir to Arunachal Pradesh, extending north of the main range into **Tibet** along the Sun Kosi river to Nyalam, in the Chumbi valley to Yadong, and in the valleys of the Manas (to Cona), Tsangpo (to Medog), Po Tsangpo (to Bomi) and Lohit (to Zayu) rivers; also the NE Indian hill states in Nagaland, Manipur and Meghalaya (Khasi hills; breeds?), and adjoining **Myanmar** (**Burma**), in the west through the Chin hills to Mount Victoria and in the northeast from the Adung valley south to at least Putao and Kambaiti (Stanford & Ticehurst 1935). In western and central **China** found in **Sichuan** (avoiding the plains of the Red Basin except in winter, and also the higher mountains in the west), southern **Gansu**, extreme southern **Ningxia Hui** (Jingyuan), southern **Shaanxi** (Qin Ling mountains), western **Hubei**, southern **Hunan**, northern **Guangxi** (Maoershan; Vuilleumier 1993), **Guizhou** and NW, west and SE **Yunnan** (north to Kunming), extending into northern **Vietnam** in NW Tonkin, where recorded only from Pakha in Laokay province (and not from the relatively well-known Cha Pa), with disjunct populations in south Vietnam on the Da Lat plateau (south to Mount Pantar, near Di Linh), and in **Taiwan**. Resident, with some limited altitudinal movements, dispersing October–March to the foothills and sometimes the adjacent plains. In Pakistan, recorded in winter from Peshawar, Islamabad, the Murree foothills at Margalla and the eastern Salt Range, and in northern India from the plains of the northern

Punjab and in Uttar Pradesh at Dehra Dun. In the eastern Himalayas, found in the Jalpaiguri duars and Bhutan foothills.

**HABITAT** Essentially a forest bird, but tolerating a very wide variety of formations, from subtropical evergreen forest through deciduous, mixed and coniferous forest to high-altitude birch and juniper. Partial to pine forest (notably Khasi Pine), especially in the Khasi hills, on Mount Victoria, in southern China (Guizhou and Sichuan) and on the Da Lat plateau in southern Vietnam. Also found in bamboo scrub, second growth, orchards, walnut groves, trees near cultivation and gardens, perhaps in more open country largely during the winter, although generally prefers edge habitats. Altitudinal range very broad. Breeds in the subtropical and temperate zones, at 1500–3170 m in the western Himalayas in Pakistan, 1200–3660 m in the eastern Himalayas and 1830–2600 m in NE Burma, and recorded on Mount Victoria at 1400–2600 m. In winter, may descend to the foothills or, in some areas, the adjoining plains, e.g. in Pakistan recorded in the eastern Salt Range at 580 m, in Bhutan recorded down to 400 m, in eastern Arunachal Pradesh noted at 500 m and in NE Burma at 315–2135 m. Throughout the range, however, often remains at higher altitudes, even in conditions of deep snowfall, and recorded in winter in Sikkim at 2680 m and in Nepal at 3900 m (Ali & Ripley 1983, although usually found below 2745 m in winter in Nepal). Elsewhere, found in SE Tibet at 1980–3650 m and in China proper in Yunnan at 1170–3960 m, Guangxi at 1500 m, Guizhou at 500–2750 m (with a nest discovered at 2400 m), Sichuan at 1100–3810 m in summer and 100 m to about 3050 m in winter, whilst in southern Shaanxi recorded at 1000–2400 m, and in Taiwan at 600–2800 m. In southern Vietnam, found in 915–1585 m.

**POPULATION** Fairly common to common, even abundant, throughout its range.

**HABITS** Found in pairs in the breeding season, otherwise in small flocks, occasionally with up to 20 together; often joins mixed-species foraging parties. Often tame; will sometimes enter habitations and frequently nests under the roofs of houses. Usually forages in the shrub layer and understorey, although also in the canopy of deciduous trees, and will cling to tree trunks. May feed on the ground, although less frequently than Great Tit, but in winter ground-foraging parties of 15–20 birds have been recorded. Food insects, flower buds, fruit and berries.

**BREEDING BIOLOGY** Season March–June; apparently year-round in Taiwan, although the majority breed there in April-June. The nest is placed in a cavity in a tree, stump, post, roadside parapet, rocky bank, wall or even the eaves and walls of houses, usually under 3 m above ground, although it may be up to 7 m high. Will utilise nestboxes. The nest, built by the female, is a pad of moss, grass, wool, hair and feathers, lined with wool or fur. Clutch 4–8: eggs white or pinkish-white, spotted and speckled reddish-brown; 16.7 x 13.1 mm (*P. m. monticolus*). Female incubates; she is fed on the nest by the male. The young are fed by both sexes. Incubation and fledging periods unknown. Single-brooded.

**DESCRIPTION** *P. m. monticolus* **Adult Male**: *In fresh plumage* (September–spring), crown, nape and border of upper mantle black, glossed blue; small white nuchal patch. Mantle, scapulars and back olive-green, upper mantle bordered yellow, rump light grey, uppertail-coverts sooty-black, longest tipped blue-black. Tail blackish, T1–T5 fringed dull violet-blue and tipped white, minutely on T1 and to largest extent on T5, outer web of T6 white, inner web broadly tipped white (see figure below). Wings sooty-black, lesser coverts fringed and tipped light grey, median coverts

*Figure 87.1  Tail of adult male* P. m. monticolus.

fringed and tipped off-white, greater coverts finely fringed blue-grey and broadly tipped white, alula narrowly fringed and tipped white, tertials fringed and more broadly tipped off-white, secondaries and inner primaries fringed dull violet-blue and tipped off-white, progressively replaced by a narrow white fringe on distal portion of P6–P3, broadening around the emarginations; P3–P5 with outer web white at extreme base adjacent to primary coverts. Cheeks and ear-coverts white. Sides of neck, lores, chin, throat, centre of breast and narrow ventral stripe black, feather fringes glossed blue. Remainder of underparts sulphur-yellow, faintly washed olive on flanks. Undertail-coverts sooty-black, broadly tipped white. Underwing-coverts and axillaries white. *In worn plumage* (spring to about August), often little different, but when very worn cap and bib duller and less glossy, grey of rump more extensive, wing and tail feathers slightly paler and browner; pale tertial fringes and flight feather tips may be completely abraded. **Bare Parts**: Iris dark brown or hazel; bill black, tip and cutting edge of lower mandible paler; legs and feet dark slate to blue-grey, claws horny-brown or blackish. **Adult Female**: As male, but bib and ventral line average less extensive and duller, sooty-black with blue gloss faint or absent, wing and tail feathers very slightly paler and browner, blue fringes to greater coverts, primaries and secondaries slightly duller and greyer, and tertial fringes, especially on longest tertial, faintly washed olive-yellow. **Juvenile Male**: As adult, but cap sooty-brown, lacking any gloss, nuchal spot pale yellow, mantle slightly duller and drabber, median- and greater-covert tips and tertial fringes washed yellow, cheeks not so pure white, bib and ventral line sooty-brown, and underparts average slightly duller yellow, washed greyish-olive. **Juvenile Female**: As juvenile male, but wing and tail feathers, cap and especially bib average slightly paler and browner, with a more intense yellow wash to the fringes of the greater coverts and tertials but duller and greyer fringes to the primaries and secondaries. **1st Adult**: As adult (see Sex/Age). **Measurements**: Wing of male 62–72, of female 61–70; tail of male 50–59, of female 45–61; bill 10.5–13; tarsus 15–20. Weight 12–16.8 g.

**MOULT**   Adult   post-breeding   complete (July–November; March in southern Vietnam). Post-juvenile partial, includes includes a variable number of tail feathers, greater coverts (usually all?) and tertials, and sometimes some flight feathers, one bird from Simla dated October is replacing P8 on both wings and P2 on one wing (July–November).

**GEOGRAPHICAL VARIATION** Rather slight, with four subspecies recognised. A cline of increasing pigmentation runs west to east (reversed slightly in the easternmost parts of the range in China), with birds from Pakistan being palest. Conventionally, two races are recognised on this cline, nominate *monticolus* in the west and *yunnanensis* in the east. There has been some debate concerning where the boundary between the two is best drawn (i.e. where there is a perceptible 'step' in the gradual change in coloration); first located in NE Burma, Paynter (1962) moved it to Nepal. The division between the races is, however, at best arbitrary and, because the difference between even the extremes of coloration is very slight, it may well be best to synonymise *yunnanensis* with nominate *monticolus*. In southern Vietnam *legendrei* is rather better marked, while *insperatus* in Taiwan differs constantly from the mainland forms, but in minor details of coloration only.

***P. m. monticolus*** Western Himalayas east to western Nepal, where intergrades with *yunnanensis*. See Description.

***P. m. yunnanensis*** Himalayas from Nepal eastwards, NE India, Burma, China and NW Vietnam. Poorly marked. As nominate *monticolus*, but upperparts slightly brighter green, underparts perhaps brighter yellow. Wing of male 62–73, of female 60.8–69; tail of male 48–65, of female 47–67.

***P. m. insperatus*** Taiwan. As *yunnanensis*, but tertials fringed blue rather than white, also broader white tips to the tertials, secondaries and greater and median coverts (see figure 87.2).

***P. m. legendrei*** Southern Vietnam on the Da Lat plateau (= 'Langbian' plateau) of southern Annam. As nominate *monticolus*, but mantle, back and scapulars distinctly duller and greyer, tertials fringed blue and broadly tipped white (i.e. as *insperatus*), white tips to median and greater coverts average narrower, ventral stripe much broader, with yellow of underparts paler, washed grey and restricted to a narrow line on the flanks. Wing 62–69, of male 65–69, of female 65–67.

**RELATIONSHIPS** Placed in the *major* group, together with Great and White-naped Tits, by Eck (1988) and Snow (1954b), the former author adding also the African grey tits. Green-backed Tit closely resembles Great Tit (notably the green-and-yellow races of the nominate *major* group of subspecies), a species which it more or less replaces at higher altitudes in the Himalayas and China. Its ecological relationships with Great Tit are, however, obscure. Although Green-backed Tit generally occurs at higher altitudes and in wetter forest, it overlaps at the lowest altitudes with Great Tit and is sometimes found in the same foraging flocks. Furthermore, in the eastern Himalayas the species is sandwiched between the lowland form of Great Tit ('Grey Tit' *P. m. nipalensis*) and the high-altitude, green-backed form (*P. m. tibetanus*), while in Sichuan it is found in the valleys (above 1830 m) alongside *P. m. minor* and on the plateau alongside *P. m. tibetanus* (Traylor 1967).

**REFERENCES** Ali & Ripley (1983), Baker (1932–33), Martens & Eck (in press), Paynter (1962), Roberts (1992).

*Figure 87.2  Wing pattern of* P. m. monticolus *(left) and* P. m. insperatus *(right): note extent of white in tertials, secondaries and greater and median coverts.*

## 88 WHITE-NAPED TIT *Parus nuchalis*                     Plate 29
Other name: White-winged Black Tit

This enigmatic tit is endemic to India, but is rare and locally distributed; the population in the south of the peninsula, the very existence of which has been doubted, has recently been rediscovered.

**IDENTIFICATION** Length 120 mm (4.75 in). Upperparts black, with a variable white nuchal patch. Much white in wings and outer tail feathers (conspicuous in flight). Cheeks and underparts white, often washed yellowish, with a broad blackish ventral line from the throat to the vent. A distinctive black and white tit, hardly likely to be confused with Great Tit. In flight, the black and white plumage pattern may recall an Oriental Magpie Robin or a male White-bellied Minivet.

**SEX/AGE** The sexes are rather similar, but the male has a more distinct blue gloss to the cap, the

Figure 88.1 Wing of adult male (left) and juvenile male (right): note distribution of white.

Figure 88.2 Tail of adult male (left) and juvenile male (right): note distribution of white.

mantle and wing-coverts are blacker with a pronounced blue gloss, the bib and ventral stripe rather darker with a slight blue gloss to the bib, and the flight feathers blacker with small white tips to all the outer primaries. Males may also, on average, have a reduced yellow wash on the underparts, but this varies individually with the state of moult and wear. Juveniles are duller than females, lacking any gloss (although they may show a glossy cap?), with a smaller white nuchal patch and less white in the wings and tail see figures 88.1 and 88.2). There are usually white tips to the outer three tail feathers only, and although the outer two pairs remain largely white they may be washed or spotted with brown. The wing pattern of the juvenile male resembles that of the adult male, although with less white in the tertials and on the fringes to the secondaries, and with the addition of white tips to the greater coverts, but the female is rather duller, with white largely confined to the base of the flight feathers. The 1st adult remains as the juvenile after the post-juvenile moult, although the cap is now glossed blue and a variable number of tertials and tail feathers are replaced with an adult-type pattern. 1st adults usually show an obvious contrast between the new tertials and the retained flight feathers; they also generally retain dull, brown, white-tipped juvenile greater coverts until the first pre-breeding moult, after which they resemble the respective adult sex, although the retained primary coverts, alula and flight feathers and any retained juvenile outer greater coverts will continue to facilitate ageing until the autumn of their second calendar-year. Otherwise, following the first pre-breeding moult, the 1st-adult male in breeding plumage resembles the adult male, although its upperparts average slightly less glossy (but still rather glossier than either adult or 1st-adult females), and its bib largely lacks any gloss. 1st-adult females have slightly paler and greyer upperparts than adult females, with the pale feather fringes more pronounced and only the cap showing a blue gloss.

**VOICE** Contact call a short phrase, comprising rather thin, trilled whistles introduced by a slightly higher, sharper and more abrupt note (*ti* or *teep*): *ti, pee-pee-pee, ti-pee-pee-pee-pee...* (or *teep, whee-whee-whee-whee*). Ali & Ripley (1983) also note the usual joyous harsh 'wheeching' notes of the Great Tit, and a bold *whew whew whew whew whew*, the last note higher-pitched.

**DISTRIBUTION AND MOVEMENTS**

Endemic to **India**, with two distinct populations. In NW India occurs in northern **Gujarat** from western Kachchh (i.e. Kutch, with recent sightings confined to Bhuj, Nakhtrana and Lakhpat districts), east and north to Disa, Palanpur and Pol, and in central and south-central **Rajasthan** from Jodhpur, Ajmer, Sambhar and Marot south to the Gujarat border and east to Jhalawar. In southern peninsular India rare and local. There are three old records. The type specimen was collected in **Andhra Pradesh**, in the Eastern Ghats west of Nellore, where said to be 'very rare'; despite a 'very special look-out for it' by the ornithological survey of the Eastern Ghats (Ali 1942) and more recent field work in the region, there have been no subsequent records from this area. Secondly, a specimen was obtained *c.* 10 km west of Bangalore, **Karnataka**. Finally, a juvenile male was collected at Satyamangalam in the Biligiri Rangana hills, northernmost **Tamil Nadu**, on 14 September 1934. After a gap of 50 years, the species was rediscovered in southern India in the 1980s, and subsequently observed in southern **Karnataka** in the region of the confluence of the Cauvery (= Kaveri) and Arkavathi rivers and in the Biligiri Rangana hills (*c.* 40 km north of Satyamangalam), in central Karnataka in the Adichunchanagiri Peacock Sanctuary, Mandya district (Subramanya *et al.* 1992), and in the Wynaad district of northern **Kerala** (Zacharias & Gaston 1993). Resident, and subject to local movements.

**HABITAT** In NW India, favours thorn scrub forest dominated by *Acacia catechu* and *A. nilotica*, perhaps especially in broken, stony or hilly country. Noted as keeping to the tops of heavily wooded hills on the Eastern Ghats (Baker 1922), and records in Karnataka and Tamil Nadu have come from hilly dry deciduous scrub forest at 375–920 m, but in Kerala noted in moist deciduous forest.

**POPULATION** Reported to be fairly common but patchily distributed in Kutch (Ali & Ripley 1983), but sparse and sporadic in northern Gujarat (Ali 1954–55) and local and uncommon in the remainder of NW India (Gaston 1984). Recent reports indicate that the species has declined drastically, owing primarily to habitat destruction, as dry thorn forest rapidly diminishes or is degraded, the latter factor leading to the removal of old trees with suitable nest holes. Rare in southern India, with only a few scattered records, and locally extinct around Bangalore, probably as a result of urbanisation (replaced there by the Great Tit). The patchiness of its distribution is probably associated with the scarcity of suitable habitat, and the gap between the northern and southern populations may similarly have resulted from the loss of scrub forest between the two regions. The species is listed as vulnerable in BirdLife International's world checklist of threatened birds (Collar *et al.* 1994).

**HABITS** Found in pairs or in family parties of 4–5; restless and reported to be shy, most easily located by its frequent musical calls. May join mixed-species foraging flocks. Noted roosting in a hole in a crossbar of a gate, a single marked bird occupying the roost in August and again the following April (i.e. perhaps over an eight-month period), the same hole having been in use about six years previously. On inspection, the bird swayed its head from side to side, the white cheeks and black ventral line creating a snake-like effect (Ali 1955). Forages in the canopy and shrub layer. Food insects and spiders.

**BREEDING BIOLOGY** Poorly known. Season in NW India May–August (especially July–August in Kutch); in southern India a pair accompanied by a recently fledged juvenile noted on 20 July. The nest, placed in a hole in a tree (usually an abandoned woodpecker excavation), 1–2 m above ground, is a rough pad of soft fibres, wool, cotton and hair. Eggs, clutch size and incubation period unknown, although a family of three young has been reported. Both sexes feed the young (Ali 1955; Ali & Ripley 1983).

**DESCRIPTION Adult Male**: *In fresh plumage* (December–April), crown, nape and upperparts, including lesser and median coverts, black, glossed blue, with a variable, although usually large, white patch on lower nape and upper mantle. Inner four tail feathers largely black, T1–T3 narrowly tipped white, T4 broadly tipped white, with outer web also white; T5–T6 largely white (see figure 88.2, p. 375). Wing-coverts black, fringes glossed blue; concealed white spot at or near tip of inner web of inner 3–5 greater coverts (not innermost). Alula and primary coverts black, fringes faintly glossed blue; inner primary coverts may also show faint subterminal white spots. Tertials largely white, basal two-thirds of inner webs and basal half of outer webs black (largely concealed). Flight feathers black, innermost secondary broadly tipped and fringed white, remainder of secondaries broadly tipped white with disjunct broad white fringes to terminal third, fringes otherwise glossed blue; base of outer webs of secondaries and P10–P3 white, white extending more narrowly to emarginations on P3–P7, and all primaries tipped white, finely so on outer wing. Lores and base of bill black, cheeks, ear-coverts and sides of neck white, sides of breast, belly and flanks creamy. Chin, centre of throat and centre of breast black, slightly glossed blue, broad sooty-black stripe extending to vent. Undertail-coverts cream, longer ones with sooty-black inner webs. Under primary coverts sooty-black, broadly tipped white, axillaries and under-wing-coverts otherwise whitish. *Following partial*

*pre-breeding moult*, body plumage fresh, yellow wash on underparts more intense, especially on sides of breast and flanks; tail and tertials new, flight feathers only slightly bleached and abraded. **Bare Parts**: Iris dark brown; bill black; legs and feet slaty-grey. **Adult Female**: In fresh plumage as male, but upperparts duller, crown with reduced blue gloss and remainder of the upperparts sooty-black, feather bases darker and faintly glossy and tips slightly paler and browner; nuchal patch averages smaller and rather narrower. Wings duller than on male, with slightly less white, wing-coverts sooty-black, fringes faintly glossed blue, white on inner webs of inner greater coverts averages more extensive, innermost secondary usually lacks complete white fringe, white on distal third of secondaries reduced or absent, and usually lacks white tips to outer primaries. Bib and ventral line much paler, sooty-brown, sides of breast and flanks with a more pronounced yellow wash. *Following partial pre-breeding moult,* yellow wash on underparts more intense. **Juvenile Male**: As adult, but crown and upperparts sooty-black, lacking blue gloss (duller even than adult female), nuchal patch smaller, washed creamy-yellow. Tail duller, white areas duller, may be washed or spotted brown, usually lacks white tips to T1–T3, white on tip of inner web of T4 reduced to a small spot, white of outer web broken or almost broken near the tip; tail feathers average slightly narrower and more pointed than the adult's. Wings duller, the dark areas sooty-brown, the pale areas washed creamy; the wing-coverts lack blue-glossed fringes, but a variable number of greater coverts broadly tipped whitish on both webs (thus white visible on closed wing), fringes of primary coverts and alula faintly glossed blue, white in the tertials confined to the tip and fringe of tt1–tt2 and to the tip only of tt3 (white areas may be washed brown), lacks white fringes to the distal quarter of secondaries, and whitish tips to outer primaries reduced (and sometimes absent on P1). Bib and ventral line sooty-brown. **Juvenile Female**: As juvenile male, but upperparts slightly duller, with more obvious diffuse paler feather fringes (i.e. as adult female but slightly paler and greyer, pale feather tips more pronounced), and less white in tail, white on outer web of T4 reduced to a narrow fringe, broken near the tip; even less white in the tertials, white confined to the tip of tt1 and the tips of the outer web only on tt2–tt3, narrower white tips to secondaries and white tips to the primaries tiny (absent on outer primaries); white in flight feathers largely confined to the basal quarter, with a fine white fringe around the emarginations of P4–P5. **1st Adult**: As juvenile, but cap glossed blue, and a variable number of tertials and tail feathers replaced with adult-type feathers (if all tertials and tail replaced, these show a marked moult contrast with the retained juvenile flight feathers). *Following the first pre-breeding moult* underparts rather yellower; male as adult male but upperparts slightly less glossy, bib with little or no gloss, while female differs from adult female as juvenile. In both sexes, tail, tertials and most or all greater coverts as adult, but alula, primary coverts, primaries and secondaries still old and worn. **Measurements**: Wing of male 64–71, of female, 66–68; tail of male 48–55 (one juvenile 44.5), of female 49–53; bill 11–13 g; tarsus 17–19.5. Weight 13, 14.5 g (Hussain *et al.* 1992).

**MOULT** Adult post-breeding complete (September–December; Ali & Ripley 1983, Vaurie 1950a). Adult pre-breeding partial, includes body, tertials, tail and a variable number of inner greater coverts (late April–May). Post-juvenile partial, includes a variable number of tertials, sometimes the tail, perhaps also the median and inner greater coverts? (late June–August). First pre-breeding partial, includes the median coverts, inner greater coverts, usually all the tail feathers and tertials and rarely 1–2 inner secondaries (late April–mid June).

**GEOGRAPHICAL VARIATION** None.

**RELATIONSHIPS** Obscure. Placed in a species-group with Great and Green-backed Tits and the African grey tits by Eck (1988).

**REFERENCES** Ali (1942, 1945, 1954-55), Ali & Ripley (1983), Baker (1922), Hussain *et al.* (1992), Subramanya *et al.* (1992), Zacharias & Gaston (1993).

---

# 89 BLACK-LORED TIT *Parus xanthogenys*       Plate 31

Other name: Yellow-cheeked Tit

---

This brightly coloured tit is a familiar member of mixed-species foraging flocks at lower altitudes in the Himalayas, whilst in peninsular India altogether duller, washed-out and rather 'dusty' birds can similarly be found in bird waves.

**IDENTIFICATION** Length 130 mm (5 in). A large tit with a conspicuous bushy crest. Rather variable in appearance, either brightly coloured and predominantly yellow and green or duller and largely greyish-olive and pale yellowish-grey. Males have a black cap and ventral stripe, whilst females and juveniles may resemble the male or may have the black replaced by dull olive (see Sex/Age and Geographical Variation). Indeed, in the Western Ghats of peninsular India individuals with black crests and black ventral stripes, black crests and green ventral stripes, and green crests and green ventral stripes may be found in the same flock. Throughout most of the range unmistakable, as no other tit combines yellowish cheeks and underparts with a prominent crest. In eastern Nepal and Darjeeling (and possibly also Sikkim), however, Black-lored Tit must be carefully distinguished from Yellow-cheeked Tit: note its smaller size, the black (not yellow) forehead and lores, plain olive-green mantle (with any blackish streaks confined to the scapulars), olive (rather than grey) rump, and yellow-washed (rather than pure white) wing spots. Hybrids between the two species have never been recorded, but could conceivably occur, and it is therefore worth paying careful attention to all tits seen in these areas; the occurrence of any intergrades would throw light on the relationships between these very similar species.

**SEX/AGE** Sexes practically alike in the Himalayas and probably indistinguishable in the field, the female differing from the male merely in having a shorter crest and slightly narrower ventral stripe. In the peninsular Indian race *aplonotus,* the female differs from the male in having a greyish-olive (rather than black) bib and ventral stripe, while in the Western Ghats race *travancoreensis* the female totally lacks black markings on the head and underparts (although the juvenile female has a black crown, and note that the polymorphism of adult females reported by Ali & Ripley 1983 was questioned by Vaurie 1950a and disproved by Unnithan 1992). The juvenile of the Himalayan race is rather similar to the adult and difficult to age, even in the hand. Compared with the adult, its crest is shorter, the cap averages duller, the tail feathers are narrower and more pointed, with the tips faintly washed olive, the fringes to the secondaries are washed olive (rather than clear mid blue-grey, but this distinction is very subtle), the bib is rather duller (sooty brown-black), smaller and more restricted, and the underparts are paler and whiter (although near the coloration of a worn adult, and note that both adults and juveniles have yellow-washed wing spots). The 1st adult resembles the adult but retains the juvenile flight feathers, which may still show an olive wash to the fringes of the secondaries. Juveniles of the peninsular race *aplonotus* resemble the respective adult sex, but their black markings are less glossy, the white tips to the greater and median coverts are washed yellow, and the white tips to the tail feathers are smaller and not so pure white. The juvenile male of the Western Ghats race *travancoreensis* resembles the adult (differing as for *aplonotus*), but the juvenile female shows a black cap and crest and dull olive-green ventral band (thus, juvenile females moult from a black cap to a greenish-olive cap in 1st-adult plumage, and note that the black-crowned juvenile of *travancoreensis* is rather different from adult female *aplonotus*, showing much less contrast on the underparts, with a sooty-black rather than glossy blue-black cap). 1st adult female *travancoreensis* resembles the adult, although it is perhaps more likely to show dark centres to the crown feathers, and may show moult contrasts in the greater coverts and retain yellow-fringed juvenile tertials.

**VOICE** Loud and musical, and closely similar to that of Yellow-cheeked Tit. Calls include *si-si, tzee-tzee-wheep-wheep-wheep, tsi-tsi-pit-tui,* and also a rather rapid, nuthatch-like rattled *ch-chi-*

*chi-chi-chi...*; alarm *tst-reet*. The song comprises various stereotyped phrases, made up of 2–3 syllables that span a broad range of frequencies, repeated several times in rapid succession, e.g. *pui-pui-tee, pui-pui-tee..., tsi-teuw, tsi-teuw...* or *tsi-wheeah-wheeah....* Occasionally, more irregular patterns or mixed phrases are given. The individual notes are relatively long and well spaced, giving the phrase a 'slow motion' recalling Green-backed Tit, although sharper (Martens & Eck in press). Song period in Nepal January–September, especially March–April.

## DISTRIBUTION AND MOVEMENTS
Endemic to the Indian subcontinent, with two disjunct populations. In the north, breeds in the foothills of the Himalayas from NW Himachal Pradesh (Chamba) in **NW India** to easternmost **Nepal**. Largely resident, but occurs as a rare winter visitor on the periphery of the breeding range. To the west, formerly bred commonly in the Murree hills, **Pakistan**, but now extirpated there as a breeding bird and the only recent sighting is from the Margalla hills in the Murree foothills at 365 m in February 1986; also recorded from the Salt Range of Pakistan. To the east, a specimen in the British Museum labelled 'Darjeeling' and dated February 1932 may have originated from eastern Nepal, but a sight record from near Darjeeling town in March 1989 confirms its occasional occurrence in **West Bengal** (N.J. Redman pers. comm.); there are no confirmed records from Sikkim. In **peninsular India**, occurs from southern Rajasthan (Mount Abu and Jhalawar) east to eastern Bihar (Parasnath Hill), south in the west through the Western Ghats to southern Kerala and SW Tamil Nadu, and in the east through the Eastern Ghats to the Godaveri river. Occurs mainly on the Deccan plateau and peninsular hills, and uncommon or absent in the coastal plains.

## HABITAT
Essentially a bird of light, open subtropical forest and forest edge, in the Himalayas in oak or pine forest, also second growth with scattered trees, cut-over scrub or well-wooded cultivation, sometimes visiting gardens. In peninsular India occurs in similarly well-wooded areas, and in the Western Ghats in evergreen habitats in open forest, mixed bamboo jungle, cardamom sholas and coffee plantations. In the Himalayas breeds at 1000–2400 m, with exceptional records in Nepal from the Dhorpatan valley at 2925 m in June and Rara at 2700 m in July. Descends in winter to 915–2135 m, and recorded at 75 m in January at Simra, Nepal. In the peninsula breeds at *c.* 600–1830 m, wandering lower in winter, and in the Western Ghats from 760–1525 m, being absent from the drier lowlands.

## POPULATION
Generally common in the Himalayas, although somewhat capricious and absent from large areas of apparently suitable habitat, and uncommon east of the Arun valley of Nepal. Frequent in the Murree hills, Pakistan, until the 1930s, but not seen since in summer despite intensive searches and apparently now only a rare winter visitor there. In peninsular India and the Western Ghats widespread and fairly common, but here, too, somewhat local and capricious.

## HABITS
Usually found in pairs or small parties, and outside the breeding season often joins mixed-species foraging flocks, although reported to be less gregarious than other tits. When agitated, raises its crest and flicks its wings and tail. Strictly arboreal, foraging largely in the canopy and mid storey, and will occasionally flycatch. Food insects, spiders and some fruit and flower buds, and frequently visits silk cotton trees for nectar.

## BREEDING BIOLOGY
Season: Himalayas, March–June, mainly April; northern peninsular India, April–August; southern peninsular India, July–October; Western Ghats, June–November. The nest is placed in a natural cavity in a tree or in an abandoned woodpecker or barbet hole, or the birds may excavate a hole in a rotten branch or stump (Baker 1932–33; Whistler 1949); occasionally sited in the roof of a building or a hole in a wall or earth bank. Nests are found up to 7 m above ground. The foundation of moss and similar materials is lined with a cup of wool, hair or fur. Clutch 4–5 (3–6): eggs white or pale pinkish, variably spotted with reddish-brown and purplish-brown, the spots sometimes concentrated at one end or large and blotchy; 17.9 x 13.2 mm (*P. x. xanthogenys*). Both sexes build, incubate and care for the young, but the incubation period is unknown. Possibly double-brooded?

## DESCRIPTION
*P. x. aplonotus* **Adult Male**: *In fresh plumage* (July–March), lores, crown, crest, nape, and border of upper mantle black, glossed blue on feather fringes, nuchal patch and tips of longer crest feathers yellow; supercilium (formed by yellow feather tips) joins nuchal spot, rather faint in front of eye. Upperparts bright yellowish olive-green, blackish centres to scapulars may show as irregular dark spots, uppertail-coverts mid grey with the blackish centres largely concealed. Tail blackish, T1–T5 fringed mid grey, outer web of T6 white, all feathers tipped white, broadest on T6 (see figure below). Wings black, lesser coverts tipped mid grey, median and greater coverts broadly tipped white (and narrowly margined yellow), alula broadly tipped white; primary coverts rather variable, often with whitish subterminal spot or white tip on outer webs, concealed inner webs largely white. Tertials broadly tipped and more narrowly fringed white, secondaries and P7–P10 fringed mid grey and broadly tipped white, widest on inner secondaries, P3–P6 broadly fringed white around emarginations, more narrowly so on distal half, P2 very finely fringed white, P1 faintly fringed white at tip of outer web; P3–P7 with base of outer web white, forming a

*Figure 89.1  Tail of adult male* P. x. aplonotus.

contrasting patch at the base of the primaries. Cheeks and ear-coverts yellow, sides of neck blackish. Throat, upper breast, and centre of lower breast and belly black, faintly glossed blue, flanks and sides of breast and belly washed olive on rear flanks, vent dull olive-yellow. Undertail-coverts dark grey, broadly fringed and tipped whitish. Thighs white. Underwing-coverts and axillaries white. *In worn plumage* (April–August), upperparts duller and greyer, with more black centres visible on scapulars; when very worn, greenish fringes to scapulars fully abraded. Nuchal and cheek patches and underparts bleached rather paler. White at tip of tail reduced, pale fringes to wing feathers reduced. **Bare Parts**: Iris brown; bill black; legs and feet slaty-blue, claws darker. **Adult Female**: In fresh plumage as male, but cap not so glossy, crest slightly shorter, and nuchal patch, cheeks, supercilium and sides of breast and belly slightly paler yellow. Throat, centre of breast and irregular narrow stripe on belly greyish-olive. Wings and tail as male, but wing spots may be very finely margined yellow; P1 lacks white tip and P2 lacks white fringe. **Juvenile Male**: As adult male, but cap slightly duller and crest much shorter; upperparts slightly duller and greyer, especially rump, with uppertail-coverts olive-grey. Tail feathers duller, with broader but less well-defined grey fringes and usually much less extensive white tips, often faint or absent on T1–T2 (on adult *c.* 10 mm of white on tip of inner web of T6, 14 mm at shaft, compared with *c.* 5 mm on juvenile). Primary coverts average more uniformly dark, although may show white subterminal spot on outer web; white spots on tips of median and greater coverts, tertial fringes and tips, and sometimes tip of alula, washed yellow; grey fringes to secondaries washed olive on distal half, wearing to dull grey; P1 usually lacks white fringe at tip, P2 usually lacks white fringe. Bib and ventral line slightly duller, browner-black, and slightly less extensive, especially on belly. **Juvenile Female**: As adult female, but secondaries fringed olive-grey (wing spots finely margined yellow, as fresh adult); tail as juvenile male. **1st Adult**: See Sex/Age. **Measurements**: Wing of male 66–78, of female 65–73; tail of male 50–61, of female 47–54; bill 10–13.7; tarsus 15–21. Weight 14.1–19.7 g.

**MOULT** Adult post-breeding complete (late October, Himalayas; August–February peninsular India; birds in body or tail moult in April and June may be in a partial pre-breeding moult?). Post-juvenile partial, includes tail, a variable number of greater coverts and tertials (usually all), and possibly the alula and a variable number of secondaries (September, Himalayas; October, December, January, April and May, peninsular India). Ali & Ripley (1983) state that the post-juvenile moult is complete, but evidence for this is lacking.

**GEOGRAPHICAL VARIATION** Marked. Three races recognised.

*P. x. xanthogenys* Himalayan foothills. As male *aplonotus*, but upperparts average slightly brighter, more yellowish-green, scapulars with more extensive black centres and narrower greenish fringes, yellow supercilium extends further forwards (to

front edge of eye), lesser coverts tipped yellowish-olive, median coverts tipped pale yellow and greater-covert tips washed pale yellow, outer webs of tertials, especially innermost, washed yellow on fringes, and cheeks, sides of neck and sides of breast slightly richer yellow. Sexes very similar; juvenile differs from adult as in male *aplonotus* (see Description). Wing of male 67–77, of female 65–74; tail of male 50–60, of female 50–55; bill 12–14; tarsus 17.5–19.

*P. x. aplonotus* Northern and eastern peninsular India, south in the western Ghats to around Pune (Mahabaleshwar, central Maharashtra). Intergrades in the southwest with *travancoreensis* (see '*xanthonotus*' below). See Description.

*P. x. travancoreensis* Southern peninsular India in the Western Ghats from SW Maharashtra (south Konkan district) southwards. Upperparts duller than in *aplonotus*, mantle rather greyish (olive-grey), cheeks very pale washed-out yellow, underparts also much duller and paler yellow, washed olive-green, flanks washed olive-grey, and smaller white tips to tail feathers. Sexes differ as in *aplonotus*, but the adult female has cap and very short crest olive-grey, concolorous with the remainder of the upperparts (although may show variable dark feather centres), eyestripe only slightly darker, and bib and ventral stripe olive-grey, contrasting little with the remainder of the underparts, which show only a faint yellow tinge at the sides of the breast. Juvenile female as adult female, but cap sooty brown-black, cheeks and sides of breast dull yellowish, and much less contrast in the underparts, with the bib olive-grey and the remainder of the underparts also sullied olive-grey; otherwise differs from adult female as in *aplonotus*. Juvenile male differs from adult male as in *aplonotus*. Bill horny-black in male and horny-brown in female, cutting edges and tip of lower mandible whitish in juvenile. Slightly larger than *aplonotus*. Wing of male 71–82.5, of female 68–76; tail of male 53–63, of female 51–57; bill 12–14; tarsus 18–21. Includes '*xanthonotus*' of the Western Ghats from south Konkan to Hassan. This name has been given to a variable population, intermediate in coloration between *aplonotus* and pure *travancoreensis*. Females have a greenish throat, and the cap varying from greenish to pure black (variations include sooty-black crown feathers narrowly fringed olive, to olive-green cap feathers with blackish feather centres or merely blackish shaft streaks). Other intermediate characters include a better-defined bib and ventral stripe, showing more contrast with the whitish-yellow cheeks and sides of the breast and belly. Female *travancoreensis* is sometimes considered to be polymorphic (e.g. Ali & Ripley 1983, following Whistler 1942): morph A similar to the male, with a black cap, eyestripe and ventral stripe (i.e. as female *xanthogenys*); morph B similar, but ventral stripe dull olive-green (i.e. as female *aplonotus*); morph C with the cap and crest dull greyish-olive with darker feather centres and shafts, and the eyestripe and ventral stripe dull greenish-olive, the latter showing little contrast with the remainder of the underparts. Vaurie (1950a) doubted the existence of polymorphism in true *travancoreensis* from the southern Ghats, and considered that the adult female has a greenish cap, bib and ventral stripe; the black-crowned, green-throated birds, so-called 'adult' females, are juveniles which have not yet started the post-juvenile moult, whilst the black-crowned, black-throated 'females' are probably wrongly sexed. As noted above, however, adult females from the broad zone of intergradation between *travancoreensis* and *aplonotus* (i.e. '*xanthonotus*') have the crown varying from greenish to black.

**RELATIONSHIPS** Placed in the *major* species group (subgenus *Parus*) and forms a superspecies with the closely related Yellow-cheeked Tit of the eastern Himalayas, southern China and South-East Asia. The ranges of the two species overlap marginally, if at all, in far-eastern Nepal: Yellow-cheeked Tit occurs west to the Mai valley in eastern Nepal, and Black-lored Tit has been recorded east to Darjeeling, but these records may refer to winter wanderers. No hybrids between the two forms are known, which together with the clear-cut differences in size and coloration, provides good reason to treat them as separate species, rather than the geographically more logical treatment of the bright Himalayan forms as one species, distinct from the duller birds in peninsular India. (See also Yellow Tit, p. 384.)

**REFERENCES** Ali (1935), Ali & Ripley (1983), Baker (1932), Paynter (1962), Vaurie (1950a), Whistler & Kinnear (1932).

# 90 YELLOW-CHEEKED TIT *Parus spilonotus*　　　　Plate 31
Other name: Black-spotted Yellow Tit

A large, showy, crested tit, with an intricate pattern of variation among the various races and ages and between the sexes.

**IDENTIFICATION** Length 140 mm (5.5 in). A large tit with a conspicuous erect, shaggy, pointed crest. Rather variable in appearance: predominantly yellow and green in the Himalayas, otherwise grey and black with contrasting yellow cheek patches. Males have a black cap and ventral stripe, whilst females and juveniles may resemble the male, or may have the bib and ventral stripe almost concolorous with the remainder of the underparts (see Sex/Age and Geographical Variation). Throughout most of the range unmistakable, as no other tit combines bold white wingbars and yellowish cheeks with a prominent crest. In eastern Nepal and Darjeeling (and possibly also Sikkim), however, Yellow-cheeked Tit must be carefully distinguished from Black-lored Tit: note its larger size, yellow (not black) forehead and lores, extensive blackish spotting on the upperparts, grey (not olive) rump and pure white (rather than yellow-washed) wingbars.

**SEX/AGE** The sexes are similar in the Himalayan race (nominate *spilonotus*), although females tend to have a slightly duller and less glossy bib and an olive wash to the fringes of the tertials and secondaries. In all other races, the sexes are distinct. In southern China (*P. s. rex*), the cap of the female is duller, the upperparts washed olive with indistinct blackish markings, the wingbars and fringes to the wing and tail feathers washed yellow or olive-yellow, and the bib and ventral line yellowish olive-grey, concolorous with the remainder of the underparts. Females of the other eastern races also differ from the male in having the bib and ventral stripe faint or almost uniform with the underparts. Juveniles of the nominate race are rather similar to adults, but their crest is shorter, cap slightly duller black, mantle and back duller, with the black areas less well defined, the greater coverts browner and tipped yellow-white, tertial fringes washed yellowish, bib duller (slightly browner than an adult female's), and underparts paler and more washed-out (dirty creamy-yellow). Juveniles of the race *subviridis* are similar, but in the Chinese race *rex* the juvenile male is much duller than the adult, with the cap and a much-reduced crest dull sooty-black, the sides of the head and nuchal spot paler yellow, upperparts much more olive, less white in the tail, wing-coverts duller and browner, wingbars faintly washed yellow, and fringes to the tertials and secondaries washed olive; the bib is sooty brown-black, the ventral line indistinct, and the remainder of the underparts dull pale olive-grey. The juvenile female is even duller, with the cap and crest slightly paler and browner, upperparts slightly paler and duller, tertials and secondaries fringed dull olive-yellow, and throat dull light grey, washed olive-yellow, concolorous with the remainder of the underparts. The 1st-adult male resembles the adult male, but the bib averages very slightly duller and less glossy, the fringes to the retained flight feathers are washed olive, and there may be a contrast between the new greater coverts and tertials and the retained juvenile primaries and secondaries. The 1st-adult female is very similar to the adult female, but the retained flight feathers may be slightly paler and browner (contrasting with the new greater coverts), the fringes averaging slightly more olive.

**VOICE** Calls rather similar to those of Great Tit, including *sit*, *si-si-si*, a lisping *tsee-tsee-tsee*, *si-si-pudi-pudi*, and *witch-a-witch-a-witch-a*, often combined with a harsh *churr-r-r-r-r-r* (which recalls Blue Tit). Song a ringing three-note motif, rapidly repeated in groups of 2–6, *chee-chee-piu*, *chee-chee-piu*, *chee-chee-piu*... or *dzi-dzi-pu*, *dzi-dzi-pu*....

**DISTRIBUTION AND MOVEMENTS** The eastern Himalayas from easternmost **Nepal** (where recorded January–April at Hanga Tham in the upper Mai valley, and also at Chisapani in the lower Mai), through NE **India** in **Darjeeling** and **Sikkim**, **Bhutan** and **Arunachal Pradesh** to the Mishmi hills. Extends north of the main range into southern **Tibet** along the Tsangpo river to at least Medog, and to Dawang (near the Bhutan border, perhaps in Arunachal Pradesh). Also NE **India** in **Nagaland**, **Manipur**, **Meghalaya** (Khasi hills), **Assam** (Cachar hills), and **Mizoram**. Found in **Myanmar** (**Burma**) in the Chin hills south to Mount Victoria, also northern Burma and in eastern Burma south through Kachin, the Shan States and Karenni to Mount Mulayait in northern Tenasserim. Breeds in southern and SW **China** in western and southern **Yunnan**, east to Kunming and Mengzi, south-central **Sichuan** (Mabian, Pingshan), southernmost **Guizhou** (Xingyi, Ceheng, Rongjiang), northern **Guangxi Zhuang** (Yaoshan, Maoershan), southern **Hunan** (Yizhang), NE **Guangdong**, NW **Fujian** and southern **Zhejiang** (Taishun; King & Zheng 1988). In South-East Asia, found in northern **Thailand** east to Loei province, **Vietnam** in NW Tonkin and on the Da Lat plateau in southern Annam, and in **Laos** in the north and on the Bolovens plateau in the south (mapped range in Laos and Burma tentative). Generally resident, although some winter dispersal, when recorded in central Fujian and in **Hong Kong**, where an increasingly regular visitor, some oversummering, and has bred. Shows some seasonal altitudinal movements.

**HABITAT** Generally light forest, especially oak or pine, also rhododendron and other evergreens, second growth with scattered trees, the neighbourhood of cultivation and, in South-East Asia, hill evergreen forest. Found in the subtropical and temperate evergreen zones, in the eastern Himalayas resident at 1200–2450 m, sometimes descending in winter, and exceptionally reported at 450 m in eastern Nepal and 500 m in eastern Arunachal Pradesh, although also collected as high as 3675 m in late December in Sikkim (Meinertzhagen 1927) and at c. 3100 m in October in western Arunachal Pradesh (Ludlow 1944). In the northeast hill states of India breeds above 1220 m, moving lower in winter, and in Burma recorded at 1400–2200 m on Mount Victoria, at 1220–2620 m in the northeast and at 1070–2135 m in the east. In southern China, noted in Sichuan at 1200 m in April, in Yunnan at 1140–3050 m, in Guizhou at 340–800 m; in northern Guangxi at 500–2000 m, in northern Guangdong at 350–500 m, in NW Fujian breeds above c. 1000 m, descending to lower altitudes in winter, and in Zhejiang at 600–700 m. In Thailand noted at 900–1675 m, and found above 800 m on the Bolovens plateau of southern Laos. In NW Vietnam occurs at 1310–1675 m and in southern Vietnam at c. 800–2285 m.

**POPULATION** Scarce and local, even rare in the eastern Himalayas, although locally common in the northeastern hill states of India and in Burma and South-East Asia. Noted as uncommon in China by Cheng (1987), but reported as common in NW Fujian (La Touche 1899–1900, 1925;

Viney 1986), northern Guangdong (Chalmers 1990) and SE Yunnan (La Touche 1925). First recorded in Hong Kong in January 1988, followed by a small influx from late October 1988 and proven breeding in 1989 and probably again in 1990 at Tai Po Ka, with a resident population at this locality.

**HABITS** Found in pairs or small parties and often joins mixed-species foraging flocks. Not shy. Usually forages in the lower canopy, and also in low trees and the shrub layer. Food largely insects, also berries and some other vegetable matter.

**BREEDING BIOLOGY** Season: Darjeeling, June; northeast hill states, late March–late June; Burma, April–May; southern China, April–June; Thailand, February–March. The nest is placed in a hole in a tree, less frequently in stone walls and rocky banks. A pad of moss, grass and leaves is lined with fur, wool and feathers, whilst 'fir flowerscales', bristles and cast snakeskin have also been recorded as nest linings. Clutch 4–6 (3–7): eggs white, spotted with shades of red and reddishbrown, with reddish-lilac undermarkings; 17.5 x 13.8 mm (*P. s. rex*; La Touche 1899–1900).

**DESCRIPTION** *P. s. rex* **Adult Male**: *In fresh plumage* (October–spring), forehead, supercilium and nuchal spot yellow. Crown, crest, sides of nape and neck and eyestripe (behind eye only) black, glossed blue, longest crest feathers tipped yellow as a continuation of the nuchal spot. Centre of upper mantle largely white, remainder of upperparts to rump mid blue-grey, distal half of mantle and scapular feathers broadly fringed blueblack, extreme tips blackish (fringes progressively reduced towards lower scapulars, creating a variable pattern of grey and black stripes). Longer uppertail-coverts blackish, broadly fringed bluegrey. Tail black, T1–T5 fringed blue-grey, outer web of T6 largely white, all feathers tipped white, most extensively on T6 (see figure 90.1). Wings black: lesser coverts broadly fringed mid blue-grey, median coverts broadly tipped white, greater coverts broadly tipped white on outer web; alula minutely tipped white; tertials narrowly fringed light grey and broadly tipped white; secondaries and P8–10 fringed blue-grey and tipped whitish, P6–P7 finely fringed blue-grey at base and very finely fringed white distally of emarginations, P3–P5 narrowly fringed white; base of outer webs of P3–P8 white (contrasting with black primary coverts). Lores, cheeks and ear-coverts yellow. Throat and breast black, lightly glossed blue, extending in broad ventral line onto centre of belly and joining black sides of the neck. Axillaries, sides of breast and border of ventral stripe pale grey-white, flanks light-mid grey. Undertail-coverts dark grey, broadly fringed and tipped white, thighs sooty-black, narrowly tipped off-white. Underwing-coverts sooty-black, broadly tipped off-white. *In worn plumage* (summer–August), lower mantle and scapulars more extensively black, wing and tail feathers abraded, especially spots at tips of tertials, bib duller, and ventral line broader, bordered whiter. **Bare Parts**: Iris brown; bill dark grey-horn or black; legs and feet slaty-blue to blue-grey. **Adult Female**: As male, but

Figure 90.1  Tail of adult male P. s. rex.

cap not so deep black, upperparts olive-grey or greyish-olive, feathers of mantle and scapulars diffusely fringed sooty with fine, slightly paler and purer grey shaft streaks (thus upperparts indistinctly scaled rather than streaked). Tail as male, but T1–T5 fringed dull olive-grey. Lesser coverts broadly tipped olive-grey, white spots at tips of median and greater coverts and tertials tinged yellow. Tertials fringed dull olive-yellow, secondaries and inner primaries fringed olive-grey. Chin, throat and remainder of underparts yellowish olive-grey, slightly paler in centre of belly and vent. In worn plumage, upperparts slightly darker and more uniform, underparts slightly duller and greyer (yellowish feather fringes abraded), when very worn, some may show a slightly darker bib as sooty feather bases revealed. **Juvenile Male**: As adult male, but cap and much- reduced crest dull sooty-black, sides of head and nuchal spot paler yellow. Mantle and scapulars sooty brown-black, broadly tipped dull mid blue-grey, washed olive overall, especially on longest scapulars. Back, rump and uppertail-coverts dark drab-grey. Tail as adult, but paler, white tips smaller and duller (sometimes absent); feathers more pointed than on adult. Lesser coverts sooty-black, tipped dull blue-grey, median and greater coverts as adult but duller and browner, white tips faintly washed yellow. White tips to tertials reduced, fringes pale olive-grey, fringes to secondaries tinged olive. Throat, breast and indistinct ventral line sooty brown-black, remainder of underparts dull light grey, washed yellow-olive, slightly paler along border of bib and ventral line. **Juvenile Female**: As juvenile male, but cap and crest slightly paler and browner, upperparts slightly duller and paler, tertials and secondaries fringed dull olive-yellow. Chin and throat dull light grey, washed olive-yellow, as remainder of underparts. **1st-Adult Male and Female**: See Sex/Age. **Measurements**: Wing 72–86, of male 76.5–86, of female 74.5–79.5; tail of male 52–69, of female 55–61.5; bill 10.5–12.5; tarsus 16–21. Weight 18–23 g.

**MOULT**  Adult post-breeding complete (August–October, NE India; August, Burma; September–October, southern China; late August–November, Thailand). Post-juvenile partial, includes tail, greater coverts and a variable number of tertials, also sometimes up to four inner secondaries? (September, Burma; September–December, southern China).

**GEOGRAPHICAL VARIATION** Marked. Two populations meet in a zone of secondary intergradation in SW China, where the eastern, grey-and-

white race *rex* meets the western, green-and-yellow nominate race. This may be a rather recent phenomenon as the resultant hybrid population is very variable. In southern Laos and southern Vietnam, the subspecies *basileus* is intermediate between *subviridis* and *rex*, and again is rather variable and may represent another recent contact; whether it is connected to the population in northern Laos is unclear. Four subspecies recognised.

*P. s. spilonotus* Eastern Himalayas and adjacent NE Burma, southern Tibet and SW China in extreme NW Yunnan (Gongshan). Sexes almost identical. Male as male *rex*, but upperparts olive-yellow, spotted or streaked with black on mantle, scapulars and back (feathers blackish with large triangular yellowish-olive tip, extreme base grey), rump slightly greyer, shorter uppertail-coverts slightly yellower; bib and ventral line average rather less extensive, sides of breast and underparts pale yellow, washed greyish-olive on flanks. Female as male, but bib sooty brown-black, lacking gloss, and fringes to tertials and secondaries faintly tinged olive. Juvenile male as adult, but cap dull, crest shorter, bib duller (slightly browner than on female) and less extensive, greater-covert and tertial fringes washed yellow. As juvenile *rex*, but upperparts olive-yellow, diffusely streaked sooty-brown, underparts pale yellow, ventral line more extensive. Wing of male 71.5–81, of female 72–79; tail of male 50–56, of female 50–57. A very variable hybrid population of *rex* x *spilonotus* is found in western Yunnan (south to Tengchong), including individuals approaching both source populations as well as *subviridis*. One such bird was named 'evanescens', but naming such hybrid populations is inappropriate. In the Gaoligong Shan, western Yunnan: wing of male 72–81, of female 68–76; tail of male 58–67, of female 57–64; weight 15–22 g. Also, birds in NE Burma are not typical *spilonotus*, males having a greener mantle (less yellowish) and greyish-olive flanks (not yellowish), thus approaching *subviridis*, but females are very similar to males, differing only as in *spilonotus*; also larger than typical *spilonotus*: wing of male 77–84; tail of male 58–63.

*P. s. subviridis* NE Indian hill states, adjacent western Burma in the Chin hills, eastern Burma south through the Shan States to northern Tenasserim, and northern Thailand; also NW Laos? Presumably intergrades with nominate *spilonotus* in northern Burma and with *rex* in Laos. Sexes differ. Male as nominate *spilonotus*, but upperparts slightly darker and more olive (yellow-olive), black on feathers reduced, upperparts more scaled and less streaked; wing spots faintly washed yellow, flanks more extensively washed greyish-olive. Female as male, but black on upperparts further reduced, mantle more uniform yellow-olive, tertial and secondary fringes washed olive, and bib and ventral line dull, reduced to olive-yellow or even absent; as female *rex*, but upperparts brighter and yellower, more obviously mottled black, underparts yellower, often with contrasting darker bib. Juvenile near juvenile nominate *spilonotus*. Wing of male 75–80, of female 72; tail *c*. 58.

**P. s. rex** Southern China from southern Yunnan (the Mekong valley) eastwards, NW Vietnam, and NE Laos south to about Xieng Khouang. Hybridises with nominate *spilonotus* in western Yunnan. See Description.

**P. s. basileus** Southern Laos on the Bolovens plateau and southern Vietnam in southern Annam. Sexes differ. Male as male *rex*, but mantle variably tinged olive (olive feather centres), sides of breast dull yellow, connecting yellow cheeks with pale yellow underparts (often whitish on belly), flanks washed pale olive-grey; as male *subviridis*, but upperparts duller and greyer, especially lower mantle and rump, underparts paler and whiter. Female as female *rex*, but underparts slightly yellower and less grey; very similar to female *subviridis*, but underparts average slightly yellower. Much individual variation in the intensity of the green and yellow hues, males from Vietnam tending to be yellower on the underparts than those from Laos. Wing 74–83.

**RELATIONSHIPS** Closely similar to Black-lored Tit of peninsular India and the western Himalayas (confusingly also often called 'Yellow-cheeked Tit'), and sometimes treated as conspecific. However, the ranges of the two species meet or possibly overlap in a small area of the eastern Himalayas and no intermediates have ever been recorded; this, together with clear-cut differences in size and plumage, suggests that they are 'good' species. On the other hand, the Himalayan races of both species show little difference between the sexes, whilst more southerly or easterly forms exhibit marked sexual dimorphism; this hints at a close relationship between nominate *spilonotus* and the nominate race *xanthogenys* of Black-lored Tit, which may yet prove to be more closely related to each other than they are to the populations of peninsular India or China and South-East Asia. Biochemical evidence could throw some light on this problem. (See also Yellow Tit, p. 384

**REFERENCES** Ali & Ripley (1983), Cheng (1987), Paynter (1962), Stanford & Mayr (1940–41), Stanford & Ticehurst (1938–39).

# 91 YELLOW TIT *Parus holsti*                                      Plate 18

Endemic to Taiwan, and with a limited range and declining habitat, this is one of the rarest tits in the world, and very little is known of its biology or ecology.

**IDENTIFICATION** Length 130 mm (5.25 in). A large, robust tit. The adult male has the forehead and lores yellow and cap and crest black, with the longer feathers of the crest and the nuchal patch whitish. Upperparts sooty-black, glossed blue-green. Tail sooty-black, variably glossed blue, with sides and tip white. Wings black, median coverts tipped off-white, greater coverts extensively white. Flight feathers black, variably glossed blue and tipped white. Cheek patches and underparts rich yellow, flanks slightly paler, vent matt black, undertail-coverts yellow-white. The female and juvenile are a little duller. Unmistakable. The only other tit on Taiwan with yellow underparts is Green-backed Tit, which has a black bib and ventral line and lacks a crest.

**SEX/AGE** Sexes differ. The female resembles the male, but has a slightly shorter crest, duller olive-green upperparts, duller tail and flight feathers, and lacks the black patch on the belly. Juvenile distinct, paler than an adult, with the upperparts, including the crest, blue-grey, washed olive on the nape and mantle; the underparts are white, only faintly washed yellow (most obviously so on the lores, chin and ear-coverts). No information on the 1st adult.

**VOICE** Calls rather Great Tit-like, including a thin *si-si-si* (or more sibilant and insect-like *tzee-tzee-tzee*) and a harsh, scolding *dz-za-za-za* (which may be given in prolonged scolds). These two calls are often combined, *si-si-si-dza-dza-dza*, and also gives similar, but more complex combinations, *tsi'tsu-tsi'tsu-dza-dza-dza*. Also *tsut, tsut* and a thinner buzzing *dzi-dzi-dzi*. Song a variety of trisyllabic motifs (sometimes four distinct syllables), each repeated 3–7 times, sometimes ringing, e.g. *tu-wich-chi, tu-wich-chi, tu-wich-chi...*, *pu-wid-zi, pu-wid-zi, pu-wid-zi...* or *pipi-chu, pipi-chu, pipi-chu...*, and sometimes more buzzing, *chich-chich-ziu, chich-chich-ziu, chich-chich-ziu...* (all are variations on the 'tea-cher' theme). Song sometimes lasts over one minute, and the female also sings, but not for so long or so melodiously as the male. Does not call often outside the breeding season (*Birds of Yü-shan National Park*).

**HABITAT** Primary broadleaved forest, occasionally primary mixed forest and open second growth. In the winter, also forest edge near human habitations. Breeds at 1000–2500 m, optimum zone *c*. 1500 m, with a nest found at 1250 m. May descend in winter to 700 m, but also recorded as high as 2500 m in the non-breeding season/winter.

**DISTRIBUTION AND MOVEMENTS** Endemic to **Taiwan**, where recorded throughout the mountainous centre of the island, north to Mount Lala (24° 43′ N, 121° 25′ E) and south to Mount Wutou (22° 42′ N, 120° 47′ E). Resident.

**POPULATION** Rather rare, although more numerous in the southern and western parts of the mountains (described as fairly common by Chang 1980, but not common in Yü-shan National Park, although known to flock fairly frequently at Hsi-t'ou, outside the park). The species may always have been uncommon, but the population has been further reduced by the felling of its preferred habitat, primary broadleaved forest, and is largely unable to occupy more marginal habitats (such as edge and scrub, as well as plantations of conifers and bamboo) owing to competition from the less specialised Green-backed Tit. Because it is a colourful bird with a pleasant song, it is also under heavy pressure from bird-catchers. The species is now considered threatened by forest destruction and other human activities, and is listed as near-threatened in BirdLife International's world check-list of threatened birds (Collar *et al.* 1994).

**HABITS** Usually found singly or in pairs, but may join mixed-species foraging flocks, although seldom more than one or two Yellow Tits per flock. Forages in the canopy and upper understorey of the forest. Observed feeding young with caterpillars.

**BREEDING BIOLOGY** Poorly known. The nest was not found until 1976 (Chang & Severinghaus 1979). Season April. The nest is placed in a cavity in a tall tree (usually hardwood?); recorded at 6 and 7.5 m above ground. The nest itself is a pad of dried leaves (including bamboo), lichens and mosses, as well as feathers. It may reuse nests year after year, adding nesting material each year (*Birds of Yü-shan National Park*). Clutch 3–4 (just two clutches reported, perhaps incomplete); eggs white, spotted and streaked with pinkish and brown, markings concentrated at the larger end; *c.* 17 x 12.5 mm.

**DESCRIPTION** **Adult Male**: *In fresh plumage* (autumn–winter), centre of forehead, crown, crest and nape black, glossed blue, longer crest feathers tipped whitish, nuchal patch whitish. Sides of neck, mantle, scapulars, back and rump black, glossed blue-green (greenish metallic-blue: Seebohm 1895). Uppertail-coverts black. Tail black, outer webs extensively fringed blue (the blue slightly iridescent, varying with the angle of the light to bright pale blue); T2–T5 with small white tips, T6 with white tip and white outer web (see figure, 91.1). Wing-coverts black, median coverts tipped dirty white, innermost greater coverts tipped and fringed dirty white, central greater coverts more broadly fringed white, forming a solid grey-white panel, outer two greater coverts fringed dull blue and tipped whitish. Alula and primary coverts black. Flight feathers black, tertials broadly fringed iridescent blue (as tail) and tipped white, secondaries similar but with smaller white tips, primaries similar but P1–P7 lack white tips and blue fringes very narrow on distal half of feathers and absent on P1–P2. Base of bill and short supercilium (to eye) yellow. Small spot in

*Figure 91.1 Tail of adult male.*

front of eye and eyering blackish. Cheeks, ear-coverts, throat and breast rich yellow, flanks extensively slightly paler and duller (with a faint grey wash), vent matt black, undertail-coverts yellow-white. Axillaries and underwing-coverts whitish, under primary coverts with blackish bases. No information on worn plumage. **Bare Parts**: Iris dark reddish-brown to brown; bill black; legs and feet grey-blue or slate. **Adult Female**: In fresh plumage, forehead, crown and crest sooty-black, glossed blue, longest feathers of crest tipped white, large white nuchal patch. Sides of crown and sides of neck, nape, mantle, scapulars, back and rump dull olive-green. Tail as male, but blue fringes slightly paler and duller (tinged grey). Median coverts dull blue-grey, tipped pale grey, greater coverts dull pale blue-grey with slightly paler grey tips and narrow olive fringes. Alula and primary coverts contrastingly sooty-black. Flight feathers as male but fringes slightly duller and a greyer blue. Supercilium and underparts as male, but lacks black patch on vent. **Juvenile**: Forehead, crown and nape blue-grey, longest feathers of crest tipped whitish. Mantle, scapulars and back blue-grey, washed olive-green. Wings and tail apparently as adult. Supercilium, cheeks and ear-coverts pale yellow, remainder of underparts white, washed pale yellow. (No specimens seen, description based on a photograph in *Birds of Yü-shan National Park*). **1st Adult**: No information. **Measurements**: Wing of male 75.5, 78, of female 72.5; tail of male 50.5, 55.5, of female 49; bill 12.5–13; tarsus 19–20. Weight: no information.

**MOULT** No information.

**GEOGRAPHICAL VARIATION** None.

**RELATIONSHIPS** Allied with Black-lored and Yellow-cheeked Tits by Snow (1954b and Eck 1988), but placed on its own in the monotypic subgenus *Machlolophus* by Thielke (1968).

**REFERENCES** Chang & Severinghaus (1979), Hachisuka & Udagawa (1951).

This small, perky tit is one of the most familiar garden birds in Britain and much of Europe. Tame and acrobatic, it has adapted well to man-made environments. The North African and Canary Islands populations are perhaps better treated as a distinct species.

**IDENTIFICATION** Length 120 mm (4.25 in). A small, rather square-headed and relatively short-tailed tit. Cap ultramarine-blue, bordered on all sides by white, while the narrow black eyestripe connects at the rear with a broad blue-black nuchal band, which in turn connects via the sides of the neck with small black bib, a dark line thus encircling the white cheek patches. Narrow band on upper mantle bluish-white, remainder of upperparts greyish-green. Tail and wing feathers fringed blue, with a broad white wingbar on the greater coverts and white tips to the tertials. Underparts yellow, with a variable narrow black ventral line on the centre of the breast. The North African populations are rather different, with the cap blue-black and the upperparts slaty-blue, whilst in the Canary Islands the cap is blackish, the upperparts slaty-blue and the underparts variably whitish. Very distinctive, and unlikely to be confused with any other species. Unusually pale leucistic Blue Tits could be mistaken for a vagrant Azure Tit, but never show the massive amounts of white in the wings and tail displayed by Azure, whilst in NE Iran care should be taken to distinguish the rather pale local race of Blue Tit from Yellow-breasted Tit, which has been recorded once in the region.

**SEX/AGE** Sexes very similar, but in the hand most adults may be sexed with practice, or with comparative material. The female averages duller blue on the crown (especially the forecrown), with a narrower and greyer nuchal band (dull, dark blue-grey, as against deep blue-black on the male), the upperparts are more grey-green (less bluish), with duller and paler fringes to the flight feathers, tail and especially wing-coverts (more greyish, less blue than the male when fresh, more turquoise when worn, compared with deep ultramarine-blue on male); the bib is greyer, and on some females the dark ventral line is restricted to a few dark grey feather tips. These differences are most marked between adult males and 1st-adult females; adult females may be much more similar to adult males (see also Geographical Variation). In the *teneriffae* group the sexes are rather more similar, and sexing is more difficult when the bird's age is unknown. The upperparts of adult males average purer grey-blue, of 1st-adult females greyer and sometimes with much green on the rump, adult females and 1st-adult males being intermediate. The black line on the sides of the neck averages narrower on females (especially 1st adults), the bib dull black (deep black on males), and the underparts of 1st adults (especially females) paler yellow than on adults, with the tail and wings slightly greyer blue, not so bright and glossy. Juvenile distinct, with the face, supercilium and nape washed-out dirty yellow and the cap, eyestripe and nuchal band hardly darker

than the upperparts, which are greenish-grey. The fringes to the tail and flight feathers are duller, more greenish-blue, and tertials and wing-coverts are duller and greyer, with greenish fringes, and the wingbar is tinged yellowish. Underparts dull yellow, with a much-reduced bib and no ventral line. In the *teneriffae* group, juveniles have the cap and stripes on the head dark grey (better defined and less olive than juveniles of the *caeruleus* group), the upperparts grey-green and the face and underparts brighter yellow, sometimes showing traces of a small greyish bib. The 1st adult is closely similar to the adult, but retains the juvenile flight feathers, primary coverts, a variable number of tail feathers and occasionally some tertials, outer greater coverts and feathers of the alula. The best ageing character is the contrast between the new bright blue greater coverts and the retained dull blue-grey juvenile primary coverts (often tinged greenish) and, if present, similar moult contrasts within the greater coverts. The primary coverts also contrast with new feathers in the alula, and look also for moult contrasts in the tail (shape, colour and wear: retained juvenile feathers average more worn, while any new inner feathers may retain a white tip until the winter). The 1st-adult female is duller than the male, but retains the relative contrasts between the new 1st adult greater coverts and old primary coverts. Her white forehead averages slightly duller and less extensive, the nuchal band narrower and duller (more grey-blue), the blue of the crown and tail duller and greyer, wingcoverts more grey-blue or cerulean-blue, bib greyer with more extensive white feather tips, dark ventral line paler grey and more irregular, and the belly more extensively white; when worn, the crown is brighter and glossier blue, but with grey feather bases visible (unlike males).

**VOICE** Varied. Characteristic call, given in excitement or alarm, a fast, hard scolding, e.g. *churrrrit*, sometimes preceded or followed by one or more high-pitched notes, *pit pit churrr, drrrrrt tit tit tit, chirrr-rr-rr...*, in which case it may be prolonged (averages higher-pitched and more slurred than similar calls of Great Tit, with the individual units less well separated). Contact call a short, high-pitched *tsee*, often in series, *tsee-tsee-tsee*. Also a fuller, more ringing *tsee-tsee-tsee, tsit* (mostly given in late winter and spring, sometimes with the last note repeated), a clear *seeseedu*, and a thin, sibilant *sissississississ*. When disturbed on the nest, gives an explosive *tufff*, whilst fledged young give a high, slightly discordant *tsee-tsee-tsee-tsee-tsee...* (very similar to Great Tit). Hawk alarm a prolonged *seeee*. The song is a clear, silvery, high-pitched trill lasting *c.* 2 seconds (higher, clearer, sweeter and less abrasive than the 'scold'), usually introduced by 1–4 high-pitched notes, thus *pee-pee-ti sihihihihihi, pee-pee-ti sihihihihihi...* (other renditions include *tsee tsee t t t t t t t*). This is repeated several times, and variants include a slower, ringing but still tremulous *psi-psi tsatsatsa, psi-psi tsatsatsa....* Other songs are the repetition of high-pitched notes, lacking tremolo, *tee-tee see-see, tee-tee see-se, psi-dada, psi-dada, psi-dada...*or *see-saw* (recalling Great Tit, but are not so ringing or incisive). Each male has a repertoire of 3–8 song types; the female also sings fairly frequently. In the *teneriffae* **group** the song is a rapid repetition of phrases made up of simple units without tremolo, *tizee tizee tizee..., tee-zay-brre tee-zay-brre..., tuz-a-pee, tuz-a-pee, tuz-a-pee...* etc., often with a rather metallic timbre (it may recall Coal Tit, but is harder and not so sweet). Within this simple structure, song is very variable, both between different populations and between males within a population, whilst each male has a repertoire of 7–19 song types. The song of birds from the Canary Islands is only partially understood by birds from Europe (see Becker *et al.* 1980). The song of the populations on Corsica and Majorca is allied with that of North Africa (Thibault 1983). Some calls are shared with the *caeruleus* group, but others are distinctive, including a variety of mate-directed calls, territorial calls, the females' calls and the aerial-predator alarm call (Schottler 1994). (Largely after Cramp & Perrins 1993, Witherby *et al.* 1944).

## DISTRIBUTION AND MOVEMENTS
Virtually endemic to the West Palearctic. Breeds in **Britain** and **Ireland** (including the Inner Hebrides, but very local in the Outer Hebrides on Lewis and Harris, and absent as a breeding bird in Orkney and Shetland), and throughout **Continental Europe**, south to the Mediterranean, including Majorca, Corsica, Sardinia, Sicily, Pantelleria, Crete and Rhodes, and north to northern **Norway** (*c.* 66° N) and **Sweden** (*c.* 65° N, and including many of the Baltic islands) and central **Finland** (irregularly northern Finland), the **Baltic Republics**, and in **Russia** to about Petrozavodsk, Yaroslavl', the Kokshaga river, Malmyzh and the southwest part of the Perm region (occasionally recorded breeding further north, at Arkhangel'sk, Mezen' and Velikiy Ustyug). The range extends east in Russia to the foothills of the Ural mountains, to Ufa, Orenburg and Ak'yar, and in the **Ukraine** south in the west to the Black Sea and Askaniya Nova, but absent from the region of the Sea of Azov, although breeds in the mountains of the southern Crimea. In southern **Russia** breeds south to Rostov and Volgograd, and along the Volga to the Caspian Sea, but absent from the Stavropol region. In northern and western **Kazakhstan** extends south to Urda and Ural'sk and along the Ural river to at least Mergenevo. Also breeds in the Caucasus, north to the Kuban' river, Prokhladnyy, Kizlyar and the Samar river. Occurs through the Transcaucasus, in **Georgia**, **Armenia** and east to the Talyshskiye mountains in extreme SE **Azerbaydzhan**. In **Iraq** occurs in the extreme northwest in the foothills of the Zagros (Amadiyah to Chwarta, but perhaps winter visitor

only?), and in adjacent **Iran** found in the Zagros mountains southeast to central Fars (around Shiraz), in the mountains of northern Azarbaijan, and in the Elburz mountains east to about Gonbad-e-Kavus and Mayamey, and in adjacent SW **Turkmenistan** in the western Kopet Dag east to Füryuza (Ashkhabad). Widespread in **Turkey**, although absent from parts of the central plateau and the southeast. In **Syria** apparently a locally numerous resident in the northwest, with breeding proven in the Jabal al Nusayriyah, and probably also breeds around Damascus (and some dispersal, e.g. to Sahyun (Latakia) in February 1976). Breeds locally in **Lebanon**, and in **Jordan**, where unrecorded since 1893 until rediscovered in the northern highlands in1984, with breeding proven in Dibbin forest in 1990 and now annual; has strayed south to about Amman (Andrews 1995). An irregular winter visitor **Israel**. Also breeds very locally in northern **Libya** in the Al Jabal al Akhdar (especially around Wadi el Kuf, Merg and Barce), and in **NW Africa** south to the northern edge of the Sahara and some of its northern oases, in northern **Tunisia** south to Nefta and Sfax, northern **Algeria** south to the Djebel Amour and in NW **Morocco** south to the Anti-Atlas. Also found throughout the **Canary Islands**. In winter found along the southern Ural river to the Caspian Sea, on the lower reaches of the Atrek river and around the southeastern shore of the Caspian Sea in SW Turkmenistan and Iran, where also recorded in the Turkmen steppes and has straggled in winter to the Rezauyeh basin, Tehran area and Mashhad. Vagrant **Malta** (*P. c. ultramarinus?*, spring 1908; *P. c. caeruleus*, October 1975), also **Cyprus**; In northern Scotland, vagrant **Fair Isle** (eight records) and irregular scarce migrant **Orkney** and **Shetland** October–May (most or all nominate *caeruleus*). Resident and generally sedentary in the south of the range, seldom moving more than 100 km, and over 95% of recoveries in Britain are within 10 km of the ringing site. Central and northern populations undertake more regular movements, usually heading south and west, and good numbers of Blue Tits from the north overwinter in the Mediterranean basin. Has been noted moving east in small numbers at the Bosporus in late September–October (Porter 1983). The numbers are rather irregular, and the passage during September–October at various migration watchpoints in the Baltic and Alpine passes varies greatly from year to year. Sometimes there may be irruptions, occasionally on a very large scale, perhaps caused by very high population levels, as in autumn 1957, when large numbers of Continental birds reached Britain in late September–October (with smaller numbers noted on return passage in late January–early May). Those breeding at higher altitudes undertake some altitudinal movements in winter (e.g. in the Caucasus and Scotland).

## HABITAT
In most of Europe found in deciduous woodland and scrub, notably oak woodland, as well as orchards, hedgerows and urban parks and gardens, in fact anywhere where there are trees with suitable cavities for nesting; although large-

ly avoiding conifers, does sometimes utilise conifer plantations (especially if there are nearby stands of deciduous trees). In the Mediterranean found in a wider variety of habitats, including broadleaved evergreen woodland, and in Corsica and in North Africa shrublands, but in northern Libya confined to montane juniper, cypress and pine, in northern Jordan to pine and oak, and in NW Syria to cedar forest. In the more arid parts of the range in SE Europe and SW Asia, confined to riverine vegetation or to man-made habitats such as shelterbelts, parks and gardens, although in the mountains of Iran found in oak woodland, and occurs in palm groves in Saharan oases. In the Canary Islands, breeds in tamarisk woodland on the arid eastern islands of Fuerteventura and Lanzarote, otherwise in montane pine and laurel forest. In the autumn and winter found in a slightly wider variety of habitats, such as *Brassica* crops and sparse scrub in steppe regions, and regularly including reedbeds. Generally found in the lowlands, but breeds at up to c. 1250 m in the Swiss Alps (and recorded in the breeding season up to 1700 m), to 1540 m in the Austrian Alps (where usually below 1000 m), up to 1370 m in SW Bulgaria and up to the treeline at 3500 m in the Caucasus, to 1525 m in Turkey, 1525 m in northern Iran and at least 2040 m in SW Iran, and to at least 1600 m in the Moyen Atlas of Morocco.

**POPULATION** Generally very common, although rare on the northern borders of the range and in the southeast. Some increase on the northern and western edges of the range: in Britain first bred Isles of Scilly in 1953 and Outer Hebrides in 1963, has spread northwards into northernmost Scotland, and into Norway from c. 1970, and expanded into southern Finland from c. 1900, with a marked increase since mid 1970s. Not particularly vulnerable to hard winters, although these cause some short-term fluctuations.

**HABITS** Restless and often tame and inquisitive, persistently flicking its wings and tail and frequently calling. May raise its nape feathers in excitement, to form a hint of a crest. Found singly and in pairs, and adults remain through the winter near their breeding territory, joining a mixed-species foraging flock (whose range includes several breeding territories). As well as the resident pairs, the flock also attracts 'nomads'. The flock begins to break up into pairs in the late winter, individual territories being gradually re-established. In the southeast of the range, flocks of several hundred have been recorded in autumn and winter. Generally monogamous, but bigamous males are not rare, especially in optimum habitats. About 75% of pairs remain together from one year to the next in cases where both members survive. Courtship feeding begins around the time of nest-site selection; formerly considered a symbolic ritual, it has now been established that the provision of high-protein food items by the male plays essential part in the nutrition of the female during the laying and incubation periods. In the winter roosts in holes (sometimes among ivy or in old nests, in urban areas in street lamps), and in the summer among foliage, although the female continues to roost in the nest hole until just before the young fledge. Forages primarily in the canopy, but also in the middle and lower storeys, concentrating on the smaller outer twigs and branches, buds and leaves, but also sometimes feeds on the ground, especially in the winter. Adept at locating hidden prey, such as small insects under bark, in leaf mines or galls, or in reed stems. Sometimes flycatches, especially in the early spring. Food largely insects and spiders, also fruits and seeds in the autumn and winter and nectar in the spring and summer. A very frequent visitor to birdtables, and well known in Britain for its habit of prising off milk-bottle tops and drinking the cream; its inquisitive nature has also resulted in putty-pecking and paper-tearing. Does not normally hoard food.

**BREEDING BIOLOGY** Season April–mid May (exceptionally from late March, and in northern Russia to early June; second clutches in Russia laid in second half of June). The nest is placed in a hole in a tree, sometimes in a wall but rarely in the ground, and readily takes to nestboxes and other artificial sites where natural holes are scarce; occasionally inside open nests of other birds or in the foundations of large nests, and several records of deep cup nests placed in tree forks (Perrins 1979). May occasionally clean out cavities and remove rotten wood. The final selection of a nest site is probably made by the female. The nest itself is a cup of moss, often with dried grass and other plant material, lined with hair, wool, fine grass, bark shavings and some feathers, built by the female alone over 5–12 days, and material may continue to be added even after the eggs hatch. Clutch in northern and western Europe 7–13 (2–19; clutches of up to 24 are probably the product of two females), 6–8 (3–10) in the Mediterranean and SW Asia, and 2–6 on the Canary Islands: eggs white, finely spotted chestnut, spots often concentrated at the broad end, with greyish undermarkings (sometimes unmarked); 15.4 x 11.9 mm (*P. c. obscurus*). Female incubates, period 12–16 days; she is fed on and off the nest by the male. The young are fed by both sexes, but brooded only by the female, and fledge after 19 (16–23) days. Two broods occasional to frequent in Continental Europe, but very rare in Britain, Corsica and Morocco.

**DESCRIPTION** *P. c. caeruleus* **Adult Male**: *In fresh plumage* (August/September to about March), forehead, supercilium and rear crown white, centre of crown ultramarine-blue, brighter and paler at the front. Narrow black eyestripe from bill to broad blue-black nuchal band, which extends in turn broadly onto the sides of the neck and more narrowly onto the lower throat below the cheek patch and to the small dull black bib on the chin and centre of the throat; feathers of bib very finely tipped white. Cheeks, ear-coverts and sides of throat white, grey feather bases may show, especially on ear-coverts. Lower nape and upper mantle off-white, feathers tipped pale blue-grey, remainder of upperparts greyish-olive or blue-green, often washed yellow on rump; longest uppertail-coverts blue. Tail dark blue, shafts black, inner webs duller and greyer, outer webs fringed brighter blue, T6 very narrowly fringed white. Wing-coverts and alula grey, broadly fringed blue, greater coverts broadly tipped white. Tertials dark grey, tipped white, outer webs washed blue and fringed yellowish-green. Inner webs of primaries, secondaries and primary coverts dark grey, outer webs blue (not P1–P2), P3–P6 very narrowly fringed grey-white distally of emarginations; all except outer primaries narrowly tipped white. Underparts sulphur-yellow, faintly washed green, feathers of central breast tipped blackish, forming a variable narrow ventral line (sometimes virtually absent), centre of belly variably whitish. Underwing-coverts and axillaries pale sulphur-yellow. *In worn plumage* (about April–August), cap, tail and wing-coverts (including primary coverts) brighter and more glossy blue, mantle and scapulars duller and greyer (less green), white tips to greater coverts, tertials and flight feathers abraded (sometimes completely so), bib darker and blacker, and underparts duller, flanks and vent tinged greyish-green, black ventral line and whitish belly more prominent. **Bare Parts**: Iris dark hazel-brown to blackish-brown; bill dark slate-grey to horn-black, cutting edges pale grey; legs and feet slate-blue. **Adult Female**: See Sex/Age. **Juvenile Male**: Forehead, supercilium, rear crown and nape dirty pale yellow. Upperparts greenish-grey, crown, eyestripe, and narrow band across nape and sides of neck as upperparts or slightly darker. Tail as adult, but averages duller blue, feathers more pointed. Wing-coverts and tertials grey, fringed greenish, greater coverts and tertials tipped yellow-white. Primary coverts grey, outer webs tinged greenish-blue, may be faintly tipped paler. Alula dark grey, finely tipped white. Flight feathers as adult, but outer webs average duller and greyer blue with a variable green tinge, especially on secondaries. Cheeks, ear-coverts and underparts pale dirty yellow, with indistinct grey bib on chin and upper throat, often not connected with 'bridle' of nape and sides of neck. No dark ventral line. When a few weeks old, yellow of head and underparts becomes paler, fore supercilium whiter, eyestripe and bridle darker, greyer and less olive. Bill as adult, but tip horn-coloured. **Juvenile Female**: As juvenile male (see Sex/Age). **1st-Adult Male and Female**: As adult, but retains a variable number of juvenile wing and tail feathers (see Sex/Age). **Measurements**: Wing of male 61–73, of female 60–69; tail of male 49–54, of female 47–52; bill 8–9.7; tarsus 16.2–18. Weight 7.5–14.7 g.

MOULT   Adult post-breeding complete (mid May–September, occasionally October, duration c. 70–80 days). Post-juvenile partial, includes variable number of tail feathers (c. 15–70% replace T1), greater coverts (c. 35–95% replace all), tertials (c. 70–90 % replace all) and feathers of alula (c. 35–80% moult all), the extent varies with season, and moult is least extensive in Britain and probably usually more extensive in southern populations (e.g. often whole tail moulted in Iberia);

very exceptionally, may also include inner 1–2 secondaries (starts at age c. 2 months, June–early October, occasionally November).

**GEOGRAPHICAL VARIATION**   Marked, with two groups of subspecies, the *caeruleus* group in Europe and the Middle East, and the *teneriffae* group in North Africa and the Canary Islands.

**THE *CAERULEUS* GROUP**   Cap and head stripes blue, mantle greenish, bill stubby. Variation slight and clinal, the intensity of yellow and blue in the plumage increasing from northeast to southwest, with a parallel increase in the extent and intensity of the black markings and decrease in the extent and purity of the white areas. Another, less obvious, cline runs at right angles, the depth of green in the plumage decreasing northwest to southeastern (Britain to Iran). Thus, the palest birds are in the east (north of the Caspian Sea and in SW Iran), the darkest in the west (British Isles and, even more so, southern Iberia and the west Mediterranean islands). Exceptions are the populations of Majorca, which have a whitish belly, and the Elburz mountains of northern Iran, which are richly coloured (like west Mediterranean birds) (Martin 1988). Nine races recognised.

*P. c. obscurus* Britain, Ireland and Channel Islands; intergrades with nominate *caeruleus* in western France. Poorly marked. As nominate *caeruleus*, but cap slightly darker blue, mantle slightly darker and greener (less blue-grey), underparts deeper and duller yellow, sullied green-grey, white tips to tertials and greater coverts slightly narrower and duller. Averages smaller. Wing of male 60–72, of female 57–66.

*P. c. caeruleus* Continental Europe south to northern Spain, Sicily, northern Greece, western and northern Turkey and the Ukraine, and east to the northern Urals (north of Perm') and Volga river. Irregular migrant September–April Britain; vagrant Sardinia (also Cyprus?). See Description. Birds from Rhine valley of Germany, Low Countries and northern France sometimes darker and duller, tending towards *obscurus*, although larger and with tips of tertials and greater coverts more extensively white. Conversely, *obscurus* from East Anglia and eastern Kent tend towards nominate *caeruleus*. Birds from Italy and Sicily tend towards *ogliastrae* in more grey-green upperparts and deeper yellow underparts.

*P. c. balearicus* Majorca. Poorly marked. As nominate *caeruleus*, but mantle slightly paler and greyer, underparts slightly paler yellow, with breast and belly more extensively white and with ventral line reduced. Wing of male 61–70, of female 64–68.

*P. c. ogliastrae* Portugal, southern Spain, Corsica and Sardinia; intergrades with nominate *caeruleus* in southern Galicia, Salamanca and Teruel (Spain). Poorly marked. Very similar to *obscurus*, but mantle slightly bluer or greyer, wing-coverts slightly darker and brighter blue, underparts purer yellow (not so greenish); sexual dimorphism reduced, females may be as bright as males. Small (as *obscurus*). Wing of male 57–66, of female 57–61.5.

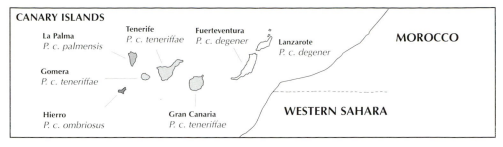

Figure 92.1 Distribution of the teneriffae group in the Canary Islands.

**P. c. calamensis** Southern Greece in the Pelopónnisos, also the Cyclades, Crete and Rhodes. Poorly marked. As nominate *caeruleus*, but smaller. Wing of male 61–67, of female 58–64.

**P. c. orientalis** SE European Russia from around the Volga river to the central and southern Urals. (Included in nominate *caeruleus* by Stepanyan 1990.) As nominate *caeruleus*, but upperparts olive-grey, tinged yellow (distinctly paler and greyer/yellower, less green), underparts paler and brighter yellow. Averages very slightly larger. Wing of male 68–71, of female 66–69.

**P. c. satunini** Crimea, Caucasus, Transcaucasia, NW Iran (Azarbaijan), eastern Turkey, Taurus mountains of southern Turkey, and Turkmenistan; also this race or *persicus* in Levant, SE Turkey (south of Taurus) and northern Iraq (synonym *georgicus*). Intergrades with nominate *caeruleus* in wide band across western Turkey, Bulgaria, northern Greece, Albania and the south and west of former Yugoslavia. Poorly marked (differences most pronounced in eastern Transcaucasia and NW Iran, the end of the cline). As nominate *caeruleus*, but upperparts olive-grey (paler and greyer, less saturated grey-green), underparts cleaner and paler yellow (slightly sullied sulphur-yellow). As *orientalis*, but upperparts fractionally darker and greyer (less yellow), underparts slightly darker, flanks a little greyer. Wing of male 61.5–70, of female 62–68.

**P. c. raddei** Northern Iran (those in Khorasan and SW Turkmenistan are paler and more similar to *satunini*). Poorly marked. Near nominate *caeruleus*, but mantle averages fractionally darker and bluer, underparts average slightly richer and cleaner yellow (thus near *ogliastrae*); also averages slightly smaller. As *satunini* but upperparts slightly darker and less grey, underparts darker and richer yellow. Wing of male 62–69, of female 59–65.

**P. c. persicus** South and SW Iran in Zagros mountains (eastwards to Fars); intergrades with *satunini* in the north (Hamadan). Relatively distinct. Pale (and palest in the southeast), upperparts bluish green-grey (slightly paler and rather greyer, less olive or greenish-yellow, than *satunini*; as *orientalis*, but much less olive-yellow), underparts variable, from uniform yellow-white to richer yellow on the breast and whitest on the belly and vent. Averages small. Wing of male 62–68, of female 62–65.

**THE *TENERIFFAE* GROUP** Cap and head stripes blackish, mantle slate to blue-grey (greenish in *ombriosus*), forehead, supercilium and cheeks pure white and bill relatively long and thin. Vocalisations distinct, and, with a clearly different ancestry, this group may merit full specific status. Six well-differentiated isolated races.

**P. c. ultramarinus** NW Africa and Pantelleria island (Italy). As nominate *caeruleus*, but forehead, narrow supercilium and hindcrown pure white, cap black with glossy dark blue feather tips, especially on forecrown, broad, distinct black eyestripe, and chin, throat and broad nuchal band extending down sides of neck to side of lower throat deep black, forming a black collar of medium width; upperparts dark blue-grey, with green (if any) restricted to rump, and tail and wingcoverts slightly brighter blue (near *ogliastrae*); greater coverts tipped white (c. 1–2 mm deep), tertials and secondaries finely tipped white; underparts slightly richer and deeper but duller yellow. Wing of male 57–68, of female 56–63.

**P. c. cyrenaicae** Libya. As *ultramarinus*, but white forehead band narrower, mantle darker and duller blue (especially upper mantle), underparts slightly darker and dingier yellow, with little or no white on belly. Averages smaller, but bill relatively thick. Wing of male 56–61, of female 56–58.

**P. c. degener** Fuerteventura and Lanzarote, eastern Canary Islands. Close to *ultramarinus*, but upperparts paler and greyer (mid–light grey, washed blue, palest on upper mantle and rump, thus less dark and bluish), black nuchal band and collar narrower, greater coverts more broadly tipped white (c. 2–3 mm deep), underparts slightly cleaner and paler yellow with more extensive whitish belly, and bill longer (also relatively thick).

**P. c. teneriffae** Gomera, Tenerife and Gran Canaria, central Canary Islands. As *degener*, but upperparts darker (slaty-blue, but not so dark and bluish as *ultramarinus*), broader black nuchal band and collar (broader than in *ultramarinus*), lacks white tips to greater coverts and white fringes to tertials greatly reduced, underparts darker yellow, with little white on belly (near *ultramarinus*), and notably, black ventral line much reduced.

**P. c. palmensis** La Palma, western Canary Islands. As *teneriffae* but duller, cap not so glossy blue (black on male, sooty-black on female), mantle and scapulars much duller and greyer, mid-dark grey, sometimes tinged green, especially on back and rump, greater coverts narrowly tipped white (c. 1 mm deep), and belly extensively white.

**P. c. ombriosus** Hierro, western Canary Islands. As *teneriffae*, but upperparts greenish, greater coverts narrowly tipped greyish-white (c. 1 mm deep) and underparts slightly darker and richer yellow.

**HYBRIDS** Regularly hybridises with Azure Tit following westward invasions of that species (see p. 393 for full details). Hybrids with Great Tit also very rarely recorded.

**RELATIONSHIPS** Forms a superspecies with Azure and Yellow-breasted Tits, the three sometimes separated from the other members of the genus *Parus* in the subgenus *Cyanistes*, characterised by their bright blue or azure coloration. The *teneriffae* group may be the most ancient (based on its song type, a repetition of note groups, typical of the genus *Parus* in general).

The *caeruleus* group derived from this, and then the Azure/Yellow-breasted complex from the *caeruleus* group, subsequently splitting into Yellow-breasted (still quite close to the *caeruleus* group of Blue Tit in coloration and song), whilst Azure Tit, lacking any yellow in the plumage, is a relatively recent offshoot, specialising in riparian forests (J. Martens *in litt.*). Martin (1988) suggests that the subgenus could be best considered as a superspecies comprising four sister-species: the *teneriffae* group ('Canarian Tit'), *caeruleus* group (Blue Tit), and Yellow-breasted and Azure Tits.

**REFERENCES** Cramp & Perrins, Grant (1979), Jenni & Winkler (1994), Martin (1988), Portenko *et al.*, (1982)Vaurie (1950a, 1957a, 1959), Witherby *et al.* (1938) .

# 93 AZURE TIT *Parus cyanus* Plate 30

This ghostly tit is an enigmatic inhabitant of willow thickets and other scrubby riverine vegetation in the taiga forests of eastern Europe and Asia. Prone to westward vagrancy, is has often hybridised with Blue Tit, and the occurrence of such hybrids puts European birdwatchers in a listing dilemma!

**IDENTIFICATION** Length 135 mm (5.25 in). A medium-large tit with a proportionally long, slightly graduated tail. Often appears slightly 'fluffy'. Head white with narrow black eyestripes that meet at the rear in a dark blue nuchal band. Upperparts blue-grey; wings slaty-blue with two broad white wingbars (prominent in flight), white tips to the primary coverts, and extensively white tertials (forming a broad white inverted 'V' on the wings). Tail black, broadly bordered with white. Underparts white with an irregular narrow blue-black ventral line. The flight is powerful and bounding, and the long tail may suggest a Long-tailed Tit or even a wagtail. The strikingly pallid, pale blue-and-white appearance is distinctive, although the plumage pattern and long tail may momentarily recall a Long-tailed Tit of one of the white-headed northern races. Great care must be taken, however, to distinguish extralimital birds from hybrids (or perhaps leucistic Blue Tits). Note Azure Tit's larger size and proportionally longer and more graduated tail, white throat (lacking a black bib), broad white wingbars and extensive white sides and tip to the tail (see also Hybrids).

**SEX/AGE** Sexes very similar and not separable in the field. In the hand, sexing is still rather difficult, but may be possible, especially in comparison with birds of known sex. Females differ from males *on average* as follows: nuchal band narrower and less regular, dull slate-black with a reduced gloss; mantle and scapulars greyer, less bluish; lesser and median coverts grey-blue rather than cyanine-blue; greater coverts, tertials and outer webs of primaries and secondaries duller slate-blue, less cyanine-blue; underparts more heavily washed greyish-cream, less pure white. Correct sexing is further complicated by age variation (see below). Juvenile as adult but greyer, especially on the crown and upperparts, with the eyestripe and nuchal band dull dark grey, and the lesser and median coverts and fringes to the greater coverts grey (not bright blue), while the underparts often lack the dark ventral line. 1st adult as adult, but retains the juvenile flight feathers, primary coverts, outer five tail feathers, and occasionally the alula or outer greater coverts. Shows slight moult contrasts between the duller blue juvenile primary coverts (and outer greater coverts, if retained) and new inner greater coverts; in the tail, the tips of T2–T5 are more pointed and worn than the fresh square-tipped T1, with the white tips of the old feathers duller and more abraded. Aging is, however, very difficult in spring and summer owing to the relatively rapid wear of fresh 1st-adult feathers. Differences between male and female as for adults, but 1st adults sometimes duller; thus, the 1st-adult male may be closely similar to an adult female, whilst the 1st-adult female has even duller blue-grey on the wing than the adult female, especially the retained juvenile feathers, which may be mainly grey.

**VOICE** Quite similar to Blue Tit, but perhaps even more varied, especially the song. Contact call, given at rest and in flight, a quiet, slurred *tirr tirr*, *tsirr-rirr* or *tsirrup* (recalling Long-tailed Tit). Also gives a hard, scolding, *chr-r-r-r-r-it* (almost sparrow-like), often preceded or followed by one or more high-pitched notes, e.g. *tsi-tsi-tsi t-t-t-t-t* or *tsit-tsi r-r-r-r-r-r* (overall rather similar to the 'churr' of Blue Tit, but perhaps slower and more deliberate in delivery); variants include more complex phrases both introduced and followed by higher, clearer notes, e.g. *tsee tsee chrrrr chi-chi-chi, tsee tsee chrrrr chi-chi-ch...*, and a rapid, trilling but 'flat' *tiddytddy-u, tiddytddy-u, tiddytddy-u...*. Other calls include a thin *sit* or *swip*, a scolding, metallic *chi-chi-chi-chi* and a similar but more conversational and nasal *tsee-tsee-tsee, tsee-tsee-tsee...* or *tsi-tsi-dzee, tsi-tsi-dzee...* (almost a chick-a-dee call?). In alarm or excitement gives a loud, merry fast *tscher-pink tscher-pink tscher-pink* (perhaps the same as the metallic *chi-chi-chi* ?). Song apparently very varied, including (i) a loud descending trill, *tii-tsi-dji-daa-daa-daa-daa* (similar to Blue Tit, but shorter, lasting *c.* 1 second, harsher and deeper, and made up of three distinct notes, rather than usually two; Cramp & Perrins 1993); (ii) a rapidly repeated *tee-tee-tee-chup-chup* (very similar to Blue Tit, Cramp & Perrins 1993); (iii) *tuwi-tee, tuwi-tee tuwi-tee* (or *dyoeez zee dyoeez zee...)* the phrase repeated 3–8 times (a 'tea-cher' phrase, in timing recalling Great Tit, but thinner and harsher); (iv) phases introduced by 1–2 sweet, high-pitched notes, e.g. *tsee-tsee chi'chi'chi chewee chi'chi'chi chewee* or *see wi dada wi dada*; (v) a relatively monotonous repetition of 2–8 'flat' units, all on one pitch, *chiu-chiu-chiu-chiu...* (recalling the song of Marsh Tit, and although Yellow-breasted Tits have a similar, but faster vocalisation, apparently completely absent from Blue Tit's vocabulary). (Partly after Cramp & Perrins 1993.)

## DISTRIBUTION AND MOVEMENTS
Central **European Russia** north to *c.* 58° N (including Gor'kiy and Perm) and south to 51° N (including Voronezh, the Vorona river, Penza and Orenburg), then through **southern Siberia**, north in the Ob' basin to 61° N, to Laryak, Tomsk and Krasnoyarsk, in the Baykal region to 55° N, and, further east, north to Dzhalinda and 52° N. In **Kazakhstan** breeds south to the northern Kyrgyz Steppes at *c.* 51° N In the northwest (including the Utva river and Aksuat) and 48° N in the northeast (to at least Borovoye, Tselinograd, Pavlodar and Semipalatinsk), then south to Lake Zaysan, in SE Kazakhstan south and west to the Chu river, and in adjacent eastern **Kyrgyzstan** west to Kara Balta (see also Geographical Variation). In **NW China** found in western and northern **Xinjiang** from the Sanju river in the eastern Kun Lun, north through Shache (= Yarkant) and the foothills of the Pamirs (Kashi), the Kok Shaal Tau, Borohoro Shan and Tien Shan east to Turpan and Hami, also the far north in the foothills of the Altai (Altay, Fuyun). Found in northern and western **Mongolia** in the western Mongolian Altai (including the southern watershed, in the Bulgan Gol, Üyönch Gol and other valleys, and the Barun-Huray depression), the Achit Nuur depression, Tesin Gol valley, the Hangayn range, and south in eastern Mongolia to the valleys of the Tuul Gol and upper Kerulen, the Hentiyn range and upper Onon valley, also the Halhïn Gol valley on the border with Nei Mongol in NE China. Scarce in winter around Ulan Bator, but abundant in autumn and especially spring in the nearby Tola river valley. Has been recorded in the Govi180ltay in October (west of the Ih Bogd Uul; Kozlova 1932-33). In Siberia, extends south to the Altai and Sayan mountains and east to the Russian Far East, in **Amurland** north to Komsomol'sk-na-Amure and Sofiysk, and south in **Ussuriland** to Lake Khanka, Kirovskiy and *c.* 44° N. Extends into adjacent **NE China** in NE **Nei Mongol** (Hailar) and **Heilongjiang** (Heihe (= 'Aihui') and Harbin). The western boundary of the range is poorly known, and although the species has bred west to Belarus' and Finland, it may possibly not occur regularly west of the Volga basin. In **Belarus'** breeds irregularly (?) in the south (breeding proved Luninets 1952, Pinsk 1964, Lel'chitsy 1987 and the Lan river, Brest region, 1989), but there is also an estimate of 400–1,000 pairs in the Poles'ye area of the Pripyat valley (M.E. Nikiforov in Snow & Perrins in prep.). Away from the breeding areas, vagrant north and west to Brest, Minsk and in the northwest to Postavy. During its periodic waves of expansion (see below), and also to a lesser extent in the autumn and winter, recorded in **European Russia** north and west to the Lake Ladoga region, St Petersburg, Vologda, Yaroslavl', Vladimir, to the Moscow region (in the north, bred in 1981–82 in the Yakhroma-Dubna lowlands, where present in 1930s and 1950s, and to the west may breed in the Moscow Meshchera), Rzhev and Smolensk. Largely resident, but some seasonal altitudinal movements, with montane populations dispersing onto the adjacent plains of Central Asia, NW China and Mongolia. Lowland populations are usually relatively sedentary, roaming in flocks during the winter over fairly short distances, usually within the breeding range. They may wander further afield, however, and undertake irregular movements, largely in autumn and spring, which may be on a large scale (flocks of several hundred individuals recorded by Dementiev & Gladkov 1966–70); in the Novosibirsk region of south-central Siberia, such large movements occur in late September–October and April, with over 18,000 moving southwest near Chany lakes in the first ten days of September 1961. When on a large scale, these periodic irruptions have led to temporary colonisation of regions outside the normal range. Azure Tit has undergone several such waves of westward expansion, consequently overlapping with Blue Tit (with which it occasionally hybridises: see Hybrids). The largest were in the 1870s and 1880s, with an intensive movement northwest into the Yaroslavl' and Vladimir regions of European Russia noted in 1882-86. The most recent westward influx was in 1968–79, with breeding recorded in Finland in 1973. These periods of expansion are followed by a retreat eastwards. Recorded once in extreme northern **Pakistan**, where perhaps a rare winter visitor: a party was noted in riverine tamarisk thickets near Misgar (36° 45' N, 72° 57' E) in northern Hunza on 20 October 1930, from which a male and female were collected (Ludlow & Kinnear 1933). Accidental **Ukraine** (including Kiev), **Latvia** (several), **Estonia**, **Finland** (first record a breeding pair at Tohmajärvi in 1973, then a mixed pair in 1975; total of 23 individuals 1973–92), **Sweden** (Säby, Frustuna, Södermanland, before 1786; Abramsäng, Blekinge, November 1983), **Denmark** (Klampenborg, Zeeland, January 1964), **Poland** (*c.* 30, October–March, including December 1977, two in March 1981, three or four Wroclaw February 1982 and March 1990, and Tarnowskie

Gory, Silesia, January 1994), **Germany** (one record, Ohrdruf, October 1821, of the race *tianschanicus*, but considered by Brensing & Barthel 1993 to have been an 'escape'), the former **Czechoslovakia** (*c*. 30, October–March), **Austria** (at least 11, but thought probably to include some hybrids and misidentified birds: brensing & Bartel 1993), **Romania**, **Yugoslavia** and **France** (Villars-les-Dombes, Ain, winter 1907/08, but possibly a fraud or hybrid). In the east, vagrant **Japan**, on Rishiri-to, off northern Hokkaido, November 1987 (Kosuki 1988). See also Hybrids.

**HABITAT** Primarily riverine thickets of willow, birch or poplar, with a mixture of trees and bushes, alongside lakes, rivers, streams and around oases, both in the southern taiga and in the northern steppe zones. Also light deciduous and mixed woodland, overgrown bushy marshland and swamp forest, Turanga groves and saxaul forest. Montane populations favour willow and larch thickets, birch forest and broadleaved undergrowth around stands of spruce or juniper (presumably near water). In autumn and winter also found in a wider variety of wooded habitats, Siberian Pea Tree thickets in semi-desert and, especially, in reedbeds, which are favoured by vagrants. Occurs at up to 1800 m in southern Siberia and 2500 m in the Tien Shan.

**POPULATION** Rather local, but very common in central Russia and not uncommon in Mongolia and Transbaykalia, and, although generally uncommon in China, in Xinjiang quite common in the plains in autumn, winter and spring (also occurring in summer, breeding around the oases) and fairly plentiful in the Tien Shan (Ludlow & Kinnear 1933). In central Siberia, a rare breeder along the Yenisey in the Minusinsk region, and rare there even on migration. Rare on the western border of the range in western Russia and Belarus'.

**HABITS** Restless and active, flicking the wings and tail, but may be difficult to see as it often remains under cover in bushes or reeds and seldom flies over open spaces; apparently less secretive during winter dispersal, although winter flocks may be restless and wary. Occurs in pairs in breeding season and in family parties in July–October, at other times sometimes also singly or in flocks of 10–15, and may join mixed-species foraging flocks. Social behaviour poorly known, but pair formation takes place in the late winter, about two months before nest-building begins, and parties roost huddled together. Forages in trees and on the ground, and in winter works reed stems from top to bottom; may flycatch. Food insects and spiders, also seeds and fruit in the autumn and winter.

**BREEDING BIOLOGY** Season: European Russia and Siberia, May; Tien Shan, May–June. The nest is placed in a hole in a tree, 1–4 m above ground, also in cavities in buildings and among rocks, and also in metal telegraph and streetlight poles. The nest is probably built by the female alone, from moss, dry grass and fur compacted into a felt-like material, and lined with fur, wool, down or cotton. Clutch 7–11 (a clutch of 5 recorded in Xinjiang by Ludlow & Kinnear 1933 may not

*Figure 93.1 Tail of adult male* P. c. cyanus.

have been complete): eggs white, sparsely marked reddish-brown, markings often concentrated at the larger end; 17.1 x 12.4 mm (*P. c. cyanus*). Female incubates, period 13–14 days. The young are fed by both parents; fledging period unknown.

**DESCRIPTION** *P. c. cyanus* **Adult Male**: *In fresh plumage* (autumn–winter), head white, crown and ear-coverts faintly tinged pale lavender-grey. Eyestripe dull black, occasionally partly concealed, extending back from the lores and joining a wide indigo-blue nuchal band. Centre of upper mantle pale grey, lower mantle, scapulars and back light-mid grey, feather tips broadly washed blue (extreme tips whitish when very fresh), lower rump off-white, and uppertail-coverts indigo-blue, tipped white. Tail blackish-grey, T1 and outer webs of T2–T4 washed indigo-blue, all feathers broadly tipped white, progressively wider towards T6 (outer webs of T5–T6 white with some grey at extreme base, and inner web of T6 white on distal two-thirds; see figure 93.1). Wing-coverts and primary coverts indigo-blue, median coverts tipped grey to off-white, greater and primary coverts very broadly tipped white (*c*. 12 mm deep on greater coverts, 4–6 mm on primary coverts). Alula indigo-blue, fringed and tipped white. Tertials white, innermost usually with concealed dark mark at base, outer two with indigo-blue base to outer web. Primaries and secondaries dark grey, outer webs of secondaries broadly fringed indigo-blue, P3–P10 fringed indigo-blue at base and white towards tip, with an increasing proportion of white towards outer wing, where P4–P6 white distally of emargination and P1–P2 entirely fringed white; all feathers tipped white, more broadly so on inner primaries and especially secondaries. Underparts, axillaries and underwing-coverts white, when very fresh faintly tinged creamy-buff, flanks faintly washed grey. Short, irregular dull black ventral line, feathers partly tipped white (blackish may be largely or completely concealed; blackish bases to throat feathers fully concealed). *In worn plumage* (from about April), white of head and underparts may be contaminated with dirt, grey feather bases may show through, especially on cheeks and throat; dark ventral line more distinct. White tips to primaries, secondaries and central tail feathers abraded, but those of greater coverts and tertials still prominent. **Bare Parts**: Iris brown to dark brown; bill dark blue-grey to horn-black, cutting edges (and tip?) paler; legs and feet grey to grey-blue or slaty. **Adult Female**: As male (but see Sex/Age). **Juvenile**: As adult, but centre of crown light grey, eyestripe indistinct, dull mid grey. Nuchal band mid-dark grey, not extending onto sides of neck. Mantle and scapulars mid-light grey, faintly tinged blue when very fresh. Tail and flight feathers as adult female, but tail feathers more pointed, fringes slightly duller blue (as fringes to primary coverts). Lesser and median coverts mid grey, greater coverts fringed grey and very broadly tipped dirty white (extent as on adult). Underparts white, washed very pale yellow or creamy; often lacks ventral line. When worn, centre of crown, nuchal band, mantle and scapulars dull ash-grey, underparts dirty cream-white. **1st Adult**: As adult (but see Sex/Age). **Measurements**: Wing of male 64.5–73, of female 63.5–71; tail 57–68, of male 59–64, of female 57–64; bill 9–10.7; tarsus 16.0–17.4. Weight 11.1-16 g (*P. c. tianschanicus*).

**MOULT** Adult post-breeding complete (late June–September). Post-juvenile partial, includes variable number of greater coverts (usually all), tertials and tail feathers (usually just T1) (July–September).

**GEOGRAPHICAL VARIATION** Slight and largely clinal. A cline of decreasing colour saturation runs eastwards from nominate *cyanus* to *hyperrhiphaeus*, the latter being replaced in the southeast by *koktalensis*, which is similar in coloration but has a distinctly larger bill. In the mountains of Central Asia *tianschanicus* is darker blue above with a pale lavender crown, whilst *yenisseensis* of southern Siberia is a very variable race and possibly of hybrid origin (the result of secondary intergradation between *hyperrhiphaeus* and *tianschanicus*). Five subspecies recognised, but the precise boundaries are disputed, especially in southern and eastern Siberia.

*P. c. cyanus* European Russia east to the basin of the middle Volga, intergrading with *hyperrhiphaeus* from c. 50–51° E. See Description. Darkest in the west, with the upperparts relatively dark blue-grey; further east, in the Volga basin and Penza, the mantle and scapulars are slightly paler and greyer, less intensely blue, but much individual variation.

*P. c. hyperrhiphaeus* Easternmost European Russia, including Bashkirskaya (east of nominate *cyanus*), western Siberia and northern Kazakhstan, east to Semipalatinsk. In the east, intergrades with *yenisseensis* between the valleys of the upper Ob' and the upper Yenisey, in the northern and western foothills of the Altai. In winter typical *hyperrhiphaeus* occurs in SE European Russia and probably this race to the central Ukraine. Poorly marked. As nominate *cyanus*, but paler. Mantle and scapulars light grey, tinged lavender, rump almost white; blue of nuchal band, wings and tail less intense, tertials more extensively white (dark restricted to blue-grey on inner web of longest), greater coverts with more extensive white tips (c. 12–13 mm deep, comprising the entire exposed portion), more white in tail. Wing of male 68–70, of female 65–65.5.

*P. c. koktalensis* Lowland of SE Kazakhstan, in the region south of Lake Balkhash, including the valleys of the Chu (northwest to at least Furmanovka), lower Ili, Karatal, and probably also

of the Aksu and Lepsa; confined to willow beds invaded by reeds, and its relatively large bill may be an ecological adaptation. Coloration intermediate between nominate *cyanus* and *hyperrhiphaeus* (or nearer latter), but bill thick with a strongly convex culmen.

*P. c. tianschanicus* SE Kazakhstan in the Tarbagatay, Dzhungarskiy Alatau, the valley of the middle and upper Ili, and Ketmen' ranges, Tien Shan of Kazakhstan and adjacent Kyrgyzstan north to Zailiyskiy and Kyrgyzskiy ranges, west to 74° E and Kara Balta in the Kyrgyzskiy Alatau, the At-Bashi valley, Naryn and the Aksay plateau; also NW China in the Tien Shan and associated ranges of Xinjiang. Recorded Pakistan. Intergrades with *yenisseensis* on the southern borders of the Lake Zaysan depression. As nominate *cyanus*, but crown and sides of head pale grey, often tinged lavender towards rear crown, upperparts darker, light-mid grey, tinged blue; white tips to greater coverts, tertials and tail feathers average less extensive, underparts slightly duller white, washed creamy, flanks tinged grey. The underparts of juveniles may be washed very pale yellow. Wing of male 62.5–73, of female 62–68; tail of male 56–63, of female 57–61. Some variation, those from the western Tien Shan with upperparts near powder-blue, whilst birds from NW China are constantly paler and greyer (as described above). The populations of the Saur mountains (easternmost Kazakhstan), northern Xinjiang (NW China, in the foothills of the Altai), Mongolia, Transbaykalia, NE China and Ussuriland are more or less intermediate and are variously placed with *tianschanicus* (e.g. Cramp & Perrins 1993; Cheng 1987) and *yenisseensis* (e.g. Stepanyan 1990).

*P. c. yenisseensis* SE Siberia from the upper Yenisey and western foothills of the Altai east to the Sea of Japan and lower Amur river. Intergrades with *hyperrhiphaeus* in the west, and with *tianschanicus* on the southern borders of the Lake Zaysan depression. Vagrants reported west to western Russia. Poorly marked. As *tianschanicus*, but averages slightly paler, head tinged pale grey, upperparts light pale grey, tinged blue (slightly paler and less blue). As nominate *cyanus*, but duller, head not pure white, upperparts greyer and less bluish (and distinctly darker than *hyperrhiphaeus*), underparts and wings near *tianschanicus*. Juveniles occasionally have pale yellow wash on breast and belly (Dementiev & Gladkov 1966–70). Wing of male 63–70, of female 62.5–68.

**HYBRIDS** Following westward range expansions, Azure Tit has hybridised with Blue Tit. During the invasions of the 1870s and 1880s, when Azure Tit spread north and west across Russia to reach the Baltic, hybrids were recorded from Minsk, St Petersburg, Moscow, Vologda, Yaroslavl', Vladimir and Orenburg (Dementiev & Gladkov 1966–70; Portenko *et al.* 1982). Such hybrids were described under many names, the oldest of which is Pleske's Tit '*P. pleskii*'. Hybrids were apparently relatively common, especially around Moscow, although Pleske (1912), the source for most statements concerning hybridisation, provides details only of seven individuals (Thielcke 1969). Azure Tit later retreated eastwards, but still overlaps broadly with Blue Tit. Hybridisation may perhaps still take place, although to a lesser extent. Indeed, after a prolonged absence of records, two hybrids were noted at St Petersburg in 1969. Hybrids may also result from the pairing of vagrant Azure Tits with local Blue Tits, and a mixed pair was noted in Finland in 1975. Records of vagrants may also involve hybrids, which have been reported from the Netherlands (Flevoland, November 1968), Poland (1973), Latvia (three records, the most recent at Pape in October 1981) and Austria (Lake Neusiedl, November 1989) and a hybrid was ringed at Landsort, in Södermanland, Sweden, in October 1991, and then controlled at Värtsilä, eastern Finland, in April 1992. Hybrid Azure x Blue Tits show a wide range of characters, with a darker cap than Azure Tit, varying from lavendergrey to blue or even black, pale greyish upperparts, much less white in the tail, with only the outer web of T6 white and T5 very finely fringed white (thus more white than Blue Tit), reduced white in the tertials and greater coverts (wingbar c. 3–5 mm deep, compared with 2–3.5 mm on Blue Tit and 12–13 mm on Azure Tit), and a gradation of patterns on the underparts, from traces of a dark collar, through a dark bib to a yellowish wash. Hybrids also occur in which the characters of one species are very slightly indicated, and these may be back-crosses with pure birds. Thus, after just a few generations, owing to the lack of reinforcements and back-crossing with Blue Tits, the hybrids presumably disappear. Azure Tit hybridises with Yellow-breasted Tit in the central Tien Shan. See p. 396 for full details.

**RELATIONSHIPS** Forms a superspecies with Blue (*caeruleus* and *teneriffae* groups) and Yellow-breasted Tits (see p. 390), and closely related to Blue Tit. Indeed, in view of hybridisation between the two, some authors consider that Blue and Azure Tits may not have achieved full specific status, and consequently unite them in a single species (e.g. Eck 1988). The vocalisations of Blue and Azure Tits are rather similar, but this is considered an 'old' character, already in existence when their common ancestor divided into two populations. Playback experiments show that Blue Tits will in certain conditions react territorially to the songs and calls of Azure Tits, especially those most similar to their own vocalisations. Thus, given a low population of one of the species (i.e. after invasions or vagrancy), pair formation may occur (Martens & Schottler 1991). Although Azure Tit seems able to invade the range of Blue Tit in northern European Russia, there are apparently ecological, behavioural or genetic factors which prevent a prolonged overlap. There is however, a long-standing zone of overlap in SE European Russia (inhabited by distinctive races of both Blue and Azure Tits, indicating that the two have been coexisting there for a prolonged period). It is therefore probably ecological factors which prevent Azure Tits from establishing themselves further north and west. Furthermore, in view of the withdrawal of Azure Tit and the disappearance of hybrids, it is likely that hybrids are selected against, a good argument for full specific status. For relationship with Yellow-breasted Tit, see that species.

**REFERENCES** Cramp & Perrins (1993), Dementiev & Gladkov (1966–70), Portenko *et al.* (1982), Vaurie (1957a, 1959).

# 94 YELLOW-BREASTED TIT *Parus flavipectus*      Plate 30

This colourful tit has a restricted range in the mountains of Central Asia and hybridises in some areas with Azure Tit, whilst a disjunct population in a remote region of northern China may be better treated as a distinct species.

**IDENTIFICATION** Length 130 mm (5 in). A medium-sized, relatively long-tailed tit (wing/tail index 80–95%; the tail is also slightly graduated). Forehead whitish, cap and upper mantle pale grey, with blackish eyestripes running back from the eye and joining at the rear in a narrow dark blue nuchal band. Lower mantle, scapulars and back mid grey, tinged blue, rump pale grey. Tail dark grey, tipped and broadly fringed white. Wings dark blue-grey, greater and primary coverts broadly tipped white, outer webs of tertials white, flight feathers broadly fringed white. Sides of head whitish, with chin and centre of throat duller and greyer, forming a ghostly bib. Breast and upper flanks yellow, remainder of underparts whitish with a fine dark ventral line from the lower breast to the belly. Juveniles are washed yellow, sometimes extensively so. The plumage may appear rather fluffy, and often raises a slight crest (cf. Blue Tit). The pale head and yellow breast band are

distinctive, although in Central Asia it is necessary to eliminate hybrids with Azure Tit. Juveniles may resemble juvenile Blue Tits, but show much more white in the wings and tail. Occasionally juvenile Azure Tits of the western race *tianschanicus* show a faint tinge of yellow on the breast, but never as pronounced as on Yellow-breasted Tit.

**SEX/AGE** Sexes similar, but males average slightly brighter, with a cleaner pale grey cap, darker and bluer upperparts and slightly richer yellow breast patch. Juvenile distinct, with the head and underparts variably washed yellow and the mantle and scapulars washed greenish; forehead, sides of crown and upper mantle pale yellow-grey, eyestripe and nuchal band paler and not so blue, and upperparts faintly tinged olive; sides of head, throat and underparts uniformly pale yellowish-white to pale yellow (there is some individual variation and some are considerably less yellow than others). 1st adult as adult, but may be duller on the head, with the forecrown, cheeks, ear-coverts and sides of throat dirty grey-white; the tips of the retained juvenile primary coverts are worn and thus smaller and duller than those of a fresh adult at same time of year.

**VOICE** Apparently more similar to Blue than Azure Tit (J. Martens *in litt.*). Common calls include a hard, scolding *trrrrit* (almost sparrow-like; sometimes a faster and more buzzing *prrrrret*), often preceded by high-pitched notes, e.g. *chi-chi-chi, trrrrrit* or *tsi-tip-i-trrrrrit*; the high-pitched notes may also be given alone, e.g. *chi-chi-chi* (the 'scold' is perhaps more similar to Blue Tit than to Azure Tit). Other calls include a conversational but nasal and scolding *tsee-tsee-tsee* (very similar to Azure Tit), and a very un tit-like and plaintive or 'sad' *chiddle-chiddle-chiddle*, mingled with finch-like trills (cf song variant iv). More complex calls of uncertain function include harsh motifs followed by more ringing, bell-like notes, e.g. *chidut chidut tsiu-tsiu, chidut chidut tsiu-tsiu tzee-tzee* (recalling Great Tit) and almost rattling motifs introduced by higher, clearer notes, e.g. *tsee chidit chiddle-ee, tsee chidit chiddle-ee...* repeated at intervals. Also a short, 'tripping' phrase *ti-di-didi*, becoming a more trilling *tidididididi* and given rather 'conversationally' (cf song variant i). Song probably rather varied, including (i) a Blue Tit-like clear, sometimes full and sometimes high-pitched trill, introduced by high-pitched notes, repeated at intervals, e.g. *tsee-tsee tisi'isi-u, tisi'isi-u, tsee-tsee-tsee tisi'isi-u...*; (ii) slightly harsh or grating phrases in a 'tea-cher' pattern, e.g. *tis-a-u, tis-a-u* (may recall Great Tit); (iii) a simple repetition of high-pitched units, *tee-tee see-see, tee-tee see-see* (with variants that are difficult to distinguish from calls, e.g. *tsee-tsee tuzit, tsee tsee tuzit*); (iv) a rapid, tremulous but 'flat' trilling *chi'chi'chi'chi'chip...*, slightly falling in pitch (recalling the Marsh Tit-like song variant of Azure Tit, but rather faster, and not present in Blue Tit's vocabulary).

**DISTRIBUTION AND MOVEMENTS** The Tien Shan, Alay system and western Pamirs of Central Asia in **Kazakhstan**, **Kyrgyzstan**, **Uzbekistan**, **Tadzhikistan** and **Turkmenistan**. In the western Tien Shan recorded in the Karatau range (breeds?), and from the Kyrgyzskiy mountains (east to Issykata and *c.* 76° E), Talasskiy, Ugamskiy and Pskemskiy ranges, south through the Susamyrtau, Chatkal'skiy, Kuraminskiy and Ferganskiy mountains to the Fergana basin. In the Alay system found from the western extremities of the Turkestanskiy, Zerav'shanskiy (Samarkand) and Gissarskiy ranges and the western slopes of the Baysunskiy range and Kugitangtau, east to the eastern Alayskiy range. In the western Pamirs breeds east to 72° E (locally slightly further east), and in SW Tadzhikistan found south to the Amudar'ya river (but in Tadzhikistan does not penetrate into the Pamirs and avoids lowland riverine habitats during the breeding season). Breeds in northern **Afghanistan**, in Badakhshan and north of the Hindu Kush (south to at least Bamian and the Salang Pass), and recorded in NW **Afghanistan** in October in Band-i-Turkestan range and may breed there (also the Paropamisus range?). Recorded in adjacent extreme NW **Pakistan** in NE Chitral, where presumably breeds, as five juveniles were collected on 26 July 1902 at Shost (36° 45' N, 72° 57' E) on Yarkhun river, where the species was apparently numerous. A widely disjunct population in north-central **China** in NE Qinghai, around Qinghai Hu (Koko Nor) on the upper Hwang He river and in the eastern Qilian Shan. Vagrant NE **Iran**, at Mashhad in February 1927. Resident, but undertakes seasonal altitudinal movements, although the extent is very variable, depending on the severity of the winter; in Tadzhikistan descends to lower woods and gardens during late August–November (sometimes later), returning late March. May also perform more irregular dispersals (similar to Azure Tit), but details sparse. Dolgushin *et al.* (1972) give details of two obtained in December 1875 on the river Talgar in the Zailiyskiy Alatau, one of the longest recorded movements from the breeding range.

**HABITAT** In Central Asia montane deciduous and mixed forests, and often found in mature valley woodland, whilst in northern Afghanistan noted in valley-bottom willow scrub at 1525 m (below juniper-covered slopes), and in northern Pakistan recorded in dense riverine scrub of stunted willow, juniper and birch. In Central Asia occurs at up to 2500 m, recorded at 3050 m in Chitral, and a single vagrant at 1220 m in NE Iran.

**POPULATION** Uncommon and often local, occurring in small discontinuous pockets in Central Asia, whilst in northern China the species is apparently rare and little known (and may not have been recorded since collected by Przevalski in the 1880s).

**HABITS** In winter found singly, in pairs, or in flocks of 3–25, sometimes joining mixed-species foraging flocks. In the Talasskiy Alatau, often roosts in Spanish Sparrow nests or in nestboxes. Forages both in the canopy of tall trees and in low bushes, especially near water. Food insects.

**BREEDING BIOLOGY** Season in Central Asia late May–early June, but probably dependent upon latitude and altitude. The nest is placed in a hole in a tree, in a rock crevice or in holes in earth banks, enlarged by the birds themselves; also uses metal telegraph and streetlight poles. The nest itself is composed of moss, dry grass, wool or fur, lined with finer hair. It is built by the female alone over a period of 4–15 days, sometimes accompanied by the male. Clutch 6–9: eggs presumably as those of Azure Tit. Female incubates. The young are fed by both sexes, and fledge after 16 days. Second broods occur, at least occasionally.

**DESCRIPTION** *P. f. flavipectus* **Adult Male:** *In fresh plumage* (September–March), forehead whitish and crown pale grey, with narrow blackish

*Figure 94.1  Tail of adult male P. f. flavipectus.*

eyestripe from bill backwards, joining narrow dark indigo-blue nuchal band (broadest at sides of neck and mantle). Upper mantle pale grey, lower mantle, scapulars and back mid grey, tinged blue, feathers very faintly tipped paler, longer scapulars and rump pale grey, longer uppertail-coverts dark blue, finely tipped white. Tail dark grey, T1 and outer webs of T2–T5 dark indigo-blue, all feathers tipped white, T1 with small and irregular white spot or streak at tip, T6 with outer web and distal half of inner web white (see figure 94.1). Lesser and median coverts mid grey, broadly fringed indigo-blue, median coverts faintly tipped paler. Greater coverts dark grey, broadly fringed dark indigo-blue and broadly tipped white (c. 7 mm deep). Primary coverts and alula dark grey-blue, primary coverts tipped whitish, alula very finely fringed and more broadly tipped whitish. Innermost tertial white with concealed dark grey base, next with basal third of inner web blackish-grey, basal three-quarters of outer web dark indigo-blue, longest tertial and secondaries blackish-grey, broadly fringed dark indigo-blue and tipped white. Primaries blackish-grey, P3–P10 fringed indigo-blue at base and white towards tip, extent of white increasing outwards; P3–P6 fringed white distally of emargination, P1–P2 narrowly fringed white. Cheeks, ear-coverts and sides of throat whitish, chin and centre of throat dirty pale grey-white (dark feather bases shine through to give very faint bib). Breast and upper flanks lemon yellow, remainder of underparts off-white, washed cream, with well-marked dull black or blue-black ventral line from lower breast to belly, lower flanks tinged grey. Axillaries and underwing-coverts pale yellow-white, marginal coverts dark slate. In worn plumage (about April–August), centre of crown white, nuchal band slightly broader, upperparts slightly duller with less of a blue 'bloom' and upper mantle irregularly blotched whitish, white tips to tail feathers abraded (may be absent on T1–T2), whitish tips to outer tertials and flight feathers abraded, underparts whiter, yellow breast patch paler and more restricted, dark ventral line more pronounced. **Bare Parts:** Iris dark brown; bill black; legs and feet dark grey. **Adult Female:** As male, but cap slightly duller, very faintly washed drab and not so white, upperparts slightly greyer and less blue (when fresh, pale powder-blue, not so dark and blue as male), breast slightly duller and paler yellow. **Juvenile:** Forehead, supercilium and rear crown pale yellowish-grey, centre of crown light grey. Eyestripe and broad nuchal band dark grey, extending onto sides of neck. Border of upper mantle pale yellowish-grey, mantle, scapulars and rump light to mid smoke-grey, faintly tinged olive. Tail as adult, but slightly duller and less blue, feathers narrower and more pointed. Lesser and median coverts as adult, faintly tipped paler. Greater coverts mid grey, fringed slightly bluer and broadly tipped whitish. Alula, primary coverts and flight feathers as adult. Cheeks, ear-coverts, throat and entire underparts uniform pale yellowish-white to pale yellow. **1st Adult:** As adult (see Sex/Age). **Measurements:** Wing of male 65–71, of female 64–66; tail of male 57–62.5, of female 55–58; bill 10.5–11.5; tarsus 16–18.5. Weight 10.6–12.3 g.

**MOULT** Adult post-breeding complete (mid July–early October). Post-juvenile partial, extent as for Azure Tit? (period unknown).

**GEOGRAPHICAL VARIATION** Three races recognised, *flavipectus* and *carruthersi* in the mountains of central Asia and *berezowskii* highly isolated in north-central China.

*P. f. carruthersi* The Alay system and western Pamirs, north and east to the Fergana basin and eastern Alayskiy mountains, and south to the Amudar'ya river; one record NE Iran. As nominate *flavipectus*, but slightly duller, crown light-mid grey, almost concolorous with upperparts, nuchal band averages slightly narrower, upperparts slightly darker and greyer, especially upper mantle (which is not obviously paler as in nominate *flavipectus*), less white in the tail, T1–T3 irregularly tipped white, T4–T6 extensively tipped white, throat darker and greyer, breast averages slightly darker yellow, and belly slightly dirtier white. Also smaller. Wing of male 62–66, of female 63; tail of male 59, 61, of female 59.

*P. f. flavipectus* The western Tien Shan, south to the Fergana basin and eastern Alayskiy mountains, northern Afghanistan and northern Pakistan. Intergrades with *carruthersi* in the southwest. See Description.

*P. f. berezowskii* North-central China. As nominate *flavipectus*, but cap and upper mantle duller, washed light lavender-grey, lacks dark eyestripe, nuchal band reduced to a narrow blue-black line, upperparts slightly duller and greyer, sides of head and chin paler and whiter, dark grey feather bases on lower throat form dusky bib, breast slightly duller yellow. Juvenile plumage apparently unknown. Wing, 62–69, of male 64–69; tail 55–60; bill 9.6–10.

**HYBRIDS** The breeding ranges of Yellow-breasted and Azure Tits do not, apparently, overlap, but where they meet in the central Tien Shan Yellow-breasted Tit (nominate *flavipectus*) hybridises with Azure Tit *P. c. tianschanicus* in the eastern parts of the Kyrgyzskiy range, c. 76° E (Stepanyan 1990). A little to the west, mixed pairs have been noted feeding young at Ala Archa gorge, Frunze, and in 1990 3–4 pairs seen here had a yellow wash on the underparts rather than a well-defined yellow patch (N. J. Redman pers. comm.). Hybrids have also been recorded from the eastern Alayskiy mountains at Gul'cha (Vaurie 1957a). Hybrids are intermediate in appearance between Yellow-breasted and Azure Tits, typically having a yellow wash on the underparts, rather than a well-defined yellow breast band. Note, however, that some juvenile Yellow-breasted may show a yellow tinge to the underparts, and so birds must be correctly aged before they can be identified as hybrids. Thus, Yellow-breasted Tit may hybridise with Azure Tit in Chitral, NE Pakistan, but this population is known only from five juveniles collected in 1902, and, given the individual variability of juvenile Yellow-breasted Tits, no firm conclusion can be reached on the status of these birds.

**RELATIONSHIPS** Forms a superspecies with Azure Tit, the pair making up a species group with Blue Tit, and sometimes placed with it in the subgenus *Cyanistes*. Yellow-breasted Tit is often considered conspecific with Azure Tit. Despite the existence of a hybrid zone, however, where they come into contact in Central Asia they appear to act as two competing species, limiting each other's range. They appear distinctly different, especially in juvenile plumage (although occasional juvenile Azure Tits of the race *tianschanicus* can show a faint yellow wash on the breast, but this may be the result of intergradation of Yellow-breasted genes). Given the substantial difference in appearance, the contact between the two species is presumably secondary and there is no evidence that the variation is clinal. Moreover, hybridisation does not prove them conspecific; Black-capped and Carolina Chickadees present a rather similar case, yet are almost always treated as distinct species (and, indeed, hybrid Azure x Blue Tits are far commoner in collections than hybrid Azure x Yellow-breasted Tits: Vaurie 1957b). Adult Yellow-breasted is superficially intermediate between Azure and Blue Tits, resembling Blue Tit in underpart coloration, and Azure Tit in the colour of the head, upperparts, wings and tail, as well as in structure. The juvenile is even more like a Blue Tit, being extensively washed yellow. A simple interpretation is that Yellow-breasted Tit arose as a consequence of hybridisation between Blue and Azure Tits, the hybrid population stabilising in a separate range. This is, however, extremely unlikely given the distributions of Blue and Azure Tits. Another possibility is that Yellow-breasted Tit is a relict of an early offshoot of the common ancestor of both Blue and

Azure Tits. Overall, given the uncertainty over the extent of hybridisation, and the possibility that Yellow-breasted Tit is closer to Blue than to Azure Tit (in its behaviour, habitat and vocalisations), it seems best to follow Stepanyan (1990) and treat it as specifically distinct. The relationship of *berezowskii* of northern China to the other races is not clear. It is separated by 2500 km of inhospitable territory from the nearest populations of Yellow-breasted Tit. It may represent a relict of a once more continuous distribution (in the past, the species' range may have extended along the slopes of the Kun Lun, Altun Shan and Nan Shan). Whatever, the two populations of Yellow-breasted Tit are now separated by a southward extension of the range of Azure Tit to the western Kun Lun. Thus, a second possibility is that *berezowskii* originated with colonists of Azure Tits from the eastern Tien Shan and Mongolia (where they have been recorded in the Govialtay in October, only half the distance of the nearest Yellow-breasted Tits), evolving rapidly to resemble Yellow-breasted Tit, or reverting to some ancestral type. Bearing in mind the uncertainty over its relationships, and its distinctive appearance (lacking the dark eyestripe common to Azure, Yellow-breasted and Blue Tits), it is possible that *berezowskii* merits full specific status (Vaurie 1957b).

**REFERENCES** Cramp & Perrins (1993) Dementiev & Gladkov (1966–70), Stepanyan (1990), Vaurie (1950a, 1957a, 1959).

# 95 VARIED TIT *Parus varius* Plate 18

This colourful tit has managed to colonise many islands in the Japanese archipelago and been used in traditional fortune-telling. It also has the dubious distinction of being the only species of tit in which an entire population is thought to be extinct.

**IDENTIFICATION** Length 100–130 mm (4–5.25 in). Forehead, lores and cheek patches pale buff to rufous, and crown and nape black with a narrow pale nuchal patch, separated from the mid grey upperparts by a rufous collar. Extensive dull black bib; remainder of underparts rufous, sometimes with a paler and buffer ventral line. A very distinctive tit, and totally unmistakable.

**SEX/AGE** Sexes similar, although the female averages slightly paler and buffer on the underparts, especially the flanks. Juvenile distinct, much duller than the adult, with the black of the head replaced by sooty olive-grey, the forehead and lores dull orange-buff, and the cheek and nuchal patches dull yellowish-buff; the entire upperparts are greyish-olive with a diffuse dull rufous border to the upper mantle; the bib is smoky-grey and the underparts pale rufous, with a pale yellow-ochre ventral line. 1st adult as adult, but retains the juvenile tail and flight feathers, usually all the tertials, and a variable number of greater coverts; the fringes of the retained wing feathers have a distinct olive tinge (although this is also shown by adults of some of the southern races), with the tips to any retained greater coverts pale rufous or buff

(bleaching paler and whiter), whilst the tail feathers average slightly narrower and very slightly more pointed than an adult's.

**VOICE** Calls include a single sharp but thin *pit*, a high-pitched *spit-spit-see-see* or *spit-see-see-see*, and full, scolding and almost sparrow-like *chi-chi-chi*. Brazil (1990) also notes the contact call as a weak *tsuu tsuu tsuu*. Has a 'chick-a-dee' call system (see Black-capped Chickadee, p. 267), combining short, high-pitched units with lower-pitched and more prolonged and nasal D notes, but the details are as yet unstudied. The shorter, higher notes include a sharp *chit* and a sharp but slightly more sibilant *stitz*, which may be run into a characteristic stuttering *stit'ti'ti'ti...*, sometimes full and almost 'stony', sometimes faint (and sometimes recalling the jangling of coins). This comprises 2–8 units which fade away in volume and sometimes rise in pitch. The harsh D note is quite variable, from a prolonged *dzeeeu* through *dzer* to a short *dza*. The shorter, higher notes and stuttering phrase may be given on their own, as may Ds, e.g. *dzer, dza-dza-dzer-dzer* or *dzer-dza-dza-dzer-dzer*. In full-blown 'chick-a-dees' D notes are given in combination with the sharp *chit*, e.g. *dza-chit't'tit* or *dza-chit*, with the sibilant *stitz*, e.g. *stitz'tit-dzer, stit-t-tit-dzer*, or with the stuttering *stit-ti-ti...*, e.g. *stit't't't't't'dza-dza-dza*; in all cases, the higher-pitched 'chick-a' components may be given before or after the D notes. The song is a repetition of complex motifs repeated relatively slowly, and is apparently rather variable, although a ringing, pure, monotonal, whistled *peee* (very similar to the 'Alpine Song' of Willow Tit) is probably a common component of song motifs. Examples include *tsre-tsre peee-triri-peee-triri-peee-triri*, the *peee-triri* motif repeated 2–3 times, and in which the introductory *tsre-tsre* has a rolling or vibrato quality and the intervening *triri* may become a more rattling *tl'l'l'l*. Another example is *peee-spit'tit, peee-spit'tit....* The race *owstoni* on the outer Izu islands has been recorded giving *chip* and *tuwee* motifs in combination, e.g. *chip, tuwee, chip-chip, tuwee, chip-chip-tuwee*, but any constant geographical variation in the song remains to be described. Austin & Kuroda (1953) also note a faint but delightfully melodious and burbling subsong given in February, otherwise song period in Japan March–June.

## DISTRIBUTION AND MOVEMENTS
Found in extreme eastern **Russia** on Iturup, Kunashir and Shikotan in the southern Kurile islands; also recorded from south Sakhalin island, where two were seen on 21 September 1976 in dense coniferous forest on the upper reaches of the Nisser'yu river (a tributary of the Pugachevka river) (Bardin 1987). In **NE China** found in eastern **Liaoning** (localities include Dandong, Caohekou and Shenyang), also SW **Jilin** (Meyer de Schauensee 1984). Also found in **southern China** in **Guangdong** in the Ba Bao Shan (northwest of Ruyuan) in October 1993 (Lewthwaite 1993) and May 1994 (G.M Kirwan & R.P. Martins *in litt.*), in an extraordinary extension of the range (but the proximity of this locality to Hong Kong suggests that the possibility of escapes from captivity cannot be excluded). In **North Korea** possibly confined to the south and west (Austin 1948 lists records for Pyongan Pukdo, Pyongan Namdo and Hwanghae Do only), but apparently widespread in **South Korea**, including Cheju and Ullung islands. Also **Taiwan**, and in **Japan** found on the major islands of **Kyushu**, **Shikoku**, **Honshu** and **Hokkaido**, where most frequent in the centre and southwest and absent from the extreme north and east (although found in the Nemuro district, SE Hokkaido, in 1987). Also occurs on Sado-shima, Oki, Tsushima, the **Goto islands** (breeds?), the **Izu Islands**, Tanega-shima and Yaku-shima in the **Osumi group**, the islands of the **Nansei Shoto** south to Iriomote, and the **Daito** (**Borodino**) **islands** (see Geographical Variation for details); and reported from Yagishiri-to off Hokkaido. Introduced into **Hawaii** in the period 1890–1931, on Kauai, Oahu, Maui and Hawaii, becoming established on Kauai and Oahu; these populations declined during the 1940s, and last reported in 1963, although may perhaps persist in the Kokee area of Kauai and the Koolau mountains of Oahu. Largely resident, but some evidence of a withdrawal in winter to lower altitudes, and also from the northern parts of the range, although the evidence for the latter is contradictory. Described as a summer visitor to Korea by Austin (1948), with a few wintering in the southern provinces of South Korea and some evidence of passage in late April/May and late October/November; Gore & Won (1971), however, described the species as resident in South Korea. Also thought to withdraw from Hokkaido in winter, moving to northern Honshu, with some evidence of passage through the Ishikari plain in SW Hokkaido in spring and autumn (Austin & Kuroda 1953; but perhaps only local movements within Hokkaido). Nevertheless, apparently resident in the far north of the range in the southern Kurile islands (Ilyashenko 1990), and in China (Cheng 1987).

## HABITAT
In Russia coniferous forest, especially Yew; in China and Taiwan open deciduous and mixed forest, and in Japan mature deciduous, mixed or subtropical evergreen broadleaved forest with dense undergrowth, also cedar and cypress plantations, but avoids pure stands of conifers. Seldom found in villages or urban areas, although in both Japan and Korea will frequent the woodland around shrines (e.g. Meiji Shrine, Tokyo) and occasionally large, well-wooded gardens. In southern Japan occurs at up to 1600 m, favouring wooded foothills, but only up to 1000 m in northern Honshu and confined to the lowlands on Hokkaido. On Taiwan found at up to 1100 m, and in Korea in the lowlands and foothills. The observations in Guangdong, southern China, were made in primary mixed forest with a bamboo understorey at *c.* 1200 m.

## POPULATION
Considered common, even locally abundant in the Kurile islands and common in Korea, but described as rare in NE China (Cheng 1987). Uncommon in northern Japan on northern Honshu and particularly Hokkaido, but common in the south, and locally very common, especially in the southern islands. Recorded densities in evergreen forest are 1–3 pairs per $km^2$ on Mount Kiyosumi in Chiba-ken (southern Honshu), 5–6 per $km^2$ on the Izu peninsula in Shizuoka-ken (southern Honshu), and 10–15 per $km^2$ on the Miyake-jima in the Izu islands. Uncommon in Taiwan. The race *orii*, endemic to Kita-daito-jima and Minami-daito-jima in the Daito islands of southern Japan, is presumed extinct, as it could not be found in 1984 or 1986 (Brazil 1990). One of the three most popular cagebirds in Japan, and also used in fortune-telling for over 200 years, this trick still being performed in the 1980s. A captive tit takes a coin from the customer, places it in a small chest, rings a bell, takes a written fortune from a miniature shrine, removes the string from the fortune, and carries it back to the customer (Brazil 1990). The effect of the cagebird trade on wild populations is unknown.

## HABITS
Can be secretive. Found singly or more often in pairs, and generally mates for life. Territories are generally maintained year-round and have relatively stable boundaries which are vigorously defended during the breeding season. In the autumn and winter, may also be found in small parties and sometimes joins mixed-species foraging flocks. Even in flocks, however, estab-

lished pairs still keep together, and they will (re-) establish a breeding territory within the flock's winter range. Forages in the canopy, among the leaves and outer twigs, flycatching and leaf-gleaning, but also feeds on the larger limbs and even the trunks of trees, and also in the understorey and on the ground. Food during the breeding season insects and spiders, in the autumn and winter nuts and berries. Nuts may be cached in the autumn, especially by the birds on Miyake-jima, for which they form the main winter food; there, nuts are also used in courtship feeding and in feeding the young in the following breeding season.

**BREEDING BIOLOGY** Season: Russia, April–May; Korea, June; Okinawa, Tsushima and Miyake-jima, from early March; south Kyushu, from early April; west Honshu, from mid April; central Honshu, from early May; Hokkaido, June. The nest is placed in a natural cavity in a tree or stub up to 6 m (–18 m) above ground. May excavate its own hole in a stump or use abandoned woodpecker holes, less frequently nestboxes or the space under the eaves of buildings. Materials include moss, and building may be undertaken largely or exclusively (?) by the female. Clutch size varies, clutches being smaller and the eggs larger on the southern islands of Japan than on mainland Japan; clutch 6–7 (3–8) eggs on the mainland, but on the Izu islands 4–8 (mean 5.4) on Kozu-shima and 3–6 (mean 3.9) on Miyake-jima: eggs white, finely spotted reddish-brown at the larger end; *c.* 18.3 x 14 mm (nominate *varius*). Female incubates, period 12–14 days. The young fledge after 17–21 days, but are fed by the parents for a further 7–20 days in mainland Japan and for 15–80 days on Miyake-jima, where young also have a more exaggerated begging posture than on the mainland. May be double-brooded in the southern parts of range, the second clutch being laid in July.

**DESCRIPTION** *P. v. varius* **Adult Male**: *In fresh plumage* (September to about March), forehead buff, crown and nape black, crown faintly glossy (occasionally, odd feathers of crown, especially forecrown, tipped mid grey or subterminally mid grey with the extreme tip rufous). Narrow off-white nuchal patch. Upper mantle chestnut-rufous, remainder of upperparts mid-dark grey, longer uppertail-coverts sometimes faintly tipped buff. Tail blackish-grey, feathers finely fringed mid grey. Wing-coverts mid grey, dark centres of lesser and median coverts fully concealed. Remainder of wing dark grey, tertials and secondaries fringed mid grey, primary coverts narrowly fringed mid grey, P3–P10 fringed mid grey, paler and narrower distally of emarginations on P3–P6. Lores and cheeks pale buff, ear-coverts off-white, tinged buff, rear ear-coverts and sides of neck whiter. Chin, throat and upper breast black (occasionally with odd rufous feather tips), line along lower border of bib creamy to pale buff, centre of breast, belly and vent pale buff, forming a variable pale ventral line, often duller towards the rear. Upper flanks chestnut-rufous, lower flanks extensively rufous, undertail-coverts pale cinnamon. Under primary coverts brownish-black, narrowly fringed off-white, remainder of underwing-coverts and axillaries

buff. *In worn plumage,* cheek patch slightly whiter, upperparts slightly duller and browner, wing and tail feathers darker and more abraded, bib slightly more extensive, and underparts rather paler and buffer. **Adult Female**: See Sex/Age. **Bare Parts**: Iris cinnamon; bill dark brown; legs and feet dark grey. **Juvenile**: Forehead and lores dull buff, crown and nape sooty-grey, washed olive, nuchal spot dull yellowish-olive. Upper mantle narrowly bordered dull rufous, remainder of upperparts dull greyish-olive. Tail as adult, but feathers very finely tipped off-white. Wings as adult, but tertials fringed greyish-olive (tinged dull rufous), primary coverts and secondaries fringed greyish-olive, greater coverts fringed greyish-olive or olive-rufous and tipped pale rufous to buff. Cheeks, ear-coverts and sides of neck yellowish-buff. Chin, throat and upper breast light grey, washed olive, flanks dull rufous, paler at rear, breast and belly pale yellow-ochre. Legs and feet appear paler than on adult, dull brownish-flesh; bill with paler cutting edges. **1st Adult**: As adult (see Sex/Age). **Measurements**: Wing of male 73.5–82, of female 73–79; tail of male 47–58, of female 46–54; bill 12–14.2; tarsus 18–21. Weight 15.9–18.2 g.

**MOULT** Adult post-breeding complete (July–September). Post-juvenile partial, includes a variable number of greater coverts and sometimes the inner tertials (September–November).

**GEOGRAPHICAL VARIATION** Nominate *varius* breeds over the bulk of the range. On the islands of southern of Japan there are two separate clines: a cline of decreasing size and increasing colour saturation on the underparts (the buff on the head changing very little) runs down the islands of the Nansei Shoto, terminating in Taiwan, whilst there is marked colour variation down the Izu chain. Nine subspecies recognised.

*P. v. varius* Kurile islands, NE China, Korea (including Cheju do and Ullung do); the main islands of Japan, also Sado, Oki, Tsushima, the Goto islands and Oshima (the innermost Izu island), and reported from Yagishiri-to. See Description.

*P. v. sunsunpi* Tanega-shima, Osumi group. Poorly marked. As nominate *varius,* but upperparts slightly darker grey and underparts slightly darker chestnut. Wing of male 73–81.

*P. v. yakushimensis* Yaku-shima, Osumi group. Rather poorly marked. As *sunsunpi,* but slightly darker, especially on forecrown and sides of head (?). Wing of male 73–80.

*P. v. amamii* The northern and central Nansei Shoto on Amami-O-shima, Tokuno-shima and Okinawa. As nominate *varius* and *sunsunpi,* but chestnut patch on upper mantle reduced or absent, mantle slightly duller grey and faintly washed olive, and underparts duller chestnut. Averages *c.* 2 mm shorter-winged and marginally longer- and stouter-billed. Wing of male 75–77.

*P. v. olivaceus* The southern Nansei Shoto on Iriomote-jima. Poorly marked? As *amamii* but upperparts perhaps more heavily washed with olive. Averages slightly smaller? Wing of male 70–74, of female 65.5–66.5.

*P. v. castaneoventris* Taiwan (also apparently

*Figure 95.1 Distribution of the various subspecies.*

this race Guangdong, southern China, although field observations showed a very extensive whitish-buff nuchal patch: perhaps an unde-scribed subspecies?). Coloration similar to *amamii* and *olivaceus*, with underparts uniform dark rufous with no pale median line and chestnut bor-der to upper mantle much reduced, but no olive tone to mantle and averages rather smaller (tiny compared with nominate *varius*). Wing of male 60–64; tail 37–41.5; bill 12.2, 11.5.

**P. v. orii** Kita-daito-jima and Minami-daito-jima in Daito-jima (Borodino islands). Well differentiat-ed. Large chestnut border to upper mantle, upper-parts distinctly tinged olive, forecrown, sides of head and underparts deep but rather dull chestnut, bill long and stout. Wing 71–79.5.

**P. v. namiyei** The inner Izu islands on To-shima, Nii-jima and Kozu-shima. Intermediate between nominate *varius* and *owstoni*. Wing of male 77–82.

**P. v. owstoni** The outer Izu islands on Miyake-jima, Mikura-jima and Hachijo-jima. The darkest race (similar to *orii* in coloration but even darker). Forehead and cheek patches rufous, nuchal patch orange-rufous, upperparts (including fringes to wing feathers) greyish-olive, underparts cinna-mon-rufous (slightly more orange than *casta-neoventris*), darkest on breast and flanks. Bill long and stout (as *orii*), but overall dimensions slightly larger, near nominate *varius*. Wing of male 80–82; tail of male 54, 55; bill 14.5.

**HYBRIDS** Hybrids with Willow Tit have been

recorded on at least six occasions: they are intermediate in appearance, but have the voice of Varied Tit, although 'finer' (Mishima 1969).

**RELATIONSHIPS** Placed in the subgenus *Sittiparus* together with the White-fronted Tit of the Philippines, although this relationship is far from certain.

**REFERENCES** AOU (1983), Austin & Kuroda (1953), Brazil (1990), Dementiev & Gladkov (1966–70), J.L. Long (1981), Vaurie (1957b, 1959).

# 96 WHITE-FRONTED TIT *Parus semilarvatus*     Plate 22

This enigmatic forest tit from the Philippines is very poorly known and was, until recently, rarely seen. At least one population may be endangered.

**IDENTIFICATION** Length 130 mm (5.25 in). A large, long-billed and long-tailed tit, blackish overall but with the lores and forehead whitish, although the white 'face' may be hard to see as the birds move high through the treetops. Depending on age and sex, the nape and undertail-coverts may also be whitish, and on Mindanao there is also a conspicuous whitish patch at the base of the primaries. A distinctive tit, very different from the Elegant Tit and recalling no other species of Philippine bird.

**SEX/AGE** Sexes distinct. Females have upperparts slightly duller than males, with the white on the nape not fully concealed, especially in northern Luzon, where it may show as small whitish spots on the back and sides of the neck; notably, the underparts are rather duller and paler, milk-chocolate brown with no gloss (blackish, glossed blue, on the male). The juvenile and 1st-adult plumages are poorly known. The juvenile male resembles the adult female, but the underparts are slightly darker brown with little or no gloss (may show a touch at the sides of the neck); in northern Luzon juveniles have a conspicuous white half-collar. 1st adult as adult, but retains the juvenile primary coverts and/or greater coverts, which are worn and bleached paler, forming a paler panel on the wing. On Mindanao the sexes apparently differ as on Luzon, the female having slightly browner and less blue-glossed upperparts and more noticeably paler brown underparts. Little information on juveniles from Mindanao, but field observations of probable juveniles indicate that they may be rather pale, mid brown, tinged dusty grey, with an off-white nuchal patch and white undertail-coverts (and sharing the white face and wing flash with the adult).

**VOICE** Poorly known, and possibly has a rather limited vocabulary. Calls include a short, high, sharp *psit* and high, thin, plaintive and rolling *tsuit*, given 1–3 times and sometimes combined with a sharper introductory note, e.g. *sit-tsuit-suit-suit* (this may recall Coal Tit). A high-pitched *tsi*, given in bouts of 1–5, e.g. *tsi-tsi-tsi-tsi*, may be one of the commoner calls. It is sometimes preceded or followed by a slightly fuller *tsre* or *tsre'e*. One or more *tsi* notes may also be introduced by a thinner and rather 'breathy' *tseeeh*, e.g. *tsee-tsi* or *tsee-tsi-tsi*, and longer series of 10–12 *tsi* units, shortening and accelerating towards the end of the series and preceded by a breathy *tseeh*, may be the song, e.g. *tseeeh, tsi-tsi-tsi-tsi'tsi'tsi'ts'ts'tsi* (the whole phrase lasting nearly 3 seconds) J. Hornskov (*in litt.*) also notes a metallic *i-i-i-i-i, tji*, slightly rising in pitch, followed by a clearer trilling *djidididiw*, the whole phrase endlessly repeated and recalling a Blue Tit.

**DISTRIBUTION AND MOVEMENTS** Endemic to the **Philippines**. Rather local. Recorded on **Luzon** from the northern Sierra Madre mountains from Cape Engano south to at least Diagopanay (16° 34' N, 122° 08' E, southern Isabela province), and in the southern Sierra Madre at Angat Dam (Rizal province), with unconfirmed reports from Quezon NP. Known also from Bataan province, from Pampanga province (Mount Arayat), and from Sorsogon province in southern Luzon. On **Mindanao** recorded from Mount Sugarloaf (Zamboanga del Sur), Mount Piapayungan (= Mount Ragang, Lanao del Sur), Mainit, Iligan City (Lanao del Norte); Manticao, (Misamis Oriental), Glan (Cotabato province), Sitio Siete, Sebu (South Cotabato), from around Davao city and from the PICOP concession, south of Bislig (Surigao del Sur). Note that McGregor (1909–10) attributed a record from Negros to the Steere Expedition, but the report of this expedition does not mention the species and there is no further information to confirm its occurrence on Negros.

**HABITAT** Forest, forest edge, relict forest patches, second growth and even occasionally scrub, at up to 1150 m; in SE Mindanao, noted in logged forest and adjacent pines at *c.* 350 m.

**POPULATION** Locally uncommon in the Sierra Madre of northern Luzon, but rare and local elsewhere. In particular, there have been few recent observations on Mindanao. Forest destruction in the Philippines is rampant and the very local distribution of the White-fronted Tit may indicate particular ecological requirements which put it especially at risk. Its small size and elusive habits may also, however, be responsible for the lack of field observations, and the species may be commoner than supposed. Listed as near-threatened in BirdLife International's world checklist of threatened birds (Collar *et al.* 1994).

**HABITS** Found singly or in pairs, sometimes in groups of up to ten, and infrequently in mixed-species foraging flocks. Feeds in the middle storey and canopy of tall forest trees, where it may move through rather rapidly or fly in, perch motionless in a fairly exposed position and then fly off for a fair distance to the next perch.

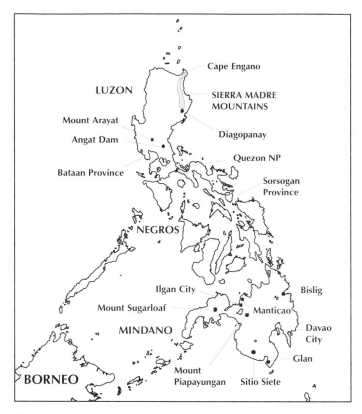

Figure 96.1 Range in the Philippines, showing localities mentioned in the text.

**BREEDING BIOLOGY** Virtually unknown. The only information is that an oviduct egg was recorded from a specimen taken in May in Zamboanga del Sur, Mindanao, whilst on Luzon a pair was noted around a hole in a tree stub c. 4 m above ground in early February on forest edge at Angat Dam in the southern Sierra Madre, and an adult was observed feeding a fledged juvenile in mid March in the northern Sierra Madre. (Most Philippine passerines breed in the period April–June.)

**DESCRIPTION** *P. s. semilarvatus* **Adult Male**: *In fresh plumage*, forehead, lores and fore cheeks buffy-white. Crown, nape, sides of neck, mantle, scapulars and rump brownish-black with a deep indigo-blue gloss (the feathers fringed deep iridiscent blue). Basal half to two-thirds of nape feathers white, but fully concealed. Tail brownish-black, feathers fringed deep blue on outer webs. Whole wing brownish-black, median and greater coverts and tertials fringed deep indigo-blue (base of primaries white, fully concealed by primary coverts). Ear-coverts and underparts brownish-black, glossed indigo-blue on ear-coverts and breast. Shorter lateral undertail-coverts grey-white. Axillaries tipped whitish, underwing-coverts whitish, washed brown, under primary coverts brownish-black, inner webs of flight feathers narrowly fringed whitish. No information on the worn plumage. **Bare Parts**: Iris light brown or brown; bill black; legs, feet and claws black. **Adult Female**: In fresh plumage upperparts as male, but averages slightly less blue-glossed and concealed white nape patch larger, extending to sides of neck (odd white flecks may be revealed). Underparts rather paler, near milk-chocolate brown with no blue fringes except on sides of neck and faintly across breast. Lateral undertail-coverts show more limited white? **Juvenile Male**: As adult female, but underparts slightly darker brown, tips of primary and greater coverts slightly paler, upperparts may have slightly more gloss. Underparts blackish-brown, perhaps slightly glossier on sides of breast. **1st Adult**: See Sex/Age. **Measurements**: Wing of male 76, 79.5, of 1st-adult male 76, of female 69, 71; tail of male 50, 51.5, of 1st-adult male 46, of female 44.5, 45; bill 13.3–14.1; tarsus 16.5–18. Weight: no information.

**MOULT** Adult post-breeding, no information. Post-juvenile partial, does not include the primary coverts and/or greater coverts (May on Luzon).

**GEOGRAPHICAL VARIATION** Moderate. Three subspecies recognised.

*P. s. semilarvatus* Southern and central Luzon north to the southern Sierra Madre mountains in Rizal province (the extent of any range gap between *snowi* and nominate *semilarvatus* is unknown). See Description.

*P. s. snowi* NE Luzon in the Sierra Madre mountains from Cape Engano south to San Mariano,

Isabela province. Male as nominate *semilarvatus*, but may average slightly duller and less glossy blue on upper- and underparts; concealed white nape patch more extensive (as female nominate *semilarvatus*), but a similar proportion of each feather white, thus fully concealed. Parkes (1971) also notes that the undertail-covert patches are more extensive, with a greater proportion of the feather white, and the inner webs of the flight feathers are more broadly fringed purer white. Female as female nominate *semilarvatus*, but white on nape more extensive (extending to the sides of the neck) and not fully concealed, small whitish spots showing in the centre of the nape and on the sides of the neck. Slightly duller above than female nominate *semilarvatus*, but in proportion to the differences shown by the male (and their underpart coloration, is at least on some, identical to that of female nominate *semilarvatus*, thus sexual dimorphism perhaps no more pronounced?); also, under primary coverts more extensively white? Juvenile male as juvenile male nominate *semilarvatus*, but white on nape extensively revealed as a narrow whitish half-collar, under primary coverts whitish and white of axillaries more extensive. Wing of male 78, 78, of 1st-adult male 76, of female 69; tail of male 47, 50.5, of 1st-adult male 47, of female 44; bill 13–14.4; tarsus 15.5–19.

**P. s. nehrkorni** Mindanao. Differs from both Luzon races in having white outer webs to the base of the primaries (not P1–P2) and outer secondaries, extending *c.* 8–10 mm beyond tips of primary coverts, forming a broad white band across the wing; axillaries more extensively white. Juveniles (?) rather pale brown, with an off-white nuchal patch and white undertail-coverts Wing, of male 78.5; tail of male 53.

**RELATIONSHIPS** Considered by Delacour & Mayr (1945) to be closely related to the Varied Tit, with a similarly long bill and white forehead and face, while the concealed white feather bases on the nape (more extensive in juvenile plumage) correspond to the white nuchal patch of Varied Tit. The two species are sometimes placed in the subgenus *Sittiparus*. Their vocalisations appear, however, to be very different. The sombre, blackish plumage is similar to that of the Dusky Tit of Central and West Africa, but this is presumably due to convergence in a similar humid tropical-forest habitat rather than to any direct relationship.

**REFERENCES** Dickinson *et al.* (1991), Parkes (1971), Poulson (in prep.).

# 97 BRIDLED TITMOUSE *Parus wollweberi*

**Plate 17**

This attractive tit is confined to a small area of the southwestern USA, where it is common, and to Mexico, and much of its biology remains a mystery.

**IDENTIFICATION** Length 130 mm (5 in). Forehead and centre of crown grey, sides of crown, nape and upper mantle and conspicuous crest black. Centre of nape and upperparts, including wings and tail, olive-grey, back and rump dull olive, tail very narrowly fringed white. 'Face' dirty white, with a blackish eyestripe and narrow black line around the rear border of the ear-coverts connecting with the rather small black bib. Underparts pale grey or off white, washed dirty yellow-buff, especially on the lower flanks, belly and undertail-coverts. When worn, the upperparts are rather plain grey. The combination of the black-and-white 'bridled' face pattern, small black bib and blackish crest is unique. Black-crested Titmouse has a plain face, whilst Mountain Chickadee lacks a crest.

**SEX/AGE** Sexes similar. Juvenile distinct, being rather duller than the adult, with the crest shorter and duller black, the face pattern duller and less well defined, and the bib pale and washed-out, with a dark grey chin and light grey upper throat being merely a shadow of the adults' full black bib; the upperparts are duller and browner, with broader pale fringes to the flight feathers, and, in the hand, the tail feathers narrower and more pointed. 1st adult as adult, but possibly shows moult contrasts in the wing.

**VOICE** Calls include a sharp, metallic *psit* and thin, high-pitched *tsit*. Most other calls appear to fall into a 'chick-a-dee'-type system (see Black-capped Chickadee, p. 267), being combinations of a handful of high-pitched units and a single stereotyped low-pitched phrase (the 'D' phrase). Although the details have yet to be studied, in this system each note may be given alone or in various combinations. The high-pitched notes include *chit*, often given alone in staccato, machine-gun-like rattles, *chit-it'it'it'it*, a thinner and more sibilant *sik*, a sharper and fuller *tsik*, mellower *tsip* and full *slip*. The D note is a short *chr*, which may be given in a short series, *chr'r* or *chr'r'*, but is more typically given in groups of 5–16 notes as a scolding, sparrow-like chatter, *chr'r'r'r'r'r'r'r*; in longer series, the initial notes may be very quickly repeated and then it settles down to a rate of *c.* 15 units per second, too fast to distinguish the individual notes. Series of D notes may be given alone, or in full-blown 'chick-a-dee' combinations, in which they are preceded (but probably never followed) by various high-pitched notes, e.g. *sik'sik'chi'chi'chr'i'r*, *chit'tit'tit'tit'tit'tit'chr'r'r* or *sik'sik'sik'slip'chr'r'r'r'r*. Song apparently stereotyped, but there are three different song types, each used in a specific context; each may be sung in bouts of up to 100 repetitions before switching to a different type. The first is a monotonous, staccato rattle, 'wooden' in tone, comprising a repetition of 5–11 *pli* motifs (formed in fact by two notes in a couplet, *p'li*, but this is barely discernible), rapidly repeated at the rate of c. 7 per second, and used spontaneously as an advertising song, *pli-pli-pli-pli-pli....* The second song type is an upward-slurred whistle, repeated 5–8 times at a rate of c. 6 notes per second, and used when countersinging against another male. The third is made up of c. 19–35 monosyllabic *chi* units given rapidly in a mellow 'wooden' trill at the rate of 12 notes per second, *chichichichichi...* (similar to some songs of Plain Titmouse of the interior *ridgwayi* group, although the rattles average longer and slower), and used when countersinging with a nearby rival and when approaching the nest. (Partly after Gaddis 1983.)

## DISTRIBUTION AND MOVEMENTS

The USA in central **Arizona** from Yavapai Co. (Juniper, Weaver and Bradshaw mountains), south of the Mogollon Rim and west to Pinal mountain (Gila Co.) and the Baboquivari mountains (Prima Co.), although local in the Lower Sonoran Zone (e.g. Camp Verde region and lower San Pedro river upstream to Aravaipa Creek; may also have bred around Tucson in 1950s). In SW **New Mexico** found in Catron Co. (San Francisco basin), Grant Co. (Cliff and Pinos Altos) and Hidalgo Co. (Peloncillo mountains). In **Mexico** found in the Sierra Madre Occidental and associated ranges in eastern **Sonora** (west to Saric, Cibuta and Opodepe), **Sinaloa** and **Nayarit**, and in western **Chihuahua** (east to Sierra del Nido, Bustillos) and **Durango**, also the central plateau in **Jalisco**, **Colima**, **Michoacan**, **Zacatecas**, **Aguascalientes**, **Guanajuato**, **Hidalgo**, **Mexico**, **Morelos** (Cuernavaca), **Puebla** and western **Veracruz** (Orizaba). Extends into the southern Sierra Madre Oriental in **San Luis Potosi** (west in the south to Xilitla), south-central **Nuevo Leon** and western **Tamaulipas**, and also into the Sierra Madre del Sur of **Guerrero** and **Oaxaca** east to Nejapa, and in interior Oaxaca north to Llanos Verde. Generally resident, but occasionally found during mid October–mid March (late September–early April) a little to the south and west of the breeding range in Arizona in Maricopa, Pinal and Pima Cos. (e.g. along the Verde, Salt, Gila, San Pedro and Santa Cruz rivers), west to Phoenix and Sacaton (but see Population). Accidental outside this range in Arizona: to lower Bill Williams river, Mohave/La Paz Cos., February–March 1977; Cataract Canyon, above Supai, Coconin Co., September 1950; and bottom of central Grand Canyon, March 1975. Also occurs casually to central-south New Mexico. Movements in Mexico poorly understood, but very occasionally recorded at lower levels in NE and north-central Sonora (e.g. Granados, Banamichi), and may also disperse to higher elevations, to at least 3200 m in central Mexico. Extremely rare vagrant **Texas**, where not on the official state checklist, although there are documented sight records that are generally accepted as being valid (DeSante & Pyle 1986): Brewster Co. in Santa Elena Canyon, Rio Grande, May 1937, Chisos mountains, c. 1937 (Oberholser 1974) and five in the Chisos Mountains in May 1981 (*Amer. Birds*, 35: 838).

## HABITAT

Breeds in montane forests of evergreen oak, pine and juniper (and sometimes American Plane) and various mixtures thereof, preferring a strong presence of oak (sometimes rather dense and scrubby). In Arizona, locally also in willow-cottonwood-mesquite at lower elevations, and in winter found in riparian willow-cottonwood, mesquite-grassland, and city parks. Breeds in the SW USA at 1525–2135 m, most commonly 1525–1830 m, occasionally wandering to 2590 m. In Mexico, recorded in Sinaloa at 610–1950 m, in southern Chihuahua at 2285 m, in Durango at up to 2590 m, and in Oaxaca at 560 m and 1830–2440 m, and general altitudinal range in Mexico 1000–3000 m.

## POPULATION

Common in Arizona (abundant in the Huachuca and Chiricahua mountains) and fairly common in New Mexico. In Mexico, generally common or fairly common. There has apparently been some expansion of the range in Arizona, where the first records for Tucson valley were in 1915/16, but with the continued destruction of riparian woodland along the Gila and lower Salt rivers now largely absent from these areas in winter (Rea 1983).

## HABITS

Tame and confiding, but perhaps less active than other tits. Territorial during the breeding season from February onwards, but once the young have fledged forms family parties, and typically found in flocks of 2–8 birds, sometimes up to 25 in the autumn. May join mixed-species foraging flocks, sometimes acting as the nucleus of such flocks. Reacts strongly to the calls (either real or imitated) of Northern Pygmy Owl. Forages predominantly in the middle storey, among branches, investigating bark crevices and hanging from twigs and small branches to examine the undersides of leaves, but seldom if ever visits the ground. Food mostly insects, and captive birds have been noted to store food in bark cracks.

## BREEDING BIOLOGY

Poorly known. Season: USA, mid April–May; Oaxaca, May. The nest is placed in a natural hole in a tree or stump, usually an oak, 0.6–8.5 m above ground, although sometimes in abandoned woodpecker excavations, and will use nestboxes. The nest itself is a foundation of leaves, lichen and forbs, mixed with plant down and lined with fur and plant down. Clutch 5–7 (perhaps as few as 3 in southern Mexico): eggs white; 16.1 x 12.6 mm. The division of labour between the sexes in nest-building and incubation is unknown; incubation and fledging periods unknown. Single-brooded?

## DESCRIPTION

*P. w. wollweberi* **Adult**: *In fresh plumage* (autumn–early winter), base of bill dirty-white, longer feathers of forehead tipped mid grey. Centre of crown mid grey, front and sides of crown blackish and feathers of crest blackish. Nape blackish, longer feathers tipped olive-grey. Mantle and scapulars olive-grey, upper mantle bordered blackish. Back and rump dull olive (citrine), uppertail-coverts olive-grey. Tail grey-brown, feathers fringed dull olive, T6 more narrowly fringed whitish. Wing coverts dull grey-brown, fringed olive-grey, very broadly so on lesser and median coverts. Alula dark grey-brown, smaller feathers very finely fringed olive-grey. Primary coverts, tertials and secondaries grey-brown, fringed olive-grey. Primaries grey-brown, fringed olive grey-white (not P2). Lores blackish, fringed dirty white towards base of bill, eyestripe blackish. Supercilium whitish, continuing around ear-coverts to join dirty white sides of neck. Cheeks and ear-coverts dirty white with blackish rear border (connecting eyestripe and bib), upper ear-coverts greyer at rear. (All white areas of face faintly washed buff.) Chin and throat blackish, line below lower border of bib dirty white (connecting with dirty white half-collar). Breast and upper flanks light grey, centre of breast washed dirty yellowish-buff. Lower flanks, belly, vent and under-tail-coverts pale dirty yellowish-buff, lower flanks washed grey. Axillaries whitish, underwing-coverts whitish, washed yellow, base of under primary coverts whitish, washed yellow, base of under primary coverts mid grey. *In worn plumage* (April–August), cap blacker (grey feather tips abrade), dark bases to feathers of cheeks and ear-coverts may show. Upperparts duller and rather greyer (less olive), wings browner, pale fringes abraded. Underparts abrade whiter, when very worn may be dull dirty-buff (dark feather bases shining through). **Bare Parts**: Iris brown; bill black; legs and feet blue-grey. **Juvenile**: As adult, but forehead and crown mid grey, tinged olive, feathers fringed slightly darker (vague scaled effect). Crest shorter, blackish-grey (as sides of crown). Nape sooty-brown, tipped pale greyish-brown, mantle to uppertail-coverts pale greyish-brown. Flight feathers dull grey-brown, tertials fringed dull olive and tipped paler, secondaries tipped dirty white, primaries fringed dirty buff-white. Lores dark grey-brown, eyestripe sooty-brown. Supercilium and sides of neck dirty white, cheeks dull buff-white, ear-coverts dirty white, sooty-brown at rear. Chin and upper throat dark grey, feathers broadly tipped pale grey, breast light grey, with no pale line below the bib. **1st Adult**: As adult. **Measurements**: Wing of male 68–70 (chord 67–70), of female 65, 67 (chord 64–64.5); tail of male 56–64, of female 55–57; bill 9.5–11.6; tarsus 15–18. Weight 8.8-11.7 g (*P. w. vandevenderi*).

**MOULT** Adult post-breeding complete (July–August). Post-juvenile incomplete, probably includes at least the tail feathers and tertials (July–August).

**GEOGRAPHICAL VARIATION** Rather slight, and at all obvious only in fresh plumage. It may be preferable to recognise just two races, *phillipsi* (including *vandevenderi*) and nominate *wollweberi* (including *caliginosus*), but here, following Phillips (1986), four races recognised.

*P. w. vandevenderi* Rea (in Phillips 1986). Arizona north of the Gila river, and SW New

Mexico. As *phillipsi*, but in fresh plumage mantle slightly darker, duller and less olive (olive-grey rather than greyish-olive), rump greyish-green, only slightly paler than back (not a paler greenish straw-yellow), and underparts darker, with a broad smoke-grey wash across the breast and flanks and whiter centre to the belly, with little or no yellowish wash (not whitish with a strong yellow wash on the belly and flanks in fresh plumage, virtually lacking a greyish tinge to breast and flanks). By January–February both races are greyer (*vandevenderi* less olive, *phillipsi* less yellowish), through to wear and fading. Occasionally atypically olive-green on upperparts, but these darker above than *phillipsi* in a comparable state of wear. Wing (chord) of male 63.5–65.5, of female 60–63.5; tail of male 59–61, of female 54–57.5.

*P. w. phillipsi* SE Arizona (south of Gila river) and the northern Sierra Madre Occidental in Chihuahua (south to c. 27° N) and Sonora; also northern Sinaloa (?). Intergrades with nominate *wollweberi* in southern Chihuahua, northern Sinaloa and Durango. As nominate *wollweberi*, but very slightly paler, also less olive (especially rump and fringes to tail feathers), and underparts slightly less yellow-tinged, more pale grey on centre of breast and belly; averages slightly smaller. Some variation within southern Arizona, the richest (brightest above, yellowest below) are from Santa Catalina mountains and Huachuca mountains, the dullest from Baboquivari mountains.

*P. w. wollweberi* Central and southern highlands of Mexico, north to Durango and Sinaloa in the west and central Nuevo Leon in the east. See Description.

*P. w. caliginosus* Sierra Madre del Sur of Guerrero and Oaxaca (also northern Oaxaca?). Poorly marked; marginally the darkest race. As nominate *wollweberi*, but upper- and underparts slightly darker and more olive.

**RELATIONSHIPS** On the basis of morphology and distribution, Thielcke (1968) placed Bridled Titmouse together with Crested and Grey-crested Tits in the subgenus *Lophophanes*. Eck (1988) agreed, placing all three in the 'species group' *cristatus*. Biochemical evidence clearly shows, however, that Bridled Titmouse, although convergent in appearance with Crested Tit, is closely related to the Tufted/Black-crested/Plain Titmouse group, subgenus *Baeolophus* (for protein relationships, see Gill *et al.* 1989; for DNA-DNA hybridisation, see Sheldon *et al.* 1992).

**REFERENCES** Bent (1946), Gaddis (1983), Phillips (1986), Phillips *et al.* (1964), van Rossem (1947).

This dull titmouse inhabits two distinct regions of western North America, the oak woods of the west coast and the pinyon-juniper of the interior. The two populations look and sound very much alike, but recent biochemical research strongly hints that they have long been separated and may be distinct species.

**IDENTIFICATION** length 150 mm (5.75 in). A rather drab titmouse with a short crest. Two distinct groups of populations. From Oregon to Baja California, the forehead and face are mottled dusty white and dull grey-brown, the upperparts, including the wings and tail, are dull grey-brown, and the underparts pale buffy-grey. In the interior west, the upperparts are rather greyer. The small crest, plain plumage and tit-like actions are distinctive. In western Texas, however, Plain Titmouse should be carefully distinguished from juvenile Black-crested Titmouse, which has a much paler cap and crest than the adult (although still dusky) but retains the characteristic cinnamon-buff flanks.

**SEX/AGE** Sexes similar. Juvenile very similar to the adult, although often with paler and buffer tips to the greater coverts and also perhaps slightly narrower and more pointed tail feathers. 1st adult as adult, but may show moult contrasts in the primaries and secondaries, sometimes replacing some inner secondaries and, more rarely, some outer primaries.

**VOICE** Very variable. In the **coastal *inornatus* group** the contact call is a soft, lisping *sip* or *sisip*. Has a characteristic but a rather variable 'chick-a-dee'-type call (see Black-capped Chickadee, p. 267), e.g. a thin *tsitsi-tzer*, *tsitsi-tzer*, *tsitsitsi-tzer-zer* or scolding *tzer-zer-zer-ze*r, given in territorial contexts and at greater intensity in alarm or excitement. A series of high-pitched notes in a short trill may also be part of the same complex of notes. In more extreme alarm gives a high, thin *see-see-see*, sometimes combined with the scolding notes. In aggressive interactions males give a slowly enunciated, subdued *wee-to* or *see-yor* and also a loud, emphatic *sisip*. In courtship, soliciting females give a soft, twittering *sit-sit-sit* (similar to the begging note of recently fledged juveniles), and if disturbed incubating females give an explosive hissing and puffing note. In the coastal *inornatus* group the song is very variable. Perhaps the commonest form is characterised by the relatively slow repetition of groups of more or less whistled stereotyped motifs at the rate of 2–4 motifs per second. These motifs may be monosyllabic, e.g. *pli*, *tui* or a rising *sweet*, or more complex combinations, e.g. *chuwi* or *pi-pi-tiu*, whilst a whistled *seetur* recalls the 'peter' motif of Tufted Titmouse. Often the introductory note is slightly sibilant or rasping, e.g. *tsri-wa* or *tsit-tsit-chiu*, or occasionally the terminal note a rasping D (as in the 'chick-a-dee'), e.g. *pi-zur*. Often motifs are made up of couplets of identical notes, e.g. *chit'it*. Each song phrase comprises groups of 1–7 motifs, e.g. *pli-pli...*, *chuwi-chuwi-chuwi-chuwi...*, *tsit-tsit-chiu*, *tsit-tsit-chiu*, *tsit-tsit-chiu...* and *chit'it-chit'it-chit'it...*, and each bout of song usually uses just one motif. Bouts of song may be made up of just

8–10 phrases or even fewer, although single and paired motifs may be given in longer bouts of over 20 phrases. The next bout of song will then typically use a different motif, and when countersinging males match their neighbours' motif. A variant song is a more rapid monotonous rattling, the units being given at *c*. 10 per second, and a common variant is a phrase made up from several high-pitched whistles followed by a trill (at *c*. 20 units per second). Each male has a repertoire of about ten different song types, and local dialects of shared song types develop which may persist for several years. Song is given largely in spring, February–May in California. (Partly after Dixon 1949, 1969.) In the **interior *ridgwayi* group** calls include a quiet but full *tup*, a thin *sit* and a rattling, scolding *chur* lasting *c*. 1 second, *chrrrrrrrrr*. Most song types of the *ridgwayi* group are built up from the repetition of motifs comprising three identical units (compared with two in the couplets sometimes given by the coastal group), the resultant motifs then being repeated at *c*. 3.5–5 per second in a slightly 'disjointed' rattle, e.g. *chi'd'd-chid'd'd-chid'd'd...*, or are rattles interspersed with clearer whistles, e.g. *chi'chi'chipu-chi'chi'chipu....* Other common song types are constructed from the rapid repetition of *c*. 7–17 simple monosyllabic units in monotonous, unmusical rattles at 10–21 notes per second, e.g. *pli'li'li'li'li'li'li...* or *chwi'wi'wi'wi'wi'wi'wi* (resembling the rattling song of the coastal group, but typically faster). Still other variations consist of the repetition of more complex motifs made up of groups of two different note types (sometimes rattles and trills at alternating higher and lower pitches). Males may have a repertoire of up to 15 different song types, but not all are distinguishable to the human ear. Typically, only one song type is used in each bout of song, and when countersinging birds will match their neighbours' song, but occasionally males will give a quiet, rambling 'subsong' combining many different song types when near the female. (Partly after Johnson 1987.)

**DISTRIBUTION AND MOVEMENTS** In the **USA**, the coastal *inornatus* group breeds from SW **Oregon**, through much of **California** west of the Sierra Nevada, although absent from the San Joaquin valley and Mojave desert (see also Geographical Variation), to **Mexico** in NW **Baja California** (south to the Sierra San Pedro Martir) and also the mountains of extreme southern **Baja California Sur** (Sierra Victoria, Sierra de la Laguna). The interior *ridgwayi* group breeds from central-southern **Oregon** (east of the Cascades in southern Lake and SE Klamath Cos.), SE **Idaho** (Cassia Co. north and east to Bonneville) and SW **Wyoming** (east to Carbon Co.), south through eastern **California** (east of the Sierra Nevada; see Geographical Variation), most of **Nevada** and

**Utah**, western **Colorado** (east to Moffat, Eagle and western Archuleta Cos.), SE **Colorado** (from Las Animas and western Baca Cos. northwest to southern Chaffee and El Paso Cos.), and westernmost **Oklahoma** in NW Cimmaron Co. in the western panhandle (with an increase in records there in autumn and winter), to westernmost **Texas** in the Guadalupe mountains (Culberson Co.), **New Mexico** west to Colfax, Lincoln, Otero and probably Quay Cos.), and most of northern and eastern **Arizona** (east to the Cerbat, Hualapai, Superstition, Galiuro and Chiricahua mountains). Extends marginally into northern **Mexico**, into the San Luis mountains of extreme NE **Sonora**. Highly sedentary, but some dispersal in the autumn, probably exclusively by juveniles, with scattered records from lowland areas adjacent to the breeding range. Recorded in eastern **Oregon** (Steens mountains, Harney Co.), SW **Idaho**, NW and SE **Wyoming**, interior southern **California** (Mecca, Riverside Co.), **Colorado** (Boulder, Jefferson, Gunnison and San Juan Cos.), **Arizona** (Santa Catalina and Rincon mountains and to the bottom of the Grand Canyon), and Trans-Pecos **Texas** (September–mid March, when additional birds in the Guadalupe mountains) and also recorded in the Davis mountains and at El Paso.

**HABITAT** The coastal *inornatus* group is found primarily in dry evergreen woodland, principally oak, sometimes with a mixture of pine, juniper or Californian Laurel. It also inhabits riparian alder, well-wooded suburban areas and chaparral, although usually only when oaks are present nearby. Generally occurs at low altitudes, from near sea level to c. 915–1100 m in northern and central California, but up to 2050 m in southern California, with some seasonal wanderings, both to lower altitudes and upslope, and in Baja California found at 500–2400 m. The interior *ridgwayi* group is more or less strictly confined to woodland of pinyon-juniper, sometimes mixed with oak, in the foothills of the Sierra Nevada and Rocky Mountains, and on low desert ranges and mesas. Also found occasionally in scrub oak woodland and in winter may wander into Ponderosa Pine, riparian woodland, willow thickets and even treeless sagebrush scrub. Occurs at 1340–2285 m in western California (wandering in winter to 2440 m), up to at least 2135 m in Arizona, and at 1400–2440 m in New Mexico.

**POPULATION** Overall fairly common, and common in California, especially in the Sacramento valley, but uncommon in Idaho, NE and southern Nevada, SW Arizona, Oklahoma and Texas. In Mexico, common in Baja California but rare in NE Sonora.

**HABITS** Drab and often rather inconspicuous, this species is more often heard than seen, and even sings from cover. The following details apply to the coastal *inornatus* group. Found singly and in pairs, and usually pairs for life, with 'divorce' being uncommon. Pairs maintain a territory year-round, the boundaries remaining remarkably stable from one season to the next (and not expanding to fill adjacent territories should these fall vacant). If one partner dies, the other remains on

territory and re-mates the following season. Territories are defended most actively in spring, with patrolling of boundaries, exchange of song and occasionally pursuit of neighbours conspicuous from late winter onwards. Pairs may temporarily join mixed-species foraging flocks as these pass through their territory, but they drop out as their boundary is reached. Family parties break up about a month after fledging, the juveniles leaving their parents' territories (and any intrusion by wandering juveniles into existing territories is resisted). Some juveniles quickly form pairs (by August), and may then occupy their own territory by the early autumn (juveniles may even have a territory as early as June), although many of these initial territories are apparently unsuitable, perhaps because of the lack of nest sites, and are abandoned the following spring. Other juveniles become 'floaters' and continue to wander or occupy marginal habitats until they find a suitable untenanted area or a single, unmated territory-owner. Generally forages in the upper storey and canopy, gleaning from bark, chipping away pieces to expose insects. Sometimes feeds on the ground, especially in winter, carrying off food items to be consumed under cover. Will visit bird feeders. Food insects, also catkins, berries, leaf buds and acorns (which are broken open with the bill), with a relatively large proportion of the diet made up of animal material. Roosts singly in natural cavities, the female roosting in the nest, sometimes from a month before the eggs are laid; also roosts in dense foliage. The only difference noted for the interior *ridgwayi* group is that it is more prone to form small winter flocks. Pair formation apparently takes place in the flocks, before the establishment of territories.

**BREEDING BIOLOGY** Season: California, late March–mid July; New Mexico, May; Baja California, late April–May. The nest is placed in tree cavities, usually in oaks, junipers or Joshua Trees, 1–3 (–11) m above ground. Often uses old woodpecker excavations, and takes readily to nestboxes and sometimes other artificial structures. May excavate or partly excavate its own nest hole in rotten wood or even an earthen bank. Often reuses the same hole. The site is chosen by the female, who also builds the nest, a pad of moss, grass, forbs and bark strips, lined with hair, fur, feathers etc. Clutch 6–8 (3–9): eggs white, sometimes very finely spotted reddish-brown; 17.4 x 13.4 mm. Female incubates (sitting very tight), period 14–16 days; she is fed on the nest by the male and also broods the nestlings. Both sexes feed the young (the male taking the greater share early in the period), which fledge after 16–21 days, but continue to be fed by both parents for 21–28 days. Single-brooded.

**DESCRIPTION** *P. i. inornatus* **Adult**: *In fresh plumage* (August onwards), feathers of forehead mid grey, tipped cinnamon-buff. Crown, crest and upperparts (including lesser and median coverts) mid brown, tinged grey, scapulars and back slightly warmer and browner, rump slightly paler and buffer (especially longer feathers). Tail dark brown, tinged grey, each feather fringed as upperparts (slightly paler on outer feathers). Wings dark brown, tinged grey; greater coverts, primary coverts, tertials and secondaries fringed as upperparts, faint paler tips to secondaries, P3–P10 fringed paler and greyer, broadest inwards of emargination on P3–P7. Lores, cheeks, supercilium and ear-coverts light grey, feathers subterminally whiter and tipped drab (giving a mottled effect). Submoustachial region and sides of neck off-white. Throat and centre of breast pale grey, remainder of underparts pale buffy-grey, rear flanks and vent slightly buffer. Thighs pale drab-grey. Axillaries and underwing-coverts whitish. *In worn plumage* (summer), fringes on wing and tail feathers abraded and may be bleached paler, underparts slightly duller (grey feather bases shining through). **Bare Parts**: Iris dark brown; bill dull brown, greyer at the sides; legs and feet dull blue-grey. **Juvenile and 1st Adult**: As adult (but see Sex/Age). **Measurements**: Wing of male 64–73, of female 67–72; tail of male 56–63, of female 55–60; bill 11.6–13.6; tarsus 19–22.5. Weight 12.6–19.2 g (*P. i. ridgwayi* 15.2–23.1 g: Grinnell *et al.* 1930).

**MOULT** Adult post-breeding complete (late May–August). Post-juvenile incomplete, includes tail, greater coverts, 2–3 tertials, sometimes the inner two secondaries and rarely the outer two primaries and their coverts (July–September).

**GEOGRAPHICAL VARIATION** Relatively slight, although falling into two basic groups, largely separated by the Sierra Nevada and Mojave desert: the grey-brown *inornatus* group in the Pacific-coast region and the grey *ridgwayi* group in the interior west. Notably, the two groups show as much genetic differentiation as separates most *species* of tit, indicating a long period of isolation. They are thought to have diverged from a common ancestor *c.* 2 million years ago (Gill & Slikas 1992). They may well be better treated as two distinct species, and further study of morphology, vocalisations and genetics, as well as investigations of their relationship in California, is clearly needed. Six races recognised, following Phillips (1986).

**THE *INORNATUS* GROUP** Pacific-coast regions of the USA and Mexico.

*P. i. sequestratus* SW Oregon (the interior coast ranges of the Rouge valley in Josephine and Jackson Cos.) and NW California (Shasta river and South Fork of Trinity river, Siskiyou and Trinity Cos.). Poorly marked. As nominate *inornatus,* but darker, also perhaps browner on upperparts (and flanks?).

*P. i. inornatus* Western California, east to the Sierra Nevada, from Mendocino Co. and the northern end of the Sacramento valley south to Santa Barbara Co. (where intergrades with *affabilis*), and the southern end of the San Joaquin valley (absent from the coastal fog belt north of Marin

Co.). See Description. Includes *'kernensis'* of Kern basin in southern Tulare and Kern Cos. and the eastern slopes of the Sierra Nevada in extreme SW Inyo Co., with upperparts apparently greyer and underparts whiter.

*P. i. affabilis* SW California from Santa Barbara and Ventura Cos. (largely absent from the coast in San Diego Co.) south to northern Baja California Norte. As nominate *inornatus,* but upperparts very slightly darker and browner (less grey), underparts rather duller, more heavily washed grey-drab (but brownish tinge may often be staining) and bill larger; close to *sequestratus,* but slightly darker (and less brown?) and bill larger. Bill 12.4–13.1. Includes *'transpositus'* of SW California, perhaps browner, and *'mohavensis'* of Little San Bernardino mountains, perhaps slightly greyer.

*P. i. cineraceus* Baja California Sur. As nominate *inornatus,* but upperparts greyer, underparts paler (the palest race), and averages smaller, especially in bill and tail. Wing of male 72, of female 71; bill 12.6, 12.9.

**THE *RIDGWAYI* GROUP** Interior western North America. Shows a mosaic of irregular non-clinal geographic variations in size and darkness of the grey tones. Larger, somewhat darker birds occur in the White mountains, California, but also in Colorado; small birds occur in the southwest, but also in Idaho; while the Utah populations are 'normal' or undifferentiated. Naming these random variations seems pointless, and perhaps better treated as a single race (Phillips 1959).

*P. i. ridgwayi* Interior western North America west to Idaho, central Nevada, SE California (the Clark, New York and Providence mountains in eastern San Bernadino Co.), Arizona and NE Sonora. As *inornatus,* but upperparts rather greyer, mid grey, washed brown or brownish-grey; fringes to wing feathers paler and greyer, fringes to tail feathers slightly greyer. Wing (chord) of male 70–75, of female 68–73.5; tail of male 56–64, of female 55.5–63.5; bill 12.8–14.1. Includes *'plumbescens'* of Arizona (except northeast), SW New Mexico and NE Sonora, supposedly darker and more lead-grey, especially on upperparts

*P. i. zaleptus* Central-southern Oregon (east of the Cascades), western Nevada (Virginia mountains, Carson City) and eastern California (in the northeast, in Modoc and Lassen Cos. and in central-eastern California in the Benton, White, Inyo, Grapevine and Panamint mountains of Mono and Inyo Cos., although these latter populations may be better placed with *ridgwayi*). Poorly marked, and probably better synonymised with *ridgwayi*. As *ridgwayi,* but in fresh plumage overall paler and cleaner grey.

**RELATIONSHIPS** Forms a superspecies with Tufted and Black-crested Titmice (see Tufted Titmouse).

**REFERENCES** Dixon (1949, 1954, 1956, 1969).

The largest tit in the New World, the Tufted Titmouse is a familiar visitor to feeders in the eastern USA. Its range has expanded steadily northwards in the 20th century, aided by the regular supplies of food provided by man in the late winter and spring.

**IDENTIFICATION** Length 155 mm (6.25 in). Forehead black, conspicuous short crest and remainder of upperparts grey. Lores pale buff, underparts whitish with rufous-buff flanks. The blackish forehead, the crest, the conspicuous large dark 'eye' (produced by the fine black eyering) set in a pale 'face', and the lack of a black bib are distinctive (other crested birds, such as Blue Jay or waxwings, are rather larger). The similarly crested Black-crested Titmouse has a whitish forehead and black cap and crest. Tufted and Black-crested Titmice hybridise in central Texas and hybrids may show a combination of characters, typically including a dark brown or rufous forehead and a sooty-grey crest. See Black-crested Titmouse for full details.

**SEX/AGE** Sexes similar. Juveniles differ from adults in their much duller and more brownish-black forehead, sooty-grey cap and crest (thus less contrast between the forehead and cap), and darker and browner upperparts; the underparts are also duller, with the breast washed grey and the belly and vent washed buff, thus showing less contrast with the rich buff of the flanks. Note that worn adults may have a duller black forehead and paler flanks, but their plumage, especially the wings and tail, is worn or moulting at a time when the juvenile is fresh. 1st adults as adult, although in the hand they may show a contrast between the new greater coverts (and sometimes new tertials) and the retained juvenile primaries, secondaries, and usually also brownish juvenile primary coverts.

**VOICE** Rather noisy. Contact calls include a 'chick-a-dee' call, a harsh, peevish *day-day-day* or *tsee-day-day-day* (sometimes coarser and lower-pitched than that of Carolina Chickadee, sometimes high, thin and fine, e.g. *tsi-tsi-dza-dza-dza*), becoming sharper and more emphatic in excitement. Another contact call is a *tsit* or *tseet*. In excitement gives a rapid *sit-sit-sit*, in anxiety a high, thin *see-see-see* (including as a hawk-alarm call). In subordination, the female gives a *zhee-zhee-zhee*. The song comprises loud whistles, which may be full and mellow and almost thrush-like in tone, or higher, clearer and more tit-like. Each phrase is made up of either a slurred monosyllabic units, e.g. *p'li, poo* or *piu*, or disyllabic motifs which fall in pitch, e.g. *wheedle, peto, pidu* or *peter*. These are repeated up to ten or so times at various speeds, sometimes almost rattling, sometimes slow and sedate: *peter-peter-peter-peter...* or *p'li-p'li-p'li-p'li-p'li...*; songs with slurred monosyllabic and disyllabic motifs are apparently equally common. Songs may be given up to 35 times a minute, and individual males may have up to 15 different song types, variations including elements that are monosyllabic (e.g. *weet*) or rise in pitch (e.g. *daytee-daytee-daytee...*) and, rarely, three-syllable elements (e.g. *peetery-*

*peetery-peetery*); more subtle variations include the length of the individual phrases, the gaps between them and the speed of delivery. Neighbouring males share many song types and often match each other's theme during bouts of countersinging, responding less strongly to a 'stranger's' song. Song is given all year, although mainly in February–September. Both sexes sing, but females much less frequently than males, and apparently in March–July only (Brackbill 1970). A confused, buzzing and warbling jumble of notes, of uncertain function, has also been recorded. (Largely after Dixon 1950.)

**DISTRIBUTION AND MOVEMENTS** In **Canada** breeds in southern **Ontario**, and in the eastern **USA** breeds from SE **Minnesota**, southern **Wisconsin**, southern **Michigan** (lower peninsula, although sparse in the northern half), central **New York** (occasionally north to Clinton and Jefferson Cos., and including Long Island), southern **Vermont** (confined to river valleys north to Lamoille and Caledonia Cos.), southern **New Hampshire** and southern **Maine** (recorded north at least to the foot of the Longfellow mountains), south to southern **Florida** (Collier Co., but absent from the coastal belt south of Cape Canaveral and Lee Co.) and the **Gulf Coast** (but rarely or never crosses coastal marshes to the coastal cheniers of Louisiana). Occurs west to eastern **Iowa**, SE **Nebraska** (Missouri valley, in Sarpy, Cass and Gage Cos.), central **Kansas** (west to Republic, Barton, Hodgeman and Clark Cos., also Finney Co.), **Oklahoma** (west to Woods, Roger Mills and Tillman Cos.; occurs locally along the eastern border of the Texas panhandle, but no definite breeding records) and central **Texas**, where the range skirts the Balcones escarpment of the Edwards plateau (see figure 100.2, p. 414). Has bred **South Dakota** (Union Co., 1931), otherwise a very rare non-breeding visitor to Grant, Yankton and Union Cos. Largely resident; ringing recoveries show that less than 1% of Tufted Tits move more than 30 km from the ringing site. Nevertheless, there are short-distance movements and wanderings, with post-breeding dispersal in September–October. Also, small numbers may move further, especially outside the breeding season, with pioneers penetrating north of the breeding range. Thus, irregular in northern **Minnesota** and **Wisconsin**, a rare winter visitor to southern **Quebec** (first recorded North-Hatley in December 1978, now a rare and irregular winter visitor, especially around Montreal, with an 'invasion' in winter 1990/91 producing c. 50 records), and vagrant **New Brunswick** (records include Fredericton, December 1983). In the south, during exceptional winters (e.g. severe drought), may also wander outside the breeding range into the range of Black-crested Titmouse, which may lead to incidents of hybridisation; in

**Texas**, such exceptional winter records come from Bexar, Coleman, San Patricio and Travis Cos.

**HABITAT** Deciduous and mixed woodlands, especially along streams, river valleys and in swamps (has a clear association with wetter areas, especially on the edge of the range), also, particularly outside the breeding season, well-wooded farmland, orchards, parkland and suburban areas with plenty of mature trees, although normally avoids small woodland patches, hedgerows and scrub. In eastern Texas, however, favours upland oak woodland and scarce in valley-bottom hardwood forests. Also occurs in coniferous forests, although at low densities, such as the Longleaf Pine woodlands of Florida and the Gulf Coast lowlands, where it favours the smaller cypress swamps within the pine woods. In all habitats during the breeding season, the presence of mature trees with suitable cavities is critical. Generally avoids higher altitudes, and not found above 610 m in the west of the range, although occurs at up to 1500 m in Tennessee and exceptionally to 1220 m in Kentucky.

**POPULATION** Generally common within breeding range, and commonest along the Ohio, Cumberland, Arkansas and Mississippi rivers, and scarce in the Ozark and Appalachian mountains. Only fairly common in Wisconsin, Michigan, Rhode Island, Massachusetts and Nebraska; uncommon in Maine, New Hampshire, Vermont and Minnesota; and rare in Ontario (where commonest in the Niagara region). Has spread northwards in 20th century. First recorded in Canada in May 1914 at Point Pelee, Ontario, with the first summer recorded at Fishers Glen in Haldimand-Norfolk RM in July 1932, probable breeding in 1936 near Hamilton and proven breeding at Sarnia in 1955. Now a rare resident in SE Ontario, with the largest concentration on the Niagara peninsula, and an estimated population of *c.* 40 pairs, but remains very rare east of Toronto. The increase in range and numbers has been very slow, apparently aided by the provision of bird feeders, especially those stocked throughout the spring, and on the northern periphery of the range commonest in areas with feeders. The range has also expanded in the Great Lakes region, westwards into Michigan's lower peninsula, north to Emmet Co. (but still commonest in the southwest, and little recent expansion), and into Wisconsin, where unknown until 1900, now regularly breeding north to St Croix, Adams and Jefferson Cos., but perhaps some recent retraction of the range. Also spread into Iowa in the early 1900s. There has been a spread into northern Pennsylvania and also in New York, where prior to the 1950s rare and local east of the Hudson river, but a major influx took place in the winter of 1954 and the species is now common and has recolonised Long Island, although still absent from the higher ground in mid state. An even more dramatic expansion has occurred in New England, into Connecticut (bred annually from 1946), Massachusetts (since 1958), southern Vermont (first bred 1975), southern New Hampshire and southern Maine (first bred 1978, with a major incursion in 1983). Now common in southern New England.

**HABITS** Active, noisy and not shy, although not so tame as Black-capped Chickadee. It is easily attracted by 'pishing' or 'squeaking', and is a familiar visitor to feeders, where it is dominant, ousting all but the Blue Jay. A conspicuous species through the winter, it is less vocal in the spring and summer and can be elusive, especially when foraging silently in the canopy of large trees. Generally found singly or in pairs, the latter being the basic social unit. Pair-bonds are formed at any season and are almost always permanent, enduring until the death or disappearance of one partner. Males are dominant over females, and occasionally will drive them from feeders etc.; this behaviour may be related to courtship chases. Within the sexes, adults dominate over young birds. In late summer after the breeding season, Tufted Titmice form family parties. Later in the autumn these disperse, and from September/October to February/March established pairs or individuals defend a territory (some young are known to stay with their parents through the autumn and winter). Disputes occur at the boundaries, involving loud calling and excited behaviour, usually from males. Occasionally, single males will intrude into a neighbour's territory, but will either quickly withdraw or be driven off by the residents. (Tufted Titmice are also pugnacious during the breeding season in defence of their territory.) Some pairs or individuals will accept other Tufted Titmice (their offspring or young birds from elsewhere) into their winter range, and they may then form flocks of up to eight birds, although most of these flocks break up each day from mid morning onwards. Tufted Titmice may also join mixed-species foraging flocks as these pass through their territory, but will not follow the flock beyond the boundary. In winter flocks of Tufted Titmice the dominant ('alpha') male and female are usually paired and will establish a breeding territory within the winter range around February–April. At the same time, the other, subordinate, tits will disperse, although they may remain within the flock's territory if they have paired with another member of the flock, to form a 'beta' pair. In such cases, the alpha pair will establish its breeding territory 3–4 weeks earlier than the beta pair (and 4–5 weeks earlier than flock members that have left the winter territory altogether). Early establishment of a breeding territory probably gives the alpha pair a distinct advantage, enabling them to produce more offspring. Roosts in cavities in trees, the female roosting in the nest from laying onwards. Forages at all levels of the vegetation, but favours the higher trees in spring and summer and, especially in winter, frequently descends to the ground; often clings to the bark of trees. Food in summer largely insects, also snails and spiders and, in late summer, fruit; the autumn and winter diet is mostly seeds and nuts, and acorns may form the bulk in November–February. Caches food in large amounts throughout the territory, storing seeds in deep bark crevices or in the ground.

**BREEDING BIOLOGY** Season in the north (Ontario, New York) early/mid May–mid June; in the west (Kansas) late March–mid June, usually late April; in the south (Texas) late March–May. The nest is placed in a natural cavity in a tree (living or dead) or abandoned woodpecker excavation, usually 1.2–6 m (0–33.5 m) above ground. Holes in rotten stumps and fence posts, nestboxes or even hollow metal poles are also occasionally used. Occasionally excavates its own cavity in very rotten wood (Jackson 1995). Sometimes the same nest is used for several years. Both sexes help to locate a suitable cavity, but the female takes the dominant role, and she builds the nest over a period of 6–11 days, continuing to add material throughout the laying period. Leaves, bark strips, moss and grass are used to fill up excess cavity space, and the cup is made of moss and leaves lined with soft materials such as hair and fur, which may be collected from live animals, sometimes humans, and even rags and string; often the nest contains a cast snakeskin. Clutch 5–7 (3–8): eggs white or creamy, finely spotted with rufous-brown; 18.4 x 14.1 mm. Female incubates, period 12–14 days; the male will occasionally feed the female on the nest, but more often off the nest. Both sexes participate in nest sanitation and feeding the young, although they are brooded largely or exclusively by the female. Fledging after 15–18 days, the juveniles continue to be fed by the adults until 6–8 weeks old. Exceptionally, two broods are raised, especially in the south of the range, when the young from the first clutch may help care for the second brood. Occasionally, unmated birds may help in feeding the young; these may be 1st adults assisting their parents.

**DESCRIPTION** Adult: *In fresh plumage* (September–March), forehead and feathers at base of upper mandible blackish, sometimes tinged rusty (there may be a conspicuous rusty border to the black forehead or extensive concealed rusty feather bases). Crown mid lead-grey, tinged brown at front, rear feathers elongated into a marked crest (exceptionally shows darker shaft streaks and very rarely blackish feather centres). Nape, sides of neck, extreme upper mantle, back, rump and lesser coverts mid lead-grey, mantle, scapulars and uppertail-coverts brownish olive-grey. Tail, tertials and median and greater coverts mid grey, feathers fringed brownish olive-grey, T6 more narrowly fringed light grey. Alula, primary coverts, primaries and secondaries dark grey, smaller feathers of alula fringed lead-grey, primary coverts, secondaries and P3–P10 fringed mid lead-grey (much finer and whiter distally of emarginations on P3–P7). Lores whitish, tinged buff, cheeks and ear-coverts pale grey. Fine well-defined black eyering, usually broken at rear. Chin, throat and breast white, washed pale drab-grey, sides of breast washed pale grey, remainder of underparts white, faintly washed buff. Flanks rich rufous-buff. Axillaries buff, underwing-coverts whitish. *In worn plumage* (April–August), black of forehead less intense, head loses blue-grey bloom and becomes more uniform with mantle, which loses brownish-olive cast. Wing and tail feathers browner, fringes on wing feathers abraded and bleached paler. Underparts more uniform, flanks paler, more buff. **Bare Parts**: Iris dark brown; bill black, or upper mandible slate-grey and lower lead-grey; legs and feet lead-grey. **Juvenile**: As adult but blackish of forehead reduced in extent and duller, brownish-black or brownish, crown and nape sooty-grey, border of upper mantle mid grey, remainder of upperparts mid grey variably washed drab-brown. Outer webs of tail feathers fringed more buff-brown. Breast washed greyer, belly and vent washed buff, flanks rich buff. When very young, legs and feet dull pinkish-buff. **1st Adult**: See Sex/Age. **Measurements**: Wing of male 77–86 (chord 72–85), of female 74–82 (chord 71–82); tail of male 65–81, of female 61.5–79; bill 12.1–13.9; tarsus 19–22.1. Weight 17.5–26.1 g.

**MOULT** Adult post-breeding complete (July–early September). Post-juvenile incomplete, includes the greater coverts, a variable number of tail feathers and often the tertials, occasionally also the innermost secondary and primary coverts, and possibly also the outermost primary (July–September).

**GEOGRAPHICAL VARIATION** Slight. Averages larger in the north, with birds from New Jersey 5–7 mm longer-winged than those from Florida, but no subspecies are recognised.

**HYBRIDS** Two hybrids with Black-capped Chickadee recorded by Cockrum (1952). See also Black-crested Titmouse.

**RELATIONSHIPS** A member of the *bicolor* superspecies together with Plain and Black-crested Titmice. All three have very similar behaviour and vocalisations. Plain Titmouse does not come into contact with the other two members of the superspecies, but the ranges of Tufted and Black-crested meet in central Texas and the two hybridise in the narrow zone of transition between their respective habitats; see Black-crested Titmouse. The *bicolor* superspecies (together with Bridled Titmouse), is genetically very distinct from other members of the genus *Parus*, and was placed in the subgenus *Baeolophus* by Thielcke (1968). Indeed, the genetic distance between it and the other members of the genus *Parus* is comparable with that distinguishing many genera of passerine birds, and there may be good reason to revive *Baeolophus* for these crested tits (see also Bridled Titmouse).

**REFERENCES** Beddall (1963), Bent (1946), Brackbill (1970), Brawn & Samson (1983), Dixon (1955), Gill *et al.* (1989).

Often treated as conspecific with Tufted Titmouse, the relationship of these two species has been intensively studied, yet even recent biochemical evidence has failed to resolve the issue.

**IDENTIFICATION** Length 145 mm (5.75 in). Forehead whitish, sometimes tinged buff or brown, cap and conspicuous long crest blackish, and upperparts mid grey, washed olive. Lores, face and underparts whitish, with orange-buff flanks. The whitish or buffy forehead, blackish cap and crest (often carried erect), conspicuous large dark eye set in a pale face and lack of a black bib are distinctive. Separated from Tufted Titmouse, by its whitish (not black) forehead, black cap and longer and fuller crest. The juvenile is rather duller and much more similar to juvenile Tufted Titmouse, but its upperparts are more brownish or olive-washed, not so clean grey, usually with a whitish forehead and a narrow dark line back from the bill (forehead brownish on Tufted Titmouse). Juveniles are separated from juvenile Plain Titmouse, a possible source of confusion in westernmost Texas, by their rufous-washed flanks. In central Texas Black-crested Titmouse hybridises with Tufted Titmouse, and hybrids typically show a rufous or brown forehead and a sooty-black or dark grey crest with variable amounts of grey (sometimes the cap is entirely grey; see Hybrids).

**SEX/AGE** Sexes rather similar, females averaging slightly duller and less glossy black on the cap and crest (but birds with a greyish crest may be hybrids with Tufted Titmouse: see below). Juvenile distinct, with the forehead drab-white, crown and crest brownish, only slightly darker than the light drab upperparts (which are rather browner than adult's), the greater coverts fringed off-white with darker centres (not uniformly grey), and the underparts duller, with the breast washed dull buff and the flanks duller cinnamon-buff. 1st adult as adult, but usually retains the juvenile secondaries and a variable number of primaries and primary coverts, which contrast with the new tertials and greater coverts.

**VOICE** Similar to that of Tufted Titmouse, although more vocal and most calls are louder, slightly sharper and more nasal. Calls include a nasal, sibilant *si-si-cha-cha* (the 'chick-a-dee' call), *pete-chee-chee-chee*, a scolding *cher-cher-cher-cher-cher-cher*, *vet vet*, *vet vet*, or *enk enk* and also a grating *redeck redeck*. Contact call a thin but full and slightly explosive *tsit* or *tseet*, in anxiety gives a high, thin *see-see-see*, and in excitement a rapid *sit-sit-sit* (all identical to calls of Tufted Titmouse). Song usually consists of 4–7 (2–10) repetitions of monosyllabic, mellow but ringing whistles at various speeds, e.g. *piu-piu-piu-piu...* or *p'lu-p'lu-p'lu...*; variants are a slurred *tyur-tyur-tyur...* and (apparently rather less frequently) disyllabic motifs, e.g. *peter, peter, peter...* with the second note higher than the first (variations with the second note of each motif lower-pitched are rather rarer than in Tufted). Individual males have repertoires of 7–12 different song types, and neighbouring males have a similar repertoire, often matching song types when countersinging, but, unlike Tufted Titmouse, they will frequently sing simultaneously. (Largely after Lemon 1968.)

**DISTRIBUTION AND MOVEMENTS** In the **USA** breeds in **Texas** on the Edwards plateau and in the Rio Grande and Nueces valleys, east and north to Young, Eastland, San Saba, Llano, Kendall, Bexar, Atascosa, Bee and Refugio Cos. (to Refugio city only), and north to Midland, Borden and Kent Cos. (and recorded Lubbock Co. in the autumn). Also a possibly disjunct population in the Texas panhandle, in the Pease river drainage in Motley, Cottle, Foard and Wilbarger Cos. and the drainage of the Prairie Dog Town fork of the Red river in Randall and Armstrong Cos., extending to SW **Oklahoma** in Harmon, Jackson and Tillman Cos. (and also recorded from Kiowa and Cotton Cos. and, in April 1985, Comanche Co.). Also occurs in Trans-Pecos Texas in the Sierra Vieja and Chisos and Davis mountains in Jeff Davis, Presidio and Brewster Cos. Range in Texas widely misrepresented in the literature (e.g. Oberholser 1974 and AOU 1957, 1983, where stated to be resident east to Houston and Grimes Co.; see Dixon 1955, Phillips 1986); this is largely the result of the confusion caused by hybridisation with Tufted Titmouse and the occasional winter wanderings of both species. Accidental Weymouth, **Massachusetts** (AOU 1983). Found in northern **Mexico** in northern **Coahuila** in the Sierra del Carmen (presumably contiguous with the population in Trans-Pecos Texas), and then the eastern slopes of the Sierra Madre Oriental and much of the coastal plain of eastern Mexico in eastern **Coahuila** (west to Sabinas, the Sierra de la Madera Sur Ocampo and Sierra San Marcos and Sierra de la Gavia (southwest and southeast of Monclova respectively)); central and eastern **Nuevo Leon** (west to Lampazos and Santa Catarina); **Tamaulipas** (west to Jaumave); the mountains of SE **San Luis Potosi** (northwest to Rio Verde and south to Tamazunchale); NE **Hidalgo** (west to Jacala and Metztitlan), and northern **Veracruz** (south to at least Papantla, including Juana Ramirez island in Lake Tamiahua); with a disjunct population in central Veracruz on the Sierra de los Tuxtlas. Also recorded, perhaps just as a vagrant, in easternmost **Chihuahua** (Santa Rica, southeast of Ojinaga) and eastern **Guanajuato** (San Miguel de Allende).

**HABITAT** Dry forest and scrub and, especially in the winter, city suburbs and shade trees in towns. Generally avoids dense tropical evergreen and montane coniferous forests. Moving from north to south, in the Texas panhandle and SW Oklahoma inhabits riparian woodland, such as cottonwood, from c. 750–1065 m. On the mesquite plains of north-central Texas, restricted to riparian woodland in the canyons and juniper-oak woodland on the slopes of adjacent mesas (with the spread of mesquite onto the prairies, Black-crested Titmouse has expanded away from the major watercourses; mesquite may, however, be a marginal habitat, with birds preferring to forage in oaks when available). On the broken hills of the southern Edwards plateau, found at up to 750 m in live oak or oak-juniper woodland. On the plains of the Rio Grande of SW Texas and the coastal plains of eastern Mexico, found in riparian woodland and, in lower densities, in semi-arid thorn scrub with mesquite (may disperse into the more arid scrubland outside the breeding season). Also recorded at c. 250 m in evergreen forest on the floodplain of the Rio Corona in western Tamaulipas. Further inland in Mexico, on the Gulf slope of the Sierra Madre Oriental, found in dry forests of pine-oak, pinyon and oak-sweetgum up to c. 1370 m, following suitable habitat along watercourses into Hidalgo to 1525 m and into the interior mountain ranges of San Luis Potosí to 1675 m. Further west, in the interior desert areas, largely montane. In the Trans-Pecos region of SW Texas found at 305–2135 m (although the lower records may be largely in winter; in the Davis mountains breeds at 1525–1675 m in riparian timber, pine and oak-juniper woodlands, in the Sierra Vieja in riparian timber, and in the Chisos mountains above 1370 m in pinyon-juniper-oak), and in adjacent NW Coahuila occurs in the Sierra del Carmen at 1460–2285 m in oak and pine-oak woodland. In the far south, recorded at 150 m in pine-oak forest in the Sierra de los Tuxtlas in Veracruz.

**POPULATION** Generally common, with high populations on the Edwards plateau and Davis mountains of Texas and the Sierra del Carmen of northern Coahuila, although very uncommon at the southern extremity of its range in the Sierra de los Tuxtlas of Veracruz. Oberholser (1974) suggests that Black-crested Titmouse has spread eastwards in Texas at the expense of Tufted Titmouse, but the boundary between the two species has remained more or less static throughout the 20th century, with no indication of an eastward expansion of Black-crested (Dixon 1990). With the spread of mesquite and the invasion of prairie by brushlands, however, more habitat may be available to Black-crested Titmouse in certain parts of the range.

**HABITS** Active and confiding, but rather less pugnacious than Tufted Titmouse. Found singly or in pairs, although in the autumn forms family parties and in the winter may form loose flocks of up to six birds. These break up by early February, when territories are established. Females are rather more vociferous during the laying period than female Tufted Titmouse, and the species is on the whole rather less secretive during the breeding season than Tufted. Recorded roosting in a clump of Spanish moss. Food insects, spiders and berries, with Pecan nuts and acorns important in the winter, and may forage in more open cover than Tufted Titmouse.

**BREEDING BIOLOGY** Season in Texas late February–early June. The nest is placed in a hole in a tree, usually living, also in stumps, posts and telephone poles. Often takes over abandoned woodpecker holes, and will use nestboxes. Nests recorded at 1–7 m above ground, and may reuse the same cavity from year to year. The nest is made of fur, wool, feathers, lichen, moss, grass, leaves and bark and, as with Tufted Titmouse, often contains a cast snakeskin; excess space in the cavity may be filled with moss. Built exclusively by the female? Clutch 6 (4–7): eggs white or pinkish-white with reddish-brown speckles, often concentrated at the larger end; 17 x 13.5 mm (*P. a. atricristatus*). Female incubates, period unknown.

**DESCRIPTION** *P. a. sennetti* **Adult Male**: *In fresh plumage* (about September–March), forehead buffy or whitish, sometimes tinged rusty; longer feathers of rear forecrown tipped blackish, sometimes a narrow black median line running back from base of bill. Crown sooty-black, rear feathers elongated in marked crest. Upperparts (including lesser coverts) mid-light grey, all except nape, upper mantle and rump tinged olive-brown; uppertail-coverts brownish-grey. Tail dark brownish-grey, T1–T5 fringed olive-grey. Wings dark brownish-grey, primary coverts narrowly fringed olive-grey, median and greater coverts, tertials, secondaries and inner primaries fringed olive-grey, P3–P7 fringed pale grey inwards of emarginations. Lores and eyering whitish. Cheeks, ear-coverts and sides of neck pale grey. Underparts off-white, washed grey on breast, flanks orange-buff, vent and undertail-coverts faintly washed buff. Axillaries buff, underwing-coverts whitish. *In worn plumage* (April–August), mantle purer grey, wing and tail feathers browner, fringes on wing feathers abraded and bleached paler, underparts duller, drabber and more uniform, flanks paler, more buff. **Bare Parts**: Iris dark; bill black; legs and feet dark bluish. **Adult Female**: As male, but cap and crest average less intensely black (sometimes grey: Phillips 1986), crest slightly shorter, flanks average slightly paler. **Juvenile**: Forehead pale grey-white, feathers variably tipped dark drab, crown, crest and nape dark drab, feathers vaguely fringed paler. Upperparts light drab. Tail, wing-coverts and tertials light greyish-drab, lesser and median coverts narrowly fringed pale buffish-grey, greater coverts narrowly fringed and tipped pale grey, tertials and tail fringed dull olive-buff, T6 narrowly and diffusely fringed off-white (tail feathers rather narrower than on adult, although not pointed). Alula and primary coverts dark greyish-drab, primary coverts narrowly fringed pale grey. Secondaries and primaries dark greyish-drab, inner secondaries narrowly fringed pale dull olive-buff, outer secondaries fringed buffish-grey, P2–P10 narrowly fringed pale grey-white, more broadly so inwards of emarginations on P3–P5. Lores, cheeks and ear-coverts pale buffish-grey. Throat and breast pale grey-white, remainder of underparts dirty white, washed dull buff, flanks washed pale cinnamon-buff. **1st Adult**: See Sex/Age. **Measurements**: Wing of male 76 (chord 70–80), of female 76 (chord 68–79); tail of male 63.5–73, of female 58.5–72; bill 11.9–13.6; tarsus 18–21.5. Weight 15.5–20.9 g.

**MOULT** Adult post-breeding complete (August). Post-juvenile incomplete, includes the greater coverts, tertials, tail, often the four outer primaries, and occasionally some inner secondaries, but usually not the primary coverts (August–December).

**GEOGRAPHICAL VARIATION** Slight, with a cline of decreasing size running north-south. Three races recognised.

*P. a. paloduro* Two populations: (i) Texas panhandle and SW Oklahoma: (ii) mountains of SW Texas in the Trans-Pecos and NW Coahuila (Sierra del Carmen), and presumably easternmost Chihuahua, wandering in winter to lower elevations (Rio Grande Village). Intergrades with nominate *atricristatus* in western Coahuila. Poorly marked. As *sennetti*, but upperparts slightly greyer, little or no rusty tinge on forehead, wing and tail feathers slightly darker and browner, underparts duller and greyer, flanks average darker; sexual dimorphism may be reduced, and crest of both sexes deeper black. Averages *c.* 4 mm longer-winged. Includes 'dysleptus', Trans-Pecos Texas and northern Coahuila, reportedly slightly paler with less olive upperparts. Wing (chord) of male 71.5–81, of female 69–77; tail of male 62–73, of female 61–70.

*P. a. sennetti* Central and southern Texas south to Brooks Co. and west to Terrell Co. Presumably intergrades with *paloduro* in western Texas. Hybridises with Tufted Titmouse on eastern boundary of range (see Hybrids). See Description.

*P. a. atricristatus* Extreme southern Texas in the lower Rio Grande valley (Starr, Hidalgo and Cameron Cos.), and Mexico (excluding range of *paloduro*). Intergrades with *sennetti* in southern Texas and northern Nuevo Leon. Poorly marked. As *sennetti*, but forehead pale buff to white, more often with a fine black central line back from the bill, crest of male averages longer and deeper black, upperparts slightly darker and in fresh plumage rather more distinctly tinged olive, underparts slightly duller, washed more greyish-buff, and flanks may be slightly brighter and more orange. Smaller, averages *c.* 4.5 mm shorter-winged. Wing of male, 64–77 (chord 65–76), of female 63–69 (chord 63–73); tail of male 56–72, female 55.5–70; bill 11.3–13.7; averages largest in interior Mexico.

**HYBRIDS** Well-marked hybrids with Tufted Titmouse occur over a rather narrow zone, around 50–100 km wide, from the coast of Texas at Corpus Christi northwards, in the west through Nueces, Live Oak, Bexar, Lampasas and Eastland Cos., and in the east through Refugio, Victoria, Bastrop, Williamson, McLennan and Tarrant Cos., to Jack and Wise Cos., with an isolated record from Concho Co. (see figure 100.3). This coincides with the junction of the moist sub-humid biotype, in which Tufted Titmouse is found in denser forest and on the floodplains, and the dry sub-humid biotype, where Black-crested Titmouse favours juniper-oak woodland. The breeding ranges of the two species do not come into contact everywhere along this zone, rather only where their preferred wooded habitats of deciduous forest and juniper-oak woodland abut (generally along NE-SW corridors). In SW Oklahoma, hybrids have been recorded from Jackson Co. (and

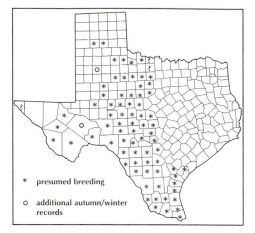

*Figure 100.1  Distribution of Black-crested Titmouse in Texas by counties.*

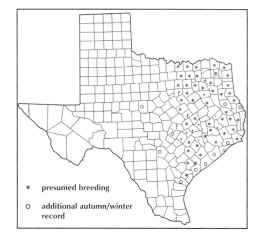

*Figure 100.2  Distribution of Tufted Titmouse in Texas by counties.*

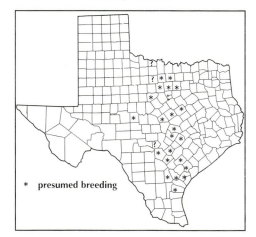

*Figure 100.3  Distribution of Tufted x Black-crested Titmouse hybrids in Texas by counties.*

probably from elsewhere within the range in Oklahoma: see Sutton 1967). Within the zone, resident birds are hybrids. 'Pure' individuals may wander into the hybrid zone or even into the range of the other species, and exceptionally, may stay to breed, e.g. an influx of Tufted Titmice into the range of Black-crested at San Antonio in 1886/87 resulted in local hybridisation. Any vagrant Tufted Titmice which remain to breed are, however, apparently assimilated into Black-crested populations by repeated back-crossing or selective removal of their offspring, or both (Dixon 1990). There are no areas where resident populations of 'pure' Black-crested and 'pure' Tufted Titmice meet and interbreed (although on the Colorado river in Bastrop and Travis Cos. individuals resembling both species, as well as hybrids, have been recorded). Hybrids vary from the parent species in two obvious respects. Firstly, the colour of the forehead may vary from black (pure Tufted) through brown and buff to pale buff or whitish (pure Black-crested). Secondly, the colour of the cap and crest varies from grey (pure Tufted) through various mixtures of grey and black, or blackish feathers fringed or tipped grey, to black (pure Black-crested, although there is some variation in the intensity of black in Black-crested, with females averaging duller). Thus, the first indication of the presence of Black-crested genes in a Tufted Titmouse is a brown forehead, whilst grey fringes to the crown feathers or a rufous forehead are an indication of Tufted genes in a Black-crested.

**RELATIONSHIPS** Forms a superspecies with Tufted and Plain Titmice, and indeed, often considered conspecific with Tufted. Dixon (1955) found that Black-crested and Tufted Titmice interbreed in a narrow zone of hybridisation in Texas. Mixed pairs are formed freely and apparently at random within the zone, irrespective of the colour of the bird's cap. On the basis of this, and the similarities in ecology and behaviour, Dixon considered them conspecific, a conclusion followed by the AOU (1983). Central Texas clearly forms a zone of secondary contact between the two titmice, where two populations, once separated, have now come together again. However, rather than a gradual intergradation of characters (to form a cline), there is a narrow hybrid zone, sometimes merely the width of a few titmouse territories. In assessing whether the two birds should be treated as one or two species, the dynamics of the hybrid zone must be considered. Should the zone be expanding, then any barriers to interbreeding are disappearing and the two forms will eventually intergrade smoothly. Should the zone contract (or remain stable), there must be barriers to interbreeding and, eventually, full reproductive isolation may be achieved. In Texas, the hybrid zone has been stable throughout the 20th century (Dixon 1990), indicating that hybrids are selected against at the margins of the zone, and, if this is the case, barriers to interbreeding may be developing, although, as Dixon reported random interbreeding, neither behaviour (e.g. voice or display) nor ecological factors seem to be hindering hybridisation. The hybrids may, however, be at a selective disadvantage. This, and the marked difference in size between Tufted and Black-crested Titmice in Texas (Tufted being c. 5 mm longer-winged), hints at rather different ecological requirements in their respective moist and humid habitats, a factor which may serve to confine the hybrids to the narrow zone where these habitats meet, the hybrids having a selective advantage in the zone of transition between the two habitat types. Turning to recent biochemical studies, Braun et al. (1984) found that the protein differences between Black-crested and Tufted Titmice, although small, were of a magnitude frequently observed between undoubtedly distinct species. They placed the separation of the two forms at c. 240,000 years ago, and suggested that the narrowness of the zone might imply a genetic barrier to introgression outside the limits of the hybrid zone. Avise & Zink (1988) and Gill & Slikas (1992) found, however, that the difference in the mtDNA between Tufted and Black-crested Titmice was relatively small and, although similar to that of other rather closely related species pairs, was smaller than the variation recorded within some single widespread species. The conflicting results may be reconciled by supposing that Black-crested and Tufted Titmice are old, long-standing species which exchanged genetic material through hybridising events in the late Pleistocene (hence their genetic similarity), with a continued, albeit limited, 'leak' of DNA across the modern hybrid zone. Hence, biochemical evidence fails to resolve the issue of specific status, and, pending a better understanding of the dynamics of the hybrid zone, it seems best to follow Sibley & Monroe (1990) and treat Tufted and Black-crested Titmice as two distinct species (see also Tufted Titmouse).

**REFERENCES** Allen (1907), Bent (1946), Dixon (1955, 1990).

# 101 YELLOW-BROWED TIT *Sylviparus modestus*          **Plate 12**

This aberrant tit is close to a leaf-warbler in general coloration, and is easy to overlook. Its strangely sporadic distribution may be a reflection of its inconspicuous appearance, or may indicate very specific habitat requirements.

**IDENTIFICATION** Length 100 mm (4 in). Small. Upperparts olive-green to greyish-olive, with a variable but often ill-defined pale olive-buff wing-bar. Narrow yellowish-white eyering. The short, bright yellow supercilium extending backwards from the eye is usually concealed (although spread in alarm or courtship), but it often shows a slight crest. The underparts vary from dull pale yellow to dull pale grey with a slight yellowish wash. With atypical plumage for a tit, in mixed-species foraging flocks it is easily overlooked among warblers, with which it shares a generally olive and yellow plumage with a contrasting yellow patch at the bend of the wing. Its short crest, when raised (often in agitation or excitement), is distinctive, however, as are the pale eyering, stubbier bill, stocky pale blue-grey legs and feet, and its lack of a prominent long pale supercilium or dark eyestripe. Distinguished from female and immature Fire-capped Tits by its crest, much less obvious single wingbar, lack of a paler rump or distinct pale tertial fringes (although the west Himalayan race does have diffuse pale tips and fringes to the tertials), and usually duller underparts. Distinguished from Green Shrike-Babbler and flowerpeckers by its daintier build, its much more slender bill, its crest and its much livelier, more acrobatic demeanour.

**SEX/AGE** Sexes similar. Juvenile very similar to the adult, although in the hand the tail feathers may average slightly narrower and more pointed, with a slightly concave tip to the inner web of T6. 1st adult as adult.

**VOICE** Apparently complex and not well understood. Contact calls include a thin but emphatic *tsit*, *psit* or *pit*, given with varying emphasis, and a fuller *chip*, *chup* or *tchup* (recalling the '*zup*' of Long-tailed Tit); these may be alternated in an irregular sequence, e.g. *psit*, *tchup*, *psit*, *psit*, *tchup*, *psit*...; and also sometimes a rapid trilling or scolding *tszizizizi*, *tszizizi*..., or *si-si-si-si-si-si*. A phrase composed of 1–5 ringing, almost metallic units, *pli-pli-pli-pli*... (or more obviously disyllabic *pili-pili-pili*...), and a phrase of 1–6 mellower, more nuthatch-like whistled units, *piu-piu-piu-piu*... or *tiu-tiu-tiu-tiu*... (sometimes repeated in faster and shriller series, containing as many as 15 units), may be the song. (Fleming 1973 notes the song as a high, squeaky *tee*, repeated 5–8 times over a 5-second period (but this was thought probably to be an alarm call by Löhrl 1981), and the alarm as a very high-pitched, buzzing *tzee-tzee*, whilst Ali & Ripley 1983 give the song as an incessant, thin, shrill *zee-zi zee-zi zee-zi*...).

**DISTRIBUTION AND MOVEMENTS** The Himalayas from western **Kashmir** in **NW India** (the Pir Panjal range and Srinagar, although may not breed in these areas) and Ladakh (where collected in 1873 both near Kharbu and at Leh in August; status in these areas unclear), east through **Himachal Pradesh**, northern **Uttar Pradesh** (Kumaon), **Nepal**, **Sikkim** and **Bhutan** to **Arunachal Pradesh** (recorded east to the Dibang valley district), extending north of the main range into SE **Tibet** along the Sun Kosi river to Nyalam and the Tsangpo river to Tangmai and Trulung (Pome district). In **NE India** found in the hills of **Nagaland**, **Manipur**, southern **Assam** in Cachar (eastern Barail range) and perhaps **Meghalaya?**, while in **Myanmar** (**Burma**) known from Mount Victoria in the southern Chin hills, the northeast (south to about Gulang) and from the Kengtung

region in the Southern Shan States. In western **China** found in central **Sichuan** in the mountains bordering the Red Basin from Guan Xian south to Xichang, including Dayi, Tianquan and Emei Shan and in NW **Yunnan** in the Gaoligong Shan, Salween-Mekong divide south to around Baoshan, Mekong-Yangtze divide and Lijiang mountains, and around Bingzhongluo ('Gomba-La'). There are also populations, possibly disjunct, in NE **Guizhou** (Jiangkou), northern **Guangxi** (Maoershan, Xing'an and Ziyuan; Vuilleumier 1993), northern **Guangdong** in the Ba Bao Shan (northwest of Ruyuan), and NW **Fujian** in the Huanggang Shan, and also reported to have been collected near Fuzhou in coastal Fujian in the winter (Caldwell & Caldwell 1931). Resident in NW **Thailand** on Doi Pha Hom Pok and Doi Inthanon, and presumably on some other high peaks with significant areas of forest above 1700 m in Chiang Mai province. In northern **Laos** recorded from Phou Bia in Tranninh in December 1946. Occurs in **Vietnam** in northern Tonkin (Fansipan) and South Annam on the Da Lat plateau. Resident, but may undertake some local dispersal (e.g. western Himalayas) and altitudinal movements.

**HABITAT** Forest, especially oaks. In the drier NW Himalayas, noted in summer in willows and Apricot orchards, wintering in Ban Oak forest, deciduous jungle and gardens. Further east in the Himalayas, breeds in oak, rhododendron and mixed forest (also pure coniferous forests?), mossy forests with plenty of epiphytes, and also in scrub near the treeline, descending in winter to evergreen and rhododendron forests and scrub. On Mount Victoria in western Burma similarly found in mossy hill evergreen forest, occasionally in adjacent pines, and recorded from hill evergreen forest in NE India, Vietnam and Thailand, but in SW China also in spruce, fir and rhododendron forest in NW Yunnan and in subalpine pines in Sichuan. Favours the temperate zone. In the western Himalayas of NW India, summers at c. 2100–3000 m and recorded in Ladakh at 3600 m, wintering from 1200 to 2400 m; in Nepal summers at 2000–2800 m, occasionally up to 3250 m, with breeding noted at 2000–2440 m, and winters at 1500–2800 m, with an exceptional autumn record at 4265 m on the Gandak-Kosi watershed (Smythies 1947). In the eastern Himalayas, recorded at 1980–3350 m in summer and 1525–3400 m in winter (in Arunachal Pradesh, undated records at 900–3100 m) and noted in SE Tibet at c. 2000–2130 m. In NE India recorded in the Naga hills above 2350 m, in western Burma on Mount Victoria at 2400–3000 m, and in NE Burma at 1830–3350 m. In SW China recorded at 1500–2800 m in Sichuan, in NW Yunnan found from 2440 m in winter to a minimum of 4270 m in summer (Greenway 1933), in Guizhou at 450–2200 m (March–April), in Guangxi at 1900 m in summer, and in the higher mountains of NW Fujian at c. 615–2000 m. In NW Thailand found at 1700–2590 m, in northern Vietnam at 2000–2800 m, in southern Vietnam at 1500–2590 m, and recorded in winter in Laos (Tranninh) around 2800 m.

**POPULATION** Generally fairly common, at least locally, although on the edges of the range, in the western Himalayas (east to the Dhaulagiri massif in central Nepal) and in NW Thailand uncommon.

**HABITS** Generally rather quiet and inconspicuous, and easily overlooked. Found singly, in pairs or in small parties in summer, but in winter often joins mixed-species foraging flocks. Forages in the canopy and mid storey, less frequently in the shrub layer, and actions include typical tit-like acrobatics, although its restless flitting through the foliage, with nervous wing-flicks, also recalls a leaf-warbler. Breeding adults feeding young are bold and fearless. Food mainly insects, but also seeds.

**BREEDING BIOLOGY** Poorly known. Season in Himalayas April–May, and recently fledged young noted on Mount Victoria on 11 May. The nest is placed in a natural cavity in a tree, 0.4–7 m above ground, with a very small entrance, a slit *c.* 17 x 45–50 mm or a more circular hole some 30 mm in diameter. It is a foundation of moss, lined with a pad of hair and fur. Clutch 4–6: eggs white. Young fed by both sexes.

**DESCRIPTION** *S. m. modestus* **Adult**: *In fresh plumage* (August–April), forehead pale greyish-olive with slightly darker feather centres, grading to olive-green on crown, sides of neck, rear ear-coverts, mantle, scapulars and back, the feathers of the crown and nape with vague darker centres. Rump and uppertail-coverts slightly brighter, more yellowish olive-green. Tail dark grey-brown, feathers fringed yellowish olive-green, broadly so at base. Wing-coverts grey-brown, lesser and median coverts broadly fringed olive-green, greater coverts fringed olive-green and with broad but diffuse pale olive-drab tips forming a broad wingbar, best defined on inner wing; dark centres on coverts almost fully concealed. Alula dark grey-brown, fringed olive-green, larger feathers pale olive-grey on outer web. Primary coverts dark grey-brown, fringed olive-green. Flight feathers grey-brown, tertials slightly paler on inner webs; tertials and secondaries fringed olive-green and diffusely tipped dull drab; P3–P10 fringed olive-green, fringes paler and present only inwards of emarginations on P3–P6, P2 fringed pale buff on outer web. Marginal wing-coverts dull pale yellow. Lores, cheeks and ear-coverts as forehead; narrow pale olive-drab eyering. Short bright yellow supercilium back from leading edge of eye. Chin pale olive-drab with slightly darker mottling. Throat, breast, sides of belly and undertail-coverts pale greyish-olive, flanks washed buffish-olive, centre of belly and vent pale grey, variably washed olive-yellow to pale buffish-yellow. Axillaries pale grey, washed olive-yellow, underwing-coverts whitish, tipped pale yellow. *In worn plumage* (May–July), upperparts duller, darker and greyer, especially head, nape and mantle (olive margins to feathers abrade); supercilium paler; wing-coverts, especially greater coverts, greyer and

browner as fringes abrade, tips to greater coverts bleached paler (dull pale grey), thus wingbar paler and narrower; fringes at base of primaries bleached paler; underparts duller and greyer with reduced yellow tones, especially in the centre of the belly and vent. **Bare Parts**: Iris dark brown; upper mandible dark horn, blue-slate at base and greyish-white at sides of distal half, lower mandible blue-slate with a dark tip; legs, feet and claws blue-grey. **Juvenile**: As adult (see Sex/Age). **1st Adult**: As adult. **Measurements**: Wing of male 52–65, of female 54–62; tail of male 32–46, of female 32–42; bill 8–10; tarsus 13–17. Weight 5–9 g.

**MOULT** Adult post-breeding complete (July in SE Tibet). Post-juvenile partial, probably not including tertials, greater coverts or tail (September in eastern Himalayas).

**GEOGRAPHICAL VARIATION** Slight. Three subspecies recognised.

*S. m. simlaensis* Western Himalayas east to Kumaon, northern Uttar Pradesh. As nominate *modestus*, but upperparts brighter and yellower, yellowish olive-green, with brighter and yellower fringes to tertials, flight feathers and tail, and tertials more obviously tipped and fringed paler; underparts brighter and yellower, washed pale yellow overall, with a slight buff tinge. Wingbar as nominate *modestus*, but shows slightly less contrast with primary coverts (marginally paler feather centres to coverts and flight feathers). Wing of male 57–61, of female 58–59; tail of male 35–40, of female 36–38.

*S. m. modestus* Himalayas from Nepal eastwards, NE India, Burma, China, north Vietnam and Thailand. See Description.

*S. m. klossi* Da Lat plateau, south Annam, Vietnam. Very similar to *simlaensis*, and perhaps best synonymised with it. Vaurie (1957b) gave details of a single bird which differed from *simlaensis* in its slightly duller and greyer, more greenish (less yellowish) upperparts and fringes to the tail feathers, and much-reduced yellow supercilium. Snow (1957) could not confirm these differences, though it is possibly smaller (wing of male 56–61, of female 55–59). Given the wide gap in distribution between *simlaensis* and *klossi*, its seems best to maintain separate subspecific names.

**RELATIONSHIPS** This aberrant tit has no close relations within the family Paridae. With its atypical coloration, with a warbler- or flycatcher-like appearance, the Yellow-browed Tit is sometimes considered to represent a 'primitive' stage in the evolution of the genus *Parus*. Indeed, Löhrl (1981), although concluding that its tit-like acrobatics and hole-nesting habits placed it with the Paridae, could not rule out a relationship with the Regulidae (goldcrests and kinglets).

**REFERENCES** Ali & Ripley (1983), Fleming (1973), Löhrl (1981).

This gaudy tit is the largest member of the family, yet can be surprisingly elusive in the canopy of tall forest trees.

**IDENTIFICATION** Length 205 mm (8 in). A very large black and yellow tit. The male has the crown and crest bright yellow (black in central Vietnam and southern Laos), the upperparts black, glossed greenish-blue on the mantle, the throat and upper breast black, and the remainder of the underparts bright yellow. The long crest is erected when excited. The female and juvenile are a little duller. A very distinctive tit, although in silhouette it may recall one of the crested bulbuls.

**SEX/AGE** Sexes marginally distinct, the female differing from the male in having the upperparts dark bottle-green rather than black, the wings blackish-brown with dull olive fringes to the coverts and flight feathers, and the sides of the head sooty-brown, washed olive, grading to yellowish olive-green on the bib. The juvenile is duller still than the female, sooty-black, lacking any gloss to the plumage, with a shorter crest and yellow-white tips to the greater coverts. The sexes are similar in juvenile plumage, juvenile males moulting from sooty olive-brown to black on the bib, females to olive. 1st adult as adult, but retains a variable number of pale-tipped juvenile greater coverts, and shows moult contrasts between the fresh tertials and the worn flight feathers, primary coverts and alula.

**VOICE** Quite noisy, with a limited repertoire of distinctive calls. Perhaps most characteristic are a flat, stony, rattling *chi-dip*, *tri-trip* or *tji-jup* and a fast, shrill, squeaky, whistled phrase, *tria-tria-tria*, *tcheery-tcheery-tcheery* or *squear-squear-squear*, given with varying emphasis but generally rising in pitch with each note. When very agitated, the rattle and some truncated squeals (*sque-u*) may be combined (the squeals then recalling the flight call of parakeets). Also gives a quiet, slightly squeaky *whit* or *quit* and a loud, abrupt, ringing *vheet* or *weet*, slightly rising and 'inquisitive' and sometimes given in couplets (this call may recall a cuckoo-shrike or bulbul). Song rather different, a series of *c.* 5 loud, clear, mellow, whistled *chiu* or *piu* units, *piu-piu-piu-piu-piu*, the phrase lasting *c.* 1.5–2 seconds and repeated at regular intervals.

**DISTRIBUTION AND MOVEMENTS** The foothills of the **Himalayas** from Rupa Tal in central **Nepal** east through **NE India** in **Darjeeling** and **Sikkim**, also **Bhutan** and **Arunachal Pradesh** and the adjacent plains of **Assam**, and **Nagaland**, **Manipur**, **Mizoram** and **Meghalaya**. Breeds in SE **Bangladesh** in the Chittagong hills and throughout most of **Myanmar** (**Burma**). In southern **China** confined to **Hainan island** and western and southern **Yunnan** (in the south in the Mekong drainage at Xishuangbanna (= Mengla area) and Simao) and SW **Guangxi Zhuang** (including Long Chow), with a disjunct population in central **Fujian** (with no records from intervening areas in Guangdong or Hong Kong). In South-East Asia, occurs throughout most of **Thailand** (although absent from the central

plains), extending south in **Malaya** to Johore (including Penang island, but not Singapore); also northern **Laos** and northern **Vietnam** in Tonkin, and in north and central Annam and southern Laos. Status in **Sumatra** enigmatic. 'Sumatra' is given as the type locality of *Melanochlora Sumatrana* by Lesson (1840) and of *Parus flavocristatus* ('isles de la Sonde') by Lafresnaye (1837), but neither specimen can now be traced. A sight record of a flock of 6–10 birds in lowland forest in Utara province in 1938, however, presumably puts the occurrence of the species on the island beyond doubt (van Marle & Voous 1988). Resident throughout the range.

**HABITAT** Deciduous, mixed deciduous and evergreen forest, with preference for light evergreen forest and edge habitats; also bamboo, scrub and second growth and large trees near cultivation. Generally found below 1200 m and throughout the range the species is usually commonest in submontane forest rather than in the lowlands. Occasionally also found in montane areas, with the highest recorded altitudes 1370 m in Nepal, 1460 m in Darjeeling, 1900 m in Sikkim, 1600 m in Arunachal Pradesh, 1680 m in Burma (Bernardmyo), in Malaya 1220 m on Bukit Fraser and 1500 m in the Cameron Highlands and 1100 m on Hainan island (recorded rarely up to 2000 m in China: Etchécopar & Hüe 1983, but in error?). In Indochina, usually found at middle altitudes and in central Annam the race *gayeti* is rarely found below 200 m, is quite common at 1400 m and has been recorded up to 1900 m.

**POPULATION** Rare in the western part of the range in the Himalayas and has declined in Nepal, where, despite reports that the species was fairly common in the late 18th century, now scarce, with few records (most frequently reported from the Churia hills in Chitwan NP). The decline is attributable to habitat destruction. A similar situation prevails in Darjeeling, but further east in the Himalayan foothills the species is still quite common. Generally uncommon in China (although fairly common on Hainan island) and no recent records in Bangladesh, but could still occur there. Very scarce and local in most of Burma, although quite common in the lower Kachin hills and Hukawng valley of northern Burma, and uncommon to locally common in Thailand and Vietnam.

**HABITS** Found in pairs and in parties of 3–12, often joining mixed-species foraging flocks. Usually feeds in the canopy, although also sometimes in the middle storey and in bamboo, and occasionally down to a few feet above ground. Despite its large size and gaudy plumage, often inconspicuous, staying in the tops of tall trees, and best located by call. Favours 'basking in the sun upon some elevated pinnacle point, answering with its loud whistling call a rival both in song and combat of some distant woodland' (Caldwell &

Caldwell 1931). Typically acrobatic, though somewhat slower than other tits. Food insects, also fruit and seeds.

**BREEDING BIOLOGY** Poorly known. Season: India, April–July; southern China (Fujian), April onwards; Burma, April–May; Thailand, April. Nest placed in a hole, crack or crevice in a tree, a pad of green mosses and leaf skeletons lined with hair, plant down and other fibres. Clutch 5–7: eggs white, variably spotted brownish-red with faint lavender or pinkish-grey undermarkings; 20.5 x 16 mm (*M. s. sultanea*).

**DESCRIPTION** *M. s. sultanea* **Adult Male:** *In fresh plumage* (autumn and winter), forehead and crown yellow, feathers of the rear crown elongated into a marked crest. Remainder of upperparts, including lesser and median coverts, black, glossed greenish-blue, especially on mantle and scapulars. Tail, greater and primary coverts and flight feathers black, glossed greenish-blue on fringes of outer webs; concealed inner webs of primaries white at base, T6 occasionally narrowly tipped white on outer web. Lores, cheeks and ear-coverts sooty-black, rear ear-coverts glossed greenish-blue. Throat and breast black, glossed greenish-blue, feathers of lower border of bib tipped yellow. Remainder of underparts yellow, thighs sooty-brown, feathers subterminally white and tipped yellow. Axillaries yellowish, marginal coverts black, under primary coverts sooty-brown, feathers subterminally white and fringed yellow, under secondary coverts white, fringed yellow. *In worn plumage* (summer), upperparts and bib slightly less glossy. **Bare Parts:** Iris brown or reddish-brown; bill black to bluish-slate, upper mandible tipped horn; legs and feet blue-grey or greenish-grey blue, claws horn-brown. **Adult Female:** In fresh plumage as male, but upperparts sooty brown-black, feathers broadly fringed dull oily-green, slightly glossy (overall impression very dark green), outer webs of tail feathers washed blue-green. Wings sooty brown-black, median coverts fringed glossy blue-green, greater coverts and tertials fringed dull olive, secondaries and inner primaries narrowly fringed dull olive-green, slightly paler inwards of emarginations on P3–P6, primary coverts very narrowly fringed glossy blue-green. Lores sooty, ear-coverts and sides of neck sooty-brown, washed olive, grading to yellowish olive-green on throat and breast; feathers of lower bib finely tipped dull yellow (dark feather bases largely concealed). **Juvenile:** As adults, but feathers of the crest shorter and rounded, upperparts sooty-black, pale feather bases revealed by 'loose' plumage. Greater coverts narrowly tipped yellow-white or off-white, most prominent on outer wing, primary coverts sometimes very finely tipped paler. Bib sooty olive-brown, yellow areas of plumage slightly paler. Sexes similar, although males may show a faint blue gloss to the upperparts and a slightly darker and browner bib. **1st Adult:** See Sex/Age. **Measurements:** Wing of male 102–115, of female 94–109; tail of male 83–99, of female 80–95; bill 15–18; tarsus 21–26. Weight 34–49 g.

**MOULT**  Adult  post-breeding  complete

(November–December, India; August–December, Thailand). Post-juvenile partial, includes tertials, tail and some or all greater coverts (July–November, NE India; August, Burma; August–October, Thailand; July–September, Malaya; August, Vietnam).

**GEOGRAPHICAL VARIATION** Overall rather slight, involving the intensity of yellow, and size. The isolated subspecies *gayeti* of central Vietnam and southern Laos, however, is very distinct, with a black cap and crest. Over the rest of South-East Asia and in southern China, a variable proportion of birds show fine black shaft streaks in the crest, and the instability of the feature, which apparently occurs almost randomly, hints at past contact between the yellow- and black-crested groups and subsequent hybridisation. Four subspecies recognised.

*M. s. sultanea* The Himalayan foothills from Nepal to Assam and south to the Kachin hills and Arakan in Burma, Yunnan in SW China, NW Thailand (south to Tak province in the west and extending into NE Thailand in Loei province), northern Laos (south to Tranninh), and northern Vietnam in NW Tonkin. See Description.

*M. s. seorsa* Southern China in Guangxi Zhuang and Fujian. Poorly marked. As nominate *sultanea*, but crest and underparts slightly paler yellow, and some individuals show fine black shaft streaks in the crest feathers. Size as nominate *sultanea*. Wing of male 103–112, of female 100–106. Central Laos (around Nape) and NE Vietnam (NE Tonkin and northern Annam south to c. 18° N) are inhabited by a variable hybrid population of *seorsa* x nominate *sultanea*, and black shaft streaks are also occasionally found in birds from northern Thailand and northern Burma.

*M. s. flavocristata* Hainan island, southern Burma and central and southern Thailand (from the southern portion of the northeastern plateau and the southwest southwards) through the peninsula to Malaya; also this race Sumatra? Intergrades with nominate *sultanea* in northern Thailand and southern Burma (Tenasserim). Poorly marked. As nominate *sultanea*, but crest averages shorter and less profuse, tail only rarely tipped white. Juveniles may show dark shaft streaks in the crest and fine white tips to the tertials and secondaries. Averages slightly smaller. Wing of male 96–109, of female 93–95; tail of male 82–95, of female 62–88. Weight 28–44 g.

*M. s. gayeti* Vietnam in central Annam around the massifs of Col des Nuages (= Hai Van Pass, 16° 12' N, 108° 90' E) and Ba Na, and the adjacent Bach Ma NP (16° 11' N, 107° 50' E), also southern Laos on the Plateau des Bolovens (Phon Set peak, above Thateng; Engelbach 1932); the species was noted, but not subspecifically identified, by Robson *et al.* (1989) in central Annam from about Hue south to around Kontum. As nominate *sultanea*, but male has forehead, crown and crest black glossed blue, and female with forehead and crown black, crest black, more faintly glossed blue (contrasting with the green tone to the upperparts). Also smaller. Wing 91–108, of male 100–106, of female 96–100: tail of male 91, of female 89.

**RELATIONSHIPS** Placed in the monospecific genus *Melanochlora* within the family Paridae, and no obvious affinities, although the black-and-yellow coloration and the conspicuous crest hint at a relationship with Black-lored and Yellow-cheeked Tits.

**REFERENCES** Baker (1932–33), Deignan (1945), Delacour & Jabouille (1931), Lekagul & Round (1991), Ripley (1982).

# 103 LONG-TAILED TIT *Aegithalos caudatus*　　　　　　　Plate 33

The most widespread of the 'long-tailed' tits, this species shows considerable geographical variation and the white-headed northern populations are prone to wander.

**IDENTIFICATION** Length 130–160 mm (5–5.75 in), of which the tail makes up 60–100 mm. A tiny, round-bodied tit with a short stubby bill and a very long, narrow tail. Plumage mainly black and white, with variable amounts of grey and pink. Much geographical variation, but essentially four groups of subspecies: northern birds with a white head and black upperparts showing some pink; European and east Asian populations similar but with blackish lateral crown stripes; and two southern groups around the Mediterranean and in China with greyish upperparts showing little or no pink, often a dark bib, and a relatively short tail. Distinctive throughout the range, the combination of small size, long tail and piebald plumage being unique. In western China, overlaps with three other species of long-tailed tit. Distinguished from Black-browed and Black-throated Tits by the narrower lateral crown stripes (which do not surround the eye in a 'bandit's mask'), dark eye and lack of a well-marked breast band, and similarly distinguished from Sooty Tit by the lack of a breast band.

**SEX/AGE** Sexes similar. Juvenile distinct, being overall darker and browner, with a darker head in which the cheeks and ear-coverts are dusky, accentuating the pale eyering, and generally only the centre of forehead and crown are whitish; the mantle and back are brown (rather than black or grey), and the pink tones in the plumage are much reduced or absent (except on Chinese birds). Juveniles are also rather short-tailed compared with adults (in the hand, the central tail feathers are very short-grown, with T1 = T5, whereas T1= T3 on adults). After the complete post-juvenile moult, 1st adults are identical to adults.

**VOICE** Very vocal. The usual contact calls are an abrupt single *ssrit*, a low, abrupt or clicking but soft and slightly slurred *zup* or *tup*, and a high-pitched, thin, but penetrating and slightly sibilant *tsee-tsee-tsee* (given especially in flight, particularly when the flock is in rapid movement, and by 'lost' individuals isolated from the main flock). In alarm or excitement, and frequently without any apparent provocation, gives a rapid trill, falling in pitch towards the end, a rippling *tsirr*, *tsirrup* or *tsirrrup*; this call is often given in combination with *tsee-tsee* phrases when the flock is moving some distance, and loud, high-intensity versions are given in conflicts between flocks. There is no territorial song, but a quiet twittering and trilling is given by both sexes, especially during aggressive

encounters with other Long-tailed Tits and during copulation. This 'song' is seldom heard, and includes the *tsee* and *tsirrrup* notes rapidly repeated in a jumbled, bubbling chatter. (Partly after Cramp & Perrins 1993.)

**DISTRIBUTION AND MOVEMENTS** Breeds in **Britain** (including the Channel Islands and sporadically on most islands in Inner Hebrides, bred Outer Hebrides in 1939, but absent Isle of Man, Orkney and Shetland), **Ireland** (absent far west) and throughout mainland Europe, north to c. 70° N in **Norway**, 67° N in **Sweden**, 63° N in **Finland** (and sporadically and locally north to 66° N), 65°N in **European Russia** and 61° N in the Urals. Breeds south to the Mediterranean, but absent from higher altitudes in the Alps and Appennines, and only a winter visitor to coastal **Yugoslavia** and parts of southern **Greece**. Resident on many Baltic islands, **Corsica** and **Sicily**, but absent on other Mediterranean islands. In **Turkey** breeds in the southern coastlands, the west and the Black Sea coastlands, with an isolated (?) population in the east around Elazig. Present **Crimea** and **Caucasus**, north to the valley of the Kuban', the Stavropol' uplands and northern foothills of the Great Caucasus, and also the Transcaucasus in **Georgia**, **Armenia** and **Azerbaydzhan**. Occurs very locally in northernmost **Iraq**, in northern and western **Iran** and in SW **Turkmenistan**. Also found in southern **Moldova**, and in southern **Ukraine** in the lower Don and to 51° N in the Ural valley. Local in the Ukraine and **SE Russia**, being generally confined to riverine vegetation along the major rivers (and very common in the lower Volga delta). Breeds east across **Siberia** north to 60–61° N (on the Yenisey sporadically north to Mirnoye at 62° 15' N), east to the Pyagina peninsula on the north coast of the Sea of Okhotsk, Kamchatka (north to c. 60° N), **Sakhalin**, and the southern **Kurile islands** (Urup, Iturup, Kunashir and Shikotan). Found south in Central Asia to the limits of the forest steppe, to 53° N in northern **Kazakhstan** and east of 72° E (in the area of the Kazakh 'melkosopochnik', i.e. low hills and gentle slopes) south to 49° N; occurs in gallery forest along the Irtysh river to Zaysan Nor, to the Saur, Tarbagatay and probably Dzhungarskiy Alatau mountains, and to the Altai and Sayan ranges. In the east, occurs south to Transbaykalia, Ussuriland and Amurland. Breeds in northern and central **Mongolia** in the Hangayn and Hentiyn ranges, also in the northwest to the north of Uvs Nuur and in the Tesin Gol valley, and in the east around Buyr Nuur, the valley of Halhïn Gol and Greater Khingan range. Also NE and central **China**, south and west to NW **Yunnan**, both **North** and **South Korea** (including Cheju island), and most of **Japan** (but absent from the islands of the Nansei Shoto). See also Geographical Variation. Birds from northern Siberia undertake regular migrations during late August–May, with some northward dispersal in autumn (when flocks of hundreds of individuals have been recorded in central Siberia), although the bulk of the movement is to the south. Thus, numbers in southern Siberia are swelled by immigrants in winter, when the species may be numerous as far south as the Zaysan depression in NE Kazakhstan (migrants have also been recorded in the Ili river valley). Numbers may also remain in the north of the species' range (or even further north than the breeding range). In NE China a regular migrant at Beidaihe, coastal Hebei, in mid October–mid November: birds may be nominate *caudatus*, *vinaceus* or intergrades, but in 1989 all were *vinaceus* and in 1990 all were nominate *caudatus*; 1990 also saw the highest total recorded at Beidaihe, 408 bird-days, thought to indicate an irruption that year (also recorded in late December 1990 in **Hong Kong**, although all Hong Kong records are presumed to involve escapes from captivity; Williams *et al.* 1991, 1992). White-headed birds occur in winter south of the breeding range in China, Japan and irregularly south to southernmost South Korea. Northern populations also perform irregular, sometimes large-scale irruptions in the west, when large numbers may reach Finland, the Baltic States and eastern Europe, and much smaller numbers appear in western Europe. These movements peak in mid October, and at least some return to the natal area in the spring. Water-crossings are, however, avoided. Those breeding in mountainous areas presumably undertake some altitudinal movements, spreading onto the adjacent foothills and plains in winter (e.g. in Hebei, NE China). Otherwise, resident throughout the range with some short-range dispersal. An irregular autumn wanderer to the Isles of Scilly (England) and Orkney, the Isle of May and the Outer Hebrides (Scotland), but only one undocumented record on Fair Isle and just two records for Shetland (four on Unst, April 1860; four at Lerwick, November 1988). A flock of 200 white-headed birds was found in the Netherlands in December 1971, but few records of white-headed northern birds in mainland Britain: nominate *caudatus* was recorded in Northumberland in November 1852, with some sight records from the east coast, and one record of *A. c. europaeus* in Kent in 1882. Accidental **Morocco** and **Tunisia**.

**HABITAT** Deciduous and mixed woodland with a well-developed shrub layer, favouring edge habitats. Also scrub, heathland with scattered trees, maquis, bushes and hedges in farmland, and riverine woodland. Avoids pure conifers in the west of the range, but noted in open forests of spruce, fir, larch and Siberian Stone Pine in central Siberia (probably especially forest edge or river-side areas where there is an admixture of broadleaved trees), and in pine forest in Yunnan, SW China. Sometimes visits well-wooded gardens, parks, temple grounds and cemeteries. In winter favours similar habitats, and also reedbeds. In Europe usually breeds below 1000 m, although found very locally up to 1800 m (e.g. in southern Austrian Alps), and ascends to 1300 m in Turkey, 1500 m in the Caucasus and at least 1830 m in Iran. In Japan occurs mainly at 500–1600 m, wandering to lower levels in winter. Also primarily montane in China, where noted at 780–1100 m (400–1800 m) in the Changbai Shan in Jilin, 500 to about 1700 m in the Qin Ling Shan in Shaanxi (also at the foot of the mountains), up to 2925 m in Gansu, 3020 m in Qinghai, 2590 m in northern Sichuan and 3050 m in Yunnan. May move to the lowlands in winter, but still present at 2835–3050 m in Yunnan in January–February.

**POPULATION** Fairly common in western Europe and in China, Korea and Japan, although scarcer towards the edge of the range in northern Scotland and western Ireland. More local and sometimes even scarce in eastern Europe and Siberia and rare on the Kamchatka peninsula, although numbers in southern Siberia are augmented in the winter by immigrants from the north of the range. In Iran, common in the Caspian lowlands but rather scarce in northern Azarbaijan and the Zagros mountains. No major changes in status apparent, although has spread north in Norway since c. 1970 and some expansion in northern Scotland, but there has been a marked decline in Sweden since the 19th century, with a similar decline probably taking place in Finland owing to modern forestry practices. Susceptible to hard winters, following which the population may decline by up to 80%. May take several years to recover from these setbacks, this perhaps due to the high loss of nests (sometimes over 50%) to predators.

**HABITS** Tame and very gregarious, for most of the year forming stable flocks of about 3–30 birds based around the parents and offspring of the previous breeding season, together with any adult 'helpers' that had been involved in raising the brood. May join mixed-species foraging flocks. Periods of quiet feeding alternate with noisy rapid movement, follow-my-leader fashion, to a new area; when traversing open areas the flock gathers together, calling excitedly, before crossing over in single file. The flight is whirring and bouncing, the speed and direction being rather irregular. Individuals separated from the flock become agitated, calling loudly and searching for their companions. Flocks may occasionally amalgamate temporarily, with groups of up to 300 individuals being reported, and where migratory it is probable that siblings migrate together. Members of the flock roost huddled together on a horizontal branch, usually in a thorny thicket, their ruffled plumage forming a ball of feathers (see figure 103.1 , p. 422). The distance between individuals depends on the temperature: on cold nights they are huddled very close (and in very cold weather, they may roost in a hole in the ground, among

*Figure 103.1 Roosting Long-tailed Tits.*

roots or even in snow holes). The position that an individual occupies in the roost plays an important part in its chances of survival, those at the ends dying first in cold weather, so dominant birds occupy the centre of the row. It has been suggested that such communal roosting is essential for survival in this tiny tit, and may be the main reason for its great sociability (Glen & Perrins 1988). The winter flock occupies a well-defended territory, the extent of which depends upon the number of birds in the group. In the late winter and early spring flocks break up, unmated females moving away and pairing with males in adjacent flocks (perhaps usually 'switching sides' during territorial disputes). Display includes a butterfly-like jerky flight in which the male (?) flies up to a height of 5–6 m, alternately fanning and closing the tail before diving vertically down; 3–4 birds may display in quick succession or even simultaneously. Each pair sets up a loosely defended territory within the area occupied by the winter flock of which the male was a member, but continues to roost with other members of the flock until the nest is sufficiently well built to be used as a roost (usually when the dome is completed). The pair then roosts in the nest until the young fledge. The flock may temporarily re-form in cold weather, whilst some individuals remain unmated in the early spring and may then be prone to wander. Forages in the shrub layer and canopy, only occasionally on the ground, delicately picking items from the surface of twigs, leaves and buds. Can hover, and sometimes flycatches. When dealing with an insect too big to swallow immediately, will hang by one foot from a twig and hold the food item in the other foot to peck at it. Food throughout the year largely invertebrates (unlike *Parus* tits), although occasionally also vegetable material in the autumn and winter; recorded drinking sap.

Seldom visits birdtables.

**BREEDING BIOLOGY** Season: mid March–June, Europe and Japan (very exceptionally, fledged young recorded early February, England: Thompson 1992); from March onwards, Iran; March–April, NE China. Most nests are placed in low thorny bushes less than 3 m above ground, but a sizeable minority are sited in a tree fork or against the trunk 6–25 m high, and also suspended among the terminal twigs of conifers, up to 35 m high; there are a few records of nests in holes in the ground. The nest itself is a compact, domed oval ball of moss, woven with cobwebs and hair, covered with up to 3,000 flakes of lichen (which provide excellent camouflage); average size 160 mm tall x 100 mm diameter, with entrance hole at one side near the top. The lining is composed of small feathers, often around 1,500, with a maximum of 2,680 recorded; feathers may continue to be added during the laying period. The nest is built by both sexes over a period of up to 33 days. Clutch 8–12 (6–15), clutches averaging largest at higher latitudes: eggs white, unmarked or with tiny reddish freckles; 14 x 10.9 mm (nominate *caudatus*). Female incubates, period 12–18 days; she is fed on the nest by the male. Both sexes care for the young, assisted by a variable number of 'helpers' (up to eight have been noted). These are often adults whose own nest has failed (the later in the breeding cycle the nest fails, the more likely the adults are to become helpers). Male and female from the failed pair do not help at the same nest; in cases where the relationship has been established, the helper has been a sibling of the male of the breeding pair (thus helping its brother to breed). Helpers significantly increase the breeding success of the pair. The young fledge after 14–18 days, and are fed by parents and helpers for at least a further 14 days, the family then remaining together throughout the winter. Single-brooded.

**DESCRIPTION** A. c. rosaceus **Adult**: *In fresh plumage* (September–April), forehead, centre of crown and nape white, irregularly spotted dark brown, sides of crown and nape dull black from just in front of the eye (occasionally from the bill) to the sides of the mantle. Upper mantle black, lower mantle and back a mixture of black and dull pink, scapulars and rump largely dull pink, feathers narrowly tipped whitish with some black feather bases revealed. Uppertail-coverts black. Tail black, T4 with distal half of outer web white, extending as a wedge onto tip of inner web, T5–T6 similar but whole outer web white (see figure 103.2 below). Lesser, median and outer greater coverts, primary coverts and alula black, inner greater coverts brown, tipped white and fringed white and pink. Tertials brown, fringed white or buff-white on outer web, secondaries dark brown, fringes as tertials but rather narrower, especially on outermost, primaries sooty-black. Lores and throat off-white, ear-coverts and sides of neck whitish, finely streaked dark brown. Breast, belly and vent off-white, washed beige, sometimes with a vague necklace of darker streaks across the upper breast formed by fine dark brown feather tips. Sides of breast, flanks and undertail-coverts pale pink, feathers tipped white. Thighs pinkish-white. Axillaries and underwing-coverts white. *In worn plumage* (May–August), white tips to scapulars and flanks abraded, these areas becoming darker pink. **Bare Parts**: Iris dark hazel, eyelid yellow to red, depending on age (yellow commonest in adult) but probably also reflecting mood; bill black; legs, feet and claws blackish-brown. **Juvenile**: Lores, forehead, ear-coverts, sides of neck, sides of crown and nape, and upperparts sooty-brown, centre of crown and nape white with some brown spots, distal half of scapulars white, tinged pink or brown. Tail black-brown, T4 with faint whitish marking on distal half of outer web, T5–T6 with outer webs brownish-white, extending slightly onto tip of inner web. Wing-coverts dark brown, inner greater coverts narrowly fringed and tipped buffish-white. Flight feathers as adult, but paler and browner, tertials more narrowly fringed white. Throat, breast and belly white, some feathers of upper breast washed brown, flanks white, washed buff, vent and undertail-coverts light russet to russet-brown. Bill black with yellowish base and tip; legs and feet dull flesh, claws brown. **1st Adult**: As adult. **Measurements**: Wing of male

*Figure 103.2  Tail of adult* A. c. rosaceus.

58–64, of female 57–61.5; tail of male 80–92, of female 72–90, well graduated, T6 42–52 shorter than T2; bill 6–8.2; tarsus 16–18. Weight 6.2–10.4 g (A. c. europaeus).

**MOULT** Adult post-breeding complete (late May–early October, duration c. 80 days). Post-juvenile complete (June–early October).

**GEOGRAPHICAL VARIATION** Complex, with 19 races recognised, divisible into four groups: the *caudatus* group in northern Europe and Asia, the *europaeus* group in southern and western Europe, NE China and Japan, the *alpinus* group in Mediterranean Europe and SW Asia, and the *glaucogularis* group in China. In the regions where the groups meet, there are extensive areas occupied by very variable populations of 'hybrids'. These areas of hybridisation (and probably the whole range of the *europaeus* group) are zones of secondary intergradation, where two populations have met relatively recently.

**THE *CAUDATUS* GROUP** Head and throat white, mantle black with a variable amount of pink.

**A. c. caudatus** Fennoscandia and NE Europe from Poland east through Siberia to Kamchatka, south to northern Mongolia, Amurland, Ussuriland, northern China in NE Nei Mongol (Hulun Nur, Greater Khingan mountains), Heilongjiang and Jilin (south to the Changbai Shan), northern North Korea (south to 40–41° N), Sakhalin, the southern Kurile islands, northern Japan on Hokkaido, Rebun-to and Rishiri-to. Occurs in winter south of the breeding range in China to NE Hebei (Weichang, Qinhuangdao) and Beijing; in Japan south to central Honshu (Chiba-ken) and irregularly south to southernmost South Korea. Intergrades with *europaeus* in Denmark, eastern Germany, southern Poland, southern Ukraine and northern Romania; intergrades with *magnus* in Korea in the area south to 38° N. As *rosaceus*, but head all white, underparts purer white, usually lacking the vague breast band, pink of flanks and belly less extensive (although brighter and purer), tertial and secondary fringes average broader, and dark in tertials sometimes reduced to a shaft streak, although tertials usually dark on inner web. Juvenile as juvenile *rosaceus*, but forehead dirty brown-white and entire underparts dirty off-white, tinged buff on belly. Wing 58–70, of male 60–68, of female 58–67; tail 80–104, of male 88–100, of female 87–99. Includes 'sibiricus' (SE Russia and the Urals east to the Pacific coast, south to NE China; head and underparts purer white, white fringes to tertials and secondaries average broader, especially on inner webs), and 'japonicus' (lower Amurland, Ussuriland, Korea, the Kurile islands, Sakhalin, and Japan; as *sibiricus*, but tertials darker).

**THE *EUROPAEUS* GROUP** Head whitish with broad blackish lateral crown stripes, mantle and throat as *caudatus* group. This group, with races in Europe and eastern Asia, may represent the relict of a formerly more continuous distribution, but is more likely to be a collection of more or less stable hybrid populations resulting from the intermingling of the *caudatus* and *alpinus/glaucogu-*

*laris* groups. Although the various races are better marked than those in the *caudatus* group, there is great individual variation and some subspecies are particularly unstable.

**A. c. rosaceus** British Isles. Well marked. See Description. Irish birds tend to show a dark-spotted gorget.

**A. c. aremoricus** Western France, east to Blois and south to about Poitou, also the Channel Islands and Ile d'Yeu. Intergrades with *taiti* in the south. Poorly marked. As *rosaceus,* but centre of crown and underparts whiter, lateral crown stripes broad and black (although not so broad as in *taiti*). Wing 58.5–61.5.

**A. c. taiti** South and SW France, including Ile d'Oléron, the Pyrénées, northern and NW Spain and Portugal south to the Tejo valley. Intergrades with *irbii* in central Spain and Portugal. Small and dark. As *aremoricus* and *rosaceus,* but lateral crown stripes broader and blacker, upperparts blacker, especially the rump, with less pink. Wing of male 56–64, of female 54–62; tail of male, 75–89, of female 72–83.

**A. c. europaeus** France and Germany south to northern Italy and the north of former Yugoslavia and east to northern Bulgaria and western Romania. Intergrades with *aremoricus* in western France, *taiti* in SW France, *italiae* on the southern slopes of the Alps, and *macedonicus* in southern Yugoslavia and southern Bulgaria. Rare migrant Estonia. Typical individuals as *rosaceus,* but brighter and paler, lateral crown stripes narrower, white crown stripe less obscured by dark spots and streaks, cheeks and ear-coverts less mottled and streaked brown, underparts paler and whiter, less often showing traces of a gorget of dark spots. Very variable: notably, the lateral crown stripe is sometimes broken or almost absent (thus resembling nominate *caudatus,* but always at least some indication of a dark stripe) or very broad, leaving only a small white patch in the centre of the crown. Wing of male 60–67, of female 56–65; tail of male 84–99, of female 80–91.5.

**A. c. macedonicus** Albania, Makedonija (former Yugoslavia), Greece and southern Bulgaria. Poorly marked. As *taiti,* but gorget better marked and eye-stripe extends further forwards, often to bill. Wing of male 59–63, of female 63.

**A. c. tauricus** Southern Crimea. Poorly marked. As *europaeus,* but lateral crown stripes blacker and better defined, mantle blacker with reduced (and paler) pink, scapulars often greyish. Wing of male 59–64.

**A. c. magnus** South Korea and Tsushima island, Japan. As *caudatus* group, but with blackish lateral crown stripes and usually a well-marked gorget of blackish spots on the breast.

**A. c. trivirgatus** Southern Japan on Honshu, Awa-shima, Sado and Oki, also Cheju island, Korea. As *europaeus,* but white areas purer white, black on upperparts restricted to upper mantle, lower mantle paler with a greater admixture of brighter pink. Wing of male 59–64.

**A. c. kiusiuensis** Shikoku, Kyushu and Yakushima, south Japan. As *trivirgatus,* but darker and gorget less distinct or lacking. Also slightly smaller. Wing of male 55–59.

**THE *ALPINUS* GROUP** Head pattern as *europaeus* group (although cheeks, ear-coverts and sides of neck streaked darker), but upperparts mainly grey with little or no pink and with blackish confined to the border of the upper mantle; often a blackish spot on the throat. Compared with the *europaeus* group, wings and especially tail shorter. Variation pronounced.

**A. c. irbii** Southern Spain, Portugal south of the Tejo valley, and Corsica. Narrow black border to upper mantle, mantle and scapulars grey, scapulars sometimes tinged pink. Wing of male 55–61, of female 55–61.5; tail of male 69–80.5, of female 69–80.

**A. c. italiae** Mainland Italy and SW Slovenija (former Yugoslavia). Intergrades with *europaeus* in the north, and unstable in northern Italy (of the *alpinus* group, the closest in appearance to the *europaeus* group). As *irbii,* but broader black border to upper mantle, lower mantle slightly darker slate-grey, scapulars more broadly tipped pink. Wing of male 54–65, of female 58–62; tail of male 74–92, of female 76.5–89.

**A. c. siculus** Sicily. As *irbii,* but lateral crown stripes duller and browner, centre of crown white, washed buff, dark border to upper mantle reduced, more brownish-black, upperparts paler and greyer, virtually lacking pink; may show vague sooty-black spot on lower throat. Wing of male 58–60, of female 56.5–60.5; tail of male 70–78, of female 70.5–79.

**A. c. tephronotus** Asia Minor. As *siculus,* but lateral crown stripes black, dark border to upper mantle lacking or reduced to a small brown spot, underparts buffish with a well-defined blackish throat spot. Juvenile as juvenile *rosaceus,* but centre of crown brownish, streaked dirty white, sides of crown slightly darker, forming ill-defined darker stripe backwards from eye, ear-coverts brownish; upper mantle and rump grey, lower mantle and scapulars dull brownish; wings paler brown, coverts finely fringed dirty-white; chin dirty white, throat and breast pale grey with some fine paler mottling; centre of belly and undertail-coverts off-white (juveniles of other races in this group broadly similar). Wing of male 56.5–63, of female 53–61; tail of male 59–77, of female 63–76.

**A. c. major** Caucasus and west and central Transcaucasia. As *siculus,* but lateral crown stripes darker, blackish-brown, centre of crown whiter (not buffish) with a few small brown streaks, border to upper mantle brown to black and varying in width, rump bright pink; breast whiter, lower belly and flanks brighter pink; dark bib on lower throat faint or absent. Wing of male 54.5–64.5, of female 55–64; tail of male 76, 84, of female 81–86.

**A. c. alpinus** SE Azerbaydzhan (Talysh and the Lenkoran' lowlands), northern Iran from Azarbaijan through the Elburz and southern Caspian districts to about Gorgan, and SW Turkmenistan in the Kopet Dag east to 58° E. As *tephronotus,* but lateral crown stripes black, centre of crown buffish-white, streaked brown, upperparts darker and more slatey, upper mantle grey mixed with some black, underparts washed buffy-brown, pink flanks showing little contrast; lower throat usually sooty. Wing of male 57.5–64.5, of female 56–62; tail of male 68–72, of female 65–70.5.

**A. c. passekii** Western Iran in the Zagros mountains from western Azarbaijan southeast to Fars. May intergrade with *tephronotus* in SE Turkey. As *tephronotus* and *alpinus,* but overall rather paler, especially the underparts, with only a faint brown wash on the belly; centre of crown white (not buff), and lacks gorget (although shows dark throat spot). Wing of male 58–63, of female 56–62.5; tail of male 61–72, of female 59–71.

**THE *GLAUCOGULARIS* GROUP** Head buffish with glossy black lateral crown stripes, upperparts grey, underparts buffy-grey with a dark bib. Juvenile distinctive. Formerly sometimes treated as a distinct species, *A. glaucogularis* ('Silver-throated Tit'), this group is sometimes united with the *alpinus* group.

**A. c. glaucogularis** Central China in the Chiang Jiang (Yangtze) valley from northern Zhejiang to Hubei (Yichang) (and west to lowlands of Sichuan?), extending north to parts of southern Shaanxi (Qin Ling mountains) and Henan. **Adult**: Forehead buff, lateral crown stripes glossy black, merging on forecrown; crown stripe and centre of nape pale buff, variably streaked blackish. Upperparts mid-dark grey, with a narrow band of pink on rump; outer scapulars tipped blackish. T1–T4/5 fringed mid grey on outer web, T3 tipped white. Lesser and median coverts and alula blackish, greater and primary coverts sooty-brown, fringed black (inner greater coverts browner, lacking pink). Flight feathers dark brown, tertials and secondaries fringed slightly paler and greyer, outer primaries blacker towards base. Lores, cheeks and ear-coverts pale drab-grey, chin, submoustachial

region and sides of neck off-white. Throat sooty-black, feathers finely tipped pale grey. Breast pale drab-grey to buffy-grey, belly slightly paler and whiter, flanks, vent and undertail-coverts clean pale pink. *In worn plumage,* flight feathers much paler and browner, fringed off-white (contrasting with primary and outer greater coverts), bib dark grey and underparts drab-grey-white. **Juvenile**: As juvenile *europaeus,* but chin, throat and breast vinous-pink, contrasting with the white submoustachial area and sides of neck, remainder of underparts washed yellow-buff. Wing of male 55–59, of female 56.5–57; tail short, of male 60–67, of female 57–70.

**A. c. vinaceus** Northern and western China in central and SE Nei Mongol (Ih Ju Lake and Chifeng), southern Liaoning, northern Hebei, NW Shandong (migrant only?), northern Shanxi, southern and central Gansu (north to Wuwei) eastern Qinghai (west to c. 100° E), mountains of central Sichuan (Baoxing), and NW Yunnan (Lijiang). Poorly marked. As *glaucogularis,* but sides of head slightly paler, bib slightly paler grey, remainder of underparts slightly paler, the breast especially less intensely washed buff, but often marked by a gorget of marginally darker and browner streaks; tail longer. Juvenile as juvenile *glaucogularis.* Averages larger. Wing of male 57–68, of female 55–67; tail of male 72–91; of female 69–86.

**RELATIONSHIPS** Although clearly allied to other members of the genus *Aegithalos*, no obvious relationship to any one member of the group.

**REFERENCES** Cramp & Perrins (1993), Gaston (1973), Glen & Perrins (1988), Stepanyan (1990), Vaurie (1959).

## 104 WHITE-CHEEKED TIT *Aegithalos leucogenys*          Plate 35

This small tit is a common resident of scrubby woodlands in eastern Afghanistan and Pakistan, but its status in India is obscure. May build winter roost nests, a habit not recorded for the well-studied Long-tailed Tit.

**IDENTIFICATION** Length 110 mm (4.25 in). A small tit with a medium-long tail. Forehead and crown cinnamon-drab, washed olive-brown at the rear and bordered on the sides of the crown by a narrow black band, which is poorly defined behind the eye. A broad white cheek patch and blackish bib, the latter tinged rusty on the lower border. Upper breast drab-grey, becoming duller and more ochre on the lower breast and belly; flanks and vent pale pinkish-buff. Upperparts light greyish olive-drab, tail brownish, fringed and tipped white. The eye is conspicuously yellow, and the bill is short and deep with (compared with White-throated Tit) a strongly arched culmen. Rather similar to Black-throated Tit (subspecies *iredalei*), but the crown stripe is cinnamon-drab rather than rufous, there is no white supercilium and the black bands on the sides of the crown are rather narrower, barely encompassing the eye.

Additionally, the chin is black, with the bib therefore extending to the bill (rather than being interrupted by a white chin as on Black-throated), and the underparts are paler and duller, lacking the pale rufous tones of Black-throated. Juveniles are more similar to juvenile Black-throated, both having a necklace of blackish streaks, but juvenile White-cheeked Tit lacks a white supercilium, and its throat is dull pale buff with some darker mottling (especially in the centre), differing little from the remainder of the underparts, rather than being contrastingly white. Overlaps with White-throated Tit in NE Pakistan and Kashmir. Adult White-cheeked Tits are easily distinguished by their cinnamon-drab, rather than white, forehead and forecrown, and also their black chin and throat. Juveniles are rather more similar, with uniform dull pale pinkish-buff underparts and a necklace of vague blackish streaks, but both adult and juvenile White-throated Tits are still separated by their white forehead and forecrown.

**SEX/AGE** Sexes similar. The juvenile is distinct, with the crown slightly paler and more buffish-drab than on the adult, the dark sides to the crown slightly narrower, although better defined at the rear, and the upperparts slightly duller and browner. Importantly, juveniles lack the black bib, both the cheek patch and the throat being pale buff, although they may show indications of a narrow dark bib on the chin and centre of the throat, which is sometimes blackish, but still overlaid with pinkish-drab feather tips. The sides of the breast are dull cinnamon-brown and remainder of underparts pale pinkish-buff, variably streaked dark brown on the upper breast.

**VOICE** May be more varied than that of, for example, Black-throated and Long-tailed Tits. Contact call *si-si-si-si*, sometimes slightly slurred or lisping towards the end, *si-si-si-sisisip*, and sometimes a fuller and mellower *see-see-see-see*; also *seeup* and a very dry *tup* (occasionally a subdued *tup-tup-tup* or *se-tu-ip* and similar 'creaky' phrases), and a short and explosive, dry buzzing *trrrt* or *trrrp*. Song or subsong a weak, rather rambling series of squeaky and piping notes.

**DISTRIBUTION AND MOVEMENTS** In NE **Afghanistan** found in Nuristan, south to the Peiwar spur of the Safed Koh range. In **Pakistan** occurs from Chitral south through Swat Kohistan, the Safed Koh, Kurram valley, Samana hills and Waziristan to the Shinghar range and Ziarat in northern Baluchistan, east to Gilgit and Baltistan in the north and to Hazara and the Margalla hills near Islamabad in the south. Found in **NW India** in the Vale of Kashmir (Kangan in the Sind valley, on the north side of the main vale; Meinertzhagen 1927). Also recorded from Garhwal, northern Uttar Pradesh (Vaurie 1959), most recently at Deodi in Nanda Devi NP (Halberg & Peterson 1984). Resident, although undertakes some seasonal altitudinal movements. In Pakistan, recorded in the winter in the Attock and Campbellpore region of the NW Punjab.

**HABITAT** Favours open scrubby forest of Holly Oak, junipers and pines, also Almond scrub at higher altitudes; avoids pure stands of Deodar (cedar). In winter may frequent the edge of cultivation, thorn scrub and riverside tamarisks. In Afghanistan found from *c.* 1220 to 2600 m, and breeds in Pakistan at *c.* 1500–3660 m, although recorded in late summer at 550 m in the Safed Koh and in winter down to 450 m at Attock. In Kashmir reported from 1525–3660 m (Fleming *et al.* 1984), although the only specific record traced is at 1800 m in late March (Meinertzhagen 1927).

**POPULATION** Common in Afghanistan, and locally common in Pakistan, although rather scarcer in Gilgit. Apparently scarce or even rare in Kashmir.

**HABITS** Found in pairs and, from late summer until about mid April, in parties of 6–12, often joining mixed-species foraging flocks. Active and restless, foraging largely in the shrub layer, although also in the crowns of Holly Oaks and well-grown junipers. Food mainly insects and spi-

ders. Winter 'roost nests' have been recorded, with one such nest under construction on 19 and 23 January in the Margalla hills, Pakistan, at 460 m. It was firmly woven into a thorny bush and decorated on the outside with white spider-egg cocoons (Roberts 1992).

**BREEDING BIOLOGY** Season late March–May. Nest, usually placed in a thorny bush, stunted Holly Oak or juniper, 1–3.5 m above ground, is an upright oval ball, *c.* 110 x 85 mm, with entrance at the side near the top, woven from moss, grass, vegetable fibres etc., bound with spiders' webs and densely lined with feathers. Both sexes collect nest material. Clutch 5–8: eggs white, sometimes faintly spotted pinkish-red at the larger end; *c.* 14.7 x 9.9 mm. Incubation period unknown, as is the role of the sexes in incubation, but both male and female feed the fledged young, which remain dependent for at least 14 days after leaving the nest.

**DESCRIPTION** **Adult**: *In fresh plumage* (September to about March), forehead dull cinnamon, crown and nape cinnamon-drab, washed greyish-drab, especially in centre. Lores and sides of crown and nape (encompassing eye) black, feathers behind eye tipped grey ('hoary') and merging into light greyish-drab on upper ear-coverts. Upperparts and wing-coverts light greyish-olive-drab. Tail mid-dark brown, T1–T4 fringed as upperparts, T4 may have small triangular whitish tip, T5–T6 with large white triangular spot at tip of inner web, extending more diffusely onto tip of outer web (see figure 104.1 below). Alula and primary coverts blackish-brown. Tertials and flight feathers mid-dark brown, fringed as upperparts. Cheeks and lower ear-coverts white, extending onto sides of neck as a white half-collar. Chin and throat blackish, lower border of bib tinged burgundy. Upper breast light drab-grey, forming an indistinct dark breast band, lower breast and belly paler and greyer, flanks and vent pale brownish-buff, variably washed pink. Axillaries and underwing-coverts white. *In worn plumage* (about March–August), upperparts duller and greyer, olive-grey. **Bare Parts**: Iris straw-yellow or grey-yellow; bill black; legs and feet pale orange-brown or pinkish-brown; claws brown. **Juvenile**: As adult, but crown slightly paler, more buffish-drab, dark stripes at sides slightly narrower, but better defined at rear (lacking greyish feather tips). Upperparts slightly duller and browner, dull cinnamon-brown. Upper ear-coverts pinkish-drab, cheeks, lower ear-coverts, sides of neck and throat pale buff; narrow bib on chin and centre of

*Figure 104.1  Tail of adult.*

throat variably darker, may be blackish with pinkish-drab feather tips. Sides of breast dull cinnamon-brown, remainder of underparts pale pinkish-buff; darker feather bases revealed, especially on breast, where variable dark brown streaks on upper breast. **1st Adult**: As adult. **Measurements**: Wing of male 56–59, of female 52–58; tail of male 45–57, of female 48–53; bill 8.6–10.5; tarsus 15.5–18.5. Weight 6–8 g.

**MOULT** Adult post-breeding complete (August–September). Post-juvenile complete (July).

**GEOGRAPHICAL VARIATION** Slight. Birds from Baluchistan average purer grey on the upperparts than those from northern Pakistan (i.e. than in Description), olive-grey wearing to light or pale grey, tinged olive, by February/March (rather than greyish olive-drab, wearing to olive-grey), the crown stripe is paler, less brown and more cinnamon-grey, thus contrasting more with the mantle; the underparts are overall slightly paler and more uniform, with a narrower, paler grey and much less obvious breast band, the remainder of the underparts being purer pink with some whitish feather tips. No subspecies are named, however.

**RELATIONSHIPS** Obscure, although the general appearance is closest to that of Black-throated Tit. Ecologically, appears to have a niche intermediate between those of the low-altitude Black-throated and the high-altitude White-throated Tit, favouring a much drier habitat than Black-throated and avoiding the moist coniferous forest favoured by White-throated Tit (Roberts 1992).

**REFERENCES** Ali & Ripley (1983), Paludan (1959), Roberts (1992).

# 105 BLACK-THROATED TIT *Aegithalos concinnus*      Plate 34
Other name: Red-headed Tit

This stunning little tit is a common bird in the Himalayas, China, Burma and Indochina, usually found in large noisy parties moving 'follow-my-leader' fashion through the undergrowth.

**IDENTIFICATION** Length 105 mm (4 in). A small tit with a medium-long tail. Crown rufous (or greyish-brown in eastern Burma and NW Thailand), bordered by black in a distinctive 'highwayman's mask' which surrounds the pale eye, whilst Himalayan birds also have a prominent white supercilium from the eye backwards. Upperparts blue-grey, wings and tail darker, the tail bordered and tipped white. Chin and submoustachial stripe white, framing the black throat, the remainder of the underparts buff or pale rufous on Himalayan birds, white with clear-cut white and rufous breast bands in China and South-East Asia. Juveniles have a whitish throat and a necklace of dark streaks across the breast. The distinctive race *annamensis*, found in southern Laos and central and southern Vietnam, has a white forehead, greyish crown, brown breast band and pinkish flanks; the throat of the adult is black, as in the other races. A brightly coloured tit, the most widespread Oriental member of the genus. The key feature of adults is the black throat, encircled by a white chin and submoustachial stripes: and of juveniles the contrast between the white chin and throat and the buffish underparts, and the necklace of blackish streaks. When the generic identity is not clear, the species may be mistaken for Black-throated Parrotbill. In the western Himalayas, overlaps with White-cheeked Tit. Adult Black-throated Tit is easily identified by its broad white supercilium, white chin separating the bill from the black throat patch, and the darker chestnut crown. Juveniles of the two species are more similar, both having a necklace of vague blackish spots or streaks, but juvenile Black-throated has a white chin and throat, contrasting with buffish underparts, rather than a dull pinkish-brown throat with some darker mottling. In the western Himalayas, Black-throated Tit also overlaps with White-throated Tit. Adults are easily separated by their chestnut forehead and forecrown (white on White-throated) and white supercilium. Juveniles are more similar, but Black-throated has the forehead and forecrown reddish-buff (not white) with a more extensive black highwayman's mask. In the eastern Himalayas, SW China and Burma, overlaps with Black-browed Tit. Adult Black-throated have the entire crown chestnut to grey-fawn and a more restricted black mask (with a white supercilium in the Himalayas), and a black throat with the chin, submoustachial stripe and sides of the neck white (rather than a narrow fawn crown stripe and extensive black sides to the crown). The breast, flanks and belly of both species are variably marked, being similarly uniform buffish in the Himalayas, and again similar in SW China and Burma, with a rufous breast band separating the white lower throat from the whitish belly. Juvenile Black-throated is separated from adult Black-browed Tit by its head pattern (as the adult), and from juvenile Black-browed Tit, which has a whitish or buffy crown stripe and underparts, by its head pattern and the contrast between its white throat and buffy underparts. In western China, separated from Sooty Tit by its chestnut crown, greyish upperparts (not brown), black highwayman's mask and, on adults, black throat.

**SEX/AGE** Sexes similar. The juvenile resembles the adult, but the cap is paler, the supercilium poorly marked, upperparts duller and browner, and most noticeably the chin and throat are off-white, separated from the remainder of the underparts (which are washed dull buff) by a line of variably prominent dark spots or streaks. 1st adult as adult after the complete post-juvenile moult.

**VOICE** Contact calls a thin *psip, psip* and a sibilant *si-si-si-si...* or *si-si-si-si-li-u.* Also a fuller *sup* or *zup* in alarm or excitement, extending into a short dry rattling *churr trrrt, trrrt,* which may be rather harsh when agitated and taken up by every member of the party. Song a repeated twittering or babbling *tir-ir-ir-ir-ir* interspersed with some well-spaced single chirps (Roberts 1992); also described as a very high, thin *tur-r-r-tait-yeat-yeat-yeat* (Fleming *et al.* 1984). Overall, vocalisations strongly recall those of Long-tailed Tit.

**DISTRIBUTION AND MOVEMENTS** Found in extreme NE **Pakistan** in the lower Kagan valley (Hazara), Murree hills and lower Neelum (Kishen Ganga) and Jhelum valleys in Azad Kashmir; does not occur in Baluchistan, NWFP or Chitral (*contra* Ali & Ripley 1983; see Roberts 1992). **NW India** in the outer Himalayas from Kishtwar (Kashmir; although absent from the Vale of Kashmir), through Himachal Pradesh, northern Uttar Pradesh, **Nepal**, Darjeeling district, **Sikkim** and **Bhutan** to Arunachal Pradesh and the Mishmi hills, extending north of the main range of the Himalayas into **Tibet** (Xizang) along the Sun Kosi river (Nyalam) and in the Tsangpo bend area around Tangmai in both the Yi'ong Tsangpo and Po Tsangpo valleys. Also the hills of **NE India** in SE Arunachal Pradesh, Nagaland, Manipur, Meghalaya (Khasi hills), southernmost Assam (Cachar hills) and Mizoram (Lushai hills), extending into western **Myanmar** (**Burma**) in the Chin hills south to Mount Victoria, and in NE Burma south through Bhamo district and the Shan States to Kayah (at least to Mawchi). In NW **Thailand** confined to Doi Pha Hom Pok on the Burmese border. In **Laos** found in the north in Tranninh and in the south on the Bolovens plateau, and in **Vietnam** in NW Tonkin and central and south Annam from Ba Na south to the Da Lat plateau. In southern **China** occurs from **Sichuan** (except the northwest), southern **Gansu**, southern **Shaanxi** (Qin Ling mountains), **Henan**, **Anhui** and southern **Jiangsu** southwards, although possibly absent from Hunan and Hubei. An irregular winter visitor **Hong Kong**, with only four records prior to 1989, but then a significant increase with widespread reports in the period September–May from the winter of 1989/90 onwards, increasing oversummering, and bred in 1992 and 1993 (cf. Yellow-cheeked Tit). Also resident **Taiwan**. Resident, with some erratic and rather limited altitudinal movements.

**HABITAT** Primarily edge habitats in broadleaved forest, especially oak, also mixed forest and sometimes Deodar (cedar) and, especially in NE India (and also southern Vietnam?), pine. In addition, found in a wide variety of wooded or bushy habitats such as scattered trees, second growth, bamboo groves, riverine scrub, bushes on open hillsides and gardens. Generally found at mid altitudes in the subtropical and temperate zones. In Pakistan occurs at 1375–2400 m and in the western Himalayas breeds at 1400–2400 m, ranging to 2700 m in Nepal and apparently to 3200 m in the eastern Himalayas (Ripley 1982; but records traced are at 1065–2440 m in Sikkim/Darjeeling, 1400–2630 m in Bhutan and 1980–2130 m in

Pome in SE Tibet). Some altitudinal movement in winter, when recorded down to 1200 m in Pakistan, at 900–3050 m in the western Himalayas, 1065–3000 m in Nepal and 600–3600 m in the eastern Himalayas (Ripley 1982; with an undated record at 400 m in Arunachal Pradesh), although does not usually descend below the breeding range except in the hardest weather. In NE India found from 1430 m to at least 2745 m, and in Burma at 915–2500 m (not uncommon 1525–2135 m); on Mount Victoria occurs at 1400–2600 m. In Thailand found at 1500–2100m, and in Vietnam found in NW Tonkin at 1400–1800 m and in Annam at 60–1980 m, with breeding noted at 600 m (C. Robson pers. comm.). Recorded in China at 75–3960 m, generally below 2000 m, in Yunnan noted as high as 3960 m in the northwest (Riley 1931), up to 3660 m in the Lijiang range and at 2745–3350 m in the Shweli-Salween divide (Gaoligong Shan) (Rothschild 1926; although noted in the Gaoligong Shan only at 1500–2500 m by Academica Sinica 1980). In Taiwan recorded at 1000–3000 m, although probably breeds largely at 1500–2400 m.

**POPULATION** Generally fairly common to abundant, although local in Bhutan and very rare on Mount Victoria.

**HABITS** Very gregarious, and usually associates in flocks, sometimes as many as 40 birds together. Often joins mixed-species foraging parties. Individuals pair off in March, but small flocks may be encountered throughout the breeding season, comprising failed breeders or non-breeders and then family parties from early broods. Restless and active, and often very tame, flocks move through an area in a 'follow-my-leader' fashion. Roosts in groups, perched on a sheltered branch within a bush. Forages mainly in the shrub layer, but also in the forest canopy. Food mainly insects, but also small seeds and fruits, especially raspberries.

**BREEDING BIOLOGY** Season: Himalayas, NE India and Burma, March–May, sometimes June; southern China, late February–May; NW Thailand, April. The nest is an oval ball of green moss, lichen, rootlets, bark scraps, hair, spiders' egg cases and vegetable down, bound together with spiders' webs, 100–150 mm tall x 95–140 mm wide with the entrance hole at the side near the top, densely lined with feathers and sometimes also wool, fur or vegetable down. Usually sited in a low tree or bush up to 3 m above ground, in a fork or woven around several twigs, nests are occasionally up to 12 m high, placed on the horizontal bough of a Deodar or at the tip of a pine branch, and have also been found in rough grass or other low, tangled vegetation. The nest is constructed over a protracted period, sometimes over two weeks, by both sexes, although the female takes the dominant role, working from inside the nest during the later stages of building. Clutch 3–6 (3–8) in Himalayas, 3 in NE India and northern Burma and 3–5 in the Chin hills of western Burma: eggs white or pale pink, variably but usually finely spotted with reddish, especially in a ring at the larger end, occasionally unmarked; 13.9 x 10.6 mm (*A. c. iredalei*). Female incubates (although male roosts in the nest), period *c.* 15–16 days. Young are fed by both sexes, and remain dependent for at least ten days after fledging. Single-brooded.

**DESCRIPTION** *A. c. iredalei* **Adult**: *In fresh plumage* (September to about March), forehead cinnamon-orange, grading to rufous on crown and nape. Broad white supercilium extending from above and behind eye to nape. Eyestripe from lores to sides of upper mantle black, encompassing the eye and broadening at the rear. Border of upper mantle ochre in centre, blackish at sides, remainder of upperparts dark blue-grey, rump tinged brownish-ochre. Tail blackish-brown, T1–T3 fringed mid-dark grey, T4–T6 with triangular white spot at tip of shaft, outer web of T6 largely white; tail graduated, T6 *c.* 15–17 mm shorter than T1 (see figure 105.1 below). Wing-coverts dark brown, lesser and median fringed dark blue-grey, greater narrowly fringed dark grey. Alula and primary coverts blackish-brown. Flight feathers dark brown, all except P1–P2 fringed mid-dark grey, although only inwards of emarginations on P3–P6. Chin and submoustachial stripe white, tinged buff. Throat black. Sides of neck and narrow band on upper breast pale buffy-white (pale collar most pronounced on eastern birds), grading to rufous-buff or salmon colour on breast, feather tips slightly paler, and to pinkish on flanks and sides of vent; centre of lower breast, belly and vent slightly paler and whiter. Axillaries and underwing-coverts very pale buff. *In worn plumage* (about April–August), cap slightly paler, some paler feather bases revealed, supercilium patchier, may be reduced to discrete flecks as white feather tips abraded. Upperparts slightly paler and less blue, wings and tail rather browner and slightly paler. Underparts paler, especially breast, and flanks more pinkish-cinnamon. **Bare Parts**: Iris yellow-white; bill black; legs and feet dull orange-brown or brownish-yellow; claws pale horn to black. **Juvenile**: As adult, but cap slightly paler and more cinnamon-rufous (feather tips paler and whitish feather bases revealed). Upperparts slightly duller and less uniform, tinged drab, border of upper mantle pale buff to off-white in centre, some dark grey feather tips on mantle. Tail as adult but slightly paler, white areas faintly washed brown. Wings as adult, but flight feathers paler and fringed buffy-brown or buff. Supercilium poorly marked, small discrete white tips; eyestripe slightly duller and browner. Throat off-white, some dark grey feather bases revealed, especially on lower border, breast off-white, grading to pale cin-

namon-orange on remainder of underparts, paler and less uniform than adult. **1st Adult**: As adult. **Measurements**: Wing of male 46–57, of female 43.5–56; tail of male 45–58, of female 43–55; bill 7–9.5; tarsus 15–17. Weight 4–9 g.
**MOULT** Adult post-breeding complete (June–September). Post-juvenile complete (July–October).
**GEOGRAPHICAL VARIATION** Marked. Six subspecies are recognised, divisible into three groups.

**THE *IREDALEI* GROUP** The Himalayas. A white supercilium and uniform pale pinkish-buff underparts, with the white breast band faint or lacking.

*A. c. iredalei* The Himalayas from NE Pakistan to the Mishmi hills, also southern Tibet in the Sun Kosi valley and Tsangpo bend area. See Description. Includes '*rubricapillus*' from Nepal eastwards, averaging slightly darker on the crown, darker and bluer on the mantle, tending to show a slightly whiter breast band, and also slightly smaller.

**THE *CONCINNUS* GROUP** NE India, Burma and China. Lacks a supercilium, but has a neat chestnut breast band and flanks, separated from the black throat by a white band, and a white centre to the lower breast and belly.

*A. c. manipurensis* NE India from SE Arunachal Pradesh (Noa Dihing valley, Changlang district (formerly eastern Tirap district) to Meghalaya and Mizoram, extending to the Chin hills of western Burma. May intergrade with *talifuensis* at the northeast end of the range. As *iredalei*, but crown slightly paler, rufous-cinnamon, supercilium reduced to a few white feather tips, breast and flanks rufous-cinnamon, separated from black throat by narrow white collar, and centre of breast and belly whitish. Wing of male 47.5–49, of female 47.5.

*A. c. concinnus* Central and eastern China (east of *talifuensis*) and Taiwan. As *manipurensis*, but crown averages slightly paler and more cinnamon, breast band averages narrower and better defined, although may be nearly broken in centre, also slightly darker and more cinnamon-rufous, and remainder of underparts whiter, pale pinkish-buff feather bases on belly and vent exposed with wear (differences reflected by juveniles). Includes '*taiwanensis*' of Taiwan, with a fractionally darker breast band. Wing of male 46–53, of female 46–49; tail of male 44–56, of female 43–50.5.

*A. c. talifuensis* NE Burma east of the Irrawaddy river, SW China in Yunnan, SW Guizhou and central and SW Sichuan (from Emei Shan southwards), NW Vietnam and northern Laos (Tranninh). Intergrades with nominate *concinnus* in central Sichuan. Poorly marked. As nominate *concinnus* (and perhaps better synonymised with the nominate form), but crown darker (slightly darker and more rufous than *manipurensis*, but not so dark as *iredalei*), some faint white flecks on rear sides of crown, and breast band and flanks darker rufous-chestnut. Wing of male 47–52, of female 44–50. Includes '*tonkinensis*' of NW Vietnam, which averages very slightly darker.

*A. c. pulchellus* Eastern Burma in the Southern Shan States and Kayah (= Karenni district); pre-

*Figure 105.1  Tail of adult* A. c. iredalei.

sumably this subspecies in NW Thailand. May intergrade with *talifuensis* in the north. As *manipurensis,* but forehead and crown light drab, no supercilium (or just a few faint white flecks), centre of lower breast and belly purer white. Juvenile as juvenile *iredalei,* but crown light drab and more contrast between white throat patch (which may show dark feather centres in centre and a necklace of dark spots on the upper breast), cinnamon breast band and flanks, and white centre of belly and vent (i.e. as difference between adults).

**THE ANNAMENSIS GROUP** Southern Indochina. Dull whitish underparts with a brown breast band and pinkish flanks (somewhat resembling Sooty Tit and the subspecies *sharpei* of Black-browed Tit).

**A. c. annamensis** Southern Laos (Bolovens plateau) and Vietnam in central and southern Annam (range presumably disjunct from those of other subspecies). Very distinctive. Forehead pale drab-grey, centre of crown mid grey, washed faintly with brown (slightly paler than the dark grey mantle), with a vague white-flecked supercilium from eye to nape; breast band mid grey-drab, flanks washed beige or light greyish-pink, centre of breast and belly dirty white. Juvenile with forehead pale dirty buff, crown as adult, chin, submoustachial stripe and sides of neck dirty buff, some dark feather centres showing on throat, breast band of dark spots, breast grey-buff with some dark feather centres, flanks washed buffy-cinnamon. Wing 47–54, of male 49–51, of female 50–52; tail of male 52.5–55, of female 51–52.

**REFERENCES** Ali & Ripley (1983), Whistler (1949).

# 106 WHITE-THROATED TIT *Aegithalos niveogularis*     Plate 34

This diminutive tit is strangely scarce and local throughout its range in the western Himalayas, and consequently rather poorly known.

**IDENTIFICATION** Length 115 mm (4.5 in). A small tit with a medium-long tail. Forehead and crown stripe white, fading to cinnamon-brown on the hindcrown and nape. The lores, cheeks and sides of the crown are black, becoming blackish-brown on the rear crown and cinnamon-brown on the rear ear-coverts, and merging into the nape and upper mantle. Upperparts greyish, washed buffish in fresh plumage, with a narrow pinkish band on the rump. Tail dark grey-brown, fringed and tipped white. Chin and throat pale grey, with the sub moustachial area and sides of the neck purer white, and clearly demarcated from the narrow cinnamon-brown breast band. Remainder of underparts beige or pale pinkish-drab. A typical long-tailed tit in shape, behaviour and voice, the key plumage feature being the white forehead and forecrown. Overlaps widely with Black-throated Tit (subspecies *iredalei*), but adult White-throated is easily distinguished by its white forehead and forecrown, white chin, throat and half-collar, and lack of a white supercilium. Juvenile Black-throated Tit is, however, more similar to White-throated, with a whitish throat, pale cinnamon-orange underparts and a necklace of indistinct blackish spots, but its forehead and forecrown are cinnamon-rufous, not white, and it has a white supercilium and a solid black 'highwayman's mask'. Juvenile White-throated Tit has dirty white underparts with a vague darker breast band, but nevertheless shows the adult's distinctive head pattern. Overlaps with White-cheeked Tit in NE Pakistan and Kashmir. Adult White-throated are easily distinguished by their white forehead and forecrown, and also the white chin, throat and half-collar (rather than a broad cinnamon-drab crown stripe and blackish chin and throat). Juvenile White-cheeked is rather more similar, with uniform dull pale pinkish-buff underparts and a necklace of vague blackish streaks, but both adult and juvenile White-throated Tits are still separated by their white forehead and forecrown. There is a narrow zone of overlap with Black-browed Tit in west-central Nepal (where both species are rare); in this area, pay careful attention to all plumage details, especially the throat pattern, as hybrids could occur. Adult White-throated are separated by their white forehead and forecrown, white chin, throat and half-collar (rather than a cinnamon-buff crown stripe, blackish chin and silvery-grey throat with blackish sides), and also have a much-reduced black mask. Juvenile Black-browed is more similar, with a pale buff to whitish crown stripe and dirty pale buff underparts, but its black mask is still much more extensive.

**SEX/AGE** Sexes similar. The juvenile is distinct, with a duller crown stripe, tinged buff on the forecrown, browner upperparts, and a buff wash to the sides of neck and submoustachial area; it also has a dull pinkish throat (rather than white), with the dark feather bases sometimes revealed, narrow and irregular breast band (and thus less contrast between the throat and breast), and sometimes faint darker bars on the remainder of the underparts. 1st adult as adult.

**VOICE** Contact call *wi* (similar to that of European Goldfinch, Whitehead 1914) and a high, rapid, repeated *tze-tze-tze* similar to call of Black-throated Tit (Fleming *et al.* 1984), also a *t-r-r-r-t* (Roberts 1992). Song a long and complicated series of phrases, not very loud or far-carrying, and comprising rapid chattering *tweet-tweet* notes interspersed with rapid, tittering *tsi-tsi-tsi* phrases and short elided warbling phrases, more complex than, and superior to, the songs of either White-cheeked or Black-throated Tits (Roberts 1992).

**DISTRIBUTION AND MOVEMENTS** In **Pakistan** found east of the Indus in the Kandia and Palas valleys of Indus Kohistan, the Kagan valley in Hazara district and the Neelum valley (= Kishen Ganga) of Azad Kashmir; although noted as occurring in Chitral by Bates & Lowther (1952), evidence is lacking. The range extends east through NW **India** in Kashmir, Himachal Pradesh (including Duala Dhar, Kulu, Simla and the Great Himalayan NP) to Garhwal in northern Uttar Pradesh (including Nanda Devi NP). In **Nepal**, extends through Rara, Jumla, the Langu valley and Dolpo to just east of the Kali Gandaki valley (Ghorepani, where recorded three times in 1981), with an exceptional record of a pair from Gosainkund, central Nepal, in April 1979. Resident, with some altitudinal movements.

**HABITAT** The coniferous zone in Deodar (cedar), spruce, fir and pine, also oak, cherry, barberry, birch forest and dwarf willows and rhododendrons at the treeline. Found at high altitudes near the upper limit of the coniferous zone. In Pakistan breeds near the treeline, with records from 3200–3400 m, in Kashmir recorded from 2440 to about 3660 m, in Uttar Pradesh occurs at up to 3700 m and in Nepal found at 2750–3965 m. Some altitudinal movement in winter, when recorded as low as 1800 m in Kashmir.

**POPULATION** Rare and local in Pakistan and Nepal (although locally common in the Langu valley of western Nepal) and uncommon to locally common in India. With a rather restricted distribution and apparently low population density, the species may be vulnerable, and listed as near-threatened in BirdLife International's world checklist of threatened birds (Collar *et al.* 1994).

**HABITS** Similar to those of other members of the genus. Found in pairs in the spring and early summer, otherwise usually in small parties, sometimes as many as 20 birds together, and may join mixed-species foraging flocks. Active, restless and often tame. 'This exquisite little bird is perhaps the doyen of the group, a gentleman among gentlemen' (Meinertzhagen 1927). Forages in the shrub layer. Food largely insects, also possibly flower buds.

**BREEDING BIOLOGY** Season May–early July. Nest an oval or pear-shaped ball of moss and cobwebs, covered with lichen and densely lined with feathers, the entrance to one side near the top. Placed in a tree or bush, in a fork 1–3 m above the ground or suspended in tree branches up to 10 m up. One record of a clutch of 4, but variation in clutch size unknown: eggs white, finely spotted pink at the broader end; c. 14.2 x 11 mm.

**DESCRIPTION** **Adult**: *In fresh plumage* (September–April), forehead and centre of crown white, merging into cinnamon-brown on central hindcrown and nape. Upperparts light-mid grey, washed cinnamon-buff on upper mantle and olive-buff on lower mantle, scapulars and back; a narrow pinkish band on rump. Tail dark grey-brown, T1–T4 fringed light grey, T4–T5 tipped white, outer web of T6 white, narrowly fringed darker towards tip, inner web with triangular white spot at tip (see figure 106.1). Lesser and

*Figure 106.1  Tail of adult.*

median coverts dark grey-brown, fringed as upperparts, greater coverts grey-brown, fringed mid grey. Alula and primary coverts dark grey-brown. Tertials brown, slightly paler and more cinnamon on inner web, fringed light grey. Secondaries and primaries dark grey-brown, fringed light grey, although fringes absent on P1–2, restricted to base on P3 and present only inwards of emarginations on P4–P6. Sides of crown and nape black, with some brown admixture at rear, and thus poorly demarcated from centre of nape and merging irregularly into the upper mantle. Lores and cheeks sooty-black, fore ear-coverts sooty-black, streaked light grey, grading into cinnamon-brown on rear ear-coverts. Sides of neck and submoustachial area white, chin and throat pale grey (dark feather bases fully concealed). Upper breast and upper flanks cinnamon-brown, clearly demarcated from throat, remainder of underparts beige or pale pinkish-drab, feather tips slightly paler and whiter, especially in centre of breast and belly. Axillaries and underwing-coverts pale pink. *In worn plumage* (May–August), forecrown may be tinged buff, upperparts slightly greyer, flight feathers and tail abraded, fringes on primaries and secondaries bleached paler, dark breast band slightly narrower, and underparts more uniformly pinkish (whitish feather tips abraded). **Bare Parts**: Iris pale brown to dark brown or reddish-brown; bill dark slate to black; legs and feet fleshy-yellow to brown, soles yellow-horn; claws dark brown or black. **Juvenile**: As adult, but forehead tinged buff, centre of forecrown pale grey, centre of rear crown and rear ear-coverts paler and more cinnamon. Upperparts browner, sooty feather bases showing on upper mantle and faint darker feather tips on remainder of upperparts. White in tail reduced, duller and tinged brown. Sides of neck, submoustachial area and throat tinged buff, chin and centre of throat dull pinkish, darker feather centres revealed. Narrow and irregular sooty-brown breast band, remainder of underparts pale pinkish-buff, darker feather tips show as faint bars on breast and belly, and darker feather bases show on upper flanks, breast and belly (these areas duller and drabber than rear flanks and vent). **1st Adult**: As adult. **Measurements**: Wing 58.5–65, of male 59.5–63, of female 58.5–60; tail of male 53–57, of female 51–54; bill 8.8–11; tarsus 16.5–18.5. Weight: no information.

**MOULT** Adult post-breeding complete (late July–October). Post-juvenile complete (July–August).

GEOGRAPHICAL VARIATION None.

RELATIONSHIPS Sometimes considered conspecific with Black-browed Tit (e.g. Vaurie 1959). It differs from that species, however, not only in plumage pattern, but also in its larger size. Recent field work has established that the ranges of the two meet and marginally overlap at the Kali Gandaki valley in west-central Nepal (possibly a greater degree of overlap: see Distribution and Movements), apparently without intergradation, and treatment as a distinct species seems fully justified. Its ecological relationship with the rather similar White-cheeked Tit, with which it overlaps from NE Pakistan to western Nepal, is problematic, although the former prefers drier, more open habitats at lower altitudes and avoids moist coniferous forest (Roberts 1992).

REFERENCES Ali & Ripley (1983), Fleming *et al.* (1984), Roberts (1992).

## 107 BLACK-BROWED TIT *Aegithalos iouschistos*     Plate 34
Other names: Rufous-fronted Tit, Black-headed Tit

With a rather limited distribution around the eastern Himalayas and in western China, this is very much the high-altitude equivalent of Black-throated Tit, able to cope with rather harsh conditions.

IDENTIFICATION Length 110 mm (4.25 in). A typical long-tailed tit in habits, size and shape, with a long, well-graduated tail. The key plumage feature is the extensive black sides to the head, including lores, supercilium, eyestripe and upper ear-coverts, totally encompassing the yellow eye. Otherwise, marked geographic variation: In the *iouschistos* group of the eastern Himalayas, the forehead and centre of the nape are cinnamon, crown stripe buff, sides of head glossy black, grading to black on the lores, cheeks and upper ear-coverts. Lower ear-coverts, cheeks and sides of neck cinnamon-buff. Narrow rufous submoustachial stripe, extending to the sides of the breast. Chin and sides of throat black (forming a diffuse inverted 'V'), centre of throat and breast silvery-grey, remainder of underparts rufous-cinnamon. Upperparts dull mid grey, tail darker grey-brown, outer feathers tipped paler. In the *bonvaloti* group of NE Burma and western China, the crown stripe is narrower and paler and the submoustachial stripe off-white. The chin and malar stripes show the same pattern of a black inverted 'V', but it is better defined, with the centre of the throat and the upper breast paler and whiter. There is a broad well-demarcated cinnamon band across the lower breast. Belly white, lower flanks and vent pinkish-cinnamon. In the *sharpei* group of SW Burma, the crown stripe is whitish, becoming cinnamon-brown at the rear, with the black bands on the side of the head relatively narrow and the ear-coverts cinnamon-brown. The sides of the neck and submoustachial stripe are white and the chin and malar stripe blackish, showing the inverted 'V' (although duller and less well defined than in other groups), with the centre of the throat and upper breast white, well demarcated from the cinnamon-brown lower breast, which, however, grades into dull pinkish-cinnamon on the belly; remainder of underparts cinnamon. The range widely overlaps that of Black-throated Tit, but Black-browed is always distinguished by its much more extensive blackish sides to the head and narrow pale crown stripe. In the eastern Himalayas and SE Tibet (*iouschistos* group), adults are also separated from the local race of Black-throated by their lack of a white supercilium or black bib . Note that juvenile Black-throated Tit lacks a black throat, having a white chin and throat, buffy underparts and a necklace of indistinct dark spots. Adult Black-browed Tits are still easily distinguished as above, but juvenile Black-browed are more similar, with the crown stripe and entire underparts whitish or pale buff, but they still have the extensive black sides to the head and lack a supercilium. In Burma and China, Black-browed Tits (*bonvaloti* group) have the crown stripe buffish or white, and the throat region is also white, contrasting with the cinnamon breast band and flanks. In this region, Black-throated Tit lacks a supercilium and shares a rufous breast band separating the white lower throat from the whitish belly, but is otherwise still separable as above. Black-browed Tits may be found together with Sooty Tits, especially in winter. The two are superficially similar (especially the duller northern race of Black-browed, *A. i. obscuratus*, which has a well-defined brown breast band and greyer chin and centre to the throat), but Sooty Tit lacks the blackish lateral crown stripes and inverted 'V' on the throat, and has pale grey, not cinnamon, cheek patches. On Mount Victoria in SW Burma, the isolated *sharpei* groups overlaps with Black-throated Tit (subspecies *manipurensis*). It is separated from Black-throated by its extensive black side to the head, narrow crown stripe, whitish throat and duller and browner breast band. There is a narrow zone of overlap with White-throated Tit in west-central Nepal (where both species are rare); hybrids are possible and careful attention to all plumage details, especially the throat pattern, is essential. Adult Black-browed is easily separated by its narrow cinnamon-buff crown stripe, much more extensive black sides to the head, throat pattern (White-throated has a white chin, throat and half-collar), and darker underparts, lacking a breast band. Juvenile Black-browed is more similar, with a pale buff to whitish crown stripe and underparts, but the black sides to its head are still much more extensive.

**SEX/AGE** Sexes similar. Juvenile distinct. In the Himalayan *iouschistos* group, the juvenile's crown stripe is paler, sides of head duller black, submoustachial area and ear-coverts pale pinkish-buff, sides of neck and entire underparts (including the throat) dirty pale buff, more cinnamon-buff on the belly and vent, with dark grey blotching and spotting, especially on the breast. In the Chinese *bonvaloti* group the sides of the head and blackish markings on the throat are duller black in the juvenile, there is no cinnamon on the upper border of the mantle, the ear-coverts are paler, more buff, contrasting less with the submoustachial stripe, throat and breast (which are washed buff), and the underparts are also buff, spotted grey, especially on the upper breast and centre of the belly, forming an irregular breast band of dark blotches. No information on juveniles of the *sharpei* group. 1st adult as adult.

**VOICE** Very similar to that of Long-tailed Tit, including a constant conversational *see-see-see-see* and *tup* or *trrup*. Fleming *et al.* (1984) note the alarm as a shrill *zeet* and *trr-trr-trr*.

**DISTRIBUTION AND MOVEMENTS** The southern flanks of the **Himalayas** from central **Nepal** (west to the Langtang valley, and rarely west to Dana and between Kalopani and Tukche in the Kali Gandaki valley; one record for the Kathmandu valley, on Phulchowki in October 1989), east through **Sikkim** and **Bhutan** to **Arunachal Pradesh**, penetrating north of the main range into SE **Tibet** (Xizang) along the Chumbi valley to Yadong, the Manas valley to around Cona (near 'Lepo'), the Subansiri valley to 'Natrampa' and 'Lung', the lower Tsangpo river to about Gyemdong (= 'Risho'; Vaurie 1972), and its tributaries the Nyang Qu to about Taizhao, Yi'ong Zangbo to Yi'ong, Po Tsangpo to Sumzom, and the Lohit river to Zayu (Gyigang); also in the region northwest of Qamdo. Found in extreme NE **Myanmar** (**Burma**), east of the Irrawaddy from Myitkyina north to the Adung valley, with a disjunct population on Mount Victoria in SW Burma. Also western **China** in central and western **Sichuan** from Muli and Batang northeast to about Baiyü in the Jinsha Jiang valley (= 'Gartoh Gompa'; Vaurie 1972), Barkam, Songpan and Guan Xian, western **Guizhou** in the Weining region, and NW **Yunnan** from Yongning south to about Dali, and including Lijiang, the Mekong-Salween divide and Gaoligong Shan, and also recorded from Kunming (perhaps a winter visitor only? Stott 1993). Resident, with some seasonal altitudinal movements.

**HABITAT** Forest undergrowth, of rose, barberry, bamboo, willow thickets and streamside tangles in stands of oak, chestnut and rhododendron, mixed forest and less commonly in pines and subalpine forests of hemlock and other conifers (especially in western China). Also similar scrubby second growth and scrub and brambles above the tree-line, with some post-breeding dispersal downwards into subtropical evergreen forest. Commoner in the drier areas north of the main range of the Himalayas than in the denser forest to the south. On Mount Victoria found in open pine forest, sometimes also oak and rhododendrons at the summit. Favours temperate and subalpine forests, and in the Himalayas found at 2700–3600 m, down to 2400 m in the autumn and winter (with undated records down to 1100 m in Arunachal Pradesh). In China, found in Guizhou at 2200–2750 m, Yunnan at 2135–4400 m, Sichuan at 700–4270 m (probably breeding at c. 2600–4000 m), and in SE Tibet at 2130–3650 m. Recorded in northern Burma at 1830–3110 m, and on Mount Victoria occurs from 2500 m to the summit at 3053 m, descending in winter to 2100 m. Seasonal altitudinal movements undoubtedly occur within the given ranges in NE Burma and China, but the species is rather hardy and rarely shuns harsh winter weather, except in the case of heavy snowfalls, when it may descend a few hundred metres. Thus, in Sikkim found in winter at 2745–3720 m, descending exceptionally to 2440 m in severe weather.

**POPULATION** Common in the Himalayas and NE Burma. Although considered uncommon in China by Cheng (1987), stated to be very common in SW Sichuan (King 1989c) and abundant in SE Tibet (Ludlow 1944, 1951).

**HABITS** Behaviour reminiscent of that of Long-tailed Tit: lively, restless and often very confiding. Occurs in parties of up to 40 individuals outside the breeding season, sometimes joining mixed-species foraging flocks (but apparently not in the same areas as Black-throated Tit). From May–July the flocks break up into pairs, but then gather again into large flocks as soon as the young are able to fly. Forages in the canopy, as well as in the shrub layer. Food insects, also some vegetable matter.

**BREEDING BIOLOGY** Season: Himalayas, May–July (?); Guizhou, SW China, May; otherwise fledged young observed in late May in SE Tibet, mating noted on 13 April on Mount Victoria, where fledged young seen in May, and males coming into breeding condition collected in northern Burma in mid March. The nest is placed in an azalea or oak 0.8–2 m above ground, although the species has also been recorded carrying nesting material into the upper branches of a large fir. The lichen-covered ball of moss and creepers, c. 93 mm high x 74 mm deep x 93 mm external diameter with the entrance hole to the side, is lined with feathers; overall, it is very similar to that of Long-tailed Tit. Clutch 4–5: eggs white; 14.4 x 10.6 mm. Both sexes incubate and feed the young (Fleming *et al.* 1984; Wu *et al.* 1986).

**DESCRIPTION** *A. i. iouschistos* **Adult**: *In fresh plumage* (September–March), forehead cinnamon, centre of crown cinnamon-buff, centre of nape cinnamon with some blackish mottling. Sides of crown and nape glossy black, merging irregularly into sides of upper mantle. Upperparts mid grey, washed olive, tinged buffish on border of upper mantle; narrow band on rump tinged pinkish-cinnamon, longer uppertail-coverts mid grey. Tail dark grey-brown, T1–T3 fringed mid grey, T4–T6 with paler outer webs, whitish shafts and off-white tips; tail well graduated, T2 longest, T6 c. 15 mm shorter (see figure, p. 435). Wing-coverts dark

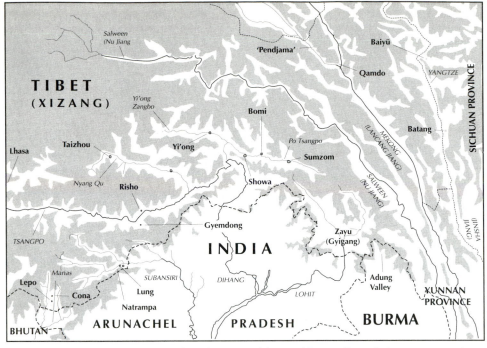

*Figure 107.1  SE Tibet, showing areas where the ranges of the* iouschistos *and* bonvaloti *groups approach one another and possibly overlap. The* iouschistos *group is found in the Himalayas and along the Tsangpo and its tributaries east to Sumzom on the Po Tsangpo. The* bonvaloti *group occurs in NE Burma and SW China, west to Zayu (Cheng 1987, who also lists* bonvaloti *for Bomi, within the range of* iouschistos). *Throughout the region the species probably breeds in the range 2600–4000 m. Shading indicates land above 4000 m above sea level.*

grey-brown, fringed as upperparts, narrowly so on greater coverts, revealing dark centres. Alula and primary coverts blackish-brown. Flight feathers greyish-brown, paler and buffer on inner webs of tertials, finely fringed mid grey (fringes absent on P1–P3, and present only inwards of emargination on P4–P6). Lores and cheeks sooty-black, grading into cinnamon-buff on ear-coverts and sides of neck. Narrow rufous or orange-rufous submoustachial stripe; chin and malar stripe sooty-black, forming an inverted 'V' (but feathers tipped paler, thus ill-defined), grading into silvery-white on throat and centre of upper breast (sooty-black feather centres shining through whitish tips). Lower border of bib orange-rufous (joining the submoustachial stripe to form a 'necklace'), remainder of underparts cinnamon-rufous, grading into pinkish-cinnamon on rear flanks, belly, vent, thighs and undertail-coverts. Axillaries and underwing-coverts pale cinnamon-buff. *In worn plumage* (April–August), crown stripe, sides of neck and border of upper mantle paler and buffer, upperparts slightly greyer, wings and tail abraded, throat slightly darker and more silvery-grey, and more contrast between orange-rufous breast band (on border of throat) and pinkish-cinnamon belly and flanks. **Bare Parts**: Iris yellow-white to lemon-yellow; bill black; legs and feet yellow-brown or fleshy-brown to reddish-brown or dark brown. **Juvenile**: As adult, but forehead cinnamon-buff, crown stripe pale buff or buffy-white, sides of

crown not so glossy black. Upperparts slightly greyer, tertials and secondaries fringed pale buff. Lores and cheeks sooty-brown, ear-coverts and submoustachial stripe pale pinkish-buff, sides of neck and remainder of underparts dirty pale buff, more cinnamon-buff on belly and vent, mid-dark grey feather centres extensively revealed, especially on breast. Bill may be paler than on adult, dark horny; iris may be grey; legs and feet average slightly paler. **1st Adult**: As adult. **Measurements**: Wing of male 55–60, of female 53–58; tail of male 48–59, of female 45–53; bill 8–10; tarsus 17–19. Weight 5–7.5 g.

**MOULT** Adult post-breeding complete (August–September). Post-juvenile complete (July–August).

**GEOGRAPHICAL VARIATION** Marked. Four subspecies recognised, divisible into three groups: the *iouschistos* group in the Himalayas, the *bonvaloti* group in NE Burma and western China, and the *sharpei* group in SW Burma. Wunderlich (1991a, b) notes that the *iouschistos* and *bonvaloti* groups almost come into contact or even perhaps replace each other altitudinally in SE Tibet in Bomi, perhaps without intergradation, and he treats them as two distinct species. Evidence for this is as yet lacking, however, and there may be no definite records of *bonvaloti* west of the Zayu river. The crucial region is the Tsangpo bend area. There are many specimen records of nominate *iouschistos* east to 95º E, and Cheng (1987) lists it for Yi'ong (on the Yi'ong Zangbo); Ludlow (1951) gives sight records from Showa on the Po Tsangpo, and Robson (1987) sight records for Sumzom on the Po Tsangpo. Cheng (1986), on the other hand, lists *bonvaloti* for Bomi, on the Po Tsangpo between these two localities. This may be an error or involve migrants or wanderers, but if the two forms are found breeding together without intergradation or hybridisation, then they would certainly have to be treated as specifically distinct.

**THE *IOUSCHISTOS* GROUP** Forehead cinnamon, chin black, submoustachial stripe and underparts variably rufous, but only a hint of a darker breast band.

**A. i. iouschistos** Himalayas from Nepal to Arunachal Pradesh, extending into SE Tibet east to *c.* 96º E. See Description.

**THE *BONVALOTI* GROUP** Chin and centre of throat as *iouschistos*, but submoustachial area and base of throat white, separated from the whitish belly by a dark breast band.

**A. i. bonvaloti** NE Burma, adjacent SE Tibet along the Lohit/Zayu valley, and western China in Yunnan, Guizhou and central and western Sichuan (from Muli north and east to Batang, Kangding and Barkam); also reported for Bomi on the Po Tsangpo in SE Tibet by Cheng (1987), and 'Pendjama', probably NW of Qamdo (Wunderlich 1991a). May intergrade with nominate *iouschistos* in the Tsangpo bend area of SE Tibet. **Adult**: As nominate *iouschistos,* but crown stripe slightly paler and narrower, more buffish, whiter on forehead. Upper mantle dull cinnamon. More white in tail, T4–T6 with larger white tips, outer web of T6 pale grey with a dusky border near the tip. Lores and cheeks sooty-black, ear-coverts cinnamon-buff (better demarcated from dark crown stripe). Submoustachial stripe off-white, sides of neck buffish. Chin and malar stripes sooty-black (more uniform and better defined), well demarcated from off-white centre of throat (white tips more extensive), lower throat and upper breast white. Upper flanks, sides of breast and band across lower breast cinnamon (as nominate *iouschistos* or slightly browner). Belly off-white, well demarcated from breast band but grading into pinkish or pinkish-cinnamon lower flanks and vent, feathers narrowly tipped white. Axillaries and underwing-coverts white. *In worn plumage,* breast band narrower and paler, more buffish-cinnamon, belly more extensively pinkish; when very worn, dark feather bases extensively exposed on breast. Iris pale yellow to yellow-white; bill black; legs yellow-brown to dark brown. **Juvenile**: Sides of crown sooty, mantle tinged buffy-brown (with no cinnamon upper border), chin and malar stripes sooty, ear-coverts buff, submoustachial stripe, throat and breast tinged buff, underparts buff, dark grey feather bases revealed, especially on upper breast and centre of belly, forming an irregular breast band of dark blotches. Averages slightly larger and proportionally longer-tailed than nominate *iouschistos*. Wing of male 50–61.5, of female 55–62; tail of male 51–64, of female 52.5–60; bill 6.5–9.5. Weight 5–8.5 g.

**A. i. obscuratus** North-central Sichuan in the mountains northwest of the Red Basin, from Tianquan, Baoxing, Guan Xian, Wenchuan and Maowen to Songpan. Probably intergrades with *bonvaloti* in the west. Inexplicably linked with *iouschistos* by Wunderlich (1991b). Poorly marked. As *bonvaloti,* but overall duller. Ear-coverts, rear crown stripe and nape darker and browner, mantle slightly browner (brownish-grey, not olive-grey), chin and centre of throat more extensively grey, with the black 'V' less well defined (?), breast band and upper flanks slightly darker and browner (more brownish-cinnamon), breast band may average narrower and better defined.

**THE *SHARPEI* GROUP** Endemic to Mount Victoria in SW Burma. Given its highly disjunct distribution (*c.* 600 km from its nearest neighbours) and distinctive appearance, it may be better treated as a distinct species, *A. sharpei* ('Burmese Tit'), recalling White-throated or even Sooty Tit. Close to White-throated Tit of the NW Himalayas, but rear crown stripe cinnamon-brown (not pinkish-brown), upper mantle cinnamon-brown (not grey), white throat not so extensive, with dark chin and malar stripes (absent on White-throated), and underparts more pinkish-cinnamon (less beige or pinkish-drab). Near *bonvaloti,* but note pattern of breast band, ear-coverts and underparts.

**A. i. sharpei** Forehead and centre of crown whitish, grading to cinnamon-brown on rear crown and nape; ear-coverts cinnamon-brown. Blackish bands at sides of crown slightly narrower, especially at rear, than on other races, contrasting less with the rear crown stripe and ear-coverts. Chin and sides of throat blackish, centre of throat and submoustachial stripe white (dark feather bases on throat paler, greyer and less extensive than on other races, fully concealed). Upper breast and sides of neck white. Well-defined cinnamon-brown breast band, centre of lower breast and belly dirty pinkish-cinnamon, feathers tipped off-white, remainder of underparts cinnamon or cinnamon-buff. White in tail as *bonvaloti*. Smaller than *bonvaloti*: nearer nominate *iouschistos,* but proportionally longer-tailed. Wing of male 54–57, of female 51–54; tail 48–52; bill 8.4–9.5; tarsus 15–19.

**RELATIONSHIPS** The four subspecies of the Black-browed Tit, together with the White-throated Tit of the western Himalayas, form a complex group which has been considered to comprise between one and four species.

**REFERENCES** Ali & Ripley (1983), Fleming *et al.* (1984), Wunderlich (1991a, b).

This poorly known tit is confined to a small area of central China, and information on its habits and breeding biology is almost entirely lacking.

**IDENTIFICATION** Length 115 mm (4.5 in). A typical long-tailed tit in size, shape and actions. Centre of crown and nape dark brown, slightly paler and greyer at the sides. Lores, supercilium and cheek patches contrastingly frosty pale grey, grading at the rear into the brown nape and demarcated below by the grey-brown moustachial stripe. Upperparts dark brown, with the rump paler and pinker, and the tail fringed and tipped white. Throat pale grey, finely streaked whiter (wearing to sooty-brown), bordered below by the white sides of the neck and upper breast, which in turn are bordered by a broad brown breast band. Belly white, rear flanks and vent pinkish, variably mottled brown or cinnamon on the flanks and white on the vent, undertail-coverts mixed brown and white. Note that the juvenile is rather different, with a white crown stripe and more boldly marked breast band. Identification straightforward, the brownish upperparts, lack of black markings on the head, silver-grey cheek patches and clear-cut dark breast band being distinctive among the long-tailed tits. Sometimes found in the same areas as Black-browed Tit (even forming mixed flocks), but that species has a richer, more rufous breast band and flanks and bold blackish lateral crown stripes. Note also that this poorly

known species could be confused with Streak-throated Fulvetta.

**SEX/AGE** Sexes similar. Juvenile distinct, with the forehead and centre of the crown white (rather than dull brown), forming a broad white crown stripe, contrastingly darker sides to the crown, pale grey cheeks with a slightly paler supercilium and a blackish wedge behind the eye, purer white throat, darker breast band and whiter underparts, lacking the pinkish flanks. No information on 1st adult, but presumably similar to the adult after the post-juvenile moult.

**VOICE** Typical of that of the genus, although perhaps not so sweet, less hesitant and more incisive than is usual. Includes single thin *sit* or *chit* notes, repeated in an irregular series and sometimes given with more emphasis as *sut*; thin, high, silvery *si-si-si, si-si, si-si-si...* phrases; a rolling *sir-rrup*; and low, rattling *chrrrr, sirrrr* or *trrrr* (harder and 'stonier' than the equivalent call of Long-tailed Tit).

**DISTRIBUTION AND MOVEMENTS** Endemic to western and central **China** and apparently confined to the mountains around the northern and western perimeters of the Red Basin. In central **Sichuan** occurs from the Min Shan and Pingwu south through Maowen and the Qionglai

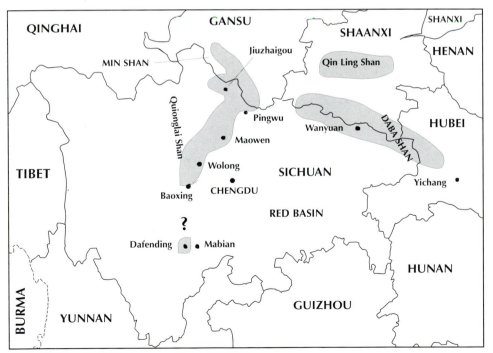

Figure 108.1 Approximate distribution in west and central China, with some localities mentioned in the text. Recorded only in the altitudinal band 1000–2600 m, Sooty Tit must be especially vulnerable to deforestation, which is rampant and devastating at these altitudes. The species is listed as near-threatened in Collar et al. (1994).

Shan range to Baoxing (where very rare; recorded by Swinhoe 1871); range includes Jiuzhaigou and Wolong Panda Reserves, and also noted at Dafending Panda Reserve, Mabian Co. (R.P. Martins pers. comm.). In adjacent southern **Gansu** found in the Min Shan, in southern **Shaanxi** in the Qin Ling Shan, and in NE **Sichuan** in the Daba Shan (Wanyuan), extending into western **Hubei**, NW of Yichang. Resident.

**HABITAT** Mixed forest with firs and well-developed deciduous scrub (such as willows and birches along the watercourses), rhododendrons and often an extensive bamboo understorey. Favours the lower parts of the coniferous/mixed-forest zone, and recorded in NW Sichuan at 1000–2600 m, at *c.* 2150 m in central-south Sichuan (July), 2440 m in southern Gansu in September and above 1000 m in southern Shaanxi, in April–October. Some evidence of altitudinal movements, as noted at 1160–1380 m in winter in Sichuan.

**POPULATION** Generally rather uncommon, and rare in southern Shaanxi. Listed as near-threatened in BirdLife International's world checklist of threatened birds (Collar *et al.* 1994).

**HABITS** Typical of the genus. After the breeding season (from June onwards) found in fast-moving family parties, with up to 40 birds recorded together. Forages in the shrub layer. Food insects and berries.

**BREEDING BIOLOGY** Poorly known. Presumed to be feeding young in the nest in Jiuzhaigou, northern Sichuan, in mid May.

**DESCRIPTION Adult**: *In fresh plumage* (September–March), forehead, centre of crown and nape, mantle, scapulars and back rich dark brown, narrow band on rump light vinous-pink, shorter uppertail-coverts cinnamon-brown. Sides of crown and nape, rear ear-coverts and moustachial stripe slightly paler and more grey-brown. Throat, lores, cheeks, supercilium and fore ear-coverts light to pale grey, grading into browner sides of crown and rear ear-coverts; throat feathers dark grey at base with fine whitish shaft streaks.

*Figure 108.2 Tail of adult.*

Tail dark brown, T1–T4 fringed mid grey, broadly so at the base, T3 sometimes with a small whitish spot at the tip of the outer web, T4–T6 with triangular whitish spot at tip of shaft, most extensive on T6, where outer web extensively white; tail graduated, T3 longest, T6 *c.* 20 mm shorter (see figure 108.2 below). Wings mid brown, alula slightly darker, secondary and primary coverts and flight feathers fringed slightly dark brown. Sides of neck and upper breast white, lower breast rich dark brown, forming a broad breast band extending to the upper flanks. Belly white, rear flanks vinous-pink, variably tipped brown or cinnamon, vent vinous-pink, feathers tipped whiter, undertail-coverts brown, broadly fringed white. Thighs brown. Axillaries whitish, underwing-coverts whitish with some faint brown feather tips. *In worn plumage*, upper mantle paler and greyer, wings and tail abraded; dark grey bases to throat feathers may be revealed when very worn. **Bare Parts**: Iris white, yellow or yellow-brown; bill, legs and feet black? **Juvenile**: Forehead and centre of crown white (grading into grey of nape at rear), sides of crown sooty brown-black, slightly paler and browner at rear and on nape. Short dark wedge or eyestripe immediately behind eye. Mantle and scapulars sooty-brown; tail sooty-black, feathers tipped white (pattern as adult?). Wings dark brown, fringes to tertials and flight feathers tinged olive. Short but broad pale grey supercilium above and behind eye, cheeks and ear-coverts slightly darker greyish. Throat, sides of neck (forming a half-collar) and upper breast white. Wide, well-defined sooty brown-black breast band. Remainder of underparts white, upper flanks washed pale grey. Eyering dull ochre; iris dull pale olive-yellow (as adult?); bill yellowish, tipped horn-brown; legs and feet dull brownish-flesh (no specimens seen; descriptions from photographs supplied by Johan Wallander, taken at Jiuzhaigou, Sichuan, in June 1988). **1st Adult**: No information. **Measurements**: Wing of male 53.5–60, of female 52.5–58; tail of male 52–62, of female 51–59; bill 7.5–8.8; tarsus 17–18.5. Weight 4–8 g.

**MOULT** Adult post-breeding complete? (September). Post-juvenile, no information; presumably complete as in other members of the genus.

**GEOGRAPHICAL VARIATION** None.

**RELATIONSHIPS** No obvious affinities to other members of the genus, although approaches in some respects the *bonvaloti* group of races (especially the race *obscuratus*) of Black-browed Tit.

**REFERENCES** Bangs & Peters (1928), Cheng

## 109 BUSHTIT *Psaltriparus minimus*    Plate 36
Other names: Black-eared, Common, Lead-coloured and Plain Bushtit

The smallest North American tit, and indeed one of the smallest North American birds. It displays a complex geographical variation, and has been treated as two or even three separate species, whilst it also has an intricate social system.

**IDENTIFICATION** Length 100–110 mm (4–4.5 in). A tiny tit with a long, graduated tail, small stubby bill, plain grey-brown upperparts, and whitish underparts variably washed grey, buff or pinkish. West-coast birds have a contrasting brown cap, the interior race a grey cap and browner ear-coverts, and a varying proportion of birds from Arizona, New Mexico and Texas southwards into Mexico and Guatemala a grey cap, olive-grey upperparts, blackish ear-coverts and richly coloured underparts. The very small size, long tail, plain plumage and gregarious habits are distinctive. Juveniles, especially recently fledged birds with short tails, could be confused with a juvenile Verdin, although the highly gregarious habits of Bushtit would preclude confusion in most cases. When full-grown, the tail of juvenile Bushtit is 46–62 mm long, compared with 43–50 mm in Verdin, but the two species are best separated by bill shape, a tiny black chisel in Bushtit compared with Verdin's large, conical bill, which is pale-based in juveniles. Bushtits also show either a brownish cap or brownish to black ear-coverts, compared with the completely plain grey head of a juvenile Verdin.

**SEX/AGE** Sexes variably distinct. The most reliable character for sexing birds is eye colour, dark brown in males of all ages and white, cream or yellow in females. Note that young juvenile females also show dark brown eyes, gradually paling through grey to whitish; the difference between the sexes in iris coloration may be perceptible in the hand a few days after fledging, but some birds may take several weeks to change eye colour. Plumage differences between the sexes show considerable geographical variation. In the interior *plumbeus* group the sexes are very similar, although males show a contrast between the white throat and upper breast and pale drab-grey underparts, females having a duller throat, contrasting less with the underparts (although a more obvious buff tinge to the belly and vent). In addition, any individual north of Mexico showing black on the ear-coverts after the post-juvenile moult is likely to be a male. In the west-coast *minimus* group the

sexes are slightly more distinct, males having a whitish throat and pinkish-drab wash on the flanks, whilst on females the throat and breast are duller, washed drab-grey. In the Mexican *melanotis* group males usually differ strikingly from females in underpart coloration, with the throat and sides of the neck white, breast and upper flanks pale vinous-grey, rear flanks extensively vinous-pink and vent and rearmost flanks buff. Females have the chin washed drab, throat and sides of the neck pale grey-white, tinged vinous-grey or pink on the lower throat and sides of the neck and grading to buff on the remainder of the underparts, deepest on the flanks and vent (paler in worn plumage). All males have the sides of the head (and often the chin) blackish, faintly glossed blue in adults, whilst on females the sides of the head vary from pale drab in northern populations to dull black on the upper and rear ear-coverts on southern birds. See Geographical Variation. In juvenile plumage, the differences between the sexes may be reduced or even absent, and are obscured by wear, otherwise juveniles are very similar to adults. In the *minimus* group the cap of juveniles is rather paler and drabber than the adults', contrasting less with the mantle. In the *plumbeus* group the juvenile is slightly duller and drabber than the fresh adult, with less contrastingly brownish ear-coverts, thus resembling a worn adult, although with fresh wing and tail feathers. The ear-coverts are variably black on some juvenile males, especially in the southern parts of the range (southern Arizona and New Mexico), where occasionally juvenile females also show black ear-coverts. In the *melanotis* group juveniles resemble the respective adult sex, but with less contrast between the cap and mantle, sometimes with drab-brown fringes to the feathers of the cap, and duller and browner wings and tail. Juvenile males have sootier-black ear-coverts and average slightly duller and buffer on the underparts than adult males; juvenile females have slightly duller and paler buff underparts than adult females and usually show a mix of black in the ear-coverts, especially on the upper and rear portions, whereas adult females vary from plain pale drab to blackish. See Geographical Variation. In the hand, juveniles of all races show loose undertail-coverts and, when very fresh, a relatively unworn tail. The most important character is, however, the length and shape of the first primary. In juveniles, it is relatively broader and more oblong (the vane tapering for less than a third of the total length), and usually longer than 15 mm from the tip to the point of insertion (see figure 109.1). In adults, the first primary is narrower and dagger-like (the vane tapering for more than half its length) and usually less

*Figure 109.1  First primary (P1) of adult (left) and juvenile (right): note shape and length.*

than 15 mm long (although 12–16 mm in *plumbeus*). 1st adult as adult after the complete post-juvenile moult.

**VOICE** Rather vocal. Contact call a moderately high-pitched, quiet, delicate but emphatic *pit* or *tsit* given in irregular series and combined with occasional, harsher, more powerful and more 'rolling' *srrit* notes. When birds are moving more rapidly, the *pit* or *srrit* notes are louder and sometimes combined with high-pitched, silvery, quavering trills (which strongly recalls Long-tailed Tit), thus *pit, pit, pit, sre-e-e-e-e-e* or *srrit, srrit, srrit, sisisi*; in anxiety when an individual is separated from the main flock, this sequence is even louder and faster. In alarm several loud, abrupt *tsit* or *psit* notes are given in rapid, monotonous succession (these notes may be a hard, rock-clicking *chik* or *click*), and when an avian predator is sighted a *sre-e-e-e-e-e*, often taken up by the whole flock in a 'confusion chorus' lasting up to 2 minutes. No song is known. (Partly after Grinnell 1903.)

**DISTRIBUTION AND MOVEMENTS** Breeds in **Canada** in SW **British Columbia** (the Vancouver region and Vancouver island north to at least Campbell river), and in the **USA** from western **Washington** (west of the Cascades, also Yakima Co.), **Oregon**, SW **Idaho** (Owyhee Co. east to at least Oneida Co.), northern **Utah**, SW **Wyoming** (notably Sweetwater Co.) and north-central **Colorado**, south to Mexico. Ranges east to western **Colorado**, where found east to western Eagle and Gunnison Cos. (rarely), the San Luis valley, and in SE Colorado from southern Chaffee and El Paso Cos. east to SW Baca Co. (has bred Boulder Co.), western **Oklahoma**, where resident in NW Cimarron Co. (also recorded rarely in Woods, Woodward, Ellis and Comanche Cos.), and **Texas**, where found in the Trans-Pecos mountains and on the western rim of the Edwards plateau and the Brazos river drainage north to Eastland Co. and east to Dallas, Travis and Bexar Cos.; also stated to be resident in the panhandle (south to Howard Co. and east to Palo Pinto Co.) by Arnold (1984), but status in much of central Texas obscure. In **California** the range includes Santa Cruz island and formerly Santa Catalina island, but absent from the higher parts of the Sierra Nevada and from much of the Mojave desert and Imperial valley; vagrant Anacapa island, August 1976. In **Arizona** absent from parts of the southwest (although breeds in the Harquahala mountains, and has bred along Salt river east of Phoenix). In **Mexico** largely montane, occurring in the Sierra Madre Occidental and central and southern highlands south to the Sierra Madre del Sur in **Guerrero** and **Oaxaca** and the mountains of **Chiapas**. Absent from most or all of the Gulf slope north of **Veracruz** and **Puebla** (although recorded from NE **San Luis Potosi** and the Sierra del Carmen in NW **Coahuila**). Also found in **Baja California Norte** and disjunctly in the mountains of southern **Baja California Sur**. In **Guatemala** breeds in the volcanic and western highlands southeast to Chimaltenango and north to San Mateo. (See also Geographical Variation; mapped range in Mexico tentative.) Resident, although some post-breeding

wanderings, e.g. to SE Wyoming, and north and east in Colorado to Larimer Co. In **Kansas**, several autumn-winter records from Morton Co. since 1976, and also recorded Ellis and Hamilton Cos. Additionally, some populations may undertake altitudinal movements, birds of the southwestern mountains moving at irregular intervals to higher altitudes or dispersing into suitable habitat in the surrounding desert lowlands in the period July–April, e.g. into the eastern watershed of the Sierra Nevada in California, in SW Arizona to the Colorado valley in La Paz and Yuma Cos., and into northern Sonora and western Texas, including the northern Texan Panhandle north to Potter Co.

**HABITAT** Generally open deciduous and mixed woodland and second growth, favouring live oak, pine-oak, juniper-pinyon pine and Coyote Brush. Prefers well-spaced large shrubs and small trees, edge habitats and valley-bottom deciduous growth in denser montane forests, and also found in sagebrush, mesquite, chaparral, scrub-oak and cedar brush, in more arid areas especially in canyons and along watercourses. Frequently enters residential areas, and outside the breeding season may wander into fir forests at higher altitudes or to desert areas, although generally avoids open desert. Capricious, it may be absent from apparently suitable habitat, or may appear and disappear unpredictably. Found from near sea level along the Pacific coast from California south to northern Baja California (where occurs up to at least 760 m), and at mid altitudes on the Edwards plateau of Texas, where recorded as low as 180 m (although breeding above c. 500 m). Otherwise, in interior USA and Mexico largely montane: found in the Californian coast range up to 1850 m, with post-breeding dispersal up to 2750 m; in the Sierra Nevada breeds at up to 2440 m (once 2930 m), dispersing as high as 3140 m; in the Rocky Mountains up to 2440 m, occasionally to 2650 m (and a July record at 3505 m in Colorado); in Arizona mainly 1220–2135 m, in New Mexico 1370–2135 m (exceptionally 2745 m), in SW Texas c. 1525–2600 m, in Baja California up to 2500 m, in interior Mexico c. 1500–3505 m (but recorded down to 1070 m), and in Guatemala 1500–3350 m.

**POPULATION** Fairly common in British Columbia. In the USA, commonest in the West Coast states (especially in the oak woodlands of the Sacramento valley and coast range of California) and in the southwest, fairly common in Nevada, Utah, Oklahoma and Texas, and uncommon in Idaho, Wyoming and Colorado. In Mexico apparently commonest in the north, in Baja California and Sonora, and rather sparser in the south (although fairly common in Oaxaca). Common in Guatemala. Has expanded its range in Oregon, northern Washington and British Columbia (on Vancouver island, first nested in 1937 and now common).

**HABITS** Active, tame and confiding; found in suburban areas and often visits birdbaths. Highly gregarious outside the breeding season; juveniles are not driven off by their parents and family parties combine to form flocks of 6–40, moving through the vegetation in a 'follow-my-leader' fashion. Flight weak, and undulating over longer distances. Once formed, flocks are very stable, with little or no interchange between groups, and contain many of the same birds from year to year; 'foreigners' are usually driven off once the flock has formed. Flocks have moderately defined territories, but boundaries may overlap and chance contacts precipitate loud calling, pursuits and fights between males. Bushtit flocks may join mixed-species foraging flocks for short periods as they move through the area. Courtship begins in the flock and involves excited contact calls, trills, and posturing, and pair-bonds are sometimes maintained from year to year. Flocks begin to break up in January and February, pairs usually nesting within their flock's winter range and maintaining poorly defined territories, although some individuals may move 3–4 km to nest and subsequently join the local flock there. Although flocks of Bushtits may be encountered throughout the breeding season, these comprise birds which have not yet completed their nest and return to the flock overnight, or adults and young from early-breeding pairs. Flocks roost in the open among dense branches, with individuals usually well spaced, but they may form a tight huddle, presumably to conserve energy. In the early stages of breeding the mated pairs return to the flock to roost, but once the outer shell of the nest is complete the breeding pair will roost in the nest. Forages by gleaning from foliage and small branches of trees and shrubs (even the finest peripheral branches), but rarely on the ground. Food insects and spiders, also seeds and fruit.

**BREEDING BIOLOGY** Season: USA, mid January–early July; Mexico, April–June; Guatemala, March–April. The nest is gourd-shaped, 165–300 mm tall x 65–100 mm in diameter, with the entrance hole usually at one side near the top. It is placed in a tree or shrub, 1.25–7.5 m above ground, sometimes as high as 15 m, suspended from the end of a single twig or branch in full view or woven around and supported by several twigs and thus more concealed. The site is apparently selected by the male. The nest is constructed by both sexes from twigs, rootlets, moss, lichen, leaves, plant down, cocoons, grass, wool, feathers and flowers, all bound together with spiders' webs. The interior is lined with a cup of plant down, hair and feathers, the birds continuing to add material until the young fledge. Nest-building takes 13–51 days, the period varying owing to the reuse of material from nests which have been lost to predation or bad weather; these may be dismantled and recycled in the same season by the building pair or by other pairs, allowing later nests to be constructed more rapidly than initial nests. Indeed, if disturbed during nest-building, laying or incubation, pairs often desert, and then may change mates and build a new nest; a single pair may make up to five nesting attempts in a single season. Occasionally, one or both partners are usurped from an active nest by other Bushtits. Clutch 5–7 (4–8, 4 being more frequent in Mexico?): eggs white, c. 13.7 x 10.1 mm (*P. m.*

*minimus*). Both sexes incubate, period 12 days (15–16 days recorded from Guatemala: Skutch 1960), and both sexes brood and feed the young, which fledge after 14–15 days (17–19 in Guatemala) and are independent after a further 8–14 days. Rarely double-brooded in coastal California, although two breeds may be more common in interior populations with a more extended breeding season. Bushtits have a complex social system, not yet fully understood. Clutches of up to 15 eggs have been recorded and probably result from two females laying in the same nest, and the species is questionably monogamous. Breeding pairs show a high tolerance of other Bushtits in their territory, allowing them to forage and even to take part in lining the nest, in incubation and in feeding the young, and sometimes permitting them to roost in the nest. These supernumeraries have been dubbed 'helpers', and are usually or always males. Ervin (1978), however, considers that such cases of helping are uncommon, one-off events that are probably the result of chance and the Bushtit's highly gregarious nature, rather than being a regular breeding strategy.

**DESCRIPTION** *P. m. plumbeus* **Adult Male**: *In fresh plumage* (September–March), upperparts mid grey, forehead tinged drab, mantle and scapulars faintly tinged olive-drab in some southern populations. Tail dark drab-grey, T1 and outer webs of T2–T5 narrowly fringed light grey, T6 with outer web and tip of inner web whitish. Lesser coverts mid grey, remainder of wing dark drab-grey, fringed mid grey, broadly so on greater coverts (dark centres fully concealed); fringes present only inwards of emarginations on P3–P6 and absent on P1–P2. Lores, cheeks and ear-coverts dull brownish-drab, sides of neck light grey. Chin white, faintly washed buff, throat and centre of breast off-white, remainder of underparts pale drab-grey. Underwing-coverts and axillaries white. In worn plumage (April–August), upperparts purer grey, wings and tail browner, grey fringes variably abraded, underparts whiter. **Bare Parts**: Iris dark brown; bill black or blackish-grey, base of lower mandible may be pale blue-grey or whitish; legs and feet brownish-black. **Adult Female**: As male, but throat averages duller, not so pure white, and a distinct buff tinge to the belly and vent. Iris white, cream or yellow. **Juvenile**: As adult, but forehead and sides of head paler and greyer, upperparts faintly washed drab, ear-coverts variably black on some juvenile males, especially in southern parts of the range (rarely also on juvenile females), wings and tail slightly paler and browner, underparts lightly washed drab. Iris dark at fledging, but rapidly becoming pale in females. **1st Adult**: As adult. **Measurements**: Wing of male 49–55 (chord 48–53.5), of female 49.5–53 (chord 48–53.5); tail of male 54.5–62, of female 51–60.5; bill 7.6–9.1; tarsus 15–16.5. Weight 5–6 g (*P. m. dimorphicus*) (Miller 1955).

**MOULT** Adult post-breeding complete (July–October, USA; June–November, Mexico). Post-juvenile moult complete (July–October, USA; July–September, Mexico).

**GEOGRAPHICAL VARIATION** Complex, with

*Figure 109.2 Head of three adult male 'P. m. lloydi', from the Chisos mountains of Texas, showing variation in extent of blackish on the lores, cheeks and ear-coverts. (After Raitt 1967)*

11 subspecies divisible into three groups: the *minimus* group of the Pacific coastal regions, the interior *plumbeus* group and the southern *melanotis* group. They meet in zones of secondary intergradation in California, Texas and northern Mexico, and are sometimes treated as three distinct species (e.g. Oberholser 1974), largely based on the now discredited theory that the *melanotis* and *plumbeus* groups overlap without interbreeding in SW Texas; in fact, the *plumbeus* and *melanotis* groups show a near-continuous gradation of characters from north to south. (Largely after Raitt 1967 and, for Mexican races, Phillips 1986.)

**THE *MINIMUS* GROUP** 'Plain' or 'Common Bushtit'. The Pacific coast region from British Columbia southwards, west of the Cascades and Sierra Nevada, to southern Baja California. Cap brown, upperparts grey or brownish-grey, ear-coverts dull brownish-drab. Variation largely clinal, involving the colour of the cap, upperparts and flanks.

*P. m. saturatus* Southern British Columbia and the Puget Sound lowlands of Washington, including Whidbey island. As nominate *minimus*, but cap darker, dark sooty-brown, mantle darker, duller and not so pure grey, dark sooty-grey, flanks darker brownish-vinaceous, especially on males. Wing (chord) of male 46.5–47, of female 47.5–48.5.

*P. m. minimus* Pacific coast region, west of the Cascades, from the Columbia river in northern Oregon, south through coastal California (west of the coast range) to Santa Barbara Co., possibly to Los Angeles Co.; also the Yakima valley of south-central Washington. Male as *plumbeus*, but crown and nape olive-brown, upperparts washed olive, contrasting strongly with the cap, underparts duller and buffer, rear flanks washed pinkish-drab or vinaceous-drab. Underparts of female average buffer than on female *plumbeus*. Wing of male 47–49, of female 45–48.

*P. m. melanurus* Coastal southern California from northern San Diego Co. (possibly north to Los Angeles Co.), south in Baja California Norte to c. 30º N. Poorly marked. As *saturatus*, but crown and nape slightly browner, contrasting more with the mantle, which is a slightly cleaner grey, flanks more drab-brown, less vinaceous-brown.

*P. m. californicus* Interior southern Oregon (Jackson, Klamath and Josephine Cos.) south in California (east of the coast range, although almost to coast in Mendocino Co.) to Kern Co. As nominate *minimus*, but crown slightly paler and warmer brown, mantle slightly paler and cleaner grey (less washed with olive), underparts whiter, flanks of male washed drab with reduced vinaceous tones. Hybridises with *plumbeus* in a narrow north-south zone in California, in the northeast in Modoc and Lassen Cos., and the south-centre in western Inyo and (?) Mono Cos. The hybrid population shows a mixture of characters (especially in cap coloration), but each individual more or less resembles one or other of the parent populations.

*P. m. grindae* Mountains of the cape district of Baja California Sur, north to c. 24º N. As *californicus* but at all ages mantle slightly paler and purer grey.

**THE *PLUMBEUS* GROUP** 'Lead-coloured Bushtit'. Mountains of interior western North America from Oregon to northern Sonora and western Texas. Upperparts grey with no contrast between the cap and mantle, although ear-coverts dull brownish-drab.

*P. m. plumbeus* Central-eastern Oregon, Idaho and Wyoming south to eastern California (eastern watershed of Sierra Nevada, also Little San Bernardino mountains), central-north Sonora, southern Arizona (including Chiricahua mountains) southern New Mexico (including Peloncillo mountains and western Texas (Guadalupe mountains)), east to western Oklahoma; recorded Yakima valley of south-central Washington. Intergrades with the race *californicus* of the *minimus* group on the eastern flank of Sierra Nevada in California (Inyo and eastern Lassen and Riverside Cos.). See Description. Some slight local variation. Upperparts faintly tinged olive in some southern populations and ear-coverts variably black on some juvenile males, especially in the southern parts of the range (not uncommon in southern Arizona and New Mexico), while individuals with a small amount of black are occasionally found north to Nevada, Utah and Colorado and exceptionally juvenile females show black ear-coverts in southern Arizona and New Mexico.

**INTERMEDIATE POPULATIONS** The 'hybrid' population between the Black-eared and Lead-coloured groups may be known as '*P. m. lloydi*' (type locality the Davis mountains of Texas), although the naming of such a population is not necessarily satisfactory (note that *lloydi* was used to designate a population of *plumbeus* characterised only by its smaller size by Phillips *et al.*

1964 and Rea 1983; the range of this smaller group does not correspond with that of *lloydi* as presently defined). In the populations of extreme SW **New Mexico** (San Luis mountains), NE **Sonora** (NE Sierra Madre east of Rio Bavispe), NW **Chihuahua** and central and western **Texas** (except Guadalupe mountains), adult males are dimorphic, either black-eared or grey-eared, the proportion of black-eared males increasing southwards. In this area, the proportion of black-eared juvenile males shows a similar southwards increase, being lowest on the Edwards plateau and reaching 100% in the Chisos mountains, and juvenile females are also dimorphic, the proportion showing black ear-coverts reaching 50% in the Chisos mountains; adult females are always grey-eared. North of this region, no adult males show black ear-coverts, and the occasional black-eared juvenile males are probably the result of the introgression of black-eared genes into northern populations. South of this area, all adult males show black ear-coverts. Within the zone, birds are rather variable. The black on the head may be restricted to a small patch on the rear ear-coverts or a narrow eye-stripe, or it may include the entire 'face' (lores, ear-coverts, submoustachial region and sides of neck) and extend in a line across the nape. All intermediate stages occur, and the face often appears mottled with black and brown. The prevalence of black shows a rough north-south cline, and there is also a slight average increase in the olive wash on the mantle and a tendency towards the brighter underpart coloration of Mexican birds. Because of the instability of these intermediate populations, where both grey-eared and black-eared birds may be found together, and a poor understanding of the variation with age and sex, Black-eared and Lead-coloured Bushtits were believed to overlap in this hybrid zone and to behave as separate species (e.g. in Chisos, Glass and Davis mountains of Trans-Pecos Texas and San Luis mountains on the New Mexico/Sonora/Chihuahua border). Various differences in habitat preferences, range and vocalisations were described, all of which are now known to be spurious. In previous accounts, the range of *plumbeus* in the north and that of *dimorphicus* in the south have been extended into the zone to a variable extent (e.g. *lloydi* was synonymised with *plumbeus* by Phillips 1986, although otherwise it is usually treated as part of the Black-eared group). Here, I follow the boundaries of the hybrid zone described in Raitt (1967); see text figure, 109.3, p. 443.

**THE *MELANOTIS* GROUP** 'Black-eared Bushtit'. Middle America from central Sonora and northern Coahuila south to central Guatemala. Variation largely clinal, with an increasing proportion of age/sex-classes in the south showing black ear-coverts and an increasing extent of black on the individuals that exhibit it, also a more intense olive wash to the mantle (and thus greater contrast with the grey crown).

**P. m. dimorphicus** Mountains of central-east and SE Sonora south to NE Sinaloa and northernmost Durango, also northern Coahuila (Sierra del Carmen). As *plumbeus*, but upperparts average slightly drabber, contrasting more with the cap. Underparts of male tinged light vinaceous-grey with a faint buff cast, deepest and most vinous on the rear flanks, showing more contrast with the white throat, and vent pale buff; female with chin washed drab, throat and breast washed light grey, tinged pink, remainder of underparts pale buff, deepest on the rear flanks and vent (as female *plumbeus*). All males have sooty-black supercilium, lores, ear-coverts, submoustachial stripe, and also often chin, adult female with ear-coverts light drab, and juvenile female dimorphic. Wing of male 46.5–51, of female 49–50.

**P. m. iulus** Mountains from Durango and (?) SE Coahuila (around Saltillo) south to southern Jalisco (Nevada de Colima), SW (?) and NW Michoacan and southern Queretaro, east to western Tamaulipas (also this race NE San Luis Potosi?). As *dimorphicus*, but upperparts mid grey, washed brownish-olive, showing marked contrast with the cap, rump more cinnamon-brown. Male has breast and belly slightly paler and whiter than *dimorphicus*, but rear flanks and vent rich cinnamon-buff. Female has belly, rear flanks and vent washed buff. All males black-eared, the black faintly glossed blue-green on adults; adult female often with sooty-black on the upper and rear ear-coverts, especially when blackish feather bases revealed in worn plumage; juvenile female with ear-coverts a mix of sooty-black and drab-brown, black most frequent on upper and rear ear-coverts. Wing of male 49–52, of female 48–49.

**P. m. personatus** Mountains of central Mexico from central Michoacan east through Mexico and southern Hidalgo to western Veracruz (including Cofre de Perote) and north to NE Puebla. As *iulus*, but mantle cinnamon-brown, contrasting strongly with the cap, rump paler and more cinnamon. Male has underparts as *iulus*, but breast and belly slightly drabber (i.e. as *dimorphicus*), thus showing less contrast with rich cinnamon-buff rear flanks and vent. Female has breast washed buff, the remainder of the underparts as female *iulus* although slightly deeper. Ear-coverts as *iulus*, but on males black may extend onto the sides of the nape in a half-collar or extend across the nape in a narrow nuchal band. Wing of male 48–51.5, of female 46–51.

**P. m. melanotis** Mountains of southern Mexico in Guerrero, Oaxaca (throughout interior and down to at least 1950 m on Pacific slope) and Chiapas (and possibly westwards coastally to SW Jalisco), also Guatemala. As *personatus*, but upperparts slightly darker and duller brown (less cinnamon, more olive), rear flanks and vent of male slightly duller cinnamon, underparts of female slightly deeper buff. All males and juvenile females black-eared; adult females have blackish upper ear-coverts and often connecting narrow black nuchal band.

**RELATIONSHIPS** The Common Bushtit 'P. minimus' and Black-eared Bushtit 'P. melanotis' were formerly considered to be separate species, but have been shown to be conspecific by Raitt (1967). They meet in a rather narrow zone of secondary intergradation around the USA-Mexico

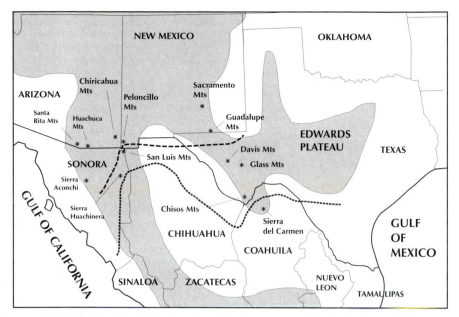

*Figure 109.3 Distribution of Bushtit in SW USA and northern Mexico. The* plumbeus *group is found north of the dashed line, and the* melanotis *group is found south of the dotted line. The intervening area is inhabited by an intermediate polymorphic population, '*P. m. lloydi*'. Note that the mapped range in Texas includes autumn and winter records. (Adapted from Raitt 1967)*

border, a relatively recent mingling of populations probably accounting for the high degree of individual variation (the so-called polymorphism). The Lead-coloured '*P. plumbeus*' and Common groups were also sometimes considered separate species; they hybridise in secondary contact in California. The genus *Psaltriparus* is very closely related to the

typical long-tailed tits in the genus *Aegithalos*; indeed, Bushtit was placed in *Aegithalos* by Snow (1967), Phillips (1986) and Rea (1983).

**REFERENCES** Bent (1946), Ervin (1975, 1977a, b, 1978 & pers. comm.), Grinnell (1903), Phillips (1986), Raitt (1967), Skutch (1987).

# 110 PYGMY TIT *Psaltria exilis*                                         Plate 36

Endemic to Java and the smallest Passerine species, this minute bird is aptly named. Inhabiting tropical forests, its gregarious habits and vocalisations are nevertheless remarkably similar to those of the Long-tailed Tit of temperate latitudes.

**IDENTIFICATION** length 85 mm (3.5 in). Head drab-brown, upperparts mid grey, tinged drab, rump purer grey. Tail drab-brown. Chin and throat light grey, mottled and bordered below by pale pinkish-buff. Sides of breast and upper flanks greyish-drab, remainder of underparts very pale dull pinkish-buff. Unmistakable. A tiny, long-tailed, nondescript tit with a short, stubby, broad-based bill.

**SEX/AGE** Sexes similar, although Kuroda (1936) noted that the female has slightly paler upperparts, with the wing and tail feathers faintly fringed paler. Juvenile and 1st adult probably similar or identical to the adult.

**VOICE** Strongly reminiscent of that of Long-tailed Tit. Most vocalisations are a combination of up to three elements: a high-pitched *si* or *sisi* (sometimes prolonged, or becoming *silililili*), a similarly

high-pitched but sibilant or even grating *srrrr*, and a soft *chip, tchip* or *sip*; e.g. *sisi-srrrr, si... tchip, tchip... sisi... tchip, tchip... sisi tchip tchip... sisi-sirrr...*, and *sip, sip, sisisi sip sip, sisisi....*

**HABITAT** Montane forest and plantations above 1000 m (occasionally down to 830 m), frequenting conifers and other open trees, often on the forest edge.

**DISTRIBUTION AND MOVEMENTS** **Indonesia**. Endemic to **Java**, where it occurs in the mountains in the west and centre of the island. Records from Gonoharjo, Gunung Unguran, and above Pancoran Tujuh, Gunung Slamat, may be the most easterly for the species (Robson 1994).

**POPULATION** Locally common (e.g. at Cibodas). On the densely populated island of Java, however, even this montane-forest endemic should be considered at long-term risk from deforestation.

443

**HABITS** Active, travelling in small flocks. Often forages at low levels. Food insects and spiders.

**BREEDING BIOLOGY** Season, West Java, March–May and August–November. The nest is a suspended pouch of leaves and grass, lined with moss, the small entrance hole being near the top (generally similar to a flowerpecker's nest). Clutch 2–3: eggs white with fine red spots.

**DESCRIPTION Adult**: *In fresh plumage,* crown, lores, cheeks, ear-coverts, nape, sides of neck and border of upper mantle drab-brown, tinged cinnamon on the forehead. Mantle, scapulars and back mid grey, tinged drab, rump purer grey, longer uppertail-coverts drab-brown. Tail drab-brown, shaft and tip of T6 slightly paler, brownish-white. Lesser coverts drab-brown, fringed mid grey, remainder of wing drab-brown with faintly greyer fringes to the greater coverts. Chin and throat light grey, feathers faintly tipped pale pinkish-buff, bordered below by a thin band of pale pinkish-buff. Sides of breast and upper flanks greyish-drab, connected across the breast by a faint narrow breast band of the same colour. Remainder of underparts, axillaries and underwing-coverts dirty whitish, washed pale pinkish-buff, base of longer under primary coverts dark brown. *In worn plumage,* fringes to flight feathers bleached paler. **Bare Parts**: Iris yellowish-white to whitish; bill greyish-horn, dark brown or black; legs and feet fleshy-yellow or yellow. **Juvenile and 1st Adult**: No information. (The 51 specimens in the Rijksmuseum van Natuurlijke Historie, Leiden, form a uniform series, without tangible plumage differences between the sexes and none is recognisable as a juvenile (e.g. by having a pale, relatively small bill): G.F. Mees *in litt.* 1990. Either there is no distinct juvenile plumage, or it is retained for only a very short period after fledging.) **Measurements**: Wing of male 40–49, of female 42–44; tail of male 38–42, of female 33–39, well graduated, with T6 6.5–10 mm shorter than T1; bill 6.3–8.9; tarsus 12–14. Weight: no information.

**MOULT** No information.

**GEOGRAPHICAL VARIATION** None.

**RELATIONSHIPS** Obscure, although behaviour and vocalisations are very similar to those of the Palearctic members of the family.

**REFERENCES** Kuroda (1936), MacKinnon (1988).

# BIBLIOGRAPHY

Note that *Bull. BOC = Bull. Brit. Orn. Club* and *JBNHS = J. Bombay Nat. Hist. Soc.*

Abdulali, H., & Unnithan, S. (1992) A catalogue of the birds in the collection of Bombay Natural History Society - 35: Troglodytidae, Cinclidae, Prunellidae, Paridae, Sittidae and Certhiidae. *JBNHS* 89: 55-71.

Academica Sinica (1980) [A Survey of the vertebrate animals of the Gaoligong Shan district: Vol. 2, Birds.] Beijing: Science Press. [In Chinese.]

Adamus, P.R. (no date) *Atlas of Breeding Birds in Maine, 1978-1983.* Augusta: Maine Dept Inland Fisheries & Wildlife.

Addicott, A.B. (1938) Behaviour of the Bush-tit in the breeding season. *Condor* 40: 49-63.

Aldrich, J.W. (1944) Notes on the races of the White-breasted Nuthatch. *Auk* 61: 592-604.

Alerstam, T., & Ulfstrand, S. (1977) Niches of tits *Parus* spp. in two types of African woodland. *Ibis* 119: 521-524.

Alexander, H.G. (1974) *Seventy Years of Birdwatching.* Berkhamsted: Poyser.

Ali, S. (1935) The ornithology of Travancore and Cochin. Pt 2. *JBNHS* 38: 60-92.

Ali, S. (1942-43) The birds of Mysore. *JBNHS* 43: 130-147, 318-341, 573-595; 44: 9-26, 206-220.

Ali, S. (1945) *The Birds of Kutch.* Bombay: Oxford Univ.

Ali, S. (1946) An ornithological pilgrimage to Lake Manasarowar and Mount Kailas. *JBNHS* 46: 286-308.

Ali, S. (1954-55) The birds of Gujarat. *JBNHS* 52: 374-458, 735-802.

Ali, S. (1962) *The Birds of Sikkim.* Delhi: Oxford Univ.

Ali, S. (1969) *Birds of Kerala.* 2nd edn. Delhi: Oxford Univ.

Ali, S. (1977) *Field Guide to the Birds of the Eastern Himalayas.* Delhi: Oxford Univ.

Ali, S. (1979a) *The Book of Indian Birds.* 11th edn. Delhi: Oxford Univ.

Ali, S. (1979b) *Indian Hill Birds.* Delhi: Oxford Univ.

Ali, S., & Ripley, S.D. (1948) The birds of the Mishmi Hills. *JRNHS* 48: 1-37.

Ali, S., & Ripley, S.D. (1983) *Handbook of the Birds of India and Pakistan together with those of Bangladesh, Nepal, Bhutan and Sri Lanka.* Compact edn. Delhi: Oxford Univ.

Ali, S., Ripley, S.D., & Biswas, B. (in press) The birds of Bhutan. *Rec. Zool. Surv. India, Occ. Pap.* 136.

Allen, F.H. (1910) Warbling song of the Boreal Chickadee. *Auk* 27: 86-87.

Allen, J.A. (1907) The *Baeolophus bicolor-atricristatus* group. *Bull. Am. Mus. Nat. Hist.* 23: 467-481.

Allport, G., Ausden, M., Hayman, P., Robertson, P., & Wood, P. (1989) *The Birds of the Gola Forest and their Conservation.* ICBP Study Report No. 38. Cambridge: International Council for Bird Preservation.

American Ornithologists' Union [AOU] (1957) *Check-list of North American Birds.* 5th edn. AOU.

American Ornithologists' Union [AOU] (1983) *Checklist of North American Birds.* 6th edn. AOU.

Amos, E.J.R. (1991) *A Guide to the Birds of Bermuda.* Bermuda: Corncrake.

Anderson, S.H. (1976) Comparative food habits of Oregon nuthatches. *Northwest Science* 50: 213-221.

Andrews, I.J. (1991) Blue Tits in Jordan. *Bull. Orn. Soc. Middle East* 27: 6-7.

Andrews, I.J. (1995) *The Birds of the Hashemite Kingdom of Jordan.* Musselburgh: author.

Andrews, R., & Righter, R. (1992) *Colorado Birds.* Denver: Denver Mus. Nat. Hist.

Andrle, R.F. (1967) Birds of the Sierra de Tuxtla in Veracruz, Mexico. *Wilson Bull.* 79: 163-187.

Andrle, R.F., & Carroll, J.R. (1988) *The Atlas of Breeding Birds in New York State.* Ithaca, New York: Cornell Univ.

Anon. (1986) European News. *Brit. Birds* 79: 284-292.

Anon. (1988) Additions and corrections to the annotated checklist of the birds of Hong Kong, 4th Edition 1986. *Hong Kong Bird Report 1987:* 28-34.

Anon. (1991) European News. *Brit. Birds* 84: 1-12.

Anon (1993a) European News. *Brit. Birds* 86: 36-47.

Anon. (1993b) European News. *Brit. Birds* 86: 278-293.

Anon. (1994) From the field. *Bull. Oriental Bird Club* 19: 65-67.

Archer, G.F., & Godman, E.M. (1961) *Birds of British Somaliland and the Gulf of Aden.* Vol. IV. Edinburgh & London: Oliver & Boyd.

Armstrong, R.H. (1990) *Guide to the Birds of Alaska.* 3rd edn. Anchorage/Seattle: Alaska Northwest Books.

Arnold, K.A. (1972) Crested Titmice from Cottle and Foard Counties, Texas. *Bull. Texas Orn. Soc.* 5: 23.

Arnold, K.A. (ed.) (1984) *The T.O.S. Checklist of the Birds of Texas.* 2nd edn. Texas Orn. Soc.

Ash, J.S., & Gullick, T.M. (1989) The present situation regarding the endemic breeding birds of Ethiopia. *Scopus* 13: 90-96.

Ash, J.S., & Miskell, J.E. (1983) Birds of Somalia, their habitat, status and distribution. *Scopus* Special Suppl. 1. Nairobi: EANHS.

Austin, G.T. (1976) Behavioral adaptations of the Verdin to the desert. *Auk* 93: 245-262.

Austin, G.T. (1977) Production and survival of the Verdin. *Wilson Bull.* 89: 572-582.

Austin, G.T. (1978a) Daily time budget of the postnesting Verdin. *Auk* 95: 247-251.

Austin, G.T. (1978b) Pattern and timing of moult in penduline tits (*Anthoscopus*). *Ostrich* 49: 168-173.

Austin, G.T., & Rea, A.M. (1971) Key to age and sex determination of Verdins. *Western Bird Bander* 46: 41.

Austin, G.T., & Rea, A.M. (1976) Recent southern Nevada bird records. *Condor* 78: 405-408.

Austin, G.T., & Smith, E.L. (1972) Winter foraging ecology of mixed insectivorous bird flocks in oak woodland in southern Arizona. *Condor* 74: 17-24.

Austin, O.L. (1948) The birds of Korea. *Bull. Mus. Comp. Zool., Harvard* 101: 1-301.

Austin, O.L., & Kuroda, N. (1953) The birds of Japan, their status

and distribution. *Bull. Mus. Comp. Zool., Harvard* 109: 279-637.

Avise, J.C., & Zink, R.M. (1988) Molecular genetic distances between avian sibling species: Long-billed and Short-billed Dowitchers, Boat-tailed and Great-tailed Grackles, and Tufted and Black-crested Titmice. *Auk* 108: 516-528.

Bagg, A.M. (1958) A variant form of the chickadee "fee-bee" call. *Mass. Audubon* 43: 9.

Baker, E.C.S. (1907) The birds of the Khasia Hills. *JBNHS* 17: 783-795, 957-975.

Baker, E.C.S. (1922) *Fauna of British India. Birds.* 2nd edn. Vol. 1. London: Taylor & Francis.

Baker, E.C.S. (1932-33) *The Nidification of Birds of the Indian Empire.* Vols 1 & 2. London: Taylor & Francis.

Balch, L.G. (1980) Mystery bird of the north: the Gray-headed Chickadee. *Birding* 12: 126-131.

Balchin, C.S. (1988) Recent observations of birds from the Ivory Coast. *Malimbus* 10: 201-206.

Bangs, O. (1921) The birds of the American Museum of Natural History's Asiatic Zoological Expedition of 1916-1917. *Bull. Amer. Mus. Nat. Hist.* 44: 575-612.

Bangs, O. (1924) A new form of *Melanochlora sultanea* from Fukien. *Proc. New England Zool. Club* 9: 23.

Bangs, O. (1932) Birds of western China obtained by the Kelley-Roosevelts Expedition. *Field Mus. Nat. Hist. Publ. (Zool. Ser.)* 18: 343-379.

Bangs, O., & Peters, J.L. (1928) Birds collected by Dr. Joseph F. Rock in western Kansu and eastern Tibet. *Bull. Mus. Comp. Zool.* 68: 313-381.

Bangs, O., & Van Tyne, J. (1931) Birds of the Kelley-Roosevelts expedition to French Indo-China. *Field Mus. Nat. Hist. Publ. (Zool. Ser.)* 18: 33-119.

Banks, R.C. (1970a) Re-evaluation of two supposed hybrid birds. *Wilson Bull.* 82: 331-332.

Banks, R.C. (1970b) Moult and taxonomy of Red-breasted Nuthatches. *Wilson Bull.* 82: 201-205.

Banks, R.C. (1978) Prealternate moult in nuthatches. *Auk* 95: 179-181.

Bannerman, D.A. (1930-51) *The Birds of Tropical West Africa.* Vols. 1-8. London: Crown Agents.

Bannerman, D.A. (1935) [Description of *Anthoscopus flavifrons waldroni*.] *Bull. BOC* 55: 131.

Bannerman, D.A. (1939) A new race of penduline tit. *Bull. BOC* 59: 41-42.

Bannerman, D.A. (1953) *The Birds of West and Equatorial Africa.* 2 Vols. London & Edinburgh: Oliver & Boyd.

Baptista, L.F., & Johnson, R.B. (1982) Song variation in insular and mainland California Brown Creepers (*Certhia familiaris*). *J. Orn.* 123: 131-144.

Bardin, A.V. (1987) [Record of Varied Tit on Sakhalin island.] *Ornitologiya* 22: 175. [In Russian.]

Barnes, J.A.G. (1975) *The Titmice of the British Isles.* Newton Abbot: David & Charles.

Bates, R.S.P., & Lowther, E.H.N. (1952) *Breeding Birds of Kashmir.* Delhi: Oxford Univ.

Bauer, H.-G. (1991) Unterschiede in der Stimme von Garten-*Certhia brachydactyla* und Waldbaumläufer *C. familiaris.* *Limicola* 5: 64-69.

Baumgart, W., & Stephan, B. (1994) Weitere Ergebnisse ornithologischer Beobachtungen in Syrien. *Mitt. Zool. Mus. Berlin* 70, Suppl. Ann. Orn. 18: 101-140. [In German.]

Beaman, M.A.S. (1986) Turkey: Bird report 1976-1981. *Sandgrouse* 8: 1-41.

Becker, P.H., Thielcke, G., & Wüstenberg, K. (1980) Versuche zum angenommenen Kontrast - verlust im Gesang der Blaumeise (*Parus caeruleus*) auf Teneriffa. *J. Orn.* 121: 81-95.

Beddall, B.G. (1963) Range expansion of the Cardinal and other birds in the northeastern states. *Wilson Bull.* 75: 140-158.

Beesley, J.S.S. (1973) The breeding seasons of birds in the Arusha National Park, Tanzania. *Bull. BOC* 93: 10-12.

Behle, W.H. (1948) Systematic comment on some geographically variable birds occurring in Utah. *Condor* 50: 71-80.

Behle, W.H. (1951) A new race of the Black-capped Chickadee from the Rocky Mountain region. *Auk* 68: 75-79.

Behle, W.H. (1956) A systematic review of the Mountain Chickadee. *Condor* 58: 51-70.

Behle, W.H., Sorensen, E.D., & White, C.M. (1985) *Utah Birds: A Revised Checklist.* Salt Lake City: Utah Mus. Nat. Hist.

Bellatreche, M. (1991) Deux nouvelles localisations de la Sittelle kabyle *Sitta ledanti* en Algérie. *L'Oiseau* 61: 269-272.

Bellatreche, M., & Chalabi, B. (1990) Données nouvelles sur l'aire de distribution de la Sittelle Kabyle *Sitta ledanti.* *Alauda* 58: 95-97.

Bennun, L.A. (1986a) Montane birds of the Bwindi (Impenetrable) Forest. *Scopus* 10: 87-91.

Bennun, L.A. (1986b) Composition of Bwindi Forest bird parties. *Scopus* 10: 108-111.

Bennun, L.A. (1991) E.A.N.H.S. Nest Record Scheme: 1985-1989. *Scopus* 13: 165-180.

Benson, C.W. (1945-48) Notes on the birds of southern Abyssinia. *Ibis* 87: 366-400, 489-509; 88: 25-48, 180-205, 287-306, 444-461; 89: 29-50; 90: 325-327.

Benson, C.W. (1960) Recent records from north-western North Rhodesia. *Bull. BOC* 80: 106-112, 114-119.

Benson, C.W., & Benson, F.M. (1977) *The Birds of Malawi.* Limbe, Malawi: Montfort Press.

Benson, C.W., Boulton, R., & Irwin, M.P.S. (1961) Some records from the Mpika and Serenje Districts, Northern Rhodesia. *Bull. BOC* 81: 3-5.

Benson, C.W., Brooke, R.K., Dowsett, R.J., & Stuart Irwin, M.P. (1971) *The Birds of Zambia.* London: Collins.

Benson, C.W., & Pitman, C.R.S (1966) Further breeding records from Zambia (formerly Northern Rhodesia) (No. 12). *Bull. BOC* 86: 21-33.

Bent, A.C. (1946) Life histories of North American jays, crows and titmice. *Bull. U.S. Natl Mus.* 191.

Bent, A.C. (1948) Life histories of

445

North American nuthatches, wrens, thrashers and their allies. *Bull. U.S. Natl Mus.* 195.

Betts, F.N. (1956) Notes on the birds of the Subansiri area, Assam. *JBNHS* 53: 397-414.

Bijnens, L., & Dhondt, A.A. (1984) Vocalisations in a Belgian Blue Tit *Parus c. caeruleus* population. *Le Gerfaut* 74: 243-269.

Binford, L.C. (1989) A distributional survey of the birds of the Mexican state of Oaxaca. AOU: *Orn. Monog.* No. 43.

Bingham, C.T. (1903) A contribution to our knowledge of the birds occurring in the Southern Shan States, Upper Burma. *Ibis* Ser. 8, 3: 584-606.

Birckhead, H. (1937) The birds of the Sage West China Expedition. *Am. Mus. Novit.* 966: 1-17.

BirdLife Österreich (1994) *Atlas of Breeding Birds in Austria - A Summary of Species Accounts.* Vienna: BirdLife Österreich.

Bison, P., & van der Laan, J. (1985) Juvenile plumage of Algerian Nuthatch. *Dutch Birding* 7: 108-109.

Blake, E.R. (1953) *Birds of Mexico.* Chicago: Univ. Chicago.

Blanford, W.T. (1873) Description of new species of *Nectarinia, Sitta*, and *Parus* from Persia and Baluchistan. *Ibis* Ser. 3, 3: 86-90.

Blanford, W.T. (1876) *Eastern Persia: An Account of the Journeys of the Persian Boundary Commission 1870-71-72. Vol. 2. The Zoology and Geology.* London: Macmillan.

Bleitz, D. (1951) Nest of Pygmy Nuthatches attended by four parents. *Condor* 53: 150-151.

Bock, C.E. (1969) Intra- vs. interspecific aggression in Pygmy Nuthatch flocks. *Ecology* 50: 903-905.

Bock, C.E., & Lepthien, L.W. (1972) Winter eruptions of Red-breasted Nuthatches in North America, 1950-1970. *Am. Birds* 26: 558-61.

Bohlen, H.D. (1978) *An Annotated Check-list of the Birds of Illinois.* Springfield: Illinois State Mus.

Bond, J. (1931) A new nuthatch from the island of Grand Bahama. *Proc. Acad. Nat. Sci. Philadelphia* 83: 389.

Bonde, K. (1981) *An Annotated Checklist to the Birds of Lesotho.* Unpubl. MS.

Bonde, K. (1993) *Birds of Lesotho.* Pietermaritzburg: Univ. Natal.

Boon, L.J.R. (1994) Hybrid Azure x Blue Tits in Europe. *Dutch Birding* 16: 232-234.

Bowles, J.H. (1909) Notes on *Parus rufescens* in western Washington. *Condor* 11: 55-57.

Brackbill, H. (1970) Tufted Titmouse breeding behaviour. *Auk* 87: 522-536.

Brandt, H. (1951) *Arizona and its Bird Life.* Cleveland, OH: Bird Res. Found.

Braun, D., Kitto, G.B., & Braun, M.J. (1984) Molecular population genetics of Tufted and Black-crested forms of *Parus bicolor. Auk* 101: 170-173.

Braun, M.J., & Robbins, M.B. (1986) Extensive protein similarity of the hybridizing chickadees *Parus atricapillus* and *P. carolinensis. Auk* 103: 667-675.

Brauning, D.W. (ed.) (1992) *Atlas of Breeding Birds of Pennsylvania.* Pittsburgh & London: Univ. Pittsburgh.

Brawn, J.D., & Samson, F.B. (1983) Winter behaviour of Tufted Titmice. *Wilson Bull.* 95: 222-232.

Brazil, M.A. (1990) *The Birds of*

Japan. London: Christopher Helm.

Brazil, M.A. (1992) The birds of the Shuangtaizihekou National Nature Reserve, Liaoning Province, P.R. China. *Forktail* 7: 91-124.

Breife, B., Hirschfeld, E., Kjellén, N., & Ullman, M. (1990) Sällsynta fåglar i Sverige. *Vår Fågelvärld* Suppl. 13.

Brennan, L.A., & Morrison, M.L. (1991) Long-term trends of chickadee populations in western North America. *Condor* 93: 130-137.

Brensing, D., & Barthel, P.H. (1993) Ein Hybride aus Lasur-*Parus cyanus* und Blaumeise *P. caeruleus* am Neusiedlersee. *Limicola* 7: 147-151.

Bretagnolle, F. (1993) An annotated checklist of birds of northeastern Central African Republic. *Malimbus* 15: 6-16.

Brewer, R. (1961) Comparative notes on the life history of the Carolina Chickadee. *Wilson Bull.* 73: 348-373.

Brewer, R. (1963) Ecological and reproductive relationships of Black-capped and Carolina Chickadees. *Auk* 80: 9-47.

Brewer, R., McPeck, G.A., & Adams, R.J. (1991) *The Atlas of Breeding Birds of Michigan.* East Lansing: Michigan State Univ.

Brichetti, P., & Di Capi, C. (1985) Distribution, population and breeding ecology of the Corsican Nuthatch, *Sitta whiteheadi* Sharpe. *Riv. ital. Orn.* 55: 3-26.

Brichetti, P., & Di Capi, C. (1987) Conservation of the Corsican Nuthatch *Sitta whiteheadi* Sharpe, and proposals for habitat management. *Biol. Conserv.* 39: 13-21.

Britton, P.L. (ed.) (1980) *Birds of East Africa.* Nairobi: EANHS.

Broadley, D.G., & Minshull, J.I. (1986) A gazetteer of African countries, their constituent parts, and their synonyms. *Arnoldia Zimbabwe* 9: 333-342.

Brosset, A., & Erard, C. (1986) *Les oiseaux des régions forestières du nord-est du Gabon. Vol. 1.* Paris: Société Nationale de Protection de la Nature.

Brown, L.H., & Britton, P.L. (1980) *The Breeding Seasons of East African Birds.* Nairobi: EANHS.

Browne, P.W.P. (1980) Birds observed near Lome, Togo in 1976 and 1977. *Malimbus* 2: 51-55.

Browne, P.W.P. (1981) New bird species in Mauritania. *Malimbus* 3: 63-72.

Browning, M.R. (1978) An evaluation of the new species and subspecies proposed in Oberholser's Bird Life of Texas. *Proc. Biol. Soc. Washington* 91: 85-122.

Browning, M.R. (1990) Taxa of North American birds described from 1957 to 1987. *Proc. Biol. Soc. Washington* 103: 432-451.

Bruce, M.D. (1975) Notes on the birds of Amami Oshima. *Bull. BOC* 95: 158-160.

Brunel, J., (1978) Les oiseaux de la région du Lang-Bian, massif montagneux de la chaine Annamitique. *L'Oiseau* 48: 53-68, 159-180.

Bruun, B., Delin, H., & Svensson, L. (1986) *Birds of Britain and Europe.* Twickenham: Country Life.

Buckley, P., & McNeilage, A. (1989) An ornithological survey of Kasyoha-Kitomi and Itwara Forests, Uganda. *Scopus* 13: 97-108.

Bull, J. (1964) *Birds of the New York Area.* New York: Harper & Row.

Bull, J. (1985) *Birds of New York State including the 1976 Supplement.* Ithaca: Cornell Univ.

Bull, J., & Farrand, J. (1977) *The Audubon Society Field Guide to North American Birds. Eastern Region.* New York: Alfred A. Knopf.

Bundy, G. (1976) *The Birds of Libya. An Annotated Checklist.* London: Brit. Orn. Union.

Bundy, G., & Warr, E. (1980) A check-list of the birds of the Arabian Gulf States. *Sandgrouse* 1: 4-49.

Burleigh, T.D. (1972) *Birds of Idaho.* Caldwell: Caxton Printers.

Burleigh, T.D., & Peters, H.S. (1948) Geographical variation in Newfoundland birds. *Proc. Biol. Soc. Washington* 61: 111-126.

Burner, E. (1976) Une nouvelle espece de l'avifaune paléarctique: la Sittelle kabyle, *Sitta ledanti. Nos Oiseaux* 33: 337-340.

Buttemer, W.A., Astheimer, L.B., Weathers, W.W., & Hayworth, A.M. (1987) Energy savings attending winter-nest use by Verdins (*Auriparus flaviceps*). *Auk* 104: 531-535.

Cadman, M.D., Eagles, P., & Helleiner, F. (1987) *Atlas of Breeding Birds of Ontario.* Univ. Waterloo.

Cai, Q. (ed.) (1987) [Birds of Beijing.] Beijing. [In Chinese.]

Caldwell, H.R., & Caldwell, J.C. (1931) *South China Birds.* Shanghai: Hester May Vanderburgh.

Campbell, B., & Lack, E. (eds) (1985) *A Dictionary of Birds.* Calton: T & AD Poyser.

Carey, G.J., & Chalmers, M.L. (1994) Report on the birds 1993. Records committee report. *Hong Kong Bird Report* 1993: 4-90.

Carley, F.L. (1988) Finding Siberian Tits. *Birding* 20: 164-165.

Carroll, R.W. (1988) Birds of the Central African Republic. *Malimbus* 10: 177-200.

Carswell, M. (1986) Birds of the Kampala area. *Scopus* special supplement No. 2. Nairobi: EANHS.

Cave, F.O., & Macdonald, J.D. (1955) *Birds of the Sudan: Their Identification and Distribution.* Edinburgh: Oliver & Boyd.

Chalmers, M.L. (1986) *Annotated Checklist of the Birds of Hong Kong.* 4th edn. Hong Kong: Hong Kong Birdwatching Soc.

Chalmers, M.L. (1990) Records committee report 1989. *Hong Kong Bird Report* 1989: 16-31.

Chang, J.W. (1980) *A Field Guide to the Birds of Taiwan.* Taichung.

Chang, W.F., & Severinghaus, S.R. (1979) Notes on the Yellow Tit *Parus holsti* of Taiwan with discovery of its nest. *Bull. BOC* 99: 54-56.

Chapin, J.P. (1932-54) The birds of the Belgian Congo. *Bull. Am. Mus. Nat. Hist.* 65, 75, 75A, 75B.

Chapin, J.P. (1958) A new pendulline titmouse from the eastern Congo forest. *Rev. Zool. Bot. Afr.* 57: 22-24.

Chaplin, S.B. (1982) The energetic significance of huddling behaviour in Common Bushtits

(*Psaltriparus minimus*). *Auk* 99: 424-430.

Chapman, F.M. (1898) Notes on birds observed at Jalapa and Las Vigas, Vera Cruz, Mexico. *Amer. Mus. Nat. Hist. Bull.* 10: 15-43.

Chapman, M.S. (1984) Identification of Short-toed Treecreeper. *Brit. Birds* 77: 262-263.

Chappuis, C. (1976) Origine et évolution des vocalisations de certains oiseaux de la Corse et des Baléares. *Alauda* 44: 475-495.

Chappuis, C. (1980) List of sound-recorded Ethiopian birds. *Malimbus* 2: 1-15, 82-98.

Chappuis, C. (1986) Revised list of sound-recorded Afrotropical Birds. *Malimbus* 8: 25-39, 79-88.

Chasen, F.N., & Kloss, C.B. (1930) On a collection of birds from the lowlands and islands of North Borneo. *Bull. Raffles Mus.* 4: 1-112.

Cheke, R.A., Walsh, J.F., & Sowah, S.A. (1986) Records of birds seen in the Republic of Togo during 1984-1986. *Malimbus* 8: 51-72.

Cheng, Tso-hsin (1973) [Birds of Tsingling Mountains]. [In Chinese.]

Cheng Tso-hsin [Zheng Zuo-xin] (1987) *A Synopsis of the Avifauna of China.* Beijing: Science Press.

Cheng, Tso-hsin, & Cheng Pao-Li (1962) [On birds from the Hsi-Shuan-Pan-Na area and vicinity in Yunnan Province. III.] *Acta Zool. Sinica* 14. [In Chinese.]

Cheng, Tso-hsin, Tan, Y.-K., & Li, Y.-H. (1965) [On the avifauna of northwestern Szechwan.] *Acta Zool. Sinica* 17: 435-450. [In Chinese.]

Cheng, Tso-hsin, Tan, Y.-K., Liang, C.-U., & Chang, C.-F. (1963) [Studies on birds of Mount Omei and their vertical distribution.] *Acta Zool. Sinica* 15: 17-335. [In Chinese.]

Cheng, Tso-hsin, Ting, W., & Wang, T. (1964) A new subspecies of the Velvet-fronted Nuthatch from Hainan - *Sitta frontalis chienfengensis* Subsp. Nov. *Acta Zootax. Sinica* 1: 1-5. [In Chinese, English summary.]

Cherry, J.D., & Cannell, P.F. (1984) Rate and timing of pre-basic moult of adult Boreal Chickadees. *J. Field Orn.* 55: 487-489.

Clancey, P.A. (1943) Notes on individual and sexual bill variation in the British Treecreeper (*Certhia familiaris britannica* Ridgway). *Ibis* 85: 41.

Clancey, P.A. (1947) On the races of *Parus palustris* Linnaeus indigenous to England and Wales. *Bull. BOC* 67: 67-69.

Clancey, P.A. (1958a) Taxonomic notes on two southern African species of Paridae. *Ibis* 100: 451-454.

Clancey, P.A. (1958b) A new name for a southern African race of Grey Tit *Parus afer* Gmelin. *Bull. BOC* 78: 133.

Clancey, P.A. (1963) *Parus afer* Gmelin. *Durban Mus. Novit.* 6: 258-60.

Clancey, P.A. (1964a) Subspeciation in the Black Tit *Parus niger. Durban Mus. Novit.* 7: 167-177.

Clancey, P.A. (1964b) *The Birds of Natal and Zululand.* Edinburgh: Oliver & Boyd.

Clancey, P.A. (1966) A catalogue of birds of the South African Sub-Region. Part III. *Durban*

Mus. Novit. 7 (11).

Clancey, P.A. (1971) A handlist of the birds of southern Moçambique. Lourenco Marques: Inst. Invest. Cientifica Mocambique Ser. A. 10: 145-302; 11: 1-167.

Clancey, P.A. (1972) The status of Parus niger carpi Mcdonald and Hall, 1957, and a regrouping of some populations of the Parus niger Vieillot, sens. strict., complex. Durban Mus. Novit. 9: 236-244.

Clancey, P.A. (1974) Subspeciation studies in some Rhodesian birds. Arnoldia (Rhodesia) 6: 1-43.

Clancey, P.A. (1975) The Austral African races of Salpornis spilonotus (Franklin). Durban Mus. Novit. 10: 206-208.

Clancey, P.A. (1979) A further race of Parus rufiventris Bocage from the middle and lower Okavango R. drainage. Durban Mus. Novit. 12: 52-54.

Clancey, P.A. (ed.) (1980) S.A.O.S. Checklist of Southern African Birds. Johannesburg: Southern African Orn. Soc.

Clancey, P.A. (1985) The Rare Birds of Southern Africa. Johannesburg: Winchester Press.

Clancey, P.A. (1989) The southern isolate of Parus rufiventris pallidiventris Reichenow, 1885. Bull. BOC 109: 134-137.

Clausen, P., & Toft, S. (1988) Mixed singers and imitation singers among Short-toed Treecreepers. Brit. Birds 81: 496-503.

Clement, F.A. (1992) Recent records of birds from Bhutan. Forktail 7: 57-73.

Cockrum, E.L. (1952) A check list and bibliography of hybrid birds of North America north of Mexico. Wilson Bull. 64: 140-159.

Collar, N.J., & Andrew, P. (1988) Birds to Watch: The ICBP World Checklist of Threatened Birds. Cambridge: International Council for Bird Preservation.

Collar, N.J., Crosby, M.J., & Stattersfield, A.J. (1994) Birds to Watch 2. The World List of Threatened Birds. Cambridge: BirdLife International.

Collar, N.J., & Stuart, S.N. (1985) Threatened Birds of Africa and Related Islands. The ICBP/IUCN Red Data Book, Part 1. 3rd edn. Cambridge: International Council for Bird Preservation/IUCN.

Collar, N.J., & Stuart, S.N. (1988) Key Forests for Threatened Birds in Africa. ICBP Monograph No. 3. Cambridge: International Council for Bird Preservation.

Colston, P.R., & Curry-Lindahl, K. (1986) The Birds of Mount Nimba, Liberia. London: Brit. Mus. (Nat. Hist.).

Conder, P. (1981) Birds of the Azraq wetland reserve, Jordan: January and February 1979. Sandgrouse 2: 22-32.

Corfiled, D.M. (1983) Birds of Islamabad, Pakistan and the Murree Hills. Islamabad: Asia Study Group.

Cox, J.H. (1989) Treecreeper (Certhiidae) nesting in western Nepal. JBNHS 86: 452-453.

Craig, A.J.F.K. (1983) Moult in Southern African passerine birds: a review. Ostrich 54: 220-237.

Cramp, S. (1963) Movements of tits in 1959 and after. Brit. Birds 56: 237-263.

Cramp, S. (ed.) (1988) The Birds of the Western Palearctic. Vol. 5.

Oxford: Oxford Univ.

Cramp, S., & Perrins, C.M. (eds) (1993) The Birds of the Western Palearctic. Vol. 7. Oxford: Oxford Univ.

Cramp, S., Pettet, A., & Sharrock, J.T.R. (1960) The irruption of tits in autumn 1957. Brit. Birds 53: 49-77, 99-117, 176-192.

Crase, F.T. (1976) Occurrence of the Chestnut-backed Chickadee in the Sierra Nevada Mountains, California. Am. Birds 30: 673-675.

Crick, H.Q.P., & Marshall, P.J. (1981) The birds of Yankari Game Reserve, Nigeria: their abundance and seasonal occurrence. Malimbus 3: 103-114.

Cyrus, D., & Robson, N. (1980) Bird Atlas of Natal. Pietermaritzburg: Univ. Natal.

Daunicht, W.D. (1991) Unterscheidungsmerkmale im Grossgefieder von Waldcerthia familiaris und Gartenbaumläufer C. brachydactyla. Limicola 5: 49-64.

David, A., & Oustalet, E.M. (1877) Les oiseaux de Chine. 2 vols. Paris: G. Masson.

David-Beaulieu, A. (1939) Les oiseaux de la région de Pleiku (haut plateau du Sud-Annam). L'Oiseau 9: 13-32, 163-182.

David-Beaulieu, A. (1939) Liste complémentaire des oiseaux du Tranninh. L'Oiseau 9: 183-186.

David-Beaulieu, A. (1940) Deuxième liste complémentaire des oiseaux du Tranninh. L'Oiseau 10: 78-85.

David-Beaulieu, A. (1944) Les oiseaux du Tranninh. Hanoi: Université Indochinoise.

David-Beaulieu, A. (1948) Notes sur quelques oiseaux nouveaux pour le Tranninh et même pour l'Indochine. L'Oiseau 18: 133-140.

David-Beaulieu, A. (1949-50) Les oiseaux de la province de Savannakhet (Bas-Laos). L'Oiseau 19: 41-84, 153-194; 20: 9-50.

Davis, C.M. (1978) A nesting study of the Brown Creeper. Living Bird 17: 237-263.

Davis, M.F. (1978) A helper at a Tufted Titmouse nest. Auk 57: 767.

Davison, G.W.H. (1992) Birds of Mount Kinabalu, Borneo. Kota Kinabalu: Natural History Publications (Borneo).

Dean, W.R.J. (1974b) Birds weights from Angola. Bull. BOC 94: 170-172.

Dean, W.R.J. (1974) Breeding and distributional notes on some Angolan birds. Durban Mus. Novit. 10: 109-125.

Dean, W.R.J. (1988) The avifauna of Angolan miombo woodlands. Tauraco 1: 99-104.

Dean, W.R.J., Huntley, M.A., Huntley, B.J., & Vernon, C.J. (1988) Notes on some birds of Angola. Durban Mus. Novit. 14: 43-92.

de Bie, S., & Morgan, N. (1989) Les Oiseaux de la Réserve de la Biosphere "Boucle du Baoulé", Mali. Malimbus 11: 41-60.

de Boer, W.F., & Legoupil, F. (1993) Observations sur la présence et l'abondance des oiseaux au Tchad. Malimbus 15: 17-23.

Deignan, H.G. (1938) A new nuthatch from Yunnan. Smiths. Misc. Coll. 97 (9): 1-2.

Deignan, H.G. (1945) The birds of northern Thailand. Bull. U.S. Nat. Mus. 186.

Deignan, H.G. (1963) Checklist of

the birds of Thailand. Bull. U.S. Nat. Mus. 226.

Delacour, J. (1927) New birds from Indo-China. Bull. BOC 47: 151-170.

Delacour, J. (1929) On the birds collected during the Fourth Expedition to French Indo-China. Ibis Ser. 12, 5: 193-220, 403-429.

Delacour, J. (1930a) On the birds collected during the Fifth Expedition to French Indo-China. Ibis Ser. 12, 6: 564-599.

Delacour, J. (1930b) Notes sur quelques oiseaux rares ou nouveaux obtenus au cours de la cinquieme expédition en Indo-Chine. L'Oiseau 11: 457-468.

Delacour, J. (1932a) Etude systématique de quelques oiseaux nouveaux ou intéressants obtenus par la VI expédition en Indochine. L'Oiseau NS 2: 419-438.

Delacour, J. (1932b) Description de deux oiseaux d'Indochine. L'Oiseau NS 2: 616-618.

Delacour, J. (1946) The name of the White-faced Titmouse of the Philippines. Auk 63: 433.

Delacour, J. (1947) Birds of Malaysia. New York: Macmillan.

Delacour, J. (1951) Commentaires, modifications et additions à la liste des Oiseaux de l'Indochine Française (suite). L'Oiseau 21: 1-32, 81-119.

Delacour, J., & Greenway, J.C. (1939) Seven new races from Indo-China. Bull. BOC 59: 130-134.

Delacour, J., & Greenway, J.C. (1940) VIIe expédition onithologique en Indochine Française. L'Oiseau 10: 1-77.

Delacour, J., & Jabouille, P. (1925) On the birds of Quangtri, Central Annam; with notes on other forms from other parts of French Indo-China. Ibis Ser. 12, 1: 209-260.

Delacour, J., & Jabouille, P. (1926) [Description of Melanochlora gayeti.] Bull. BOC 46: 5-6.

Delacour, J., & Jabouille, P. (1927) Recherches ornithologiques dans les provinces du Tranninh (Laos), de Thua-Thien et de Kontoum (Annam) et quelques autres régions de l'Indochine Française. Arch. Hist. Nat. (Paris) 3: i-xii, 1-216.

Delacour, J., & Jabouille, P. (1928-29) On the birds collected during the Third Expedition to French Indo-China. Ibis Ser. 12, 4: 23-51, 285-317; 5: 193-220, 403-429.

Delacour, J., & Jabouille, P. (1930) Description de trente oiseaux de l'Indochine Française. L'Oiseau 9: 393-408.

Delacour, J., & Jabouille, P. (1931) Les oiseaux de l'Indochine Française. 4 vols. Paris: Exposition Coloniale Internationale.

Delacour, J., & Mayr, E. (1945) Notes on the taxonomy of the birds of the Philippines. Zoologica 30: 105-117.

Delacour, J., & Mayr, E. (1946) Birds of the Philippines. New York: Macmillan.

Delacour, J., & Vaurie, C. (1950) Les mésanges charbonnières (Revision de l'espèce Parus major). L'Oiseau 20: 91-121.

Delin, H., & Svensson, L. (1988) Photographic Guide to the Birds of Britain and Europe. London: Hamlyn.

Dementieff, G., & Heptner, W. (1932) Contributions à l'ornithologie de la Russie (suite). IV - Notes sur les races géo-

graphiques de Cyanistes cyanus. Alauda 4: 284-291.

Dementiev, G.P., & Gladkov, N.A. (eds) (1966-70) Birds of the Soviet Union. 6 vols. Jerusalem: Israel Program for Scientific Translations.

Demey, R., & Fishpool, L.D.C. (1991) Additions and annotations to the avifauna of Cote d'Ivoire. Malimbus 12: 61-86.

Demey, R., & Fishpool, L. (1994) The birds of Yapo Forest, Ivory Coast. Malimbus 16: 100-122.

DeSante, D., & Pyle, P. (1986) Distributional Checklist of North American Birds. Vol. 1: United States and Canada. Lee Vining, California: Artemisia.

Desfayes, M., & Praz, J.C. (1978) Notes on habitat and distribution of montane birds in southern Iran. Bonn. zool. Beitr. 29: 18-37.

Devillers, P. (1976) Observations ornithologiques de printemps au Garhwal, Himalaya Indien. Le Gerfaut 66: 221-249.

Dhondt, A.A., & Hublé, J. (1969) Een geveal van hybridisatie tussen een glanskopmees female (Parus palustris) en een matkopmees male (Parus montanus) te Gent. Le Gerfaut 59: 374-77.

Dickinson, E.C. (1966) An account of the Doi Inthanon Expedition 1963. Nat. Hist. Bull. Siam Soc. 20: 279-292.

Dickinson, E.C., Kennedy, R.S., & Parkes, K.C. (1991) The Birds of the Philippines. An Annotated Check-list. Tring: Brit. Orn. Union.

Dickinson, J.C. (1953) Report on the McCabe collection of British Columbia birds. Bull. Mus. Comp. Zool. 109: 123-205.

Diesselhorst, G., & Martens, J. (1972) Hybriden von Parus melanolophus und Parus ater im Nepal-Himalaya. J. Orn. 113: 374-390.

Dinsmore, J.J., Kent, T.H., Koening, D., Petersen, P.C., & Rossa, D.M. (1984) Iowa Birds. Ames: Iowa State Univ.

Dixon, K.L. (1949) Behaviour of the Plain Titmouse. Condor 51: 110-136.

Dixon, K.L. (1950) Notes on the ecological distribution of Plain and Bridled Titmice in Arizona. Condor 52: 140-141.

Dixon, K.L. (1954) Some ecological relations of chickadees and titmice in central California. Condor 56: 113-124.

Dixon, K.L. (1955) An ecological analysis of the interbreeding of crested titmice in Texas. Univ. California Publ. Zool. 54: 125-206.

Dixon, K.L. (1956) Territoriality and survival in the Plain Titmouse. Condor 58: 169-182.

Dixon, K.L. (1962) Notes on the moult schedule of the Plain Titmouse. Condor 64: 134-139.

Dixon, K.L. (1963) Some aspects of social organisation in the Carolina Chickadee. Proc. 13th Int. Orn. Congr. 1: 240-258.

Dixon, K.L. (1969) Patterns of singing in a population of the Plain Titmouse. Condor 71: 94-101.

Dixon, K.L. (1972) Attack calls and territorial behaviour of the Mountain Chickadee. Proc. 15th Int. Orn. Congr.: 640-641.

Dixon, K.L. (1978) A distributional history of the Black-crested Titmouse. Am. Midl. Nat. 100: 29-42.

Dixon, K.L. (1985) Mountain Chickadee through the seasons. Utah Birds 1: 65-69.

Dixon, K.L. (1989) Contact zones of avian congeners on the southern Great Plains. Condor 91: 15-22.

Dixon, K.L. (1990) Constancy of margins of the hybrid zone in titmice of the Parus bicolor complex in coastal Texas. Auk 107: 429-431.

Dixon, K.L., & Gilbert, J.D. (1964) Altitudinal migration in the Mountain Chickadee. Condor 66: 61-64.

Dixon, K.L., & Martin, D.J. (1979) Notes on the vocalizations of the Mexican Chickadee. Condor 81: 421-423.

Dixon, K.L., & Stefanski, R.A. (1965) An evaluation of the song of the Black-capped Chickadee. Amer. Zool. 5: 693.

Dixon, K.L., & Stefanski, R.A. (1970) An appraisal of the song of Black-capped Chickadee. Wilson Bull. 82: 53-62.

Dixon, K.L., Stefanski, R., & Folks, F.N. (1970) Acoustic signals in the mating of Mountain and Black-capped Chickadees. Auk 87: 322-328.

Dolan, B. (1938) Zoological results of the second Dolan expedition to western China and eastern Tibet, 1934-36. Part 1- Introduction. Proc. Acad. Nat. Sci. Phil. 40: 159-184.

Dolgushin, I.A., Korelov, M.N., Kuz'mina, M.A., Gavrilov, E.I., Kovshar', A.F., & Borodikhin, I.F. (1972) [The birds of Kazakhstan.] 4. Alma-Ata: Nauka. [In Russian.]

Dorn, J.L., & Dorn, R.L. (1990) Wyoming Birds. Cheyenne: Mountain West.

Dorofeev, A.M., Parfenov, V.I., & Sushchenya, L.M. (eds) (1993) [Red data book of the Republic of Belarus'.] Minsk: Belaruskaya Entsyklapedyya. [In Belorussian.]

Dowsett, R.J. (ed.) (1989) Enquête faunistique dans la Fôret du Mayombe et check-liste des oiseaux et des mammifères du Congo. Tauraco Res. Rept No. 2.

Dowsett, R.J. (ed.) (1990) Enquête faunistique et floristique dans La Fôret de Nyungwe, Rwanda. Tauraco Res. Rept No. 3.

Dowsett, R.J. (1993) Afrotropical avifaunas: annotated country checklists. In Dowsett, R.J., & Dowsett-Lemaire, F. (eds) (1993).

Dowsett, R.J., & Dowsett-Lemaire, F. (eds) (1991) Flore et faune du Bassin du Kouilou (Congo) et leur exploitation. Tauraco Res. Rept No. 4.

Dowsett, R.J., & Dowsett-Lemaire, F. (eds) (1993) A contribution to the distribution and taxonomy of Afrotropical and Malagasy Birds. Tauraco Res. Rept No. 5.

Dowsett, R.J., & Forbes-Watson, A.D. (1993) Checklist of Birds of the Afrotropical and Malagasy Regions. Vol. 1: Species limits and distribution. Liège, Belgium: Tauraco.

Dowsett-Lemaire, F., & Dowsett, R.J. (1991) The avifauna of the Kouilou basin in Congo. In Dowsett, R.J., & Dowsett-Lemaire, F. (eds) (1991).

Dowsett-Lemaire, F., Dowsett, R.J., & Bulens, P. (1993) Additions and corrections to the avifauna of Congo. Malimbus 15: 68-80.

Dresser, H.E., & Delmar Morgan, E. (1899) On new species of birds obtained in Kan-su by M. Berezovsky. Ibis Ser. 7, 5: 270-277.

Dubois, P.J., & Yésou, P. (1991) Les oiseaux rares en France.

Bayonne: Editions Raymond Chabaud.

Ducey, J.E. (1992) Nebraska Birds: Breeding Status and Distribution. Omaha: Simmons-Boardman.

Dunajewski, A. (1934) Die eurasiatischen Formen der Gattung Sitta Linn. Act. Orn. Mus. Zool. Polonici 1: 181-251.

du Pont, J.E. (1971) Philippine Birds. Greenville, Delaware: Delaware Mus. Nat. Hist.

Duquet, M. (1995) Un hybride probable Mésange nonette Parus palustris x M. charbonnière Parus major. Ornithos 2: 93.

Durand, A.L. (1972) Landbirds over the North Atlantic: unpublished records 1961-65 and thoughts a decade later. Brit. Birds 65: 428-442.

Duvall, A.J. (1945) Distribution and taxonomy of the Black-capped Chickadees of North America. Auk 62: 49-69.

Duyck, B.E., McNair, D.B., & Nicholson, C.P. (1991) Dirt-storing behaviour by White-breasted Nuthatches. Wilson Bull. 103: 308-309.

Dyer, M., Gartshore, M.E., & Sharland, R.E. (1986) The birds of Nindam Forest Reserve, Kagoro, Nigeria. Malimbus 8: 2-20.

Dymond, J.N. (1991) The Birds of Fair Isle. Shetland: author.

Earle, R., & Grobler, N. (1987) First Atlas of Bird Distribution in the Orange Free State. Bloemfontein: Nat. Mus.

Eck, S. (1977) Vergleichende Messungen an Kohlmeisen, Parus major. Beitr. Vogelkd. Leipzig 23: 193-228.

Eck, S. (1979) Geographischer Parallelismus und intraspezifische Gruppenbildungen bei Nonnenmeisen (Parus palustris) und paläarktischen Weidenmeisen (P. atricapillus). Orn. Jahrb. Mus. Hein. 4: 19-37.

Eck, S. (1980a) Intraspezifische Evolution der Graumeisen. Zool. Abh. Staatl. Mus. Tierkde Dresden 36: 135-219.

Eck, S. (1980b) Parus major - ein Paradebeispiel der Systematik? Falke 27: 385-392.

Eck, S. (1982) Merkmalsgradation und Selektion bei paläaearktischen Weidenmeisen, Parus atricapillus. Mitt. Zool. Mus. Berlin 58: 137-144.

Eck, S. (1984a) Mehrjährige Paarbindung und Flügellänganzunahme bei der Nonnenmeise (Parus palustris). Ber. Vögel. Hiddensee 5: 95-97.

Eck, S. (1984b) Eine unbeschriebene Weidenmeise (Parus atricapillus) aus dem östlichen Nordamerika? Zool. Abh. Staatl. Mus. Tierkde Dresden Vol? 71-73.

Eck, S. (1987a) Eine auffällig gefärbte Blaumeise (Parus caeruleus) im Erzgebirge. Zool. Abh. Staatl. Mus. Tierkde Dresden 15: 109-110.

Eck, S. (1987b) Zum Gesang der Weidenmeise (Parus atricapillus) des Böhmerwaldes (Sumava, CSSR). Zool. Abh. Staatl. Mus. Tierkde Dresden 14: 161-162.

Eck, S. (1988) Gesichtspunkte zur Art-Systematik der Meisen (Paridae). Zool. Abh. Staatl. Mus. Tierkde Dresden 43: 101-134.

Eck, S. (1990) Alpenmeisen in der CSR noch in Polen. Der Falke 3: 87-91.

Eck, S., & Piechocki, R. (1977) Eine Kontaktzone zwischen den bokharensis-Subspezies und den major-Subspezies der Kohlmeise, Parus major, in der Südwest-Mongolei. Mitt. Zool. Mus. Berlin 53: 127-136.

Eckman, J. (1979) Coherence, composition and territories of winter social groups of the Willow Tit Parus montanus and the Crested Tit P. cristatus. Ornis Scand. 10: 56-68.

Eckman, J. (1989) Ecology of non-breeding social systems of Parus. Wilson Bull. 101: 263-288.

Ehrlich, P.R., Dobkin, D.S., & Wheye, D. (1988) The Birder's Handbook: A Field Guide to the Natural History of North American Birds. New York: Fireside.

Elder, W.H. (1985) Survivorship in the Tufted Titmouse. Wilson Bull. 97: 517-524.

Elgood, J.H. (1977) Forest birds of southwest Nigeria. Ibis 119: 462-480.

Elgood, J.H., Heigham, J.B., Moore, A.M., Nason, A., Sharland, R.E., & Skinner, N.J. (1994) The Birds of Nigeria. An Annotated Check-list. 2nd edition. Tring: Brit. Orn. Union.

Elkins, K.C. (1982) A Checklist of the Birds of New Hampshire. Concord: Audubon Soc. New Hampshire.

Ely, C.A. (1962) The birds of southeastern Coahuila, Mexico. Condor 64: 34-39.

Engelbach, P. (1932) Les oiseaux du Laos Méridional. L'Oiseau 2: 439-498.

Erard, C., & Etchécopar, R.D. (1970) Contribution à l'etude des oiseaux de l'Iran. (Résultats de la Mission en Iran 1967.) Mém. Mus. natn. Hist. nat. (A) 66.

Ernst, S. (1991) Über den Gesang der Weidenmeise Parus montanus im östlichen Altai. Monticola 6: 178-182.

Erskine, A.J. (1977) Birds in boreal Canada: communities, densities and adaptations. Canadian Wildl. Serv. Rep. Ser. 41.

Ervin, S. (1975) Iris coloration in young bushtits. Condor 77: 90-91.

Ervin, S. (1977a) Flock size, composition, and behaviour in a population of Bushtits. Bird-Banding 48: 97-109.

Ervin, S. (1977b) Nest appropriation and mate replacement in the Bushtit. Auk 94: 598-599.

Ervin, S. (1978) Bushtit helpers: accident or altruism. Bird Behav. 1: 93-97.

Etchécopar, R.D., & Hüe, F. (1970) Les oiseaux du Proche et du Moyen Orient de la Méditerranée aux contreforts de l'Himalaya. Paris: Éditions N. Boubée & Cie.

Etchécopar, R.D., & Hüe, F. (1983) Les oiseaux de Chine, de Mongolie et de Corée. Passereaux. Paris: Sociéteé Nouvelle des Éditions Boubée.

Evans, T.D., Dutson, G.C.L., & Brooks, T.M. (eds) (1993) Cambridge Philippines Rainforest Project 1991. Final Report. BirdLife International Study Report No. 54. Cambridge: BirdLife International.

Farmer, R. (1979) Checklist of the birds of the Ile-Ife area, Nigeria. Malimbus 1: 56-64.

Felt, A.C. (1967) Ageing Mountain Chickadees. Western Bird

Bander 42: 3.

Ficken, M.S. (1981) What is the song of the Black-capped Chickadee? Condor 83: 384-386.

Ficken, M.S. (1990a) Vocal repertoire of the Mexican Chickadee I. Calls. J. Field Ornithol. 61: 380-387.

Ficken, M.S. (1990b) Vocal repertoire of the Mexican Chickadee II. Song and song-like vocalisations. J. Field Ornithol. 61: 388-395.

Ficken, M.S., & Ficken, R.W. (1987) Bill-sweeping behaviour of a Mexican Chickadee. Condor 89: 901-902.

Ficken, M.S., Ficken, R.W., & Witkin, S.R. (1978) Vocal repertoire of the Black-capped Chickadee. Auk 95: 34-48.

Ficken, M.S., Hailman, E.D., & Hailman, J. (1994) The chick-adee call system of the Mexican Chickadee. Condor 96: 70-82.

Ficken, M.S., & Nocedal, J. (1992) Mexican Chickadee. In, Poole, A., Stettenheim, P., & Gill, F. (eds) The Birds of North America, No. 8 . Philadelphia: Academy of Natural Sciences; Washington: Amer. Orn. Union.

Finnis, R.G. (1961) Song variation in the Great Tit, Parus major newtoni. Bull. BOC 81: 21-26.

Fishpool, L.D.C. (1993) New bird records from Budongo and Kifu forests, Uganda, with an addition to the East African avifauna. Scopus 17: 37-39.

Fleming, R. L. (1973) Notes on the nest and behaviour of the Yellow-browed Titmouse, Parus modestus (Burton). JBNHS 70: 326-329.

Fleming, R.L., Sr, Fleming, R.L., Jr, & Bangdel, L.S. (1984) Birds of Nepal. 3rd edn. Kathmandu: Avalok.

Flint, V.E., Boehme, R.L., Kostin, Y.V., & Kuznetsov (1984) A Field Guide to the Birds of the USSR. Princeton: Princeton Univ.

Fomin, V.E., & Bold, A. (1991) [Catalogue of the birds of the Mongolian People's Republic.] Moscow: Nauka. [In Russian.]

Forbush, E.H. (1925-29) Birds of Massachusetts and other New England States. 3 vols. Boston: Mass. Dept Agriculture.

Forbush, E.H., & May, J.B. (1939) A Natural History of American Birds of Eastern and Central North America. New York: Bramhall House.

Formozov, N.A., Kerimov, A.B., & Lopatin, V.V. (1993) [New hybridisation zone of the Great Titmouse and Parus bokharensis in Kazakhstan and relationships in forms of Parus major superspecies.]. In Rossolimo, O.L. (ed.) [Hybridisation and the problem of species in vertebrates.] Arch. Zool. Mus. Moscow State Univ. 30: 118-146. [In Russian.]

Fosse, A. (1992) Algerian Nuthatch plumages. Birding World 5: 234.

Fosse, A., & Vaillant, G. (1982) A propos de la couleur de la calotte chez la Sittelle kabyle (Sitta ledanti). Alauda 50: 228.

Frade, F. (1951) Catalogo das Aves de Mocambique. Lisbon: Ministero das Colonias.

Frandsen, J. (1982) Birds of the South Western Cape. Sloane Park (South Africa): Sable.

Frank, G., & Voous, K.H. (1969) Vangst van Parus 'pleskii' in Nederland. Limosa 42: 201-204.

Frankis, M.P. (1991) Krüper's Nuthatch Sitta krueperi and

Turkish Pine *Pinus brutia*: an evolving association? *Sandgrouse* 13: 92-97.

Franzreb, K.E. (1985) Foraging ecology of Brown Creepers in a mixed-coniferous forest. *J. Field Ornithol.* 56: 9-16.

Fraticelli, F. (1985) Bagno tra il fogliame del Rampichino, *Certhia brachydactyla*. *Riv. ital. Orn.* 55: 192.

Fraticelli, F. (1989) Commenti sulla determinazione del Rampichino *Certhia brachydactyla* in una zona mediterranea. *Avocetta* 13: 57-59.

Friedmann, H., Griscom, L., & Moore, R.T. (1950-57) *Distributional Check-list of the Birds of Mexico*. Cooper Orn. Club, Pacific Coast Avifauna Nos 29 & 33.

Fu, T., Gao, W., & Song, Y. (1984) [Birds of Changbai Mountains.] Changchun: Northeast Normal Univ. [In Chinese.]

Fuggles-Couchman, N.R. (1984) The distribution of, and other notes on, some birds of Tanzania. *Scopus* 8: 1-17.

Gabrielson, I.N., & Jewett, S.G. (1940) *Birds of Oregon*. Corvallis, Oregon: Oregon State Coll.

Gabrielson, I.N., & Lincoln, F.C. (1959) *The Birds of Alaska*. Washington, DC: The Stackpole Co., Harrisburg, PA & Wildlife Management Institute.

Gaddis, P.K. (1983) Differential usage of song types by Plain, Bridled and Tufted Titmice. *Ornis Scand.* 14: 16-23.

Gaddis, P.K. (1985) Structure and variability in the vocal repertoire of the Mountain Chickadee. *Wilson Bull.* 97: 30-46.

Gaines, D. (1988) *Birds of Yosemite and the East Slope*. Lee Vining (Calif.): Artemisia.

Gantlett, S.J.M. (1985) *A Checklist of the Birds of the Isles of Scilly*. Author.

Gantlett, S. (1994) 1993: The Western Palearctic year. *Birding World* 7: 24-37.

Gao, Wie. (1978) [On the breeding behaviour and feeding habits of the Black-headed Nuthatch.] *Acta Zool. Sinica* 24: 260-268. [In Chinese.]

Garrett, K., & Dunn, J. (1981) *Birds of Southern California: Status and Distribution*. Los Angeles: Los Angeles Audubon Soc.

Gartshore, M.E. (1989) *An Avifaunal Survey of Tai National Park Ivory Coast*. ICBP Study Report No. 39. Cambridge: International Council for Bird Preservation.

Gaston, A.J. (1973) The ecology and behaviour of the Long-tailed Tit. *Ibis* 115: 330-351.

Gaston, A.J. (1979) Roosting behaviour of flocks of the Crested Black Tit (*Parus melanolophus*). *JBNHS* 76: 517-518.

Gaston, A.J. (1984) Is habitat destruction in India and Pakistan beginning to affect the status of endemic passerine birds? *JBNHS* 81: 636-641.

Gaston, A.J., Garson, P.J., & Pandey, S. (1993) Birds recorded in the Great Himalayan National Park, Himachal Pradesh, India. *Forktail* 9: 45-57.

Gatter, W. (1988) The birds of Liberia (West Africa). A preliminary list with status and open questions. *Verh. orn. Ges. Bayern* 24: 689-723.

Gatter, W., & Mattes, H. (1979) Zur Populationsgrösse und Ökologie des neuentdeckten Kabylenkleibers *Sitta ledanti* Vielliard 1976. *J. Orn.* 120: 390-405.

Gaugris, Y. (1976) Additions à l'inventaire des oiseaux du Burundi (décembre 1971-décembre 1975). *L'Oiseau* 46: 273-289.

Gaugris, Y., Prigogine, A., & Vande Weghe, J.-P. (1981) Additions et corrections à l'avifaune du Burundi. *Le Gerfaut* 71: 3-39.

Gehlbach, F.R., Dillon, D.O., Harrell, H.L., Kennedy, S.E., & Wilson, K.R. (1976) Avifauna of the Rio Corona, Tamaulipas, Mexico: Northeastern limit of the tropics. *Auk* 93: 53-65.

Georgi Orn. Soc. Checklist Committee (1986) *Annotated Checklist of Georgia Birds*. Occ. Papers No. 10, Georgia Orn. Soc.

Germain, M., & Cornet, J.-P. (1994) Oiseaux nouveaux pour la République Centrafricaine ou dont les notifications de ce pays sont peu nombreuses. *Malimbus* 16: 30-51.

Géroudet, P. (1976) A propos de la Sittelle kabyle. *Nos Oiseaux* 33: 340-342.

Gibbons, D.W., Reid, J.B., & Chapman, R.B. (compilers) (1993) *The New Atlas of Breeding Birds in Britain and Ireland: 1988-1991*. London: T & AD Poyser.

Gill, E.H.N (1923-25) A description of the nests and eggs of the common birds occurring in the plains of the United Provinces. *JBNHS* 28: 1069-1074; 29: 107-116, 334-344, 757-768, 963-970; 30: 273-284.

Gill, F.B., Funk, D.H., & Silverin, B. (1989) Protein relationships among titmice (*Parus*). *Wilson Bull.* 101: 182-197.

Gill, F.B., Morstrom, A.M., & Mack, A.L. (1993) Speciation in North American chickadees: 1. Patterns of mtDNA genetic divergence. *Evolution* 47: 195-212.

Gill, F.B., & Slikas, B. (1992) Patterns of mitochondrial DNA divergence in North American crested titmice. *Condor* 94: 20-28.

Ginn, P.J., McIlleron, W.G., & Milstein, P. le S. (compilers) (1989) *The Complete Book of Southern African Birds*. Cape Town: Struik Winchester.

Giraudoux, P., Degauquier, R., Jones, P.J., Weigel, J., & Isenmann, P. (1988). Avifaune du Niger: Etat des connaissances en 1986. *Malimbus* 10: 1-140.

Glase, J.C. (1973) Ecology of social organisation in the Black-capped Chickadee. *Living Bird* 12: 235-267.

Glen, N.W., & Perrins, C.M. (1988) Co-operative breeding by Long-tailed Tits. *Brit. Birds* 81: 630-641.

Gochfeld, M. (1977) Plumage variation in Black-capped Chickadees: is there sexual dimorphism? *Bird-Banding* 48: 62-66.

Godfrey, W.E. (1950) Birds of the Cypress hills and Flotten Lake regions, Saskatchewan. *Bull. Nat. Mus. Canada* 120: 1-96.

Godfrey, W.E. (1951) Geographical variation in the Boreal Chickadee east of the Rockies. *Canadian Field Nat.* 65: 22-26.

Godfrey, W.E. (1959) Notes on Newfoundland Birds. *Bull. Nat.*

*Mus. Canada* 172: 98-111.

Godfrey, W.E. (1986) *The Birds of Canada*. Rev .edn. Ottawa: Natl Mus. Nat. Sci.

Goenka., D & Pandit, H. (1987) The Indian Grey Tit (*Parus major*) on an abandoned honey comb. *JBNHS* 84: 218.

Gompertz, T. (1961) The vocabulary of the Great Tit. *Brit. Birds* 54: 369-394, 409-418.

Gompertz, T. (1968) Results of bringing individuals of two geographically isolated forms of *Parus major* into contact. *Vogelwelt (Beiheft)* 1: 63-92.

Gong, Huisheng, & Deng, Fengming (1993) [On the avifauna of Niubeiliang nature reserve, Shaanxi.] *Sichuan J. Zool.* 12: 27-29. [In Chinese.]

Gonzales, P.C., & Rees, C.P. (1988) *Birds of the Philippines*. Manilla: Haribon Foundation.

Goodman, S.M., Meininger, P.L., Baha El Din, S.M., Hobbs, J.J., & Mullié, W.M. (eds) (1989) *The Birds of Egypt*. Oxford & New York: Oxford Univ.

Gore, M.E.J. (1990) *Birds of the Gambia. An Annotated Checklist*. 2nd edn. Tring: Brit. Orn. Union.

Gore, M.E.J. (1994) Bird records from Liberia. *Malimbus* 16: 74-87.

Gore, M.E.J., & Won, P. (1971) *The Birds of Korea*. Seoul: Roy Asiatic Soc., & Taewon.

Gosler, A. (1993) *The Great Tit*. London: Hamlyn.

Gosler, A.G., & King, J.R. (1989) A sexually dimorphic plumage character in the Coal Tit *Parus ater* with notes on the Marsh Tit *Parus palustris*. *Ringing and Migration* 10: 53-57.

Graber, B. (1990) Siberian Tits. *Birding* 22: 193.

Grant, C.H.B., & Mackworth-Praed, C.W (1942) Notes on East African Birds. *Bull. BOC* 63: 43-47.

Grant, C.H.B., & Mackworth-Praed, C.W (1948) Notes on East African Birds. *Bull. BOC* 68: 74-77.

Grant, P.R. (1975) The classical case of character displacement. *Evol. Biol.* 8: 237-337.

Grant, P.R. (1979) Ecological and morphological variation of Canary Island Blue Tits, *Parus caeruleus* (Aves: Paridae). *Biol. J. Linnean Soc.* 11: 103-129.

Gray, A.P. (1958) *Bird Hybrids*. Bucks, England.

Green, A.A. (1983) The birds of Bamingui-Bangoran National Park, Central African Republic. *Malimbus* 5: 17-30.

Green, A.A. (1984) The avifauna of the Al Jawf region, northwest Saudi Arabia. *Sandgrouse* 6: 48-61.

Green, A.A. (1990) The avifauna of the southern sector of the Gashaka-Gumti Game Reserve, Nigeria. *Malimbus* 12: 31-51.

Green, A.A., & Carroll, R.W. (1991) The avifauna of Dzanga-Ndoki National Park and Dzanga-Sangha Rainforest Reserve, Central African Republic. *Malimbus* 13: 49-66.

Green, A.A., & Sayer, J.A. (1979) The birds of Pendjari and Arli National Parks (Benin and Upper Volta). *Malimbus* 1: 14-28.

Green, M.J.B. (1986) The birds of the Kedarnath Sanctuary, Chamoli District, Uttar Pradesh: status and distribution. *JBNHS* 83: 603-617.

Greenway, J.C. (1933) Birds from Northwest Yunnan. *Bull. Mus. Comp. Zool.* 74: 109-168.

Greenway, J.C. (1967) Family Sittidae. In Paynter, R.A. (ed.), *Check-list of Birds of the World*. Vol. 12. Cambridge, Mass.: Mus. Comp. Zool.

Greig-Smith, P.W. (1978) The formation, structure and function of mixed-species insectivorous bird flocks in west African savanna woodland. *Ibis* 120: 284-295.

Grimes, L.G. (1987) *The Birds of Ghana. An Annotated Checklist*. London: Brit. Orn. Union.

Grimmett, R., & Taylor, H. (1992) Recent observations from Xinjiang Autonomous Region, China, 16 June to 5 July 1988. *Forktail* 7: 139-146.

Grinnell, J. (1903) Call notes of the bush-tit. *Condor* 5: 85-87.

Grinnell, J. (1904) The origin and distribution of the Chestnut-backed Chickadee. *Auk* 21: 364-382.

Grinnell, J. (1937) An overlooked synonym of the Chestnut-backed Chickadee. *Condor* 39: 255.

Grinnell, J., Dixon, J., & Linsdale, J.M. (1930) Vertebrate natural history of a section of northern California through the Lassen Peak region. *Univ. Calif. Publ. Zool.* 35.

Grinnell, J., & Miller, A.H. (1944) *The Distribution of the Birds of California*. Berkeley: Cooper Orn. Club.

Grossman, A.F., & West, G.C. (1977) Metabolic rate and temperature regulation of winter acclimatized Black-capped Chickadees *Parus atricapillus* of interior Alaska. *Ornis Scand.* 8: 127-138.

Grubb, T.C., & Pravosudov, V.V. (1994) Tufted Titmouse (*Parus bicolor*). In Poole, A., & Gill, F. (eds), *The Birds of North America*, No. 86. Philadelphia: Academy of Natural Sciences; Washington: Amer. Orn. Union.

Grzybowski, J.A., Arterburn, J.W., Carter, W.A., Tomer, J.S., & Verser, D.W. (1992) *Date Guide to the Occurrences of Birds in Oklahoma*. Oklahoma Orn. Soc.

Guggisberg, C.A.W. (1986) *East African Birds*. Vol. 2. Sapra Safari Guide No. 6. Nairobi: Mount Kenya Sundries.

Güntert, M., Hay, D.B., & Balda, R.P. (1988) Communal roosting in Pygmy Nuthatch: a winter survival strategy. *Proc. Int. Orn. Congr.* 19: 1964-1972.

Hachisuka, M. (1930) Contributions to the birds of the Philippines, No. 2. Orn. Soc. Japan Suppl. 14: 141-222.

Hachisuka, M., & Udagawa, T. (1951) Contributions to the ornithology of Formosa, Part 2. *Q. J. Taiwan Mus.* 4: 1-180.

Haffer, J. (1977) Secondary contact zones of birds in northern Iran. *Bonner Zoologische Monographien* No. 10.

Haffer, J. (1989) Parapatrische Vogelarten der paläarktischen Region. *J. Orn.* 130: 475-512.

Haftorn, S. (1972) Hypothermia of tits in the Arctic winter. *Ornis Scand.* 3: 153-166.

Haftorn, S. (1973) Lappmeisa *Parus cinctus* i hekketiden: forplantning, stemmeregister og hamstring av næring. *Sterna* 12: 91-155.

Hailman, J.P. (1989) The organization of major vocalizations in the Paridae. *Wilson Bull.* 101: 305-343.

Halberg, K., & Peterson, I. (1984)

Himalaya 1978-87: observation of birds, mammals and some reptiles. Unpublished.

Hall, B.P. (1960) Variation in the African Black Tits, *Parus niger* and *Parus leucomelas*. *Ibis* 102: 116-123.

Hall, B.P., & Moreau, R.E. (1970) *An Atlas of Speciation in African Passerine Birds*. London: Brit. Mus. (Nat. Hist.).

Hall, B.P., & Traylor, M.A. (1959) The systematics of the African grey tits, *Parus afer* and *Parus griseiventris*. *Bull. BOC* 79: 42-46.

Hall, K.J. (1984) Identification of Willow Tit. *Brit. Birds* 77: 117-118.

Halleux, D. (1994) Annotated bird list of Maventa Prefecture, Guinea. *Malimbus* 16: 10-29.

Hammond, N., & Everett, M. (1980) *Birds of Britain and Europe*. London: Pan.

Hampton, R.R., & Sherry, D.F. (1992) Food storing by Mexican Chickadees and Bridled Titmice. *Auk* 109: 665-666.

Harding, D.P., & Harding, R.S.O. (1982) A preliminary list of birds in the Kilimi area of northwest Sierra Leone. *Malimbus* 4: 64-68.

Harrap, S. (1991) The Hainan nuthatch. *Bull. Oriental Bird Club* 13: 35-36.

Harrap, S. (1992a) Identification of Short-toed Treecreeper. *Birding World* 5: 10-16.

Harrap, S. (1992b) Little known West Palearctic birds: Algerian Nuthatch. *Birding World* 5: 154-156.

Harrington, H.H. (1909) A list of the birds of the Bhamo district of Upper Burma. *JBNHS* 19: 107-128, 299-313.

Harris, A., Tucker, L., & Vinicombe, K. (1989) *The Macmillan Field Guide to Bird Identification*. London: Macmillan.

Harrison, C. (1978) *A Field Guide to the Nests, Eggs and Nestlings of North American Birds*. Glasgow: Collins.

Harrison, C. (1982) *An Atlas of the Birds of the Western Palearctic*. London: Collins.

Harrison, H.H. (1979) *A Field Guide to Western Birds' Nests*. Boston: Houghton Mifflin.

Harrison, J. (1968) The occurrence of *Certhia familiaris macrodactyla* C.L. Brehm in the British Isles. *Bull. BOC* 88: 148-150.

Harrison, J.M. (1935) A note on *Certhia familiaris* and *C. brachydactyla*. *Ibis* Ser. 13, 5: 419-421.

Harrison, J.M. (1946) Some remarks upon *Parus major newtoni* Prazak and *Parus major major* L. *Bull. BOC* 66: 24-28.

Harrison, J.M. (1946) Continental Great Tit in Kent. *Brit. Birds* 39: 153.

Hartert, E. (1902) On birds from Pahang, eastern Malay Peninsula. *Novit. Zool.* 9: 537-580.

Hartert, E. (1903-10) *Die Vögel der paläarktischen Fauna*. 1. Berlin.

Hartert, E. (1905) [Description of *Sitta frontalis palawana*.] *Bull. BOC* 16: 11-12.

Hartert, E., & Steinbacher, F. (1933) *Die Vögel der paläarktischen Fauna. Ergänzungsband*. (2). Berlin.

Harvey, W.G. (1990) *Birds in Bangladesh*. Dhaka: Univ. Press.

Hawbecker, A.C. (1948) Analysis of variation in western races of the White-breasted Nuthatch. *Condor* 50: 26-39.

Heaton, A.M. (1979) Birds of the Parc National de la Benué. *Malimbus* 1: 146-147.

Heaton, A.M., & Heaton, A.E. (1980) The birds of Obudu, Cross River State, Nigeria. *Malimbus* 2: 16-24.

Heim de Balsac, H. (1976) Commentaires sur la découverte d'un élément imprévu de la faune paléarctique. *Alauda* 44 (3, suppl. spec.): 353-355.

Heimerdinger, M.A. (1955) A possible case of polymorphism in the Lead-colored Bush-tit. *Wilson Bull.* 67: 133.

Heintzelmann, D.S., & Mac Clay, R. (1971) An extraordinary autumn migration of White-breasted Nuthatches. *Wilson Bull.* 83: 129-131.

Heinzel, H., Fitter, R., & Parslow, J. (1974) *The Birds of Britain and Europe with North Africa and the Middle East*. 3rd edn. London: Collins.

Hellebreckers, W.P.J., & Hoogerwerf, A. (1967) A further contribution to our oological knowledge of the island of Java (Indonesia). *Zool. Verh.* 88: 1-164.

Hellmayr, C.E. (1911) In Wytsman, P. (ed.), *Genera Avium.* 16. Munich.

Hemmingsen, A.M. (1951) Observations of birds in north eastern China. 1. *Spolia Zool. Musei Hauniensis* 11: 1-227.

Hemmingsen, A.M., & Guildal, J.A. (1968) Observations of birds in northeastern China, especially the migration at Pei-tai-ho beach. II. Special part. *Spolia Zool. Musei Hauniensis* 28: 1-326.

Henry, G.H. (1971) *A Guide to the Birds of Ceylon*. 2nd edn. Oxford: Oxford Univ.

Herholdt, J.J., & Earlé, R.A. (1986) Ashy Tit and Pied Barbets roosting in a sandbank. *Ostrich* 57: 64.

Hertz, P.E., Remsen, J.V., & Zones, S.I. (1976) Ecological complementarity of three sympatric parids in a California oak woodland. *Condor* 78: 307-316.

Higuchi, H. (1975) Comparative feeding ecology of two geographical forms of the Varied Tit, *Parus varius varius* in southern Izu Peninsula and *P. v. owstoni* in Miyake I. of the Izu Is. *Tori* 1975: 15-28.

Higuchi, H. (1976a) Comparative study of the breeding of mainland and island subspecies of the Varied Tit, *Parus varius*. *Tori* 1976: 1-20.

Higuchi, H. (1976b) Home range and pair duration in the Varied Tit *Parus varius*. *Tori* 1976: 69-80.

Hildén, O. (1983) A hybrid *Parus ater x P. montanus* found in Finland. *Ornis Fennica* 60: 58-61.

Hildén, O., & Ketola, H. (1985) A mixed pair of *Parus cinctus* and *P. montanus* nesting in Kuusamo. *Ornis Fennica* 62: 26.

Hill, B.G., & Lein, M.R. (1988) Ecological relations of sympatric Black-capped and Mountain chickadees in southwestern Alberta. *Condor* 90: 875-884.

Hinde, R.A. (1952) The behaviour of the Great Tit *Parus major* and some related species. *Behav. Suppl.* 2. Leiden.

Hinde, R.A. (ed.) (1969) *Bird Vocalizations*. Cambridge: Cambridge Univ.

Hirschfeld, E. (1984) Problem att i fält skilja trädkryparen *Certhia familiaris* och trädgårdsträdkryparen *Certhia brachydactyla*.

Vår Fågelvärld 43: 21-26.

Hirschfeld, E. (1985) Further comments on treecreeper identification. *Brit. Birds* 78: 300-302.

Hobson, W. (1964) Notes on the Corsican nuthatch (*Sitta whiteheadi*, Sharpe). *Oologists' Record* 38: 22-25.

Hockley, P.A.R., Underhill, L.G., Neatherway, M., & Ryan, P.G. (1989) *Atlas of the Birds of the Southwestern Cape*. Cape Town: Cape Bird Club.

Hoffmann, T.W. (1989) Notes on the status and distribution of some birds in Sri Lanka as listed by S.D. Ripley (1982) "A Synopsis of the Birds of India and Pakistan, together with those of Nepal, Bhutan, Bangladesh and Sri Lanka". *JBNHS* 86: 7-16.

Hollom, P.A.D., Porter, R.F., Christensen, S., & Willis, I. (1988) *Birds of the Middle East and North Africa*. Calton: Poyser.

Holmes, P.R. (1986) The avifauna of the Suru River Valley, Ladakh. *Forktail* 2: 21-41.

Holyoak, D.T., & Seddon, M.B. (1990) Distributional notes on the birds of Benin. *Malimbus* 11: 128-134.

Hopwood, J.C., & Mackenzie, J.M.D. (1917) A list of birds from the north Chin Hills. *JBNHS* 25: 72-91.

Hornskov, J. (1989) Some observations in Hainan province, P.R. China. Unpublished.

Hornskov, J. (1991) Some bird observations at Laoye Shan, east Qinghai Province, China. *Hong Kong Bird Report* 1990: 179-182.

Houck, W.J., & Oliver, J.H. (1954) Unusual nesting behaviour of the Brown-headed Nuthatch. *Auk* 71: 330-331.

Hovel, H. (1987) *Check-list of the Birds of Israel*. Tel Aviv Univ. & Soc. Protection of Nature in Israel.

Howell, S.N.G., & Webb, S. (1995) *A Guide to the Birds of Mexico and Northern Central America*. Oxford: Oxford Univ.

Huang, Qiang, Huang, Yongzhao, & Deng, Heli (1993) [Report of a survey of birds of Pingshan county, Sichuan.] *Chinese J. Zool.* 3: 20-26. [In Chinese.]

Hubbard, J.P. (1970) Mensural separation of Black-capped and Carolina Chickadees. *EBBA News* 33: 211-213.

Hussain, S.A., Asad Akhtar, S., & Tiwari, J.K. (1992) Status and distribution of White-winged Black Tit *Parus nuchalis* in Kachchh, Gujarat, India. *Bird Conservation International* 2: 115-122.

Hutchinson, C.D. (1989) *Birds in Ireland*. Calton: T & AD Poyser.

Ilyashenko, V. Yu. (1990) Pp. 32-35 in Nazarenko, A.A., & Nazarov, Yu. N. (eds) [Ecology and distribution of birds in the south of the Far East.] Vladivostok. [In Russian.]

Inglis, C.M. (1901-04) The birds of the Madhubani subdivision of the Darbhanga District, Tirhut, with notes on species noticed elsewhere in the district. *JBNHS* 13: 621-631; 14: 132-139, 362-371, 554-563, 764-771; 15: 70-77, 337-343; 16: 70-75.

Inglis, C.M., Travers, W.L., O'Donel, H.V., & Shebbeare, E.O. (1920) A tentative list of the vertebrates of the Jalpaiguri District, Bengal. *JBNHS* 26: 819-[...], 988-999, 27: 151-162.

Ingram, C. (1913) A few remarks on the European Certhiidae. *Ibis* Ser. 10, 1: 545-550.

Inskipp, C. (1989a) The ornithological importance of Khaptad National Park, Nepal. *Forktail* 5: 49-60.

Inskipp, C. (1989b) *Nepal's Forest Birds: Their Status and Conservation*. ICBP Monograph No. 4. Cambridge: International Council for Bird Preservation.

Inskipp, C., & Inskipp, T. (1991) *A Guide to the Birds of Nepal*. 2nd edn. London: Christopher Helm.

Inskipp, C., & Inskipp, T.P. (1993a) Birds recorded during a visit to Bhutan in autumn 1991. *Forktail* 8: 97-112.

Inskipp, C., & Inskipp, T.P (1993b) Birds recorded during a visit to Bhutan in spring 1993. *Forktail* 9: 121-143.

Irvin, L. (1960) Birds of Anaktuvuk Pass, Kobuk, and Old Crow. Washington D.C.: *U.S. Nat. Mus., Bull.* 217.

Irwin, M.P.S. (1956) On the geographical variation in bill size of *Parus afer* in relation to habitat. *Bull. BOC* 76: 114-115.

Irwin, M.P.S. (1959) The specific relationship of *Parus afer* and *Parus griseiventris*. *Bull. BOC* 79: 46-48.

Irwin, M.P.S. (1963) A new race of *Anthoscopus caroli* (Sharpe) from the Zambesi valley. *Bull. BOC* 83: 2-4.

Irwin, M.P.S. (1981) *The Birds of Zimbabwe*. Harare: Quest.

Isenmann, P., & Guillosson, J.-Y. (1993) Simultaneous bigamy by Short-toed Treecreepers. *Brit. Birds* 86: 371.

Ivanow (1940) *Oiseaux du Tadjikistan*. Moscow.

Jackson, F.J. (1899, 1902) List of birds obtained in British East Africa. *Ibis* Ser. 7, 5: 587-639; Ser. 8, 2: 33-96, 611-643.

Jackson, J.A. (1938) *The Birds of Kenya Colony and the Uganda Protectorate*. London: Gurney & Jackson.

Jackson, J.A. (1995) Tit for tat. *Birder's World* February 1995: 16-20.

Jacobs, P., Mahler, F., & Ochando, B. (1978) A propos de la couleur de la calotte chez la Sittelle Kabyle (*Sitta ledanti*). *Aves* 15: 149-153.

Jamdar, N. (1987) An interesting feeding behaviour of the Whitecheeked Nuthatch (*Sitta leucopsis*). *JBNHS* 84: 443.

Jamdar, N., & Price, T. (1990) Simla Black Tit *Parus rufonuchalis* and Rufousbellied Crested Tit *Parus rubidiventris* breeding sympatrically in Kashmir. *JBNHS* 87: 302-303.

James, D.A., & Neal, J.C. (1986) *Arkansas Birds, their Distribution and Abundance*. Fayetteville: Univ. Arkansas.

James, R.D. (1991) *Annotated Checklist of the Birds of Ontario*. 2nd edn. Toronto: Royal Ontario Mus.

Järvinen, A. (1987) A successful mixed breeding between *Parus cinctus* and *P. montanus* in Finnish Lapland. *Ornis Fennica* 64: 158-159.

Järvinen, A. (1989) More mixed breedings between *Parus cinctus* and *P. montanus* in Finnish Lapland. *Ornis Fennica* 66: 123.

Järvinen, A., Ylimaunu, J., & Hannila [...] A mixed nesting pair *Parus montanus* and *P. cinctus* in Finnish Lapland. *Ornis Fennica* 62: 25-26.

Jellis, R. (1977) *Bird Sounds and [...]*

*their Meaning.* London: BBC.

Jenni, L., & Winkler, R. (1994) *Moult and Ageing of European Passerines.* London: Academic Press.

Jensen, J.V., & Kirkeby, J. (1980) *The Birds of the Gambia.* Aros Nature Guides.

Jewett, S.G., Taylor, W.P., Shaw, W.T., & Aldrich, J.W. (1953) *Birds of Washington State.* Seattle: Univ. Washington.

Johnsgard, P.A. (1979) *Birds of the Great Plains.* Lincoln & London: Univ. Nebraska.

Johnson, L.S. (1987) Pattern of song type use for territorial defence in the Plain Titmouse *Parus inornatus. Ornis Scand.* 18: 24-32.

Johnson, S.R., & Herter, D.R. (1989) *The Birds of the Beaufort Sea.* Anchorage: BP Exploration (Alaska) Inc.

Johnston, D.W. (1971) Ecological aspects of hybridizing chickadees (*Parus*) in Virginia. *Am. Midl. Nat.* 85: 124-134.

Jones, A.E (1947-48) The birds of Simla and adjacent hills. *JBNHS* 47: 117-125, 219-249, 409-432.

Jonsson, L. (1992) *Birds of Europe with North Africa and the Middle East.* London: Christopher Helm.

Jourdain, F.C.R. (1911-12) Notes on the ornithology of Corsica. *Ibis* Ser. 9, 5: 189-208, 440-458; 6: 63-82, 314-332.

Kale, H.W., & Maehr, D.S. (1990) *Florida's Birds: A Handbook and Reference.* Sarasota: Pineapple.

Karasov, W.H., Brittingham, M.C., & Temple, S.A. (1992) Daily energy and expenditure by Black-capped Chickadees (*Parus atricapillus*) in winter. *Auk* 109: 393-395.

Katholi, C. (1966) Titmouse postjuvenal molt. *EBBA News* 29: 200.

Kattl, M., Singh, P., Manjrekar, N., Sharma, D., & Mukherjee, S. (1992) An ornithological survey in eastern Arunachal Pradesh, India. *Forktail* 7: 75-89.

Kaufman, K. (1990) *Advanced Birding.* Boston: Houghton Mifflin.

Keith, S., & Gooders, J. (1980) *Collins Bird Guide.* London: Collins.

Keith, S., Twomey, A., Friedmann, H., & Williams, I. (1969) The avifauna of the Impenetrable Forest, Uganda. *Am. Mus. Novit.* 2389.

Kennerley, P.R. (1987) A survey of the birds of the Poyang Lake Nature Reserve, Jiangxi Province, China, 29 December 1985-4 January 1986. *Hong Kong Bird Report* 99: 97-111.

Kilham, L. (1968) Reproductive behaviour of White-breasted Nuthatches. I. Distraction display, bill-sweeping, and nest hole defence. *Auk* 85: 477-492.

Kilham, L. (1971) Roosting habits of White-breasted Nuthatches. *Condor* 73: 113-114.

Kilham, L. (1972a) Reproductive behaviour of White-breasted Nuthatches. II. Courtship. *Auk* 89: 115-129.

Kilham, L. (1972b) Death of Red-breasted Nuthatch from pitch around nest hole. *Auk* 89: 451-452

Kilham, L. (1973) Reproductive behaviour of the Red-breasted Nuthatch. I. Courtship. *Auk* 90: 597-609.

Kilham, L. (1974) Covering of

stores by White-breasted and Red-breasted Nuthatches. *Condor* 76: 108-109.

Kilham, L. (1975) Association of Red-breasted Nuthatches with chickadees in a hemlock cone year. *Auk* 92: 160-162.

Kilham, L. (1981) Agonistic behaviour of the White-breasted Nuthatch. *Wilson Bull.* 93: 271-274.

King, B. (1984) Bird notes from the Anyemaquen Shan range, Qinghai Province, China. *Le Gerfaut* 74: 227-241.

King, B. (1987a) Some bird observations at Pangquanguo Reserve in west central Shanxi Province in NE China. *Hong Kong Bird Report* 1984/1985: 112-114.

King, B. (1987b) Some notes on the birds of the Yi Shan area of NW Jiangxi Province, China. *Hong Kong Bird Report* 1984/1985: 115-119.

King, B. (1989a) Birds observed at Huang Nian Shan, Mabian county, southern Sichuan, China. *Forktail* 4: 63-68.

King, B. (1989b) Birds observed at Dafengding Panda Reserve, Mabian county, southern Sichuan, China. *Forktail* 4: 69-76.

King, B. (1989c) Some bird observations at Kangwu Liangsi, southwest Sichuan Province, China. *Hong Kong Bird Report* 1988: 102-110.

King, B., Abramson, I.J., Keith, A.R., Weiss, W.J., & Carrott, J. (1973) Some new bird records for Burma and Thailand. *Nat. Hist. Bull. Siam Soc.* 25: 157-160.

King, B., Dickinson, E.C., & Woodcock, M. (1975) *A Field-guide to the Birds of South-East Asia.* London: Collins.

King, B., & Han Lianxian (1991) Field notes on the birds recorded from the Simao area in south central Yunnan Province, China. *Hong Kong Bird Report* 1990: 172-178.

King, B., & Liao Wei-ping (1989) Hainan Island Bird Notes. *Hong Kong Bird Report* 1988: 80-101.

King, B., & Zheng Guangmei. (1988) Preliminary list of the birds of Wuyanling Natural Reserve in southern Zhejiang Province, China. *Hong Kong Bird Report* 1987: 93-102.

King, J.R. (1990) Sexual dimorphism of Marsh Tit. *Brit. Birds* 83: 510.

King, J.R. (1994) An undescribed plumage character of the Irish Coal Tit *Parus ater hibernicus.* *Bull. BOC* 114: 174-176.

King, J.R., & Griffiths, R. (1994) Sexual dimorphism of plumage and morphology in the Coal Tit *Parus ater. Bird Study* 41: 7-14.

Kinnear, N.B. (1929) On the birds collected by Mr. H. Stevens in northern Tonkin in 1923-24. *Ibis* Ser. 11, 4: 107-150, 292-344.

Kinnear, N.B. (1934) On the birds of the Adung Valley, North-East Burma. *JBNHS* 37: 347-368.

Kinnear, N.B. (1935) Correct names for the Indian Tree-Creepers. *Ibis* Ser. 13, 5: 604-605.

Kinnear, N.B. (1936) [Description of *Sitta castanea tonkinensis.*] *Bull. BOC* 56: 70-71.

Kirwan, G. (1992) Around the region. *Bull. Orn. Soc. Middle East* 29: 35-48.

Kleinschmidt, O. (1932-33) Fremde Formenkreise des Namenkreises Spechtmeise (*Sitta*). Berajah (Halle a.S.).

Kleinschmidt, O., & Weigolds, H. (1922) Zoologische Ergebnisse

der Walter Stötznerschen Expeditionen nach Szetschwan, Osttibet und Tschili. 1. Corvidae, Certhiidae, Sittidae, Paridae, Cinclidae. *Abh. Ber. Zool. u .Anthro-Ethn.* Dresden 15: 1-18.

Kluijver, H.N. (1951) The population ecology of the Great Tit, *Parus m. major* L. *Ardea* 39: 1-135.

Kniprath, E. (1967) Untersuchungen zur Variation der Rückenfärbung der beiden Meisen *Parus montanus* und *Parus palustris.* *J. Orn.* 108: 1-46.

Knorr, O.A. (1957) Communal roosting of the Pygmy Nuthatch. *Condor* 59: 398.

Koelz, W. (1939) New birds from Asia, chiefly from India. *Proc. Biol. Soc. Washington* 52: 61-82.

Koster, S.H., & Grettenberger, J.F. (1983) A preliminary survey of birds in W Park, Niger. *Malimbus* 5: 62-72.

Kosuki, K. (1988) The first record of *Parus cyaneus* from Japan. *Strix* 7: 297-298.

Kovshar', A.F. (1976) [On ecology of Dzungarian Tit.] *Vestn. Zool., Kiew* 1976: 34-39. [In Russian.]

Kozlova, E.V. (1932-33) The birds of South-West Transbaikalia, Northern Mongolia and Central Gobi. *Ibis* Ser. 13, 2: 316-347, 405-438, 576 596; 3: 59-87, 301-332.

Krebs, J.R. (1977) Song and territoriality in the Great Tit. Pp. 47-62 *in* Stonehouse, B., & Perrins, C.M. (eds) ,*Evolutionary Ecology.* London: Macmillan.

Krebs, J.R., Ashcroft, R., & Webber, M. (1978) Song repertoires and territory defence in the Great Tit (*Parus major*). *Nature* 271: 539-542.

Kumerloeve, H. (1958) Sur la présence en Asie mineure de la Sittelle naine de Krüper (*Sitta canadensis kruperi* Pelzeln). *Alauda* 26: 81-85.

Kumerloeve, H. (1967-69) Recherches sur l'avifaune de la République Arabe Syrienne essai d'un aperçu. *Alauda* 35: 243-266; 36: 1-26, 190-207; 37: 43-58, 114-134, 188-205.

Kuroda, N. (1931) The second lot of bird-skins from south Manchuria. *Tori* 7: 42-46.

Kuroda, N. (1936) *Birds of the Island of Java II. Passeres.* Tokyo: author.

Laarksonen, M., & Lehikoinen, E. (1976) Age determination of Willow and Crested Tits *Parus montanus* and *P. cristatus. Ornis Fennica* 53: 9-14.

Labzyuk, V.I., Nazarov, Yu. N., & Nechaev, V.A. (1971) Pp. 52-78 *in* Ivanov, A.I. (ed.) [Ornithological researches in the south of the Far East.] Vladivostok. [In Russian.]

Lack, D. (1969) Tit niches in two worlds; or homage to Evelyn Hutchinson. *Am. Naturalist* 103 (929): 43-49.

Lack, D. (1971) *Ecological Isolation in Birds.* Oxford & Edinburgh: Blackwell Scientific Publications.

Lack, D., & Lack, E. (1958) The nesting of the Long-tailed Tit. *Bird Study* 5: 1-19.

Lack, P. (compiler) (1986) *The Atlas of Wintering Birds in Britain and Ireland.* Calton: T & AD Poyser.

Lafresnaye, De. (1837) Mésange à Huppe Jaune. *P. flavo-cristatus. Mag. Zool.* Paris 7: 89-90.

Lamarche, B. (1980-81) Liste com-

mentée des Oiseaux du Mali. *Malimbus* 2: 121-158; 3: 73-102.

Lamarche, B. (1988) *Liste commentée des oiseaux de Mauritanie.* Nouakchott: Assoc. Nat. Sah., & Ouest-Afr.

Land, H.C. (1970) *Birds of Guatemala.* Wynnewood (Pennsylvania): Livingston.

Laskey, A.R. (1957) Some Tufted Titmouse life history. *Bird Banding* 28: 135-145.

Latimer, W.A. (1977) A comparative study of the songs and alarm calls of some *Parus* species. *Z. Tierpsychol.* 45: 414-433.

La Touche, J.D.D. (1899-1900) Notes on the birds of North-west Fohkien. *Ibis* Ser. 7, 5: 169-210, 400-431; 6: 34-60.

La Touche, J.D.D. (1920-21) Notes on the birds of north-east Chihli in north China. *Ibis* Ser. 11, 2: 629-671, 880-920; 3: 3-48.

La Touche, J.D. (1923a) [Notes on the tits of the *Parus commixtus* group.] *Bull. BOC* 43: 101-104.

La Touche, J.D. (1923b) [Description of *Sylviparus modestus ricketti.*] *Bull. BOC* 43: 104-105.

La Touche, J.D.D. (1923-24) On the birds of South-east Yunnan, S.W. China. *Ibis* Ser. 11, 5: 300-332, 369-415, 629-645; 6: 284-307.

La Touche, J.D.D. (1925) *A Handbook of the Birds of Eastern China.* Vol. 1. London: Taylor & Francis.

Laughlin, S.B., & Kibbe, D.P. (eds) (1985) *The Atlas of Breeding Birds of Vermont.* Hanover & London: Univ. of New England.

Lawson, W.J. (1961) Comments on the geographical variation in Carol's Penduline Tit *Anthoscopus caroli* in southern Africa. *Bull. BOC* 81: 149-150.

Leberman, R.C. (1973) A study of Tufted Titmouse weights. *EBBA News* 36: 34-38.

Ledant, J.P. (1977) La Sittelle kabyle (*Sitta ledanti* Vielliard), espèce endémique montagnarde récemment découverte. *Aves* 14: 83-85.

Ledant, J.P. (1978) Données comparées sur la Sittelle Corse (*Sitta whiteheadi*) et sur la Sittelle Kabyle (*Sitta ledanti*). *Aves* 15: 154-157.

Ledant, J.P. (1981) Conservation et fragilité de la forêt de Babor, habitat de la Sittelle kabyle. *Aves* 18: 1-9.

Ledant, J.P., & Jacobs, P. (1977) La Sittelle kabyle (*Sitta ledanti*): données nouvelles sur sa biologie. *Aves* 14: 233-242.

Ledant, J.P., Jacobs, J.-P., Jacobs, P., Mahler, F., Ochando, B., & Roché, J. (1981) Mis à jour de l'avifaune algérienne. *Gerfaut* 71: 295-398.

Ledant, J.P., Jacobs, P., Ochando, B., & Renault, J. (1985) Dynamique de la forêt du mont Babor et préférences écologiques de la Sittelle kabyle *Sitta ledanti. Biol. Conserv.* 32: 231-254.

Lee, T.-H., Cheng, S.-W., & Cheng, Tso-hsin (1965) [Avifaunal studies of the Yuh-shuh Autonomous Region, Chinghai Province.] *Acta Zool. Sinica* 17: 217-229. [In Chinese.]

LeFevre, R.H. (1962) *The Birds of Northern Shantung Province, China.* Pennsylvania: author.

Le Fur, R. (1981) Notes sur l'avifaune algérienne 2. *Alauda* 49: 295-299.

Légendre, M. (1932) *Monographie des Mésanges D'Europe. Encyclopédie Ornithologique*

VI. Paris: Paul Lechevalier.

Lekagul, B., & Cronin, E.W. (1974) *Bird Guide of Thailand.* Bangkok: Association for the Conservation of Wildlife.

Lekagul, B., & Round, P.D. (1991) *A Guide to the Birds of Thailand.* Bangkok: Saha Karn Bhaet.

Lemon, R.E. (1968) Coordinated singing in the black-crested tit-mice. *Canad. J. Zool.* 46: 1163-1167.

Leonovich, V.V., & Veprintsev, B.N. (1986) [New faunistic records for Sakhalin.] *Ornitologiya* 21: 137. [In Russian.]

Ler, P.A. (ed.) (1989) [Rare vertebrates of the Soviet Far East and their protection.] Leningrad: Nauka. [In Russian.]

Lesson, R.P. (1840) Oiseaux rares ou nouveaux de la collection du Docteur Abeillé, à Bordeaux. *Rev. Zool.* 2 (1839): 40-43.

Leven, M.R. (1993) Velvet-fronted Nuthatches in Hong Kong. *Hong Kong Bird Report* 1992: 188-191.

Lewington, I., Alström, P., & Colston, P. (1991) *A Field Guide to the Rare Birds of Britain and Europe.* London: HarperCollins.

Lewis, A., & Pomeroy, D. (1989) *A Bird Atlas of Kenya.* Rotterdam/Brookfield: A.A. Balkema.

Lewis, V. (1985) Voices of Willow Tit and Marsh Tit. *Brit. Birds* 78: 197-198.

Lewthwaite, R. (1993) Birds recorded at Ru Yang NR (Ba Bao Shan), Guangdong Province, PRC. 9-13 October 1993. Unpublished MS.

Li, D.-H., & Wang, Z.-X. (1979) [New records of subspecies of Chinese birds from Xizang.] *Acta Zootax. Sinica* 4: 190-191. [In Chinese.]

Li, G., Liu, L., Zhang, R., & Zhang, Q. (1976) [On the avifauna of Boaxing, Sichuan.] *Acta Zool. Sinica* 22: 101-114. [In Chinese.]

Li, G.Y., Zheng, B.L., & Liu, G.Z. (1982) *Fauna Sinica. Aves.* Vol. 13. Passeriformes (Paridae-Zosteropidae). Beijing: Science Press. [In Chinese.]

Li, Guiyuan, Zhang, Qingmao (1989) [Avifauna of Wangland nature reserve, Pingwu County, Sichuan.] *Sichuan J. Zool.* 8: 17-20. [In Chinese.]

Li, Guiyuan, Zhang, Qingmao *et al.* (1994) [On the avifauna of Laba He nature reserve, Tianquan County, Sichuan.] *Sichuan J. Zool.* 13: 57-66. [In Chinese.]

Liao, W.-p. (1983) [The birds and mammals of Hainan Island.] Beijing: Science Press. [In Chinese.]

Ligon, J.S. (1961) *New Mexico Birds and Where to Find Them.* Albuquerque: Univ. New Mexico.

Limbert, M. (1984) Vagrant races of Willow Tit in Britain. *Brit. Birds* 77: 123.

Lippens, L., & Wille, H. (1976) *Les Oiseaux du Zaïre.* Tielt: Lanoo.

Livesey, T.R. (1933) Nidification of the Giant Nuthatch (*Sitta magna* Wardlaw Ramsay). *JBNHS* 36: 993.

Lobkov, E.G. (1986) [The breeding birds of Kamchatka.] Vladivostok: Far East Science Centre of the Acadamy of Sciences of the USSR. [In Russian.]

Löhrl, H. (1960, 1961) Vergleichende Studien über Brutbiologie und Verhalten der

Kleiber *Sitta whiteheadi* Sharpe und *Sitta canadensis.* Parts I and II. *J. Orn.* 101: 245-264; 102: 111-132.

Löhrl, H. (1962) Artkennzeichen von *Sitta krüperi. J. Orn.* 103: 418-419.

Löhrl, H. (1963) The use of bird calls to clarify taxonomic relationships. *Proc. 13th Int. Orn. Congr.*: 544-552.

Löhrl, H. (1964) Verhaltensmerkmale der Gattungen *Parus* (Meisen), *Aegithalos* (Schwanzmeisen), *Sitta* (Kleiber), *Tichodroma* (Mauerläufer) und *Certhia* (Baumläufer). *J. Orn.* 105: 153-181.

Löhrl, H. (1966) Zur Biologie der Trauermeise (*Parus lugubris*) (mit Bemerkungen über die Untergattung *Poecile*). *J. Orn.* 107: 167-186.

Löhrl, H. (1967) Zur verwandtschaftlichen Stellung von *Cephalopyrus flammiceps* auf Grund des Verhaltens. *Bonn. Zool. Beitr.* 18: 127-138.

Löhrl, H. (1968) *Tiere und wir.* Berlin: Ullstein.

Löhrl, H. (1975) Brutverhalten und Jugendentwicklung beim Mauerläufer (*Tichodroma muraria*). *J. Orn.* 116: 229-262.

Löhrl, H. (1981) Zur Kenntnis der Laubmeise, *Sylviparus modestus. J. Orn.* 122: 89-92.

Löhrl, H. (1987) Haltung und Zucht der Schmuckmeise *Parus venustulus. Gefiederte Welt* 111: 121-123.

Löhrl, H. (1988) Zur Taxonomie, Brutbiologie und Mauser der Schmuckmeise *Parus venustulus* Swinhoe, verglichen mit *Sylviparus modestus* und *Parus ater. Bonn. Zool. Beitr.* 39: 7-17.

Löhrl, H., & Thielcke, G. (1969) Zur Brutbiologie, Ökologie und Systematik einiger Waldvögel Afghanistans. *Bonn. Zool. Beitr.* 20: 85-98.

Löhrl, H., & Thielcke, G. (1973) Alarmlaute europäischer und nordafrikanischer Tannenmeisen (*Parus ater ater, P. ater atlas, P. ater ledouci*) und der Schwarzschopfmeise (*P. melanolophus*). *J. Orn.* 114: 250-252.

Long, J.L. (1981) *Introduced Birds of the World.* Newton Abbot & London: David & Charles.

Long, R. (1981) Review of birds in the Channel Islands, 1951-80. *Brit. Birds* 74: 327-344.

Lönnberg, E. (1924) Notes on some birds from Kansu, China. *Ibis* Ser. 11, 6: 308-328.

Loskot, V.M. (1982) *Parus hyrcanus* Sar. et Loud.: A distinct species. *In* Gavrilov, V.M., & Potapov, R.L., *Ornithological Studies in the USSR.* Moscow: Zool. Inst., USSR Academy of Sciences.

Loskot, W.M (ed.) (1987) *Parus hyrcanus* (Sarudny et Loudon). *In* Dathe, H., & Neufeldt, I.A., *Atlas der Verbreitung paläarktischer Vögel.* 14 (3). Berlin.

Loskot, W.M., Sokolow, E.P., & Wunderlich, K. (1991) *Sitta tephronota* Sharpe. *In* Dathe, H., & Neufeldt, I.A. *Atlas der Verbreitung palaarktischer Vögel.* 17. Berlin.

Louette, M. (1981) *The Birds of Cameroon: An Annotated Check-list.* Brussels: Paleis der Academiën.

Louette, M., & Prévost, J. (1987) Passereaux collectés par J. Prévost au Cameroun. *Malimbus* 9: 83-96.

Lowe, W.P. (1933) A report on the

birds collected by the Vernay Expedition to Tenasserim and Siam. *Ibis* Ser. 13, 3: 259-283, 473-491.

Lowery, G.H. (1974) *Louisiana Birds.* 3rd edn. Baton Rouge: Louisiana State Univ.

Ludlow, F. (1927-28) Birds of the Gyantse neighbourhood, southern Tibet. *Ibis* Ser. 12, 3: 644-659; 4: 51-73, 211-232.

Ludlow, F. (1937) The birds of Bhutan and adjacent territories of Sikkim and Tibet with notes by N.B. Kinnear. *Ibis* Ser. 14, 1: 1-46, 249-293, 467-504.

Ludlow, F. (1950) The birds of Lhasa. *Ibis* 92: 34-45.

Ludlow, F. (1951) The birds of Kongbo and Pome, south-east Tibet. *Ibis* 93: 547-578.

Ludlow, F., & Kinnear, N.B. (1933-34) A contribution to the ornithology of Chinese Turkestan. *Ibis* Ser. 13, 3: 240-259, 440-473, 658-694; 4: 95-125.

Ludlow, F., & Kinnear, N.B. (1944) The birds of southeastern Tibet. *Ibis* 86: 43-86, 176-208, 348-389.

Lunk, W.A. (1952) Notes on variation in the Carolina Chickadee. *Wilson Bull.* 64: 7-21.

McCallum, D.A., Gaunt, S.L.L., & Gill, F.B. (1994) Does the Père David's Tit have the most primitive vocal repertoire among the chickadees? *Parus International* 4 (2): 12.

McCallum, D.A., Gill, F.B., & Gaunt, S.L.L. (in prep.) Habitat overlap among *Parus* species of western China.

Macdonald, D.W., & Henderson, D.G. (1977) Aspects of the behaviour and ecology of mixed-species bird flocks in Kashmir. *Ibis* 119: 481-493.

Macdonald, J.D. (1957) *Contribution to the Ornithology of Western South Africa.* London: British Museum.

Macdonald, J.D., & Hall, B.P. (1957) Ornithological results of the Bernard Carp/Transvaal Museum Expedition to the Kaokoveld, 1951. *Ann. Transvaal Mus.* 23: 1-39.

Macdonald, M.A., & Taylor, I.R. (1977) Notes on some uncommon forest birds in Ghana. *Bull. BOC* 97: 116-120.

Macfarlane, A.M. (1978) Field notes on the birds of Lebanon and Syria, 1974-1977. *Army Bird-watching Soc.*, per. pub. 3.

McGregor, R.C. (1909-10) *A Manual of Philippine Birds.* Manilla: Bureau Science.

Mack, A.L., Gill, F.B., Colburn, R., & Spolsky, C. (1986) Mitochondrial DNA: A source of genetic markers for study of similar passerine bird species. *Auk* 103: 676-681.

Mackenzie, P. (1979) Birds of the Calabar area. *Malimbus* 1: 47-54.

MacKinnon, J. (1988) *Field Guide to the Birds of Java and Bali.* Yogyakarta: Gadjah Mada Univ.

MacKinnon, J., & Phillips, K. (1993) *A Field Guide to the Birds of Borneo, Sumatra, Java and Bali. The Greater Sunda Islands.* Oxford: Oxford Univ.

Mackworth-Praed, C.W., & Grant, C.H.B. (1960) *Birds of Eastern and North Eastern Africa (African Handbook of Birds. Series 1).* Vol. II. 2nd edn. London & New York: Longman.

Mackworth-Praed, C.W., & Grant, C.H.B. (1963) *Birds of the Southern Third of Africa*

(African Handbook of Birds. Series 2). Vol. II. London & New York: Longman.

Mackworth-Praed, C.W., & Grant, C.H.B. (1973) *Birds of West Central and Western Africa (African Handbook of Birds. Series 3).* Vol. II. London & New York: Longman.

McLaren, M.A. (1975) Breeding biology of the Boreal Chickadee. *Wilson Bull.* 87: 344-354.

McLaren, M.A. (1976) Vocalisations of the Boreal Chickadee. *Auk* 93: 451-463.

Maclean, G.L. (1993) *Roberts' Birds of Southern Africa.* 6th edn. London: New Holland.

McNair, D.B. (1983) Brown-headed Nuthatches store pine seeds. *Chat* 47: 47-48.

McNair, D.B. (1984) Clutch-size and nest placement in the Brown-headed Nuthatch. *Wilson Bull.* 96: 296-301.

McWhirter, D.W. (1985) Bird nesting data from Okinawa island. *Tori* 33: 123-125.

Madge, S.C. (1978) Birds of the Salang Pass, Central Afghanistan. *Bull. Orn. Soc. Middle East* 1: 2-5.

Mallon, D.P. (1987) The winter birds of Ladakh. *Forktail* 3: 27-41.

Mann, C.F. (1985) An avifaunal study in Kakamega Forest, Kenya, with particular reference to species diversity, weight and moult. *Ostrich* 56: 236-262.

Manolis, T. (1977) Foraging relationships of Mountain Chickadees and Pygmy Nuthatches. *Western Birds* 8: 13-20.

Marshall, J.T. (1957) Birds of pine-oak woodland in southern Arizona and adjacent Mexico. Berkeley, California: Cooper Orn. Soc. *Pacific Coast Avifauna* No. 32.

Martens, J. (1971) Artstatus von *Parus rufonuchalis* Blyth. *J. Orn.* 112: 451-458.

Martens, J. (1975) Akustische Differenzierung verwandtschaftlicher Beziehungen in der *Parus* (*Periparus*)-Gruppe nach Untersuchungen im Nepal-Himalaya. *J. Orn.* 116: 369-433.

Martens, J. (1981) Lautäusserungen der Baumläufer des Himalaya und zur akustischen Evolution in der Gattung *Certhia. Behaviour* 77: 287-318.

Martens, J. (1992) Die holarktischen Weidenmeisen (*Parus atricapillus* s.l.) - Gesangsdifferenzierung und Ausbreitungsgeschichte. *Verh. Dtsch Zool. Ges.* 85,1: 190.

Martens, J. (1993) Lautäußerungen von Singvögeln und die Entstehung neuer Arten. *Forschungsmagazin der Johannes Gutenberg-Universität Mainz* 2/93: 34-44.

Martens, J. (in press) Vocalizations and speciation of Palearctic birds. In Kroodsma & Miller (eds), *Ecology and Evolution of Acoustic Communication in Birds.*

Martens, J., & Eck, S. (in press) Towards an ornithology of the Himalayas. Ecology, systematics and vocalisations of Nepal birds. *Bonn. Zool. Monogr.*

Martens, J., Ernst, S., & Petri, B. (in press) Reviergesänge ostasiatischer Weidenmeisen (*Parus montanus*) und ihre mikroevolutive Ableitung. [Territorial songs and intraspecific evolution of east Asian Willow Tits (*Parus montanus*)]. *J. Orn.*

Martens, J., & Gebauer, A. (1993) Bemerkungen zu Biologie,

Stimme und Verwandtschaft der Weissbrauenmeise (*Parus superciliosus*). *Zool. Abh. Staatl. Mus. Tierkde Dresden* 47: 213-222.

Martens, J., & Nazarenko, A.A. (1993) Microevolution of eastern Palearctic Grey Tits as indicated by their vocalisations (*Parus* [*Peocile*]: Paridae, Aves). 1 *Parus montanus*. *Z. zool. Syst. Evolut.-forsch.* 31: 127-143.

Martens, J., & Schöttler, B. (1991). Akustische Barrieren zwischen Blaumeise (*Parus caeruleus*) und Lasurmeise (*Parus cyanus*)? *J. Orn.* 132: 61-80.

Martin, J.-L. (1988) *Variation géographique, adaptation et spéciation: l'exemple de Parus caeruleus (Aves)*. Académie de Montpellier, Université des Sciences et Techniques du Languedoc. Thesis.

Martin, J.-L. (1991) Patterns and significance of geographical variation in the Blue Tit (*Parus caeruleus*). *Auk* 108: 820-832.

Martin, J.-L., & Pitocchelli, J. (1991) Relation of within-population phenotypic variation with sex, season and geography in the Blue Tit. *Auk* 108: 833-841.

Martins, R.P. (ed.) (1989) Turkey Bird Report 1982-6. *Sandgrouse* 11: 1-41.

Masterson, A. (1970) Notes on the Spotted Creeper. *Honeyguide* 61: 35-37.

Matthews, W.H., & Edwards, V.S. (1944) *A List of the Birds of Darjeeling*. Darjeeling: authors.

Matthysen, E., & Adriaensen, F. (1989) Notes on winter territoriality and social behaviour in the Corsican Nuthatch *Sitta whiteheadi* Sharpe. *Alauda* 57: 155-168.

Matthysen, E., Gaunt, S.L., & McCallum, D.A. (1991) A note on the vocalisations of the Chinese Nuthatch. *Wilson Bull.* 103: 706-710.

Mauersberger, G. (1960) *Certhia brachydactyla* Brehm. In Stresemann, E. & Portenko, L.A. (eds), *Atlas der Verbreitung paläarktischer Vögel*. 1. Berlin.

Mauersberger, G. (1983) Taxonomische Probleme der mongolischen Avifauna. *Mitt. Zool. Mus. Berlin* 59, Suppl. Ann. Orn. 7: 47-83.

Mauersberger, G. (1989) Zur Ernährungsweise des Chinesenkleibers, *Sitta villosa* Verreaux. *Acta ornithoecol.* 2: 79-86.

Mauersberger, G., & Stephan, B. (1967) *Parus cristatus* L. In Stresemann, E., Portenko, L.A., & Mauersberger, G. (eds), *Atlas der Verbreitung paläarktischer Vögel*. 2. Berlin.

Mayr, E. (1938) The birds of the Vernay-Hopwood Chindwin Expedition. *Ibis* Ser. 14, 2: 277-320.

Mayr, E. (1956) Gesang und Systematik. *Beitr. Vogelk.* 5: 112-117.

Mayr, E., & Amadon, D. (1951) A classification of recent birds. *Am. Mus. Novit.* 1496: 1-42.

Mayr, E., & Short, L.L. (1970) Species taxa of North American birds. *Pub. Nuttall Ornith. Club* 9: 1-127.

Mead, C.J. (1975) Variation in some characters of three Palearctic Certhia species. *Bull. BOC* 95: 30-39.

Mead, C.J., & Wallace, D.I.M. (1976) Identification of European treecreepers. *Brit. Birds* 69: 117-131.

Mearns, E.A. (1916) On the geographical forms of the Philippine Elegant Titmouse, *Pardaliparus elegans* (Lesson),

with descriptions of three new subspecies. *Proc. U.S. Nat. Mus.* 51: 57-65.

Medway, Lord, & Wells, D.R. (1976) *The Birds of the Malay Peninsula. Vol. 5: Conclusion, and Survey of Every Species*. London: H.F. & G. Witherby.

Mees, G.F. (1970) On some birds from southern Mexico. *Zool. Meded.* 44: 237-245.

Mees, G.F. (1986) A list of the birds recorded from Bangka Island, Indonesia. *Zool. Verhand.* 232: 1-176.

Meigs, J.B., Smith, D.C., & Van Buskirk, J. (1983) Age determination of Black-capped Chickadees. *J. Field Orn.* 54: 283-286.

Meinertzhagen, R. (1920) Notes on the birds of Quetta. *Ibis* Ser. 11, 2: 132-195.

Meinertzhagen, R. (1927) Systematic results of birds collected at high altitude in Ladak and Sikkim. *Ibis* Ser. 12, 3: 363-421, 571-633.

Meinertzhagen, R. (1928) Some biological problems connected with the Himalaya. *Ibis* Ser. 12, 4: 480-533.

Meinertzhagen, R. (1938) On the birds of northern Afghanistan. *Ibis* Ser. 14, 2: 480-520, 671-717.

Meinertzhagen, R. (1947a) On the British forms of *Certhia familiaris* Linnaeus. *Bull. BOC* 68: 26.

Meinertzhagen, R. (1947b) On the Western European forms of *Aegithalos caudatus* (Linneaus). *Bull. BOC* 68: 26-28.

Meinertzhagen, R. (1951) Some relationships between African, Oriental, and Palearctic genera and species, with a review of the genus *Monticola*. *Ibis* 93: 443-459.

Meise, W., Schönwetter, M., & Stresemann, E. (1937) Aves Beikianae. Beiträge zur Ornithologie von Nordwest-Kansu nach den Forschungen von Walter Beck in den Jahren 1926-1933. *J. Orn.* 85: 37-576.

Melville, D.S., & Galsworthy, A.C. (1991) The 1989/90 Penduline Tit 'invasion' of Hong Kong. *Hong Kong Bird Report* 1990: 149-154.

Ménégaux, A., & Didier, R. (1913) Etude d'une collection d'oiseaux recueillie par M. Albert Pichon au Yunnan occidental. *Revue Française d'Ornithologie* 5: 97-103.

Mengel, R.M. (1965) *The Birds of Kentucky*. Am. Orn. Union, Orn. Monographs No. 3.

Merritt, P.G. (1978) Characteristics of Black-capped and Carolina Chickadees at the range interface in northern Indiana. *Jack-Pine Warbler* 56: 171-179.

Merritt, P.G. (1981) Narrowly disjunct allopatry between Black-capped and Carolina Chickadees in northern Indiana. *Wilson Bull.* 93: 54-66.

Mey, E. (1988) Herbstdaten zur Mongolischen Avifauna. [Autumn data on the Mongolia bird fauna.] *Mitt. Zool. Mus. Berlin* 64, Suppl. Ann. Orn. 12: 79-128.

Meyer de Schauensee, R.M. (1946a) On two collections of birds from the Southern Shan States, Burma. *Proc. Acad. Nat. Sci. Phil.* 98: 99-122.

Meyer de Schauensee, R.M. (1946b) On some forms of *Parus major* found in eastern and southern Asia. *Notulae Naturae (Acad. Nat. Sci. Phil.)* 169: 1-9.

Meyer de Schauensee, R.M.

(1984) *The Birds of China*. Washington D.C.: Smithsonian Institution.

Miller, A.H. (1943) A new race of Brown-headed Chickadee from northern Washington. *Occas. Papers. Mus. Zool. Louisiana State Univ.* 14: 261-263.

Miller, A.H. (1946) Endemic birds of the Little San Bernardino Mountains, California. *Condor* 48: 75-79.

Miller, A.H. (1955) The avifauna of the Sierra del Carmen of Coahuila. *Condor* 57: 154-178.

Miller, A.H., & Storer, R.W. (1950) A new race of *Parus sclateri* from the Sierra Madre del Sur of Mexico. *J. Wash. Acad. Sci.* 40: 301-302.

Miller, A.H., Friedmann, H., Griscom, L., & Moore, R.T. (eds) (1957) Distributional check-list of the birds of Mexico. Berkeley, California: Cooper Orn. Soc. *Pacific Coast Avifauna* No. 23.

Miller, R.C. (1921) The flock behaviour of the Coast Bush-tit. *Condor* Vol?: 121-127.

Minock, M.E. (1971) Social relationships among Mountain Chickadees (*Parus gambeli*). *Condor* 73: 118-120.

Mishchenko, Yu. V. (1982) [On the taxonomic relationships of *Parus major intermedius* (Zarudny) with tits of adjoining regions ] *Vestnik Zool.* (5): 35-42.

Mishchenko, Yu. V. (1983) [New data on the bird fauna of the Kopet-Dagh.] *Vestnik Zool.* (5): 87-88.

Mishima, T (1969) An example of *Parus varius* x *P. atricapillus* a pale phase of *Emberiza spodocephala*. *Misc. Rep. of the Yamashina Inst. for Ornithol.* 5: 676-678.

Monga, S.G., & Naoroji, R.K. (1983) Birds of the Rajpipla forests - South Gujarat. *JBNHS* 80: 575-612.

Monroe, B.L., Stamm, A.L., & Palmer-Ball, B.L. (1988) *Annotated Checklist of the Birds of Kentucky*. Kentucky Orn. Soc.

Monson, G., & Phillips, A.R. (1981) *Annotated Checklist of the Birds of Arizona*. 2nd edn. Tucson: Univ. Arizona.

Moore, W.S. (1977) An evaluation of narrow hybrid zones in vertebrates. *Quart. Rev. Biol.* 52: 263-277.

Morel, G.J., & Morel, M.-Y. (1988) *Liste des oiseaux de Guinée*. *Malimbus* 10: 143-176.

Morel, G.J., & Morel, M.-Y. (1990) *Les oiseaux de Sénégambie*. Paris: ORSTOM.

Morley, A. (1953) Field observations on the biology of the Marsh Tit. *Brit. Birds* 46: 233-238, 273-287, 332-346.

Morris, P.I. (1992) Feeding behaviour of Marsh Tit. *Brit. Birds* 85: 313-314.

Morse, D.H. (1967) Foraging relationships of Brown-headed Nuthatches and Pine Warblers. *Ecology* 48: 94-103.

Morse, D.H. (1968) The use of tools by Brown-headed Nuthatches. *Wilson Bull.* 80: 220-224.

Morse, D.H. (1970) Ecological aspects of some mixed-species foraging flocks of birds. *Ecological Monographs* 40: 119-168.

Mosher, J.I., & Lane, S. (1972) A method of determining the sex of captured Black-capped Chickadees. *Bird-Banding* 43: 139-140.

Mountfort, G., & Ferguson-Lees,

I.J. (1961) Observations on the birds of Bulgaria. *Ibis* 103: 443-471.

Mumford, R.E., & Keller, C.E. (1984) *The Birds of Indiana*. Bloomington: Univ. Indiana.

Murray, B.G., & Jehl, J.R. (1964) Weights of autumn migrants from coastal New Jersey. *Bird Bander* 35: 253-63.

Nash, S.V., & Nash, A.D. (1988) An annotated checklist of the birds of Tanjung Puting National Park, central Kalimantan. *Kukila* 3: 93-116.

National Geographic Society (1983) *Field Guide to the Birds of North America*. Washington: National Geographic Soc.

Nazarenko, A.A. (1988) In Litvinenko, N.M. (ed.) [Rare birds of the Far East and their protection.] Vladivostok. [In Russian.]

Neufeldt, I.A., & Wunderlich, K. (1984) *Sitta krueperi* Pelzeln. In Dathe, H., & Neufeldt, I.A. *Atlas der Verbreitung palaarktischer Vögel*. 12. Berlin.

Newby, J.E. (1979-80) The birds of the Ouadi Rimé-Ouadi Achim Faunal Reserve: a contribution to the study of the Chadian avifauna. *Malimbus* 1: 90-109; 2: 29-49.

Newman, K. (1988) *Newman's Birds of Southern Africa*. Updated. Johannesburg: Southern Book Publishers.

Newman, K. (1989) *Newman's Birds of Botswana*. Southern Book Publishers.

Nikolaus, G. (1987) *Distribution Atlas of Sudan's Birds with Notes on Habitat and Status*. Bonner Zoologische Monographien Nr. 25. Bonn: Zoolog. Forschungsinst. u. Museum Alexander Koenig.

Nikolaus, G. (1989) Birds of south-ern Sudan. *Scopus* Special Supplement No. 3. Nairobi: EANHS.

Norris, R.A. (1958) Comparative biosystematics and life history of the nuthatches *Sitta pygmaea* and *Sitta pusilla*. Univ. Calif. Publ. Zool. 56: 119-300.

Nowicki, S. (1989) Vocal plasticity in captive Black-capped Chickadees: the acoustic basis and rate of call convergence. *Anim. Behav.* 37: 64-73.

Oates, E.W. (1889) *Fauna of British India, Birds*. Vol. 1. London: Taylor & Francis.

Oberholser, H.C. (1897) Critical notes on the genus *Auriparus*. *Auk* 14: 390-394.

Oberholser, H.C. (1903) A synopsis of the genus *Psaltriparus*. *Auk* 20: 198-201.

Oberholser, H.C. (1917) Critical notes on the eastern subspecies of *Sitta carolinensis* Latham. *Auk* 34: 181-187.

Oberholser, H.C. (1947) Two races of the Bridled Titmouse. *Fieldiana Zool.* 31: 87-93.

Oberholser, H.C. (1974) *The Bird Life of Texas*. Vol. 2. Austin: Univ. Texas.

Odum, E.P. (1942) Annual cycle of the Black-capped Chickadee. 3. *Auk* 59: 499-531.

Ogilvie-Grant, W.R. (1906) [Type description of *Sitta corea*.] *Bull. BOC* 16: 87-88.

Ogilvie-Grant, W.R. (1910) Ruwenzori Expedition Reports. 16 Aves. *Trans. Zool. Soc. London* 19.

Ogilvie-Grant, W.R., & La Touche, J.D.D. (1907) On the birds of the island of Formosa. *Ibis* Ser. 9, 1:

151-198.

O'Halloran, K.A., & Conner, R.N. (1987) Habitat use by Brown-headed Nuthatches. *Bull. Texas Orn. Soc.* 20: 7-13.

Oustalet, M.E. (1897) Notice sur quelques oiseaux de la Chine occidentale. *Bull. Mus. Nat. Hist. Paris* 3: 208-211.

Padron, F.P. (1986) *The Birds of the Canary Islands.* 3rd edn. Aula de Cultura del Excmo. Cabildo Insular de Tenerife.

Palmer-Ball, B., & Haag, W.R. (1989) First reported nesting of Brown Creeper in Kentucky. *Kentucky Warbler* 65: 77-78.

Paludan, K. (1959) On the birds of Afghanistan. *Videnkabelige Meddelelsev* 122: 1-332.

Pandey, S., Joshua, J., Rai, N.D., Mohan, D., Rawat, G.S., Sankar, K., Katti, M.V., Khati, V.S., & Johnsingh, A.J.T. (1994) Birds of Rajaji National Park, India. *Forktail* 10: 105-114.

Parkes, K.C. (1958) A revision of the Philippine Elegant Titmouse (*Parus elegans*). *Proc. Biol. Soc. Wash.* 71: 95-106.

Parkes, K.C. (1963) Additional notes on the Philippine Elegant Titmouse, *Parus elegans. Bull. BOC* 83: 148-150.

Parkes, K.C. (1971) Taxonomic and distributional notes on Philippine birds. *Nemouria* 4: 1-67.

Parkes, K.C. (1973) Annotated list of the birds of Leyte Island, Philippines. *Nemouria* 11: 1-73.

Parkes, K.C. (1987) Sorting out the Chickadees in Southwestern Pennsylvania. *Pennsylvania Birds* 1: 105-106.

Parkes, K.C. (1988a) Sorting out the Chickadees in Southwestern Pennsylvania. *Birding* 20: 308-310.

Parkes, K.C. (1988b) The Ontario specimen of Carolina Chickadee. *Ontario Birds* 6: 111-114.

Payne, R.B. (1986) Birds songs and avian systematics. *In* Johnston, R.F. (ed.), *Current Ornithology.* Vol. 3. New York: Plenum.

Paynter, R.A. (1952) Birds from Popocatépetl and Ixtaccíhuatl, Mexico. *Auk* 69: 293-301.

Paynter, R.A. (1962) Taxonomic notes on some Himalayan Paridae. *JBNHS* 59: 951-956.

Paynter, R.A. (ed.) (1967) Check-list of Birds of the World. Vol. 12. Cambridge, Mass.: Mus. Comp. Zool.

Paz, U. (1987) *The Birds of Israel.* London: Christopher Helm.

Pearson, D.J. (1983) East African Bird Report 1981. *Scopus* 5: 129-153.

Pearson, D.J. (1984) East African Bird Report 1983. *Scopus* 7: 105-135.

Pearson, D.J. (1987) East African Bird Report 1985. *Scopus* 9: 145-159.

Pearson, D.J. (1988) East African Bird Report 1986. *Scopus* 10: 117-132.

Pearson, D.J. (1990) East African Bird Report 1988. *Scopus* 12: 105-126.

Peck, G.K., & James, R.D. (1987) *Breeding Birds of Ontario Nidiology and Distribution.* Vol 2. Passerines. Toronto: Royal Ontario Museum.

Perrins, C.M. (1979) *British Tits.* London: Collins.

Persson, O., & Ohrström, P. (1989) A new avian mating system: ambisexual polygamy in the Penduline Tit *Remiz pendulinus. Ornis. Scand.* 20: 105-111.

Peterjohn, B.G., & Rice, D.L. (1991) *The Ohio Breeding Bird Atlas.* Columbus: Ohio Department of Natural Resources.

'Peters' = Paynter, R.A. (ed.) (1967) *Check-list of Birds of the World.* Vol. 12. Cambridge, Mass.: Mus. Comp. Zool.

Peterson, R.T., Mountfort, G., & Hollom, P.A.D. (1993) *Birds of Britain and Europe.* 5th edn. London: HarperCollins.

Phillips, A.R. (1959) The nature of Avian species. *J. Arizona Acad. Sci.* 1: 22-30.

Phillips, A.R. (1966) Further systematic notes on Mexican birds. *Bull. BOC* 86: 125-131.

Phillips, A.R. (1986) *The Known Birds of North and Middle America. Part 1: Hirundinidae to Mimidae; Certhiidae.* Denver, Colorado: Denver Mus. Nat. Hist.

Phillips, A., Marshall, J., & Monson, G. (1964) *The Birds of Arizona.* Tucson: Univ. Arizona.

Piechocki, R., & Bolod, A. (1972) Beiträge zur Avifauna der Mongolei. Teil II. Passeriformes. *Mitt. Zool. Mus. Berlin* 48: 41-175.

Piechocki, R., Stubbe, M., Uhlenhaut, K., & Sumjaa, D. (1982) Beiträge zur Avifauna der Mongolei. *Mitt. Zool. Mus. Berlin Suppl. Ann. Orn.* 6: 58: 3-53.

Pinto, A.A. da Rosa, & Lamm, D.W. (1953) Contribution to the study of the ornithology of Sul do Save (Mozambique). *Separata das Mem. Mus. Dr Alvaro de Castro* No. 2.

Pitts, T.D. (1976) Fall and winter roosting habits of Carolina Chickadees. *Wilson Bull.* 88: 603-610.

Pleske, T. (1912) Zur Lösung der Frage, ob *Cyanistes pleskei* Cab. eine selbständige Art darstellt, oder für einen Bastard von *Cyanistes caeruleus* (Linn.) und *Cyanistes cyanus* (Pallas) angesprochen werden muß. *J. Orn.* 60: 96-109.

Poole, C. (compiler) (1994) Around the Orient. *Bull. Oriental Bird Club* 20: 15-23.

Portenko, L.A. (1955) [A review and taxonomic assessment of the forms of Palearctic Penduline Tits [*Remiz pendulinus* (L.)]. *Trudy Zool. Inst. Akad. Nauk SSSR* 18: 459-492. [In Russian.]

Portenko, L.A., & Stübs, J. (1977) *Certhia familiaris* L. *In* Dathe, H., & Neufeldt, I.A. *Atlas der Verbreitung palaarktischer Vögel.* 6. Berlin.

Portenko, L.A., Stübs, J., & Wunderlich, K. (1982) *Parus caeruleus* L. und *Parus cyanus* Pallas eingeschlossen die *flavipectus*-Gruppe. *In* Dathe, H., & Neufeldt, I.A. *Atlas der Verbreitung palaarktischer Vögel.* 10. Berlin.

Portenko, L.A., & Wunderlich, K. (1980) *Certhia himalayana* Vigors. *In* Dathe, H., & Neufeldt, I.A., *Atlas der Verbreitung palaarktischer Vögel.* 9. Berlin.

Portenko, L.A., & Wunderlich, K. (1984) *Parus major* L. *In* Dathe, H., & Neufeldt, I.A., *Atlas der Verbreitung palaarktischer Vögel.* 12. Berlin: Lieferung.

Porter, R.F. (1983) The autumn migration of passerines and near-passerines at the Bosphorus, Turkey. *Sandgrouse* 5: 45-74.

Potter, E.F., Parnell, J.F., & Teulings, R.P. (1980) *Birds of the Carolinas.* Chapell Hill: Univ. North Carolina.

Post, W., & Gauthreaux, S.A. (1989) *Status and Distribution of South Carolina Birds.* Charleston: Charleston Mus.

Pough, R.H. (1949) *Audubon Western Bird Guide.* New York: Doubleday.

Pough, R.H. (1957) *Audubon Land Bird Guide.* New York: Doubleday.

Poulson, M.K. (in prep.) The status and conservation of threatened birds in the Sierra Madre mountains, northern Luzon, the Philippines. *Bird Conserv. International.*

Pravosudov, V.V. (1993) Breeding biology of the Eurasian Nuthatch in northeastern Siberia. *Wilson Bull.* 105: 475-482.

Pravosudov, V.V. (in press) Social organisation of the Nuthatch *Sitta europaea asiatica. Ornis Scand.*

Pravosudov, V.V., & Grubb, T.C. (1993) White-breasted Nuthatch (*Sitta carolinensis*). *In* Poole, A., & Gill, F., (eds), *The Birds of North America,* No. 54. Philadelphia: Academy of Natural Sciences; Washington D.C.: Amer. Orn. Union.

Price, T.D. (1979) The seasonality and occurrence of birds in the Eastern Ghats of Andhra Pradesh. *JBNHS* 76: 379-422.

Prigogine, A. (1957) Trois nouveaux oiseaux de l'est du Congo belge. *Rev. Zool. Bot. Afr.* 55: 39-46.

Pulich, W.M. (1988) *The Birds of North Central Texas.* College Station: Texas A+M Univ.

Pyle, P., Howell, S.N.G., Yunick, R.P., & DeSante, D.F. (1987) *Identification Guide to North American Passerines.* Bolinas, CA: Slate Creek.

Pym, A. (1985) Bill coloration of treecreepers. *Brit. Birds* 78: 303.

Rabbitts, B., & Vinicombe, K.E. (1978) Wallcreeper wintering in Somerset. *Bristol Orn.* 11: 17-20.

Radke, E.L., Craig, A.M., & McCaskie (1988) Bushtit (*Psaltriparus minimus*). *Western Bird Bander* 43: 5.

Raitt, R.J. (1967) Relationships between Black-eared and Plain-eared forms of Bushtits (*Psaltriparus*). *Auk* 503-528.

Rand, A.L. (1972) Nest-entrance modification in the nuthatches. *Auk* 89: 450-451.

Rand, A.L., & Fleming, R.L. (1957) Birds of Nepal. *Fieldiana Zool.* 41: 1-218.

Rand, A.L., Friedmann, H., & Traylor, M.A. (1959) Birds from Gabon and Moyen Congo. *Fieldiana Zool.* 41: 221-411.

Rand, A.L., & Rabor, D.S. (1960) Birds of the Philippine Islands: Siquijor, Mount Malindang, Bohol, and Samar. *Fieldiana Zool.* 35: 221-441.

Rand, A.L., and Rabor, D.S. (1967) New birds from Luzon, Philippine Islands. *Fieldiana Zool.* 51: 85-89.

Rea, A.M. (1983) *Once a River: Bird Life and Habitat Changes on the Middle Gila.* Tucson: Univ. Arizona.

Redman, N. (1981) Birds in central Afghanistan. *Bull. Orn. Soc. Middle East* 7: 2-4.

Redman, N.J., Lambert, F., & Grimmett, R. (1984) Some observations of scarce birds in Nepal. *JBNHS* 81: 49-53.

Reed, T.M. (1979) A contribution to the ornithology of the Rishi Ganga valley and the Nanda Devi Sanctuary. *JBNHS* 76: 275-282.

Ridgway, R. (1904) The birds of North and Middle America: adescriptive catalogue. Part 3. *Bull. U.S. Nat. Mus.* 50.

Riley, J.H. (1926) A collection of birds from the provinces of Yunnan and Szechwan, China, made for the National Geographic Society by Joseph F. Rock. *Proc. U.S. Nat. Mus.* 70: 1-70.

Riley, J.H. (1930) Birds collected in Inner Mongolia, Kansu, and Chihli by the National Geographic Society's Central-China Expedition under the direction of F.R. Wulsin. *Proc. U.S. Nat. Mus.* 77: 1-39.

Riley, J.H. (1931) A second collection of birds from the provinces of Yunnan and Szechwan, China, made for the National Geographic Society by Joseph F. Rock. *Proc. U.S. Nat. Mus.* 80: 1-91.

Riley, J.H. (1938) Birds from Siam and the Malay Peninsula in the United States National Museum collected by Drs. Hugh M. Smith and William L. Abbott. *U.S. Nat. Mus. Bull.* 172: i-iv, 1-581.

Ripley, S.D. (1952) A collection of birds from the Naga Hills. *JBNHS* 50: 475-514.

Ripley, S.D. (1959) Character displacement in Indian nuthatches (*Sitta*). *Postilla, Yale Peabody Mus. Nat. Hist.* 42: 1-11.

Ripley, S.D. (1961) Some bird records from northern Burma with a description of a new subspecies. *JBNHS* 58: 279-283.

Ripley, S.D. (1982) *A Synopsis of the Birds of India and Pakistan, together with those of Nepal, Bhutan, Bangladesh and Sri Lanka.* 2nd edn. Bombay & Delhi: Bombay Nat. Hist. Soc. & Oxford Univ.

Ripley, S.D., & Beehler, B.M. (1991) Notes on birds from the Upper Noa Dihing, Arunachal Pradesh, Northeastern India. *Bull. BOC* 111: 19-28.

Ripley, S.D., Beehler, B.M., & Krishna Raju, K.S.R. (1987) Birds of the Visakhapatnam Ghats, Andhra Pradesh. *JBNHS* 84: 540-559.

Rippon, G. (1897) An additional list of birds obtained at Kalaw, Southern Shan States, during April and May, 1896. *Ibis* Ser. 7, 4: 1-5.

Rippon, G. (1901) On the birds of the Southern Shan States, Burma. *Ibis* Ser.8, 4: 523-561.

Rippon, G. (1903) [Description of *Aegithaliscus talifuensis*.] *Bull. BOC* 14: 18.

Rippon, G. (1904) [Descriptions of new birds from the southern Chin Hills, Burma.] *Bull. BOC* 14: 83-84.

Rippon, G. (1906) [Descriptions of *Sylviparus saturatior* and *Certhia victoriae*.] *Bull. BOC* 16: 87.

Rising, J.D. (1968) A multivariate assessment of interbreeding between the chickadees, *Parus atricapillus* and *P. carolinensis. Syst. Zool.* 17: 160-169.

Rising, J.D. (1983) The Great Plains hybrid zones. *In* Johnston, R.F. (ed.), *Current Ornithology.* Vol. 3. New York: Plenum.

Ritchison, G. (1981) Breeding biology of the White-breasted Nuthatch. *Loon* 53: 184-187.

Ritchison, G. (1983) Vocalisations of the White-breasted Nuthatch. *Wilson Bull.* 95: 440-451.

Robbins, C.S. (1980) Predictions of future Nearctic landbird vagrants to Europe. *Brit. Birds* 73: 448-457.

Robbins, C.S., Brünn, B., & Zim, H.S. (1966) *Birds of North America*. New York: Golden.

Robbins, M. (1989) What's your name, my little chickadee? *Birding* 21: 205-207.

Robbins, M.B., Braun, M.J., & Tobey, E.A. (1986) Morphological and vocal variation across a contact zone between the chickadees *Parus atricapillus* and *P. carolinensis*. *Auk* 103: 655-666.

Robbins, M.B., & Easterla, D.A. (1992) *Birds of Missouri*. Columbia & London: Univ. Missouri.

Robbins, S.D. (1991) *Wisconsin Birdlife*. Madison: Univ. Wisconsin.

Roberts, T.J. (1991, 1992) *The Birds of Pakistan*. Vol. 1 Regional Studies and Non-passeriformes; Vol. 2 Passeriformes: Pittas to Buntings. Karachi: Oxford Univ.

Robinson, H.C. (1928) *The Birds of the Malay Peninsula*. II: The Birds of the Hill Stations. London: Witherby.

Robinson, H.C., & Kloss, C.B. (1918) Results of an expedition to Korinchi Peak, Sumatra. II. Birds. *J. Fed. Malay States Mus.* 8: 81-284.

Robinson, H.C., & Kloss, C.B. (1919) On birds from South Annam and Cochin China. *Ibis* Ser. 11, 1: 392-453, 565-625.

Robinson, J.C. (1990) *An Annotated Checklist of the Birds of Tennessee*. Knoxville: Univ. of Tennessee.

Robson, C.R. (1986) Recent observations of birds in Xizang and Qinghai provinces, China. *Forktail* 2: 67-82.

Robson, C. (compiler) (1994) From the field. *Bull. Oriental Bird Club* 20: 55-61.

Robson, C.R., Eames, J.C., Wolstencroft, J.A., Nguyen Cu & Truong Van La (1989) Recent records of birds from Viet Nam. *Forktail* 5: 71-97.

Robson, C.R., Eames, J.C., Nguyen Cu & Truong Van La (1993a) Further recent records of birds from Viet Nam. *Forktail* 8: 25-52.

Robson, C.R., Eames, J.C., Nguyen Cu & Truong Van La (1993b) Birds recorded during the third BirdLife Forest Birds Working Group expedition in Viet Nam. *Forktail* 9: 89-119.

Rodriguez De Los Santos, M. (1985) Notes on Short-toed Treecreepers from southern Spain. *Brit. Birds* 78: 298-299.

Rogacheva, H. (1992) *The Birds of Central Siberia*. Husum: Husum Druck-u. Verlagsges.

Root, R.B. (1964) Ecological interactions of the Chestnut-backed Chickadee following a range expansion. *Condor* 66: 229-238.

Root, T. (1988) *Atlas of Wintering North American Birds*. Chicago: Univ. Chicago.

Rothschild, Lord (1921) On a collection of birds from west-central and north-western Yunnan. *Novit. Zool.* 28: 14-67.

Rothschild, Lord (1923) On a third collection of birds made by Mr. George Forrest in North-West Yunnan. *Novit. Zool.* 30: 247-267.

Rothschild, Lord (1926) On the avifauna of Yunnan, with critical notes. *Novit. Zool.* 33: 189-343.

Round, P.D. (1983) Some recent bird records from northern Thailand. *Nat. Hist. Bull. Siam Soc.* 31: 123-138.

Round, P.D. (1984) The status and conservation of the bird community in Doi Suthep-Pui National Park, north-west Thailand. *Nat. Hist. Bull. Siam Soc.* 32: 21-46.

Round, P.D. (1988) *Resident Forest Birds in Thailand: Their Status and Conservation*. ICBP Monograph No. 2. Cambridge: International Council for Bird Preservation.

Rowley, J.S. (1966) Breeding records of birds in the Sierra Madre del Sur, Oaxaca, Mexico. *Proc. West. Found. Vert. Zool.* 1: 107-204.

Rowley, J.S. (1984) Breeding records of land birds in Oaxaca, Mexico. *Proc. West. Found. Vert. Zool.* 2: 74-224.

Ruiz-Campos, G., & Quintana-Barrios, L. (1991) First mainland record of the Red-breasted Nuthatch from Baja California, Mexico. *Western Birds* 22: 189-190.

Rustamov A.K. (1958) [The birds of Turkmenistan 2.] Ashkhabad: Publishing House of the Acadamy of Sciences of the Turkmen SSR. [In Russian.]

Safford, R.J., Duckworth, J.W., Evans, M.I., Telfer, M.G., Timmins, R.J., & Chemere Zewdie (1993) The birds of Nechisar National Park, Ethiopia. *Scopus* 16: 61-80.

Salvan, J. (1967-69) Contribution a l'étude des oiseaux du Tchad. *L'Oiseau* 37: 255-284; 38: 53-85, 127-150, 249-273; 39: 38-69.

Sankaran, R. (1994) Ornithological survey of Nanda Devi National Park, India. *Forktail* 10: 115-130.

Sasvari, L. (1980) Different responsiveness of Indian and European Great Tits (*Parus major mahrattarum, P. m. major*) to acoustic stimuli. *J. Orn.* 121: 391-396.

Saunders, N., & Saunders, F. (1989) *Birds of Maryland and the District of Columbia: A County Check-List*. Colesville: privately published.

Schäfer, E. (1938) Ornithologische Ergebnisse zweier Forschungsreisen nach Tibet. *J. Orn.* 86: 1-349.

Schäfer, E., & Meyer de Schauensee, R.M. (1938) Zoological results of the second Dolan expedition to western China and eastern Tibet, 1934-1936. Part II, - birds. *Proc. Acad. Nat. Sci. Phil.* 40: 185-260.

Schaldach, W.J. (1963) The avifauna of Colima and adjacent Jalisco, Mexico. *Proc. West. Found. Vert. Zool.* 1: 1-100.

Schaller, G.B. (1993) *The Last Panda*. Chicago & London: Univ. Chicago.

Schels, C. (1990) Breeding records from southern Somalia. *Scopus* 14: 28-29.

Schmidl, D. (1982) *The Birds of the Serengeti National Park Tanzania*. London: Brit. Orn. Union.

Schnebel, G. (1972) Die Okologie der Baumläufer (*Certhia brachydactyla* und *Certhia familiaris*) in Ostniedersachsen. *Vogelwelt* 93: 201-205.

Schottler, B., & Martens, J. (1991) Akustische Differenzierung der Blaumeisen (*Parus caeruleus*) der Kanarischen Inseln. *Verh. Dtsch. Zool. Ges.* Tübingen 1991: 448-449.

Schottler, B., & Martens, J. (1992) Alarmrufe kanarischer Blaumeisen (*Parus caeruleus*) - ein Beitrag zur intraspezifischen Diversität. *Verh. Dtsch. Zool. Ges.* 85,1: 192.

Schottler, B., & Henning, F. (1993) Lautäußerungen von *Parus fasciiventer* in Zentralafrika (Aves: Paridae). *Bonn. zool. Beitr.* 44: 63-68.

Schottler, B. (1994) Songs and calls of Canary Island Blue Tits (*Parus caeruleus*) - variability, geographic differentiation and colonization history. *Parus International* 4 (2): 9-10.

Schouteden, H. (1956) De Vogels van Belgisch Congo en van Ruanda-Urundi. Vol. 4. *Ann. Koninklijk Mus. Belgisch Congo Tervuren (Belgie)* (Ser. 4) 4: 1-236.

Schouteden, H. (1960) Faune du Congo Belge et du Ruanda-Urundi. Vol. 5 Oiseaux, Vol. 3. *Ann. Koninklijk Mus. Belgisch Congo Tervuren (Belgie)*: 7-328.

Schouteden, H. (1961) La faune ornithologique des districts de la Tschuapa et de L'Equateur. *Mus. Roy. Afr. cent. Tervuren. Doc. Zool.* 1.

Schouteden, H. (1962a) La faune ornithologique du territoire de Mushie (district du Lac Leopold II). *Mus. Roy. Afr. cent. Tervuren. Doc. Zool.* 2.

Schouteden, H. (1962b) La faune ornithologique des districts de la Mongala et de L'Ubangi. *Mus. Roy. Afr. cent. Tervuren. Doc. Zool.* 3.

Schouteden, H. (1963a) La faune ornithologique des districts du Bas-Uele et du Haut-Uele. *Mus. Roy. Afr. cent. Tervuren. Doc. Zool.* 4.

Schouteden, H. (1963b) La faune ornithologique du district de L'Ituri. *Mus. Roy. Afr. cent. Tervuren. Doc. Zool.* 5.

Schouteden, H. (1964) La faune ornithologique de la province du Kasai. *Mus. Roy. Afr. cent. Tervuren. Doc. Zool.* 6.

Schouteden, H. (1965a) La faune ornithologique de la province de Kwango. *Mus. Roy. Afr. cent. Tervuren. Doc. Zool.* 8.

Schouteden, H. (1965b) La faune ornithologique des territoires de Dilolo et Kolwezi de la province du Katanga. *Mus. Roy. Afr. cent. Tervuren. Doc. Zool.* 9.

Schouteden, H. (1966a) La faune ornithologique du Rwanda. *Mus. Roy. Afr. cent. Tervuren. Doc. Zool.* 10.

Schouteden, H. (1966b) La faune ornithologique du Burundi. *Mus. Roy. Afr. cent. Tervuren. Doc. Zool.* 11.

Schouteden, H. (1969) La faune ornithologique du Kivu II. Passereaux. *Mus. Roy. Afr. cent. Tervuren. Doc. Zool.* 15.

Schouteden, H. (1971) La faune ornithologique de la Province du Katanga. *Mus. Roy. Afr. cent. Tervuren. Doc. Zool.* 17.

Schroeder, D.J., & Wiley, R.H. (1983a) Communication with shared song themes in Tufted Titmice. *Auk* 100: 414-424.

Schroeder, D.J., & Wiley, R.H. (1983b) Communication with repertoires of song themes in Tufted Titmice. *Anim. Behav.* 31: 1128-1138.

Scott, R.E. (1976) Short-toed Treecreeper at Dungeness. *Brit. Birds* 69: 508-509.

Seebohm, H. (1895) On some new and little-known species of birds from Formosa *Ibis* Ser. 7, 1: 211-213

Semenchuk, G. P. (ed.) *The Atlas of Breeding Birds of Alberta*. Edmonton: Fed. Alberta Naturalists.

Serle, W. (1965) A third contribution to the ornithology of the British Cameroons. *Ibis* 107: 230-246.

Serle, W., & Morel, G.J. (1977) *A Field Guide to the Birds of West Africa*. London: Collins.

Severinghaus, S.R., & Blackshaw, K.T. (1976) *A New Guide to the Birds of Taiwan*. Taipei: Mei Ya Publications.

Severinghaus, S.R., Kuo-wei Kang & Alexander, P.S. (1970) *A Guide to the Birds of Taiwan*. Taipei: The China Post.

Shackford, J.S., & Patti, S.T. (1986) Black-capped Chickadee in Oklahoma. *Bull. Oklahoma Orn. Soc.* 19: 25-27.

Sharpe, R.B. (1888-89) On the ornithology of North Borneo *.Ibis* Ser. 6, 1: 63-85, 185-205, 265-283, 409-443; 2: 1-24, 133-149, 273-292.

Shaw, Tsen-Hwang, A.M. (1936) *The Birds of Hopei Province*. II. Zoologica Sinica, Ser. B. The Vertebrates of China. Vol. 15. Peking: Fan Memorial Inst. Biol.

Sheldon, F.H., Slikas, B., Kinnarney, M., Gill, F.B., Zhao, E., & Silverin, B. (1992) DNA-DNA hybridisation evidence of phylogenetic relationships among major lineages of *Parus*. *Auk* 109: 173-185.

Sherry, D.F. (1989) Food storing in the Paridae. *Wilson Bull.* 101: 289-304.

Shirihai, H. (in press) *The Birds of Israel*. London: Academic Press.

Short, L.L. (1969) Taxonomic aspects of avian hybridisation. *Auk* 86: 84-105.

Short, L.L. (1973) Notes on Okinawan birds and Ryukyu island zoogeography. *Ibis* 115: 264-267.

Short, L.L., Horne, J.F.M., & Muringo-Gichuki, C. (1990) Annotated Check-list of the birds of East Africa. *Proc. West. Found. Vert. Zool.* 4: 61-246.

Shull, B., Grettenberger, M., & Newby, J. (1986) Recent observations of W National Park (Niger). *Malimbus* 8: 23-24.

Sibley, C.G. (1970) A comparative study of the egg-white proteins of passerine birds. *Bull. Peabody Mus. Nat. Hist. Yale Univ.* 32: 1-131.

Sibley, C.G., & Ahlquist, J.E. (1985) The phylogeny and classification of the passerine birds, based on comparisons of the genetic material, DNA. Pp. 83-121 in Ilyichev, V.D., & Gavrilov, V.M. (eds), *Proc. 18th Int. Orn. Congr. Moscow 1982* Moscow: Nauka Publ.

Sibley, C.G., & Ahlquist, J.E. (1990) *Phylogeny and Classification of Birds. A study in Molecular Evolution*. New Haven & London: Yale Univ.

Sibley, C.G., Ahlquist, J.E., & Monroe, B.L. (1988). A classification of the living birds of the world based on DNA-DNA hybridisation studies. *Auk* 105: 409-423.

Sibley, C.G., & Monroe, B.L. (1990) *Distribution and Taxonomy of Birds of the World*. New Haven & London: Yale Univ.

Sibley, C.G., & Monroe, B.L. (1993) *A Supplement to Distribution and Taxonomy of Birds of the World*. New Haven & London: Yale Univ.

Sien, Y., Pan, Y., Wang, T., Yang, L., & Cheng, Tso-hsin (1973) [New records of Chinese birds from Yunnan and Tibet.] *Acta Zool. Sinica* 19: 420. [In Chinese.]

Simon, S.W. (1960) Occurrence

and measurements of Black-capped Chickadees at Monkton, Md. *EBBA News* 23: 11-12.

Sinclair, I., Hockey, P., & Tarboton, W. (1993) *Illustrated Guide to the Birds of Southern Africa*. London: New Holland.

Sinclair, J. C. (1987) *Ian Sinclair's Field Guide to the Birds of Southern Africa*. London: Collins.

Singh, P. (1994) Recent bird records from Arunachal Pradesh. *Forktail* 10: 65-104.

Skead, C.J. (1959) A study of the Cape Penduline Tit *Anthoscopus minutus minutus* (Shaw & Nodder). *Ostrich Sup.* 3: 274-288.

Skutch, A.F. (1935) Helpers at the nest. *Auk* 52: 257-273.

Skutch, A.F. (1960) Life histories of Central American birds. 2. Berkeley, California: Cooper Orn. Soc., *Pacific Coast Avifauna* 34.

Skutch, A.F. (1987) *Helpers at Birds' Nests*. Iowa City: Univ. Iowa.

Small, A. (1994) *California Birds: Their Status and Distribution*. Vista: Ibis.

Smith, H.C., Garthwaite, P.F., & Smythies, B.E. (1940) Notes on the birds of Nattaung, Karenni. *JBNHS* 41: 577-593.

Smith, H.C., Garthwaite, P.F., & Smythies, B.E. (1943) On the birds of the Karen Hills and Karenni found over 3,000 feet. *JBNHS* 43: 455-474, 44: 60-72, 221-232.

Smith, P.W. (1986) 'Pishing' technique. *Brit. Birds* 79: 138-139.

Smith, S.M. (1972) Roosting aggregations of Bushtits in response to cold temperatures. *Condor* 74: 478-479.

Smith, S.M. (1984) Flock switching in chickadees: why be a winter floater? *Amer. Nat.* 123: 81-98.

Smith, S.M. (1989) Black-capped Chickadee summer floaters. *Wilson Bull.* 101: 344-349.

Smith, S.M. (1991) *The Black-capped Chickadee. Behavioural Ecology and Natural History*. Ithaca & London: Cornell Univ.

Smith, S.M. (1993) Black-capped Chickadee. *In* Poole, A., Stettenheim, P., & Gill, F. (eds.), *The Birds of North America*, No.39. Philadelphia: Academy of Natural Sciences; Washington: Amer. Orn. Union.

Smith, S.T. (1972) Communication and other social behaviour in *Parus carolinensis*. *Publ. Nuttall Orn. Club* No. 11.

Smithe, F.B. (1975) *Naturalist's Color Guide*. New York: Am. Mus. Nat. Hist.

Smythies, B.E. (1947) Some birds of the Gandak-Kosi watershed including the pilgrom trail to the sacred lake of Gosainkund. *JBNHS* 47: 432-443.

Smythies, B.E. (1949) A reconnaissance of the N'Mai Hka drainage, northern Burma. *Ibis* 91: 627-648.

Smythies, B. (1957) An annotated checklist of the birds of Borneo. *Sarawak Mus. J.* 7: i-xv, 523-818.

Smythies, B.E. (1981) *The Birds of Borneo*. 3rd edn. Kota Kinabalu & Kuala Lumpur: Sabah Soc. & Malayan Nature Soc.

Smythies, B.E. (1986) *The Birds of Burma*. 3rd (revised) edn. Liss, Hants, & Pickering, Ontario: Nimrod Press & Silvio Mattacchione.

Snow, D.W. (1954a) The habitats of Eurasian tits (*Parus* spp.) *Ibis* 96: 565-585.

Snow, D.W. (1954b) Trends in

geographical variation in Palearctic members of the genus *Parus*. *Evolution* 8: 19-28.

Snow, D.W. (1955) Geographical variation in the Coal Tit, *Parus ater* L. *Ardea* 43:195-226.

Snow, D.W. (1956) The specific status of the Willow Tit. *Bull. BOC* 76: 29-31.

Snow, D.W. (1957) 'Supplementary notes'. Pp. 36-43 *in* Vaurie, C., Systematic notes on Palearctic birds. No. 27 Paridae: the Genera *Parus* and *Sylviparus*. *Am. Mus. Novit.* 1852: 1-43.

Snow, D.W. (1967) Families Paridae, Remizidae *in* Paynter, R.A. (ed.),*Check-list of Birds of the World*. Vol. 12. Cambridge, Mass.: Mus. Comp. Zool.

Snow, D.W. (ed.) (1971) *The Status of Birds in Britain and Ireland*. Oxford, London & Edinburgh: Blackwell Scientific Publications.

Snow, D.W., & Perrins, C.M. (in prep.) [Material in preparation for a revised edition of BWP.]

South Dakota Ornithologists' Union (1991) *The Birds of South Dakota*. 2nd edn. Aberdeen: NSU.

Stanford, J.K., & Mayr, E. (1940-41) The Vernay-Cutting Expedition to northern Burma. *Ibis* Ser. 14, 4: 679-711; 5: 56-105, 213-245, 353-378, 479-518.

Stanford, J.K., & Ticehurst, C.B. (1935) Notes on some new or rarely recorded Burmese birds. *Ibis* Ser. 13, 5: 38-65, 249-279.

Stanford, J.K., & Ticehurst, C.B. (1938-39) On the birds of northern Burma. *Ibis* Ser. 14, 2: 65-102, 197-229, 391-428, 599-638; 3: 1-45, 211-258.

Stepanyan, L.S. (1983) [Superspecies and sibling species in the avifauna of the USSR.] Moscow: Nauka. [In Russian.]

Stepanyan, L.S. (1990) [Conspectus of the Ornithological Fauna of the USSR.] Moscow: Nauka. [In Russian.]

Stephens, D.A., & Sturts, S.H. (1991) *Idaho Bird Distribution*. Pocatello: Idaho Mus. Nat. Hist.

Stevens, H. (1923-25). Notes on the birds of the Sikkim Himalayas. *JBNHS* 29: 503-518, 723-740, 1007-1030; 30: 54-71, 352-379, 664-685, 872-893.

Steyn, P. (1974) A confiding creeper. *Bokmakierie* 26: 80-82.

Stone, W. (1933) Zoological results of the Dolan West China Expedition. *Proc. Acad. Nat. Sci. Phil.* 85: 165-222.

Stott, R.D.W. (1993) Birds new to the Kunming Area. *Hong Kong Bird Report* 1992: 167-175.

Stresemann, E. (1929a) Neue Formen aus Nord-Kansu III. *Orn. Monatsberichte* 37: 74-75.

Stresemann, E. (1929b) Eine Vogelsammlung aus Kwangsi. *J. Orn.* 77: 323-337.

Stresemann, E., & Heinrich, G. (1940) Die Vögel des Mount Victoria. *Mitt. Zool. Mus. Berlin* 24: 153-264.

Subramanya, S., Prasad, J.N., & Karthikeyan, S. (1992) Recent records and notes on Whitewinged Black Tit *Parus nuchalis* Jerdon from southern India. Paper submitted to International Council for Bird Preservation Biodiversity Project in the Orient.

Sultana, J., Gauci, C., & Beaman, M. (1975) *A Guide to the Birds of Malta*. Valletta: Malta Orn. Soc.

Sutton, G.M. (1967) *Oklahoma Birds*. Norman: Univ. Oklahoma.

Svensson, L. (1992) *Identification Guide to European Passerines*. 4th edn. Stockholm: author.

Swarth, H.S. (1914) The California forms of the genus *Psaltriparus*. *Auk* 31: 499-526.

Swinhoe, R. (1871) A revised catalogue of the birds of China and its islands, with descriptions of new species, references to former notes, and occasional remarks. *Proc. Zool. Soc. London*: 337-423.

Sydeman, W.J. (1989) Effects of helpers on nestling care and breeder survival in Pygmy Nuthatches. *Condor* 91: 147-155.

Sydeman, W.J., Güntert, M., & Balda, R.P. (1988) Annual reproductive yield in the cooperative Pygmy Nuthatch (*Sitta pygmaea*). *Auk* 105: 70-77.

Tan, B.C., Li, Z.-H., & Lin, P.-C. (1988) The Hainan-Mindoro connection, an obscure pathway for plant migration in Southeast Asia. *Nat. Hist. Bull. Siam Soc.* 36: 7-15.

Tan, Y.-K., & Cheng, Tso-hsin (1964) [On the vertical distribution of birds on Mt. Yu-lung, northwestern Yunnan.] *Acta Zool. Sinica* 16: 295-314. [In Chinese.]

Tanner, J.T. (1952) Black-capped and Carolina Chickadees in the southern Appalachian Mountains. *Auk* 69: 407-424.

Tarbell, A.T. (1983) A yearling helper with a Tufted Titmouse brood. *J. Field Orn.* 54: 89.

Tarboton, W.R. (1981) Cooperative breeding and group territoriality in the Black Tit. *Ostrich* 52: 216-225.

Tarboton, W.R., Kemp, M.I., & Kemp, A.C. (1987) *Birds of the Transvaal*. Pretoria: Transvaal Museum.

Taverner, P.A. (1940) Canadian status of the Long-tailed Chickadee. *Auk* 57: 536-541.

Taylor, C. (1989) *Checklist to the Birds of Sonora and the Sea of Cortéz, including Barranca del Cobre*. Portal, Arizona: Borderland Productions.

Taylor, P.B. (1983) E.A.N.H.S. Nest record scheme: 1982. *Scopus* 6: 129-143.

Taylor, W.K. (1970a) Some taxonomic comments on the genus *Auriparus*. *Auk* 87: 363-366.

Taylor, W.K. (1970b) Molts of the Verdin, *Auriparus flammiceps*. *Condor* 72: 493-496.

Taylor, W.K. (1971.) A breeding biology study of the Verdin, *Auriparus flaviceps* (Sundevall) in Arizona. *Amer. Midl. Nat.* 85: 289-328.

Temminck, C.J. (1821) *Recueil d'Oiseaux* [*Planches Coloriées*]. Vol. IV. livr. 12, pl. 72.

Temple, S.A., & Cary, J.R. (1987) *Wisconsin Birds. A Seasonal and Geographical Guide*. Univ. Wisconsin.

Terres, J.K. (ed.) (1980) *The Audubon Society Encyclopedia of North American Birds*. New York: Knopf.

Thayer, J.E., & Bangs, O. (1912) Some Chinese vertebrates, Aves. *Mem. Mus. Comp. Zool.* 40: 137-200.

Thibault, J.-C. (1983). *Les oiseaux de la Corse*. Ajaccio: Parc Naturel Régional de La Corse.

Thielcke, G. (1962) Versuche mit Klangattrappen zur Klärung der Verwandtschaft der Baumläufer *Certhia familiaris* L., *C. brachydactyla* Brehm und *C. americana* Bonaparte. *J. Orn.* 103:

266-271.

Thielcke, G. (1968) Gemeinsames der Gattung *Parus*. Ein bioakustischer Beitrag zur Systematik. *Beiheft der Vogelwelt* 1: 147-164.

Thielcke, G. (1969) Geographic variation in bird vocalisations. Pp. 311-342 *in* Hinde, R.A., (ed.), *Bird Vocalisations*. Cambridge: Cambridge Univ.

Thielcke, G. (1972) Waldbaumläufer (*Certhia familiaris*) ahmen artfremdes Signal nach und reagieren darauf. *J. Orn.* 113: 287-296.

Thielcke, G. (1988) An examination of Tree Creeper *Certhia familiaris* song for character displacement and vocal convergence in areas sympatric and allopatric with Short-toed Tree Creeper *Certhia brachydactyla*. *Acta Ornithol.* (Warsaw) 24: 75-83.

Thiollay, J.-M. (1985) The birds of the Ivory Coast: status and distribution. *Malimbus* 7: 1-59.

Thom, V.M. (1986) *Birds in Scotland*. Calton: T & AD Poyser.

Thomas, W.W. (1964) *A Preliminary List of the Birds of Cambodia*. Unpublished.

Thompson, B. (1992) Recently fledged Long-tailed Tits in February. *Brit. Birds* 85: 618-619.

Thompson, H.N., & Craddock, W.H. (1902) Notes on the occurrence of certain birds in the Southern Shan States of Burma. *JBNHS* 14: 600.

Thompson, M.C., & Ely, C. (1992) *Birds in Kansas*. Vol. 2. Lawrence: Univ. Kansas.

Thompson, P.M., Harvey, W.G., Johnson, D.L., Millin, D.J., Rashid, S.M.A., Scott, D.A., Stanford, C., & Woolner, J.D. (1993) Recent notable bird records from Bangladesh. *Forktail* 9: 12-44.

Thönen, W. (1962) Stimmgeographische, ökologische und verbreitungsgeschichtliche Studien über die Mönchsmeise (*Parus montanus* Conrad). *Orn. Beobachter* 59: 101-172.

Thönen, W. (1972) *Parus montanus* und *Parus atricapillus*: song variation and systematics. *Proc. XV Int. Orn. Congr., The Hague* 697: 696.

Thormin, T.W., & Tull, E.C. (1980) The ex-Gray-headed Chickadee. *Birding* 12: 62-64.

Ticehurst, C.B. (1933) Notes on some birds from southern Arakan. *JBNHS* Vol?: 920-937.

Ticehurst, C.B. (1939a) On the invalidity of *Certhia victoriae*. *Ibis* Ser. 14, 3: 158.

Ticehurst, C.B. (1939b) Additional information on northern Burmese birds. *Ibis* Ser 14, 3: 768-770.

Todd (1963) *Birds of the Labrador Peninsula and Adjacent Areas*.

Toops, C., & Dilley, W.E. (1986) *Birds of South Florida*. Conway, Arkansas: River Road.

Traylor, M.A. (1949) Notes on some Veracruz birds. *Fieldiana Zool.* 31: 269-275.

Traylor, M.A. (1961) A new race of *Parus funereus* (Verreaux). *Bull. BOC* 81: 3.

Traylor, M.A. (1963) *Check-list of Angolan Birds*. Comp. Diam. Angola, Museo do Dundo, Lisbon.

Traylor, M.A. (1967) A collection of birds from Szechwan. *Fieldiana Zool.* 53: 1-67.

Tucker, L. (1984) Possible use of bill colour in separating Short-toed Treecreeper and Treecreeper.

*Brit. Birds* 77: 263-264.

Tufts, R.W. (1986) *Birds of Nova Scotia*. 3rd edn. Halifax: Nimbus/Nova Scotia Mus.

Turner, D.A. (1977) Status and distribution of the East African endemic species. *Scopus* 1: 2-11.

Turner, D.A. (1991) East African Bird Report 1989. *Scopus* 13: 137-164.

Turner, D.A. (1992) East African Bird Report 1990. *Scopus* 14: 129-158.

Tyler, J.D. (1989) Black-crested Titmouse in Comanche County, Oklahoma. *Bull. Oklahoma Orn. Soc.* 22: 28.

Tymstra, Y.R. (1993) Some bird observations from the lower Apsuwa River, East Nepal. *Forktail* 8: 53-64.

Udvardy, M.D.F. (1977) *The Audubon Society Field Guide to North American Birds. Western Region*. New York: Alfred A. Knopf.

Ulfstrand, S. (1960) A new subspecies of *Anthoscopus caroli* (Sharpe 1871) from western Tanganyika Territory. *Bull. BOC* 80: 11-13.

Unnithan, S. (1992) Plumages, female dimorphism and polymorphism of the endemic Indian species *Parus xanthogenys*. *JBNHS* 89: 126-128.

Urban, E.K. (1980) *Ethiopia's Endemic Birds*. Addis Ababa: Ethiopian Tourism Commission.

Urban, E.K., & Brown, L.H. (1971) *A Checklist of the Birds of Ethiopia*. Addis Ababa: Haile Sellassie I Univ.

van den Berg, A.B. (1982) Plumages of Algerian Nuthatch. *Dutch Birding* 4: 98-100.

van den Berg, A.B. (1985) Photospot 11. Algerian Nuthatch. *Brit. Birds* 78: 265-268.

van den Berk, V. (1991) Visible migration of Sparrowhawk *Accipiter nisus* and Penduline Tit *Remiz pendulinus* in southern Turkey. *Sandgrouse* 13: 101-102.

van Marle, J.G., & Voous, K.H (1988) *The Birds of Sumatra. An Annotated Check-list*. Tring: Brit. Orn. Union.

van Marle, J.G., Voous, K.H., & Wattel, J. (1973) Kortsnavelboomkruiper en andere noordoost-Europese gasten in 1971-72. *Limosa* 46: 63-66.

van Rossem, A.J. (1935) A note on the color of the eye of the Bushtit. *Condor* 37: 254.

van Rossem, A.J. (1945a) A distributional survey of the birds of Sonora, Mexico. *Occ. Papers Mus. Zool. Louisiana State Univ.* No. 21.

van Rossem, A.J. (1945b) Two races of the Bridled Titmouse. *Fieldiana Zool.* 31: 87-92.

van Someren, Dr. (1921) [Descriptions of *Anthoscopus rocatii taruensis* and *Parus niger purpurascens*.] *Bull. BOC* 41: 112.

Vaughan, R. (1991) *In Search of Arctic Birds*. London: Poyser.

Vaurie, C. (1950a) Notes on some Asiatic titmice. *Am. Mus. Novit.* 1459: 1-66.

Vaurie, C. (1950b) Notes on some Asiatic nuthatches and creepers. *Am. Mus. Novit.* 1472: 1-39.

Vaurie, C. (1951) Adaptive differences between two sympatric species of nuthatches (*Sitta*). *Proc. Xth Int. Orn. Congr.*

*Uppsala*: 163-166.

Vaurie, C. (1952) Additional systematic notes on the titmice of the *Remiz pendulinus* group (Aves). *Am. Mus. Novit.* 1549: 1-5.

Vaurie, C. (1957a) Systematic notes on Palearctic birds. No. 26 Paridae: the *Parus caeruleus* complex. *Am. Mus. Novit.* 1833: 1-15.

Vaurie, C. (1957b) Systematic notes on Palearctic birds. No. 27 Paridae: the genera *Parus* and *Sylviparus*. *Am. Mus. Novit.* 1852: 1-43.

Vaurie, C. (1957c) Systematic notes on Palearctic birds. No. 28 The families Remizidae and Aegithalidae. *Am. Mus. Novit.* 1853: 1-21.

Vaurie, C. (1957d) Systematic notes on Palearctic birds. No. 29 The subfamilies Tichodromadinae and Sittinae. *Am. Mus. Novit.* 1854: 1-26.

Vaurie, C. (1957e) Systematic notes on Palearctic birds. No. 30 The Certhiidae. *Am. Mus. Novit.* 1855: 1-14.

Vaurie, C. (1959) *The Birds of the Palearctic Fauna: Passeriformes*. London: Witherby.

Vaurie, C. (1972) *Tibet and its Birds*. London: Witherby.

Venning, F.E.W. (1912) Some birds and birds' nests from Haka, Chin Hills. *JBNHS* 21: 621-633.

Vere Benson, S. (1970) *Birds of Lebanon and the Jordan Area*. Cambridge: International Council for Bird Preservation.

Vernon, C.J. (1978) Breeding seasons of birds in deciduous woodland at Zimbabwe, Rhodesia, from 1970 to 1974. *Ostrich* 49: 102-115.

Vernon, C.J., & Dean, W.R.J. (1975) On the systematic position of *Pholidornis rushiae*. *Bull. BOC* 95: 20.

Vielliard, J. (1976) La Sittelle kabyle. *Alauda* 44 (3, suppl. spec.): 351-352.

Vielliard, J. (1978) Le Djebel Babor et sa Sittelle *Sitta ledanti* Vielliard 1976. *Alauda* 46: 1-42.

Vielliard, J. (1976) Remarques complémentaires sur la Sittelle kabyle *Sitta ledanti* Vielliard 1976. *Alauda* 48: 139-150.

Vincent, J. (1933, 1935) The birds of Northern Portuguese East Africa. Comprising a list of, and observations on, the collections made during the British Museum Expedition of 1931-32. *Ibis* Ser. 13, 3: 611-652; 5: 1-37, 355-397, 485-529, 707-762.

Viney, C. (1986) WWF HK visit to north-west Fujian Province, P.R.C. 28 May-7 June 1986. Unpublished.

Viney, C. (1987) Observations on the birds of Nan Kun Shan Nature Reserve, Guangdong Province, China. *Hong Kong Bird Report 1984/1985*: 79-96.

Viney, C., & Phillipps, K. (1983) *Birds of Hong Kong*. 3rd edn. Hong Kong: Govt Printer.

Virkkala, R. (1990) Ecology of the Siberian Tit *Parus cinctus* in relation to habitat quality: effects of forest management. *Ornis Scand.* 21: 139-146.

Virkkala, R., & Liehu, H. (1990) Habitat selection by the Siberian Tit *Parus cinctus* in virgin and managed forests in northern Finland. *Ornis Fennica* 67: 1-12.

von Jordans, A. (1923) Ueber seltenere und über fragliche Vogelformen meiner Sammlung. *Falco Suppl.*, 8-26.

von Jordans, A. (1970) Die westpalaearktischen Rassen des

Formenkreises *Parus major* (Aves, Paridae). *Zool. Abh. Staatl. Mus. Tierkde Dresden* 31: 205-225.

Voous, K.H. (1960) *Atlas of European Birds*. Nelson.

Voous, K.H. (1977) *List of Recent Holarctic Bird Species*. London: Brit. Orn. Union.

Voous, K.H., & van Marle, J.G. (1953) The distributional history of the Nuthatch, *Sitta europaea* L. *Ardea* 41 (extra): 1-68.

Vuilleumier, F. (1993) Notes on birds observed in beech (*Fagus*) forests in the Maoershan Natural Reserve, Guangxi Autonomous Region, China. *Bull. BOC* 113: 152-166.

Vuilleumier, F., & Mayr, E. (1987) New species of birds described from 1976 to 1980. *J. Orn.* 128: 137-150.

Waite, T.A. (1987a) Vigilance in the White-breasted Nuthatch: effects of dominance and sociality. *Auk* 104: 429-434.

Waite, T.A. (1987b) Dominance-specific vigilance in the Tufted Titmouse: effects of social context. *Condor* 89: 932-935.

Waite, T.A., & Grubb, T.C. (1987) Dominance, foraging and predation risk in the Tufted Titmouse. *Condor* 89: 936-940.

Walsh, J.F. (1987) Records of birds seen in north-eastern Guinea in 1984-1985. *Malimbus* 9: 105-122.

Wang, Y.J. (1986) [Protected birds of Shanghai.] Shanghai: Xue Lin Publishing. [In Chinese.]

Ward, R. (1966) Regional variation in the song of the Carolina Chickadee. *Living Bird* 5: 127-150.

Ward, R., & Ward, D.A. (1974) Songs in contiguous populations of Black-capped and Carolina Chickadees in Pennsylvania. *Wilson Bull.* 63: 344-356.

Wardlaw Ramsay, R.G. (1884) Contributions to the ornithology of the Philippine islands - On two collections of birds from the vicinity of Manilla. *Ibis* Ser. 5, 2: 330-335.

Warren, R.L.M., & Harrison, C.J.O. (1973) Type-Specimens of Birds in the British Museum (*Natural History*). Vol. 3, *Systematic Index*. London: Brit. Mus. (Nat. Hist.).

Waterman, J. (1989) A case of polyandry in the Black-capped Chickadee. *Wilson Bull.* 101: 351-353.

Webster, D. (1984) Richardson's Mexican collection: birds from Zacatecas and adjoining states. *Condor* 86: 204-207.

Webster, J.D. (1986) 'Certhia *americana* Bonaparte'. In Phillips, A.R., *The Known Birds of North and Middle America. Part 1: Hirundinidae to Mimidae; Certhiidae*. Denver, Colorado: Denver Mus. Nat. Hist.

Weigolds, H. (1922) Zoologische Ergebnisse der Walter Stötznerschen Expeditionen nach Szetschwan, Osttibet und Tschili. 3. Muscicapidae. *Abh. Ber. Zool. u. Anthro-Ethn. Dresden* 15: 23-34.

Wetmore, A. (1941) Notes on birds of the Guatemalan highlands. *Proc. U.S. Nat. Mus.* 89: 523-581.

Whistler, H. (1925) [Description of *Cephalopyrus flammiceps satu-ratus*.] *Bull. BOC* 45: 15.

Whistler, H. (1930) The birds of the Rawal Pindi District, N.W. India. *Ibis* Ser. 12, 6: 67-119,

247-279.

Whistler, H. (1942) New birds from Asia, chiefly from India. *JBNHS* 43: 33-38.

Whistler, H. (1944-45) Materials for the ornithology of Afghanistan. *JBNHS* 44: 505-19; 45: 61-72, 105-122, 280-301, 462-485.

Whistler, H. (1949) *Popular Handbook of Indian Birds*. 4th edn. London & Edinburgh: Oliver & Boyd.

Whistler, H., & Kinnear, N.B. (1932) The Vernay scientific survey of the Eastern Ghats (Ornithological section). [Part 1] *JBNHS* 35: 505-524.

White, C.M.N. (1945-46) The ornithology of the Kaonde-Lunda Province, Northern Rhodesia. *Ibis* 87: 11-25, 185-202, 309-345; 88: 68-103, 206-224, 505-512.

White, C.M.N. (1963) *A Revised Check List of African Flycatchers, Tits, Tree creepers, Sunbirds, White-eyes, Honey eaters, Buntings, Finches, Weavers and Waxbills*. Lusaka: Govt Printer.

White, C.M.N. (1968) Taxonomic notes on African birds. *Bull. BOC* 88: 30-31.

White, C.M.N., & Bruce, M.D. (1986) *The Birds of Wallacea (Sulawesi, the Moluccas & Lesser Sunda Islands, Indonesia). An Annotated check-list*. London: Brit. Orn. Union.

Whitehead, C.H.T. (1909) On the birds of Kohat and Kurram, northern India. *Ibis* Ser 9, 3: 90-134, 214-284.

Whitehead, C.H.T. (1914) Some notes on the birds of the Kaghan Valley, Hazara, North West Frontier Province. *JBNHS* 23: 104-109.

Wickham, P.F. (1929-30) Notes on the birds of the Upper Burma hills. *JBNHS* 33: 800-827; 34: 46-63, 337-349.

Wilbur, S.R. (1987) *Birds of Baja California*. Berkeley: Univ. California.

Wild Bird Society of Japan (1982) *A Field Guide to the Birds of Japan*. Tokyo: Wild Bird Soc. Japan.

Wilder, G.D., & Hubbard, H.W. (1938) Birds of Northeastern China. Peking Nat. Hist. Bull.; Handb. No. 6. Peking.

Wildlife Conservation Society of Jilin Province (1987) [Jilinsheng Yesheng Dongwu Tujian (Niao Lei).] Shenyang: Jilin Science and Technology Press. [In Chinese.]

Wilkinson, R., & Beecroft, R. (1985) Birds in Falgore Game Reserve, Nigeria. *Malimbus* 7: 63-72.

Williams, A.J. (1988) *Popular Checklist of the Birds of South West Africa/Namibia*. Windhoek: Dept Agriculture & Nature Conservation.

Williams, J.B., & Batzlie, G.O. (1979) Winter diet of a bark-foraging guild of birds. *Wilson Bull.* 91: 126-131.

Williams, J.G., & Arlott, N. (1980) *A Field Guide to the Birds of East Africa*. London: Collins.

Williams, M.D., Carey, G.J., Duff, D.G., & Xu, W. (1992) Autumn bird migration at Beidaihe, China, 1986-1990. *Forktail* 7: 3-55.

Williams, M., & Dorner, J. (1991) Changes in numbers of migrants recorded at Beidaihe. *China Flyway* 2,1 (Spring 1991): 22-27.

Williams, M.D., Hsu Weishu,

Holloway, S.J., & Christensen, J.H. (1991) Observations of birds at Beidaihe, autumn 1990. *China Flyway* 2,1 (Spring 1991): 2-21.

Winterbottom, J.M. (1959) A new subspecies of *Anthoscopus minutus* (Shaw & Nodder) from Cape Province. *Bull. BOC* 79: 152.

Winterbottom, J.M. (1964) Report on the birds of Game Reserve No. 2. *Cimbebasia* 9: 2-75.

Winterbottom, J.M. (1966a) Results of the Percy Fitzpatrick Institute of African Ornithology-Windhoek State Museum joint ornithological expeditions. 3. The birds of the Okavango valley. *Cimbebasia* 15: 2-78.

Winterbottom, J.M. (1966b) Results of the Percy Fitzpatrick Institute of African Ornithology-Windhoek State Museum joint ornithological expeditions. 5. Report on the birds of the Kaokoveld and Kunene River. *Cimbebasia* 19: 3-71.

Winterbottom, J.M. (1971) *A Preliminary Check List of the Birds of South West Africa*. Windhoek: S.W.A. Scientific Soc.

Wisemann, A.J. (1969) The geographically erratic chickadees. *Inland Bird Banding News* 41: 164-168.

Witherby., H.F. (1903) An ornithological journey to Fars, Southwest Persia. *Ibis* Ser. 8, 3: 501-571.

Witherby, H.F. (1907) On a collection of birds from western Persia and Armenia. *Ibis* Ser. 9, 1: 74-110.

Witherby, H.F. (1910) On a collection of birds from the south coast of the Caspian Sea and the Elburz mountains. *Ibis* Ser. 9, 4: 491-517.

Witherby, H.F. (1937) [Notes on Corsican Nuthatch.] *Bull. BOC*

58: 4-6.

Witherby, H.F., Jourdain, F.C.R., Ticehurst, N.F., & Tucker, B.W. (1938) *The Handbook of British Birds.* Vol. 1. London: Witherby.

Wolters, H.E. (1975-82) *Die Vögel der Erde*. Hamburg & Berlin: Paul Parey.

Won, P.O. (1969) *An Annotated Checklist of the Birds of Korea*. Seoul: Forest Research Institute.

Won, P. (1993) [A field guide to the birds of Korea.] Seoul: Kyo-Hak Publ. [In Korean.]

Wood, D.S. (1992) Color and size variation in eastern White-breasted Nuthatches. *Wilson Bull.* 104: 599-611.

Wood, D.S., & Schnell, G.D. (1984) *Distributions of Oklahoma Birds*. Norman: Univ. Oklahoma.

Wood, H., & Finn, F. (1902) On a collection of birds from Upper Burmah. *J. Asiatic Soc. Bengal*

Wood, H., & Finn, F. (1902) On a collection of birds from upper Burmah. *J. Asiatic Soc. Bengal* 71: 121-131.

Wu, Z., Lin, Q., Yang, J., Liu, J., & Wu, L. (1986) [The avifauna of Guizhou.] Guiyang: Guizhou People's Publishing House. [In Chinese].

Wunderlich, K. (1982) *Parus lugubris* Temminck. In Dathe, H., & Neufeldt, I.A., *Atlas der Verbreitung paläarktischer Vögel*. 10. Berlin.

Wunderlich, K. (1983a) *Sitta whiteheadi* Sharpe. In Dathe, H., & Neufeldt, I.A., *Atlas der Verbreitung paläarktischer Vögel*. 11. Berlin.

Wunderlich, K. (1983b) *Sitta ledanti* Vielliard. In Dathe, H., & Neufeldt, I.A., *Atlas der Verbreitung paläarktischer Vögel*. 11. Berlin.

Wunderlich, K. (1986) *Sitta neumayer* Michahelles. In Dathe, H., & Neufeldt, I.A., *Atlas der*

*Verbreitung paläarktischer Vögel*. 12. Berlin.

Wunderlich, K. (1988a) *Sitta leucopsis* Gould. In Dathe, H., & Neufeldt, I.A., *Atlas der Verbreitung paläarktischer Vögel*. 15. Berlin.

Wunderlich, K. (1988b) *Certhia nipalensis* Blyth. In Dathe, H., & Neufeldt, I.A., *Atlas der Verbreitung paläarktischer Vögel*. 15. Berlin.

Wunderlich, K. (1989a) *Aegithalos niveogularis* (Gould). In Dathe, H., & Neufeldt, I.A., *Atlas der Verbreitung paläarktischer Vögel*. 16. Berlin.

Wunderlich, K. (1989b) *Aegithalos leucogenys* (Moore). In Dathe, H., & Neufeldt, I.A., *Atlas der Verbreitung paläarktischer Vögel*. 16. Berlin.

Wunderlich, K. (1989c) *Parus melanolophus* Vigors. In Dathe, H., & Neufeldt, I.A., *Atlas der Verbreitung paläarktischer Vögel*. 16. Berlin.

Wunderlich, K. (1991a) *Aegithalos bonvaloti* Oustalet. In Dathe, H., & Neufeldt, I.A., *Atlas der Verbreitung paläarktischer Vögel*. 17. Berlin.

Wunderlich, K. (1991b) *Aegithalos iouschistos* (Hodgson). In Dathe, H., & Neufeldt, I.A., *Atlas der Verbreitung paläarktischer Vögel*. 17. Berlin.

Wunderlich, K. (1991c) *Cephalopyrus flammiceps* (Burton). In Dathe, H., & Neufeldt, I.A., *Atlas der Verbreitung paläarktischer Vögel*. 17. Berlin.

Yamashina, Y. (1982) *Birds in Japan: A Field Guide*. New Edition. Tokyo: Shubun International.

Ye, Xiaodi, & Wang, Zuxiang (1993) [The fauna, conservation and management of avian

resource of Mengda forests of Xunhua County, Qinghai.] *Chinese J. Zool.* 28: 18-20. [In Chinese.]

Yen, K.Y. (1933-34) Les oiseaux du Kwangsi (Chinese). *L'Oiseau* 3: 204-243, 615-638, 755-788; 4: 24-51, 297-317, 489-507.

Yen, K.Y. (1934) Eine Vogels ammlung aus Kwei-chow (China). *J. Orn.* 82: 381-398.

Yen, K.-Y., & Chong, L.-T. (1937) Notes additionelles sur l'avifaune du Kwangsi. *L'Oiseau* 7: 546-553.

Yunich, R.P. (1984) An assessment of the irruptive status of the Boreal Chickadee in New York State. *J. Field Orn.* 55: 31-37.

Zacharias, V.J., & Gaston, A.J. (1993) The birds of Wynaad, southern India. *Forktail* 8: 11-23.

Zeranski, J.D., & Baptist, T.R. (1990) *Connecticut Birds*. Hanover: Univ. New England.

Zhao, Z. (ed.) (1985) [The avifauna of Changbai mountain.] Changchun: Jilin Science and Technology Press. [In Chinese.]

Zhao, Z., et al. (no date) [Report of migratory birds survey in the Jilin province.] Yangji (Jilin): Yanbian People. [In Chinese.]

Zheng, Z., Li, D., Wang, Z.,Jiang, Z., & Lu, T. (1983) [The avifauna of Xizang.] Beijing: Science Press. [In Chinese.]

Zhikang, W., Zhumei, L., Zhigang, Y., & Hong, J. (1994) Tuoda (also Toada or Tuode) forest farm. *Bull. Oriental Bird Club* 19: 26-29.

Zink, R.M., & Remsen, J.V. (1986) Evolutionary processes and patterns of geographic variation in birds. In Johnston, R.F. (ed.), *Current Ornithology*. Vol. 3. New York: Plenum.

# SOUND RECORDINGS

Brigham, M. (1994) *Bird Sounds of Canada*. Manotick, Ontario: Great Wildlife Recordings.

Chappuis, C. (1979) *Les Oiseaux de l'Ouest Africain*. Disc 10. Sylviidae (fin) et Paridae. Sound Supplement to *Alauda* 47: 195-212.

Cornell Laboratory of Ornithology/Interactive Audio (1990) *A Field Guide to Bird Songs. Eastern and Central North America*. 3rd edn. Boston: Houghton Mifflin.

Cornell Laboratory of Ornithology/Interactive Audio (1992) *A Field Guide to Western Bird Songs*. 2nd edn. Boston: Houghton Mifflin.

Gibbon, G. (1991) *Southern*

*African Bird Sounds*. Durban: Southern African Birding.

Gillard, L. (1983) *Southern African Bird Calls*. Johannesburg: Gillard Bird Cassettes.

Kabaya, Tsuruhiko (1990) *Wild Birds Living in Japan*. 5 CDs. Nippon Columbia. [A re-issue of *Japanese Nature and Birds* 1977.]

Keith, G. S., & Gunn, W.W.H (1971) *Birds of the African Rain Forests*. Ontario: Federation Ontario Naturalists & AMNH.

Keller, G.A. (1988) *Bird Songs of Southeastern Arizona and Southern Texas*. Coos Bay, Oregon: Sora Record.

Kettle, R., & Ranft, R. (compilers & eds) (1992) *British Bird Sounds*

on CD. London: The British Library.

Lewis, V.C. (1984) *A Sound Guide to British Tits*. Lyonshall, Herts: V.C. Lewis.

Mild, K. (1987) *Soviet Bird Songs*. Stockholm: Krister Mild.

Mild, K. (1990) *Bird Songs of Israel and the Middle East*. Stockholm: Krister Mild; bioacoustics.

National Geographic Society/ Library of Natural Sounds, Cornell Laboratory of Ornithology (1986) *Guide to Bird Sounds*.

Roché, J.C. (1985) *'The Bird Walker'. A Dictionary of Bird Sounds from Britain, Europe and North Africa*. Viens (France): L'Oiseau Musicien.

Roché, J.C. (1990) *All the Bird Songs of Europe*. La Mure (France): Sittelle.

Sander, T.G. (producer) (1989) *Bird Songs of California. Selected Bird Songs from the Sierras to the Pacific*. Wilderness Recordings.

Smith, S.W. (1994) *Bird Recordings from the Gambia*. Lymington, Hants: S.W. Smith.

Smith, S.W. (1994) *Bird Recordings from Java, Bali & Sumatra*. Lymington, Hants: S.W. Smith.

Walton, R.K., & Lawson, R.W. (1990) *Birding by Ear. A Guide to Bird-song Identification. Western North America*. Boston: Houghton Mifflin.

# APPENDICES

## APPENDIX A: SCIENTIFIC NAMES OF BIRDS MENTIONED IN THE TEXT

American Cliff Swallow — *Hirundo pyrrhonota*
Atlantic Canary — *Serinus canaria*
barbet — Capitonidae sp.
Bearded Tit — *Panurus biarmicus*
bee-eater — *Merops* sp.
bittern — Botaurinae sp.
Black-throated Parrotbill — *Paradoxornis nipalensis*
Blue Jay — *Cyanocitta cristata*
Blue Magpie — *Urocissa erythrorhyncha*
bluebird — *Sialia* sp.
Brambling — *Fringilla montifringilla*
Buff-bellied Warbler — *Phyllolais pulchella*
bulbul — Pycnonotidae sp.
Chipping Sparrow — *Spizella passerina*
Common Chaffinch — *Fringilla coelebs*
Common Magpie — *Pica pica*
Common Reed Bunting — *Emberiza schoeniclus*
Common Starling — *Sturnus vulgaris*
Common Whitethroat — *Sylvia communis*
coot — *Fulica* sp.
crombec — *Sylvietta* sp.
crossbill — *Loxia* sp.
cuckoo-shrike — *Coracina* sp.
Dunnock — *Prunella modularis*
Eurasian Jay — *Garrulus glandarius*
Eurasian Tree Sparrow — *Passer montanus*
European Goldfinch — *Carduelis carduelis*
European Greenfinch — *Carduelis chloris*
European Robin — *Erithacus rubecula*
flowerpecker — Dicaeidae sp.
Gold-billed Magpie — *Urocissa flavirostris*
Goldcrest — *Regulus regulus*
Great Spotted Woodpecker — *Dendrocopos major*
Green Shrike-Babbler — *Pteruthius xanthochlorus*
Green Hylia — *Hylia prasina*
House Sparrow — *Passer domesticus*
kinglet — *Regulus* sp.

leaf-warbler — *Phylloscopus* sp.
Lesser Honeyguide — *Indicator minor*
Oriental Magpie Robin — *Copsychus saularis*
Maxwell's Black Weaver — *Ploceus albinucha*
Northern Beardless Tyrannulet — *Camptostoma imberbe*
Northern Pygmy-Owl — *Glaucidium gnoma*
parakeet — *Psittacula* sp.
Red-backed Shrike — *Lanius collurio*
Red-throated Pipit — *Anthus cervinus*
redstart — *Phoenicurus* sp.
River Warbler — *Locustella fluviatilis*
roller — *Coracias* sp.
sapsucker — *Sphyrapicus* sp.
Severtzov's Tit-warbler — *Leptopoecile sophiae*
Spanish Sparrow — *Passer hispaniolensis*
Spotted Flycatcher — *Muscicapa striata*
Square-tailed Drongo — *Dicrurus ludwigii*
Streak-throated Fulvetta — *Alcippe cinereiceps*
Stripe-throated Yuhina — *Yuhina gularis*
sunbird — Nectariniidae sp.
Tree Pipit — *Anthus trivialis*
wagtail — *Motacilla* sp.
waxwing — *Bombycilla* sp.
weaver — Ploceidae sp.
Western Black Flycatcher — *Melaenornis edoioides*
Whiskered Yuhina — *Yuhina flavicollis*
White-bellied Minivet — *Pericrocotus erythropygius*
Whimbrel — *Numenius phaeopus*
Willow Warbler — *Phylloscopus trochilus*
Winter Wren — *Troglodytes troglodytes*
Wood Warbler — *Phylloscopus sibilatrix*
woodcreeper — Dendrocolaptinae
woodpecker — Picidae sp.
Yellow-bellied Eremomela — *Eremomela icteropygialis*
Yellow-vented Eremomela — *Eremomela flavicrissalis*

## APPENDIX B: SCIENTIFIC NAMES OF PLANTS MENTIONED IN THE TEXT

acacia — *Acacia* sp.
alder — *Alnus* sp.
Aleppo Pine — *Pinus halepensis*
Algerian Chestnut-leaved Oak — *Q. castaneifolia* var. *incana* (syn. *Q. afares*)
Algerian Fir — *Abies numidica*
Algerian Oak — *Quercus canariensis*
Almond — *Prunus dulcis*
Apricot — *Prunus armeniaca*
ash — *Fraxinus* sp.
aspen — *Populus* sp.
American Aspen — *Populus tremuloides*
Atlas Oak — *Quercus tlemcenensis* (syn. *Q. faginea* ssp. *tlem cenensis*)
Atlas Cedar — *Cedrus atlantica* (syn. *C. libani* ssp. *atlantica*)
American Elm — *Ulmus americana*
American Plane — *Platanus occidentalis* (also known as 'sycamore')
Arizona Cypress — *Cupressus arizonica*
azalea — *Rhododendron* sp.
Balsam Fir — *Abies balsamea*

bamboo — Poaceae sp. (subfamily Bambusoideae)
Ban Oak — *Quercus leucotrichophora* (*Q. incana*)
barberry — *Berberis* sp.
bayberry — *Myrica* sp.
beech — *Fagus* sp.
birch — *Betula* sp.
Bird Cherry — *Prunus padus*
Bishop Pine — *Pinus muricata*
Black Pine — *Pinus nigra*
Black Spruce — *Picea mariana*
Blue Pine — *Pinus wallichiana*
bramble — *Rubus* sp.
buckthorn — *Rhamnus* sp.
bulrush — *Typha* sp. (also known as cattail)
California Laurel — *Umbellularia californica*
Camelthorn — *Acacia erioloba*
cassava — *Manihot* sp.
casuarina — *Casuarina* sp.
Catclaw Acacia — *Acacia greggii*
Caucasian Fir — *Abies nordmanniana*

459

| Common name | Scientific name |
|---|---|
| Caucasian Spruce | Picea orientalis |
| cedar | Cedrus sp. |
| cherry | Prunus sp. |
| chestnut | Castanea/Castanopsis sp. |
| cholla | Opuntia sp. |
| Cilician Fir | Abies cilicica |
| Coast Redwood | Sequoia sempervirens |
| Common Beech | Fagus sylvatica |
| Cork Oak | Quercus suber |
| Corsican Pine | Pinus nigra |
| cottonwood | Populus sp. |
| Coyote Brush | Baccharis pilularis |
| Creosote Bush | Larrea tridentata |
| cypress | Cupressus/Chamaecyparis sp. |
| Deodar | Cedrus deodara |
| Douglas Fir | Pseudotsuga menziesii |
| Downy | Oak Quercus pubescens |
| Edible Seed Pine | Pinus gerardiana |
| elder | Sambucus sp. |
| elm | Ulmus sp. |
| Engelmann Spruce | Picea engelmannii |
| eucalyptus | Eucalyptus sp. |
| Eurasian Aspen | Populus tremula |
| European Hornbeam | Carpinus betulus |
| European Silver Fir | Abies alba |
| European Wild Olive | Olea europaea |
| fir | Abies sp. |
| Giant Sequoia (or Sierra Redwood or Wellingtonia) | Sequoiadendron giganteum |
| hackberry | Celtis sp. |
| Hazel | Corylus avellana |
| heather | Erica/Calluna sp. |
| hemlock | Tsuga spp. |
| hickory | Carya sp. |
| Himalayan Fir | Abies webbiana = spectabilis |
| Holly Oak or Holm Oak | Quercus ilex |
| honeysuckle | Lonicera sp. |
| hornbeam | Carpinus sp. |
| hydrangea | Hydrangea sp. |
| idigbo | Terminalia sp. |
| Incense-cedar | Calocedrus decurrens |
| Indian Horse Chestnut | Aesculus indicus |
| live oak | Quercus sp. (typically Q. agrifolia in California and Q. virginiana in Texas) |
| Jeffrey Pine | Pinus jeffreyi |
| Joshua Tree | Yucca brevifolia/Yucca sp. |
| juniper | Juniperus sp. |
| Khasi Pine | Pinus kesiya |
| larch | Larix sp. |
| laurel | Lauraceae sp. |
| Lebanon Cedar | Cedrus libani |
| Loblolly Pine | Pinus taeda |
| Lodgepole Pine | Pinus contorta |
| Longleaf Pine | Pinus palustris |
| mahobohobo | Baikiaea sp. |
| mango | Mangifera sp. |
| maple | Acer sp. |
| mavuda | Cryptosepalum sp. |
| Maritime Pine | Pinus pinaster |
| mesquite | Prosopis sp. |
| milk vetch | Astragalus sp. |
| mistletoe | Loranthaceae/Viscaceae sp. |
| Monterey Pine | Pinus radiata |
| mountain mahogany | Cercocarpus sp. |
| mulberry | Morus sp. |
| mutemwa | Baikiaea sp. |
| oak | Quercus sp. |
| olive | Olea sp. |
| Osier | Salix viminalis |
| Paloverde | Parkinsonia florida |
| Peanut | Arachis hypogaea |
| Pecan | Carya illinoinensis |
| pine | Pinus sp. |
| pinyon pine | Pinus edulis / P. monophylla / P. cembroides (also eight other rarer species) |
| pistachio | Pistacia sp. |
| podocarp | Podocarpus sp. |
| Poison Ivy | Rhus radicans |
| Ponderosa | Pine Pinus ponderosa |
| poplar | Populus sp. |
| raspberry | Rubus sp. |
| reed | Phragmites sp. |
| reedmace | see bulrush |
| rhododendron | Rhododendron sp. |
| rose | Rosa sp. |
| sagebrush | Artemisia spp. (shrubby sp; used mainly in America) |
| salt cedar | see tamarisk |
| Salt Tree | Halimodendron halodendron |
| saxaul | Haloxylon sp. |
| Scots Pine | Pinus sylvestris |
| Sessile Oak | Quercus petraea |
| Shisham | Dalbergia sissoo |
| Shortleaf Pine | Pinus echinata |
| Siberian Pea Tree | Caragana arborescens |
| Siberian Stone Pine | Pinus sibirica |
| silk cotton tree | Ceiba sp. or Bombax sp. |
| spruce | Picea sp. |
| Stone Pine | Pinus pinea |
| Sugar Maple | Acer saccharum |
| sweetgum | Liquidambar sp. |
| tamarisk | Tamarix sp. |
| tamerack | Larix sp. |
| teak | Tectona sp. |
| Turanga | Populus euphratica |
| Turkish Pine | Pinus brutia |
| walnut | Juglans sp. |
| West Himalayan Spruce | Picea morinda |
| willow | Salix sp. |
| witch-hazel | Hamamelis sp. |
| wormwood | Artemisia vulgaris/A. spp. (non-shrubby species) |
| Yew | Taxus baccata |

# INDEX

Figures in bold refer to plate numbers.